SECOND EDITION

LEGAL RESOURCE

for

SCHOOL HEALTH SERVICES

A reference regarding legal issues impacting school health. The second edition of *Legal Resource for School Health Services* provides new chapters, completely updated and more comprehensive information on 60 topics that school health services programs and school nurses encounter, addresses legal implications, and presents legal resources and references that can be applied to practice and policy development.

Editors
Cheryl A. Resha, EdD, MSN, RN, FNASN, FAAN
Vicki L. Taliaferro, BSN, RN, NCSN-E

Legal Consultant
Katherine J. Pohlman, MS, JD, Nurse Attorney

SCHOOLNURSE.COM
Your School Health Connection

SchoolNurse.com
P.O. Box 558
Midlothian, VA 23113

LEGAL RESOURCE FOR SCHOOL HEALTH SERVICES
Copyright © 2024 SchoolNurse.com

ISBN-13: 978-1-7348295-3-2
ISBN-10: 1-7348295-3-2

Phone: 615-419-3241

DISCLAIMER

Many hours of research went into the creation of this book, and the authors worked diligently to provide accurate and up-to-date information. However, laws change on a regular basis, and interpretations of law can also vary significantly. This publication is intended to provide a comprehensive overview of a wide variety of legal topics related to the practice of school nursing. The information in this book should not be considered legal advice, and readers should understand that court decisions and legislative actions that occur every day may render particular laws or legal concepts invalid or outdated. In addition, legal analysis depends very heavily upon the fact patterns to which a law or legal concept is applied, and sometimes even the smallest change in a fact can result in a completely different finding of law.

The jurisdiction in which an issue occurs also plays a large role in the applicability and interpretation of any particular law or legal concept. Thus, this work is not intended to replace case-specific research or legal counsel, and no representations, warranties, or guarantees, express or implied, are made as to the accuracy, adequacy, reliability, relevancy, completeness, suitability, or applicability of the information found within this book. All information should be independently verified prior to use in practice.

SchoolNurse.com, the editors, legal consultant, authors, or reviewers do not assume responsibility for or accept liability regarding any error, omission, or inaccuracy of law or fact in the information contained within this work. Readers should seek independent legal counsel before relying on any part of this work. To the maximum extent permitted by law, SchoolNurse.com, its editors, legal consultant, and contributing authors and reviewers also do not assume any responsibility for or accept liability regarding any loss, damage, or injury, financial or otherwise, suffered by any person acting or relying on information contained in or omitted from this work.

This publication provides links to several 3rd party websites. These links have been provided for convenience only and may be subject to updates, revisions, or other changes by the entities controlling or owning those sites. The inclusion of the link does not imply that the publisher, editors, legal consultant, authors, or reviewers endorse the content or the site operator. Likewise, this publication cites many reference materials. Endorsement of such works, their authors, publishers, or organizations with which they are affiliated should not be implied.

FOREWORD

I am honored to have been invited to again author the foreword for the updated edition of this valuable resource for school nurses, administrators, and attorneys. As legal counsel for the National Association of School Nurses, I have been involved in legal issues related to school nursing and school health services for over 35+ years.

The legal landscape associated with healthcare continues to increase in complexity over the past several decades, and even more so in the school setting. Once our legal system recognized the rights of medically complex students to receive education in the least restrictive environment and receive the supportive services they need to do so, the responsibilities of the licensed professionals who provide those services expanded. Unfortunately, the violence and divisiveness that characterizes our current culture have increasingly infected the school environment also and further complicated an already challenging legal landscape.

Those professionals must be knowledgeable about a myriad of laws and regulations, both state and federal, that pertain to the services they provide. Those laws are scattered throughout the federal and state codes and administrative rules—not simply located in the sections of the law directly related to professional licensure or education. And at times, the school district policies and procedures adopted to comply with the mandates of those various laws conflict with those governing nursing practice, creating ethical and legal dilemmas for school nurses.

The challenge of providing school health services within tight budget constraints creates pressure to delegate to unlicensed assistive personnel responsibilities that might otherwise be provided by licensed school nurses. Because nurse practice acts and related regulations differ from state to state with respect to delegation, school nurses must make sure that school district delegation policies do not require actions that violate those practice acts.

Because of the complexity involved, few of the many legal dilemmas that arise in the school health setting lend themselves to black and white answers. When working through the many shades gray, those involved should seek input from trusted advisors and turn to reliable resources. The *Legal Resource for School Health Services* is a valuable asset and much-needed addition to that collection of resources.

Katherine J. Pohlman, MS, JD, RN
Nurse Attorney and Consultant

ABOUT THIS BOOK

School nursing services are comprehensive and uniquely address students' health and safety needs individually and in populations, as a component of their role incorporates community/public health nursing. School nurses' work focuses directly on three areas: health services, health education, and a healthy school environment. Their services require diverse knowledge including, but not limited to, pediatric/adolescent health, infectious diseases, mental health, chronic diseases, and emergency care. School nurses can influence the health and safety aspects of schools. They can provide leadership to a district's or campus' whole school, whole child, whole community model that, in addition to health services, health education, and the healthy school environment, addresses mental health and social services, nutrition services, physical activity, family and community involvement, and staff health promotion/services.

Inherent in providing these services and in the daily activities of school nurses and school health programs are legal issues that school health services must address in order to provide care to children safely and safeguard the schools' accountability for student well-being and the individual school nurse's professional licensure. This resource serves as a reference for school nurses. It can assist them, their administrators, school boards, and consulting attorneys to identify legal topics, develop policies and procedures, and implement strategies for safe student care. This manual offers brief summaries of a variety of legal considerations that schools and school nurses encounter but is not intended to substitute for any legal consultation nor serve as the sole resource on legal topics.

Legal Resource for School Health Services was developed through the cooperative efforts of school nurse experts, nurse attorneys, education attorneys, and public health attorneys. Compliance with health, education, and employment law is of utmost importance for school health services programs. Still, it can often be complicated and layered with state and local district laws and policies. We hope this reference provides information, explanations, and resources that can assist school health services programs in meeting their legal obligations, providing safe care, and respecting the rights of children while protecting schools and school nurses. It is important to note that in some situations/content areas, there is no legal guidance or laws that direct safe practice. The authors present "best practices" based on acceptable clinical guidelines or practice models in those situations.

LAWS

As depicted in the algorithm below, the legal framework for practice begins with the federal and state constitutions, federal and state laws, federal and state regulations, case law, and finally, non-regulatory guidance, such as recommendations from federal and state health and education departments.

SOURCES OF LAW

Erin D. Gilsbach, Esquire (2017)

1st Amendment – Free Speech, Freedom of Religion, Free Association

4th Amendment – Prohibits Unreasonable Search and Seizure by Govt. (incl. public schools)

5th Amendment – Due Process Rights

14th Amendment – "Equal Protection Clause" – Equal Opportunities & Equal Treatment

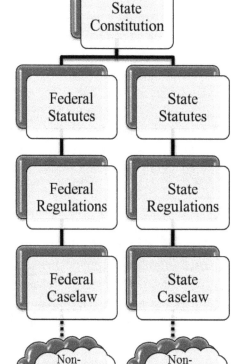

State constitutions establish right to free public education

Includes such statutes as:
- IDEA
- PPRA
- FERPA
- ESSA/ESEA
- Section 504
- McKinney-Vento
- Civil Rights Act of 1964

Includes State Nurse Practice Act (or the equivalent) – statutes regulating the practice of nursing

Rules promulgated by federal agencies pursuant to statutory authority – provides more detailed rules re: compliance with federal statutes, such as those listed, above

Rules promulgated by state agencies pursuant to statutory authority – includes state Dept. of Health / state Board of Nursing (or their equivalents) – requirements for licensure / standards of nursing practice

Interprets law based upon specific facts in a case

Interprets law based upon specific facts in a case

- Office of Civil Rights (OCR) Letters
- Family Policy and Compliance Office (FPCO) Letters
- Office of Special Education Programs (OSEP) Letters

Guidance issued by agencies such as:
- State Dept. of Health
- State Dept. of Education
- State Dept. of Public Welfare

Not law, but persuasive to courts

Often issued by same agency tasked with enforcing the law

DESCRIPTION OF LEGAL RESOURCES FOR SCHOOL HEALTH SERVICES

The book is divided into six sections:

School Nurse Practice Issues
Laws/Policy
Nursing Care
Nursing Coordination
Staff Services
Beyond the Public School

Each chapter follows a prescribed format:

Description of the Issue
Background
Implications for School Nurse Practice
Conclusion
Resources
References

In some cases, the authors provided additional information, which is included in chapter appendices. In other chapters, outside authors provide some practical tips on the topic and are included as an addendum with credit to the outside author noted.

The process for developing a chapter included recruiting and selecting authors who have expertise in the area through specialized practice as presenters, authors on the topic, or instructors. Authors provided drafts of their chapters to the editors, who reviewed and made suggestions for changes throughout the development of the chapter. Each chapter went through blind reviews by both school nurse and legal content experts (i.e., school nurses, state school nurse consultants, school nurse educators, health educators, education attorneys, health-related attorneys, or nurse attorneys). The final chapters were once again reviewed and finalized by the editors and the legal consultant.

TERMINOLOGY

Child find: The term "child find" is not formally identified in Section 504 of the Rehabilitation Act of 1973; however, Section 504 does call for the need to identify and determine eligibility for children with disabilities; therefore, "child find" in quotes is used not a formal term but as a way to express the intent to find children in need of services.

Healthcare Provider: This term addresses all terms used for healthcare providers: physicians, practitioners, doctors, dentists, those with prescriptive authority, etc.

LEGAL RESOURCE FOR SCHOOL HEALTH SERVICES

IDEA/IDEIA: The **Individuals with Disabilities Education Act (IDEA)** has undergone multiple amendments and reauthorizations in the decades since its initial passage. Most recently, the IDEA was reauthorized as the Individuals with Disabilities Education Improvement Act (IDEIA) in 2004. The original acronym continues to be used colloquially, and for practical purposes, we refer to the legislation in its most recent form as the IDEA throughout the book; however, on occasion, IDEIA is also used.

School(s): The term school in this book refers to "public" schools. When the term is related to non-public, private, or parochial schools, it will be specifically identified as such.

School District: Different terms are used throughout the country to describe school entities, i.e., school system, school jurisdictions, and school campus. Throughout this book will use the term "school district."

School Nurse: For this book, the term school nurse is used for a licensed registered nurse (RN). Under some state laws, school nurses are required to obtain special certification from their state departments of education, which may mean additional credits and/or experience. Licensed Nurse Practitioners and RNs without school nurse certification may assist "school nurses," but they cannot replace them, and they do not count towards the state minimum for school nurses. Licensed Practical Nurses (LPNs) or Licensed Vocational Nurses (LVNs) often are hired as school nurses and, in most states, are required to work in a team relationship with a RN. The differences vary across states, so we have used the term broadly for simplicity.

We welcome your suggestions for future editions and wish you success in safely caring for our nation's children. You may contact us at *www.schoolnurse.com*.

Cheryl A. Resha, EdD, MSN, RN, FNASN, FAAN, Editor
Vicki L. Taliaferro, BSN, RN, NCSN-E, Editor
Katherine Pohlman, MS, JD, RN, Legal Consultant
Robert Andrews, Publisher
SchoolNurse.com
PO Box 558, Midlothian, VA 23113
615-957-7638
www.schoolnurse.com

ACKNOWLEDGEMENTS

As editors, we would like to extend our sincere gratitude to the authors and reviewers of this book. Each spent many hours researching the topic, writing, and reviewing materials which significantly contributed to the development of this resource. As you review this book, it will become obvious that each chapter was authored by experts who were both passionate and knowledgeable about their subject matter. Not unlike other large endeavors, this work is clearly one that was successfully completed due to the collective efforts of many.

We would also like to take this opportunity to thank our publisher, Robert Andrews, for his support and commitment to providing school health services personnel with needed resources.

Finally, we would like to thank our families, especially Bonnie and Mike, for their support during this process.

CONTRIBUTORS

AUTHORS

Andrea Adimando, DNP, MS, APRN, PMHNP-BC, BCIM

Dr. Andrea Adimando is an Associate Professor of Nursing at Southern CT State University (SCSU). In addition to her teaching and administrative responsibilities, Dr. Adimando practices as a Board-Certified Family Psychiatric & Mental Health Nurse Practitioner (PMHNP-BC) in various outpatient and acute care settings in Connecticut, specializing in the care of children and adolescents with psychiatric and behavioral disorders. Prior to becoming a certified nurse practitioner, Dr. Adimando worked as a pediatric nurse on a school-aged medical/surgical unit at Yale New Haven Children's Hospital. Throughout her 18+ years of practice, she has worked collaboratively with school systems, including therapeutic and residential schools, both as a psychiatric consultant and as part of comprehensive evaluation and treatment planning for her own clients.

Dori Pagé Antonetti, Esquire

Dori Pagé Antonetti is a member of Shipman & Goodwin's School Law Practice Group where she represents a wide range of educational institutions, including both public and independent K-12 schools in a variety of education and employment law matters. In her day-to-day representation of clients, Dori draws on her unique experience as a former educator and labor relations hearing review officer. Dori has extensive experience in policy development and review and regularly advises schools on matters related to compliance with state and federal family and medical leave laws, disability-related laws, and other health-related issues that arise in the school context. Dori enjoys staying abreast of legal developments that have a significant impact on schools, most recently advising schools on policies and procedures related to supports and protections for transgender and gender non-conforming students and student immunization requirements. Dori also currently serves as an adjunct professor at the University of Connecticut Neag School of Education.

LEGAL RESOURCE FOR SCHOOL HEALTH SERVICES

Martha D. Bergren, PhD, RN, NCSN, PHNA-BC, FNASN, FASHA, FAAN

Martha Dewey Bergren is nationally certified in school nursing and advanced public health nursing, and her areas of expertise include legal issues, leadership, population health, nurse-sensitive outcome indicators, and informatics. She is currently Executive Editor of The Journal of School Nursing and Clinical Professor Emerita at the University of Illinois-Chicago College of Nursing. She has numerous publications in peer-reviewed journals and book chapters on school nursing, population health, legal issues, and privacy. She is a fellow in the American Academy of Nursing, the National Association of School Nurses, and the American School Health Association.

Cheryl Blake, MSN, RN, NCSN

Cheryl Blake has worked as a school nurse for the last 23 years at Trinity School of Durham in North Carolina. She is currently serving as the Past Chair for the Private, Independent, and Parochial School Nurses (PIPSN), a Special Interest Group of the National Association of School Nurses. Cheryl currently serves as the President of the Sandhills Region for the School Nurse Association of North Carolina.

Jane C. Boyd, MSN, RN, NCSN

Jane Boyd is a retired State School Nurse Consultant with over 37 years as a registered nurse and over 21 years of experience in school nursing practice. From 2016-2019 she was the Delaware State School Nurse Consultant. She is a member of the Technology Committee of the National Association of State School Nurse Consultants. She was a reviewer for the 10th edition of the School Nurse Resource Manual. She is currently a Graduate Nursing Adjunct Faculty at Wilmington University.

Edie Brous, MS, MPH, BSN, JD, RN, FAAN

Ms. Brous is a Nurse Attorney in private practice concentrating in professional licensure representation and nursing advocacy. She has practiced in major litigation law firms representing nurses at all levels of practice, physicians, other healthcare professionals, hospitals, and pharmaceutical companies. Edie is admitted to practice before the bars of the state courts of New York, New Jersey, and Pennsylvania, the Southern and Eastern Districts of the New York Federal Courts, and the United States Supreme Court. She is a member of many bar associations and nursing organizations and was the 2011 president of The American Association of Nurse Attorneys. Ms. Brous has an extensive clinical and managerial background in OR, Emergency, and Critical Care Nursing. In addition to her law degree, she holds master's degrees in public health and in Critical Care Nursing from Columbia University. She has been part-time faculty at Columbia University and has held adjunct faculty positions at several universities teaching legal aspects of nursing. Ms. Brous has lectured and published extensively on legal issues for nurses and co-authored the textbook *Law and Ethics for Advanced Practice Nurses*. She is the 2008 recipient of the Outstanding Advocate Award, the 2017 Outstanding Litigation Section Member Award, and the 2020 Outstanding Solo Practice Section Member Award from The American Association of Nurse Attorneys.

Mariann F. Cosby, DNP, MPA, RN, CEN, NE-BC, LNCC, CLCP, CCM, MSCC, CSN, FAEN

Dr. Mariann F. Cosby of Sacramento, California, is a California Credentialed School Nurse whose nursing career spans 43 years. It is woven with an overlap of 25 years of traditional emergency department stretcher-side and nursing manager roles and 31 years of non-traditional emergency practice settings, including school nursing, correctional nursing, and community-based pediatric and geriatric programs. Her past employment included various clinical, management, teaching, and consulting positions in hospitals, nursing schools, and community-based statewide programs. Although recently semi-retired, she continues her 32-year legal nurse consultant practice as an expert witness and consultant. As the owner of MFC Consulting, Mariann offers a variety of services to attorneys who benefit from her broad nursing background on complex nursing malpractice and a variety of other civil and criminal cases. Mariann holds several national professional certifications and credentials. As a certified life care planner for 20 years, she develops and critiques life care plans, medical cost projections, and past medical bills for reasonable value. Dr. Cosby has presented on topics related to emergency nursing practice, legal nurse consulting, and writing for publication at state, national, and international conferences. She is published in multiple peer-reviewed journals and nursing textbooks, including three chapters in the 2020 fourth edition of the American Association of Legal Nurse Consultants Principles and Practices and in two compendium eBooks, all editions including the upcoming fourth edition of School Nursing: A Comprehensive Text, and in 2023 a chapter on Emergency Nursing Practice: Traditional and Non-Traditional Settings and Organizations that include emergency nursing practice in the educational setting. From 2016 to 2018, she was the editor of the Journal of Nurse Life Care Planning. In 2020, she was inducted as a Fellow into the Academy of Emergency Nursing in recognition of her outstanding and enduring contributions to the advancement of emergency nursing. Dr. Cosby volunteers her time serving on numerous professional boards and working committees charged with updating international standards of practice and finding solutions to current practice issues. Dr. Mariann F. Cosby can be reached at mfcconsulting3@gmail.com.

Deborah D'Souza-Vazirani, DrPH

Deborah D'Souza-Vazirani DrPH, is currently serving as the Program Evaluation Director at the National Association of School Nurses (NASN). She has led NASN's *Champions for School Health* program for the duration of the project – an initiative that focused on increasing vaccine access, confidence, and equity in school-required vaccinations and the pediatric COVID-19 vaccine. She has over 25 years of program evaluation and program management experience in public health with a focus on health disparities research and advancing health equity in marginalized communities, working in both the private and government sectors and as a hospital administrator.

Linda Davis-Alldritt, MA, BSN, RN, FNASN, FASHA

Linda Davis-Alldritt is Past President of the National Association of School Nurses and is currently an independent school health services consultant. Linda was educated in California. She has a Master's degree in Sociology from California State University Long Beach, a Baccalaureate Degree in Nursing from California State University Sacramento, and a Baccalaureate Degree in Sociology from the University of California Davis. She holds credentials from the California Commission on Teacher Credentialing in school nursing, administrative services, and community college teaching. She has been a nurse for 38 years, including ten years as a school nurse administrator and 16 years as the State School Nurse Consultant for the California Department of Education. Linda is a past president of the California School Nurses Organization (CSNO) and a past president of the National Association of State School Nurse Consultants (NASSNC). She has received several awards, including CSNO School Nurse of the Year, NASSNC Outstanding State School Nurse Consultant, and California Public Health Association Public Health Leadership Award. Linda is a fellow of NASN and the American School Health Association (ASHA). She is a published author, including journal articles and the chapter on school health funding for both editions of the NASN textbook: "School Nursing: A Comprehensive Text." Linda currently lives in Helsinki, Finland, with her husband of 50 years.

Sandi Delack, Med, BSN, RN, NCSN-E, FNASN

Sandi Delack is a nationally certified school nurse and a National Association of School Nursing fellow. She was employed for 31 years in the field, serving as a RI Certified School Nurse Teacher and Health Services Coordinator before retiring in 2019. She is currently an independent school health consultant and national speaker on the topics of interest of infection control, vector-borne illness, and Individualized Healthcare Plans for school nurses. Sandi has served as President of the National Association of School Nurses, President of the National Board for Certification of School Nurses, and Vice President of the Accreditation Board for Specialty Nursing Certification. Her passions include advocacy, leadership, and legal issues, and she has authored numerous peer-reviewed articles.

Joan Edelstein, DrPH , MSN, RN

Dr. Joan Edelstein has extensive experience as a clinician and educator in maternal/child health as well as community health and school nursing. She was a Professor of Nursing for 22 years at San Jose State University. After leaving academia, she worked for Oakland Unified School District as School Nurse, Asthma Specialist through a CDC Controlling Asthma in American Cities Project grant, where she helped develop and implement the evidence based Kickin' Asthma program for middle and high school students. She then became Health Services Coordinator for the Oakland Unified School District through a jointly funded position with the Alameda County Public Health Department, successfully implementing model policies to support student and staff health. As a current faculty member, Dr. Edelstein teaches several courses in the School Nurse Credential Program at California State University Sacramento and was part of a team to develop the newly approved School Nurse Credential Program at San Francisco State University. She coordinates and leads the biweekly Alameda County school nurse meeting in collaboration with the Alameda County Office of Education and assists school nurses statewide in developing district policy to advocate for student health. Dr. Edelstein was a recipient of the CSNO Excellence in School Nursing, Bay Coast award in 2020.

Patricia Endsley, MSN, RN, NCSN

Dr. Patricia Endsley is a full-time school nurse at Wells High School in Wells, Maine. In addition, she is the Program Chair of the MEd in School Nurse Education at Cambridge College, Boston, MA. Dr. Endsley is also an online adjunct instructor for Arizona College of Nursing's Tucson, AZ Campus. Dr. Endsley's nursing career spans 38 years in the outpatient, obstetric, and school nursing specialties. She has a special interest in qualitative research which includes school nurse workload. emergency preparedness, and student wellness.

Ingrid Hopkins Duva, PhD, RN

Dr. Ingrid Duva is an Assistant Professor at the Nell Hodgson Woodruff School of Nursing at Emory University. Dr. Duva has worked previously as a school nurse and is currently conducting research on emotional regulation and well-being in students in Georgia. Previously funded by the AHRQ, Veteran›s Health Administration, and Sigma Theta Tau, Dr. Duva led studies examining nurse care coordination in a variety of settings, the nurses› role in diabetes care, and changing scope of registered nurse practice in primary care. A nurse for more than 30 years, prior roles include pediatric staff nurse, operations leadership, administration, and regulatory compliance within the healthcare system. An active member of several professional organizations, she authored a chapter on leadership for the American Nurses Association (ANA) publication: *Care Coordination: The Game Changer - How nursing is revolutionizing quality care* (2014). Dr. Duva is also a certified Community Resiliency Model Teacher and a board member of the non-profit organization: Community Resiliency Model GA (crmgeorgia.org).

John E. Freund, III, Esquire

Attorney Freund is the chairman of the Education Law Practice Group at King Spry Herman Freund & Faul in Bethlehem, PA.

Marlene S. Garvis, JD, MSN, BSN, BA

Marlene entered the practice of law following a successful career in nursing. She practiced at Jardine, Logan & O'Brien, PLLP, for most of her legal career, where she was a partner and held many leadership positions in the firm. She has also had several leadership positions in the legal community, including President of the Minnesota Women Lawyers, the Hennepin County Bar Foundation, and the Hennepin County Bar Association; Chair of the Battered Women's Legal Advocacy Project; and Chair of the Federal Bar Association Health Law Section. She is currently on the Advisory Board of the Minnesota Woman Lawyers, a Vice Chair of the American Bar Association Health Law Section Nurses and Allied Health Professionals, and Secretary of the Federal Bar Association, Health Law Section and Chair of the Membership Committee. Marlene is also on the Board of Directors of the American Association of Nurse Attorneys, where she currently serves as Treasurer, and the Beyond Pink Foundation Leadership Board, where she currently serves as Secretary. Marlene is a Life Fellow of the American Bar Foundation and a Founding Fellow of the Hennepin County Bar Foundation. Since January 2015, Marlene has practiced in her own law firm in Minnetonka, Minnesota, where she represents clients in consultation, litigation, and administrative proceedings on Health Care Law and Professional Licensure, Health Care Law Consultation, Licensing, Discipline and Regulatory Matters, Litigation, Consultation, and Appellate Matters. She has represented clients before the Boards of Nursing, Medical Practice, Psychology, Behavioral

Health and Therapy, Social Work, Marriage and Family Therapy, and Physical Therapy; as well as on appeals at the Minnesota Department of Human Services and the Office of Administrative Hearings. Marlene has an AV® Preeminent Rating in the distinguished legal directory, Martindale-Hubbell®, and was selected to the 2014-2022 Minnesota Super Lawyers lists. She can be reached at marlene@marlenegarvis.com.

Erin D. Gilsbach, JD, MEd, BA

An experienced speaker at the state and national levels on issues regarding education and education law, Erin Gilsbach is the CEO of EdLaw Interactive, a unique online learning tool designed to provide educators, school nurses, and school leaders with access to high-quality, low-cost training in the area of school law. Atty. Gilsbach is an experienced speaker at the state and national levels, and she works with schools throughout Pennsylvania and nationwide, consulting on legal issues, assisting in the development of legally defensible policies and procedures, and providing professional development in the area of school law. In her practice, she frequently provides professional development for school nurses and school nurse organizations on current and high-liability issues related to school law and nursing. Atty. Gilsbach is a past president of the PA School Boards Association (PSBA) Solicitors Association, and she has served on the board of the NSBA Council of School Attorneys (COSA). She is a frequent author and presenter with NSBA, COSA, the National Business Institute, the Pennsylvania School Boards Association, LRP Publications, the LRP Institute, and the Pennsylvania Bar Institute. She has written two books on students with disabilities and health-related needs for LRP publications. Prior to entering private practice, she served for over two years at the Pennsylvania Department of Education's Office of Chief Counsel.

Timothy E. Gilsbach, Esquire, JD, BA

Timothy E. Gilsbach is an attorney with Fox Rothschild in Blue Bell, concentrating his practice in education law and special education law. He has represented school districts, charter schools, and intermediate units through numerous IEP meetings and litigated dozens of special education matters, from administrative due process hearings to appeals through the Federal District Courts and Court of Appeals. He also advises clients on a wide variety of other educational law issues, including FERPA, student discipline, and the use of medical marijuana in schools. Mr. Gilsbach is admitted to practice law in Pennsylvania and New Jersey. He was named a Pennsylvania Super Lawyer "Rising Star" for three years, from 2012 to 2014, and a Pennsylvania Super Lawyer from 2017 through 2020 and again in 2022 by Super Lawyer Magazine in the area of school law. Mr. Gilsbach earned his Juris Doctorate from Dickinson School of Law of Pennsylvania State University and his Bachelor of Arts in Political Science from Messiah College.

Shirley Countryman Gordon, PhD, RN, NCSN, AHN-BC, HWNC-NC, SGAHN

Dr. Shirley Countryman Gordon is a Professor of Nursing at Florida Atlantic University (FAU), where she founded and has continuously directed the Head Lice Treatment and Prevention Project since 1996. Professionally, Dr. Gordon has over 40 years of experience as a registered nurse and nurse educator. Dr. Gordon is an active member of many professional organizations, including the National Association of School Nurses, and is an invited member of the International Phthiraptera Congress of lice experts. Dr. Gordon has authored national and international articles and publications regarding school nursing and student health. She was the first to define and focus attention on persistent head lice infestations, conceptualize head lice as a family phenomenon, and identify early nursing interventions. Her theory, Shared Vulnerability, has been used around the world to study social morbidity associated with caring for children experiencing persistent head lice infestations.

Jenny M. Gormley, DNP, MSN, RN, NCSN

Jenny Gormley has 36 years of experience as a registered nurse, with the last 23 years in school health, and is a nationally certified school nurse. Dr. Gormley is currently the Director of the Northeastern University School Health Academy (NEUSHA), providing in-person workshops and conferences, virtual webinars, and recorded learning opportunities for school nurses and their colleagues across the U.S. and globally to support student health, safety, and achievement. Prior to NEUSHA, she worked for the Hudson Public Schools as Director of Health, Nursing, and Safety, where she completed and developed training with local law enforcement and administrators on planning for and responding to a violent intruder. In this role, she also coordinated the Youth Risk Behavior Survey, using results to plan curriculum and programs to address student reports of violence and mental health risk behaviors. Dr. Gormley started her career in school health as an elementary nurse and per diem school nurse. Dr. Gormley served on the Massachusetts School Nurse Organization (MSNO) board as President (2018-2020) and continues as advocacy committee member and regional co-chair. Dr. Gormley was awarded the Doctor of Nursing Practice degree from Northeastern University in 2018, publishing her scholarly work on the development of an educational program to increase school nurse advocacy for student health, safety, and school attendance at the local level in the Journal of School Nursing. She received the 2022 National Association of School Nurses Outstanding School Nurse Educator of the Year award and the 2023 Anne Sheetz Leadership award from MSNO. In 2023, Dr. Gormley was inducted into the National Academy of School Nurses.

Kathleen A. Hassey, DNP, MEd, BA, BSN, RN

Kathy Hassey received a BA in Biology, then her Bachelor of Science in Nursing from Boston University. She received her master's in education in School Health in 2001. She has been a Registered Nurse for 42 years and initially worked at Mount Auburn Hospital and Deaconess Waltham Hospital. She moved into the school health specialty in 1999 as the Director of Health Services for the Hudson Public School system until 2005. Ms. Hassey was the Director of the NEU School Health Institute at Northeastern University and is now the Director of the Northeastern University School Health Academy (NEUSHA), providing conferences and continuing education for School Nurses in all 50 states and 21 countries. She has taught graduate courses such as *"Legal and Ethical Issues in School Nursing"* and *"Leadership Skills for School Nurses"* since 2003. She presently teaches *Leadership in School Health* for Cambridge College *and taught Leadership Skills in School and Community Health and Health Impacts on Academics* for Canisius College for several years. She was President of the Massachusetts School Nurse Organization (MSNO) 2007-2009 and was the MSNO NASN Director for Massachusetts (2014-2016) and served on the NASN Executive Committee. Ms. Hassey completed her DNP in 2018, and she received the NASN School Nurse Educator of the Year in 2023.

Denise Herrmann, DNP, RN, CPNP, FNASN

Denise has her Doctorate in Nursing Practice and is a Certified Pediatric Nurse Practitioner specializing in children with special health needs. Denise has been with the Minnesota Department of Health (MDH) since June 2019 and in the role of State School Health Consultant since April 2020. In this role, she provides technical assistance, consultation to school nurses and leaders, education and training on various school health and school nursing topics and leads the MDH School Health Services website https://www.health.state.mn.us/people/childrenyouth/schoolhealth/index.html with content writing and resource links. Denise's career spans over 40 years, with 23 years as a school nurse and pediatric nurse practitioner, where she provided care to students of all ages and abilities. Denise has served as President of the School Nurse Organization of Minnesota (SNOM) and was MN School Nurse of the Year in 2005. She was inducted into the National Association of School Nurses (NASN) Academy of Fellows in 2007. She holds membership in SNOM, and NASN and is also a member of the National Association of State School Nurse Consultants, the National Association of Pediatric Nurse Practitioners, and the American Academy of Pediatrics.

Annie Hetzel, MSN, RN, NCSN

Annie Hetzel is the Washington Office of the Superintendent for Public Instruction (OSPI) School Health Services Consultant, having joined this position during the pandemic in October 2020. She is a registered nurse with 32 years of experience in hospital, home care, and school nursing. Prior to joining OSPI, she worked as a School Nurse Corps Administrator for the Puget Sound region for 5 years, providing school nurse support and managing school safety services. She is a member of the School Nurse Organization of Washington (SNOW) and currently serving as Vice-President of the National Association of State School Nurse Consultants.

Julie Jaquays, Esquire

Julie Jaquays is a member of Shipman & Goodwin's School Law Practice Group. She advises public school districts on a variety of general education, special education and labor and employment issues. Julie focuses her practice on special education matters and disputes, student discipline, and the Connecticut Freedom of Information Act. She also serves on the firm's Model Policy Committee, which provides a comprehensive set of model policies and administrative regulations for Connecticut boards of education and charter schools. Prior to joining Shipman & Goodwin, Julie was a Judicial Intern to the Honorable Jeffrey Alker Meyer for the United States District Court for the District of Connecticut.

Kathleen H. Johnson, DNP, RN, NCSN-E, PHNA-BC, FNASN, FAAN

Dr. Katie Johnson is Affiliate Faculty in Population Health Nursing at the University of Washington (UW), and Mentor Faculty for the Washington Office of the Superintendent of Public Instruction. Prior to joining UW, Dr. Johnson worked as the Manager of Student Health Services in Seattle Public Schools, supervising 90 nurses serving 54,000 students. She briefly served as Interim State Consultant for WA while completing her DNP in Community Health Systems Nursing. She holds fellowships as RWJ Executive Nurse Fellow, Johnson & Johnson School Health Leadership Fellow, is a National Academy of School Nursing Fellow, and the American Academy of Nursing. She served on the National Board for Certification of School Nurses and is a founding member of the NASN Step Up! Be Counted, and Every Student Counts! data collection programs, and the Center for School Health Innovation and Quality. Katie presents and publishes on school health records systems and data to support advocacy for students and to advance school nursing practice.

Pamela Kahn, MPH, RN

Pamela Kahn served for over 17 years as the Coordinator for Health and Wellness for the Orange County Department of Education in California. In this capacity, she acted in an advisory position regarding health programs and healthcare to the 28 public school districts in the county. She worked closely with the school nurses and many community and private agencies to provide the 500,000 students in Orange County with the health services they need to succeed in school. Pamela retired from this position in May 2023. Prior to this, she served as a credentialed school nurse for 12 years in the Anaheim Union High School District. She belongs to many professional organizations, including the National Association for School Nurses, and has held many positions in the California School Nurses Organization, including that of President. She has been published in Nursing World magazine, the Journal of School Nursing, and Congenital Cardiology Today. She has contributed a chapter to the 2nd edition of "School Nursing: A Comprehensive Text". She received the Nurse.com 2012 Nursing Excellence Award in Advancing and Leading the Profession and was named the 2013 Cypress College Alumni of the Year. She continues to teach in various capacities, including for CSU Sacramento, and travels the state providing professional development for numerous school-based programs.

Linda S. Kalekas, MSN, RN, NCSN

Linda Kalekas has over 46 years of critical care, ambulatory care, and school health experience. She is currently employed as a nursing administrator for the Clark County School District (CCSD), the fifth-largest school district in the country. Ms. Kalekas maintains a business providing expert legal and educational nursing consultant services. She is a national instructor for the School Emergency Triage Training (SETT) program sponsored by the National Association of School Nurses (NASN) and served as the secondary author in the revision of the SETT manual. For over a decade, Ms. Kalekas served as an Emergency Management liaison between CCSD and the Clark County Multi-Agency Coordination Center (CC-MACC). As liaison, she worked on real-world disaster events such as the "1 October" Mass Casualty Incident (MCI) in Las Vegas and all phases of COVID-19 pandemic operations to ensure effective collaboration between Clark County, Southern Nevada Health District, and Clark County School District.

Ms. Kalekas graduated from Muhlenberg Hospital School of Nursing and Union County College in New Jersey, earning a Diploma in Nursing and an Associate in Science Degree in 1977. She is an honors graduate of Arizona State University, receiving a Bachelor of Science in Nursing, cum laude, in 1987. She is an honors graduate of the University of Nevada, Las Vegas, receiving a Master of Science in Nursing (MSN) degree with an emphasis in nursing education in 2008. She earned post-graduate certifications in School Safety: Emergency Preparedness in Schools in 2010 and Educational Technology in 2011 from Southern Utah University. She maintains professional certifications, including NCSN and PHTLS. Ms. Kalekas is an active member of the National Association of School Nurses and the Nevada State Association of School Nurses.

Linda J. Khalil, MSEd, BSN, RN, SNT

Linda Khalil received her Bachelor of Science in Nursing from the University of Wisconsin-Eau Clair in 1979, and her Master of Science in Education at Nazareth College in Pittsford, NY in 2000. From 1996-2011, she provided school nursing and health education as a NYS certified K-12 School Nurse Teacher in Pittsford, NY. In this role, she provided leadership in coordinated school health, emergency planning, and technology use. In 2011, she assumed directorship of the New York State Center for School Health (NYSCSH), a statewide technical assistance center funded by the New York State Education Department. As Director, Linda reviewed and provided recommendations on school health guidelines; researched and supported best practices in school health; and provided consultation to school health professionals, school districts, and community organizations in promoting quality nursing services and school health education programs. Linda is committed to nurturing the next generation of school nurse leaders. Upon her retirement from NYSCSH in 2021, she established a consulting service where she assists NYS school nurses and school districts optimize school health services in alignment with Federal, State, and local mandates.

Rebecca King, MSN, RN, NCSN-E

Rebecca King is currently the Director of Nursing for the Delaware Department of Public Health. Professionally, Rebecca has 36 years of experience as a registered nurse. For 18 years, as a nationally board-certified school nurse, she worked in schools serving populations from kindergarten through 12th grade. Additionally, she is an adjunct faculty at Immaculata University, Immaculata, PA. She is an active member of the Delaware School Nurses Association (DSNA) and the National Association of School Nurses (NASN), where she has held multiple leadership roles. She is the co-author of the NASN position document on naloxone (2015) and a member of the NASN naloxone workgroup that created the Naloxone Toolkit for School Nurses (2016). She is a 2012 Fellow from the Johnson & Johnson School Health Leadership Institute at Rutgers University Center of Alcohol and Drug Abuse Studies. Rebecca is a board member of the Delaware grassroots organization "atTAcK addiction". Former Delaware Governor Jack Markell appointed her in 2016 to the Delaware Overdose Fatality Review Commission. Rebecca spends time locally and nationally presenting on the topic of substance use disorder and the use of naloxone in communities. Rebecca was the Delaware School Nurse of the Year in 2007. Other awards include the 2014 Caron Medical Professionals Award for the Greater Philadelphia area, the 2008 Delaware Nurses Association Excellence in Nursing Award for Community Nursing, and the 2006 Nemours Vision Award Winner for Excellence in Child Health Promotion and Disease Prevention. Rebecca received two Governor's Volunteer awards (2004 for community education and 2014 with "atTAcK addiction").

Maria D. Krol, DNP, RNC-NIC, ACUE

Dr. Krol is an Associate Professor and Chairperson of the School of Nursing at Southern Connecticut State University. She is the Founder and Past President of the CT Chapter of the National Association of Hispanic Nurses. Dr. Krol has over 30 years of experience working in the areas of maternal newborn health and nursing education. In 2015 Dr. Krol developed a study abroad program to Cusco, Peru. In 2020 she developed the SCSU Summer Nursing Symposium introducing nursing to underrepresented minority students. Her areas of interest in research are diversity, inclusion, and improving the cultural humility of undergraduate nursing students. She has published peer-reviewed articles on student activities to improve cultural humility. Dr. Krol has received recognition for her work in improving access. In 2023 she received the Top Owl Award for her Social justice initiatives. In 2014 CT NAHN recognized her with an Award for Leadership, and in 2012 the Association of Hispanic Healthcare Executives awarded Dr. Krol with the "Hospital Executive of the Year"- Leaders Advancing Health Equity. She is the recipient of the 2019 Nightingale Awards for Excellence in Nursing.

Kimberly Lacey, DNSc, MSN, RN, CNE, CNL

Dr. Kimberly Lacey is an Associate Professor at the Southern Connecticut State University (SCSU) School of Nursing, where she has been faculty since 2004. A registered nurse for 39 years she has degrees from Northeastern University (BSN) and Yale University (MSN Cardiovascular Clinical Specialist and DNSc in Chronic Illness). Dr. Lacey is a Certified Nurse Educator through the National League for Nursing and a Certified Clinical Nurse Leader (American Association of Colleges of Nursing). She has extensive experience in medical-surgical cardiovascular and peripheral vascular diseases, public/community health, home care, ambulatory care, group homes, and school nursing, caring for high-risk and vulnerable individuals, families, and communities. In collaboration with colleagues from the Connecticut Center for Nursing Workforce (formerly the Connecticut League for Nursing), she developed an online introductory course for registered nurses new to home health care, which she taught for several years. Dr. Lacey has held several leadership positions in a variety of clinical settings and served as a consultant for home health care and community organizations. As lead community health faculty at SCSU for several years, Dr. Lacey has been instrumental in expanding clinical experiences aimed at broadening students' learning experiences as well as exposure to diverse and underserved populations in the Greater New Haven area and along the Connecticut shoreline. In addition to her teaching responsibilities, Dr. Lacey has served in a variety of volunteer and appointed leadership positions at SCSU, most recently as the Director of Assessment, Quality Improvement, and Curriculum Development.

Dawn Lambert, PhD, MSN, RN

Dr. Lambert is an Assistant Professor of Nursing in the Wehrheim School of Nursing at Millersville University of Pennsylvania. In addition to her teaching responsibilities, Dr. Lambert is the School Nurse Certification Program Coordinator and serves as Faculty Co-Chair for the university Institutional Review Board. She has over thirty (30) years of nursing experience in a variety of practice areas, including school nursing. Dr. Lambert is passionate about educating school nurses and has devoted much of her career in academia over the past 15 years to advocating for the specialty practice area of school nursing and creating educational programs and courses to support currently practicing and future school nurses. She is an active member of the National Association of School Nurses, the Pennsylvania Association of School Nurses and Practitioners, and Sigma Theta Tau International.

Julia Lecthenberg MSN, RN, NCSN-E

Julia Lecthenberg has over 17 years of experience as a school nurse. She is a member of several professional organizations, including the National Association of School Nurses and Sigma Theta Tau International. She is a nationally certified school nurse and a Johnson and Johnson School Health Leadership Fellow. Julia's school nursing experience includes district-level consultative services in an urban school district, preschool through 12th grade. Julia has authored and contributed to articles regarding school nursing and student health. She is committed to providing quality health services in the academic setting. She actively advocates for safe school nurse practice and quality school health programs at the national and state level.

Suzanne Levasseur, MSN, APRN, CPNP, NCSN

Suzanne Levasseur is currently the Supervisor of Health Services for Westport Public Schools in Westport CT. She also works in private practice as an APRN. Professionally, Suzanne has over 25 years of experience in school health and is the past President of the Association of School Nurses of Connecticut. Suzanne has authored and contributed to articles and publications regarding Pediatric and Perinatal Nursing, school nursing, and student health.

Rosale Lobo, PhD, RN, CNS

Rosale Lobo has been a nursing professional for 37 years. She earned a MSN in 1989 (Hunter College, NY) as a Pediatric Clinical Nurse Specialist. Dr. Lobo worked in multiple pediatric settings (community, home care, and education). She moved into the adult homecare space as a direct care nurse, then an administrator. Lobo Consulting Group, LLC (2004 – 2015), partnered with law firms nationwide in support of injured patients. During this time, Dr. Lobo became a staunch advocate for nurses and their naivete of healthcare policy and the changing scope of documentation and adverse events. This passion allowed Dr. Lobo to write a book and speak nationally (2008 – 2021) to thousands of nurses and healthcare facilities on nursing woes and methods to mitigate unfortunate nursing outcomes. Dr. Lobo is the Nursing Lab Coordinator at Southern Connecticut State University. Her most important accomplishments are being a wife and mother to her three amazing young men.

Marc C. Lombardi, Esquire

Marc Lombardi is chair of Shipman & Goodwin's Privacy, Cybersecurity, and Data Innovation Practice Group. With more than 20 years of privacy law experience, Marc provides clients strategic business advice on all aspects of information policy and data governance, including privacy, cybersecurity, data incident response, and data asset management. Marc regularly advises on compliance with federal and state privacy laws, including the Health Insurance Portability and Accountability Act (HIPAA), the Gramm-Leach-Bliley Act (GLBA), state data privacy and breach notification laws, as well as international data privacy and transfer regulations such as the EU General Data Protection Regulation (GDPR). Prior to joining Shipman, Marc served as Deputy General Counsel of the Yale New Haven Health System, encompassing a broad range of subject matter areas, including HIPAA, data privacy and security, compliance, and corporate transactions. Because Marc began his career as a software architect, he brings a wealth of knowledge of both legal compliance issues along with software, technology, and data processing to his clients in highly regulated industries such as health care, education, insurance, public utilities, and banking.

Kathleen Maguire, DNP, RN

Dr. Kathleen Maguire is currently retired from full-time School Health Services. Dr. Maguire has previously been the District Nurse Coordinator for Wissahickon School District (WSD). Prior to WSD, Dr. Maguire worked for the Philadelphia School District as the Coordinator of Nursing Services and a Certified School Nurse for almost nineteen years. Dr. Maguire also served on the Pennsylvania Governor's Commission on Children and Families. Professionally, Dr. Maguire has over 43 years of registered nurse experience and continues to remain active in the National Association of School Nurses (NASN), the Pennsylvania Association of School Nurses and Practitioners (PASNAP), and the PA League of Nursing. Dr. Maguire has received both the Certified School Nurse of the Year and Administrator of the Year awards from PASNAP. Dr. Maguire was recognized in May 2017 with the Gwynedd Mercy University School of Nursing Excellence Award. Dr. Maguire has presented numerous school and public health conference presentations for NASN, PASNAP, and the American Public Health Association. Currently, Dr. Maguire is an adjunct faculty at Holy Family University School of Nursing and Allied Health Services, teaching Nursing and Health Promotion courses.

Carol Marchant, JD

Carol A. Marchant is an attorney serving as the deputy division counsel for Prince William County Public Schools in Manassas, Virginia. Following a federal clerkship, she began representing school divisions in several states both in private practice and as in-house counsel. She advises school boards and school administrators on legal issues affecting services to students, including parent and student rights issues, student discipline, student services, and special education. Ms. Marchant has also served as an adjunct instructor in the graduate educational leadership programs for the University of Virginia and George Mason University teaching school law to aspiring school administrators. Ms. Marchant received her Juris Doctorate from the University of Wisconsin Law School.

Kelly Martinez, EdD, MSN, APRN, FNP-C

Dr. Kelly Martinez is an Assistant Professor in the Department of Nursing at Southern Connect State University (SCSU). In addition to her teaching responsibilities, Dr. Martinez is a Board-Certified Family Practice Nurse Practitioner (FNP) and maintains a clinical practice as a hospitalist in a community hospital in Middletown, Connecticut, specializing in hospital medicine. Prior to becoming and FNP, Dr. Martinez was a Registered Nurse since 2002 holding nursing positions in medical-surgical units, adult critical care, telemetry, cardiovascular care (open heart units), pediatric intensive care unit, pediatric cardiac catheterization laboratory, and pediatric transport care team. Dr. Martinez sits on several boards and committees at various levels.

Lynne P. Meadows, MSN, RN, FNASN

Lynne P. Meadows, MSN, RN, FNASN has over 36 years of nursing and healthcare experience. Lynne currently serves as the Director of District Health Services for Fulton County School System in Atlanta, GA, where she has served in the role since the program's inception in 2000. She was named the 2011 School Nurse Administrator of the Year by the Georgia Association of School Nurses and named the 2017 Nurse Administrator of the Year by March of Dimes. She has received several awards and recognitions at the local, state, and national levels for contributing to advancing the practice of school nursing. Lynne serves and participates on several healthcare and community boards, also on the local, state, and national levels. She was just recently inducted as a Fellow in the National Association of School Nurses. Lynne's work focuses on supporting pediatric and women's health initiatives, being a working champion for school nurses and school health services, advocating for health equity, diversity, and inclusion, and other efforts aimed at improving the quality of life specifically for those most in need.

Alicia Mezu, MSN/ED, BSN, RN

Alicia Mezu is currently the School Nurse Consultant for the Maryland State Department of Education and the Lead School Health Services Specialist within the Division of Student Support, Academic Enrichment, and Educational Policy. Prior to joining the MSDE, Alicia worked as a school nurse in the Baltimore County Public Schools and is very active with the national and state nurses' professional associations, i.e., the National Association of School Nurses and the Maryland Association of School Health Nurses. Professionally, Alicia has twenty-eight (28) years of experience in the field of nursing. Prior to becoming a registered nurse, Alicia worked as a research biologist and conducted various biological research projects related to HIV/AIDS, breast cancer, pharmacology, and other chronic disease studies.

Lisa Minor, EdD, MSN, RN, CNE

Dr. Lisa Minor currently resides in Mechanicsville, Virginia, which is just outside of Richmond and has been a registered nurse for a little over 35 years. She has been married for 34 years to her husband David and has two grown married children. Her son Chris is married to his wife, Nicole, and her daughter Sloan is married to her husband, Kalub. Dr. Minor is currently a tenured Associate Professor in the Department of Nursing at Longwood University, where she teaches pharmacology and maternal–newborn nursing while providing clinical assistance in the fields of community health and psychiatric nursing. In an effort to keep up her clinical skills, she still works PRN at the bedside on the Mother-Baby unit in a hospital based in Richmond. She graduated from Radford University in 1987 with a Bachelor of Science in Nursing, a Master of Science in Nursing Education in 2007 from Walden University, and her Doctorate in Higher Education and Adult Learning in 2012, also from Walden University. Dr. Minor has held numerous positions in nursing, including orthopedics, OB, pediatrics, community health, and school nursing. She entered school nursing in 1999 as a school nurse in an elementary school until 2006. In 2006 she accepted the position as the Health Services Coordinator for school nursing until 2013, at which time she moved to her current position at Longwood University. During her time with Hanover County and while at Longwood, she has given numerous presentations in school nursing, community health, coordinated school health, supervising and evaluating school nurses. She also assisted the School Nurse Institute Partnership (SNIP) in the development of a school nurse evaluation tool. Her doctoral dissertation revolved around school nursing, coordinated school health, and the role of the school nurse and school nurse supervisor in enhancing the academic success of students in the school setting.

Brenna L. Morse, PhD, FNP-BC, NCSN, CNE, PMGT-BC, FNASN, FAAN

Dr. Morse is board-certified as a family nurse practitioner, nationally certified school nurse, nurse educator, pain management nurse, and is a fellow in the National Academy of School Nursing. She is currently a full-time nurse academic with an appointment as an associate professor in the Massachusetts General Hospital Institute of Health Professions and remains in clinical practice as a nurse practitioner at Boston Children's Hospital. Previous professional experiences include appointment as an associate professor with tenure at the University of Massachusetts Lowell and work as a registered nurse across community settings with children and families. She is also the past president and member of the board of directors for the National Board for Certification of School Nurses and a member of the Accreditation Board for Specialty Nursing Certification board of directors.

Ann O. Nichols, MSN, RN, FNASN

Ann Nichols is an Independent Consultant in School Nursing and School Health. Her current projects support NASN grants as the Subject Matter Expert for the PCORI Dissemination Initiative and the NASN Consultant for the 'Every Student Counts' data initiative. She is also the Program Manager for North Carolina DHHS ARPA School Health Team Workforce grant. Ann served as the North Carolina State School Health Nurse Consultant until 2021. She completed her undergraduate degree in nursing at Duke University and her MSN at the University of Cincinnati in Family and Child Health with a dual minor in Nursing Education and Nursing Administration. Ann has contributed to the profession through a 40+ year career in school nursing, child health clinical practice, public health nursing, and undergraduate nursing education and has published research articles and other resources for school nurses. Her awards include NASSNC's Outstanding State Consultant of the year, NCAPHNA Distinguished Public Health Nurse, 2020 Great 100 Nurse, The NC Order of the Long Leaf Pine, and she is a 2022 Fellow of the National Academy of School Nursing. Ann is proud to have mentored, precepted and taught many nurses who practice today in a profession that serves the greater good.

Lynette Ondeck, MEd, BSN, RN, NCSN

Lynnette Ondeck is currently a School Nurse Corps Administrator for the Northwest Educational Service District (NWESD). Prior to joining the NWESD, Lynnette worked as the district nurse for the Nooksack Valley School District. She has been active in her professional organization, the School Nurse Organization of Washington (SNOW) and the National Association of School Nurse (NASN). Lynnette has 33 years of school nursing experience and is the immediate past Vice President of NASN. Lynnette serves on several state and regional boards and is the current chair of the North Sound Oral Health Local Impact Network. She is passionate about school nursing and advocates to promote this specialty of nursing practice.

William (Bill) Patterson Jr., MPA, RN

Bill Patterson is currently a School Nurse Consultant for the State of Hawaii, Department of Education (HIDOE). Prior to joining the HIDOE, Bill worked for the State of Hawaii Department of Health as the Supervisor of the Children with Special Health Needs Program and as a field Public Health Nurse. Through Public Health Nursing, Bill first encountered school health and school nursing, which became his "cause" or passion. Professionally, Bill has over twenty-five (25) years of experience in the medical and nursing fields and is an active member of both the National Association of School Nurses (NASN) and the National Association of State School Nurse Consultants (NASSNC) - currently serving on the Board of Directors as Treasurer.

Krista M. Pendergast, EdD, RN, CNE

Dr. Prendergast is an assistant professor of nursing at Southern Connecticut State University, New Haven, CT. She is certified by the National League for Nursing as a Certified Nurse Educator. Practice experience includes medical-surgical nursing, critical care, and long-term care-assisted living. Dr. Prendergast has ten years of full-time faculty experience in the Connecticut State Colleges and Universities system. Teaching interests include the topic of medical surgical nursing and the application of this knowledge in the classroom, clinical, and simulation settings. Other interests include the use of active learning strategies such as simulation and case studies to assist students with the synthesis and application of their learning. Dr. Prendergast has recently provided presentations and poster presentations on the effectiveness of debriefing strategies used in simulation.

Frances Penny, PhD, RN, MPH, MSN, IBCLC, CNL

Dr. Penny is an Associate Professor of Nursing at Southern Connecticut State University (SCSU) in New Haven, CT, where she is the Director of the Doctorate in Education in Nursing Education. She is also an Adjunct Assistant Professor at Georgetown University. She is teaching graduate and undergraduate students and a range of courses, including evidence-based practice, maternal child health, public health, leadership, nursing theory, and nursing interventions. In addition, she has been a practicing nurse for over 30 years in Pediatrics and Maternal and Child Health, as well as an International Board-Certified Lactation Consultant (IBCLC). She has published peer-reviewed research in lactation and maternal and child Health. Her areas of practice as a pediatric nurse include cardiology, transplant, trauma, neurology, oncology and endocrinology, pediatric intensive care, neonatal intensive care, home health, and school health. She also holds a master's in public health. She has worked in healthcare consulting in Washington, D.C., as well as a director of public health programs and a research nurse at multiple academic institutions.

Katherine J. Pohlman, MS, JD, Nurse Attorney

Katherine J. Pohlman has served as legal counsel to the National Association of School Nurses since 1986. She has practiced healthcare law, medical malpractice defense litigation, and professional licensure defense and served as a risk manager and in-house counsel at healthcare and insurance companies. Over the years, Katherine also served in a variety of nursing positions, including clinical, management, and faculty. As a nurse attorney, coach, and consultant, Katherine's passion is advocating for, counseling, and coaching healthcare providers regarding their legal rights, practice, and professional & personal well-being. She's an integrative practitioner who works within a holistic perspective, taking into consideration body, mind, and spirit. Find more at katherinejpohlman.com

Emily Poland, MPH, RN, NCSN

Emily Poland is currently the School Nurse Consultant for the Maine Department of Education and leader of the Coordinated School Health Team within the Office of School and Student Supports. Prior to joining the MDOE, Emily worked as a school nurse in the Maine public school system and was active with her professional organization, the Maine Association of School Nurses. Professionally, Emily has twenty-four (24) years of experience in the nursing field and is the past president of the National Association of State School Nurse Consultants (NASSNC). She was elected and serves her community on her local school board. In addition to her passion for school health and education, she is a supporter of visual and performing arts opportunities for youth.

Suzanne Putman, MEd, BSN, RN

Suzanne Putman is a Nurse Consultant-Special Education in Michigan. She earned her Bachelor of Science degree in nursing from Oakland University and her Master of Education specializing in school nursing from Cambridge College. She has over 30 years of maternal-child nursing experience, including 20 years of experience as a school nurse consultant for students with moderate-severe cognitive and physical impairments. Additionally, Suzanne acts as Clinical Faculty for Oakland University in the community setting.

Jacquelyn M. Buige Raco, MSN, MEd, CSN, CSSHS

Jacquelyn M. Buige Raco has been a practicing registered nurse for 30 years and certified school nurse for 17 years. She has experience as a pediatric bone marrow transplant nurse, certified school nurse, district nurse supervisor, university lecturer, university school health education program director, and conference speaker. She co-serves as the Pennsylvania School Nurses and Practitioners (PASNAP) board's Southwest region representative. She has been honored as PASNAP's 2010 Southeast Region School Nurse of the Year, PASNAP's 2021 Southeast Region School Nurse Administrator of the Year, PASNAP Conference 2022 Keynote Speaker, and the National Association of School Nurses (NASN) 2022 Pennsylvania School Nurse Administrator of the Year. Her passion for nursing and education fuels her to establish improved statewide school nurse education programming and professional development opportunities.

Kathy L. Reiner, MPH, BSN, RN

Kathy Reiner is currently a School Nurse Consultant and member of the Health Services Management Team for the Aurora Public School District in Aurora, CO. Previously, she worked in the public health arena in the study of communicable diseases and injury epidemiology. In that role, Ms. Reiner authored and contributed to articles regarding head injury and infectious diseases. Professionally, Ms. Reiner has 20 years' experience as a school nurse and 10 years as a public health researcher. She is currently the Colorado Director to the National Association of School Nurses and has been actively involved in her State School Nurse organization, serving on the Executive Board and as the Legislative chair for 2010-15.

Cheryl Resha, EdD, MSN, RN, FNASN, FAAN

Dr. Cheryl Resha, Professor Emerita and former Department Chair, retired from Southern Connecticut State University (SCSU) in 2021. Dr. Resha began her career in pediatric nursing at the Children's Hospital of Philadelphia and eventually transitioned to school nursing, first at the local level and then at the Connecticut State Department of Education as a Bureau Manager and state school nurse consultant. Dr. Resha has provided leadership and advocacy for school nurses and safe school nursing practice at the local, state, and national levels. She was inducted as a Fellow in the National Academy of School Nursing in June 2012. Dr. Resha has co-edited, authored, and contributed to articles and publications regarding school nursing, such as the *School Nursing: Scope and Standards of Professional Practice (2nd, 3rd, and 4th eds.)*, the *School Nurse Resource Manual*, and the *Legal Resource for School Health Services*. In October 2022, Dr. Resha was inducted as a Fellow in the American Academy of Nursing.

Jeannie Rodriguez, PhD, RN, C-PNP/PC

Dr. Rodriguez is an Associate Professor at the Emory University Nell Hodgson Woodruff School of Nursing and Specialty Director of the Pediatric Primary Care Nurse Practitioner Program. Dr. Rodriguez is an experienced clinician-scientist who has been a pediatric nurse for almost 30 years and a pediatric nurse practitioner for over 20 years. Her current clinical practice focuses on school-based healthcare. Dr. Rodriguez has worked to establish relationships with several local schools and school systems in Georgia to meet critical healthcare needs on-site. She is committed to community-based care that meets children and their families where they live, work, and play.

LEGAL RESOURCE FOR SCHOOL HEALTH SERVICES

Joanne F. Roy, PhD, MSN, RN

Dr. Joanne F. Roy is an Associate Professor of Nursing at Southern Connecticut State University (SCSU), New Haven, CT. She has earned Clinical Nurse Leader (CNL) designation through the Commission on Nursing Certification of the American Association of Colleges of Nursing. Dr. Roy has worked as a professional nurse for over 35 years in a variety of capacities within the practice and academic settings. Presently, in addition to her teaching responsibilities within the undergraduate, graduate, and doctoral programs of nursing at SCSU, Dr. Roy is also the Director of the RN to BSN program at the university. Prior to joining the faculty at SCSU, Dr. Roy held regional leadership roles within nursing education and professional development within local and regional healthcare systems. Dr. Roy has a dedicated commitment to advancing the ongoing professional development and life-long learning of nurse leaders, front-line nurses and the interprofessional team through strong and collaborative academic practice partnerships.

Brooke E.D. Say, Esquire

Ms. Say is the Chair of Stock & Leader's School Law Group and represents school districts in Central Pennsylvania. In her school practice, she has developed expertise in advising on special education, disability, discipline, school health, investigatory, and civil rights matters. She counsels her clients through internal compliance audits and defends them in administrative hearings and federal litigation. In more recent years, she has served as an expert witness in special education matters and a court-appointed certified mediator in the U.S. District Court for the Middle District of Pennsylvania. She regularly presents for the PA Exceptional Children's Conference (ECC), Lehigh University, Pennsylvania School Board Association, and Pennsylvania Bar Institute workshops and across the United States for state-based conferences. In 2012 and for eight consecutive years, Attorney Say was named to the Pennsylvania Rising Stars list as one of the top up-and-coming attorneys. Additionally, she was the recipient of the Legal Intelligencer, Lawyers on the Fast Track in 2015. In 2020, she was awarded the Central Pennsylvania Business Journal's Women of Influence award. Attorney Say is an alum of Messiah University and the Dickinson School of Law of the Pennsylvania State University.

Wendy L. Sellers, RN, MA

Wendy L. Sellers, RN, MA, CSE, FASHA has been a passionate advocate for student health for more than 35 years. She is a registered nurse with a master's degree in Family and Consumer Sciences. As the founder and president of Health 4 Hire, Inc./Puberty: The Wonder Years, Ms. Sellers provides a variety of consulting services, including training, public speaking, and writing. Wendy has taught thousands of educators how to teach sex education and presents sessions on effective sex education at state and national conferences. Wendy advocates for skills-based, comprehensive sex education that starts early, involves parents, and meets students' needs. Wendy is known nationally for creating *Puberty: The Wonder Years* and co-authoring the *Michigan Model for Health*. She also reviews manuscripts for the *American Journal of Sexuality Education*. Wendy was named 2014 National Health Coordinator of the Year by the American School Health Association (ASHA). This award is bestowed for exceptional service in school health coordination. Wendy served on the ASHA Board of Directors and chaired the Advocacy and Coalitions Committee during 2017-18. ASHA named her a fellow in 2019. The Society of State Leaders of Health and Physical Education honored Wendy with the 2021 Russ Henke Service Award, and Wendy currently serves on their Board of Directors. Ms. Sellers completed the Sexual Health Certificate Program at the University of Michigan and is an AASECT Certified Sexuality Educator. Wendy is a graduate of the Goldman Sachs 10,000 Small Businesses program.

Robin Adair Shannon, DNP, RN, NCSN, FNASN

Dr. Robin Adair Shannon is a Clinical Associate Professor at the University of Illinois Chicago College of Nursing. She has worked as a school nurse in diverse urban and suburban school districts across all grade levels. Robin authored NASN's *Model for Developing School Nursing Evidence-based Clinical Guidelines,* among other publications. She is also privileged to be a co-editor of the National Association of School Nurses' *School Nursing: A Comprehensive Textbook, 3rd ed.* (2019). Robin has served on the National Board for Certification of School Nurses and is a Fellow of the National Academy of School Nurses.

Vicki L. Taliaferro, BSN, RN, NCSN-E

Vicki L. Taliaferro is a school nurse consultant and editor of *School Nurse Digest* (a weekly newsletter for school nurses) and *Administrator's Risk Alert* (a bi-monthly newsletter for school nurses, administrators, and attorneys). She was the lead editor for the *School Nurse Resource Manual* - 2010, 2013, 2016, and 2020. She has authored articles, school nurse text chapters, position papers, and state and local guidelines on school health topics and initiatives. She was a consultant to the National Association of School Nurses and was their coordinator of professional practice documents. As a State School Nurse Consultant with the Maryland State Department of Education for ten years, she provided technical advice to state school nursing leadership, developed state guidelines & policies, and assisted with the development of Board of Nursing curriculums for delegation and medication administration. She served on numerous commissions and coordinated an annual School Health Interdisciplinary Program – a multi-disciplinary professional development weeklong training for school staff. Additionally, she is a member of the National Assn. of State School Nurse Consultants, having served as president and in other officer positions.

Rachel Torres, DNP, RN, PHNA-BC

Rachel J. Torres is a nationally certified advanced public health nurse, and her areas of expertise include health policy, maternal-child health, leadership, and social justice. Dr. Torres is currently an Assistant Professor for California State University East Bay nursing program and a public school nurse administrator. She has had a very interesting career working in so many different areas of nursing at the bedside, in the community, as a program manager, and as an educator. Dr. Torres was also a nurse in the U.S. Army Reserves where she provided public health nursing and policy expertise in civil-military affairs.

Antoinette Towle, EdD, PNP-BC, SNP-BC

Dr. Towle is an Associate Professor at Southern Connecticut State University, New Haven, CT, USA. She is an American Nurse Credentialing Center (ANCC) Board Certified Advanced Practiced Registered Nurse (APRN) in Pediatric and School Health specialty areas. Dr. Towle has worked as a professional nurse for over 30 years, in a variety of capacities (Administrator, Manager, Director, Case Worker, APRN, RN, and Educator) and within a wide variety of healthcare settings (schools, residential settings for children and the elderly, veterans' hospitals, Insurance companies, federal and privately funded medical offices and hospitals, and community healthcare agencies). Presently, teaching full-time to graduate and undergraduate nursing students focus on nursing leadership, understanding, respecting, and appreciating cultural diversity, health promotion, and integrating these key components into clinical practice. Dr. Towle is the first to create and continues to lead a nursing study abroad program for students at the University to Jamaica, China, and Armenia.

Christopher Tracy, Esquire

Christopher Tracey is a member of Shipman & Goodwin's School Law Practice Group. He advises schools and public school districts in diverse areas of school law, with particular experience in special education, education reform, and budgetary and finance matters. Chris has expertise in the area of contracting. His work includes the development of business, enrollment, admissions, food service, and transportation contracts. Chris assists districts who find themselves navigating the fast-paced and heavily regulated digital landscape, analyzing and drafting contracts with educational software and app developers that comply with federal law and Connecticut's nuanced Student Data Privacy laws. Chris also maintains a thriving special education practice, advising a variety of schools and school districts in all areas of legal compliance related to the education of students with disabilities, including representation in dispute resolution activities and due process proceedings. Prior to practicing law, Chris worked as an educational policy researcher at Harvard University and several other prominent research organizations, and he taught at an alternative high school for at-risk Yup'ik youth in Southwestern Alaska.

Sharonlee Trefry, MSN, RN, NCSN, FNASN

Sharonlee Trefry is a retired State School Nurse Consultant for nine years after 18 years as a school nurse in public and private schools. Community health is a lifelong passion. She is a state and national leader and is active in the National Association of State School Nurse Consultants. Sharonlee is a part-time professional and community volunteer.

Jo Volkening, MSEd, BSN, RN, PEL/IL-CSN, NCSN

Jo Volkening is a state and national board-certified school nurse currently with Naperville 203 school district in Illinois. She belongs to the National Association of School Nurses and the Illinois Association of School Nurses. Over the past several years, as IASN's Member Inquiry Specialist, she has provided initial assistance and support for inquiries from school nurses and administrators throughout the state of Illinois. Ms. Volkening has been employed in healthcare for over 30 years, initially as a paramedic and instructor for EMTs. She is presently an instructor and course coordinator for the Illinois EMS for Children program *School Nurse Emergency Care Course.* This three-day course is presented throughout the state and teaches school nurses the essential skills and knowledge base to treat pediatric emergencies within the school environment. Ms. Volkening regularly provides subject matter expertise for review and revision of the SNEC course curriculum and manual, now in its seventh edition. In 2021, she collaborated in the development of a narrated online version of the SNEC course that was implemented to provide a self-study option.

Terry Woody, BSN, RN, NCSN

Terry Woody has been a registered nurse for over 40 years. Many of those years were spent working in acute care. She has spent the last 18 years in school health. Although she has enjoyed every nursing job she has held, school health is her first love. She first worked as a middle school and elementary school nurse and for the past 10 years as the School Health Coordinator overseeing 24 schools in Hanover County, Virginia. She received her bachelor's degree in nursing from Virginia Commonwealth University. She completed a specialty program at VCU, School Nurses as Professional Partners: Supporting Educational Outcomes for Students with Low-Incidence Disabilities (SNAPP). She is a member of the Sigma Theta Tau International Honor Society of Nursing and the National Association of School Nurses. She previously served on the Executive Board of the Virginia Association of School Nurses as a District Director and Chairman of the Legislative Committee.

Gwen J. Zittoun, Esquire

A member of Shipman's robust School Law Practice Group, Gwen Zittoun represents the firm's 100+ boards of education and public school districts in legal matters related to student data privacy and confidentiality, contracts and board policies, Title IX compliance, special education, and general education matters. She frequently supports school districts in special education mediations, due process hearings, and federal court actions and provides legal counsel on a variety of special education issues. She also supports schools in Office for Civil Rights complaints and Title IX investigations. Gwen's commitment to education is evidenced by her decade-long role as an Adjunct Professor of the University of Connecticut's Neag School of Education, where she educated students on general and special education law.

REVIEWERS

Martha D. Bergren, PhD, RN, NCSN, PHNA-BC, FNASN, FASHA, FAAN
Executive Editor, The Journal of School Nursing
Clinical Professor Emerita, University of Illinois-Chicago College of Nursing
Illinois

Jane Boyd, MSN, RN, NCSN
Retired State School Nurse Consultant, Delaware
National Association of State School Nurse Consultants, Technology Member
Delaware

Edie Brous, MS, MPH, BSN, JD, RN, FAAN
Nurse Attorney
Edith Brous, Esq., PC
New York, New Jersey, and Pennsylvania

Joan Cagginello, MS, BSN, RN
Clinical Faculty, Quinnipiac University, School of Nursing
Connecticut

Sheila Caldwell, BSN, RN, CSN, FNASN
New Jersey School Nurse
NEA ESPQ SISP Fellow
New Jersey

Annie Carver, Esq.
Staff Attorney
Project HEAL (Health, Education, Advocacy, and Law) at Kennedy Krieger Institute
Maryland

Pamela Chambers, DNP, EJD, MSN, CRNA, FAANA
Assistant Professor, Nurse Anesthesia Program
College of Nursing
Rosalind Franklin University of Medicine and Science
Illinois

Tyler Cochran, JD, BA
Legal Advocate
Project HEAL (Health, Education, Advocacy, and Law) at Kennedy Krieger Institute
Maryland

Robin Cogan, MEd, RN, NCSN, FNASN, FAAN
The Relentless School Nurse
New Jersey

Ann Connelly, MSN, RN, LSN, NCSN
Supervisor, School Nursing and Early Childhood Health Programs
Ohio Department of Health
Ohio

Leigh E. Dalton, Esquire, PhD
School Law Attorney
Stock and Leader, Attorneys at Law
Pennsylvania

Máireád Day Lopes, MSN, RN, NCSN
Director, School-Based Health Center Program
Massachusetts Department of Public Health
Massachusetts

Stephanie G. Denya, MPH, RN, NCSN
Associate Director of Health & Human Services
Meriden Department of Health & Human Services
Connecticut

Carolyn Dolan, JD, MSN, FNP-BC, PPCNP-BC, SANE-A, SANE-P, PI HRSA-SANE/ANE Grant
Professor
University of South Alabama Baldwin Campus
Alabama

Carey R. Driscoll, CPNP, APRN, CDE
Pediatric Nurse Practitioner
Diabetes and Endocrinology
Connecticut Children's Medical Center
Connecticut

Nancy Dube, MPH, BSed, RN
School Nurse Consultant, Retired
Maine

Joan Edelstein, DrPH, MSN, RN
School Nurse Educator; School Health Policy
Consultant
School Nurse Credential Program, California State
University, Sacramento
California

Bonnie J. Edmondson, EdD, MS
Professor Emerita
School Health Education
Southern Connecticut State University

Patricia Endsley MSN, PhD, RN, NCSN
Wells High School Nurse
Past President, Maine Association of School
Nurses (2018-2020)
Program Chair, M.Ed. School Nurse Education,
Cambridge College (Boston, MA)
Maine

Maureen Fearon, MSN, APRN, FNP-BC
Pediatric Endocrinology and Diabetes
Connecticut Children's Medical Center
Connecticut

Marie Foley, PhD, RN
Dean and Professor
College of Nursing
Seton Hall University
New Jersey

Mary Ann Gapinski, MSN, RN, NCSN-E
Director of School Health Services (Retired)
MA Department of Public Health
Massachusetts

Aimee Greer, Esquire
Aimee Greer, RN, BSN, Esq.
The Law Office of Aimee Greer, Esq.
New York

Marlene S. Garvis, JD, MSN, BSN, BA
Marlene S. Garvis, LLC
Minnesota

Timothy E. Gilsbach, Esquire, JD, BA
Fox Rothschild LLP
Pennsylvania

Lorali Gray, MEd, BSN, RN, NCSN-E
School Nurse Organization of Washington Board
of Directors
Johnson & Johnson School Health Leadership
Fellow
Washington

Denise Herrmann DNP RN CPNP FNASN
Child Family Health / Maternal Child Health
School Health Coordinator
Minnesota

Annie Hetzel, MSN, RN, NCSN
School Health Services Consultant
Student Support
Office of Superintendent of Public Instruction
(OSPI)
Washington

Janis Hogan BUS, RN, NCSN
NASN Advisory Board member
Leadership Exchange for Adolescent Health
Programs (LEAHP)
Maine

Karen Hollowood, MSEd, BSN, RN
State School Nurse Consultant
Supervisor of Education Programs
Statewide Foster Care Point of Contact
Office of Student Support Services
New York State Education Department
New York

Evilia A Jankowski, MSA, BSN, RN, NCSN
State School Nurse Consultant
Michigan Department of Health and Human
Services
Michigan Department of Education
Michigan

Alison Jochen Ed.D, RN, CSN, M.Ed.
Assistant Teaching Professor
Ross and Carol Nese College of Nursing
The Pennsylvania State University
Pennsylvania

Lisa Kern MSN, RN, NCSN
Director Florida Association of School Nurses
Florida

Linda J. Khalil, MSEd, BSN, RN, SNT
School Health Consultant | Khalil Consulting LLC
NYS Certified Women-Owned Business Enterprise
(M/WBE)
New York

Rebecca King, MSN, RN, NCSN
Retired Nursing Director, Delaware Division of
Public Health (10/19)
Board President, KIDS COUNT Delaware
Board Member, Mom's House of Wilmington
Education and Prevention Committee Co-Chair, DE
Behavioral Health Consortium
Founding Board of Directors "atTAcK addiction"
Delaware

Justin Knight, Attorney
Perry, Guthery, Haase & Gessford, P.C., L.L.O.
Nebraska

Donna Kosiorowski, MS, RN, NCSN-E
School Health Consultant
Connecticut

**Patricia Krin, MSN, MS, RN, FNP-BC- Ret.,
NCSN-E, FNASN**
School Health Consultant
Connecticut

Dawn Lambert, PhD, RN
Assistant Professor and School Nurse Program
Coordinator
Wehrheim School of Nursing
Millersville University of Pennsylvania
Pennsylvania

Mallory Legg, Esq.
Director
Project HEAL (Health, Education, Advocacy, and
Law) at Kennedy Krieger Institute
Maryland

Suzanne Levasseur, MSN, APRN, CPNP
Supervisor of Health Services
Westport Public Schools
Connecticut

Phyllis Lewis, MSN, BSN, RN, FNP, FCN, FASHA
Retired School Nurse Consultant and School Board member
Indiana

Kerri McGowan Lowrey, J.D., M.P.H.
Deputy Director and Director for Grants & Research
The Network for Public Health Law – Eastern Region Office
University of Maryland Francis King Carey School of Law
Maryland

Ruth Ellen Luehr, DNP, RN, Licensed School Nurse, PHN, NCSN, FNASN
Consultant - Nursing Services in the School and Community
Minnesota

Alicia Mezu, MSN/Ed, BSN, BS, RN
Lead Health Services Specialist
Maryland State Department of Education
Maryland

Judith Morgitan, MEd, BSN, RN, CSN
Health Services Department Chair
Perkiomen Valley School District
Pennsylvania

Brenna Morse, PhD, FNP-BC, NCSN, CNE, PMGT-BC, FNASN, FAAN
Associate Professor, Nursing
Massachusetts General Hospital Institute of Health Professions
Massachusetts

Luanne Mottey
Law trainee
Project HEAL (Health, Education, Advocacy, and Law) at Kennedy Krieger Institute
Maryland

Monica Murphy
Managing Attorney
Disability Rights Wisconsin (retired)
Wisconsin

Barbara Obst, MSEd, BSN, RN, NCSN
Nurse Coordinator of Kennedy Krieger Therapeutic Foster Care
Kennedy Krieger Institute
Maryland

Bill Patterson, MPA, RN
School Nurse Consultant
Office of Student Support Services
Medicaid Reimbursement Section
State of Hawaii, Department of Education
Hawaii

Mandy Pennington, MSN, RN
Supervisor, School Health
Red Clay Schools
Delaware

Emily Poland, MPH, RN, NCSN
School Nurse Consultant
Coordinated School Health
Office of School and Student Supports
Maine Department of Education
Maine

Karen Robitaille, MBA, MSN, RN, NCSN
Director, School Health Services
Bureau of Community Health and Prevention
Massachusetts Department of Public Health
Massachusetts

LEGAL RESOURCE FOR SCHOOL HEALTH SERVICES

Herbert Z. Rosen, Esquire
Berchem Moses PC
Connecticut

Brooke E.D. Say, Esquire
School Law Attorney
Stock and Leader, Attorneys at Law
Pennsylvania

Brad Schimel, BA, JD
Prior State Attorney General
Circuit Court Judge
Wisconsin

Sally Schoessler, MSEd, BSN, RN, AE-C
School Health Consultant & Project Manager
Pennsylvania

Jennifer Sherman, JD
Legal Advocacy Fellow
American Diabetes Association
Washington, D.C.

Colleen Schultz, MEd, CSN RN
Director, Division of School Health
Pennsylvania Department of Health
 Bureau of Community Health Systems
Pennsylvania

Gail Trano, BSN, RN, CSN
SCHOOL HEALTH HELP Consulting
School Nurse/ Health Educator Pre-K - 12
PPSN Discussion List Monitor
NYS Epinephrine Resource Nurse
New York

Sharonlee Trefry, MSN, RN, NCSN, FNASN
Retired School Nurse Consultant
Vermont

H. Estelle S. Watts, DNP, RN, NCSN
State School Nurse Consultant
Office of Healthy Schools
Mississippi Department of Education
Mississippi

Nick Webb, RN, DNP, ESQ
Nurse Attorney
Law Office of Nicholas R. Webb
California

Lee Wells, J.D., PhD, CDBC, CPDT-KA, CADT
Certified Animal Behavior Consultant
California

Jennifer Wessel, JD, MPH
Senior Policy Analyst/ Data Privacy Officer
Arkansas Center for Health Improvement
Arkansas

Anita Wheeler, MSN, RN
State School Nurse Consultant-Retired
Texas

Wendy A. Williams, BSN, RN, NCSN
State School Nurse Consultant
School Nursing/Health Services Program & Office
of School Health and Safety
Women, Children, and Family Health
 Division of Public Health, Department of Health
Alaska

J. Craig Wilson, JD, MPA
Director of Health Policy
Arkansas Center for Health Improvement
Arkansas

LEGAL RESOURCE FOR SCHOOL HEALTH SERVICES

Louise Wilson, MS, BSN, RN, Licensed School Nurse, NCSN
School Nursing and Health Services Consultant
WI Department of Public Instruction
Wisconsin

Susan Zacharski, MEd, BSN, RN, FNASN
School Nurse Consultant
Michigan

TABLE OF CONTENTS

Nursing Coordination

School Staff Interactions

Beyond the Public School Walls

TABLE OF CONTENTS by subject

SCHOOL NURSE PRACTICE ISSUES

The following section of the book is dedicated to discussing the legal and ethical underpinnings of school nurse practice. Some topics included are Licensure, Malpractice, Scope and Standards of Practice, Safe School Nurse Staffing, and Documentation. This section outlines nursing practice in the unique setting of pre-K to 12 schools. Often school nurses are independent practitioners in this non-traditional health arena. These chapters guide a school nurse's understanding of how the sub-specialty of school nursing is aligned with a more traditional nursing role and how to address the unique needs of school nursing practice.

Chapter 1

PROFESSIONAL LICENSURE AND PRACTICE IN THE SCHOOL SETTING

Edith Brous, MS, MPH, JD, RN, FAAN

Licensure is the process by which boards of nursing grant permission to an individual to engage in nursing practice after determining that the applicant has attained the competency necessary to perform a unique scope of practice. Licensure is necessary when regulated activities are complex and require specialized knowledge, skill, and independent decision-making. The licensure process determines if the applicant has the necessary skills to safely perform a specified scope of practice by predetermining the criteria needed and evaluating licensure applicants to determine if they meet the criteria (National Council of State Boards of Nursing [NCSBN], 2023a).

DESCRIPTION OF ISSUE

School nurses face unique challenges because they are employed by academics, administrators, or educators who commonly do not appreciate professional licensure regulations or scope of practice restrictions. Unlike nurses who work in most other settings, school nurses are likely to report to a person who is not another nurse, so they often do not understand clinical standards of care or legal aspects of nursing practice. For this reason, it is essential that school nurses be fully familiar with the Nurse Practice Act (NPA) or other nursing regulations in the states in which they practice and take adequate steps to protect their licenses.

Many nurses have misinformation about licensure or the steps they should take to safeguard their livelihoods. School nurses are particularly vulnerable to this knowledge deficit because they work in isolation and are less likely to interact continuously with other nurses. It is never an effective defense to argue that you did not understand that your actions were considered unethical or illegal, or that they constituted professional misconduct (i.e., ignorance of the law is never a defense). Nursing boards issue licenses and renewal certificates with the expectation that nurses have familiarized themselves with the state's standards of professional conduct and hold them accountable for violations.

BACKGROUND

Nurses are more likely to be disciplined by the board of nursing than they are to be sued for malpractice. Healthcare professionals are reported to the National Practitioner Data Bank (NPDB) – an electronic repository that tracks information on medical malpractice payments and adverse actions such as licensure discipline or the loss of privileges or credentials (US Department of Health and Human Services [USDHHS], 2023). In 2021, a total of 12,200 registered nurses were reported to the NPDB. Of those, only 299 were reported for medical malpractice payments. The remaining 12,499 were reported for adverse actions. Contrast this with physicians reported to the NPDB during the same time period. Of the 11,537 physicians reported to the NPDB, 5,885 were reported for malpractice payments and only 5,652 for adverse actions (USDHHS, 2023). Nurses Service Organization data from 2019 indicated that nurses were 62 times more likely to be involved in an adverse licensing action than a medical malpractice payment (NSO, 2020). Disciplinary action on a license can be more damaging to a career than a lawsuit because it can separate a nurse from practice, result in collateral consequences, or even permanently terminate one's livelihood and permission to hold oneself out as a nurse.

It is important to understand how nursing regulation works and separate common misperceptions from reality regarding licensure:

Common Misperceptions

Someone else is "working under my license" or "working on my license."

Licenses are not transferable. The state issues a professional nursing license to one person, and only that person is authorized to practice using that license. School nurses might supervise others, but the people they supervise are not working under or on the school nurse's license. School nurses might delegate to others, but the people to whom they delegate are not working under or on the school nurse's license. Only the school nurse is working on the school nurse's license. The school nurse is responsible for what and to whom he or she delegates but is not responsible for anyone else's practice but their own.

A state cannot discipline my license if I don't renew it.

In some states, a license, once issued, is good for the lifetime of the licensee. It is accompanied by a registration certificate which must be renewed periodically to continue in practice. It is the registration certificate that lapses or expires, but the license itself remains valid unless it is annulled, surrendered, or revoked. Some states indefinitely retain jurisdiction over the licensee, regardless of the registration status, meaning the state can continue to discipline a license even if the nurse has not renewed the registration. In other states, the license itself expires, ending the state's jurisdiction over the nurse who is no longer a licensee.

I am covered to do something as long as a doctor, or my supervisor orders me to do it.

Nurses are responsible for adhering to their legal scope of practice and standards of care. Physicians cannot override the NPA and order a nurse to exceed the lawful scope of practice. Principals or school administrators cannot override state regulations and order a school nurse to violate the law. They also cannot mandate that nurses violate acceptable standards of nursing care or ethical codes of conduct.

School nurses who violate state practice acts or nursing standards cannot defend themselves to the nursing board by saying the healthcare provider ordered it or the school told them to do so. Nurses are held responsible for adhering to legal and ethical requirements as stated by the National Council of State Boards of Nursing, "[T]he responsibilities of a licensed nurse include knowledge of, and adherence to, the laws and rules which govern nursing as outlines in the nurse practice act and regulations" (NCSBN, 2023b).

IMPLICATIONS FOR SCHOOL NURSE PRACTICE

Each state has its own set of laws and regulations. Many states incorporate nursing regulations under a single statute called the NPA. Other states imbed nursing law in health law, business law, or other regulatory schemes. This chapter refers to nursing law as the NPA. The board of nursing is responsible for enforcing the NPA by investigating and disciplining nurses who violate the law. It is important to know not only what the law says but how the nursing board interprets that law. For instance, the NPA might specifically state that a nurse must possess moral character. It is important to know that the board of nursing considers a criminal conviction to be a reflection of a nurse not meeting that moral character requirement. The following are some specific implications for school nurses based on laws and BON interpretations.

Scope of Practice and Delegation

The legal definition of nursing practice varies considerably from state to state. The school nurse must know what is within the scope of practice not only for their own role but also for anyone to whom they delegate. What a school nurse can or cannot delegate to another Registered Nurse, a Licensed Practical or Vocational Nurse, or to unlicensed personnel also depends on specific state laws.

Nursing boards (not education departments) regulate nursing practice; state practice acts (not school districts) determine what nurses can and cannot delegate. The National Association of School Nurses (NASN) notes that the nursing process itself cannot be delegated. Delegation in the school setting is an assignment by a *school nurse* (NASN, 2022). School nurses assign the performance of selected tasks to others who are competent to perform the task. Unlicensed assistive personnel (UAPs) must be trained, supervised, and evaluated in the performance of those tasks. State laws can be specific on what UAPs may and may not do. Some states do not permit the delegation of medication at all; some permit the administration of emergency medications, and some permit the administration of all medications, including insulin. It is particularly important for the school nurse to know what is and is not allowed with medication administration.

Compare, for example, the way three different states address delegation and supervision. Pennsylvania specifically does not permit school nurses to delegate nursing functions to unlicensed persons. It spells out that school administrators do not have the authority to delegate nursing functions such as medication administration:

Registered Nurses licensed in Pennsylvania may NOT delegate nursing functions to unlicensed persons... School administrators do not have the authority to delegate nursing functions, *such as medication administration....* An educator holding a valid Pennsylvania certificate as a K-12 Principal is qualified to perform the following: ... Supervision and direction of certified and non-certified staff persons required for school operation **exclusive of directing health services controlled by the Nurse Practice Act.**" ... Paraprofessionals serving as health room aides or other non-professional school district employees shall not be directed to engage in health-related activities reserved exclusively for licensed professionals and controlled by the Nurse Practice Act or other medically related laws" (Pennsylvania Department of Health, 2023).

By contrast, South Carolina provides a specific advisory about medications in school settings which states that RNs or LPNs assigned to a school in consultation with an RN may "select, train, determine competency and evaluate unlicensed school personnel in the provision of treatments and administration of medications that may be required to meet a specific student's needs in the event that a *medical emergency* occurs when a licensed nurse is not readily available" (SC BON, 2019). Specific guidance is provided in determining the training appropriateness, selection of UAPs, training and determining competency, and evaluation.

Virginia permits UAPs to administer medications and provides explicit instructions with specific training for the administration of insulin and glucagon. UAPs must also demonstrate an understanding of HIPAA/FERPA and necessary documentation. Because the Virginia Nurse Practice Act does not permit nurses to delegate medication administration, the school administrator designates the UAP to administer medications in the absence of the nurse. A Registered Nurse or licensed physician must provide the training and feedback. The guidance provides required training modules and specifies who can and cannot refuse to provide health care services, including medication administration (VA DOE, 2023).

It is critical to know if the law permits the delegation. If such delegation is not within the legal scope of practice for the school nurse's license, the analysis ends, and the school nurse does not perform the delegation. If the law does permit the delegation, the school nurse proceeds with the analysis. North Carolina provides a four-step decision tree which is provided in APPENDIX Delegation (NC BON, 2022).

It is essential that school nurses maintain training records for those to whom they are delegating to document evidence of adequate education and competency assessment. School district policies must be in place to support the delegation, and the school nurse must have the ability to supervise the delegatee. While the delegatee is responsible for their own performance, the school nurse is legally and ethically responsible for the decision to delegate to that person. The NCSBN and the American Nurses Association (ANA) Joint Position Statement on Delegation states, "[T]he licensed nurse must determine when and what to delegate based on the practice setting, the patient's needs and condition, the state/jurisdiction's provisions for delegation, and the employer policies and procedures regarding delegating a specific responsibility" (NCSBN/ANA, 2019). The position statement refers nurses to the Five Rights of Delegation - the right task, right circumstance, right person, right communication, and right supervision.

A study by the Institute of Safe Medication Practices (ISMP) noted that medication errors are three times more likely when UAPs administer medications than when nurses do (ISMP, 2012). A Journal of Pediatric Pharmacology and Therapeutics article warns schools that "[U]sing untrained school staff to administer medications in schools can increase both risk and liability" (Butler et al., 2020). Even with vigilant selection, training, and monitoring, medication administration by unlicensed personnel is error-prone, particularly in pediatric populations (Phan et al., 2020). As the Virginia Department of Education notes, "[E]ven with the best training, a UAP cannot be expected to provide the level of nursing care that licensed professional nurses attain through advanced education" (VA DOE, 2020).

(*Please see Chapter 4 for more information on delegation*).

Practice Under Level of Preparation

Nurses should not practice in a role under their level of preparation and licensure if that can be avoided, and they must be very careful to stay within the role they are assigned when they do. "Scope creep" can be difficult to avoid and create liability. RNs, for example, are not permitted to diagnose or prescribe. An advanced practice nurse working as an RN must limit patient assessments to those within the RN role and not creep into diagnosis. An RN working as a health assistant must avoid performing RN-level assessments while in that role. If health assistants are not permitted to administer medications, the RN cannot do so while working as a health assistant. School nurses are cautioned to look carefully at job descriptions and limit their practice to what is included in their assigned role, which can be extremely difficult to do during emergencies.

Nurses will be held accountable for the standards of their highest level of preparation, regardless of their assigned role. An advanced practice nurse still has the education and expertise of an advanced practice nurse, even when working as an RN. In the event of a malpractice lawsuit, the standard used to judge the nurse will be what a reasonable advanced practice nurse would do in the same or similar circumstances, not what a reasonable advanced practice nurse *working as an RN* would do in the same or similar circumstances. The nurse then, is only being paid for functioning as an RN but still maintains the liability of an advanced practice nurse. RNs being used as health assistants create the same problem. That nurse is going to be held to the standard of an RN.

School nurses should check with their individual state boards to determine the licensure implications of functioning below their preparation level and confer with their professional liability insurance companies about coverage implications when doing so.

Conflict Between School District and Professional Obligations

The school nurse can have conflicting responsibilities. On the one hand, the nurse is an employee who reports through a chain of command in the workplace. On the other hand, the nurse is a licensed professional who is responsible to a regulatory agency that oversees his or her practice. When the school district's expectations are at odds with what the nursing board would find acceptable, the school nurse can be placed in a challenging situation.

School administrators do not always understand the standards of practice to which the nurse will be held. Nor do they always appreciate the rules of professional conduct by which nursing licenses can be disciplined. When school nurses are told to do something that violates the NPA, or that is inconsistent with acceptable nursing practice, or with the ethical code of conduct for nursing, they must explain why they cannot follow those directives. This can create conflict with the employer, but such conflict is preferable to engaging in professional misconduct or unsafe practice.

"My boss told me to." "That's what we have always done," or "The healthcare provider said so," are not effective defenses in a nursing board investigation. The mission of the nursing board is to protect the public. If a nursing board believes a school nurse has engaged in unsafe or unethical practice, it will impose discipline on that nurse's license regardless of the fact that the school nurse was following a healthcare provider's orders or a school administrator's directions.

(*Please see Chapter 55 for more information on employee conflict resolution*).

Privacy Issues

School nurses may be employed in schools subject to federal laws - either the Family Educational Rights and Privacy Act (FERPA), the Health Insurance Portability and Accountability Act (HIPAA), or both, and state privacy laws. Generally, FERPA applies to agencies and institutions that receive federal funds under programs administered by the US Department of Education. FERPA covers most public schools.

Schools subject to FERPA cannot disclose *education* records or personally identifiable information from education records without parental or eligible student's written consent (an eligible student is at least 18 or attends a postsecondary institution at any age.) *Education* records under FERPA include student health records; however, *treatment records* of eligible students are not available to anyone other than professionals providing treatment to the student (Electronic Code of Federal Regulations, 2022). Generally, *education* records are those that are shared outside of the treatment context, such as immunization or Individuals with Disabilities Act (IDEA) records. *Treatment* records are used only for treatment, such as medical and psychological treatment, and are not shared. School nurses should seek guidance when unsure if the records can be shared as educational records or must be protected as treatment records.

Private and religious schools generally do not get US Department of Education funds and are therefore not subject to FERPA. Schools not subject to FERPA can be subject to HIPAA. HIPAA can apply to a school if the school employs healthcare professionals or provides a health clinic, therefore becoming a *healthcare provider*, and if it conducts electronic transactions related to health care, making it a *covered entity*. Like FERPA, schools subject to HIPAA cannot disclose protected health information without written consent.

(*Please see Chapter 12 for more information on FERPA/HIPAA*).

IDEA and individual state law also address privacy and confidentiality. Faculty and school staff other than healthcare providers should only be able to access healthcare material if they have a legitimate need to know specific information, and this must be determined on a case-by-case basis. Some specific information, such as anaphylactic allergies or dietary restrictions, can be communicated without sharing the health record itself.

In all cases, school nurses must be cautious in disclosing student health information. The NASN Code of Ethics recognizes the importance of privacy in the school nurse's role (NASN, 2021) and provides resources on HIPAA/FERPA and data privacy (NASN, 2020). Nurses who violate patient privacy rights can face disciplinary action by the nursing board.

Nurses who misuse social media expose themselves to misconduct charges for privacy as well as professional boundary violations. Discussing a student on any of these platforms is unacceptable, even when redacting student identifiers. Personal relationships outside of the provider/patient relationship are viewed with suspicion. The nurse/student relationship exists solely for the benefit of the student. "Friending," "following," or otherwise connecting with students on social media platforms can create the appearance of unhealthy boundaries and lead to licensure discipline. Texting medical information or taking photographs with personal devices can also lead to charges of privacy violations.

(*Please see Chapter 51 for more information on social media*).

<u>Field Trips</u>

Field trips require planning and coordination, particularly for students with health needs. Federal laws provide students with special needs the right to participate in these experiences. The school nurse must play an active role in assessing and planning the health needs of students during times when they will not be on school premises.

Some states permit unlicensed personnel to administer medications. The school must have clear policies on who the qualified personnel are, how they are trained and supervised, what medications can be administered, and how parental or guardian written consent is obtained. These policies must be consistent with the state's

NPA. In states that do not permit nurses to delegate this function or where such delegation cannot be safely performed, a nurse might be required to accompany the student on the trip (NASN, 2019).

If the field trip is planned for a state where the school nurse is not licensed, the nurse must contact that state's board of nursing to receive permission to practice there. When in another state, the school nurse must know and abide by that state's scope of practice and laws, regardless of what is permitted in the nurse's home state. Nurses who practice in states participating in the Nursing Licensure Compact (NLC) can practice in other compact states but must still do so within that state's regulations. For school nurses engaging in telehealth, it is important to realize that professional licensing boards consider the practice to be occurring where the *patient* is located, not where the clinician is located:

As the organizations representing the state and territorial licensing boards in the United States that regulate the practice of medicine, pharmacy, and nursing, the Federation of State Medical Boards (FSMB), National Association of Boards of Pharmacy (NABP), and National Council of State Boards of Nursing (NCSBN) affirm that in a consumer protection model, health care practice occurs where the recipient of health care services is located (Tri-Regulator, 2014).

Some students might be able to self-administer medications. The school must also have clear policies regarding the self-administration of medications that is consistent with the student's individual medication plan and the written orders of a licensed prescriber.

(*Please see Chapter 59 for more information on school-sponsored trips*)

Licensure Protection Strategies

Professional Liability Insurance

School nurses should not fall prey to the many false claims about malpractice insurance:

- I don't need it because my employer covers me.
- I am more likely to be sued if I have a policy.
- Juries give higher awards if they know you are insured.
- It's too expensive.
- If I have my own policy, my employer won't cover me.
- I have immunity, so I can't be sued.
- I'm retired or not currently in practice, so I don't need it.

These reasons are all inaccurate. As stated earlier, the greater risk for nurses is being disciplined by licensing boards than being sued for malpractice. In general, employer policies do not cover nurses for disciplinary defense, so school nurses need policies that offer that coverage. Employer policies also do not cover nurses for anything that happens off the job.

It is not true that nurses are more likely to be named in lawsuits if they have malpractice policies. Plaintiff's lawyers do not have malpractice insurance information when they file complaints. They will obtain that information in the discovery phase of the lawsuit, and there might be strategic reasons to keep a party in or let a party out of a lawsuit based upon insurance coverage, but it does not determine if a person is named in the suit. Juries do not have insurance information, so having a policy does not figure into deliberations.

Insurance premiums for registered nurses (RNs) are quite inexpensive for the coverage they provide and are business expenses that might be deducted during tax preparation. One of the reasons the premiums are low is that a personal liability insurance company provides *secondary coverage* for employed nurses. The employer remains responsible for employees' actions, so it provides *primary* coverage. Employer coverage is not voided by having a personal policy. Personal policies are only *primary coverage* for nurses who are unemployed or self-employed, and those rates are higher.

The rates for nurse practitioners (NPs) are higher than for RNs because NPs have additional risk exposure from diagnosis and prescription but remain substantially lower than those for physicians. Immunity does not apply in many circumstances, and even when it does, the legal arguments have to be made by counsel so the nurse will still incur attorney expenses. There is no immunity for nursing board investigations. Even when retired or not working, the standard school nurses will be held to differs from the standard a layperson will be held to. The nursing board does not care if the nurse is retired or not currently in practice. The mission of the nursing board is to protect the public, which can result in discipline on a license in any case.

When the board of nursing investigates nurses, they should be represented by attorneys experienced in licensure defense. Being uninsured can make that financially difficult or impossible. Nurses spend a great deal of time, money, and energy obtaining their credentials and experience. They need to protect that investment.

Portfolio

When defending against a board of nursing allegation of professional misconduct, providing evidence of a history of safe practice and ethical conduct can be helpful. Nurses should ask for copies of any performance appraisals or evaluations they receive along with copies of letters of reference or recommendation, thank you letters from students and their families, awards, publications, public speaking, volunteer or public interest work, or anything else that speaks to professional accomplishments. Membership in professional organizations, subscriptions to professional journals, and certificates of completion for continuing education and specialty certifications can demonstrate a commitment to continuing education and competency. Keeping all those documents in a folder, along with licenses, registration certificates, insurance policies, and records, will make them accessible should a defense become necessary.

Stay Informed About Nursing Law

Nursing boards have websites that publish advisory opinions, practice alerts, frequently asked questions, and position papers. The discipline of a licensed professional is public information, so charges and penalties against nurses are also published on nursing board websites. School nurses should go to the websites periodically to review the NPA in their state. Knowing the law and regulations is essential to being compliant. It is crucial to be familiar with the Code of Ethics published by professional nursing organizations.

Review the definitions of professional misconduct and the scope of practice for all providers. Keeping a copy of the regulations in the school nurse's office can be convenient as a reference when having disputes with the school administration about what is and is not permitted. When conflict arises, seek the opinion of the nursing board or a licensure attorney in your state. If the conflict between what the school district wants you to do and what the nursing board allows you to do cannot be resolved, you must abide by the nursing board's definition of professional conduct. School nurses must explain that they are not insubordinate but cannot follow a certain directive without violating the law or exposing the student to unsafe nursing practice. Put such concerns in writing and maintain a copy for your own files.

Keep Records

Maintain copies of correspondence with administrators where safety issues are addressed or concerns are voiced about the conflict between job expectations and nursing law or standards. Keep records of education provided to people you train in medication administration, seizure precautions, response to asthma attacks or allergies, or anything related to health care. The records should include the information that was imparted, materials used, an assessment of proficiency, return demonstrations, and periodic supervision. Keep copies of any correspondence with the nursing board where you have sought clarification, an advisory opinion, or requested permission to attend an out-of-state field trip.

If You Are Investigated by The Board of Nursing

Nursing boards generally advise licensees that they are under investigation by calling the nurse on the telephone or sending the nurse a letter. In some states, the investigator might physically come to the nurse's home or place of employment. Nurses should tell investigators that they will cooperate in the investigation but cannot make statements or answer questions without an attorney being present. Obtain counsel immediately and refrain from having direct contact with the board. Investigations are adversarial proceedings, and nurses do not have the presumption of innocence or the due process rights they assume are in place. Having an attorney from the beginning of the process is preferable to trying to hire one after the case is in progress or after the damage has been done.

Inform your professional liability insurance company of the investigation as soon as you receive notice. Notification is required to trigger coverage. The insurance company can provide a referral to a licensure defense attorney. Do not use a lawyer without specific experience in licensure defense before the nursing board. It is an area of practice that requires specific expertise, and attorneys who practice in other arenas are not equipped to represent you adequately. Licensure defense attorneys can also be found through The American Association of Nurse Attorneys (TAANA, 2022), local or state bar associations, collective bargaining units, and professional nursing organizations.

Do not apply for licensure in another state until the matter is fully resolved in your home state. Disciplinary action in one state does cause *reciprocal discipline* or discipline in other states. Receiving a license in another state can also lead to discipline in that other state. Make sure the licensure defense attorney representing you know of any other licenses you have ever held in any other states so reporting requirements can be met in those states. The requirement to report out-of-state discipline might still be in place, even if your registration lapsed years ago.

Take care of yourself emotionally. The experience of being investigated by the nursing board is stressful. If you are employed during the process, it can be challenging to function safely at work if you are sleep-deprived or distracted by anxiety. Get stress counseling if necessary and engage in whatever sleep hygiene measures are effective so you are well-rested. The American Holistic Nurses Association (AHNA, 2023) offers self-care and stress management resources.

CONCLUSION

A nursing board investigation is a stressful experience, even if no charges are ultimately filed, or the matter is ultimately dismissed without discipline. Having good practice habits, maintaining competency in current, evidence-based standards, keeping accurate records, and understanding the Nurse Practice Act, the scope of practice, definitions of professional misconduct, and state regulations can reduce your exposure to being under investigation. Having a professional liability insurance policy, keeping a portfolio, and obtaining counsel immediately if you are the subject of a complaint, can increase your chances of a good outcome if that does happen.

RESOURCES

American Nurses Association. (2015). *Code of ethics for nurses with interpretative statements.* Nursesbooks.org.

American Nurses Association. (2021). *Nursing scope and standards of practice, 4th edition*. Nursesbooks.org.

North Carolina Board of Nursing. (2022.) *Decision Tree for Delegation to UAP*. https://www.ncbon.com/myfiles/downloads/position-statements-decision-trees/delegation-to-uap-decision-tree.pdf

and see APPENDIX.

Case Law

Electronic Code of Federal Regulations (2022) Title 34, Education, Subtitle A, Chapter 1, Part 99, *The Family Educational Rights and Privacy Act* (FERPA). https://www.ecfr.gov/current/title-34/part-99

REFERENCES

American Holistic Nurses Association. (2023). *Holistic stress management for nurses*. http://www.ahna.org/Resources/Stress-Management

Butler, S. M., Boucher, E. A., Tobison, J. & Phan, H. *Medication use in schools: Current trends, challenges, and best practices, Journal of Pediatric Pharmacology and Therapeutics* 2020; 25(1), 7-24. https://www.ncbi.nlm.nih.gov/pmc/articles/PMC6938291/

Electronic Code of Federal Regulations. (2022). *Title 34, Education, Subtitle A, Chapter 1, Part 99, The Family Educational Rights and Privacy Act* (FERPA). https://www.ecfr.gov/current/title-34/part-99

Institute for Safe Medication Practices. (2012). *Fewer school nurses leads to greater medication errors.* www.consumermedsafety.org/medication-safety-articles/item/550-fewer-school-nurses-leads-to-greater-medication-errors

National Association of School Nurses. (2018). *Nursing delegation in the school setting.* https://www.nasn.org/nasn-resources/resources-by-topic/delegation

National Association of School Nurses. (2019). *School-sponsored trips, role of the school nurse* (Position Statement). https://www.nasn.org/nasn-resources/professional-practice-documents/position-statements/ps-trips

National Association of School Nurses. (2020). *HIPAA and FERPA.* https://www.nasn.org/nasn-resources/resources-by-topic/school-health-documentation/hipaa-ferpa

National Association of School Nurses. (2021). *Code of ethics.* https://www.nasn.org/RoleCareer/CodeofEthics

National Council of State Boards of Nursing and American Nurses Association. (2019). *Joint statement on delegation.* https://www.nursingworld.org/practice-policy/nursing-excellence/official-position-statements/id/joint-statement-on-delegation-by-ANA-and-NCSBN/

National Council of State Boards of Nursing. (2023a). *About nursing licensure.* https://www.ncsbn.org/nursing-regulation/licensure.page

National Council of State Boards of Nursing. (2023b). *Components of nursing licensure.* https://www.ncsbn.org/nursing-regulation/licensure.page

North Carolina Board of Nursing. (2022). *Decision tree for delegation to UAP.* HYPERLINK https://www.ncbon.com/vdownloads/position-statements-decision-trees/decision-tree-delegation-to-uap.pdf

Nurses Service Organization. (2020). *Nurse Spotlight: Defending your license.* https://www.nso.com/getmedia/2c55d7fb-e661-4991-b302-fa441ccf975a/CNA_CLS_NURSE20_SL_061120p3_CF_PROD_ASIZE_ONLINE_SEC.pdf

Pennsylvania Department of Health. (2023). *Nurse practice issues in the school setting: Caseload/delegation.* https://www.health.pa.gov/topics/school/Pages/Delegation.aspx

Phan, H., Butler, S. M., Tobison, J., & Boucher, E. (2020). Medication use in schools, *Journal of Pediatric Pharmacology and Therapeutics*, 2020; 25(2): 163-166. https://www.ncbi.nlm.nih.gov/pmc/articles/PMC7025751/

South Carolina Board of Nursing. (2019). *Advisory opinion # 50, administration of medications in school settings* https://llr.sc.gov/nurse/AdvisoryOp/AO50.pdf

The American Association of Nurse Attorneys (TAANA). (2022). *Attorney referral.* http://taana.org/referral

Tri-Regulator (Federation of State Medical Boards, National Association of Boards of Pharmacy, National Council of State Boards of Nursing). (2014). *The Tri-regulator collaborative position statement on practice location for consumer protection.* https://www.ncsbn.org/papers/the-triregulator-collaborative-position-statement-on-practice-location-for-consumer-protection

United States Department of Health & Human Services. (n.d.). *NPDB national practitioner data bank.* https://www.npdb.hrsa.gov/topNavigation/aboutUs.jsp

Virginia Department of Education. (2020). *Medication administration school nurse's guide: a training manual for unlicensed public school employees Virginia Department of Education 2020.* https://www.vdh.virginia.gov/content/uploads/sites/58/2021/01/DOEMedication-administrations-manual.pdf

Virginia Department of Education. (2023) *Diabetes management in schools: manual for unlicensed personnel.* https://www.doe.virginia.gov/programs-services/student-services/specialized-student-support-services/school-health-services/school-health-guidance-resources

DECISION TREE FOR DELEGATION TO UAP

NCBON
North Carolina Board of Nursing

P.O. BOX 2129
Raleigh, NC 27602
(919) 782-3211
FAX (919) 781-9461
Nurse Aide II Registry (984) 238-7697
www.ncbon.com

Step 1 of 4: Assessment and Implementation

Is the task within the scope of practice for a licensed nurse (RN/LPN)? → **No** → **Stop!** Do not delegate to UAP.

↓ Yes

Is the activity allowed by the Nursing Practice Act, Board Rules, Statements, or by any other law, rule or policy? → **No** → **Stop!** Do not delegate to UAP.

↓ Yes

Is RN assessment of client's nursing care needs complete? → **No** → **Stop!** RN to complete assessment, then proceed with consideration of delegation.

↓ Yes

Is the RN/LPN competent to make delegation decisions? *Nurse is accountable for the decision to delegate, to implement the steps of the delegation process, and to assure that the delegated task is appropriate based on individualized needs of each client which includes stability, absence of risk of complications, and predictability of change in condition. The delegating nurse must be competent to perform the activity.* See (A) and (B) pg. 2 → **No** → **Stop!** Do not delegate to UAP.

↓ Yes

Is the task consistent with the rules for delegation to UAP? Must meet all the following criteria:
- Frequently recurs in the daily care of a client or group of clients
- Is performed according to an established sequence of steps
- Involves little to no modification from one client care situation to another
- May be performed with a predictable outcome
- Does not inherently involve ongoing assessment, interpretation, or decision making which cannot be logically separated from the procedure(s) itself; and
- Does not endanger the client's life or well being.

→ **No** → **Stop!** Do not delegate to UAP.

↓ Yes

Is the UAP properly trained and validated as competent by an RN to accept the delegation? → **No** → **Stop!** Do not delegate until evidence of education and validation of competency available, and then reconsider delegation; otherwise do not delegate.

↓ Yes

Does the capability of UAP match the care needs of the client? See (A) and (B) pg. 2 → **No** → **Stop!** Do not delegate until the nurse has evaluated capability of UAP matches the care needs of the client.

↓ Yes

Are there written agency policies, procedures, and/or protocols in place for this task? → **No** → **Stop!** Do not proceed without evaluation of need for policy, procedures and/or protocol or determination that it is in the best interest of the client to proceed with delegation in urgent or emergency situations.

↓ Yes

Is appropriate supervision available? See (C) (D) (E) pg. 3 → **No** → **Stop!** Do not delegate to UAP.

↓ Yes

Proceed with delegation.

The UAP is responsible for accepting the delegation, seeking clarification of and affirming expectations, performing the task correctly and timely communicating results to the nurse. Only the implementation of a task/activity may be delegated. Assessment, planning, evaluation and nursing judgment cannot be delegated. **Delegation is a client and situation specific activity in which the nurse must consider all components of the delegation process for each delegation decision.** Specific direction by the nurse (RN, LPN) to UAP when assisting the nurse with a task or nursing activity and under the <u>direct visual supervision</u> of the nurse is not considered delegation.

Page 1 of 3

IMPORTANT COMPONENTS FOR DELEGATION TO UAP

Prior to proceeding to Step 2, consider the following:

Delegation is a process of decision-making, critical thinking and nursing judgment. Decisions to delegate nursing tasks/activities to UAP are based on the RN's assessment of the client's nursing care needs. The LPN may delegate nursing tasks/activities to UAP under the supervision of the RN. Additional criteria that must be considered when determining appropriate delegation of tasks include, but are not limited to:

(A) Variables:	(B) Use of critical thinking and professional judgment for The Five Rights of Delegation:
<ul><li>Knowledge and skill of UAP</li><li>Verification of clinical competence of UAP</li><li>Stability of the client's condition which involves predictability, absence of risk of complication, and rate of change</li><li>Variables specific for each practice setting:<ul><li>The complexity and frequency of nursing care needed by a given client population</li><li>The proximity of clients to staff</li><li>The number and qualifications of staff</li><li>The accessible resources</li></ul></li><li>Established policies, procedures, practices, and channels of communication which lend support to the types of nursing activities being delegated, or not delegated, to UAP</li></ul>	1. Right Task – the task must meet all of the delegation criteria 2. Right Circumstance – delegation must be appropriate to the client population and practice setting 3. Right Person – the nurse must be competent to perform the activity and to make delegation decisions, the nurse must ensure the right task is being delegated to the right person (UAP) and competence has been validated by an RN, and the delegation is for the individualized needs of the client 4. Right Communication – the nurse must provide clear, concise instructions for performing the task 5. Right Supervision – the nurse must provide appropriate supervision/monitoring, evaluation, and feedback of UAP performance of the task

Step 2 of 4: Communication - Communication must be a two-way process

The nurse:	The UAP:	Documentation by nurse and UAP (as determined by facility/agency policy) is:
<ul><li>Assesses the UAP's understanding of:<ul><li>Task to be performed and expectations of performance of tasks</li><li>Information to report including client specific observations, expected outcomes and concerns</li><li>When and how to report/record information</li></ul></li><li>Communicates individualized needs of client population, practice setting, and unique client requirements</li><li>Communicates and provides guidance, coaching, and support for UAP</li><li>Allows UAP opportunity for questions and clarification</li><li>Assures accountability by verifying UAP accepts delegation</li><li>Develops and communicates plan of action in emergency situations</li><li>Determines communication method between nurse and UAP</li></ul>	<ul><li>Asks questions and seeks clarification</li><li>Informs the nurse if UAP has never performed the task or has performed it infrequently</li><li>Requests additional training or guidance as needed</li><li>Affirms understanding and acceptance of delegation</li><li>Complies with communication method between nurse and UAP</li><li>Reports care results to nurse in a timely manner</li><li>Complies with emergency action plans</li></ul>	Timely, complete and accurate documentation of provided care:<ul><li>Facilitates communication with other members of the health care team</li><li>Records the nursing care provided.</li></ul>

Page 2 of 3

Step 3 of 4: Supervision and Monitoring – The RN supervises the delegation by monitoring the performance of the task and assures compliance with standards of practice, policies and procedures. The LPN supervision is limited to on-the-job assurance that tasks have been performed as delegated and according to standards of practice established in agency policies and procedures. Frequency, level, and nature of monitoring vary with the needs of the client and experience of the UAP.

(C) The nurse takes into consideration the:	(D) The nurse determines:	(E) The nurse:
▪ Client's health stability, status, and acuity ▪ Predictability of client response to interventions and risks posed ▪ Practice setting and client population ▪ Available resources ▪ Complexity & frequency of nursing care needed ▪ Proximity of clients to staff ▪ Number and qualification of staff ▪ Policies, procedures, & channels of communication established	▪ The amount/degree of supervision required ▪ Type of supervision: direct or indirect ▪ The Five Rights of Delegation have been implemented: 1. Right Task 2. Right Circumstances 3. Right Person 4. Right Directions and Communications 5. Right Supervision and Evaluation	▪ Maintains accountability for nursing tasks/activities delegated and performed by UAP ▪ Monitors outcomes of delegated nursing care tasks ▪ Intervenes and follows-up on problems, incidents, and concerns within an appropriate timeframe ▪ Nursing management and administration responsibilities are beyond LPN scope of practice. To assure client safety, the LPN may need authority to alter delegation or temporarily suspend UAP per agency policy until appropriate personnel action can be determined by the supervising RN. ▪ Observes client response to nursing care and UAP's performance of care ▪ Recognizes subtle signs and symptoms with appropriate intervention when client's condition changes ▪ Recognizes UAP's difficulties in completing delegation activities

Step 4 of 4: Evaluation and Feedback – Evaluate effectiveness of delegation and provide appropriate feedback

- Evaluate the nursing care outcomes:
  - (RN) Evaluate the effectiveness of the nursing plan of care and modify as needed
  - (LPN) Recognize the effectiveness of nursing interventions and propose modifications to plan of care for review by the RN
- Evaluate the effectiveness of delegation:
  - Task performed correctly?
  - Expected outcomes achieved?
  - Communication was timely and effective?
  - Identify challenges and what went well
  - Identify problems and concerns that occurred and how they were addressed
- Provide feedback to UAP regarding performance of tasks/activities and acknowledge the UAP for accomplishing the task

References:
G.S. 90-171.20 (7)(d) & (i) and (8) (d) Nursing Practice Act
21 NCAC 36.0221 (b) Licensed Required
21 NCAC 36.0224 (a) (b) (c) (d) (e) (f) (i) & (j) Components of Nursing Practice for the Registered Nurse
21 NCAC 36.0225 (b) (c) (d) (e) (f) Components of Nursing Practice for the Licensed Practical Nurse
21 NCAC 36.0401 (c) Roles of Unlicensed Personnel

American Nurses Association Decision Tree for Delegation by Registered Nurses, 2012
Joint Statement on Delegation ANA and NCSBN Decision Tree for Delegation to Nursing Assistive Personnel, 2019
National Council of State Boards of Nursing Decision Tree – Delegation to Nursing Assistive Personnel, 2005

Origin: 5/2000; Revised 4/2007, 9/2013, 9/2022; Reviewed 2/2013, 9/2018

Reprinted with permission

Chapter 2

MALPRACTICE / PROFESSIONAL LIABILITY

Edith Brous, MS, MPH, JD, RN, FAAN

Healthcare is a challenging industry and is experiencing an increase in the frequency of higher professional liability verdicts. Nursing professionals should be cognizant of a greater risk of professional liability claims settling for higher than anticipated amounts relative to historic averages (CNA HealthPro and Nurses Service Organization [NSO], 2020).

DESCRIPTION OF ISSUE

When healthcare costs increase, payouts for malpractice claims also increase to provide adequate compensation for damages and the need for continuing medical care. The fear of liability, however, far exceeds the reality for nurses in all areas of practice. Despite constant rhetoric about a "malpractice crisis" "runaway juries" or "frivolous lawsuits," most nurses will complete their careers without ever being named in a malpractice lawsuit. This chapter discusses the elements required for a nurse to be sued for malpractice and tips for further reducing school nurses' low exposure.

As of May 2021, the US Bureau of Labor Statistics reported 3,047,530 employed professional Registered Nurses (RNs) in the United States (US Department of Labor, 2022). If nurses were the frequent target of medical malpractice lawsuits, one would expect a significant percentage of that 3 million or so nurses to be involved in cases that resulted in payments to plaintiffs (persons bringing the suit). However, the National Practitioner Data Bank reports for the entire calendar year of 2021 that only 299 RNs in the United States were reported because of a malpractice payment (United States Department of Health and Human Services, n.d.).

For school nurses, in particular, the risk is exceptionally low. The largest medical malpractice insurance provider for nurses -Nurses Service Organization (NSO) – provided a claims study evaluating paid claims for nurses between 2015 and 2019 by specialty and location (CNA Health Pro & NSO, 2020). School nursing did not even appear as a distinct category. As uncommon as it is for school nurses to be individually named in medical malpractice lawsuits, it is still important to understand the elements of a suit and engage in exposure reduction strategies.

BACKGROUND

It is important to distinguish between *negligence, malpractice, and wrongful death*. Negligence is a *lay* standard. What would a reasonably prudent *person* have done in the same or similar circumstances? A person is negligent if he or she does not exercise the care that a reasonably prudent person would have exercised. Malpractice and wrongful death are *professional* standards. What would a reasonably prudent *nurse* have done in the same or similar circumstances? The distinction is significant because procedural requirements to file the lawsuit can differ depending on whether the suit is negligent, malpractice, or wrongful death. Statutes of limitation can be different as well (the time limit during which the person must bring the suit). Most importantly, the standards by which the defendant (the person accused) is judged depend upon how the complaint is framed.

While specifics may vary from state to state, for a plaintiff to bring a medical malpractice or wrongful death lawsuit against a school nurse, he or she must successfully demonstrate four elements – duty, breach, cause, and harm:

Duty: Duty is the duty of reasonable care. A nurse has a duty to provide care that is consistent with professional standards. The element of duty is established as soon as the nurse/patient relationship is created.

Breach: A nurse breaches his or her duty to a patient by departing from the standards of care. Unlike negligence, which is a lay standard, an expert witness is required to demonstrate this element. The expert witness must testify to the standard of practice and must also testify that the nurse deviated from the acceptable standards of practice by doing something a reasonably prudent nurse in the same or similar circumstances would not have done (an act) or by not doing something a reasonably prudent nurse would have done in same or similar circumstances (an omission).

Cause: The plaintiff must demonstrate that the nurse's departure from standards *proximately* caused the injury he or she sustained. This can be either a "but for" standard, meaning the injury would not have occurred *but for* the nurse's departure, or a "substantial factor" standard, meaning there might have been other, independent forces at play. However, the nurse's departure from acceptable standards of practice played a substantial role in causing the patient to be injured.

Harm: The purpose of a lawsuit is to compensate a plaintiff for damages, so there must be actual damages to compensate. A nurse cannot be sued for potential or theoretical harm to a patient, but only because a patient was, in fact, injured. Patients can be harmed in ways that cause physical, emotional/psychological, and financial damage.

Student nurses are held to the same standards of practice as licensed professional nurses and can be named in malpractice lawsuits. For this reason, many clinical settings and schools require student nurses to maintain their own professional liability insurance. Although claims against student nurses are infrequent, the consequence of students being unsupervised while performing complex nursing care of high acuity patients is that student nurse cases result in the highest-paid claims of all nursing license levels (CNA HealthPro and NSO, 2020).

If a student nurse makes a clinical error in which a patient is harmed, there can also be a liability for the precepting nurse or clinical instructor. Because students do not have the clinical competence of experienced nurses, the preceptor or instructor must assess the student's ability and properly delegate and supervise the student's practice. Many student-nurse errors result from inadequate instructor communication (Freeman, 2020; Valiee, 2018).

(Please see Chapter 11 for more information on supervision of student nurses).

The elements of duty, breach, cause, and harm are demonstrated in a 2019 Sixth Circuit case. In *Meyers v. Cincinnati Board of Education*, eight-year-old Gabriel Taye was a third-grade student subject to escalating bullying since first grade. On January 24, 2017, another student grabbed and yanked him toward the wall. Taye lost consciousness and collapsed to the floor, where he was then taunted and kicked by more than a dozen other students. The assistant principal, Jeffrey McKenzie, found Taye unresponsive on the floor. He did nothing to assist the child, and by the time the school nurse, Margaret McLaughlin, arrived, Gabriel had been unconscious for more than seven minutes. Nurse McLaughlin examined him but did not call 911, as was policy. An hour after Taye regained consciousness, McLaughlin called his mother. Although the nurse testified that she called the mother and told her to take the child to the hospital (del Valle, 2018), the complaint alleged that the nurse told the mother that Gabriel had" fainted" and that he did not require further medical attention because he was alert, and his vital signs were stable.

When Gabriel returned home from school, he told his mother that he could not remember what had happened to him but had fallen, and his stomach hurt. His stomach pain continued, and he started experiencing nausea and vomiting, so his mother took him to the hospital. Because she had never been informed that Gabriel had been attacked and unconscious for more than seven minutes, his mother told the doctors that he had passed out. Because the doctors did not know he had sustained a head injury, they discharged him with a diagnosis of stomach flu. He stayed home from school the following day.

When he returned to school on January 26, 2017, two boys attacked him again. Nothing happened when he reported this to a teacher. That day, when he came home from school, Gabriel hanged himself from the top of his bunk bed with a necktie. His mother found him hanging and unresponsive and began CPR. A neighbor came to help, and his mother called 911, but the paramedics were unable to resuscitate him.

The administratrix of the estate and his parents filed a lawsuit in federal court against the school and several specific individuals, including the school nurse. They alleged wrongful death, intentional infliction of serious emotional distress, negligent infliction of emotional distress, loss of consortium, and failure to report child abuse. The defendants argued that they should be dismissed on the grounds of immunity. However, this was denied because the court found their conduct to be reckless and demonstrated conscious disregard or indifference to a known risk of harm. Circuit Judge Bernice Bouie Donald stated, "[T]his Court finds their behavior, as alleged, to be egregious and clearly reckless, thus barring them from the shield of government immunity" (Meyers v. Cincinnati Board of Education, p. 875).

Had the case proceeded to trial, the plaintiffs would need to demonstrate that Nurse McLaughlin had a **duty** to Gabriel. This element would be easily demonstrated by establishing the nurse/patient relationship the school nurse had with the students. The duty would be the duty of reasonable care – what a reasonably prudent school nurse would do in the same or similar circumstances.

They would next need to demonstrate that Nurse McLaughlin **breached** her duty by departing from the standard of care. This would also be easily demonstrated by providing a copy of the policy requiring that she call 911 when she did not do so. An expert witness could also establish that failing to provide accurate and thorough information to his mother was a breach of her duty. A reasonably prudent school nurse in the same or similar circumstances would have informed Gabriel's mother that he had sustained a head injury with a significant loss of consciousness.

The more difficult element would be causation. The plaintiffs would need to show that the nurse's failure to call 911 or appropriately notify his mother of the situation was why he died. The death of an eight-year-old by his own hand certainly demonstrates actual **harm**. However, an expert would need to convince a jury that had the nurse acted differently, Gabriel would not have taken his own life – that his suicide was **caused by** her departure from standards (breach) or that her departure from standards **was a substantial factor** in his suicide.

On June 2, 2017, the school district held a press conference announcing that the case was being settled. The proposed settlement included a 3 million dollar payment to Gabriel's family and a commitment to enact anti-bullying measures with two years of oversight (Mitchell, 2021; Simko-Bednarski, 2021).

Because school nurses are employees, most medical malpractice lawsuits will target the school district as the employer. The nurse might be individually named as well. The elements for the nurse will remain the same – the plaintiff will need to demonstrate that the nurse had a **duty**; that he/she **breached** that duty by departing from acceptable standards of practice; that the breach was the **cause** of an injury; and that there were actual damages (**harm**).

Note: This case illustrates the need for school nurses to be vigilant in monitoring for and responding to bullying. School nurses should also be actively involved in planning and implementing the school district's policies and procedures for combating harassment and bullying (including cyberbullying.)

(Please see Chapter 52 for more information on violence/bullying).

IMPLICATIONS FOR SCHOOL NURSE PRACTICE

Interpersonal Skills

The most important action the school nurse can take is to develop good interpersonal communication skills. Multiple studies have indicated that there is no more effective risk-reduction strategy in decreasing liability exposure (Console, 2022; Scott, 2019; SPC Health, 2022;). Adverse events are far less likely to result in litigation when healthy provider/patient relationships exist. Students and their families are more reluctant to file lawsuits when they trust the school nurse. Transparency, trust, accountability, respect, and apologies can reduce litigation (Wisenberg Brin, 2018).

Professional Liability Insurance

School nurses should maintain personal insurance policies and not rely upon their employers for professional liability coverage. Employer policies do not cover nurses for any actions that arise from events that are unrelated to the scope of their employment. Employer policies do not generally cover school nurses for licensure defense or other administrative actions. Because school nurses are more likely to be in a position of reporting to a person who does not understand the scope of practice limitations or clinical standards of practice, it is particularly important to have adequate insurance protection. In addition to malpractice lawsuits, licensed professionals have liability exposure in other arenas for which they need coverage.

School policies typically name the school district as the insured party, not the individual school nurse. The school nurse is an employee of the insured party, not the named insured or protected party. School nurses should review the insurance policy to determine if he or she is an additional insured. If the school nurse is not a named insured, he or she will not be protected. It is also important to know if the policy only covers malpractice or if the school nurse is also protected for administrative and licensure defense. In any case, the school nurse should still maintain their own policy.

The attorney representing the school district in a lawsuit represents the best interests of their client - the *school*, not the nurse. The focus is on dismissing, settling, or trying the case, not protecting the nurse's career. Some malpractice attorneys are not familiar with the administrative and licensure implications for the school nurse. Without individual coverage, the school nurse is not adequately represented or protected.

Immunity

One reason school nurses give for not having their own professional liability insurance is the belief that they are protected from exposure by way of "immunity" because a school district employs them. Although each state provides some shelter from liability for public schools, the degree and nature of that legal protection varies widely. Some states offer very narrow protection, while others provide a broader shield. Whether or not immunity applies in a given situation depends on several factors specific to the case and state law.

It is essential to understand that "governmental immunity" or "sovereign immunity" is a defense that can be asserted in answering a complaint but does not prevent a lawsuit from being filed. Immunity does not mean that a school nurse cannot be sued. The nurse will still have to defend the lawsuit and make the legal arguments that immunity applies. This is true for charitable immunity, Good Samaritan immunity, Official immunity, or any other form of immunity. There is no immunity from lawsuits. Immunity only provides some protection from the extent to which a school nurse or a school district can be held liable for damages.

Legal analysis is necessary to determine if any immunity protection applies. Many questions must be answered. What does the specific state statute say regarding immunity protections? Is the immunity *absolute* or *qualified*? Was the negligence *simple negligence* or *gross negligence*? Was the function *ministerial* or *discretionary*? Are the actions *governmental* or *proprietary*? Do circumstances place the case under one of the exceptions to the immunity statute? What is the school's insurance coverage? Has the school district *waived* immunity? Was the student injured in an area used for educational or recreational activities? Was there malicious intent on the part of the defendants? Was the care rendered in a setting that provided proper and necessary medical equipment? Did the defendant have a duty to render assistance? Was the care rendered in a manner that could be considered the scene of an accident or emergency? The analysis can be complicated and contentious.

Even if successful, the expense of defending the suit on immunity grounds can be considerable. **Most importantly for nurses, there is no immunity whatsoever from nursing board investigations that can accompany the lawsuit.**

Maintain Clinical Competency

Unlike nurses who work in hospitals or many other settings, school nurses practice in isolation, without the availability of immediate and on-site consultation. Standards of care change and the school nurse's isolation can result in outdated practices. To further reduce liability exposure, **it is critical that school nurses maintain competency and update their skills to reflect current, evidence-based standards.** Continuing education, membership in professional organizations, subscriptions to professional journals, and participation in conferences can assist the school nurse in practicing in accordance with the standards of care as they would be judged in a malpractice lawsuit. **Policies and procedures should be updated to reflect practices consistent with industry standards.**

(Please see Chapter 3 for more information on the scope and standards of practice).

Documentation

In a medical malpractice lawsuit, the best evidence, and sometimes the only evidence that can be used to defend against the allegations, is found in the medical record. If the student's health record demonstrates that the school nurse adhered to the standards of practice, it is difficult for a plaintiff to prove that he or she breached a duty. As previously discussed, without a breach of duty, the elements of causation and harm become irrelevant. Records that establish compliance with organizational policies, care plans, and prescriber's orders can prove that the school nurse acted in the same way another reasonably prudent school nurse would have acted in the same or similar circumstances.

When documenting assessments and interventions, it is necessary to chart in a manner that allows the re-creation of an accurate sequence of events and picture of the student. Vague terms like "moderate" and "copious" should be avoided when measurable terms can be used instead. Specifically, identify people by last name rather than referring to titles such as "MD", "parents", or "teacher." Use entire dates, including the year and times, including am or pm. Document all communications or attempts to contact administrators, parents/guardians, or other providers about student concerns. In documenting communication with students, capture the presence of any witnesses to the conversation, the student's level of consciousness at the time, and the student's ability to understand and repeat the information.

Pursue concerns to resolution and document that you engaged the chain of command. Failure to rescue or failure to observe and report claims can be made if the record does not demonstrate that the nurse escalated concerns. Documentation must accurately reflect the evaluation and treatment of the student, and the records must be maintained in a manner that preserves their credibility. An example of problematic documentation and record-keeping practices is illustrated in *KRS v. Bedford Community School District* (SD Iowa 2015).

K.R.S. was a special education student at the defendant school district in 2012, where he was subjected to bullying. On several occasions, he saw the school nurse with complaints of headaches and reported to her that players had thrown footballs at his head. He also demonstrated double vision and expressed concern that he had a concussion. He stated that the double vision had started after being hit in the head with the footballs. On one occasion, the school nurse advised KRS to inform his grandmother, but she did not notify the football coach. On another occasion, she documented that she spoke with the grandmother, who agreed to take KRS to the doctor, but again, she did not notify the football coach.

Four days after his last visit with the school nurse, KRS was taken to the emergency room with balance problems, headache, neck pain, and visual problems. An MRI revealed a mass in his head, and he was admitted to the hospital, where a cavernous malformation was detected. He was advised against contact sports, provided an eye patch, and told to stay out of school for two to three weeks. Less than two weeks later, he was readmitted with a recurrence of hemorrhage requiring surgery. He was placed in a medically induced coma, and after two weeks of hospitalization, he was transferred to a rehabilitation facility with permanent brain damage.

A lawsuit against the school district was brought on behalf of KRS, in which the school nurse was individually named. Several claims were made, including violations of the Rehabilitation Act (§ 504 claims), breach of fiduciary duty, intentional infliction of emotional distress, and failure to remove from athletic competition. The claim against the school nurse was negligence in failing to provide reasonable medical care.

The school nurse was deposed on two occasions. At the first deposition, she testified that it was her practice to keep a spiral notebook which she used as a daily log. She wrote notes about student visits by hand into that notebook, then later transcribed the notes into an electronic medical record (EMR). At the end of the school year, she destroyed the spiral notebook. At the end of this particular school year, however, she had kept the pages related to KRS. She brought those pages to the deposition, which were marked as exhibits. During one of KR S.'s visits to her office, she believed she had mistakenly written the wrong encounter date in the log but had not corrected it upon transcribing it into the EMR.

During the discovery period of the lawsuit, it was revealed that what she had provided as "original" records at her deposition, in fact, were records she had re-created from the EMR after losing the original records. This compromised her credibility as a witness and the credibility of the medical records. Most importantly, it harmed the defense in the case. The school district made a *motion for summary judgment*, an application to the court asking to dismiss the case. Such motions are granted when there are no facts in dispute. The court denied this motion because of the school nurse's documentation and record-keeping practices:

> As for the claim that Nurse Schuelke failed to provide reasonable medical care, it is undisputed that KRS visited her on at least two occasions complaining of headache and double vision, which he said started after he was hit in the head with footballs. Because of the credibility issues arising from her duplication of lost notes, however, the dates when Nurse Schuelke saw KRS are disputed; indeed, all her testimony at this stage is tarnished by the "lost notes" issue. In resistance to the summary judgment motion, the plaintiff has included a report from their nursing expert witness Martha Dewey Bergren which criticizes how Nurse Schuelke responded to KRS's complaint of headaches in connection with football practice in several respects. The court cannot determine credibility issues on summary judgment, and there is a debate in the record about the adequacy of Nurse Schuelke's practices concerning KRS. Based on this summary judgment record, the court finds disputed facts preclude the entry of summary judgment in favor of the defendants on the plaintiff's negligence claims... (KRS v. Bedford Community School District, 2015, pp.23-24).

The trial lasted a week, and the jurors found both the school and the school nurse negligent for failing to notify the coaches that KRS might have a concussion and for not making sure he saw a physician after being seen by the school nurse (Bleier, 2015). He was awarded $991,832 (Nelson, 2015). About $140,000 was for medical expenses, and the remainder was for damages for pain and suffering, loss of mind and body, and loss of future earnings (Elliott, 2015).

Note: This case also illustrates why school nurses should not rely upon "immunity" to practice without professional liability insurance and how complicated the analysis of whether or not immunity applies can be. The defendants argued that they were entitled to immunity under state law because they performed *discretionary* functions exempting them from claims. The state law defined discretionary functions as those that involved an element of choice or discretion and provided protection if public policy concerns, social, economic, or political considerations drove such discretionary judgment.

In this case, the court said that all defendants met the first part of this test in that they all exercised professional judgment. The school failed, however, to convince the court of the second prong of this analysis:

> Defendants do not identify any social, economic, or political consideration as a basis for the coaches' permitting KRS to participate in football after he complained of a headache (which, for purposes of this motion, the court will assume occurred) or for Nurse Schuelke's decision to have KRS report his headaches to his grandmother and to accept his word he was not participating in practices instead of reporting KRS's complaints to the coaches (K.R.S. v. Bedford Community School District, 2015, p. 24).

(Please see Chapter 9 for more information on documentation).

If Named in a Suit

Employers have what is referred to as *vicarious liability* for the actions of their employees, which means a school district can be held responsible for a school nurse's acts or omissions within the course of the school nurse's employment. Students harmed by a school nurse's negligence can hold the nurse personally responsible, but they can also hold the school district responsible as the school nurse's employer.

Because school nurses are employees, it will generally be the employer who is notified of a lawsuit by being served with a *summons with notice* or a *summons and complaint*. Occasionally, however, employees are directly served with these documents. If directly notified that you have been named in a suit, you should immediately inform your school's legal department so a timely answer can be served on your behalf.

Whether directly served or notified by the school that you have been named in a lawsuit, inform your private insurance company immediately. Your policy is likely to have a clause requiring you to report as soon as you are aware of a claim even if it is the school that will be defending you. Consult an attorney who can advise you on the lawsuit's licensure and other administrative implications. Ask your private insurance for a referral to a licensure defense attorney when you notify them of the lawsuit.

Avoid discussing the matter with anyone other than the attorney who will be representing you. Conversations with others can be discoverable if they are not privileged and can unintentionally create adverse witnesses. Additionally, if you have inadvertently made a statement against your own interest, it can be used to damage you. Resist the temptation to make personal copies of records, accident reports, statements, or other documents. Doing so can violate school policies, privacy laws, and professional conduct rules. Do not keep personal logs, diaries, or journals that detail experiences related to student care or adverse events. They can be discoverable in litigation. Even when redacting identifiers, they can also violate privacy laws or professional standards.

CONCLUSION

Most school nurses will complete their entire careers without ever being involved in a medical malpractice lawsuit. Staying insured, maintaining clinical competency, documenting adequately, and cultivating healthy relationships with sound interpersonal communication skills can reduce liability exposure even further.

RESOURCES

Justia (2022). All topics in Education Law Resource Center. https://www.justia.com/education/sitemap/

Case Law

KRS v. Bedford Community School District, 109 F.Supp.3d 1060 (S.D. Iowa 2015). https://casetext.com/case/krs-v-bedford-cmty-sch-dist

Meyers v. Cincinnati Bd. of Educ., 983 F3d 873 (6th Cir. 2020). https://law.justia.com/cases/federal/appellate-courts/ca6/18-3974/18-3974-2020-12-29.html

REFERENCES

Bleier, E. (2015, May 12). Jury awards high school football player who suffered a concussion but was allowed to continue practicing $ 1 million in largest high school head injury payout in history. *Daily Mail.com*. https://www.dailymail.co.uk/news/article-3078682/Jury-awards-injured-high-school-football-player-1M.html

CNA/Nurses Service Organization (2020). Nurse professional liability exposure claim report: 4th Edition. https://www.nso.com/getmedia/499d682c-6855-46fb-b6b1-c12da2d7ea23/CNA_CLS_NURSE20_061120p2_CF_PROD_ONLINE_SEC.pdf

Console, R. (2022). Bad bedside manner or medical malpractice? *The National Law Review*, December 14, 2022, https://www.natlawreview.com/article/bad-bedside-manner-or-medical-malpractice

del Valle, L. & Jorgensen, S. (2017). Parents of 8-year-old who hanged himself file lawsuit against Cincinnati schools, CNN August 8, 2017. https://www.cnn.com/2017/08/07/us/gabriel-taye-school-lawsuit/index.html

ELLIOTT, D. (2015, MAY 12). JURY AWARDS HS ATHLETE NEARLY $1 MILLION IN HEAD INJURY CASE. *Yahoo Sports*. https://www.yahoo.com/tv/bp/jury-awards-h-s--athlete-nearly--1-million-in-head-injury-case-145741413.html

Freeman, M., Dennison, S., Giannotti, N., and Voutt-Goos, M.J. (2020). An evidence-based framework for reporting student nurse medication incidents: errors, near misses and discovered errors. *Quality Advancement in Nursing Education*, *6* (3), Article 4. https://doi.org/10.17483/2368-6669.1233

Mitchell, M. (2021). CPS board approved settlement in Gabriel Taye bullying case, *The Enquirer*, June 7, 2021. https://www.cincinnati.com/story/news/2021/06/07/cps-board-approves-settlement-gabriel-taye-bullying-case/7587648002/

Nelson, A. (2015, May 12). Former Iowa HS Football player nearly $1m; nurse didn't respond properly to concussion-like symptoms. *World Herald*. http://www.livewellnebraska.com/consumer/former-iowa-hs-football-player-nearly-m-nurse-didn-t/article_505471b1-88b9-535a-9685-459b2fc2879a.html

Scott, S. (2019). Strong physician-patient relationships improve care, ward off malpractice suits, *AAP News*, July 23, 2019. https://publications.aap.org/aapnews/news/13647

Simko-Bednarski, E. (2021). Cincinnati school district to settle lawsuit filed by parents of bullied boy who hanged himself, CNN June 5, 2021. https://www.cbs58.com/news/cincinnati-school-district-to-settle-lawsuit-filed-by-parents-of-bullied-boy-who-hanged-himself

SPC Health. (2022). 5 ways clear communication helps avoid medical malpractice, August 18, 2022. F Brin https://www.scp-health.com/blog/5-ways-clear-communication-helps-avoid-medical-malpractice/

U.S. Department of Education, Office for Civil Rights. (2010). Free Appropriate Public Education for Students with Disabilities: Requirements Under Section 504 of the Rehabilitation Act of 1973. http://www.ed.gov/about/offices/list/ocr/docs/edlite-FAPE504.html

United States Department of Health and Human Services. (n.d.). National practitioner data bank. *NPDB Research Statistics.* https://www.npdb.hrsa.gov/resources/aboutStatData.jsp

United States Department of Labor Statistics (2022). Occupational employment and wage statistics, 29-1141 Registered Nurses. https://www.bls.gov/oes/current/oes291141.htm

Vailee, S., Fathi, M. & Shahoei, R. (2018). Nursing students' errors and their causes: a qualitative exploration of clinical instructors' perspectives, *Patient Safety & Quality Improvement Journal*, November 2018. https://www.academia.edu/67578428/Nursing_Students_Errors_and_Their_Causes_a_Qualitative_Exploration_of_Clinical_Instructors_Perspectives

Wisenberg Brin, D. (2018). The best response to medical errors? Transparency. *AAMC News*, January 15, 2018. https://www.aamc.org/news-insights/best-response-medical-errors-transparency

Chapter 3

SCOPE, STANDARDS AND COMPETENCIES FOR SCHOOL NURSING:
IMPLICATIONS FOR SCHOOL NURSE PRACTICE

Joanne Roy, PhD, MSN, RN
Rosale Lobo, PhD, MSN, RN
Cheryl Resha, EdD, MSN, RN, FNASN, FAAN

DESCRIPTION OF ISSUE

The scope and standards of nursing, and subsequently the related competencies, guide the professional practice for all nursing. For school nurses, including school nurse consultants and graduate-level nurses working with school communities, the *School Nursing: Scope and Standards of Practice* (2022) specifically provides the framework for nursing care within schools and school communities. The scope describes who, what, where, when, why, and how of school nursing and the standards are the authoritative statements of nursing practice and professional expectations (American Nurses Association [ANA], 2021). Competencies are objective measures of the standards and are a way to demonstrate nursing knowledge, skill, and behaviors regarding standards of practice.

School nurses have a social and professional obligation to practice within and to the full extent of the scope and standards of practice. Legally school nurses can and should use the *School Nursing: Scope and Standards of Practice* to guide what they do every day for all healthcare consumers within the school community. For school nurses, the healthcare consumer "includes not only the student, but also those influencing students such as the family, school community, the larger surrounding community, aggregates within the school population, or the entire school population" (National Association of School Nurses [NASN], 2022, p. 102)

Adhering to the scope and standards of practice, along with individual state laws and nurse practice acts, can support safe practice, promote high-quality care, guide nurses to successfully meet the various roles and responsibilities of school nursing, and minimize the risk of malpractice claims, as well as discipline by boards of nursing. The standards of practice can be useful to establish in a legal setting that the standard of care was met, i.e., that another nurse with similar education and experience in similar circumstances would have provided the same care. The scope and standards of practice can also serve as the basis for job descriptions, supervision, evaluation guidelines, and direct negotiations for union contracts.

BACKGROUND

History

As stated above, the scope and standards of nursing practice describe nursing practice. In 1973, the ANA published the first standards for the practice of nursing and subsequently invited specialty areas of nursing to develop standards unique to their area of practice within the context of ANA's overarching scope and standards of school nursing practice were published and now the standards of school nursing practice

---

*Original authors: Cheryl Resha, EdD, MSN, RN, FNASN & Stephanie Knutson, MSN, RN (2017)

have undergone several revisions (Resha, 2019). According to Resha, despite the view that standards are authoritative statements of practice, standards are intentionally broad and need examples and details to make them specific and understandable for nurses (2019, p.34). Therefore, in addition to standards, competencies serve as the measure of knowledge, skills, and behaviors that become understandable to school nurses and the public.

Educating school nurses about their practice, the standards, and the resources available to them is a priority to promote safe care for students and avoid liability from negligence or charges of professional misconduct by the nursing board from how prudent school nurses would function in a similar situation. It is important to remember "a standard of care is defined as what a reasonably prudent person would do under the same or similar circumstance" (Resha, 2019, p. 34).

NASN (2021) describes the broad and evolving role of the school nurse as including elements of leadership, community/public health, care coordination, and quality improvement. With this expanding and evolving role, the scope and standards of practice are revised every five years to keep up with changing trends. To foster high-quality care, school nurses need to stay up to date with practice changes, revisions to the scope and standards of practice, and emerging evidence that supports best practices.

School Nursing: Standards of Practice and Professional Performance

STANDARD 1. ASSESSMENT

The school nurse collects pertinent data and information relative to the student, family, group, school community, or population.

STANDARD 2. DIAGNOSIS

The school nurse analyzes the assessment data of the student, family, group, school community, or population to describe actual or potential diagnoses.

STANDARD 3. OUTCOMES IDENTIFICATION

The school nurse identifies measurable expected outcomes for a plan individualized to the student, family, group, school community, or population.

STANDARD 4. PLANNING

The school nurse develops a collaborative course of action that prescribes strategies to attain expected, measurable outcomes that student, family, group, school community, or population.

STANDARD 5. IMPLEMENTATION

The school nurse executes an agreed upon plan/interventions for student, family, group, school community, or population.

STANDARD 5A. COORDINATION OF CARE

The school nurse aligns care for student, family, group, school community, or population.

STANDARD 5B. HEALTH TEACHING AND HEALTH PROMOTION

The school nurse employs strategies to improve health and safety of students, family, group, school community, or population.

STANDARD 6. EVALUATION

The school nurse systematically appraises progress toward attainment of student and school population goals and outcomes.

STANDARD 7. ETHICS

The school nurse integrates ethics in all aspects of practice.

STANDARD 8. ADVOCACY

The school nurse demonstrates advocacy in all roles and settings.

STANDARD 9. RESPECTFUL AND EQUITABLE PRACTICE

The school nurse practices with cultural humility and inclusiveness.

STANDARD 10. COMMUNICATION

The school nurse effectively conveys information in all areas of practice.

STANDARD 11. COLLABORATION

The school nurse collaborates with students, families, and key stakeholders.

STANDARD 12. LEADERSHIP

The school nurse leads within the professional practice setting and the profession.

STANDARD 13. EDUCATION

The school nurse seeks knowledge and competence that reflects current nursing practice and promotes innovative, anticipatory thinking.

STANDARD 14. SCHOLARLY INQUIRY

The school nurse integrates scholarship, evidence, and research findings into practice.

STANDARD 15. QUALITY OF PRACTICE

The school nurse contributes to quality nursing practice.

STANDARD 16. PROFESSIONAL PRACTICE EVALUATION

The school nurse evaluates one's own and others' school nursing practice.

STANDARD 17. RESOURCE STEWARDSHIP

The school nurse utilizes appropriate resources to plan, provide, and sustain evidence-based nursing services that are safe, effective, financially responsible, and used judiciously.

STANDARD 18. ENVIRONMENTAL HEALTH

The school nurse practices in a manner that advances environmental safety, justice, and health.

(NASN, 2022, p. 57-58. Reprinted with permission. All rights reserved).

Use of Standards

According to Resha (2019), standards can be used as a framework to inform many aspects of school nurse practice. The use of the school nursing standards serves as the foundation for orientation to the role of school nursing, the development of job descriptions, as well as the guide for an evaluation/job performance system that further validates the significance of those standards as a guide for practice (NASN, 2022; NASN, 2018b; Resha, 2019). NASN (2018b) suggests, "to promote proficiency, professionalism and quality improvement initiatives, supervision and evaluation of school nurse performance should support the specific roles and responsibilities necessary to promote the health, safety, and learning of individual students and unique school communities" (pp. 1); the use of school nursing standards promote just that.

The standards have also served to educate others on the role of school nurses. In an environment where school nurses often work as the sole healthcare provider alongside non-healthcare administrators and staff, there are times when conflict occurs regarding what care can be provided and by whom. The scope and standards of school nursing practice have served to help articulate the unique and professional role of the school nurse (Resha, 2019).

Standards can serve to inform policies and procedures within a school district or at a state level. Policies are broad statements regarding specific activities, such as medication administration, immunization requirements for entrance into school, and care of ill or injured students, and approved by a governing board, usually the board of education. Procedures or protocols are the details behind the policy and specifically outline how the policy is operationalized.

Finally, the standards provide a structure for quality improvement to continuously evaluate and promote best practices regarding the overall district or statewide practice of school nursing. If the standards are used to develop the policies and procedures, they are also useful in the evaluation of procedures and overall health services as well as quality improvement efforts (Resha, 2019). For example, a school district can examine Standard 13: Education, and recommend that a goal for their school nurses would be to have all of their school nurses become nationally certified.

IMPLICATIONS FOR SCHOOL NURSE PRACTICE

Nursing Preparation

School nurses practice in environments that offer opportunities to make important decisions that may have a lasting impact on the lives of students. School nurses are usually the sole healthcare professional in school environments and contribute significantly to the development of school health policies and programs. Practicing within the Framework for 21st Century School Nurse Practice provides school nurses with reference to the 5 principles: Standards of Practice, Care Coordination, Leadership, Quality Improvement, and Community/ Public Health (NASN, 2021) (ASCD & CDC, 2014).

An example of this need to base care on standards is exemplified in the following case:

K.R.S. v. Bedford Community School District, No. 4:13-cv-00147 (S.D. Iowa, 2015)

In this case, a lawsuit was brought against a school nurse and the school district for not alerting the football coaches nor the grandmother about a student's continued complaints of headaches and vision difficulties following a prank where teammates threw footballs at his head while he was sitting on the sideline during a practice. The student told the nurse that he had been hit on the head with a football and was concerned that he might have a concussion. The student returned to the school nurse for continued complaints of headaches and blurred vision, yet no notifications occurred. The suit also claimed that the school should be held responsible for the student's need to consult with a physician and follow up with his grandmother to make sure that he saw a doctor. Had the nurse alerted his coaches and grandmother to a possible concussion after his first visit to the nurse's office, he could have been evaluated immediately, preventing the blood clot and resulting brain damage. Ultimately the case was settled in favor of the student and grandmother, and that the school nurse departed from the standards of care and should have notified both the coaches and family to ensure follow-up with the physician. This case also emphasizes the importance of the standards for documentation.

(See Chapter 2 for more information regarding professional malpractice).

Nurses who choose to enter the specialty of school nursing may not be proficient in all the national school nursing standards (NASN, 2022). School nurses may initially be surprised by and unprepared for the degree of autonomy their specialty provides them. However, regardless of their prior experiences, educational preparation, or the diverse conditions under which school nurses work, they must understand that they are legally responsible and accountable for practicing and adhering to the school nursing scope and standards of practice. Specifically, *Standard* 13, *Education*, states that "the school nurse attains knowledge and competence that reflects current nursing practice…" (NASN, 2022, p. 86). NASN (2022) further acknowledged that all practicing school nurses must uphold commonality of conduct and gains towards proficiency in competencies.

School nurses who take part in continuous education will remain up to date with the standards for best practice. According to Hsieh, Chen, and Chang (2018) "evidence-based practice (EBP) has become the standard for provisions of the best patient care in the clinical system" (p. 1). School nurses are seeing an increasingly diverse population with complex needs, and staying current with standards ensures the best outcome for students (Hsiehet al., 2018).

Suggested Strategies

Participating in professional development activities can lead to proficiency in school nursing competencies. Professional development should be intentional and goal-directed, as opposed to random. Nurses who plan and manage such activities to acquire current knowledge and skills are more likely to provide safe and effective nursing care (Miambo et al., 2021). Sound knowledge of the scope and standards that are implemented in daily school nursing practice is required to demonstrate compliance with these standards of practice in malpractice and nursing board cases.

In line with the Robert Wood Johnson Foundation's Initiative on *The Future of Nursing* 2020-2030, "School nurses are front line health care providers, serving as a bridge between the health care and education systems and other sectors" (National Academy of Science, 2020, p.10). School nurses engage with students who face social and economic disparities like food insecurity and homelessness. Environmental circumstances impact a student's mental and physical ability to engage in educational activities. For some students, their only access to healthcare may be the school nurse. Engaging in theoretical as well as clinically focused professional development activities can minimize knowledge deficit and improve student health outcomes. It can also maximize the nurse's potential and job satisfaction. Therefore, professional school nurses must also engage in self-evaluation to gauge their competencies and self-reflective processes to gain insights that lead to the creation of specific plans to meet their professional development needs.

Practicing school nurses must take the necessary steps to align their job-related responsibilities, job descriptions, and employee evaluations with the *School Nursing: Scope and Standards of Practice* (NASN, 2022). Continuous preparation to meet competencies are reinforced when formal documentation of school nursing role and responsibilities (i.e., job descriptions and employee evaluations) are supported with the well-recognized standards of practice.

(Please see Chapter 6 for more information on school nurse evaluation).

Creating a portfolio highlighting professional skills, knowledge and accomplishments is another way school nurses can remain current with practice standards. Participating in conferences with school administrators to discuss the portfolio validates professional practice standards for the school nurse. This method is used in education and allows the school nurse to demonstrate competency for the dynamic responsibilities occurring in their daily practice, especially when they are often supervised by non-nursing administrators (Wallin & Rothman, 2020).

Finally, the use of recommended decision-making processes will assist school nurses to know that they are functioning within their scope of practice. In collaboration with other nursing groups, the National Council of State Boards of Nursing (NCSBN) recently developed a decision-making tool to guide practicing nurses through making informed decisions. The algorithm (APPENDIX) helps practicing nurses provide care within their scopes of practice (Ballard et al., 2016).

Working in Interprofessional Teams

School nurses who practice in elementary and secondary schools must know, understand, and abide by relevant education and nursing/health laws and regulations. Federal laws such as the Individuals with Disabilities Education Improvement Act (IDEIA), the Americans with Disabilities Act (ADA), the McKinney-Vento Homeless Assistance Act, as well as state education and health laws are specific to educational environments. State nurse practice acts, and laws specific to school nursing practice must be considered along with federal and state education laws when creating, implementing, and evaluating nursing and healthcare services provided to students. Laws also vary across states in terms of what nursing and health practices are allowed in school environments. For example, certain medication administration, screening, or school enrollment practices permitted in one state may be illegal in another state. Delegation of nursing activities to unlicensed assistive personnel also varies from state to state.

(*See Chapter 4 on delegation and Chapter 1 on professional licensure for more information*).

> *The case of the American Nurses Association (ANA) v. Torlakson, 57 Cal.4th 570 (Cal. App. 2014), provides an example of the variations of state laws. In California, unlicensed personnel may administer insulin. This is not the case in other states. The ANA sued the California Superintendent of Public Instruction and Department of Education regarding the authorization of school employees, other than school nurses, to administer insulin to students (citation, p.1). The objection was that the 2007 Legal Advisory constituted the unauthorized practice of nursing and was a violation of the nurse practice act. The California Supreme Court decided that the California Nursing Practice Act and California law did not prohibit school personnel other than licensed healthcare providers to administer medication, therefore, unlicensed school personnel could administer insulin to students (Ass'n v. Torlakson (Cal. App. 2014)).*

Educational and health-related individualized plans are one way of documenting services provided to students by members of the school's interprofessional teams. These teams rely on school nurses to contribute their health and nursing expertise to the development of legally binding student plans, such as Individualized Education Plans (IEP) or Section 504 Plans. With knowledge and a clear understanding of how to apply education and nursing/health laws in school environments, boards of education can provide a defense in legal action.

> *In Begley v. City of New York, 111 A.D. 3d5 (2013), parents of a developmentally delayed student, who died after suffering an anaphylactic reaction at a non-public school, failed to establish that the local department of education (DOE) was responsible for the actions of an independently contracted nurse. In this case, the related services agreement documented in the student's IEP expressly stated that it (1) was an agreement between the parent and the independent nurse for nursing services approved by DOE; (2) required the nurse to carry her own professional liability insurance; and (3) further reiterated that current DOE employees could not provide such services under that contract. The court ruled in favor of the DOE due to the language provided in the student's IEP.*

Standard 11 of the *School Nursing: Scope and Standard of Practice*, which is titled Collaboration, emphasizes team and interprofessional interaction and states that the school nurse "Partners with students, families, stakeholders, and members of the interprofessional team to create, implement, and evaluate a comprehensive plan for change that leads to positive outcomes and quality care" (NASN, 2022, Competency 11.7, p. 81) Not only is participation in interprofessional teams a competency benchmark but according to *Standard 10 on Communication*, it is expected that professional school nurses must also understand regulations so they can effectively communicate and convey accurate information in a responsible manner that protects the rights of students, parents, and the local DOE.

Suggested Strategies

By participating in mentorships, school nurses can gain new knowledge and guidance from experts in their field. These professional relationships with an expert school nurse can provide a learning and development partnership that can assist the newer school nurse to close the knowledge gap, especially related to school and district policies unique to the school nurse role. Transitioning from a hospital or other clinical setting to an educational environment often requires knowledge and skills that may only be available or acquired through professional relationships with school nurse leaders and colleagues with expertise in school nursing practices.

NASN (2022) defines mentoring as "a power-free...relationship using skills similar to coaching with the goal of professional development" (p. 104). School nurses should consider a mentor both within and outside the school nursing profession. This additional engagement by school nurses with other disciplines can serve to educate members of the interprofessional team about their valuable role as the health expert in the school community while at the same time building professional relationships.

Joining professional associations is another way of creating professional relationships. Professional organizations facilitate collaboration and keep members up to date with trends and advance specific to the specialty practices of the profession. This engagement provides a place of connection with stakeholders and government entities associated with contemporary practice. (Yonkaitis et al., 2021) Additionally, the benefits of becoming a member of a local, regional, or national nurses' association include opportunities for enhanced networking, access to career resource information, current events, and best practice updates while staying connected to colleagues with similar specialty, such as school nursing.

Aligning School Nursing Practice with School District's Goals and Priorities
Experienced school nurses know and understand the importance of aligning the health goals of students with school district goals and priorities. As public health nurses, school nurses may encounter situations and circumstances where the prioritization of health goals outweighs an immediate educational activity. The professional nurse is relied on to apply, abide by, and reference appropriate laws and regulations when necessary. Boards of Education have a legal duty to educate students, but they also have a legal duty of care to protect students from harm through safe, preventative, and direct care measures and when necessary, provide emergency care in cases of injury or accidents. School nurses, as the primary or sometimes only healthcare professional in the school environment, must be knowledgeable in applying the scope and standards of school nursing practice that includes:

- communicating with students and parents/guardians;
- conducting health promotion activities;
- collaborating with the appropriate local public health and emergency crisis teams;
- connecting with the school physician;
- knowing and following the chain of command; and
- communicating well thought-out information that assists school leaders in making decisions that ensures the health and safety of students.

A school nurse's decision to remove a child from the classroom can be disruptive to the educational process. Ramifications may include the need to make up hours of instruction missed by students with IEPs, reallocating staff, rescheduling, or canceling school events, and contacting parents/guardians, to name a few. However, there may be occasions that require interruption of the school program, such as to conduct screening tests for students, or in the case of an epidemic. School nurses must then use appropriate competencies such as those outlined in Standards one through six, including assessment, planning, implementation strategies, coordination of care; and then, using critical thinking skills, communicate information that promotes and supports a functioning, healthy and safe learning experience, and environment for students.

> *One important district goal and priority is school attendance by students. Chronic absence is recognized as a national crisis as it is directly linked to exacerbating achievement gaps and dropout rates (Attendance Works, 2022). Fortunately, chronic absence may be reduced when school communities, families and community partners work together to remove barriers that inhibit attendance to school by students and engage in effective practices for improved student attendance. School nurses, as an expert in health and integral member of the school team, can help address absenteeism by leveraging the five pronged approach: "engage students and parents, recognize good and improved attendance, monitor school attendance data and practice, provide personalized early outreach, and develop programmatic response to barriers" (NASN, 2018a, p. 1). These engagement by school nurses demonstrates how school nursing practice can be aligned with school district goals and priorities.*

Suggested Strategies

Developing school health policies, protocols, and procedural guidelines that impact student health outcomes and school nursing practice is another important role of the school nurse. When circumstances do not allow for active engagement in the creative process, school nurses must be vigilant in lending their expertise by reviewing policies, etc., that have been developed and revisiting existing student individualized plans. These actions should be ongoing throughout each school year.

Participating in crisis and emergency school teams is another important responsibility of the school nurse. School nurses advocate for safety by participating in the development of school safety plans to address bullying, school violence, and the full range of emergency incidents that may occur at school (NASN, 2019). In addition to providing a nursing, medical, and healthcare perspective, school nurses promote access to care, connect students and families to community services, and are aware of community resources and therefore a critical part of the crisis and emergency teams.

Finally, in addition to aligning with district goals and priorities, school nurses should engage in strategies to ensure that health programs and services are aligned with the scope and standards of practice. The use of ongoing evaluation and quality improvement efforts can help the school nurse assess areas of strength and those in need of improvement. The Scope of School Nursing Practice Tool (SSNPT) can be utilized to assess standards of practice within the context of the Framework for 21st Century School Nursing (White et al., 2021). Examining and documenting quality improvement efforts is an effective strategy in promoting safe practice.

(Also see Disaster Preparedness Chapter 43 for more information on standards of practice during public health emergencies).

CONCLUSION

The scope and standards of practice serve as the guide and provide authoritative statements on standards of care for all school nurses. In the absence of federal, state, or local laws, the professional standards become the "standard of care" which can be used to determine if a school nurse acted in a way that reflects best practices, competent care, health promotion, and safety for all. Becoming educated on the standards and using them to guide job descriptions, orientation, evaluation, professional development, policies, and quality improvement is key to promoting high-quality, evidence-based healthcare services in the school.

RESOURCES

American Nurses Association (2016). Nursing Administration: Scope and Standards of Practice 2nd Ed. Author

American Nurses Association (2015) Code of Ethics for Nurses with Interpretive Statements. Author.

National Association of School Nurses (2021). NASN Code of Ethics. https://www.nasn.org/nasn-resources/resources-by-topic/codeofethics

National Association of School Nurses. The framework for 21st century school nursing. Author. https://www.nasn.org/nasn-resources/framework

Case Law

Am. Nurses Ass'n v. Torlakson (Cal. App. 2014)

Begley v. City of N.Y., 111 A.D.3d 5 (2013)

K.R.S. v. Bedford Community School District, 109 F.Supp.3d 1060 (2015)

REFERENCES

American Nurses Association (2021). *Nursing: scope and standards of practice.* (5th ed.). Author.

Attendance Works. (2022). *Why attendance matters for the healthcare provider.*https://www.attendanceworks.org/wp-content/uploads/2019/06/For-Health-Care-Providers_May-2022_finalv1.pdf

Ballard, K., Haagenson, D., Christiansen, L., Damgaard, G., Halstead, J., Jason, R., Joyner, J., O'Sullivan, A., Silvestre, J., Cahill, M., Radtke, E.& Alexander, M. (2016). Scope of practice decision-making framework. *Journal of Nursing Regulation, 7*(3), 19-21.http://dx.doi.org/10.1016/S2155-8256(16)32316-X

Hsieh P-L, Chen S-H, Chang L-C. School Nurses' Perceptions, Knowledge, and Related Factors Associated with Evidence-Based Practice in Taiwan. *International Journal of Environmental Research and Public Health.* 2018; 15(9):1845. https://doi.org/10.3390/ijerph15091845

Mlambo, M., Silén, C. & McGrath, C. (2021). Lifelong learning and nurses' continuing professional development, a meta-synthesis of the literature. *BMC Nursing, 20*(62). https://doi.org/10.1186/s12912-021-00579-2

National Academies of Sciences, Engineering, and Medicine. (2021). *The future of nursing 2020-2030: Charting a path to achieve health equity.* The National Academies Press. https://doi.org/10.17226/25982

National Association of School Nurses. (2022). *School Nursing: Scope and Standards of Practice* (4th ed.). Author.

National Association of School Nurses. (2018a). *School nurses: An integral member of the school team addressing chronic absenteeism* (Position Statement). Author. https://www.nasn.org/nasn-resources/professional-practice-documents/position-statements/ps-absenteeism

National Association of School Nurses. (2018b). *Supervision and evaluation of the school nurse* (Position Statement). Author.https://www.nasn.org/nasn-resources/professional-practice-documents/position-statements/ps-supervision

National Association of School Nurses. (2019). *Emergency preparedness* (Position Statement). Author. https://www.nasn.org/nasn-resources/professional-practice-documents/position-statements/ps-emergency-preparedness

National Association of School Nurses. (2021). *The framework for 21st century school nursing*. Author. https://www.nasn.org/nasn-resources/framework

National Association of School Nurses. (2022). *School nursing: Scope and standards of practice* (4th ed.). Author.

Resha, C. (2019). Standards of practice. In J. Selekman, R.A.Shannon, & C.F. Yonkaitis (Eds.), *School nursing: A comprehensive text* (3rd ed., pp. 31-49). F.A. Davis Company.

Wallin, R., & Rothman, S. (2020). A framework for school nurse self-reflection and evaluation. *NASN School Nurse, 35*(1), 35-40. https://doi.org/10.1177/1942602X19852295

White, K., Davis, D., & Maughan, E. (2021). Development and validation of an instrument to measure scope of practice in school nurses. *Journal of Advanced Nursing, 77*(7),3226–3237. https://doi.org/10.1111/jan.14867

Yonkaitis, C., Madura, K., & Vollinger, L. (2021). School Nursing Associations: Restructuring for Contemporary Practice. *NASN School Nurse, 36*(5), 284-290. https://doi.org/10.1177/1942602X21992860

Chapter 4

PROCESS FOR DELEGATION IN THE SCHOOL SETTING

Kimberly Lacey, DNSc, MSN, RN, CNE, CNL

Krista Prendergast, EdD, MSN, RN, CNE

Cheryl Resha, EdD, MSN, RN, FNASN, FAAN

DESCRIPTION OF ISSUE

Delegation is an essential skill and is defined as "the transfer of a nursing activity, skill, or procedure to a delegatee… and allows the delegatee to perform a specific nursing activity, skill, or procedure that is beyond the delegatee's traditional role and not routinely performed" (American Nurses Association (ANA) and National Council of State Boards of Nursing (NCSBN), 2019, p. 2). In school nursing, delegation occurs when the school nurse transfers the nursing activity, skill, or procedure to another person, often to another licensed nurse or unlicensed assistive personnel (UAP), such as an administrator, teacher, paraprofessional or health aide (National Association of School Nurses [NASN], 2018).

To ensure safe practice, and ultimately safe care for all children, school nurses are responsible for the delegation of any nursing care or activity in the school setting and on school-sponsored trips. This requires knowledge and understanding of the profession's guidance on delegation, their specific state's nurse practice act (NPA) related to delegation of nursing activities, other applicable state laws related to unlicensed personnel in schools (e.g., specific medication or screening laws), district policies, and communication and collaboration among all stakeholders (ANA, 2012; NASN, 2018; & ANA & NCSBN, 2019).

BACKGROUND

Children with medical complexity have significant chronic health conditions that involve multiple organ systems, substantial health service needs, major functional limitations, and high health resource use (Murphy et al., 2020). This complexity of care is also required at school. The incidence of chronic conditions has also grown; according to the Centers for Disease Control and Prevention (CDC), approximately 40% of children have at least one chronic condition and require daily management (CDC, 2021; NASN, 2022a). As the incidence of children with chronic or special healthcare condition grows, so does the legal responsibility of schools to ensure access to a free, appropriate public education (FAPE) for all children under Section 504 of the Rehabilitation Act of 1973 [Section 504], the Americans with Disability Act [ADA] or Individuals with Disabilities Education Act [IDEA] (ADA National Network, 2018).

According to the 2017 NASN School Nurse Survey, there are variations across the country regarding staffing patterns (i.e., one school nurse per school building, one school nurse responsible for more than one school building, and some schools with no school nurse) as well as the number of students per building (Willgerodt et al., 2018). Regarding school coverage, "43.7% of school nurses were assigned to only one building, 18.2% covered two school buildings, and 37.7% covered more than two buildings…additionally, 73.6% report using non-health-care-trained professional personnel (e.g., school administrative staff, teachers) to support health

---

*Original author: Cheryl Resha, EdD, MSN, RN, FNASN (2017)

services" (Willgerodt et al., 2018, pp. 236-237). In addition, many school nurses report no clinical supervision, and only about one-third of the school nurses in a national survey reported having a registered nurse as a supervisor (NASN, 2019b). These staffing patterns, workloads, and availability of nursing supervision can, at times, impede the delivery of health services.

In the modern healthcare environment, "fiscal constraints, nursing shortages, and increases in patient care complexity have cultivated an environment in which delegation is necessary. If appropriately used, delegation can significantly improve patient care outcomes" (Barrow & Sharma, 2022, para. 13). In schools, the growing healthcare needs and staffing patterns coupled with the need to ensure FAPE and provide the health services to students on and off campus makes delegation a valid consideration to meet the health needs of children in schools. However, delegation comes with challenges. Overcoming the challenges and successfully using delegation to provide health care in schools requires a clear understanding of the key definitions, one's state NPA and any associated state board of nursing (BON) regulations or declaratory rulings or opinions. Other pertinent federal and state laws (e.g., Section 504, IDEA, and state medication laws), and acceptable standards of care for the delegation from professional nursing organizations, such as ANA & NCSBN (2019), NASN (2018), NASN (2022b) and NCSBN (2016) must also be considered. If students are traveling out of state on school-sponsored trips, school nurses should also be familiar with the destination state's NPA and regulations on the delegation to UAPs (NASN, 2019a).

Definitions

Accountability: "to be answerable to oneself and others for one's own choices, decisions and actions as measured against a standard..." (ANA, 2015, p. 41)

Assignment: "the routine care, activities, and procedures that are within the authorized scope of practice of the RN, LPN/LVN or part of the routine function of the UAP" (ANA & NCSBN, 2019, p. 2)

Assistive Personnel (AP): Any assistive personnel trained to function in a supportive role, regardless of title, to whom a nursing responsibility may be delegated. This includes but is not limited to certified nursing assistants or aides (CNAs), patient care technicians, CMAs, certified medication aids, and home health aides (formerly referred to as "unlicensed" assistive personnel [UAP]) (ANA & NCSBN, 2019, p 2).

Delegatee: The person accepting the responsibility to perform a specific nursing activity (NCSBN & ANA, 2019).

Delegated Responsibility: "A nursing activity, skill, or procedure that is transferred from a licensed nurse to a delegatee" (ANA & NCSBN, 2019, p. 2).

Delegator: "One who delegates a nursing responsibility. A delegator may be APRN, RN, or LPN/LVN, if state NPA allows" (NCSBN & ANA, 2019, p. 2)

Licensed Nurse: A licensed nurse includes APRNs, RNs, and LPN/VNs. In some states/jurisdictions, LPN/ VNs may be allowed to delegate (ANA & NCSBN, 2019, p. 2).

Case Review

The case of *Mitts vs. Hillsboro Union High School* (1987) is one of the most well-documented opinions regarding delegation and school health services and, in some ways, has set the stage for current practices. In the Mitts vs. Hillsboro case, the paraprofessional (in this case Ms. Mitts) sued the school in court after the school principal directed her to perform clean intermittent catheterization (CIC) on a student with spina bifida. The parents initially trained the paraprofessional. After carrying out the duty for a period of time, she was provided additional training and supervision on a monthly basis by the school nurse. The essence of the suit was the paraprofessional's claim that she was not competent to perform the CIC.

The case was brought to the Oregon court system; however, the court then asked the Oregon Board of Nursing for an opinion on the case. The key outcomes of the board's declaratory statement provide an analysis of current practices in school nursing. First, depending on state law, CIC can be delegated to a UAP **only** after the licensed nurse has assessed the healthcare needs, the stability of the client, the competency of the UAP to perform the activity, and deemed it safe for the UAP to carry out the nursing activity. Second, the principal did not have the authority to delegate a nursing activity to a UAP. Third, because he assessed the health needs and delegated care, **he was practicing nursing without a license.** In addition, since the UAP accepted the assignment from the principal, the UAP was also found to be practicing nursing without a license. Finally, although the school nurse had the authority to delegate after an appropriate assessment, the board also found that the nurse neglected to conduct the initial assessment and assumed a supervisory role after the delegation occurred, which is not an acceptable standard of practice (Mitts vs. Hillsboro, 1987).

It is evident that delegation is an acceptable practice in nursing. *However, it is **the nurse**, and not administrators, other school personnel, or directives, that guides the process and is accountable for the outcomes of the nursing care provided.*

Delegation guidelines (2019) can be applied to:
- APRNs delegating to RNs, LPN/LVNs, and UAPs;
- RNs delegating to LPN/LVNs and UAPs; and
- LPN/LVNs delegating to UAPs.

It is important to note that these guidelines do not apply to RNs to RNs or LPN/LVNs to LPN/LVNs; this is considered a handoff of assignment (ANA & NCSBN, 2019).

Delegation Model

The national guidelines for nursing delegation, including a Delegation Model presented by NCSBN (2019), include dynamic and overlapping concepts of delegation.

The Delegation Model (Figure 1) outlines the employer/nurse leader's responsibilities along with those for the delegating nurse and delegatee. The employer/nurse leader role in school nursing might be the school nurse supervisor (who is a registered nurse) or the lead school nurse for the district or building when there is no nursing supervisor. Because of the autonomous role of school nursing and the varying staffing patterns for school health services, the lead school nurse often holds a dual role as the employer/nurse leader and the nurse delegating to UAPs.

In addition to the overlapping spheres depicting the responsibilities of these three roles are the key concepts of two-way communication, the delegation process and UAP competency, and training and education with the ultimate goal of public protection. Inherent in this model continues to be the *Five Rights of Delegation* (task, circumstance, person, direction and communication, and supervision and evaluation) (NCSBN, 2019).

Delegation Model

Employer/Nurse Leader Responsibilities
- Identify a nurse leader
- Determine nursing responsibilities that can be delegated, to whom, and in what circumstances
- Develop delegation policies and procedures
- Periodically evaluate delegation process
- Promote positive culture/work environment

Communicate information about delegation process and delegatee competence level

Training and Education

Public Protection

Licensed Nurse Responsibilities
- Determine patient needs and when to delegate
- Ensure availability to delegatee
- Evaluate outcomes of and maintain accountability for delegated responsibility

Two-way Communication

Delegatee Responsibilities
- Accept activities based on own competence level
- Maintain competence for delegated responsibility
- Maintain accountability for delegated activity

Figure 1. NCSBN (2016). Delegation Model. ©2016 National Council of State Boards of Nursing. Reprinted with permission. All rights reserved.

Although there are national guidelines developed by an expert panel outlining the delegation process of nursing activities to other licensed nurses and UAPs, there is not a universal law governing delegation. The individual state NPAs and state laws continue to address to whom and, in some cases, what, nursing activities, skills, and procedures may be delegated (NCSBN, 2019).

School nurses often use delegation as an effective tool to ensure FAPE and access to needed healthcare services for students. However, there is still concern among school nurses regarding what a school nurse can and cannot delegate; what is recommended for safe delegation practices; who can assume responsibility for nursing activities, and who is liable if there is an error. The following section outlines implications for school nurses and suggested strategies to use when school nurses delegate nursing care to other licensed nurses or UAPs in the school setting.

IMPLICATIONS FOR SCHOOL NURSE PRACTICE

State Nurse Practice Acts and Other Pertinent State Laws

School nurses have the responsibility to themselves, other school staff who assume responsibility for nursing activities and students to be knowledgeable of state laws regarding the delegation of nursing activities to other licensed nurses (i.e., LPN/LVNs) and UAPs. Most states include delegation laws, regulations, and declaratory rulings under the auspices of the state BON and the state NPAs. The NCSBN provides a link to every state BON on their website for easy access finding this information at
https://www.ncsbn.org/membership/us-members/contact-bon.page

Some states' NPAs are very specific and identify which activities may be delegated to UAPs, while other state NPAs may only outline what aspects of the nursing process may be delegated rather than provide a list of tasks. For example, the Connecticut Board of Examiners for Nurses (CBEN) issued a *Declaratory Ruling* on delegation to unlicensed personnel (1995), which clearly identifies that only nursing tasks, skills, or procedures that do not require nursing judgment are allowed to be delegated, and these activities would fall under the implementation phase of the nursing process. This might include blood glucose monitoring for a stable student with type 1 diabetes, where a school nurse would train and supervise a UAP conducting blood glucose testing for a young student. However, the UAP would not be able to determine the next steps after obtaining the blood glucose reading without a written protocol or care plan (CBEN, 1995), which remains in place today on the CBEN current website.

National guidelines, most state NPAs, and declaratory rulings also emphasize that only the delegating nurse can determine what may be delegated, that the nurse is responsible to determine the competency of the UAP to carry out the nursing activity, and that no other aspect of the nursing process may be delegated, i.e., assessment, diagnosis, planning or evaluation may not be delegated (NCSBN & ANA, 2019; NASN, 2018).

Some state BONs are silent on delegation within the NPA. In these situations, school nurses will need to review other state laws that may inform their decisions and follow acceptable standards of care, such as the delegation process outlined by school nursing professional organizations (NASN, 2022b; NCSBN & ANA, 2019).

Finally, as mentioned above, school nurses also need to be knowledgeable of other state laws that may allow or prohibit certain nursing activities or procedures that can be delegated to other licensed nurses or UAPs. Some examples of these state laws, outside of the BON rulings or NPAs, include individual state educational or health laws on medication administration, administration of emergency epinephrine or inhalers, and blood glucose monitoring. For example, many states allow UAP in schools to administer medication to students in the absence of the school nurse.

Delegation versus Assignment

Delegation is the transfer of responsibility for a nursing activity, skill, or procedure from a licensed nurse to another licensed nurse or UAP, and the activity is beyond the traditional and routine role for this person. In this situation, the nurse retains accountability for the activity. The delegatee is responsible for carrying out the task properly and according to the direction provided by the nurse (ANA, 2012; NASN, 2018). For example, in many states, the administration of an epinephrine auto-injector (aka EpiPen®) to a child identified with a life-threatening food allergy may be delegated to a UAP in school or for off-campus events (Asthma and Allergy Network, n.d.). The school nurse trains the UAP, the school nurse determines the UAP to be competent to perform the activity by return demonstration with a trainer injector and accurate understanding of the emergency care plan indicating when to administer the auto-injector. The UAP is also able to verbalize when to contact the Emergency Medical System and what information should be communicated back to the school nurse following every off-campus event.

One common question that arises from retaining accountability for the activity is the question of liability (i.e., allegations of malpractice or discipline by the BON) if the delegatee makes an error in performing the activity. If the delegating nurse followed all the acceptable practices of delegation (see delegation process section) and has documentation of those practices, the school nurse would have a defense for any allegations of improper delegation and supervision. If, however, the school nurse did not conduct a comprehensive assessment and provide adequate training, supervision, evaluation, and documentation, both the school nurse and the delegatee would be responsible for the error (NCSBN & ANA, 2019).

The assignment is the transfer of the responsibility and accountability of the activity from the licensed nurse (APRN or RN) to another licensed nurse (e.g., LPN/LVN) or UAP, and the activity is part of their traditional role. For example, the RN may assign the LPN/LVN to perform a routine gastrostomy tube feeding after the RN conducted the assessment and developed the IHP. In this case, the LPN/LVN is likely to have had training/ education on this activity as part of their basic education or certification (NSCBN & ANA, 2019). Another example is when a licensed nurse can assign a health assistant (UAP) that works routinely in the school health office to take the temperature of all students who come in with the chief complaint of a stomachache or sore throat. The health assistant is responsible for obtaining the temperature, competently carrying out the task, and reporting the results to the school nurse. The well-developed job description or list of responsibilities is helpful in distinguishing between assignment and delegation. Another distinguishing characteristic between delegation and assignment is delegation is for a specific student and a specific task after an individualized assessment by the nurse vs an assignment where the task can be performed for a group of students (e.g., taking vital signs).

While there is no argument that both delegation and assignment require supervision and assurance by the registered nurse that the task is completed correctly, the key difference is if the activity (i.e., assignment) is within their scope of practice for an LPN/LVN or routine responsibilities as a UAP (NCSBN & ANA, 2019). If it is an assignment, then the person carrying out the activity is both responsible and accountable for the activity. For many school nurses, this distinction is important, particularly if they are not on-site for daily supervision and evaluation of the activity.

Delegation versus Training

Another question around delegation often occurs when the school nurse is contracted by a neighboring district or company (e.g., transportation company) where they are not employed to train staff on certain nursing or health activities. In these situations, if state laws allow the UAP to carry out the task, e.g., medication administration, then the school nurse (contracted) may be considering conducting a "professional activity," which is defined as providing education or training. Therefore, it may not be considered delegation as there is no ongoing relationship or assessment regarding delegating the activity and it is not "patient" specific (Herschel et al., 2005). In states that do not allow UAPs to perform a task, the act of the school nurse teaching the task to the UAP would be in violation of the state's nursing law. It is important to know what each state does and does not permit, as well as how the state defines delegation, assignment, etc. The Wisconsin Department of Education (2019) articulates the difference as "training is the process of providing general health information to others regarding a health skill, condition, injury, medication, or procedure. It can be done in a group or individual setting. If the training is specific to a certain student's health care needs, medications, and procedures, then the training is part of the process of delegation" (p. 10).

School nurses who provide the education are responsible to determine that the trainee is competent to perform the task at the end of the training or educational workshop (like a student/teacher relationship vs a nurse/patient relationship). This may include conducting a "teach-back" or some other form of assessment. "*Teach Back* is generally defined as a procedure during which the patients describe the information they have been taught, using their own words, to confirm their understanding of the information. Many authors have expanded the definition to include additional components considered central to performing this skill" (Anderson et al, 2020, p. e95). In the situation described above, the contracted school nurse should maintain an attendance list, a copy of the training outline and materials used, and documentation of the successful completion of the competency assessment (perhaps through the use of a checklist).

> **Best Practice for Documentation of Educational Trainings**
>
> The school nurse should maintain:
>
> Attendance List
>
> Training Curriculum
>
> Training Materials
>
> Competency checklist or record of successful teach-back for each participant

It is important to note that a case study regarding professional activity vs. delegation presented in Herschel et al. (2005) was an examination of Connecticut law, regulations, NPA, and rulings related to a nurse consultant in a childcare setting; and ultimately, the Board of Nursing did confirm that these situations were more akin to professional activity than delegation. While this is useful in establishing precedent, and activities like training school personnel in neighboring school districts are more likely professional activities, **each school nurse engaging in "professional activities" should review their state laws, regulations, and BONs to determine their stand on these issues.**

Delegation Policies

Policies are effective tools to provide clarity to an issue, ensure effective decision-making, standardize care, and provide education to those less familiar with the intent and purpose of the issue and in this case, delegation (Kahlil, 2023; NASN, 2018; NCSBN & ANA, 2019). School nurses straddle nursing and education laws, regulations, and practices; therefore, having clear policies can avoid nurse practice violations (Kahlil, 2023; NASN, 2022b). Lowe et al. (2022) conducted a systematic review and meta-synthesis on medication administration practices in schools across the U.S. including delegation. They found that inconsistencies in policies and procedures in state regulations and nurse practice acts remain a concern. They emphasize that national guidelines for medication administration in schools and off-campus activities are necessary to protect schools, nurses, UAP, and children. This is particularly important as the presence of UAPs in schools and children with complex medical problems in schools increases.

The school nurse or school nurse supervisor is a critical member of the team developing and continuously reviewing any policies related to student health. Policy statements are broad statements of the issue and guide what is expected of the organization (Kahlil, 2023; NCSBN & ANA, 2019). For example, a policy on delegation may state that:

- The school nurse initiates and guides the delegation of nursing activities.
- The school nurse follows procedural guidelines set forth by the professional organizations (ANA, NASN) and state boards of nursing responsible for nursing licensure, the scope of practice, nursing care, and the safety of care delivery.
- The school nurse is responsible for the supervision of the delegation of care.
- The school nurse may terminate the delegation of nursing activities at any time if there is a concern for the safety of the student or delegatee or if it is ineffective in meeting the student's healthcare outcomes.

Policies are substantiated with legal references and should be reviewed at least every three years and any time a new law or regulation is enacted. Finally, policies should not be confused with procedures or protocols that are much more detailed and may include all the necessary steps in the delegation process (Kahlil, 2023).

Delegation Process

After reviewing the applicable laws and district policy and determining that delegation is an option in the particular state and for the school nurse, the delegation process would begin with an assessment of the student, the creation of a student health plan, and needed health services. Delegation is a complex process. Barriers to effective delegation can be avoided by utilizing the following steps:
- Assure that you remain within your scope of practice.
- Understand the level of competency of the delegatee.
- Communicate your expectations and specific instructions.
- Understand to whom you should delegate.
- Understand when it is appropriate to delegate.
- Use delegation experiences to provide education to the delegatee and learn from the delegatee; and
- Express your appreciation to the delegatee for their work. (Anderson, 2018)

Prior to delegating an activity to another, the school nurse would begin a formal assessment process using the *Decision Tree: Nursing Delegation in the School Setting* (APPENDIX, NASN, 2018) and the *Five Rights of Delegation* (Anderson, 2018; NASN, 2018; NCSBN & ANA, 2019) to determine if delegation for a specific situation/activity is safe and appropriate.

PROCESS FOR DELEGATION IN THE SCHOOL SETTING

Assessment

The assessment would include a thorough review of the student's health needs and IHP to determine what nursing activities or procedures may need to be delegated to ensure the student is safe and their healthcare needs are met during the school day and school-sponsored trips. Following this review, the school nurse would then review the *Five Rights of Delegation* [Table 1] (NASN, 2018; NCSBN & ANA, 2019).

Table 1 Five Rights of Delegation

Right Task	Is the activity within the designee's job description? Is it allowed by law and in your policy? Can the necessary training be provided?
Right Circumstance	Is the student's condition stable? Is the care predictable?
Right Person	Does the delegatee have the skills and knowledge to carry out the task? Does the delegatee demonstrate the competencies needed to carry out the task?
Right Direction and Communication	Is there a specific Individualized Healthcare Plan (IHP) or emergency care plan (ECP) that outlines the care for the student? Is there specific communication for both the initial instructions and ongoing opportunities for two-way communication? Is the delegatee willing to accept the responsibility? How will data on the student's condition be collected and shared with the delegator? Does the delegatee understand that they cannot make any decisions and must consult with the delegating nurse for additional guidance?
Right Supervision and Evaluation	How will supervision occur? What frequency and mode of evaluation? How will the delegatee communicate any immediate or emergency concerns? Is the delegating nurse able to respond as needed? Is all information related to the activity documented?

Adapted from NASN, 2018; NCSBN & ANA, 2019

In addition to the *Five Rights*, the school nurse needs to consider what documents are available to guide safe care and would provide written direction for the delegated tasks, such as IHPs, ECPs, and nursing protocols.

Communication

The achievement of positive outcomes in healthcare requires a team approach which is enhanced through effective communication and delegation procedures (Wagner, 2018). The provision of clear instructions when delegating activities to others is essential. This includes reviewing the delegated assignment and responsibilities to the delegatee. Specific information regarding the student's condition, their care requirements, and information that should be reported back to the licensed nurse should be communicated to the delegatee (NCSBN & ANA, 2019).

Following the initial communication and instructions, ongoing two-way communication is needed to maintain open lines of communication between the delegating nurse and the delegatee for questions, reinforcement, and supervision. The licensed nurse should instruct the delegatee to provide regular communication regarding patient status (NCSBN & ANA, 2019). These instructions should include when and what the delegatee should communicate, how the delegate should respond to an emergency, and how the delegatee should provide documentation (NASN, 2018).

Supervision/Evaluation

Supervision and evaluation of the delegation process vary depending on the student's condition, complexity, and stability. Variability also occurs based on the delegatee's skill, the proximity to the nurse, and the need for additional training and support (NCSBN & ANA, 2019). For example, the delegation of blood glucose monitoring may have two very different supervision and evaluation plans based on the fluctuations in their daily blood glucose numbers, their age, and their cognitive abilities. It may also vary based on the delegatee's prior knowledge and education of the activity. A delegatee who is familiar with and performed blood glucose monitoring for another student in the past may be more comfortable implementing this particular student's plan than someone who has never performed blood glucose monitoring before. Regardless of these variations, every supervision and evaluation plan should include the following elements for all delegatees:

- specified amount of supervision time needed, based on the complexity of the activity and the delegatee's skill.
- onsite evaluation of delgatee's competence and written documentation (NASN, 2018).
- licensed nurses follow up with the delegatee after the delegated activity is completed.
- licensed nurse evaluation of student's condition after the delegated activity is completed; and
- licensed nurse feedback to the nurse leader regarding the delegation process and challenges regarding delegatee competence or inability to make good decisions and judgments. (NCSBN & ANA, 2019)

Documentation

Documentation of the delegation process helps protect the school nurse if his/her actions are ever called into question. Generally, in a court of law, it can be argued if it was not documented, it was not done (Burke, 2023). This concept, which is true in the care a nurse provides, is also true in the nurse's process of delegation.

According to Attorneys Scott and Bubert (2012), documentation should include:

1. the rationale for determining that a particular nursing activity could be safely delegated to another licensed nurse or UAP;
2. the rationale used to determine the competency of the other person that will allow for safe care and delegation based on the client's condition;
3. how the activity, task, or procedure was taught;
4. the teaching outcome;
5. the content and materials provided to the delegatee;
6. evidence that the delegatee understood any risks in performing the activity and what to do should any adverse events occur;
7. evidence that the delegatee understands that they are only allowed to perform the task on the specific client and is not intended to be transferred to another client;
8. how frequently the client should be assessed regarding continued delegation; and
9. how frequently the delegatee should be evaluated on performing the task? (p.214)

In addition to documentation of the delegation process and training provided, the delegating nurse should have a written IHP and ECP (if appropriate) for the student and a nursing protocol for the activity. Adair Shannon & Kubelka (2013a; 2013b) also recommend the use of procedural checklists as a teaching and documentation tool. Using a checklist makes it clear the steps needed to complete the activity and the sequence of the steps to complete it and document it appropriately.

Finally, documentation of the supervision and evaluation should be included in the process. Notations should be made regarding the student's condition and response to the intervention (e.g., stability of condition, tolerance of activity, etc.) and the delegatee's performance and comfort with the activity. The checklist could serve as a documentation tool assessing continued competence and proper technique (Adair Shannon & Kubelka, 2013a; NASN, 2018; NCSBN & ANA, 2019).

Education and Training
Delegation is a complex process that necessitates comprehensive knowledge and training for all parties, i.e., the school community, the delegating nurse, and the delegatee (NASN, 2018).

Delegation doesn't simply go from one person to another. Developing and documenting policy is the first step to avoiding conflicts in the process. The second step is determining whom this policy will affect, educating them, and educating the entire school community that the policy exists (e.g., there is a policy about who can administer medications). All teaching staff need to know this policy, so they do not unwittingly accept medication from a parent who tells the teacher, "Susan needs to take this at lunch". This will help avoid unnecessary conflict between parents, school administrators, delegates, and nurses (NASN, 2018; NCSBN & ANA, 2019).

Education of the delegating nurses ideally begins in basic nursing education and continues throughout their careers (NASN, 2022). To effectively delegate, school nurses need knowledge of all the areas previously outlined (e.g., state laws, national guidelines, district policies, etc.). Nurses can obtain this knowledge through:
- their professional organizations,
- their direct nursing supervisor (if available),
- formal education, such as webinars and conferences, and
- developing networks and mentors of more experienced or seasoned nurses
- frequently review their nursing board website for rules and updates
  (NASN, 2022).

According to Ciocco (2020), "Delegation is an art and a skill that can be developed and honed into one of the most effective professional management strategies any registered nurse (RN) can use" (para. 1).

The delegating nurse is directly responsible for the education of another licensed nurse or UAP. Although parents/guardians may provide insight into unique needs or techniques for their child, the lead nurse (in this case, the school nurse) is responsible for the training of the delegatee in accordance with acceptable standards of care (Mitts v. Hillsboro, 1987; NASN, 2018; NCSBN & ANA, 2019). The education of the delegatee includes the steps needed to carry out the nursing activity, perhaps using a checklist or procedural guideline (Adair Shannon & Kubelka, 2013b; NASN, 2018), demonstration of competency to carry out the activity; and a communication plan for routine supervision and evaluation as well as what to do in the event of an urgent or emergency situation.

One acceptable strategy for observing competency is the use of the *teach-back* or return demonstration method, where the delegating nurse demonstrates the activity, and then the delegatee performs the activity under the direct supervision of the delegating nurse. This method allows for accurate and direct observation of the skill, the opportunity for immediate feedback and correction if needed, and questions and answers that the delegatee may have in performing the skill/activity (Anderson et al., 2020; NCBSN & ANA, 2019).

A qualitative study by Schofield (2018) showed that each theme: delegation, administration, education-training, monitoring healthcare needs, role confusion, and work overload, affected the other. Education of all staff members, including administration, school nurses, paraprofessionals, and teachers was one of the strategies discussed in this study to resolve issues negatively impacting effective delegation. Examples of education beyond student-specific information included the education of teachers and paraprofessionals in basic nursing skills, activities of daily living such as feeding and toileting, monitoring of physiologic parameters such as vital signs, management of equipment, and development of interpersonal skills (Schofield, 2018). This study highlights the ongoing education and training needed for delegation in the school setting.

Strategies to Safely Delegate in Schools

- Know your state nurse practice act and other pertinent state and federal laws that would inform your decision to delegate.
- Advance your knowledge and confidence regarding delegation.
- Develop or participate in the development of a school district policy on delegation and procedural guidance.
- Participate in the ongoing review of the policy.
- Follow the delegation process, including the use of the decision-making tree and the five rights of delegation.
- Provide necessary and ongoing training, including the use of teach-back methods to document the competency of the UAP.
- Implement and floor a two-way communication plan (between the delegating nurse and the delegatee) for routine questions and supervision as well as emergency situations.
- Establish and follow a clear method for supervision and evaluation, including the competency and accuracy of the performed task/activity by the UAP as well as the stability and outcomes of the student's health condition.
- Document, document, document.
- Maintain records.

CONCLUSION

Delegation is needed in all healthcare delivery systems, including school health. Adequate preparation at all levels (organization, nurse, delegatee, and student) is required for delegation to be a safe and effective tool in providing health care to students in schools. Furthermore, delegation should be based on standards of care, state laws, and national evidence-based guidelines. Delegation should never be used as a substitute for the school nurse but may be a complementary practice that allows all students access to education and allows the school nurse to provide more complex nursing care that requires critical thinking and nursing judgment.

(Please also see Chapter 1 for more information regarding professional licensure).

RESOURCES

American Nurses Association. (2012). *Principles of Delegation*. Nursesbooks.org.

Idaho Nurse Delegation Toolkit. (2023). https://www.idhca.org/nurse-delegation-toolkit/

National Association of School Nurses. (2018). *Principles for Practice: Nursing Delegation to Unlicensed Assistive Personnel in the School Setting*.

National Council of State Boards of Nursing. (2023). Delegation. https://www.ncsbn.org/1625.htm

State Board of Nurses: The National Council of State Boards of Nursing provides a link to each state's Board of Nursing at https://www.ncsbn.org/contact-bon.htm

Wisconsin Department of Public Instruction (2019). *Use of Delegation in the School Setting.* https://dpi.wi.gov/sites/default/files/imce/sspw/pdf/Use_of_Delegation_in_the_School_Setting_2019.pdf

Case Law

Mitts, Carol v. Hillsboro Union High School district 3-8 Jt et al., Washington County Circuit Court Case 87-1142C (1987).

NSO: Nurse Case Study: Wrongful delegation of patient care to unlicensed assistive personnel https://www.nso.com/Learning/Artifacts/Legal-Cases/Wrongful-delegation-of-patient-care-to-unlicensed

REFERENCES

American with Disabilities Act, National Network. (2018). Disability Rights Laws in Public Primary and Secondary Education: How do they relate? https://adata.org/factsheet/disability-rights-laws-public-primary-and-secondary-education-how-do-they-relate

Adair Shannon, R. & Kubelka, S. (2013a, July). Reducing the risks of delegation: Use of procedure skills checklist for unlicensed assistive personnel in schools, part 1. *NASN School Nurse, 28*(4), 178-181. https://doi.org/10.1177/1942602X1348988

Adair Shannon, R. & Kubelka, S. (2013b, September). Reducing the risks of delegation: Use of procedure skills checklist for unlicensed assistive personnel in schools, part 2. *NASN School Nurse, 28*(5), 222-226. https://doi.org/10.1177/1942602X13490030

American Nurses Association. (2012). *Principles of delegation*. Nursesbooks.org.

American Nurses Association. (2015). *Code of ethics with interpretive statements.*Nursesbooks.org.

Anderson, A. (2018). Delegating as a new nurse. *American Journal of Nursing, 118*(12), 51–55. https://doi.org/10.1097/01.NAJ.0000549691.41080.6c

Anderson, K.M., Leister, S., De Rego, R. (2020). The 5Ts for teach back: An operational definition for teach-back training. *Health Literacy Research and Practice*; 4(2): e94-e103. https://www.ncbi.nlm.nih.gov/pmc/articles/PMC7156258/pdf/hlrp0420anderson.pdf

Asthma and Allergy Network. (n.d.). *School stock epinephrine laws.* http://www.allergyasthmanetwork.org/advocacy/current-issues/stock-epinephrine/

Barrow JM, Sharma S. (2022, July 25). Five Rights of Nursing Delegation. In: StatPearls. Treasure Island (FL): StatPearls Publishing. https://www.ncbi.nlm.nih.gov/books/NBK519519/

Burke, A (2023). Assignment, Delegation and Supervision: NCLEX-RN. [webpage]. https://www.registerednursing.org/nclex/assignment-delegation-supervision/#evaluating-effectiveness-staff-members-time-management-skills

Centers for Disease Control and Prevention. (2021). *Managing chronic conditions*. https://www.cdc.gov/healthyschools/chronicconditions.htm

Connecticut Board of Examiners for Nursing. (1995). *Delegation by licensed nurses to unlicensed assistive personnel* (Declaratory Ruling). https://portal.ct.gov/-/media/Departments-and-Agencies/DPH/dph/phho/Nursing_Board/Guidelines/unlicensedapdecrulpdf.pdf

Heschel, R. T., Crowley, A. A., & Cohen, S. S. (2005). State policies regarding nursing delegation and medication administration in child care settings: a case study. *Policy, politics & nursing practice*, *6*(2), 86–98. https://doi.org/10.1177/1527154405275884

Kahlil, L. (2023). Considerations when developing school health services policies. In C. Resha & V. Taliaferro (Eds.), *Legal Resource for School Health Services* (2nd ed.). Schoolnurse.com

Lowe, A. A., Gerald, J. K., Clemens, C., Gaither, C., & Gerald, L. B. (2022). Medication Administration Practices in United States' Schools: A Systematic Review and Meta-synthesis. *The Journal of school nursing: The official publication of the National Association of School Nurses*, *38*(1), 21–34. https://doi.org/10.1177/10598405211026300

Murphy, N.A., Alvey, J., Valentine, K.J., Mann, K., Wilkes, J., Clark, E.B. (2020, August). Children With Medical Complexity: The 10-Year Experience of a Single Center. *Hospital Pediatrics*; 10 (8): 702–708. https://doi.org/10.1542/hpeds.2020-0085

National Association of School Nurses. (2018). *Principles for practice: Nursing delegation to unlicensed assistive personnel in the schools setting*. Author. https://www.nasn.org/nasn-resources/resources-by-topic/delegation

National Association of School Nurses. (2019a). *School-sponsored trips, role of the school nurse* (Position Statement). Author. https://www.nasn.org/nasn-resources/professional-practice-documents/position-statements/ps-trips

National Association of School Nurses. (2019b). *Supervision and evaluation of the school nurse* (Position Statement). https://www.nasn.org/nasn-resources/professional-practice-documents/position-statements/ps-supervision

National Association of School Nurses (2022a). Chronic Health Condition Management. Web Resources. https://www.nasn.org/nasn-resources/resources-by-topic/chronic-health-condition-management

National Association of School Nurses. (2022b). *School nursing: Scope and standards of practice* (4th ed.). NASN.

National Council of State Boards of Nursing. (2016). National guidelines for nursing delegation. *Journal of Nursing Regulation, 7*(1), 5-14. https://www.ncsbn.org/nursing-regulation/practice/delegation.page

National Council of State Boards of Nursing & American Nurses Association. (2019). National guidelines for nursing delegation [Position Paper]. Authors. https://www.nursingworld.org/~4962ca/globalassets/practiceandpolicy/nursing-excellence/ana-position-statements/nursing-practice/ana-ncsbn-joint-statement-on-delegation.pdf

Schofield, S. L. (2018). *A qualitative case study on delegation of school nursing practice: school nurses, teachers, and paraprofessionals perspectives.* Rowan Digital Works Theses and Dissertations, 2491. https://rdw.rowan.edu/etd/2491

Scott, L. R., & Bubert, J. S. (2012). Legal issues related to school nursing practice: The foundation. In J. Selekman (Ed.), *School nursing: A comprehensive text* (2nd ed., pp. 196–224). F. A. Davis Company.

Wagner, E. A. (2018). Improving patient care outcomes through better delegation-communication between nurses and assistive personnel. *Journal of Nursing Care Quality*, *33*(2), 187–193. https://doi.org/10.1097/NCQ.0000000000000282

Willgerodt, M.A., Brock, D. M., & Maughan, E.M. (2018). Public school nursing practice in the United States. *The Journal of School Nursing, 34*(3), 232-244. https://doi.org/10.1177/1059840517752456

Wisconsin Department of Public Instruction. (2019). *Use of delegation in the school setting.* https://dpi.wi.gov/sites/default/files/imce/sspw/pdf/Use_of_Delegation_in_the_School_Setting_2019.pdf

Decision Tree: Nursing Delegation in the School Setting

Does the state's Nurse Practice Act allow delegation?	NO – Cannot delegate YES – Can delegate
Does school policy support training and supervision of the UAP by the school nurse?	NO – Cannot delegate YES – Can delegate
Has a healthcare provider ordered the healthcare task?	NO – Cannot delegate YES – Can delegate
Does the school nurse have the competence to train the UAP on the nursing task?	NO – Cannot consider delegation YES – Can proceed with delegation
Does the student's IHP – based on the nursing assessment, in combination with the healthcare provider's orders -outline the nursing tasks required to help meet the student's health goals?	NO – Cannot delegate YES – Can delegate
Does the nursing care task meet the criteria of delegation? (Right task) • Not complex • Part of the student's routine plan of care, whether at school or at home. • Follows an established sequence of steps. • Does not require modification. • Has a predictable outcome. • Does not involve assessment, judgment, interpretation of results, or decision-making by the UAP.	NO – Cannot delegate YES – Can delegate
Did the nursing assessment of the student's health status and health goals identify any unique needs that may deem delegation inappropriate? (Right circumstance)	NO – Cannot delegate YES – Can delegate
Is an appropriate, competent, and willing UAP available? (Right person)	NO – Cannot delegate YES – Can delegate
Is the school nurse able to develop the UAP training, implement the training, provide a written sequence of steps for the nursing task, and evaluate competence? (Right direction and communication)	NO – Cannot delegate YES – Can delegate
Is there a communication plan between the UAP and the school nurse in place? (Right direction and communication)	NO – Cannot delegate YES – Can delegate
Can the school nurse provide ongoing supervision of the UAP and evaluation of the student's health outcomes? (Right supervision and evaluation)	NO – Cannot delegate YES – Can delegate
For out-of-state school-sponsored events: • Are both the home and visiting states members of The Nurse Licensure Compact? *	NO – Cannot delegate YES – Can delegate
Does the visiting state allow delegation to UAP?	NO – Cannot delegate YES – Can delegate

Reprinted with permission, © National Association of School Nurses, 2018
*The Nurse Licensure Compact enables multistate licensure for nurses. For more information:
https://www.ncsbn.org/nlc.htm

Chapter 5

SUPERVISION OF SCHOOL NURSES

Lisa Minor, EdD, MSN, RN, CNE*
Terry Woody, BSN, RN, NCSN*

DESCRIPTION OF ISSUE

Schools throughout the United States recognize that students need better access to healthcare and a healthier environment to grow, learn, and thrive. Aside from states where school nursing is required, this recognition is one of the primary reasons many school systems throughout the United States employ registered nurses to provide health services and assistance in the school setting. "School nurses are often the first to identify and address student behavioral health concerns and serve as an early warning system for children and families in crisis or otherwise at risk of abuse and neglect. School nurses support and care for students with special healthcare needs/chronic conditions through care management and direct care, including medication administration and health procedures. School nurses are often the sole healthcare provider in a school setting" (National Association of School Nurses [NASN], 2022, p.1). School nurses function within the nursing standards of care and promptly follow orders that a physician or other healthcare provider provides. Although school nurses are trained and licensed healthcare providers in the school setting, nursing/medical personnel often do not supervise them. According to the National Association of School Nurses (NASN School Nurse, 2020, pp. 49-50), the nature of this supervision can create conflicts and legal concerns: "[M]any school nurses are supervised and evaluated by non-nursing personnel such as school administrators who may have limited understanding of the role of the registered nurse in the school setting" (NASN School Nurse, 2020, pp. 49-50). It is not uncommon for school nurses to be supervised by the school principal or have non–nursing supervisors with no medical knowledge.

There are situations to meet the health needs of children, school nurses may choose to delegate some of the healthcare tasks to unlicensed staff when appropriate. The delegation process requires a sound knowledge of laws and education and supervision of those staff selected to perform the tasks.

(*For more information on Delegation, please refer to Chapter 4*).

This chapter will address two issues 1) the need for school nurses to be supervised and evaluated by someone with sound clinical knowledge and a strong clinical background, and 2) the responsibility of the school nurse to select, train, and supervise unlicensed staff to provide delegated tasks.

BACKGROUND

The school nurse's professional responsibility is to ensure the safety and well-being of the students in their care. The impact on the school district as an employer is multifactorial; they may be liable for the retention of unsatisfactory employees or negligent in the supervision of staff because the supervising administrator lacks the clinical expertise to know if a nursing task is being done correctly. This premise also holds for school

---

*Original authors: Tia Campbell, MSN, RN, NCSN, FNASN & Lisa Minor, RN, MSN, EdD (2017)

administrators who designate an employee to serve as unlicensed assistive personnel (UAP). Because most school administrators have no medical or clinical knowledge, they cannot be sure that the task delegated to the UAP is appropriate, being taught properly, or if the UAP is competent to perform the task. If the school administrator designates someone to perform a task and does not allow time for proper training by the school nurse, there can be legal ramifications for the school system and staff members involved.

In the school setting, the school nurse is responsible for meeting the students' health needs. Whether a medical emergency or routine care, school nurses must use their knowledge, critical thinking skills, and proper decision-making to successfully handle the emergency. Additionally, the school nurse is accountable for the delegation to and supervision of UAPs.

IMPLICATIONS FOR SCHOOL NURSE PRACTICE

Supervision of Registered Nurses by Non-Clinical Personnel

Prior to the passage of Section 504 of the Rehabilitation Act (Section 504) and Individuals with Disabilities Education Act (IDEA), many school health offices were covered by UAPs or even a parent volunteer, who would provide very basic first aid and occasionally administer medication to students. In these situations, it was common and more acceptable for non-clinical personnel to supervise these UAPs or volunteers because neither the UAP nor the parent volunteer was a licensed healthcare provider. The use of unlicensed personnel still exists in some cases in school systems where a registered nurse is not present. However, students with more significant health needs are now attending public school, which under Section 504 and IDEA, may require skilled nursing care on a daily basis. And yet, even with more specialized nursing care needed in the school setting, school nurses are not mandated in most states. According to Willgerodt, Brock, & Maughan (2018), almost 60 percent of schools in the United States do not have full-time nurses (pp. 232-244). Although not statutorily mandated in most states, many school systems have decided to employ registered nurses to meet the needs of those requiring specialized nursing care when in the school setting. "The American Academy of Nursing believes that all students must have daily access to a full-time school nurse who is part of a comprehensive health care and education system and is supportive by health and education dollars" (Maughan et al., 2018, p. 95).

> Registered nurses in the school setting are unique because they are often the only health professional in a building that otherwise focuses on academics and instruction. School administration must understand that even though non-clinical personnel can supervise school nurses regarding their professionalism, communication, and work ethic, they are not technically qualified or able to supervise clinical skills or determine safe practice effectively. "Clinical supervision and evaluation of nursing practice require nursing knowledge and skill" (NASN School Nurse, 2020, p. 50).

Because school administrators may not fully understand the legal scope of practice of the school nurse, they may ask school nurses to divulge confidential information or complete tasks not within, and many times beyond, the scope and standards of practice for a school nurse, which could put the school system at increased risk for legal ramifications. "It is important that school administrators understand that only the nursing profession, via state nurse practice acts, defines the scope of nursing practice..." (Combe & Clarke, 2019, p. 946).

School nurses' clinical performance should be supervised by a nurse professional with the knowledge and skill to effectively oversee the clinical qualifications of the school nurse, as well as have the legal authority to supervise, which means an active nursing license. According to Davis, Lynch, & Davis (2020), school nurses operate under a completely different scope of practice than school administrators (who are not licensed as a nurse), making it difficult for principals to effectively supervise the day-to-day activities of the school nurse (pp. 95-110).

Supervision of School Nurses: Educating on the Scope of Practice

Adequate supervision of school nurses is essential to ensure that the school nurse appropriately meets the scope and standards of practice, whether providing direct care to a student or supervising UAP. Nurses can assist unlicensed supervisors with understanding the scope of practice. Practice guidelines are based on individual state nurse practice acts and national standards; therefore, the nurse must be clear when explaining their role to the school administration. "Principals may not be fully aware of the scope of the school nurse role, and therefore it is incumbent on the school nurse to describe the school nurse role and to use data to explain and support the structure of the current school health program" (Duff, 2019, p, 71). Without these explanations, a non-clinical supervisor might otherwise determine that the school nurse is competent to make judgment calls or provide direction to the UAP when the nurse may lack the competency to provide safe care or necessary skills for safe delegation.

Potential Strategies to Promote Supervision of the School Nurse

To address the challenge of a non-licensed supervisor overseeing the clinical practice of a school nurse, educating the non-licensed administrator on the scope of practice of the school nurse and possible legal implications (e.g., consequences of negligent supervision, practicing without a license, and the liability of retaining unsatisfactory employees) is a beginning.

In addition to education, possible solutions for supervision include:
- Allow self-evaluation, providing evidence of meeting clinical standards of practice.
- Contract with someone with a clinical background to provide supervision of the school nurse (such as an experienced school nurse or school nurse administrator).
- Contract for a licensed nurse to complete an audit of school nursing records.
- Provide an annual observation by a licensed nurse in the school setting.
- Partner with a clinical supervisor (school nurse administrator if available) to evaluate and supervise the clinical component and support the school administrator in evaluating or supervising the professional component of the school nurse's performance (e.g., communication and professionalism).

Delegation and Supervision of UAPs

"Delegation of nursing tasks to unlicensed assistive personnel (UAPs) in school settings continues to be a necessary yet challenging practice. Although the practice of delegation to UAPs in schools, as in other healthcare settings, is necessary due to limited resources and increasing healthcare needs, it remains essential to provide students with healthcare that is safe and high in quality "(Resha, 2010, para. 1). School nurses may delegate nursing tasks as appropriate if UAPs are carefully selected, trained, and supervised by the school nurse. State nurse practice acts clearly articulate that unlicensed school administrators may not delegate a nursing task to

UAPs. The school nurse must communicate to the school administration their responsibility in the delegation process, what they can and cannot delegate to UAP, and supervision requirements. This includes the school nurse's participation in the selection of the UAP and the responsibility to train and supervise the UAP. School nurses must also be very careful to document any training given to UAP and what has been observed when supervising the UAP for a particular procedure.

The following examples at Consumermedsafety.org (2022) demonstrate how errors can be made when unlicensed assistive personnel are delegated nursing tasks without proper supervision and safe procedures are not in place.

- A kindergartner was taken to the hospital on the first day of school. A teacher's aide accidentally gave him another child's medicine. The child became drowsy after he was given Catapres (clonidine), a blood pressure medication sometimes used to treat children who have attention deficit hyperactivity disorder (ADHD).
- An eighth-grade student with ADHD was suddenly not responding to his methylphenidate (Ritalin). He began developing new symptoms and ended up unconscious in the emergency department. The school nurse was unavailable the prior week, so the school secretary gave the children their medicine. For three days, the secretary accidentally gave the eighth-grade student another student's methadone, a powerful narcotic pain medicine with serious side effects. The medicines were kept in envelopes with only the generic names, methylphenidate, and methadone, handwritten on the outside, not the student's name. Both medicines start with m-e-th and are taken in similar doses.
- A school office secretary did not require a child to wash his hands before diabetes testing. This resulted in an abnormally high blood sugar level because the child had jelly on the finger used to test the blood. The child received too much insulin and experienced signs of very low blood sugar.
- A 10-year-old girl with asthma and food allergies collapsed and died in a Washington school. She had arrived at school short of breath. Her sister ran to the office to get help. A plan detailing emergency treatment was on hand. There was also a supply of the girl's asthma medicine, a rescue inhaler in case of an asthma attack, and an epinephrine injector for an allergic reaction. However, the nurse was only at that school a few days a week, and that day was not one of them. Filling in as a "health clerk" was a former lunch server and playground supervisor with no formal medical training. The rescue inhaler was never given to the child. When the child finally collapsed to the floor, paramedics were called. But the child did not receive an emergency epinephrine injection, nor did anyone attempt any form of CPR (cardiopulmonary resuscitation). She died from an acute asthma attack.
- Another child died after having a seizure at home and hitting his head. When checking the child's school medication card, a part-time school nurse noticed that in the weeks before his death, the child had missed nearly half of his regular doses of anti-seizure medicine because the office staff filling in during her absence had not called the child into the office to give him his medicine.

Case Law

Trebatoski v. Ashland School District

In CTL ex rel. Trebatoski v. Ashland School District, 742 F.3d.524 (7th Cir. 2014), an elementary school Type I diabetic student's parents had worked with the school to develop a Section 504 Plan for their son's care during the school day. One of the requirements included that three staff members, along with the school nurse, be trained in his care and fully understand what was to be done with his medical needs. According to the case, the school division only had one fully trained individual for the student: the school nurse. On one occasion, the school nurse had to be out for the day, and the school nurse supervisor, who had not been trained for this particular student's needs, took over. Even though the school nurse tried to explain what was expected for this student, the supervisor ignored the nurse's recommendations. The school nurse supervisor, on the day in question, made several inappropriate decisions and did not adequately follow the plan of care. The student's blood sugars elevated, and proper measures were not taken to correct the hyperglycemia.

When the school nurse returned, she questioned the school nurse supervisor about the inappropriate decisions. The school nurse supervisor informed the principal about being questioned by the school nurse. The principal reacted by reprimanding the school nurse because he did not understand the seriousness, ramifications, and concerns presented on the school nurse's behalf. As time progressed, no measures were made on behalf of the school administration to train two more individuals to meet the requirements listed in the Section 504 Plan. Because the principal, as the school administrator and ultimate supervisor of the school nurse when in the school setting, did not have proper clinical knowledge, he allowed the problems to continue, which put the student at risk. The principal did not understand the importance of the Section 504 plan and did not intervene when inappropriate decisions were made in the care of the student, which resulted in a lawsuit. While it was clear that there was some violation of the Section 504 plan, the district was able to successfully defend against a claim of intentional discrimination under Section 504 through an appeal to the 7th Circuit.

Yeckleyv. Willoughby-Eastlake City Schools Board of Education

In a case filed in December 2022, *Yeckley v. Willoughby-Eastlake City Schools Board of Education, et al., 1:22-cv-02330 (Dec. 28, 2022),* claims that her eighth-grade daughter was taken to the nurse's office where a nurse's aide allegedly forced her to strip down to only her underwear while looking for a vape pen after she was instructed to do so by the middle school's school nurse, who was not present at the time and although licensed did not supervise the UAP's actions. The complaint claims that the district never trained the aide to properly conduct searches and had no business doing so.

CONCLUSION

School nurses are often the sole health professional in the building, and they are accountable for their practice. It is most important for the school nurse to have supervision from a licensed Registered Nurse to promote safe practice and competency. In the situation with a non-nurse school administrator supervising, there must be additional input from a nursing professional, a process for peer review, or self-evaluation. Without ensuring that the registered nurses in the school setting are clinically competent and skilled in the supervision of UAP, the administrator could be held liable for unsafe care. In the worst case, the unlicensed administrator/supervisor could be accused of practicing nursing without a license. School nurses must advocate for themselves and be accountable for their actions.

School nurses must make certain that school administrators clearly understand the scope and standards of practice for school nurses, individual state nurse practice acts, individual state laws pertaining to delegation, and what can and cannot be delegated to UAP. It is also of utmost importance that school nurses explain to school administration why they cannot effectively supervise the clinical knowledge and skill of the nurse. According to Davis, Lynch, & Davis (2020), the school nurse must be the expert on healthcare laws and guidelines determined at the local, state, and federal levels and guide administrators in decision-making (p. 102). If school nurses, school administration, and school systems work together by putting proper clinical supervision in place, school districts can be more effective in meeting the health needs of students, keeping them healthy, and in doing so, promoting students to excel academically.

RESOURCES

National Association of School Nurses (2022). Student access to school nursing services (Position Statement). https://www.nasn.org/nasn-resources/professional-practice-documents/position-statements/ps-access-to-services

National Association of School Nurses (2023). Supervision and evaluation of the school nurse (Position Statement).

https://www.nasn.org/nasn-resources/professional-practice-documents/position-statements/ps-supervision

Case Law

Yeckley v. Willoughby-Eastlake City Schools Board of Education, et al., Case: 1:22-cv-02330 Doc #:1 N.D. Ohio, 2022), https://tennesseestar.com/wp-content/uploads/2023/01/1-COMPLAINT-12.28.22.pdf

CTL ex rel. *Trebatoski v. Ashland School District, 742 F.3d.524* (7th Cir. *2014).*

REFERENCES

Combe, L., & Clarke, Y. (2019). Management of school health staff. In J. Selekman, Shannon, & Yonkaitis (Eds.), *School nursing: A comprehensive text* (3rd ed., p. 946). F.A. Davis Company.

Consumermedsafety.org. (2022), Fewer school nurses lead to greater medication errors. https://www.consumermedsafety.org/safety-articles/fewer-school-nurses-leads-to-greater-medication-errors

Davis, C.R., Lynch, E.J. & Davis, P. A. (2020). The principal and the school nurse: Conditions and conceptual model for building a successful and vital professional relationship. *Planning and Changing 50*(1/2), 95-110. https://education.illinoisstate.edu/downloads/planning/Davis_50.1-2.pdf

Duff, C. (2019). Frameworks and models for school nursing practice. In J. Selekman, Shannon, & Yonkaitis (Ed.), *School nursing: A comprehensive text* (3rd ed., p.71). F.A. Davis Company.

Maughan, E., Cowell, J., Engelke, M., Mccarthy, A. M., Bergren, M., Murphy, K., Barry, C., Krause-Parello, C., Luthy, K. B., Kintner, E. & Vessey, J. (2018). The vital role of school nurses in ensuring the health of our nation's youth. *Nursing Outlook*, *66*(1), 94-96. https://doi.org/10.1016/j.outlook.2017.11.002

National Association of School Nurses (2022). *Student access to school nursing services*. (Position Statement). https://www.nasn.org/nasn-resources/professional-practice-documents/position-statements/ps-access-to-services

NASN School Nurse. (2020). *Supervision and evaluation of the school nurse*, *35*(1), 49-50. https://journals.sagepub.com/doi/epdf/10.1177/1942602X19890469

Resha, C. (2010**).** Delegation in the school setting: Is it a safe practice? OJIN *OJIN: The Online Journal of Issues in Nursing*, *15*(2), Manuscript 5. https://doi.org/10.3912/OJIN.Vol15No02Man05

Willgerodt, M.A., Brock, D. M., & Maughan, E.M. (2018). Public school nursing practice in the United States. *The Journal of School Nursing, 34*(3), 232-244. https://doi.org/10.1177/1059840517752456

ADDENDUM

Practical Resolutions to the Nurse Supervision Problem

Brooke E. D. Say, Esquire*

As detailed in the preceding chapter, it is expected that a school nurse and his/her supervisor will, at some point, conflict in their supervisory and professional relationship. The administrative supervisor will ask the school nurse to do or not do something that the school nurse feels is in opposition to the requirements of her nursing license or nursing standards. The school nurse may attempt to exercise her discretion in an area where there is administrative overlap. Conflict over what is delegation of nursing duties versus personal care assistant duties is one such example. Students are impacted if the school nurse and administrative supervisor remain at loggerheads. Therefore, school nurses need to anticipate the need for a way to resolve these conflicts before they even happen in order to balance the required supervision and the responsibility of a nurse license. The school nurse and administrator should proactively outline the following resolution options, to be used progressively or in conjunction: (1) consultation with state-wide issued manuals for school nursing; (2) consultation with an outside administrator and nurse from another school; (3) contact with an outside nurse evaluator used for annual evaluations of the nurse; (4) contact with the school solicitor for advice; (5) contact the school nursing department or other nursing authority for the state, to seek counsel and guidance on standards of care and current law; and (6) only when other such steps have failed or when there is an immediate risk of harm without reporting, the nurse makes a report to the state nursing authority.

Steve M. Cohen, Ed. D, President and Managing Partner of the Labor Management Advisory Group located in Kansas City, who has an extensive background in both education and business and whose wife and sister are both nurses, has some practical advice regarding how nurses could approach this sensitive topic with their employers. "The school nurse should advise, in polite and professional terms, that the official has wandered into an area where the official is unauthorized to operate. The nurse should provide the administrator with documentation that supports the position that it is inappropriate and perhaps illegal to do what has been or is attempting to be done." Dr. Cohen further advises, "I would point out that by taking this action, the administrator is incurring liability for him/herself and for the district that is unnecessary and could be a job killer or even a career killer." Importantly, he urges school nurses to come prepared not only with a message of potential liability but also potential solutions that will demonstrate that, while the school nurse's foremost concern is for the safety of the students, they are also committed to finding practical solutions. "My suggestion is to not simply say 'no' but, rather, to seek to deploy a course of action that achieves a win/win. Anyone can say no and appear irksome and unaccommodating. The person who works toward getting to 'yes' without violating fiduciary obligations demonstrates that they are trying to accommodate." This approach is both practical and positive, and it achieves the desired goal: ensuring the safety and security of the students and preventing the unauthorized practice of nursing: "[a]t the end of the day, the most important factor in this decision-making is the health and safety of the students. All legal, regulatory, and employment requirements should be interpreted in light of their needs."

Original author: Erin Gilsbach, JD (2017)

Chapter 6

PERFORMANCE EVALUATION OF SCHOOL NURSES

Lisa Minor, EdD, MSN, RN, CNE*
Terry Woody, BSN, RN, NCSN*

DESCRIPTION OF ISSUE

Conversations with school nurses across the United States and abroad express concern due to the lack of evaluation or evaluation by personnel unqualified to assess nursing skills. Many nurses are evaluated utilizing tools used for unlicensed school personnel, which simply address attendance, dress, punctuality, and the like. Some school nurses express frustration that they are not viewed as professionals for evaluation purposes. Some, but not all, states require that a school nurse be a registered nurse. However, a supervising registered nurse must oversee the unlicensed personnel in all states. Those registered nurses in the school setting should be evaluated by someone with medical knowledge and medical background to effectively evaluate the skills of the registered nurse in that setting. "Many school nurses are supervised and evaluated by non-nursing personnel such as school administrators who have limited understanding of the role of the registered nurse in the school setting" (National Association of School Nurses [NASN] School Nurse, 2020, p. 49). In districts without clinical nursing supervisors, it is challenging to receive clinically based feedback in the form of an evaluation because non-nursing personnel are unaware of a school nurse's scope and practice, making it difficult to evaluate true nursing competence adequately. "Competence in nursing practice requires evaluation by the individual nurse (self-assessment), nurse peers, nurse supervisors, mentors, or preceptors" (National Association of School Nurses [NASN], 2018, p. 1).

BACKGROUND

A recent literature review showed a gap for, and development of, standards-based evaluation tools and clinical evaluation related to the specific legal implications posed for school nurses and school systems on the topic of school nurse evaluations.

The school nurse is responsible for ensuring that their practice meets standards for safety and is based on evidence and current best practice. The ultimate goal of the evaluation process is to document competence, provide a plan for correcting any deficiencies, and support staff in performing and achieving their full potential. According to the position statement from NASN (NASN School Nurse, 2020), a registered nurse specializing in school nursing should evaluate school nursing competency and performance.

The literature is clear that evaluation tools should be standards-based. The school nurse should be aware of the specialty's scope of practice and professional performance. Evaluation tools should address specific competencies within the scope of practice. "Performance review and evaluation is a quality management process that provides employees with recognition for good performance and specific guidance for needed performance improvements. An effective performance review system motivates, gives direction, establishes expected contributions, and identifies educational needs" (Combe & Clarke, 2019, p. 947). Lacking the

---

*Original authors: Tia Campbell, MSN, RN, NCSN, FNASN & Lisa Minor, RN, MSN, EdD (2017)

educational background, understanding of health laws, licensure requirements, and practice issues of school nurses, educational administrators are not qualified to evaluate the clinical practice of the school nurse. They would be unable to provide direction or guidance in this field since they are not healthcare professionals. "Clinical supervision and evaluation of nursing practice require nursing knowledge and skill. Evaluation of school nurse practice by school nurses is crucial to promote safe, high-quality, competent care for all school children and their school communities" (NASN School Nurse, 2020, p. 50).

IMPLICATIONS FOR SCHOOL NURSE PRACTICE

Documenting Competence

Evaluations provide the organization with documentation that the employee meets stated job standards. Therefore, the school nurse evaluation tool must be specific to school nurse standards of practice. "Evaluation of competence involves using tools to capture subjective and objective data about the individual's knowledge and actual performance. Those tools should be appropriate for the specific school nursing situation and the desired outcome of the competence evaluation" (NASN Scope and Standards of Practice (2022, p. 32). When school districts fail to utilize a standards-based evaluation tool, they miss the opportunity to document that their nurse meets established criteria. If litigation ensued, the district might have itself without sufficient admissible evidence to "prove" that the nurse was competent to perform job-related duties. Along with the importance of a proper evaluation tool that should be used to evaluate school nursing competence, school nurses can also solidify their competence by showcasing their accomplishments through the use of a portfolio that can be used during the evaluation process. According to Wallin and Rothman (2020), demonstrating competence using portfolios during the evaluation process can help school administrators better understand the school nurse's role and what is needed to demonstrate competence (p. 36).

Ensuring Quality Practice

Evaluation serves to ensure quality practice in the school setting. Performance appraisals offer opportunities to evaluate nursing practice in relation to school nursing standards and develop a plan of action to improve any noted deficits, which is why the evaluation by a non-nurse is ineffective. By properly evaluating school nurses and developing ways to enhance school nurse competency, better outcomes can be promoted for our students. "The competency of the school nurses can influence the health outcomes of the school members, so an effective strategy is needed to develop and improve school nurses' competency (Shin & Roh, 2020, p. 246). According to NASN Scope and Standards of Practice (2022), the evaluation should use subjective and objective data about the school nurse's knowledge and competence using proper evaluation tools, including but not limited to portfolios, observation, performance evaluation, and skills (pp.32-33).

Standards-Based Evaluation Tools

For districts that do not employ a nurse supervisor, the NASN has developed standards of practice and professional performance for school nurses. Several states or localities have developed standards-based evaluation tools or are, by law, prohibiting a school nurse from being supervised or evaluated by non-nurse personnel. The following are three examples. In 2017, Washington State Legislature, under chapter 18.79 RCW, states that school nurses can be evaluated only by a registered nurse or advanced practice nurse; it also states that a school nurse can be supervised by non-nurse personnel but not in matters related to the practice of nursing (Washington State Legislature, 2017). The School Nurse Institute Partnership in Virginia developed a standards-based evaluation tool that closely mirrors the mandated state teacher evaluation tool (Southall et al., 2017). This approach promotes ease of use by non-clinical administrators and allows the school nurse to provide concrete evidence of having met the standards of practice. A school nurse evaluation tool was developed by the Colorado Department of Education and practitioners across Colorado (2016) using categories and guidelines to assist school nurses in looking at best practices to meet or exceed standards of practice.

Impact on Employers

It behooves the school system to ensure that the school nurse is providing safe and effective care to students that conforms to state laws governing the practice of nursing, local policy, and established clinical guidelines. "By providing a standardized and objective method of documentation, the performance review serves as a quality assurance tool for employers responsible for decisions regarding employee promotion or termination" (Combe & Clarke, 2019, p. 947).

The most common challenges to acceptable evaluation practices are the lack of a clinical supervisor and educational administrators who fail to understand that they lack the skills to evaluate school nursing practice. An important step in addressing this deficit is educating the non-medical/nursing administrator on the scope of practice of the school nurse and the possible legal implications of non-medical/nursing administrators evaluating school nurses (negligent supervision, practicing without a license, and the liability of retaining unsatisfactory employees). Advocating for a standards-based evaluation tool and the ability to provide evidence of having met the standards of practice is certainly within the power of the individual nurse.

Robust school nurse evaluation methods should include both a clinical and an educational component. School nurses must demonstrate to those providing an evaluation that they are competent and sound in their decision to ensure the health and well-being of any and all students they encounter. "The use of portfolios in conjunction with an evaluation tool can help a non-nurse evaluator better understand school nursing practice" (Wallin & Rothman, 2020, p. 36.) A portfolio can help the school nurse showcase his or her accomplishments and quality of work.

Strategies for Evaluation

To promote annual school nurse evaluation:
- Read and understand the *School Nursing: Scope and Standards of Practice.*
- Provide ongoing education for non-clinical school nurse administrators on the scope of practice, licensure, and laws guiding school nursing practice.
- Advocate for a clinical nurse supervisor or a designated lead nurse to provide clinical input on evaluations.
- Contribute to a standards-based evaluation tool if one does not exist in your district (search the internet for existing tools and seek permission to modify if you need a place to start).
- Document annual personal and professional goals.
- Conduct an annual self-evaluation of practice based on the *School Nursing: Scope and Standards of Practice,* especially if you do not receive a formal evaluation.
- Engage in peer review if no formal evaluation is provided.

- Work to establish policies for the annual evaluation of school nurse practice by a registered professional school nurse based on the job description, scope, and standards of practice.

CONCLUSION

The legal implications of evaluating school nursing practice include promoting a competent workforce, avoiding non-nurse administrators practicing nursing without a license, and negligent supervision. Like all school employees, school nurses deserve the opportunity to discuss their clinical performance based on laws and acceptable standards. If a non-medical/nursing administrator evaluates the nurse, additional input from an evaluator with clinical expertise is needed. Without clinical input from a licensed practitioner, the administrator runs the risk of being found to be practicing without a license. In addition, without knowledge of nursing practice, the administrator may unknowingly breach the state nurse practice act when making assignments or designating medical tasks to unlicensed personnel.

School nurses are responsible for evaluating their professional practice and educating administrators on the laws that govern nursing and the scope and standards of school nursing practice. Furthermore, the school nurse must advocate for a professional-level evaluation process. Using a standards-based evaluation tool and advocating for a clinical evaluator to contribute to the evaluation process will help ensure appropriate feedback is received to promote the safe and effective care of children in the school setting. This can also document the attainment of professional goals, outcome measures, and benchmarks for the school nurse.

RESOURCES

Colorado Department of Education. (2016). Colorado state model evaluation system for specialized

service professionals: Practical ideas guide for evaluating school nurses.
https://www.cde.state.co.us/educatoreffectiveness/practical_ideas_guide_schoolnurses

National Association of School Nurses. (2023). Supervision and evaluation of the school nurses (Position Statement).
https://www.nasn.org/nasn-resources/professional-practice-documents/position-statements/ps-supervision

REFERENCES

Colorado Department of Education. (2016). *Colorado state model evaluation system for specialized service professionals: Practical ideas guide for evaluating school nurses*. https://www.cde.state.co.us/educatoreffectiveness/practical_ideas_guide_schoolnurses

Combe, L., & Clarke, Y. (2019). Management of school health staff. In J. Selekman, Shannon, & Yonkaitis (Ed.), *School nursing: A comprehensive text* (3rd ed., p. 946). F.A. Davis Company.

National Association of School Nurses. (2022). *School nursing: Scope and standards of practice* (4th ed.). National Association of School Nurses.

National Association of School Nurses. (2018). *Supervision and evaluation of the school nurse* (Position Statement). https://www.nasn.org/nasn-resources/professional-practice-documents/position-statements/ps-supervision

NASN School Nurse. (2020). Supervision and evaluation of the school nurse. *NASN School Nurse, 3*(1), 49-50. https://journals.sagepub.com/doi/epdf/10.1177/1942602X19890469

Shin, E.M., & Roh, Y.S. (2020). A school nurse competency framework for continuing education. (2020). *Healthcare 2020, 8*(3), 246. https://doi.org/10.3390/healthcare8030246

Southall, V.H., Wright, J.B., Campbell, T., Bassett, M.K., Strunk, J.A., & Trotter, S.E. (2017). School nurse evaluation: Developing a tool that both school nurses and administrators can use. *NASN School Nurse, 32*(2),87-90. https://doi.org/10.1177/1942602X16684848

Wallin, R.L., & Rothman, S. (2020). A new framework for school nurse self-reflection and evaluation. *NASN School Nurse,35*(1),35-42. https://doi.org/10.1177/1942602X19852295

Washington State Legislature. (2017). RCWs > Title 28A > Chapter 28A.210 > Section 28A.210.305. https://app.leg.wa.gov/rcw/default.aspx?cite=28A.210.305

Chapter 7

CONSIDERATIONS WHEN DETERMINING SAFE SCHOOL NURSE STAFFING

Ann O. Nichols, MSN, RN, NCSN, FNASN*

DESCRIPTION OF ISSUE

School nursing is a specialized practice of nursing that protects and promotes student health, facilitates optimal development, and advances academic success (NASN, 2022). A specialized practice nurse is generally a seasoned professional nurse who has developed the competence and knowledge required of the specialty setting. Determination of adequate numbers and types of nursing staff for patient safety and optimal outcomes is often a challenging process in many settings, including school nursing.

The American Nurses Association describes common models of staffing while saying that no single model works for all situations in all settings. However, the primary elements to consider include factors related to the consumer of nursing care (students), characteristics of the nursing staff and other care providers, workplace culture, working environment, and outcomes from program evaluations (ANA, 2020). Within any chosen staffing model, care delivery options are also considered since every nursing staff member may not be qualified to provide all required activities needed. Among others, common care delivery modalities known to most school nurses include primary nursing, requiring an all-Registered School Nurse (RN) staff, and team nursing, which may involve nurses with a variety of credential types performing activities for the same patients based on licensure and competence.

School nurse staffing models vary widely in the United States in both credentialing of staff and workload assignments. Selection of a model for school nursing may, unfortunately, sometimes be driven by funding availability over other relevant factors. As with other practice settings, school nurse staffing is also impacted by additional challenges such as public health crises (COVID19 pandemic), shortages of qualified candidates for hire, and aging of the experienced nurse workforce (American Association of Colleges of Nursing (AACN), 2022). These conditions have focused increased attention on school nurse staffing and workload as gaps and lack of guiding evidence for staffing decisions have been exposed. The competitive market for qualified nursing staff may become even more challenging since the United States Department of Labor has determined that employment needs will grow for nurses at the rate of 9% per year, with a gap of 275,000 nurses by 2030 (Hadad, 2022).

Regardless of the staffing model schools or school systems selected, student safety and health for access to education are always the primary concerns.

BACKGROUND

Early models for school health services largely depended on ratios of school nurses to students to address mandated nursing services for students with special health care needs. These federal laws included the Rehabilitation Act of 1973, Section 504 of the Rehabilitation Act, the Individuals with Disabilities Education

---

*Original author: Laurie G. Combe, MN, RN, NCSN (2017)

Improvement Act (IDEIA, 2004,2017), and the 2015 Every Student Succeeds Act (ESSA). IDEIA and ESSA cite the school nurse as Specialized Instructional Support Personnel responsible for leading student chronic disease management. These laws guarantee all students access to free and appropriate public education, including the health services necessary for students with complex health needs to access the educational process.

Beginning in the 1970s, the National Association of School Nurses (NASN) (2015), the American Academy of Pediatrics (AAP) (2016), and Healthy People 2020 (US Department of Health and Human Services [USDHHS], 2014) supported school nurse to student ratios of 1:750 for healthy students, 1:225 for students requiring daily nursing services, 1:125 for students with complex health needs, and 1:1 for students requiring continuous nursing services. However, these ratio recommendations were not evidence-based, even though they may represent a resource-based starting point for making decisions regarding school nurse staffing (Jameson et al., 2020). NASN (2020) identifies other factors that should be considered and are aligned with the ANA recommendations. These include:

- Safety, medical acuity, and health needs of students.
- Characteristics and considerations of the school population stemming from social determinants of health.
- Characteristics of the school nurse and other team members; and
- School and district culture and context that impact the delivery of nursing services (NASN, 2020).

Healthy People 2030 set a goal to increase the proportion of students with access to a full-time school nurse (USDHHS, Office of Disease Prevention and Health Promotion, n.d.). School nurse staffing models should take a multi-faceted workload approach that analyzes all factors while recognizing that little exists in data or validated tools to assist at present.

A few states provide a legal mandate for certified school nurses, but many require that a school nurse simply meet state nursing licensure requirements. In making decisions regarding nurse staffing and student safety, it is essential to ensure the competence of individual nursing staff. This includes expectations of the work assignment and the unique knowledge required within a specialty area of practice. NASN provides numerous resources on the expected roles and responsibilities of the professional school nurse through Clinical Practice Guidelines and Position Statements on practice issues. These school nurse expectations should be considered when hiring and assigning competent staff. State and local education and experience requirements for positions and credentials such as certification can provide objective evidence in this area. Particularly in the absence of a state system, national certification through the National Board for Certification of School Nurses (NBCSN) should be considered. NBCSN states validation of school nurse knowledge and skills as an outcome of certification (NBCSN, 2023).

Staffing models may consist of staff combinations that include all registered nurses (RN), a blend of RNs and RN extenders such as licensed practical/vocational nurses (LPN/LVN) or Unlicensed Assistive Personnel (UAP), LVN/LPN only staffing, or UAP only staffing (Willgerodt et al., 2018). Table 1 demonstrates the results of the National Association of School Nurses' 2017 survey related to school nurse licensure types in care delivery models.

Table 1: Licensure-Related Staffing Patterns (Willgerodt et al., 2018)

RN	RN + LPN	LPN	No Nurse
69.5%	13.6%	4.7%	11.4%%

The National Association of State School Nurse Consultants (NASSNC) represents state school health nurse consultants, both active and retired, in states that employ one. At the time of this writing, 36 states employed one or more state consultants. NASSNC completes an annual survey of membership that includes a question regarding the state minimum credential requirements for a school nurse in that state. Table 2 demonstrates the responses to this survey question. Eight reporting states that do not have licensure or certification requirements also do not have a mandate for schools to employ a school nurse, nor do they have a definition for a school nurse. Fourteen states reported legislative mandates requiring nursing in schools, while 19 states reported no such mandates. Of the 33 states responding, 25 (75%) require licensure as a Registered Nurse, 11 (33%) require a BSN, with 14 (42%) accepting a non-nursing bachelor's degree. Two states noted a minimum LPN/LVN licensure requirement, while three states have additional mandatory requirements (beyond BSN) upon hire. Individual state requirements for credentialing are an important factor to consider in addressing school nurse staffing models and delivery of care.

Table 2: Minimum requirements for school nurse licensure or certification (Wolfe et al., 2023)

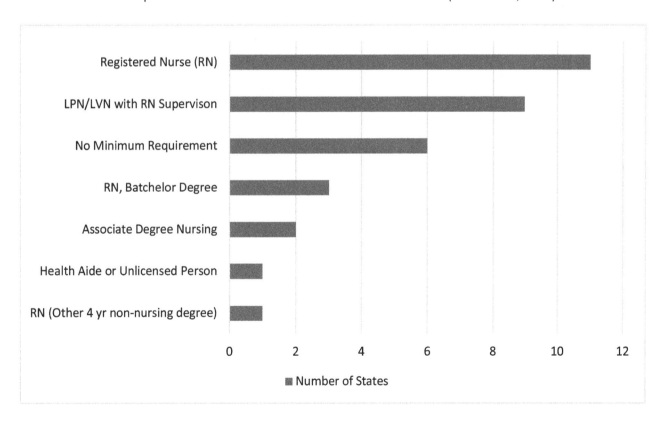

IMPLICATIONS FOR SCHOOL NURSE PRACTICE

For the purposes of this discussion, the term *school nurse(s)* will be used to designate both school nurses practicing on school campuses and school nurses with dedicated administrative duties. School nurses are expected to meet practice standards as set forth by federal education and disability laws, national professional nursing organizations, state boards of nursing (BON), applicable executive orders, local law, and employer policy and procedure (NASN, 2021). School nurses serve as the bridge between health care and education and encounter "unique *legal, policy, funding, and supervisory issues that may also have ethical dimensions*" (NASN, 2020, p.22). It is each nurse's professional and legal responsibility to be familiar with laws, standards, and ethical considerations that impact their practice and to assure compliance in nursing assignments.

National Standards and Law

In making decisions regarding staffing for health care in schools, it is critical to be consistent with professional standards and legal requirements, both state and national. National standards of practice for school nurses are set forth in *School Nursing: Scope & Standards of Practice, 4th ed.* (NASN, 2022), *Nursing Administration: Scope & Standards of Practice* (ANA, 2016), the *Code of Ethics for Nurses with Interpretative Statements* (ANA, 2015), *and the NASN Code of Ethics* (NASN, 2021). The aforementioned documents note the obligation of nurses to:

1) promote a culture of safety in their workplace
2) advocate for the health and safety of patients
3) assign and accept only those responsibilities for which the nurse or assignee possesses skill, competence, and workload capacity (ANA, 2015; NASN, 2022; ANA, 2016).

These foundational documents establish that "the standard of care is what an ordinary prudent professional nurse would provide under the same or similar circumstances" (Resha, 2019, p. 34) and may be called into evidence during a board of nursing or legal proceedings surrounding the delivery of school nursing care (Brous, 2019, p. 151). Nurses are "accountable and responsible for the quality of their practice" as established through law and professional standards (Sherman & Cohn, 2019, para. 5). Therefore, it is incumbent upon school nurses to familiarize themselves with the tenets of these documents, use them as a guide for continuous improvement of nursing practice, and update when they change.

Equally important is that school nurses understand the impact of federal education laws, rules, and regulations on school nurse practice. School nurses advocate for student access to education as guaranteed by Section 504 of the Rehabilitation Act of 1973 and ESSA (2015).

As such, school nurses are essential team members who serve several functions, which include:

1) identify and participate in the evaluation of students for qualifying health status
2) develop Plans of Care as appropriate to student need
3) recommend accommodations and services
4) train and supervise assistive personnel
5) provide Inservice training on health conditions and care
6) participate in transition planning
7) evaluate the effectiveness of health-related components of student plans
   (Halbert & Yonkaitis 2019, p. 169; NASN 2018)

State Statutes and Nurse Practice Acts

Knowledge and understanding of state nurse practice regulations and rules are imperative for school nursing staff, who often work very independently within a non-healthcare-oriented setting. State regulations may be accessed through the National Council of State Boards of Nursing (NCSBN). All nursing practice within the United States is further guided by legal constructs delineated in individual state Nurse Practice Acts (NPA) and the associated rules and regulations set forth to interpret the NPA (NCSBN, 2019). While carrying equal weight under the law, NPAs, and the rules and regulations authorize the formation and composition of boards of nursing; protect nursing titles; set forth requirements for nursing education and licensure; outline the nursing scope and standards of practice; **define parameters for safe practice**; and provide the grounds for violations, disciplinary action, and remedies (Russell, 2017). As in other nursing practice arenas, commitment to the patient is the priority for the school nurse (NASN, 2021). Therefore, school nurses can be held accountable and liable by regulatory bodies when failing to act consistently with existing regulations and standards, regardless of employer. *(See Chapter 2 for information on professional liability).*

Local School or District Policy

School nurse regulations and standards can provide the foundation for school health policy and related protocols and procedures (Resha, 2019). Having these in place provides a structure for school nursing activities, defines expectations for quality practice, creates a local standard of care for school

> *Because healthcare **policy constantly changes, nurses must always have a seat and a voice at the table (Schaeffer & Haebler, 2019).***

communities, and provides legal protection for school systems and their employees (Costante, 2013).

Local school policy that impacts the delivery of care and school nursing practice should continually be developed or revised with the collegial participation of school nurses. Many sources may be consulted in determining needed policies, including reviewing current policies in place, identifying recent issues poorly informed by current policy, reviewing policies developed by comparable school districts, consulting the Center for Disease Control's Healthy School website, and reviewing current literature.

Many state boards of nursing also recognize the importance of policies and procedures for nurses. Boards of nursing direct nurse employer agencies to establish them, and many of the directives produced by a board of nursing may also include the caveat that an action should be within the scope and be allowed by agency policy and procedure. School employers are not health care agencies and need the input of a knowledgeable school nurse to be informed about the requirements for school nursing policies and procedures and the content of those. The following is an example of something that might be included in a policy on 'Identification of Students with Health Care Needs.' Most state boards of nursing deem unlicensed individuals, including school administrators, to be unqualified to independently make decisions regarding the healthcare needs of students and nursing service needs. In recognition of this, the IDEA requires that a qualified member of that related service evaluate a student's level of need for related services. Nursing is a related service under IDEA (IDEA, 2004). The developed policy should reflect this expectation of IDEA and a board of nursing.

Assessing for the Provision of Safe Student Care

The structure created by standards, laws, nurse practice acts, and good local policies/procedures supports the safe provision of care in the school setting and helps to create a structure for school nursing practice. These are essential supports for safe staffing but do not address staffing numbers. While NASN advises that every student should have access to a school nurse every day, the position statement also points to assessing the needs of students and the school community to determine specific staffing credentials and numbers for safe care (NASN, 2020).

It is well documented that advances in health care have contributed to the increasing number and acuity of students attending school with complex health needs (Cohen & Patel, 2014). Models of nurse workload assessment can help direct decisions on the numbers and types of school health staff needed to meet needs and deliver safe care. Acuity models are workload-based models. Ascertaining student health acuity is essential to determining appropriate levels of staffing and safe delivery of care based on the need for continuous, daily, or periodic nursing care and supervision. Staffing decisions may be more accurately made by applying a full school population-based acuity model that allows the inclusion of the needs of the entire school population in an assessment in addition to individual student acuity (Daughtry & Engelke, 2018). An example of an assessed need for a school population might be the lack of healthcare providers in the community for referral and regular care. This can impact the nurse's workload through the extended effort required to secure care for any situation.

An acuity-based model for nurse staffing may include factors such as those listed in Table 3 but should be based on the factors assessed as indicative of the school or district for which decisions are made.

Table 3. Student Acuity Tool for School Nurse Assignment (SATSNA).

Indicator	Weighted Percent (%)
Free and reduced lunch	30
NC ABC results from performance composite	30
Limited English proficiency (LEP)	10
English as a second language (ESL)	10
Identified health conditions	10
Invasive medical procedures	10

Note. ESL and LEP were combined into one indicator based on data after the first year that demonstrated these indicators were highly correlated.

The use of assessment and decision-making models and tools, such as an acuity model, can assist in determining staff needs to provide safe and appropriate care. The Plan-Do-Study-Act (PDSA) Model illustrated in Table 4 is another example of when current staffing concerns do not present an immediate pressing safety issue for students or legal concern for the school nurse. It can be utilized to explore possible staffing improvements in the local system (US Department of Health and Human Services: Agency for Healthcare Research and Quality, 2020).

Table 4: Plan-Do-Study-Act Model (USHHS: AHRQ, 2020, Institute for Healthcare Improvement, 2017)

Plan	Develop a plan to test a scenario and collect the data
Do	Pilot the plan on a small sample
Study	Analyze the data
Act	Create an action plan based on modifications identified during the test.

The PDSA model is an outcome evaluation model that allows testing of decisions made to assure the desired outcome. It incorporates ANA's recommendation to include program evaluation data in school nurse staffing decision-making. A particular outcome may be expected from a staffing change, such as school nurses will be able to provide case management services more often for students with poorly controlled asthma as a result of certain staff changes. PDSA fosters an ability to determine if the change does produce the desired student outcome. It can answer the questions:

- What are we trying to accomplish?
- How will we know that a change is an improvement?
- What changes can we make that will result in improvement?

For additional assistance in staffing models, the American Nurses Association's *Principals for Nurse Staffing (ANA, 2020)* is also a recognized resource in determining nurse staffing needs.

Nursing Delegation

Many school nurses and their employers support the NASN position that students deserve everyday access to the services of a registered, professional school nurse (NASN 2022). Depending on the staffing model and delivery of care modality utilized, that registered nurse may or may not provide all aspects of health care for all assigned students. If nurse salaries are competitive, yet the demand for registered nurses exceeds the local supply, a team approach using nurse extenders must be considered. Even with extenders, a Registered Professional School Nurse who is the leader of a team must be accessible and accountable to assigned students and will still provide the activities that are within the scope of the Registered Nurse. In the absence of nurse extenders, the school nurse may be placed in the position of dealing with an unmanageable workload and possible unsafe care situations with an inability to complete all requirements of practice, such as full documentation of care, adequate assessment, and planning for complex students, and meeting continuing competency education needs.

Nurse extenders are those staff who perform activities and procedures that fall into the scope of nursing practice but can be performed by someone other than an RN when allowed by the state BON and the assessed condition and situation of the student. Nurse extenders include licensed practical nurses/licensed vocational nurses (LPNs/LVNs), and unlicensed personnel such as nursing assistants, nurse aides, some paraprofessionals, and trained school staff. LPNs and LVNs have a scope of practice defined by the state of licensure. Care activities consistent with their scope can be assigned to the LPN/LVN job description. Unlicensed staff performing health care procedures usually do so as a part of a delegation process. Staff providing care as a nurse extender must receive supervision and assurance of competency in the assigned or delegated tasks. Therefore, the school nurse requires a good understanding of the scope and practice of both themselves as the RN and the nurse extender positions. During the COVID19 pandemic, with its associated shortage of nurses, some school nurses experienced their first opportunity to provide school health services with a team that included nurse extenders.

The North Carolina School Health Program Manual includes a section on the use of nurse extenders (NCDHHS, 2022). Table 5 is excerpted from the manual and provides examples of nursing activities with allowed scope in North Carolina for each credential type. School nurses should always confirm practice regulations with their state boards of nursing since practice regulations vary across states.

Table 5: Staffing Healthcare in Schools (NCDHHS, 2022)

School Staff	Registered Nurse (RN) (Bolded activities may only be completed by the RN)	School Nurse Extender (Require ongoing practice supervision and direction from RN)	
.		Licensed Practical Nurse/ Licensed Vocational Nurse (LPN/LVN)	Unlicensed Assistive Personnel (UAP)
Activity			
Health Care Plans (IHP/ EAP/504/IEP)	Develop, implement and evaluate health plans. Update with changes.	Implement health plans under RN direction/supervision. Report student progress to RN.	Complete assigned tasks per training and protocol under the supervision of the school nurse.
Medication	Review orders and assess for clarity and need at school. Monitor expected student response and side effects. Manage medication administration process in the school setting. Provide training and ensure the competence of staff.	Administer ordered medications as assigned by RN per local policy. Report student responses and concerns to the school nurse. May teach medication administration but may not determine competence.	Administer ordered medications as directed by RN per local policy. Report student responses and concerns to the school nurse.
Health Room Visits	Assess student needs and ability to remain in school. Provide care to students with illness or injury. Train staff and ensure competence to provide basic care and first aid.	Follow structured guidelines and protocols to care for students with illness or injury. Notify the school nurse of visits and follow-up needs.	Provide help in a limited manner for students with illness or injury (Call parent, call 911, bandage). Notify the school nurse of visits and follow-up needs.
Special Health Procedures	Assess student needs and determine procedure steps in school. Complete ordered medical procedures. Assign tasks, train, and supervise LPN/UAP and assure competence.	Complete ordered procedures per policy under the supervision of the RN. Assign tasks, train, and supervise UAP's completing procedures. They may not determine competence. Report student responses or concerns to RN.	Complete assigned ordered procedures per policy under the supervision of the school nurse. Report concerns to the school nurse.
Health Screening and Follow-up	Perform student screening. Perform rescreens that determine referral needs. Follow up to ensure care was received.	Perform student screening per policy, if trained. Report results to RN for referral and follow-up.	Perform student screening per policy, if trained. Report results to RN for referral and follow-up.
Health Care Related Staff training	Develop staff training following local policies. Complete standardized staff training and assure competence.	Assist with staff training as assigned by RN. Audit medication and procedure records as assigned.	Attend training as needed. May not train other staff.

Reprinted with permission of NCDHHS, Division of Child & Family Wellbeing, School Health Unit.

As allowed by state law, the school nurse may decide that delegation to a UAP is a tool that can be utilized to meet student healthcare needs (NCSBN & ANA, 2019). The use of delegation allows the school nurse to manage some aspects of student and school needs through nurse extenders, thus expanding coverage for the assignment of the professional school nurse. *School Nursing: Scope and Standards of Practice* (NASN, 2022) defines delegation as "the assignment of the performance of a nursing activity to unlicensed assistive personnel or from a registered nurse to a licensed practical/vocational nurse…. Accountability remains with the registered nurse; state laws and regulations and school regulations must be followed; and standards of nursing practice must be upheld" (p. 100). While the delegation of some nursing functions can extend the reach of the school nurse, the nurse must be cautious in their application of the delegation process, considering the Five Rights of Nursing Delegation as listed in Table 6.

Table 6: Five Rights of Nursing Delegation (NCSBN & ANA)

Right task: The activity falls within the delegatee's job description or is included as part of the established written policies and procedures of the nursing practice setting. The facility needs to ensure the policies and procedures describe the expectations and limits of the activity and provide any necessary competency training.
Right circumstance: The health condition of the patient must be stable. If the patient's condition changes, the delegatee must communicate this to the licensed nurse, and the licensed nurse must reassess the situation and the appropriateness of the delegation.
Right person: The licensed nurse along with the employer and the delegatee is responsible for ensuring that the delegatee possesses the appropriate skills and knowledge to perform the activity.
Right directions and communication: Each delegation situation should be specific to the patient, the licensed nurse and the delegatee. The licensed nurse is expected to communicate specific instructions for the delegated activity to the delegatee; the delegatee, as part of two-way communication, should ask any clarifying questions. This communication includes any data that need to be collected, the method for collecting the data, the time frame for reporting the results to the licensed nurse, and additional information pertinent to the situation. The delegatee must understand the terms of the delegation and must agree to accept the delegated activity. The licensed nurse should ensure that the delegatee understands that she or he cannot make any decisions or modifications in carrying out the activity without first consulting the licensed nurse.
Right supervision and evaluation: The licensed nurse is responsible for monitoring the delegated activity, following up with the delegatee at the completion of the activity, and evaluating patient outcomes. The delegatee is responsible for communicating patient information to the licensed nurse during the delegation situation. The licensed nurse should be ready and available to intervene as necessary. The licensed nurse should ensure appropriate documentation of the activity is completed.

Local school policy and procedure must include procedural guidance to school nurses and UAPs related to nursing delegation and oversight during unfilled school nurse absences. The UAP must have unlimited access to nurse consultation regarding delegated tasks. This may be accomplished using onsite school nurses, school nurse administrators, experienced lead school nurses, or assignment of "buddy" campuses where school nurses share information about the health needs of their students. Regardless of the support system provided, clear lines of communication must be established and documented in a readily accessible format. In the rare situation when the school nurse is absent, and a nurse substitute cannot be secured, the student's parents should be made aware of the lack of a school nurse and offered the options of providing the care themselves or keeping the student at home. This ensures the student's safety but should be a last resort when all other options are exhausted.

School nurses should always be knowledgeable about the requirements for various licensure-level providers in their state, including their role in delegation, assignment, oversight, and supervision. School systems and school nurses must exercise caution when assigning UAPs to perform nursing procedures. For example, an Oregon principal directed the UAP to perform clean, intermittent catheterization for a new student in one case. The parent trained the UAP while the school nurse was present to answer questions. The school nurse did not provide written direction to the UAP but did provide periodic supervision as directed by the school district. The court consulted the Oregon Board of Nursing (BON) to determine if the nursing procedure could be legally delegated to a UAP (*Mitts, C. v. Hillsboro Union High School District, 1987).* The BON found that the principal had practiced nursing without a license in assigning a nursing procedure to the UAP. The BON also disciplined the school nurse for accepting the principal's assignment and failing to comply with BON regulations related to delegation, including nursing assessment to determine the rightness of the delegation (Schwab & Gelfman, 2001/2005). *(See Chapter 4 for more information on delegation).*

Other Staffing Concerns

School nurses may encounter staffing situations that they consider unsafe or do not align with their legally defined scope of practice. When school nurses accept an assignment, they are obligated to provide nursing care that aligns with law and standards. If confronted with unsafe staffing or scope of practice concerns, the school nurse must advocate for safe patient care, report unsafe staffing situations, and request assistance in writing (ANA, 2015; Schwab & Gelfman, 2001/2005). Scope of practice, staffing, and other client safety concerns must be addressed directly and through appropriate organizational channels.

The Texas NPA (2013) and the Texas Administrative Code (TAC), Rule 217.20 (2013), allow a nurse who determines that an assignment is unsafe to declare *safe harbor* and request <u>a peer review</u> of the practice concern. A good faith declaration of *a safe harbor*, made in writing before the nurse begins the assignment, provides the following protections to the nurse:

(1) may not be disciplined or discriminated against for making the request,
(2) may engage in the requested conduct pending the peer review,
(3) is not subject to the mandatory reporting requirement for unsafe practice, and
(4) may not be disciplined by the board for engaging in that conduct while the peer review is pending (TX NPA, 2013).

Safe harbor protection is unique to nurses in Texas; however, nurses in other states might benefit from asking a peer school nurse for an assessment when confronted with a safety concern. Nurse response to these situations will vary by state, and the school nurse should be familiar with the state of employment expectations.

Ethical and professional dilemmas are created as the school nurse weighs duty to the client and impacts on nursing licensure and future employment. If the school nurse is unable to secure the changes needed for a safe healthcare environment, the duty to resign may be the only resort (ANA, 2015; NASN, 2022). The resignation must be given with adequate notice so the school nurse can avoid a charge of abandonment. For example, the North Carolina BON defines abandonment as the act of coming on duty, accepting an assignment, and then abandoning the patient without arranging the continuation of care. "The focus in nursing law and rules is on the relationship and responsibility of the nurse to the client, not to the employer or employment setting" (NC BON, 2019, p. 3). Connecticut and Oregon also provide specific guidelines to assist nurses and their employers determine if abandonment occurred (Connecticut Board of Examiners for Nurses, 2002; Oregon State Board of Nursing, 2020). Nurses should consult their state NPA to determine actions that may constitute patient abandonment.

Competence as a Consideration for Staffing

The ANA defines competency as "an expected level of performance that integrates knowledge, skills, abilities, and judgment" (ANA, 2018, p.3). School nurses are self-directed, self-regulating, and individually accountable for their practice (NASN, 2022). While expectations place the assurance of competence in care primarily on the school nurse who self-assesses competence, the employer also expects assurance. As a component of licensure, many states require evidence of continuing competence and reflective practice for licensure. An example is provided by the North Carolina Board of Nursing (NCBON, 2023), which requires specific contact hours (or equivalent) and employment for licensure renewal.

The concept of **Novice to Expert** states that two to three years of experience in the same practice specialty is generally required for a nurse to be competent (Brenner, 1984). As a consideration for staffing, the competence of the individual nurse is critical when considering assignments and needed support. The complexity of the school nurse role and practice setting creates challenges for orientation activities and access to peers. The school nurse is most often the only healthcare professional in a school (NASN, 2022). A strong orientation plan can serve a purpose in verifying essential skill competency for new school nurses (Combe & Clark, 2019).

Despite orientation and experience, a student with special healthcare needs may present with a new procedure that is unfamiliar to the nurse. The nurse must be supported in expressing a lack of competence, and a protocol outlining the steps toward attaining competence should be in place. As with any learner, these may include a review of written material, a review of video demonstration, an observation of a peer performing the skill, and a return demonstration to a peer. Relationships with local medical practices and schools of nursing may be of help. The nurse should not be put in a position of refusal to complete the skill without continuing education. This situation can be avoided by a policy that allows planning and preparation time for students with complex health issues who are new to a school or have a new procedure. In a 1999 decision, the Office of Civil Rights ruled that a school may delay admission for up to ten school days if needed for proper planning or training of school staff (Seattle, 1999). Including this time in a policy allows the school nurse to achieve competence in the activity.

Once trained, the nurse is expected to complete the procedure as ordered. Acceptable reasons for not doing so include the belief that the procedure will harm the student or having reason to believe that the order was written by a provider not qualified to do so. Otherwise, the nurse may be found in breach of duties and may be subject to employer repercussions or state board of nursing discipline for failing to provide ordered care (Brent, 2015).

Job Assignment Not Congruent with Licensure

Schools may offer nurses employment for positions aligned with a scope of practice that is not consistent with licensure. That may be an advanced practice registered nurse (ARPN) as a school nurse or registered nurse (RN) in jobs intended for LPN/LVN or UAP.   Similarly, LPN/LVN may be offered jobs as UAP. While the state NPA requires the nurse to practice to the full extent of their licensure, the employer's job description may limit the nurse's ability to function as an ARPN, an RN, or an LPN/LVN. Schools may also employ nurses in teaching positions with no job description duty to respond as would be required of a nurse. To fulfill the standard of the NPA may require the nurse to violate the standard set forth by the employer for the position, and vice versa (Schwab & Gelfman, 2001/2005). It is not possible to separate a nurse's knowledge, expertise, and level of accountability from the license. Nurses who practice under these circumstances receive compensation well below that expected for licensed nurses and perpetuate employer expectations of a high level of care for less than adequate pay. They may also place themselves at risk for liability. The school nurse should consult with their state BON for guidance about using their credentials to document care and possible exposure of the nurse's license to liability. The use of school nursing staff in a position not congruent with licensure is not advised as a part of a staffing model. *(See Chapter 2 for more information on professional liability).*

Addressing School Healthcare Concerns

Nurses are often the last healthcare providers to stand between safety and error for their students (Zoinierek, 2012). Clear, direct, and specific communications between all stakeholders are essential to sustaining a culture of safety in schools in any staffing model. School nurses should follow the chain of command when communicating concerns about student safety. Depending on employer organizational structures, the school nurse's immediate chain of command may be an education, medical, or nursing administrator. School nurses must be cognizant that education and medical administrators may not fully understand nursing education preparation or the legal constraints of the NPA and its associated Rules and Regulations. Organizational policies and procedures should provide a structure through which nurses can express safety concerns without fear of retaliation and a method to test proposed strategies for staffing improvement.

The Situation, Background, Assessment, Response (SBAR) model is one method of communication that provides a proactive process to address critical situations before error and inadequate care occur. SBAR allows objectively presenting and discussing problems and potential solutions, thereby allowing all parties to seek solutions (Coolen et al., 2020). SBAR delivers concise communication to promote collaborative relationships with key stakeholders and influence decisions.

Table 7 demonstrates the steps of the SBAR communication model.

Table 7: SBAR Communication Model (Horgan, 2013)

Situation	A brief statement of the current concern
Background	Set the scene with a concise review of the current practice concern, including relevant student/situation data, historical data
Assessment	Statement of interpretation of the situation and professional conclusions
Response	Offer recommendation(s) for resolution of the practice concern

School nurses must proactively develop and adopt formal procedures for addressing practice concerns related to staffing or other issues. These processes require training and case study testing so that school nurses are familiar with the process, have an opportunity to role-play crisis communication with school administrators and other stakeholders and anticipate critical staffing situations that may arise. Meetings and discussions with the administration about issues of concern may be primarily verbal. However, the school nurse should always maintain notes regarding meeting content, expressions of concerns, and administration response. These can be shared with those present as additional documentation of issues and the decided outcomes and serve as evidence of the school nurse's expression of concern. All written documentation, including memos and copies of emails regarding the issue, should be retained. When conditions persist despite sharing with others, the nurse should regularly send written updates and not rely on one instance of communication as sufficient. If persistent, unsafe situations may benefit from discussion with the state BON.

CONCLUSION

Many, often competing, factors impact staffing for the safe delivery of health care to students. Staffing decisions must be made in an intentional manner that meets the assessed needs while being responsive to resource constraints. Without an assessment of the actual staffing required for safe care, the school nurse relies only on perception and anecdotes. Administrators may genuinely be unaware of the challenges faced by current staff and the inadequacy to ensure safe student care. Nurses who find themselves providing substandard care due to low staffing must provide clear, factual, written evidence. Resignation may be the only outcome for some if the evidence is met with little response.

Nursing codes of ethics, scope, standards of nursing practice, and state NPA outline nurses' professional responsibility to protect the safety of their patients. School nurses must have a working knowledge of these and keep abreast of changes over time. Because unsafe staffing conditions result in nursing error and ineffective care, it is incumbent upon the school nurse to advocate for staffing needs via the established chain of command, institutional practices, and respective NPA statutes/rules (ANA, 2015; Zolneirek, 2012). School nurses must familiarize themselves with problem-resolution models to facilitate rapid response in staffing crises. Continuous improvement of nursing skills and knowledge in an environment that allows a manageable workload is essential to safe, competent care and is the responsibility of every school nurse.

RESOURCES

National Council of State Boards of Nursing (2023). Find your nurse practice act. https://www.ncsbn.org/policy-gov/npa-toolkit/npa.page

North Dakota Board of Nursing (2019). *Abandonment* (Practice Guidance). https://www.ndbon.org/Practice/PracticeGuidance/Abandonment.asp

Nursing Service Organization (2017). When to refuse an assignment https://www.nso.com/Learning/Artifacts/Articles/when-to-refuse-an-assignment

REFERENCES

American Academy of Pediatrics. (2016). The role of the school nurse. *Pediatrics*, *137*(6), 34-39. https://doi.org/10.1542/peds.2016-0852

American Association of Colleges of Nursing. (2022, October). *The nursing shortage.* Fact Sheet. Author. https://www.aacnnursing.org/news-information/fact-sheets/nursing-shortage

American Nurses Association. (2015). *Code of ethics for nurses with interpretative statements.* Nursesbooks.org.

American Nurses Association. (2016). *Nursing administration: Scope and standards of practice* Nursebooks.org.

American Nurses Association. (2018). *ANA leadership competency model.* https://www.nursingworld.org/~4a0a2e/globalassets/docs/ce/177626-ana-leadership-booklet-new- final.pdf

American Nurses Association. (2020). *Principles for nurse staffing* (3rd ed.). American Nurses Association. https://cdn2.hubspot.net/hubfs/4850206/PNS3E_ePDF.pdf

Brenner, P. (1984). From novice to expert, excellence and power in clinical nursing practice. Addison-Wesley Publishing Company.

Brent, J. N., (2015, July 3), Can a nurse be terminated or demoted for not doing a task she is uncomfortable performing? *Nurse.com.* https://www.nurse.com/blog/can-a-nurse-be-terminated-or- demoted-for-not-doing-a-task-she-is-uncomfortable-performing/

Brous, E. (2019). The law and school nursing practice. In J. Selekman, R.A. Shannon, & C. F. Yonkaitis (Eds.), School nursing: A comprehensive text (3rd ed., p. 151). F. A. Davis & Co.

Combe, L. & Clark, Y. (2019). Management of school health staff. In J. Selekman, R.A. Shannon, & C. F. Yonkaitis (Eds.), *School nursing: A comprehensive text* (3rd ed., p. 942). A. Davis & Co.

Cohen, E., & Patel, H. (2014). Responding to the rising number of children living with complex chronic conditions. CMAJ: Canadian Medical Association journal = journal de l'Association medicale

Canadienne, 186(16), 1199–1200. https://doi.org/10.1503/cmaj.141036

Connecticut Board of Examiners for Nurses (2002). *Patient abandonment guidelines for APRN's, RN's, and LPN's.* https://portal.ct.gov/-/media/Departments-and-Agencies/DPH/dph/phho/Nursing_Board/Guidelines/Patientabandpdf.pdf

Coolen, E., Engbers, R., Draaisma, J., Heinen, M. & Fluit, C. (2020). *The use of SBAR as a structured communication tool in the pediatric non-acute care setting: bridge or barrier for interprofessional collaboration?* https://doi.org/10.1080/13561820.2020.1816936

Costante, C. C. (Ed.). (2013). School nurse administrators: Leadership and management. National Association of School Nurses.

Daughtry D, Engelke, M.K. (2018). Demonstrating the relationship between school nurse workload and student outcomes. The Journal of School Nursing, 34(3),174-181. https://doi.org/10.1177/1059840517725790

DeMitchell, T. A. (n.d.). Education law: In loco parentis. http://usedulaw.com/345-in-loco-parentis.html

Every Student Succeeds Act of 2015, Pub. L. No. 114-95 § 114 Stat.

Haddad, L.M., Annamaraju, P & Toney-Butler, J. (2022, February 22). Nursing shortage. StatPearls. StatPearls Publishing. https://www.ncbi.nlm.nih.gov/books/NBK493175/

Halbert, L., & Yonkaitis, C.F. (2019). Federal laws protecting students with disabilities. In J. Selekman, R.A. Shannon, & C. F. Yonkaitis (Eds.), School nursing: A comprehensive text (3rd ed., p. 161). F. A. Davis & Co.

Horgan, M. (2013). Communication is key. World of Irish Nursing & Midwifery, 21(1), 46-47. MedMedia Limited.

Individuals with Disability Education Improvement Act (2004), 20 USC 1400 et seq.

Institute for Healthcare Improvement. (2017). How to improve: Science of improvement-testing change. http://www.ihi.org/resources/Pages/HowtoImprove/ScienceofImprovementTestingChanges.aspx

Jameson BE, Anderson LS, Endsley P. Identification of Workload Measurement Indicators for School Nursing Practice. The Journal of School Nursing. 2022;38(3):287-298. doi:10.1177/1059840520946833

Mitts, Carol v. Hillsboro Union High School district 3-8 Jt et al., Washington County Circuit Court Case 87-1142C (1987).

National Association of School Nurses. (2015). School nurse workload: Staffing for safe care (Position Statement). Silver Spring, MD: Author.

National Association of School Nurses. (2018). IDEIA and Section 504 teams – The school nurse as an essential team member (Position Statement). Author. https://www.nasn.org/nasn-resources/professional-practice-documents/position-statements/ps-ideia

National Association of School Nurses. (2020). School nurse workload: Staffing for safe care (Position Statement). Author. https://www.nasn.org/nasn-resources/professional-practice- documents/position-statements/ps-workload

National Association of School Nurses. (2021). Code of ethics. Author. https://www.nasn.org/nasn-resources/resources-by-topic/codeofethics

National Association of School Nurses. (2022). School nursing scope and standards of practice (4th ed.). Author.

National Association of School Nurses. (2022). Student access to school nursing services (Position Statement). Author. https://www.nasn.org/nasn-resources/professional-practice-documents/position-statements/ps-access-to-services

National Board for Certification of School Nurses. (2023). Why Certify? Author. https://www.nbcsn.org/why- certify/

North Carolina Board of Nursing. (2019). Staffing and patient/client safety. https://www.ncbon.com/myfiles/downloads/position-statements-decision-trees/staffing-and-client-patient-safety.pdf

North Carolina Board of Nursing. (2023). Continuing competence requirements. https://www.ncbon.com/licensure-listing-continuing-competence

National Council of State Boards of Nursing and American Nurses Association. (2019). National guidelines for nursing delegation. https://www.ncsbn.org/public-files/NGND-PosPaper_06.pdf

North Carolina Department of Health and Human Services. (2022). *School Nursing Practice.* North Carolina School Health Program Manual, Chapter C, Section 1, pp. 4-5. https://www.dph.ncdhhs.gov/wch/cy/schoolnurses/manual.htm

North Carolina Department of Health and Human Services. (2023). *Healthcare teams in the school setting.* https://www.dph.ncdhhs.gov/wch/cy/schoolnurses/healthcareteams.htm

Oregon State Board of Nursing (2020). *Patient abandonment.* https://www.oregon.gov/osbn/documents/IS_PatientAbandonment.pdf

Plan-Do-Act (PDSA) Directions and Examples. (2020). Agency for Healthcare Research and Quality, Rockville, MD. https://www.ahrq.gov/health-literacy/improve/precautions/tool2b.html

Rehabilitation Act of 1973, 29 USC § 504

Resha, C. A. (2019). Standards of school nursing practice. In J. Selekman, R.A. Shannon, & C. F. Yonkaitis (Eds.), *School nursing: A comprehensive text* (3rd ed., p. 34). F. A. Davis & Co.

Russell, K. A. (2017). Nurse practice acts guide and govern: Update 2017. Journal of Nursing Regulation, 8(3), 18– 25. https://www.ncsbn.org/publicfiles/2017_NPA_Guide_and_govern.pdf

Schwab, N.C. & Gelfman, M.H.B. (Eds.). (2001/2005). *Legal issues in school health services.* Sunrise River Press.

Schaeffer, R., & Haebler, J. (2019, August). Nurse leaders: Extending your policy influence. Nurse Leader, 17(4). https://www.sciencedirect.com/science/article/abs/pii/S1541461219301491

Seattle (WA) Public Schools, 31 IDELR 193 (OR).

Sherman, R. O., & Cohn, T. M. (2019). Promoting professional accountability and ownership. *American Nurse Today, 12*(2). https://www.myamericannurse.com/promoting-professional-accountability-ownership/

Texas Administrative Code, Title 22, Part 11, Chapter 217, Rule § 217.20. (2012). Safe harbor peer review for nurses and whistleblower protections. https://www.bon.texas.gov/rr_current/217-20.asp.html

Texas Board of Nursing. (2013). Nurse practice act, nursing peer review, & licensure compact Texas occupations code and statutes regulating the practice of nursing. http://www.statutes.legis.state.tx.us/Docs/OC/htm/OC.301.htm

U.S. Department of Health and Human Services. (2014). *Healthy People 2020, educational and community-based programs.*

U.S. Department of Health and Human Services, Office of Disease Prevention and Health Promotion. (n.d.). Increase the proportion of secondary schools with a full-time registered nurse — AHR08, *School Nurse. Healthy People 2030.* https://health.gov/healthypeople/objectives-and-data/browse-objectives/schools/increase-proportion-secondary-schools-full-time-registered-nurse-ah-r08

U.S. Department of Health and Human Services, Agency for Healthcare Research and Quality. (2020). *Plan-do- study-act (PDSA) cycle.* https://www.ahrq.gov/health-literacy/improve/precautions/tool2b.html

Willgerodt, M. A., Brock, D. M., & Maughan, E. D. (2018). Public school nursing practice in the United States. Journal of School Nursing, 34(3), 232-244. https://doi.org/10.1177/1059840517752456

Wolfe, L. C., Davis-Alldritt, L., Schultz, C., & Boyd., J. C. (2023, March). *2021 state of the states' report: NASSNC annual states report.* [Unpublished manuscript]. National Association of State School Nurse Consultants.

Zolnierek, C. (2012). Speak to be heard: Effective nurse advocacy. *American Nurse Today, 7*(10). https://www.americannursetoday.com/speak-to-be-heard-effective-nurse-advocacy/

Chapter 8

RESEARCH IN SCHOOL HEALTH

Ingrid Hopkins Duva, PhD, RN

DESCRIPTION OF ISSUE

Because school health covers a myriad of issues, the school setting offers a ripe opportunity for health research. Moreover, students in schools represent a significant cross-section of our nation. Thus, the services and scope of school health are rapidly increasing. Nurses are uniquely positioned at the crux of this intersection between school services and health research. The nurse's role in research may have many different variations, and all are important. School nurses are in an ideal position to lead their own investigations, collaborate with other researchers and facilitate the management of research studies, or even participate in studies led by others, such as public health researchers. At the very least, school nurses are accountable for evidence-based practice and, therefore, should be able to access and interpret research findings and translate those findings into practice.

Legal issues arising from conducting, participating in, or using research by nurses in schools are rare. If documented disputes exist, those legal cases are difficult to locate, much less to interpret. However, the school setting is subject to federal regulations governing ethical research and the safe treatment of children in an educational or school setting. Understanding how these regulations affect informed consent, privacy, and parental oversight is necessary for the nurse involved in research in this setting. As a research setting, the school is complex but can be navigated. This chapter provides a review of the basic legal obligations that accompany research to enhance the school nurse's ability to protect those in their care and, at the same time to contribute more fully to the future health and wellness of this population.

BACKGROUND

Ethical conduct is a consideration for all types of research experiments or studies. Ethical considerations in the conduct of school health research must meet a high standard of obligations. Therefore, basic human subjects' protection is required. According to the U.S. Department of Health and Human Services (USDHHS) regulations at 45 CFR 46, students are considered vulnerable if they are under the age of 18 (Protection of Human Subjects, 2018). Students are also vulnerable because a school is considered an institutional setting, so those in authority positions may influence their participation in research (Gordon, 2020). Legal guidelines exist so that at least minimal ethical standards of behavior are upheld. At a minimum, these essential protections assure autonomous decision-making (respect for persons), beneficence, and justice for all research participants (Protection of Human Subjects, 2018).

Current legal protections for research participants arose from poor ethical conduct by researchers dating back to the early 20th century. The Nuremberg war crime trials in Germany (1945-1947) judged physicians and scientists to have participated in unethical conduct. Biomedical experiments on concentration camp prisoners included various tests of human endurance, fully expecting that death and disability may be the outcome for the participants. These inhumane acts led to the Nuremberg Code, providing international and national guidelines for the ethical treatment of research subjects (Houser, 2018). The Nuremberg Code was the prototype for current legal protections in the form of specific informed consent requirements to participate in research experiments (USDHHS, 1979).

The Tuskegee Study conducted by the U.S. government began in 1932 to follow the natural disease progression of syphilis and continued into 1972. Participants in this study were not informed of their diagnoses and did not sign informed consent. New treatments for syphilis were withheld from approximately 400 black participants in the study. (Houser, 2018). Soon after the conclusion of this study, the federal government commissioned a report to outline the basic ethical principles and to provide guidance for research involving human subjects. The Belmont Report (named after the conference center hosting most meetings deliberating this issue) outlines the fundamental ethical principles of autonomy, beneficence, and justice. The Belmont report was published in the Federal Register on April 18, 1979, and was meant to serve as a guide for resolving ethical problems associated with research involving human subjects. This report informed The Common Rule (45 CFR 46). The Common Rule, formally known as the Federal Policy for the Protection of Human Subjects, was first published in 1991. It forms a set of regulations that provide the basic ethical principles for conducting research involving human subjects. The Common Rule is now codified in Title 45 of the Code of Federal Regulations, Part 46 (45 CFR 46).

Unfortunately, ethical violations in research are not limited to historical cases. Examples of more recent unethical conduct can easily be found with a quick scan through the ethics chapter of a current nursing research textbook. To address the ongoing concern that all biomedical or behavioral research studies involving human subjects meet legal and ethical requirements, institutions that conduct or host research are required to have a human subject's review committee (also referred to as an Institutional Review Board [IRB]) to approve and monitor research activities (Protection of Human Subjects, 2018). Proposed research must be submitted to the institution's IRB (for public schools, research approval occurs at the district level) or the partnering academic research institution's IRB prior to initiation of the study. This process is in place to further promote ethical compliance, functioning as the oversight for the ethical conduct of studies. Informed consent and IRB approval are legal protections for research subjects.

Additionally, research supported or conducted by a federal department or agency requires IRB approval and legal protection. All public schools meet this requirement unless the research meets one of the exemptions outlined in the regulations, such as de-identified educational testing data. These same principles of protection should still be applied in school research regardless of whether a formal approval process is in place.

Further federal guidelines exist to protect students' civil rights in public education settings. An in-depth discussion of those laws and statutes goes beyond the scope of this chapter. However, a cursory introduction helps frame the context for the additional complexities and nuances unique to research in the school setting. First, the Family Educational Rights & Privacy Act (FERPA) protects the rights and privacy of student information and education records (FERPA, 2012). FERPA applies to all schools that receive federal funds under an applicable U.S. Department of Education program. The Healthcare Insurance Portability and Accountability Act (HIPAA), passed in 1996, addresses the documentation, sharing, and privacy of health information in electronic health records (HIPAA, 1996). Only persons with a legitimate interest should access student information, whether health or education information and this access should be documented (FERPA, 2012; HIPAA, 1996).

The Protection of Pupils Rights Act (PPRA) may also be relevant to research (Protection of Pupils Rights Act, 2016). This law allows parents to preview student education materials (in eight specific areas noted later in this chapter). It may be interpreted to mean that any survey instruments, interviews, or assessments in these specific areas included in a study should be accessible to the parents. This section defines children as persons up to the age of 21 if enrolled in eligible programs (defined in PPRA §98.1 (a) or (b), or as determined under state law). Because parents typically need to provide informed consent for children 18 years of age or under, compliance with PPRA may be accomplished through the informed consent process. However, the researcher should recognize these as two separate and distinct requirements.

Private schools that do not receive federal funding generally do not fall under the same legal obligations unless the research is federally funded. Still, the school nurse in the private setting should also ensure appropriate school approvals are obtained, and student protections are in place. Still, the school nurse in the private setting should also ensure appropriate school approvals are obtained, and student protections are in place. Typically, approval processes that the school board or authorized administration must execute would be outlined in the school's policies or operational regulations. A student/parent (guardian) handbook, or similar documentation, expresses these policies as a contract between the school and the students and governs what student information is shared with parents/guardians.

IMPLICATIONS FOR SCHOOL NURSE PRACTICE

In addition to regular duties, school nurses are professionals responsible for initiating and supporting efforts toward improving the care of and health outcomes for students (American Nurses Association, 2015). According to the National Association of School Nurses (NASN), "School nurses utilize research data as they advocate and illustrate the impact of their role on meaningful health and academic outcomes" (NASN, 2016, p.49). Although less common, depending on education level, position, and setting, school nurses facilitate and can lead systematic investigations to increase professional knowledge and advance the science of school health. Based on current evidence, formal research is needed to ensure school nurses deliver care to students and school communities and document the cost-benefit to schools providing professional nursing services (Maughan et al., 2018). Knowledge gaps related to practice exist, and professional guidance also exists in this endeavor. The National Association of School Nurses (NASN) publishes an annual list of school health research priorities (Bergren, 2021). For example, the 2022 NASN research priorities reflect the current knowledge gaps:

- Addressing Health Equity and Social Determinants of Health
- Disaster Preparedness and Public Health Emergency Response
- Funding for School Health
- Implementation Science
- School Nursing Practice
- School Nursing Workforce
- School Nursing Well-Being

The likelihood that the school nurse will become involved in research is rising. Many factors contribute to this, including but not limited to the following:

- The changing healthcare environment and more healthcare responsibilities fall on the school as a community provider and health system safety net (Centers for Disease Control [CDC], 2017)

- The characteristics of students are changing; up to 40% have a documented chronic condition requiring more health services at school (CDC, 2022)
- The complexity of care is increasing, driving the need for more education, coordination of care, and support (Maughan et al., 2018),
- The COVID-19 pandemic. Renewed focus on communicable disease care and surveillance,
- Social Determinants of Health and health inequity in this population.

In addition to acute care needs, the pandemic highlighted a relationship between health and education and the significance of inequity to poorer outcomes (National Academy of Science, Engineering, and Medicine (NASEM), 2021).

The Every Student Succeeds Act (ESSA) was reauthorized in 2021, encouraging funding for support roles in education (such as nurses) to create healthier school environments for greater student success, particularly in Title 1 schools that have more low-income students (ESSA, 2016). Children living below the poverty level are disproportionately affected by chronic illness. Schools may play a critical role in bridging healthcare quality gaps by improving access to care for many children (CDC, 2017; Leroy et al., 2017). School nurses are addressing increasingly complex care needs for their students, and public attention to school health is rising, resulting in more research opportunities for this setting. Focused education or refreshers on the requirements of research, partnering with research-oriented organizations (such as schools of nursing or government agencies), and finding mentors specific to nursing research is important for school nurses to ensure the science grows and, at the same time, students are appropriately protected.

Research Determination

Differentiating informal and formal research is essential. The **first step** to determining any legal obligations related to a research study and the use of data is to determine if a study is formal research. Systematic inquiry using disciplined methods to answer questions or solve problems is the scientific research method. What distinguishes formal research is the purpose: to generate new or validate existing knowledge (Gray & Grove, 2021). For example, data collected during the routine examination of a student to improve the process of providing daily health services locally to a group of students does not qualify as formal research (Fleming, 2013). Data obtained during the course of practice can and should be used to improve practice. Investigation into published research findings and improved outcomes can and should be implemented if applicable to the local context. However, even if these activities were approached in a systematic manner, they may not be considered formal research if the conclusions are not intended to be generalized or applied universally. Therefore, the purpose of a study is critical to establish the necessary threshold for applying the legal research considerations discussed here. This may pose a learning curve for some school nurses. The process will benefit from partnering with experts, i.e., health scientists or nurses with PhDs from local hospitals, healthcare facilities, or universities. Differentiating research used for quality improvement from formal research is the first step to understanding legal obligations.

Practice example:

> *A survey for collecting information on dietary habits within the school setting may not meet the research threshold if the study intends to improve internal school processes (such as self-serve lunch lines). It may directly benefit the survey participant (improved food choices), and the results may be shared locally (within the school itself or with district administrators). This survey could be part of an improvement initiative, not a formal research study.*
>
> *Alternately, a survey used for collecting information on dietary habits within the school setting (either provided alone or as part of a larger or more comprehensive study) could meet the research threshold: If the study intends to gain knowledge, knowledge gained will not benefit the participating student, and the results of the study will be shared with a broad audience, the basic legal obligations accompanying research may apply.*

Institutional Review Board (IRB)

The **second step** for the school nurse, considering the responsibility for research conducted in the school setting or informing school nursing practice, is to be responsible and ethical. Most research conducted in schools involves human subjects, and therefore IRB approval is required. The IRB is comprised of a group of individuals charged with protecting the rights, safety, and welfare of human subjects. This group provides an added layer of oversight to "human subjects" research, assuring ongoing safety for all participants (Protection of Human Subjects, 2018). The IRB approval is a requirement for all federally funded organizations and most funding agents for research studies. Larger school districts may have their own IRB in place and a policy directing the researcher through an approval process with the school district or collaborating academic institution. Smaller or independent schools may rely on collaborating organizations for the IRB process. When no IRB is available because a study is small, unfunded, or not sponsored by the federal government, a local research review process should be in place to ensure the appropriate ethical considerations. The nurse can contact the administration to be referred to the appropriate contact for their school.

The nurse's obligation to protect their students and ensure the ethical conduct of research varies according to role and purpose. At the least, the nurse should look for a statement or acknowledgment of IRB approval in the guiding research publications or practice guidelines if evaluating research findings or translating evidence to practice. School nurses who facilitate or participate in the study should have a copy of the IRB approval (or study number for reference) and can contact the appropriate IRB committee with questions or to confirm approval. Notification of approval should be easily identified on any research study announcements and consent forms. Additionally, nurses working solely as collaborators or data collectors for a study (conducted by a person or entity within or outside the school district) should keep a copy of the study's protocol and documentation of the collaborator's IRB approval.

Nurse investigators, those conducting or leading studies themselves, submit their research protocol directly to the applicable review process, either an IRB or an approved oversight committee. There are three types of IRB review, depending on the level of risk to the participants, typically requiring a greater length of time in this order: exempt, expedited, or full board review. Exempt studies do not require approval because it falls into one of the exempt categories in the federal IRB regulations. For example, this would apply when the study does not meet the research definition, or the consent process would present a greater risk to the participant. Expedited reviews are for the category of research studies that present no more than minimal risk and so do not need a full IRB board to convene. Typically, the review is conducted by one reviewer, and so is completed more quickly. Full board reviews are for complex studies, and so need the expertise and perspective of multiple board members to evaluate the risk involved to the participants. IRB approval is needed in advance of data collection, but oversight of the study is ongoing; updates and reviews of the research may periodically occur throughout the course of the study. During project planning, the nurse investigator should consider that some time is needed to go through the IRB approval process. Collaborating with experienced researchers may smooth the process and can help avoid delays.

Informed Consent Requirements

Unless strictly limited to unidentifiable data, most research studies in schools will fall under the human subject's category and require informed consent. Through the human subjects' review process, the IRB will approve the type and extent of consent required from research participants developed by the primary investigator. There may be exceptions to the informed consent requirement, particularly in educational settings. For example, research involving normal education practices, or the use of standard educational test scores may not need informed consent because the intervention is part of standard practice. Alternately, some research does not require a signature consent. Of course, the participants still need to be informed.

An alteration to required consent common in the school setting is passive parental consent instead of active consent. Passive consent requires a parent or guardian to sign and return a form only if they refuse to allow their child to participate in research or a particular study. This practice may improve the process of implementation but is only used if there is no more than minimal risk to the student/participant. There are also instances where a waiver of documented consent may be appropriate.

For some research studies, implied consent may be justified, meaning that participation is sufficient to indicate agreement on the participant's part after becoming informed. For example, an implied consent process may be approved if obtaining documented consent will present a barrier to student participation (therefore limiting the benefit of the research to a certain population of students). This need for implied consent has been documented by investigators, particularly in alternative school environments that may have more transient students or less contact with parents and guardians (Johnson et al., 2016). Keep in mind that the decision to waive signed consent for a research study is not up to the individual investigator, researchers must maintain the requirement to meet the basic elements of informed consent, and for either an exemption or a waiver of any kind, documentation will need to be on record.

Formal research studies requiring student participation will likely be categorized as research including children. Children are a special class of research participants with unique considerations and protections. For human subject research, the regulation defines children as "persons who have not attained the legal age for consent to treatment or procedures involved in the research, under the applicable law of the jurisdiction in which the research will be conducted" (Protection of Human Subjects, 2009, 45 CFR 46.402(a)). The age determination for adulthood may vary in some states or locales or depending on the medical treatment under consideration but typically is 18 years or older. The most recent NIH update, effective January 2016, classified children as ages 18 or younger (NIH, 2015). The process for consenting students, particularly children, may have the most implications for a collaborating school nurse. For a child to participate in research, one or more parent/guardian(s) must consent.

Additionally, for the school-age child who is capable, assent is required. This means that the child must also be informed of the basic elements of consent, including what the study is about and any risks or benefits, and then agree to participate in the research. Cases in which a child would typically not be required to agree to research include those where the risk is minimal or where there may be a direct personal benefit to the child. The need for this documented agreement from the child is determined based on a sliding scale, weighing the risk (harm, discomfort, or threat to well-being) of participating against the benefit that may be experienced. Again, the need for documented consent or student assent is governed by federal regulation and approved locally by the IRB.

Practice Example:

> *Consider the dietary survey used above. If deemed research by the IRB, informed consent will be required. However, if the risk of participation is low or requiring signed/witnessed consent may limit participation, then consent may be implied through the students' voluntary participation. Study participants are informed of the study purpose, risks, and how to withdraw participation, and this process is documented.*
>
> *In other cases, such as a study with an intervention or a survey that might impose some determined risk to a participant, the informed consent process will be documented, and each participant's consent will be required in writing. In the school setting, students may need to document assent, and the parent/legal guardian would sign consent. This process is documented and approved by the IRB or local research review authorities. Informed consent is required to meet human subject research requirements.*

Privacy and Confidentiality

Participating in research studies should not compromise student privacy rights. Privacy is concerned with individual identification, and so the concern is that information does not link back to or identify an individual. Therefore, the organization of documents pertaining to any ongoing or recently concluded research study is another important step to consider. Storing sensitive data and the study documents that include this data must be addressed in the protocol. Any forms and data collected from study participants must be kept locked or safeguarded when not in use. Electronic data should be encrypted and stored in a password-protected file.

Students' educational and health information is confidential. Confidentiality is concerned with the data from the study. Only those school staff with a job-related purpose should have access to those documents, educational or health data. For example, a school nurse (regardless of the employer) would need parental (for minors) and school permission to use test scores or healthcare data for research or anything other than caring for the student.

Diligent access logs need to be kept. Even the approved school staff who access documentation or raw data need to log their access, including their name, title, date and need to know. When school staff access a student's health or education data because of their need to know, their legal access is still limited to just that portion of information or data that applies. Student data may not be shared outside of the need to know without prior approval, informed consent, and, if applicable, an approved data use or data sharing agreement (FERPA, 2012).

Surveys, Instruments, or Assessments

The Protection of Pupils Rights Act (PPRA) found at 20 U.S.C.A. § 1232h contains an inspection and consent requirement of instructional materials. This federal statute applies to any educational institution receiving federal funds. It may implicate student health studies using surveys or educational material and adds another layer of legal oversight unique to research in student health settings. Under PPRA, all instructional materials in the eight categories below, used in conjunction with any survey, evaluation, or analysis as part of any applicable program, must be made available for inspection by the minor's parent or guardian (20 U.S.C.A. 1232h(a)). PPRPA also mandates an additional informed consent requirement for eight categories of sensitive information (20 U.S.C.A. 1232h(b)). Those categories are:

1. Political affiliations or beliefs of the student or the student's parent;
2. Mental or psychological problems of the student or the student's family;
3. Sex behavior or attitudes;
4. Illegal, anti-social, self-incriminating, or demeaning behavior;
5. Critical appraisals of other individuals with whom respondents have close family relationships;
6. Legally recognized privileged or analogous relationships, such as those of lawyers, physicians, and ministers;
7. Religious practices, affiliations, or beliefs of the student or student's parent; or
8. Income (other than that required by law to determine eligibility for participation in a program or for receiving financial assistance under such program).

Any survey, evaluation, or analysis of any information covered by these eight categories requires informed parental consent, not just the right to inspect the actual material. Without informed parental consent, the minor student is not required to submit to any analysis, evaluation, or survey covering any material involving information dealing with these eight categories.

The regulation includes a list of policies that the local educational agency must set forth to protect student privacy, parental access to information, and physical examinations. If the state or local educational agency has policies that meet the specifications of the regulations as of January 8, 2002, then the agency needs to provide parents with notification of these policies in accordance with the notification provision contained in the statute.

Notably, the regulation does not provide a private cause of action for individuals who feel that their rights have been violated. This means that an individual cannot use the law itself as a tool to sue the entity or individual who violates it. The federal government enforces compliance, and it expressly states that in order for assistance under PPRA to be terminated, there must be a finding that there was a failure to comply, as compliance cannot be gained through voluntary means. Assuming the violating agency agrees to comply, it is unlikely that an enforcement action could do any real harm to the local or state agency (the school or school nurse). Just the same, this compliance is an essential aspect of properly administered school-based research.

Therefore, in addition to assuring IRB approval, the school nurse should confirm the district policy and that it complies with the PPRA.

Practice example:

Under PPRA, the survey regarding dietary habits within the school setting intended to improve the internal school process could require parental notification even though it does not serve the purpose of education or research. Parental notification letters offer the parent or legal guardian an opportunity to take action with a written statement to opt –out their student, with no justification, and assure no ramifications to the student.

Likewise, a student survey about daily dietary habits within the school setting provided as part of a comprehensive research study on student performance may require that the school notify parents/ legal guardians of their right to request prior viewing of any invitation to participate, survey instruments being used, or other accompanying information given to the student related to the study.

The Center for Disease Control's Youth Risk Behavior Surveillance is an example of a survey high school students complete that includes questions about their diet but is part of a comprehensive study. According to the USDHHS/CDC (2019), their own IRB approved the protocol for the national survey, but local procedures were followed for parental permission (UDHHS/CDC, 2019). This implies that, because there is sensitive information collected, not only were parent notification letters sent to all students asked to complete this survey, but informed consent was needed. The local IRB or research board may have approved implied consent because student participation in the survey is voluntary and anonymous. The school nurse can and should access the locally approved protocol before administering the survey and assure compliance with parent permission procedures before initiating data collection.

CONCLUSION

The scope of nursing research in a public education setting has not been extensively discussed in courts. Limitations on the number of student participants, the appropriate level of consent, the types of studies that can or cannot be conducted, or even the length of studies have not spawned enough litigation to give clear guidance on these issues. To conduct or facilitate a legally "compliant" formal research study, the school nurse must abide by basic research principles of informed consent, private health and academic information protection, and any other fundamental research controls. Local, state, or tribal laws may provide additional protections to human subjects of research. Additionally, state school nurse consultants at the state health or education departments may be a resource to school nurses regarding research questions. To use data to improve individual practice or student outcomes, the school nurse must abide by all applicable guidelines to protect student privacy, confidentiality, and, if sensitive information is involved, appropriate informed consent. To conduct or facilitate a legally "compliant" formal research study, the school nurse will need IRB approval and further follow basic research principles of informed consent, protection of private health and academic information, and any other fundamental research controls. While school nurses may have qualified immunity for discretionary actions taken in the course and scope of their nursing care duties, the law is less clear on what liability protection a school nurse may have in the context of conducting or facilitating a research study, particularly an unauthorized study or one without appropriate consent.

Therefore, before the study begins, the school nurse should ensure the school district has authorized the study and has also agreed to indemnify and hold harmless the research team from and against any lawsuits, claims, or damage demands arising from the study's performance. The nurse should make absolutely certain that the research team is covered by insurance as an additional insured under the insurance policy issued to the school district not only for any school-related medical care being provided but also for any claims arising out of the research study itself. In most instances, this insurance coverage is handled through the school's legal department and is documented via a contract between the school and the collaborating research institutions.

In summary, the general legal considerations for the school nurse involved in research are:

1. Determination of the research as formal research.
2. In the private setting, just as in the public setting, the school nurse will need to investigate applicable school policies before initiating or participating in any research.
3. Obtain a copy of the research proposal, including a protocol for participant recruitment, type of consent, and document/ data management and dissemination plan with IRB approval documented.
4. Knowledge of the proper consenting procedures, assuring necessary parental notifications.
5. Depending on the age of the research subjects and the nature of the study, the school nurse may be responsible for obtaining assent from the subjects themselves (even though, as minors, they cannot give informed consent).
6. Student confidentiality and privacy are protected by securing student data and meeting all school health documentation rules.
7. Compliance with any data management, storage, or sharing plan, including all study materials and documentation after the conclusion of the study.

Also, see Table 1.

Table 1

Legal Consideration	Resource
Determination of formal research	Expert consultation, e.g., Doctoral prepared RNs or Health Services Researchers
Protection of Human Subjects	Collaborating institution IRB. Local school, district, university, or state IRB regarding protocol approval.
Compliance with federal regulations governing the school's protection of students.	The local school, district, and state policies and administrative team.
Compliance with private school rules, regulations, and parent contracts.	Private school policies, administration, and governing board.
Respect for students and consideration for equal, representative access to study participation.	Collaborating institution IRB. Local school, district, university, or state IRB regarding consent/assent procedures.
Privacy and confidentiality for students (including documentation management).	Collaborating institution IRB. Local school, district, university, or state IRB regarding consent procedures. The local school, district, and state policies and administrative team

RESOURCES

45 CFR (2021). Title 46 – Protection of human subjects.

Mosca, N.W. (2007). Research tidbits: When research involves human subjects: The institutional review board. *NASN Newsletter, 22***(2), 8–9.** https://doi.org/10.1177/104747570702200204

National Association of School Nurses. Research Priorities.
https://www.nasn.org/research/research-priorities

National Association of School Nurses. Research agenda and research grants.
https://www.nasn.org/research/research-grants

National Institutes of Health (NIH). *Research involving human subjects*.
https://grants.nih.gov/policy/humansubjects.htm

National Institute of Nursing Research (NINR). Grant development and management resources.
https://www.ninr.nih.gov/researchandfunding/fundingopportunities

National Research Act, Pub. Law 93-348 (1974).
https://www.congress.gov/bill/93rd-congress/house-bill/7724

U.S. Department of Health and Human Services/ Centers for Disease Control and Prevention. (2019). Youth risk behavior surveillance- United States, 2019. Morbidity and Mortality Weekly Report. 69(1), 1-88. https://www.cdc.gov/healthyyouth/data/yrbs/pdf/2019/su6901-H.pdf

U.S. Department of Health and Human Services (HHS). Office for human research protections.
http://www.hhs.gov/ohrp/regulations-and-policy/guidance/faq/children-research/index.html

REFERENCES

American Academy of Pediatrics. (2021, January). *Consensus statement on the core tenets of chronic condition management in schools.* https://publications.aap.org/aapnews/news/17434

American Nurses Association. (2015). *Code of ethics for nurses.* American Nurses Publishing.

Best, N.C., & McCabe, E.M. (2023). Learning from the past and moving forward: Implementing school nursing research priorities. *The Journal of School Nursing 39*(1), 3-5. https://doi.org/10.1177/10598405221143495

Bergren, M.D. (2021). School nursing research priorities. The Journal of School Nursing. 37(1), 5. https://doi.org/10.1177/1059840520975614" https://doi.org/10.1177/1059840520975614

Centers for Disease Control. (2017). *Research brief: Chronic health conditions and academic achievement.* https://www.cdc.gov/healthyschools/chronic_conditions/pdfs/2017_02_15-CHC-and-Academic-Achievement_Final_508.pdf

Centers for Disease Control and Prevention. (2019). Youth risk behavior surveillance- United States, 2019. *Morbidity and Mortality Weekly Report.* 69(1), 1-88. https://www.cdc.gov/healthyyouth/data/yrbs/pdf/2019/su6901-H.pdf

Centers for Disease Control and Prevention (2022, May). *Chronic Disease Fact Sheet: Healthy Schools* (Fact Sheet). https://www.cdc.gov/chronicdisease/resources/publications/factsheets/healthy-schools.htm

Every Student Succeeds Act of 2015, Pub. L. No. 114-95 § 114 Stat. 1177 (2015-2016). https://www.congress.gov/bill/114th-congress/senate-bill/1177/text

Family Educational Rights and Privacy Act, 20 U.S.C. § 1232g; 34 CFR Part 99 (1974 & rev 2012). https://www.govinfo.gov/content/pkg/CFR-2013-title34-vol1/pdf/CFR-2013-title34-vol1-part99.pdf

Fleming, R. (2013). Demystifying the differences in using data to improve individual practice versus publishing research findings. *School Nurse, 28*(5), 237–238. http://doi.org/10.1177/1942602X13494847

Gordon, B. (2020). Vulnerability in research: Basic ethical concepts and general approach to review. *The Oschner Journal, 20*(1), 34–38. https//doi.org/10.31486/toj.19.0079

Gray, J.R., & Grove, S.K. (2021). *Burns and Grove's The practice of nursing research: Appraisal, synthesis, and generation of evidence* (9th ed.) Saunders Elsevier.

Health Insurance Portability and Accountability Act, P.L. No 104-191, 110 Stat. 1938 (1996).

Houser, J. (2018). *Nursing research: Reading, using, and creating evidence* (4th ed). Jones & Bartlett Learning.

Johnson, K.E., Morris, M., Rew, L., & Simonton, A.J. (2016). A systematic review of consent procedures, participation rates, and main findings of health-related research in alternative high schools from 2010 to 2015. *The Journal of School Nursing, 32*(1), 20-31. https://doi.org/10.1177/1059840515620841" https://doi.org/10.1177/1059840515620841

Krause-Parello, C.A. (2013). An overview of nursing research and relevance to school nursing practice. *NASN School Nurse, 28*(6), 294-296. http://doi.org/10.1177/1942602X13502675" http://doi.org/10.1177/1942602X13502675

Leroy, Z.C., Wallin, R., & Lee, S. (2017). The role of school health services in addressing the needs of students with chronic health conditions. *Journal of School Nursing, 33*(1),64–72. http://doi.org/10.1177/1059840516678909. Epub 2016 November 21.

Maughan, E.D., Cowell, J., Engelke, M., McCarthy, A.M., Bergren, M.D., Murphy, K., Barry, C., Krause-Parello, C.A., Luthy, B., Kintner, E.K., & Vessey, J.A. (2018). The vital role of school nurses in ensuring the health of our nation's youth. *Nursing Outlook, 66* (2018), 94–96. https://doi.org/10.1016/j.outlook.2017.11.002" https://doi.org/10.1016/j.outlook.2017.11.002

National Academies of Sciences, Engineering, and Medicine (2021). *The future of nursing 2020-2030: Charging a path to achieve health equity.* The National Academies Press. https://doi.org/10.17226/25982

National Association of School Nurses. (2015). *The Patient Protection and Affordable Care Act: The role of the school nurse* (Position Statement). Author.

National Association of School Nurses. (2016). Framework for 21st century school nursing practice. *NASN School Nurse, 31*(1), 45-53. https://doi.org/10.1177/1942602X15618644

National Institutes of Health. (2009 rev 2015). *NIH policy and guidelines on the inclusion of children as participants in research involving human subjects* (NOT-OD-16-010). https://grants.nih.gov/grants/guide/notice-files/not98-024.html

Protection of Human Subjects, (2018). https://www.hhs.gov/ohrp/regulations-and-policy/regulations/45-cfr-46/index.html

Protection of Pupils Rights Act, 20 U.S.C.A. § 1232h (2016). https://www.govinfo.gov/app/details/USCODE-2021-title20/USCODE-2021-title20-chap31-subchapIII-part4-sec1232h

Tanner, A.L. and Stanislo, K. (2022). School nursing research and nursing implementation priorities. The *Journal of School Nursing*, 38(6). 500-501. https://doi.org/10.1177/10598405221123231

Underwood, J.M., Brener, N., Thornton J., Harris, W.A., Bryan, L.N., Shanklin, S. L., Deputy, N., Roberts, A.M., Queen, B., Chyen, D., Whittle, L., Lim, C., Yamakawa, Y., Leon-Nguyen, M., Kilmer, G., Smith-Grant, J., Demissie, Z., Everett Jones, S., Clayton, & H., Dittus, P. (2021).Overview and methods for the youth risk behavior surveillance system — United States, 2019. *MMWR Supplement, 69*(1), 1–10. http://dx.doi.org/10.15585/mmwr.su6901a1

U.S. Department of Health and Human Services, Office for Human Research Protections. (1979). National Commission for the Protection of Human Subjects of Biomedical and Behavioral Research. *The Belmont Report: Ethical principles and guidelines for the protection of human subjects of research.* https://www.hhs.gov/ohrp/regulations-and-policy/belmont-report/index.html

Chapter 9

SCHOOL HEALTH DOCUMENTATION AND IMPLICATIONS FOR DATA COLLECTION

Katie Johnson, DNP, RN, NCSN-E, APHN-BC, FNASN, FAAN

Due to the length of this chapter, the following outline provides an overview of the chapter content:

BACKGROUND

- Importance of Documentation
- What to Document
- Standardized Nursing Languages
- Documentation Formats
- Standards and Quality
- Meaningful Use of Documentation
- Electronic Documentation Systems
- Recommendations from Research

IMPLICATIONS FOR SCHOOL NURSE PRACTICE

- Standardized Language
- Documentation Formats
- Data Ethics
- Quality of Documentation
- Accuracy of Documentation
- Meaningful Use of Data
- Impact of Effective Documentation

DESCRIPTION OF ISSUE

Concise and accurate documentation of healthcare services in the school setting is critical to ensuring seamless and effective communication throughout the student's academic journey, promoting safe and continuous care and providing legal protections for both the nurse and the school district. Aggregated data derived from nursing documentation has the power to develop evidence for practice, create effective policy, and drive quality of care. The following describes guidance on elements of documentation, documentation formats, quality standards, and reporting of school health data.

Nursing documentation is "the record of nursing care that is planned and given to individual patients and clients by qualified nurses or by other caregivers under the direction of a qualified nurse," promoting "structured, consistent, and effective communication between caregivers" (Urquhart et al., 2009, p. 1; Wang et al., 2011 p. 1859). Effective documentation promotes safe, legal, individualized care that is coordinated across caregivers and settings. It is "essential to the provision of safe, quality, and effective evidence-based care" (McCarthy et al., 2019, p. 491) and an "essential element of safe, quality, evidence-based nursing practice" and "a necessary and integral aspect of the work of registered nurses in all roles and setting" (American Nurses Association [ANA], 2010, p. 3).

In the school setting, the primary purposes of documentation are to describe the clinical history of the student's care and treatment, to allow for continuity of care, and to provide evidence that the nurse has discharged their duties of care (Griffith, 2016). Experts describe its purpose as "...communication, quality assurance, legal responsibilities, reimbursement, diagnosis and research, assessment and evaluation, education, statistics, and healthcare planning" (Folio 3, n.d.). Effective reporting of documentation supports the development of evidence for practice and advocacy. Nursing documentation includes "patient care documents, assessments of processes, and outcome measures across organizational settings" (ANA, 2010, p. 6). It serves to "monitor performance" and compliance with standards by providers and healthcare facilities (ANA, 2010, p. 6).

Effective documentation requires attention to a variety of standards, including nursing standards of care; accurate, adequate, and timely recording of care; and effective use of the information collected in the student record.

BACKGROUND

Importance of Documentation

The National Association of School Nurses (NASN) emphasizes the importance of documentation throughout the nursing process as a standard of nursing practice (NASN, 2022b). Nursing documentation has been described as defining "the nature of nursing itself" and being a "repository of knowledge" that supports the visibility of the work, decision-making, and outcomes of nursing care (Jefferies et al., 2010, p. 113). Legal expert, Richard Griffith, states, "in litigation, the outcome is not based on truth, but on proof," supporting the nursing adage that "if it is not documented, it was not done;" this reminds nurses that "records are never neutral – they will either support you or condemn you" (Griffith, 2016, p. 408).

Legal experts support this concept indicating that "...effective communication, documentation, and post-incident procedures, proper care may be defended, and unnecessary exposure avoided" (Newfield, 2006, p.

247). Newfield also advises that "clear, consistent, and reasonably thorough" documentation can be more effective than "more" documentation that is ambiguous or documents that are inconsistent from one record to another (Newfield, 2006, p. 248). Quality documentation "requires thought about the language used, confidence about the care provided, and a willingness to critically examine the record… to ensure it effectively represents the care provided." This is important considering the likelihood of an extended time between care, any litigation that may be brought, and the number of patients served by individual nurses (Newfield, 2006, p. 249; NSO, n.d.-a; Wortham & Maag, 2019).

Critical examination of the record at the time of recording limits the risk from the presumption that documentation is clear when it actually contains ambiguities (Newfield, 2006). Ambiguities could result in challenges during the legal process when the recall is clouded by the length of time between care and litigation. Legal experts describe the success or failure of litigation based on the completeness, timeliness, and accuracy of the health practitioner's documentation. Wortham & Maag advise that "every piece of information that is entered – or not entered… could become evidence" where "quality [documentation}…can make the nurse appear competent…or careless" (p.4).

The importance of documentation is further emphasized in the many ways it is used to support safe and legal care.

Effective documentation:

- Provides a legal record of care
- Chronicles the history of care and the student's needs
- Supports communication with other members of the school team
- Supports continuity of care, and
- Allows for the evaluation of care

When aggregated and analyzed, it also supports the:

- Development of evidence for effective practice
- Understanding of population health needs, and
- Identification of critical nursing-sensitive student outcomes which hold implications for policy, research, and resource allocation

What to Document

Prudent documentation reflects the nursing process and communicates the application of nursing judgment in the following:

1) assessment and identification of a nursing diagnosis,
2) nursing interventions, and
3) outcomes of nursing care demonstrating adherence to nursing regulations, professional practice, and performance standards.

This also includes:

- Abnormalities
- Changes in condition
- Clinical Problems
- Adverse findings
- Changes in the plan of care and reason for the change
- Outcomes after the intervention
- Family responses
- Relevant social issues
- Medication records
- Care declined by clients
- Medical orders – acknowledged, implemented, and evaluated
- Health status of the patient
- Patient's perception of their health, and
- Communication with other health professionals (ANA, 2010; Blair & Smith, 2012; Griffith, 2007; Jefferies et al., 2010; Koch, 2014; NSO, n.d.-b; Prideaux, 2011).

Complete documentation also includes information about any dissent with other team members about the care provided. The recorded note of the dissent contains factual accounting (vs. criticism) of the events leading to the dissent, the nurse's rationale for disagreement, and subsequent action taken (Griffith, 2015). This would include the nurse's accounting of their communication regarding dissent with those in authority.

Failure to adequately document creates risks related to

- Legal fact-finding
- Affecting the "legal rights, claims, and defenses" of patients and health care providers
- Liability for health care organizations and providers (ANA, 2010, p. 6)

Standards and Quality

The quality of documentation is essential to ensure effective communication of the student's care across caregivers and settings. The records also afford legal protection to the nurse and clarity for the district in case of a dispute over care. Quality in nursing documentation is "patient centered, based on the nurse's clinical decision and includes a description of all nursing interventions, follows the principles of logic and continuity, is written in real-time, describes different aspects of the treatment performed, and complies with legal requirements" (Nool et al., 2022, p. 5). Experts recommend that nurses "document defensively" (NSO, n.d. -b). Quality documentation reflects the nurse's critical thinking and application of the nursing process.

High-quality documentation is:
- Accessible
- Accurate, relevant, and consistent, not falsified
- Auditable

- Clear, concise, and complete
- Legible/readable
- Thoughtful
- Timely, contemporaneous, and sequential
- Reflective of the nursing process
- Retrievable on a permanent basis in a nursing-specific manner (ANA, 2010, p. 12; NSO, n.d.-a).

To achieve quality, it is recommended that nurses:

- Document care as close to the time of rendering as possible (contemporaneously);
- Document risks or problems and the nurse's intervention in response;
- Ensure accuracy of record without falsification;
- Ensure all notes are appropriately attributed or linked to the author of the note;
- Ensure notes are clear with the date and time of entry included, and contain no unnecessary jargon or abbreviations;
- Ensure notes are fact-based – not speculative;
- Avoids gaps and criticism;
- Demonstrates care coordination and delegated care;
- Includes response to care, as well as nonadherence to care;
- Are secure; and
- Avoid copy and paste features; and if used sparingly and with care (Griffith, 2016; NSO, n.d.-a; NSO, n.d.-b; NSO, n.d.-c).

Documentation that occurs contemporaneously with care enhances the perception of accuracy, quality, and reliability (Griffith, 2016). Documentation should be completed by the individual providing the care – this includes care provided by unlicensed persons - unless the information in that record is clearly attributed to the person providing care. However, documentation created directly by the person providing care holds more credibility in legal questions than secondhand reports. In the event of a need to change a record (e.g., error, wrong record, etc.), Griffith also points out that any alteration of a record after the fact could be taken as a cover-up of wrongdoing. Therefore, a single line through a paper entry that allows the error to be legible, with the word "error" and the nurse's initials, is an appropriate method to correct errors in paper records. Records are dated and signed and follow the previous entry. Document changes or additions made after the initial entry should state a "late entry" with the writer's signature and date. With any changes to a record, it must be clear who made the changes, what the changes were, and when they were made. Electronic documentation systems should provide overwrite protection that does not allow entries to be deleted but supports the correction of errors, an audit log that records changes in the record, and durability and authentication of the author of the record (Johnson & Guthrie, 2012). (*See Chapter 10 for more information on School Health Records.*)

Poor documentation is affected by workload, inefficient documentation forms, use of local abbreviations or terminology that are not well-understood, inadequate resources, and workplace culture (NSO, n.d.-c; Okaisu et al., 2014). Recommendations to improve nursing documentation included appropriate forms to support nursing workflow and a healthy work culture that included "authentic leadership, meaningful recognition, skilled communication, and appropriate staffing," as well as professional development in documentation (Okaisu et al., 2014, p. 5). Training and aligning documentation structures with the nursing process has been identified as a way to improve quality by many experts (ANA, 2022; Bruylands et al., 2013; Gale et al., 2023; Kay et al., 2023; Laukvik et al., 2022; Malabusini, 2023; Munroe et al., 2021; Nool et al., 2022; Paterson et al., 2023; Rossi et al., 2022; Ting et al., 2021). Nursing leaders can support effective documentation by "translating the results" of quality documentation, emphasizing its value in "helping colleagues" in their work, and its impact on ethical, quality nursing care (Bogeskov & Grimshaw-Aagaard, 2019).

The importance of quality in documentation is evidenced by the volumes of literature addressing it (ANA, 2010; Behairy et al., 2023; Charalambous & Goldberg, 2016; DeGroot et al., 2022; Eshel et al., 2023; Futterman et al., 2023; Jaekel et al., 2022; Kay et al., 2023; Laukvik et al., 2022; McCarthy et al., 2019; Munroe et al., 2021; Nool et al., 2022; Paterson et al., 2023; Rossi et al., 2022; Ting et al., 2021; Wang et al., 2011). Findings from a systematic review of the quality of nursing documentation revealed incomplete documentation on psychosocial, cultural, and spiritual aspects of care, patient teaching, and nursing assessment of the patient's quality of life, knowledge deficits, and pain. Other deficits included the inaccurate use of nursing diagnoses and interventions and a lack of coherence in the steps of the nursing process. Recommendations to address these issues included the use of electronic documentation systems, the use of standardized terminology, prompts in the EHR to improve comprehensiveness, and education in the documentation of the nursing process (Wang et al., 2011).

Multiple studies and systematic reviews have shown the value of EHRs to documentation quality (McCarthy et al., 2019; Ting et al., 2021). Other studies have found that user-friendly programs and quality indicators (DeGroot et al., 2019; 2022) contribute to effective documentation. A mixed methods study of community nurses identified that the type of documentation affected their perception of the burden of documentation – documentation describing nursing care of patients was viewed as less burdensome than "organizational documentation" such as billing or staffing records (DeGroot et al., 2022). In addition, ethical issues have emerged related to the burden of time for documentation and the "fair distribution of goods" among patients (i.e., time devoted to nursing care) vs. time spent documenting, as well as balancing harm between effective communication with the care team and patient autonomy over what is documented (Jorgensen & Kollerup, 2022).

Barriers to patient safety related to documentation include individual, social, organizational, and technological factors (Valderaune et al., 2016). To support quality, (Bruylands et al., 2013) summarized the literature on the value of diagnostics on the quality and quantity of documentation and recommended "Guided Clinical Reasoning" as a tool to promote quality documentation (Bruylands et al., 2013, p. 164). The guide focused on the integration of critical thinking and reflection on the nursing process using clinical case studies. They recommended that professional development in documentation include guided clinical reflection, electronic documentation systems, and support in standardized terminologies. Professional development in documentation for new nurses focused on documenting the critical thinking behind their care.

Wang and colleagues (2011) identified audit tools that addressed three dimensions of documentation:
1) structure,
2) process, and
3) content.

The authors noted that the quality of the content of nurses' documentation is interpreted to align with the quality of nursing care provided. They also note that thorough documentation of the nursing process demonstrates nursing knowledge and skill in the application of clinical reasoning. Blair & Smith (2012) noted the frequent absence of documentation demonstrating nurses' critical thinking. The Nursing and Midwifery Content Audit Tool (NMCAT) demonstrated both content and interrater reliability, which focused on both legal components of documentation and content (Johnson et al., 2010).

Clinical reasoning is essential to the nursing process and must be reflected in the documentation. It reflects "the cognitive processing performed by RNs when collecting and analyzing patient information, evaluating the significance of this information, weighing alternative actions, achieving positive patient outcomes, and reflecting upon care delivery" (Laukvik et al., 2022, p. 223). The complexity of clinical reasoning becomes evident when the components are broken apart and analyzed:

- Data analysis – interpreting information
- Deliberation – rumination or processing of information
- Heuristics – informal thinking strategies
- Inference – speculation on the meaning based on evidence
- Metacognition – reflexive thinking or analyzing the quality of thinking
- Logic – clarity, and consistency of analysis
- Cognition – perception or awareness of one's own reasoning process
- Information processing – organizing data in the context of the problem
- Intuition – insight independent of reasoning, often based on experience

Using these components in a think aloud study (Laukvik et al., 2022) analyzed how experienced nurses plan care and how they document that care.
1) Nurses used the nursing process to support reasoning while planning and documenting nursing care. Their clinical reasoning focused on information exchange about the care they provided – what and how to document.
2) RNs "used all clinical reasoning attributes during care planning and documentation" and most frequently used inference, information processing, and cognition. Information processing appeared in their retrieval, organization, and recording of data gathered during their care. Cognition appeared in consideration of clients' "individual needs and preference" (Laukvik et al., 2022, p. 227). Inference was used to determine what they needed to communicate.
3) Nurses moved iteratively through the nursing process and used multiple reasoning attributes when documenting. Information processing, cognition, deliberation, logic & inference were used to document assessment and implementation. Implementation & evaluation utilized information processing, cognition, deliberation, heuristics, logic, and inference.

It is clear that nurses use critical thinking in processing how to deliver quality care; the challenge comes in how that critical thinking is represented in their documentation. Recommendations include EHR functions that synthesize relevant assessment information and support the workflow and iterative nature of the nursing process (Laukvik et al., 2022). Using large quantities of aggregated data can be developed into clinical decision support to be embedded into the record.

Standardized Nursing Languages

Norma Lang described the importance of standardized variables to collect nursing data in 1992: "...if we cannot name it, we cannot control it, finance it, teach it, research it, or put it into public policy" (Clark & Lang, 1992, p. 109). Standardized nursing languages allow nurses to describe and document their care using common terminology that aligns with and supports the nursing process. "Standardized nursing languages provide common definitions of nursing concepts and allow theory-based and comparable nursing data to emerge" from the record (Wang et al., 2011, p. 1859). Many studies support documentation that aligns with the nursing process to reduce the burden of documentation (ANA, 2010; Ferdousi et al., 2021; DeGroot et al., 2022; Laukvik et al., 2022; Malabusini, 2023; Nool et al., 2022; Rossi et al., 2022).

Most nursing languages have been "mapped" or aligned with computer codes used in medical, billing, and other health services that allow similar concepts to be machine (computer) aggregated (ANA, 2022). Machine aggregation supports the seamless exchange of data between healthcare systems and a broader analysis of the patient's care - integrating data from many providers for a holistic view of the patient's care. Standardized nursing languages support "continuity in the patient care process by harmonizing concepts across disparate organizations" and systems (ANA, 2022, p. 17). A variety of standardized nursing languages exist, including NANDA, NOC and NIC, Omaha, ICNP, and Clinical Care Classification, which are available in the *Nursing Informatics: Scope and Standards of Practice* (ANA, 2022; Coenen, 2003).

Nursing languages translate facts of nursing care into "linguistic descriptions" that "make reality describable" (Malabusini, 2023, p. 1). Documenting with standardized nursing languages is an "effective way to promote the identification of nurses' specific contribution" (Malabusini, 2023, p. 2) – which becomes more important as the financial implications of bringing visibility to nursing care become more evident. The use of natural language processing (NLP) is gaining more attention as electronic methods of capturing data become more sophisticated. Using artificial intelligence and machine analysis, NLP is the ability of computers to "convert text into machine-readable structured data" (ANA, 2022, p. 21). Considerations for "nursing pure terminology" should:

- "...describe nursing activities as faithfully as possible according to the practical context in which they occur;
- Describe nursing activities in a way that conforms to the chosen conceptual model;
- Keep pace with changing approaches to personhood and health issues;
- Focus on meanings generated within nursing care between people involved, improving person-centeredness" (Malabusini, 2023, p. 6)

As data analytics advance, the use of EHRs and standardized languages will be essential in ensuring that student health data is visible in the greater healthcare system.

Documentation Formats

Many formats provide a structure to promote clear, accurate, and intelligible documentation. These include a chronological narrative of the events of student care, an orderly review of body systems, or a problem-oriented approach based on the nursing process (Blair & Smith, 2012). The nursing process provides the most widely accepted structure for nursing documentation, assuring a full description of the student's condition, the nursing interventions addressing the reason for care, and the outcomes related to those interventions (Blair & Smith, 2012). Some common nursing documentation formats include SOAPIER, Focus charting, and Gordon's Functional Health Pattern.

The most recommended format is SOAPIER, which follows the nursing process (DeGroot et al., 2022; Nicholson & Johnson, 2020).

- Subjective data – statements of the student or family;
- Objective data – what the nurse observes or measures;
- Assessment – the nurse's conclusion in the form of a nursing diagnosis based on the data available;
- Plan – of the expected outcomes and actions to achieve those outcomes;
- Implementation of the plan;
- Evaluation of the outcomes of the plan; and
- Revision of the plan based on any differences between the plan and the outcomes.

Focus charting promotes improved accessibility and data flow around specific problems. Documentation using focus charting uses the DAR technique:

- Data – subjective and objective information that includes the assessment, signs and symptoms, and nursing diagnosis;
- Action – describing the nursing interventions that include planning and implementation; and
- Response – describing the student's response to interventions corresponding to the nurse's evaluation of the outcomes of interventions (Blair & Smith, 2012).

Gordon's Functional Health Pattern Framework (GFHP) is another tool to support complete documentation that reflects "nursing clinical judgment and make[s] nursing care visible" (Rossi et al., 2022, p. 72). Use of the GFHP addresses the idea that ICD 10 codes used in medicine do not "consistently capture the patient's human response to illness (a core focus of nursing care) and other phenomena of concern such as health maintenance and recovery from illness," which "makes it difficult to see, measure, and compare the health concerns" that are the focus of nursing care (Rossi et al., 2022, p. 73). There are 11 GFHPs – each with several subcategories as well as a review of physical systems:

- Health Status Perception and Management
- Nutrition
- Elimination
- Exercise/activity
- Sleep/rest
- Sexuality/reproductive

- Cognitive/Perceptual
- Self-concept/self-perception
- Coping/stress tolerance
- Roles/relationships
- Values/beliefs. (Rossi et al., 2022, p. 74)

Other structures include:

VIPS – Values, Individual's needs/care, Perspective, Supportive (social psychology);

WIPS – Well-being, Integrity, Prevention, Safety, which is a Swedish model for documentation;

HOAP – History, Observation, Assessment, Plan; and

PES – Problem, Etiology, Symptoms (DeGroot et al., 2019).

Rubrics also exist for verbal communication to improve patient outcomes. These include HIRAID and SBAR. HIRAID is a pneumonic to describe the History, Identify Red flags, Assessment, Interventions, Diagnostics, Reassessment, and Communications (Munroe et al., 2021). SBAR addresses the Situation – Background-Assessment-Recommendation (Kay et al., 2023). A variation on SBAR is ISBAR – Introduction, Situation, Background, Assessment, Recommendation (Paterson et al., 2023).

Meaningful Use of Documentation

Documentation – particularly that developed in electronic systems - holds great value in reporting health quality at both the individual and population levels.

Effective reporting:

- Tracks progress and trends;
- Is actionable;
- Accountable;
- Asset focused;
- Important;
- Has a plausible theory;
- Is reliable and valid;
- Accessible; and
- Is values-based (Flores, Davis, & Culross, 2007).

The meaningful use of patient information from documentation is an outgrowth of healthcare reform. It is designed to address the poor outcomes of U.S. health care identified by the Institute of Medicine, the National Academies (Institute of Medicine Committee on Quality of Health Care in America [IOM], 2000; Institute of Medicine [IOM], 2010a; 2010b; 2012; National Academies of Sciences, Engineering, and Medicine [NASEM], 2021). Meaningfully using the data contained in nursing documentation to report on and analyze health care and systems enhances the value of the information it contains, allowing it to move beyond a static electronic file cabinet (Johnson & Bergren, 2011) into actionable patient care knowledge (ANA, 2022). When the information is aggregated and analyzed over time for an individual or across populations, it becomes knowledge that drives evidence for practice as described in the Data-Information- Knowledge- Wisdom (DIKW) model *(See Chapter 10 for more information on DIKW)* (ANA, 2022). According to the Office of the National Coordinator for Health Information Technology (ONC), using records meaningfully will:

- Improve quality, safety, and efficiency, and reduce health disparities;
- Engage patients and family;
- Improve care coordination, and population and public health; and
- Maintain privacy and security of patient health information" (ONC, 2019, MIPS section).

Electronic Documentation Systems

Accomplishing meaningful use requires the use of electronic documentation systems as well as the use of standardized terminology to aggregate and report on data effectively. Standardized terminology supports the machine (computer) aggregation of similar data elements. Data elements can then be reported and analyzed to develop evidence for practice using the DIKW Model (ANA, 2022). Electronic documentation systems allow access by multiple appropriate stakeholders – for example, to enhance the implementation of concussion practices (Mylabathula et al., 2022). Electronic documentation systems have been shown to improve the quality of documentation, decrease errors, improve compliance with documentation requirements, and reduce time on documentation (McCarthy et al., 2019). In addition, they support the aggregation of data to support the identification of nurse-sensitive outcomes – essential to increase the visibility and value of school nursing interventions (McCarthy et al., 2019).

Well-designed electronic documentation systems impact the quality of "documentation, patient safety, quality of treatment, communication, treatment management, nursing tasks, and hospital resources" (Ferdousi et al., 2021, p. 64) to:

- Facilitate and improve information access, quality, and the speed of documentation
- Promote patient safety - increasing accuracy, reducing errors,
- Promote quality of treatment, improved decision-making, monitoring, quality, and patient satisfaction
- Improve communication between departments, with enhanced privacy, and security
- Enhances treatment and management - coordinated care, reduced treatment time, improved treatment processes
- Improve efficiency of nursing tasks – reduced workload, reduced time for tasks, facilitated reporting
- Improve hospital resources – improves planning & organizing, reduces the time for repetitive tasks
- Improve quality & design of clinical information systems – software speed, ease of use, ease of learning, flexibility, relevance to nursing, and well-designed interface (Ferdousi et al., 2021, p. 62)

In another study, Donabedian's Structure / Process / Outcomes quality improvement rubric was used to analyze the use of EHRs (Rossi et al., 2022).

- Structure
  - Supports included: efficiency, prompts to enter complete data; practice alerts; and the ability to track patient responses to interventions
  - Challenges included: limited consistency in elements of the record, limited connection to nursing workflow, fragmented displays

- Process
  - Supports included: improvements in standardization, the potential to reduce documentation time; mining data to advance nursing knowledge
  - Challenges included: difficulty documenting the human and lived experience of the patient, inconsistencies in how the record was displayed across sections; practice alerts did not always reflect the complete record
- Outcomes
  - Supports included: better compliance with regulatory requirements
  - Challenges included: limited access to records across providers; an overwhelming number of sometimes redundant choices; failure to capture care transitions; limited inclusion of patient experience (Rossi et al., 2022)

Opportunities to improve the use of EHRs included:

- More integration of information across record sections to reduce redundant documentation
- Less duplication of information (i.e., enter once-use many times)
- The potential of Big Data to demonstrate the value of nursing care in the attainment of patient outcomes
- Need for mentoring in using EHR to strengthen clinical reasoning and capture patient complexity (Rossi et al., 2022)

Recommendations from Research

In summary, many studies of nursing documentation support the following strategies to improve quality and reduce the burden of recording nursing care and patient responses:

- Alignment with the nursing process (DeGroot et al., 2019; 2022)
- Interoperability between organizations and systems that provide patient care to improve care coordination (DeGroot et al., 2022)
- Entering data once with use many times to decrease duplication of data entry (DeGroot et al., 2022)
- Use of standardized nursing languages and mapping to standardized languages in other professional domains (DeGroot et al., 2019; 2022; Eshel et al., 2023)
- Standardized tools support quality, efficiency, and completeness of documentation in common care processes and improved implementation of clinical guidelines (Aktas et al., 2018; Futterman et al., 2023)
- Algorithms to support clinical decision support that can be developed from structures for common data collection aggregated from many records (Eshel et al., 2023; Wysocki & Maughan, 2019)
- Training to support effective documentation
  - Use of Plan-Do-Study-Act was used in multiple studies with success (Behairy et al., 2023; Jaekel et al., 2022; Kay et al., 2023)
  - Training that is "multipronged and delivered in a manner that allows nurses to integrate EHRs into their daily routines and clinical workflows" (Ting et al., 2021, pp. 5–6)
- Efficient and streamlined documentation systems that integrate nursing feedback; support clinical workflow; capture nursing decision-making; and decision-making that individualizes the patient/ provider partnership (Paterson et al., 2023)

- While few tools exist to evaluate the quality of documentation – particularly digital records- some have been used with success. These include:
  - Physician Documentation Quality Instrument (PDQI-9) (Eshel et al., 2023)
  - Quality of Nursing Diagnosis, Interventions, Outcomes (Q-DIO) (McCarthy et al., 2019)
  - D-Catch (DeGroot et al., 2019)

IMPLICATIONS FOR SCHOOL NURSE PRACTICE

Appropriate documentation protects the student, the nurse, and the school district. The importance of complete and accurate documentation is reinforced in the frequency with which it is identified in the *School Nursing: Scope and Standards of Practice* – the professional and legal standard for all school nurses (NASN, 2022b) as well as the broader *Nursing: Scope and Standards of Practice* (ANA, 2021). Additionally, the Nursing Code of Ethics implies the importance of documentation in its references to accountability, communication, and contributions to research and practice standards (Fowler, 2015).

Failure to document according to standards can put the student at risk for poor outcomes from inadequate communication and care coordination and put the nurse and the school district at risk for litigation. State nurse practice acts and medical records acts, the *School Nursing: Scope and Standards of Practice* (NASN, 2022b), ANA guidance (ANA, 2010), and billing requirements drive standards for documentation. Nurses should ensure that their documentation provides evidence of the critical thinking that directed their care and demonstrates that the nurse has discharged their duty of care. School nurses should be familiar with their scope and standards of practice, the nurse practice act, and medical records acts in the state in which they practice. For example, the Washington Nurse Practice Act states that documentation "shall communicate significant changes in the client's status to appropriate members of the healthcare team... in a timely manner... the nursing care given and the client's response to that care" (WAC, 1997/2022) (Washington Administrative Code, 246-840-700 §§ (3) (b) 2004). In the event of a question about the outcomes of care, documentation that reflects those standards will provide supporting evidence of quality care.

Standardized Language

Using standardized languages and formats that are universally accepted and reflect standards of care allows the integration of school health information into the student's broader health record, reflects the professional care provided in schools, and allows for effective aggregation and reporting across systems. School nurses have a unique role as providers of not only individual care but care of populations (Bergren, 2017). This complex population-level data available in student health documentation makes using EHRs and standardized nursing terminologies "essential to representing nursing in the documentation of patient care and the continued evolution of the nursing body of knowledge" (ANA, 2022, p. 15). Standardized languages that use the nursing process provide nurses with a "cognitive map" to support critical thinking and effective care (von Krough et al., 2005, p. 276). For example, when a student presents to the health room, the nurse assesses the student's symptoms and identifies a nursing diagnosis. That diagnosis leads to a set of desired outcomes for the student, which appear in the EHR in a dropdown menu. The selection of the outcomes by the nurse further prompts the selection of appropriate interventions to achieve desired outcomes that appear in a dropdown menu.

Further, when a specific medical diagnosis such as asthma is entered, additional decision support is triggered in the EHR, prompting reminders to enter rescue inhalers, peak flow measures, and symptom triggers for the student. As population-level research related to student health matures, clinical decision support using standardized languages can be built into the electronic health record. Using standardized languages allows student health data in nursing records to be used meaningfully across multiple systems and to support policy, evidence for practice, research, and resource allocation.

School Nurses in Washington State have developed standardized codes to be used in their EHRs that address chronic conditions; medication administration; and health room reasons for the visit, interventions (by RNs and UAPs), and dispositions (Washington School Nurse Data Workgroup [WSNDW], 2023). The codes have been integrated into the EHRs at the state level and are used by most districts in Washington. The Workgroup was started in 2005 as part of a Department of Health program to monitor flu outbreaks using absenteeism in schools. The group meets periodically to review and revise codes to fit practice needs. Their goal is "promoting consistency in school nursing data by using standardized coding to give common language to use in nurse documentation" (WSNDW, 2023, para. 1).

Documentation Formats

Several formats, as previously noted, can guide the school nurse in quality documentation, including SOAPIER, focus charting, DAR, and others.

An editorial in the Annals of Internal Medicine (Sequist, 2015, p. 315) promotes the value of "longitudinal management of conditions across settings and providers," suggesting the importance of the accessibility of all child health records into one record of care. This concept aligns with the longitudinal nature of school health records. Promoting access by the student's medical provider to the records kept at school ensures that the full picture of the student's health is available for care planning. SOAPIER and problem-oriented (focused) documentation methods have been used across healthcare disciplines and thus are formats that can be readily utilized across the care continuum, including acute and ambulatory care (Nicholson & Johnson, 2020).

Issues such as parental refusal to consent to information sharing must be respected under the Family Educational Rights and Privacy Act (FERPA) (USDE, 2021). Using principles of cultural humility to build trust with the family, along with guidance on how information sharing promotes their child's continuity of care, may help the parent move toward greater information sharing (Foronda et al., 2016). While FERPA is silent on information sharing related to medication or treatment administration, the Health Insurance Portability and Privacy Act (HIPAA) allows for provider-to-provider information sharing (USDE, 2021). Under this provision, a school nurse may request clarification on medical orders but cannot share educational information without parental consent. (*See Chapter 12 for more information on FERPA and HIPAA.*)

Focus charting may be an effective documentation rubric for school nurses in that it reflects the reasons for interventions, which in the school setting are often focused on a specific student health problem (Nicholson & Johnson, 2020). Blair's team (2012) modified the DAR focus to AIE – Assessment, Intervention, and Evaluation, in which the documentation focuses on a specific, identified problem. The authors found that this method allowed rapid aggregation of specific problems within an individual record or across many patients in a practice.

They found that AIE focus charting was easily understood and quickly adopted by the majority of nursing staff. This method proved its value in the timeliness of a response to an infectious disease outbreak allowing infections to be quickly and easily identified across the patient population. In addition, documentation of the course of the infection was more readily tracked within an individual patient record. Given the longitudinal and population-based aspects of school nursing, focus charting may allow rapid analysis of both the individual student and the school or district health issues and risks.

Data Ethics

Nurses and their administrators who use data based on their documentation have a duty to use that data ethically (ANA], 2014; 2015; 2021; NASN, 2022b) - educational data ethics also require this (National Center for Education Statistics [NCES], 2010). This duty is reinforced in federal privacy laws described in the Family Education Rights and Privacy Act (FERPA) and the Health Insurance Portability and Accountability Act (HIPAA) (U.S Department of Education [USDE], 2021; U.S. Health and Human Services [USHHS], 2022). This includes attention to privacy, confidentiality, and security of the data collected. (*See Chapter 10 for more information on privacy, confidentiality, and security*.) School nurses should review the *Forum Guide to Data Ethics* to ensure ethical use (NCES, 2010). The Privacy and Technical Assistance Center (PTAC) of the USDE (n.d.) has additional resources to support the privacy and security of data. Care should be taken to ensure that reported totals are large enough that individual students cannot be identified in the data. This ensures that student privacy is maintained and records are held confidentially. The *Forum* guides educators in using data in a manner that supports student well-being, is valid (accurately represents the true events), reliable (is consistent), accurate, timely, and cost-effective (NCES, 2010). FERPA requires the consent of the parent/guardian to release personally identifiable information on students except in certain situations. Aggregated, de-identified data does not require consent to release (Code of Federal Regulations PART 99 - Family Educational Rights and Privacy, 1988/2000, (b)(1) section; Network for Public Health Law [NPHL], 2020).

Quality of Documentation

The quality of documentation is important not only to demonstrate the quality of school nursing care but to ensure effective and accurate communication of the student's concerns, nursing interventions, and the outcomes of care. Audit tools could be used to measure the quality of nursing documentation and, when used in a timely manner, can also support feedback to the nurse to improve the quality of their care. Glasper (2011) recommends using the CIA Standard to ensure that records are Clear, Intelligible, and Accurate. Griffith (2015; 2016) recommends that nurses perform a 5-minute personal audit of their records addressing:

- Completeness – duty of care discharged, all care documented, including consent, immunizations, and explanation of risk;
- Accuracy – details of the factual basis of any opinion; and
- Clarity – understandable by non-health readers, avoidance of abbreviations and jargon, detailed enough to clearly represent the status of the student and the care given.

Accuracy of Documentation

FERPA allows parents "the right to request that inaccurate or misleading information in his or her child's education records be amended," however "this right cannot be used to challenge a grade, an individual's opinion, or a substantive decision made by a school about a student" (USDE, 2020, p. 1). Nursing documentation is a legal record that cannot be altered without the risk of appearing to conceal misconduct (Cornell University Law School, 2002). The USDE (2020) further advises that if there is a dispute about the accuracy of the nurse's documentation, the parent may submit an amendment to the note that includes the parent's comments, the parent's name, relationship, the section of notes disputed, and the date submitted. *(See Chapter 12 for more information on FERPA/HIPAA.)*

Meaningful Use of Data

The variety of conditions, large caseloads, and longitudinal data collected over the years of a student's school attendance produce volumes of data that are too broad and complex for the human mind to process effectively (Amatayakul, 2009). However, using standardized languages that are collected and stored electronically and software that allows the data to be reported from multiple perspectives allows it to be analyzed for a deeper meaning to promote child health and standards of care. Nurses can then process the data into manageable chunks to provide the individual student's care and further aggregate it into population-level data at the school, district, state, or national level. Using data collected in the day-to-day documentation of school nurses in this way provides a unique population-level view of the health of school-age children (Bergren, 2017; Johnson & Bergren, 2011).

Aggregating these large amounts of data and reporting them in meaningful ways reflects the standards of school nursing practice by providing information for research; evidence-based practice; collaboration; advocacy; and communication across silos of care (NASN, 2022b). FERPA permits the use of aggregated data if an individual cannot be identified in the data (Code of Federal Regulations PART 99 - Family Educational Rights and Privacy, 1988/2000; NPHL, 2020).   Aggregating the data in their documentation allows the nurse to use it meaningfully. It moves beyond a mere static record of care to become information, knowledge, and wisdom (ANA, 2022; Johnson & Bergren, 2011). It allows the information entered into the record once to be used many times to support care and build evidence for practice. For example, immunization dates entered and analyzed at the individual student level are used to determine that student's immunization compliance. In a meaningful-use environment, immunization dates are then aggregated with school-level data to determine if there is a school risk from vaccine-preventable illnesses. They can be further aggregated to monitor the history of immunization compliance over several years to understand district immunization patterns. The dates that represent data on an individual's immunization status hold additional power when combined and analyzed in this way. The same concept can be applied to data on chronic conditions, playground injuries, and other population health issues routinely managed by school nurses.

Collecting data meaningfully allows a student's school health data to be integrated into the broader universe of their electronic health record in acute and ambulatory care settings, thus maximizing the coordination of care and minimizing silos of information. Electronic transfer of data using standardized languages in an EHR minimizes human error through transcription errors and is particularly useful for the precision of medication orders and immunization dates.   It contributes to the efficient and safe care of students across systems and ensures that students outside the traditional healthcare systems have their needs equitably represented. It promotes the visibility of school nursing interventions and holds implications for resource allocation.

Over 95% of children ages 6 – 17 years attend public schools in the United States (ChildStats: Forum on Child and Family Statistics, 2021; NCES, 2023). School nurses' documentation represents students with chronic health conditions and screening and episodic care of well students. The data collected by school nurses daily in the course of their normal documentation represents true population data. It provides a window into the prevalence of childhood chronic conditions and children's health status (Stanislo, 2023). Every school nurse can identify their students with Type I Diabetes and describe the parameters of their care. Every school nurse can identify students with life-threatening allergies and describe every dose of epinephrine they have administered to save lives. Despite this, the true prevalence of these conditions among school-aged children and many other low-frequency but potentially life-threatening conditions can only be estimated in many child health databases. The documentation of school nurses provides the only evidence of the prevalence of these conditions for children and youth attending school – making these records invaluable to promote child health.

To that end, the NASN has developed a nationally standardized school health dataset called *National School Health Dataset: Every Student Counts!* that uses aggregated, de-identified data collected from the daily documentation of school nurses across the United States. The data is used to describe student health needs, the resources to address those needs, and the nursing-sensitive student outcomes of nursing interventions (Stanislo, 2023). Resources to support data collection and reporting are included on the NASN website (NASN, 2023).

Impact of Effective Documentation

Effective reporting of school health data is student-focused, organized for easy understanding, and considers the audience's perspective when reported. Considerations for effectively framing reports using nursing data may include:
- A description of the health needs of students vs. the size of a school nurse's caseload and resources available for care.
- Data reports can be organized along the NASN's Framework for 21st Century School Nursing Practice (NASN, 2022a) or a chronological account of a student's care to another provider or the student's parent/ guardian.
- When used within the confines of proper consent and confidentiality standards as outlined in The *Forum's Data Ethics* guidance, aggregated data can provide information to advocate for student health for various stakeholders (NCES, 2010). For instance,
  - The school board may be interested in how documentation supports compliance with federal and state statutes or district policy.
  - Medical providers will be interested in an individual student's progress.
  - The principal of a school may be interested in the academic impacts of a nurse's health program – how instruction in respiratory hygiene or handwashing has reduced absenteeism.
  - Risk management, legal and budget departments will be interested in documentation to support their missions.
  - Federal and community stakeholders may be interested in the documentation that describes equity, resource distribution, and academic impact of school nursing work and its impact on population levels.

The extraordinary value of the information in school nursing records is realized when quality records are maintained in systems that allow that information to be aggregated, analyzed, and reported while preserving student privacy.

CONCLUSION

Documentation in school nursing practice is essential to ensure continuity of care over the student's school career and to support the nurse in demonstrating that appropriate care was delivered. It is the foundation for data that supports research, child health policy, and evidence for practice. Quality documentation describes the school nurse's critical thinking as the nursing process is applied to the care of students.

Documentation of the nursing process is important for legal, research, and care coordination purposes. A variety of formats support effective documentation, including SOAPIER and problem-oriented methods. Data from documentation in electronic records using standardized variables supports the meaningful use of records and holds the potential to create evidence for practice, inform policy and improve care coordination across settings and over time. School nurses particularly benefit from electronic systems and standardized variables to improve school nursing interventions' visibility and promote school-age children's health.

RESOURCES

- ANA Principles for Nursing Documentation http://www.nursingworld.org/~4af4f2/globalassets/docs/ana/ethics/principles-of-nursing-documentation.pdf
- The Forum Guide to Data Ethics http://nces.ed.gov/pubs2010/2010801.pdf
- National School Health Dataset: Every Student Counts! https://www.nasn.org/research/everystudentcounts
- Framework for 21st Century School Nursing http://www.nasn.org/Framework
- NASN Documentation Resources https://www.nasn.org/nasn-resources/resources-by-topic/school-health-documentation
- NSO Dos & Don'ts of Documentation https://www.nso.com/Learning/Artifacts/Articles/Do-s-and-Don-ts-of-Documentation
- The Five Legal Requirements for Nursing Documentation https://experience.care/blog/5-legal-requirements-for-nursing-documentation/
- Washington State Standardized Health Codes https://www.esd123.org/services/school_health/washington_school_nurse_data_workgroup

REFERENCES

Aktas, O. N., Kao, L. M., Hoyt, A., Siracusa, M., Maloney, R., & Gupta, R. S. (2018). Development and implementation of an allergic reaction reporting tool for school health personnel: A pilot study of three Chicago schools. *Journal of School Nursing*, *35*(5), 316–324. https://doi.org/10.1177/1059840518777303

Amatayakul, M. K. (2009). *Electronic healthcare records: A practical guide for professionals and organizations* (4th ed., vol. 20). American Health Information Management Association.

American Nurses Association. (2010). *Principles for nursing documentation: Guidance for Registered Nurses*. nursingworld.org. https://www.nursingworld.org/~4af4f2/globalassets/docs/ana/ethics/principles-of-nursing-documentation.pdf

American Nurses Association. (2014). *Professional role competence* [Position Statement]. nursingworld.org. https://www.nursingworld.org/globalassets/practiceandpolicy/nursing-excellence/ana-position-statements-secure/nursing-practice/professional-role-competence.pdf

American Nurses Association. (2015). *Code of Ethics for Nurses*. Author.

American Nurses Association. (2021). *Nursing: Scope & standards of practice* (4th ed.).

American Nurses Association. (2022). *Nursing informatics: Scope and standards of practice* (3rd ed.).

Behairy, M., Alenchery, A., Cuesta-Ferrino, C., Bhakta, H., & Mayas-Santiago, A. (2023). Increasing language interpreter services use and documentation: A quality improvement project. *Journal for Healthcare Quality, 45*(1), 19–26. https://doi.org/10.1097/JHQ.0000000000000366

Bergren, M. D. (2017). School nursing and population health: Past, present, and future. *Online Journal of Issues in Nursing, 22*(3). https://doi.org/10.3912/OJIN.Vol22No03Man03

Blair, W., & Smith, B. (2012). Nursing documentation: Frameworks and barriers. *Contemporary Nurse, 41*(2), 160–168. https://doi.org/110.5172/conu.2012.41.2.160

Bogeskov, B. O., & Grimshaw-Aagaard, S. L. S. (2019). Essential task or meaningless burden? Nurses' perceptions of the value of documentation. *Nordic Journal of Nursing Research, 39*(1), 9–19. https://doi.org/10.1177/2057158518773906

Bruylands, M., Paans, W., Hediger, H., & Muller-Staub, M. (2013). Effects on the quality of the nursing care process through an educational program and use of electronic nursing documentation. *International Journal of Nursing Knowledge, 24*(3), 163–170. https://doi.org/10.1111/j.2047-3095.2013.01248.x

Charalambous, L., & Goldberg, S. (2016). 'Gaps, mishaps, and overlaps .'Nursing documentation: How does it affect care? *Journal of Research in Nursing, 21*(8), 638–648. https://doi.org/10.1177/1744987116678900

ChildStats: Forum on Child and Family Statistics. (2021). *POP1 child population: Number of children (in millions) ages 0–17 in the United States by age, 1950–2021 and projected 2022–2050*. childstats.gov. https://www.childstats.gov/americaschildren/tables/pop1.asp

Clark, J., & Lang, N. (1992). Nursing's next advance: An internal classification for nursing practice. *International Nursing Review, 39*(4), 109–111.

Code of Federal Regulations PART 99 - Family Educational Rights and Privacy, 34 Part 99.31 U.S.C. § (b)1 (1988 & rev. 2000). https://www.ecfr.gov/current/title-34/subtitle-A/part-99

Coenen, A. (2003). The International Classification for Nursing Practice (ICNP) Program: Advancing a unifying framework for nursing. *Online Journal of Issues in Nursing, 8*(2), 1–13. https://doi.org/10.3912/OJIN.Vol8No02PPT01

Cornell University Law School. (2002). *18 U.S. Code § 1519 - Destruction, alteration, or falsification of records in Federal investigations and bankruptcy*. https://www.law.cornell.edu/uscode/text/18/1519

DeGroot, K., DeVeer, A. J., Munster, A. M., Francke, A. L., & Paans, W. (2022). Nursing documentation and its relationship with perceived nursing workload: A mixed-methods study among community nurses. *BMC Nursing, 21*(34), 1–12. https://doi.org/10.1186/s12912-022-00811-7

DeGroot, K., Triemstra, M., Plans, W., & Francke, A. L. (2019). Quality criteria, instruments, and requirements for nursing documentation: A systematic review of systematic reviews. *Journal of Advanced Nursing, 75*, 1379–1393. https://doi.org/10.1111/jan.13919

Eshel, R., Bellolio, F., Boggust, A., Shapiro, N. I., Mullan, A. F., Heaton, H. A., Madsen, B. E., Homme, J. L., Iliff, B. W., Sunga, K. L., Wangsgard, C. R., Vanmeter, D., & Cabrera, D. (2023). Comparison of clinical note quality between an automated digital intake tool and the standard note in the emergency department. *American Journal of Emergency Medicine, 63*, 79–85. https://doi.org/10.1016/j.ajem.2022.10.009

Ferdousi, R., Arab-Zozani, M., Tahamtan, I., Rezaei-Hachesu, P., & Dehghani, M. (2021). Attitudes of nurses towards clinical information systems systematic review and meta-analysis. *International Nursing Review, 68*, 59–66. https://doi.org/10.1111/inr.12603

Folio 3. (n.d.). *What are the 5 legal requirements for nursing documentation?* digital health.folio3.com. Retrieved June 6, 2023, from https://digitalhealth.folio3.com/blog/5-legal-requirements-for-nursing-documentation/

Foronda, C., Baptiste, D., Reinholdt, M. M., & Ousman, K. (2016). Cultural humility: A concept analysis. *Journal of Transcultural Nursing, 27*(3), 210-217. http://dx.doi.org/10.1177/1043659615592677

Flores, L. M., Davis, R., & Culross, P. (2007). Community health: A critical approach to addressing chronic diseases. *Preventing Chronic Disease, 4*(4), 1–6. http://www.cdc.gov/pcd/issues/2007/oct/07_0080.htm

Fowler, M. D. (2015). *Guide to the code of ethics for nurses: Interpretation and application.* Nursebooks.org.

Futterman, I., Friedmann, H., & Haberman, S. (2023). NLP - a tool to address documentation gaps and improve revenue. *American Journal of Obstetrics and Gynecology,* S656. https://doi.org/10.1016/j.ajog.2022.11.1104

Glasper, A. (2011). Improving record keeping: Important lessons for nurses. *British Journal of Nursing, 20*(14), 886. https://doi.org/10.12968/bjon.2011.20.14.886

Griffith, R. (2007). The importance of earnest record keeping. *Nurse Prescribing, 5*(8), 364. https://doi.org/10.12968/npre.2007.5.8.363

Griffith, R. (2015). Understanding the Code: Keeping accurate records. *British Journal of Community Nursing, 20*(10), 511–514. https://doi.org/10.12968/bjcn.2015.20.10.511

Griffith, R. (2016). For the record: Keeping detailed notes. *British Journal of Nursing, 25*, 408–409. https://doi.org/10.12968/bjon.2016.25.7.408

Institute of Medicine. (2010a). *For the public's health: The role of measurement in action and accountability* (Institute of Medicine). National Academies Press. http://www.nationalacademies.org/hmd/Reports/2012/For-the-Publics-Health-Investing-in-a-Healthier-Future.aspx

Institute of Medicine. (2010b). *The future of nursing: Leading change, advancing health.* National Academies Press. http://books.nap.edu/openbook.php?record_id=12956&page=R9

Institute of Medicine. (2012). *Health IT and patient safety: Building safer systems for better care* (National Academy of Sciences). National Academies Press. http://www.nap.edu/catalog/13269/health-it-and-patient-safety-building-safer-systems-for-better

Institute of Medicine Committee on Quality of Health Care in America. (2000). *To err is human: Building a safer health system.* National Academies Press. https://doi.org/10.17226/9728

Jaekel, C., Becker, D. P., & Voss, Y. (2022). Use of PDSA Cycles to increase aspiration risk and swallow screening documentation in the hospitalized general medical patient care population. *Journal of Nursing Care Quality, 38*(1), 89–96. https://doi.org/10.1097/NCQ.0000000000000664

Jefferies, D., Johnson, M., & Griffiths, R. (2010). A meta-study of the essentials of quality nursing documentation. *International Journal of Nursing Practice, 16*, 112–124. https://doi.org/10.1111/k.1440-172X.2009.01815.x

Johnson, K. H., & Bergren, M. D. (2011). Meaningful use of school health data. *The Journal of School Nursing, 27*, 102–110. https://doi.org/10.1177/1059840510391095

Johnson, K. H., & Guthrie, S. (2012). Harnessing the power of student health data: Selecting, using, and implementing electronic school health documentation systems. *NASN School Nurse, 27*(1), 27–33. https://doi.org/10.1177/1942602X11429828

Johnson, M., Jefferies, D., & Langdon, R. (2010). The Nursing and Midwifery Content Audit Tool (NMCAT: A short nursing documentation audit tool. *Journal of Nursing Management, 18*, 832–845. https://doi.org/10.1111/j.1365-2834.2010.01156x

Jorgensen, L., & Kollerup, M. G. (2022). Ethical dilemmas in nursing documentation. *Nursing Ethics, 29*(2), 485–497. https://doi.org/10.1177/09697330211046654

Kay, S., Unroe, K. T., Lieb, K. M., Kaehr, E. W., Black urn, J., Stump, T. E., Evans, R., Klepfer, S., & Carnahan, J. L. (2023). Improving communication in nursing homes using Plan-Do-Study-Act cycles of an SBAR training program. *Journal of Applied Gerontology, 42*(2), 194–204. https://doi.org/10.1177/07334648221131469

Koch, G. (2014). Going back to basics: Documentation. *Oregon Board of Nursing Sentinel*, 14–15. http://epubs.democratprinting.com/publication/?i=214579

Laukvik, L. B., Rotegard, A. K., Lyngstad, M., Slettebo, A., & Fossum, M. (2022). Registered nurses' reasoning process during care planning and documentation in the electronic health records: A concurrent think-aloud study. *Journal of Clinical Nursing, 32*, 221–233. https://doi.org/10.1111/jocn.16210

Malabusini, C. (2023). 'Sono solo parole': Facing challenges entailed in developing and applying terminologies to document nursing care. *Nursing Philosophy, 24*. https://doi.org/10.1111/nup.12383

McCarthy, B., Fitzgerald, S., O'Shea, M., Condon, C., Harnett-Collins, G., Clancy, M., Sheehy, A., Denieffe, S., Bergin, M., & Savage, E. (2019). Electronic nursing documentation interventions to promote or improve patient safety and quality care: A systematic review. *Journal of Nursing Management, 27*, 491–501. https://doi.org/10.1111/jonm.12727

Munroe, B., Curtis, K., Fry, M., Shaban, R. Z., Moules, P., BMath, T.-K. E., Ruperto, K., Couttie, T., & Considine, J. (2021). Increasing accuracy in documentation through the application of structured emergency nursing framework: A multisite quasi-experimental study. *Journal of Clinical Nursing, 31*, 2874–2885. https://doi.org/10.1111/jocn.16115

Mylabathula, S., C. M., Mylabathula, S., Colantinio, A., Guttmann, A., & Tator, C. H. (2022). Concussion public policy in elementary and high schools in Ontario, Canada: A cross-sectional survey to examine implementation compliance, barriers, and facilitators. *Journal of School Health, 93*, 14–24. https://doi.org/10.1111/josh.13245

National Academies of Sciences, Engineering, and Medicine. (2021). *The Future of Nursing 2020-2030: Charting a Path to Achieve Health Equity.* The National Academies Press. https://doi.org/10.17226/25982

National Association of School Nurses. (2022a). *Framework for 21st century school nursing practice.* https://www.nasn.org/portals/0/resources/21stCenturySchoolNurseFramework2015onepager.pdf

National Association of School Nurses. (2022b). *School nursing: Scope and standards of practice* (4th ed.). Author.

National Association of School Nurses. (2023). *National School Health Dataset: Every Student Counts!* nasn.org. https://www.nasn.org/research/everystudentcounts/uniform-data-points

National Center for Education Statistics. (2010). *The forum guide to data ethics.* nces.ed.gov. https://nces.ed.gov/pubs2010/2010801.pdf

National Center for Education Statistics. (2023). *Racial/ethnic enrollment in public schools.* https://nces.ed.gov/programs/coe/indicator/cge/racial-ethnic-enrollment#:~:text=During%20the%20coronavirus%20pandemic%2C%20enrollment,fall%202020%20and%20fall%202021.&text=Total%20enrollment%20is%20projected%20to,year%20of%20projected%20data%20available).

Network for Public Health Law. (2020). *Data sharing guidance for school nurses.* networkerphl.org. https://www.networkforphl.org/wp-content/uploads/2020/01/Data-Sharing-Guidance-for-School-Nurses-with-Appendices-1-23-2020.pdf

Newfield, J. S. (2006). Documentation: Focusing on better rather than more. *Home Health Care Management and Practice*, *18*(3), 247–249. https://doi.org/10.1177/1084822305284301

Nicholson, C., & Johnson, K. H. (2020). Unlocking the power of school nursing documentation. *NASN School Nurse*, *35*(4), 203–207. https://doi.org/10.1177/1942602X20928053

Nool, I., Parm, L., & Ojasoo, M. (2022). The quality of nursing documentation and standardized nursing diagnoses in the children's hospital electronic nursing records. *International Journal of Nursing Knowledge*, *34*, 4–12. https://doi.org/10.1111/2047-3095.12363

NSO. (n.d.-a). *Documentation on trial: 9 ways to protect your agency.* NSO.org. Retrieved June 6, 2023, from https://www.nso.com/Learning/Artifacts/Articles/Documentation-on-trial-9-ways-to-protect-your-age

NSO. (n.d.-b). *Defensive documentation: Steps nurses can take to improve their charting and reduce their liability.* NSO. org. Retrieved June 6, 2023, from https://www.nso.com/Learning/Artifacts/Articles/Defensive-Documentation-Steps-Nurses-Can-Take-to-Improve-Their-Charting-and-Reduce-Their-Liability

NSO. (n.d.-c). *Abbreviations in documentation: A shortcut to disaster for nurses.* NSO.org. Retrieved June 6, 2023, from https://www.nso.com/Learning/Artifacts/Articles/Abbreviations-in-Documentation-A-shortcut-to-disaster-for-Nurses

Office of the National Coordinator of Health Information Technology. (2019). *Meaningful use.* healthit.gov. https://www.healthit.gov/topic/meaningful-use-and-macra/meaningful-use

Okaisu, E. M., Kalikwani, F., Wanyana, G., & Coetree, M. (2014). Improving the quality of nursing documentation: An action research project. *Curationis*, *38*(1). https://doi.org/10.4102/cyratuibus,v37i1.1251

Paterson, C., Roberts, C., & Bail, K. (2023). 'Paper care not patient care': Nurse and patient experiences of comprehensive risk assessment and care plan documentation in hospital. *Journal of Clinical Nursing*, *32*, 523–538. https://doi.org/10.1111/jocn.16291

Prideaux, A. (2011). Issues in nursing documentation and record-keeping practice. *British Journal of Nursing*, *20*(22), 1450–1454. https://doi.org/10.12968/bjon.2011.20.22.1450

Rossi, L., Butler, S., Coakley, A., & Flanagan, J. (2022). Nursing knowledge captured in electronic health records. *International Journal of Nursing Knowledge*, *34*, 72–84. https://doi.org/10.1111/2047-3095.12365

Sequist, T. D. (2015). Clinical documentation to improve patient care. *Annals of Internal Medicine*, *162*(4), 315–316. https://doi.org/10.7326/M14-2913

Stanislo, K. J. (2023). Revisiting the National School Heath Data Set: Every Student Counts! *NASN School Nurse*, *38*(1), 26–30. https://doi.org/10.1177/1942602X221137519

Ting, J., Garnett, A., & Donelle, L. (2021). Nursing education and training on electronic health record systems: An integrative review. *Nurse Education in Practice*, *55*, 1–7. https://doi.org/10.1016/j.nepr.2021.103168

U.S. Department of Education. (n.d.). *Request PTAC training or technical assistance.* studentprivacy.ed.gov. Retrieved June 25, 2023, from https://studentprivacy.ed.gov/request-ptac-training-or-technical-assistance

U.S. Department of Education. (2020). *The Family Educational Rights and Privacy Act: Guidance for parents.* student privacy.ed.gov. https://studentprivacy.ed.gov/sites/default/files/resource_document/file/FERPAGuidanceForParents.pdf

U.S. Department of Education. (2021). *Family Education Rights & Privacy Act - FERPA*. https://www2.ed.gov/policy/gen/guid/fpco/ferpa/index.html

U.S. Health and Human Services. (2022). *The HIPAA privacy rule*. hhs.gov. https://www.hhs.gov/hipaa/for-professionals/privacy/index.html

Urquhart, C., Currell, R., Grant, M. J., & Hardiker, N. R. (2009). Nursing record systems: effects on nursing practice and healthcare outcomes. *Cochrane Databased of Systematic Reviews*, (1). https://doi.org/10.1002/14651858.CD002099.pub2

Valderaune, V., Bjerkan, J., & Olsen, R. M. (2016). Patient safety through documentation: Barriers identified by healthcare professionals and students. *Injury Prevention*, *22*(Suppl2), A77. https://doi.org/10.1136/injuryprev-2016-042156.211

von Krough, G., Dale, C., & Nadin, D. (2005). A Framework for Integrating NANDA, NIC, and NOC in electronic patient records. *Journal of Nursing Scholarship*, *37*(3), 275–281. https://doi.org/10.1111/j.1547-5069.2005.00047.x

Wang, N., Hailey, D., & Yu, P. (2011, January 22). Quality of nursing documentation and approaches to its evaluation: A mixed-method systematic review. *Journal of Advanced Nursing*, 1858–1875. https://doi.org/10.1111/j.1365-2648.2011.05634.x

Washington Administrative Code, Standards of nursing conduct or practice 246-840-700(3)(b) (1997 & rev. 2022). https://app.leg.wa.gov/wac/default.aspx?cite=246-840-700&pdf=true

Washington School Nurse Data Workgroup. (2023). *Washington School Nurse Data Workgroup*. esd123.org. https://www.esd123.org/services/school_health/washington_school_nurse_data_workgroup

Wortham, J., & Maag, C. (2019). *Good documentation is a nurse's best defense* [Conference summary]. voice.ons. org. https://voice.ons.org/conferences/good-documentation-is-a-nurses-best-defense

Wysocki, R., & Maughan, E. D. (2019). Using data to tell your health story. *NASN School Nurse*, *34*(5), 274–277. https://doi.org/10.1177/1942602X19865327

Chapter 10

SCHOOL HEALTH RECORDS

Katie Johnson, DNP, RN, NCSN-E, APHN-BC, FNASN, FAAN

DESCRIPTION OF ISSUE

School health records are comprised of the documentation developed and collected by school nurses, or other educational personnel in the absence of the school nurse, in the course of their work with students. They include health-related documents and files that address a variety of purposes, are contained in various formats, and are subject to multiple federal, state, and local regulations. The complexity of school health records is reflected in the wide variation of management requirements. This chapter will address the types of records, the formats they are contained in, and the requirements for privacy, storage, access, and reporting. Proper documentation of health information is addressed in Chapter 9.

Records are increasingly managed electronically, allowing information to be entered once and used many times, allowing access to persons in the school who have a legitimate educational interest (i.e., need to know) about the student's health issues, and facilitating reporting and analysis from multiple perspectives to improve population and student health. School health records in paper and electronic formats provide legal protection for the nurse and the district in documenting the specific care given to students.

School nurses are bound ethically and legally to protect student records related to privacy, security, and loss. At the same time, they must advocate for student health needs by effectively using records to communicate with student care teams and other stakeholders. Federal and state statutes and rules protect student and family rights to confidentiality, access, and correction of student records. Statutes also drive the kinds of information that need to be kept in student records – for example, to demonstrate compliance with the Individuals with Disabilities in Education Act [IDEA – special education] (U.S. Department of Education [USDE], 2017a), the Americans with Disabilities Act Amendment Act (ADAAA – Section 504) (USDE, Office for Civil Rights, 2016), and state nurse practice acts. School districts may also have requirements for records as directed in policies and procedures.

As the health expert in an educational environment, school nurses must navigate the complexity of school health records, know records requirements, and how to demonstrate compliance.

BACKGROUND

Improving Healthcare Quality

Over the last several decades, efforts have focused on interventions to improve healthcare quality. These include the implementation of electronic health records (EHRs), the Quintuple Aim, the growth of nursing informatics, using health data meaningfully, the emergence of Big Data, interoperability of documentation systems, and efforts to standardize the variables and definitions of the terms to describe the delivery of nursing care (i.e., standardized nursing languages).

Electronic Health Records

In 2000 and 2001, the Institute of Medicine (IOM - now the National Academy of Medicine) released two groundbreaking reports on the state of healthcare in the United States. In *To Err is Human: Building a Safer Health System*, the Committee on Quality of Health Care in America reported that about 98,000 people died from medical errors in hospitals – greater numbers than the more publicized deaths at that time (Institute of Medicine Committee on Quality of Health Care in America [IOM], 2000). In addition, the IOM released *Crossing the Quality Chasm: A New Health System for the 21st Century,* which called for fundamental changes to address the healthcare quality gap (IOM, 2001). In 2004, the Office of the National Coordinator for Health Information Technology (ONC) was established to address healthcare quality, costs, and complexity. Efforts to improve the U.S. healthcare system included technology and electronic health records (EHRs) (Blumenthal, 2009). The goal was for the broad use of information technology to "... improve the quality of health care, prevent medical errors, reduce health care costs, increase administrative efficiencies, decrease paperwork, and expand access to affordable health care" (U.S. Health and Human Services [USHHS], 2022a, p. 1). An infrastructure for health information technology that allows communication across systems of care providers (interoperability) was considered fundamental to the coordination of care.

Benefits of Electronic Documentation Systems

1. EHRs allow instant, secure access by authorized users to: the variety of health care records on an Individual patient,
2. evidence-based tools for clinical decision-making and
3. the platform to automate and streamline the coordination of care (ONC, 2023a).

EHRs promote improved:
- Patient Care
- Patient Participation
- Care Coordination
- Diagnostics & Patient Outcomes
- Efficiencies and Cost Savings (ONC, 2023a).

For patients, the benefits include:
- Reduction in duplicative "paperwork"
- Access to up-to-date-data by the healthcare team
- Coordination of care among multiple providers
- Reduction in unnecessary tests and procedures
- Direct access to their own healthcare record (ONC, 2023a, Benefits of health IT section)

The American Nurses Association (ANA) and the National Association of School Nurses (NASN) support the use of electronic records to decrease barriers, increase access, improve outcomes, and increase patient engagement (ANA, 2022; NASN, 2019). A variety of federal statutes and regulations drive the quality of EHRs in the hospital and clinic setting that include requirements for certification (ONC, 2020).

Quintuple Aim

Soon after these IOM reports, and the development of regulations for EHRs, Donald Berwick established the Institute for Healthcare Improvement (IHI, 2023a). The IHI developed a framework for healthcare quality called the Triple Aim and endorsed the use of EHRs to achieve quality improvements. The Triple Aim is a systems approach to improving healthcare delivery that focuses on three elements:

- Improving the patient experience of care (including quality and satisfaction)
- Improving the health of populations
- Reducing the per capita cost of health care (IHI, 2023b)

The Triple Aim has evolved into the Quadruple and Quintuple Aim, expanding the goals to include workforce well-being and safety, and advancing health equity (Nundy et al., 2022). The Quintuple Aim is especially relevant for large populations such as children in Pre-Kindergarten-12 schools.

Nursing Informatics

Nurses stepped up to the goal of improving healthcare through Nursing Informatics. Nursing informatics "integrates nursing science with multiple information and analytical sciences to identify, define, manage and communicate data, information, knowledge and wisdom in nursing practice" (Healthcare Information & Management Systems Society [HIMSS], 2019). Nurse informaticists provide much of the technical support and training in the use of EHRs, transform "...data into needed information," and leverage "technologies to improve health and health care equity, safety, quality, and outcomes" (ANA, 2022, p. 3).

The framework used to transform data from nursing documentation is called the DIKW Model, which includes Data – Information – Knowledge – Wisdom (ANA, 2022, p. 11). For example, discrete data points such as 12, 200, 2,7, and 7.1 are merely a string of numbers. These data points become information when the context is added: 12 noon; 200 mg/dL of blood sugar; 27 grams of carbohydrate; and A1c 7.1. When set in the context of the nurse's knowledge of diabetes, a plan of care can be developed. When the nurse synthesizes the knowledge about an individual's diabetes care, combines it with knowledge of their past history, and the nurse's experience providing care for others with diabetes, wisdom emerges to support effective nursing care and the development of evidence for practice.

Big Data

"**Big Data**" refers to the structured and unstructured information in multiple, large, complex data sets that can be compiled and aggregated to better understand phenomena (Wilson et al., 2017). When the "n" or members of a sample for the study is "all" of the population (vs a carefully designed sample), the potential to better understand the connections between and variations among subsets of a population become possible (Warren, 2017). Population-level datasets then become not only a collection of information but data to be analyzed and reported to create new knowledge.

Terminology

Meaningful Use of Data

Using data meaningfully means moving past documentation as a static (often unused) element to a dynamic tool for promoting better care for individuals and populations (Johnson et al., 2012).

Interoperability

Interoperability is the ability to "seamlessly exchange data and information between two or more disparate information systems" (ANA, 2022, p. 67). Interoperability allows for the coordination of care across multiple settings that previously may have relied on the patient to coordinate – for example, between a hospital and a stand-alone clinic. Including mechanisms for interoperability in school health records with the broader health care documentation systems would allow the inclusion of the child health data that school nurses collect and increase the visibility of school nurses' support of child health.

Standardized Variables in Nursing

Standardized languages are the common terminology and definitions that allow the machine aggregation necessary to support research, describe nursing care, and improve patient outcomes.

An example is the common terminology and definitions used in the *Nationally Standardized School Health Dataset: Every Student Counts!* (National Association of School Nurses [NASN], 2023). Common terminology and definitions of terms are essential to allow computers to compile and report data from many sources. For example, if every nurse in a school district used different terms to describe a health condition such as asthma, the work required to compile all students with asthma would be too costly. Using one term – asthma – defined in a specific way – "students with a diagnosis of **asthma** from a health care provider" (as NASN does in its national dataset) improves the ability to report on the work of school nurses.

Aggregating information using standardized languages also allows for the development of the evidence needed for practice.

Privacy, Confidentiality, and Security of Records

Assuring the privacy, confidentiality, and security of student health information is a duty upheld by both nursing codes of ethics (ANA, 2015; NASN, 2021) and the *School Nursing: Scope and Standards of Practice* (NASN, 2022).   **Privacy** is the right of an individual to determine which information they disclose and to understand how their health information is used (U.S. Health & Human Services [USHHS], 2023). **Confidentiality** is a duty of healthcare professionals to assure that disclosed information will be kept private unless permission to disclose is obtained from the patient (DeBord et al., 2018). **Security** addresses the "policies, procedures, software and/or hardware designed to ensure that data in information systems are protected against accidental or inappropriate destruction, alteration, or access" (Chou & Sengupta, 2008, p. 37). All three areas must be considered when addressing the collection and storage of student health information, regardless of the method used to manage information. (See Table 2 below for more information).

Federal Regulations: FERPA and HIPAA

While most nurses are aware of the Health Insurance Portability and Accountability Act (HIPAA), which addresses the privacy and security of personally identifiable health information in the healthcare setting, the Family Educational Rights and Privacy Act (FERPA) regulates the privacy and security of education data. FERPA defines education records as those that "contain information directly related to a student and which are maintained by an educational agency or institution or by a party acting for the agency or institution" (USDE, Privacy Technical Assistance Center [PTAC], 2014, p. 4). Therefore, in most cases, once a health or patient record moves from a healthcare setting (such as a medical or other provider's office) to the school, it becomes an education record and is subject to FERPA.

Family Educational Rights and Privacy Act (FERPA)

FERPA was enacted in 1974 (predating HIPAA by more than two decades). It addressed the rights of parents/ guardians and eligible students to (1) inspect and review student records; (2) request a correction to records; and (3) require consent before releasing any information from an educational record (USHHS & USDE, 2019, p. 4). FERPA "applies to educational agencies and institutions that receive Federal funds under any program administered by the U.S. Department of Education" (USHHS & USDE, 2019, p. 3).

FERPA specifically addresses students' education records and defines them as records that are:
(1) directly related to a student, and
(2) maintained by an educational agency or institution or by a party acting for the agency or institution (USHHS & USDE, 2019, p. 4).

This includes immunization and records "maintained by an education agency or institution (such as by an elementary or secondary school nurse)" (USHHS & USDE, 2019, p. 4). Special education records also fall under FERPA, although broader confidentiality provisions are required under IDEA (USHHS & USDE, 2019, p. 4). Post-secondary institutions have other requirements for managing student health data (USHHS & USDE, 2019, p. 4).

FERPA allows disclosing personally identifiable student information to persons with a "legitimate educational interest" (USHHS & USDE, 2019). FERPA also applies to health records created by a third-party contractor "acting for a FERPA-covered elementary or secondary school" (USHHS & USDE, 2019, p. 9). These parties must comply with the regulations regarding disclosure, and their use must be "under the direct control of the agency or institution" (National Center for Education Statistics [NCES], 2010, p. 15). Information may also be disclosed without prior written consent "to appropriate parties in connection with an emergency, if these parties' knowledge of the information is necessary to protect the health or safety of the student or other individuals" (USHHS & USDE, 2019, p. 4).

The National Center for Education Statistics (NCES) identifies security measures for staff with access to personally identifiable information, including background checks, privacy, data protection training, signed confidentiality pledges, and agreement to uphold relevant regulations (NCES, 2010). In general, sharing personally identifiable student information is not permitted; however, there are exceptions, as noted in Table 1.
Sharing school directory information without consent is permissible, provided that parents/guardians are notified and have a reasonable opportunity to refuse (USDE, 2021). Directory information includes "the student's name, address, telephone number, date and place of birth, honors and awards, and dates of attendance" (USDE, 2021, p. 1). Schools may also release de-identified data without permission if the size of the reported data is large enough to prevent an individual from being identified (USDE, n.d.). The NCES also has guidance on Data Ethics (NCES, 2010).

Table 1

FERPA Information Categories (NPHL, 2020; USDE, 2021)

Type	Definition	Parental Consent Required
Directory Information	Student's name, address, telephone number, date and place of birth, honors and awards, and dates of attendance	No, but parents may opt-out
Personally Identifiable Information (PII)	Information with specific identifiers that goes beyond directory information	Yes, except for those with a "legitimate educational interest" and certain others, including to comply with a judicial order or with appropriate officials in health and safety emergencies
Non-Personally Identifiable Information	Aggregated, de-identified information	No, often used for research, program evaluation, and quality improvement

FERPA Disclosure exceptions to the prior written consent include:
- School officials with a legitimate educational interest;
- Other schools to which a student is transferring;
- Specified officials for audit or evaluation purposes;
- Appropriate parties in connection with financial aid to a student;
- Organizations conducting certain studies for or on behalf of the school;
- Accrediting organizations;
- To comply with a judicial order or lawfully issued subpoena;
- Appropriate officials in cases of health and safety emergencies; and
- State and local authorities within a juvenile justice system, pursuant to specific state law (USDE, 2021, p. 1)

FERPA Application to Private Schools

Private schools that do not accept funds from the USDE are not subject to FERPA but may be subject to HIPAA if they transmit health data electronically. However, records of a student from a FERPA-covered entity receiving services from a private school are subject to FERPA even if the records of their classmates are not covered under FERPA (USHHS & USDE, 2019). For example, the records of a student enrolled in a private school who qualifies to receive special education services through a public school are covered by FERPA. Records maintained by a post-secondary institution are also subject to different rules under FERPA (USHHS & USDE, 2019). *(See Chapter 12 for more information on FERPA).*

Health Insurance Portability and Accountability Act (HIPAA)

As described previously, education records in public elementary and secondary schools include those maintained by school nurses – even if they have been created by school nurses who are employees of a hospital or public health agency. Because the records of school nurses are education records, they are explicitly subject to FERPA (USHHS & USDE, 2019). While HIPAA does not apply directly to student records, it is helpful to have a fundamental understanding of this federal statute, as most healthcare providers who provide information to schools will be required to comply with its regulations. HIPAA was enacted in 1996 and has undergone several revisions since that time. Its goals were to adopt national standards for electronic healthcare transactions and protect health information privacy (U.S. Health and Human Services Office for Civil Rights [USHHS OCR], 2021).

HIPAA addresses "protected health information" held by "covered entities" and consists of information on an individual's physical or mental health condition, provision of care, and payment information by which an individual can be identified (USHHS, 2022b, p. 1). Covered entities include healthcare providers who conduct business electronically, a healthcare clearinghouse, or a health plan (ONC, 2015). HIPAA allows healthcare providers to share information with other healthcare providers without consent for treatment purposes, including the administration of medication (ONC, 2015, p. 11).
(Please see Chapter 12 for more information on HIPAA).

Data Stewardship

Data stewardship is an obligation by the organization and employees to ensure that education data is:

- Accurate, complete, timely, and relevant
- Collected, maintained, used, and disseminated in ways that respect privacy and ensure confidentiality
- Utilized to support evaluation and monitoring of educational progress and programs goals
- Accuracy is prioritized to assure access to individual student rights and educational opportunities (NCES, 2010).

Security of records requires physical security – locked from access by unauthorized persons, maintained in a manner that keeps records intact, shielded from inadvertent review by others, and inclusion of an audit log (system to track who accessed the record, any changes made to the record, who made those changes, and when the changes were made) (Griffith, 2016). Security of school health records is important to assure compliance with federal and often state requirements. Fundamental safeguards include:

- Not sharing passwords;
- Not leaving student records unattended;
- Logging off when the student information system is not in use;
- Maintaining locked records for confidential and personally identifiable information;
- Assuring that consent to share records is obtained and that the individual providing consent understands what information is being kept and with whom it will be shared;
- Assuring that private information is disclosed only to those who have a legitimate educational interest;
- Ensuring that records are accurate;
- Maintaining knowledge of and compliance with local and federal statutes and policies regarding information sharing and data management; and
- Assuring data is used as it was intended (Beach & Oates, 2014, p. 48)
- Using caution when sharing personally identifiable information over email (USDE, 2016)
- Assuring data security in the event of disasters and other threats (USDE, n.d.-c)
- Avoiding the use of personal cell phones for transmitting PII (NPHL, 2020-b)

Electronic records should be equipped with features that ensure confidentiality and security, particularly if stored on a laptop that is moved from school to school. This includes the strategies outlined below in Table #1. The USDE cautions that when PII is disclosed without consent, only the "minimum amount ... necessary for the intended purpose" should be disclosed (USDE, 2023, p. 4).

Table 2

Strategies for Security and Confidentiality of Electronic Documentation Systems (Bergren, 2001/2005, cited by Johnson & Guthrie, 2012, p. 32). Reprinted with permission.

System Elements	Description	Purpose
Partitioning	Separates sections of the record from other sections (ex., health from food service)	If assigned by appropriate role, can prevent school personnel with no legitimate educational interest from accessing health records
Rejection	Refuses access to a user who attempts to log on with an incorrect password too many times	Forces an unauthorized user to interact with school authorities to prevent inappropriate access
Audit of access	Records a user's trail of access through the system to limit unnecessary viewing of the record	Allows a record of who accessed what information on which date to allow the analysis of their legitimate interest
Overwrite protection	Assures that there is no unauthorized alteration of the record	The record remains intact to provide a legally admissible record. Errors and updates can be entered with appropriate notation. Any changes to the record are discoverable for legal purposes.
Password Security	Secure requirements, i.e., must contain symbols, be a certain length, use capital and lower-case letters, and need to maintain secrecy	Limits access by unauthorized personnel
Business Practices	**Description**	**Purpose**
Security policy	Written policy on compliance with confidentiality and roles associated with access; and responsibilities of various roles	Allows school personnel with access to FERPA-protected data to understand their responsibilities for data security
Access	Limited to specific individuals based on role	Limits access to those with legitimate educational interest
Employee Education	Regarding appropriate management of security and confidentiality	Allows school personnel with access to FERPA-protected data to understand their responsibilities to protect student information
Confidentiality Agreement	Related to the use of the data	Provides school officials and school employees to have clarity in roles and responsibilities for protecting student information.
Communication with the IT department	Regarding security requirements for healthcare records	Allows school personnel to communicate requirements for health information; and IT staff to promote appropriate use of electronic records.

Legal Issues	Description	Purpose
Authentication	Legally recognized electronic signature of the entry into the record – often a log of the username	Limits access by unauthorized personnel and acts as a "signature" for data entry. Sharing usernames and passwords undermines authentication
Durability	Appropriate retention and maintenance of the data	Records are maintained in their original in accordance with federal, state, and district policies
Secure storage	Protects the data from loss or damage due to disaster or theft	Usually includes daily backup of data to a remote location in the event the record storage facility is destroyed in disasters or through theft
Admissibility	The record can be verified as being produced in the normal course of business with a log of the date and time the record was entered or changed	Allows the nurse to use their documentation to legally defend their care in a court case.
Audit log	Log of changes to the data that provides evidence that the record is the original entry and has not been changed or manipulated	Required to be used in a legal defense.

Data Governance and Data Stewardship

Data governance is defined as the practices that support critical organization-wide decision-making for data assets to meet regulatory requirements and achieve organization objectives (ONC, n.d.). Bergren (2019) identifies key actions for school nurses to ensure appropriate data governance:

- Know who is identified as the district data steward.
- Know the district data governance committee and request that a health services representative is included.
  - Consider volunteering to serve on this committee.
- Be aware of and understand state data regulations, policies, and procedures.
- Understand and use the district data policies and procedures.
- Build their own data literacy and knowledge.
- Use the resources of the U.S. DE Privacy and Technical Assistance (PTAC) Center.

Public Health Access to Health Data

Recognizing the importance of school health data to effective public health surveillance, intervention, and prevention activities, the Association of State and Territorial Health Officials (ASTHO, 2019) has developed FERPA and HIPAA guidance on the exchange of personally identifiable information from student records. Areas which ASTHO has identified that school data has the potential to impact public health include (1) outbreaks of infectious illness, (2) immunization tracking, (3) prevalence of chronic and environmental conditions, (4) success of injury prevention activities, (5) trending of health status such as obesity rates, (6) surveillance of toxic environmental exposures such as lead, and (7) identification of disease outbreaks related to disasters or emergencies (ASTHO, 2019, p. 1). The complexity of data sharing between schools and public health has value yet is subject to complex and sometimes challenging regulations. The Network for Public Health Law (NPHL) has developed *Data Sharing Guidance for School Nurses* that addresses many of these issues (NPHL, 2020-a).

Rights of Minors to Consent

In general, parents have a right to access and make decisions about their minor child's care. A minor's ability to consent for care is complex and varies by their state, age, marital status, and type of medical care (School House Connection, 2023).

In 2009, the Agency for Healthcare Research and Quality (AHRQ) and the ONC described three circumstances where the minor has authority to control their health information:
- "When state or other law does not require the consent of a parent or other person before a minor can obtain a particular healthcare service, and the minor consents to the healthcare service;
- when a court determines, or other law authorizes someone other than the parent to make treatment decisions for a minor; or
- when a parent agrees to a confidential relationship between the minor and the healthcare provider" (AHRQ & ONC, 2009, Chapter 3 p. 11)

The report by AHRQ and ONC outlines state regulations on minors' access to their healthcare records. It includes access by minors to their own records acknowledging that there are complications related to the age of consent for confidential care, including care for substance abuse, sexual health, and mental health (AHRQ & ONC, 2009). The reports differentiated between the rights of parents to be notified vs. having access to their minor child's records related to confidential care. The guidance did not address the issues of parental access to their child's education record as protected by FERPA. However, it identified the complexity of parental access to records related to confidential care for minors and the impact of electronic records on that issue. Generally, "when a minor lawfully consents to healthcare without the permission of the minor's parents, the HIPAA Privacy Rule defers to state laws with respect to whether the healthcare provider must or may notify the parents…or provide access to health information related to such treatment" (AHRQ & ONC, 2009, Chapter 1 p. 2). HIPAA and FERPA both protect the right of the individual to access and amend records kept by the institution on the patient or student (AHRQ & ONC, 2009).

The inexactness of the guidance from HIPAA on the rights of minors requires that nurses be familiar with and have resources regarding HIPAA and minor consent rules in their state. To address the variability in access to their minor child's records, the American Academy of Pediatrics recommends that the EHR systems reflect the child's age with regard to system privacy protection features (AHRQ & ONC, 2009, Chapter 3, p. 17). *(See Chapter 15 for more information on the rights of minors).*

Records Retention and Destruction of Health Information

The retention and destruction of records containing health information are driven by the "availability of timely, relevant data and information for patient care purposes; to meet federal, state, and local legal requirements; and to reduce the risk of legal discovery" (American Health Information Management Association [AHIMA], 2013, p. 1). AHIMA provides guidance for healthcare entities that describes the following considerations to drive minimum record retention schedules:

- "Ensure patient health information is available to meet the needs of continued patient care, legal requirements, research, education, and other legitimate uses of the organization.
- Include guidelines that specify what information is kept, the time period for which it is kept and the storage medium on which it will be maintained (e.g., paper, microfilm, optical disk, magnetic tape)
- Include clear destruction policies and procedures that include appropriate methods of destruction for each medium on which information is maintained" (AHIMA, 2013, p. 1)

Rules related to the retention of healthcare records are governed by state statutes (AHRQ & ONC, 2009). The Centers for Medicare and Medicaid (CMS) recommends the retention of medical records for a minimum of seven years based on their requirements (CMS, 2022). While FERPA does not provide specific requirements for data retention or destruction (U.S.DE, Privacy and Technical Assistance Center [PTAC], 2014), similar consideration for the retention of school health records is prudent given the potential for minors' right to access their records after they reach the age of 21 years. Nurses are advised to check their state statutes for the most current guidance on records retention. PTAC provides guidance on best practices for data destruction (USDE, Privacy & Technical Assistance Center, 2014).

IMPLICATIONS FOR SCHOOL NURSE PRACTICE

Types of School Health Records School nurses maintain many records describing student health and the care provided. These include:

- Healthcare delivery records;
- Individualized and emergency health plan records;
- Communication with other providers, parent/guardian(s), and students;
- Medication records;
- Health Screenings;
- Immunization records;
- Special education and Section 504 records;
- Staff training records;
- Accident, incident and injury records; and
- Personal notes

(Please see the index for several other chapters related to medication administration, health screenings, immunizations, IDEA/ADA, staff training, accident, incident, and injury records that offer more detailed information on these subjects).

Nursing Care Delivery Records

Nursing care records should reflect the nursing process, standards of care, and the critical thinking that went into that care. The care should be documented contemporaneously (at the time that care is given) and by the person providing the care. Appropriately documenting care assures that all health and educational team members can coordinate to deliver student-centered healthcare and that the nurse and the district demonstrate that they have discharged their duty for care. *(See Chapter 9 for more information on school health documentation).* The record of healthcare also includes communication with students, parent/guardian(s), and other members of the school/healthcare team and the individualized health plans (IHPs) developed by the nurse. In addition to the documentation of care by the school nurse, unlicensed assistive personnel (UAPs) should also document the care they administer (Bergren, 2021).

Individualized Health Plan Records (IHPs)

IHPs, including emergency care plans, contain important information on the school nurse's guidance to school staff on the care to be given for a student's health condition. The IHP demonstrates the nurse's discharge of their duty of care in the event that any questions arise. Updates to the care plan should be documented with the date and reasons any change in the care plan was made. The NASN describes the importance of IHPs (2020).

Communication with Other Providers, Parent/Guardian(s), and Students

Communication, including referrals made to other providers, should be recorded to clarify who was contacted and what information and recommendations have been provided. Many electronic documentation systems include dropdown menus that list the parent/guardian and emergency contacts. Bergren outlines the importance of communication in school nursing data (2016).

Medication Records

Medication records are especially important parts of the school health record. As with medication administration in any setting, the importance of documentation is reflected in the six rights of medication administration as identified in the NASN evidence-based clinical practice guideline (Bergren, 2021). These include:
- RIGHT Student;
- RIGHT Medication;
- RIGHT Dose;
- RIGHT Route;
- RIGHT Time; and
- RIGHT Documentation (Bergren, 2021, pp. 16–18)

The right documentation includes promptly documenting medication as it is administered to prevent double dosing. Documentation of administered medications is required of all caregivers (i.e., licensed providers or UAPs) who are delegated to administer medications. Medication refusal and medication errors should also be documented, as well as the notification of parents (Bergren, 2021). In addition, documentation of medication counts upon receipt of the medication, as well as routine counts of controlled medications and medications that are disposed of, wasted, lost, or stolen, is required (Bergren, 2021).

Screening Records

State statutes often require vision, hearing, dental, body mass index (BMI), scoliosis, lead, and other health screenings. Appropriate record management demonstrates compliance with those statutes, including proper consent and maintaining privacy and confidentiality. When managed in electronic systems, screening reports provide the opportunity to better understand student health status, care needs, and population health issues.

Screening records should include the date of the screening, the results, and the completion status of screening referrals – such as a completed physical examination by a professional and any treatment prescribed, e.g., glasses, etc. Communication with parents regarding the screenings and the outcomes of the screening process should be documented.

Immunization Records

Immunization records demonstrate compliance with state school attendance requirements related to the spread of vaccine-preventable diseases. Records should be maintained over the student's school career to allow assessment of the risk of illness individually and in the overall school population in the event of an outbreak. Complex algorithms to determine compliance with state statutes and the Advisory Committee on Immunization Practices (ACIP) guidelines make electronic immunization data management more efficient. Many states maintain immunization registries that collect immunization administration data, organize it by the patient, analyze it for compliance with recommended immunization schedules, and report on recommendations for due dates to complete an immunization series. Using electronic systems in this way promotes effective population-level care and the efficient use of vaccine supplies. It demonstrates compliance with statutes and allows monitoring of population health in the event of a disease outbreak. The HIPAA Privacy Rule "permits a covered health provider to disclose proof of immunization directly to a school that is required by law to have such proof prior to admitting a student, with the oral or written agreement of the parent or guardian" (USHHS, 2013, para. 1). The CDC provides additional information on Immunization Information Systems (CDC, 2019-a & 2019-b). *(See Chapter 44 for more information on Immunizations).*

Special Education Records

The Individuals with Disabilities in Education Act (IDEA) requires that specific information be documented, including the effects of health issues on the student's academic progress (USDE, 2017b). Health components of special education records may include vision and hearing screening results, recommendations for accommodations by the student's healthcare provider, health and developmental history, nursing assessment of the student's health and current needs, and the indication for any nursing or health services required to allow the student to access their federally protected right to a free and appropriate public education (FAPE). Electronic programs document compliance with the procedural rules for IDEA. Billing records are most often associated with nursing or health services that are provided as part of a student's special education. Nursing documentation is often a component of that billing record. The NASN (2023) provides guidance on the nurse's role in special education and Section 504 teams.

Staff Training Records

Records describing the training of school staff for medication delegation and individual student emergency care planning should include the date, content of the training, and the names and signatures of the trainer and the trainee(s). Documentation of staff training is required to demonstrate appropriate delegation processes and compliance with statutes. Ongoing supervision of delegated tasks must also be documented and describe the trainee's verbal and demonstrated understanding of the skill of administering medications and individual student emergency care and the dates of ongoing supervision. The ANA and the National Council of State Boards of Nursing (NCSBN) provide guidance on delegation (ANA & NCSBN, 2019). *(See Chapter 4 and Chapter 54 for more information on Delegation and Staff Training).*

Accident, Incident, and Injury Records

Accident, incident, and injury records are comprised of factual documentation of an accident, incident, or injury that occurs while the student is in the custody of the school. Quality incident reporting creates the data needed to address quality improvement issues (Joint Commission, 2018). Creating a culture of safety in which incidents and errors are reportable allows the organization to identify hidden risks that could be addressed (Fetherston, 2015). The report is completed by the person who witnessed the injury *or* provided immediate care and should include the name of the individual injured, date of birth, date and time of the incident, brief factual report of the incident, names of witnesses, harm caused, action taken at the time of the incident, and the name of the person reporting the incident (Fetherston, 2015). If the school nurse did not witness the incident, the school nurse should include their documentation of any follow-up care, contact with the student's parent/guardian(s) or medical providers. The school nurse may assist the witness (staff member) in completing the form if the witness is unfamiliar with accident and injury reports. Wasted, lost, or stolen medications should be reported as incidents (Bergren, 2021). Accident, incident and injury reports should not be documented in the student record but forwarded to the risk management department under district policies and procedures. *(See Chapter 40 for more information on Accident and Injury Reporting).*

Personal Notes

Personal notes are those "kept in the sole possession of the maker of the records, are used only as a personal memory aid, and are not accessible or revealed to any other person except a temporary substitute for the maker of the records" (USDE, n.d.-b, p. 1). While personal notes may be exempt from FERPA protections, nurses should be aware that their notes have the potential to be subpoenaed.

Management of School Health Records

Student health records may be managed on paper or electronic systems – although the convenience and security of electronic records make them the increasingly common choice of nurses and school districts. Paper records may be state, district, or nurse-developed forms that act as a prompt for complete documentation. Electronic records can be self-developed in software programs such as Microsoft Word®, Excel®, or Access®; stand-alone school nursing software; or as a health module in a student information system (SIS) (Johnson & Guthrie, 2012). Each method has benefits and risks (See Table 3 below for a Comparison of Documentation Systems).

Table 3

Comparison of Documentation Systems (Johnson & Guthrie, 2012, p. 30). Reprinted with permission.

System	Opportunities	Threats
Paper	Inexpensive, simple to use, high control over access	Records can be easily lost; only one user at a time; the record can be inaccessible for remote documentation; does not allow for rapid, systematic entry of data, lacks the ability to aggregate, sort, or query data; and does not identify who has accessed the health information.

System	Opportunities	Threats
Self-developed files in Microsoft Word, Excel, or Access	Less expensive; little training required.	Can be destroyed if the computer crashes or is corrupted; questionable legal protection related to admissibility; only one user at a time; does not authenticate who entered data or identify who accessed information.
Health module in a school-wide student information system (SIS)	Benefits of electronic documentation; access to education data; uses database technology to analyze and report on data; can allow direct communication with education staff; no extra training for non-health staff required	Often do not use nursing languages; requires technical support; requires training; may not address nursing-specific documentation needs.
Commercial school nursing software	Often use nursing languages; benefits of electronic documentation; use database technology to analyze and report on data.	Difficult to compare health interventions with education outcomes; requires technical support; requires training; may not allow direct communication with education staff; increases the number of programs to purchase & train for; using a separate system for health decreases communication of data between users of the systems.
Access to an electronic health record in a hospital or clinic	Use nursing languages; benefits of electronic documentation; uses robust database technology to analyze and report on data; promotes care coordination across the continuum of care.	Difficult to compare health interventions with education outcomes; requires technical support; requires training; may not allow direct communication with education staff; using a separate system for health decreases communication of data between users of the systems.

Electronic Documentation Systems in Schools

Electronic documentation systems hold great value in helping school nurses organize and report the volumes of information they create during their daily care of students. As in other healthcare settings, the use of electronic records by school nurses is important to support efficient documentation of compliance with legal standards of care. Documentation of care is enhanced with appropriate electronic systems built to support the nursing process and evidence-based practice.   Using school health data to support care decisions assures the inclusion of real-time entry of medication use, description of student symptoms and response to care, and the professional assessment by a school nurse to establish a data-driven treatment plan.   Screens for data entry in electronic health records can be programmed to prompt data entry and can even require that data be entered in specific fields to support complete and timely documentation. The NASN takes the position that "all [school nurses] should have access to a software platform for student electronic health records (EHRs) that includes nursing language/medical terminology and complies with standards of confidentiality" (NASN, 2019, p. 1).

Electronic documentation systems allow school nurses to aggregate and report on the data in student health records to better understand not only the history of the student's health needs but also understand the population of students they serve – regardless of whether that population is special education students, students with special healthcare needs, or district and state level populations of students.   In fact, the volume and complexity of data that school nurses collect on students in their large caseloads over the many years of a student's school career make it a challenge to use that data effectively to promote individual and population health unless electronic documentation systems are used to sort and analyze data.

It is important that school nurses promote the use of electronic school health documentation systems that are interoperable with the student's other healthcare records to assure that the "breadth, depth and pervasiveness of school health data" is available to support care coordination (Johnson & Guthrie, 2012, p. 104). Healthcare provider software compatible with the school's software allows collaboration and data sharing (are interoperable) with providers in the acute and ambulatory care settings. Interoperable records improve the accessibility of care records and reduce the expense and risk of error from multiple human data entry events.

Using EHRs meaningfully – using standardized languages with the ability to be interoperable with other systems – improves the safety and efficiency of care for children. Interoperability with a children's hospital and clinic records, for example, can improve communication of critical details to reduce hospital readmissions, improve continuity of care, and facilitate medication management. The outcomes of care coordinated across school and clinic include improved school attendance for students, reduced interruptions in employment for parents/guardians, reduced cost of child healthcare for society, and improved academic outcomes (Baker et al., 2022; Basch, 2011; Wang et al., 2014). Some acute and ambulatory healthcare systems allow school nurses to access their student's electronic health record with the permission of the student's parent/guardian(s) with improvements in care coordination, improved accuracy and efficiency of sharing health information, increased visibility of the school nurse as a member of the health care team (Baker & Gance-Cleveland, 2021).

Multiple studies describe problems with care coordination of children with Down Syndrome, neurodevelopmental disabilities, low income youth with special health care needs, the mental health of caregivers, and others, as well as in perceptions by caregivers on the communication between school and health care provider, and care coordination (Cosgrove et al., 2023; Gail et al., 2022; Geffel et al., 2022; Mirzo et al., 2022; Van Orne, 2022; Willgerodt et al., 2020; Yu et al., 2020). Improved communication and coordination of care across systems is one of the benefits of interoperable EHRs and could greatly improve the healthcare of students with special healthcare needs, especially those whose health is threatened by social determinants of health.

Another benefit of electronic systems is the confidentiality of logging health room visits. Under FERPA, parents have a right to review any records kept on their child – including a log of health room activity. If another parent requests the log to obtain access to information on their own student's record, and the health room visit log that contains information on multiple students, a paper log-in may not adequately protect another student's privacy. If a record is subpoenaed, it must be presented without redacting other students' private health room visits. An individual student's privacy may be at risk even if no information other than the student's name and reason for the visit is kept on a health room log of visits. Previous student health complaints entered into the log should not be visible to subsequent students in the health office.

Individual student healthcare records should be used to assure the privacy of individual students. Electronic health records can enhance privacy by allowing individual students to log themselves into the health room, capturing the date and time and potentially the reason for their visit through the use of the student's unique student ID and password. Electronic documentation systems that aggregate student log-ins on a screen seen only by the nurse can allow the nurse to triage students for care yet maintain the privacy of an individual student's reason for the visit.

While paper systems limit direct access to healthcare information, electronic systems can improve the confidentiality and security of healthcare records through a variety of measures, as described in Table 2 above (page 3). For example, EHRs can partition access to the various parts of the system based on role-specific permissions. This means that the system can be set to only allow those staff identified as nurses to access health records or to only allow dietary specialists to access student lunch accounts. In addition, an audit log, where the system keeps track of who accesses the record and the date and time that any changes are made, can result in tighter control over access to student records. The log of who accesses the record meets FERPA requirements to maintain a record of where education records were disclosed. For these reasons, knowledge of fundamental security measures needed for health records and participation in the processes to select and implement an electronic documentation system are important responsibilities of school nurses.

Selecting an Electronic Documentation System

Just like the rights for medication administration and delegation, there are five rights for EHR systems. These include:
- Right Clinical Data – complete, accurate, meaningful;
- Right Presentation – human computer interface is efficient & effective in capturing & displaying data, information, and knowledge;
- Right Decision – clinical decision support that is context-sensitive, tailored to the user, based on current evidence, and allows documentation of override reasons;
- Right work processes – efficient and effective processes that integrate workflows; and
- Right Outcomes – value-driven, quality, and cost (Amatayakul, 2009, p. 175).

In order to create an electronic health information system that meets the needs of its constituents, assures compliance with legal requirements, and promotes sustained use after installation, foundational elements need to be in place to assure adoption is most effective:
- An advisory committee that represents end-users;
- Data points and vendor selection standards developed by end-users;
- An information technology infrastructure;
- A competitive selection process;
- Training for staff;
- A strong on-site vendor presence during implementation;
- Involved leaders and partners (project champions) that are required to be on-site during key implementation points; and
- Sustainability of training resources for new staff (Robert Wood Johnson Foundation, 2011).

Implementing Electronic Documentation Systems

Implementation of electronic health systems is improved with training on the use of the system.   A hybrid training model that incorporates online learning, face-to-face instruction, and support from superusers – early adopters of technology – can guide their colleagues' integration of the new system. Technical support in implementing electronic records improved nurses' knowledge and attitudes toward using electronic systems and compliance with documentation requirements, completeness, and accuracy. Training for using the EHR demonstrates an organization's commitment to the safe and effective use of the system.

Other Considerations with EHRs

For all student records, a parent's right to access their child's healthcare records may be complicated by the minor's rights to assent to care, which vary from state to state.   School nurses should be familiar with their state's laws related to parental access to records for confidential student healthcare.

While some companies market electronic health records to schools and even offer them at no cost to a district, school nurses should carefully consider the ethical implications of the data requests of parents by these companies, the implications of sharing data, and the assurance of parents' understanding how their student's data is used (Wilburn, 2018). As an advocate, the school nurse can help parents understand the implications of sharing their child's data to be used by the EHR company. Parents need to understand their rights under FERPA and be guided to ask how the EHR company will use their child's data, how securely it will be stored, and who will have access to it.

The rapid development and ubiquitous presence of smartphones and other personal devices have led to increased use but limited guidance on the safety of both health applications and retention of student information on nurses' personal devices (Eysenbach & Buis, 2020). The NPHL advises against using personal cell phones unless there is written consent from parents, and the cell phone uses encryption to keep the information secure. Even then, this practice is concerning. School districts should provide school nurses with district cell phones or laptops that have appropriate encryption features that allow more secure transmission. The NPHL has developed guidance for school nurses on the many issues related to data privacy (NPHL, 2019, p. 4).

Security of Electronic Documentation Systems in Schools

Information Technology (IT) has brought new benefits and challenges to school health records that impact the confidentiality and security of those records. The rising use of electronic documentation systems brings the enhanced capacity to collect and analyze population-level school health data. However, it comes with new risks through email hacking, malware, and unauthorized users. Security of electronic data includes protection against cyber threats to "unauthorized access, use and disclosure" to protect data "confidentiality, integrity, and availability" (HIMSS, 2023a). While strong measures on the national and organizational level exist to protect health information in traditional healthcare settings (USHHS, 2023), electronic school health records systems have limited standards to promote healthcare level protection of data. This leaves "school nurses with limited IT experience, and school IT and administrators with little knowledge of health IT requirements" to select school documentation systems" (Johnson, 2017, p. 6). School nurses must build their skills in data stewardship.

HIPAA Implications for Schools

HIPAA comes into play for a school nurse when requesting records. The NPHL (2020) states, "HIPAA allows health care providers to disclose protected health information without parental consent or authorization for treatment purposes. Likewise, a school nurse may (under FERPA) communicate with a student's outside health care provider to clarify that provider's treatment orders" (NPHL, 2020, p. 4). They recommend that school nurses obtain parents' permission to exchange information for any students with a nursing care plan. The resource list contains information on training for the security of school information systems.

School nurses need to use discretion in determining which personally identifiable information to disclose and to whom(NCES, 2010). Considering the sensitivity of information (e.g., physical and mental health information, disciplinary information) as well as the potential harm to the student if it were released can guide the nurse in protecting student information (NCES, 2010). Fair Information Practice Principles that include the minimization of shared information are applicable (Federal Privacy Council, n.d.). Nurses are encouraged to contact their district's Data Governance Committee for additional support.

Big Data in School Nursing

The data in school nurses' documentation is truly an example of Big Data. It contains information on students who are well and those with chronic health conditions and is the most comprehensive child health dataset in the U.S. – true population health data. Using machines to analyze data requires standardized reporting nationally – using the same variables, with the same definitions, in the same order so that trends and patterns can be identified. This Big Data can then be used to identify student health needs, clarify how school nursing impacts child health, and influence local, state, and national healthcare policy and spending. EHRs provide the opportunity to better understand social determinants of health (SDOH) and utilize "tools that allow for efficient, effective, and accurate data collection, analysis, and reporting" at the population level (ANA, 2022, p. 70). To meet this need, the National Association of School Nurses has created the *National School Health Dataset: Every Student Counts!* (Stanislo, 2023) which aggregates de-identified data from contributing school nurses in the U.S.

As population-level research related to student health matures, clinical decision support can be built into the EHR based on the population-level data contained in school nursing documentationFor example, when the diagnosis of asthma is entered, EHR decision support tools can prompt reminders to enter rescue inhalers, peak flow measurement, and symptom triggers for the student. Prompts and decision support mechanisms inherent in electronic documentation systems support and record the nursing judgment behind the care provided and promote the efficient and thorough documentation required to demonstrate appropriate healthcare.

CONCLUSION

School nurses stand at the intersection of both the health and education sectors and have a legal obligation to use student health data to support the health and well-being of their students while protecting the privacy, confidentiality, and security of that information. As such, they generate records that must consider the requirements of both sectors. Federal statutes, such as FERPA and HIPAA, protect the privacy and security of student health information that must be balanced against the legitimate educational interests of school staff providing direct care to students. Managing the veracity, volume, and velocity of the information they oversee requires EHRs. The school nurse's maintenance and safeguarding of student health records is a critical professional obligation.

RESOURCES

DATA SHARING

- Data Privacy in School Nursing: Navigating the Complex Landscape of Data Privacy Laws (Part I). Network for Public Health Law https://www.networkforphl.org/wp-content/uploads/2019/12/Data-Privacy-in-School-Nursing-Navigating-the-Complex-Landscape-of-Data-Privacy-Laws-Part-1-1.pdf

- Data Privacy in School Nursing: Navigating the Complex Landscape of Data Privacy Laws (Part II) Network for Public Health Law https://www.networkforphl.org/wp-content/uploads/2020/01/Data-Privacy-in-School-Nursing-Part-II-1-23-2020.pdf

- Data Sharing Agreement Checklist for IDEA Part C and Part B 619 Agencies and Programs Privacy Technical Assistance Center https://ideadata.org/resources/resource/1468/data-sharing-agreement-checklist-for-idea-part-c-and-part-b-619-agencies

- Data Sharing Guidance for School Nurses – Network for Public Health Law

- Data Stewardship – National Center for Education Statistics https://nces.ed.gov/pubs2011/2011602.pdf

- Data Stewardship: Managing Personally Identifiable Information in Electronic Student Education Records https://nces.ed.gov/pubs2011/2011602.pdf

- Forum Guide to Data Ethics https://nces.ed.gov/pubs2010/2010801.pdf

- Public Health and Schools Toolkit https://healthystudentspromisingfutures.org/wp-content/uploads/2019/07/Public-Health-Access-to-Student-Health-Data-_-State-Public-Health-_-ASTHO.pdf

- Transparency Best Practices for Schools and Districts https://studentprivacy.ed.gov/sites/default/files/resource_document/file/LEA%20Transparency%20Best%20Practices%20final.pdf

ELECTRONIC HEALTH RECORDS

- Guide to Privacy and Security of Electronic Health Information. (2015). https://www.healthit.gov/sites/default/files/pdf/privacy/privacy-and-security-guide.pdf

- Interoperability in Healthcare – Health Information Management Systems Society. (n.d.) https://www.himss.org/resources/interoperability-healthcare?gclid=CjwKCAjwiOCgBhAgEiwAjv5whP4TIZSpMn2fCEu5pvPBnJMFK_VkSghTrXhYlw6nMzUxwYGzuGCNaBoC2GcQAvD_BwE

- ONC Health IT Playbook – Office of the National Coordinator for Health Information Technology. (2019). https://www.healthit.gov/playbook/electronic-health-records/

- NASN Position Statement: Electronic health records: An essential tool for school nurses to keep students healthy. (2019). https://www.nasn.org/nasn-resources/professional-practice-documents/position-statements/ps-electronic-health-records

- NASN 2021 School nursing evidence-based clinical practice guideline: Medication administration in schools. nasn.org. https://learn.nasn.org/courses/33787

FEDERAL PRIVACY LAWS – FERPA & HIPAA

- Comparison of FERPA and HIPAA Privacy Rule for Accessing Student Health Data https://www.cdc.gov/phlp/docs/hipaa-ferpa-infographic-508.pdf
- Disclosure of Student Immunizations to Schools https://www.hhs.gov/hipaa/for-professionals/privacy/guidance/student-immunizations/index.html
- FERPA: Frequently Asked Questions https://studentprivacy.ed.gov/frequently-asked-questions
- HHS - FERPA & HIPAA http://www.hhs.gov/hipaa/for-professionals/faq/ferpa-and-hipaa
- Joint Guidance on the Application of the Family Educational Rights and Privacy Act (FERPA) and the Health Insurance Portability and Accountability Act of 1996 (HIPAA) to Student Health Records https://studentprivacy.ed.gov/resources/joint-guidance-application-ferpa-and-hipaa-student-health-records
- Protection of Pupil Rights Amendment - https://studentprivacy.ed.gov/training/what-protection-pupil-rights-amendment#:~:text=The%20Protection%20of%20Pupil%20Rights%20Amendment%2C%20or%20PPRA%2C%20is%20a,use%20of%20personal%20information%20for
- Student Immunizations https://www.hhs.gov/hipaa/for-professionals/privacy/guidance/student-immunizations/index.html
- Health Information & Privacy: FERPA and HIPAA | CDC https://www.cdc.gov/phlp/publications/topic/healthinformationprivacy.html
- HIPAA for Professionals https://www.hhs.gov/hipaa/for-professionals/index.html
- Joint Guidance on the Application of FERPA and HIPAA to Student Health Records https://www.hhs.gov/hipaa/for-professionals/special-topics/ferpa-hipaa/index.html
- FERPA and HIPAA FAQ https://www.hhs.gov/hipaa/for-professionals/faq/ferpa-and-hipaa/index.html
- Family Education Rights and Privacy Act FERPA – USDE https://www2.ed.gov/policy/gen/guid/fpco/ferpa/index.html
- Frequently asked questions: Electronic documentation systems in schools. https://journals.sagepub.com/doi/epdf/10.1177/1942602X18814735
- U.S. Department of Education – Family Educational Rights and Privacy Act: Guidance for School Officials on Student Health Records https://studentprivacy.ed.gov/resources/family-educational-rights-and-privacy-act-guidance-school-officials-student-health-records
- U.S. Department of Education Videos on best practices for student privacy https://studentprivacy.ed.gov/content/videos

- U.S. Department of Education Online Training Modules
  https://studentprivacy.ed.gov/content/online-training-modules

- U.S. Department of Education Recorded Webinars
  https://studentprivacy.ed.gov/content/recorded-webinars

- Network for Public Health Law Family Educational Rights and Privacy Act
  https://www.networkforphl.org/wp-content/uploads/2020/01/Snapshot-FERPA_final1.pdf

SECURITY

- Data Security: Top Threats to Data Protection – U.S. Department of Education Privacy and Technical Assistance Center https://studentprivacy.ed.gov/sites/default/files/resource_document/file/Issue%20 Brief%20Data%20Security%20Top%20Threats%20to%20Data%20Protection_0.pdf

- Guide to Privacy and Security of Electronic Health Information https://www.healthit.gov/sites/default/ files/pdf/privacy/privacy-and-security-guide.pdf

- Technical Training or Assistance – U.S. Department of Education Privacy and Technical Assistance Center https://studentprivacy.ed.gov/request-ptac-training-or-technical-assistance

- Data Destruction - https://studentprivacy.ed.gov/sites/default/files/resource_document/file/Best%20 Practices%20for%20Data%20Destruction%20(2014-05-06)%20%5bFinal%5d_0.pdf

REFERENCES

Agency for Healthcare Research and Quality & Office of the National Coordinator of Health Information Technology. (2009). *Privacy and security solutions for interoperable health information exchange: Report on state medical record access laws* [RTI Project Number 0209825.000.015.100].

Amatayakul, M. K. (2009). *Electronic healthcare records: A practical guide for professionals and organizations* (4th ed., Vol. 27). American Health Information Management Association.

American Health Information Management Association. (2013). *Retention and destruction of health information.* library.ahima.org. Retrieved 2013, from https://library.ahima.org/PB/RetentionDestruction#.ZG0Lmi_MJpQ

American Nurses Association. (2015). *Code of ethics for nurses with interpretive statements* (2nd ed.). Author.

American Nurses Association. (2022). *Nursing informatics: Scope and standards of practice* (3rd ed.).

American Nurses Association & National Council of State Boards of Nursing. (2019). *National guidelines for nurse delegation.* https://www.nursingworld.org/~4962ca/globalassets/practiceandpolicy/nursing-excellence/ana-position-statements/nursing-practice/ana-ncsbn-joint-statement-on-delegation.pdf

Association of State and Territorial Health Officials. (2019). *Public health and schools toolkit.* healthy students https://healthystudentspromisingfutures.org/wp-content/uploads/2019/07/Public-Health-Access-to-Student-Health-Data-_-State-Public-Health-_-ASTHO.pdf

Baker, C., & Gance-Cleveland, B. (2021). Linking school nurses with health care systems using EHRs: An integrative review. *Journal of School Nursing, 37*(1), 28–40. https://doi.org/110.1177/1059840520913323

Baker, C. L., Ozkaynak, M., Ziniel, S. I., Harpin, S. B., & Makic, M. F. (2022). Systems of communication in school-nurse led care coordination: A concept analysis. *Nursing Forum, 57*(6), 1536–1544. https://onlinelibrary.wiley.com/doi/10.1111/nuf.12824

Basch, C. E. (2011). Healthier students are better learners: High quality, strategically planned, and effectively coordinated school health programs must be a fundamental mission of schools to help close the achievement gap. *Journal of School Health, 81*, 650–662. https://doi.org/10.1111/j.1746-1561.2011.00632.x

Beach, J., & Oates, J. (2014, May 7). Maintaining best practice in record-keeping and documentation. *Nursing Standard, 28*(36), 45–50. https://doi.org/10.7748/ns2014.05.28.36.45.e8835

Bergren, M. D. (2016). The feasibility of collecting school nurse data. *Journal of School Nursing, 32*(5), 337–346. https://doi.org/10.1177/1059840516649233

Bergren, M. D. (2019). Data governance and stewardship. *NASN School Nurse, 34*(3), 149–151. https://doi.org/10.1177/1942602X19838798

Bergren, M. D. (2021). *School nursing evidence-based clinical practice guideline: Medication administration in schools* [Clinical Guideline]. https://learn.nasn.org/courses/33787/documents/50343

Blumenthal, D. (2009, December 30). Launching HITECH. *New England Journal of Medicine.* https://doi.org/10.1056/NEJMp0912825

Centers for Disease Control and Prevention. (2019-a). *About immunization information systems.* https://www.cdc.gov/vaccines/programs/iis/about.html

Centers for Disease Control and Prevention. (2019-b). *IIS technical guidance..* https://www.cdc.gov/vaccines/programs/iis/technical-guidance/index.html

Center for Medicare and Medicaid. (2022). *Medical record maintenance & access requirements* https://www.cms.gov/files/document/mln4840534-medical-record-maintenance-and-access-requirements.pdf

Chou, D., & Sengupta, S. (2008). Infrastructure and security. In T. H. Payne (Ed.), *Practical guide to clinical computing systems* (vol. 37, pp. 37–78). Academic Press.

Correa-de-Araujo, R. (2017). Balancing data access and utilization: Federal Big Data initiative and relevance to health disparities research. In C. W. Delaney, C. A. Weaver, J. J. Warren, T. R. Clancy, & R. L. Simpson (Eds.), *Big Data-Enabled Nursing* (pp. 227–243). Springer.

Cosgrove, B., Knafl, K., & Van Riper, M. (2023). A mixed methods analysis of care coordination needs and desirable features of an M-Health application to support caregivers of children with down syndrome. *Journal of Pediatric Health Care, 37*, 30–39. https://doi.org/10.1016/j.pedhc.2022.08.002

DeBord, J., Burke, W., & Dudzinski, D. M. (2018). *Confidentiality.* depts.washington.edu. https://depts.washington.edu/bhdept/ethics-medicine/bioethics-topics/detail/58

Eysenbach, G., & Buis, L. (2020). Nurses' use of personal smartphone technology in the workplace: Scoping review. *JMIR Mhealth Uhealth, 8*(11), e18774. https://doi.org/10.2196/18774

Federal Privacy Council. (n.d.). *Fair information practice principles (FIPPs).* fpc.gov. Retrieved June 25, 2023, from https://www.fpc.gov/resources/fipps/

Fetherston, T. (2015). The importance of critical incident reporting - and how to do it. *Community Eye Health, 29*(90), 26–27.

Gail, V. N., Buchhalter, J., Antonelli, R. C., Richard, C., Yohemas, M., Lachuk, G., & Gibbard, W. B. (2022). Improving care for families and children with neurodevelopmental disorders and co-occurring chronic health conditions using a care coordination intervention. *Journal of Developmental and Behavioral Pediatrics*, *43*(8), 444–453. https://journals.lww.com/jrnldbp/Fulltext/2022/11000/Improving_Care_for_Families_and_Children_with.2.aspx

Geffel, K. M., Lombardi, B. M., Yu, J. A., & Bogen, D. (2022). Prevalence and characteristics of providers' care coordination communication with schools. *Academic Pediatrics*, *22*(7), 1184–1191. https://doi.org/10.1016/j.acap.2022.01.009

Griffith, R. (2016). For the record: Keeping detailed notes. *British Journal of Nursing*, *25*, 408–409. https://www.magonlinelibrary.com/doi/abs/10.12968/bjon.2016.25.7.408

Healthcare Information & Management Systems Society. (2019, July 3). *What is nursing informatics?* Retrieved April 8, 2021, from https://www.himss.org/resources/what-nursing-informatics

Health Information Management Systems Society. (2023-a). *Cybersecurity in healthcare.* https://www.himss.org/resources/cybersecurity-healthcare

Health Information Management Systems Society. (2023-b). *Interoperability in healthcare.* https://www.himss.org/resources/interoperability-healthcare

Institute for Healthcare Improvement. (2023a). *History*.https://www.ihi.org/about/Pages/History.aspx

Institute for Healthcare Improvement. (2023b). *Overview of the IHI Triple Aim.* https://www.ihi.org/Topics/TripleAim/Pages/Overview.aspx

Institute of Medicine Committee on Quality of Health Care in America. (2000). *To err is human: Building a safer health system*. National Academies Press. https://nap.nationalacademies.org/catalog/9728/to-err-is-human-building-a-safer-health-system

Institute of Medicine Committee on Quality of Health Care in America. (2001). *Crossing the quality chasm: A new health system for the 21st Century*. National Academies Press. https://doi.org/10.17226/10027

Johnson, K. H. (2017). Healthy and ready to learn: School nurses improve equity and access. *OJIN: The Online Journal of Issues in Nursing*, *22*(3 Manuscript 1). https://ojin.nursingworld.org/MainMenuCategories/ANAMarketplace/ANAPeriodicals/OJIN/TableofContents/Vol-22-2017/No3-Sep-2017/Healthy-and-Ready-to-Learn.html

Johnson, K. H., & Guthrie, S. (2012). Harnessing the power of student health data: Selecting, using, and implementing electronic school health documentation systems. *NASN School Nurse*, *27*(1), 27–33. https://doi.org/10.1177/1942602X11429828

Johnson, K. H., Bergren, M. D., & Westbrook, L. O. (2012). The promise of standardized data collection: School health variables identified by states. *Journal of School Nursing*, *28*(2), 95–107. https://doi.org/10.1177/1059840511426434

Joint Commission. (2018). *Sentinel event alert*. jointcommission.org. https://www.jointcommission.org/-/media/tjc/documents/resources/patient-safety-topics/sentinel-event/sea_60_reporting_culture_final.pdf

Landstrom, G. L. (2017). Big data impact on transformation of healthcare systems. In C. W. Delaney, C. A. Weaver, J. J. Warren, T. R. Clancy, & R. L. Simpson (Eds.), *Big data-enabled nursing* (pp. 253–263). Springer.

Mirzo, M., Keating, E., Krisher, A., & Pinto, J. (2022). Care coordination experiences of low-income parents of children and youth with special health care needs: An exploratory study. *Journal of Health Care for the Poor and Underserved*, *33*(4), 1925–1948. https://doi.org/10.1353/hpu.2022.0146

National Association of School Nurses. (2019). *Electronic health records: An essential tool for school nurses to keep students healthy.* https://www.nasn.org/nasn-resources/professional-practice-documents/position-statements/ps-electronic-health-records

National Association of School Nurses. (2020). *Use of individualized healthcare plans to support school health services*https://www.nasn.org/nasn-resources/professional-practice-documents/position-statements/ps-ihps

National Association of School Nurses. (2021). *NASN code of ethics..* https://www.nasn.org/nasn-resources/professional-topics/codeofethics

National Association of School Nurses. (2022). *School nursing: Scope and standards of practice* (4th ed.). Author.

National Association of School Nurses. (2023). *National School Health Dataset: Every Student Counts!* nasn.org. https://www.nasn.org/research/everystudentcounts/uniform-data-points

National Association of School Nurses. (2023). *IDEIA and Section 504 teams - The school nurse as an essential team member..* https://www.nasn.org/nasn-resources/professional-practice-documents/position-statements/ps-ideia

National Center for Education Statistics. (2010). *Data stewardship: Managing Personally Identifiable Information in electronic student education records.* nces.ed.gov. https://nces.ed.gov/pubs2011/2011602.pdf

National Forum on Education Statistics. (2010). *The Forum guide to data ethics* (NFES 2010-801). Government Printing Office. https://www.nejm.org/doi/full/10.1056/NEJMp0912825

Network for Public Health Law. (2019). *Data privacy in school nursing: Navigating the Complex landscape of data privacy laws (Part 1).* networkforphl.org. https://www.networkforphl.org/_asset/tzqw3y/Data-Privacy-in-School-Nursing-Navigating-the-Complex-Landscape-of-Data-Privacy-Laws-Part-1.pdf

Network for Public Health Law. (2020-a). *Data sharing guidance for school nurses.* https://www.networkforphl.org/wp-content/uploads/2020/01/Data-Sharing-Guidance-for-School-Nurses-with-Appendices-1-23-2020.pdf

Network for Public Health Law. (2020-b). *Data privacy in school nursing: Navigating the complex landscape of data privacy laws (Part II).* Networkforphl.org. https://www.networkforphl.org/wp-content/uploads/2020/01/Data-Privacy-in-School-Nursing-Part-II-1-23-2020.pdf

Nundy, S., Cooper, L. A., & Mate, K. S. (2022). The Quintuple Aim for health care improvement: A new imperative to advance health equity. *Journal of the American Medical Association, 327*(6), 521–522. https://doi.org/10.1001/jama.2021.25181

Office of the National Coordinator for Health Information Technology. (n.d.). *Data governance.* Retrieved June 26, 2023, from https://www.healthit.gov/playbook/pddq-framework/data-governance/

Office of the National Coordinator for Health Information Technology. (2015). *Guide to privacy and security of electronic health information.* https://www.healthit.gov/sites/default/files/pdf/privacy/privacy-and-security-guide-chapter-2.pdf

Office of the National Coordinator for Health Information Technology. (2019a). *Advancing care information reporting.* https://www.healthit.gov/topic/federal-incentive-programs/MACRA/MIPS/advancing-care-information-reporting

Office of the National Coordinator for Health Information Technology. (2019b). *ONC Health IT playbook.* https://www.healthit.gov/playbook/electronic-health-records/

Office of the National Coordinator for Health Information Technology. (2020). *Certification standards and regulations.* https://www.healthit.gov/topic/certification-ehrs/certification-standards-and-regulations

Office of the National Coordinator for Health Information Technology. (2022). *Certification of health IT.* https://www.healthit.gov/topic/certification-ehrs/certification-criteria

Office of the National Coordinator for Health Information Technology. (2023a). *Benefits of EHRs.*
https://www.healthit.gov/topic/health-it-and-health-information-exchange-basics/health-information-exchange

Office of the National Coordinator for Health Information Technology. (2023b). *Interoperability / TEFCA.*
https://www.healthit.gov/topic/interoperability

U.S. Department of Education, Privacy Technical Assistance Center. (2014). *Data sharing agreement checklist for IDEA Part C and Part B 619 agencies and programs.* https://dasycenter.sri.com/downloads/DaSy_papers/DaSy_Data_ Sharing_Agreement_Checklist_Acc.pdf

U.S. Department of Education, Privacy and Technical Assistance Center. (2014). *Best practices for data destruction.* https://studentprivacy.ed.gov/sites/default/files/resource_document/file/Best%20Practices%20for%20Data%20 Destruction%20(2014-05-06)%20%5bFinal%5d_0.pdf

Robert Wood Johnson Foundation. (2011). *School health connection goes electronic: Developing a health information management system for New Orleans' school-based health centers.* http://www.rwjf.org/content/dam/farm/ reports/program_results_reports/2011/rwjf71528

School House Connection. (2023). *State laws on minor consent for routine medical care.* schoolhouse connection.org.
https://schoolhouseconnection.org/state-laws-on-minor-consent-for-routine-medical-care/

Stanislo, K. J. (2023). Revisiting the National School Heath Data Set: Every Student Counts! *NASN School Nurse, 38*(1), 26–30. https://doi.org/10.1177/1942602X221137519

U.S. Department of Education. (n.d.-a). *Request PTAC training or technical assistance.* https://studentprivacy.ed.gov/ request-ptac-training-or-technical-assistance

U.S. Department of Education. (n.d.-b). *What records are exempted from FERPA?* https://studentprivacy.ed.gov/faq/ what-records-are-exempted-ferpa

U.S. Department of Education. (n.d.-c). *Request PTAC training or technical assistance.* studentprivacy.ed.gov. Retrieved June 25, 2023, from https://studentprivacy.ed.gov/request-ptac-training-or-technical-assistance

U.S. Department of Education. (2016). *Email and student privacy.* https://studentprivacy.ed.gov/training/email-and-student-privacy

U.S. Department of Education. (2017a). *IDEA Individuals with Disabilities Education Act: Sec 300. 321 IEP team.*
https://sites.ed.gov/idea/regs/b/d/300.321

U.S. Department of Education. (2017b). *Sec. 300.311 Specific documentation for the eligibility determination..*
https://sites.ed.gov/idea/regs/b/d/300.311

U.S. Department of Education. (2021). *Family Educational Rights and Privacy Act (FERPA).* ed.gov.
https://www2.ed.gov/policy/gen/guid/fpco/ferpa/index.html

U.S. Department of Education, Office for Civil Rights. (2016). *Parent and educator resource guide to Section 504 in public elementary and secondary schools.* https://www2.ed.gov/about/offices/list/ocr/docs/504-resource-guide-201612.pdf

U.S. Department of Education, Privacy Technical Assistance Center. (2015). *Data security: Top threats to data protection.*
https://studentprivacy.ed.gov/sites/default/files/resource_document/file/Issue%20Brief%20Data%20 Security%20Top%20Threats%20to%20Data%20Protection_0.pdf

U.S. Department of Education, Privacy Technical Assistance Center. (2014). *Data sharing agreement checklist for IDEA Part C and Part B 619 agencies and programs.* https://dasycenter.sri.com/downloads/DaSy_papers/DaSy_Data_ Sharing_Agreement_Checklist_Acc.pdf

U.S. Department of Education, Privacy and Technical Assistance Center. (2014). *Best practices for data destruction.* studentprivacy.ed.gov. https://studentprivacy.ed.gov/sites/default/files/resource_document/file/Best%20 Practices%20for%20Data%20Destruction%20(2014-05-06)%20%5bFinal%5d_0.pdf

U.S. Department of Education. (2023). *Family Educational Rights and Privacy Act: Guidance for school officials on student health records.* https://studentprivacy.ed.gov/sites/default/files/resource_document/file/The%20 Family%20Educational%20Rights%20and%20Privacy%20Act%20Guidance%20for%20School%20Officials%20 on%20Student%20Health%20Records.pdf

U.S. Department of Education, Privacy Technical Assistance Center. (2022). *Local Education Agency website student privacy transparency reviews final report.* https://studentprivacy.ed.gov/sites/default/files/resource_document/ file/Local%20Education%20Agency%20Website%20Student%20Privacy%20Transparency%20Reviews%20 Final%20Report.pdf

U.S. Department of Health and Human Services. (2013). *Student immunizations.* https://www.hhs.gov/hipaa/for-professionals/privacy/guidance/student-immunizations/index.html

U.S. Department of Health and Human Services & U.S. Department of Education. (2019). *Joint guidance on the application of the Family Education Rights and Privacy Act (FERPA) and the Health Insurance Portability and Accountability Act of 1996 (HIPAA) to student health records (Updated 2019).* studentprivacy.ed.gov. https://studentprivacy.ed.gov/sites/default/files/resource_document/file/2019%20HIPAA%20FERPA%20 Joint%20Guidance%20508.pdf

U.S. Health and Human Services. (2022a). *Health information technology.* https://www.hhs.gov/hipaa/for-professionals/ special-topics/health-information-technology/index.html

U.S. Health and Human Services. (2022b). *The HIPAA privacy rule.* https://www.hhs.gov/hipaa/for-professionals/ privacy/index.html

U.S. Health and Human Services Office for Civil Rights. (2021). *HIPAA for professionals.* https://www.hhs.gov/hipaa/for-professionals/index.html

U.S. Health & Human Services. (2023). *Summary of the HIPAA Privacy Rule.* https://www.hhs.gov/hipaa/for-professionals/privacy/laws-regulations/index.html

Van Orne, J. (2022). Care coordination for children with medical complexity and caregiver empowerment in the process: A literature review. *Journal for Specialists in Pediatric Nursing, 27*(3), 1. https://onlinelibrary.wiley.com/ doi/10.1111/jspn.12387

von Krough, G., Dale, C., & Nadin, D. (2005). A Framework for Integrating NANDA, NIC, and NOC in electronic patient records. *Journal of Nursing Scholarship, 37*(3), 275–281. https://doi.org/10.1111/j.1547-5069.2005.00047.x

Wang, L. Y., Vernon-Smiley, M., Gapinski, M. A., Desisto, M., Maughan, E., & Sheetz, A. (2014). Cost-benefit study of school nursing services. *JAMA Pediatrics, 168*, 642–648. https://jamanetwork.com/journals/jamapediatrics/ fullarticle/1872779

Warren, J. J. (2017). A big data primer. In C. W. Delaney, C. A. Weaver, J. J. Warren, T. R. Clancy, & R. L. Simpson (Eds.), *Big data-enabled nursing,* (pp. 33–57). Springer.

Wilburn, A. (2018). Nursing informatics: Ethical considerations for adopting electronic records. *NASN School Nurse, 33*(3), 150–153. https://doi.org/10.1177/1942602X17712020

Willgerodt, M., Johnson, K. H., & Helmer, C. (2020). Enhancing care coordination for students with Type 1 Diabetes. *Journal of School Health, 90*, 651–657. https://doi.org/10.1111/josh.12912

Wilson, M. L., Weaver, C. A., Proctor, P. M., & Beene, M. S. (2017). Big data in healthcare: A wide look at a broad subject. In C. W. Delaney, C. A. Weaver, J. J. Warren, T. R. Clancy, & R. L. Simpson (Eds.), *Big data enabled nursing: Education, research and practice* (pp. 11–29). Springer.

Yu, J. A., Henderson, C., Cook, S., & Ray, K. (2020). Family caregivers of children with medical complexity: Health-related quality of life and experiences of care coordination. *Academic Pediatrics*, *20*, 1116–1123. https://doi.org/10.1016/j.acap.2020.06.014

Zhang, T., Wu, X., Peng, G. Q. Z., Chen, L., & Cai, Z. (2021). Effectiveness of standardized nursing terminologies for nursing practice and healthcare outcomes: A systematic review. *International Journal of Nursing Knowledge*, *32*, 220–228. https://doi.org/10.1111/2047-3095.12315

Chapter 11

STUDENT NURSES: SCHOOL NURSE PRECEPTOR RESPONSIBILITIES

Dawn Lambert, PhD, RN

DESCRIPTION OF ISSUE

School nurses have valuable knowledge and experiences to share with undergraduate and graduate nursing students. Experiential learning opportunities in the school setting are essential for preparing students in the specialty practice area of school nursing. School nurses are positive role models for students at all levels of education and a valuable resource in the educational process. For school nurses serving in the preceptor role to have a positive experience when partnering with student nurses, it is essential to have a signed agreement or contract with the university (i.e., the school of nursing [SON]), clear goals and objectives from the university for the student experience, and guidance on ways to lessen exposure to liability concerns when in the preceptor role. This formal agreement/contract may go by various terminology like Memorandum of Understanding (MOU) or Letter of Agreement (LOA), but conceptually it's a legally enforceable document. For the purposes of this chapter, MOU will be used to reflect this formal agreement/contract.

BACKGROUND

In the United States, each state and territory has a governmental agency, usually called a board of nursing (BON), that establishes standards and regulations for nursing education and practice. To this end, school nurse preceptors must be familiar with their state nurse practice act and state laws, rules, and regulations that provide the legal foundation for nursing practice. Additionally, school nurses must follow the professional standards for the profession of nursing and specialty practice area of school nursing, which guide the application of knowledge to practice. The American Nurses Association (ANA) has established the Nursing: Scope and Standards of Practice (2021). The ANA has approved the School Nursing Scope and Standards of Practice developed by the National Association of School Nurses (NASN, 2022).

In addition to understanding the regulations and standards that govern and guide their practice, school nurses must also understand their role as a preceptor when that additional responsibility is required of them. In the preceptor role, school nurses are called upon to teach, mentor, assess learning, and provide feedback to nursing students (L'Ecuyer et al., 2018). Some challenges school nurses face in the preceptor role include lack of orientation, time constraints, and unclear expectations of the role. It is essential for schools of nursing and academic nurse educators who are placing students in school health settings to establish an agreement (MOU) with clear expectations for the student placement, provide orientation to the school nurse preceptor as well as ongoing support throughout the practicum experience.

IMPLICATIONS FOR SCHOOL NURSE PRACTICE

There are many benefits and challenges associated with the role of precepting nursing students, especially in the school health setting. Some benefits include providing exposure to nursing roles and experiences that students may not have had previous exposure to, expanding the profession of school nursing, and enjoying personal satisfaction from sharing valuable knowledge and insight. Some challenges include a lack of understanding of academic and clinical faculty expectations for a particular student/nursing program and additional demands on already limited time and resources. Furthermore, some school nurse preceptors may have concerns and confusion about the legal aspects of their role in providing experiential learning opportunities for nursing students.

Nurse Practice Act/Scope and Standards

School nurses must be familiar with their state nurse practice act. Each state defines supervision, delegation, roles, and responsibilities differently. Additionally, school nurses must thoroughly understand *Nursing: Scope and Standards of Practice* and the specialty publication *School Nursing: Scope and Standards of Practice.*

Nursing License

Regarding litigation, it is essential to remember that student nurses and licensed nurses are held accountable to the same standards of nursing care when providing care (Pozgar, 2020). It is a common misnomer that student nurses are practicing "under the license" of their faculty or preceptor. This phrase attempts to describe the accountability for practice and authority of a BON to discipline an individual based upon their ownership of their nursing license. Only the person named on the license is practicing "under" that license (Brooks, 2017). The academic nursing faculty and nursing preceptor are responsible for ensuring the student is supervised appropriately regarding their current education and skill level. School nurses being asked to supervise student nurses should receive clear information about the current level of education, expectations for the experience, and the level of responsibility the student will have during the precepted experience (Willey, 2018). The preceptor or faculty member may be liable for a student's action or failure to act, especially if the preceptor or faculty member had not intervened when necessary or failed to provide appropriate supervision or instruction (Brooks, 2017).

Professional Liability Insurance

It is strongly recommended that school nurses obtain their own professional liability insurance. While school nurses may be protected under their employer's insurance, this may not always be the case if negligence or failure to supervise a student properly is a factor (Brooks, 2017; Willey, 2018). The professional liability policies need to also include coverage for licensure defense matters, as opposed to simply professional negligence, since the reality is that the risk of licensure defense for nurses is much greater than malpractice lawsuits.

(*Please refer to Chapter 2 for more information on professional liability*).

Policies and Procedures

School nurses should ensure that all policies and procedures related to school nursing practice in their district/ building are up to date and based on current evidence. They should be familiar with the policies and procedures and confirm that the academic faculty and student understand them, know where to locate them during the clinical experience, and have the opportunity to ask clarifying questions about the policies and procedures. School nurses should know the process and procedure for student placement in the district/building for the clinical experience. Usually, a formal agreement between the school district and the academic institution/school of nursing is required. These documents are often standardized and approved by the legal counsel of both parties. School nurses must verify that this agreement is in place prior to students engaging in the practicum experience. Knowing and following the policies is often the best protection against a lawsuit.

Communication

Before beginning the practicum experience, school nurses should communicate with the academic clinical faculty and students to determine the expectations for the practicum and the student's learning needs. Clear communication with the academic institution/school of nursing is essential to ensure that necessary documentation, including a MOU and required clearances, is in place prior to the start of the practicum experience. It is also important that school nurse preceptors obtain a copy of the student's course syllabus, including the learning objectives, and that they discuss any required or suggested practicum experiences with the student and faculty.

As students begin their practicum experiences, school nurses should assess students for their level of competency/comfort prior to delegating a task. Competency and comfort will vary depending on the student's educational level and degree program. For example, a graduate nursing student with ten years of experience in an acute care setting will likely have high confidence in assessing a student experiencing shortness of breath. A student in a pre-licensure program will need much more guidance, support, and verification of assessment findings. In another example, the academic faculty member should be present for students who have not demonstrated competency in immunization administration in order for the student to participate in a school-based immunization clinic. This is a higher-level skill, and the school nurse may not have time to provide the appropriate level of supervision for the students giving immunizations due to the other demands simultaneously placed on school nurses during special clinics. Additionally, some state SON regulations may prohibit student nurses from administering medication/immunizations unless under the direct supervision of the academic faculty member.

Documentation

School nurses should also carefully document to protect themselves from legal liability concerns (Willey, 2018). Prior to the practicum experience, school nurses should verify their school policy and the partnering educational institution's policy for supervision of documentation or signing notes. If the partnering institution requires the academic faculty to be there to sign a note or other documentation record, an alternative opportunity can be given to the student to practice the skill. For example, if the academic/clinical faculty is required to co-sign a student's documentation and the faculty is not available, the student could practice documentation in a way that does not involve the actual student record. The school nurse preceptor could then provide feedback on that learning activity without violating policies while providing the student with a valuable learning experience.

(For additional information, please refer to Chapter 1 for more information on licensure and Chapter 2 for more information on malpractice and professional liability).

CONCLUSION

School nurses have a valuable role in partnering with educational institutions to provide experiential learning opportunities to undergraduate and graduate students. In addition to providing knowledge and mentorship, school nurses have the opportunity to reflect on their early days in the specialty practice area of school nursing and encourage students to consider school nursing practice. Although the legal aspects of partnering with an educational institution to precept a student nurse may seem daunting, proper preparation and consideration of these legal aspects can decrease the potential prospect of liability in the preceptor role. Mentoring undergraduate and graduate students is essential to advancing the professional nursing practice specialty in school health.

RESOURCES

National Association of School Nurses. (2018). *The role of the 21st century school nurse (*Position Statement). NASN.

REFERENCES

American Nurses Association. (2021). *Nursing: Scope and standards of practice* (4th ed). American Nurses Association.

Brooks, K. L. (2017). Issues of liability: The myth of another working under the nurse's license. *New Mexico Nurse, 62*(3), 5. https://www.nursingald.com/articles/18652-issues-of-liability-the-myth-of-another-working-under-the-nurse-s-license

L'Ecuyer, K. M., von der Lancken, S., Malloy, D., Meyer, G., & Hyde, M. (2018). Review of state boards of nursing rules and regulations for nurse preceptors. *Journal of Nursing Education, 57*(3), 134 -141. http://doi.org/10.3928/01484834-20180221-02

National Association of School Nurses. (2022). *School nursing: Scope and standards of practice* (4th ed.). National Association of School Nurses.

Pozgar, G. D. (2020). *Legal and ethical issues for health professionals* (5th ed.) Jones and Bartlett Learning.

Willey, J. (2018). Legal implications for student nurses and preceptors. *DNA Reporter, 43*(2), 5. http://nursingald.com/articles/20580-legal-implications-for-student-nurses-and-preceptors

LAWS/POLICIES

The following section of the book is dedicated to discussing the educational and health laws related to school health. Some topics included are Family Educational Rights and Privacy Act, Health Insurance Portability and Accountability Act, Individuals with Disabilities Education Act, Child Protection laws, and Do Not Attempt to Resuscitate statutes and policies.

This section is foundational to understanding the context for health services and standards at a broad level. Primarily federal standards and laws are described and set the stage for many individual state and local laws, regulations, and policies. Having a foundational knowledge of these topics will allow the reader to identify conflicts and potential concerns quickly, understand overlaps, and help avoid legal errors.

Chapter 12

FAMILY EDUCATIONAL RIGHTS AND PRIVACY ACT ("FERPA")/HEALTH INSURANCE PORTABILITY AND ACCOUNTABILITY ACT ("HIPAA")

Attorney Marc C. Lombardi*

Attorney Gwen J. Zittoun*
Shipman & Goodwin LLP

DESCRIPTION OF ISSUE

The confidentiality of student records within the educational environment is a topic fraught with legal and practical implications that present a constant struggle for school nurses, administrators, and other school personnel. While the importance of maintaining the confidentiality of personally identifiable information (PII) cannot be emphasized enough, it must be balanced in the school environment with the need for educational professionals to have access to information necessary to appropriately and effectively educate students and the right of parents/guardians and eligible students to access education records.

The Federal Educational Rights and Privacy Act (FERPA) and the Health Insurance Portability and Accountability Act (HIPAA) are the two major federal laws addressing the confidentiality of school or health records. While state laws may also address confidentiality requirements and include stricter requirements than federal law, state law cannot conflict with federal law. HIPAA is widely known and understood to be the law governing medical records, while FERPA protects the confidentiality and integrity of students' education records. **However, what is surprising to many is that, as a general rule (to which there is always an exception), HIPAA does not apply to student health records. Rather, FERPA governs the confidentiality and access to all education records, which includes student health records, when a school district creates or maintains, and receives them.**

BACKGROUND

FERPA - At A Glance

Congress enacted FERPA in 1974 for the purposes of protecting the confidentiality of, and providing access to, education records of students (34 CFR § 99.2). FERPA requires that educational institutions in receipt of federal funding from the U.S. Department of Education (USDE) maintain the confidentiality of personally identifiable information (PII) within education records and permit parental access to inspect and correct such records. An educational institution that does not receive federal funding from the USDE is not subject to the requirements of FERPA. Private elementary and secondary schools that do not receive such funding may not be required to comply with FERPA but may be guided by state laws and principles of contract and negligence in their management of student records (34 C.F.R. § 99.1). For example, a private school may -- but is not required by federal law to -- include aspects of the FERPA rules in its enrollment contracts and student handbooks, thereby creating a contractual obligation to comply with this aspect of federal law.

*Original authors: Attorney William J. Roberts & Attorney Gwen J. Zittoun with acknowledgment to Attorney Laura A. Fisher for her research and writing assistance (2017)

FERPA is administered by the Student Privacy Policy Office (SPPO), formerly known as the Family Policy Compliance Office (FPCO), in the USDE (20 U.S.C. § 1232g). The SPPO accepts complaints related to the application of FERPA and issues letters to interested parties explaining the law's applicability to individual factual scenarios. In 2010, the USDE created the Privacy Technical Assistance Center ("PTAC") within the SPPO to serve as a resource to school personnel and other stakeholders concerning FERPA compliance and other student privacy matters. While schools risk the loss of federal funding for failure to comply with FERPA's requirements, a parent or eligible student does not have the right to sue an educational institution for an alleged violation of FERPA (*Gonzaga University v. Doe* (2002), holding that parent/guardian(s) and eligible students have no private right of action to enforce FERPA).

FERPA contains two explicit provisions:
1. Mandates the confidentiality of PII in education records, subject to limited exceptions for disclosure (20 U.S.C. § 1232g(b)); and
2. Grants parents (parents include "a natural parent, a guardian, or an individual acting as a parent in the absence of a parent or a guardian," 34 C.F.R. § 99.3) the right to inspect and review education records of their students and make corrections where the records are inaccurate, misleading, or otherwise in violation of privacy rights of students (20 U.S.C. § 1232g(a)(2)).

This parental right of access applies to both custodial and non-custodial parents. Both parents have full access rights under FERPA unless and until the school district is provided evidence of the revocation of that right by a court order, state statute, or legally binding document (34 C.F.R. § 99.4). These rights of access and amendment transfer to the student upon attainment of the age of eighteen or enrollment in a postsecondary institution (making the student an "eligible student" under FERPA, 20 U.S.C. § 1232g(d)).

Importantly, FERPA's confidentiality provision is limited to education **records**, which are defined rather broadly as records that are directly related to a student and maintained by an educational agency or institution or by a party acting for the agency or institution, which may include a health department providing school nurse services (34 C.F.R. § 99.3). If the student information is not actually documented (for example, if the information is provided verbally or by observation and is not otherwise included in a document), it is not covered by FERPA. The definition of education records excludes those kept in the sole possession of the maker, which are only used as a personal memory aid and are not accessible or revealed to any other person except an individual serving as a temporary substitute. However, if the owner of the document reveals the document to any other individual, the document may be considered an education record if it meets the other criteria contained in the definition (34 C.F.R. § 99.3).

Interestingly, it is not the education records themselves that FERPA protects, but the PII included within those records. Indeed, under some circumstances, schools may be required to produce education records pursuant to a state's public records law; however, any PII must be redacted from those records prior to disclosure unless an exception applies. Under FERPA, PII includes the following: a student's name, birth date, address, parents' names, and mother's maiden name. PII also includes information linked or linkable to a specific student that would lead a reasonable person within the school community to know the student's identity (34 C.F.R. § 99.3). Finally, PII also includes student-specific information relating to a "targeted request." A school district is prohibited from releasing documents, even if cleaned of identifying information, to an individual who the school "reasonably believes knows the identity of the student to whom the education record relates" (34 C.F.R. § 99.3, See the definition of "personally identifiable information" at (g)).

Schools must notify parents and eligible students annually of their rights under FERPA. Specifically, schools must notify parents and eligible students of the right: to inspect and review education records and the procedures to do so; to seek amendment of records the parent or eligible student believes are inaccurate and the procedures to so do; to consent to disclosures of education records, except to the extent that FERPA authorizes disclosure without consent; and to file a complaint with SPPO concerning potential violations. Schools must also provide annual notice to parents of the types of student information that it releases publicly. This type of student information, commonly referred to as "directory information," is addressed later in this chapter. Additionally, federal law requires that parents be notified that the school routinely discloses names, addresses, and telephone numbers to military recruiters upon request, subject to a parent's request not to disclose such information without written consent. Finally, this notice must include that disclosure of PII without consent is permitted to school officials with a legitimate educational interest, the criteria for determining who constitutes a school official, and what constitutes a legitimate educational interest.

HIPAA - At A Glance

HIPAA is a federal law that, among other things, governs the use, disclosure, maintenance, and protection of patient health information. In the context of HIPAA, patient information (also referred to as protected health information or "PHI") is defined broadly to include virtually any record certain individuals or entities maintain about a person's past, present, or future health care, health status or payment for healthcare services (45 C.F.R. § 160.103). However, HIPAA does not apply to every entity in the healthcare field.

HIPAA applies to only those individuals and entities known as *"covered entities"* and their respective *"business associates."* It is important to note that unless a person or entity meets one of these very technical definitions, they are not subject to HIPAA and are not required to comply with its voluminous rules and regulations.

A covered entity is a health insurance plan, a healthcare clearinghouse (i.e., an intermediary information processor), or a healthcare provider that conducts certain transactions, such as electronic billing for patient services (45 C.F.R. § 160.103). However, a healthcare provider that is not paid for providing services in the normal course of business or does not transmit information electronically in connection with reimbursement-related transactions is not a covered entity and is not required to comply with HIPAA. A business associate is a vendor of a covered entity that creates, receives, maintains, or transmits PHI for or on behalf of the covered entity during the course of the services it provides (45 C.F.R. § 160.103). For example, a physician's practice may provide PHI to a lawyer or consultant for compliance work or may utilize a cloud storage company to maintain patient records. In these examples, the lawyer, consultant, and cloud storage company would be business associates of the physician and, therefore, subject to HIPAA.

For those subject to HIPAA, its rules and requirements can be grouped into three categories:
*   The first is the *"Privacy Rule,"* which is an extensive set of regulations governing how covered entities and business associates may use and disclose PHI and establishing the rights individuals have to access, amend, restrict access to, and obtain information about their PHI.

- The *"Security Rule"* establishes the physical, technical, and administrative safeguards a covered entity and business associate must utilize in order to protect the confidentiality and integrity of the electronic PHI they maintain.
- The third component is the *"Breach Notification Rule."* This regulation defines when an inadvertent or unauthorized use or disclosure of PHI constitutes a data breach and sets forth how a covered entity or business associate must react when such a breach is discovered, including providing notice to impacted individuals, the media, and governmental authorities (45 C.F.R. §§ 164.400-414).

In the normal course, HIPAA's privacy, security, and breach notification rules do not apply to the student health records created or maintained by schools. Often, a school is not a HIPAA-covered entity because it does not perform HIPAA transactions (such as electronically billing an insurer) or because the student health records it maintains do not contain information constituting PHI. In recognition of FERPA, HIPAA specifically excludes from its scope any information that is also student health information contained within education records protected by FERPA. In other words, if FERPA applies to a particular record, HIPAA does not. Section 3 of this chapter will discuss exceptions to the general rule and present several instances in which HIPAA may apply in the public school setting.

IMPLICATIONS FOR SCHOOL NURSE PRACTICE

The management of student records impacts the daily practice of school nurses. While school nurses must keep in mind the need to maintain the confidentiality of education records, they must also address the need for other school professionals and parents to have access to those records under certain circumstances.

School personnel are encouraged to review their school district policies and any applicable state requirements concerning student confidentiality and student records and to review the specific procedural requirements of FERPA. The vast extent of this law runs beyond the scope of this chapter. However, simply put, for schools to disclose PII from education records that are within the purview of FERPA, either a parent or an eligible student must consent explicitly in writing to the disclosure, or one of several statutory exceptions to the consent requirement must apply (20 U.S.C. §§ 1232g(b)(1) -(2)). As with many laws, the exceptions under FERPA are extensive and may impact the day-to-day work of school nurses.

Confidentiality

1. *No Access by Third Parties without Parental Consent*

> Under FERPA, disclosure of PII, outside of directory information, within education records is authorized only when parents or eligible students provide written consent to the disclosure or a statutory exception applies (20 U.S.C. § 1232g (b)(1) -(2); 34 C.F.R. § 99.30). The signed, dated, written consent must specify which records may be disclosed, the purpose of the disclosure, and the party to whom the disclosure may be made (34 C.F.R. § 99.30(b)).

> As related to this limitation on disclosure, FERPA requires schools to institute security protections to prevent the unauthorized release of PII (34 C.F.R. § 99.31(1)(ii)). Schools must, either physically or electronically, prevent access to third parties and school professionals who do not have a legitimate educational interest in the PII. Practically, this means securing paper records in locked or otherwise

restricted locations and including password protection or other security measures on electronically-stored information. School nurses should take further steps to protect PII, specifically as related to discussing or reviewing confidential information in areas where third parties may be present, whether while on the telephone, using the computer, or providing treatment to students.

2. *Exceptions to Parental Consent*

FERPA includes a variety of narrowly tailored exceptions to the general confidentiality requirement. If an exception applies, parental consent is not required prior to the release of PII contained within education records, although some exceptions require parental notification or review of records being disclosed. Some of these exceptions include disclosure to another school where the student seeks or intends to enroll; in connection with financial aid applications; to a state official pursuant to statute; pursuant to a court order or subpoena; to accrediting institutions; and to organizations conducting studies for or on behalf of educational agencies to develop, validate, or administer predictive tests, administer student aid programs, or improve instruction (34 C.F.R. § 99.31).

Subject to certain exceptions, schools must maintain a record of each request for access to and each disclosure of PII from the education records of each student, as well as the names of state and local educational authorities and federal officials and agencies listed in 34 C.F.R. § 99.31(a)(3) that may make further disclosures of PII from students' education records **without consent**. The school must maintain this record with the student's education records as long as the education records are maintained.

Schools do not have to record disclosures of PII from education records that were made to:
1) the parent or eligible student;
2) a school official under § 99.31(a)(1);
3) a party with written consent from the parent or eligible student;
4) a party seeking directory information; or
5) a party seeking or receiving records in accordance with the provisions in FERPA related to disclosures pursuant to certain types of subpoenas or court orders as set forth in § 99.31(a)(9)(ii)(A)-(C). See § 99.32(d).

Explanations and examples of the most commonly used exceptions for school nurses are provided below (**note:** a complete explanation of the entire list of exceptions goes beyond the scope of this chapter and may require reviewing resources provided or consultation with the school district administration and legal counsel).

a. Legitimate Educational Interest

The most commonly used exception is disclosure to school officials, including teachers, within the school whom the school has determined to have legitimate educational interests in the PII (34 C.F.R. § 99.31(a)(1)(i)(A)). The applicable statute or regulations do not define the term school official; however, the SPPO generally interprets the term to include parties such as professors, instructors, administrators, health staff, counselors, and others. Contractors, consultants, volunteers, or other parties to whom the school has outsourced institutional services may also be considered school officials if they meet additional elements provided by the regulations (34 C.F.R. § 99.31(a)(1)(i)(B)). School officials are generally deemed to have legitimate educational interests when they need to review an education record as part of their professional responsibilities (FPCO, Letter to Anonymous, 2017). Care must be taken to ensure that such officials obtain access only to those education records in which they have a legitimate educational interest (34 C.F.R. § 99.31(a)(1)(ii)).

Most importantly, this exception allows a teacher, administrator, counselor, school nurse, or other school professional access to a student's PII if that individual has a legitimate professional interest in viewing the information. For example, a teacher attending a meeting pursuant to Section 504 of the Rehabilitation Act ("Section 504") for a student with a peanut allergy may have a legitimate educational interest in reviewing that student's health information, as that teacher would be required to participate in the meeting and understand the nature of the student's health issues relative to the student's educational needs. Also, members of an individualized education program (IEP) team may have a legitimate educational interest in reviewing a psychiatric evaluation for a student identified with an emotional disturbance. Schools and individuals working within the school should ensure that appropriate safeguards are used to protect education records; however, all school professionals must be aware that other professionals within the school are able to access education records without parent consent if such access is legitimately related to the performance of the individual's professional responsibilities.

While recognizing the importance of monitoring proper access to and disclosure of students' education records, it is also necessary to balance those interests in complying with other education laws. Specifically, while schools must ensure the confidentiality of student information, schools must also comply with laws such as the Individuals with Disabilities Education Act, Section 504, and the Americans with Disabilities Act. Compliance with these laws generally requires implementing educational programs and accommodation plans specific to the unique needs of students. Schools must ensure that appropriate staff have access to the student-specific information necessary to effectively meet student needs.

b. Parents of Dependent Students

Once a student reaches age eighteen or attends a postsecondary institution, that student becomes eligible under FERPA, and the rights transfer to the eligible student. This includes the right to access (and request amendment of) the student's education records. Significantly, however, Congress recognized that with this shift in rights comes serious concern by parents about losing access to educationally related information concerning their children. Thus, another exception. FERPA expressly permits disclosure of education records to parents of dependent students, as defined by the Internal Revenue Code (34 C.F.R. § 99.31(a)(8)). If a parent claims a child on the parent's tax returns after the student turns eighteen, the school may release the student's education records to that parent without the student's written consent. As a practical matter, most students at the secondary level are still claimed as dependents by their parents; thus, although the student can access and request amendment of their record, parents may continue to have access to the records.

c. Health and Safety Emergencies

FERPA has always generally included an exception for the disclosure of PII in the case of a health or safety emergency, which was previously narrowly construed (34 C.F.R. § 99.31(a)(10)). In 2008, however, FERPA was amended to clarify that an educational agency or institution may disclose PII from an education record to appropriate parties, including parents of an eligible student, in connection with an emergency if knowledge of the information is necessary to protect the health or safety of the student or other individuals (34 C.F.R. § 99.36(a)). In determining whether such disclosure is necessary for health or safety reasons, the school may consider the totality of the circumstances pertaining to a threat to the health or safety of a student or other individuals (34 C.F.R. § 99.36(c)). If it is determined that there is an articulable and significant threat to the health or safety of a student or other individuals, the school may make the disclosure necessary to protect the health or safety of those involved (34 C.F.R. § 99.36(c)). As long as there is a rational basis for the school's determination of an articulable and significant threat, and the school has documented the articulable threat, the USDE will not substitute its own judgment for the educational agency with regard to the decision to release PII (34 C.F.R. § 99.36(c)). The USDE discusses additional confirmation of this in guidance letters and by the USDE's commentary on the federal regulations (See SPPO, Letter to Anonymous, 2021 discussing the health and safety emergency exception in the context of the COVID-19 pandemic; and 73 Fed. Reg. 74.838, 2008, states that threats need not be verbal but must be articulable by institution when it makes and records the disclosure).

The importance of this exception cannot be underscored enough. A health and safety emergency may include, for example, a significant medical issue concerning an individual student. School officials may inform emergency responders, police, and fire personnel of any appropriate PII for the health and safety of that student. This may include the student's medical information (allergies, chronic conditions, etc.), parent(s) name(s), address, etc. This exception may also be applicable in a school-wide crisis or significant threat where the health and safety of all students is at issue. Schools should be cautious, however, to ensure that emergency personnel receive PII only if this or another exception is applicable rather than as a convenience.

d. Directory Information

Provided that the district has designated certain types of information to be directory information, a school is permitted to release such information to a third party without parent consent. Directory information is information contained in a student's educational record that would not generally be considered harmful or an invasion of privacy if disclosed (34 C.F.R. § 99.3). Examples of directory information include a student's name, address, telephone listing, electronic mail address, photograph, place and date of birth, major field of study, grade level, enrollment status, dates of attendance, participation in officially recognized activities and sports, weight, and height of members of athletic teams, degrees, honors, and awards received, and the most recent educational agency or institution attended (34 C.F.R. § 99.3). Directory information does not generally include a student's social security number or student identification number (But see 34 C.F.R. § 99.3 under the definition of directory information (c)(1) and (2)).

Importantly and as addressed earlier in this chapter, the school must provide proper notice to parents of the designation of information as directory information and allow parents the opportunity to opt out of such release (34 C.F.R. § 99.37). Thus, for example, while a school may publish student names and awards received in the town newspaper without parent consent (e.g., honor roll list), the school is prohibited from putting the name and award of a student in the newspaper if the student's parent has opted-out of the release of such information (FPCO, Letter to Jett, 2012, which outlined procedures for designation and parental opt-out provisions with regard to directory information).

Access

Under FERPA, parents or eligible students have the right to access the student's education records upon request. FERPA does not require that parents or eligible students receive copies of education records, although state laws may include such provisions. The school must provide the requesting party the opportunity to inspect and review the education records within 45 calendar days of receiving a request, being mindful that shorter timelines may apply for special education records under state law (34 C.F.R. § 99.10(a)and(b)). The educational agency must also respond to reasonable requests for explanations and interpretations of the education records (34 C.F.R. § 99.10(c)). This provision, in practice, generally requires a school district to provide access to parents to any document that directly relates to the student and is maintained by the school district. This includes a student's health records. The access and confidentiality rights under FERPA belong to the parents or eligible students, and, as discussed earlier, a parent may continue to have the right to access student records even after a student turns eighteen under certain circumstances. Of note, FERPA does not apply to information a school official observes that is not otherwise documented in a student's education record (SPPO, Privacy Technical Assistance Center, FERPA Frequently Asked Questions). In those instances, FERPA would not protect the release of information about a student that was obtained through the school official's personal knowledge or observation.

Similarly, FERPA does not include any provisions concerning the role of a school professional in maintaining confidentiality of information received directly from a student. State laws and professional codes of ethics may spell out a professional's obligation to maintain as confidential some information relayed from a student. School nurses and other school health-related professionals must balance the need to maintain the confidence of and build relationships with students with the requirements of FERPA, mandatory reporting obligations relative to abuse and neglect, as well as standards of practice and liability. While state laws/guidance and certain privacy rights (e.g., legal rights of minors) may come into play, FERPA does not require that a school professional maintain, as confidential from a parent, information that a school professional observes or receives directly from a student. For example, if a student were to inform a school nurse that the student intends on running away from home, FERPA does not prohibit the school nurse from informing the student's parents, even if the information is included in an education record.

If the education records at issue contain information pertaining to more than one student, the parent or eligible student may inspect and review only the specific information about their child (34 C.F.R. § 99.12(a)). School professionals may be required to redact education records before sharing them with the parents of a second student, as those parents only have the right to see the information relevant to their child, absent consent from the other parent. If information directly relating to a second student (or multiple students) cannot be redacted or segregated without destroying the meaning of the record, then the parent is permitted to review and inspect the record as a whole, including information concerning the second student (SPPO, Letter to Wachter, 2017 opining that, where multiple students were involved in a hazing incident visible in part on a surveillance video and the school could not redact student information, the video was an education record of each student about whom the video was directly related.

Amendment

Parents and eligible students also have the right to request amendment of education records where those records are inaccurate or misleading or are a violation of the student's rights of privacy (34 C.F.R. § 99.20(a)). The school must consider a request to amend and, if it decides not to amend in accordance with the request, must inform the parents or eligible student of their right to a hearing on the issue within a reasonable time (34 C.F.R. § 99.20(c)). If the educational agency, as a result of the hearing, deems the information to be inaccurate, misleading, or otherwise in violation of the privacy rights of the student, it shall amend the record accordingly and inform the parent or eligible student of such amendment in writing (34 C.F.R. § 99.21(b)(1)). If, after the hearing, the school affirms its decision not to amend the records, the parents or student have the right to insert into the record a statement outlining their views (34 C.F.R. § 99.21(b)(2)). If such a statement is placed into the records, it must be maintained as long as the record is maintained, usually in accordance with state statute or regulation concerning record retention (34 C.F.R. § 99.21(c)). The school district must then disclose the parent statement with the associated education record whenever that education record is disclosed (34 C.F.R. § 99.21(c)(2)).

When Does HIPAA Come into Play?

As discussed previously, in general, the practice of the traditional school nurse employed by the school is not subject to HIPAA. While the school nurse may be subject to state law or codes of professional ethics governing patient confidentiality, neither the school nor the nurse is obligated to comply with the HIPAA Privacy Rule with respect to the student health information maintained in education records covered by FERPA. However, there are scenarios in which school nurses must be aware of HIPAA's requirements and, in some instances, may even be subject to them.

1. Interactions with Healthcare Professionals

    The most common instance in which school nurses encounter HIPAA is when medical records of a student must be provided by a healthcare provider to the school. Generally, a healthcare provider is prohibited from disclosing a patient's medical records to a third party, including the school, without first obtaining a HIPAA-compliant authorization from the patient (45 C.F.R.

§ 164.508). State laws may also require specific consent for certain types of information, including behavioral health, sexually transmitted disease or infection, genetic, or substance abuse information. While many healthcare providers will require the use of their own forms, schools should consider adopting their own authorization form in compliance with HIPAA and applicable state law, which can be distributed to students, families, and healthcare providers. This may facilitate the receipt of a student's medical records from a provider.

Despite the general rule, there are two instances in which a healthcare provider may disclose a student's PHI to a school nurse <u>without</u> first receiving a HIPAA-compliant authorization. **First, HIPAA permits a healthcare provider to disclose a student's health information to school nurses, physicians, or other healthcare providers for purposes of treating the student** unless state law (as noted above) requires consent, even for treatment purposes (45 C.F.R. § 164.506(c)(2)). HIPAA defines treatment broadly, and this exception would permit, for example, a healthcare provider to discuss a student's medication regime with the school nurse who will administer the medications without first obtaining an authorization (45 C.F.R. § 164.501). School nurses familiar with this exception can remind healthcare providers of their treatment role at the school and educate providers on their right to disclose student information without an authorization which may save valuable time when information is needed quickly, but an authorization cannot be obtained.

The second exception relates to school immunization records. HIPAA permits a healthcare provider to disclose immunization records of a student directly to a school without a HIPAA compliant authorization if the school is required by law to have such records prior to admitting the student and the student's parent or guardian agrees to the disclosure (45 C.F.R. §164.512(b) (1)(vi)). If the student is an adult or emancipated minor, the agreement of the student is required. Although typically a written authorization is required by HIPAA, the agreement in the context of immunization records may be verbal and does not need to be signed or include the numerous elements necessary to constitute a HIPAA-compliant authorization (45 C.F.R. §164.512(b)(1)(vi)). When disclosing immunization records pursuant to this exception, the healthcare provider may disclose the records to whomever the parent or school designates. Unlike disclosures for treatment purposes, immunization records need not be provided to a specific healthcare provider within the school.

Schools wishing to take advantage of the flexibility offered by the immunization records exception may consider the development of educational materials for healthcare providers to inform them of the exception and its relationship to information needed by schools (i.e., the school is required by law to have such records prior to admitting the student). Schools may also develop a protocol to assist in obtaining the "agreement" required by the exception or forms that would allow a healthcare provider to document such agreement.

2. School-Based Health Centers

In the typical school-based health center arrangement, a healthcare provider (often a community clinic or hospital) establishes healthcare services on school premises to treat or provide specific services to students. These arrangements often present several HIPAA-related challenges for school nursing staff.

School staff must be cognizant of the center's status as a distinct entity that is permitted to share a student's PHI only in accordance with HIPAA and state law, as outlined above. Accordingly, a school-based health center's disclosures of PHI to the school will be limited to instances of treatment or when an authorization has been executed. While it may appear from the student's perspective that the school and the healthcare provider are integrated within the school-based health center – they are not. Therefore, it is important to maintain logical and physical separation between the school and the healthcare provider. This is essential because the provider is subject to HIPAA and the school staff are not, while the school is subject to FERPA and the provider is not. To avoid inadvertent disclosures of PHI, think of the healthcare provider as a "tenant" may help encapsulate or "firewall" the services provided within the school-based health center.

In addition, the school must carefully consider the administrative services it will provide in support of the school-based health center. Specifically, a school must be aware that providing certain services may make the school a HIPAA "business associate" and thus subject to HIPAA's privacy, security, and breach notification rules. For example, if a school were to volunteer to maintain the center's medical records in a school closet, the school would be a business associate. Further, if the school agreed to shred documents containing PHI from the center (e.g., lab test results and billing information), the school would be a business associate. Schools should exercise caution to avoid performing the functions of a business associate under these arrangements to avoid becoming subject to the burdensome requirements of HIPAA because of the relative ease with which a school may be deemed a business associate in this context. (*Please see chapter 47 for more information on SBHCs*).

3. Schools as Covered Entities

While unusual, it is important to acknowledge that as schools expand beyond their traditional healthcare functions and extend the healthcare services they provide to a broader population, it is possible that such schools will be, in part, subject to HIPAA. This is most likely to occur if a school provides health care services and bills a third-party payer for reimbursement for such services. For example, if a school were to provide related services to a student with an IEP and bills Medicaid for such services, the school is considered a "covered entity" because it transmits PHI electronically when submitting a claim for reimbursement (a transaction for which HHS has adopted a transaction standard). Therefore, as a covered entity, the school's healthcare transactions must comply with the HIPAA Transactions and Code Sets Rule (or Transactions Rule). However, even if a school is a covered entity and must comply with the Transactions Rule, as long as the school only maintains health information within "education records" under FERPA, the school is not required to comply with HIPAA's Privacy Rule because FERPA "education records" are explicitly excluded from the definition of "protected health information" under HIPAA.* It is important to keep in mind, however, FERPA's privacy requirements <u>do apply</u> and require written consent from a parent or guardian before disclosing information to Medicaid for purposes of reimbursement. (* See references).

Alternatively, if a school operates a mental health clinic or audiology program that is open to members of the public and bills third-party payers for the services provided, the school would be a HIPAA "covered entity" with respect to that particular program and must comply with all of HIPAA's requirements with respect to the health information of non-students that it creates. Schools contemplating providing services in this manner should consider the implications of compliance with HIPAA and strategies for minimizing the application of HIPAA to the school's operations. Such strategies may include designation as a hybrid entity or carving out HIPAA-covered components in school policies and procedures (45 C.F.R. § 164.105(a)(1)).

CONCLUSION

The maintenance of student confidentiality must be a priority within the school environment. Under limited circumstances, FERPA and HIPAA provide rules on how schools must handle student education records, PII and PHI. School nurses should use these rules to guide their practice, understanding that state law and school district policies and procedures may also come into play in the management of student education records.

RESOURCES

> See:
> ADDENDUM #1- School Nurse Strategies for Protecting Student Privacy
> ADDENDUM #2 Exceptions to Education Records under FERPA

Student Privacy Policy Office: https://studentprivacy.ed.gov/about-us

Student Privacy Policy Office, Privacy Technical Assistance Center: https://studentprivacy.ed.gov/

Student Privacy Policy Office, Privacy Technical Assistance Center, *Frequently Asked Questions:* https://studentprivacy.ed.gov/frequently-asked-questions

United States Department of Education - Protecting Student Privacy: https://studentprivacy.ed.gov/?utm_content=&utm_medium=email&utm_name=&utm_source=govdelivery&utm_term=

United States Department of Health and Human Services, Health Information Privacy: http://www.hhs.gov/hipaa/

Wright's Law - Special Education Caselaw: http://www.wrightslaw.com/caselaw.htm

Case Law

Family Educational Rights and Privacy Act, 20 U.S.C. § 1232g; 34 C.F.R. § 99.1 <u>et seq.</u>

Student Privacy Policy Office. (2021). Letter to Anonymous, 121 LRP 19451

Family Policy Compliance Office. (2017). Letter to Anonymous, 117 LRP 41927

Family Policy Compliance Office. (2012). Letter to Jett, 112 LRP 58495

Student Privacy Policy Office. (2017). Letter to Wachter, 118 LRP 16524

Gonzaga University v. Doe, 122 S. Ct. 2268 (2002)

Health Insurance Portability and Accountability Act of 1996, 45 C.F.R. § § 160, 162 and 164

REFERENCES

HIPAA Omnibus Rulemaking, 78 Fed. Reg. 5566 - 5702 (2013, January 25). www.gpo.gov/fdsys/pkg/FR-2013-01-25/pdf/2013-01073.pdf

HIPAA Privacy Rule, 65 Fed. Reg. 82462 – 82829. (2000, December 28). www.hhs.gov/sites/default/files/ocr/privacy/hipaa/administrative/privacyrule/prdecember2000all8parts.pdf

HIPAA Privacy Rule Modifications, 67 Fed. Reg. 53182 – 53273. (2002, August 14). www.hhs.gov/sites/default/files/ocr/privacy/hipaa/administrative/privacyrule/privrulepd.pdf

HIPAA Security Rule, 68 Fed. Reg. 8334 – 8381. (2003, February 20). www.hhs.gov/sites/default/files/ocr/privacy/hipaa/administrative/securityrule/securityrulepdf.pdf

*United States Department of Public Health and Human Services and United States Department of Education. (2019). *Joint guidance on the application of the Family Educational Rights and Privacy Act (FERPA) and the Health Insurance Portability and Accountability Act of 1996 (HIPAA) to student health records.* https://www.hhs.gov/sites/default/files/2019-hipaa-ferpa-joint-guidance.pdf

ADDENDUM #1

School Nurse Strategies for Protecting Student Privacy

Martha Dewey Bergren, DNS, RN, NCSN, APHN-BC, FNASN, FASHA, FAAN

Meeting the privacy requirements for students' personally identifiable health information is an important responsibility for a school nurse. School nurses must balance the need to keep a student healthy against the unnecessary release of information. In addition to developing an understanding of the Family Education Rights and Privacy Act (FERPA) and Health Insurance Portability and Accountability Act (HIPAA) requirements, three strategies will decrease anxiety when sharing information while protecting student privacy.

First, plan ahead. Before the school year begins, prepare the FERPA release or exchange of information authorizations for any student with a care plan or receiving medications or treatments during the school day. Standards of nursing practice demand that the nurse be able to communicate with a provider who has input into the student's plan of care or who has prescribed treatments or medication. If the exchange of information has been signed proactively, there will be no delay when a consultation is needed.

Second, partner with parents/guardians to ensure that the plan of care is communicated with all who are charged with the student's safety or who must respond if a student's condition exacerbates. Parents/guardians should participate in the plan of care, including weighing in on who should receive the plan.

Third, when asked to aggregate health data, be sure to strip all identifiers from the report:

- Name
- Address
- Date and place of birth
- Telephone numbers
- Fax number
- Email address
- Social Security Number
- Medical record number
- Health plan beneficiary number
- Account number
- Student number
- Certificate or license number
- Any vehicle or other device serial number
- Web URL
- Internet Protocol (IP) Address
- Finger or voice print
- Photograph
- Any other characteristic that could uniquely identify the individual

The Department of Education Privacy Technical Assistance Center (PTAC) provides guidance on student privacy practices and steps for deidentification (PTAC, 2013).

School nurses have many resources to appropriately safeguard student privacy. In addition to the Department of Education PTAC, the National Association of School Nurses (NASN) provides student privacy webinars and other resources readily available on the NASN website (NASN, n.d.). If your state has a state school nurse consultant, they can provide assistance in meeting federal and state-specific privacy laws (National Association of State School Nurse Consultants, n.d.). With preparation and prudence, school nurses are well-equipped for the challenge of protecting their students' privacy.

REFERENCES

National Association of School Nurses. (2020). *HIPAA and FERPA*. NASN. https://www.nasn.org/nasn/nasn-resources/professional-topics/school-health-documentation/hipaa-ferpa

National Association of State School Nurse Consultants. (n.d.). *Welcome to the National Association of State School Nurse Consultants*. https://nassnc.clubexpress.com/

Privacy Technical Assistance. (2013). *Data deidentification: An overview of basic terms*. U.S. Department of Education, Privacy Technical Center. http://ptac.ed.gov/sites/default/files/data_deidentification_terms.pdf

U.S. Department of Health and Human Services. (2022). *Guidance regarding methods for de-identification of protected health information in accordance with the Health Insurance Portability and Accountability Act (HIPAA) Privacy Rule*. https://www.hhs.gov/hipaa/for-professionals/privacy/special-topics/de-identification/

ADDENDUM #2

Exceptions to "Education Records" under FERPA

Erin D. Gilsbach, Esquire, 2017

A school may maintain some records that contain personally identifiable information but are specifically exempted from the definition of "education records" under FERPA. Those records are:

1. **Sole-Possession Records.** To qualify as a sole-possession record, the record must be:
   a. Used only as a personal memory aid; and
   b. Not be accessible or revealed to any person other than a temporary substitute.

2. **Law Enforcement Records.** Some schools have law enforcement units, such as school resource officers (SROs), the officers of which have full law enforcement authority, including the authority to conduct a criminal investigation and arrest. Records from school law enforcement are exempt only if they are:
   a. Created by a law enforcement unit;
   b. Created for law enforcement purposes; and
   c. Maintained by the law enforcement unit.

3. **Employment Records.** There are times when an employee's file may contain personally-identifiable information about a student, such as a worker's compensation claim that resulted after an employee intervened in a fight between two students. Employment records that contain PII are not "education records" subject to FERPA if they:
   a. Are made and maintained in the normal course of business;
   b. Relate exclusively to the individual in that individual's capacity as an employee; and
   c. Are not available for use for any other purpose.
      *Student employment records *are* "education records" subject to FERPA.

4. **Post-Attendance Records.** Any records that a school has received after a student graduates or transfers out of a school, if they are not directly related to the individual's attendance as a student, are not considered education records.

5. **Peer-Graded Scores.** Scores/grades on peer-graded papers are not education records until the teacher has recorded them.

6. **Treatment Records.** There is also an exception for what are commonly termed 'treatment records,' although this exception typically does not apply at the K-12 level. For the 'treatment records' exception to apply:
   • The student must be 18 or older or attending a postsecondary school;
   • Made or maintained by a physician, psychiatrist, psychologist, or other recognized professional or paraprofessional acting in his or her professional capacity or assisting in a paraprofessional capacity;
   • Made, maintained, or used only in connection with the treatment of the student; and
   • Disclosed only to individuals providing the treatment.

It is important to note that, for the purpose of this definition, "treatment" does not include remedial educational activities or activities that are part of the program of instruction at the agency or institution, such as those that would be maintained as part of a student's records.

Chapter 13

EDUCATION LAW FOR CHILDREN WITH DISABILITIES:

THE INDIVIDUALS WITH DISABILITIES EDUCATION ACT (IDEA) AND SECTION 504 OF THE REHABILITATION ACT OF 1973 (SECTION 504)

Attorney Christopher A. Tracey*
Attorney Dori P. Antonetti*
Attorney Julie Jaquays*
Shipman & Goodwin LLP

DESCRIPTION OF ISSUE

Schools foster the development of society's next generation by providing environments where students have the opportunity to progress intellectually, socially, and emotionally. In providing such environments, all students should be afforded an equal opportunity to progress. As recently as fifty years ago, many students with disabilities were denied access to public education, placed in segregated classrooms, or otherwise not provided with adequate support for their needs. Since that time, two federal laws—Section 504 of the Rehabilitation Act of 1973 (Section 504) and the Individuals with Disabilities Education Act (the IDEA)—have been enacted to ensure access to a public education for individuals with disabilities. Both laws impose affirmative duties upon schools that receive federal funds, requiring them to promptly identify, evaluate, and address the individual needs of students with disabilities to ensure equal access to education.

Enacted in 1973, Section 504 was the first federal civil rights law prohibiting discrimination against individuals with disabilities. Section 504 applies generally to programs and entities receiving federal financial assistance, including schools. Two years after the passage of Section 504, the IDEA was enacted to protect the rights of students with certain qualifying disabilities. The original acronym IDEA continues to be used colloquially, and for practical purposes, we refer to the legislation in its most recent form (as reauthorized by Congress in 2004) as the IDEA throughout this chapter. The IDEA provides federal funding to states and school districts in exchange for compliance with certain mandates. The primary intent of the IDEA is to provide students with qualifying disabilities of eligible age with educational services and supports so that they are able to gain meaningful educational benefit from public education at no expense to their parent(s)/guardian(s).

School nurses play an important role in ensuring that children with disabilities receive appropriate services and support in accordance with the IDEA or Section 504. This chapter provides a summary of the IDEA and Section 504. It also outlines legal obligations; discusses practical implications for school nurses working with students with disabilities; summarizes possible legal challenges that may arise under the IDEA and Section 504; and offers insight in response to frequently asked questions.

---

* Original authors: Attorney Alyce L. Alfano, Attorney Melika S. Forbes, & Attorney Laura A. Fisher (2017)

BACKGROUND

IDEA—At a Glance

The IDEA imposes obligations on states and local educational agencies regarding the education of children with qualifying disabilities who, by reason of their disabilities, require special education and, in some cases, related services. The IDEA regulations define *special education* as "specially designed instruction, at no cost to the parents/[guardians], to meet the unique needs of a child with a disability" (34 C.F.R. § 300.39). In order to qualify for services under the IDEA, a student must be identified under one of the following federal eligibility categories: autism; deaf-blindness; developmental delay (applicable to younger children only, as specifically delineated under state law); emotional disturbance; hearing impairment, including deafness; intellectual disability; multiple disabilities; orthopedic impairment; other health impairment (which often includes ADD/ADHD); specific learning disability; speech or language impairment; traumatic brain injury; and visual impairment, including blindness (34 C.F.R. § 300.8). Notably, states may recognize qualifying disabilities in addition to those included in federal regulations.

The IDEA requires local educational agencies to offer eligible students a free and appropriate public education (FAPE). The United States Supreme Court first analyzed this standard in *Board of Education v. Rowley* (1982). Under *Rowley,* the inquiry for determining whether a school district provided a student with a FAPE is two-fold. The first inquiry is whether the local educational agency complied with the IDEA's procedural requirements. The second inquiry asks the substantive question of whether "the [Individualized Education Program (or, as abbreviated, "IEP," a document which is described further below)] developed...[is] reasonably calculated to enable the child to receive educational benefits" (Board of Education v. Rowley, 1982).

More recently, in *Endrew F. v. Douglas County School District* (2017), the Supreme Court refined the FAPE standard by ruling that school districts must provide an educational program "reasonably calculated to enable a child to make progress appropriate in light of the child's circumstances" — a standard which the Court instructed is "markedly more demanding than the 'merely more than *de minimis' [educational benefit]* test" that had been applied by certain courts. Importantly, the *Endrew F.* Court did not overturn *Rowley.* Rather, the *Endrew F.* decision sets forth a general standard and underscores the necessarily fact-specific nature of each case. Each student with a disability has unique needs and circumstances; therefore, there can be no bright-line rule governing precisely which educational supports or services satisfy the FAPE standard in every case. In reaching its conclusion, the *Endrew F.* Court reiterated that the IDEA does not "guarantee any particular level of education" and that it "cannot and does not promise any particular educational outcome."

Moreover, the *Endrew F.* Court retained the "reasonably calculated" qualification and explained that it "reflects a recognition that crafting an appropriate program of education requires a prospective judgment by school officials" based on the specific facts related to a student and informed by school officials' expertise and input from the parents or guardians. The *Endrew F.* Court emphasized that "[a]ny review of an IEP must appreciate that the question is whether the IEP is *reasonable*, not whether the court regards it as ideal." In its decision, the *Endrew F.* Court underscored the deference owed to school officials in the development of an appropriate IEP in explaining that such "deference is based on the application of expertise and the exercise of judgment by school authorities." The IDEA "vests these officials with responsibility for decisions of critical importance to the life of a disabled child" (Endrew F. v. Douglas County School District, 2017).

With the above standards in mind, the IDEA requires that a planning team (known federally as an IEP team but which may be referred to in some jurisdictions by other names) develop an eligible student's individualized education program (IEP), a document which sets forth the manner in which the local educational agency will provide the student with a FAPE. The IEP team is required by law to consist of certain individuals: the parent(s)/guardian(s); a regular education teacher; a special education teacher; a representative of the school system able to make decisions on behalf of the system (such as an administrator); someone to interpret any relevant evaluation results (for example, a speech and language pathologist or an occupational therapist); and, at the discretion of the parent/guardian(s) or school district, other individuals who have knowledge or special expertise regarding the child (20 U.S.C. § 1414(d)(1)(B)). A school nurse will often be part of the IEP team when the student has health-related needs or takes medication. The student will also be included as part of the IEP team in appropriate circumstances (34 C.F.R. § 300.321).

Among other responsibilities, the IEP team is responsible for planning evaluations, reviewing evaluation results, and determining eligibility for special education and related services. When health issues are or may be implicated, the school nurse should assist in planning and determining what type of evaluation(s) should be recommended. Additionally, the school nurse should analyze relevant documentation and help in designing the appropriate IEP for students with health needs. The determination of whether a student qualifies for special education programming and services or whether the student qualifies instead for a Section 504 Plan (described below) will never be solely the school nurse's responsibility. Rather, the determination of eligibility and the development of IEPs are the responsibility of the IEP team as a whole. Elements of the IEP include the student's present levels of academic and functional performance; measurable goals and objectives; criteria for measuring progress towards the mastery of the goals and objectives; the extent, if any, to which the student will not participate with non-disabled children; the special education and related services and supplementary aids and services to be provided to the student, as well as frequency, location, and duration of such services; accommodations and modifications; IEP team recommendations and prior written notice of any changes to the IEP; and transition services, when appropriate and applicable (34 C.F.R. § 300.320).

In determining a student's educational program and placement, a central task of the IEP team, the team must determine what constitutes the least restrictive environment ("LRE") for that student. The IDEA's LRE requirement mandates that qualifying students be educated with non-disabled peers to the maximum extent appropriate (34 C.F.R. § 300.114). In other words, whenever possible, a student must be educated in regular education classrooms with supplemental aids and services. Only when this is not appropriate considering the student's needs, may the student be educated along a continuum of progressively more restrictive environments (for example, self-contained classrooms or private special education schools). There is no threshold amount of 'mainstreaming' required by the IDEA, and courts are deferential to educational professionals about what constitutes the LRE for a particular student.

Section 504—At a Glance

Section 504 is a federal civil rights law that prohibits discrimination against individuals with disabilities in programs or activities that receive federal financial assistance. It provides that "[n]o otherwise qualified individual with a disability ...shall, solely by reason of...[a] disability, be excluded from the participation in, be denied the benefits of, or be subjected to discrimination under any program or activity receiving [f]ederal financial assistance…" (29 U.S.C. § 794). The IDEA and Section 504 both protect individuals with disabilities, but they are not co-extensive. Whereas the IDEA provides protections to a subset of students with certain qualifying disabilities, Section 504 more broadly provides protections to any individual—whether or not a student—who satisfies the legal definition of a person with a disability. An individual is protected by Section 504 if such an individual has a physical or mental impairment that substantially limits one or more major life activities. Additionally, individuals may qualify under Section 504 if they have a record of such an impairment or are regarded as having such an impairment (34 C.F.R. § 104.3).

Section 504's protections are intended to be construed broadly in favor of expansive coverage. Its accompanying regulations instruct that determining whether an individual qualifies for protection under Section 504 does not require extensive analysis and that the term *major life activity* does not impose a strict standard nor require that the activity be of central importance to daily life (*See* 28 C.F.R. § 35.108(c)(2)). Moreover, the regulations use broad language to define the terms *physical impairment* and *mental impairment*. Under Section 504, *physical impairment* means "any physiological disorder or condition, cosmetic disfigurement, or anatomical loss affecting one or more … body systems;" while *mental impairment* means "any mental or psychological disorder" (34 C.F.R. § 104.3). As such, the list of impairments that satisfy these broad definitions is wide-ranging and extensive in scope. In addition, whether an impairment substantially limits a major life activity must be determined without

> A non-exhaustive list of recognized impairments includes: orthopedic, visual, speech and hearing impairments; cerebral palsy; epilepsy; muscular dystrophy; multiple sclerosis; cancer; heart disease; diabetes; intellectual disabilities; emotional illnesses such as depression, bipolar disorder, etc.; learning disabilities such as dyslexia; ADHD; HIV; tuberculosis; drug addiction; and alcoholism.

regard to the ameliorative effects of mitigating measures such as medication, medical supplies and equipment, except for ordinary eyeglasses or contact lenses. As noted above, Section 504 applies to a large pool of individuals, but this chapter will focus on Section 504's applicability to students in the education context.

Section 504 also requires schools to provide students with disabilities with a FAPE (34 C.F.R. § 104.33). However, Section 504's definition of a FAPE is different from the standard set forth under the IDEA. Under Section 504's regulations, to ensure the provision of a FAPE, schools must provide "regular or special education and related aids and services that (i) are designed to meet individual educational needs of handicapped persons as adequately as the needs of non-handicapped persons are met and (ii) are based upon adherence to procedures that satisfy the requirements of [the Section 504 regulations]" (34 C.F.R. § 104.33). Section 504 also requires that schools accommodate students with disabilities in other aspects of school programs and activities, including sports, extracurricular activities, and field trips (34 C.F.R. § 104.37). In effect, Section 504 requires schools to level the playing field for students with disabilities so that they have educational opportunities equal to their non-disabled peers.

Schools have an affirmative duty under Section 504 to identify and evaluate students and must provide eligible students equal access to education (34 C.F.R. § 104.35). Although this legal obligation does not rest on any singular school employee, a school nurse can be an essential member of the multidisciplinary team (Section

504 team) charged with fulfilling the school's obligations under Section 504. Accordingly, it is important that school nurses understand their roles and responsibilities regarding participation in Section 504 teams.

IMPLICATIONS FOR SCHOOL NURSE PRACTICE

School nurses are essential school personnel who, through assessment, observation, and implementation of treatment or other services or supports, help to ensure that the health needs of all students are addressed while in the school environment. Indeed, IDEA and Section 504 place significant obligations on school nurses that many nursing preparation programs may not address. As noted above, the IDEA and Section 504 require school districts to promptly identify and evaluate students who may be eligible for protection under either law. Although school nurses may be called to serve as a member of a student's IEP or Section 504 team to assist in the evaluation of a student, a school nurse's obligation under both laws begins prior to a student's referral to an IEP or Section 504 team.

Role and Responsibilities

While the language of the IDEA and Section 504 places responsibility on the amorphous "school district" or "program," both laws have been interpreted to require individual school employees to refer students believed to have a qualifying disability (in the case of the IDEA) or a disability (under Section 504) to the appropriate multidisciplinary evaluation team (*See, e.g.*, Rodiriecus L. v. Waukegan School District No. 60, 1996, and Board of Education of Fayette County, KY v. L.M., 2007). Therefore, school nurses must be vigilant in identifying students who demonstrate health needs that could trigger the IDEA or Section 504 requirements. School nurses must immediately notify the school's Special Education or Section 504 Coordinator of their observations and, where appropriate, refer the student for evaluation to determine whether the student is eligible for protection under the law. It is important to recognize that the information that forms the basis of the referral may come directly from a parent/guardian or an external healthcare provider, or it may be based on the school nurse's observation of and interaction with the student. Regardless of the source of information, the duty to identify students with disabilities promptly and refer such students for evaluation is of primary importance.

In some cases, a student being evaluated will not have a health-related need or disability. In such a case, it is unlikely that a school nurse would serve as a member of the multidisciplinary team evaluating or planning for the student. However, where there is knowledge, suspicion, a claim, or even the possibility that a student has a health-related need or disability, the school nurse should participate as a member of the IEP or Section 504 team. As an IEP team or Section 504 team member, the school nurse shares responsibility with the other team members to meet the IDEA and Section 504 requirements.

To comply with applicable legal requirements, the team must first make an eligibility determination. Although eligibility determinations are team decisions, cases where health-related needs or disability are at issue may require a significant contribution from the school nurse. The team members will rely on the school nurse's expertise to help them understand the student's health-related needs during the evaluation process. The school nurse will likely be called upon to assess the student's health-related needs or disability, interpret medical documentation, and communicate with external healthcare providers. Simply put, the school nurse will serve as a "translator" for team members who lack medical expertise but need to understand medical information in order to make an informed eligibility determination and understand how the health condition may affect the student's ability to benefit from or access the student's educational program. Thus, a school nurse's role, at the outset, is to come prepared with any data or documentation regarding the student's health needs. It may be advisable that the school nurse share such information prior to the meeting, if possible, to allow for a more productive and efficient discussion during the meeting, provided that all applicable decisions must be made during, not in advance of, the meeting.

If a student with a disability, including but not limited to a disability that includes health-related needs, is found eligible under the IDEA or Section 504, the multidisciplinary team moves forward to the planning phase. As noted above, both the IDEA and Section 504 mandate that schools develop an appropriate plan—IEP or Section 504 Plan, respectively—to address the individual needs of an eligible student. Despite that shared goal, the substantive standard to satisfy the above requirement is different under each law. With respect to an IEP, the law requires an annual written plan, the IEP, which sets forth the detailed requirements described earlier in this chapter.   In contrast, Section 504 does not require a written plan; however, as a best practice, schools should, and usually do, provide a written plan as an accountability measure and to clearly document the decisions of the team. Written Section 504 Plans typically include descriptions of the qualifying disability, services, and supports (including setting, frequency, and duration) and the accommodations to be implemented for the student.

While the IEP team as a whole tackles the academic, developmental, social, and emotional needs of the student, the responsibility of addressing the healthcare needs of the student falls primarily on the school nurse. The school nurse uses available data and documentation (or requests additional information needed) to accomplish the following:
1) determine the healthcare needs of the student;
2) recommend or conduct healthcare evaluations and assessments, as appropriate;
3) determine and recommend the appropriate healthcare services and supports required by the student to access the student's education;
4) provide input, based on nursing expertise, regarding the appropriateness of services and supports under consideration by the team;
5) determine whether, and to what extent, parent, student, or non-nursing staff healthcare training is required;
6) draft individualized healthcare plans ("IHPs") and emergency care plans ("ECPs"), where appropriate; and
7) draft measurable and appropriate healthcare annual IEP goals and objectives, where appropriate.

To accomplish these tasks, the school nurse may need to consult with the parent(s)/guardian(s), student, and external healthcare providers, such as treating physicians, mental health counselors, pediatricians, or psychiatrists. In instances where consultation with an external party is required, it is critical that the school nurse receive written parental consent to disclose the student's personally identifiable information. As detailed in *Chapter 10, School Health Records,* this consent should be obtained prior to any discussion or the release of student-related information or records.

Following the development of an appropriate plan of services and supports summarized in a written IEP or Section 504 Plan and assuming parental agreement, the law requires the school to implement the plan with fidelity. As a first step, the written plan must be disseminated to each team member, including the parent(s)/ guardian(s) and school personnel who work with the student. While this dissemination is not usually the school nurse's responsibility, a school nurse serving as a team member must obtain a copy of the finalized plan, which may include an attached IHP or ECP, and must review it to determine the nurse's responsibilities. IEP and Section 504 Plans may require school nurses to provide training to parent(s)/ guardian(s), students, and educators; administer health services and supports; supervise personnel administering health services and supports; consult and collaborate with parent(s)/guardian(s), school-based staff, or external healthcare providers at regular intervals; and assist in planning and implementing a student's accommodations to allow for participation in sports, special events such as field trips, and extracurricular activities.

In accordance with applicable legal requirements, school nurses should document their periodic monitoring and maintain detailed and accurate records of the implementation of IDEA or Section 504 services, supports, and training. School nurses must monitor the progress of eligible students for the duration of the relevant plan. The laws also impose a duty to reconvene the IEP or Section 504 team for the following purposes:

- Annual review of the student's progress towards IEP goals and objectives and development of a new IEP based on the current evaluative information (IDEA only);
- Triennial review of the student's continued need for specialized instruction (IDEA only);
- Periodic review to ensure the student's Section 504 Plan is appropriate and determine whether any changes are necessary (Section 504 only);
- Change in the student's educational placement; or
- Request for a meeting by a team member, including the parent/guardian(s).

Thinking Ahead— Legal Peril under Special Education and Disability Laws

Parents who disagree with the identification, educational plan, or services being offered to their child through an IEP or Section 504 Plan may pursue legal remedies to address their concerns. Understanding the legal avenues available to parent(s)/guardian(s) under both the IDEA and Section 504 will assist a school nurse in preparing to assist with or participate in a school district's defense. It is important to remember that under both IDEA and Section 504, a school nurse (or any other individual school employee) will not incur liability in their individual capacity. Rather, under both laws, parent(s)/guardian(s) bring legal action against a school district as a whole.

IDEA

Due Process: Under the IDEA, parents/guardians may file for a due process hearing to pursue their disagreement with a school district over the identification, evaluation, educational placement, or provision of a FAPE to their child (34 CFR § 300.507). While school districts may also file due process hearing requests, it is much more common for parents/guardians to generate hearing requests. The request for a due process hearing must be in writing and contain certain components such as the student's name, the nature of the problem, related facts, and a proposed resolution (34 CFR § 300.508). Each state's educational agency has procedures for processing due process complaints and must ensure that the opposing party receives a copy of the complaint, that an impartial hearing officer is appointed, and that a timely hearing ensues in which both parties may be represented by attorneys (34 CFR § § 300.508-511).

Due process hearings are administrative hearings that are similar in form to trials. Both sides have the opportunity to present documents as exhibits to be reviewed by the hearing officer, who acts as the judge. Both sides also present witnesses who are questioned, provide direct testimony relevant to the issues, and are subject to cross-examination by the opposing party.

The school nurse may be called upon to assist the district in gathering all of the relevant health and medical documentation regarding the student in question for submission as evidence. Maintaining consistently clear, organized, and up-to-date records will benefit both the district and the school nurse in preparing for a hearing. The school nurse may also be asked to consult with administrators and the school district's attorney to explain their interaction with a student or the parent(s)/guardian(s) and the school nurse's perspective on the health issues involved in the dispute. Finally, the school nurse may be called as a witness by the school district's attorney or by the attorney for the parent(s)/guardian(s) to testify under oath in response to questions about the student and the situation at hand. Although this does not happen for school nurses frequently, it can be nerve-wracking when it does. The school district's attorney should and probably will prepare the school nurse for questioning by reviewing both the content and the testimonial process in advance of providing testimony at the hearing. The result of a due process hearing is a written decision by the hearing officer, which the parties must follow if it is not appealed.

Prior to the hearing, the law requires the parties to try to resolve their differences through a Resolution Meeting or a mediation process (34 C.F.R. § 300.510). These meetings are negotiation sessions, sometimes facilitated by a neutral party, to assist the school district and the parent/guardian(s) in trying to reach an agreement on the outstanding issues. The school nurse may be asked to assist in gathering any relevant documentation to assist the administration and the school district's attorney in preparing for the negotiation session. Depending upon the nature of the dispute and the extent to which health issues are involved, the school nurse may also be asked to be present at the session to assist in understanding the facts and helping to craft workable solutions. A successful dispute resolution process results in a written agreement guiding the parties' relationship going forward for a given period.

State Complaint

The IDEA provides that every state's primary educational agency establish a written procedure for the filing of complaints (34 C.F.R. § 300.151). Thus, each state has its own process for receiving, reviewing, and responding in writing to a parent's complaint regarding an alleged violation of their child's rights to special education identification, evaluation, or programming. Similar to due process complaints, these are most commonly filed by parents. However, organizations may also file complaints on behalf of a given student or group of students. School districts are notified of the complaint and are given an opportunity to respond both verbally and in writing. The school nurse's role in assisting with a response to a state complaint is similar to their role in responding to a due process complaint. Again, the school nurse may be asked to gather any relevant health and medical documentation regarding the student. Thus, once again, it is critical to keep clear and up-to-date records. The school nurse may also be asked to explain to the school district's administration, attorney, or the state complaint investigator, the school nurse's understanding of the facts and perspective on the student's health needs. However, in the context of a state complaint, the school nurse will not have to testify under oath. At the conclusion of the state complaint investigation, the investigator issues a written report of findings. If it is found that certain corrective actions are required on the part of the school district (such as new procedures for recordkeeping or additional staff training relating to student health or nursing issues), the school nurse will be informed of these actions and will participate in implementing them.

Section 504

Office for Civil Rights Complaints: When parent(s)/guardian(s) disagree with a student's Section 504 Plan or its implementation, the parent(s)/guardian(s) may file a complaint with the federal Office for Civil Rights ("OCR"). OCR is the arm of the United States Department of Education responsible for enforcing civil rights laws and protecting against discrimination on the basis of disability, among other things. Each area of the country has a regional OCR office that receives and processes complaints. Filing an OCR complaint is a relatively simple process for a parent and does not require the assistance of an attorney. In addition, there is no charge to the party filing the complaint. Once OCR receives a complaint, it decides whether the discrimination alleged falls within its jurisdiction. If so, OCR contacts the school district via written letter to explain that a complaint has been filed, provides an overview of the complaint, and requests specific, detailed data and documentation from the school district. If the student has health issues, the school nurse will typically be an integral part of the school team responding to the OCR complaint. The school nurse will be responsible for gathering and compiling all related documentation for the response. If the school nurse has had regular interaction with the student or the parent(s)/guardian(s), the school nurse will likely be asked to recount those interactions in response to OCR's inquiries eliciting such information. Depending upon the extent to which OCR pursues its investigation of the complaint, OCR may request interviews with specific employees, including the school nurse. In the event such a request is made, the school administration and the school district's attorney will arrange the interview, which is usually telephonic, and help to prepare the school nurse for it. The result of an OCR investigation may be a determination or mutual agreement that certain training or other protocols must be put into place. In that event, the school nurse would be informed of the results of the investigation to know what actions to implement.

Section 504 Hearing

Under Section 504, parents also have the right to request a hearing by an impartial hearing officer to address their concerns with a student's Section 504 Plan or its implementation. While parents infrequently choose this path, school districts are required to inform parents that the process is available and to provide an impartial hearing officer if requested. In a Section 504 hearing, the school nurse's role is similar to their role at a due process hearing under IDEA. The nurse would likely be responsible for assisting in gathering all health and medical records in the school's possession, acting as a consultant and advisor to the administration and the school district's attorney, and potentially testifying at the hearing.

Frequently Asked Questions

In preparing to write this resource and address the real concerns of school nurses, the editors and authors polled school nurses to solicit questions that arise related to school nurse participation in IDEA and Section 504 implementation. A few of the most frequently posed questions, with responses, are provided below. Please note that these are examples not to be construed as specific legal advice applicable to any particular facts or case.

1. Should nurses be part of the Section 504 planning process?

    ANSWER: As expressed throughout this chapter, when a student has a health-related condition necessitating a Section 504 Plan, the school nurse will be an integral and necessary part of the planning team and will be responsible for educating necessary staff about the health-related components of the plan and assisting in its implementation.

2. If a Section 504 Plan states that a Registered Nurse will check a student's blood sugar or perform another nursing task, does that bind the district to allow *only* the school nurse to complete that task?

    ANSWER: The short answer is yes. If a plan is so specific as to identify the qualifications of the individual implementing a component of the plan, it must be followed as written. Written IEPs or Section 504 Plans must be strictly adhered to. Thus, it is best practice to broaden the language of the plan to say, for example, "registered nurse, or other qualified individual."

3. Should IHPs be attached to a student's IEP if a student has both?

    ANSWER: While the IDEA does not require this, it is strongly recommended that the IHP be attached to the IEP. In that way, any individual who is reading the IEP has full knowledge of the student's complete needs and plan. Please note that this does not mean that the IHP is legally incorporated into the IEP itself; therefore, the IHP can be revised with parental and medical input without the need to convene a formal IEP meeting.

4. Does a student need a Section 504 Plan if the student has an existing IEP and IHP?

    ANSWER: A student eligible under the IDEA is not required to have a Section 504 Plan in addition to an IEP, even though the student is also protected by Section 504. The sound development and implementation of an IEP satisfies the Section 504 FAPE standard (34 CFR 104.33(b)(2)).

5. Is it helpful/appropriate for Section 504 Plans to be specific as to the appropriate medical order/ protocol for a student?

    ANSWER: Typically, specific medical order/protocol is not contained in the Section 504 Plan but rather in the student's IHP, which can be included by reference for clarity. It is not usually appropriate or helpful to have specific medical protocols in a plan that would be disseminated to staff beyond the school health professionals. The law does not, however, prohibit this information from being included on a student's Section 504 Plan if it is helpful or appropriate in an individual circumstance.

6. Does a nurse potentially have individual legal liability for a plan if the school nurse has expressed his or her professional opinion and the team disagrees?

    ANSWER: Individual liability for school employees, including school nurses, does not accrue under either IDEA or Section 504. These laws allow parents to pursue legal remedies from a public school district as a whole, not from employees in their individual capacity (*See, e.g.,* 20 U.S.C. § 1415; 34 C.F.R. § 104.36).

7. Could a student's IEP or Section 504 Plan include specialized transportation and potentially require a nurse to ride that transportation with them?

ANSWER: **Yes.** Under the IDEA, nursing services and/or specialized transportation are related services that may be incorporated into a student's IEP if required (34 C.F.R. § 300.320(a)(4)). Similarly, it is possible that a student's health needs require that the student's Section 504 Plan have these accommodations. Due to practical and logistical considerations, it would typically be a contracted nurse rather than a school nurse serving in this role.

8. What is the chain of command regarding the implementation of plans for students with healthcare needs?

ANSWER: Each school district has its own internal structure that dictates who on a student's team is that student's "go-to" person or case manager. Ultimately, the director of special education, Section 504 coordinator, or head of pupil personnel/student services is the individual responsible for the coordination of the student's IEP plan. Importantly, when there are healthcare needs involved, the school nurse will be a key voice in implementing and monitoring the implementation of the student's plan. In legal situations, as described above, the school nurse may also be called upon to present, interpret, and answer questions regarding the healthcare plan documentation and implementation.

CONCLUSION

School nurses are the individuals within a school system with primary responsibility for the healthcare implications of an eligible student's IEP or Section 504 Plan. As key members of the team, school nurses bring their nursing training and knowledge to help shape and implement an eligible student's plan. School nurses are key members of IEP and Section 504 teams and, as such, they should be familiar with the legal aspects of both laws.

RESOURCES

> See Addendum: The School Nurse's Role in the Identification Process for a 504 Plan and The School Nurse's Role on the 504 Team

U.S. Department of Education Office for Civil Rights, *Parent and Educator Resource Guide to Section 504 in Public Elementary and Secondary Schools* (2016), available at https://www2.ed.gov/about/offices/list/ocr/docs/504-resource-guide-201612.pdf

Wright's Law, Special Education Caselaw, http://www.wrightslaw.com/caselaw.htm

REFERENCES

Board of Education v. Rowley, 458 U.S. 176 (1982)

Board of Education of Fayette County, KY v. L.M., 478 F.3d 307 (6th Cir. 2007)

Endrew F. v. Douglas County School District RE-1, 137 S. Ct. 988 (2017)

Rodiriecus L. v. Waukegan School District No. 60, 90 F.3d 249 (7th Cir. 1996)

Section 504 of the Rehabilitation Act of 1973, 29 U.S.C. § 794, 34 C.F.R. § 104.1 *et seq.*

The Individuals with Disabilities Education Act, 20 U.S.C. § 1400 *et seq.*, 34 C.F.R. § 300.1 *et seq.*

ADDENDUM # 1
The School Nurse's Role on the 504 Team
Annie Hetzel, MSN, RN, NCSN

Introduction:

The intersection of education and disability laws is complex. Each law has similar processes, but they are governed by different legislation. Some students may qualify under both IDEA and 504 with accommodations that are incorporated into the IEP. Other students with health conditions may only require health accommodations under 504. Neither IDEA or Section 504 provide explicit detail for implementation, leaving districts to create policies and procedures that may omit the role of the school nurse. The National Association of School Nurses' position statement on IDEA posits that "The school nurse is the team member qualified to evaluate the health needs of the student, many of which may not be apparent without a thorough health assessment. If health-related barriers are not recognized, appropriately interpreted, and addressed, those students risk academic failure" (NASN, 2023). As such, every child with a disability or at risk of health-related learning barriers benefits from the participation of a school nurse on the 504 and IEP team.

Q: Should the school nurse be a member of the 504 team?

A. Section 504 law does not provide a high level of detail for program implementation and specificity regarding the composition of the school 504 team. As a result, there may be a lack of clarity about the school nurse's role and level of involvement. Each district must develop a procedure to evaluate students to measure areas of educational needs. Tests used must be validated and administered by trained personnel best suited to implement evaluations and design 504 plans for each student (USDE, 2016). While no specific list exists of who should be on a team, school nurses are often the only school personnel who can provide health expertise and an understanding of the impact that health may have on student access to education. As such, school nurses are essential members of the 504 team.

Q. What preparation is needed for a school nurse to be a member of the 504 team?

A. All school nurses should have a basic understanding of education law (NASN, 2023), such as IDEA and 504. Some states require specific credentials or licensure for school nurses. School nurses should seek educational opportunities about Section 504 and the implications for the provision of health services in schools, whether it is mandated by local regulations or not. Such training may be available from the state Department of Education, State School Nurse Consultant, or school nurse organization.

Q. What is the school nurse's responsibility as part of the team?

A. In the IEP and 504 teams, school nurses review the health history of students to identify health concerns that may impact a student's ability to access their education and refer students who may need accommodations to the team. School nurses ensure that vision and hearing screenings and appropriate referrals are completed to reduce barriers related to visual or auditory deficits. As members of the team, school nurses determine what health accommodations and adaptations are needed to support student learning, if any (Younkaitis & Crespo, 2023). The nurse provides vital information regarding known health conditions. They may also identify undiagnosed concerns based on information shared by team members during the evaluation and make applicable referrals for medical follow-up and support.

Q: Should the school nurse have access to 504 plans?

A. School nurses potentially interact with every student in the school in the provision of primary health services such as health screenings, health education, and first aid that may be impacted by student disabilities. School nurses are frequently the only individuals in schools licensed and qualified to perform health evaluations in schools (NASN, 2023). For this reason, school nurses must have access to student 504 plans regardless of their role on the team.

Q: Is it appropriate for the school nurse to be a designated coordinator of the 504 team?

A. In the Parent and Educator Resource Guide to Section 504 in Public Elementary and Secondary Schools, the U.S. Department of Education Office of Civil Rights describes the role of the Section 504 Coordinator to include informing staff about 504 policy, procedures, and practices to ensure compliance with 504 responsibilities. The leadership of the 504 team requires a professional who can interpret the implications of an educational evaluation and applicable academic accommodations. While school nurses are valuable members of the 504 and IEP teams for their health expertise (Fleming & Willgerodt, 2017), their ability to take the designated coordinator role depends on their knowledge of education law and ability to interpret evaluation data and determine educational accommodations. Additionally, school nurses' position within the health services team and level of direct student care responsibilities, including caseload, may impact their ability to dedicate adequate time and resources to coordinating the 504 team. In some districts, the leadership of the 504 team may be shared between specialists based on their professional expertise. In such instances, school nurses may coordinate 504 planning for students with complex healthcare needs, while counselors or school psychologists are responsible only for students needing educational accommodations.

School nurses may need to advocate with their administrative leadership for an appropriate level of participation in the 504 team. A foundational understanding of Section 504 law and its application by the school team and the role of the team coordinator will aid school nurses in obtaining optimal inclusion.

REFERENCES

Fleming, R., & Willgerodt, M.A. (2017, September 30). Interprofessional collaborative practice and school nursing: A model for improved health outcomes. *OJIN: The Online Journal of Issues in Nursing*, *22*(3) Manuscript 2. https://doi.org/10.3912/OJIN.Vol22No03Man02

National Association of School Nurses. (2023, Revised). *IDEIA and section 504 teams - The school nurse as an essential team member* (Position Statement). https://www.nasn.org/nasn-resources/professional-practice-documents/position-statements/ps-ideia

Shannon, R. A., & Yonkaitis, C. F. (2017). The role of the school nurse in the special education process; Part 2: Eligibility determination and the individualized education program. *NASN School Nurse,32*(4), 249-254. https://doi.org10.1177/1942602X17709505

U.S. Department of Education, Office for Civil Rights. (2016). *Parent and educator resource guide to Section 504 in public elementary and secondary schools.* https://www2.ed.gov/about/offices/list/ocr/docs/504-resource-guide-201612.pdf

Yonkaitis, C.F., & Crespo E. (2023). Legal Issues 101: Students with disabilities. *NASN School Nurse, 2020,* (0). https://doi.org/10.1177/1942602X221146756

Chapter 14

MCKINNEY-VENTO HOMELESS ASSISTANCE ACT

Julia Lechtenberg, MSN, RN, NCSN-Emeritus

DESCRIPTION OF ISSUE

Homelessness is a serious issue that can significantly affect a student's academic success. In 1987, in response to increasing and widespread homelessness, President Ronald Reagan signed into law the McKinney-Vento Homeless Assistance Act (the "Act"). The Act was the first piece of major federal legislation that addressed the needs of the homeless and the education of homeless children and youth, thereby facilitating the removal of barriers to a homeless child's academic success (National Coalition for the Homeless, 2006). One of the Act's main goals is to ensure that homeless children and youth have equal access to the same free and appropriate public education as provided to other children and youth (U.S. Department of Education [USDE], 2018).

The Act has been amended several times since its inception. The Act was reauthorized in December 2015 when President Obama reauthorized the Elementary and Secondary Act via the Every Student Succeeds Act (ESSA, 2015). The *McKinney-Vento Homeless Assistance Act,* as amended by the *Every Student Succeeds Act*:

- Emphasizes the identification of homeless children and youths, including requirements that State Educational Agencies and Local Education Agencies (LEAs) provide training and professional development opportunities for staff (SchoolHouseConnection, 2020).
- Requires that State Coordinators monitor LEAs in coordination with local district liaisons to ensure the enforcement of the McKinney-Vento Act (USDE, 2018).
- Ensures that the eligibility of a student's homelessness be determined based on the definition set forth by the U.S. Department of Housing and Urban Development (National Center for Homeless Education [NCHE], 2020).
- Focuses on school stability by allowing homeless students to stay in their school of origin for the duration of their homelessness if it is in the student's best interest (ESSA, 2015).
- Removes barriers to accessing academic programs and extracurricular activities for qualifying homeless students, such as charter and magnet school, summer school, vocational and technical education, advance placement courses, and online learning programs.
- Mandates that school districts reserve Title I, Part A funds to be used for the education or support of homeless students (i.e., academic tutoring or social work services due to domestic violence.
- Expands current transportation services from grades K–12 to include district-run public preschools and Head Start programs.
- Provides a dispute resolution process, such that if a dispute arises between the school district and the parent/guardian of a homeless student, the school district must immediately enroll the student and provide necessary transportation until the dispute is resolved, including through the appeal process.

As most recently reauthorized, the Act defines homeless children and youth as:
  (2) The term "homeless children and youths" –
    (A) mean individuals who lack a fixed, regular, and adequate nighttime residence (within the meaning of [42 U.S.C. § 11302(a)(1)]); and

(B) includes -

(i) children and youths who are sharing the housing of other persons due to loss of housing, economic hardship, or a similar reason; are living in motels, hotels, trailer parks, or camping grounds due to the lack of adequate alternative accommodations; are living in emergency or transitional shelters; or are abandoned in hospitals.

(ii) children and youths who have a primary nighttime residence that is a public or private place not designed for or ordinarily used as a regular sleeping accommodation for human beings (within the meaning of [42 U.S.C. § 11302(a)(2)(C)]).

(iii) children and youths who are living in cars, parks, public spaces, abandoned buildings, substandard housing, bus or train stations, or similar settings.

(iv) migratory children (as defined in [20 U.S.C. § 6399]) who qualify as homeless because they are living in the circumstances described in clauses (i) through (iii) (42 U.S.C. § 11434a (2).

Unaccompanied children and youth are not specifically referenced in the McKinney-Vento definition of homeless. However, the term unaccompanied youth is defined in the Act as "a homeless child or youth not in the physical custody of a parent or guardian" [42 U.S.C. § 11434a (6)] (NCHE, 2021, p. 2).

BACKGROUND

Homelessness is a pervasive social issue that seriously influences a student's educational experience. Causes of homelessness are numerous and include poverty, unemployment, lack of affordable housing, illness, and natural disasters (National Library of Medicine [NLM], 2021). Homelessness may impact school attendance, and significant absenteeism has tangible impacts on a student's education. For example, students who are not in school often have difficulty learning. In addition, chronic absenteeism negatively affects standardized test scores, grade-level retention rates, and, ultimately, graduation rates (USDE, 2019).

A stigma is associated with homelessness, making it difficult to identify homeless individuals and families. Provisions in the Act require school districts to identify homeless children and youth and provide appropriate transportation and education to homeless students. School districts are required to designate a district homeless coordinator, otherwise known as a local education agency (LEA) liaison ("liaison") (42 U.S.C. § 11432(g)(1)(J)(ii)). The LEA liaison is charged with enforcing the Act's requirements, including:

- identifying homeless children and youth within the school district.
- ensuring that homeless children and youths enroll in and have a full and equal opportunity to succeed in district schools.
- ensuring that homeless families, children, and youths receive educational services for which such families, children, and youths are eligible (e.g., Head Start and Early Head Start programs, Even Start programs, preschool programs administered by the district, and referrals to healthcare services, dental services, mental health services, and other appropriate services).
- informing the parents or guardians of homeless children and youths about their children's educational and related opportunities.
- providing public notice of the educational rights of homeless children and youths (42 U.S.C. § 11432(g)(6)(A)).

- reserving funds from the LEA's Title I, Part A allocations for services to homeless students. The services must be reasonable and necessary to assist homeless students to take advantage of educational opportunities.

An effective LEA liaison should be empathetic to the needs of the homeless, have good communication skills, be familiar with community resources, and have experience working with vulnerable students (Washington Office of Superintendent of Public Instructions, 2020). The role of the liaison may be assigned to an existing school district employee to perform along with their other duties. School nurses possess many of the necessary traits making them potential candidates for the position; however, time constraints often interfere with the efforts needed for the school nurse to provide continual support to homeless students at the district level. Nonetheless, school nurses can assist a school district in several ways to meet its responsibilities under the Act.

IMPLICATIONS FOR SCHOOL NURSE PRACTICE

Identification of Students

Identifying homeless students is the first step in providing necessary academic, health, and community resources to remove barriers to learning. District identification of homeless students can be challenging because students and parents may try to hide their homeless situations. School nurses can help identify homeless students because school nurses provide a nurturing environment, the school nurse may be the student's only resource for health care, and the school clinic is a safe haven that homeless students may frequent. Using keen assessment skills and open communication, the school nurse may be the first person to identify a homeless student. Warning signs include:

- Missing immunization and medical/health records
- Poor hygiene (may wear same clothes several days)
- Food insecurity (hungry - may hoard food)
- Poor health (respiratory issues, skin rashes, etc.)
- Unmet dental or vision needs
- Emotional and behavioral challenges
- Transportation issues
- High absenteeism and tardiness
- Falling asleep in class (NCHE, n.d.)

School Entry

School districts are required to enroll homeless children immediately and permit them to attend, even if they lack appropriate documentation such as immunization or medical records, proof of residency, guardianship documentation, or special education paperwork (USDE, 2022). The school nurse can be instrumental in securing immunization and medical records as quickly as possible by contacting the students' previous schools to obtain missing medical and immunization records. If a child or youth needs to obtain immunizations or other required health records, the enrolling school must immediately refer the parent, guardian, or unaccompanied youth to the LEA liaison, who must assist in obtaining the immunizations, screening, or immunization and other health records (NCHE, 2020).

Access to Care

Homeless students may have unmet dental and medical needs due to limited access to care. Homeless children and youth nationally often have a higher incidence of chronic diseases, wound infections, pneumonia, and substance abuse (NLM, 2021). They often lack medical insurance and appropriate transportation, limiting access to much needed medical and psychiatric care.

The school nurse can coordinate with the district's liaison to utilize Title 1, Part A funds to pay for needed health services such as immunizations, medical and dental services, vision exams and eyeglasses, hearing aids, and social work services (NCHE, 2020). The school nurse should collaborate with the LEA liaison and staff members to identify homeless students with chronic health diseases and unmet health needs, link these students to necessary local resources, and assist parent/guardian(s) complete medical forms and health insurance applications.

Mental Health Concerns

According to the American Psychological Association (2022), homelessness significantly impacts a child's overall physical and mental health. Homelessness is a traumatic experience, and homeless children and youth often experience anxiety and stress related to homelessness, including feelings of sadness and hopelessness. Homeless children and youth frequently struggle with low self-esteem and depression, putting them at higher risk of destructive behaviors. In the 2019 Youth Risk Behavior Survey, homeless high school youth were four times more likely to attempt suicide than their housed peers (SchoolHouseConnection, 2021). Homeless children and youth will often need mental health services; schools can utilize Title 1, Part A funds for needed social work services for these individuals (NCHE, 2020).

(For additional information on suicide, see Chapter 38)

CONCLUSION

Homelessness is a serious issue that negatively influences a student's life and significantly impacts their academic success. The McKinney-Vento Homeless Assistance Act guarantees homeless students a free and appropriate education and provides them the right to enroll, attend, and succeed in school (USDE, 2018). When implementing the central features of the Act, school nurses, in collaboration with the LEA liaison and the school community, can identify and provide necessary resources to ease the detrimental effects of homelessness and allow homeless students to achieve academic success.

RESOURCES

Institute for Children, Poverty and Homelessness
http://www.icphusa.org/
(212) 358-8086

National Alliance to End Homelessness
www.endhomelessness.org
202-638-1526

National Association for the Education of Homeless Children and Youth
http://naehcy.org/
855-446-2673

National Call Center for Homeless Veterans Hotline
http://www.va.gov/homeless/nationalcallcenter.asp
1-877-4AIDVET

National Center for Homeless Education
http://center.serve.org/nche/
1-800-308-2145

National Center for Homeless Education
Common Signs of Homelessness
https://nche.ed.gov/wp-content/uploads/2019/12/Common-Signs-of-Homelessness.pdf

National Center for Homeless Education
Homeless Liaison Toolkit
http://center.serve.org/nche/downloads/toolkit2/toolkit.pdf

Federal Register
McKinney-Vento Education for Homeless Children and Youths Program
https://www.federalregister.gov/articles/2016/03/17/2016-06073/mckinney-vento-education-for-homeless-children-and-youths-program

National Association for the Education of Homeless Children and Youth: https://naehcy.org/
Department of Education's Education for Homeless Children and Youth Program:
https://www2.ed.gov/programs/homeless/index.html

National Center for Homeless Education. (2021). *Determining eligibility for McKinney-Vento rights and services.* https://nche.ed.gov/wp-content/uploads/2018/10/det_elig.pdf

Legal References

ESSA – Legislation: Bill summaries, text, and U.S. Department of Education Guidance and Regulations
http://www.naehcy.org/essa-legislation-bill-summaries-text-and-us-department-education-guidance-and-regulations

Every Student Succeeds Act, 20 U.S.C. § 6301 (2015). https://www.congress.gov/bill/114th-congress/senate-bill/1177

McKinney-Vento Homeless Assistance Act (42 U.S.C. § 11431 et seq.)
STATUTE-101-Pg482.pdf (congress.gov)

McKinney-Vento Homeless Assistance Act
Reauthorized December 10, 2015, by Title IX, Part A of the Every Student Succeeds Act
(Effective October 1, 2016)
https://nche.ed.gov/wp-content/uploads/2020/02/NewMV2015clean.pdf

REFERENCES

American Psychological Association. (2022). *Exploring the mental health effects of poverty, hunger, and homelessness on children and teens.* https://www.apa.org/topics/socioeconomic-status/poverty-hunger-homelessness-children#:~:text=Homelessness%20can%20have%20a%20tremendous%20impact%20on%20children%2C,their%20pets%2C%20their%20belongings%2C%20and%20other%20family%20members

Every Student Succeeds Act (ESSA). (2015). *Every Student Succeeds Act of 2015*, Pub. L. No. 114-95 § 114 Stat. 1177 (2015-2016). https://www.congress.gov/114/plaws/publ95/PLAW-114publ95.pdf

National Center for Homeless Education. (n.d.). *Common signs of homelessness.* https://nche.ed.gov/wp-content/uploads/2019/12/Common-Signs-of-Homelessness.pdf

National Center for Homelessness Education. (2021). *Determining eligibility for McKinney-Vento rights and services.* https://nche.ed.gov/wp-content/uploads/2018/10/det_elig.pdf

National Center for Homeless Education. (2020). *Homeless liaison toolkit / 2020 edition.* https://nche.ed.gov/homeless-liaison-toolkit/

National Coalition for the Homeless. (2006). *McKinney-Vento act.* https://nationalhomeless.org/publications/facts/McKinney.pdf

National Library of Medicine. (2021). *Homeless health concerns.* https://medlineplus.gov/homelesshealthconcerns.html

SchoolHouseConnection. (2020). *McKinney-Vento Act: Quick reference.* https://schoolhouseconnection.org/mckinney-vento-act

SchoolHouseConnection. (2021). *Student homelessness: Lessons from the Youth Risk Behavior Survey (YRBS).* https://schoolhouseconnection.org/student-homelessness-lessons-from-the-youth-risk-behavior-survey-yrbs/

U.S. Department of Education. (2022). *A Brief History of The McKinney-Vento Act.* https://nche.ed.gov/wp-content/uploads/2018/12/ehcy_profile.pdf

U.S. Department of Education. (2019). *Chronic absenteeism in the nation's schools.* https://www2.ed.gov/datastory/chronicabsenteeism.html

U. S. Department of Education. (2018). *Education for homeless children and youths program non-regulatory guidance.* https://oese.ed.gov/files/2020/07/160240ehcyguidanceupdated082718.pdf

Washington Office of Superintendent of Public Instruction. (2020). *Designating a local homeless education liaison: A guide for school district administrators in Washington.* https://www.k12.wa.us/sites/default/files/public/homelessed/pubdocs/liaisonbrief.pdf

Chapter 15

MINORS' RIGHTS TO CONFIDENTIAL HEALTH SERVICES

Pamela Kahn, MPH, RN

DESCRIPTION OF ISSUE

The issues of minor confidentiality and consent are two of the most sensitive areas that school nurses must handle in their work with children and adolescents. Understanding the federal and state laws that govern these issues is essential, as is the need for the school nurse to be aware of the rapidly changing landscape of these laws. The school nurse is charged with making certain that a student receives the appropriate physical and mental health services. The nurse must be knowledgeable about the laws and regulations guiding who has the ability to consent to certain services and how to protect the confidentiality of health information.

This chapter offers a general overview of minor confidentiality and consent regulations. Numerous and complex laws and statutes govern the privacy of healthcare information, and these laws and statutes vary by state. Therefore, it is important to consult an attorney in one's state when faced with specific legal questions.

BACKGROUND

Over the past 30 years, the range of health services that minors may consent to has expanded significantly. These include sexual and reproductive care, mental health services, and substance abuse treatment. In most states, laws granting the ability to consent independently to specified health services, including HIV and other sexually transmitted infection (STI) services, pregnancy care, adoption, or medical care for a child, apply to minors aged 12 and older (Guttmacher Institute, 2023a). However, some states describe certain cases in which minors may consent – only those who are married, pregnant, or already parents; and four states have no relevant statutes, regulations, or case law. Nearly every state allows parents who are minors to make health care and other important decisions for their children. Most states, at the time of writing, require parental involvement in a minor's abortion; however, many states allow minors to obtain contraceptive, prenatal, and sexually transmitted infections services without parental consent (Guttmacher Institute, 2023a).

The laws that are most pertinent to school nurses who work with students are:
1) the Health Insurance Portability and Accountability Act (HIPAA) medical privacy rules- Health Insurance Portability and Accountability Act of 1996, Public Law 104-191 (see also Centers for Disease Control and Prevention [CDC], 2022)
2) the Family Educational Rights and Privacy Act (FERPA)- 20 U.S.C. § 1232g; 34 CFR Part 99 (U.S. Department of Education [USDE], 2021)
3) Title X of the Public Health Services Act - PHS Act, codified at 42 U.S.C. §§300 to 300a (see also Congressional Research Service, 2022)
4) the Child Abuse Prevention and Treatment Act- Victims of Child Abuse Act Reauthorization Act of 2018 (P.L. 115-424) (see also USDHHS, 2020)
5) state privacy laws and minor consent laws

HIPAA and FERPA are federal laws that limit the sharing of personal health information and protect the privacy of the records. In general, HIPAA pertains to the disclosure of information maintained by certain covered entities, including healthcare providers, whereas FERPA addresses the disclosure of information in education records that schools maintain.

The Health Insurance Portability and Accountability Act of 1996 (HIPAA) Privacy Rule

Congress passed HIPAA in 1996 to create standards that nationally protect the privacy of healthcare records. The HIPAA Privacy Rule took effect in 2003, establishing a federal floor of privacy protections for healthcare consumers. These rules limit how providers can use patients' medical information and are designed to govern the disclosure of protected health information. The Privacy Rule applies only to covered entities and not to all persons or institutions that collect individually identifiable health information. Covered entities are defined in the HIPAA Rule as

1) health plans,
2) healthcare clearinghouses, and
3) healthcare providers who electronically transmit health information concerning transactions for which HHS has adopted standards. Covered entities can be institutions, organizations, or persons (Health Insurance Portability and Accountability Act of 1996, Public Law 104-191; Centers for Medicare & Medicaid Services, 2022).

The Family Educational Rights and Privacy Act (FERPA)

Congress passed FERPA in 1974 with the intent to protect the privacy of educational records while at the same time assuring parental access to these same records. A parent's right to access their child's health records is much broader under FERPA than HIPAA. HIPAA states explicitly that its rules do not apply to health information held in an educational record; this information is subject to FERPA. Therefore, HIPAA and FERPA will never apply to the same information simultaneously. FERPA applies to educational agencies or institutions that receive federal funds from programs administered by the U.S. Department of Education. This includes public schools, school districts or local educational agencies, and postsecondary institutions such as colleges and universities. Generally, elementary and secondary private and parochial schools do not receive federal funding and, as such, are not subject to FERPA. FERPA also applies to agencies and organizations that consult or contract with an education agency (under certain circumstances) and to any person acting for such an agency, including school nurses, teachers, and principals. (20 U.S.C. § 1232g; 34 CFR Part 99; National Center for Youth Law [NCYL], 2018). For example, if a school nurse is hired by the local health department and assigned to a public school, the health records created by that nurse would remain part of the educational record and be subject to FERPA, not HIPAA. *(Please refer to Chapter 9 on documentation for further discussion regarding which agency school health records fall under).*

FERPA protects educational documents that contain information on a student and are maintained by an educational agency or institution or by a person acting for the agency/institution, such as school nurses who provide services at school sites but are hired by hospitals or health departments (USDE/DHHS, 2019). These documents may include immunization records, Individualized Education Program (IEP) documentation, and medical records that are part of a student's file. FERPA does not include oral communications or personal records that are kept in the sole possession of the maker, are used only as a personal memory aid, and are not accessible or revealed to any other person except as a temporary substitute for the maker of the record (20 U.S.C. § 1232g; 34 C.F.R. § 99.3; see also USDE, n.d.).

The definition of education records excludes those kept in the sole possession of the maker, which are only used as a personal memory aid and are not accessible or revealed to any other person except an individual serving as a temporary substitute. However, if the owner of the document reveals the document to any other individual, the document may be considered an education record if it meets the other criteria contained in the definition (20 U.S.C. § 1232g, 34 C.F.R. § 99.3).

FERPA requires that written permission is obtained before releasing any information in the educational record. Most often, a parent or guardian would sign for the release of records; however, once students reach the age of 18, they may sign their own release forms.

Exceptions to FERPA allow some records to be released without written release. For example, directory information that includes student name, address, telephone listing, date/place of birth, major field of study, participation in officially recognized activities and sports, weight and height of members of athletic teams, dates of attendance, degrees, and awards received, and the most recent previous educational agency or institution attended by the student may be shared with the general public after the school district has followed certain procedures defined in FERPA (20 U.S.C. § 1232g; 34 CFR Part 99; see also USDE, n.d.). Another exception allows for the sharing of information with school officials in the same school who have a "legitimate educational interest" in the information once the appropriate policies are in place at the district level. Exceptions to FERPA also exist during emergencies and for school transfers. For example, a school official generally has a legitimate educational interest if the official needs to review an education record to fulfill his or her professional responsibility (USDE, n.d.).

There are some situations in which student health information may not be considered an educational record and is therefore not subject to FERPA:

> Personal notes that a nurse has maintained regarding a student's health. These notes must be kept only as memory aids, must remain in the sole possession of the writer, are not used to replace, or avoid normal documentation, and are shared with nobody except a temporary substitute for the maker of the record (20 U.S.C. § 1232g; 34 C.F.R. § 99.3; see also California School-Based Health Alliance [CSBHA], 2023a).

> A "treatment record" may exist for students 18 years or older or those attending an institution of postsecondary education. A treatment record is defined as a record made or maintained by a physician, psychiatrist, psychologist, or other recognized professional or paraprofessional acting in their professional capacity. These records must be made, maintained, and used only in connection with the treatment of the student and disclosed only to individuals providing the treatment. For example, treatment records would include health or medical records that a university psychologist maintains only in connection with the provision of treatment to an eligible student and health or medical records that the campus health center or clinic maintains only in connection with the provision of treatment

to an eligible student. Treatment records also would include health or medical records of an eligible student in high school if the records otherwise meet the above definition. (USDHHS/USDE, 2019). FERPA gives parents the right to inspect and review their student's educational records. If a student is provided health care services, and the school nurse notes this in the student files, this information becomes part of the educational record, and as such, parents have a right to see it. This is true even in states where healthcare providers are allowed to withhold such information from parents because there is a conflict between FERPA and state law; FERPA usually prevails (The Network for Public Health Law, 2020).

Note that when treatment records are disclosed to someone other than "those persons providing treatment," then the records become educational records and are no longer considered treatment records excluded from FERPA (USDHHS/USDE, 2019). (*For more information on HIPAA and FERPA, please see Chapter 12*).

State Laws

There exists a variety of state laws that govern minor confidentiality and consent. These fall in the category of minor consent laws, medical records laws, professional licensing laws, funding program requirements, and education laws.

Whether a minor can or cannot consent to health care depends on that state's laws and regulations. Each state has specific laws addressing the ability of a minor to obtain care without the consent of a parent or guardian. State laws take into consideration both the status of the minor, such as emancipated minors, those who live apart from parents, those who are married, pregnant, or parenting, as well as the type of care that is given, such as emergency, reproductive services, mental health or drug/alcohol (American Academy of Pediatrics [AAP], n.d.) Often there are limitations on minors' ability to consent to mental health services (e.g., type of care, providers that are covered, number of visits, the age of the minor, number of visits, and health professionals who are covered).

Some states have laws in that explicitly require that a minor's health information be disclosed to a parent. The regulations allow the healthcare provider to disclose the information in these cases. Conversely, if state law prohibits disclosing information to a parent, the regulations do not allow a healthcare provider to disclose it. If the state or other law is silent on the question or permits disclosure (but does not require it), the provider is given the discretion to decide whether to grant parent access to the minor's health information (Guttmacher, 2023b).

When FERPA and state laws or regulations conflict, FERPA preempts state law. If a local education agency (LEA) believes that there is an existing conflict between the requirements under state law and its ability to comply with FERPA, the LEA must notify the USDE's Family Policy Compliance Office. (Colorado Association for School-Based Health Care [CASBHC], n.d.).

Emancipation

Depending on state law and other considerations, emancipation usually occurs at 18, the usual age of majority. An emancipated minor may be defined as a person who is not legally an adult but is no longer dependent upon their parent(s) (Cornell, 2022). State requirements for emancipation prior to the age of majority differ. However, in most cases, a minor may become emancipated by getting married, joining the military, having a child (whether married or not), leaving home, and becoming self-sufficient, or by court order. An emancipated minor may sign legally binding contracts, give medical consent, and otherwise function as an adult in society.

The minimum age in most states at which a minor can petition a court for emancipation is 16; however, some states, such as California, allow those as young as 14 to file a court petition for emancipation (Cornell Law School, Legal Information Institute, 2022). In most states, it is possible to become emancipated without filing a petition, but the options are limited and often require a parent or legal guardian's permission. <u>The school nurse needs to become familiar with the laws regarding minor emancipation in the state where they practice.</u>

The HIPAA Privacy Rule and Adolescents

HIPAA, unlike FERPA, defers to state law on matters of minor consent. Under HIPAA, a minor has more power to control and limit the release of their health records than under FERPA (CASBHC, n.d.) Generally, a parent is allowed, via HIPAA, access to their minor child's medical records when state or other law allows. However, the AAP (n.d.) lists three exceptions to the HIPAA Privacy Rule that may preclude parents from accessing records or granting access to others.

- When parent consent is not required by state or other law and the minor consented to their own care.
- When a court directs that a minor receive care.
- When, with parent agreement, a confidential relationship exists between the healthcare provider and the minor.

HIPAA has special privacy protections for minors. One of these allows minors to request that healthcare providers and healthcare plans confidentially communicate with the minor by email rather than by phone or at a place other than their home. Minors may also request that the plan or provider limit disclosure related to treatment, payment, or healthcare operations that normally would take place. Responses to these requests may vary by provider and plan, depending upon the type of request and to whom the request is made (Guttmacher, 2023b).

The HIPAA privacy rule allows a healthcare provider or plan to deny access to health records to parents who they suspect have subjected the minor to abuse, neglect, or domestic violence or in situations when treating the parent as the personal representative could endanger the minor. The privacy rule also allows a provider or plan to disclose a minor's health information to help prevent or diminish an imminent threat to the health and safety of the person or the public (Guttmacher, 2023b). Providers should consult with legal counsel when considering denying access to records under these privacy protections.

The HIPAA Privacy Rule allows a healthcare provider to disclose a student's protected health information to a school nurse, physician, or other healthcare provider for treatment purposes without the authorization of the student's parent or the student. A physician would be able to discuss healthcare needs, medication orders, and other issues concerning the student's care while at school with the school nurse. The school nurse, though, is governed by FERPA and, as such, would be limited in what he/she would be able to share with the physician (USDHHS, 2013). A healthcare provider not employed by the school district and subject to HIPAA may share confidential medical information with other healthcare providers for referral and treatment purposes without needing a signed release. However, if this information is shared with others who are not health professionals, including teachers and other school staff, a HIPAA-compliant consent form is required before any information may be disclosed (NCYL, 2018).

Federal Substance Abuse Confidentiality Requirements and HIPAA

Confidentiality requirements for federally assisted alcohol and drug abuse treatment programs are regulated by federal law and regulations that outline under what limited circumstances information about the client's treatment may be disclosed with and without the client's consent. These confidentiality requirements are often more restrictive than HIPAA regulations, and providers must follow the more stringent confidentiality protection (USDHHS, 2004). Generally, federally subsidized substance abuse treatment programs under 42 C.F.R., Part 2 cannot disclose information without written consent. The minor's signed consent is required before health information can be released to anyone, including a parent or legal guardian (Substance Abuse and Mental Health Services Administration, 2023). The NCYL (2014) lists conditions under which a program or individual may share information with a parent without obtaining prior written consent:
- The minor's situation poses a substantial threat to the life or physical well-being of the minor or another.
- The threat may be reduced by communicating relevant facts to the minor's parents; **and**
- The minor lacks the capacity because of extreme youth or a mental or physical condition to make a rational decision on whether to disclose to the parents.

Almost all states have implemented laws that allow minors to consent to treatment for substance abuse. School staff are encouraged to familiarize themselves with the laws pertaining to this consent for their specific states and the confidentiality laws that apply to treatment programs that are not federally funded.

The Federal Title X Family Planning Program

The Federal Title X of the Public Health Service Act was created in 1970 to provide free or low-cost family planning and related health services available to eligible individuals, including adolescents. Regulations require that Title X-funded services are available to all adolescents, regardless of age. If services are wholly or partly funded by Title X, minors of any age or marital status may consent to these services, and the provision of these services is not dependent upon parental consent or notification. The laws governing Title X-funded programs guarantee the confidentiality of patient information, including that of minor patients. Covered entities are prohibited from disclosing or granting access to parents without the minor's authorization (NCYL, 2011).

In cases where state law requires parental consent or notification for services, Title X providers must allow adolescents to obtain Title X services with their own consent. Family planning services funded through other federal programs, such as Medicaid, are governed by different confidentiality rules but provide protections for adolescents related to confidential contraceptive care.

IMPLICATIONS FOR SCHOOL NURSE PRACTICE

Privacy and Confidentiality Considerations

The complexity and variability of laws surrounding minor confidentiality and consent require that the school nurse to be knowledgeable about all applicable local, state, and federal laws. Nurses must consider a student's age, their emancipation status, the type of services that the student is seeking, etc., and determine how federal and state laws govern these various situations. School nurses must always keep in mind the goal of protecting the privacy of a student while at the same time avoiding illegal or unethical disclosure of health information. It is important for the school nurse to consider the difference between adhering to laws regarding confidentiality and respecting a student's privacy and when it may be acceptable to violate said privacy. Privacy may be defined as the right of the student to keep information about themselves from being disclosed without their permission (Institute of Education Sciences, National Center for Educational Statistics, n.d.). Confidentiality means that the information disclosed by a student will be maintained in a confidential manner to the extent allowable by law and will not be disclosed to anyone without the student's consent (CURA, 2023). Permission to disclose confidential information should always be obtained directly from the student.

Support Systems

School nurses are obligated to protect the confidentiality of students and their parent/guardian(s). At the same time, nurses face the challenge of encouraging communication between these students and their parent/guardian(s) in a way that is respectful of the student's need for privacy and recognizing the support that parent/guardian(s) can provide to their child in most situations. Where there are real and potentially dangerous consequences to talking with parent/guardian(s) (i.e., family violence, potential homelessness), school nurses can encourage students to look to other adults such as extended family members, social workers, clergy, and others who may be able to offer support. When possible, school nurses should review with minors and parents the limits of confidentiality and document all informed consent discussions. Publicizing information in their office and other public spots on campus on the rights of minor confidentiality may encourage students to seek health care even when they are unable to speak to family members or other adults.

While a school nurse may feel that confidentiality is in the student's best interest, laws and regulations may prevent the nurse from guaranteeing this protection. In such situations, the school nurse may want to consider referring the student to a Title X-funded clinic or other facility that can better meet the student's needs. The critical point is that if students are not assured access to confidential health care, they may simply stop seeking the needed services. School nurses need to be aware of surrounding clinics and their policies around confidentiality.

Protection of School Records

A school nurse whose records are subject to FERPA cannot promise students that their education records containing health information will be kept confidential. Under FERPA, parents or guardians have access to the education records of their unemancipated minor children, including any health information contained in those records (USDHHS/USDE, 2019).

However, FERPA contains no obligation that schools notify parents about services that the minor has received without the parent's consent. If the nurse is holding information about the "minor consent" health information only in their personal notes (sole possession), these notes are not considered part of the education record and, as such, are not subject to the rules of FERPA. FERPA does not cover health information in oral form or personal notes. However, once these records are shared with anyone other than a temporary substitute for the maker, they become part of the education file and are subject to FERPA (CSBHA, 2023a).

It is important to note that HIPAA states explicitly that its rules do not apply to health information held in an educational record; this information is subject to FERPA. Therefore, HIPAA and FERPA will never apply to the same information at the same time. However, state medical confidentiality laws do not have this same exception. Therefore, state confidentiality law can apply to health information in an education record subject to FERPA. If FERPA and state law provide conflicting guidance pertaining to disclosure or protections, legal counsel should be sought regarding which rule to follow (CSBHA, 2023b).

School-Based Health Centers and Confidentiality

Schools that operate school-based health centers (SBHCs) must pay close attention to the interaction between HIPAA and FERPA regulations for services the student may obtain at such centers. Depending upon whether the program or provider is considered an "educational agency "or the agent of the educational agency determines if the records of the school health program are subject to HIPAA or FERPA rules. The "Joint Guidance" issued by the U.S. Department of Health and Human Services and the U.S. Department of Education (USDHHS/USDE, 2019) provides some case examples that may be used to determine which federal law applies; unfortunately, there is no clear-cut checklist to determine where a program might fit. SBHC records are not subject to FERPA "if the center is funded, administered and operated by or on behalf of a public or private health, social services, or other non-educational agency or individual." In such a case, the records would be subject to HIPAA, even if the services were being provided on school grounds, since the SBHC would not be acting on behalf of the school. Conversely, if the SBHC is funded, administered, and operated by or on behalf of a school or educational institution, the records are considered "education records" and are subject to FERPA (CSBHA, 2023b). If in doubt, the provider is recommended to seek legal counsel regarding which federal law governs school health records and staff. (*Please see Chapter 47 for more information on school-based health centers*).

CONCLUSION

An important guiding principle in the school setting that should be considered is that confidential health information should be shared on a need-to-know basis only, and this sharing is in the interest of keeping a student safe and functioning to their highest capacity in the educational setting. Licensed staff (i.e., the school nurse) are responsible for educating all non-licensed staff on the appropriate sharing of health records and informing non-licensed staff of the laws governing such records' disclosure.

Federal and state laws and other rules and regulations at the district or school level govern minor confidentiality and consent to care. School nurses need to be knowledgeable regarding applicable state minor consent and privacy laws and state health privacy laws in general. Additionally, the nurse needs to consider the institution's culture where they are employed, ensuring that school and district administrators are informed regarding the federal and state legal guidelines and support the important balance of parental and minor's rights.

MINORS' RIGHTS TO CONFIDENTIAL HEALTH SERVICES

When considering minor consent and confidentiality, the school nurse must honor both the legal and ethical obligations of a nurse to the patient.

> Please see APPENDIX: "Minors May Consent to" and see Chapter 26 for more information on consent to healthcare.

RESOURCES

American Academy of Pediatrics & Healthy Foster Care America. (n.d.) *Confidentiality Laws Tip Sheet.*

https://www.aap.org/en-us/advocacy-and-policy/aap-health-initiatives/healthy-foster-care-america/Documents/Confidentiality_Laws.pdf

Center for Adolescent Health & The Law. https://www.cahl.org/

Guttmacher Institute https://www.guttmacher.org/

National Center for Health Law http://teenhealthlaw.org/

Gudeman, R., & Madg, S. (n.d.) *The Federal Title X Family Planning Program: Privacy and Access Rules for Adolescents* Retrieved from National Center for Youth Law http://youthlaw.org/publication/the-federal-title-x-family-planning-program-privacy-and-access-rules-for-adolescents1/

REFERENCE

43 C.F.R., Part 2. https://www.ecfr.gov/current/title-42/chapter-I/subchapter-A/part-2

American Academy of Pediatrics. (n.d.). *Confidentiality laws tip sheet*. Retrieved 7-3-23 from https://downloads.aap.org/AAP/PDF/Foster%20Care/Confidentiality_Laws.pdf

California School-Based Health Alliance. (2023a). *FERPA: an overview for California school health professionals.* https://www.schoolhealthcenters.org/resources/sbhc-operations/student-records-consent-and-confidentiality/california-guide/ferpa-basics/

California School-Based Health Alliance. (2023b). *Key points about HIPAA and FERPA in California.* https://www.schoolhealthcenters.org/resources/sbhc-operations/student-records-consent-and-confidentiality/california-guide/key-points-about-hipaa-and-ferpa-in-california/

Centers for Disease Control and Prevention. (2022). *Health insurance portability and accountability act of 1996 (HIPAA).* https://www.cdc.gov/phlp/publications/topic/hipaa.html

Centers for Medicare & Medicaid Services. (2022). *Are you a covered entity?* https://www.cms.gov/Regulations-and-Guidance/Administrative-Simplification/HIPAA-ACA/AreYouaCoveredEntity

Child Abuse Prevention and Treatment Act- Victims of Child Abuse Act Reauthorization Act of 2018 (P.L. 115-424)

Colorado Association for School-Based Health Care. (n.d.). *Understanding minor consent and confidentiality in Colorado.* Retrieved 7-3-23 from https://coloradoearlycolleges.org/wp-content/uploads/CEC_Files/CEC_Douglas_County Documents_Forms/ALL_DouglasCountySites/MinorConsentforTreatmentinColorado.pdf

Congressional Research Service. (2022). *Title X family planning program.* https://crsreports.congress.gov/product/pdf/IF/IF10051

Cornell Law School Legal Information Institute (2022). *Emancipated minor.* https://www.law.cornell.edu/wex/emancipated_minor"https://www.law.cornell.edu/wex/emancipated_minor

CURA Network. (2023). *Privacy v. confidentiality.* Loyola University Chicago. https://www.luc.edu/cura/forparentsandfamilies/privacyvconfidentiality/

Family Educational Rights and Privacy Act (FERPA)- 20 U.S.C. § 1232g; 34 CFR Part 99, https://www.ecfr.gov/current/title-34/subtitle-A/part-99/subpart-A/section-99.3

Guttmacher Institute. (2023a). State laws and policies. *An overview of consent to reproductive health services by young people.* https://www.guttmacher.org/state-policy/explore/overview-minors-consent-law

Guttmacher Institute (2023b). *The HIPPA privacy rule and adolescents: Legal questions and clinical challenges.* https://onlinelibrary.wiley.com/doi/10.1363/3608004

Health Insurance Portability and Accountability Act (HIPAA) medical privacy rules- Health Insurance Portability and Accountability Act of 1996, Public Law 104-191

Institute of Education Sciences, National Center for Education Statistics. (n.d.). A primer for privacy. Retrieved on 7/26/23 at https://nces.ed.gov/pubs97/p97527/Sec1_txt.asp

National Center for Youth Law. (2014). *California minor consent and confidentiality laws.* https://www.careinnovations.org/wp-content/uploads/2017/10/CA_Minor_Consent__Confidentiality_Laws.pdf

National Center for Youth Law. (2018). *HIPAA or FERPA? A primer on sharing school health information in California.* https://www.courts.ca.gov/documents/BTB25-2O-01.pdf

The Network for Public Health Law. (2020, January). *Data privacy in school nursing; navigating the complex*

landscape of data privacy laws (part II). https://www.networkforphl.org/wp-content/uploads/2020/01/Data-Privacy-in-School-Nursing-Part-II-1-23-2020.pdf

Substance Abuse and Mental Health Services Administration. (2023). Substance abuse confidentiality regulations.

https://www.samhsa.gov/about-us/who-we-are/laws-regulations/confidentiality-regulations-faqs

Title X of the Public Health Services Act - PHS Act, codified at 42 U.S.C. §§300 to 300a

U.S. Department of Education. (n.d.). *Protecting student privacy; 34 CFR part 99 – family educational rights and privacy.* Retrieved 7-3-23 from https://studentprivacy.ed.gov/ferpa

U.S. Department of Education. (2021). *Family rights and privacy act (FERPA).* https://www2.ed.gov/policy/gen/guid/fpco/ferpa/index.html

U.S. Department of Health & Human Services. (2004). *The confidentiality of alcohol and drug abuse patient records regulation and the HIPAA privacy rule: implications for alcohol and substance abuse programs.* https://www.samhsa.gov/sites/default/files/samhsapart2-hipaacomparison2004.pdf

U.S. Department of Health & Human Services. (2013). *Does the HIPAA privacy rule allow a health care provider to disclose protected health information (PHI) about a student to a school nurse or physician?* https://www.hhs.gov/hipaa/for-professionals/faq/517/does-hipaa-allow-a-health-care-provider-to-disclose-information-to-a-school-nurse/index.html

U. S. Department of Health & Human Services. (2020). *The child abuse prevention and treatment act.* (CSAPTA). https://www.acf.hhs.gov/cb/law-regulation/child-abuse-prevention-and-treatment-act-capta

U.S. Department of Health and Human Services & U.S. Department of Education. (2019). *Joint guidance on the application of the Family Educational Rights and Privacy Act (FERPA) and the Heath Insurance Portability and Accountability Act of 1996 (HIPAA) to student health records.* https://studentprivacy.ed.gov/sites/default/files/resource_document/file/2019%20HIPAA%20FERPA%20Joint%20Guidance%20508.pdf

U.S. Department of Health & Human Services. (2022). *What constitutes a "serious and imminent" threat that would permit a health care provider to disclose PHI to prevent harm to the patient, another person, or the public without the patient's authorization or permission?* https://www.hhs.gov/hipaa/for-professionals/faq/3002/what-constitutes-serious-imminent-threat-that-would-permit-health-care-provider-disclose-phi-to-prevent-harm-patient-public-without-patients-authorization-permission/index.html

APPENDIX

MINORS MAY CONSENT TO:

STATE	CONTRACEPTIVE SERVICES	STI SERVICES	PRENATAL CARE	ADOPTION	MEDICAL CARE FOR MINOR'S CHILD	ABORTION SERVICES
Alabama	All[†]	All[*]	All	All	All	Parental Consent
Alaska	All	All	All		All	▼ (Parental Notice)
Arizona	All	All		All		Parental Consent
Arkansas	All	All[*]	All		All	Parental Consent
California	All	All	All	All		▼ (Parental Consent)
Colorado	All	All	All	All	All	Parental Notice
Connecticut	Some	All		Legal counsel	All	All
Delaware	All[*]	All[‡]	All[*]	All	All	Parental Notice[‡]
Dist. of Columbia	All	All	All	All	All	All
Florida	Some	All	All		All	Parental Consent and Notice
Georgia	All	All[*]	All	All	All	Parental Notice
Hawaii	All[*,†]	All[*,†]	All[*,†]	All		
Idaho	All	All[†]	All	All	All	Parental Consent
Illinois	Some	All[*]	All	All	All	
Indiana	Some	All		All		Parental Consent
Iowa	All	All				Parental Notice
Kansas	Some	All[*]	Some	All	All	Parental Consent
Kentucky	All[*]	All[*]	All[*]	Legal counsel	All	Parental Consent
Louisiana	Some	All[*]		Parental consent	All	Parental Consent
Maine	All*	All[*]	All*			All
Maryland	All[*]	All[*]	All[*]	All	All	Parental Notice
Massachusetts	All	All	All		All	Parental Consent
Michigan	Some	All[*]	All[*]	Parental consent	All	Parental Consent
Minnesota	All[*]	All[*]	All[*]	Parental consent	All	
Mississippi	Some	All	All	All	All	Parental Consent
Missouri	Some	All[*]	All[*]	Legal counsel	All	Parental Consent

STATE	CONTRACEPTIVE SERVICES	STI SERVICES	PRENATAL CARE	ADOPTION	MEDICAL CARE FOR MINOR'S CHILD	ABORTION SERVICES
Montana	All*	All*	All*	Legal counsel	All	Parental Notice‡
Nebraska	Some	All				Parental Consent
Nevada	Some	All	Some	All	All	▼ (Parental Notice)
New Hampshire	Some	All†	Some	AllΩ		Parental Notice
New Jersey	Some†	All*,β	All*	All	All	▼ (Parental Notice)
New Mexico	All	All	All	All		▼ (Parental Consent)
New York	All	All	All	All	All	
North Carolina	All	All	All			Parental Consent
North Dakota		All†	ξ*	All		Parental Consent
Ohio		All		All		Parental Consent
Oklahoma	Some	All*	All*	All†	All	Parental Consent and Notice
Oregon	All*	All	All*,‡			
Pennsylvania	All†	All	All	Parental notice	All	Parental Consent
Rhode Island		All		Parental consent	All	Parental Consent
South Carolina	All	All	All	All	All	Parental Consent‡
South Dakota	Some	All				Parental Notice
Tennessee	All	All	All	All	All	Parental Consent
Texas	Some	All*	All*			Parental Consent and Notice
Utah	Some	All	All	All	All	Parental Consent and Notice
Vermont	Some	All		All		
Virginia	All	All	All	All	All	Parental Consent and Notice
Washington	All	All†	All	Legal counsel		
West Virginia	Some	All	Some	All		Parental Notice
Wisconsin		All				Parental Consent
Wyoming	All	All		All		Parental Consent and Notice
TOTAL	27+DC	50+DC	33+DC	28+DC	30+DC	2+DC

Notes: "All" applies to all individuals or to those at a specified age (such as 12 or 14) and older. "Some" applies to specified categories of young people (those who have a health issue, or are married, pregnant, considered mature). Totals include only those states that allow all individuals to consent.

▼ Permanently enjoined by court order; law not in effect.

* Physicians may, but are not required to, inform the young person's parents.

† Applies to individuals 14 and older. Hawaii allows individuals aged 14 and older to consent to STI care and allows all individuals, regardless of age, to consent to HIV/AIDS care.

‡ The abortion law in Delaware and Montana applies to individuals younger than 16. Oregon's prenatal care law applies to individuals at least 15 years old. South Carolina's abortion law applies to those younger than 17.

Ω A court may require parental consent.

β New Jersey allows all individuals, regardless of age, to consent to STI care and allows individuals aged 13 or older to consent to HIV/AIDS care.

ξ Individuals younger than 18 may consent to prenatal care in the first trimester and the first visit after the first trimester. Parental consent required for all other visits.

Source: Guttmacher Institute, An overview of minors' consent law, *State Laws and Policies (as of June 1, 2023),* 2023. Retrieved 7-3-23 from https://www.guttmacher.org/state-policy/explore/overview-minors-consent-law.

Chapter 16

LEGAL PROCEEDINGS – SUBPOENAS, LAWSUITS, AND INVESTIGATIONS

Marlene S. Garvis, JD, MSN*

DESCRIPTION OF ISSUE

While rare, there may be occasions where a school nurse will be called to testify in a legal proceeding, produce documents pursuant to a court order, participate in a criminal investigation, and even respond as a named party in a lawsuit. This chapter provides basic information describing each of these processes, highlights best practices, and outlines a school nurse's options and legal obligations regarding each proceeding.

BACKGROUND

In order to better understand the implications of this topic for school nurse practice, the following basic information is important to know:

Subpoenas: A subpoena is a document used to summon witnesses or the submission of evidence before a court or other legal proceeding. There are generally three types of subpoenas:
- subpoenas that require testimony (also referred to as "*subpoena ad* testificandum");
- subpoenas that require the production of documents for a legal proceeding (also referred to as "*subpoena duces tecum*"); and
- subpoenas that require both testimony and the production of documents.

The legal process for issuing and complying with subpoenas can vary depending upon the law applicable in the related court's jurisdiction. In many states, in order to be valid, a subpoena must be issued and signed by a judge or court official. <u>Where a judge or court official does not sign a subpoena, the school nurse should seek legal counsel to verify that the document is a lawfully issued subpoena.</u>

Lawsuits – Civil lawsuits generally commence when one party files a formal written complaint with a court. Typically, a complaint must identify the accused party (the "defendant" in the case), allege facts establishing a cause of action, and identify the legal theory or cause of action that serves as the basis of the case being brought by the accuser (the "plaintiff" in the case).

Investigations – Many different types of investigations may occur within a school. This chapter addresses investigations of students by law enforcement, child welfare officials, and US Immigration and Customs Enforcement (ICE). Child neglect or abuse investigations are typically the most commonly encountered by school nurses, but other law enforcement investigations also occur in schools.

---

*Original author: Erin Gilsbach, Esquire (2017)

IMPLICATIONS FOR SCHOOL NURSE PRACTICE

Student Confidentiality and Subpoenas

The issuance of a lawful subpoena is one situation in which a school is permitted to disclose personally identifiable information from student records under the Family Educational Rights and Privacy Act ("FERPA") (34 CFR §99.31(a)(9)(i)). In such cases, however, unless the court has specifically ordered that the information regarding the subpoena not be disclosed to the parents, the school is legally required to "make a reasonable effort to notify the parent" (or the student, if the student is at least eighteen years old) before complying with the subpoena. The purpose of doing this is to give the parent (or eligible student) time to seek protective action (FERPA at 34 CFR §99.31(a)(9)(ii)). As discussed in *Chapter 11* regarding confidentiality, a "parent," under FERPA, is defined as "a parent of a student and includes a natural parent, a guardian, or an individual acting as a parent in the absence of a parent or a guardian" (FERPA, 20 U.S.C. §1232g; 34 CFR §99.3).

Subpoenas Requiring the Production of Documents

Upon receipt of a subpoena to produce school-related documents, such as student records, school nurses should immediately notify their supervisor or building administrator. Because such a subpoena involves the potential release of education records, which FERPA governs, the school may need to take necessary action to notify parents (see the above discussion regarding "Student Confidentiality and Subpoenas") and confirm the subpoena's validity. Because nursing/health records are student records governed by FERPA's confidentiality and disclosure requirements, rather than medical records governed by HIPAA's privacy rule (*see Chapter 12, Family Education Rights and Privacy Act and Health Insurance Portability Accountability Act; see also* US Departments of Education and Health and Human Services, 2019/2008), FERPA's notice provision, explained above, would apply.

Right to Counsel / Seeking the Advice of Counsel upon Receipt of Subpoena to Testify

While it may not always be necessary, individuals served with a subpoena to testify in a court proceeding may also have the right to have counsel present (typically at their own expense unless they have insurance), depending upon the state and type of court (federal or state) in which the matter is brought. For example, the Federal Administrative Procedure Act grants the right to representation by counsel where a subpoena to appear is issued. The federal rule states: "[a] person compelled to appear in person before an agency or representative thereof is entitled to be accompanied, represented, and advised by counsel or, if permitted by the agency, by other qualified representatives. A party is entitled to appear in person or by, or with counsel in an agency hearing" (Federal Administrative Procedure Act, 5 USC §555(b), 1946).

Anytime a school nurse is served with a subpoena related to either the school nurse's employment or a student in the school, the school nurse should seek the advice of legal counsel (i.e., the school board attorney or a privately retained attorney – see commentary below) to ascertain whether the subpoena is valid, was properly served, and whether the testimony poses any potential personal liability for the school nurse. Sometimes, an attorney's involvement can eliminate the need for testimony by offering a written document or student records instead. If nothing else, the school nurse's attorney can contact the subpoenaing party's legal counsel and obtain more information about what that party expects to ask or elicit from the school nurse. This information can be beneficial both in the school nurse's preparation for testimony and to the school nurse's peace of mind knowing what will be expected of their testimony and what to anticipate in the legal proceeding. Legal counsel can also be beneficial when a school nurse is being called to testify in a court outside of their local area. Attorneys can often facilitate witness testimony via video conferencing or telephone conferencing.

The school nurse may not need to hire private counsel for these purposes. Suppose the school nurse is a member of a collective bargaining unit ("union") or other representative organization. In that case, a staff attorney may be responsible for providing this type of legal counsel. In some cases, where the subpoena is related to custody or other matter that does not appear to present a conflict of interest, with the permission of the school administration, the school's legal counsel may be able to provide legal counsel to the school nurse and the school. Because school attorneys often represent the school in employment matters as well as general consulting matters, a school nurse should not seek counsel from the school's attorney in cases that involve allegations of misconduct on the part of the school nurse, potential malpractice claims, or other potential liability that may have employment implications. (*Please see Chapter 2 for more information regarding malpractice*).

If the school nurse believes that he or she would be best served by hiring private counsel, or if the school nurse is unable to obtain access to an attorney through the union or school district, the school nurse should consult with private counsel and a limited consult on this type of matter can usually be done for a set fee. Based upon that information, the school nurse can then better determine whether to continue to retain private counsel or whether the risk of potential liability is small enough that the risk outweighs the expense of private attorney representation.

Technical Issues Regarding Issuance of Subpoena

Each state has its own rules regarding the requirements for serving someone with a subpoena, and rules regarding matters brought in state court may differ from those that apply to federal court proceedings. Consultation with an attorney who practices in the jurisdiction in question can verify that a subpoena and its service are valid. Unless the issue poses a significant threat of liability to the school nurse, seeking to have a subpoena quashed on a technicality, such as improper service, is usually not possible or cost-effective since most courts allow parties to "cure" (a legal term meaning "correct" or "fix") procedural defects through proper re-service. In addition, minor spelling errors in a name or address, where the intended recipient is clear and where the subpoena reached the intended recipient despite such errors, are generally insufficient to invalidate the subpoena.

Subpoenas Requiring an Individual to Testify in Child Custody Case

Many subpoenas issued to school nurses require the appearance of the school nurse as a witness in a child custody matter. In such cases, the parent calling the school nurse as a witness often believes that the school nurse has information that is helpful to their case (or harmful to the other parent's case) and will cause the judge to award custody in their favor. Custody cases in which school nurses are called to testify are generally cases involving custody of a child with health-related needs. The parent may seek to have the school nurse testify as to which parent has been more engaged in addressing the student's health-related needs in the school setting or which parent appears to be more knowledgeable about the student's health condition. In some cases, the parent calling the school nurse to testify may seek to have the school nurse testify about a conversation that the school nurse had with the student or treatment provided by the school nurse in the school health office that may be significant to the custody issue at hand.

When providing testimony, the school nurse should focus on factual statements and avoid hypothesizing or answering hypothetical questions to which the answer may change depending upon surrounding circumstances. For instance, a school nurse should consult nursing entries in the student health record to answer the question of which parent communicates with the school most often or addresses medical needs, such as changes in medication, most frequently. School nurses should avoid or be cautious about answering questions for which they do not have first-hand factual information, such as, "which parent is most concerned about the child's medical well-being?" While the school nurse may have an opinion on this question, he or she likely possesses no factual information regarding quantifying either parent's concern.

Subpoena to Testify in Child Abuse Case

Another circumstance frequently arises for school nurses is a subpoena to testify in a child abuse or endangerment case. School nurses are often on the front lines of child abuse reporting and investigation in schools due to their medical/health expertise. School nurses are legally mandated child abuse reporters in most states, and it is common for teachers, administrators, and other school employees to seek the opinion or advice of a school nurse in a case of suspected abuse. As a result, school nurses are usually called to testify in child abuse cases more often than their non-medical colleagues. Due to the highly protective immunity that is afforded to mandated reporters under most state laws, testimony in these types of criminal matters generally poses few legal issues and, unlike custody matters, where the student's health records are likely to be sufficient, a school nurse's testimony regarding the nature and extent of the injury to the child can be invaluable in the prosecution of a child abuse case.

It is a good idea for school nurses to be familiar with the immunity provisions in their state's law related to mandated child abuse reporting and participating in a legal proceeding regarding the abuse of a child so that they can be fully informed as to whether they should seek legal counsel in cases where they are called as witnesses in child abuse cases. This information is often readily available through the state health department, state nursing organizations, and collective bargaining units. Due to the strong protections afforded to reporters and witnesses in most states, testifying in a child abuse case generally does not pose a legal liability to the school nurse as a witness. However, if the school nurse has any questions about this, the nurse should seek legal counsel to discuss the situation before testifying.

During testimony, school nurses should limit testimony to that of which they have factual knowledge and avoid making assumptions, suppositions, or hypotheses. For instance, in a child abuse case where a child suffers from chronic and untreated head lice, the school nurse could testify to the fact that the student has lice, when the school nurse became aware of the lice, what treatments the school nurse recommended, and what notifications and information were communicated to which parent on which date and by what means (phone call, meeting, email, note home, etc.). In most cases where both parents have partial custody, and the student lives with each parent for part of the week, it is unlikely that the school nurse would have sufficient information to be able to opine or hypothesize about in which household the lice problem exists, whether it is limited to only one household or is a problem in both, or which parent(s) may be at fault for the issue.

There may be other pertinent facts of which the school nurse has knowledge, such as if the condition clears up every time the mother is away on business. For example, whether the child stays with the father for extended periods of time but then the lice recur when the mother returns, and the child resumes the regular custodial arrangement. Testimony should be based upon factual assertions, not generalizations or hypotheses. In the example described above, a school nurse should not be offering her opinion that the head lice infestation "was probably the mother's fault." If there is a factual basis behind such a broad statement, it is the underlying set of facts upon which such an opinion could be made to which the school nurse should testify, not a conclusion for which no specific facts have been given.

Responding to a Lawsuit

Being served with a complaint as a named defendant in a legal action can be alarming, but in most cases, there is little likelihood that the individual defendants in an action that is truly against the school itself will remain in the case for long. This is due to the heightened tort claims protections afforded to school employees in most states and the fact that most federal and state laws applicable to schools do not permit a cause of action against individual defendants. Upon a school nurse's receipt of a complaint in which he or she is a named defendant, the school nurse should immediately obtain legal counsel to determine the next steps. Where the complaint involves the school or conduct that occurred when the school nurse was acting in their official capacity as a school nurse, the school nurse should also immediately notify the school administration.

Depending upon the nature of the action and the school nurse's individual circumstances, the school nurse may be able to use counsel that might be available through a collective bargaining unit if that is a service offered as part of membership. Otherwise, the school nurse will need to secure private legal counsel. Either way, it is important to seek legal counsel as quickly as possible after being notified of direct involvement with a lawsuit since the timeline for filing motions, responding to the complaint, and taking other necessary legal action has already begun. The school nurse's attorney can provide legal counsel regarding when and how to notify the school of the action, identify the information that the attorney will need to defend the case, or, ideally, how the attorney can have the school nurse removed from the case as a named defendant.

Litigation Hold

Any time there is pending litigation, litigation is threatened, or someone reasonably suspects that litigation is imminent, there generally is an obligation to perform a "litigation hold," which means that all evidence potentially related to such litigation must be maintained and may not be destroyed. For example, if a parent informs the school nurse that he is going to hire a lawyer to address a particular issue with legal action against the school or the school nurse individually, that may be sufficient to initiate a "litigation hold." Wherever a school nurse is aware of litigation or has reason to believe that there may be a lawsuit in the future, the school nurse should communicate that information directly to the school's administration and request guidance regarding preserving records.

Investigations

Schools are involved in numerous types of investigations of students by state and federal child welfare and law enforcement agencies, and some are more common than others. The nature of the investigation and investigator governs which laws are applicable in any given situation. Regardless of the nature or type of investigation, school nurses should immediately contact the school's administration whenever an investigator requests or demands personally identifiable student information.

Criminal Investigations

School nurses may be called upon to participate in a criminal investigation. Although there are some specific exceptions to FERPA's written parental consent requirement related to investigations by the US Department of Homeland Security, personally identifiable information about students may only be shared with police in a criminal investigation if there is a valid judicial order, such as a search warrant or subpoena, and in most cases, parents must be notified prior to compliance. Prior to sharing any student information with police or participating in a criminal investigation, school nurses should notify the school administration to ensure that all necessary protocols are followed.

Many schools have School Resource Officers, or "SROs," who assist with school safety. School resource officers have dual school and law enforcement roles. When a school resource officer asks to share personally identifiable information about a student, the school nurse should discuss the request with a school administrator. When an SRO requests the information in their law enforcement capacity, a valid warrant must be produced.

Child Abuse Investigations

School nurses are frequently asked to participate in child abuse investigations. Depending upon applicable state law, child abuse investigations may be conducted by local police, county child welfare agencies, or another entity. FERPA does not contain a specific exception to the written consent requirements for disclosures of student information in child abuse investigations. It does contain a "health or safety emergency" exception, however, which permits schools to disclose education records where there is an imminent threat to the health or safety of the child or others. In examining the issue, the Family Policy Compliance Office (FPCO), which is the federal office responsible for interpreting and enforcing FERPA, deemed that provision to not be applicable, as a matter of course, to mandated child abuse, due to the fact that a blanket release of information in cases where a school employee knows of or suspects that a child may be subject to abuse is overly broad for the "health or safety emergency" exception. The FPCO did conclude, however, that the Federal Child Abuse Prevention, Adoption and Family Services Act of 1988 ("CAPAFSA"), which amended the Child Abuse Prevention and Treatment Act ("CAPTA") supersedes FERPA. See 42 U.S.C. §§ 5106a(b)(1)(A) and 5106a(b)(4)(A) and 45 CFR 1340.14(c)). CAPTA requires disclosing and re-disclosing information concerning child abuse and neglect to entities determined by the state to need the information. Thus, federal guidance dictates that school employees may disclose personally identifiable information related to potential child abuse to the entities responsible for conducting child abuse investigations, which may include child protective services agencies and law enforcement. When informed about such investigations, the school nurse should request guidance from the school administration on how to respond to investigators' requests.

Immigration and Customs Enforcement (ICE)/Immigration Investigations

The law does not prohibit the Immigration and Customs Enforcement (ICE) from conducting investigations and arresting or detaining undocumented students in schools; however, the Department of Homeland Security has issued a policy statement stating that it "can accomplish . . . [its] enforcement mission without denying or limiting individuals' access to needed medical care, children access to their schools, . . . and more." (Policy

Memorandum, US Department of Homeland Security, October 27, 2021). While federal policy may change at any time, it is important for the school nurse to seek legal counsel if confronted with a situation that affects children's access to their schools.

Unlike child abuse investigations, no exception to FERPA's nondisclosure requirement exists for ICE investigations. Thus, any request for records by ICE would require a warrant or other judicial order. As with regular law enforcement investigations, school nurses should immediately inform their school administration regarding any requests for education records by ICE. Where no warrant or judicial order is produced, the school should seek legal counsel for assistance. Likewise, the school nurse should consult legal counsel if a warrant is produced, but its meaning is ambiguous.

CONCLUSION

While school nurses may not be required to deal with subpoenas, lawsuits, or investigations by law enforcement or other agencies on a regular basis, it is important for them to understand the legal issues involved and their rights and obligations under the law. In some instances, including situations where there is a question regarding what laws apply and what would constitute a legally defensible course of action, school nurses should seek legal counsel, either through the school, through their collective bargaining unit, if available/applicable, or privately.

> Please also see Chapter 2- Malpractice/Professional Liability.

RESOURCES

Administrative Procedure Act [PUBLIC LAW 404—79TH CONGRESS]. (1946).
https://www.justice.gov/sites/default/files/jmd/legacy/2014/05/01/act-pl79-404.pdf

Family Educational Rights and Privacy Act (FERPA) US Department of Education. (2021).
https://www2.ed.gov/print/policy/gen/guid/fpco/ferpa/index.htmlx

Family Education Rights & Privacy Act (FERPA) Regulations. US Department of Education. (2022).
https://www2.ed.gov/policy/gen/reg/ferpa/index.html?exp=6

Summary of Laws Related to Child and Adolescent Mental Health (2020), Public Health Informatics Institute.
https://phii.org/wp-content/uploads/2020/08/Summary-of-Laws-Related-to-CAMH.pdf

45 CFR § 1340.14 - Eligibility requirements. - Content Details - CFR-2014-title45-vol4-sec1340-14 (2014).
https://www.govinfo.gov/app/details/CFR-2014-title45-vol4/CFR-2014-title45-vol4-sec1340-14

REFERENCES

Child Abuse Prevention, Adoption and Family Services Act of 1988 ("CAPAFSA"), 42 USC §§ 5106a (b)(1)(A) and 5106a(b)(4)(A) and 45 CFR 1340.14(c).

Child Abuse Prevention and Treatment Act ("CAPTA"), 42 USC §§ 5106a(b)(1)(A) and 5106a(b)(4)(A). See 45 CFR 1340.14(c).

Family Educational Rights and Privacy Act ("FERPA"), Public Law 100-294, 20 USC §1232g, 34 CFR §§991, et seq. (1974). See also 20 USC §1232g, 34 CFR Part 98 (Protection of Pupil Rights Amendment and 34 CFR Part 99 (Family Education Rights and Privacy). Full Text of Regulations can be found at the US Department of Education's website: http://www2.ed.gov/policy/gen/reg/ferpa/index.html?exp=6.

Federal Administrative Procedure Act ("APA"), 5 USC §551 et. seq. (1946).

US Department of Homeland Security, Bureau of Customs and Border Protection. (October 27, 2021). *Memorandum from Alejandro N. Mayorkas, Secretary. Guidelines for enforcement actions in or near protected areas.* https://www.dhs.gov/sites/default/files/publications/21_1027_opa_guidelines-enforcement-actions-in-near-protected-areas.pdf

US Departments of Education and Health and Human Services. (December 2019, Update to 2008 Report). *Joint Guidance on the Application of the Family Educational Rights and Privacy Act (FERPA) and the Health Insurance Portability and Accountability Act of 1996(HIPAA) to Student Health Records,* Washington, DC https://rems.ed.gov/docs/2019%20HIPAA%20FERPA%20Joint%20Guidance.pdf

Chapter 17
PARENTAL RIGHTS, CUSTODY AGREEMENTS AND PROTECTION FROM **ABUSE ORDERS**
Brooke E.D. Say, Esquire*

Due to the length of this chapter, the following outline provides an overview of the chapter content:

Determining **Who** Has the Legal Authority

Determining **What** is the legal question?

What law, if any, applies to this situation?

- The right/authority to view records or receive confidential information from records

- The right/authority to make medical decisions/consent to non-emergency medical treatment on behalf of a child

- The right/authority to make general educational decisions on behalf of a child.

- The right/authority to consent to special education services (including related services that may involve the school nurse) under the IDEA.

- The right/authority to take physical possession of the child.

- The right/authority to provide emergency care/services to a child.

How do laws identified define "parent" or assign rights?

FERPA

Custody Laws and Power of Attorney

Power of Attorney

Custody

IDEA

Handling Disagreements between Divorced and Separated Parents

Emancipated Students / Students over Age 18

Protection from Abuse Orders (Restraining Orders)

---

*Original author : Erin D. Gilsbach, Esquire (2017)

PARENTAL RIGHTS, CUSTODY AGREEMENTS & PROTECTION FROM ABUSE ORDERS

DESCRIPTION OF ISSUE

This chapter is designed to assist school nurses in identifying the legal parental authority rights in several different situations. It sets forth a process by which school nurses will be able to recognize a legal issue in each scenario quickly, identify the applicable law, and indicate who has parental or decision-making authority in that situation. The chapter also discusses the implications of custody agreements and protection from abuse orders (e.g., restraining orders) in the school setting. **Due to the complexity of these issues, please see chapter contents to search for a topic for this specific chapter.**

BACKGROUND

School nurses encounter students from a wide array of backgrounds and families - students whose parents are divorced, who live with individuals other than their parents, who are in the foster care system, whose parents are incarcerated, who are living on their own, or who are homeless, etc. It is often difficult to know what rules apply in different situations. For example, can a step-parent view a child's school health records? Can a grandparent with whom a child is living (but without legal custody) agree to nursing-related services in an Individualized Education Plan (IEP)? What happens when divorced parents disagree? What rights do foster parents have? Issues related to a child's family can be tricky, not only because of the many different types of families and living situations involved but also because of the number of different state and federal laws that could potentially be implicated. This chapter provides a practical approach for school nurses to use in determining who has rights with regard to a child and what role non-parents may play in the child's education.

IMPLICATIONS FOR SCHOOL NURSE PRACTICE

Determining Who Has the Legal Authority

Different laws grant different rights to different people. What makes this issue truly tricky, though, is the fact that the term "parent" is used in several different school and state law contexts, including Family Education Rights and Privacy Act (FERPA), the Individuals with Disabilities Education Act (IDEA), and state custody laws. The definition of parent is different for each. To reach a legally correct conclusion, school nurses must think critically about the issue at hand. Three fundamental questions must be asked whenever issues regarding parental rights and authority arise:

---

1. *What is the legal issue?*
2. *What law, if any, applies to this situation?*
3. *How do laws identified in question 2 define "parent" or assign rights?*

As stated above, the answers to the questions are not as important in the long term as the ability to identify and carefully frame, with precision, the questions to be answered. Applicable laws may change based on jurisdiction or time period. However, mastering the analytical process of narrowing the scope of an issue from a generalized fact pattern presented during a school nurse's duties to a narrowly tailored query regarding applicable laws specific to a particular legal issue is the more relevant and important goal. It is also a skill that, once mastered, can be used repeatedly with successful results.

While this resource book was designed for the express purpose of providing school nurses, school administrators, and school attorneys with much-needed information on the law, limitations apply to any legal resource, no matter how thorough and well-drafted. As the introductory materials of this book point out, the law is geographically specific and temporally specific. Different states have different laws, and laws are constantly changing. Thus, while this section provides helpful information regarding the substance of the laws themselves, the more important purpose of this chapter, in general, and this section, specifically, is to assist school nurses in breaking down the issues and identifying the questions that need to be answered.

To better explain in more concrete terms the analytical process required for making legally defensible decisions regarding custody and other issues related to family law, the following scenario will be addressed throughout the remainder of this section:

> *Pursuant to the accommodations set forth in a student's Section 504 Plan, the school nurse communicates with the student's mother on a weekly basis by phone to let her know how the student is doing, communicate any concerns, and answer any questions the student's mother may have. Their phone calls occur regularly every week on the same date and at the same time. The parent calls the school nurse's direct line, which the nurse typically provides only in cases where direct communication is necessary. All other calls are transferred to the school nurse's office by the main office. One week, the school nurse is surprised to find that the student's grandmother had called instead of mom. She called the school nurse's direct line at the correct time on the correct date and explained that the mother (her daughter) asked her to participate in this phone conference on her behalf while she was away on business. She tells the school nurse that the mother is away for an extended business trip and that she will be gone for the next three weeks. She explains that since the child's father died a few years ago, she has been assisting her daughter with childcare whenever she is away. She also explains that the mother has left her a copy of the student's Section 504 Plan in the event that she needs to reference it. The grandmother is not able to provide contact information for the mother during her trip since the mother is "overseas" and does not have cell phone access. However, she has a note scrawled in the mother's handwriting that states, "I hereby give my mother, Ida Kenner, power of attorney over my children and full parental rights while I am gone."*
>
> *Because she was not expecting to speak with the grandmother, and she is uncertain whether she can disclose the student's information to the student's grandmother, the school nurse kindly informed the grandmother that she would need to return her call. They establish a suitable time later that day. The school nurse then checks her records and the records in the student's main office file. The mother has never provided the school with a consent form permitting the student to disclose information from the student's records with the grandmother. The school nurse now needs guidance as to whether she can share this information or, if not, what would be legally required to allow her to do so.*

In regular daily practice, the school nurse would likely consult with a member of the administration, who would probably be able to provide her with direction as to what she should do in this circumstance. However, we will use this scenario to go through the 3-step-analysis process presented here to provide a concrete example of how to analyze parental authority and custody-related legal issues.

Question 1: What is the legal question?

<u>The following discussion is not an exhaustive list.</u> Because there are so many different laws that apply to schools, and because the school's obligations, as well as the law's definition of "parent," as described above, varies significantly depending upon the law in question, a nurse must first clarify the legal issues that are posed by a given fact pattern. The graphic below identifies some of the most common legal issues addressed by schools and school nurses*, and the sections below provide an analysis of each issue identified.

*Note that this is certainly not an exhaustive list of family/custody-related legal issues that nurses will encounter by any means. For instance, *Chapter 21* discusses "do not attempt to resuscitate" orders (DNARs), which generally require a combination of parental authority, state approval, and other potential factors, such as wearing a state-issued wristband or other wearable DNAR notice.

The legal issue in the scenario presented above is one that schools face regularly: when dealing with confidential student records issues, who has the right to access a student's records? In this case, the school nurse is aware that the mother, before she left, did not expressly sign a consent form to permit the grandmother to have the records. However, the mother provided all the necessary information to enable the grandmother to participate in the weekly phone conferences in her absence, and she provided the grandmother with a copy of the Section 504 Plan. The school nurse is aware that FERPA applies not only to the student's records themselves but also to discussions involving information from those records.   If written consent is not required, can the mother's consent be implied by her actions of notifying the grandmother of the standing appointment and providing her with the necessary information to participate in her absence? If not, is it possible that the grandmother could actually fall within FERPA's definition of "parent," at least while she is the temporary full-time caregiver for the student?

What does the school nurse specifically need to know in this context?

1. Is the "Power of Attorney" note a valid transfer of decision-making rights under the law?
2. What constitutes parental "consent" to have access to a student's records under FERPA?
   a. Is written consent required?
   b. If not, do the facts in this scenario effectively establish legal consent under FERPA?
3. Could the grandmother qualify as a "parent" under FERPA for the purposes of being granted access to the student's records?

Question 2: What law, if any, applies to this situation?

Both state and federal laws must be considered when deciding what law applies in a particular situation. In addition, the type of school entity is important. For instance, a private school that does not receive any federal funding is not subject to many federal laws, such as the IDEA and FERPA. Private schools may be treated differently under state laws as well. Likewise, states may impose different requirements on public charter schools than on private and public school districts. Therefore, an understanding of the specific type of institution and the laws that apply to it is essential to answering these questions thoroughly and accurately.

As with many aspects of the law, knowing the *questions* to ask is the most essential part of the process. In the first step of the process, the issues were identified. Now, the appropriate applicable laws need to be identified. Knowing the issues allows the questions regarding applicable law to be far more exact. Adding the additional key components of federal vs. state and type of school (private, public, public charter, cyber charter, etc.) allows the questions to be framed with accurate precision. *What federal confidentiality laws apply to a charter school that receives federal funding? What state confidentiality laws apply to charter schools in my state? Is there a difference between the confidentiality standards set forth for charter schools in my state and those required of public school districts?* If the questions have been framed with this level of detail, obtaining the answers becomes a much simpler process, and there may be several readily available resources that can help with the answers.

The following few paragraphs provide helpful information regarding applicable laws for each of the "Common Legal Issues in the School Setting."

The right/authority to view records or receive confidential information from records

The school nurse in the scenario knows that FERPA is the federal law that addresses student confidentiality and records access. (As stated in *Chapter 12* of this book, FERPA, not HIPAA, governs the confidentiality of student health records.)   The school nurse would also need to determine whether any state laws apply in this situation. Some states do not have state-specific laws addressing confidentiality, others have some, and still, others may be heavily regulated and have many additional requirements. In addition, even within a particular state's laws, there may be variation depending upon the type of school entity (school district, public charter, private school, etc.), as discussed above. The school, in the scenario presented here, is in Pennsylvania, which, at the time of publication of this book, does not have any additional state confidentiality laws that would apply to this situation. Therefore, school nurses in Pennsylvania would be addressing the issue with regard to one primary law: FERPA.

Legal custody issues come into play, too, however. In the scenario above, the mother assigns to the grandmother, in a handwritten note, "power of attorney" and the right to make decisions on behalf of her children. Is this a valid transfer of rights/authority? This issue will be explored in greater detail in the "Custody" section when answering Question #3 below.

Some of the other laws that might be implicated by the common legal issues that school nurses encounter are set forth in the graphic "Common Legal Issues in the School Setting" above. Remember that legal jurisdiction (geographical location) and type of entity will always factor into a legal analysis of applicable laws.

The right/authority to make medical decisions/consent to non-emergency medical treatment on behalf of a child

The issue of who can consent to medical treatment is state-specific, so the answer will vary based on specific state custody law requirements and statutes regarding medical decision-making. Many states, however, include medical decision-making in legal custody rights (see the discussion regarding Question 3, below for a discussion of the difference between legal and physical custody). While parental custody is a state law issue, most states differentiate among the different types of custody in the same manner.

The right/authority to make general educational decisions on behalf of a child

In most states, educational decision-making goes hand-in-hand with medical decision-making, which generally accompanies legal custody, as discussed above. As with medical decision-making, this is a state-specific issue, so it is possible that there may be additional state laws that apply. However, absent any other legal authority, the right to make general educational decisions about a child typically follows legal custody rights. Legal custody can be, and is often, shared between parents (who may or may not have similar and corresponding rights of physical custody).

The right/authority to consent to special education services (including related services that may involve the school nurse) under the IDEA

The IDEA has a very specific provision that deals with this issue, which will be discussed in more detail below. In short, however, the IDEA provides a hierarchical chain of authority in which the individual(s) that are highest on the chain has (have) the authority (34 C.F.R. § 300.30) when "acting as the parent." A detailed explanation of the IDEA's chain of authority is provided below.

The right/authority to take physical possession of the child

State law may answer this question directly; however, parents are typically permitted to identify specific individuals who may pick up their child from school. In cases of divorced parents, however, the law varies from state to state. In some states, the non-custodial parent is not permitted to take possession of a child. In other states, custody agreements are legal documents that bind only the parties to the custody action, not the schools. Thus, if a school has no reason to believe that releasing the child will result in harm, the school may release a student to a non-custodial parent (but arguably should not do so without notice to the custodial parent). Arguably, this release would be permissible for a parent with partial or shared physical custody rights, even when it is not that parent's designated "day." In the event that the school is aware of an outstanding protection from abuse (PFA) order against a specific individual, however, that puts the school on notice that releasing the child to the individual against whom the PFA has been issued. In most states, the school will be prohibited, by law, from doing so. Even where there is no specific legal prohibition, there may be a general liability if a school releases a child to an individual against whom a PFA has been issued. In all such cases, schools should refrain from releasing the child to such individual or should contact their legal counsel.

The right/authority to provide emergency care/services to a child

The provision of emergency care/services to a child extends to several individuals under a variety of legal theories. First and foremost, any individual providing or attempting to provide life-saving emergency care to a child is likely protected under a state's Good Samaritan laws. These actions would include emergency care teachers, administrators, and other school employees provide. Although there are usually some limitations to the types of care a layperson could provide and still be protected under those laws, their protections are typically expansive. It is important to note, however, that state law may carve out special exceptions for certain types of emergency care, such as specific requirements for the use of portable defibrillators (see the *Centers for Disease Control [2019] resource on "Public* Access Defibrillation (PAD) State Law Fact Sheet" for a more expansive discussion of this topic), so it is crucial that school employees understand the parameters of their state Good Samaritan laws.

Additionally, schools in most states have *in loco parentis* (*the legal responsibility of some person or organization to perform some of the functions or responsibilities of a parent*) authority over children while the children are in school. Some states have explicit *in loco parentis* statutes, while, in others, the *in loco parentis* authority has been established through common law (case law). While a school's *in loco parentis* authority is generally limited to the educational context and what is necessary for the school to receive during the school day, the provision of emergency care generally falls under that authority.

The provision of emergency care by school nurses, pursuant to responsibilities often set forth in statutes, is also generally permitted. While school nurses, as medical professionals, are held to a higher standard of care and, thus, often are not protected by the typical Good Samaritan law, their background and licensure enable them to provide emergency care effectively and lawfully. Finally, first responders, such as emergency medical technicians (EMTs) and emergency room medical personnel, have the authority to provide life-saving care to students without parental permission. While there are, of course, some exceptions set forth under the law for medical personnel, such as instances when a lawfully issued DNAR order is in effect, the authority of a first responder or emergency medical team to provide life-saving medical services/treatment is well-established.

Question 3: How do laws identified in question 2 define "parent" or assign rights?

Determining who is granted rights under each of the laws identified above and those granted under applicable state laws is the crux of this chapter. Most laws governing schools and school records assign the rights to the student's parents. This is complicated by the fact that different laws define "parent" differently, both on the state and federal levels, and the definitions are often quite technical and sometimes counterintuitive. For example, under some laws, a family friend who is watching a child during a parent's extended business trip can legally constitute a "parent," while others relying on strict legal assignations and court orders, limit the definition to mean only a natural parent or an individual who has obtained parental or guardian status through a court order.

As with the section above, while this resource provides information regarding the parameters of the term "parent" in some of the commonly applicable federal school laws, it is the framing of the questions themselves, as well as the more generalized understanding of the different contexts and circumstances in which the questions will arise, that is ultimately the most important part of the process. For instance, once the nurse decides that the specific issue at hand involves rights granted to parents under the IDEA, for example, determining who is a "parent" under the IDEA is a simple and straightforward process, as described below. The hard part is framing the questions.

FERPA

FERPA's definition of "parent" is directly at issue in the scenario presented above. In that scenario, the school nurse knows, from reading Chapter 12 of this book, that FERPA has a very broad definition of parent. FERPA's definitions state that "parent means a parent of a student and includes a natural parent, a guardian, or an individual acting as a parent in the absence of a parent or a guardian." (34 CFR § 99.3). In this situation, it is clear that the grandmother is a "parent" under FERPA since she is watching the student in the mom's absence. She is "acting as a parent in the absence of a parent," so she falls within FERPA's definition of "parent." Because of that, she can have the same access to the student's educational records that the child's natural parent would have. The nurse may release the information and discuss the student's records without restriction. No written consent is necessary during the time the parent is away (when the grandparent is "acting as a parent in the absences of the parent."). When the parent returns and is "acting as a parent," the school may no longer treat the grandparent as the parent unless the grandparent meets the scenario outlined below by the U.S. Department of Education. However, it is important to remember that, in this scenario, the school nurse is dealing only with federal law because no other state law applies. Applicable state laws should always be considered in addition to this federal law.

Under this liberal definition of "parent," there are many commonly encountered individuals whose relationship with a child places them squarely within FERPA's definition of "parent." The U.S. Department of Education has determined that a parent is *absent* "if he or she is not present in the day-to-day home environment of the child" (FPCO 2004). Where an individual has day-to-day access to a child, such as a step-parent who is married to the parent with primary physical custody (FPCO 2004), an adult sibling who lives alone with a school-aged child, a neighbor with whom the child is living, and, as in this example, caregivers who are watching the children when the parent(s) are not available, they might fit the definition of a parent under FERPA. In the scenario presented, the definition of "parent" under FERPA gives the grandmother the authority to view and hear what is contained within the student's records, not the "power of attorney." There is no need for the school to prove that the parent *intended* for the grandmother to be able to have access to the information in the student's records. The mere fact that the grandmother is currently acting as the parent in the absence of the biological parent gives the grandmother the right to view the records, independent of the mother's intention.

It is important to note that parents do not have the right to refuse or withhold consent from another qualifying individual. For instance, a child's mother cannot prohibit the school from releasing information to the father's girlfriend or wife from a subsequent marriage where the father has already provided valid consent or where such an individual meets the definition of "parent" under FERPA (FPCO 2004). In the scenario provided here, even if she wanted to, the mother could not prohibit the grandmother from having rights under FERPA because the grandmother falls within the definition of "parent ."The mother's intentions do not change the legal analysis regarding who is a parent. In cases involving divorced parents, however, particularly where there is significant animosity between the parents, it is often simpler for the school to obtain written consent for a new spouse or significant other to have access to the records than it is to explain that they might have a status of "parent" under FERPA.

Where this consent is obtained, however, schools still need to understand whether an individual falls within the definition of "parent" under FERPA, regardless of whether consent by a biological parent has been obtained. This is because those who meet the definition of "parent" are entitled to all the parental *rights* afforded under FERPA. Those individuals for whom a parent has provided consent to have access to the records but who do not meet FERPA's definition of "parent" do not have a *right* to such access (or any other parental right afforded under FERPA). That consent merely means that the school *may* lawfully disclose the information, but it is not *required* to do so. Thus, where a biological parent refuses to give consent or is not present to do so, such refusal or inaccessibility does not alter who has parental rights under FERPA. In addition, individuals who meet the definition of "parent" under FERPA do not have the authority to challenge or prohibit access to a student's records by another individual where a "parent" has provided specific, FERPA-compliant written consent for another individual to have access to a student's records (FPCO 2004).

CUSTODY LAWS AND POWER OF ATTORNEY

Power of Attorney

First, let us consider the mother's scrawled note, allegedly giving the grandmother power of attorney and authorizing her to make decisions, including educational decisions, on behalf of her children. Many states have some form of temporary Power of Attorney for Childcare, whereby a transfer of power of attorney would be permissible if properly executed. For instance, Arizona Revised Statute 14-5104 states that a parent or a guardian of a minor or incapacitated person, through a properly executed Power of Attorney, may delegate to another person, for a period not exceeding six months, any powers the parent may have regarding care, custody or property of the minor child or ward, except the power to consent to marriage or adoption of the minor. In Arizona's case, however, "properly executed" means signed, witnessed, and notarized. Thus, mom's note falls short under this law.

In Ohio, however, the circumstances under which a grandparent can receive a Power of Attorney for childcare purposes are much more complicated, as several different laws apply to grandparents. For instance, Ohio Revised Code §3109.65 provides a solution for the situation where a child is living with a grandparent and the child's parents cannot be found. This temporary solution is not the same as legal custody. However, it allows the grandparent to do necessary things for the child, such as enrolling the child in school, taking the child to the healthcare provider, etc. Pursuant to Ohio Revised Code §3109.67, Ohio's caretaker affidavit can also be utilized without attempting to locate the parent, but only if: 1.) If paternity has not been established regarding the child's father; 2.) If the child is currently under an existing custody order; 3.) If the parent subject to the custody order is prohibited from receiving notice of relocation; or 4.) If a parent's rights have been permanently terminated by a court of competent jurisdiction, pursuant to Chapter 2151 of the Ohio Revised Code.

In other states, such as Colorado, power of attorney for childcare petitions is not legally binding if they are signed only by the parties, witnesses, and a notary. Instead, Colorado requires that all powers of attorney for childcare petitions be approved and signed by the Court (Colorado Revised Statutes 15-14-201 and 15-14-202). In these types of states, the mother's note would certainly not be sufficient to satisfy the legal requirements for a Power of Attorney.

To properly determine whether the mother's "Power of Attorney," in the scenario presented above, has any legal legitimacy, school nurses should be familiar with their state's laws regarding powers of attorney for childcare purposes. If the childcare provider, grandma, in this instance, has a legally valid power of attorney, then the school nurse would need to ascertain the scope of that document. Does it provide educational decision-making rights? Does it fully transfer all parental rights for a limited period? What are the permissions and limitations of that document? If the school nurse has any questions, or if a parent or caregiver is asserting that the caregiver has more rights than it appears he or she legally possesses, the school nurse should discuss the situation with the building administrator and, if necessary, obtain a legal opinion from the school's legal counsel.

In the scenario provided here, however, the grandmother's "power of attorney" is not legally sufficient or binding in states where Court involvement or approval is required. Since she meets the definition of "parent" under FERPA even without a valid power of attorney, though, the analysis remains the same. The grandmother is permitted to view the records and hear the informational updates, but not due to a legally recognized power of attorney status, but rather under FERPA's plain-language definition of "parent."

Custody

School nurses should always have access to a copy of any recent custody orders when in place for a child/family. This will allow the school nurse to make fully informed decisions regarding releasing a student during the school day, who has medical decision-making authority, and who is able to make educational decisions.

There are generally two types of custody: *Legal* and *Physical*. Within those types, there can be shared/joint custody or sole custody.

Legal custody generally refers to the right to make major decisions on behalf of a child, including educational, medical, and religious decisions. In essence, it generally includes basic parental rights *other than* physical custody.

Physical custody typically describes who has actual physical possession of the child.

In most states, **joint** legal custody is the default, even where one parent may be granted sole physical custody. **In joint legal custody**, both parents always have legal custodial rights. This is different from **joint physical custody**, which divides the rights. With joint physical custody, one parent has physical custody on certain days of the week or week cycles, and the other has physical custody on the others. Other terminology that is often used in describing custodial relationships includes **supervised custody**, where a non-custodial parent is permitted to have supervised visitations, and **primary physical custody**, where one parent has custody the majority of the time and the other parent has much more limited periods of custody, such as on weekends or holidays (see "partial" or "shared" physical custody, below). Different states have different specific laws and rules regarding custody, and custody definitions vary from state to state. For instance, Figure 1 below contains Pennsylvania's legal custody terms and definitions:

Custody and Grandparents Visitation Act – 23 Pa. C.S.A. 5301 et seq.
PA custody definitions, which can be found at 23 Pa. C.S.A. § 5322, are as follows:

- **"Legal custody."** The right to make significant decisions on behalf of the child, including, but not limited to, medical, religious, and educational decisions.
- **"Shared legal custody."** The right of more than one individual to legal custody of the child.
- **"Sole legal custody."** The right of one individual to exclusive legal custody of the child.
- **"Physical custody."** The actual physical possession and control of a child.
- **"Primary physical custody."** The right to assume physical custody of the child for the majority of the time.
- **"Partial physical custody."** The right to assume physical custody of the child for less than a majority of the time.
- **"Shared physical custody."** The right of more than one individual to assume physical custody of the child, each having significant periods of custodial time with the child.
- **"Supervised physical custody."** Custodial time during which an agency or an adult designated by the court or agreed upon by the parties monitors the interaction between the child and the individual with those rights.
- **"Sole physical custody."** The right of one individual to exclusive physical custody of the child.

Figure 1

From a practical perspective, the most important determination for a school nurse will be determining who has "legal custody." This is because, as stated above, the parents with "legal custody" generally have the legal right to make legal, educational, and medical decisions on behalf of the child. Where the parents have provided documentation regarding custody arrangements or termination of custody orders, it is typically not difficult to identify where a parent's legal custody has been terminated. The termination of legal custody is a significant issue that courts do not take lightly. Courts are widely more in favor of leaving legal custody intact wherever possible. Termination of legal custody is still typically treated differently than termination of the right of access to education records under FERPA. A parent would rarely lose a FERPA right of access to education records under FERPA, even if they have no legal or physical custody rights.

* See generally Somerville Board of Education v. Manville Board of Education, 167 N.J. 55 (2001); Roxbury Township Board of Education v. West Milford Board of Education, 283 N.J. Super. 505 (App. Div. 1995); F.C. v. Rockaway Township Board of Education, OAL Dkt. No. EDS 11128-04 (January 12, 2005) 2005 WL 327290 (N.J. Admin.); L.T. ex rel. C.T. v. Denville Township Board of Education, OAL Dkt. No. EDS 5899-03 (October 27, 2004).

Knowing who has "physical custody" is important when deciding to release the child at the end of the school day and sending the child home early due to illness or other reasons. In some states, such as New Jersey, schools are legally required to abide by physical custody orders, which parents provide. * In other states, such as Pennsylvania, while schools generally try to give deference to what is set forth within the physical custody agreement, schools are not parties to the agreements themselves and are, therefore, not bound by them (*23 Pa. CS 5406*). PA law states that *child custody determinations made by a PA court bind only those individuals who have been served proper notice as parties to the legal action or those who have "submitted to the jurisdiction of the court and who have been given an opportunity to be heard."* Because of the obligations of schools regarding the enforcement of custody agreements, all school employees – including school nurses – must understand their specific obligations under state law regarding custody agreements.

Custody and Medical Decision-Making

Consent to non-emergency medical treatment is generally reserved for parents with legal custody. In Pennsylvania, parents with legal custody have the right to make educational decisions on behalf of their child regardless of physical custody (23 Pa C.S.A. §5322).   In Utah, the default rule is that parents with legal custody have the right (and obligation) to make medical decisions; however, in that state, divorced parents are legally required to develop a parenting plan, which may transfer the decision-making authority between the parents (Utah Code Ann §§30-3-10.7 to 10.9). For example, although both parents have legal custody, which generally grants medical decision-making rights, the parents could agree, in the parenting plan, that the mother will have the medical decision-making rights. The father will have educational decision-making rights. Thus, in that state, since the parental plan is mandatory for all parents as a condition of the granting of the divorce, schools should request that a copy of such plan be maintained on file, and school nurses should be familiar with the decision-making authority of each parent. Where no plan is provided, the school nurse should assume that both parents have medical decision-making authority.

IDEA

The IDEA federal regulations, at 34 CFR § 300.30, present a hierarchy of who can be considered a "parent" under that law.   The individual on the highest level of the hierarchy is considered to be the lawful "parent" and is afforded the rights under the IDEA (when "acting as" parent). It is only where there is no one "acting as" the parent that meets the first definition that the IEP team looks to the second tier, and so on. The hierarchy is as follows:

IDEA "Parent" Hierarchy

1. A child's biological or adoptive parent

2. A foster parent, unless state law, regulations, or contractual obligations prohibit a foster parent from acting as a parent

3. A guardian is generally authorized to act as the child's parent or authorized to make educational decisions

4. An individual acting in the place of the biological or adoptive parent who is living with a child or an individual who is legally responsible for the child's welfare

5. A surrogate parent who has been appointed in accordance with the IDEA and federal regulations.

Where More Than One Person Qualifies Under This List:

The IDEA regulations, in 34 C.F.R. § 300.30, state that when a biological or adoptive parent attempts to assert rights under the law and more than one party qualifies as a parent, pursuant to this list, the biological or adoptive parent "trumps" and is presumed to be the parent unless the biological/adoptive parent does not have the legal authority to make educational decisions for the child. If a judicial decree or order identifies a specific person(s) to act as the "parent" or to make educational decisions on behalf of the child (often an aspect of "Legal Custody"), then that person is deemed the "parent." Unless the courts have revoked legal custody involving educational decision-making, both biological parents have rights under the IDEA.

Physical custody, or the lack thereof, has no bearing on a parent's rights under the IDEA. Even where a parent lives far from the student and has no physical custody rights, they are still a "parent" for the purposes of the IDEA unless his/her legal rights, or at least the educational decision-making component of them, have been terminated. Schools sometimes encounter this issue with regard to a parent who has been incarcerated. Such parents, unless their educational decision-making rights have been legally terminated, still retain the rights afforded to them under the IDEA.

Where a "Parent" Cannot be Found

Where no one qualifies as a "parent" under 1-4 of this list, the IDEA requires that a surrogate be judicially appointed to represent the interests of a child and act as a parent for the purposes of special education programming and IDEA decision-making. The court order must identify a specific person (20 U.S.C. 1415(b)(2); 34 CFR 300.30(b)(2)), and the judicially appointed surrogate may not be an employee of the district or any other agency involved in the education or care of the child (20 U.S.C. 1415(2)(A); 34 C.F.R. 300.519)). The IDEA regulations clarify, however, that being paid by the agency solely for the purpose of being a surrogate does not make the individual an "employee" for the purposes of the IDEA and, therefore, does not prohibit such an individual from serving as a surrogate (34 C.F.R. 300.519).

Handling Disagreements between Divorced and Separated Parents

Another very common issue that schools face is the issue of disagreements between divorced and separated parents. The above 3-step analysis can also be useful in those types of cases. Consider the following scenario:

A school nurse who regularly works with a medically fragile student receives the following letter, signed by the student's mother:

I do not give permission for Wendy Smith to have any information related to my child, including any educationally or medically related information. I further prohibit the school from meeting with Ms. Smith or contacting her regarding my child. Ms. Smith has no legal relationship with my child and does not have any legal right to my child's information or any legal authority to act in the capacity of a parent to my child. Please feel free to contact me if you have any questions.

The school nurse is aware that the child's parents have recently been through a very difficult divorce and custody battle. She also knows that the parents share custody, with the child living at her father's house every other week. Wendy Smith is her father's girlfriend, who lives with the father.

Let us look at this issue and determine what obligations the school has and what parental authority the mother and the father's girlfriend have with regard to the student. Begin with the 3 steps outlined above.

Step 1: What is the Legal Issue?

There are two legal issues in this scenario:

1. Does the mother have the authority to restrict the father's girlfriend's access to the student's information?
2. Does the father's girlfriend have the right to access the information as a "parent"?

Step 2: What Laws Apply?

Since this scenario deals exclusively with access to information from within the student's file, FERPA is the law that applies.

Step 3: How does the applicable law define "parent"?

FERPA's definitions state that "parent means a parent of a student and includes a natural parent, a guardian, *or* an individual acting as a parent in the absence of a parent or a guardian" (34 CFR § 99.3). In this case, the student lives with their dad and Ms. Smith every other week. It could certainly be argued that Ms. Smith acts as the student's mother in her mother's absence. However, suppose the school asks the father to sign a records release to permit Ms. Smith unlimited access to the student's records through written consent. In that case, the issue is clear, and the father has exercised his right under FERPA to grant written permission for Ms. Smith. While the definition of "parent" and the written consent form signed by the father leads to the same result – indicating to the mother that Ms. Smith is able to access the educational records via the father's written consent is often less confrontational to explain than explaining to the mother that Ms. Smith is a "parent," under the law, for the purposes of FERPA. As discussed above, one parent has no right or authority to override another parent under FERPA. Thus, the mother has no legal right to prohibit Ms. Smith from seeing the records if the father has expressly consented. As also discussed in the "FERPA" section above, the school should be aware, however, of whether Ms. Smith truly falls within the definition of "parent" under FERPA since that would afford her all of the parental rights under FERPA, not simply to be able to have knowledge of the student's records.

Now, if the issue were one regarding decision-making authority under the IDEA or Section 504, there would be a different outcome. As set forth in the chart above, the IDEA establishes specific requirements for who has the authority to make educational decisions on behalf of a child. That authority *always* lies with the biological or adoptive parents. Only when those individuals cannot be contacted would the school need to or be permitted to look further. Ms. Smith, while she may meet the definition of "parent" to view education records under FERPA, does not have the authority to make decisions regarding the student's IEP. Likewise, Section 504 does not contain the same broad definition of "parent" as FERPA. Thus, the decision-making afforded to a "parent" under that law would be afforded to a biological parent or legal guardian.

Emancipated Students / Students over Age 18

The concept of "emancipation" is also a state law concept that varies significantly from state to state. With most school-related laws, however, the state law concept of emancipation plays little to no role in the parental rights question. Rather, each specific law sets forth its own requirements regarding what happens when a student becomes "emancipated." For instance, under FERPA, the parental rights transfer to the student once the student turns 18 or attends a post-secondary school (34 CFR §99.3(6)). Until then, all parental rights remain with the individual who falls within the definition of "parent" under FERPA, regardless of the student's emancipation status according to state law or any other applicable laws.

Regarding FERPA, however, it is important to note that there is a broadly applicable exception to the consent requirement applicable for students who are still in high school but have turned 18. That broad exception pertains to situations where "[t]he disclosure is to parents, as defined in §99.3, of a dependent student, as defined in section 152 of the Internal Revenue Code of 1986." In short, this generally means that the disclosure is to the parents of a student whom the parents claim on their taxes. The full qualifications of IRC Section 152, however, are set forth below:

> **(c) QUALIFYING CHILD**   For purposes of this section—
>
> **(1) IN GENERAL** The term "qualifying child" means, with respect to any taxpayer for any taxable year, an individual—
>> **(A)** who bears a relationship to the taxpayer described in paragraph (2),
>> **(B)** who has the same principal place of abode as the taxpayer for more than one-half of such taxable year,
>> **(C)** who meets the age requirements of paragraph (3),
>> **(D)** who has not provided over one-half of such individual's own support for the calendar year in which the taxable year of the taxpayer begins, and
>> **(E)** who has not filed a joint return (other than only for a claim of refund) with the individual's spouse under section 6013 for the taxable year beginning in the calendar year in which the taxable year of the taxpayer begins.
>
> **(2) RELATIONSHIP**   For purposes of paragraph (1)(A), an individual bears a relationship to the taxpayer described in this paragraph if such individual is—
>> **(A)** a child of the taxpayer or a descendant of such a child, or
>> **(B)** a brother, sister, stepbrother, or stepsister of the taxpayer or a descendant of any such relative.
>
> **(3) AGE REQUIREMENTS**
> **(A)In general** For purposes of paragraph (1)(C), an individual meets the requirements of this paragraph if such individual is younger than the taxpayer claiming such individual as a qualifying child and—
>> **(i)** has not attained the age of 19 as of the close of the calendar year in which the taxable year of the taxpayer begins, or
>> **(ii)** is a student who has not attained the age of 24 as of the close of such calendar year.

Under the IDEA, an "emancipated" student is contemplated in the hierarchical definition of "parent" discussed above. If a student, regardless of age, did not have any of the described relationships in #s 1-4 below, the school would be required to seek an educational surrogate for the student. Since students are eligible for IDEA services through graduation or until age 21, whichever comes first, it is not uncommon for students to be considered "emancipated" under state law but still require an educational surrogate for the purposes of ensuring that the student's needs are being met through the IDEA programming. In most cases, both the student and the surrogate will be asked to sign off on the IDEA documentation.

A state's legal age of consent will apply for matters that do not involve the IDEA or FERPA, such as medical decision-making by an 18-year-old student. Again, while this varies from state to state, most states establish the age of legal adulthood as age 18 to waive rights, assume liability, and make personal decisions. However, school nurses should check their state's specific laws to determine what rights (if any) transfer to a student when they turn 18. Indeed, in some states, the age of legal adulthood can be 17 (or younger) in cases where the student is living on his/her own and caring for him/herself.

Protection from Abuse Orders (Restraining Orders)

Protection from Abuse orders (PFAs) are mandates issued by the court that prohibit an individual from abusing another individual. They are generally issued where there is a history or threat of abuse. Terminology varies from state to state regarding what constitutes "abuse," the label assigned to a specific state's version of a protective order (e.g., PFAs, restraining orders, protective orders, etc.). In addition, a state may have more than one type of protective order available. For instance, a state may offer a PFA for domestic violence, a restraining order for stalking/harassing behavior, etc.

For domestic violence related PFAs, state law often requires that there must be a special relationship between the parties, such as a family member, members of the same household, etc. This relationship can extend to in-laws or neighbors in some states. PFAs/Restraining Orders are generally tailored by the court to serve the purpose necessary to protect the victim. A PFA/Restraining Order may contain all or some of the following provisions:
- Prohibit physical proximity, generally ordering the abuser to stay a minimum number of feed/yards away from the victim and the victim's home, job, school, vehicle, etc.
- Prohibit communication, including calling, texting, emailing, etc.
- Permit only peaceful communication for very limited reasons, which may include child visitation or supervised visitation.
- Require the surrender of any firearms and prohibit the purchase of firearms.
- Require the abuser to attend counseling.
- Grant possession of the household to the victim (temporary or long-term)
- Require the abuser to pay support to the victim.
- Prohibit contact with minor children.

Penalties for violation of a PFA/Restraining order can range from a contempt of court charge, which generally involves a fine; to a criminal misdemeanor; to a felony, for repeat violations or more serious threats. PFAs/ Restraining Orders are subject to the "Full Faith and Credit Clause" of the U.S. Constitution (U.S. Constitution, Article IV, Section 1), which means that if a victim with a valid PFA/Restraining Order moves to a different state, the PFA/Restraining Order must be honored by the police of the new state. School nurses aware of situations involving domestic violence, particularly where the court has issued protective orders, must be vigilant for potential signs of child abuse, as domestic violence often strongly correlates to situations where child abuse is prevalent (Anselmi, 2011).

CONCLUSION

It is important for school nurses to understand the legal issues at play in any given family-related scenario and to be able to systematically analyze those issues to determine who has parental authority and to make sure that all necessary protocols are being followed with regard to PFAs and custody orders.

RESOURCES

Case Law

F.C. v. Rockaway Township Board of Education, OAL Dkt. No. EDS 11128-04 (January 12, 2005) 2005 WL 327290 (N.J. Admin.).

L.T. ex rel. C.T. v. Denville Township Board of Education, OAL Dkt. No. EDS 5899-03 (October 27, 2004).

Roxbury Township Board of Education v. West Milford Board of Education, 283 N.J. Super. 505 (App. Div. 1995).

Somerville Board of Education v. Manville Board of Education, 167 N.J. 55 (2001).

REFERENCES

Anselmi, K. (2011). Domestic violence and its implications on child abuse. *Nurse Practitioner, 36*(11), 15–17. https://doi.org/10.1097/01.NPR.0000406490.90252.60

Colorado Revised Statutes, Sections 15-14-201-202.

Family Educational Rights and Privacy Act (FERPA), 20 U.S.C. § 1232g; 34 CFR Part 99. (1974).

Family Policy and Compliance Office (FPCO) (2004). *Letter to parent re: Disclosure of education records to stepparents*https://www2.ed.gov/policy/gen/guid/fpco/ferpa/library/hastings082004.html

Individuals with Disability Education Improvement Act (2004), 20 U.S.C. 1400 et seq.; 34 C.F.R. *§§ 300.30, 300.519.*

Centers for Disease Control and Prevention. (2019). *Public access defibrillation (PAD) state law fact sheet.* https://www.cdc.gov/dhdsp/policy_resources/pad_slfs.htm

Ohio Revised Code, §3109.65, 67.

Pennsylvania Code, Custody and Grandparents Visitation Act – 23 Pa. C.S.A. *§*5301 et seq.; *§*5406.

U.S. Constitution, Article IV, Section 1.

U.S. Internal Revenue Code of 1986, 26 U.S.C. *§*152.

Utah Code Ann., **§§30-3-10.7** to 10.9.

Chapter 18

SCHOOLS' LEGAL RESPONSIBILITY FOR SCHOOL HEALTH SERVICES

Linda Davis-Alldritt, MA, BSN, RN, FNASN, FASHA

You can't educate a child who isn't healthy, and you can't keep a child healthy who isn't educated.
Former U.S. Surgeon General Dr. Joycelyn Elders

DESCRIPTION OF ISSUE

When parents send their children to school, they do so with the expectation that the school will provide education and keep their children safe and healthy during the process. Schools have legal, ethical, and moral responsibility for the provision of school health services. Overarching federal laws require that schools provide needed health services by qualified health professionals for children with disabilities. Corresponding state laws, United States Supreme Court rulings, and lower court decisions reinforce this obligation. A large variety of other state laws require schools to provide a variety of school health services, including physical health assessments, communicable disease surveillance and immunization compliance, chronic health conditions management, episodic care, and managing health emergencies.

BACKGROUND

Overview

Increasing numbers of students with a myriad of chronic conditions attend our public schools. It is conservatively estimated that over 40 percent of students have physical or mental health conditions, and 20 percent of students have obesity (American Academy of Pediatrics [AAP], 2016; Centers for Disease Control and Prevention [CDC], 2021; National Association of School Nurses [NASN], 2023c; National Center for Chronic Disease Prevention and Health Promotion [NCCDPHP], 2022; National Center for Educational Statistics [NCES],2022a), all of which may affect/influence their ability to effectively benefit from their educational opportunities. Unaddressed health problems create major barriers to students' ability to learn and achieve their full potential as students and as adults. There is no doubt that health and education are inextricably linked. It is also clear that investment in school health services and programs is time and money well spent both in terms of educational and health outcomes (Basch, 2011; Wang et al., 2014).

Federal and state laws and several court decisions guarantee the right of students with disabilities to have equal access to all school programs in the least restrictive environment. Schools also may face liability when unmet health problems interfere with student learning and safety. Additionally, as the number of students with chronic health conditions has increased, lawmakers have increasingly obligated schools with unfunded healthcare mandates. Too often, when education dollars are limited, school health services are viewed as expendable luxuries, unconnected to society's general health and welfare, to be cut when school budgets must be reduced (Wang et al., 2014).

Despite federal, state, and case laws upholding the rights of students to school health services, there continue to be significant numbers, at least 20 percent, of students and their families who report not receiving needed physical and mental health services at school (Allison et al., 2019; Brener et al., 2007a; NCES, 2022b; Whitney & Peterson, 2019). There is clearly a need for improved school health services (Brener et al., 2007b).

School nurses have the qualifications and skills to intervene with and coordinate care for acute, chronic, and potential health conditions. School nurses provide health education and promote wellness and prevention activities. They are liaisons between the education community and the healthcare community, and they connect students, staff, families, and healthcare providers and advocate for a healthy and safe school environment. School nurses increase the ability of students and families to adapt to health and social stressors and help to mitigate educationally relevant health disparities by collaborating with school and community support services to provide high-quality school health services (Basch, 2011; CDC, 2015; NASN, 2022).

As champions for student health and safety, school nurses must educate key stakeholders and decision-makers about student health issues and advocate for compliance with federal and state laws and regulations, ultimately leading to improved student health. In so doing, school nurses also help reduce school liability by promoting and assisting with implementing adequate and appropriate school health services (NASN, 2020a).

Brief History and Literature Review

A brief history of schools' legal responsibility for school health services and a brief literature review on the topic follow in Appendices A and B.

IMPLICATIONS FOR SCHOOL NURSE PRACTICE

What School Health Services Are Schools Responsible to Provide?

Three overarching federal laws guarantee the rights of all students, including those with disabilities, to attend public school. These laws are:
- Education of the Handicapped Act (P.L. 91-230) of 1970, reauthorized as Education for All Handicapped Children Act of 1975, reauthorized and renamed the Individuals with Disabilities Education Act (IDEA) in 1990 and reauthorized as the Individuals with Disabilities Education Improvement Act (IDEIA) of 2004;
- Rehabilitation Act of 1973, Section 504; and
- Americans with Disabilities Act (ADA) of 1990, which was reauthorized as the ADAAA of 2008.

The IDEA/IDEIA is the basis of how schools in all states provide special education and related services for eligible students from birth through their 21st year. The law requires public schools to evaluate children with disabilities, develop an education plan (now known as the individualized education program (IEP)), provide a free and appropriate public education (FAPE) in the least restrictive environment (LRE), and provide due process with an impartial hearing when there is a conflict between the school district and the parents of children with disabilities. Regarding children's health, the law requires that schools provide a broad range of services that enable eligible students to access educational opportunities just as non-disabled students have access.

The statute, 20 USC § 1401, defines child with a disability as a child "with intellectual disabilities, hearing impairments (including deafness), speech or language impairments, visual impairments (including blindness), serious emotional disturbance (referred to in this chapter as "emotional disturbance"), orthopedic impairments, autism, traumatic brain injury, other health impairments, or specific learning disabilities; and who, by reason thereof, needs special education and related services" (20 USC § 1401). This definition also includes children with other health impairments, such as reduced strength or stamina due to acute or chronic health conditions. (NCES, 2022a).

For younger children aged three through nine years (or any subset of that age range, including ages three through five years), a child with a disability may, at the discretion of the state and the local educational agency, include a child experiencing developmental delays, as defined by the state and as measured by appropriate diagnostic instruments and procedures, in one or more of the following developmental areas:
- physical;
- cognitive;
- communication;
- social or emotional; or
- adaptive; and
- who consequently needs special education or related services (20 USC § 1401).

In the 2020-2021 school year, there were over 7.2 million students – approximately 15 percent of the total public school enrollment – who qualified for special education and related services and over 1 million (15 percent of those qualifying for special education) who were eligible as being "other health impaired" (NCES, 2022a).

The school nurse is the only team member who is qualified to interpret medical records, evaluate the student's healthcare-related service needs, develop individualized health plan (IHP) and emergency care (ECP) plans, and assist the team in developing the IEP to appropriately accommodate the student's health needs, and evaluate the effectiveness of the plan's health-components, making revisions as necessary. Thus, with the help of the school nurse on the IEP, the student can participate in the school educational program (NASN, 2020b).

Under the IDEIA, children with disabilities are identified by specified criteria and thorough assessment by a multidisciplinary team of professionals who are knowledgeable about the student (Dang, 2010; NASN, 2023b). The team should include at least one regular education teacher, one special education teacher, a school representative, such as an administrator, the student's parent or guardian, and related specialists, including the school nurse when the nurse's specialty will be discussed (Halbert & Yonkaitis, 2019). The school nurse is the only team member who is qualified to interpret medical records, evaluate the student's healthcare-related service needs, develop individualized health plan (IHP) and emergency care (ECP) plans, and assist the team in developing the IEP to appropriately accommodate the student's health needs, and evaluate the effectiveness of the plan's health-components, making revisions as necessary (NASN, 2020b; NASN, 2022). Thus, with the help of the school nurse on the IEP, the student is enabled to participate in the educational program at school. (Halbert & Yonkaitis, 2019; Yonkaitis & Shannon, 2019; Zimmerman, 2013; Zirkel, 2009). The nurse develops the ECP from the information in the IHP (Zimmerman, 2013).

Depending on the student's needs, the school nurse may be identified on the IEP as a direct or related service. In these cases, the school nurse must supply information describing for the IEP the types of services to be provided and the frequency and duration of the services. The student's IHP may be attached to the IEP, thereby providing the rationale for the health services the student will receive at school. When the IEP specifies needs for nursing services according to the IHP, and the student is Medicaid eligible, the direct care services provided by the nurse may be reimbursable under the state's Medicaid program (Halbert & Yonkaitis, 2019; NASN, 2023a).

IDEIA also requires school districts to identify, locate, and evaluate all previously unidentified children, ages birth through age 21, with disabilities, regardless of the severity of the disability, who may need special education services. This process is known as "child find." The requirement applies to all children who live within a state, including students attending private and public schools, children whose families are highly mobile, migrant children, homeless children, foster children, and state wards (IDEIA, 20 U.S.C. sec. 1400 et. seq. (2004)). Infants and children, from birth up to three years old with disabilities are served through Early Childhood Intervention programs where healthcare practitioners evaluate the infant or toddler for delays and deficits in social, emotional, physical, cognitive, communication, and adaptive development and meet any needs through the development of an individualized family services plan (IFSP) which focuses on daily routines and family activities. At ages three to five years, children with disabilities may be enrolled in public school early childhood education classes (Halbert & Yonkaitis, 2019). As students with disabilities reach high school, transition planning for adulthood should begin and take into account the student's interests, strengths, and goals (Bargeron et al., 2015). While the student's IEP ends at age 22 (or younger if the state where the child resides specifies) and the student's Section 504 Plan lasts as long as the student is enrolled, the anti-discrimination protections of Section 504 last for life (Halbert & Yonkaitis, 2019). The school nurse is in an ideal position to help students and families through all these phases (NASN, 2019).

The amendments in the 2004 reauthorization take into account disparities between schools that serve primarily white students and have mostly white teachers, mislabeling and higher dropout rates for minority students with disabilities, disproportionate rates of minority students in special education compared to the overall student population, and discrepancies in the numbers of minority students referred and actually receiving services in special education. The amendments also require that individual student's response to evidence-based interventions, or Response to Intervention (RTI), be thoroughly assessed to determine if the student has a learning disability (NASN, 2023b).

The Individuals with Disabilities Education Improvement Act (IDEIA) of 2004 also clarifies the role of the school nurse by stating, "School health services and school nurse services means health services that are designed to enable a child with a disability to receive FAPE as described in the child's IEP. School nurse services are services provided by a qualified school nurse. School health services are services that may be provided by either a qualified school nurse or other qualified person" (IDEIA, 20 U.S.C. sec. 1400 et. seq. [2004]). *(See Chapter 13 for more information on Education Law for Children with Disabilities).*

Rehabilitation Act of 1973, Section 504 – extends civil rights to all persons (including those covered under IDEIA and adults) with mental or physical disabilities that substantially limit one or more major life activities, prohibits discrimination against persons with disabilities, requires the development of individualized accommodation plans (also known as Section 504 Plans), requires that any accommodations be 'reasonable,' and requires access for individuals with disabilities to federally funded programs and activities, including schools and jobs, if the person is otherwise qualified (Galemore & Sheetz, 2015; Halbert & Yonkaitis, 2019; Sampson & Galemore, 2012). Because this law covers all individuals with disabilities, it is important for students with disabilities to understand what accommodations they need as they transition to adulthood (Halbert & Yonkaitis, 2019).

As stated, Section 504 protects all persons with disabilities. A student with one of the defined disabilities under IDEA and who needs an IEP is covered by Section 504, but rather than a Section 504 Plan, the student will have an IEP and an IHP, as needed. A student with a disability other than one of those defined by IDEA or who does not need special education services to achieve academically may be eligible for a Section 504 Plan. Determination of Section 504 eligibility must be made to the Section 504 team, which is comprised of parents and persons who are knowledgeable about the disability, the student and the student's eligibility for accommodations, and the appropriate accommodations to fit the student's needs (Galemore & Sheetz, 2015; Halbert & Yonkaitis, 2019). School nurses are vital members of the Section 504 team. The school nurse must be prepared to speak to how the student's disability impacts major life activities and recommend accommodations supporting the student's school success (Halbert & Yonkaitis, 2019; NASN, 2023b).

Americans with Disabilities Act of 1990 – This law expands the scope of the rights guaranteed by the Rehabilitation Act of 1973 in that it prohibits discrimination against persons with disabilities in all aspects of public life, including employment, education, transportation, and in all public and private venues that are generally accessible and open to the public. This law has been reauthorized as the ADAAA of 2008. The ADAAA amendment to the definition of disability also amends the Section 504 definition. The changes include impairments that substantially limit one or more major life activities, including caring for oneself, performing manual tasks, seeing, hearing, eating, sleeping, walking, standing, lifting, bending, speaking, breathing, learning, reading, concentrating, thinking, communicating, and working.

The amendments also include coverage of episodic or in-remission impairments that, when active, can substantially limit one or more major life activities. The ADAAA (2008) states that the listed activities are examples and not a complete list of what may be included as major life activities (ADAAA, 2008). Additional changes resulting from the reauthorized ADAAA of 2008 are shown in Table 1.

Table 1. **Other changes in the amended ADAAA of 2008**

Other major bodily functions covered by the 2008 amendments include:	The amended law also states that mitigating measures have no bearing on determining whether a disability qualifies under the law. The mitigating measures include:
<ul><li>Functions of the immune system</li><li>Normal cell growth</li><li>Digestive, bowel, bladder, neurological, brain, respiratory, circulatory, endocrine, and reproductive functions</li></ul>	<ul><li>Medication</li><li>Medical supplies</li><li>Equipment or appliances</li><li>Low vision devices (other than eyeglasses and contact lenses)</li><li>Prosthetics</li><li>Hearing aids</li><li>Cochlear implants or other implantable hearing devices</li><li>Mobility devices</li><li>Oxygen therapy equipment and supplies, Assistive technology</li><li>Reasonable accommodations,</li><li>Auxiliary aids</li><li>Learned behavioral or adaptive neurological modifications</li></ul>

Zirkel (2009) suggests that, for the school nurse, the expansion of impairments and major bodily functions provides increased possibilities for conditions like sleep apnea, colitis, Crohn's disease, and irritable bowel syndrome to be covered by the ADAAA, 2008. The broadening of the definition of major life activities in the ADAAA, 2008, the addition of temporary or episodic impairments, and the requirement that mitigating factors may no longer be considered mean that students who previously were ineligible now may qualify under Section 504, as a person with a disability (Sampson & Galemore, 2012; Office of Civil Rights, 2020b; Zirkel, 2009). Zirkel (2009) also suggests that school nurses should be prepared for increasing requests to assist Section 504 teams in determining if individual students meet the expanded eligibility standards under Section 504. Recognizing this, school nurses will also contribute to "legally defensible and practically feasible answers" about the school's responsibility to provide health services for the increased numbers of eligible students under Section 504 (Zirkel, 2009, p. 260).

In response to the ADAAA, 2008, and parent complaints to the Office of Civil Rights (OCR), Zirkel et al. (2012) recommended that all students who currently have an individualized health plan (IHP) be screened in order to determine Section 504 eligibility under the school district's 'child find' obligations, and further evaluated if the screening results so indicate. School nurses clearly have a significant role in the screening and evaluation process (NASN, 2023b; Zirkel et al., 2012). While it is recommended that every student with a disability should have an IHP (Halbert & Yonkaitis, 2019), some children with disabilities may not have IHPs. School districts must be aware that 'child find' obligations remain intact (Zirkel et al., 2012). With the amendments of ADAAA, 2008, school districts may need to revise their Section 504 eligibility process and include the school nurse in that process to make "individualized but more expansive determinations" about Section 504 eligibility (Zirkel et al., 2012, p. 426).

In relationship to school health services in response to ADAAA, 2008 and Section 504, Zirkel et al. made the following recommendations for school nurses:
- Stay current with changes to Section 504 and student health conditions.
- Prioritize students with life-threatening conditions: regularly review emergency care plans, 504 Plans, and student safety measures.
- Screen all individual healthcare plans, student attendance, and health office visits.
- For student evaluation, obtain parental consent and necessary medical information, complete the evaluation process promptly, and give parents Section 504 procedural safeguards notice.
- Proactively discuss and determine as a team the student's need for accommodations and related aids and services according to Section 504's FAPE standards.
- Document and, as needed, consult with other professionals.
  [Adapted from Zirkel et al., 2012, pp. 430-431.]

(See Chapter 13 for more information on Education Laws for Children with Disabilities).

State Laws and School District Policies Mandating School Health Services

Special education legislation and court cases like *Irving Independent School Dist. V. Tatro* reinforce that schools in all states have a responsibility to provide nursing services (Maughan & Troup, 2011). In contrast with federal legislation related to school health services for students with disabilities, state laws, regulations, and school district policies, while varying widely, provide details and guidance for the provision of multiple services for all students. All states authorize some health services in school settings and some mandate specific health services. Determination of which health services are provided in schools and how they are delivered generally is left to local boards of education. Several states and many school boards mandate health services personnel to be in schools, typically school nurses and occasionally other qualified health professionals, such as school physicians. Most states do not require a school nurse in every school. School health professionals must meet state professional licensure requirements to provide health services, but the requirements for school nurses vary from state to state. School nurses need to be familiar with the laws governing their practice, including their state nurse practice act and the particular state and school district policies that authorize or require school health services.

Most states mandate some type of school-wide monitoring and screenings by the school nurse, such as vision screenings and other types of school entrance immunizations (Maughan & Troup, 2011). School testing and screening requirements typically cover five major areas (CDC, 2008):
- Communicable diseases, such as tuberculosis;
- Chronic conditions, such as hearing loss, vision problems, developmental delays, and scoliosis;
- Injuries and unhealthy behaviors, such as tobacco use;
- Monitoring child abuse or neglect; and
- Height, weight, and body mass index (BMI) screening.

In some states, testing and screening requirements are uniformly applied to all public schools in the state. Other states give discretion to local school districts regarding certain conditions. The timing and process for health testing and screening vary widely across states and school districts. Some health conditions are screened periodically, and others are screened only once in the student's career in the school district. Students are tested for other health conditions, especially communicable diseases such as tuberculosis, only when symptomatic indications warrant testing (CDC, 2008).

Many school districts require students to undergo a pre-participation physical examination for sports or other extracurricular activities. Students not meeting the stated requirements may not be permitted to participate in these activities. Drug testing is a prerequisite for participating in sports in some states. While random drug testing for students is controversial, the courts have upheld the requirement (CDC, 2008).

Like their federal counterparts, corresponding state laws guarantee access to appropriate health services for students with special healthcare needs.

Medication administration to students is a standard component of school health services. IDEIA (2004), Section 504, and ADAAA (2008) require schools to accommodate students whose asthma qualifies as a disability; however, federal law leaves the governance of student self-administration to the states (Findlaw, 2016). In 2004, Congress authorized preferential federal funding for states that permit students to possess and self-administer asthma inhalers, which resulted in most states authorizing these practices. Under these laws, students may carry their inhalers for self-medication as provided in their asthma management plans. Additionally, some states permit school districts to develop local policies that allow students to possess and administer epinephrine auto-injectors, glucagon, insulin, or other medications. (CDC, 2008). It is incumbent on the school nurse to become aware of the applicable state laws, regulations, and district policies that govern medication administration to and for students. *(See Chapter 33 for more information on medication administration in schools).*

In loco parentis - When students come to school, schools assume custody of students and, simultaneously, students no longer enjoy the protection of their parents. Essentially, schools act instead of the parent or in place of the parent. The Latin term for this role is –*"in loco parentis."* In modern usage, the term has evolved from being a right of coercion or restraint used to discipline students to becoming an obligation or duty of school officials to protect students. School officials hold authority over students due to *loco parentis* and have a concurrent duty to protect the students. Several aspects of "in loco parentis" have been tested in the courts, for example, *Tinker v. Des Moines Independent Community School District* (1969), *Hazelwood School District v. Kuhlmeier* (1987), *Vernonia School District v. Acton* (1995), and *Board of Education, Pottawatomie County v. Earls* (2002).

Consent for Treatment/Services

Some states' laws and school district policies control the process for obtaining consent for treatment in the school setting. Some states require parental consent for all or most school health services offered to minors. Other states permit minor students to access health services without parental consent. All states' consent provisions permit exceptions if a student's health is in immediate danger and parental consent cannot be obtained (CDC, 2008). In these situations, and similar situations, school personnel may cite *in loco parentis* to justify their actions (Figure 1). *(See Chapter 26 for more information on parental consent for treatment)*

Staffing: What is safe staffing for the school health office?

In the late 1970s, in response to federal legislation guaranteeing the rights of all students to attend public school, including those students with disabilities, NASN recommended, and the American Nurses Association (ANA), as well as other organizations, endorsed a school nurse-to-student ratio, which over the years evolved to a ratio of 1:750. However, given the increasing numbers of students with chronic health conditions and disabilities who now attend school and need specialized nursing care, **utilizing a fixed workload ratio is no longer appropriate, adequate, or in compliance with federal and state laws to meet today's students' highly complex healthcare needs** (American Nursing Association, 2020; NASN, 2020a; NASN, 2022; Nikpour & Hassmiller, 2017). Since 2015, the position of the NASN has been that student health, safety, and learning ability will improve with daily access to a school nurse, and to best meet student health and safety needs, school nurse workloads must be based on individual student and community health data (NASN, 2020a).

Evidence from recent studies demonstrates that appropriate school nurse staffing is associated with improved student attendance and academic performance (Allison et al., 2019; Brous, 2019; Martinez, 2016; NASN, 2020a), improved vaccination rates, illness reduction, and improved management of chronic disease (Baisch et al., 2011; NASN, 2020a). Other studies have shown that when school nurses are on campus, hundreds of hours each year are gained by administrators and teachers who are able to attend to student education rather than student health problems (Baisch et al., 2011; Hill & Hollis, 2012; NASN, 2020a). Additionally, adequate school nurse staffing is cost-effective – for every dollar expended on school nursing, at least $2.20 is saved – and full-time school nurses reduce medical costs and contribute to the productivity of teachers and parents (Wang et al., 2014).

However, nationally, approximately 52 percent of schools have a full-time school nurse, 32 percent of schools have a part-time school nurse, and 16 percent of schools do not have a school nurse (NCES, 2015). Inadequate school nurse staffing may contribute to negative outcomes for students and schools. Inadequate staffing reduces the quality of care for students, raises stress for school nurses, and impacts school nurse job satisfaction, all of which may lead to nurse turnover and increased costs to school districts (NASN, 2020a). Inadequate staffing, or no school nurse staffing at all, also raises questions about who is providing required school health services to students who need them, their qualifications, and who is supervising them to ensure student safety (Combe & Clark, 2019). In districts with inadequate staffing, school nurses must help school decision-makers understand the critical importance of safe and adequate staffing to protect the students and reduce liability for the district (Gormley, 2019).

Determining adequate nurse staffing is a complex process (ANA, 2020; NASN, 2020a) that requires identifying the individual student's acuity level and healthcare needs, as well as assessing the social determinants of the community's health, that is, the social and economic conditions that impact the health outcomes of individuals within the community (CDC, 2015). In determining staffing, adherence to individual state nurse practice acts and other related state laws must also be determined. School nurses are in key positions to educate school administrators regarding safe and adequate staffing for students with special healthcare needs (Dang, 2010). Sometimes, a school nurse will permit an unimmunized child in school or will not comply with nursing practice responsibilities because the school administrator said it was *okay not to comply*. This action would not be appropriate since school nurses have a legal and ethical responsibility to comply with their state nurse practice act, other applicable state laws, and patient/client care standards. For adequate school nurse staffing to be in place, the NASN (2020a) recommends:

- *Continuing research develops evidence-based tools using a multifactorial health assessment approach for evaluating factors influencing student health and safety.*
- *Developing staffing and workload models that support this evidence.*
- *In addition to the number of students covered, staffing for school nursing coverage must include acuity, social needs of students, community/school infrastructure, and characteristics of nursing staff.* (NASN, 2020a)

(See Chapter 7 for more information on safe school staffing).

CONCLUSION

Federal laws require schools to provide the necessary health services for students with disabilities in order for these students to receive an appropriate education. Schools must also provide services for other students with acute or episodic health problems. Schools are mandated to provide health services by federal or state legislation or risk and liability reduction. Other health services, including health screenings and immunizations, are generally accepted as belonging in the schools due to access and efficiency, or if mandated by state law, rather than with liability. Because schools are where children are, schools are frequently viewed as the logical place for population-based health prevention (Allensworth et al., 1997)

School nurses knowledgeable of federal and state laws related to working with students with disabilities, chronic illnesses, or other difficulties will make important contributions to these students' health and academic achievement. School nurses are responsible for understanding the laws, referring students who may be eligible for accommodations or special education services, and participating on school teams that determine eligibility for services covered by Section 504 and IDEIA (NASN, 2023b).

When providing health services for students, school nurses must be cognizant of their state nurse practice act, position and policy documents, and best practice guidelines, particularly the *School Nursing: Scope and Standards of Practice, 4th Edition* (2022). These documents set the standard of practice for school nursing and school healthcare delivery.

School nurses identify and address student health issues that impact school performance and are adept at navigating educational and medical systems (AAP, 2016; Baisch et al., 2011). School nurses have both opportunity and professional duty to advocate for compliance with federal and state laws related to school health services as well as district, state, and federal policies that support healthy school programs and environments (Halbert & Yonkaitis, 2019; Hoxie-Setterstrom & Hoglund, 2011NASN, 2020a).

RESOURCES

American Academy of Pediatrics. (2022, April 26). *Bright Futures*. Author. https://www.aap.org/en/practice-management/bright-futures

American Diabetes Association. (2012). Diabetes Care in the School and Day Care Setting. Diabetes Care 2012 Jan; 35(Supplement 1). https://diabetesjournals.org/care/article/35/Supplement_1/S76/26210/Diabetes-Care-in-the-School-and-Day-Care-Setting" https://diabetesjournals.org/care/article/35/Supplement_1/S76/26210/Diabetes-Care-in-the-School-and-Day-Care-Setting

Maternal Child Health. (2023, February). National survey of children's health (NSCH). Health Resources and Services Administration. https://mchb.hrsa.gov/data-research/national-survey-childrens-health" https://mchb.hrsa.gov/data-research/national-survey-childrens-health

Substance Abuse and Mental Health Services Administration (SAMHSA). http://www.samhsa.gov/

LEGAL REFERENCES

- Americans with Disabilities Act (ADA) 42 U.S.C. § 12101 (1990).
- ADA Amendments Act of 2008 (ADAAA) 42 USCA § 12101 (2008).
- Child Nutrition and WIC Reauthorization Act, Pub. L. No. 108-265, § 204, 729 (2004).
- Developmental Disabilities Assistance and Bill of Rights Act, Pub. L. No. 106-402, § 101 1680 (2000).
- Education for All Handicapped Children Act, Pub. L. No. 94-142, § 20 USC 1401. (1975).
- Elementary and Secondary Education Act, 20 U.S.C. 6301 et seq. (1965).
- Every Student Succeeds Act (ESSA), Public Law No: 114-95 (2015)
- Family Educational Rights and Privacy Act (FERPA), 20 U.S.C.S. § 1232g (1974).
- Health Insurance Portability and Accountability Act (HIPAA), Privacy Rule P.L. 104-191 (1996).
- Healthy, Hunger-Free Kids Act, Pub. L. 111–296. (2010).
- Individuals with Disabilities Education Improvement Act (IDEIA), 20 U.S.C. sec. 1400 et. seq. (2004).
- McKinney-Vento Homeless Education Assistance Improvements Act, 42 U.S.C.S. 11431 et seq. (2001).
- Mental Health Parity and Addiction Equity Act (MHPAEA), 29 U.S.C. sec. 1185a et. seq. (2008)

- o Patient Protection and Affordable Care Act (ACA), P.L. 111-148 (2010).
- o Protection of Pupil Rights Amendment (PPRA), 20 U.S.C.S. § 1232h (1978).
- o School Access to Emergency Epinephrine Act, H.R. 2094 — 113th Congress (2013). 42 U.S.C.sec. 280g(d) (2013)
- o Section 504 of the Rehabilitation Act, 29 U.S.C. § 701 et seq. (1973).

Case Law

Board of Education of the Hendrickson Central School District v. Amy Rowley, Supreme Court of the United States 458 US 176. (1982)

Board of Education, Pottawatomie County v. Earls, 536 U. S. 822, 122 S. Ct. 2559, 153 L. Ed. 2d 735 (2002).

Brown v. Board of Education of Topeka, 347 U.S. 483 (1954).

Cedar Rapids Community School District v. Garret F., Supreme Court of the United States 526 U.S. 66 (1999).

Hazelwood School District et al. v. Kuhlmeier et al., 484 U.S. 260 (1988).

Sacramento City Unified School District v. Rachel H., U.S. Court of Appeals for the Ninth circuit, 14 F.3d 1398 (1994).

Irving Independent School Dist. v. Tatro, 468 US 883, 104 S. Ct. 3371, 82 L. Ed. 2d 664 - Supreme Court, (1984).

Mills v. Board of Education, 348 F. Supp. 866 (D.D.C. 1972)

Pennsylvania Association for Retarded Children (Parc) v. Commonwealth of Pennsylvania, 334 F. Supp. 279 (E.D. PA 1972).

Tinker v. Des Moines Independent Community School District, 393 U.S. 503, 89 S. Ct. 733, 21L. Ed. 2d 731. (1969).

Vernonia School District v. Acton, 515 U.S. 646, 115 S. Ct. 2386, 132 L. Ed. 2d 564 (1995).

W. B. v. Matula, 67 F.3d. 484, 3rd Cir. (1995).

REFERENCES

Allensworth, D., Lawson, E., Nicholson, L., & Wyche, J., (Eds.). (1997). School health services. In *schools and health: Our nation's investment* (Committee on Comprehensive School Health Programs in Grades K-12, Institute of Medicine, 153-236, Chapter 4). National Academies Press https://www.nap.edu/read/**5153**/chapter/6.

Allison, M.A., Attisha, E., Lerner, M., De Pinto, C.D., Beers, N.S., Gibson, E.J., Gorski, P., Kjolhede, C., O'Leary, S.C., Schumacher, H. & Weiss-Harrison, A. (2019). The link between school attendance and good health (Policy Statement). Council on School Health. *Pediatrics, 143*(2): e20183648. https://doi.org/10.1542/peds.2018-3648

American Academy of Pediatrics. (2016). Role of the school nurse in providing school health services (Policy Statement). Council on School Health. *Pediatrics, 121*(5), 1052-1056. https://doi.org/10.1542/peds.2016-0852

American Nurses Association. (2020). *ANA's principles for nurse staffing* (3rd ed.). https://cdn2.hubspot.net/hubfs/4850206/PNS3E_ePDF.pdf

Baisch, M.J., Lundeen, S.P., & Murphy, M.K. (2011). Evidence-based research on the value of school nurses in an urban school system. *Journal of School Health, 81*(2), 74-80. https://doi.org/10.1111/j.1746-1561.2010.00563.x

Bargeron, J., Contri, D., Gibbons, L.J., Ruch-Ross, H.S., & Sanabria, K. (2015). Transition planning for youth with special health care needs (YSHCN) in Illinois schools. *The Journal of School Nursing, 31*(4), 253-260. https://doi.org/10.1177/1059840514542130

Basch, C. E. (2011). Healthier students are better learners: High-quality, strategically planned, and effectively coordinated school health programs must be a fundamental mission of schools to help close the achievement gap. *Journal of School Health*, Special Issue, *81*(10), 650–662. https://doi.org/10.1111/j.1746-1561.2011.00640.x

Brener, N.D., Weist, M., Adelman, H., Taylor, L., & Vernon-Smiley, M. (2007a). Mental health and social services: Results from the school health policies and programs study 2006. *Journal of School Health, 77*(8), 486–499. https://doi.org/10.1111/j.1746-1561.2007.00231.x

Brener, N.D., Wheeler, L., Wolfe, L.C., Vernon-Smiley, M., & Caldart-Olson, L. (2007b). Health services: Results from the school health policies and programs study 2006. *Journal of School Health, 77*(8): 464–485. https://doi.org/10.1111/j.1746-1561.2007.00230.x

Brous, E. (2019). *The law and school nursing practice*. In J. Selekman, R.A. Shannon, & C. Yonkaitis (Eds.), *School nursing: A comprehensive text* (3rd ed., pp. 257-283). F.A. Davis Company.

Centers for Disease Control and Prevention. (2008). A CDC review of school laws and policies concerning child and adolescent health. *Journal of School Health, 78*(2), 69–128. https://onlinelibrary.wiley.com/doi/epdf/10.1111/j.1746-1561.2007.00272_4.x

Centers for Disease Control and Prevention. (2015). Healthy schools: Components of the whole school, whole community, whole child (WSCC): http://www.cdc.gov/healthyschools/wscc/components.htm

Centers for Disease Control and Prevention. (2021, October 20). *Healthy schools: Managing chronic health conditions*. http://www.cdc.gov/healthyschools/chronicconditions.htm

Combe, L. & Clark, Y. (2019). Management of school health staff. In J. Selekman, R.A. Shannon, & C. Yonkaitis (Eds.), *School nursing: A comprehensive text* (3rd ed., pp. 154-171). F.A. Davis Company.

Dang, M.T. (2010). The history of legislation and regulations related to children with developmental disabilities: implications for school nursing practice today. *The Journal of School Nursing, 26*(4), 252-259. https://doi.org/10.1177/1059840510368162

Findlaw. (2016, June 20). *Self-administration of medication: common provisions*. https://www.findlaw.com/education/school-safety/common-provisions-on-schools-administering-medications-and.html

Galemore, C.A. & Sheetz, A.H. (2015). IEP, IHP, and Section 504 primer for new school nurses. NASN School Nurse, 30(2): 85-88. https://doi.org/10.1177/1942602X14565462

Gormley, J. M. (2019). School nurse advocacy for student health, safety, and school attendance: Impact of an educational activity. *Journal of School Nursing, 35*(6), 401–411. https://journals.sagepub.com/doi/10.1177/1059840518814294

Halbert, L.-A. & Yonkaitis, C.F. (2019). Federal laws protecting students with disabilities. In J. Selekman, R.A. Shannon, & C. Yonkaitis (Eds.), *School nursing: A comprehensive text* (3rd ed., pp. 154-171). F.A. Davis Company.

Hill, N.J. & Hollis, M. (2012). Teacher time spent on student health issues and school nurse presence. The Journal of School Nursing, 28(3), 181-186. https://doi.org/10.1177/1059840511429684

Hoxie-Setterstrom, G. & Hoglund, B. (2011). School wellness policies: Opportunities for change. *The Journal of School Nursing, 27*(5), 330-339. https://doi.org/10.1177/1059840511409755

Martin, E.W., Martin, R., & Terman, D.L. (1996). The legislative and litigation history of special education. *The Future of Children, 6*(1), 25-39. https://www.princeton.edu/futureofchildren/publications/docs/06_01_01.pdf

Martinez, A.K. (2016). *School attendance, chronic health conditions and leveraging data for improvement: Recommendations for state education and health departments to address student absenteeism.* National Association of Chronic Disease Directors. https://chronicdisease.org/resource/resmgr/school_health/nacdd_school_attendance_and_.pdf

Maughan, E. & Troup, K.D. (2011). The integration of counseling and nursing services into schools: A comparative review. *The Journal of School Nursing, 27*(4): 293-303. https://doi.org/10.1177/1059840511407778

National Association of School Nurses. (2019). *Transition planning for students with healthcare needs* (Position Statement). Author. https://www.nasn.org/nasn-resources/professional-practice-documents/position-statements/ps-transition

National Association of School Nurses. (2020a). *School nurse workload: Staffing for safe care* (Position Statement). Author. https://www.nasn.org/nasn-resources/professional-practice-documents/position-statements/ps-workload

National Association of School Nurses. (2020b). *Use of individualized healthcare plans to support school health services* (Position Statement). Author. https://www.nasn.org/nasn-resources/professional-practice-documents/position-statements/ps-ihps

National Association of School Nurses. (2022). School nursing: Scope and standards of practice (4th ed.). Author.

National Association of School Nurses. (2023a). *Equitable reimbursement for school nursing services* (Position Statement). Author. https://www.nasn.org/nasn-resources/professional-practice-documents/position-statements/ps-reimbursement

National Association of School Nurses. (2023b). *IDEIA and Section 504 Teams - The school nurse as an essential team member* (Position Statement). Author. https://www.nasn.org/nasn-resources/professional-practice-documents/position-statements/ps-ideia

National Center for Chronic Disease Prevention and Health Promotion. (2022, May 23). *Healthy schools*. Centers for Disease Control and Prevention. https://www.cdc.gov/chronicdisease/resources/publications/factsheets/healthy-schools.htm

National Center for Educational Statistics. (2022a). Fast facts: Students with disabilities. U.S. Department of Education, Institute of Education Sciences. http://nces.ed.gov/fastfacts/display.asp?id=64

National Center for Educational Statistics. (2015). *Percentage of schools with full-time and part-time school nurses, by school characteristics: 2015–16*. National Teacher and Principal Survey U.S. Department of Education, Institute of Education Sciences. https://nces.ed.gov/surveys/ntps/tables/ntps1516_20032002_s1n.asp

National Center for Education Statistics. (2022b). Prevalence of mental health services provided by public schools and limitations in schools' efforts to provide mental health services. *Condition of Education*. U.S. Department of Education, Institute of Education Sciences. https://nces.ed.gov/programs/coe/indicator/a23

Nikpour, J. & Hassmiller, S. (2017). A full-time nurse for every school: a call to action to make It happen. *NASN School Nurse, 32*(5), 290-293. https://journals.sagepub.com/doi/epdf/10.1177/1942602X17723920

Sampson, C. H., & Galemore, C. A. (2012). What every school nurse needs to know about Section 504 eligibility. *NASN School Nurse, 27*(2), 88-93. https://doi.org/10.1177/1942602X12437879

Wang, L.Y., Vernon-Smiley, M., Gapinski, M.A., DeSisto, M., Maughan, E., & Sheetz, A. (2014). Cost-benefit study of school nursing services. *Journal of the American Medical Association Pediatrics*, *168*(7), 642-648. https://doi.org/10.1001/jamapediatrics.2013.5441

Whitney, D.G., & Peterson, M.D. (2019). US National and State-Level Prevalence of Mental Health Disorders and Disparities of Mental Health Care Use in Children. *Journal of the American Medical Association Pediatrics*. 173(4):389–391. doi:10.1001/jamapediatrics.2018.5399

Yonkaitis, C.F. & Shannon, R.A. (2019). Health and education plans for students with special healthcare needs. In J. Selekman, R.A. Shannon, & C. Yonkaitis (Eds.), *School nursing: A comprehensive text* (3rd ed., pp. 172-199). F.A. Davis Company.

Zimmerman, B. (2013). Student health and education plans. In J. Selekman (Ed.), *School nursing: A comprehensive text (2nd ed., pp.* 284–314). F.A. Davis.

Zirkel, P.A. (2009). History and expansion of Section 504 student eligibility: Implications for school nurses. *The Journal of School Nursing*, *25*(4), 256-260. https://doi.org/10.1177/1059840509336930

Zirkel, P.A., Granthom, M.R., & Lovato, L. (2012). Section 504 and student health problems: The pivotal position of the school nurse. *The Journal of School Nursing*, *28*(6), 423-432. https://doi.org/10.1177/1059840512449358

APPENDIX A

Brief History

The century-long history of school health services in the United States is rooted in 19th-century Europe, where school medical inspections were mandated by royal command in France in 1837 and soon adopted in most European countries, Egypt, and South America (Wold, 2005). Following those examples many years later, American school medicine and health reformers in the 1890s began pushing for medical inspections of poor immigrant children who lived in the deplorable conditions of inner-city slums (Tyack, 1992). Medical inspections, the resulting exclusion of children with contagious conditions from school, and escalating school absenteeism led New York City School District to hire the first U.S. school nurse, Lina Rogers, in 1902 (Maughan & Troup, 2011). After World War I and the realization that many draftees had correctable physical defects, the National Education Association declared that health was among its seven primary principles of education (Kort, 2006). Between 1918 and 1921, most states passed school laws requiring health and physical education (Kort, 2006). From the early 1920s, as health services were increasingly located in public schools, priorities were increasingly debated, with school health relegated to a lower priority (Kort, 1984; Maughan & Troup, 2011).

Since funding for public schools came primarily from local property taxes, there were great disparities in all school services – both education and health – and many population sectors had no school services at all (Tyack, 1992). Some relief for school health services came in the mid-1960s with the authorization of the *Elementary and Secondary Education Act of 1965*, which enabled school administrators to hire school nurses (Maughan & Troup, 2011). Still today, despite laws permitting school districts to receive Medicaid reimbursement for healthcare services to eligible students at rates considerably lower than those permitted for private practitioners, schools' legal obligations to provide health services remain underfunded. The burden to provide school health services rests primarily with the education system, and there is little acknowledgment that school health services, which serve approximately 97 percent of school-age children and youth, are part of the overall general healthcare system (CDC, 2022).

Historically, persons with physical or mental disabilities, in most cultures, have been subjected to discrimination of every sort for thousands of years, and only recently have they been moved into the mainstream (Martin et al., 1996). Throughout most of the 20th century, schools in the United States provided minimal, if any, services to students with disabilities, and many of these children, particularly those with developmental disabilities, were institutionalized (Dang, 2010) or kept at home. In most states, state laws permitted school administrators to deny school enrollment to any student who was considered, by the administrator, to be uneducable (Martin et al., 1996). Some school districts admitted students with disabilities but provided no special services, and other such students were put into special programs that were inadequate or inappropriate for the student's needs (Martin et al., 1996).

In the mid-1950s, the landmark United States Supreme Court case, *Brown v. Board of Education* (1954), which ended legal segregation in public schools and paved the way for integration, was a major civil rights victory. Following the authorization of the Civil Rights Act of 1964, in 1965, Congress authorized funding through the Elementary and Secondary Education Act (ESEA) of 1965 to schools for educationally disadvantaged children from low-income families (Halbert & Yonkaitis, 2019). In 1966, ESEA was amended to allow school districts to apply to the federal government for funding to educate handicapped children, and in 1970, ESEA was further amended to include Part B: The Education of the Handicapped Act (EHA) (Halbert & Yonkaitis, 2019). *Brown v. Board of Education (1954)*, the Civil Rights Movement, and the subsequent versions of ESEA provided the impetus for three important pieces of federal legislation which have significantly impacted the educational rights of persons with disabilities and provided some of the basis for education's responsibility for school health services. These federal laws include the **Rehabilitation Act (1973), Section 504, and Education for All Handicapped Children Act (1975)** which was reauthorized and renamed in 1990 as the Individuals with Disabilities Education Act (IDEA), then reauthorized in 2004 as the Individuals with Disabilities Education Improvement Act (IDEIA) of 2004, and **Americans with Disabilities Act (ADA) (1990)** which was reauthorized in 2008 as the ADA Amendments Act (ADAAA) of 2008. (Please refer to Chapters 12 and 13 for more information on these federal laws).

REFERENCES

Centers for Disease Control and Prevention. (2022). *School health profiles 2020: characteristics of health programs among secondary schools*. https://www.cdc.gov/healthyyouth/data/profiles/pdf/2020/cdc-profiles-2020.pdf

Dang, M.T. (2010). The history of legislation and regulations related to children with developmental disabilities: Implications for school nursing practice today. *The Journal of School Nursing, 26*(4), 252-259. https://doi.org/10.1177/1059840510368162

Halbert, L.-A. & Yonkaitis, C.F. (2019). Federal laws protecting students with disabilities. In J. Selekman, R.A. Shannon, & C. Yonkaitis (Eds.), *School nursing: A comprehensive text* (3rd ed., pp. 154-171). F.A. Davis Company.

Kort, M. (2006). The delivery of primary health care in American public schools, 1890-1980. In J.G. Lear, S.L. Isaacs, & J.R. Knickman (Eds.), School health services and programs, (pp. 41-55). San Francisco, CA: Jossey-Bass.

Kort, M. (1984). The delivery of primary health care in American public schools, 1890-1980. *Journal of School Health,* 54 (11), 453-457. https://onlinelibrary.wiley.com/doi/epdf/10.1111/j.1746-1561.1984.tb08912.x

Martin, E.W., Martin, R., & Terman, D.L. (1996). The legislative and litigation history of special education. *The Future of Children*, 6(1), 25-39. https://www.princeton.edu/futureofchildren/publications/docs/06_01_01.pdf

Maughan, E. & Troup, K.D. (2011). The integration of counseling and nursing services into schools: A comparative review. *The Journal of School Nursing, 27*(4): 293-303. https://doi.org/10.1177/1059840511407778

Tyack, D. (1992). Health and social services in public schools: Historical perspectives. *The Future of Children, 2*(1): 19-31. https://doi.org/10.2307/1602459   Princeton University. https://www.jstor.org/stable/1602459?seq=1#page_scan_tab_contents

Wold, S. J. (2005). School health services: History and trends. In N.C. Schwab & M.H.B. Gelfman (Eds.), *Legal issues in school health services: A resource for school administrators, school attorneys, and school nurses* (pp. 7-54). Authors Choice Press.

APPENDIX B

Brief Literature Review

Reviewing the literature leaves no doubt about the responsibility school districts, schools, and school personnel have for providing school health services. There are many references to the three overarching federal laws - Rehabilitation Act (1973); Section 504, Education for All Handicapped Children Act (1975); and Americans with Disabilities Act (ADA) (1990) - that obligate schools to provide services (Allensworth et al., 1997; Brener et al., 2007a; Brous, 2019; Caldart-Olson & Thronson, 2013; CDC, 2008; Halbert & Yonkaitis, 2019; Krin & Taliaferro, 2012; Maughan & Troup, 2011; NASN, 2023b; Sampson & Galemore, 2012; Zirkel, 2009; Zirkel et al., 2012). The U.S. Department of Education's Office of Civil Rights (USDE-OCR) provides online compliance guidance related to federal statutory requirements under the ADAAA of 2008 and the Rehabilitation Act (1973), Section 504, for states and school districts (USDE-OCR, 2020a; USDE-OCR, 2020b).

Additionally, there are many more references to very specific health services covered by these three main federal laws and guidance on the meaning and impact of other federal and state statutes related to specific health conditions. For example, Sicherer et al. (2010) advise that federal laws protect the legal rights of students with severe life-threatening allergies. The Patient Protection and Affordable Care Act (ACA) of 2010 improves access to care for youth who have chronic physical health conditions, as well as mental health concerns (National Conference of State Legislatures [NCSL], 2015). Students who have diabetes are entitled to health services at school, as well as an individualized health assessment (American Diabetes Association, 2012; Jackson et al., 2015); additionally, Jackson et al. (2015) advise about state-specific laws that protect school staff who assist students with diabetes care. In response to two federal laws related to reducing childhood obesity, the Healthy, Hunger-Free Kids Act of 2010, and the earlier Child Nutrition and WIC Reauthorization Act of 2004, states and school districts have turned to school nurses to assist with the implementation of these laws (Hoxie-Setterstrom & Hoglund, 2011). All states have enacted laws that include basic health requirements that support academic performance and school attendance (CDC, 2008; Dean et al., 2014).

Other related topics reviewed in the literature include:
- The incidence of chronic physical and mental health conditions in student populations.
- The history of school health services.
- Laws and support for addressing student mental health.
- Availability or lack of access to school health services.
- School health policy development.
- Fiscal support or funding problems related to the delivery of school health services.
- The roles of the school nurse.

For the above topics, see references in Table 1 below.

Table 1. Other related topics reviewed include:

Topic	Citations
The incidence of chronic physical and mental health conditions in student populations	(AAP, 2016; CDC, 2021; Conners et al., 2022; Dang, 2010; Martinez, 2016; NASN, 2020a; NASN, 2023c; National Center for Chronic Disease Prevention and Health Promotion (NCCDPHP), 2022; Office of Disease Prevention and Health Promotion (ODPHP), n.d.)
The history of school health services	(Dang, 2010; Kort, 2006; Martin et al., 1996; Maughan & Troup, 2011; Tyack, 1992)
Laws and support for addressing student mental health	(AAP, 2016; Langley, 2010; Lohan, 2006; NASN, 2023c; NCSL, 2015; Silverman et al., 2016; Centers for Medicare & Medicaid Services, 2013; Weist et al., 2007)
Availability or lack of access to school health services	(AAP, 2016; Brener et al., 2007a; Brener et al.,2007b; CDC, 2015; CDC, 2022; Langley et al., 2010; NASN, 2023c; NCSL, 2015; ODPHP, n.d.)
School health policy development	(Brener et al., 2007a; Brener et al., 2007b; CDC, 2022; Jones et al., 2015; Krin & Taliaferro, 2012)
Fiscal support or funding problems related to delivery of school health services	(Allensworth et al., 1997; CDC, 2008; Cruden et al., 2016; Jordan et al., 2022; Maughan, & Troup, 2011; NASN, 2023a)
The roles of the school nurse	(Allensworth & Kolbe, 1987; AAP, 2016; Bargeron et al., 2015; Caldart-Olson & Thronson, 2013; CDC, 2008; CDC, 2015; Dang, 2010; Dean et al., 2014; Halbert & Yonkaitis, 2019; Hoxie-Setterstrom & Hoglund, 2011; Krin & Taliaferro, 2012; Lohan, 2006; NASN, 2020a; NASN, 2022; NASN, 2023c; Sampson & Galemore, 2012; Wang et al., 2014; Zirkel, 2009; Zirkel et al., 2012)

REFERENCES

Allensworth, D.D. & Kolbe, L.J. (1987). The comprehensive school health program: Exploring an expanded concept. *Journal of School Health, 57*(10), 409–412. https://doi.org/10.1111/j.1746-1561.1987.tb03183.x

Allensworth, D., Lawson, E., Nicholson, L., & Wyche, J., (Eds.). (1997). School health services. In *Schools and health: Our nation's investment* (Committee on Comprehensive School Health Programs in Grades K-12, Institute of Medicine, 153-236, Chapter 4). National Academies Press https://www.nap.edu/read/**5153**/chapter/6.

American Academy of Pediatrics. (2016). Role of the school nurse in providing school health services (Policy Statement). Council on School Health. *Pediatrics, 121*(5), 1052-1056. https://doi.org/10.1542/peds.2016-0852

American Diabetes Association. (2012). Diabetes care in the school and day care setting (Position Statement). *Diabetes Care, 35*(Supplement 1), S76-S80. https://doi.org/10.2337/dc12-s076

Bargeron, J., Contri, D., Gibbons, L.J., Ruch-Ross, H.S., & Sanabria, K. (2015). Transition planning for youth with special health care needs (YSHCN) in Illinois schools. *The Journal of School Nursing, 31*(4), 253-260. https://doi.org/10.1177/1059840514542130

Brener, N.D., Weist, M., Adelman, H., Taylor, L., & Vernon-Smiley, M. (2007a). Mental health and social services: Results from the school health policies and programs study 2006. *Journal of School Health*, *77*(8), 486–499. https://doi.org/10.1111/j.1746-1561.2007.00231.x

Brener, N.D., Wheeler, L., Wolfe, L.C., Vernon-Smiley, M., & Caldart-Olson, L. (2007b). Health services: Results from the school health policies and programs study 2006. *Journal of School Health*, *77*(8): 464–485. https://doi.org/10.1111/j.1746-1561.2007.00230.x

Brous, E. (2019). *The law and school nursing practice*. In J. Selekman, R.A. Shannon, & C. Yonkaitis (Eds.), *School nursing: A comprehensive text* (3rd ed., pp. 257-283). F.A. Davis Company.

Caldart-Olson, L. & Thronson, G. (2013). Legislation affecting school nurses. In J. Selekman (Ed.), *School nursing: A comprehensive text* (2nd ed., pp. 225–256). F.A. Davis.

Centers for Disease Control and Prevention. (2008). A CDC review of school laws and policies concerning child and adolescent health. *Journal of School Health*, *78*(2), 69–128. https://onlinelibrary.wiley.com/doi/epdf/10.1111/j.1746-1561.2007.00272_4.x

Centers for Disease Control and Prevention. (2015). Healthy schools: Components of the whole school, whole community, whole child (WSCC): http://www.cdc.gov/healthyschools/wscc/components.htm

Centers for Disease Control and Prevention. (2021, October 20). *Healthy schools: Managing chronic health conditions*. http://www.cdc.gov/healthyschools/chronicconditions.htm

Centers for Disease Control and Prevention. (2022). *School health profiles 2020: characteristics of health programs among secondary schools*. https://www.cdc.gov/healthyyouth/data/profiles/pdf/2020/cdc-profiles-2020.pdf

Centers for Medicare & Medicaid Services. (2013, January 16). [Letter to State Health Official & State Medicaid Director] on application of the Mental Health Parity and Addiction Equity Act to Medicaid MCOs, CHIP, and Alternative Benefit (Benchmark) Plans]. U.S. Department of Health & Human Services, https://www.medicaid.gov/Federal-Policy-Guidance/downloads/SHO-13-001.pdf

Conners, E.H., Moffa, K., Carter, T,, Crocker, J., Bohnenkamp, J.H., Lever, N.A., & Hoover, S.A. (2022). Advancing mental health screening in schools: Innovative, field-tested practices and observed trends during a 15-month learning collaborative. Psychology in the Schools. 59(6). 1135-1157. https://doi.org/10.1002/pits.22670

Cruden, G., Kelleher, K., Kellam, S. & Brown, C.H. (2016, August 16). Increasing the delivery of preventive health services in public education. *American Journal of Preventive Medicine*, *52* (4) Supplement 2, 158-167. https://doi.org/10.1016/j.amepre.2016.07.002 https://www.ajpmonline.org/article/S0749-3797(16)30250-1/fulltext

Dang, M.T. (2010). The history of legislation and regulations related to children with developmental disabilities: Implications for school nursing practice today. *The Journal of School Nursing, 26*(4), 252-259. https://doi.org/10.1177/1059840510368162

Dean, B.B., Kindermann, S.L., Carson, T., Gavin, J., Frerking, M., & Bergren, M.D. (2014). Healthy kids: An assessment of program performance and participation. *The Journal of School Nursing, 30*(6), 430-439. https://doi.org/10.1177/1059840514527622

Halbert, L.-A. & Yonkaitis, C.F. (2019). Federal laws protecting students with disabilities. In J. Selekman, R.A. Shannon, & C. Yonkaitis (Eds.), *School nursing: A comprehensive text* (3rd ed., pp. 154-171). F.A. Davis Company.

Hoxie-Setterstrom, G. & Hoglund, B. (2011). School wellness policies: Opportunities for change. *The Journal of School Nursing, 27*(5), 330-339. https://doi.org/10.1177/1059840511409755

Jackson, C.C., Albanese-O'Neill, A., Butler, K.L., Chiang, J.L., Deeb, L.C., Hathaway, K., Kraus, E., Weissberg-Benchell, J., Alan L. Yatvin, A.L., & Siminerio, L.M. (2015). Diabetes care in the school setting: A position statement of the American Diabetes Association. *Diabetes Care*, 38(10), 1958-1963. https://doi.org/10.2337/dc15-1418

Jones, S.E., Brener, N.D., & Bergren, M.D. (2015). Association between school district policies that address chronic health conditions of students and professional development for school nurses on such policies. *The Journal of School Nursing*, 31(#), 163-166. https://doi.org/10.1177/1059840514547275

Jordan, P., Dwyer, A., DiMarco, B. & Johnson-Green, M. (2022, May 17). *How Medicaid can help schools sustain support for students' mental health*. Georgetown University Health Policy Institute: Center for Children and Families. https://ccf.georgetown.edu/2022/05/17/how-medicaid-can-help-schools-sustain-support-for-students-mental-health/

Kort, M. (2006). The delivery of primary health care in American public schools, 1890-1980. In J.G. Lear, S.L. Isaacs, & J.R. Knickman (Eds.), School health services and programs, (pp. 41-55). San Francisco, CA: Jossey-Bass.

Krin, P. & Taliaferro, V. (2012). Establishing policies and procedures: The core of school nursing practice. In C. Costante (Ed.), *School nurse administrators: Leadership and management,* (pp. 339-362). National Association of School Nurses.

Langley, A.K., Nadeem, E., Kataoka, S.H., Stein, B.D., & Jaycox, L.H. (2010). Evidence-Based Mental Health Programs in Schools: Barriers and Facilitators of Successful Implementation. *School Mental Health,* 2(3): 105–113. https://doi.org/10.1007/s12310-010-9038-1

Lohan, J.A. (2006). School nurses' support for bereaved students: A pilot study. *The Journal of School Nursing*, 22(1): 48-52. https://doi.org/10.1177/10598405060220010801

Martin, E.W., Martin, R., & Terman, D.L. (1996). The legislative and litigation history of special education. *The Future of Children*, 6(1), 25-39. https://www.princeton.edu/futureofchildren/publications/docs/06_01_01.pdf

Martinez, A.K. (2016). *School attendance, chronic health conditions and leveraging data for improvement: Recommendations for state education and health departments to address student absenteeism.* National Association of Chronic Disease Directors. https://chronicdisease.org/resource/resmgr/school_health/nacdd_school_attendance_and_.pdf

Maughan, E. & Troup, K.D. (2011). The integration of counseling and nursing services into schools: A comparative review. *The Journal of School Nursing,* 27(4): 293-303. https://doi.org/10.1177/1059840511407778

National Association of School Nurses. (2020a). *School nurse workload: Staffing for safe care* (Position Statement). Author. https://www.nasn.org/nasn-resources/professional-practice-documents/position-statements/ps-workload

National Association of School Nurses. (2022). School nursing: Scope and standards of practice (4th ed.). Author.

National Association of School Nurses. (2023a). *Equitable reimbursement for school nursing services* (Position Statement). Author. https://www.nasn.org/nasn-resources/professional-practice-documents/position-statements/ps-reimbursement

National Association of School Nurses. (2023b). *IDEIA and Section 504 Teams - The school nurse as an essential team member* (Position Statement). Author. https://www.nasn.org/nasn-resources/professional-practice-documents/position-statements/ps-ideia

National Association of School Nurses. (2023c). *Safe, supportive, equitable schools* (Position Statement). Author. https://www.nasn.org/nasn-resources/professional-practice-documents/position-statements/ps-safe

National Center for Chronic Disease Prevention and Health Promotion. (2022, May 23). *Healthy schools*. Centers for Disease Control and Prevention. https://www.cdc.gov/chronicdisease/resources/publications/factsheets/healthy-schools.htm

National Conference of State Legislatures. (2015). *Mental health benefits: State laws mandating or regulating*. Author. http://www.ncsl.org/research/health/mental-health-benefits-state-mandates.aspx

Office of Disease Prevention and Health Promotion. (n.d.). *Healthy People 2030*. U.S. Department of Health and Human Services. https://health.gov/healthypeople/objectives-and-data/browse-objectives

Sampson, C. H., & Galemore, C. A. (2012). What every school nurse needs to know about Section 504 eligibility. *NASN School Nurse, 27*(2), 88-93. https://doi.org/10.1177/1942602X12437879

Sicherer, S.H., Mahr, T., & American Academy of Pediatrics/The Section On Allergy and Immunology. (2010). Management of food allergy in the school setting (Clinical Report). *Pediatrics, 126*(6), 1232-1239. doi:10.1542/peds.2010-2575

Silverman, B., Chen, B., Brener, N., Kruger, J., Krishna, N., Renard, P., Romero-Steiner, S.& Avchen, R.N. (2016). School district crisis preparedness, response, and recovery plans — United States, 2012. *Morbidity and Mortality Weekly Report (MMWR), 65*,949–953. http://dx.doi.org/10.15585/mmwr.mm6536a2

Tyack, D. (1992). Health and social services in public schools: Historical perspectives. *The Future of Children, 2*(1): 19-31. https://doi.org/10.2307/1602459   Princeton University. https://www.jstor.org/stable/1602459?seq=1#page_scan_tab_contents

U.S. Department of Education, Office of Civil Rights. (2020a). Frequently asked questions about Section 504 and the education of children with disabilities. U.S. Department of Education. http://www2.ed.gov/print/about/offices/list/ocr/504faq.html

U.S. Department of Education, Office of Civil Rights. (2020b). Questions and answers on the ADA Amendments Act of 2008 for students with disabilities attending public elementary and secondary schools. U.S. Department of Education. http://www2.ed.gov/about/offices/list/ocr/docs/dcl-504faq-201109.html

Wang, L.Y., Vernon-Smiley, M., Gapinski, M.A., DeSisto, M., Maughan, E., & Sheetz, A. (2014). Cost-benefit study of school nursing services. *Journal of the American Medical Association Pediatrics, 168*(7), 642-648. https://doi.org/10.1001/jamapediatrics.2013.5441

Weist, M.D., Rubin, M., Moore, E., Adelsheim, S., & Wrobel, G. (2007). Mental health screening in schools. *Journal of School Health, 77*(2): 53–58. https://doi.org/10.1111/j.1746-1561.2007.00167.x

Zirkel, P.A. (2009). History and expansion of Section 504 student eligibility: Implications for school nurses. *The Journal of School Nursing, 25*(4), 256-260. https://doi.org/10.1177/1059840509336930

Zirkel, P.A., Granthom, M.R., & Lovato, L. (2012). Section 504 and student health problems: The pivotal position of the school nurse. *The Journal of School Nursing, 28*(6), 423-432. https://doi.org/10.1177/1059840512449358

Chapter 19

CONSIDERATIONS WHEN DEVELOPING SCHOOL HEALTH SERVICES POLICIES

Linda Khalil, MSEd., BSN, RN, SNT*

DESCRIPTION OF ISSUE

Policies and procedures are essential to effective organization management. They provide a roadmap for decision-making, streamline internal processes, promote efficiency, and reduce personal, professional, and institutional risk. Education policies in the United States are based on a variety of federal, state, and local laws, mandates, regulations, and funding streams. Most education policies are decided at the state and local levels (U.S. Education Department [USDE], 2021). All fifty states require levels of school health services provided to students (USDE, 2021, p.2).

School nurses have a professional obligation to understand the laws, regulations, and school policies related to their practice within the school setting, as well as create and make recommendations for policies that promote the best clinical nursing practice, optimal health, and healthy environments and remove barriers to learning. To accomplish this, school nurses must be familiar with their school district's language and processes for policy development, adoption, monitoring, and evaluation. In addition, nurses must be aware of the legal and ethical issues that can occur when school health services policies are not aligned with the nurse practice act in their state. While school nurses engage in policy work in both public and private sectors at national, regional, and state levels, this chapter will focus on how school health services policies support evidence-based school health services practice at the school district level and the implications for school nurses. The term school health services will be used synonymously with school nursing services.

BACKGROUND

Because school nurses work in the education arena, any discussion of policy must first begin with education policy in general. Most education policies are decided at the state and local levels through state education departments or city, county, or district-level school boards, which are also called boards of education (BOE) or local education authorities (LEA). LEAs provide leadership and establish and approve the policies by which local schools are governed in compliance with state and federal laws. After a policy is approved by the LEA, the superintendent (who may also be called the district administrator) is typically responsible for developing the administrative regulations needed to implement the policy (National School Boards Association, n.d.).

Each district has a unique process for developing, reviewing, approving, implementing, and sharing policies. Districts must provide an opportunity for policy review and public comment before BOE adoption. In addition, approved policies must be publicly available and reviewed regularly. The policy should state the frequency of the review and the process for updating. Some districts maintain a paper-based manual; however, many have moved to posting the manual online via the district website. Some districts subscribe to online board policy management services through their state school board associations or third-party vendors who assist in monitoring, updating, and publishing policies to assure they align with federal, state, or local laws, mandates, contractual changes, or best practices.

---

*Original author: Lee-Ann Halbert, EdDc, JD, RN, MSN, CNM., NCSN (2017)

Terms Used in Health Services Policy Development

One challenge for those engaging in policy work is that the terms policy, regulation, standard, and guideline can mean different things to different organizations. In addition, health services policies may contain terms specific to the practice of nursing, such as the term protocol. Understanding what the terms mean to the organization in which the school nurse is employed is the first step in understanding the policy process. Most districts include a definition of terms within their policy and procedure on policy adoption and a specific process for policy development, approval, implementation, dissemination, and schedule for updating or review.

Policies describe the position and values of an organization on a given subject and share why the policy was created, what is required, and to whom the policy applies. The American Academy of Pediatrics (AAP) TEAMS (Training, Education, Assistance, Mentorship, and Support to Enhance School Health Services) *Guidance for Schools on Developing Health Services Policies* defined a policy as:

> A general principle, a guide for decision-making, or a rule adopted by the board of education. A policy is typically a broad outline of what should be done and is legally binding. School health policies define the structure of a health services program and guide staff in providing optimal care while avoiding problems; offer direction and guidance for health services provided within the school district; set expectations for students, parents, staff, and administrators; and provide consistency and continuity across the district and reflect laws and regulations. (AAP, 2022, para. 2-3)

Administrative or Superintendent's rules or regulations describe when, how, and by whom the policy will be implemented and enforced. They may include specific procedures, sample forms, or checklists,
Some BOEs vote to adopt regulations, while others leave the regulations in the hands of the superintendent, the district's chief school administrator. Regulations may be reviewed to comply with the law and align with board policy.

Policies and regulations specific to school health services may also include nursing protocols. Protocols represent the framework for the management of a specific disorder or clinical situation. Protocols are typically developed by health services leadership and include specific instructions or a sequence of steps (procedures) for assessing and managing a particular clinical issue. *School Nursing: A Comprehensive Text* defines a protocol as "an operational guideline for the implementation of a policy and guides decision-making. The term protocol is sometimes used interchangeably with "clinical guidelines" (Resha, 2019, p. 47). Policies and protocols are most likely to use

> **Note: Protocols and procedures cannot be implemented without a policy in place.**

the *Standards* for their development in guiding school nurses and districts (Resha, 2019). The most current standards for school nursing are the National Association of School Nursing (NASN) *School Nursing: Scope and Standards 4th Edition* (2022).

Simply restated: Nursing protocols and procedures provide the details of how a health services policy should be implemented.

Diagram of Terms Related to Education and Nursing Policy Creation and Implementation

Guidelines
Additional
Recommenda-
tions

Nursing Procedures
Step by Step
Description for
Implementing a
Protocol

**Nursing Protocols| Clnical
Guidelines** Written, Agreed
Upon Framework for
Managing Clinical Situations

Standards
Provide Measurable Criteria That
Identify Levels
of Knowledge or Performance
Competency

Board of Education Rules & Regulations
Describe When, How, and By Whom the Policy
Will Be
Implemented | Enforced

Board of Education Policies
Provide a Broad Statement of an Organization's High-Level
Expectations and Values
Share Why a Policy Was Created, What is Required, and to
Whom the Policy Applies

**National, State, Local Laws| Statutes|Rues & Regulations, State
and Local School Boards**
Provide Authority and Basis for Policies and Regulations

This diagram shows that policies provide the foundation upon which all other items rest.

Other terms used in both education and nursing include standards and guidelines. Merriam-Webster (2023) describes a standard as "something set up and established by authority as a rule for the measure of quantity, weight, extent, value, or quality." In education, standards are used as a basis for curriculum design and evaluation. School nursing standards include professional practice and performance standards, which provide authoritative statements of the duties, critical thinking, actions, and behaviors nurses are expected to perform. (NASN, 2022).

The American Nurses Association (ANA) develops nursing standards that apply to all nurses. These standards serve as a template for creating the specialty standards for school nursing (NASN, 2022). Although the standards shared in the *NASN School Nursing Scope and Standards of Practice,* 4th Edition are not laws, they carry significant weight because "they describe a competent level of school nursing practice and professional performance" (NASN, 2022, p.8). Clinical practice guidelines provide evidence-based practice recommendations for high-quality care (Shannon, 2018). (Please see Chapter 3 for more information on the scope and standards.)

State education and health departments may also develop school health services guidelines based on federal and state laws and regulations for use by school health personnel and administrators. Local educational agencies should review these guidelines with their district counsel as necessary to incorporate the guidance within their district policies. The process for developing a new policy or reviewing a current policy typically includes the following steps (AAP, 2022):

- **Identify the need for a policy** by assessing the issue and why it is a problem. Determine if there is new data, a new recommendation for best practice, a legal mandate, or other requirement that must be addressed.
- **Determine whether a policy is necessary and appropriate** by asking these questions:
  - Does the issue affect the entire school district?
  - Does it need to be addressed at the policy level, or is an overarching policy already in place, and a new or updated protocol or procedure would be more appropriate?
  - Does the district have the necessary resources to implement the policy?
  - Is there evidence, best practice, or law to guide policy development?
- **Determine your role in the policy process** and identify the specific steps and requirements for passing policy in your school district. This may be accomplished by meeting with the Superintendent and reviewing the BOE documents on policy development.
- **Gather resources** to inform the policy, including examples from other school districts; guidance from local, state, and national organizations; research articles; relevant laws and regulations; related policies and protocols; and relevant information from employee contracts, job descriptions, and employee guidelines.
- **Collect input** from other school nurses, the school physician or medical director, district leadership, staff, parents, students, public community members, public health, community healthcare providers, and others who will be affected or have the expertise to share.
- **Draft the policy or provide expert recommendations** according to district procedures, following the style and format used in the district.
- **Obtain feedback from stakeholders and revise** as needed.
- **Submit for review and approval** with an explanation of what the policy does, why it is needed, and the connection to educational outcomes. This may be provided in person or in writing.

Once approved, a plan for sharing and implementing the policy to move it from paper to practice must be put in place. This may require training for the staff or stakeholder groups. These steps closely replicate the nursing process: assessment, diagnosis, planning, implementation, and evaluation. The school **board should review and update policies** and regulations on a scheduled basis to assure they continue to align with updates in laws or mandates and practices.

When policies do not work *for* them, people work *around* them. Policy non-compliance is usually due to inadequate training, unclear communication, and policies that contradict laws, regulations, or other policies. Any of these issues create health, safety, and legal risks for the school district and individuals.

IMPLICATIONS FOR SCHOOL NURSES

School nurses must be familiar with board policies and regulations to assure that they align with state nurse practice acts and that their practice aligns with the policy. School nurses have a critical role in ensuring that schools effectively address issues related to the health and well-being of children and have a professional obligation to create and recommend policies for school nursing practice. The NASN position statement: *Healthy Communities -The Role of the School Nurse* states that "registered professional school nurses should work across sectors, professions, and disciplines to build a culture of health and improve student and community health outcomes by providing leadership, advocacy, care coordination, critical thinking, and mitigation of barriers to health" (NASN,2023, para. 1). This cross-sector work includes school nurses' participation in the review, creation, and evaluation of school health services policies impacting the students and families they serve.

Standard 15, "Quality of Practice," in *NASN School Nursing Scope and Standards of Practice 4th Ed.* includes the responsibility of school nurses to "provide regular and critical review and evaluation of policies, procedures, and guidelines to improve the quality of health care and the delivery of school health services" (NASN, 2022, p. 90). Additional references to policy are embedded throughout the other 17 NASN standards, as they serve as a cornerstone of professional nursing practice.

Irving states that "formalized, written school health services policies and procedures fulfill several important purposes that increase safety and reduce liability," which include:

- Promote compliance with laws, regulations, and statutes (e.g., Family Educational Rights and Privacy Act [FERPA], Health Insurance Portability and Accountability Act [HIPAA], Individuals with Disabilities Education Act [IDEA], Section 504 of the Rehabilitation Act, The Occupational Safety and Health Administration [OSHA]).
- Facilitate adherence to recognized professional practices and reduce practice variation.
- Standardize practices across multiple schools within a single district.
- Serve as a resource for staff, particularly new personnel.
- Reduce reliance on memory, which, when overtaxed, is a major source of human errors or oversights (Irving, 2014).

The article *Nursing Policies and Protocols Do Nurses Really Use Them?* stated that: "Nursing policies and protocols exist to promote high-quality, safe, and effective nursing practice; however, there is little evidence demonstrating how nurses actually use them to inform their everyday, routine practice." (Kelly et al., 2021, para. 1). The article concluded that organizations should make policies and protocols succinct, current, and easily accessible. Although this research was not specific to school nursing, it indicated that most nurses access policies and protocols once a month or more; the greatest barrier to more frequent access was the length of the policy or protocol (Kelly et al., 2021).

School nurses are responsible for reading school policies and understanding the implications for nursing practice, and acting accordingly. However, school nurses cannot follow policies they do not know. It is incumbent on school districts to train staff upon hire and notify staff when policies are updated so they can review them. It is incumbent upon school nurses to request this if it is not already in place.

While a strong working knowledge of laws and district policies related to school health services makes the school nurse a valuable asset to the district and community, professional ignorance can have significant personal and professional consequences (Dayton, 2019). Non-compliance with policy can result in repercussions not only at the district level but also at the state board of nursing, in civil or criminal charges, or with loss of employment.

As shared by NASN, "School nurses straddle health and education laws, regulations, and policies. They must interpret and integrate them with those pertaining to the practice of professional nursing" (2022, p. 10). Because school nurses practice in a system focused on education, they face unique policy, funding, and supervisory issues. These issues can have both legal and ethical implications. A nurse's first duty is to provide safe student care, regardless of setting, situation, or institutional policy (NASN, 2022, p.73).

Nursing professionals will encounter challenging situations that present ethical dilemmas throughout their careers. Some of the greatest challenges for school nurses occur when district policy conflicts with or violates laws or their state nurse practice act. The nurse is then placed in an untenable position. Below are some examples of issues related to potential law-district policy conflicts:

- School nurse (RN) or Licensed Practical Nurse (LPN) job descriptions indicate job responsibilities outside the scope of practice.
- Non-compliance with the state Nurse Practice Act (NPA).
- Non-compliance with minor consent and confidentiality laws.
- Approval or use of marijuana or other non-FDA-approved medications in the school setting.
- Acceptance or implementation of Do Not Attempt to Resuscitate (DNAR) orders.

Many of the other chapters in this book address these issues and discuss the important role of policy as the basis for determining school nurses' actions.

The NASN Code of Ethics (the Code) indicates that issues encountered by the school nurse related to policies may include "unsafe student-to-nurse workloads, accountability for care delegation, documentation expectations that do not align with the standards of nursing practice and attempts by non-licensed school administrators to direct practice" (NASN, 2021, para. 2). Even though the Code relates to ethics and not the law, attorneys could turn to it for evidence that a nurse's behavior did not meet the standards of nursing practice that outline and describe a competent level of care for registered nurses to follow.

These types of situations are stressful and challenging. It is important that school nurses understand their district policy process for responding to conflicts with policies and potential repercussions that could occur for actions they may take. If the school nurse is placed in a situation where there is a direct conflict between a school policy and legal requirements, they should follow district procedures for reporting the issue, typically notifying their supervisor or superintendent. If the school nurse is part of the teacher's association or another union or arbitrating body, there is typically a process in place to address this issue. They can also contact their state school nurse consultant or state school nursing organization for support. If no district actions are taken, and the situation would cause the nurse to violate the state NPA, they can contact the state's Nursing Regulatory Body (NRB), also called the State Board of Nursing (BON). NRBs/BONs are the jurisdictional governmental agencies in the 50 states, the District of Columbia, and four U.S. territories responsible for the regulation of nursing practice. Each state and territory also has an NPA, the law that determines the legal requirements for nursing practice and earning a nursing license. The nursing scope of practice describes the tasks or actions that the Nurse Practice Act authorizes for nurses (National Council of State Boards of Nursing, n.d.)

Ultimately, a conflict between policy and law that cannot be resolved may require a school nurse to consider seeking legal advice for guidance and potentially leaving that job for other employment. (*Please see Chapter 55 for more information on employee conflicts*).

BUILDING SCHOOL NURSE CAPACITY IN SCHOOL HEALTH SERVICES POLICY DEVELOPMENT AND USE

School board members and district administrators often recognize that the district's policies need updating but do not know where to start. School nurses can use this opportunity to share their unique health expertise in reviewing the district's school health services policies to identify topics (including those mandated by law) that are missing or need updating due to changes in the law or clinical guidance. This may seem daunting for those who have not been involved in policy work before, and school nurses may feel they lack the capacity (generally defined as the ability to use and understand information to make a decision and communicate any decision made). Specific to public health, the CDC defines capacity as the "information, skills, resources, abilities, and supports needed to develop, evaluate, and sustain a public health initiative" (CDC, 2021).

School nurses' capacity can be intentionally built by developing and strengthening their skills and abilities and providing resources for leadership development and collaboration. At an individual level, examples of capacity-building activities include training and mentorships. Developing competencies and skills in school health policy work is an important goal for school nurses, as the absence of school nurse participation leaves school health services policies to those without the knowledge to assure they align with federal and state laws related to nursing practice, health and safety, inclusion, and equity.

Reviewing how school nurses use school health services policies to guide practice within their district and identifying barriers affecting the frequency with which nurses use them can provide a vital first step in engaging in policy advocacy. Opportunities for school nurses to increase their understanding of and capacity in this area include:

- **Locate BOE policies** and review the index to understand how the manual is organized. Health services policies are typically within the section titled 'Students.'
- **Read the policies** pertinent to the practices of school health services, noting any nursing implications which may need follow-up.

- **Attend school board meetings** (in person or virtually) or read the minutes on the district's website. Attending BOE meetings or reading the minutes can help school nurses better understand the policy process and provide an awareness of which policies impact school health services both directly (i.e., a policy on delegation of medication administration) or indirectly (i.e., a policy on field trips).
- **Review an individual health services policy** that is under consideration by the board before the board meeting at which it is to be acted upon and provide written review comments.
- **Request professional development** to support policy work with colleagues and identify school health policies that are not aligned with the state's nurse practice act or current clinical guidelines. This can be done onsite in the district or via technology.
- **Review** the health services content of the district's policy manual on a section-by-section basis and provide the district with policy updating suggestions.
- **Inform school administration** of policy gaps and, with approval, prepare policy revision drafts for the district's review.
- **Collaborate with other school nurses** within the district and those in neighboring districts to share professional practice standards. Obtaining input from aligned health professionals such as school health educators and school counselors can increase the nurses' "voice ."Consulting peer-reviewed resources and requesting input or review from the school medical advisor or director can provide additional opportunities to incorporate evidence-based practices to guide decision-making.
- **Utilize the resources and expertise** of local and state school nursing associations, the NASN, and the National Association of State School Nurse Consultants (NASSNC) to increase your understanding of policy creation and obtain policy resources.
- **Utilize online and print resources** such as those provided within this chapter, including the *NASN School Nursing- Scope and Standards of Practice, 4th Edition,* for developing school health services policies that provide optimal care while protecting and promoting student health, facilitating optimal development, and advancing academic success (NASN, 2022).
- **Investigate funding** that can be used to advance policies and practices related to school health services practice. The Every Student Succeeds Act (ESSA) provides opportunities for advocacy surrounding school nursing-sensitive indicators of student success (Blackborow et al., 2018).

CONCLUSION

School health services policies inform professional nursing practice in creating an environment of consistent, high-quality, evidence-based care while promoting student health and safety and reducing personal and professional liability risks for school nurses and school districts. School nurses have a professional obligation to understand the laws, regulations, and school policies related to their practice within the school setting. School nurses should also create and make recommendations on policies related to school nursing practice that supports students' and families' abilities to adapt to health and social stressors, such as chronic health conditions or social and economic barriers to health.

To be an effective policy advocate, it is important to understand how education systems are organized and who has the authority to create, adopt and approve policies and terms used in those policies. Policies must be reviewed and updated to maintain alignment with federal and state laws and regulations and other applicable policies. Because school health services policies are based on relevant laws and regulations and set the standard of expectation by the BOE, it is advisable to have them reviewed by district counsel. Policy work is a team event. Collaborating with other stakeholders is the key to the successful development of school health services policies, processes, and practices that inform, protect, and improve the lives of students and their families.

RESOURCES

Publications

***Policy & Politics in** Nursing and Health Care, 8th Edition*
(2020). Mason, D. J., Perez, A., McLemore, M.R., & Dickson, E. (Eds.).
This text on nursing action and activism contains insights from approximately 150 expert contributors who share a wide range of topics on policies and politics that help to develop an understanding of nursing leadership and political activism. It is available in both print and eBook from the publishers and other online booksellers. 680 pages.

***Milstead's Health** Policy & Politics: A Nurse's Guide, 7th Edition*
(2021). Short, N.M.
Focused on policymaking and the impact it has on nursing and healthcare. This text is an excellent resource for nursing students and other healthcare professionals who want to expand their knowledge about the policy process, from agenda setting through policy and program evaluation. While focused at the federal and state levels, the content can be adapted to the local level. 300 pages.

Temkin, D., Piekarz-Porter, E., Lao, K., Nuñez, B., Steed, H., Stuart-Cassel, V., & Chriqui, J. (2021, February 19). *State policies that support healthy schools.* Child Trends. https://www.childtrends.org/publications/state-policies-that-support-healthy-schools

University of Wisconsin Policy Library. (2022). *Is it a policy, procedure, or guideline?* https://development.policy.wisc.edu/2022/06/01/is-it-a-policy-procedure-or-guideline/

Websites

American Academy of Pediatrics-Council on School Health (COSH)
https://www.aap.org/en/patient-care/school-health/
The AAP Council on School Health (COSH) is composed of pediatricians, and allied health professionals, including nurses who seek to promote school health policies and practices that ensure the health and safety of school-aged children and adolescents. AAP membership is not required to access the School Health page, which contains policy statements, reports, and guidelines. Two key resources include:

- **AAP Health Services Assessment Tool for Schools (HATS)**
- https://www.schoolhealthteams.org/
- The HATS is a self-assessment tool that school districts and states can use to assess the quality and comprehensiveness of school health services policies and protocols. The tool provides benchmarks that districts can work toward.

- **AAP TEAMS Enhancing Health Services for Schools**

- https://www.aap.org/en/patient-care/school-health/teams-enhancing-school-health-services/
- The Enhancing School Health Services through Training, Education, Assistance, Mentorship, and Support (TEAMS) project provides training, resources, and technical assistance to school districts and states interested in strengthening policies, practices, and infrastructure related to school health services. TEAMS emphasizes the use of school health services policy and protocol to drive long-term sustainable change.

American School Health Association (ASHA)
https://www.ashaweb.org/
ASHA is a multidisciplinary organization made up of administrators, counselors, dietitians, nutritionists, health educators, physical educators, psychologists, school health coordinators, school nurses, school physicians, and social workers. They offer resources on creating policies related to maintaining or improving school health services that support coordinated school health approaches such as the Whole School, Whole Community, Whole Child (WSCC) model.

Centers for Disease Control and Prevention (CDC)
https://www.cdc.gov/healthyyouth/policy/
The CDC Division of Adolescent and School Health, National Center for HIV/AIDS, Viral Hepatitis, STD, and TB Prevention (DASH), contains a section titled: *Adolescent and School Health Policy*, with resources on policy guidance, process development and analysis tools, and school health policy resources, including the School Health Index, School Health Policies and Practices Study, and School Health Profiles.

Child Trends
https://www.childtrends.org/?s=school+policy
Child Trends is the nation's leading research organization focused exclusively on improving the lives of children and youth by conducting independent research and partnering with practitioners and policymakers to apply that knowledge. They have authored several resources related to trauma-informed policy implementation in schools that foster equity and inclusion.

National Association of Chronic Disease Directors (NACDD)
https://chronicdisease.org/page/SchoolHealthPubs/
NACDD connects more than 3,000 chronic disease practitioners to advocate for preventive policies and programs, encourage knowledge sharing, and develop partnerships for health promotion. Public health professionals are experts who are often not familiar with the systems, structure, language, policies, and priorities in schools. Their guide *Speaking Education's Language: A Guide For Public Health Professionals Working in the Education Sector* (2013) provides a roadmap for effective collaboration.

National Association of State Boards of Education (NASBE)
http://www.nasbe.org/healthy_schools/hs/index.php
NASBE maintains a School Health Policy Database, searchable by state, enabling school nurses to determine what laws and regulations are in place related to school health services, which can be used to inform policy work at the school district level. The newest update was released in February 2021. It encompasses both

codified and non-codified policies enacted as of September 2019 (proxy for the school year 2019-2020) for 200 variables across the 10 WSCC domains, as well as a category capturing references to the WSCC model itself.

National Association of School Nurses (NASN)

http://www.nasn.org

NASN maintains a library of Professional Practice Documents containing Position Statements, Briefs, and Endorsed Statements on issues affecting school nursing. They are supported by evidence, regulations, law, or best practice reports on quality care and can be valuable resources for those creating or evaluating school health policies. NASN membership is not required to view and download these documents, which are available on the NASN website. Additional resources are available within the NASN Advocacy, Education and Events, and Resources sections of their website, including NASN's Framework for 21st Century Nursing Practice™, which identified policy development under the heading of Leadership.

National Association of State School Nurse Consultants (NASSNC)

https://nassnc.clubexpress.com/

A majority of states have state school nurse consultants, many of whom have distributed sample policy and procedure manuals from their state department of health or education or both to guide the development and delivery of health services in local settings.

School Health Associates

https://schoolhealthassociates.com/

School Health Associates provides resources and professional development for school nurses on school nurse procedures and protocols, including The Wisconsin Improving School Health Services (WISHeS) Project, which focuses on building school staff competency. One of their resources is a webinar released in 2021 titled Policy, Procedure, and Protocol: The School Nurse's Role in Development and Review.

REFERENCES

American Academy of Pediatrics. (2022). *TEAMS (Training, Education, Assistance, Mentorship and Support to Enhance School Health Services: Guidance for schools on developing health services policies.* https://www.aap.org/en/patient-care/school-health/teams-enhancing-school-health-services/guidance-for-schools-on-developing-health-services-policies/

Blackborow, M., Clark, E., Combe, L., Morgan, J., & Tupe, A. (2017). There's a new alphabet in town: ESSA and its implications for students, schools, and school nurses. *NASN School Nurse. 33*(2),116-122. https://doi.org/10.1177/1942602X17747207

Centers for Disease Control. (2021, March 5). *Policy Implementation.* https://www.cdc.gov/policy/polaris/policyprocess/implementation/index.html

Dayton, J. (2019). Preface. In J. Dayton, (Author), *Education law: Principles, policies, and practice (*2nd ed., pp. xi-xv*).* Wisdom Builders Press.

Irving, A. (2014). Policies and procedures for healthcare organizations: A risk management perspective. *Patient Safety and Quality Care (e-newsletter).* http://www.psqh.com/analysis/policies-and-procedures-for-healthcare-organizations-a-risk-management-perspective/

Kelly, U., Edwards, G., Shapiro, & Susan E. (2021, July/September). Nursing policies and protocols do nurses really use them? *Journal of Nursing Care Quality 36*(3), 217-222. https://doi.org/10.1097/NCQ.0000000000000532

Gereige, R.S., & Zenni. E.A. (Eds.). (2016). *School health policy & practice* (7th ed. Revised). American Academy of Pediatrics. https://doi.org/10.1542/9781581108453

Merriam Webster Online Dictionary. (2023). *Legal definition of standard.* https://www.merriam-webster.com/dictionary/standard

National Association of School Nurses. (2020, June 3). Framework for 21st century school nursing practice clarifications and updated definitions. *NASN School Nurse, 35*(4), 225-233. https://doi.org/10.1177/1942602X20928372

National Association of School Nurses. (2021*). NASN code of ethics.* https://www.nasn.org/nasn-resources/resources-by-topic/codeofethics

National Association of School Nurses. (2022). *School nursing: Scope and standards of practice* (4th ed.).

National Association of School Nurses. (2023). *Healthy communities- the role of the school nurse* (Position Statement). https://www.nasn.org/nasn-resources/professional-practice-documents/positionstatements/ps-healthy-communities

National Council of State Boards of Nursing. (n.d.) *About U.S. nursing regulatory bodies. Retreived* https://www.ncsbn.org/nursing-regulation/about-nursing-regulatory-bodies.page

National School Boards Association. (n.d.). *Public education frequently asked questions.*

https://www.nsba.org/About/Public-Education-FAQ

National Association of State Boards of Education. (2021). *State policy database on school health.* http://statepolicies.nasbe.org/health/

Resha, C. (2019). Standards of school nursing practice. In J. Selekman, R.A. Shannon, & C. F. Yonkaitis, (Eds.). *School nursing: A comprehensive text* (3rd ed., pp. 31-50). F.A. Davis Company.

Shannon, R.A. (2018). School nursing EBP clinical guidelines: what they are and are not, and why they matter. *NASN School Nurse, 33*(2):104-105. https://doi.org/10.1177/1942602X17753602

U.S. Education Department. (2021, June 15). *The federal role in education.* https://www2.ed.gov/about/overview/fed/role.html"https://www2.ed.gov/about/overview/fed/role.html

Chapter 20

RESPONSIBILITIES IN THE SCHOOL SETTING FOR CHILD PROTECTION

Kathy L. Reiner, MPH, BA, BSN, RN, AE-C, FNASN*

DESCRIPTION OF ISSUE

One of the most challenging roles for school nurses is protecting students from child maltreatment while supporting families to reduce the risk of further harm. Federal legislation, governmental agencies, and literature utilize the terms "child abuse and neglect" and "child maltreatment," therefore, this document will use the terms interchangeably, depending upon the source. Federal legislation lays the groundwork for state laws on child maltreatment by identifying a minimum set of acts or behaviors that define child abuse and neglect (Child Welfare Information Gateway, 2019a). All states and U.S. territories have laws to protect children from child abuse, the criteria needed for outside intervention, and identifying mandated reporters (Child Information Welfare Gateway, 2021; Gordon & Selekman, 2019; Taliaferro & Resha, 2020; National Association of School Nurses [NASN], 2023). School district policies and procedures should reflect state-specific requirements and the defined roles of school personnel for recognizing and reporting child abuse and neglect (Laubin et al., 2013).

The World Health Organization (WHO) (2022) emphasized that child maltreatment is a global problem with serious life-long consequences. In recent years, federal legislation has been passed to protect children from sex trafficking and female genital mutilation, also considered child maltreatment. The integration and coordination of social service, legal, health, mental health, domestic violence services, education, and substance abuse agencies and community-based organizations are imperative to prevent, identify, and respond to the complex problem of child abuse (Child Abuse Prevention and Treatment Act [CAPTA], 2019a).

BACKGROUND

Definitions

One of the critical pieces of child maltreatment legislation is the Child Abuse Prevention and Treatment Act (CAPTA), which was most recently reauthorized in 2010 (CAPTA, 2019). Legislation to reauthorize CAPTA was introduced in May 2021, titled the CAPTA Reauthorization Act of 2021. At the time of this writing, the act is still funded; however, the reauthorization has yet to be passed (Senate Committee on Health, Education, Labor and Pensions, 2021). CAPTA (2019) defines the term 'child abuse and neglect' as "any recent act or failure to act on the part of a parent or caretaker, which results in death, serious physical or emotional harm, sexual abuse or exploitation, or an act or failure to act which presents an imminent risk of serious harm" (p. 4). The definition of a child is a person under 18 years of age (Child Welfare Information Gateway, n.d.-a).

Each state must comply with the general definition of child maltreatment under CAPTA. However, it is critical for school nurses to know that each state also provides its own definition of maltreatment within civil and criminal statutes, generally including definitions of neglect, physical abuse, sexual abuse, and emotional abuse (Child Welfare Information Gateway, n.d.-a). It is also critical that school nurses know the requirements of

---

* Original author: Patricia K. Bednarz, RN, MN, FNASN (2017)

these statutes. School nurses can access individual state statutes at the Child Welfare Information Gateway (n.d.-c).

The Centers for Disease Control and Prevention (CDC, 2022a) defines child maltreatment as any act or series of acts of commission or omission by a parent or other caregiver that results in harm, potential for harm, or threat of harm to a child. Acts of commission included physical abuse, sexual abuse, and psychological abuse (CDC, 2022a). Acts of omission included physical, emotional, medical, and dental neglect, educational neglect, inadequate supervision, and exposure to violent environments (CDC, 2022a). The CDC (2022b) emphasized the need for a consistent definition to monitor the incidence of child abuse and neglect and to examine trends over time. The Child Information Welfare Gateway (2019a) provides information about recognizing the signs and symptoms of child abuse and neglect.

Prevalence

The U.S. Department of Health & Human Services, Administration for Children and Families, Administration on Children, Youth and Families, Children's Bureau (USDHHS, 2023) reported that in 2021, U.S. state and local child protective services (CPS) received a national estimate of 3,987,000 total referrals of children being abused or neglected. The USDHHS (2023) further reported that of the child victims, 76.0 percent of victims are neglected, 16.0 percent are physically abused, 10.1 percent are sexually abused, and 0.2 percent are sex trafficked. Other data reported by the USDHHS (2023) indicated that in 2021, a nationally estimated 1,820 children died from abuse and neglect at a rate of 2.46 per 100,000 children in the population. Age was shown to be an important factor for child abuse as 27.8% of victims were ages two and under, with children younger than one year having the highest rate of victimization (25.3 per 1,000 children) (USDHHS, 2023). The perpetrators were found to be parents (90.6%), relative(s) (5.6%), unmarried partner(s) of parent (3.3%), and "other(s)" (3.1%) (USDHHS, 2023).

Child Trafficking

Victims of child trafficking rarely self-identify due to shame or fear, being under the control of their trafficker, or inability to recognize themselves as a victim (United States Department of Education [USDE] 2021). Some children are more vulnerable to being trafficked. They may have a history of running away from home, truancy, child maltreatment, involvement with CPS or the juvenile justice system, multiple sexually transmitted infections (STI), pregnancy, or substance use or abuse problems (Child Welfare Information Gateway, 2023). Trafficking is child abuse. The Trafficking Victims Protection Act of 2000 (U.S. Department of State, 2000) defined sex and labor trafficking. It clarified that inducing a child under 18 to engage in commercial sex or to provide involuntary labor or services is illegal regardless of whether force, fraud, or coercion is involved. Many states have their own definitions of commercial sexual exploitation and sexually exploited children that will impact how children are treated (victims or delinquents). However, the number of states with "safe harbor" laws that provide coordinated services to child trafficking survivors, decrease or eliminate punitive measures for minors involved, and increase penalties for traffickers of children is increasing (Shared Hope International, 2023). School nurses, in collaboration with the school community, law enforcement, child protective services, community-based providers, and social services, can increase public awareness of human trafficking and assist with developing protocols for intervention (NASN, 2022b). The USDE (2021) indicated that one effective way to combat child sex and labor trafficking is to recognize and approach it as a public health problem. It presents a framework for trafficking prevention (p. 11), defining primary, secondary, and tertiary prevention tiers.

Female Genital Mutilation

Female genital mutilation (FGM) involves partial or total removal of the external female genitalia or other injury to the female genital organs for non-medical reasons (WHO, 2023). FGM is a federal crime and a form of child abuse and, therefore, a reportable event (U.S. Department of Justice [DOJ], 2023). The number of girls in the United States younger than 18 years of age at risk for FGM in 2012 was 199,000, an increase of more than four times compared to previous estimates (Goldberg et al., 2016). This increase is thought to be a result of the rise in the number of immigrants from FGM-practicing countries living in the United States (Goldberg et al., 2016). Novak (2016) emphasized the need for school nurses to understand FGM's cultural, legal, and social consequences. As of April 2023, 41 states have laws addressing FGM that can be found at https://www.equalitynow.org/us_laws_against_fgm_state_by_state/.

Legal Framework for Child Protection

School nurses need to understand that states specify what can be defined as child maltreatment in their jurisdiction and provide specific reporting standards. CAPTA requires each state to have provisions or procedures for requiring certain individuals to report known or suspected instances of child abuse and neglect. The Child Welfare Information Gateway (2019b) publication Mandated Reporters of Child Abuse and Neglect collected information regarding mandatory reporting laws for all states and found that all states and most territories identify the professionals required to report instances of suspected child maltreatment in statute. The professionals most often mandated to report across the States include school staff. While the circumstances under which a mandatory reporter must make a report vary, a report must be made when the reporter suspects or has reason to believe that a child has been abused or neglected.

The Child Welfare Information Gateway (n.d.-b) provides a resource identifying federal legislation affecting child welfare. The involvement of educators in reporting child abuse and neglect is guided by federal standards and regulations and mandated by state and local laws, which identify what is required of the educator and how that obligation is to be fulfilled.

IMPLICATIONS FOR SCHOOL NURSE PRACTICE

Prevention, early identification, intervention, and care of child maltreatment are critical to student's physical/emotional well-being and academic success (NASN, 2023). School nurses are essential members of the school team that collaborates to prevent and manage child maltreatment and have the expertise to recognize early signs of child maltreatment and to assess, identify, intervene, report, refer, and follow up on children in need (NASN, 2023).

School nurses need to understand that they are among those legally required to report suspected child maltreatment and that, as mandated reporters, they must make the decision to report regardless of what the supervisor or building administrator may say (Gordon & Selekman, 2019). It is not, however, the school nurse's responsibility to conduct the investigation to determine whether maltreatment exists (Gordon & Selekman, 2019).

All jurisdictions have statutory provisions to maintain the confidentiality of abuse and neglect records (Child Information Welfare Gateway, 2019b). School nurses should verify their individual state requirements for reporting child maltreatment as they vary from state to state.

School nurses should work collaboratively with other school personnel and community partners to prevent child maltreatment and provide education, including upstream efforts and evidence-based prevention strategies such as protective factor approaches such as community support, parenting competencies, and economic opportunities (Child Welfare Information Gateway 2020).

School nurses can follow the NASN Framework for the 21st Century School Nursing Practice to prevent and manage child maltreatment (NASN, 2016). Community/public health, leadership, care coordination, quality improvement, and standards of practice are the framework's fundamental principles and provide the foundation for the specialty practice of school nursing. The Framework, School Nursing: Scope and Standards of Practice (2022a), and the NASN position statement, *Prevention and Management of Child Maltreatment* (NASN 2023), together establish the basis and set the standards for school nurses to lead as vital team members in the prevention and management of child maltreatment.

Scope and Standards of School Nursing Practice

- School nurses must adhere to ethical, federal, state, and district laws, policies, and guidelines (NASN, 2022a).
- School nurses identify student, family, and community strengths and abilities (NASN, 2022a).
- School nurses advocate for students and the school community's rights, health, and safety (NASN 2022a).
- School nurses advocate for policies, procedures, programs, services, and practices that promote health, prevent harm and improve equitable access to care for culturally diverse students and families (NASN 2022a).
- School nurses apply laws and regulations pertaining to privacy and confidentiality to all communications (NASN 2022a).
- School nurses develop health policies, procedures, and programs in collaboration with school administrators and other stakeholders (NASN 2022a).
- School nurses must know the law for the exchange of information with those who have services appropriate to the investigation and treatment of Female Genital Mutilation/Cutting and an understanding of local immigration policies and practices to provide accurate counsel for students and families (Novak, 2016).

Policy Development and Implementation

- Work with school administrators to ensure school district policies and procedures are in accordance with state law and reflect the clearly defined roles and responsibilities of school personnel related to recognizing and reporting suspected abuse and neglect (AAP, 2022, Laubin et al., 2013). *(See Chapter 19 for more information on developing school policies.)*

- Be aware that state agencies, such as the department of child protection or a department of education, may publish guidelines for schools that should be used in staff training and development of policies and procedures (Laubin et al., 2013).
- Know the school or district's policies and procedures for reporting child maltreatment (Taliaferro & Resha, 2020).
- Work with school administrators to develop policies about how to respond to disclosure about child trafficking. The USDE (2021) identified the importance of developing and clearly articulating district- or school-wide policies and protocols for identifying a suspected victim or responding to a disclosure from a suspected victim of child trafficking. School districts may consider developing a protocol similar to that used for reporting child abuse or sexual assault (USDE, 2021). The school policy should include assessment for safety concerns, immediate notification of school authorities, maintenance of confidentiality, documentation of the conversations, and filing of a report to the child protective services. The USDE (2021) provided a sample protocol for schools regarding child trafficking at https://www2.ed.gov/documents/human-trafficking/human-trafficking-americas-schools.pdf
- Be knowledgeable about the problem of female genital mutilation and have a coordinated plan to protect and treat students affected by this procedure (Anderson, 2020).

Documentation

- Record the questions asked and answers given, as well as the sources for all the information (Gordon & Selekman, 2019).
- Document the exact statements used by the child and parent/guardian. Do not document interpretations of the child's statements (Gordon & Selekman, 2019).
- Use a body diagram noting all cutaneous lesions by size, location, and color. Avoid trying to "date" markings (Glick et al., 2016).
- Document subjective and objective findings, interventions, and a follow-up plan (Taliaferro & Resha, 2020).
- Follow school district/fiduciary guidelines for retaining records of child abuse reporting and documentation (Taliaferro & Resha, 2020).

Surveillance

- Know the characteristics that may increase the likelihood of a child being maltreated as described by WHO (2023) that include:
    1. Being under age four or an adolescent.
    2. Being unwanted or failing to fulfill the expectations of parents.
    3. Having special needs.
    4. Crying persistently.
    5. Having abnormal physical features.
    6. Having an intellectual disability or neurological disorder.
    7. Identifying or being identified as lesbian, gay, bisexual, transgender, or queer.
- Identify students who have been abused and neglected. Gordon & Selekman (2019) indicated that students see the health office as a safe haven, and frequent visits may indicate that the child is a victim.

Children seen in the health office should routinely be assessed for malnutrition, body hygiene, and suspicious injuries.

- Know the potential indicators of trafficking and exploitation described by the National Center for Missing and Exploited Children (2020) include:
    1. History of emotional, sexual, or other physical abuse.
    2. Signs of current physical abuse and/or sexually transmitted diseases.
    3. History of running away or current status as a runaway.
    4. The inexplicable appearance of expensive gifts, clothing, or other costly items.
    5. Presence of an older boyfriend/girlfriend.
    6. Drug addiction.
    7. Withdrawal or lack of interest in previous activities.
    8. Gang involvement.
- Understand that male and female victims of sex trafficking and commercial exploitation of children may present for medical care for a variety of reasons related to trauma, infection, reproductive issues, and mental health problems (Greenbaum et al., 2023).

Prevention

- Build protective factors (Child Welfare Information Gateway, 2020)
- Educate and support staff regarding the signs and symptoms of child maltreatment (Taliaferro & Resha, 2020).
- Advocate and refer parent/guardian(s) to effective programs that support parent/guardian(s) and teach positive parenting skills, such as home visiting programs by nurses to provide support, education, and resources (WHO, 2022).
- The Child Welfare Information Gateway provides general resources and tips for parents at: https://www.childwelfare.gov/topics/preventing/promoting/protectfactors/protective-factors-toolkit/tipsheets/
- Assist teen parents in accessing a primary care setting with a multidisciplinary treatment team (Govender et al., 2019).

Direct Care

- Understand that the immediate concern is to ensure that the student is safe and that any urgent or life-threatening medical conditions are addressed (Sabella, 2016).
- Support the victims of child maltreatment. Support is one of the protective factors that assist children in building positive self-esteem and understand their right to basic needs of food, clothing, shelter, health care, safety, and affection (Gordon & Selekman, 2019, p.811)
- Listen to what the student is saying, be supportive and nonjudgmental, remain calm, and assure the student they were right in telling the nurse (Sabella, 2016).
- Assess any immediate safety concerns, understanding that this information cannot be kept in confidence.
- Explain to the student that information will not be discussed with other students but must be reported if anything could harm the student or others (Gordon & Selekman, 2019).
- Consider that sexual exploitation carries an additional stigma and should be handled with great care and discretion.

Collaborative Communication

- Follow state and school district mandatory guidelines for reporting child abuse/neglect (Taliaferro & Resha, 2020). Some state statutes will specify the type of information to submit in a report of suspected child maltreatment, such as student's name, age, gender, and address; parent's name and address; nature and extent of the injury or condition observed; prior injuries and when observed; actions taken by the reporter (e.g., talking with the child); where the act occurred; reporter's name, location, and contact information.
- Link and refer victims and families to community resources (Taliaferro & Resha 2020). Refer children who have been abused to healthcare professionals who specialize in working with children who have been abused (Sabella, 2016).
- Collaborate with community organizations to raise awareness and reduce incidence (NASN, 2023).
- Work to establish/improve systematic collaboration and a trustful relationship with Children's Protective Services (NASN, 2023).

Social Determinants of Health and Health Equity

- Work toward a comprehensive approach that recognizes the diversity of ethnic, cultural, and religious beliefs and traditions that may impact child-rearing patterns while not allowing the differences in those beliefs and traditions to enable abuse or neglect (CAPTA, 2019).
- Understand the student populations that may be at more risk for child maltreatment. "African-American children, American Indian children, Alaska native children, and children of multiple races and ethnicities experience the highest rates of child abuse or neglect" (CAPTA, 2019) (p.3). The USDHHS (2023) reported that in 2021 American Indian or Alaska Native children had the highest rate of victimization at 15.2 per 1,000 children in the population of the same race or ethnicity, and African American children have the second highest rate at 13.1 per 1,000 children in the population of the same race or ethnicity.
- Understand that recent research indicates that not all parents who experienced childhood maltreatment will perpetrate child abuse or neglect and that most parents who experienced maltreatment will not abuse or neglect their own children (The Child Welfare Information Gateway, n.d.-d)
- Understand that, as with all sensitive and important meetings in the school, a family member, friend, or student should not be used for interpretation (Novak, 2016)

WARNING

Red Flags

Detailed and lengthy questions used for screening child sexual abuse are best left to those with appropriate training and credentials (Sabella, 2016). A nurse may be well-intentioned but may find that in a court of law, they could be accused of asking leading questions (Sabella, 2016).

RESPONSIBILITIES IN THE SCHOOL SETTING FOR CHILD PROTECTION

CONCLUSION

Protecting students from child maltreatment requires knowledge about federal, state, and local law; school district policies and procedures; community resources; and current research that identifies emerging issues and strategies for intervention. School nurses can identify students at risk for child maltreatment and intervene on behalf of them to help them reach academic success and remain safe in their home and community environment.

RESOURCES

Child Information Welfare Gateway (2019a). *What is child abuse and neglect? Recognizing signs and symptoms.* Washington, DC: U.S. Department of Health and Human Services, Children's Bureau. Retrieved from https://www.childwelfare.gov/pubPDFs/whatiscan.pdf

Childhelp National Child Abuse Hotline is staffed 24 hours a day, seven days a week, with professional crisis counselors with access to a database of 55,000 emergency, social service, and support resources. All calls are anonymous. Contact them at 1.800.4.A.CHILD (1.800.422.4453).

National Association of School Nurses and the American Nurses Association (2022). *School Nursing Scope & Standards of Practice (4th ed.).* Author.

National Child Traumatic Stress Network provides information in English and Spanish to parents whose children have been sexually abused. Information can be found at https://www.nctsn.org/what-is-child-trauma/trauma-types/sexual-abuse.

Polaris Project is a national resource for those who have been trafficked or forced into prostitution and need help getting out. Information can be found at www.polarisproject.org

REFERENCES

American Academy of Pediatrics. (2022). *Guidance for Schools on Developing Health Services Policies.* https://www.aap.org/en/patient-care/school-health/teams-enhancing-school-health-services/guidance-for-schools-on-developing-health-services-policies/

Anderson, K. (2020). Female genital mutilation/cutting in the United States and how educators can help. Crystal City, VA: National Center on Safe Supportive Learning Environments. https://safesupportivelearning.ed.gov/sites/default/files/NCSSLE-FGM-C-FactSheet-508.pdf

Centers for Disease Control and Prevention. (2022a*). Child abuse and neglect prevention.* https://www.cdc.gov/violenceprevention/childabuseandneglect/index.html

Centers for Disease Control and Prevention. (2022b). *Preventing child abuse and neglect fact sheet.* https://www.cdc.gov/violenceprevention/pdf/can/CAN-factsheet_2022.pdf

Child Abuse and Prevention Treatment Act as Amended by P.L. 115-271. (2019). The CAPTA reauthorization Act of 2010 (42 U.S.C. 5101 et seq; 42 U.S.C. 5116 et seq). https://www.acf.hhs.gov/sites/default/files/documents/cb/capta.pdf

Child Welfare Information Gateway. (2023). *Human trafficking and child welfare: A guide for caseworkers*. U.S. Department of Health and Human Services, Administration for Children and Families, Children's Bureau. https://www.childwelfare.gov/pubs/trafficking-caseworkers/

Child Welfare Information Gateway. (2021). *Links to state and tribal child welfare law and policy*. U.S. Department of Health and Human Services, Children's Bureau. *https://www.childwelfare.gov/pubPDFs/resources.pdf*

Child Welfare Information Gateway. (2020). *Protective factors approaches in child welfare*. U.S. Department of Health and Human Services, Administration for Children and Families, Children's Bureau. https://www.childwelfare.gov/pubPDFs/protective_factors.pdf

Child Welfare Information Gateway. (2019a). *What is child abuse and neglect? Recognizing signs and symptoms*.: *U.S.* Department of Health and Human Services, Children's Bureau. https://www.childwelfare.gov/pubPDFs/whatiscan.pdf

Child Welfare Information Gateway. (2019b). *Mandatory reporters of child abuse and neglect. State Statutes. U.S. Department of Health and Human Services, Children's Bureau*. from https://www.childwelfare.gov/pubPDFs/manda.pdf

Child Welfare Information Gateway. (n.d.-a). *Definitions of child abuse and neglect*. U.S. Department of Health and Human Services, Children's Bureau. Retrieved July 23, 2023, from https://www.childwelfare.gov/topics/can/defining/

Child Welfare Information Gateway. (n.d.-b). *Federal laws. U.S. Department of Health and Human Services, Children's Bureau*. Retrieved on 7/24/2023 from https://www.childwelfare.gov/topics/systemwide/laws-policies/federal/

Child Welfare Information Gateway. (n.d.-c). *Mandatory reporters of child abuse and neglect. State Statutes. U.S. Department of Health and Human Services, Children's Bureau*. Retrieved on 7/23/2023 from https://www.childwelfare.gov/topics/systemwide/laws-policies/state/

Child Welfare Information Gateway. (n.d.-d). *Intergenerational cycle of child abuse and neglect*. U.S. Department of Health and Human Services, Children's Bureau. Retrieved on 7/24/2023 from *https://www.childwelfare.gov/topics/can/impact/consequences-can/abuse/.*

Equality Now. (2023). *US Laws against FGM-State by State*. https://www.equalitynow.org/us_laws_against_fgm_state_by_state/

Glick, J.C., Lorand, M.A., & Bilka, K.R. (2016). Physical abuse of children. *Pediatrics in review, 37*(4), 146-158. https://doi.org/10.1542/pir.2015-0012

Goldberg, H., Stupp, P., Okoroh, E., Besera, G., Goodman, D. and Danel, I. (2016). Female genital mutilation/cutting in the United States: Updated estimates of women and girls at risk, 2012.external icon. *Public Health Reports, 131*, 1–8. https://doi.org/10.1177/003335491613100218

Gordon, S.C. & Selekman, J., (2019). Student victimization. In J. Selekman, R.A. Shannon, & C. Yonkaitis (Eds.), *School nursing: A comprehensive text* (3rd ed., pp. 805-819). F.A. Davis Company.

Govender, D., Naidoo, S., & Taylor, M. (2019). Nurses' perception of the multidisciplinary team approach of care for adolescent mothers and their children in Ugu, KwaZulu-Natal. *African journal of primary health care & family medicine, 11*(1), e1–e11. https://doi.org/10.4102/phcfm.v11i1.1936

Greenbaum, J., Kaplan, D., Young, J., Council on Child Abuse and Neglect, & Council on Immigrant Child and Family Health (2023). Exploitation, labor and sex trafficking of children and adolescents: Health care needs of patients. *Pediatrics, 151*(1), e2022060416. https://doi.org/10.1542/peds.2022-060416

Laubin, M., Schwab, N.C., & Doyle J. (2013). Understanding the legal landscape. In C. Costante, (Ed.) *School Nurse administrators: Leadership and management,* (pp.459-519). National Association of School Nurses.

National Association of School Nurses. (2023). *Prevention and management of child maltreatment* (Position Statement). Author. https://www.nasn.org/nasn-resources/professional-practice-documents/position-statements/ps-child-maltreatment

National Association of School Nurses. (2022a). School Nursing: Scope and Standards of Practice (4ᵗʰed.). Author.

National Association of School Nurses (2022b). Human trafficking. *NASN School Nurse;37*(2),106-108. https://doi.org/10.1177/1942602X211066655

National Association of School Nurses. (2016). Framework for the 21ˢᵗ century school nursing practice. *NASN School Nurse. 31*(1), 45-53. https://doi.org/10.1177/1942602X15618644

National Center for Missing and Exploited Children. (2020). *Child sex trafficking.* https://www.missingkids.org/theissues/trafficking

Novak. B. (2016). The school nurse's role in addressing female genital mutilation. *NASN School Nurse, 31*(5),286-291 https://journals.sagepub.com/doi/10.1177/1942602X16648193

Sabella, D. (2016). Revisiting child sexual abuse and survivor issues. *American Journal of Nursing, 116*(3), 48–54. https://journals.lww.com/ajnonline/Abstract/2016/03000/CE__Mental_Health_Matters__Revisiting_Child_Sexual.22.aspx

Senate Committee on Health, Education, Labor and Pensions. (2021). HELP Committee Advances Bipartisan Child Abuse Prevention and Treatment Act. https://www.help.senate.gov/chair/newsroom/press/help-committee-advances-bipartisan-child-abuse-prevention-and-treatment-act

Shared Hope International (2023). *The Future of Safe Harbor.* https://reportcards.sharedhope.org/safeharbor/

Taliaferro, V., & Resha, C. (Eds.). (2020). Child maltreatment. *School Nurse Resource Manual: Evidence-based guide to practice,* (10ᵗʰ ed., pp. 530-534). SchoolNurse.com

U.S. Department of Education, Office of Safe and Supportive Schools. (2021). *Human trafficking in America's schools: What schools can do to prevent, respond, and help students to recover from human trafficking* (2nd ed.). U.S. Department of Education.

U.S. Department of Health & Human Services, Administration for Children and Families, Administration on Children, Youth and Families, Children's Bureau. (2023). *Child maltreatment 2021.* https://www.acf.hhs.gov/cb/data-research/child-maltreatment.

U.S. Department of Justice. (2023). *Justice department and federal partners recognize zero tolerance day for female genital mutilation.* https://www.justice.gov/opa/pr/justice-department-and-federal-partners-recognize-zero-tolerance-day-female-genital

U.S. Department of State. (2000). *Victims of Trafficking and Violence Protection Act of 2*000. http://www.state.gov/j/tip/laws/61124.htm

World Health Organization. (2022). *Child maltreatment.* http://www.who.int/mediacentre/factsheets/fs150/en/

World Health Organization. (2023). *Female genital mutilation.* https://www.who.int/news-room/fact-sheets/detail/female-genital-mutilation

Chapter 21

DO NOT ATTEMPT TO RESUSCITATE IN THE SCHOOL SETTING

Suzanne Putman, MEd, BSN, RN

DESCRIPTION OF ISSUE

A growing number of students routinely attend school with complex, chronic diseases and serious illnesses, including terminal and irreversible conditions. Medical advances in the diagnosis and treatment of chronic diseases, which were once considered fatal, are now effectively treated, allowing school-aged children and adolescents to live longer. While federal law supports school attendance by students with complex health needs, managing those needs can be challenging. As the health needs of students who attend school with chronic diseases and serious illnesses continue to grow, the likelihood that a school district will be asked to honor a *Do Not Attempt to Resuscitate* (DNAR) order increases. The sensitivity of this issue, the variation of legal guidelines between states, and the interests of those involved make this a complex, challenging issue for school nurses. The paucity of information on this topic as it relates to school health and school nurse practice further makes this a difficult policy for school nurses to implement. It is important to note as a policy is developed that, at minimum, the team does an annual review of the DNAR and protocol, and appropriate staff training is provided. Information needed to plan for the student with a DNAR order will be addressed in this chapter.

Understanding the terminology used when planning care for end-of-life decisions is important. In the school setting, non-medical staff may view a DNAR order as "doing nothing" rather than providing supportive comfort care without prolonging the life-limiting condition. Allow Natural Death (AND) is another term that may be used. The shift toward palliative care brings about orders for comfort care referred to as Medical or Physician Orders for Life Sustaining Treatment (MOLST or POLST) (Zacharski et al., 2013). A POLST would include code status orders along with guidance related to medical interventions in the event of a life-threatening clinical event related to a medical condition, and "it also helps ensure that decisions are made within the context of serious illness when the burdens and benefits of available treatments are more likely to be known" (Hickman et al., 2021. Para. 4). As a resource, the non-profit organization National POLST provides quality standards and support. Nearly every state has a program based on this model. It is important to note that these forms vary in content and application, particularly in relation to students younger than 18 years (Linebarger et al., 2022).

BACKGROUND

The 2020-21 school year data revealed that 7.2 million public school students received special education and related services under IDEA. Of these, 15 percent were classified with other health impairments, having limited strength, vitality, or alertness due to chronic medical conditions.

Additionally, two percent of students receiving services had multiple disabilities, including hearing impairments, orthopedic impairments, visual impairments, traumatic brain injuries, and deaf-blindness (National Center for Education Statistics, 2022). Adelman (2010) asserts that there is an increase in "out-of-hospital" DNAR orders, particularly among children and adolescents with terminal illnesses (2010). In the inpatient setting, there is a growing number of deaths of pediatric patients with medical complexity.

Additionally, more families are deciding to provide end-of-life care in the home setting for these vulnerable children (Linebarger et al., 2022). Lastly, a policy statement issued by the American Academy of Pediatrics (AAP, 2010/2016) reports that each day there are 3900 school-aged children within six months of dying from a chronic condition (2010).

Despite this overwhelming evidence of the prevalence of students with chronic health conditions in the school setting, a frequently cited study reports that only a small percentage (20 percent) of school districts have a policy or procedure in place for honoring DNAR orders (Kimberly et al., 2005a). According to Weise (2010), the American Journal of Bioethics for commentary made this study available. This discussion sparked comments that underscore why a DNAR order for a student can be a sensitive issue when presented to a school district. Concerns surfaced regarding legal liability, the non-medical school staff's ability to make a critical medical judgment, and the potentially traumatic impact on staff and students. The vulnerability, rights, and duty to protect students with life-limiting conditions from painful and ineffective interventions were also of concern. Others agreed with honoring the DNAR order that end-of-life decisions that had been made with thorough consideration by the parent/guardian(s) and their healthcare provider should not be taken lightly and are in the child's best interest. This study continues to be widely referred to in the literature review.

The AAP (2010/2016) points out that laws regarding honoring DNAR requests in schools differ between states and that there are challenges in honoring a DNAR outside of the inpatient healthcare setting. In an article published by Zacharski et al. (2013), fears of liability, lack of school nurses, and moral distress were factors of concern, stating that "school administrators, staff and school nurses feel uncomfortable and ill-prepared when confronted by DNAR discussions" (p. 72). Yet, White (2005) points out that in the study by Kimberly et al. (2005b), "the authors overlook the pivotal role that the school nurses play with respect to DNAR orders as well as the delivery of school healthcare in general" (p. 83). Kimberly et al. (2005b), in response to the selected commentaries, "emphasized a fundamental point of regret for not stressing in the article, namely the crucial role that school nurses play in caring for these children" (White, 2005, para. 2).

The AAP (2010/2016) identifies the school nurse as the pivotal person in facilitating the development of an Individualized Healthcare Plan (IHP) and Emergency Care Plan (ECP), which communicates the plans for end-of-life care for an individual student in the school setting. The Individuals with Disabilities Education Act [IDEA] (2004) is the federal law that provides eligible students with q disabilities the right to a free appropriate public education (FAPE). There is a question as to whether the spirit of the law requires schools to make accommodations for the DNAR. Courts have consistently supported the "parent's right to make decisions on behalf of a minor child" (Deutch, 2015, p. 15). Additionally, competing interests (parent/guardian(s), medical community, school boards, school administrators, and teachers' unions) can make this a particularly difficult policy to implement. Traditionally, in the medical setting, there is a multidisciplinary team approach to decisions about implementing a DNAR order, which is often lacking in the educational setting. It is important for the school nurse to understand these varied issues and keep the medical, developmental, social, and spiritual needs of the student foremost when planning for care. Educating school staff on terminology and interventions, as outlined in the emergency care plan, can help ease apprehension.

IMPLICATIONS FOR SCHOOL NURSE PRACTICE

The role of the school nurse is multi-faceted. The purpose of this section is to provide standards and considerations for the school nurse caring for the student with a DNAR request for the school setting. Areas discussed include legal issues, standards of care, policy/procedure considerations, and psychosocial implications for the child and family.

Legal Issues

"*In loco parentis*" is terminology that frequently appeared in the literature review. This doctrine goes back as far as 1769, when it was determined that some amount of parental authority was delegated to the schoolmaster. Currently, *in loco parentis* stipulates that educators "act in the place of the parent when the child has been placed in the care and custody of the school" (DeMitchell & Thompson, 2017, p. 6). Adelman explains further, stating that this does not extend to medical decisions and that medical treatments for a minor child are at the parents' judgment and not for the school district or teacher to decide. This can be complicated because the *in loco parentis* doctrine allows educators to make decisions in the child's best interest in emergency situations (2010).

Engel, Favini, & Sindelar (2014) maintain that "laws cannot and do not attempt to address every special healthcare need or every school situation. They leave room for interpretation that…can frustrate and confuse education personnel, families, and lawyers" (p. 37). According to Mawdsley & Mawdsley (2010), courts tend to support the parents' wishes related to DNAR in cases involving minor children in the clinical setting. Legal issues for the school nurse are complex when dealing with DNAR orders.

In 2022, Weiler, Birnbaum, and Westbrook published a comprehensive review of state statutes and school district policies in relation to DNAR and minors in the school setting. The authors report that as of 2021, there is no federal guidance related to DNAR for terminally ill minor children attending school. In response to this, some states have enacted their own statutes to address this issue. Additionally, the authors examined eight local educational agency (LEA) policies and identified a common theme - to honor minors' DNAR orders. It was also required in all policies reviewed that students with DNAR orders have an Individualized Health Plan (IHP). This publication includes a breakdown of statutes by state and LEAs and is a valuable resource for school nurses.

Considerations include:

- Review the state nurse practice act and any other state and federal laws or regulations pertaining to implementing a DNAR in schools.
- Development of an ECP and an IHP for the student with a DNAR.
- Consider eligibility for IEP or Section 504 plan.
- Staff education and training on implementing the ECP, especially in the absence of the school nurse.
- Recognition of parental rights for DNAR for their child.
- Care of other students who may witness the death of the child.
- Emotional support for school staff not familiar or comfortable with DNARs in school.

Key Considerations

Not only does the nurse working in the school setting have to be aware of the nurse practice act in the state the Registered Nurse (RN) is practicing in, but state and federal regulations also need to be considered, including those related to education law. To responsibly implement care for a medically fragile student, the school nurse must be aware of legal obligations that may impact that care. Because the needs of medically fragile students are complex, "there is ambiguity around professional and legal liability" in the delivery of care in the school setting (Rehm, 2002, p. 83). Rehm goes on to say that although much of the litigation related to medically fragile students in schools is access related, we must also consider liability related to quality-of-care standards and "issues of responsibility for care rendered by non-healthcare personnel in school settings" (p. 82). The AAP agrees, stating that the school nurse may not be available at the time of arrest, secondary to staffing needs, and that non-medical trained school staff may be the first to respond. As with any ECP, it is vital to train school staff on a plan that outlines the implementation of the DNAR. Adelman further expands on the important role of the school nurse, stating that they are pivotal in coordinating care, providing treatment, assessing the student, and are responsible for the maintenance of the DNAR record (Adelman, 2010).

The IDEA (2004, 34 CFR §300.114(a)(2)(i)) requires that children with disabilities are educated in the least restrictive environment (LRE) to the maximum extent appropriate. Key points of IDEA are that the student's disability must impact education, determining their eligibility for special education and related services. Related services include transportation and rehabilitative therapies such as speech, occupational and physical therapy, and counseling (Engel et al., 2014; Raymond, 2009). It was not until the 2004 reauthorization of IDEA that "school nurse services" was included in the list of related services (Mandlawitz & Brubaker, 2009). If the student does not qualify for special education services under IDEA, Section 504 of the Rehabilitation Act is another federal law that supports programming for students with a disability within the school.

Legal Cases/References

- Deutch et al. (2015) discussed legal authority related to DNAR orders in a paper prepared for the National School Boards Association.

- In *Lewiston, Maine Public Schools* (1994), the Office for Civil Rights (OCR) became involved after a parent submitted a DNAR request to the school district. Although there was no court ruling in this case, OCR wrote an advisory letter. Several notable recommendations can be gleaned from this case. A multidisciplinary team should address the DNAR request and develop the individualized ECP. Deciding whether to honor a DNAR should be made on a case-by-case decision by the multidisciplinary team after considering all aspects of the case. A multidisciplinary team consists of persons knowledgeable about the student, including the student's parent, healthcare provider, and appropriate school personnel. In Lewiston, OCR determined that the manner in which this plan was developed compared generally with the approach approved by OCR in developing programs for students with disabilities. The plan was based on expert medical and other relevant information about the student. It was appropriately documented, required a second medical opinion, and was of limited duration, ensuring that it would be reevaluated periodically.

- In Massachusetts, the court ruled that the school must honor the DNAR order in *ABC and DEF School v. Mr. and Mrs. M* (1997). In this case, the court cited the constitutional right to privacy and the parents' right to refuse medical treatment for their medically fragile minor child, and the school was ordered to honor the DNAR.

- In *1994, Maryland Attorney General J. Joseph Curran* issued an opinion on whether a school must accept and honor a DNAR order:

     The opinion notes, "state courts, which generally decide matters concerning the family, give great deference to parental decisions involving minor children" (p. 248). The opinion indicates that schools must accept a DNAR order, concluding that "school officials have no legal basis for substituting their judgment for that of the parents and the physician" (p. 260). The Attorney General also offers opinions on other concerns that schools have raised. The ECP must clearly outline the medical treatment and support that are to be given, including comfort care. Staff must be notified of the DNAR and appropriately trained. It was opined that a school employee that does not honor the DNAR could be held liable for battery and other torts (p. 261). The Attorney General also addressed calling 911, stating that it would be part of an emergency procedure and does not constitute medical treatment or violate the DNAR order (p. 264-265). Curran also commented on the school staff's concern regarding the effect on and potential liability to other students for emotional distress resulting from a student's death at school. The opinion was that it was highly unlikely that a court would entertain a claim of emotional harm (p. 265). Including provisions for the other students in the classroom in the ECP, such as removing the students from the classroom, is recommended.

- In support of honoring DNAR orders in schools, Adelman (2010) cites medical autonomy and quotes Kimberly, "common law establishes the constitutional right to make reasonable healthcare decisions on behalf of their children, decisions that may include physician-approved DNR orders for certain pediatric patients with terminal illnesses" (p. 200).

- In relation to IDEA, Florida's Department of Education aligns honoring the DNAR with the provision of related services (Adelman, 2010).

- Although the case *Cedar Rapids Community Sch. Dist. v. Garrett F.* does not directly address DNAR orders, DeMitchell & Thompson (2017) discuss how this case highlights the "duty owed for foreseeable harm" and the need to provide services, including continuous care (p. 303). Mawdsley & Mawdsley (2010) also refer to this case stating the court's opinion was that the provision of comprehensive services "could be required of school districts under the IDEA to assure students a free and appropriate public education [FAPE]" (p. 76).

- Lastly, the AAP advocates for creating legal standards that support schools and school staff and protect them from liability while honoring a DNAR order. Massachusetts is one state with clearly outlined regulations related to DNAR in schools.

Other Considerations

In addition to legal considerations, it is important to consider the developmental and social needs of the student. Selekman & Ness (2019) comment that children want to be with their peers, and even if their participation is limited, "The student and their family may prefer the student to be with their friends and actively engaged, even if it is only to watch from a wheelchair.» (p. 496). Bioethicist and pediatrician Weise (2010) remarks that palliative care for children with life-limiting conditions has become an expected part of pediatric care. The shift toward palliative care brings about orders for comfort care (Zacharski et al., 2013). Further, there are positive effects for the child, even at the end of life, to attend school, eliminating isolation and offering social opportunities with peers.

Additionally, it is important to note the minimal effectiveness of CPR (less than 10% survival rate) away from the healthcare setting (AAP, 2010/2016; Jayaram et al., 2015; Weise, 2010; Zacharski et al., 2013). The AAP and the National Education Association, in 1994, set guidelines about foregoing CPR for children and adolescents, stating, "It is ethically acceptable to forego CPR when it is unlikely to be effective or when the risks outweigh the benefits, including the parents and child's assessment of the child's quality of life" (p. 1073). For many students with life-limiting conditions, the risk of CPR or other aggressive treatment could be ineffective or outweigh the benefits.

Key Strategies for the School Nurse

- Identifying laws related to DNAR directives in the educational setting (general counsel at the state department of education is a good resource).
- The formation of a multidisciplinary team, including school and community members, is recommended when drafting a policy and creating a plan for response to honoring a DNAR.
- Using multidisciplinary teams aligns with regulations related to IDEA and Section 504 planning.
- The student support team may include school administrators, teachers, school social workers, school psychologists, school counselors, and others, along with the school nurse.
- Transportation staff should also be included on the team, and accommodations for care needed for the student during transport to school must be included in the ECP.
- The parent/guardian is an important part of the support team, and the team can extend to include community members such as the healthcare provider, palliative care, and EMS staff.
- Recognize and identify the role of any siblings if they are in the same building as the student.
- The school nurse should obtain a release of information and carefully review the DNAR to ensure it is complete.

DNAR Order

The DNAR order should provide clear and specific directives for school nurses to implement should the student experience cardiac or respiratory arrest. According to Zacharski et al. (2013), DNAR requirements differ between states. The AAP policy statement (2010/2016) states, "DNAR orders should be implemented in the context of palliative care, including plans for managing pain and other symptoms" (p. 1073).

Many states have a state Emergency Medical Services (EMS) Do Not Resuscitate form that must be completed. Researching state School Health Guidelines for potential forms and resources is also helpful. Some schools may have a specific order form for the school. That form may include the following information:

- School
- Student's name and date of birth
- Physician's name/telephone/address
- Specific instructions regarding:
  - ✓ Withholding cardiopulmonary resuscitation (CPR), artificial ventilation, or other related life-sustaining procedures in the event of cardiac or respiratory arrest of the child
  - ✓ Palliative care measures (control of bleeding, airway maintenance, appropriate nutrition, control of pain, positioning for comfort, and other measures to ensure general comfort and use of prescription medications)
  - ✓ Other measures (suctioning and oxygen administration)
- A statement that the EMS system (911) will be activated in response to a real or perceived emergency at school
- Who should be notified in the event of cardiopulmonary arrest
- Requirements for renewal of the order
- Physician signature and state license number
- Parent/guardian signature

Whenever possible, the use of the state form is advisable.

DNAR Guidelines

Relatively few school districts have a policy in place that address DNAR orders. School districts should proactively create a policy, so they are prepared when presented with a DNAR request. The literature encourages the inclusion of comfort measures and other supportive care into the ECP (AAP, 2010/2016; Antommaria, 2017; Deutch et al., 2015; National Association of School Nurses [NASN], 2023, Zacharski et al., 2013). Comfort measures include holding the student, keeping the student warm, positioning for comfort and other needed care, oxygen, suctioning, Heimlich maneuver for choking, and control of bleeding and pain. The ECP should clearly outline these palliative measures (AAP, 2010/2016; Selekman & Ness, 2019). The ECP should be highly individualized and developed with input from the support team.

In addition to palliative measures, the plan should include a copy of the DNAR, clearly explaining the role of staff members, and outline classroom management, including privacy concerns. The ECP should also explain the plan for the other students should an emergency arise in the classroom (e.g., take the students to another location, outlining by whom and where, who to notify, etc.). The school nurse should work with the healthcare provider or palliative care team on a plan for transporting the student should an urgent situation arise. The ECP should specify if the team should call 911 or use another form of transportation. It is recommended that the EMS/transport company be notified of the DNAR and incorporate their input, particularly regarding communication in an emergency, into the plan. The plan must clearly outline these details in a step-by-step fashion. Emergency notification numbers of the parent/guardian also need to be included in the ECP. The support team should review the plan, and the healthcare provider who wrote the DNAR order should sign it.

If the student has an IEP or Section 504 plan, note the ECP and DNAR in the document. As the school health professional, the school nurse has a unique role in coordinating the care of the student with a DNAR order with the parent/guardian, the school, and the medical community.

DNAR Guidelines should include the following steps:

- ☐ A careful review of all required DNAR order forms
- ☐ Obtain release of information
- ☐ Organize multidisciplinary team meetings, including transportation
- ☐ Review of state law and district policy
- ☐ Create a protocol for notification of EMS, family, healthcare provider, palliative care staff
- ☐ Note DNAR in IEP or Section 504 plan
- ☐ Advise use of DNAR bracelet for out-of-hospital if indicated by state guidelines
- ☐ Conduct student assessment
- ☐ Assess staffing needs
- ☐ Identify staff training needs
- ☐ Develop an Emergency Care Plan (ECP)
- ☐ Documentation of training of identified school staff. Training should include a review of the DNAR, the ECP, and staff roles.

Components of Emergency Care Plan

- ☐ Original copy of DNAR order
- ☐ Disease-directed interventions and symptom control
- ☐ Comfort measures
- ☐ Clearly explain staff roles, including transportation considerations
- ☐ Classroom management, including a plan for other children in the room or nearby should the student's health status change, including privacy considerations and a code that elicits a quick response from staff members
- ☐ Emergency notification numbers for parent/guardian, healthcare provider, and palliative care contact
- ☐ The plan should have an expiration date and be reviewed a minimum of annually by the multidisciplinary team
- ☐ The plan should be signed by the same healthcare provider that wrote the DNAR order and the parent/guardian

CONCLUSION

A question frequently asked by school nurses is how to handle a DNAR when schools and parents disagree on implementation. **Proactively developing a DNAR policy is highly recommended**. Creating a multidisciplinary team, educating school staff, and sharing information, both from medical and educational resources (such as those noted by the National School Boards Association) may be helpful. Staff members should be reassured that care will not be withheld completely and that comfort and other measures will be given as outlined in an individualized plan. It can also be beneficial to develop a list of supports and resources.

DO NOT ATTEMPT TO RESUSCITATE IN THE SCHOOL SETTING

RESOURCES

American Academy of Pediatrics. (2010, Reaffirmed August 2016). Policy Statement-Honoring Do-Not-Attempt Resuscitation Requests in Schools. This includes a helpful table outlining the components of a DNAR order. http://pediatrics.aappublications.org/content/pediatrics/125/5/1073.full.pdf

Do Not Attempt Resuscitation (DNAR): Planning for the Child in School. (2013). Helpful checklist covering every aspect of planning for the care of a student with a DNAR order, including role of the crisis team. *NASN School Nurse, 28*(2), 71-75. https://doi.org/10.1177/1942602X12472540https://doi.org/10.1177/1942602X12472540

Massachusetts Children with "Do Not Resuscitate" or "Comfort Care" Orders in the School Setting. https://www.mass.gov/doc/dnr-policy-*107pdf/download*

National Association of School Nurses. 2023. Position Statement-Do Not Attempt Resuscitation (DNAR)-The Role of the School Nurse. https://www.nasn.org/nasn-resources/professional-practice-documents/position-statements/ps-dnar

National POLST form (2021): https://www.jamda.com/article/S1525-8610%2821%2900418-7/fulltext

National School Boards Association checklist (2015): https://cdn-files.nsba.org/s3fs-public/file/16_c_Do_Not_Resuscitate_DNR_Orders_A_Checklist_School_Districts.PDF?NMmIKChczNkGvwqUpiaR6hVwehfYlhLs

Case Law

Lewiston, Maine, Pub. Sch., 21 IDELR 83 (OCR 1994)

ABC and DEF School v. Mr. and Mrs. M, 26 IDELR (LRP) 1103 (Super. Ct. Mass., 1997)

Cedar Rapids Community Sch. Dist. v. Garrett F., 526 U.S. 66 (1999)

Opinion on DNR. 79 Md. Op. Atty. Gen. 244 (Opinion No. 94-028, 1994)

REFERENCES

Adelman, J. (2010). The school-based do-not-resuscitate order. *DePaul Journal of Health Care Law, Winter*, 197-214. http://via.library.depaul.edu/jhcl/vol13/iss2/3

American Academy of Pediatrics. (2010, Reaffirmed August 2016). Policy statement: Honoring do-not-attempt resuscitation requests in schools. *Pediatrics*, *125(5)*, 1073-1077. https://doi.org/10.1542/peds.2010-0452

Antommaria, A. (2017). Do-not-attempt-resuscitation orders. In L.B. Zaoutis & V.W. Chiang (Eds.), *Comprehensive Pediatric Hospital Medicine, 2nd ed*. McGraw Hill.

Bethell, C. D., Kogan, M.D., Strickland, B.B., Schor, E.L., Robertson, J., & Newacheck, P. (2011). A national and state profile of leading health problems and health care quality for US children: Key insurance disparities and across-state variations. *Academic Pediatrics, 11(3), 22-33.* https://doi: 10.1016/j.acap.2010.08.011

Brenner, N.D., Wheeler, L., Wolfe, L.C., Vernon-Smiley, M. & Caldart-Olson, L. (2007, October). Health services: Results from the school health policies and programs study 2006. *Journal of School Health, 77*(8), 464-485. https://doi.org/10.1111/j.1746-1561.2007. 00230.x

Carnevale, F.A., Rehm, R.S., Kirk, S. & McKeever, P. (2008). What we know (and do not know) about raising children with complex continuing care needs. *Journal of Child Health Care, 12*(4), 4-6. https://doi.org/10.1177/136749350808

DeMitchell, T. A., & Thompson, W. C. (2017). Do Not Attempt Resuscitation orders in our schools: The unthinkable ethical dilemma for educators. *Rutgers Journal of Law & Public Policy*, *14*(3), 285–312. https://rutgerspolicyjournal.org/jlpp/wp-content/uploads/sites/26/2017/12/Vol.-14-Is.-3.pdf

Deutch, J.M., Martin, L.G., & Mueller, J. A. (2015). *Managing students with health issues: Section 504 plans, DNR orders and contagious diseases.* https://cdn-files.nsba.org/s3fs-public/file/16_FINAL_Deutch_Martin_Managing_Students_with_Health_Issues_Paper.pdf?hXFC9ZaGKn_7f5xaVnOdp6gdTCPI1KCZ

Donoghue, E. A., & Kraft, C. A. (2019). Planning for Emergencies. In *Managing chronic health needs in child care and schools: A quick reference guide* (pp. 45–49). American Academy of Pediatrics.

Engel, M., Favini, P.M., & Sindelar, T. (2014). Legal issues in the education of students with special health care needs. In S. Porter, M. Haynie, P. Branowickil, & J.S. Palfrey (Eds.), *Supporting students with special health care needs: Guidelines and procedures for schools,* (3rd ed.) (pp. 37-64). Paul H. Brooks Publishing.

Heller, K.W., Fredrick, L.D., Best, S., Dykes, M.K., & Cohen, E.T. (2016). Specialized health care procedures in schools: Training and service delivery. *Exceptional Children, 66*(2), 173-186. https://doi.org/10.1177/001440290006600203

Hickman, S. E., Steinberg, K., Carney, J., & Lum, H. D. (2021). Polst is more than a code status order form: Suggestions for appropriate POLST use in long-term care. *Journal of the American Medical Directors Association*, *22*(8), 1672–1677. https://doi.org/10.1016/j.jamda.2021.04.020" https://doi.org/10.1016/j.jamda.2021.04.020

Individuals with Disability Education Improvement Act (2004), 20 U.S.C. 1400 et seq.

Jayaram, N., McNally, B., Tang, F., & Chan, P. S. (2015). Survival after out-of-hospital cardiac arrest in children. *Journal of the American Heart Association*, *4*(10). https://doi.org/10.1161/jaha.115.002122

Kimberly, M.B., Forte A.L., Carroll, J.M., & Feudtner, C. (2005a, Winter). Pediatric do-not-attempt-resuscitation orders and public schools: A national assessment of policies and laws. *American Journal of Bioethics, 5*(1), 59-65. https://doi.org/10.1080/15265160590900605

Kimberly, M. B., Forte, A. L., Carroll, J. M., & Feudtner, C. (2005b). A response to selected commentaries on pediatric do-not-attempt-resuscitation orders and public schools: A national assessment of policies and laws. *American Journal of Bioethics*, *5*(1), 19-W21. https://doi.org/10.1080/15265160590944102

Linebarger, J. S., Johnson, V., & Boss, R. D. (2022). Guidance for pediatric end-of-life care. *Pediatrics*, *149*(5). https://doi.org/10.1542/peds.2022-057011

Linebarger, J. S., Flaherty, E. G., Gavril, A. R., Idzerda, S. M., & Leventhal, J. M. (2017). Guidance on forgoing life-sustaining medical treatment. *Pediatrics*, *140*(3). https://doi.org/10.1542/peds.2017-1905

Mandlawitz, M.R., & Brubaker, C.R. (2009). School nurses and the IDEA: Ensuring students are ready to learn. *NASN School Nurse, 24*(2), 71-74.

Mawdsley, R. D., & Mawdsley, J. L. (2010). The use of do not resuscitate (DNR) orders in schools in the United States of America (US). *International Journal of Law and Education*, *15*(2), 71–85. https://www.anzela.edu.au/assets/ijle_vol_15.2_-_5_mawdsleys.pdf

National Association of School Nurses. (2023) -*Do not attempt resuscitation (DNAR)-the role of the school nurse* (Position statement). https://www.nasn.org/nasn-resources/professional-practice-documents/position-statements/ps-dnar

National Center for Education Statistics. (2022). Students with disabilities. Condition of education. *U.S. Department of Education, Institute of Education Sciences.* https://nces.ed.gov/programs/coe/indicator/cgg

Raymond, J.A. (2009). The integration of children dependent on medical technology into public schools. *The Journal of School Nursing, 25*(3), 186-193. https://doi.org/10.1177/1059840509335407

Rehm, R.S. (2002, March). Creating a context of safety and achievement at school for children who are medically fragile/technology dependent. *Advances in Nursing Science, 24*(3), 71-84. https://doi.org/10.1097/00012272-200203000-00008

Selekman, J., & Ness, M.. (2019). Do not resuscitate orders. In J. Selekman, R.A. Shannon, & C. F. Yonkaitis, (Eds.). School nursing: A comprehensive text (3rd ed., p. 496- 498). F.A. Davis Company.

Taliaferro, V. & Resha, C. (Eds.). (2020). Do not attempt resuscitation. *2020 School nurse resource manual* (pp. 474-477). School Health Alert.

van Dyck, P.C., Kogan, M.D., McPherson, M.G., Weissman, G.R. & Newacheck, P.W. (2004, September).

Prevalence and characteristics of children with special health care needs. *Archives of Pediatrics & Adolescent Medicine, 158*(9),884-890. https://doi.org/10.1001/archpedi.158.9.884

Wang, K.-W.K. & Barnard, A. (2004). Technology-dependent children and their families: A review. *Journal of Advanced Nursing, 45*(1), 36-46. https://doi.org/10.1046/j.1365-2648.2003.02858.x

Weiler, S., Birnbaum, M., & Westbrook, P. (2022). An examination of state statutes and school district policies addressing minors with do not resuscitate orders. *Educational Policy*, 089590482211202. https://doi.org/10.1177/08959048221120278

Weise, K. L. (2010). Do-not-attempt-resuscitation orders in public schools. *American Medical Association Journal of Ethics, 12*(7), 569-572. https://doi.org/10.1001/virtualmentor.2010.12.7.pfor1-1007https://doi.org/10.1001/virtualmentor.2010.12.7.pfor1-1007

White, G. (2005). Nurses at the helm: Implementing DNAR orders in the public school setting. *American Journal of Bioethics, 5*(1), 83-85. https://doi.org/10.1080/152651690928006

Zacharski, S., Minchella, L., Gomez, S., Grogan, S., Porter, S., & Robarge, D. (2013). Do not attempt resuscitation (DNAR) orders in school settings: Special needs nurses review current research and issues. *NASN School Nurse, 28*(2), 71-75. https://doi.org.10.1177/1942602X12472540

Chapter 22

PARENT REFUSAL AND NON-RESPONSIVENESS

Brooke E.D. Say, Esquire*

DESCRIPTION OF ISSUE

School nurses often encounter parents who are non-responsive to requests for information or medical documentation for their child. In addition, some parents may refuse to permit particular nursing services. This chapter provides helpful information for school nurses whena dealing with these challenging situations and legally-defensible best practices regarding communication and documentation related to this issue.

BACKGROUND

One of the most challenging things for a school nurse to face is to encounter a child who needs or may need medical/health services, but not be able to provide them (or provide them properly) due to lack of medical information from the healthcare provider or lack of permission from the parent. Such situations may have legal implications for both the school and the nurse. Should the school nurse report the situation to child services as potential child abuse? Does the school have an obligation to conduct a medical evaluation of the student? If so, what are the parameters of that obligation? Some solutions to these issues lie within the law, but most are simply a matter of good communication and documentation practices.

IMPLICATIONS FOR SCHOOL NURSE PRACTICE

Parent Non-Responsiveness

When a school nurse is aware of a medical or health-related issue that requires nursing services, parental cooperation is imperative. However, most school nurses have encountered situations where a parent simply does not respond to the school nurse's communications or fails to bring in medications or necessary medical devices. In these cases, where a parent is not refusing nursing treatment (which is discussed in a later section of this chapter) but, instead, is simply non-responsive to the school nurse's or school's attempts to obtain the medication, medical orders or other information, it is crucial that the school nurse determine the cause of the non-responsiveness.

A parent's non-responsiveness may be the result of several very different situations. The section below serves as a guide in determining the cause of the non-responsiveness, beginning with the most basic. School nurses should attempt to rule out basic factors that may be causing the non-responsiveness, such as communication issues, comprehension or language barriers, misunderstandings, and family/home issues, and other equity issues such as homelessness (NASN, 2022, Standard 10 Communication).

The chart below identifies a process based on a series of questions, which can be used to rule out these basic factors or, where necessary, identify and address them. The summary bullet points beside each question are discussed in greater detail below.

---

*Original author: Erin D. Gilsbach, Esquire (2017)

PARENT REFUSAL AND NON-RESPONSIVENESS

	Question	Action
1.	Is the parent receiving the communication from the school?	• Verify contact information. • Try different methods of communication. • Consider potential residency/homelessness issues. • Talk to the child (age appropriate).
2.	Does the parent understand what is being requested?	• Put it in writing (email, letter, etc.) • Make sure the request is clear and fully explained. • Investigate whether language barriers may exist (and, if so, address them).
3.	Does the parent understand the importance of the information or items to the school?	• Meet with or call the parent to discuss. • Put reasons in writing. • Request an administrator to contact the parent.
4.	Does the nurse have a legal obligation to obtain a medical evaluation for the student?	• If necessary, for 504/IDEA identification or provision of Free Appropriate Public Education (FAPE). • It should be a team decision. • Consider seeking a fact-specific legal opinion.
5.	Can/should the nurse communicate with the child's physician directly?	• A nurse has the right to communicate directly with a physician's office about an existing medical order or note to ensure the nurse can properly administer the doctor's orders, under an exception to HIPAA. • Even without a signed FERPA consent, HIPAA permits clarification between treating medical professionals without additional documentation/consent from the parent. • More communication is always better. • If there is no existing order or physician note for clarification, FERPA consent should be sought. • Consider requesting FERPA consent at the start of each school year.
6.	Can/should this parent's conduct be reported as potential neglect/child abuse?	• Possibly, if the issue is not resolved through the above process. • Child abuse is a state-specific standard. • Nurses may have mandatory reporting obligations.
7.	Should a student's refusal of services be addressed outside of the nursing suite?	• Convene the Section 504/ Individualized Education Program (IEP) team to discuss the non-compliance, including as a behavior. • Document non-compliance. • If the student does not have a Section 504 Plan or IEP, consider whether they should have one. • Contact the healthcare provider to provide insight or suggestions that may help alleviate the issue.

Communication logs, nursing notes, and other forms of documentation should be used to document the information obtained through these inquiries. This documentation may be important to show that the nurse and the school acted in accordance with best nursing standards and legal requirements if a lawsuit is filed.

Throughout this section, the following scenario will be used to discuss each of the questions that should be addressed:

> *A parent of a 2nd grader who has just transferred into the school indicates on her child's school enrollment forms that the child has asthma and is prescribed an emergency albuterol inhaler. The school nurse does not receive any additional information regarding the child's asthma, and the parent has not brought in the medication. The child has been sent to the school nurse's office on two separate occasions due to shortness of breath and wheezing. The school nurse called the home several times to speak with the parent, but no one answered. She has sent home numerous letters and requests for medication but has received no response. She has advised the playground supervisors to limit the child's physical activity until they are able to obtain more information from the parent.*

QUESTION # 1: IS THE PARENT RECEIVING THE COMMUNICATION FROM THE SCHOOL NURSE/SCHOOL?

To determine this, the school nurse will need to verify (and document) the contact information on file and the contact information being used to communicate with the parent. Sometimes the issue may be as simple as an inadvertent clerical or typographical error in the contact information. Additionally, a parent may not be receiving communication due to a change in living arrangements or a change in telephone number or email address. If a parent fails to respond to any nurse communications, consider whether one of these issues may be present. First, check the information being used (the number being dialed, the email or physical address being used, etc.) against the student's records.

If that has been done, and there is no indication of a typo or a misdialed number, the school nurse should inquire of the student's educational team what methods of parent communication are working for them, determine any upcoming conferences or appointments at the school where the nurse might join the opportunity, and request front-office staff to notify the nurse immediately if the parent is in the building. Then, the nurse should attempt to communicate with the parent using various forms of communication that other educational team members utilized successfully.

If there are no clues on how to connect to the parent, the nurse should scaffold her approach. For instance, if prior communication has generally been attempted or conducted by phone, the school nurse should follow up with an email, text message, or other messaging platform that the parent is responsive to. If that is not successful, the school nurse should send written correspondence to the

Tips for Communicating with Parents

All communication with parents regarding the health needs of a child should be documented. Where a parent is non-responsive, the documentation should include information regarding the verification of the contact information being used. Sometimes the nurse may have reason to know, without a doubt, that there is no error in the method of communication or that the communication is reaching its intended recipient. Some instances of this would be when the nurse calls and leaves messages on a voicemail containing a pre-recorded message by the parent or when the nurse is simply hitting the "reply" button on an email the parent sent. Nurses should carefully document the specifics of these situations in order to provide those important details. For instance, in addition to documenting in a nursing note, "called parent at 2:15 pm and left message regarding need to bring in student's medication," the nurse should add: *"student's mother's voice was on voicemail recording."* This documents the additional crucial information that the nurse is contacting the parents directly.

address on file stating the issue, asking the parent to contact the school nurse, and providing information on at least two methods of possible communication (phone number and email address are preferable for ease of communication, but a fax number and mailing address could also be provided).

If all attempts have been made, and there is still no indication as to whether the parent is receiving the information, either investigate or ask the appropriate office or individual at the school to investigate whether the parent's information needs to be updated due to a change in address, phone number, email, etc. The registration office may have updated information if the family moved or provided the school with a new phone number. The school's McKinney-Vento coordinator, responsible for ensuring compliance with the law protecting homeless students, may be aware of housing issues. The school social worker might attempt a home visit or reach out through other networks. Depending upon the student's age, they may also be able to provide information regarding updated contact information, living arrangements, or even whether the parent has been receiving the communications from the school nurse. The child may also be able to provide insight into the potential reasons why the parent may not be responsive.

> *Scenario: In the scenario described above, the school nurse does not know, for sure, whether her calls or letters are reaching the parent. No voicemail picks up to tell her it is the correct number, and she has received no response to her letters. She verifies the information with her own records. The number and address she used are the same ones she has in her files. She then verifies the information with the main office and checks whether they have an alternative number or address in the student's main office file. There is no indication that either the number or the address are incorrect.*

QUESTION # 2: DOES THE PARENT UNDERSTAND WHAT IS BEING REQUESTED?

Another basic consideration is whether the parent understands what is being requested by the school. Putting the request in writing can help ensure that the request is clearly communicated. Written communication also provides a documented record of the efforts made by the school to reach out to the parents. School nurses should take steps to ensure that the parent does not have any language issues or other barriers to understanding the request. Public schools have a legal obligation under Title VI of the Civil Rights Act of 1964 and the Equal Educational Opportunities Act (EEOA, 1974) as well as for parent participation purposes for students with disabilities under Section 504 of the Rehabilitation Act and the Individuals with Disabilities Education Act, to ensure that they can communicate with parents whose first language is not English and who have limited English proficiency. All communications with the parent should encourage them to contact the school nurse directly if they have any questions or want additional information. Most schools require parent/guardian(s) to fill out a "Home Language Survey" or otherwise provide information about their home language at the time of registration, and this documentation is maintained in the student's permanent file.

In addition to assuring the parent is able to understand the language in which communications are written, it is also important that they understand the content and context of the message. Communications should be reviewed for literacy level with a goal of having communications at a 6th – 8th-grade level. Even parents with good literacy skills may struggle with health-related terms. There are many resources for assessing and creating communications. The Centers for Disease Control and Prevention (CDC), the National Institutes for

Health, and the U.S. National Library of Medicine offer resources and online health literacy courses for health professionals. See the Resources section below for more information.

> *Scenario:* *The school nurse learns that both English and Spanish are spoken in the home. She then checks with the front office staff, who confirms that they often send forms home in Spanish, pursuant to the father's request.* The school nurse *does have Spanish language medication forms, so she completes one of those and sends it home. She decides that, for future communications, she will inquire whether it might be helpful for the parents to have an interpreter attend the meetings or provide translation services for phone calls. Unfortunately, despite these efforts, the parents continue to be non-responsive.*

QUESTION # 3: DOES THE PARENT UNDERSTAND THE IMPORTANCE OF THE INFORMATION OR ITEMS TO THE SCHOOL?

In some cases, a parent may understand the actual request being made but may not understand the importance of the information or items being requested. For instance, a mother may understand that the school is requesting that she bring in emergency epinephrine for her child, who has been diagnosed with a life-threatening food allergy, but she may not understand that it is critically important for her to provide it for her child. If the school has a written policy that requires each building and bus to be stocked with a dose of emergency epinephrine, she may be relying upon that medication if/when her child has an allergic reaction. Her reliance on the school's stock emergency epinephrine may be due, in part, to the fact that her insurance company does not cover a second dose of the medication for the student while he is at school. She may not have disclosed this information to the school nurse. Because of that, the school nurse was unable to discuss with her the importance of having designated emergency medication for this student. In this case, the school nurse and the parent each have important information the other needs. The school nurse does not understand the parent's reasons for non-compliance with a simple medication request, and the parent does not understand the importance of having a specifically designated epinephrine auto-injector for her child.

For questions 2 and 3 above, a meeting may be necessary to discuss the matter with the parent, ensure that the parent fully understands the request being made, and address any concerns or misconceptions the parent may have. In the scenario above, a meeting between the parent and the school nurse would be quite helpful because it would allow the school nurse to discuss the parent's reasoning and allow the school nurse to understand what additional information needs to be communicated to the parent.

If a parent is not responsive to requests for a meeting or phone conference or is not willing to participate in a conference, the school nurse should notify the school's administration. The parent may be more responsive to a building administrator's requests to meet. Whatever the case, the school nurse should be prepared to address complications that arise in the parent relationship, whether because of equity issues, miscommunication, or developmental factors. "One of the most basic elements of human interaction is the ability to communicate. Communication, particularly in high-intensity environments such as health care, is not merely the transaction of words. Effective communication requires an understanding of the underlying context of the situation, an appreciation for the tone and emotions of a conversation, and accurate information. When implemented consistently, the principles relating to effective communication can bridge the figurative divide of 'you vs. me' and ensure a reliable and dynamic means of relaying information and feedback (ANA, n.d., pg. 2)."

> *Scenario: The school nurse requests that the parents come in for a meeting to discuss the matter. Once the school nurse understands the parents'' perspective, she can address the parents' concerns more directly and help the parent understand that, while the school does stock emergency doses of the medication, there is no guarantee that it will be available when the child needs it. The school nurse may also be able to provide parents with contacts and resources if the parent cannot afford a second dose of the medication for school. This meeting may be very beneficial in addressing the parent's non-responsiveness.*

> *The school nurse makes several attempts to communicate with the parents by phone and email. She also sends a handwritten note asking them to call her and schedule a meeting. (She makes sure that the note is also translated into Spanish.) She does not receive a response. Concerned about the child's health, the school nurse requests a meeting with the building principal to discuss her concerns and determine what else can and should be done.*

QUESTION # 4: DOES THE SCHOOL HAVE A LEGAL OBLIGATION TO OBTAIN A MEDICAL EVALUATION FOR THE STUDENT?

Suppose a school nurse knows that information regarding a child's medical condition is needed, and the parent does not have this information or has not provided it. In that case, the school may be required to obtain it under Section 504 or the IDEA. The Office of Civil Rights (OCR) has ruled that if the school suspects a student has a disability that would qualify the student for Section 504 eligibility but needs more medical information, a medical assessment must be provided at no cost to the parent (OCR 1993). If the medical information that the school is seeking is for a temporary condition, there is likely no Section 504 issue and, thus, no obligation to obtain the information at the school's expense. Where the information is related to a non-temporary condition that satisfies the eligibility requirements under Section 504, however, the school needs to consider whether there is a requirement for the school to obtain the information.

A school may be obligated to obtain its own medical report where the parents prevent access to the student's medical providers or medical information. Schools cannot simply argue that the parents have restricted or thwarted their efforts to obtain medical information if the district has not sought to obtain its own medical information. In one case, a hearing officer concluded that both the parent *and* the district impeded the collaborative Individualized Education Program (IEP) process, where the parent refused to provide access to her child's medical provider, and the district failed to seek an independent medical assessment. *Oconee*

From the Case Files:

Courts are increasingly placing medical evaluation obligations on public schools. In one New Jersey case, the court held that a district failed to facilitate a medical evaluation of a child after she began to exhibit noticeable signs of autism. *Millburn Twp. Bd. of Educ. v. J.S.O. and K.S.O.*, 63 IDELR 229 (D.N.J. 2014). Likewise, in a New Mexico case, it was determined that a charter school violated the IDEA, where it failed to seek its own medical assessment to confirm that a student had Tourette's syndrome. In that case, the student had been erroneously classified as having an emotional disturbance.

Ralph J. Bunche Acad., 114 LRP 46982 (SEA NM 08/09/14)

County Sch. Dist., 8 GASLD 72 (SEA GA 2014). Thus, regardless of the parent's actions or inactions, the school may have a legal obligation to obtain a medical evaluation of the student.

Whether a medical evaluation is required at school expense is a question for the school's special education department or Section 504 team, which should include the school nurse in these cases or at least the school nurse's input. The special education department or Section 504 team (or Section 504 evaluators if the student is not yet eligible) will need to determine whether the information is necessary for the school to be able to determine the child's eligibility and appropriate accommodations to enable the student to access the school and its programs. Medical assessments are only necessary if they are needed to determine eligibility or if a Free Appropriate Public Education (FAPE) cannot be provided without additional information (OCR 1993). Due to the issue's significance, it is prudent to seek a legal opinion from the school's legal counsel in such cases before deciding on eligibility to determine whether a medical evaluation is necessary or legally advisable. Depending on the state regulations governing the actions of the Section 504 evaluation team, a parent's consent may be required to initiate a medical evaluation. Practically, no physician will likely evaluate a student without a parent's consent.

> *Scenario: The school does not necessarily need medical information; it needs the student's prescribed medication. Even if the school were to evaluate this student, school officials would not be able to obtain medication for the student. Thus, the school nurse needs to determine what else she can do to address the situation. She considers whether speaking to the healthcare provider may be of help. If the student no longer uses the medication, that would be valuable information to the school.*

QUESTION # 5: CAN/SHOULD THE SCHOOL NURSE SPEAK TO THE CHILD'S HEALTHCARE PROVIDER DIRECTLY?

A nurse has the right to communicate directly with a physician's office about an existing medical order or note to ensure the nurse can properly administer the doctor's orders, under an exception to HIPAA. 45 C.F.R. §164.512(b)(1)(vi). In some instances, a school nurse needs to communicate with a student's healthcare provider regarding a student's medication or diagnosis. For instance, a student may have a healthcare provider's note that requires clarification. The healthcare provider is able to provide such clarification under HIPAA because HIPAA permits such clarification between treating medical professionals without additional documentation/consent from the parent. Unfortunately, there is no similar exception to FERPA's consent requirement.

If the school nurse has a parent signed FERPA consent on file for the student, the school nurse would also be permitted to share information with the healthcare provider. For this reason, it is an exemplary practice for school nurses to request FERPA consent at the beginning of each school year for all the students on their caseloads. The FERPA form should include consent to speak to the student's healthcare providers on an ongoing basis throughout the school year regarding issues related to the student's school-related medical needs, including medication administration/modifications, interpretation of medical orders, and general health-related concerns.

Even if the school nurse does not have written parental consent to share information with the student's healthcare provider, the school nurse may still request clarification from the healthcare provider on the note. In that conversation, however, the nurse would be precluded from sharing any information the school nurse has about the student with the healthcare provider. Even so, although it would be a one-sided conversation, the healthcare provider may still be able to provide helpful and necessary information regarding the services needed by the student. If the school nurse is unable to make phone contact, the school nurse could send a written explanation of what is needed and
why it is important to the school.

Written communications sometimes get a better response since the healthcare provider is able to quickly view and assess what is needed without engaging in a discussion where privacy concerns may be at issue. However, before sending such a written request/explanation, the nurse should ensure that there are no privacy concerns with doing so (seeking clarification without revealing information) and acting only if the nurse has permission, via valid FERPA consent, to release student information to the healthcare provider. Even if the nurse only has the ability to proceed under HIPAA, the provider should be able to expand upon the basic note to outline recommended care instructions in the situation that the parent does not provide medication.

> *Scenario: In this case, the school nurse, as a matter of procedure, has all parents sign FERPA consent forms at the beginning of the year, which allows her to communicate with the students' healthcare providers. Therefore, when she contacts the student's healthcare providers to clarify a medical order or better understand a provider's description of a student's needs, she can also share information with them. The nurse confirms with this student's healthcare provider that the student does, indeed, need her medication and that the student has had several life-threatening asthma attacks in the last year where she was unable to breathe and needed to be taken to the emergency room.*

QUESTION # 6: CAN/SHOULD THIS PARENT'S CONDUCT BE REPORTED AS POTENTIAL NEGLECT/CHILD ABUSE?

If the school nurse has taken all the steps above, and the parent is still non-responsive, the nurse should consider whether the non-responsiveness rises to the level of suspected child abuse. Each state's child abuse definitions and mandatory reporter requirements differ, so the nurse would need to assess the situation in light of applicable state child abuse laws. Because so many steps have been taken to rule out and address communication issues, misunderstandings, financial issues, family/home issues, etc., the nurse may likely conclude that the non-responsiveness rises to the level of child abuse. While the definition of abuse varies from state to state, a parent's failure to communicate with or provide necessary medical information to the school will likely meet the definition of neglect. Some states also include failure to provide necessary medical services as a type of child abuse. If the parent's actions or inactions fall within the definition of child abuse, the school nurse, as a mandatory reporter, would be required to report them.

> **Scenario:** *Now that the school nurse is better aware of the student's medical condition and her need for the inhaler, she is extremely concerned. Since the parents needed to take her to the emergency room several times this year for breathing issues, they are certainly aware of her need for this life-saving medication. She has tried everything she could to engage the parents and get them to provide the medication, to no avail. Their refusal to communicate with her or bring in the medication poses a serious risk to the child.*

Parents, generally, have the legal authority to make medical decisions on behalf of their child. (*For a more expansive discussion on the issue of parental authority, see Chapter 17.*) Under the IDEA, parents have the right to refuse to consent to special education services (and in some states, parent consent is required to proceed with a written Section 504 plan). However, where a parent refuses to consent to school nurse services and where the withholding of that service would result in harm to the child, the school nurse should take all possible steps to speak to or meet with the parent to discuss the seriousness of the implications of the parent's refusal. Where the parent continues to refuse to consent to services, and where such services are necessary for the child's well-being, document the refusal and contact the building administrator. The school nurse may be required to report the situation, pursuant to the school nurse's mandatory reporting obligations, as potential child abuse.

QUESTION # 7: SHOULD A STUDENT'S REFUSAL OF SERVICES BE ADDRESSED OUTSIDE OF THE NURSING SUITE?

Where a student is non-compliant with requirements related to nursing services, the student's Section 504 or IEP team should be re-convened to determine whether the accommodations need to be modified. The team should review the reasons for non-compliance and identify possible behavioral supports that may be necessary to ensure that the student receives the necessary medical services that they need. The team should document the student's ongoing non-compliance. If the student does not have a Section 504 Plan or IEP, the school should consider whether they should have one. If the student requires nursing services for a non-temporary physical or mental impairment, the student likely qualifies under at least Section 504. *(See Chapter 12 regarding Section 504 eligibility).* The Section 504 or IEP Team, which would include the parent/guardian(s), would then be able to address the problem as a group, providing whatever modifications or supports are necessary to ensure that the student receives the appropriate medical services.

When the team meets to review the reasons for the student's refusal/non-compliance, the team should consider common issues that may cause refusal. These may include embarrassment to being singled out when needing to leave class to receive medication; disappointment at missing a key social period, such as the beginning of lunch or recess; or even frustration at missing a portion of the class and risk falling behind. These common issues can be readily addressed through proper planning and adjusting the student's schedule for nursing services. Where the basis for refusal is unclear, the team may wish to consider inviting the student into the meeting and discussing their concerns with them. Where it may be necessary or helpful, the student's healthcare provider can be contacted to provide insight or suggestions that may help alleviate the issue.

Tips for Documenting Communication with Parent/Guardian(s)

All communication with parents regarding a child's medical/health needs should be documented. Where a parent/guardian is non-responsive, the documentation should include information regarding the verification of the contact information being used. Sometimes the school nurse may have reason to know, without a doubt, that there is no error in the method of communication or that the communication is reaching its intended recipient. Examples include where the school nurse is calling and leaving messages on a voicemail containing a pre-recorded message by the parent or where the school nurse is simply hitting the "reply" button on an email the parent sent. School nurses should carefully document the specifics of these situations to provide those important details. For instance, in addition to documenting the nursing note in the health record ("called parent at 2:15 pm and left message regarding the need to bring in student's medication"), the school nurse should add: *"student's mother's voice was on voicemail recording."* This documents the additional crucial information that the school nurse is contacting the parents directly.

Emails have the added benefit of providing their own documentation if they are maintained. However, that documentation only lasts as long as the email is maintained. If the school nurse does not purposely save the email, and it simply exists in the school nurse's school email in or out-box, the school nurse has little control over how long and how that email is maintained is outside of the control of the school nurse. The email may be deleted from the server due to a long-standing or new email destruction policy (many schools only maintain their non-saved emails for 30-60 days). Thus, where an email can serve as documentation that the information was sent to the intended recipient, the school nurse should take specific steps to save that email in order to preserve it for documentation purposes.

In addition, certain email software/provider functions may not provide sufficient information to document that the email was sent using the "reply" feature, which would negate the documentation benefits discussed above. For example, Microsoft Outlook has a function that disables the email chain feature on reply emails. When a sender replies to an email, the original email or email chain is not automatically included in the new email. Only the sender's current message is included in the new email, even though it is sent in response to one or more previous emails. While this feature has many legal-

EMAIL TIPS

Strings of email conversations can often be lengthy. They may include several different recipients at different points on the email chain's timeline, which can lead to the accidental disclosure of information to an unintended recipient. Extended email chains that bounce around a school and possibly back and forth with the parents pose a heightened potential that the email will contain information that a future recipient may not be entitled to see, such as information regarding other students. Such email "conversations" also pose the risk that staff members will be too informal in their communications, forgetting that they are creating a record that may potentially be available for the parent's review pursuant to the Family Educational Rights and Privacy Act (FERPA). Such informality may lead to haphazard documentation and, at worst, communication that could be taken the wrong way by the parent and possibly be offensive.

These scenarios can be avoided if school employees use the feature, if their systems support it, of removing the email chain from all replies or forwarded emails. In the alternative, where such a feature is not available on the email program being used, a quick and reliable workaround is to simply make a point of beginning each email as a new email and refrain from using the "reply" and "forward" functions unless the communication necessitates doing so (and even then, only after thoroughly reviewing all the information being disclosed within the email chain).

defensibility benefits (see text box), it would not achieve the purpose of documenting that the email was sent as a reply because the original email would not be included. If such a feature is used, additional documentation would be required. The documentation could take a number of different forms, but a simple entry in the nursing notes is sufficient if it is done with specificity. For instance, instead of documenting "emailed parent" in the student health record, the school nurse should specify "emailed parent on [date] by replying to parent's email from [date]." Alternatively, a printout or electronically saved copy of the email sent, with an added note indicating that it was sent as a reply to the original email and giving the date and time of the original email, provides similar documentation.

Texting is not recommended as a method of communication with parent/guardian(s) unless there are emergency or urgent reasons to do so (e.g., no other means have worked to communicate with parent). It is difficult to document and save text messages in a manner that provides sufficiently comprehensive information, such as the date and time of the message; the context of the message, which may include a history of previous messages; texted responses to the specific message; and the actual text of the message. Collecting all this information regarding a text and documenting it properly is cumbersome and time-consuming, which increases the possibility that it will become overlooked in the fast-paced bustle of a school nurse's day. While methods such as screen capturing and preserving the texting log available through the cellular provider may, and should, be employed to preserve this information if a parent does communicate via text messaging, email communication is a far superior method of written communication.

The content of text messages is also problematic. Typos, spelling errors, and unintended word choices abound in texting. Voice-to-text and auto-complete features often insert unintended word choices, which may go uncorrected and could further confuse the meaning of the communication. Such errors may result in a plausible but unintended meaning, or they may result in an undecipherable message. In addition to errors, the nature and brevity of text messages make the substance of a text message easy to misinterpret, even if there are no typos or errors.

Another significant issue with texting is requiring the parent/guardian to have the school nurse's cell phone number. This is generally not recommended unless the school nurse has a school-issued phone or a messaging application for this purpose. Providing a parent/guardian with access to a personal, private cell phone opens a host of issues, including parents having access to the school nurse after school hours. A school-issued phone should be used if the school nurse wishes to provide a cell phone number. In such a case, the school nurse should establish clear parameters with the parents about the uses of the phone for communication purposes and should inform the parent that the phone is used only for school-related communication and that the school nurse does not have access to the phone after hours. Even with these precautions, however, texting poses practical and legal challenges, and school nurses should be cautious when considering using texting as a mode of communication with parent/guardian(s). When texting becomes urgently necessary, if the parent has a texting relationship established with another school team member, that member can initiate communication on the nurse's behalf- to get the parent's attention to initiate other modes of communication (such as email).

Many schools have policies regarding the use of texting by school employees and personal cell phones for school-related communications. School nurses should always refer to their school's policy regarding texting before considering using text messages to communicate with students or parents.

CONCLUSION

When a school nurse encounters a non-responsive parent, the school nurse should follow the steps outlined in this chapter to eliminate any potential communication issues or language barriers. Many issues may be resolved by determining if the parent understands the request and how to comply. School nurses should remember that pursuant to Section 504 and the IDEA, the school may have an obligation to obtain a medical evaluation of a child. When a parent refuses a life-saving medication or acts in other ways that pose concern for the student's safety, the school nurse may have a legal obligation, as a mandated reporter, to report such conduct as potential child abuse.

Regarding student refusals, school nurses should reconvene the Section 504 or IEP team to discuss the reasons for the student's refusal/non-compliance and develop a plan to address the issue.

RESOURCES

American Family Physician. *Health Literacy: The Gap Between Physicians and Patients* (2005). http://www.aafp.org/afp/2005/0801/p463.html

Centers for Disease Control and Prevention. *Health Literacy (2021).* https://www.cdc.gov/healthliteracy/developmaterials/guidancestandards.html

Centers for Disease Control and Prevention. *Health Literacy -Find Training.* https://www.cdc.gov/healthliteracy/gettraining.html

Centers for Disease Control and Prevention. (2009). *Simply Put-A guide for creating easy-to-understand materials.* https://www.cdc.gov/healthliteracy/pdf/simply_put.pdf

National Institutes of Medicine. (2021). *Clear communication. Clear & simple.* https://www.nih.gov/institutes-nih/nih-office-director/office-communications-public-liaison/clear-communication/clear-simple

National Library of Medicine. *An Introduction to Health Literacy* https://www.nnlm.gov/guides/intro-health-literacy

U.S. Department of Education. *Protecting Student Privacy – FERPA.* https://studentprivacy.ed.gov/node/548/

Case Law

Letter to Veir, 20 IDELR 864 (OCR 1993)

Millburn Twp. Bd. of Educ. v. J.S.O. and K.S.O., 63 IDELR 229 (D.N.J. 2014)

Shelby S. v. Conroe Independent School District, 45 IDELR 269 (5th Cir. 2006), cert. denied, 109 LRP 47876, 549 U.S. 1111 (2007)

REFERENCES

American Nurses Association, AONE. (n.d.) ANA/AONE principles for collaborative relationships between clinical nurses and nurse managers. The Voice of Nursing Leadership. https://www.aonl.org/sites/default/files/aone/collaboration-clinical-nurses-principles.pdf

Equal Educational Opportunities Act, 20 U.S.C. §1701, et. seq. (1974)

Health Insurance Portability and Accountability Act, 45 C.F.R. 164.512(b)(1)(vi)

Individuals With Disabilities Education Improvement Act of 2004 -20 U.S.C. sec. 1400 et. seq. (2004)

National Association of School Nurses. (2022), School nursing scope and standards of practice, 4th Ed., pages 79-80. Author.

Oconee County Sch. Dist., 8 GASLD 72 (SEA GA 2014)

Ralph J. Bunche Acad., 114 LRP 46982 (SEA NM 08/09/14)

Section 504 of the Rehabilitation Act of 1973 (29 U.S.C.), 28 CFR 35.104.

Title VI of the Civil Rights Act of 1964 (Title VI), 42 U.S.C. §2000d, *et. seq.* (1964)

NURSING CARE

The following section of the book is dedicated to the nursing care provided in the pre-K to 12 educational setting (i.e., schools). Some topics include Chronic Health Conditions, Physical Examination of Children, Medication Administration in Schools, the Use of Naloxone, and Suicide/Threatening Harm.

This section is not a "how to care or treat" students, but rather the legal implications that may be present when providing such care or conducting examinations or screenings. There are many other resources available to school nurses on clinical procedures and nursing care actions. An important consideration that grounds this section is utilizing clinical guidelines if they exist. The first chapter of this section highlights clinical guidelines, their application to school nursing, and their value as an evidence-based practice.

Chapter 23

EVIDENCE-BASED PRACTICE CLINICAL GUIDELINES FOR SCHOOL NURSES
ROBIN ADAIR SHANNON, DNP, RN, NCSN, FNASN

Evidence-based practice (EBP) clinical guidelines support school nurses in delivering high quality health care to students and school communities. Melnyk & Fineout Overholt (2015, p. 12) define EBP clinical guidelines as "specific practice recommendations grouped together that have been derived from a methodologically rigorous review of the best evidence on a specific topic." The National Association of School Nurses' (NASN) *Framework for 21ˢᵗ Century School Nursing Practice* (2016) holds that EBP clinical guidelines support the health of students as an integral component of *School Nursing Standards of Practice*, which envelop all dimensions and competencies of the specialty. As reflected in NASN's (2022) research priorities, clinical practice guidelines are important tools of implementation science to move the best available evidence toward better outcomes for students. Many of the chapters in this section outline best practices for the care of students and, where available, includes published clinical guidelines. This chapter is meant to bring attention to the importance of their use in practice.

The National Guideline Clearing House (NGC) was instituted by the Agency for Healthcare Research and Quality (AHRQ) under the U.S. Department of Health and Human Services in 1997 as a repository for rigorously developed clinical practice guidelines. The mission of the National Guideline Clearing House "was to provide physicians and other health care professionals, health care providers, health plans, integrated delivery systems, purchasers and others an accessible mechanism for obtaining objective, detailed information on clinical practice guidelines and to further their dissemination, implementation, and use" (AHRQ, 2018a, para, 3). Thousands of clinical guidelines from medicine, nursing, and other disciplines that met the stringent AHRQ criteria which were updated in 2014. According to AHRQ (2018b, para.3), the National Guideline Clearinghouse inclusion criteria were as follows:

1. The clinical practice guideline contains systematically developed statements, including recommendations intended to optimize patient care and assist physicians and/or other healthcare practitioners and patients in making decisions about appropriate healthcare for specific clinical circumstances.
2. The clinical practice guideline was produced under the auspices of a medical specialty association; relevant professional society; public or private organization; government agency at the Federal, State, or local level; or health care organization or plan. A clinical practice guideline developed and issued by an individual(s) not officially sponsored or supported by one of the above types of organizations does not meet the inclusion criteria for NGC.
3. The clinical practice guideline is based on a systematic review of evidence as demonstrated by documentation of each of the following features in the clinical practice guideline or its supporting documents.
    a. An explicit statement that the clinical practice guideline was based on a systematic review.
    b. A description of the search strategy that includes a listing of database(s) searched, a summary of search terms used, and the specific time period covered by the literature search, including the beginning date (month/year) and end date (month/year).

    c. A description of study selection that includes the number of studies identified, the number of studies included, and a summary of inclusion and exclusion criteria.

    d. A synthesis of evidence from the selected studies, e.g., a detailed description or evidence tables.

    e. A summary of the evidence synthesis (see 3d above) included in the guideline that relates the evidence to the recommendations, e.g., a descriptive summary or summary tables.

NB (nota bene): A guideline is not excluded from NGC if a systematic review was conducted that identifies specific gaps in the evidence base for some of the guideline's recommendations.

4. The clinical practice guideline or its supporting documents contain an assessment of the benefits and harms of recommended care and alternative care options.

5. The full text guideline is available in English to the public upon request (for free or for a fee). Upon submission of the guideline to NGC, it also must be noted whether the systematic review or other supporting documents are available in English to the public upon request (for free or for a fee).

6. The guideline is the most recent version published. The guideline must have been developed, reviewed, or revised within the past five years, as evidenced by appropriate documentation (e.g., the systematic review or detailed description of methodology).

Unfortunately, funding for AHRQ ended in July 2018 during the Trump Administration, and the National Guideline Clearinghouse was closed (AHRQ, 2018). Summaries and some full text versions of clinical guidelines from the National Guidelines Clearinghouse are archived by a non-profit group, the Alliance for the Implementation of Clinical Practice Guidelines (2020). Nevertheless, the AHRQ clinical guideline criteria continue to define expectations for EBP clinical practice guideline (CPG) development. The creation and dissemination of clinical guidelines is now incumbent on professional specialty associations, such as NASN, private healthcare institutions, and organizations, such as the ECRI Guidelines Trust (2023).

Evidence-based practice clinical guidelines entail the following components: rationale; specifics on the health condition and etiology; a systematic search, synthesis, and appraisal of the literature, and relevant recommendations for practice. Due to the strength of rigorously derived practice recommendations, EBP clinical guidelines are often used in the development of healthcare policies, protocols, and procedures (AGREE Next Steps Consortium, 2017).

School nursing practice should be evidence-based. However, school nurses have historically faced barriers to implementing EBP, including lack of access to the nursing and health sciences databases; heavy work demands and inadequate time to search and read the literature; limited education in identifying the level, strength, and quality of evidence; and underdeveloped skills in synthesizing the evidence into relevant practice recommendations (Maughan & Yonkaitis, 2017).

NASN recognized that EBP clinical guidelines were needed to help reduce these barriers. In response, *A Model for Developing Evidence-based School Nursing Clinical Practice Guidelines* (Shannon & Maughan, 2019) was created to meet the rigorous criteria of the National Guidelines Clearing House. The NASN Model for Developing Evidence-based School Nursing Clinical Practice Guidelines is designed to:

offer school nurse scholars, pediatric clinical specialists, school health content experts, and school nursing leaders a professional structure, standardized process, and rigorous methodology to create evidence-based CPGs for school nursing practice under the auspices of NASN. The goal of CPGs for the specialty of school nursing is to ensure that strong evidence-based practice recommendations are accessible to improve health, well-being, and educational outcomes for students with special healthcare needs (Shannon & Maughan, 2019, p.8).

Developing clinical guidelines for school nursing practice is a rigorous professional and academic team exercise that involves highly educated school nurses and child health experts. It also entails systematic review by clinical subject matter experts and clinical practice guideline criteria experts. As of 2021, NASN has published clinical guidelines on students with seizures and epilepsy (Lepkowski & Maughan, 2019), students with type 1 diabetes (Wilt & Jameson, 2021), and medication administration in schools (Bergren, 2021). New clinical guidelines are in development, and more are being planned.

School health/nursing research requires academic/community partnerships between universities and public/private schools. School nurses, who know their students and school communities best, can collaborate with PhD and DNP-prepared school nurses and medical and allied health scientists to meet the challenges of conducting well-designed research studies in the unique arena of school health. One challenge of note is that special protections must be afforded to reduce risks to children as research subjects (Office for Human Research Protections, 2023). Because children are considered a vulnerable population, the amount of randomized controlled clinical trials involving nursing interventions for students is very limited. Although the practice recommendations of school nursing clinical guidelines are derived from the best available evidence— the quality, level, and strength of that evidence are more likely to be based on case-control, cohort, or qualitative studies; systematic or integrative reviews of the literature; reference texts, case reports, legal mandates, clinical manuals, or expert opinion. Evidence for clinical practice guidelines is also commonly extrapolated from the scientific literature in related nursing, medical, and health sciences fields such as pediatrics, mental health, sociology, child development, and education.

CONCLUSION

Systematically developed EBP clinical guidelines inform school nurses of best practices when making decisions in caring for students based on the best available evidence. School nurses should base care on the recommendations/guidance when CPG exists. Advanced degree school nurses are encouraged to partner with NASN in the development of future EBP clinical guidelines on behalf of quality school nursing care and improved health outcomes for students with special healthcare needs.

RESOURCES

AGREE Next Steps Consortium. (2017, December). *Appraisal of Guidelines for Research and Evaluation II: The AGREE II Instrument.* https://www.agreetrust.org/wp-content/uploads/2017/12/AGREE-II-Users-Manual-and-23-item-Instrument-2009-Update-2017.pdf

Agency for Healthcare Research and Quality. (2018a). *About NGC and NQMC: National Guideline Clearinghouse.* U.S. Department of Health and Human Services. https://www.ahrq.gov/gam/about/index.html

Agency for Healthcare Research and Quality. (2018b). *National Guideline Clearing House: Inclusion criteria.* U.S. Department of Health and Human Services. https://www.ahrq.gov/gam/summaries/inclusion-criteria/index.html

Alliance for the Implementation of Clinical Practice Guidelines. (2020). https://aicpg.org/

ECRI Guidelines Trust (2023). https://www.ecri.org/solutions/ecri-guidelines-trust

National Association of School Nurses. (2016). Framework for 21st century school nursing practice. *NASN School Nurse, 31*(1), 45-53. https://doi.org/10.1177/19426002X15618644

National Association of School Nurses. (2022, July). *NASN research priorities 2022.* https://www.nasn.org/research/research-priorities

Office for Human Research Protections. (2023). *Children: Information on special protections for children as research subjects.* U.S. Department of Health and Human Services. https://www.hhs.gov/ohrp/regulations-and-policy/guidance/special-protections-for-children/index.html

Shannon, R.A., & Maughan, E.D. (2019). *A model for developing evidence-based clinical practice guidelines for school nursing.* National Association of School Nurses. https://learn.nasn.org/courses/14542

REFERENCES

Lepkowski, A.M., & Maughan, E.D. (2018, December). *School nursing evidence-based clinical practice guideline: Students with seizures and epilepsy.* https://learn.nasn.org/courses/8992

Bergren, M.D. (2021, August). *School nursing evidence-based clinical practice guideline: Medication administration in schools.* https://learn.nasn.org/courses/33787

Wilt, L., & Jameson, B. (2018, December). *School nursing evidence-based clinical practice guideline: Students with type 1 diabetes.* https://learn.nasn.org/courses/37660

Maughan ED, Yonkaitis CF. (2017). What does evidence-based school nursing practice even mean? Get a CLUE. *NASN School Nurse,32*(5),287-289. https://doi.org/10.1177/1942602X17724420

Melnyk, B. M. & Fineout-Overholt, E. (2015). Making the case for evidence-based practice and cultivating a spirit of inquiry. In Melnyk, B. M. & Fineout-Overholt, E. (Eds.), *Evidence-based practice in nursing and healthcare: A guide to best practice,* (pp. 3-23). Walters Kluwer.

Shannon, R. A. (2018). School nursing EBP clinical guidelines: What they are and are not, and why they matter. *NASN School Nurse*, 3(2), 104-105. https://doi.org/10.1177/1942602X1775360

Chapter 24

CHRONIC HEALTH CONDITIONS

Jacquelyn M. Buige Raco, MSN, MEd, CSN, CSSHS*

DESCRIPTION OF ISSUE

The American Academy of Pediatrics defines chronic conditions as "conditions persisting over a period of time that requires health care and/or limit activities of daily living" (American Academy of Pediatrics [AAP], 2021, p.8). The AAP (2021) states that approximately 25% of children have a chronic condition. Conditions include but are not limited to asthma, diabetes, epilepsy, food allergy, obesity, oral health, and mental health disorders (AAP, 2021). The COVID-19 pandemic's social and economic factors contributed to the inability and inequity of families to obtain routine healthcare assessments and address mental health effects. As a result, school children require increased support for physical and mental health conditions in the classroom (APA, 2021).

Condition	Prevalence in Children
Asthma	8.5%
Diabetes	0.4%
Epilepsy and seizure disorders	0.7%
Food allergy	7.6%
Mental health concerns	13-20%
Obesity	18.5%
Oral health: Untreated tooth decay	13%
Multiple chronic conditions	6%

(APA, 2021)

Students with chronic conditions may be eligible for services by implementing Section 504 of the Rehabilitation Act and the Individuals with Disabilities Education Improvement Act (IDEIA, formerly IDEA). The school nurse is a vital member of the team that identifies and assesses students with health concerns to determine if accommodation is needed. The school nurse acts as a case manager to assist students with chronic conditions to effectively manage their health and decrease barriers to academic performance and school engagement (National Association of School Nurses [NASN], 2021). This can include daily management of the student's health condition, establishing safety plans to respond to a student health emergency, and providing education and training to the school staff and students on how to care for the student's health condition. Additionally, if a school nurse has delegated procedures and treatments to unlicensed assistive personnel (UAP), the nurse retains accountability and must ensure adequate supervision and monitoring. (*See Chapter 4 for more information on delegation*).

---

*Original author: Teresa DuChateau, DNP, RN, CPNP (2017)

BACKGROUND

Several federal laws impact the school nursing practice and care of students with chronic conditions in the school setting. These include:

- The Americans with Disabilities Act of 1990 (ADA)
- The Americans with Disabilities Act Amendment Act of 2008 (ADAAA) (*42 U.S.C. § 12102*)
- Section 504 of the Rehabilitation Act of 1973 (Rehabilitation Act of 1973 [§504], 2000)
- Individuals with Disability Education Improvement Act [IDEIA], 2004
- The Family Educational Rights and Privacy Act (FERPA) (20 U.S.C. § 1232g)
- The Health Insurance Information Portability and Accountability Act (HIPAA)
- IDEIA Child Find (IDEIA, 2004; § 300.111)

The Americans with Disabilities Act (ADA) of 1990. The ADA was passed by Congress in 1990. The ADA is "a civil rights law that prohibits discrimination against individuals with disabilities in all areas of public life, including jobs, schools, transportation, and all public and private places that are open to the general public "(ADA National Network, 2017, p.1).

> *No individual shall be discriminated against on the basis of disability in the full and equal enjoyment of the goods, services, facilities, privileges, advantages, or accommodations of any place of public accommodation by any person who owns, leases (or leases to), or operates a place of public accommodation (sec302 a).*

> *Public accommodation includes: places of lodging, places serving food or drink, places of entertainment, places of public gathering, retail businesses, service providers, public transportation depots, libraries and museums, parks, all schools, social service agencies, places of exercise or recreation (sec 301 7). Very little is not covered by this list, notable exceptions being private clubs and religious organizations (Bishop & Jones, 1993, p.4).*

The Americans with Disabilities Act Amendment Act of 2008 (ADAAA). The ADAAA was enacted on September 25, 2008, and became effective on January 1, 2009. The ADAAA is reinstating a "broad scope of protection" by expanding the definition of "disability." Congress found that persons with many types of impairments – including epilepsy, diabetes, multiple sclerosis, major depression, and bipolar disorder – had been unable to bring ADA claims because they were found not to meet the ADA's definition of "disability" (U.S. Equal Employment Opportunity Commission, n.d.), hence the need for the amendment.

The Individuals with Disabilities Education Improvement Act (2004), often referred to as IDEIA or IDEA, includes specific provisions for identifying and evaluating students who may need special education services (National Association of School Nurses [NASN], 2023). In 1997, Congress amended the Education for All Handicapped Children Act of 1975 by replacing it with the Individuals with Disabilities Education Act (IDEA). IDEA was reauthorized in 2004 with changes, creating the Individuals with Disabilities Education Improvement Act (IDEIA). IDEIA is the primary source of federal funding to states for identifying and educating children between the ages of three and twenty-one with disabilities. IDEIA obligates school districts to offer children with disabilities a "free, appropriate public education" or FAPE. This means that local school districts must develop and pay for an educational program tailored to the individual needs of the student with a disability. This plan is known as an Individualized Education Plan or IEP. (*See Chapter 13 for more information*).

The following chart outlines the fourteen disability categories that qualify as a disability under IDEIA.

Autism	Multiple disabilities
Deaf-blindness	Orthopedic impairment
Deafness	Other health impairment
Developmental delay	Specific learning disability
Emotional disturbance	Speech or language impairment
Hearing impairment	Traumatic brain injury
Intellectual disability	Visual impairment, including blindness

(Dragoo, 2020).

The **IDEIA Child Find** requires that "all children with disabilities residing in the State, including children with disabilities who are homeless children or are wards of the State, and children with disabilities attending private schools, regardless of the severity of their disability, and who are in need of special education and related services, are identified, located, and evaluated" (34 C.F.R. 300.311(a)(1)). So not only must schools provide services under IDEA, but they also must identify children if their condition is known to them.

Some students with chronic conditions may qualify for **Section 504 of the Rehabilitation Act (Section 504).** An individual is protected by Section 504 if they have a physical or mental impairment that substantially limits one or more of their major life activities (34 C.F.R.§ 104.3).

> *The Section 504 regulatory provision at 34 C.F.R. 104.3(j)(2)(i) defines a physical or mental impairment as any physiological disorder or condition, cosmetic disfigurement, or anatomical loss affecting one or more of the following body systems: neurological; musculoskeletal; special sense organs; respiratory, including speech organs; cardiovascular; reproductive; digestive; genito-urinary; hemic and lymphatic; skin; and endocrine;*

Lawrence J. Altman, Esquire (2017)

Do school nurses play a role in liability prevention under Section 504's "Child Find" provision?

YES! Under the Individuals with Disabilities Education Act and Section 504 of the Rehabilitation Act, schools have an obligation under what is referred to as "Child Find" or identification and eligibility to locate and then assess any child that school staff believes might be disabled under the IDEA or Section 504. To illustrate, if the school nurse is made aware that a student uses an Inhaler to help when the child has an asthma attack, then the school has been made aware that this child might have a Section 504 disability. That student should undergo a Section 504 eligibility determination and accommodations implemented by the school due to her asthma, such as the ability to carry her inhaler with her, the development of an emergency plan, and notification of her teachers and other relevant staff members of her disability-related day-to-day and emergency needs through the dissemination of the student's Section 504 Plan.

or any mental or psychological disorder, such as mental retardation, organic brain syndrome, emotional or mental illness, and specific learning disabilities. The regulatory provision does not set forth an exhaustive list of specific diseases and conditions that may constitute physical or mental impairments because of the difficulty of ensuring the comprehensiveness of such a list.

Section 504 prohibits schools that receive federal funding from discriminating against a student because of disability in academic and non-academic activities, such as school field trips and extracurricular activities. Under Section 504, "FAPE consists of the provision of regular or special education and related aids and services designed to meet the student's individual educational needs as adequately as the needs of nondisabled students are met "(U.S. Department of Education [USDE], 2020, para. 2).

A medical diagnosis of an illness does not automatically mean a student can receive services under Section 504, nor is Section 504 eligibility dependent upon a formal medical diagnosis. The illness/condition must cause a substantial limitation on the student's ability to learn or another major life activity. Other sources to be considered, along with the medical diagnosis, include aptitude and achievement tests, teacher recommendations, physical condition, social and cultural background, and adaptive behavior (USDE, 2020).

The **FERPA (Family Education Rights and Privacy Act)** is a federal law administered by the Student Privacy Policy Office in the USDE. FERPA (20 U.S.C. § 1232g; 34 CFR Part 99) applies to educational agencies and institutions that receive funds under the USDE. It protects the confidentiality of and provides certain parental rights regarding their children's education records. Education records are generally defined as records that are "directly related to a student and maintained by an educational agency or institution or by a party acting for the agency or institution." Exemptions to the definition of "education records" include law enforcement unit records and records which are kept in the sole possession of the maker of the records (USDE, 2023). (*See Chapter 12 for more information*).

The **HIPAA (Health Insurance Portability and Accountability Act)** was enacted to improve the efficiency and effectiveness of the healthcare system by establishing national standards and requirements for electronic healthcare transactions. The law was also developed to protect the privacy and security of individually identifiable health information. HIPAA excludes educational records covered by FERPA (U.S. Department of Health and Human Services & USDE, 2019). "HIPPA's privacy, security, and breach notification rules do not apply to health care records created or maintained by schools" (Roberts & Zittoun, 2017, p. 127). However, school nurses need to be familiar with HIPAA since many healthcare providers need to follow HIPAA requirements, impacting their ability to obtain needed records without the proper release of information forms. (*See Chapter 12 for more information*).

In addition to the aforementioned federal laws, states may also have laws that impact the care of students with chronic conditions, most commonly the **nurse practice act (NPA)**. The NPA varies in each state, but it typically outlines the profession's legal scope of practice, the state's standards of nursing, types of titles and licenses, requirements for licensure and grounds for disciplinary action, other violations, and possible remedies. A state may also have administrative rules or regulations developed by the board of nursing (BON). These rules and regulations are developed to clarify or make the law more specific. The rules and regulations developed by the BON must be consistent with the NPA and cannot go beyond it. These rules and regulations undergo a process of public review before enactment. Once enacted, rules and regulations have the full force and effect of law (Russell, 2017, p.19).

A state's NPA may stipulate what tasks a nurse may delegate to a UAP. The NPA may also regulate which medications can be delegated to UAPs in the school setting. This can make it extremely challenging for school nurses since, in some states, nurses may be able to delegate the administration of glucagon but not the administration of insulin. At times the state's NPA is in direct conflict with other state regulations and statutes. "State boards of nursing and individual state legislatures differ greatly in the intricate wording of statutes, rules, and regulations, creating difficulty establishing an understanding of the laws and whether they violate state NPAs" (Wilt & Foley, 2011, p.188). School nurses should consult with legal counsel, their state BON and/ or professional practice organization when discrepancies exist for guidance.

In addition to the federal laws that impact the care of students with chronic conditions, school nurses need to be aware of the state statutes and regulations that affect school district policy and practices related to student health and safety. *(See chapters 12, 13, and 4 for more detailed information on education laws, FERPA/HIPAA, and delegation).*

IMPLICATIONS FOR SCHOOL NURSE PRACTICE

Schools are responsible for providing for students' safety when attending school and school-sponsored events. One of the most significant challenges for school nurses is the increasing number of students with chronic health conditions and the lack of adequate school nurse services in many school districts. Although every school is recommended to have a full-time school nurse (American Academy of Pediatrics, 2016; NASN, 2022), many school districts have inadequate school health services. Only 39.3% of schools employ full-time school nurses (Willgerodt et al., 2018). The lack of school health staff does not mitigate the school's responsibility to provide a safe learning environment for students with health concerns.

Students with disabilities or underlying health conditions must be given an equal opportunity to participate in academic, non-academic, and extracurricular activities. One of the most vital roles of a school nurse is to assess students to determine their health status and health needs and to evaluate potential accommodation needs. Various plans are used in the educational setting to support student health, safety, and success (NASN, 2020). The school nurse is the only school professional qualified to develop healthcare plans (Yonkaitis & Shannon, 2019, p. 173). The Individualized Healthcare Plan (IHP) is "developed by the school nurse for the school nurse" (NASN, 2020, para.3). The IHP outlines the nursing care plan for the student and can be used to demonstrate the application of the school nurse standards of care. The IHP informs other school health plans, such as the Emergency Action Plan or EAP (Yonkaitis & Shannon, 2019, p. 179). The EAP clearly and briefly outlines the responsibilities of the school staff in an emergency (Yonkaitis & Shannon, 2019, p. 184).

School nurses provide nursing care in schools and must promote educational access (Johnson, 2022). Educational plans such as 504 Plans and Individualized Education Plans (IEPs) are also informed by the IHP. 504 Plans and IEPs are created through a multidisciplinary team approach (Yonkaitis & Shannon, 2019, p.173). The school nurse is the qualified member of the team positioned to meet the student's healthcare needs (NASN, 2023).

CONCLUSION

By nature of their position, school nurses are leaders within the school setting. School nurses are in a key position to educate school leaders about the needs of students with chronic health conditions. It is imperative that school nurses are educated on the federal and state laws that impact the care of students with chronic conditions so they can inform teachers, school leaders, and healthcare providers about the legal rights of students with chronic conditions. As healthcare leaders, school nurses must be aware of federal and state laws that affect their practice and the care of students in the school setting. School nurses must advocate for the rights and needs of students and speak up when the appropriate accommodations and safeguards are not in place.

RESOURCES

Helping the Student with Diabetes Succeed. A Guide for School Personnel.
https://diabetes.org/sites/default/files/2020-02/NDEP-School-Guide-Full-508.pdf

Joint Guidance on the Application of the Family Educational Rights and Privacy Act (FERPA) and the Health Insurance Portability and Accountability Act of 1996 (HIPAA) To Student Health Records.
https://studentprivacy.ed.gov/sites/default/files/resource_document/file/2019%20HIPAA%20FERPA%20Joint%20Guidance%20508.pdf

Legal Rights of Children with Epilepsy in School and Child Care. An Advocate's Manual. 2nd ed.
https://epilepsyode3.prod.acquia-sites.com/sites/default/files/atoms/files/Legal-Rights-of-Children-with-Epilesy-in-School-and-Child-Care.pdf

Legal Rights of Students with Diabetes
http://main.diabetes.org/dorg/PDFs/Advocacy/Discrimination/education-materials/legal-rights-of-students-with-diabetes/legal-rights-of-students-with-diabetes.pdf

U.S. Equal Employment Opportunity Commission (EEOC). Questions and Answers on the Final Rule Implementing the ADA Amendments Act of 2008.
https://www.eeoc.gov/laws/guidance/questions-and-answers-final-rule-implementing-ada-amendments-act-2008

U.S. Department of Education. Protecting Student Privacy: What records are exempted from FERPA?
https://studentprivacy.ed.gov/faq/what-records-are-exempted-ferpa

Case Law

CASES	DATA	ISSUE	DECISION
San Francisco Unified School District, 5 ECLPR 377 (SEA CA 2002)	3 1/2-year-old M w/multiple disabilities.	P requested that SD address S's healthcare needs involving the management of seizures. SD argued that prolonged seizures were "medical emergencies" beyond the scope of their obligations.	For P: SD must provide health services, and aides under the supervision of a qualified nurse may evaluate seizures, administer and monitor medication, and administer ventilation intervention if needed.
Silsbee Independent School District, 25 IDELR 1023 (SEA TX 1997)	7-year-old M w/PD	SD argued that training staff in resuscitation techniques and seizure was "medical training" not required under the IDEA. P argued that such training is necessary to provide "related services" and that a full-time nurse must always be available.	For P: Staff training in resuscitation and seizure management is related to services to assist S in benefiting from special education instruction.
Gerber Union Elementary School District, 26 IDELR 199 (SEA CA 1997)	12-year-old M w/ SED	P sought to compel the district to provide the 1:1 services of an aide specifically named in an interim IEP. SD argued that the aide was not adequate to provide the services the S needed but would provide another trained adult with S at all times.	For P: The aide explicitly named on the IEP was an integral part of the IEP, and continued services were necessary to ensure the stability of S's program.
Hingham Public Schools, 33 IDELR 292 (SEA MA 2000)	5-year-old F w/Angelman Syndrome, a neurological disorder resulting in severe learning difficulties and seizure disorders.	P argued that S's IEP called for a 1:1 aide with professional status and experience, but the assigned aide did not have those credentials. S's doctor recommended that due to S's severe learning problems, the aide must have a master's degree and experience to maximize learning. SD stated that the proposed aide is committed and relates well to S, thus meeting the professional status requirements. S is benefiting from the current aide, so a master's and experience were not necessary.	For P: Since IEP called for an aide with professional credentials, SD failed to comply and provide agreed-upon services. Although S would not require an aide with professional qualifications as long as supervising teacher is experienced, since IEP specified such credentials, the aide must meet those specifications.
Mobile County Board of Education, 34 IDELR 164 (SEA AL 2001)	16-year-old M w/ MD	P alleged that S suffered physical injuries due to inadequate protection by the SD. S was attacked and injured by three Ss riding the bus. SD insisted that the aide was not furnished to foster S's greater independence by having him ride the bus without an adult accompanying him.	For P: Concomitant to the responsibility to provide transportation to permit children to attend appropriate special education programs is the obligation to provide a safe environment for students transported. An aide should have been assigned to accompany the S.

CASES	DATA	ISSUE	DECISION
Board of Education of the City of New York, 28 IDELR (SEA NY, 1998)	8-year-old M w/ OHI, Tourette's Syndrome, and ADHD.	P contended that IEP was inadequate due to the failure to train S's teacher, paraprofessional, classmates, and other school personnel. SD argued that IEP, as proposed, was appropriate.	For P: SD must provide training for S's teacher, paraprofessional, related service providers, & classmates. Initial and "update" training to be provided as necessary.
CTL v. Ashland Sch. Dis., 743 F.3d 524 (7th Cir. 2014).	Elementary-aged M w/ Type 1 diabetes	P argues that SD intentionally discriminated against their son by hiring hard to work with staff and failed to accommodate him in the classroom by not training an additional two staff members as diabetes personnel and refusing to deviate from insulin dosage calculator.	For SD: the school's choices did not make the student unsafe or denied him benefit of public education nor did they intentionally discriminate against S.

Note. M male; F female; P parent; SD school district; S student; MD mental disability; OHI other health impaired; PD physical disability; LPN licensed practical nurse; RN registered nurse; SED serious emotional disturbance.

References:

Etscheidt, S. (2005). Paraprofessional services for students with disabilities: A legal analysis of issues. *Research & Practice for Persons with Severe Disabilities, 30*(2), 60–80. https://doi.org/10.2511/rpsd.30.2.60.

Findlaw. (2023). CTL Trebatoski v. Ashland School District, 743 F. 3d 524 (7th Cir. 2014). https://caselaw.findlaw.com/court/us-7th-circuit/1657913.html

REFERENCES

ADA National Network. (2017). *An overview of the Americans with Disabilities Act.* https://adata.org/sites/adata.org/files/files/ADA_Overview_final2017.pdf

American Academy of Pediatrics. (2016, June). Role of the school nurse in providing school health services (Policy Statement). *Pediatrics,137*(6), e20160852.Originally published online on May 23, 2016. https://doi.org/10.1542/peds.2016-0852

Americans with Disabilities Act Amendments. (2010). *42 U.S.C. § 12102.* http://www.ada.gov/pubs/adastatute08.htm

Bishop, P. C., & Jones, A. J. (1993). Implementing the Americans with Disabilities Act of 1990: Assessing the variables of success. *Public Administration Review, 53*(2), 121–128. https://doi.org/10.2307/976704

Center for Parent Information and Resources. (2022). *Categories of disability under IDEA.* https://www.parentcenterhub.org/categories/

Dragoo, K. E. (2020, October 12). The Individuals with Disabilities Education Act: A comparison of state eligibility. *Congressional Research Service Reports.* https://crsreports.congress.gov/product/pdf/R/R46566

Etscheidt, S. (2005). Paraprofessional services for students with disabilities: A legal analysis of issues. *Research and Practice for Persons with Severe Disabilities, 30*(2), 60–80. https://doi.org/10.2511/rpsd.30.2.60

Family Educational Rights and Privacy Act of 1974, 20 U.S.C. § 1232g (1974).
https://www.law.cornell.edu/uscode/text/20/1232g

Health Insurance Portability and Accountability Act H.R. 3103 — 104th Congress: Health Insurance Portability and Accountability Act of 1996. https://www.govtrack.us/congress/bills/104/hr3103

Individuals with Disability Education Improvement Act (2004), 20 U.S.C. 1400 et seq. http://idea.ed.gov/download/statute.html

Johnson, K., (2022, September 30). Care of students with disabilities in schools: A team approach. *OJIN: The Online Journal of Issues in Nursing (27)3. https://www.doi.org/10.3912/OJIN.Vol27No03Man02*

National Association of School Nurses. (2020). *Use of individualized healthcare plans to support school health services* (Position Statement). Author. https://www.nasn.org/nasn-resources/professional-practice-documents/position-statements/ps-ihps

National Association of School Nurses. (2022). Student access to school nursing services (Position Statement). Author. https://www.nasn.org/nasn-resources/professional-practice-documents/position-statements/ps-access-to-services

National Association of School Nurses. (2023). *IDEIA and Section 504 teams - The school nurse as an essential team member* (Position Statement). Author. https://www.nasn.org/nasn-resources/professional-practice-documents/position-statements/ps-ideia

Rehabilitation Act of 1973, 29 U.S.C. § 504. https://www.dol.gov/agencies/oasam/centers-offices/civil-rights-center/statutes/section-504-rehabilitation-act-of-1973

Roberts, W.J. & Zittourn, G.J. (2017). Family Education Rights and Privacy Act ("FERPA")/Health Insurance Portability and Accountability Act ("HIPAA'). In C.A. Resha & V.L. Taliaferro (Eds.), *Legal resource for school health services* (pp. 125-135). SchoolNurse.com

Russell, K.A. (2017, October). Nurse Practice Acts guide and govern: Update 2017. *Journal of Nursing Regulation, 8 (3),* 18–25. https://www.ncsbn.org/public-files/2017_NPA_Guide_and_govern.pdf

U.S. Department of Education. (2020). *Protecting students with disabilities.* https://www2.ed.gov/about/offices/list/ocr/504faq.html

U. S. Department of Education. (2023, March 8). *An eligible student guide to the Family Educational Rights and Privacy Act (FERPA).* https://studentprivacy.ed.gov/sites/default/files/resource_document/file/An%20Eligible%20Student%20Guide%20to%20FERPA_0.pdf

U.S. Department of Health and Human Services & U. S. Department of Education. (2019). *Joint guidance on the application of the Family Educational Rights and Privacy Act (FERPA) and the Health Insurance Portability and Accountability Act of 1996 (HIPAA) to student health records.* https://rems.ed.gov/docs/2019%20HIPAA%20FERPA%20Joint%20Guidance.pdf

U.S. Department of Education. (2017, May 3). *Child Find.* Part 300/ B / 300.111 / a /1. https://sites.ed.gov/idea/regs/b/b/300.111

U.S. Equal Employment Opportunity Commission. (n.d.). *The Americans with Disabilities Act Amendments Act of 2008.* https://www.eeoc.gov/statutes/americans-disabilities-act-amendments-act-2008

Willgerodt, M.A., Brock, D. M., & Maughan, E.D. (2018). Public school nursing practice in the United States. *Journal of School Nursing, 34*(3), 232-244. https://doi.org/10.1177/1059840517752456

Wilt, L. & Foley, M. (2011). Delegation of Glucagon® in the school setting: A comparison of state legislation. *The Journal of School Nursing, 27*(3), 185-196. https://doi.org/10.1177/1059840511398240

Yonkaitis, C. F., & Shannon, R. A. (2019). Health and education plans for students with special healthcare needs. In J. Selekman, R.A. Shannon, & C.F. Yonkaitis (Eds.), *School nursing: A comprehensive text (3rd ed.*, pp.172–201). F A. Davis.

ADDENDUM 1

Kathleen Maguire, DNP, RN

Differences Between Section 504 and IDEA and School Nursing Implications

	IDEA (IEP)	Section 504	School Nursing Implication
Governance	Individuals with Disabilities in Education Act (IDEA) Education Law	Section 504 of the Rehabilitation Act of 1973, overseen by the Office of Civil Rights (OCR)	
Age	School-aged children	Covers individuals over a lifespan	
Eligibility Category	1. autism; 2. deaf-blindness; 3. deafness; 4. developmental delay (applicable to 3-5-year-old children only); 5. emotional disturbance; hearing impairment; intellectual disability; multiple disabilities; orthopedic impairment; other health impairment (which often includes ADD/ADHD); 6. physical impairment; specific learning disability; speech or language impairment; 7. traumatic brain injury; and 8. visual impairment, including blindness	• Student who does not need special education or qualifies for special education and related services under IDEA • A physical or mental impairment substantially limiting a major life activity: walking, seeing, eating, breathing, learning Please note: the list of impairments substantially limiting a major life activity has been interpreted very expansively and that the "walking, seeing, etc....." listed are simply examples.	Examples: *Physical or Mental Impairment* • Neurological • Musculoskeletal • Respiratory • Digestive • Endocrine • Emotional • Specific learning disability • Immune disorder *Major life activity:* • Concentrating • Communicating • Bowel or bladder dysfunction • Thinking *Other:* • Temporary injuries caused by accidents • Asthma • Allergies • Diabetes • Communicable disease • *It is important to note that a "medical diagnosis does not automatically mean a student receives services under Section 504" (USDE, 2020, question 24).
Requirement	Disability adversely affects education	Barriers to accessing education	

	IDEA (IEP)	Section 504	School Nursing Implication
Identification	Child Find: Identify, evaluate, and determine eligibility for special education services.	Identify and determine eligibility for Section 504 accommodations	Refer children for IEP or Section 504 for evaluation if the school nurse suspects the need for services.
Process	The full school team completes the comprehensive evaluation. Informed consent of the parent is required.	Impairment documentation from various sources: healthcare provider, parental input, and evaluation data. Team decision does not require the written consent of the parent.	Gathering information from multiple sources as appropriate to identify health history and potential health needs in school
Participation	• Multidisciplinary team of which school nurse is a member • Parent/Guardian	• Multidisciplinary team • Parent /Guardian • School nurse	Coordinate and collaborate with primary care providers and parents to gather appropriate mental or physical health documentation. Assessment of student health status Development of: • Individualized Healthcare Plan • Individualized Emergency Action Plan
Plan	Individualized Education Plan • Specialized instruction by adapting content or delivery method of instruction	Section 504 • Accommodations • Equal access	*Examples of accommodations:* • Qualified interpreters • Adaptive writing tools • Assistive devices such as crutches, wheelchair, or walker • Medication administration or health procedure at school (such as blood glucose monitoring or G-tube feeding • Other nursing services, such as monitoring and implementation of emergency plan for seizures • Assistance in note-taking • Calculators or computers • Auditory support • Extra set of textbooks • Alternative test style • Modified workload • Untimed test • Breaks between classes • Adaptive gym • Adaptive desk • Elevator key

	IDEA (IEP)	Section 504	School Nursing Implication
Evaluation	At least once every three years upon parental or teacher request.	Periodic May be temporary	Participation in reevaluation as appropriate
Placement	May be a combination of special and regular education services. Related services: speech, nursing hearing, physical or occupational therapy	Most commonly in a regular school classroom with related services or accommodations	Consult with appropriate school personnel to provide a safe school environment.
Discipline	The disciplinary process for identified students involves the first step of a manifestation determination PPT. The decision by special hearing if disability caused the action. Development of a Functional Behavior Plan	The disciplinary process for identified students involves the first step of a manifestation determination Section 504 meeting. There is an exclusion for certain 504 students. No punishment or discrimination based on disability	Support ongoing interaction with the multidisciplinary team, parent or guardian, and healthcare provider.

Reference:

United States Department of Education. (2020, January 10). *Protecting students with disabilities.*
https://www2.ed.gov/about/offices/list/ocr/504faq.html

Chapter 25

MILD TRAUMATIC BRAIN INJURY (CONCUSSION) MANAGEMENT

Jeannie Rodriguez, PhD, RN, PNP/PC*

DESCRIPTION OF ISSUE

Definition

A mild traumatic brain injury (mTBI) is defined as "an acute brain injury resulting from mechanical energy to the head from external physical forces including one or more of the following:

- confusion or disorientation,
- loss of consciousness for 30 minutes or less,
- post-traumatic amnesia for less than 24 hours, or
- other transient neurological abnormalities such as focal signs, symptoms, or seizure;
- a Glasgow Coma Scale score of 13–15 after 30 minutes post-injury or later upon presentation for healthcare" (Carroll et al.,2004; Lamba-Brown et al.,2018).

Further, a mTBI is due to a direct blow to the head, face, neck, or other body parts that transmit force to the head (McCrory et al., 2017). This trauma results in functional neuropathological changes reflected, causing short-term neurological impairment with or without a loss of consciousness, although impairment in some may be prolonged (McCrory et al., 2017).

Terms such as "concussion," "minor head injury," and "mTBI" have been used to describe this entity; however, the CDC (Lamba-Brown et al.,2018) recommended in its most recent guidelines the use of the term mTBI. Other organizations, including the American Academy of Pediatrics (AAP), continue to use the term "concussion" in their guidelines (AAP, 2021).

Prevalence

It is difficult to determine exact statistics on the incidence and prevalence of mTBIs due to the lack of current descriptive research in this area, as well as the underreporting of mTBIs and the increase in sporting activities for children outside of school, such as private sports organizations and clubs, as well as a variety of recreational activities (Institute of Medicine [IOM] and National Research Council [NRC], 2014). In 2020, 6.8% of children 0-17 years had reported ever having symptoms of a mTBI, with increasing percentages reported with increasing age (2% ages 0-5 years, 5.8% 6-11 years, 12.2% 12-17 years) (Black & Zablotsky, 2021). Additionally, 3.7% of children reported receiving a diagnosis of mTBI or brain injury by a health care professional, with increasing percentages reported with increasing age (0.9% ages 0-5 years, 2.1% 6-11 years, 8.3% 12-17 years) (Black & Zablotsky, 2021).

A recent report collected information from three national databases. It estimated that between 1.1 and 1.9 million children, equal to or under 18 years old, sustained what they described as a *sports-and recreation-related concussion* annually (Bryan et al., 2016). The incidence and reporting of mTBI related to sports

---

Original authors: Cameron Traut, MS, BSN, RN, PEL-IL, NCSN and Nancy L. Dube, MPH, BSEd, RN (2017)

participation have increased, likely due to both a true increase due to more opportunities to engage in sports for youth and an increase in overall awareness of the seriousness of mTBIs by medical professionals, coaching, and school staff, and the lay public (Halstead et al., 2018). According to a clinical report by the AAP (Halstead et al.,2018), American tackle football has the highest reported incidence of mTBI in both male and female sports. The high-contact boys' lacrosse, ice hockey, and wrestling sports also convey high risk. For girls' sports, higher risk occurs with lacrosse, field hockey, and basketball (Halstead et al.,2018). Other causes of mTBIs include non-sport-related mechanisms of injury, such as falls, altercations, motor vehicle accidents, skating/longboarding, water/snow skiing, and other recreational activities (IOM & NRC, 2014).

BACKGROUND

As far back as the late 1800s through the early 20th century, mTBIs have been recognized as a serious medical condition. American football played a significant role in mTBI prevention and care evolution due to the number of significant and sometimes life-threatening injuries (Stone et al., 2014). The first collegiate sports organization (predecessor to the National Collegiate Athletics Association [NCAA]) was formed in 1906 as a response to President Roosevelt's concerns about safety in collegiate sports. The NCAA followed in 1933 with directives for colleges stating that after sustaining a mTBI/head injury, players must rest for 48 hours before returning to practice or play. In 1937, the American Football Coaches Association recommended that head-injured players be removed from play immediately (Waldron, 2013). An article in the *New England Journal of Medicine* (Thorndike, 1952) advised players experiencing three mTBIs to leave the sport permanently for their health and safety. Since then, there have been many articles, studies, controversies, and evolving research into the long-term effects of mTBI, including the effect on young students.

As research on the pathophysiology of a mTBI continues to evolve, models of care and treatment continue to progress as well. For example, it is no longer acceptable for a player to return directly to play and school following an mTBI. A period of observation for signs and symptoms would be appropriate, and if present, the student should be evaluated by a healthcare professional experienced in mTBI management (CDC, 2019). Although most students recover from a mTBI within three weeks (Halstead et al.,2013), how quickly they improve depends on many factors. These factors include duration of symptoms, age, pre-existing health conditions (both physical and mental), and compliance with recommended interventions for self-care after the injury. Most students who have had a mTBI experience symptoms that tend to impede their ability to perform daily activities, including work, academics, and interacting with family and friends during recovery (Halstead et al.,2018).

Signs and symptoms of a mTBI can be divided into five categories; somatic, vestibular, oculomotor, cognitive, emotional, and sleep (Halstead et al.,2018). Somatic findings can include headaches, nausea, or vomiting (Halstead et al.,2018). Youth with vestibular and oculomotor symptoms may exhibit visual and hearing problems and dizziness (Halstead et al., 2018). Cognitive signs and symptoms may include confusion, difficulty concentrating, and remembering (Halstead et al.,2018). Students with emotional symptoms may experience irritability and appear more emotional than usual (Halstead et al.,2018). Finally, sleep signs and symptoms may include drowsiness or fatigue and sleeping too much or too little (Halstead et al.,2018). Headache is the most frequently reported symptom, followed by dizziness, difficulty concentrating, and confusion (Halstead,

2018). As stated above, school nurses and staff must be aware that a loss of consciousness is not a required symptom of an mTBI (Halstead et al.,2018; McCrory et al.,2017).

Physical and cognitive rest is very important after a mTBI because it helps the brain to heal. First, the student who has suffered a suspected mTBI should be immediately removed from play. Ignoring the symptoms and trying to "tough it out" often worsen symptoms and prolongs recovery. Only when the symptoms have reduced significantly, in consultation with a healthcare professional, should the student slowly and gradually return to daily activities, such as work or school. If symptoms worsen, return, or new symptoms develop as activity increases, this may require the student to slow the return to activity and increase rest (Halstead et al.,2018). Prolonged school removal is not recommended and may be harmful. However, when students return to school following a mTBI, they may require academic accommodation. School nurses should collaborate with teachers and staff to ensure that affected students have the appropriate modifications in place (Halstead et al.,2018).

Legal Issues

All 50 states and the District of Columbia have a Return to Play law (CDC, 2015). Most of the state laws and regulations generally have three items in common:

1) any athlete suspected of having sustained a concussion must immediately be removed from play;
2) the athlete may not be returned to action the same day or may only return the same day if cleared by a healthcare professional; and
3) athletes, parents, coaches, physical education educators, and referees are required to have some form of concussion awareness and education training.

In most states, these laws apply to both public and private schools (SHAPE America, 2017).

Some state laws and regulations contain additional requirements, including mandates for specific athletic department personnel to complete an annual concussion education course, implement school-based neurocognitive baseline testing, and student-athletes and parents/guardians be provided with concussion education materials along with signing a concussion information form. The full text of each state law may be accessed through the National Conference of State Legislatures website, Legislative News, Studies and Analysis | National Conference of State Legislatures (ncsl.org) (NCSL, 2023).

Recently, there have been court decisions related to concussions in schools. The courts often looked at the "duty of reasonable care." Case decisions against the school districts were based on a number of factors, including the lack of training or proper supervision during activities that led to injury. Some of the cases also included coaches independently returning students to activity without the student being cleared by a licensed healthcare professional (Anderson, 2014).

Situations of potential concern for the school nurse occur when the school policy is not implemented correctly or completely. Glassman & Holt (2011) share examples of "liability theories" which have been used in litigation:

1) "The school has no protocol and should." Concussion protocols are part of the standard of care now, with most states having laws requiring some type of protocol or policy.

2) "School protocol is flawed." If the protocol is not aligned with commonly recommended protocol templates, this is a potential liability.
3) "School did not follow protocol," which speaks for itself (p. 29).

Other liabilities noted in litigation examples have been:
1) issues with unsafe field of play/equipment conditions;
2) "failure to refer" to healthcare professionals;
3) "inadequate provision of information to other care providers"; and
4) "negligent supervision" of coaches or referees during the competition (Glassman & Holt, 2011, p. 30).

Some Examples of Recent Case Law

1. *In 2022, Shane Skillpa filed a lawsuit against the West Mifflin Area School District alleging that coaches and other parties had a duty to recognize the injury that he suffered during football practice drills in 2009 that resulted in a cracked helmet and a duty to hold Mr. Skillpa out of additional drills. The jury found in favor of the school district viewing the case through the concussion protocols available in 2009 when the coach's duties of coaches were defined differently than in 2022, and the science of concussion was less established. However, this case demonstrates that actions from years ago may still be a basis for legal claims (NFHS, 2023a).*

2. *In 2021, a settlement was reached in the case Martin v. Hermiston School District for an undisclosed amount of money. Originally filed in 2018, the lawsuit alleged that coaches and athletic trainers failed to recognize symptoms of a traumatic brain injury and reinserted the player back in the game. Further, at subsequent games, the sophomore high school student suffered additional blows to the head resulting in extensive medical problems. The suit also alleged that the student's parents were never informed of the injury, concussion protocols mandated by the state were not followed, and the student-athlete was not administered appropriate cognitive testing to determine if he could safely return to play (NFHS, 2023b).*

3. *In 2019, a settlement for $60,000 was reached in Platt v. Cedar Falls Community Schools. In this case, a junior varsity softball team member was struck in the head by a bat during practice while picking up balls near the batter. Allegedly the team had enough helmets for varsity players but not junior varsity players. The filings in this suit alleged that the defendants failed to fulfill their duties of specific supervision and provision of protective athletic equipment. This case illustrates that school athletic personnel must exercise caution when there is a foreseeable risk of injury, i.e., when students are crowded together swinging athletic equipment (NFHS, 2023c).*

4. *According to the 2014 Sports Law Year-in-Review by the National Federation of High Schools (Green, 2015), a Montana court approved a $300,000 settlement in Rouchleau v. Three Forks School District in 2009. This case involved a traumatic brain injury suffered by a high school football player who allegedly was returned to action prematurely after suffering a concussion during practice. The original filings in the suit claimed that shortly after being diagnosed with a concussion, the school's coaches allowed the player to return to action without written clearance by a licensed medical professional as*

mandated by the state's concussion protocol law and that the student-athlete then sustained a helmet-to-helmet hit, rendering him unconscious, resulting in permanent brain damage.

5. *Another lawsuit (Green, 2015) was filed against a school district and soccer coach, alleging premature return to action after a concussion in violation of the duty of reasonable care to evaluate student-athletes for incapacities, including return-to-action protocols after an injury. In M.U. v. Downingtown (PA) Area School District, the pleadings contended that a 14-year-old female soccer player, while attempting to strike a header, suffered a concussion when the girl's face collided with another player's head. The suit asserted that she was removed from the game for a few minutes and, despite exhibiting multiple indicia of a concussion, was allowed to return to action, where she suffered another head-to-head hit resulting in a "second impact syndrome" traumatic brain injury. The suit invoked the state's concussion protocol law, which required that student-athletes who show signs of a concussion be immediately removed from play, cannot return to play the same day, and may return to action only after clearance from a licensed medical professional.*

6. *A 2012 lawsuit (Schoepfer-Bochicchio, & Dodds, 2015) addressed the school nurse's "duty of care." A football player at an Iowa high school with a known neuro-vascular condition sustained a concussion in October 2012. After the injury, the student-athlete visited the nurse several times with complaints of headaches and double vision during class. The school nurse failed to report these complaints or the pre-existing condition to his coaches, and the student continued to participate in football. In November 2012, the student underwent brain surgery, was comatose post-operatively, and subsequently was permanently disabled, requiring assistive devices to walk. The school nurse and district were sued and found liable for being negligent in the school nurse's duty of care as she did not report the symptoms to a coach or the student's guardian or refer the student to a healthcare provider.*

IMPLICATIONS FOR SCHOOL NURSE PRACTICE

Conflicts can occur between school nurses and coaches, administrators, athletic directors, teaching staff, parent/guardian(s), and students regarding physical activity and sports participation. These conflicts are not new to school nurses. It is vital for the school nurse to ensure the "duty of safe care" through knowledge and implementation of the language of state laws, district policies, and the best practice guidelines provided by national organizations such as the CDC Heads Up Program, National Association of School Nurses (NASN), National Federation of High Schools (NFHS), and others. The school nurse has the knowledge to address and inform relevant staff members and caregivers about these issues.

The changing culture surrounding mTBI management presents a challenge for school nurses. The school nurse assumes many roles within mTBI care management in the school setting:

1) coordinator of individual student care,
2) mTBI oversight committee member or leader,
3) injury prevention, advocacy, and
4) gatekeeper.

MILD TRAUMATIC BRAIN INJURY (CONCUSSION) MANAGEMENT

As with many other acute and chronic health conditions, the school nurse should coordinate the district's response to mTBI management by advocating for prevention and care coordination (NASN, 2016a). The NASN Framework for 21st Century School Nursing Practice (2016b) can be used when describing the school nurse's role in mTBI management.

Care coordination: The school nurse coordinates the care of the student with a mTBI by working with the multidisciplinary team, including educators and outside-of-school healthcare professionals, regarding returning to school and physical activity/sports.

Leadership: The school nurse is a key leader in forming and participating in the school or district's mTBI oversight committee and developing the district mTBI protocol.

Community/Public Health: The school nurse, as relevant to the unique practice settings in a school environment, is the gatekeeper in regard to adhering to state and local laws and policies, best practices, referrals to appropriate medical care, and identifying preventative measures in mTBI care.

Quality Improvement: The school nurse documents care, monitors prevalence, collects data, and continually evaluates protocols, care, and management (NASN, 2016b).

The foundation for decision-making lies within each state's legal policy, starting with the nurse practice act and the nurse's education and training as a clinician.
- The school nurse must know their state's nurse practice laws, current research, and evidence-based practices.
- Each state also has a set of rules enacted by its state boards of education which may affect the coordination of care in a school.
- The school nurse must be familiar with special education law at the federal and state level, as some students with prolonged symptoms will qualify for a Section 504 Plan or an individualized education plan (Zirkel & Eagan Brown, 2015).
- Sources for state legal mandates related to healthcare policy are the states/ boards of education and health departments (Shannon & Gerdes, 2016).
- All 50 states now have concussion laws that contribute to determining the course of care and management for all students (NCSL, 2015). These laws vary from state to state, and school nurses must be well-informed about the details of their own state's concussion laws.
- At the district level, the school nurse must be knowledgeable about the district board policies and how these policies relate to the district's concussion protocol (Shannon & Gerdes, 2016).

Along with the state nurse practice act and other state policies that elaborate on the care of specific health conditions, nursing education and training lay the foundation for any professional nursing decision made regarding patient care and management. The professional school nurse is expected to have competent clinical nursing skills and be knowledgeable of the most current research and evidence-based practice related to school health and the specialty of school nursing (Resha, 2019). In the ever-changing environment of mTBI care and management, it is critical for the school nurse to have the current research and evidenced-based information readily accessible.

Protocols/Policies

School nurses have a complex set of laws, rules, and guidelines which must be acknowledged and constantly incorporated into their care (Resha, 2019). This is well illustrated in the decision-making process when caring for a student with a concussion, which includes the development of protocols, procedures, and policies addressing mTBI management in the school (Zirkel & Eagan Brown, 2015).

A protocol or policy for mTBI care and management should be in place at the individual school or the district level. Some states dictate what should be in place and offer model policies. The school nurse plays a critical role in the development of this protocol or policy. It is also important to know the difference between policy and protocol. A policy is a formal written statement detailing the particular action to be taken in a particular situation that is contractually binding (University of Wisconsin-Madison [UWM], Health Sciences, 2016).

A protocol is an agreed framework outlining the care that patients will receive in a designated area of practice (UWM, 2016). Protocols are procedural statements written and used by nurses that outline the standard of practice for assessing and managing a specified clinical problem and authorize practice activities. Nursing protocols vary according to the level of education and licensure of the nurse who will implement the protocol (Shannon & Gerdes, 2016).

To elaborate, a protocol is a more general but still descriptive set of procedures, less binding than policy, and more interpretive or flexible regarding how the procedures are implemented. Protocols, also called clinical guidelines, are typically evidence-based and define the process of implementing policy and law. Since policies must always be school board-approved, they are typically less flexible and very binding (Resha, 2019).

CONCLUSION

In summary, the role of a school nurse in mTBI care has many facets. It is guided by following a decision-making checklist when developing policy and protocols and when faced with challenging scenarios within mTBI management and care in the school setting. Laws, board policies, protocols, standards of care, and best practice are the cornerstone of the decision-making process for a school nurse. Professional organizations provide position statements on a variety of issues and care, as well as access to current research, trends in practice, and expert practitioners.

Decision-Making Checklist:
1. Federal Laws
2. State Laws
3. State nurse practice act
4. State board of health policies/regulations
5. State board of education policies/regulations
6. Local school district policy
7. Current nursing standards for best practice
   a. School nursing: Scope and Standards of Practice (NASN)
   b. Nursing: Scope and Standards of Practice (ANA)
8. Current evidence-based research
9. Professional organizations (i.e., NASN, state school nurse organizations, ASHA)
10. Examples of litigation/liability cases

MILD TRAUMATIC BRAIN INJURY (CONCUSSION) MANAGEMENT

The safety and health of the student remain the priority and focus of care as long as the school nurse reviews and incorporates these guiding principles and legal documents into all levels of their plan and practice.

Please see ADDENDUM: Concussion Law Theories of Liability.

RESOURCES

Centers for Disease Control and Prevention. (2021). HEADS UP to Schools: School Nurses. https://www.cdc.gov/headsup/schools/nurses.html

National Association of School Nurses. (2021). Concussions: School Based Management. https://www.nasn.org/nasn-resources/professional-practice-documents/position-statements/ps-concussions

The Network for Public Health Law. (n.d.). *The role of school nurse in managing students with mild brain injury (concussion)*. https://www.networkforphl.org/wp-content/uploads/2019/12/School-Nurses-Mild-Brain-Injury-Fact-Sheet_FINAL-with-post-edit-comments_KML-002_FINAL.pdf

Children's Healthcare of Atlanta. (n.d.). Community and School Resources for Concussion. https://www.choa.org/medical-services/concussion/community-and-school

American Academy of Pediatrics. (2021). Concussion. https://www.aap.org/en/patient-care/concussion

Nationwide Children's Hospital. (n.d.). A School Administrator's Guide to Academic Concussion Management. https://www.nationwidechildrens.org/specialties/concussion-clinic/concussion-toolkit/a-school-administrators-guide-to-academic-concussion-management

School Health Associates. (2021). Concussions. schoolhealthassociates.com

National Federation of High Schools (2015). *Sports medicine*. https://www.nfhs.org/resources/sports-medicine/

Public School Works (March 21, 2023). The Legal Implications of Concussions in Schools: What Superintendents Need to Know. The Legal Implications of Concussions in Schools: What Superintendents Need to Know - PublicSchoolWORKS

Case Law

Strough v. Bedford Community School District. (2012). http://www.iasd.uscourts.gov/sites/default/files/4-13-cv-147-HCA%20Strough%20v.%20Bedford%20Community%20School%20District%20et%20al.pdf

Martin et al. v Hermiston School District. (2018). Martin et al. v. Hermiston School District 8R et al., No. 2:2018cv02088 - Document 38 (D. Or. 2020):: Justia.

Rouchleau v Three Forks School District. (2014). 53bdbe93dd596.pdf.pdf (townnews.com).

M.U. v Downington High School. (2015). M.U. v. Downingtown High Sch. E., Civil Action No. 14–04877. - Federal Cases - Case Law - VLEX 884651540

REFERENCES

American Academy of Pediatrics. (2021). *Concussion.* https://www.aap.org/en/patient-care/concussion/

Anderson, P. (2014). *Legal issues surrounding concussions in youth and high school sport: Finding a standard of care.* [PowerPoint slides]. https://law.marquette.edu/assets/sports-law/pdf/Anderson.711.pdf

Black, LI & Zablotsky, B. (2021). Concussions and brain injuries in children: United States, 2020. NCHS Data Brief, Number 423, November 2021 . https://www.cdc.gov/nchs/data/databriefs/db423.pdf

Bryan, M.A., Rowhani-Rahbar, A., Comstock, R.D., & Rivara, F. (2016). Sports- and recreation-related concussions in US Youth. *Pediatrics, 138*(1), 1–8. https://doi.org./10.1542/peds.2015-4635

Carroll, L.J., Cassidy, J.D., Holm, L, Kraus, J., Coronado, V.G., WHO Collaborating Centre Task Force on Mild Traumatic Brain Injury. (2004). Methodological issues and research recommendations for mild traumatic brain injury: the WHO Collaborating Centre Task Force on Mild Traumatic Brain Injury. *Journal of Rehabilitative Medicine, 43 suppl*, 113–125.https://doi.org./10.1080/16501960410023877

Centers for Disease Control and Prevention. (2019). CDC Heads Up: A Fact Sheet for School Nurses https://www.cdc.gov/headsup/pdfs/schools/tbi_factsheet_nurse-508-a.pdf

Centers for Disease Control and Prevention (2015). *Sports concussion policies and laws.* https://www.cdc.gov/headsup/policy/index.html

Glassman, S.J. & Holt, B.J. (2011). Concussions and student-athletes: Medical-legal issues in concussion care and physician and school system risks. *New Hampshire Bar Journal, 52*(3), 26-35. https://www.nhbar.org/uploads/pdf/BJ-Autumn2011-Vol52-No3-Pg26.pdf

Green, L. (2015). *2014 Sports law year-in-review.* Indianapolis, IN: National Federation of Sports. http://www.nfhs.org/articles/2014-sports-law-year-in-review/

Halstead, M.E., McAvoy, K., Devore, C.D., Carl, R., Lee, M., Logan, K., & Council on Sports Medicine and Fitness, Council on School Health. (2013). Returning to learning following a concussion. *Pediatrics, 132*(5),2018-2967, https://doi.org/10.1542/peds.2013-2867

Halstead, M.E., Walter, K.D., Moffatt, K., & Council on Sports Medicine and Fitness. (2018). Sport-related concussion in children and adolescents. *Pediatrics, 142*(6), e20183074. https://doi.org/10.1542/peds.2018-3074

Institute of Medicine (IOM) and National Research Council. (2014). *Sports-related concussions in youth: Improving the science, changing the culture.* National Academies Press. http://www.ncbi.nlm.nih.gov/books/NBK169016/

Lumba-Brown, A., Yeates ,K.O., Sarmiento, K., Breiding, M.J., Haegerich, T.M., Gioia, G.A., Turner, M., Benzel, E.C., Suskauer, S.J., Giza,C.C., Joseph, M., Broomand C, Weissman B, Gordon W, Wright DW, Moser RS, McAvoy K, Ewing-Cobbs,L., Duhaime, A.C., Putukian, M., Holshouser, B., Paulk, D., Wade, S.L., Herring, S.A., Halstead, M., Keenan, H.T., Choe, M., Christian,C.W., Guskiewicz, K., Raksin, P.B., Gregory, A....& Timmons, S.D. (2018). Centers for Disease Control and Prevention guideline on the diagnosis and management of mild traumatic brain injury among children. *JAMA Pediatrics, 172*(11),e182853. https://doi.org/10.1001/jamapediatrics.2018.2853

McCrory P, Meeuwisse, W., Dvorak, J., *et al.* (2017). Consensus statement on concussion in sport—the 5th international conference on concussion in sport held in Berlin, October 2016. *British Journal of Sports Medicine;51,*838-847. https://doi.org/10.1136/bjsports-2017-097699

National Association of School Nurses. (2021). Concussions: School Based Management [Position Statement]. Neuman, L., Landry, J., Haapala, L., & Griffin, C. https://www.nasn.org/nasn-resources/professional-practice-documents/position-statements/ps-concussions

National Conference of State Legislatures. (2015). *Traumatic brain injury legislation*. http://www.ncsl.org/research/health/traumatic-brain-injury-legislation.aspx

National Federation of State High School Associations. (2023a). 2022 *sports law year-in-review*. https://nfhs.org/articles/2022-sports-law-year-in-review/

National Federation of State High School Associations. (2023b*). 2021 sports law year-in-review*. https://www.nfhs.org/articles/2021-sports-law-year-in-review/

National Federation of State High School Associations. (2023c).*2019 sports law year-in-review*. https://www.nfhs.org/articles/2019-sports-law-year-in-review/

Resha, C.A. (2019). Standards of School Nursing Practice. In J. Selekman, R. Adair Shannon, & C. F. Yonkaitis (Eds.), *School Nursing: A Comprehensive Text* (3rd ed., pp. 31–50). F.A. Davis Company

Schoepfer-Bochicchio, K. & Dodds, M. (2015). *Concussion lawsuit examines school nurse's duty of care.* http://www.athleticbusiness.com/civil-actions/concussion-lawsuit-examines-school-nurse-s-duty-of-care.html

SHAPE America, Society of Health, and Physical Educators. (2017). Concussion: State legislation and policy. https://www.shapeamerica.org/MemberPortal/standards/guidelines/Concussion/state-policy.aspx

Shannon, R.A. & Gerdes, J.H. (2016). *Developing school health policies, protocols, and procedures? Help please!* [PowerPoint slides]. Presentation at the NASN 2015 Annual Conference, June 24, 2015.

Stone, J.L., Patel, V., & Bailes, J. (2014). The history of neurosurgical treatments of sports concussion. *Neurosurgery, 75,* S3-S23. https://doi.org/10.1227/NEU.0000000000000488

Thorndike, A. (1952). Serious recurrent injuries of athletes; contraindications to further competitive participation. *New England Journal of Medicine, 247*(15), 554-556. https://doi.org/10.1056/NEJM195210092471504

University of Wisconsin-Madison, Health Sciences (2016). *Nursing resources: Standard, guideline, protocol, policy.* Ebling Library. http://researchguides.ebling.library.wisc.edu/c.php?g=293229&p=1953402

Waldron, T. (2013, July). *The NCAA's history with concussions: A timeline.* https://thinkprogress.org/the-ncaas-history-with-concussions-a-timeline-530a8c5af0df#.i0qyx94ns

Zirkel, P.A. & Eagan Brown, B. (2015). K-12 students with concussions: A legal perspective. *The Journal of School Nursing, 31*(2), 99-109. https://doi.org/10.1177/1059840514521465

ADDENDUM

Concussion Law Theories of Liability

Erin D. Gilsbach, Esquire, 2017

Typically, four different types of concussion-related legal actions are brought by parents against school districts. They are:

- **Tort Claims** – most common in states with weak tort claims protections, but these cases can also be brought in states with strong tort claims protection if the parents are alleging that the harm was intentional.
- **Section 504** – While concussions are generally temporary in nature and, therefore, do not qualify under Section 504, each situation must be considered individually. Since concussions can vary widely, Section 504 evaluation teams will consider the length, nature, and degree of a concussion.
- **Section 1983 / State-Created Danger** – Under this theory of law, parents have a very high burden, but some concussion cases have been successful. To prevail, parents need to prove:
  - the harm ultimately caused was foreseeable and fairly direct;
  - a state actor acted with a degree of culpability that shocks the conscience;
  - a relationship between the state and the plaintiff existed; and
  - a state actor affirmatively used his or her authority in a way that created a danger to the citizen, or that rendered the citizen more vulnerable to danger than had the state not acted at all.
- **Concussion Law Compliance** – Many states now have laws setting forth specific obligations for schools with regard to concussion.

Chapter 26

CONSENT FOR HEALTHCARE SERVICES

Marlene S. Garvis, JD, MSN*

DESCRIPTION OF ISSUE

School districts provide both educational and healthcare services to a diverse student population spanning the school-age years. In education, parental rights to consent and make decisions for their minor child generally goes without question. In school health, however, school nurses often navigate challenging legal and ethical dilemmas of parental and minor consent. Some complex situations can put school nurses, administrators, and other staff in the middle of sensitive adolescent and parental debate creating risk for liability over consent for services or treatment. School nurses, school health staff, and administrators must be knowledgeable or know where to find assistance in understanding relevant parental and minor consent laws in their state.

Providing emergency care, conducting school health surveys, communicating with outside providers, administering medication, health care during a disaster, and school health research are issues facing school nurses as they interact with children and their parents. Further, statutes and minor case law in any given state have added to the legal and ethical implications for policy and practice in a school setting. Examples include referral for a myriad of healthcare services, release from school when ill, student photographs, random drug screening, privacy, and confidentiality of counsel with students, and the subsequent documentation and records management. Minors seeking counsel or care for reproductive health issues, sexually transmitted infections, mental health concerns, HIV/AIDs, drug and alcohol treatment, and services can put school nurses, administrators, and other staff in the middle of sensitive parental and minor debate creating risk for liability over consent for services or treatment. While a minor's legal ability to consent to sensitive healthcare services has expanded greatly over the years, consent to healthcare services continues to be fraught with legal and ethical questions regarding minors and their rights to autonomy and decision-making capacity (Guttmacher Institute, 2023). Legally balancing minor autonomy and parental responsibility is a topic of continued debate and, over time, one of the most controversial and challenging issues facing federal, state, and local policymakers. Laws that govern minors' consent belong to the states and can differ widely. (See Guttmacher Institute State-by-State Policy Status Table in Appendix below). More recently, the *Dobbs v. Jackson* U.S. Supreme Court decision (Dobbs v. Jackson Women's Health Organization, 597 U.S., 142 S. Ct. 2228 [2022]) has affected the laws and policies of several states regarding choice for minors.

State laws take into consideration both the status of the minor; such as emancipated minors, those who live apart from parents, those who are married, pregnant, or parenting, as well as the type of care that is given, such as emergency, reproductive services, mental health, or drug/alcohol (AAP, n.d.). It is also necessary for minors and school staff to understand any differences between general medical care and specific clinical services such as contraception, pregnancy, HIV/AIDS, and abortion.

---

* Original author: Lorali Gray, MEd, BSN, RN, NCSN (2017)

BACKGROUND

School nurses deliver health care and nursing services to students within the National Association of School Nurses (NASN) Framework for 21st Century School Nursing Practice (NASN, 2016). Within this Framework, the key principle *Standards of Practice* have two components that directly relate to consent; code of ethics and standards of practice. Ethical care and practice protect parental rights and a minor's dignity, autonomy, rights, and confidentiality within the complex intersection of health, education, and nursing laws (American Nurses Association [ANA], 2015; NASN 2021). Diverse student needs and abilities, such as developmental age, mental capacity, homelessness, poverty, foster placement, age of majority, emancipation, mature minor, or marital status, further complicate consent for care.

Regardless of these complexities, school nurses are accountable and liable for ensuring proper consent from the parent, legal guardian, or student for any medical or nursing care provided at school. They also have an obligation to fully inform the healthcare provider, parent, or student of any unique clinical or environmental issues that could impact the outcome of any care or treatment in the school setting (Davis & Fang, 2023; AAP, 2016b).

To better understand the complexities of parental and minor consent, a literature review was conducted to explore scholarly work for history, definitions, and legal and ethical relevance to school health and nursing.

History of Minor Consent

Early American law regarding minors was based on the viewpoint that children were property and had no rights. Additionally, with the emergence of the legal principle "age of majority," it was believed that anyone under the age of majority (age 16-18 in most states) was not capable of consenting to matters about their health care (Cohn et al., 2001/2005). This was generally understood to mean that parent/guardian(s) were responsible for providing consent for health care for their child until either the age of majority or the child's emancipation. While the law has traditionally considered minors incompetent to consent, most states have implemented laws recognizing adolescents' ability to consent to medical care in specific situations. Examples include court-ordered emancipation, situational emancipation, and very specific types of treatment the adolescent is seeking, such as reproductive care and abortion (Davis & Fang, 2023).

The 1970s hallmarked the legality of abortion largely due to *Roe v. Wade,* 410 U.S. 113, 93 S. Ct. (1973). In 1977 the *Carey v. Populations Services International* decision, 426 U.S. 918, 96 S. Ct. 2621 (1976), allowed the legal sale of contraceptives to minors and supported the privacy of reproductive health services (Guttmacher Institute, 2022). Dobbs v. Jackson Women's Health Organization, 597 U.S., 142 S. Ct. 2228 (2022) changed this dramatically (see Position Statement of AAP, June 24, 2022, Reaffirming adolescents' right to comprehensive, confidential reproductive health care).

Nationally, over the past 30 years, the legal ability of a minor to consent to reproductive care, mental health services, and alcohol and drug treatment significantly expanded. (*See Chapter 15, Minor Consent Laws for an overview of minor consent laws across the United States*). The Dobbs decision overturned the longstanding precedent established in Roe vs. Wade, affirming the constitutional right to abortion. (See Baden & Driver, 2023).

Over time, the development of these laws recognizes that although parental involvement in critical healthcare services to minors is desirable, healthcare trends have shown that minors needing confidential services will forgo important treatment if forced to involve their parents (AAP, 2022b; Advocates for Youth, 2016) Therefore, preventing poor health outcomes and reducing unwanted pregnancies and disease became a big reason for the expansion of a minor's ability to consent for care. In addition, the associated support and protection of a minor's developing autonomy is a fundamental goal of pediatric health care (AAP, n.d.).

Today, minor children are no longer legally considered property. Because some policymakers, healthcare providers, and school nurses do not agree on the level of minor decision-making capacity, the legal environment remains dynamic. There remains a lack of consistency in both the definition and the laws surrounding the complexity of consent, even though it has been more than 800 years since the first recorded age of consent laws (Robertson, 2016). Like all civil liberties, society continues to debate and adjust to changing societal norms. Attention remains to policy and practice when providing health care to minors, balancing parents' responsibility, and the developing autonomy of minors to consent. (*See Chapter 15 for more information on minor consent.*)

Definitions

To better understand the many types of consent and the complex nature of both their application and relevance to school health, nursing services, and decision-making, they must first be defined.

According to AAP (2016c), "Informed consent incorporates three duties: disclosure of information to patients and their surrogates, assessment of patient and surrogate understanding of the information and their capacity for medical decision-making and obtaining informed consent before treatments and interventions" (p.2). In a school setting, this is considered the approval given by a parent or guardian to a school official based on full disclosure of relevant facts by the school official.

Written, informed consent from the parent/guardian is required for student participation in sports, after-school extracurricular activities, the exchange or release of education records, specialized nursing services such as catheterization, physical assessment, physical examinations, other medical treatments, or non-routine services (Pohlman & Schwab, 2005). Providing special education or Section 504 services for students with disabilities also requires informed, voluntary, and written parental consent that can be withdrawn at any time (The Individuals with Disabilities Education Act [IDEA], Section 504 of the Rehabilitation Act of 1973). Most districts have a policy regarding parental informed consent to take and use photographs or video images of students at school. Georgia and New Jersey passed legislation in 2010 and 2011 making it illegal for anyone other than the parent to videotape their child. In January 2023, Florida passed the "Parental Rights in Education Law" which requires parental written permission for the simplest health care i.e., band aids and icepacks.

Implied consent, on the other hand, is assumed rather than stated. When parents send their children to school, they are giving "implied" consent to routine school health and nursing services provided to their children, such as illness and injury care, vision and hearing screening, and individualized healthcare plans (IHPs). Parents are usually informed of these services through published policies, handbooks, websites, and programs and services available to students during the school day. Parental consent is implied when a school nurse makes a home visit or conducts a health history assessment to gather relevant student health information (Michigan School Nurse Guidelines and Resources, 2016). In addition, most states allow the treatment of minors in a life-threatening emergency when a parent or guardian is unavailable to provide consent. In these situations, consent is implied or presumed (Benjamin, 2018).

Finally, it is important to understand the distinction between passive and active consent. *Passive consent* occurs when a person has been informed and is considered to agree unless the parent specifically refuses to allow a student to participate (they "opt-out"). This type of consent is used in schools related to sexual health education and for some student health surveys where all students participate unless the parent opts out their student. The benefits of passive consent are less cost and labor for the district, increased response rates, and a more representative sample of students participating.

Active consent, however, requires written permission and involves a person's willingness to participate by agreeing to a specific service or program, such as student health questionnaires. For example, California Education Code Section 51513 requires parent or guardian to give active consent prior to administering the *California Healthy Kids Survey* to students; while Section 51938(b) allows passive consent for parents to "opt-out" of comprehensive sexual health education and HIV prevention education. In addition, the U.S. Department of Health and Human Services (USDHHS) (n.d.) notes that active consent is common when a parent consents for their student to participate in school health research. Sometimes in school health research, a parent may consent with the student's assent. In this circumstance, assent means voluntary agreement. Conversely, dissent occurs if a parent decides on behalf of the student and the student disagrees with it. (*See Chapter 8 for more information on research in school health.*)

Relevance to School Health/School Nursing

School nurses uphold a protective relationship with the students they serve, acting "in loco parentis," in place of, or standing in for, the parent (Loschiavo, 2023). This is also a traditional legal concept describing the authority of a school official or other individual to act in the place of an absent parent (Cornell University Law School/ Legal Information Institute, 2023b). Given this responsibility, school nurses are often confronted with the question of who can legally provide consent for a student's healthcare treatment and services and under what circumstances. Is it the parent, guardian, or the minor? To address this question, school nurses must consider the student's age, the parental relationship, legal guardianship, the situation requiring consent (e.g., is it a health or safety emergency), and the federal, state, and local laws regarding minors' consent. According to Brous (2019), school nurses need to analyze each individual situation in light of federal, state laws/regulations and their district policies. Legal and risk management consultation may be necessary to manage associated liability concerns. (*See Chapter 17 for more information on parental rights.*)

In determining who can legally provide consent, the student's age will be key in understanding this. Students under the age of majority require parental consent to participate in various school activities and programs. For these children, consent is solely the responsibility of the parent/guardian. Although adolescents, in the eyes of the law, have limited decision-making capacity, there are some exceptions to requiring parental consent. Some states' long-standing exceptions include life-threatening medical emergencies, with no time to obtain parental consent, age of majority, and the mature minor rule. The most common exception allows school nurses and administrators the authority to summon an ambulance in a life-threatening emergency for a child of any age.

Based on Emergency Medical Treatment and Labor Act (EMTALA), the American College of Emergency Physicians state that adolescents can consent to emergency medical care if waiting for parental consent increases the risk of harm. However, if the situation is medically urgent rather than life-threatening, consent from the parent must be obtained (Benjamin, 2018). In some states, child protective services or local law enforcement may have the authority to consent to evaluating and treating any child or youth in cases of suspected abuse or neglect (AAP, 2016; 2022).

Other exceptions occur at the age of majority when a student becomes a legal adult. This means the student can legally perform most tasks reserved for parents, including signing school-related forms, absence notes, medication forms, permission slips to participate in school activities, or permission slips to release themselves from school. This also includes the approval to disclose confidential health records. Additionally, students who have been granted legal emancipation from their parents or guardian at an earlier age have the same rights as a student who has reached the age of majority. An emancipated minor is usually under the age of 18, is living financially independently from his or her parents, is married, or is serving in the military (Davis & Fang, 2023). State laws governing the emancipation of minors and the age of majority can be found in Cornell University Law School's Legal Information Institute (2022).

Additionally, another exception related to student age is the mature minor rule. This rule is an ethically derived legal principle. It acknowledges that the adolescent is developmentally capable of both understanding and has the capacity to consent to specific health services without permission from the parent (Davis & Fang, 2023). These laws describe an age when a minor can legally consent to specific healthcare services such as contraception, abortion, mental health, drug and alcohol, or HIV/AIDs treatment. However, parental consent in most states continues to be required for general medical care even though the minor is considered cognitively "mature" (Davis & Fang, 2023). However, a student might not be legally competent to consent due to mental illness, chronic disability, or institutionalization. School nurses serving these students must be aware that in these circumstances, the parent or guardian must give consent.

Parental relationships are also critical in determining who can provide consent. School nurses interact with many types of families and must be ready to apply legal and ethical practices to situations where parents are separated, divorced, have joint legal custody, or have limited authority per a state court order. In these situations, which parent has the legal authority to consent to treatment must be determined, and how each parent is involved in the decision-making process. (*See Chapter 17, Parental Rights, Custody Agreements and Protection from Abuse Orders.*)

Likewise, parents who are deceased, deported, incarcerated, or debilitated leave some students without any parental care. In other cases, the student's biological parent is no longer in the picture due to neglect, abuse, or trauma (Briner, 2015). This contributes to "unaccompanied youth" described as homeless, runaway, sexually exploited, and trafficking youth. In some states, this also includes a growing population of unaccompanied immigrant minors, the vast majority of whom are escaping violence (Ataiants et al., 2018). The federal McKinney-Vento Homeless Assistance Act of 1987 requires that homeless, unaccompanied children and youth be enrolled in school immediately, even without a parent/guardian. This, however, creates concerns when a school nurse needs to refer these students for healthcare services. They face issues of consent for care, transportation, and payment. (*See Chapter 14 Homeless/McKinney-Vento Homeless Assistance Act*). An example of legislation addressing this concern is Washington State's homeless students-educational outcomes legislation. It states, in part, as follows:

RCW 7.70.065 Informed consent—Persons authorized to provide for patients who do not have capacity—Priority—Unaccompanied homeless minors

> *(1) As allowed by RCW 7.70.06,5 (2) Informed consent for health care, including mental health care, for a patient who is under the age of majority and who is not otherwise authorized to provide informed consent, may be obtained from a person authorized to consent on behalf of such a patient...and*
> *(b)(i) Informed consent for health care on behalf of a patient who is under the age of majority and who is not otherwise authorized to provide informed consent may be obtained from a school nurse, school counselor, or homeless student liaison when:*
> *(A) Consent is necessary for nonemergency, outpatient, primary care services, including physical examinations, vision examinations and eyeglasses, dental examinations, hearing examinations and hearing aids, immunizations, treatments for illnesses and conditions, and routine follow-up care customarily provided by a health care provider in an outpatient setting, excluding elective surgeries.*

Finally, the involvement of grandparents, other caregivers, guardian ad litem, or foster parents can further complicate questions of consent. Depending upon the applicable state law, a natural or biological parent may retain some or all consent rights/authority in cases where a child is placed within the foster system. When a guardian ad-litem is appointed, state law or a judicial decree governs the consent and decision-making authority such guardian may have, if any, and such authority may be dramatically different from case to case. Consent for medical care within this system is often more complicated (Legal Information Institute, Cornell Law School, 2023a).

When considering the relevance of consent to school nursing practice, delivering respectful, equitable, age-appropriate care, and reducing liability is based on an understanding of federal, state, and local law. While many of these laws do not specifically address consent in school settings, they are applicable and must be considered in developing school district policies and practices.

IMPLICATIONS FOR SCHOOL NURSE PRACTICE

Challenges

The specialty of school nursing has unique legal and ethical challenges related to parental consent, minor consent, and confidentiality of adolescent health care. School nurses interact with families, adolescent populations, and individual students in delivering multiple, complex, controversial healthcare services and consultation; interactions that also require communication and relationships with parents, school administrators, and other healthcare professionals. It can be difficult for school nurses to understand and stay current on health and education law, nursing practice standards, and the scope of nursing practice in a school setting, let alone communicate the intricacies and application of minor consent laws to parents and school administrators.

School nurses often find themselves in the middle of questions and concerns about consent for care. There are many examples:

- active versus passive consent,
- pregnancy testing,
- drug and toxicology screening at school,
- students refusing to take prescribed medication,
- Do Not Attempt to Resuscitate orders (DNAR),
- photographs of child abuse, rashes or injuries,
- parents refusing to sign consent for the nurse to communicate with a healthcare provider,
- school health research,
- care requested by a parent that does not meet standards of nursing practice,
- sexual health and alcohol and drug treatment referrals,
- mental health services, and
- releasing students from the health room.

Other than general first aid, most health care is implemented per healthcare provider order, parental input, or a nursing care plan. COVID-19 has increased the challenges for school nurses (NASN,2023).

Challenges of consent also go hand-in-hand with privacy, confidentiality, and the subsequent documentation of care. This includes exchanging or releasing records to and from outside healthcare providers and their protection under state or federal law. To minimize these challenges, school nurses must understand practice implications and potential unintended consequences of their decisions on students' health and well-being. (*See Chapter 22 for more information on parental refusal and non-responsiveness.*)

Legal Implications

School nurses practice independently in a complex legal environment. This is due in part to the isolation from other healthcare professionals, the wide variety of job responsibilities, and the conflict between education law and policy that guide school districts and health law and policy that guide nursing practice. Additionally, as seen during the 2019 COVID-19 pandemic, many conflicts between federal, state, and local mandates result in differing school health policy standards and requirements across the country (AAP, 2016a; 2022a).

Both law and legal principles impact care and consultation related to consent and nursing practice. According to Loschiavo (2023), three classifications of law have legal implications for school nurses: criminal, civil, and administrative law.

- Criminal law provides evidence of a crime. Examples of criminal law related to school nursing include fraudulently tampering with records, practicing without a license, using illegal drugs, diverting drugs, and failing to report suspected child neglect or abuse.

- <u>Civil law</u> affects the legal status of individuals or groups. It addresses an alleged offense such as a breach of duty or confidentiality, negligence, or violation of a minor's right to consent. The Family Educational Rights and Privacy Act (FERPA) governs school records, and the Health Insurance Portability and Accountability Act (HIPAA) that protects the confidentiality of health records are examples of civil law.

- <u>Administrative law</u> determines the regulation, interpretation, and enforcement of state licensing and related laws. State boards of nursing, and administrative bodies are responsible for regulating nursing practice and have the authority to enforce nurse practice laws when there is a violation, such as the failure to meet state standards of nursing practice.

Nurses must be aware of three legal principles related to consent: liability, negligence, and malpractice. (*See Chapter 2 for more information on malpractice.*)

Day-to-day decisions school nurses make related to consent not only have legal and ethical consequences for school nursing practice, but they may also result in poor health outcomes for the minor, such as delayed emergency medical care or treatment and consultation for a sexually transmitted infection, mental illness, substance abuse, or abortion. An example of this decision-making is *Arnold v. Board of Education of Escambia County*, Alabama, 754 F. Supp 853 (S.D. Ala. 1990):

> In *Arnold, a* civil rights action was brought against the school counselor, vice-principal, and school board, alleging that the student involved had been coerced into having an abortion.

> While the final ruling favored the school and that the student made her own decision regarding having an abortion, the case highlights the legal and ethical challenges that may arise related to consent.

Strategies and Solutions

School nurses must be aware of the potential liability risk inherent in their role in the school setting. Solutions to avoid legal and ethical pitfalls surrounding consent are not always clear or direct. However, to minimize the risk, there are a number of proactive strategies that school nurses can implement:

- <u>Be informed of federal, state, and local laws</u>. School nurses have an ethical responsibility to be aware of the federal, state, and local laws regarding parental consent, minor consent, and nursing standards in the state where they practice and how they apply to public or private school systems. Given the conflict that can often occur between the provisions of these laws, it is critical that school nurses communicate concerns in writing to their school administrators and proper legal authorities. This may include requesting legal interpretation by a state attorney general or an attorney selected by the nurse.

- <u>Be knowledgeable of the district's policies and procedures</u>. Understanding school district policies and procedures that guide school health services and nursing care are important risk management tools and assist in providing safe care (NASN, 2022). Policies can cover many school practices that include or overlap with consent concerns. Examples include student privacy and searches, the confidentiality of health records, emergency treatment, photographing or videotaping students, sharing student information, students' rights and responsibilities, and pregnant and parenting teens. School district policies and procedures should be reviewed regularly to stay current. They generally reflect legal mandates, so compliance and alignment with nursing practice are imperative. (*See Chapter 19, Developing School Health Policies for more information.*)

- Practice within the scope of the nursing license and job description. It is important to practice within the scope of both a nursing license and school district job description, keeping both current and reflective of the school nurse's work and caseload. While a nursing license may encompass a broad range of professional responsibilities, a job description could be more restrictive within the school setting. Job descriptions, based on school nursing standards, are considered a local standard of care by courts of law to which a school nurse would be held accountable in a civil breach of duty case (Resha, 2019). Job descriptions may also include statements such as "other duties as assigned." This does not mean that nurses can take direction to provide services outside their scope of practice. Brent (2013) states that school nurses must adhere to state nursing practice laws regardless of guidance or "permission" from well-meaning healthcare providers or school administrators to do otherwise to avoid professional liability. Nurses, who are employed by outside agencies to provide services in schools, must comply with their employer's and the district's policies, all while functioning within their scope of nursing practice (Shannon & Minchella, 2015).

- Seek guidance from leaders and experts in school nursing. State education departments often have a school health services and nursing consultant that can provide guidance, resources, and support in resolving legal and ethical dilemmas. In addition, joining a professional state school nurse organization can provide opportunities for education, collegial support, and guidance related to standards of care and the need for school nurses to consider individual liability insurance coverage. (*See Chapter 1 for more information on professional licensure.*)

- Attend professional development opportunities. State education and nursing laws and regulations can be ever-changing. Minor consent laws can undergo ongoing scrutiny with likely, periodic revisions critical to school nursing practice. School nurses must stay up-to-date on these changes to ensure their practice reflects current law, practice, and knowledge. This can be accomplished by attending appropriate professional development opportunities, collaborating with local American Academy of Pediatrics chapters, and consulting with district legal counsel and risk management partners (NASN, 2022).

- Build relationships with students and families. Building relationships with students and families to gain trust and respect is important. Involve adolescents in planning their care, allowing autonomy and participation in decision-making within the law, school district policy, and developmental ability. Where language barriers exist, use a trained medical interpreter to obtain informed consent (AAP, 2016, 2022b).

- Obtain adequate consent. Obtaining adequate consent from the appropriate person and the subsequent documentation of that consent is essential to support decisions made in providing nursing care. In the case of minor consent, each situation needs to be assessed individually and will likely need legal counsel and risk management guidance to determine the definition of a minor within each state's laws and regulations. Coleman-Lambelet & Rosskopf (2013) also note that healthcare providers must ensure the safekeeping of records pertaining to minor maturity and the consent process in case of litigation.

- <u>Document appropriately and maintain confidentiality.</u> Accurately and promptly document all care and services rendered and the student's response to the care and services. This documentation demonstrates that standards of practice were followed. Documentation includes all attempts and communications to contact parent/guardian(s), school administrators, and healthcare providers, as well as unsafe practices. Furthermore, it is critical to maintain confidentiality in both the provision of care and the subsequent documentation. (*See Chapter 9 for more information on documentation.*)

- <u>Use ethical practices when conducting school health research</u>. Regarding school research, ethicists consider students a vulnerable population (Gordon, 2020). If school health services research is conducted, using ethical protocols per the standards and requirements of an Institutional Research Board (IRB) will safeguard participating students and the nurse's liability. Together with proper documentation of consent, overall risk will be decreased. (*See Chapter 8 for more information on research in school health.*)

The best protection against liability, according to Brous (2019), is to be knowledgeable about and adhere to relevant federal, state, and local laws and regulations, have a systematic method to perform job functions, and have a system of documenting that reflects the work performed.

CONCLUSION

It is clear from the literature and case law that consent in the school setting is multifaceted and must be considered individually in light of federal and state law, nursing regulations, nursing standards, and related school district policies and procedures.

Due to the complexities of health and education law and the subsequent implications for liability, school nurses and other district staff must be informed about federal, state, and local laws that impact parental and minor consent in the school setting. In these situations, the district and the school nurse should consult their legal counsel and risk management team for guidance as the day-to-day practice may be ahead of the law; however, many times, there are no clear answers. A growing body of literature suggests that to make sound decisions, school districts should:

- promote school nurse professional development
- use risk management strategies
- implement appropriate policies and procedures
- focus on student needs
- promote good relationships with both students and parents;
- understand ethical and legal parameters of school nursing practice
- know how, where, and when to request and access assistance

School nurses who are well-informed regarding parental and minor consent can provide leadership to safeguard student health. By doing so, they are practicing within their scope and standards and can help protect against the school district and school nurse liability (NASN, 2022). Minimizing risk also involves adhering to professional standards of practice and working with district administrators to develop sound policies and procedures. The best protection for school nurses is information, communication, and documentation.

RESOURCES

American Bar Association Center on Children and the Law
ABA Center on Children and the Law
1050 Connecticut Ave NW, Suite 400
Washington, D.C. 20036
Phone: 202-662-1740; 202-662-1000
Fax: 202-662-1755
ctrchildlaw@americanbar.org

Protects children's rights through advocacy, reform, policy, research, evaluation, training, and legal practice.

National Center for Youth Law
Financial Center Building
1212 Broadway, Suite 600
Oakland, CA 94612
Phone: 510- 835-8098
Fax: 510-835-8099
info@youthlaw.org

Non-profit law firm that provides pro-bono support and resources to legal services programs, organizations, community groups and healthcare professionals representing low-income children.

Office for Civil Rights
U.S. Department of Health and Human Services
200 Independence Avenue, SW
Room 509F, HHH Building
Washington, D.C. 20201
Toll-free: (800) 368-1019
TDD toll-free: (800) 537-7697
OCRPrivacy@hhs.gov

Protects fundamental non-discrimination and health information privacy rights by educating communities and investigating civil rights and patient health and safety complaints.

MINOR CONSENT LAWS-STATE BY STATE

Resources

State Laws on Minor Consent for Routine Medical Care. SchoolHouse Connection (January 2023). https://schoolhouseconnection.org

State-by-State Variability in Adolescent Privacy Laws. American Academy of Pediatrics (June, 2022). https://www.aap.org

State Laws that Enable a Minor to Provide Informed Consent to Receive HIV and STD Services. Centers for Disease Control and Prevention (October 2022). https://cdc.gov

Case Law

Arnold v. Board of Education of Escambia County Alabama, 754 F. Supp 853 (S.D. Ala. 1990)

Cales v. Howell Public Schools, 635 F. Supp. 454 (E.D. Mich. 1985)

Carey v. Populations Services International decision, 426 U.S. 918, 96 S. Ct. 2621 (1976)

Curtis v. School Committee of Falmouth, 652 N.E. 2d 580 (Mass. 1995)

Dobbs v. Jackson Women's Health Organization, 597 U.S. _, 142 S. Ct. 2228 (2022)

Little v. Little, 576 S.W.2d 493 (Tex. Ct. Civ. App. 1979)

Moule v. Paradise Valley Unified Sch. Dist., 863 F. Supp. 1098 (D. Ariz. 1994)

Odenheim v. Carlstadt-East Rutherford Reg. Sch. Dist., 510 A.2d 709 (N.J. Super. Ct. 1985)

Ohio v. Akron Center, 497 U.S. 502, 110 S. Ct. 2972, (1990)

Planned Parenthood v. Casey, 505 U.S. 833, 112 S. Ct. 2791 (1992)

Roe v. Wade, 410 U.S. 113, 93 S. Ct. (1973)

Vernonia School District 47J v. Acton, 515 U.S. 646, 115 S. Ct. 2386 (1995)

REFERENCES

Ataiants, J., Cohen, C., Riley, A.H., Tellez Lieberman, J., Reidy, M.C., & Chilton, M. (2018). Unaccompanied children at the United States border, a Human Rights Crisis that can be addressed with policy change. Journal of Immigrant Minor Health. doi: 10.1007/s10903-017-0577-5. https://www.ncbi.nlm.nih.gov/pmc/articles/PMC5805654/

American Academy of Pediatrics. (n.d.). *Confidentiality laws tip sheet*. Retrieved 8-3-23 from https://downloads.aap.org/AAP/PDF/Foster%20Care/Confidentiality_Laws.pdf

American Academy of Pediatrics, Council on School Health. (2016a). *School health: Policy and practice,* (7th ed., p.3). https://shop.aap.org/school-health-policy-and-practice-7th-edition-paperback/

American Academy of Pediatrics, Council on School Health. (2016b). Role of the school nurse in providing school health services. https://doi.org/10.1542/peds.2016-0852

American Academy of Pediatrics, Committee on Bioethics. (2016c). Informed consent in decision-making in pediatric practice. Pediatrics, *138*(2), e20161484. https://doi.org/10.1542/peds.2016-1484

American Academy of Pediatrics. (2022a). *COVID-19 guidance for safe schools and promotion of in-person learning*. https://www.aap.org/en/pages/2019-novel-coronavirus-covid-19-infections/clinical-guidance/covid-19-planning-considerations-return-to-in-person-education-in-schools/

American Academy of Pediatrics. (2022b, June, 24). *AAP supports adolescents' right to comprehensive, confidential reproductive health care*. https://www.aap.org/en/news-room/news-releases/aap/2022/aap-supports-adolescents-right-to-comprehensive-confidential-reproductive-health-care/

American Nurses Association (ANA). (2015). *Code of ethics for nurses with interpretive statements*. https://www.nursingworld.org/codeofethics

Baden, K. & Driver, J. (2023). *The state abortion policy landscape one year post-Roe*. Guttmacher Institute. https://www.guttmacher.org/2023/06/state-abortion-policy-landscape-one-year-post-roe

Benjamin, L. (2018). Handling unaccompanied minors in the emergency department. Physician's Weekly, December 16, 2018). https://www.physiciansweekly.com/handling-unaccompanied-minors-in-the-emergency-department/

Brent, N. J. (2013). The state nurse practice act, nursing ethics and school nursing practice. *Avoiding Professional Liability Bulletin*. https://cphins.com/the-state-nurse-practice-act-nursing-ethics-and-school-nursing-practice/

Briner, L. (2015). *Responding to sexual exploitation and trafficking of youth modules*. Center for Children and Youth Justice. https://ccyj.org/wp-content/uploads/2019/11/Responding-to-the-Sexual-Exploitation-and-Trafficking-of-Youth-1.pdf

Brous, E. (2019). The law and school nursing practice. In J. Selekman, R. Adair Shannon, & C. F. Yonkaitis (Eds.), *School Nursing: A Comprehensive Text* (3rd ed., pp. 136–153). F.A. Davis Company.

Cohn, S.D., Gelfman, M. H. B., & Schwab, N.C. (2005). Adolescent issues and rights of minors. In N.C. Schwab & M.H.B. Gelfman (Eds.), *Legal issues in school health services* (pp. 231-260). Sunrise River Press.

Coleman-Lambelet, D. & Rosoff, P.M. (2013). The legal authority of mature minors to consent to general medical treatment. *Pediatrics, 131*(4), 786-793. https://doi.org/10.1542/peds.2012-2470

Cornell University Law School/ Legal Information Institute. (2022). *Emancipation of minors' laws*. Retrieved 8-8-23 from https://www.law.cornell.edu/wex/table_emancipation

Cornell University Law School/Legal Information Institute (2023a). Guardian ad litem. Retrieved on 8-8-23 from https://www.law.cornell.edu/wex/guardian_ad_litem

Cornell University Law School/ Legal Information Institute. (2023b). *In loco parentis*. Retrieved 8-8-23 from https://www.law.cornell.edu/wex/in_loco_parentis

Davis, M., & Fang, A. (2023, May 1). *Emancipated minor*. StatPearls Publishing. https://www.ncbi.nlm.nih.gov/books/NBK554594/

Gordon, B. (2020). Vulnerability in research: Basic ethical concepts and general approach to review. *The Oschner Journal, 20*(1), 34–38. https//doi.org/10.31486/toj.19.0079

Guttmacher Institute. (2022). *Access to comprehensive reproductive health care is an adolescent health issue*. https://www.guttmacher.org/article/2022/11/access-comprehensive-reproductive-health-care-adolescent-health-issue

Guttmacher Institute. (2023). An overview of consent to reproductive health services by young people. https://www.guttmacher.org/state-policy/explore/overview-minors-consent-law

Individuals with Disabilities Education Act, 20 U.S.C. § 1400 *et seq.*, 34 C.F.R. § 300.1 *et seq.*

Loschiavo, J. (2023). *Fast facts for the school nurse (4h ed.).* Springer Publishing Company, LLC.

Michigan School Nurse Guidelines and Resources. (2016). *The school nurse's role in protecting and understanding informed and minor consent in the school setting.* http://nursingnetwork-groupdata.s3.amazonaws.com/NASN/Michigan_ ASN/Guideline_Resources/Quality%20Improvement/School%20Nurses%20role%20in%20protecting%20and%20 understanding%20minorconsent%2009.20.16.pdf

McKinney–Vento Homeless Assistance Act of 1987 (Pub. L. 100-77, July 22, 1987, 101 Stat. 482), 42 U.S. Code § 11301.

National Association of School Nurses. (2016). Framework for 21st century school nursing practice. *NASN School Nurse, 30*(4), 218-231. https://doi.org/10.1177/1942602X15589559

National Association of School Nurses. (2021). *School nursing: Code of ethics.* https://www.nasn.org/nasn-resources/resources-by-topic/codeofethics

National Association of School Nurses. (2022). *School nursing: Scope and standards of practice* (4th ed.), Author.

National Association of School Nurses. (2023). The COVID-19 pandemic and chronic health conditions - the school nurse role in promoting health equity. https://learn.nasn.org/courses/29717#

Pohlman, K., & Schwab, N. (2001). Consent and release. *The Journal of School Nursing, 17*(3), 162-165.   https://doi. org/10.1177/10598405010170030801

Resha, C.A. (2019). Standards of school nursing practice. In J. Selekman, R. Adair Shannon, & C. F. Yonkaitis (Eds.), *School Nursing: A Comprehensive Text* (3rd ed., pp. 31-50). F.A. Davis Company

Robertson, S. (2016). Age of consent laws in children and youth in history. https://chnm.gmu.edu/cyh/teaching-_modules/230

Section 504 of the Rehabilitation Act of 1973, 29 U.S.C. § 794, 34 C.F.R. § 104.1 *et seq.*

Shannon, R.A., & Minchella, L. (2015). *Students requiring personal nursing care in school: Nursing care models and a checklist for school nurses.* https://doi.org/10.1177/1942602X15569781

U.S. Department of Health & Human Services. (n.d.). *informed consent FAQS.* Retrieved 8-4-23 from https://www. hhs.gov/ohrp/regulations-and-policy/guidance/faq/informed-consent/index.html"https://www.hhs.gov/ohrp/ regulations-and-policy/guidance/faq/informed-consent/index.html

Washington State. (2022). RCW 7.70.065.Informed consent—Persons authorized to provide for patients who do not have capacity—Priority—Unaccompanied homeless minors. 2021 c 270. https://app.leg.wa.gov/rcw/default. aspx?cite=7.70.065

Minors May Consent to:

STATE	CONTRACEPTIVE SERVICES	STI SERVICES	PRENATAL CARE	ADOPTION	MEDICAL CARE FOR MINOR'S CHILD	ABORTION SERVICES
Alabama	All[+]	All[*]	All	All	All	Parental Consent
Alaska	All	All	All		All	▼ (Parental Notice)
Arizona	All	All		All		Parental Consent
Arkansas	All	All[*]	All		All	Parental Consent
California	All	All	All	All		▼ (Parental Consent)
Colorado	All	All	All	All	All	Parental Notice
Connecticut	Some	All		Legal counsel	All	All
Delaware	All[*]	All[*]	All[*]	All	All	Parental Notice[‡]
Dist. of Columbia	All	All	All	All	All	All
Florida	Some	All	All		All	Parental Consent and Notice
Georgia	All	All[*]	All	All	All	Parental Notice
Hawaii	All[*,+]	All[*,+]	All[*,+]	All		
Idaho	All	All[+]	All	All	All	Parental Consent
Illinois	Some	All[*]	All	All	All	
Indiana	Some	All		All		Parental Consent
Iowa	All	All				Parental Notice
Kansas	Some	All[*]	Some	All	All	Parental Consent
Kentucky	All[*]	All[*]	All[*]	Legal counsel	All	Parental Consent
Louisiana	Some	All[*]		Parental consent	All	Parental Consent
Maine	All*	All*	All*			All
Maryland	All[*]	All[*]	All[*]	All	All	Parental Notice
Massachusetts	All	All	All		All	Parental Consent
Michigan	Some	All[*]	All[*]	Parental consent	All	Parental Consent
Minnesota	All[*]	All[*]	All[*]	Parental consent	All	
Mississippi	Some	All	All	All	All	Parental Consent
Missouri	Some	All[*]	All[*]	Legal counsel	All	Parental Consent
Montana	All[*]	All[*]	All[*]	Legal counsel	All	Parental Notice[‡]
Nebraska	Some	All				Parental Consent
Nevada	Some	All	Some	All	All	▼ (Parental Notice)

CONSENT FOR HEALTHCARE SERVICES

STATE	CONTRACEPTIVE SERVICES	STI SERVICES	PRENATAL CARE	ADOPTION	MEDICAL CARE FOR MINOR'S CHILD	ABORTION SERVICES
New Hampshire	Some	All[†]	Some	All[Ω]		Parental Notice
New Jersey	Some[†]	All[*,β]	All[*]	All	All	▼ (Parental Notice)
New Mexico	All	All	All	All		▼ (Parental Consent)
New York	All	All	All	All	All	
North Carolina	All	All	All			Parental Consent
North Dakota		All[†]	ξ[*]	All		Parental Consent
Ohio		All		All		Parental Consent
Oklahoma	Some	All[*]	All[*]	All[†]	All	Parental Consent and Notice
Oregon	All[*]	All	All[*,‡]			
Pennsylvania	All[†]	All	All	Parental notice	All	Parental Consent
Rhode Island		All		Parental consent	All	Parental Consent
South Carolina	All	All	All	All	All	Parental Consent[‡]
South Dakota	Some	All				Parental Notice
Tennessee	All	All	All	All	All	Parental Consent
Texas	Some	All[*]	All[*]			Parental Consent and Notice
Utah	Some	All	All	All	All	Parental Consent and Notice
Vermont	Some	All		All		
Virginia	All	All	All	All	All	Parental Consent and Notice
Washington	All	All[†]	All	Legal counsel		
West Virginia	Some	All	Some	All		Parental Notice
Wisconsin		All				Parental Consent
Wyoming	All	All		All		Parental Consent and Notice
TOTAL	27+DC	50+DC	33+DC	28+DC	30+DC	2+DC

Notes: "All" applies to all individuals or to those at a specified age (such as 12 or 14) and older. "Some" applies to specified categories of young people (those who have a health issue, or are married, pregnant, considered mature). Totals include only those states that allow all individuals to consent.

▼ Permanently enjoined by court order; law not in effect.

* Physicians may, but are not required to, inform the young person's parents.

† Applies to individuals 14 and older. Hawaii allows individuals aged 14 and older to consent to STI care and allows all individuals, regardless of age, to consent to HIV/AIDS care.

‡ The abortion law in Delaware and Montana applies to individuals younger than 16. Oregon's prenatal care law applies to individuals at least 15 years old. South Carolina's abortion law applies to those younger than 17.

Ω A court may require parental consent.

β New Jersey allows all individuals, regardless of age, to consent to STI care and allows individuals aged 13 or older to consent to HIV/AIDS care.

ξ Individuals younger than 18 may consent to prenatal care in the first trimester and the first visit after the first trimester. Parental consent required for all other visits.

Source: Guttmacher Institute, An overview of minors' consent law, *State Laws and Policies (as of June 1, 2023),* 2023. Retrieved 8-3-23 from https://www.guttmacher.org/state-policy/explore/overview-minors-consent-law.

Chapter 27

MANAGEMENT OF DIABETES

Linda Davis-Alldritt, MA, BSN, RN, FNASN, FASHA

DESCRIPTION OF ISSUE

Diabetes management at school and during school-sponsored activities requires education, training, and preparation to keep students healthy and safe. Given the increasing incidence and prevalence of type 1 and type 2 diabetes in school-age children and youth, it is increasingly likely that most, if not all, school nurses will care for students who have diabetes at some point in their careers. School nurses are key to coordinating care and helping students effectively and safely manage their diabetes at school (Breneman et al., 2015). The school nurse is usually the lead staff member in the school setting responsible for coordinating and providing care for students with diabetes (Centers for Disease Control and Prevention [CDC], 2022c). Consequently, school nurses must use all available tools at their disposal and become familiar with the overarching federal and state laws, district policies, best practices, and nursing standards of care for students with diabetes.

Diabetes is one of the most common chronic childhood diseases. In 2019, approximately 283,000 of all people under the age of 20 years had either type 1 (244,000 youth) or type 2 (39,000 youth), according to the CDC (2022a). This means that about one of every 300 students in the United States has diabetes. While the precise number of school-age children with type 2 diabetes is uncertain, the prevalence of type 2 in this age group is increasing (CDC, 2022a). Globally, and in the United States, the incidence of both type 1 and type 2 diabetes in people under 20 years of age is increasing (World Health Organization [WHO], 2022; CDC, 2021).

In diabetes, blood glucose levels are above normal because the body cannot effectively use and store glucose. There are three main types of diabetes: type 1, formerly referred to as juvenile diabetes or insulin-dependent diabetes; type 2, which used to be called adult-onset diabetes or non-insulin-dependent diabetes; and gestational diabetes (CDC, 2022c).

Effective management of diabetes requires maintaining blood glucose levels within the individual's target range. Consequently, diabetes must be managed continuously, 24 hours a day, seven days a week. For school-age children and adolescents, the ongoing diabetes treatment regimen impacts the student's daily schedule and, if needed accommodations are not made, may affect the student's ability to have equal access to all school-related activities. Blood glucose levels outside the target range result from an imbalance between food, activity, medication, and illness and may result in hypoglycemia or hyperglycemia. Hypoglycemia, low blood glucose level, must be treated immediately and, if untreated, will quickly progress and can be fatal. Hyperglycemia, a high blood glucose level, is associated with diabetic ketoacidosis (DKA), and if untreated, over time, can lead to long-term complications, including death.

While hyperglycemia and hypoglycemia can affect cognitive functioning and, as a result, school performance, even small fluctuations in blood glucose levels can impact the student's concentration, learning ability, ability to provide self-care, and perform daily living tasks, including walking, talking, and eating. For students with diabetes to be safe at school and fully participate in all school activities, effective diabetes care at school is essential (National Institute of Health: National Institute of Diabetes and Digestive and Kidney Diseases, 2020). Unfortunately, despite federal and state laws guaranteeing protections for all students with disabilities, including diabetes, some students with diabetes continue to be denied services and support at school (Jackson et al., 2015; Schwartz et al., 2010).

BACKGROUND

Based on 2019 data, an estimated 18,291 people under 20 years are newly diagnosed with type 1 diabetes each year, and 5,758 children and adolescents aged 10 to 19 years are annually diagnosed with type 2 diabetes (CDC, 2022a). The incidence of type 1 and type 2 diabetes has increased dramatically in people under age 20 in the United States. Between 2001 and 2017, the number of people in this age group with type 1 grew by 45 percent, and those with type 2 increased by 95 percent. In this age group, the new diagnosis of type 1 was highest for white and black children and youth, and the new diagnosis of type 2 was highest for black and Hispanic children and youth (CDC, 2021). Although there are many theories as to why type 1 diabetes is increasing worldwide, to date, none of the theories have been proven, and researchers have yet to determine what triggers the immune system to attack the beta cells in the pancreas. Researchers believe that the cause of type 1 diabetes is a combination of as-yet-unknown environmental and genetic factors (Zorena et al., 2022). Currently, there is no cure for type 1 diabetes. Treatment for type 1 diabetes includes taking insulin, monitoring blood glucose levels, eating healthy foods, counting carbohydrates, exercising regularly, and maintaining a healthy weight (American Diabetes Association [ADA], 2022).

With increasing obesity rates in children and adolescents, type 2 diabetes is becoming more common among people under 20, particularly minorities (CDC, 2021; National Institutes of Health, 2017). In the U.S., type 2 diabetes is most common among Native Americans, African Americans, Hispanic Americans, and Asian Americans/Pacific Islanders (CDC,2022a). Incidence rates for type 2 diabetes are higher among individuals aged 10–19 years than in younger children (CDC, 2022a). A progressive disease, type 2 diabetes, usually begins with insulin resistance. Overweight and obesity are clear risk factors for type 2 diabetes. Achieving and maintaining a healthy weight is essential to managing type 2 diabetes. This includes lifestyle changes in eating habits and increasing physical activity levels. Making healthy food choices and getting regular exercise are critical to success. Children and teens with type 2 diabetes may also take medication (CDC, 2022c).

Older teens and teens who are pregnant or parenting should be aware that diabetes can develop during pregnancy. This type of diabetes is called gestational diabetes and is caused by hormones present during pregnancy. Pregnancy hormones can cause a shortage of insulin, called insulin resistance. Generally, gestational diabetes is self-limiting, such that once the baby is born, this type of diabetes usually goes away. However, a woman who has had gestational diabetes has an increased risk of developing diabetes as she gets older. Additionally, the baby of this pregnancy is at increased risk for developing obesity and type 2 diabetes, thus leading to increases in both the incidence and prevalence of that disease. Effective management of gestational diabetes includes monitoring blood glucose levels, eating a healthy diet, regular physical activity, and taking medication, if needed, to control blood glucose levels (CDC, 2022c; Mayo Clinic, 2022).

Regardless of the type of diabetes the student has, thanks to federal and state laws guaranteeing the right of all students to attend school and participate fully and safely in all school-sponsored activities, most of these young people are in school. To be most successful, maximize their school experience, and maintain blood glucose control, they need assistance from trained, knowledgeable staff and a safe school environment (American Association of Diabetes Educators, 2016; ADA, 2022). Each student with diabetes lives with the constant challenge of managing and adapting to this chronic disease that impacts many, if not all, parts of their being. Fortunately, most students with diabetes are treated fairly, with respect, and receive the care and accommodations they are rightfully entitled to at school. Unfortunately, some students with diabetes experience discrimination due to their condition, violation of their rights to proper care and full inclusion, and their safety and health put at risk.

IMPLICATIONS FOR SCHOOL NURSE PRACTICE

To optimize academic achievement, safety, and long-term health for students with diabetes, appropriate care at school is vital (Jackson et al., 2015). The results of the Diabetes Control and Complications Trial identified a significant link between blood glucose control and subsequent diabetes complications, with tight or glycemic control reducing the complication risk. Achieving glycemic control requires frequent blood glucose checks, monitoring nutrition intake, adherence to a medication regimen requiring multiple daily insulin injections or the use of an infusion pump, and regular physical activity (Jackson et al., 2015; Wyckoff, 2019). Failing to provide reasonable, as well as necessary, health and safety accommodations may have legal consequences for the school district and possibly for the school nurse (Zirkel et al., 2012). When school staff are not adequately trained and supervised to respond to student health needs safely and effectively in both emergent and non-emergent situations, there is a risk of increased liability for the school district and school nurse, as well as increased morbidity and possibly mortality (Shannon & Kubelka, 2013a & b), for the student with diabetes.

Safe and effective care of students with diabetes, based on the nursing process, requires assessment, planning, coordination of interventions, and evaluation by the school nurse (NASN, 2022a). When the student with diabetes enters school, they will need an individualized healthcare plan (IHP) and an emergency care plan (ECP) developed by the school nurse in collaboration with the student and family, and based on the healthcare provider orders or diabetes medical management plan (DMMP). The IHP is both a clinical practice document and an administrative document grounded in the nursing process (NASN, 2020). Depending on the student's needs, the school nurse should provide input to an evaluation for either special education or Section 504 accommodations. As outlined in the IHP and DMMP, the school nurse helps the student to self-manage their diabetes and eventually take on increasingly more responsibility for self-care (Jackson et al., 2015; Jackson & Albanese-O'Neill, 2016; NASN, 2020). At the same time, staff must be trained to provide the student with emergency care when needed and non-emergent care, depending on state laws (ADA, 2022).

Advocating for Compliance with Federal and State Laws, and District Policies

Three federal laws protect the rights of school-age children with disabilities, which includes diabetes, to have the care they need while at school. These laws include:

- Section 504 of the Rehabilitation Act (1973) (Section 504);
- The Education for All Handicapped Children Act (1975) reauthorized in 2004 as the Individuals with Disabilities Education Improvement Act (IDEIA) of 2004; and
- The Americans with Disabilities Act (ADA) (1990) was reauthorized in 2008 as the ADA Amendments Act (ADAAA) of 2008.

These three laws protect individuals with disabilities from exclusion and discriminatory treatment at school, work, and in the community (Disability Rights Education & Defense Fund, 2016). Under these laws, schools are required to provide services and reasonably accommodate the special needs of students with diabetes and other disabilities so that these students have the same access to educational opportunities as all other children (Jackson et al., 2015; Jacquez et al., 2008). These laws also require that students with diabetes be individually assessed and that any identified needed accommodations should be documented in writing in either a Section 504 Plan, an Individualized Education Program (IEP) if the child has additional educational needs, or other written accommodations plans (Jackson et al., 2015). Under these federal and corresponding state laws, and based on evaluation results, it is intended that the needs of students with diabetes and other disabilities be provided at the student's usual school with as minimal disruption as possible to the school and the student while permitting the student to have full participation in all school activities (Jackson et al., 2015; Jackson, & Albanese-O'Neill, 2016).

While all states have laws corresponding to the three overarching federal laws, many states have passed diabetes-specific laws permitting unlicensed school personnel to provide care to students with diabetes. In these states, to ensure safe and effective care for children with diabetes, school nurses should train and clinically supervise such personnel. Some state laws prohibit unlicensed non-nursing school personnel from administering medications, particularly injectable medications, such as insulin and glucagon. Despite such state laws, school districts still must comply with federal requirements and provide students with diabetes-appropriate and necessary health services in order for those students to be safe and to fully participate in the classroom and all school-sponsored programs and activities, such as field trips, recess, sports, detention, school parties, school dances, and before-school and after-school programs and clubs (Jackson et al., 2015).

In addition to the requirement to adhere to federal and state laws, it is critical that school districts adopt policies and regulations for diabetes care at schools that align with the state's nurse practice act (NPA) and national diabetes management standards and guidelines. School administrators responsible for reviewing and developing district policies for board of education adoption are often unfamiliar with laws and best practices relating to nursing practice, the delegation of care tasks, and diabetes management. The standard of care is a significant factor, along with relevant laws, including the state NPA, expert testimony, and professional organization position statements, used by the courts in professional liability cases (Brous, 2019; Pohlman, 2005). Consequently, it is imperative that school nurses be included as team members on district policy development committees when school healthcare decisions are being made (NASN, 2022b). *(Please see Chapter 13 for more information on Education Laws for Children with Disabilities).*

Identifying and Serving Children with Diabetes

The IDEIA (2004) requires school districts to find and assess all previously unidentified students with disabilities, including diabetes, who may be eligible for special education services. This requirement is known as 'child find.' The requirement applies to all children and youth through age 21 who live within a state. Additionally, in response to the broadening of ADA 2008, and subsequent Office of Civil Rights (OCR) complaints, Zirkel et al. (2012) recommend screening all students with IHPs for Section 504 eligibility in compliance with the school district's "child find" obligations. If the screening results indicate the school nurse should recommend further evaluation by the Section 504 team. School nurses have an important role in the identification, screening, and evaluation process for "child find" (Zirkel et al., 2012).

Once students are identified as having diabetes, it is important to inform the family about their role in helping the school to help their child with diabetes remain safe and healthy at school. The 2022 ADA's *Helping the Student with Diabetes Succeed: A Guide for School Personnel* provides a list of actions families can follow to help ensure their child's successful school experience. Both the family and the student's healthcare team should work together to provide the school nurse or the school administrator, if the school does not have a school nurse, with the information necessary to allow students with diabetes to fully and safely participate in all school activities (Jackson et al., 2015).

ACTIONS FOR PARENTS/GUARDIANS
From *Helping the Student with Diabetes Succeed: A Guide for School Personnel*

Before the start of the school year, provide the school with the child's medical orders (DMMP) and permit the school and the child's healthcare providers to share medical information necessary for the child's safety at school.

Provide the school with accurate and current emergency contact information and keep the information updated.

Attend and participate in the initial and annual meetings of the school health team to discuss implementing the medical orders in the child's DMMP and review the services the child may need.

Participate in developing a Section 504 Plan, other education plans, or IEP.

Provide specific information to the school health team about the child's diabetes and the performance of diabetes care tasks at home.

Inform the school nurse or designated school staff about any changes in the child's health status or medical orders.

Notify the school nurse prior to the student attending school so proper staff training and communication can occur if the student uses an insulin pump.

Provide and maintain all supplies and equipment necessary for implementing the child's health care and education plans, including blood glucose monitoring equipment and Wi-Fi access for continuous glucose monitors (CGM), supplies for insulin administration and urine and blood ketone testing, snacks, quick-acting glucose products, and a glucagon emergency kit.

Consult with the school nurse to monitor supplies, replenish them, and refill or replace expired supplies as needed.

Provide and maintain all supplies and equipment necessary to accommodate the child's long-term needs (72 hours) in case of a disaster or emergency.

Inform appropriate school staff (school nurse, principal, teachers, coaches, and others) when the child plans to participate in school-sponsored activities, including field trips.

Adapted from American Diabetes Association (ADA), 2022, with supplemental information from Brown, 2016; Butler & Wyckoff, 2012; Colorado Department of Education (CDE), 2022.

Annual Notification to Parents/Guardians

The families of children with diabetes should be informed, annually and in writing, of their rights and responsibilities related to medication administration at school. Typically, such information is included in required annual notices and activities that school districts send to the families of all students in districts. Four issues that should be addressed in the annual notice and school district policy relate to medication administration, the delegation of nursing tasks, the provision of necessary supplies and equipment, and the use of service animals:

- An order authorizing parents/guardians to adjust insulin doses to be included in the student's individualized provider's order or DMMP to enable school nurses to make needed adjustments within the scope of the order or DMMP in collaboration with parents/guardians.
- In most states, unlicensed persons cannot delegate nursing tasks to school employees.
- Just as it is the responsibility of parents/guardians to provide the school with needed medication for students with diabetes, it is also the parent's responsibility to provide needed supplies for medication delivery, urine and ketone testing, blood glucose monitoring, and a quick-acting carbohydrate to treat hypoglycemia.
- According to the United States Department of Justice and the ADA, schools, like other state and local government agencies, must make "reasonable modifications" in policies to accommodate students with diabetes who rely on a service animal for assistance (U.S. Department of Justice, 2015). *(See Chapter 49 for more information on service animals).*

In dealing with these issues and in formulating responses to parents/guardians who desire to give medication change orders to school personnel, including school nurses, it is important to review the state NPA, the state Medical Practice Act, and other related state laws related to who can prescribe medications including dosing in schools.

Planning Care and Services for Students with Diabetes

Each student with diabetes should have a DMMP or orders from their diabetes healthcare provider that provides medical orders addressing all facets of routine and emergency diabetes management for each child. The DMMP includes nutrition, insulin or other diabetes medication, including insulin to carbohydrate ratios and correction doses, and physical activity; school schedule; social and cultural factors; glucose monitoring with CGM or meter; symptoms and action required for hypoglycemia or hyperglycemia; and the students level of self-management and need for assistance. Intrinsic to the DMMP is the provision of support for the student to transition to diabetes self-management as age and skill appropriate and in accordance with the student's diabetes provider's order and parental consent (ADA, 2022).

The school nurse uses the DMMP and additional assessment information to develop the IHP in collaboration with the student, family, and diabetes care team. While the DMMP and school nursing practice and judgment guide how the school nurse will care for students' health needs in schools, the IHP identifies the individualized health goals that the school nurse will help the student achieve each year with the outcome of promoting self-management when appropriate. The IHP describes the student's daily health needs, outlines diabetes management strategies for school personnel, informs educational plans, such as Section 504 Plans and IEPs, identifies personnel obligations to assist with diabetes care and effectively help the student achieve their goals, and promotes academic success. IHP development cannot be delegated to a licensed practical/vocational nurse (LPN/LVN) or unlicensed assistive personnel (UAP) because the IHP is based on the nursing process in accordance with the individual state NPA (NASN, 2022a; NASN, 2020). The needs of the student with diabetes will be outlined on the IHP and include blood glucose monitoring either via the finger stick method or with a continuous glucose monitor (CGM), unlimited access to bathrooms and water, administration of insulin or oral medication, and unrestricted access to food or snacks as needed (Jacquez et al., 2008). In addition to the IHP, the school nurse develops an individualized ECP, based on the IHP, for each student with diabetes, coordinates educating school staff about symptoms of hyperglycemia and hypoglycemia, and distributes copies of the ECP to all regular and substitute teachers who are responsible for the student at school and at school-sponsored activities (ADA, 2022; Jacquez et al., 2008; NASN, 2020). The ECP is a confidential document that must be made accessible to personnel responsible for the student.

If it is determined that the student is eligible for either a Section 504 Plan or an IEP, the school nurse is often the only member of the school team qualified to interpret medical records, assess the student's healthcare needs, develop the IHP and ECP, and assist the team in writing an education plan that appropriately accommodates the student's health needs. Depending on the student's healthcare needs, the school nurse may be listed on the IEP or Section 504 Plan as a direct or related service. When this is the case, the school nurse needs to supply information about the types, frequency, and duration of the health services to be provided. Attaching the student's IHP to the Section 504 Plan or IEP provides the rationale for receiving health services at school. Necessary nursing services specified in the IEP, in accordance with the IHP, may be reimbursable under the state's Medicaid program if the student is Medicaid eligible (Department of Health and Human Services and Centers for Medicare and Medicaid Services, 2022; Galemore & Sheetz, 2015; NASN, 2023a). When the IEP or Section 504 Plan is due for review, the school nurse is the only team member qualified to evaluate the effectiveness of the plan's health components and make necessary revisions (Galemore & Sheetz, 2015; Yonkaitis & Shannon, 2019; Zirkel, 2009).

Ensuring That Needed Services Are Delivered

While approximately half of the nation's schools have a full-time school nurse, it is the position of NASN that students will be safer, healthier, and better able to learn with daily access to a school nurse (NASN, 2023a; Willgerodt et al., 2018). To compensate for inadequate school nurse staffing, nurses must help administrators understand the significance of safe and adequate staffing to protect students with diabetes and reduce liability to the district. Determining safe and adequate school nurse staffing is complex (American Nurses Association [ANA], 2020; NASN, 2023a) and requires a nursing assessment of the acuity level and healthcare needs of individual students and identification of the social determinants of the community's health, such as the social and economic conditions that impact community members' health outcomes (CDC, 2022d).

Delegating in Accordance with State NPA and Student Needs

Delegation is a tool that can be useful in meeting the needs of children with diabetes at school. The ANA defines delegation as "transferring the responsibility of performing a nursing activity to another person while retaining accountability for the outcome (ANA, 2012). The delegation of nursing tasks at school when based on the ANA definition of delegation, and if allowed by the state NPA, other state laws and regulations, and professional nursing standards and guidelines. When allowed by law, delegation must be done only if it is safe for the student.

Training and supervision are part of the delegation. Delegating healthcare tasks to UAP creates professional, ethical, and legal questions for all nurses. The delegating school nurse must train, clinically supervise and evaluate the UAP to determine if the person is capable and competent to safely and effectively perform the delegated tasks. The school nurse determines the level and frequency of supervision unless state law dictates otherwise. The school nurse must document delegatees' delegation, training, supervision, and evaluation. *(See Chapter 4 for additional information on delegation and Chapter 55 for additional information on conflict with administration).*

Providing appropriate care for students with diabetes requires the school nurse and a small group of non-clinical school staff to understand diabetes and be trained in diabetes management and the treatment of diabetes emergencies in accordance with the student's individualized DMMP. Trained, knowledgeable, and caring school personnel will help the student avoid dangerous hypoglycemic episodes and achieve the glycemic control needed to reduce the risks of diabetes complications (Jackson et al., 2015). The UAP needs regular training programs and booster sessions to reinforce learning, particularly because sentinel events do not regularly occur in the school setting. Having written policies, protocols, and ECP in conjunction with training programs for UAP will ensure safe and appropriate care for students with diabetes (Wilt & Foley, 2011).

School staff training on diabetes care must convey sensitivity to the realities and frustrations for children and adolescents living with a disease requiring the continuous balancing of a wide range of self-care behaviors. Staff must avoid being judgmental about the blood glucose reading as being "good or bad" and instead approach it objectively as an opportunity for the student to help problem solve. The frustration for these students can be exacerbated by challenges at school in getting the help they need.

The 2022 ADA Guide outlines three levels of training:
- Level 1. Diabetes Overview and Recognizing and Responding to Emergency Situations
  - Train all school personnel in the following:
    - Overview of diabetes
    - Recognition and response to hypoglycemia and hyperglycemia
    - Who to contact in a diabetic emergency
- Level 2. Diabetes Basics and Emergency Response
  - Train teachers and other school personnel who have responsibility for the student with diabetes during the school day in the following:
    - Level 1 content plus an expanded overview of diabetes
    - Specific instruction on the ECPs for Hypoglycemia and Hyperglycemia
    - Activating Emergency Medical Services in a diabetes emergency
    - Roles and responsibilities of individual staff members
    - Impact of hypoglycemia or hyperglycemia on behavior and learning
    - Tips and planning needed for the classroom and for special events
    - The student's health care and education plans
    - Legal rights of students with diabetes

- Level 3. General and Student-Specific Diabetes Care Tasks
  - o   Train designated diabetes personnel in the following:
    - Level 1 and Level 2 content and training
    - General training on diabetes care tasks specified in the student's DMMP.
    - Student-specific training, using the student's equipment and supplies for each diabetes care task
    - Individualized training on the student's pump and continuous glucose monitor
    - Documentation of the performance of all care tasks
    - Plans for ongoing performance evaluation of trained diabetes personnel

Adapted from the ADA (2022), *Helping the Student with Diabetes Succeed: A Guide for School Personnel.*

Promoting Self-Management

From the time diabetes is diagnosed, self-management is a primary goal. For youth with type 1 diabetes, four additional general goals are (1) normal growth and development; (2) glycemic control; (3) minimizing short and long-term complications; and (4) positive psychosocial adjustment. Effective self-management will accomplish all the goals. (Jackson & Albanese-O'Neill, 2016; Wyckoff, 2019). School nurses are uniquely positioned to encourage and reinforce self-management techniques and principles to students with diabetes because the school nurse sees these students on a regular, generally daily basis. To ensure student safety, the student's diabetes provider and parent/guardian must provide consent, and the school district policies should include a requirement for the nurse to assess and provide input to the student's capability and competence to perform self-administration. Policies requiring authorization from the licensed healthcare provider and parent/guardian consent should mirror those governing all other medications.

Federal laws, IDEIA (2004), Section 504, and ADAAA, along with corresponding state laws, protect the rights of students to have access to a school nurse or trained non-clinical staff to provide care in accordance with the student's individualized DMMP. Students should be permitted to carry their diabetes supplies, including glucagon, and self-administer insulin at school when they have the capability to do so. Glucagon may be self-carried, but when needed, in a severe hypoglycemia emergency, the student will not be able to self-administer due to cognitive impairment and will need trained personnel to administer the medication (ADA, 2022; Jackson et al., 2015). Trained personnel should know where glucagon is stored and have immediate access to glucagon. Educating students with diabetes on self-management and insulin self-administration is fundamental to the care coordination that school nurses provide. Self-administration of insulin and self-treatment of mild to moderate hypoglycemia, when the student possesses the needed level of maturity and skill as determined by their diabetes provider and parent/guardian, is supported by healthcare experts because quick treatment of symptoms helps to reduce the effects of the disease and may prevent a hypoglycemia/hyperglycemia emergency episode. Additionally, self-administration leads to self-care competence, student independence, and improved self-esteem (ADA, 2022; Jackson & Albanese-O'Neill, 2016; Wyckoff, 2019).

Effective diabetes care depends on self-management. Ongoing diabetes self-management education and support are key to helping young people and their families learn about diabetes, sustain behavioral changes, and adjust to the reality of a chronic illness (Wyckoff, 2019). Most individuals with diabetes eventually become responsible for all aspects of routine care, including blood glucose monitoring, insulin or other medication administration, recognition and prompt treatment of hypoglycemia and hyperglycemia, and carbohydrate counting. As the more basic aspects of self-care are mastered, the individual with diabetes learns how to balance food and medication intake with physical activity and other variables affecting blood glucose levels. For students, an age-appropriate, competency-related level of responsibility for self-management must be allowed while the young person is in school (Jackson & Albanese-O'Neill, 2016). A multidisciplinary team most effectively coordinates diabetes self-management education and support. School nurses are vital members of the student's diabetes healthcare team and, in schools, are the leaders of the school health team (Yonkaitis & Shannon, 2019; NASN, 2023b).

Anticipating Transition Planning

As young people with diabetes transition into emerging adulthood, the supportive infrastructure of the family's care and supervision of diabetes management frequently lessens. As a result, glycemic control may sometimes deteriorate; there are increased risks of acute complications; psychosocial, emotional, and behavioral challenges occur; and there is an increased risk of chronic complications. During this challenging time, the ADA recommends a supportive transition plan that anticipates upcoming changes (NASN, 2022a; Chiang et al., 2016). The most effective is comprehensive and coordinated planning beginning in early adolescence or, at the latest, before the transition date for the emerging adult to seamlessly move from pediatric to adult health care (Jackson & Albanese-O'Neill, 2016). During the adolescent years, with parental consent, the school nurse can help facilitate transition planning by providing online tools from NASN and ADA and by writing into the student's IHP nursing interventions that promote "independent decision making related to healthy lifestyle choices and diabetes self-care" (Bobo & Butler, 2010, p. 115).

Arranging for Care/Medication Administration/Emergency Plans for Field Trips and Other Away from School Activities

Emergencies

When there is an emergency, the school nurse and other trained school personnel must be prepared to provide care to students with diabetes at school and at all school-sponsored activities in which a student with diabetes participates in accordance with the student's individualized DMMP (ADA, 2022).

In an emergency or disaster, planned action is required to protect lives from the effects of unexpected events (Gereige et al., 2022; Shannon & Guilday, 2019). Typically, disasters occur with little or no, warning. The degree of disaster preparation directly affects the outcome. When disaster hits a school, local and regional emergency response resources may be overwhelmed, or first responders' arrival may be delayed. However, minutes into a disaster, a student with diabetes may need juice, glucose tablets, or a glucagon injection to reverse hypoglycemia (Butler & Wyckoff, 2012; Wyckoff, 2019).

School nurses need to participate in disaster planning and practice drills before a disaster occurs. School nurses can serve on community planning groups assessing resources and the school's ability to manage a disaster, developing disaster plans, and coordinating disaster drills to test these plans. School nurses are instrumental in identifying the individual disaster preparedness needs of students and school staff with diabetes (Butler & Wyckoff, 2012). The ECPs for students with special healthcare needs, including diabetes, must be a part of the school's broader disaster plan. Students with diabetes need additional disaster-preparedness planning, including medication, food, and water availability during a prolonged lockdown or shelter-in-place (Gereige et al., 2022; Shannon & Guilday, 2019). *(See Chapter 43 for additional information on disaster planning).*

Emergency Medication

Many states have laws permitting UAP to be trained to respond to diabetes and other chronic disease emergencies. In these states, school districts that do not train UAP or stock authorized emergency medicine may be liable and found negligent for being unprepared for emergencies.

Diabetes and several other chronic diseases can rapidly cause life-threatening emergencies. Quick access to glucagon is linked to saving lives. Like all medication administration, glucagon administration may be regulated by state law and school district policy. The school nurse should develop an IHP and ECP for all students with medical orders for glucagon or glucose tablets specifying the response needed for the student in case of an emergency. When a hypoglycemic episode occurs, it is critical that school district policies permit school staff to provide appropriate care for the student with diabetes, including glucagon administration by a school nurse or trained staff member, and that access to the student's emergency medication is immediate (Wyckoff, 2019). School district policies and procedures should specify the location where the glucagon or glucose tablets are stored, the staff member(s) responsible for accessing and administering the medication, the staff member responsible for replacing outdated medication, and the staff member responsible for administering the medication on field trips and at other school-sponsored events. Additionally, the school nurse should train and supervise school staff who should be assigned as "first responders" for students with diabetes who experience hypoglycemia (Allen et al., 2012; American Academy of Pediatrics, 2009; McCaughey et al., 2020; Wyckoff, 2019).

Field Trips, Summer Programs, Before and After-School Programs, Camps

Students with diabetes are entitled by federal and related state laws to have equal opportunity to participate fully in all school-sponsored programs and activities, including before- and after-school programs, field trips, camps, and summer programs. Students with diabetes may not be excluded, even if providing their full participation creates logistical or fiscal challenges. Without regard to venue or season of the year, relevant legal and clinical standards of safe medication administration apply. Students who require nursing or healthcare services at school will minimally require the same level of care during school-sponsored activities away from school. For students with diabetes to prevent hypoglycemia, target blood glucose ranges and insulin requirements may need to be changed depending on the activity. To ensure the health and safety of all students with diabetes participating in extended day and away-from-campus activities, planning for these events should begin well ahead of the intended date and include the school nurse in all the planning phases. The planning should start with an assessment by the school nurse of the activity (intensity, duration), location of the activity, the need for assistance, and communication with the parents/guardian and healthcare provider (ADA, 2022; Erwin et al., 2014; NASN, 2022a; Wyckoff, 2019).

State-to-state differences in laws pertaining to nursing practice create challenges for the care of students with diabetes on out-of-state field trips (Erwin et al., 2014). These challenges are somewhat reduced for school nurses who are licensed in the Nurse Licensure Compact (NLC), as the NLC permits registered nurses (RN) and LPN/LVNs to practice across NLC state lines (NCSBN, n.d.). Navigating practice licensure issues may be more cumbersome for school nurses licensed in non-Compact states. To further complicate matters, the NLC does not cover Advanced Practice RNs (APRNs) or UAP (NCSBN, n.d.). Well before any away-from-school activity, and especially well ahead of out-of-state field trips involving students with diabetes, school nurses must review applicable state laws and regulations, including those pertaining to delegation in the states to be visited. The U.S. State Department provides guidance for out-of-country field trips (Erwin et al., 2014).

Field trips have become an increasingly important part of most schools' curricula. Student health and safety is a high priority. The school nurse must facilitate communication involving pertinent school staff, parents/guardians, and the student and oversee healthcare preparations for the trip. Planning for extended field trips should include the following actions:

Keeping Students with Diabetes Safe on School Field Trips
Travel with a copy of the student's IHP, ECP, and phone numbers
Train staff in recognizing and treating hypoglycemia, hyperglycemia, and other diabetes care tasks (as permitted by state NPA and school policy).
Determine the level of assistance and supplies necessary for blood glucose monitoring.
Determine the level of assistance, and supplies necessary, for insulin administration.
Establish a plan for proper insulin storage.
Pack food/snack items (extra snacks may be needed for increased activity).
Pack fast-acting carbohydrates, such as glucose gel or a glucagon kit, to be available in case of hypoglycemia.
Investigate the state laws, regulations, and the scope of nursing practice in the state(s) to be visited, if the field trip is out of state.

Adapted from Erwin et al., 2014 and Wyckoff, 2019

(See Chapter 59 for additional information on school-sponsored trips).

CONCLUSION

Ever-increasing numbers of students with both type 1 and type 2 diabetes attend school each day. Students with diabetes require coordination of diabetes care tasks, including insulin or oral medication administration, blood glucose monitoring, meal planning (including carbohydrate counting), and treatment of hypoglycemia and hyperglycemia. Federal and state laws require schools to safely and appropriately accommodate the health services needs of students with diabetes safely and appropriately at school and during school-sponsored activities outside regular school hours. School nurses provide care coordination, support safe and effective diabetes management for students with diabetes at school and during school-sponsored activities, and reduce liability risks for themselves, school staff, and the school district by developing, implementing, and evaluating IHPs for all students with diabetes (McClanahan, & Weismuller, 2015; NASN, 2022a; Wyckoff, 2019). School nurses also document the delegation, training, supervision, and evaluation of UAP and LPN/LVN to provide care and comply with the state NPA and related state laws, standards of practice and care, and school district policy.

Students with diabetes are entitled to receive appropriate diabetes management in school, with minimal disruption to these routines. In accordance with federal and state laws, students should have the opportunity, when developmentally and cognitively appropriate, to self-manage all aspects of diabetes care at school, including, but not limited to, performing blood glucose monitoring, administering insulin, having unrestricted access to meals/snacks/water/bathroom, managing hypoglycemia (with trained personnel prepared to provide glucagon treatment, if required) and hyperglycemia, and fully participating in all school-sponsored activities (ADA, 2022; Chiang et al., 2016; Wyckoff, 2019).

RESOURCES

Please see APPENDIX # 1: Brief History and APPENDIX # 2: Brief Literature Review

American Diabetes Association. (2012). *Sample Section 504 Plan.* http://main.diabetes.org/dorg/PDFs/Advocacy/Discrimination/504-plan.pdf

American Diabetes Association. (2023). *Training Resources for School Staff.* https://diabetes.org/tools-support/know-your-rights/safe-at-school-state-laws/training-resources-school-staff

American Diabetes Association. (2022). NEW! Diabetes Medical Management Plan. https://diabetes.org/tools-support/know-your-rights/safe-at-school-state-laws/written-care-plans/diabetes-medical-management-plan

American Diabetes Association Website: http://www.diabetes.org/

American Diabetes Association. (n.d.). *Fast Facts - Data and Statistics About Diabetes*. http://professional.diabetes.org/content/fast-facts-data-and-statistics-about-diabetes/?loc=dorg_statistics

Joslin Diabetes Center: www.joslin.org

Juvenile Diabetes Research Foundation Website: http://jdrf.org/

Legal References

- o Americans with Disabilities Act (ADA) 42 U.S.C. § 12101 et seq (1990).
- o ADA Amendments Act of 2008 (ADAAA) 42 USCA § 12101 (2008).
- o Child Nutrition and WIC Reauthorization Act, Pub. L. No. 108-265, § 204, 729 (2004).
- o Developmental Disabilities Assistance and Bill of Rights Act, Pub. L. No. 106-402, § 101 1680 (2000).
- o Education for All Handicapped Children Act, Pub. L. No. 94-142, § 20 USC 1401. (1975).
- o Elementary and Secondary Education Act, 20 U.S.C. 6301 et seq. (1965).
- o Every Student Succeeds Act (ESSA), Public Law No: 114-95 (2015)
- o Family Educational Rights and Privacy Act (FERPA), 20 U.S.C.S. § 1232g (1974).
- o Health Insurance Portability and Accountability Act (HIPAA), Privacy Rule P.L. 104-191 (1996).

- o Healthy, Hunger-Free Kids Act, Pub.L. 111–296. (2010).
- o Individuals with Disabilities Education Improvement Act (IDEA), 20 USC et seq., 64 (2004).
- o McKinney-Vento Homeless Education Assistance Improvements Act, 42 U.S.C.S. 11431 et seq. (2001).
- o Mental Health Parity and Addiction Equity Act (MHPAEA), (2008).
- o Patient Protection and Affordable Care Act (ACA), P.L. 111-148 (2010).
- o Protection of Pupil Rights Amendment (PPRA), 20 U.S.C.S. § 1232h (1978).
- o School Access to Emergency Epinephrine Act, H.R. 2094 — 113th Congress (2013).
- o Section 504 of the Rehabilitation Act, 29 U.S.C. § 701 et seq. (1973).

Case Law

- o American Nurses Assn. v. Torlakson (2013), Cal.4th, No. S184583. (2013).
- o Cedar Rapids Community School District V. Garret F., Supreme Court of the United States 526 U.S. 66 (1999).
- o Mitts v. Hillsboro Union High School District, (1987).

REFERENCES

Allen, K., Henselman, K., Laird, B., Quiñones, A., & Reutzel, T. (2012). Potential life-threatening events in schools involving rescue inhalers, epinephrine autoinjectors, and glucagon delivery devices: Reports from school nurses. *The Journal of School Nursing, 28*(1), 47-55. https://doi.org/10.1177/1059840511420726

American Academy of Pediatrics. (2009). Guidance for the administration of medication in school (Policy Statement). *Pediatrics, 124*(4), 1244-1251. https://doi.org/10.1542/peds.2009-1953

American Association of Diabetes Educators. (2016*). Management of children with diabetes in the school setting* (Position Statement). https://www.diabeteseducator.org/docs/default-source/practice/practice-documents/position-statements/management-of-children-with-diabetes-in-the-school-setting.pdf?sfvrsn=f3ab8c58_8

American Diabetes Association. (2022). *Helping the student with diabetes succeed: A guide for school personnel.* Author. https://diabetes.org/sites/default/files/2022-11/School-guide-final-11-16-22.pdf

American Nurses Association. (2012). *Principles for delegation by registered nurses to unlicensed assistive personnel (UAP)*. https://www.nursingworld.org/~4af4f2/globalassets/docs/ana/ethics/principlesofdelegation.pdf

American Nurses Association. (2020). *ANA's principles for nurse staffing* (3rd ed.). https://cdn2.hubspot.net/hubfs/4850206/PNS3E_ePDF.pdf

Bobo, N. & Butler, S. (2010). The transition from pediatric to adult diabetes health care. *NASN School Nurse, 25*(3): 114-115. " https://journals.sagepub.com/doi/10.1177/1942602X10363735

Breneman, C.B., Heidari, K., Butler, S., Porter, R.R., & Wang, X. (2015). Evaluation of the effectiveness of the H.A.N.D.S. program: A school nurse diabetes management education program. *The Journal of School Nursing, 31*(6), 402-410. https://journals.sagepub.com/doi/10.1177/1059840514568895

Brous, E. (2019). The law and school nursing practice. In J. Selekman, Shannon, & Yonkaitis (Eds.), *School nursing: A comprehensive text* (3rd ed., p.p. 136-153). F.A. Davis Company.

Brown, C. (2016). 21st-century diabetes: Technology leads the way. *NASN School Nurse, 31*(5), 254-256. https://journals.sagepub.com/doi/10.1177/1942602X16661198

Butler, S. & Wyckoff, L. (2012). Addressing the emergency preparedness needs of students with diabetes. *NASN School Nurse. 27*(3), 160-162. https://journals.sagepub.com/doi/10.1177/1942602X12442571"https://journals.sagepub.com/doi/10.1177/1942602X12442571

Centers for Disease Control and Prevention. (2021, August 24). *New research uncovers concerning increases in youth living with diabetes in the U.S.* [Press release]. U.S. Dept of Health and Human Services. https://www.cdc.gov/media/releases/2021/p0824-youth-diabetes.html

Centers for Disease Control and Prevention. (2022a, June 29). *National diabetes statistics report: prevalence of diagnosed diabetes.* U.S. Dept of Health and Human Services. https://www.cdc.gov/diabetes/data/statistics-report/diagnosed-diabetes.html

Centers for Disease Control and Prevention. (2022b, July 19). *Diabetes report card 2021.* U.S. Dept of Health and Human Services. https://www.cdc.gov/diabetes/library/reports/reportcard.html

Centers for Disease Control and Prevention. (2022c, October 25). *Diabetes basics.* U.S. Dept of Health and Human Services. https://www.cdc.gov/diabetes/basics/index.html

Centers for Disease Control and Prevention. (2022d, December 8). *Social determinants of health at CDC.* U.S. Dept of Health and Human Services. https://www.cdc.gov/about/sdoh/index.html

Chiang, J.L., Kirkman, M.S., Laffel, L.M., & Peters, A.L. (2016). Type 1 diabetes through the life span: a position statement of the American Diabetes Association. *Diabetes Care, 37,*2034–2054. http://care.diabetesjournals.org/content/37/7/2034.long

Colorado Department of Education. (2022). *Standards of care for diabetes management in the school setting & licensed child care facilities.* http://www.coloradokidswithdiabetes.org/wp-content/uploads/2022/09/2022-SOC-Final-083122-1.pdf

Department of Health and Human Services and Centers for Medicare and Medicaid Services. (2022). *CMCS informational bulletin - Information on school-based services in Medicaid: Funding, documentation and expanding services.* https://www.medicaid.gov/federal-policy-guidance/downloads/sbscib081820222.pdf

Disability Rights Education & Defense Fund. (2016). *Laws.* https://dredf.org/legal-advocacy/laws/

Erwin, K., Clark, S., & Mercer, S.E. (2014). Providing health services for children with special health care needs on out-of-state field trips. *NASN School Nurse, 29*(2), 84–88. https://journals.sagepub.com/doi/full/10.1177/1942602X13517005

Galemore, C.A., & Sheetz, A.H. (2015). IEP, IHP, and Section 504 primer for new school nurses. *NASN School Nurse, 30*(2), 85-88. https://journals.sagepub.com/doi/10.1177/1942602X14565462

Gereige, R.S., Gross, T., & Jastania, E. (2022). Individual medical emergencies occurring at school. Council On School Health and Committee On Pediatric Emergency Medicine (Policy Statement). *Pediatrics.* 150 (1): e2022057987. https://doi.org/10.1542/peds.2022-057987

Jackson, C. C. & Albanese-O'Neill, A. (2016). Supporting the student's graduated independence in diabetes care. *NASN School Nurse, 31*(4): 202–204. https://journals.sagepub.com/doi/10.1177/1942602X16651749

Jackson, C.C., Albanese-O'Neill, A., Butler, K.L., Chiang, J.L., Deeb, L.C., Hathaway, K., Kraus, E., Weissberg-Benchell, J., Yatvin, A., & Siminerio, L.M. (2015). Diabetes care in the school setting: A position statement of the American Diabetes Association. *Diabetes Care*, *38*(10): 1958-1963. https://doi.org/10.2337/dc15-1418

Jacquez, F., Stout, S., Alvarez-Salvat, R., Fernandez, M., Villa, M., Sanchez, J., Eidson, M., Nemery, R., & Delamater, A. (2008). Parent perspectives of diabetes management in schools. The Diabetes Educator, 34(6), 996-1003. https://doi.org/10.1177/0145721708325155

Lakhtakia, R. (2013). The history of diabetes mellitus. *Sultan Qaboos University Medical Journal, 13*(3), 368–370. https://www.ncbi.nlm.nih.gov/pmc/articles/PMC3749019/

Mayo Clinic. (2022, April 9). *Gestational diabetes: diagnosis and treatment.* https://www.mayoclinic.org/diseases-conditions/gestational-diabetes/diagnosis-treatment/drc-20355345

McCaughey, R.A., McCarthy, A.M., Maughan, E., Hein, M., Perkhounkova, Y. & Kelly, M.W. (2020). Emergency medication access and administration in schools: a focus on epinephrine, albuterol inhalers, and glucagon. *The Journal of School Nursing, 38*(4): 326–335. https://doi.org/10.1177/1059840520934185"https://doi.org/10.1177/1059840520934185

McClanahan, R. & Weismuller, P.C. (2015). School nurses and care coordination for children with complex needs: An integrative review. *The Journal of School Nursing, 31*(1), 34–43. https://journals.sagepub.com/doi/10.1177/1059840514550484

National Association of School Nurses. (2019). *Emergency preparedness* (Position Statement). Author. https://www.nasn.org/nasn-resources/professional-practice-documents/position-statements/ps-emergency-preparedness

National Association of School Nurses. (2022a, April). *Diabetes in children.* Author. https://www.nasn.org/nasn-resources/resources-by-topic/diabetes

National Association of School Nurses. (2022b). School nursing: scope and standards of practice (4th ed). Author.

National Association of School Nurses. (2020). *Use of individualized healthcare plans to support school health services* (Position Statement). Author. https://www.nasn.org/nasn-resources/professional-practice-documents/position-statements/ps-ihps

National Association of School Nurses. (2023a). Equitable reimbursement for school nursing services (Position Statement). Author. https://www.nasn.org/nasn-resources/professional-practice-documents/position-statements/ps-reimbursement

National Association of School Nurses. (2023b). *IDEIA and Section 504 teams - The school nurse as an essential team member* (Position Statement). Author. https://www.nasn.org/nasn-resources/professional-practice-documents/position-statements/ps-ideia

National Council of State Boards of Nursing & American Nurses Association. (2019). *National guidelines for nursing delegation* (Joint Statement). https://www.ncsbn.org/public-files/NGND-PosPaper_06.pdf

National Council of State Boards of Nursing. (n.d.). *Nurse licensure compact.* https://www.nursecompact.com/

National Council of State Boards of Nursing, (n.d.). *Nurse license compact FAQs: How does the NLC pertain to APRNs?* https://www.ncsbn.org/compacts/nurse-licensure-compact/nlc-faqs.page

National Institutes of Health. (2017, April 13). *Rates of new diagnosed cases of type 1 and type 2 diabetes on the rise among children, teens: fastest rise seen among racial/ethnic minority groups.* [Press release]. https://www.nih.gov/news-events/news-releases/rates-new-diagnosed-cases-type-1-type-2-diabetes-rise-among-children-teens

National Institutes of Health: National Institute of Diabetes and Digestive and Kidney Diseases. (2020a). *Diabetes in children and teens.* https://www.niddk.nih.gov/health-information/health-communication-programs/ndep/living-with-diabetes/youth-teens/Pages/index.aspx

National Institutes of Health: National Institute of Diabetes and Digestive and Kidney Diseases. (2020b). *Helping the student with diabetes succeed.* Author. https://www.niddk.nih.gov/health-information/professionals/clinical-tools-patient-management/diabetes/helping-student-diabetes-succeed-guide-school-personnel

Pohlman, K. J. (2005). Legal framework and financial accountability for school nursing practice. In N. C. Schwab, & M. H. B. Gelfman, (Eds.), *Legal issues in school health services,* (pp. 95-121). Authors Choice Press.

Polonsky, K.S. (2012). The past 200 years in diabetes. *The New England Journal of Medicine*, *367*, 1332-1340. https://doi.org/10.1056/NEJMra1110560

Resha, C. (2010). Delegation in the school setting: Is it a safe practice?" *OJIN: The Online Journal of Issues in Nursing*, *15*(2), Manuscript 5. https://doi.org/10.3912/OJIN.Vol15No02Man05

Schwartz, F.L., Denham, S., Heh, V., Wapner, A., & Shubrook, J. (2010). Experiences of children and adolescents with type 1 diabetes in school: Survey of children, parents, and schools. *Diabetes Spectrum, 23*(1), 47-55. https://diabetesjournals.org/spectrum/article/23/1/47/33326/Experiences-of-Children-and-Adolescents-With-Type

Shannon, R.A. & Guilday, P. (2019). Emergency and disaster preparedness and response for schools In J. Selekman, Shannon, & Yonkaitis (Eds.), *School nursing: A comprehensive text* (3rd ed., p.p. 457–477). F.A. Davis Company.

Shannon, R.A., & Kubelka, S. (2013a). Reducing the risks of delegation: Use of procedure skills checklists for unlicensed assistive personnel in schools, part 1. *NASN School Nurse, 28*(4), 178-181. https://journals.sagepub.com/doi/abs/10.1177/1942602X13489886"https://journals.sagepub.com/doi/abs/10.1177/1942602X13489886

Shannon, R.A., & Kubelka, S. (2013b). Reducing the risks of delegation: Use of procedure skills checklists for unlicensed assistive personnel in schools, part 2. *NASN School Nurse, 28*(5), 222-226. https://journals.sagepub.com/doi/10.1177/1942602X13490030

U.S. Department of Justice. (2015). *Frequently asked questions about service animals and the ADA.* https://archive.ada.gov/regs2010/service_animal_qa.pdf

Willgerodt, M.A., Brock, D.M. & Maughan, E.D. (2018). Public school nursing practice in the United States. *The Journal of School Nursing, 34*(3), 232-244. https://doi.org/10.1177/1059840517752456

Wilt, L., & Foley, M. (2011). Delegation of glucagon in the school setting: A comparison of state legislation. *The Journal of School Nursing, 27*(3), 185–196. https://journals.sagepub.com/doi/10.1177/1059840511398240

Wilt, L., & Jameson, B. (2021). *School nursing evidence-based clinical practice guideline: students with type 1 diabetes.* NASN Learning Center. https://learn.nasn.org/courses/37660

World Health Organization. (2022, September 16). *Diabetes.* https://www.who.int/news-room/fact-sheets/detail/diabetes

Wyckoff, L. (2019). Students with diabetes. In J. Selekman, Shannon, & Yonkaitis (Eds.), *School nursing: A comprehensive text* (3rd ed., p.p. 575–602). F.A. Davis Company.

Yonkaitis, C.F. & Shannon, R.A. (2019). Health and education plans for students with special healthcare needs. In J. Selekman, R.A. Shannon, & C.F. Yonkaitis (Eds.), *School nursing: A comprehensive text* (3rd ed., p.p. 172-199). F.A. Davis Company.

Zirkel, P.A. (2009). History and expansion of Section 504 student eligibility: Implications for school nurses. *The Journal of School Nursing, 25*(4): 256–260. https://doi.org/10.1177/1059840509336930

Zirkel, P. A., Granthom, M. F., & Lovato, L. (2012). Section 504 and student health problems: The pivotal position of the school nurse. *The Journal of School Nursing, 28*(6), 423–432. https://doi.org/10.1177/1059840512449358

Zorena, K., Michalska, M., Kurpas, M., Jaskulak, M., Murawska, A., & Rostami, S. (2022). *Environmental factors and the risk of developing type 1 diabetes-old disease and new data.* https://doi.org/10.3390/biology11040608

APPENDIX # 1

Brief History

Diabetes, one of the earliest identified chronic diseases, was first documented around 1500 B.C.E. by the ancient Egyptians. Most sources agree that the term "diabetes," meaning "siphon," was used by the Greek physician Aretaeus in the first century C.E. to describe the frequent urination and extreme thirst associated with the disease. In fifth century C.E. India, Sushruta, a physician, and the surgeon Charaka identified two types of diabetes, based on observations of the age of onset, the weight of the patient, and longevity after diagnosis, which were much later named type 1 and type 2. The famous Persian physician Avicenna (980–1037 C.E.) observed and recorded in *The Canon of Medicine* the progression and complications of diabetes. The word "mellitus," meaning "honey sweet," was added in 1675 by Thomas Wills in England when he rediscovered the sweetness of the urine and blood of patients with diabetes, first identified by Sushruta and Charaka over 1000 years earlier. One hundred years later, in 1776, Matthew Dobson in England was able to measure an excess concentration of glucose in the urine of patients with diabetes (Canadian Diabetes Association, 2016; Lakhtakia, 2013; Polonsky, 2012; Zajac et al., 2010). In 1855, Claude Bernard, the French father of modern physiology, established the role of the liver in glycogenesis and asserted that diabetes is due to excess glucose production (Jörgens & Grüsser, 2013; Zajac et al., 2010). Mering and Minkowski (Austria) discovered the role of the pancreas in the pathogenesis of diabetes in 1889. Later, this discovery was the basis of insulin isolation and clinical use by Dr. Frederick Banting and Charles Best at the University of Toronto, Canada, in 1921 (Canadian Diabetes Association, 2016).

Throughout the history of diabetes, various remedies and diets have been prescribed for patients. In 1916, Boston's Elliot Joslin compiled a textbook, The Treatment of Diabetes Mellitus, reporting that mortality in patients with diabetes was lowered due to fasting and regular exercise. Over the next five decades, Joslin's continued research established him as a leading diabetes expert (American Diabetes Association [ADA], 2013; Canadian Diabetes Association, 2016). Prior to the 1920s, there were no effective medications for diabetes management. Consequently, diabetes was a fatal disease (White, 2014).

This changed dramatically in 1921, when Banting and Best, with the support of John J.R. Macleod, isolated and successfully injected a depancreatized dog with insulin (ADA, 2013; Canadian Diabetes Association, 2016; Zajac et al., 2010). After working with James Collip to purify insulin, in January 1922, Leonard Thompson, a 14-year-old charity patient in Toronto, Canada, was the first human to be injected with insulin. The insulin treatments were successful, allowing Thompson to live 13 more years until he died at age 27 from pneumonia. News of insulin spread to the United States, and in August 1922, the daughter of U.S. Secretary of State Charles Evans Hughes, Elizabeth Evans Hughes, age 13, barely able to walk and weighing 45 pounds, went to Toronto for insulin treatment. Elizabeth's response to insulin therapy was immediate. She had a productive life and died at age 73 in 1981 (Canadian Diabetes Association, 2016; Zajac et al., 2010). In 1922, Eli Lilly and Company became the first company to produce insulin commercially. In October 1923, Banting and Macleod were awarded the Nobel Prize for the discovery of insulin – they shared their prize with Best and Collip (ADA, 2013; Canadian Diabetes Association, 2016; Zajac et al., 2010).

In 1940, the ADA was founded and began to address the increasing incidence of diabetes and the complications associated with diabetes. Throughout the decades after the discovery of insulin, advances were made in many areas of diabetes care and management that ultimately improved the quality and length of life for people with diabetes. These advancements include medications to treat diabetes and hypoglycemia, meal planning based on calories, carbohydrates, protein, and fat in each serving of food, testing strips for urine and blood, standardized syringes, glucose meters and insulin pumps, pancreas transplant surgeries, advanced research on the pathophysiology of diabetes, implementation of tight control, and new classes of drugs for people with type 2 diabetes (ADA, 2013; Canadian Diabetes Association, 2016; Zajac et al., 2010).

While life was getting better medically for people with diabetes after the discovery of insulin and the many subsequent advancements in diabetes management, the passage of federal civil rights legislation after World War II, and particularly the authorization of three overarching federal laws in the second half of the twentieth century and the first decade of the twenty-first century, protected the rights of all people with disabilities, including the right of all school-age children to have a free and appropriate public education (FAPE) in the least restrictive environment (LRE). These laws are the Rehabilitation Act (1973), Section 504; Education for All Handicapped Children Act (1975) which was reauthorized in 2004 as the Individuals with Disabilities Education Improvement Act (IDEIA) of 2004; and Americans with Disabilities Act (ADA) (1990) which was reauthorized in 2008 as the ADA Amendments Act (ADAAA) of 2008. All fifty states have subsequently passed corresponding state laws guaranteeing the rights of individuals with disabilities. Landmark court rulings, such as *Cedar Rapids Community Sch. Dist. v. Garret F., 119 S. Ct. 992* U.S. (1999), reinforced the rights of students with disabilities to health services at school. Prior to these laws, persons with disabilities, including individuals with diabetes, were subjected to discrimination, frequently denied access to public education, and, if they were granted access, were provided no supportive services to meet their special health or educational needs (Martin et al., 1996). Unfortunately, not all school districts understand their obligations under these federal laws, and according to several reports, families and students with disabilities still report either not receiving needed health services or receiving inadequate health services (Jackson et al., 2015; Jacquez et al., 2008; Schwartz et al., 2010).

REFERENCES

American Diabetes Association. (2013). *History of diabetes*. http://www.diabetes.org/research-and-practice/student-resources/history-of-diabetes.html

Canadian Diabetes Association. (2016). *History of diabetes*. http://www.diabetes.ca/about-diabetes/history-of-diabetes

Jackson, C.C., Albanese-O'Neill, A., Butler, K.L., Chiang, J.L., Deeb, L.C., Hathaway, K., Kraus, E., Weissberg-Benchell, J., Yatvin, A., & Siminerio, L.M. (2015). Diabetes care in the school setting: A position statement of the American Diabetes Association. *Diabetes Care, 38*(10): 1958-1963. https://doi.org/10.2337/dc15-1418

Jacquez, F., Stout, S., Alvarez-Salvat, R., Fernandez, M., Villa, M., Sanchez, J., Eidson, M., Nemery, R., & Delamater, A. (2008). Parent perspectives of diabetes management in schools. The Diabetes Educator, 34(6), 996-1003. https://doi.org/10.1177/0145721708325155

Jörgens, V., & Grüsser, M. (2013). Happy birthday, Claude Bernard. *Diabetes, 62*(7), 2181–2182. https://doi.org/10.2337/db13-0700

Martin, E.W., Martin, R., & Terman, D.L. (1996). The legislative and litigation history of special education. *The Future of Children, 6*(1): 25-39. https://www.princeton.edu/futureofchildren/publications/docs/06_01_01.pdf

Schwartz, F.L., Denham, S., Heh, V., Wapner, A., & Shubrook, J. (2010). Experiences of children and adolescents with type 1 diabetes in school: Survey of children, parents, and schools. *Diabetes Spectrum, 23*(1), 47-55. https://diabetesjournals.org/spectrum/article/23/1/47/33326/Experiences-of-Children-and-Adolescents-With-Type

White, J.R. (2014). A brief history of the development of diabetes medications. *Diabetes Spectrum, 29*(3), 82-86. https://www.ncbi.nlm.nih.gov/pmc/articles/PMC4522877/

Zajac, J., Shrestha, A., Patel, P., & Poretsky, L. (2010). The main events in the history of diabetes mellitus. In L. Poretsky (Ed.), *Principles of Diabetes Mellitus* (pp. 3-16). Springer International Publishing. https://doi.org/10.1007/978-0-387-09841-8_1

APPENDIX # 2

Brief Literature Review

The incidence and prevalence of both type 1 and type 2 diabetes are increasing for children and youth in the United States (CDC, 2022a; National Institutes of Health, 2017) and for all ages globally (World Health Organization [WHO], 2022). Rates differ between the sexes, age, and race or ethnicity (CDC, 2022a).

The WHO has reported that it is likely that maternal obesity and maternal diabetes will increase the prevalence of type 2 diabetes in future generations (WHO, 2022). School nurses should be aware of the risk factors and symptoms for type 2 diabetes to reduce the prevalence of that disease for those children not born with type 2 diabetes resulting from maternal obesity and maternal diabetes.

Several articles review the broadening of federal protections for persons with disabilities, the specific inclusion of diabetes as a qualifying condition for services and accommodations under federal law, and conclude - without a doubt - that schools have a legal requirement to provide services for children with diabetes (Halbert & Yonkaitis; 2019; Jackson et al., 2015; Jacquez et al., 2008; National Association of School Nurses [NASN], 2023b; Schwartz et al., 2010; Zirkel, 2009). Zirkel et al. (2012) advise that to ensure students' rights to appropriate health services at school are maintained, school nurses must understand the legal processes governing these rights and school districts' responsibilities to provide services. Despite federal laws corresponding to state laws, and subsequent case law, some students with diabetes, and their families, report challenges receiving services at school (Jackson et al., 2015; Jacquez et al., 2008; Schwartz et al., 2010).

Several articles address effective diabetes management at school and provide general recommendations for school nurses, school districts, and parents/guardians (NASN, 2022a; Chiang et al., 2016; Jacquez et al., 2008;). In an article about school nurses and care coordination, McClanahan, & Weismuller (2015) provide an integrative review of "six core essentials of nurse-provided care coordination," which include collaboration, communication, the nursing process in planning care, continuous coordination, clinical expertise, and complementary components (McClanahan, & Weismuller, 2015, p. 34). Critical elements necessary for providing vital services that keep the student with diabetes safe at school are planning and documentation and the use of the student's diabetes medical management plan (DMMP) (CDC, 2022c; Jackson & Albanese-O'Neill, 2016; Wilt & Jameson, 2021); the development of individualized healthcare plans (Galemore & Sheetz, 2015; NASN, 2020; Yonkaitis & Shannon, 2019;) and emergency plans for in-school emergencies and away from school activities, such as field trips (Brown, 2016; Butler & Wyckoff, 2012; NASN, 2014; NDEP, 2016). Part of diabetes management requires supporting the student to independence (Jackson & Albanese-O'Neill, 2016;) and assisting the student with the transition from student to adulthood (NASN, 2022a; Chiang et al., 2016; Jackson & Albanese-O'Neill, 2016).

Because approximately half of all schools in the United States have a full-time school nurse, and because the number of children with chronic health conditions continues to increase, delegation to licensed practical or licensed vocational nurses (LPN/LVN) and unlicensed assistive personnel (UAP) is a reality in many schools. For the health and safety of the student and risk reduction for the school district and school nurse, delegation of nursing tasks to LPN/LVNs or UAP requires that the delegating nurse train the delegate in accordance with both the relevant state nurse practice act (NPA) and the standards established by the profession (American Nurses

Association, 2012; NASN, 2022b), as well as the medical community. Several training tools meet professional standards (Breneman et al., 2015; NASN, 2022b).

Additional resources

American Diabetes Association. (2023). 14. Children and adolescents: standards of care in diabetes—2023. *Diabetes Care 2023*; 46(Supplement_1), pp. 230–253. American Diabetes Association. https://doi.org/10.2337/dc23-S014

REFERENCES

American Nurses Association. (2012). *Principles for delegation by registered nurses to unlicensed assistive personnel (UAP)*. https://www.nursingworld.org/~4af4f2/globalassets/docs/ana/ethics/principlesofdelegation.pdf

Breneman, C.B., Heidari, K., Butler, S., Porter, R.R., & Wang, X. (2015). Evaluation of the effectiveness of the H.A.N.D.S. program: A school nurse diabetes management education program. *The Journal of School Nursing, 31*(6), 402-410. https://journals.sagepub.com/doi/10.1177/1059840514568895

Brown, C. (2016). 21st-century diabetes: Technology leads the way. *NASN School Nurse, 31*(5), 254-256. https://journals.sagepub.com/doi/10.1177/1942602X16661198

Butler, S. & Wyckoff, L. (2012). Addressing the emergency preparedness needs of students with diabetes. *NASN School Nurse. 27*(3), 160-162. https://journals.sagepub.com/doi/10.1177/1942602X12442571

Centers for Disease Control and Prevention. (2022a, June 29). *National diabetes statistics report: prevalence of diagnosed diabetes.* U.S. Dept of Health and Human Services. https://www.cdc.gov/diabetes/data/statistics-report/diagnosed-diabetes.html

Centers for Disease Control and Prevention. (2022b, July 19). *Diabetes report card 2021.* U.S. Dept of Health and Human Services. https://www.cdc.gov/diabetes/library/reports/reportcard.html

Centers for Disease Control and Prevention. (2022c, October 25). *Diabetes basics.* U.S. Dept of Health and Human Services. https://www.cdc.gov/diabetes/basics/index.html

Chiang, J.L., Kirkman, M.S., Laffel, L.M., & Peters, A.L. (2016). Type 1 diabetes through the life span: a position statement of the American Diabetes Association. *Diabetes Care, 37*,2034–2054. http://care.diabetesjournals.org/content/37/7/2034.long

Galemore, C.A., & Sheetz, A.H. (2015). IEP, IHP, and Section 504 primer for new school nurses. *NASN School Nurse, 30*(2), 85-88. https://journals.sagepub.com/doi/10.1177/1942602X14565462

Halbert, L.A. & Yonkaitis, C.F. (2019). Federal laws protecting children and youth with disabilities in the schools. In J. Selekman, Shannon, & Yonkaitis (Eds.), *School nursing: A comprehensive text* (3rd ed., p.p. 154-171). F.A. Davis Company.

Jackson, C.C., Albanese-O'Neill, A., Butler, K.L., Chiang, J.L., Deeb, L.C., Hathaway, K., Kraus, E., Weissberg-Benchell, J., Yatvin, A., & Siminerio, L.M. (2015). Diabetes care in the school setting: A position statement of the American Diabetes Association. *Diabetes Care, 38*(10): 1958-1963. https://doi.org/10.2337/dc15-1418

Jacquez, F., Stout, S., Alvarez-Salvat, R., Fernandez, M., Villa, M., Sanchez, J., Eidson, M., Nemery, R., & Delamater, A. (2008). Parent perspectives of diabetes management in schools. The Diabetes Educator, 34(6), 996-1003. https://doi.org/10.1177/0145721708325155

McClanahan, R. & Weismuller, P.C. (2015). School nurses and care coordination for children with complex needs: An integrative review. *The Journal of School Nursing, 31*(1), 34-43. https://journals.sagepub.com/doi/10.1177/1059840514550484

National Association of School Nurses. (2020). *Use of individualized healthcare plans to support school health services* (Position Statement). Author. https://www.nasn.org/nasn-resources/professional-practice-documents/position-statements/ps-ihps

National Association of School Nurses. (2022a, April). *Diabetes in children.* Author. https://www.nasn.org/nasn-resources/resources-by-topic/diabetes

National Association of School Nurses. (2023b). *IDEIA and Section 504 teams - The school nurse as an essential team member* (Position Statement). Author. https://www.nasn.org/nasn-resources/professional-practice-documents/position-statements/ps-ideia

National Institutes of Health. (2017, April 13). *Rates of new diagnosed cases of type 1 and type 2 diabetes on the rise among children, teens: fastest rise seen among racial/ethnic minority groups.* [Press release]. https://www.nih.gov/news-events/news-releases/rates-new-diagnosed-cases-type-1-type-2-diabetes-rise-among-children-teens

Schwartz, F.L., Denham, S., Heh, V., Wapner, A., & Shubrook, J. (2010). Experiences of children and adolescents with type 1 diabetes in school: Survey of children, parents, and schools. *Diabetes Spectrum, 23*(1), 47-55. https://diabetesjournals.org/spectrum/article/23/1/47/33326/Experiences-of-Children-and-Adolescents-With-Type

Wilt, L., & Jameson, B. (2021). *School nursing evidence-based clinical practice guideline: students with type 1 diabetes.* NASN Learning Center. https://learn.nasn.org/courses/37660

World Health Organization. (2022, September 16). *Diabetes.* https://www.who.int/news-room/fact-sheets/detail/diabetes

Yonkaitis, C.F. & Shannon, R.A. (2019). Health and education plans for students with special healthcare needs. In J. Selekman, R.A. Shannon, & C.F. Yonkaitis (Eds.), *School nursing: A comprehensive text* (3rd ed., p.p. 172-199). F.A. Davis Company.

Zirkel, P.A. (2009). History and expansion of Section 504 student eligibility: Implications for school nurses. *The Journal of School Nursing, 25*(4), 256–260. https://doi.org/10.1177/1059840509336930

Zirkel, P. A., Granthom, M. F., & Lovato, L. (2012). Section 504 and student health problems: The pivotal position of the school nurse. *The Journal of School Nursing, 28*(6), 423–432. https://doi.org/10.1177/1059840512449358

Chapter 28

PHYSICAL EXAMINATION OF CHILDREN AND ADOLESCENTS IN A SCHOOL SETTING

Andrea Adimando, DNP, MS, PMHNP-BC, BCIM

DESCRIPTION OF ISSUE

Conducting a physical exam of a child is part of the day-to-day operations for school nurses as they address student health concerns and follow the nursing process. While an expected task in many health settings, exams in the school setting may present a risk for liability. Understanding legal principles will support the school nurse in delivering care safely, inclusively, and legally defensibly. The decision regarding the extent of a child's physical exam requires careful consideration by the school nurse. There are legal ramifications for both (1) performing unnecessary or inappropriate physical exams or (2) neglecting to perform an exam in an appropriate or timely manner to properly assess a child who may need emergency or outside healthcare services. Evaluation of case law may assist nurses in the decision-making process. This chapter discusses select cases, both state and federal, and general recommendations for providing safe, appropriate, patient-centered care.

School nurses make important decisions concerning the health and well-being of the students they serve each day. When children present with acute concerns, the school nurse must decide what assessment procedures they will use to best assess and manage the situation. Sometimes, the assessment may include a brief or comprehensive physical exam to select and implement appropriate treatment or referral. Given that physical exams involve the nurse inspecting, palpating, percussing, and auscultating the child's physical body, this is a decision that the nurse must consider carefully. The school nurse should avoid potential legal ramifications resulting from performing unnecessary violations of the child's autonomy or privacy and charges of negligence related to not fully assessing the child. A school nurse can use clinical practice guidelines, their state's nurse practice act (NPA), guidelines from the school nurse's certifying body and other clinical guidelines, clinical judgment, experience, and familiarity with relevant cases in order to make an informed decision regarding the need for an extent of physical examination of a child in a school-based setting.

BACKGROUND

Physical Examinations

The physical health of a student can undoubtedly contribute to the student's academic and social functioning within the school setting. Ideally, a school nurse should be aware of the medical history of each student – including immunization status, current or resolved health diagnoses, physical abilities, adversities or challenges, etc. - prior to engaging in any form of clinical assessment of the student in order to perform safe, patient-centered care. An awareness of the child's medical history typically comes from school physicals performed by the primary healthcare provider at regular, established intervals. In addition, parent/guardian(s) may provide information related to the student's previous medical history, current health status, and other conditions the student may experience more transiently. These forms of data can assist the school nurse in making accurate and patient-specific assessments of current health status.

Regardless of documented or known health conditions, students may present to the school health office with acute complaints or concerns that warrant further investigation during the school day. Depending on the nature of the complaint, the nurse may need to perform a problem-focused or a more global examination of the student when they seek care in the health office. The primary purpose of an exam of this type would be to 1) assess the imminent health status of the student, 2) assess the level of contagiousness of the student's potential ailment, 3) assess the level of function of the student to determine whether they can continue within the school setting, and 4) to communicate to the student and parent/guardian any current health concerns and recommendations for follow up care.

Legal Considerations

All children are entitled to certain rights, including patients' rights. Before physically examining children in a school setting, the school nurse must be familiar with state and federal laws and regulations, including applicable professional practice standards.

Consent

The school nurse has an ethical duty to ensure that the student who is examined in the school setting has given informed consent prior to any form of treatment, including but not limited to physical examination (Cohn et al., 2001/2005; Coverdale, 2011; Hootman et al., 2001/2005). Informed consent not only consists of the permission to treat the child, given by the parent/guardian and assent – referring to the consent given from a minor who cannot legally consent due to age – from the child/adolescent, but also is given under the assumption that the care provided will be safe and appropriate according to the current clinical practice guidelines. An exception to informed consent is only in a health or safety emergency when obtaining consent may delay treatment, which could cause harm to the child. When informed consent cannot be obtained due to an emergent situation, the school nurse should treat the child as indicated under the principle of *implied consent*. Some state statutes allow persons to operate *"in loco parentis"* – in place of a parent – under certain circumstances. In such states, this principle can be applied to the school setting should the student need care without obtaining prior parental consent (Maggiore, 2009).

Parental consent should be sought before evaluating minors under 12-14 years (depending on the particular state's laws), except in an emergent case that may pose an imminent and significant health threat to the child (Cohn et al., 2005). In many areas of nursing and medicine, however, an adolescent of 16 or 17 years is considered competent enough to give informed consent to examination and treatment. State laws and guidelines typically dictate this competence and whether or not awaiting parental consent (vs. solely obtaining consent from the adolescent in question) would cause undue delay in medical assessment or care and potentially cause harm to said adolescent. However, in non-emergent situations, it would be highly prudent of the school nurse to attain consent from the parent/guardian(s) of the adolescent concurrently with the assent of the minor wherever possible.

In the school setting, this is often established by passive consent, meaning that the parent is giving consent for the nurse to treat the child for routine matters unless otherwise specified or opted out. Schools often provide annual notification of some sort (whether it be an electronic communication, mailing, or school handbook) notifying parents of the services the school nurse provides, as well as the means for notifying the school should a family wish to opt out of these (or any specific) services. Regardless of passive or implied consent, asking for consent and receiving the student's permission is always considered best practice, even when the child is under the age of majority.

Constitutional and Legal Considerations

The Fourth Amendment of the U.S. Constitution protects individuals from unreasonable searches, calling such searches a violation of the individual's reasonable expectation of privacy (U.S. Const. amend. XIV). The school nurse must give extra consideration to this notion, as an examination – especially that of a strip-search type, such as in the case of suspected contraband or other similar safety concerns - that is perceived to be unnecessary may, in fact, constitute a violation of the Fourth Amendment. Further, another person's unpermitted "touching" may constitute battery.

Related Cases

Hearring v. Sliwowski. *In the case of Hearring v. Sliwowski (2013), a student (B.H.) complained of genital burning to her school nurse. The student's mother was called and reported a history of bladder infections in this student. The student was not examined at this time. However, when the student returned two days later with the same complaint, the school nurse brought the student (as well as the school secretary as a witness) to a private bathroom and visually inspected her genital area for any signs of irritation or infection. B.H.'s mother, who claimed that her child's 4th amendment right to be free from unnecessary searches was violated, brought suit against the school nurse shortly after this examination. Though she was initially found to have violated the student's 4th amendment rights by the district court, a court of appeals reversed the case, ruling that the nurse was entitled to qualified immunity, as no prior precedent of this type had been set. Qualified immunity is a legal term used to describe the protection of state or government employees from individual liability or civil lawsuits provided that their actions do not violate a clearly established law or constitutional rights of an individual, about which a reasonable person would have known (Schott, 2012). The court ruled that the school nurse's visual examination of B.H.'s genitals was not a strip-search type search with the intent of finding contraband but was a realistic and appropriate attempt to assess and diagnose a medical condition based on her prior complaints ("Hearring v. Sliwowski," 2013).*

Madden v. Hamilton County Department of Education. *In this case, the parent of a minor child (5 years old at the time) notified her child's school in writing of the presence of a latent congenital herpes simplex virus in her genital area. Three months later, the mother was contacted and asked to pick up her child from school and provide a letter stating that she was medically cleared to return to school despite an active lesion on her foot. When the mother inquired about how this lesion was found, it was brought to her attention that the school nurse had been conducting visual exams of the student's entire body daily for several weeks under the direction of her superiors. The student's mother filed suit against the school and the nurse, alleging that the school did not ask for permission to examine the student from her parents despite contact numbers being readily available. National and state guidelines prohibited the school nurse from medically examining students' genitals without parental consent or the presence of a medical emergency. As it was determined that no emergency was present, the daily examinations were deemed to have violated this student's Fourth Amendment rights to be free from unnecessary searches and unwanted medical treatment.*

Similarly, it was also determined that "a schoolchild's right to personal security and bodily integrity manifestly embraces the right to be free from sexual abuse at the hands of a public school employee. The substantive component of the Due Process Clause protects students against abusive governmental power as exercised by a school."("Doe v. Claiborne Cnty., Tenn.," 1996; "Hearring v. Sliwowski," 2013). These exemplary cases demonstrate the caution the school nurse must take when considering the purpose and the extent of an examination. Genital exams, particularly if conducted without parental knowledge or consent, must be contemplated circumspectly with the risks of liability weighed against the benefit to the student.

(Please refer to Chapter 2, Malpractice/Professional Liability, for more information.)

IMPLICATIONS FOR SCHOOL NURSE PRACTICE

Challenges and Considerations

Given the nature of the school nurse's role, they may frequently face the task of determining whether it is appropriate to conduct a physical exam or whether it is better to defer this exam to an outside provider.   This can be challenging, as there may be legal implications for either course of action. In some cases, a complete physical assessment may be perceived as unnecessary or inappropriate, while not performing an adequate examination may be perceived as negligence in others. In one case, Schluessler v. Independent School District (1989), a nurse was charged with negligence after failing to appropriately assess a child having an asthma attack, leading to a delay in receiving appropriate emergency care. The court determined that "School nurses have a higher duty of care than hospital nurses to make an assessment of the need for emergency services" (Schluessler v. Independent School District 200, et al.., 1989). School nurses have the essential duty of recognizing emergencies and providing appropriate follow-up care and referral in these situations (Schwab & Gelfman, 2001/2005). This level of assessment and critical thinking may warrant a brief or comprehensive physical exam, especially to rule out trauma, significant injury, or the need for emergency management of symptoms. Therefore, it is essential for the school nurse to use their best judgment, based on education, experience, and clinical guidelines, to determine the level of examination necessary to appraise the clinical urgency of the situation and the need for further emergent evaluation or treatment.

While fear of liability may factor into a school nurse's decision to examine a child, case precedence tends to favor the school nurse (and school districts), as concluded in a review of legal liability versus professional responsibilities and roles. Based on this 2019 review, professionalism, clinical judgment, and adherence to best practice standards of care should be the primary guidelines for school nurses (Zirkel, 2019).

Practice Recommendations

In considering the outcomes of the aforementioned cases involving either inappropriate physical examinations performed by the nurse or negligence at the hands of the school nurse, general recommendations for future school nurse practice include:

1. Examination of a student's genitalia should generally be avoided when possible due to potential legal or psychological consequences, as supported by the aforementioned cases. When a school nurse, exercising their professional judgment, finds that a genital examination should, in fact, be performed within the school setting and not deferred to an external/primary healthcare provider at a later date and time (such as in the case of blunt or acute trauma to the area or significant pain or discomfort that is prohibitive to the student's functioning, or the potential for a surgical emergency or condition that may exceed the capabilities of the school health office), the examination should be done in the presence of another adult, preferably of the same gender as the child (or, in the case of a transgender or nonbinary child, an adult carrying the preferred gender of the child), and with verbal consent from one of the child's legal guardians.

2. Physical examinations should be as problem-focused and brief as possible within the school setting, without compromising adequate assessment of the complaint or concern of the student, and thorough enough to rule out any other possible antecedents. The examination should be limited to the potentially affected body system(s) based on the student report and the nurse's professional judgment wherever possible.

3. Clothing removal should be kept to a minimum wherever possible to protect the privacy and rights of the student in question. Gowns and proper drapery should be provided to the student, allowing him or her to cover the body areas that are not immediately being examined.

4. An adult witness should be present for physical examinations that require the student to disrobe wherever possible. This adult should preferably be the same gender as the student unless the student specifically verbalizes otherwise in front of two witnesses.

5. Parental consent should be obtained wherever possible without compromising the student's immediate health. This may be in the form of a global consent form sent to all parents at the beginning of the school year, indicating that students may be examined based on their acute complaints on a routine or emergent basis or verbal consent obtained from the parent immediately prior to an examination. If there is not adequate time or means to obtain verbal consent from a parent, a nurse should use their best judgment in physically examining students without this consent and should be able to provide an adequate rationale for performing this examination without said consent. For example, the rationale may include the risk of harm to the student or other students should said examination not occur immediately.

6. Informed consent or assent for younger children should always be obtained from the student in question, regardless of the student's age. In some states, a student aged 16 or above may be able to provide informed consent as an adult in certain situations, which would eliminate the need for parental consent. However, even in such states, involving the parent when possible remains good practice so long as the student is comfortable and agreeable to parental involvement. If a student refuses an examination, the nurse should not proceed unless refraining from assessment/examination would cause imminent danger to the student.

7. Examination techniques should follow appropriate nursing guidelines related to the age, mental health status, physical health status, and acute health status of the child in question to ensure that the exam is as pleasant and non-traumatic as possible (Hockenberry & Wilson, 2015). These will vary based on the age and developmental level of the child in question; however, school nurses should have a general knowledge of examination techniques and sequences appropriate to children of all ages and backgrounds.

    If school staff or the school nurse suspect signs of sexual or physical abuse, the nurse should take measures to ensure the child's immediate safety as the primary priority. The school nurse should then file a report with the child protective service department in the particular state in conjunction with any other concerned staff members. The school nurse should take special care not to examine the child unless absolutely necessary for the child's immediate health and safety to avoid impeding any forensic investigation that may take place at the request of the child protective service agency. Should the agency(s) request a medical exam be performed as part of the investigation, the child should be referred to his or her primary care provider or to the local emergency room where there is a higher likelihood of competent and trained providers to perform such an exam.

8. School nurses should also be aware of any U.S. Department of Education (USDE) or state statutes which require photography as part of a maltreatment or neglect investigation. While typically parental consent is required for photographing a child, some DOE statutes (for example, New York City) require that photographs must be taken of any visible signs of trauma in connection with suspected child abuse or maltreatment, as follows:
    i.   A trained staff member must take photographs in a private setting that best serves the interest and privacy of the child.
    ii. Where feasible and appropriate, the child should be taken to the nurse's office or the school's medical room for photographs.
    iii. If a school nurse is not assigned to the building or a nurse is not available for a reasonable time, or the principal/designee determines that the child's best interest would be served by another staff member taking photographs, the principal/designee will ask the designated liaison or another trained staff member to take the photographs.

    While all state/city DOE regulations vary (and some do not issue specific guidance), the majority require photos to be taken on the city or state-owned devices, as opposed to personal devices of the school nurse, disallow for the photographing of genitalia, and require the photographer to be specifically trained in this process. School nurses must be aware of and well-versed in their individual regions' policies before engaging in any form of photographic documentation of suspicions of abuse or injuries. While photos and videos are generally protected under FERPA, photos and videos created or maintained by law enforcement or for the purposes of law enforcement are not considered educational records and may be forwarded to the police without the consent of the student or parent (U.S. Department of Education, 2023).

9. Regarding anything that may resemble a "strip search," typically defined as removing a person's clothing to permit a visual inspection of areas of the body that are not visible while the person is

robed, school nurses must be cautious and prudent in their clinical judgment. While state law varies, the nurse must be aware that strip searches can be traumatic for children and adolescents, leading to negative psychological sequellae, shame, and other signs and symptoms of trauma (Americanbar.org, 2021). A prior U.S. Supreme Court case concluded that searches of students should be conducted in a manner reasonably related to the objectives of the search and should not be excessively intrusive in light of the age and sex of the student and the nature of the infraction. The primary finding of the court was that although the Fourth Amendment applies to searches in schools, the more lenient standard of reasonable suspicion takes precedence over the ordinary standard of probable cause (New Jersey vs. TLO, 1985). It is essential that the school nurse remain vigilant about individual school district policies regarding strip-searching, many of which expressly prohibit strip-searching of any kind, and some of which allow only in situations where not doing so poses a significant and imminent threat to the student or others.

In addition to these generalized recommendations, school nurses should be aware of any state-specific guidelines, laws, or regulations that may warrant further consideration when deciding to physically examine a child in the school setting, as well as any district or school-related policies that may vary from one organization or location to another. It is ultimately the nurse's responsibility to be aware of these factors to make safe and appropriate decisions in the best interest of the students they are assessing and treating.

CONCLUSION

A school nurse's decision as to whether or not to examine a child in a school-based health setting should be carefully considered. Special consideration should be given to 1) the particular complaint or concern of the student, including whether or not this complaint/concern can be deferred to an outpatient provider for assessment or requires more imminent follow-up; 2) whether or not the school nurse has verbal or written consent to examine the child from the child's legal guardian and assent from the child themselves; 3) whether the situation is emergent in that the child may be placed in undue harm's way should the examination not take place by the school nurse in the school setting; and 4) any applicable state regulations or guidance around this issue in the school nurse's particular state of practice. Familiarity with legal cases relevant to physical assessment in the school setting can help the nurse determine differentiating factors in legally appropriate versus legally inappropriate exams. Conversely, the decision not to examine a patient may result in a claim of negligence for delaying treatment, such as in the case of an acute emergency that is not properly diagnosed or treated due to insufficient assessment of the student. With careful consideration, a school nurse can perform appropriately-timed and adequately thorough physical exams to maintain student safety, support appropriate treatments and referrals, and maximize the student's continued engagement in academic and social experiences in the school setting.

RESOURCES

Please see ADDENDUM #1: The Protection of Pupil Rights Act (PPRA)– Physical Exams /Screenings and ADDENDUM #2: Email Confirmation of Verbal Consent

State Nurse Practice Acts

Case Law

Doe v. Claiborne Cnty., Tenn., 103 F.3d 495, 506 (6th Cir. 1996)

Hearring v. Sliwowski, No. 712 F.3d 275, 712 F.3d 275 (6th Cir 2013)

Madden v. Hamilton City Dept. of Education, 1:13-CV-377 (E.D. Tenn. Aug. 9, 2016)

New Jersey v. T. L. O., 469 U. S., at 342, 345 (Supreme Court 1985)

Poe v. Leonard, 282 F.3d 123 (2d Cir. 2002)

Schluessler v. Independent School District 200, et al., No. MM89-14V (105196) MM89-14V (105196) (Dakota District Court 1989)

REFERENCES

Americanbar.org (2021). Preventing strip searches of children and youth: A guide for advocates. https://www.americanbar.org/content/dam/aba/publications/litigation_committees/childrights/strip-search-supplement-ct.pdf

Cohn, S. D., Schwab, N. C., & Gelfman, M. H. B. (2005). Adolescent issues and rights of minors. In N. C. Schwab & M. H. B. Gelfman (Eds.), *Legal Issues in school health services: A resource for school administrators, school attorneys, school nurses,* (pp. 231-261). Author's Choice Press.

Coverdale, G. (2011). Promoting the health of school-aged children: An ethical perspective. In G. M. Brykczynska & J. Simons (Eds.), *Ethical and Philosophical Aspects of Nursing Children and Young People,* (pp. 66-77). John Wiley & Sons.

Hockenberry, M. J., & Wilson, D. (2015). *Wong's nursing care of infants and children* (10th ed.). Elsevier Mosby.

Hootman, J., Schwab, N. C., Gelfman, M. H. B., Gregory, E. K., & Pohlman, K. J. (2005). In N. C. Schwab & M. H. B. Gelfman (Eds.), *Legal Issues in school health services: A resource for school administrators, school attorneys, school nurses,* (pp. 175-178). Author's Choice Press.

Maggiore, W. A. (2009). Providing EMS care for children when parents are absent. *Journal of Emergency Medical Services (JEMS).* https://www.jems.com/administration-and-leadership/providing-ems-care-children-wh-0/

Schott, R. G. (2012). Qualified immunity: How it protects law enforcement officers. *FBI Law Enforcement Bulletin.* https://leb.fbi.gov/2012/september/qualified-immunity-how-it-protects-law-enforcement-officers

Schwab, N. C., & Gelfman, M. (2005). *Legal issues in school health services: A resource for school administrators, school attorneys, school nurses.* Author's Choice Press.

U.S. Constitution, Amendment XIV. http://www.usconstitution.net/xconst_Am14.html

U.S. Department of Education (2023). *Protecting student privacy.* https://studentprivacy.ed.gov/faq/faqs-photos-and-videos-under-ferpa

Zirkel P. A. (2019). Physical exams: Legal liability (versus professional norms). *NASN School Nurse (Print), 34*(5), 270–273. https://doi.org/10.1177/1942602X19846641

ADDENDUM # 1

The Protection of Pupil Rights Act (PPRA)– Physical Exams /Screenings

Erin D. Gilsbach, Esquire, 2017

The PPRA requires local education agencies to develop and adopt policies in consultation with parents regarding the administration of physical examinations or screenings that the school may administer to a student and requires prior parental notice for certain types of physical examinations or screenings. This law would not apply in instances where the physical examination is in response to a particular medical need of the child that requires prompt attention. The PPRA provision only applies to:

(iii) Any nonemergency, invasive physical examination or screening that is—
    (I) required as a condition of attendance;
    (II) administered by the school and scheduled by the school in advance; and
    (III) not necessary to protect the immediate health and safety of the student or of other students 20 U.S.C. § 1232h(c)(1)(D).

ADDENDUM # 2

Email Confirmation of Verbal Consent

Reviewed by Cheryl Resha, EdD, MSN, RN, FAAN, FNASN

Erin D. Gilsbach, Esquire, 2017

An excellent practice that can be used in many different contexts is an email response to verbal consent from a parent. When a parent has authorized consent for a particular nursing service in a time-sensitive situation (written consent should be obtained in situations that are not time-sensitive), such as a physical exam, the parent's verbal consent should be followed up via email. At the time of verbal consent, the nurse should indicate that he/she will send a follow-up email. The email should thank the parent for speaking with the nurse and confirming what was discussed, including verbal consent. Suppose the parent receives the email and does not respond. In that case, it can be inferred that they agree with the substance (similar to passive consent for other school notifications when the parent responds only if refusing the activity). In a legal action, it would be very difficult for a parent to argue the facts, as stated in the email, if the parent did not raise the issue when the email was sent.

Chapter 29
MANAGEMENT OF HEAD LICE (PEDICULOSIS)
Shirley C. Gordon, PhD, RN, NCSN, AHN-BC, HWNC-BC

DESCRIPTION OF ISSUE

Head louse infestation (known as *pediculosis*) is a pandemic, communicable condition. Caused by the Pediculus Humanus Capitis (head louse), pediculosis is humans' most prevalent parasitic infestation (Hodgdon et al., 2010). Head louse infestations are highly stigmatized in many countries, including the United States (U.S.).

School nurses have the responsibility of protecting the community of children, educators, caregivers, support staff, and others from exposure to communicable diseases/conditions. When head louse infestations occur in the community (schools, daycare centers, and camps), strong emotional reactions from parents, teachers, staff, and community members can occur. The community expects school nurses and other healthcare providers to respond with evidence-based approaches to diagnosis, treatment, and transmission prevention. This chapter provides an overview of head lice, focusing on legal considerations in managing head louse infestations in school settings.

BACKGROUND

Head lice have existed since antiquity, and the relationship between humans and head lice is complex. Evidence of human and head lice cohabitation includes the discovery of desiccated lice and nits on Egyptian mummies and ivory nit combs dating back to the 12th and 13th centuries BC (Mumcuoglu & Zias, 1989). Attitudes toward louse infestations have changed over time. For example, in the 18th century, louse infestations were common and thought to provide protection against childhood disease (Drisdelle, 2010).

Despite the long history between humans and head lice, infestations remain prevalent worldwide (Hodgdon et al., 2010; Nolt e al., 2022). Reliable prevalence data on the number of head lice infestations occurring each year in the U.S. is unavailable. However, the Centers for Disease Control (CDC) reports that an estimated 6-12 million cases occur each year in children aged 3-11 (CDC, 2019b).

Despite low morbidity, head louse infestations impose significant social and financial costs on children and families. The cost of treating head louse infestations is high. The most recent comprehensive cost analysis conducted in the U.S. indicates we spend an estimated $500 million dollars each year to combat head lice (Gur & Schneeweiss, 2009)). This estimate considers consumer costs (including treatment products), lost wages, and school system expenses. Overdiagnosis and mismanagement of head louse infestations contribute to high social and financial costs (Pollack et al., 2000).

All ages and socio-economic groups experience head louse infestations. However, children aged 3-11 and their family members are predominantly affected (CDC, 2019b). As a result, 35.6 million children enrolled in pre-K through the 8th grade (National Center for Education Statistics, 2022) and their families are at increased risk for head louse infestations.

Factors influencing our understanding of which groups of people are largely affected include the negative impact of stigma on willingness to disclose the condition and seek help, the vigilance of school personnel in identifying head lice, and the absence of a systematic, national prevalence data collection system.

Experts believe the number of head louse cases is increasing in England and the United States, despite efforts to effectively treat and control transmission (Mumcuoglu et al., 2020). Emerging resistance to available pediculicides is a major contributing factor. In a recent study, researchers explored the prevalence of the kdr-type mutation (knockdown resistance allele frequencies) and permethrin resistance in head lice samples collected from around the country (Yoon et al., 2014). New York, Oregon, New Mexico, North Dakota, New Jersey, and Minnesota were the only states where selected head lice samples did not demonstrate 100% resistance to permethrin. This new resistance evidence informs treatment recommendations. However, it is important to note that resistance patterns vary across geographic locations, and head louse samples in this study did not represent all regions in each state. Therefore, local resistance patterns remain difficult to determine with certainty.

Interestingly, lockdowns, school closures, and physical distancing during the recent COVID-19 Pandemic may have reduced the transmission of head lice. Researchers in France and Israel documented significant decreases in the sale of head lice treatment products in response to COVID-19 mitigation strategies. Further studies are needed to assess the short and long-term impact of social behavior changes on the transmission of head louse infestations (Launay et al., 2022; Mumcuoglu et al., 2022).

Biology

Our understanding of head louse biology directs school management policies and educational programs. Adult head lice are about the size of a sesame seed (CDC, 2019a). They are ectoparasites with a fused thoracic plate and six segmented legs (Meinking et al., 2011). The louse uses claws at the end of each leg to hold onto hair strands and quickly move through hair. The shape of the claw varies, and experts believe claw shape contributes to host selection. For example, head lice with a rounded claw shape prefer hair strands with a similar shape. The claws also limit the ability of the louse to crawl effectively on surfaces other than hair. Respiratory spiracles are located on each side of the thorax. As a protective mechanism, the louse closes the spiracles when exposed to water and other liquids. Head lice do not have wings or hind legs at any time during their development. Therefore, they are not able to jump, hop or fly (CDC, 2020).

Head lice have mouthparts designed to pierce the skin, inject saliva containing vasodilatory and anticoagulation properties, and suck capillary blood directly from the host's scalp (Meinking et al., 2011). Head lice feed every 2-3 hours and "die of starvation and desiccation if feeding does not occur within the first hour after hatching" (p. 1545) and usually survive less than 24 hours away from the human host (Noltet al., 2022). Sources at the CDC (2019a) suggest head lice die within 1-2 days when removed from the human host.

Head lice can adapt to the hair and skin coloring of the human host. For example, it is common for head lice found on persons with blond hair to be lighter in color than lice found on persons with dark brown or black hair (Meinking et al., 2011; CDC, 2019a). Color variation also occurs in response to feeding patterns. Lice that have recently fed will be darker in color. The ability to adapt to their surroundings makes lice more difficult to see and increases the likelihood of an inaccurate diagnosis.

In addition, most lice experts agree that viable eggs are generally found within 6mm or ¼ inch from the scalp (CDC, 2019a). However, Meinking (1999) reported the presence of viable eggs several inches from the scalp in warm, humid climates.

Life Cycle

The life cycle of the head louse has implications for treatment recommendations and school management policies. Therefore, school nurses must understand the life cycle stages and share this understanding with families. The APPENDIX provides a detailed description of the complex life cycle of the head louse presented by the Centers for Disease Control (CDC, 2019a).

Transmission

Head lice are transmitted primarily through prolonged close head-to-head contact. *The prevalence of head lice varies by age, geographic location, and culture* (Burkhart & Burkhart, 2007; Pollack & Norton, 2022). *Head lice survive away from a person for less than one day* (Pollack & Norton, 2022). Indirect transmission through exposure to brushes, combs, and hats used or worn by persons with active infestations occurs infrequently (Burkhart & Burkhart, 2007). For example, researchers have reported that lice found on combs are often dead or injured, making establishing an infestation on a new host unlikely (Chungeet al., 1991).

Head lice live only on the human host and do not infest the environment, such as carpets, furniture, and mattresses. For example, Speare et al. (2003) found live lice on only 4% of the pillowcases used by research volunteers with active head louse infestations. While the researchers suggested indirect transmission was possible, this study did not determine the transmission rate from pillowcases. However, in a later descriptive study, Gordon (2007a) reported sleeping in bed with more than one person as a risk factor for children experiencing persistent head lice. The researcher reported head-to-head transmission during sleep as the most likely transmission mode. Some experts recommend that persons who sleep in the same bed as those diagnosed with active infestations should be treated prophylactically (CDC, 2019c).

Environmental cleaning approaches (effective in controlling body lice), including vacuuming car seats, upholstery, bed linens, and clothing that cannot be washed in hot settings over 1300 F, etc., which include vacuuming car seats, upholstery, bed linens, and clothing that cannot be washed in hot settings over 130⁰ F, etc. are often recommended to prevent head louse transmission (CDC, 2019c). However, there is no evidence to support the effectiveness of environmental cleaning in controlling head lice, and a focus on cleaning may contribute to myths surrounding associations between head lice, poor hygiene, and filthy environments.

Family caregivers are often concerned about transmission between family members and pets. Because head lice are species-specific, they do not infest family pets (cats, dogs, birds, guinea pigs, etc.). Therefore, transmission of head lice does not occur between humans and pets (CDC, 2013; Nolt et al., 2022).

Prevalence

The head louse is an equal opportunity parasite. They infest all socio-economic groups (Nolt et al., 2022) and most ethnic groups (Meinking, 1999). In the United States, head lice are frequently found among Whites, Asians, Hispanics, and North, Central, and South American Indians (Meinking et al., 2011). In the past African

Americans were excluded from prevalence estimates because the infestation prevalence was only 0.3% of African American children (Juranek, 1977). More recently, researchers suspect the American head louse has adapted to the host hair structure as a result of increased travel between countries. This adaptation has resulted in more African American children being infested with head lice (Meinking et al., 2011; McCall et al., 2022).

Research studies exploring prevalence rates demonstrate mixed results regarding gender, hair length, and type. Indicating gender, hair length, and hair type are not significant risk factors in contracting head lice infestations (Canyon & Speare, 2016) but are factors in identification and treatment efficacy (Mumcuoglu et al., 2006). Researchers report that prevalence variations are most likely due to social norms and behaviors rather than the physical characteristics of the host (Canyon & Speare, 2016).

For reasons that are not entirely clear, some students and families develop head louse infestations that persist for weeks, months, or years. Gordon (1999, 2007a) defined persistent head lice as the diagnosis of an active infestation three times in 6 weeks that is not amenable to treatment. Factors contributing to persistent head lice include:

- Treatment failure from emerging resistance, improper use of treatment products, or treatments that target a specific life cycle phase.
- Failure to treat.
- Auto-re-infestation from viable eggs left on the hair.
- Re-infestation through contact with persons experiencing active infestations (often someone in the immediate family who is asymptomatic).

Effects on the Host

Itching (pruritus) is the hallmark symptom of head lice infestations. Researchers estimate that 50% of the population develops sensitivity to the saliva injected by the louse during feeding. Depending on host sensitivity, itching may be absent or manifest as mild to severe. In sensitive persons, *itching may appear 4-6 weeks after the first infestation and sooner after a repeat infestation* (CDC, 2019). Allergic reactions presenting as small erythematous macules or papules may occur at feeding sites in people who are sensitive, and bullae may occur in highly allergic individuals (Marks et al., 2019).

Scratching in response to intense itching at feeding sites or in response to treatment products *may* result in skin excoriations on the scalp. Scalp excoriations can also occur due to the inappropriate, forceful use of plastic and metal nit combs, which are distinguishable by their linear appearance. Breaks in the skin from louse bites and excoriations serve as portals through which louse feces and bacteria can enter the host and cause secondary infection. Symptoms of secondary infection include low-grade fever, lymphadenopathy, itchy skin, and red sores with a yellow crust (impetigo). In rare, extreme cases, anemia may occur (Perez et al., 2022).

In a study by Gordon (2007b), caregivers perceived scratching from head lice-associated itching as a stigmatizing characteristic in school settings. Some participants reported keeping their children home until itching resolved to avoid having their children suffer targeting, bullying, and social trauma. Parents may also confuse itching caused by scalp irritation from treatment products as a symptom of continuing infestation. As a result, parents continue the use of treatment products in an attempt to eliminate head lice. A continuous itch-treatment cycle, illustrated in Figure 1, can lead to parent frustration, misuse of treatment products, and unsafe treatment strategies.

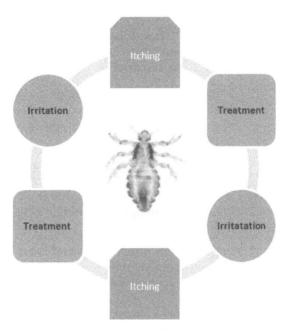

Figure 1: Itch-treatment Cycle. © 2015 Gordon. Reprinted with permission.

Individuals experiencing head lice infestations may also complain of fatigue and irritability, referred to as "feeling lousy" (Meinking et al., 2011). Sleep disruption from nighttime louse activity may contribute to fatigue and irritability.

Misconceptions and Myths

Many misconceptions and myths surround head lice transmission, treatment, and prevention. Table 1 identifies common misconceptions and myths, corresponding truths, and supporting references. School nurses should focus individual family and community education on dispelling common misconceptions and myths and promoting the safe treatment and prevention of head lice.

Table 1 **Misconceptions and Myths**

Misconception and Myths	Truths	Supporting Reference
Head lice spread easily in the classroom	Prolonged head-to-head contact is the major mode of head lice transmission. Only 1 in 10 transmissions occur in schools. Ninety percent of transmissions occur in the community. School nurses should encourage contact tracing of close family and community contacts to identify potential sources of head lice transmission.	Pollack & Norton, 2022 CDC, 2019b Maunder, 1985
Head lice spread by sharing brushes, combs, hats, helmets, or headphones with someone who has lice.	Fomite (inanimate object) transmission is RARE. Prevention efforts should focus on educating parents to identify head lice infestations early and initiate safe, effective treatment.	Nolt et al., 2022 CDC, 2019b
Head lice spread by taking selfies.	Lice spread by prolonged, direct head-to-head contact. There is no evidence to suggest teens are acquiring head lice infestations by taking selfie photographs or that there is an increase in the teen prevalence rate in the U.S.	Pollack, 2014
Lice can jump or fly from person to person.	Lice do not have wings or hind legs and, therefore, cannot jump, hop, or fly.	CDC, 2020 Meinking et al., 2011
You can get head lice from pets.	Head lice are species-specific. Animals, including pets, do not share head lice with humans. Pets should not be treated for head lice.	Nolt et al., 2022
Extensive environmental cleaning of the classroom or home is necessary to eradicate head lice and prevent transmission.	Head lice live and lay eggs on the human host. They do not infest the environment. Environmental sprays are not effective and increase pesticide exposure unnecessarily. Clean hair care items and bedding used by persons who are infested	Speare, Thomas, & Cahill, 2002 CDC, 2013 Nolt et al., 2022
Poor *personal* hygiene causes head lice.	Having head lice is not reflective of being dirty or having poor hygiene.	Nolt et al., 2022
Head lice are a sign of poor parenting and/or child neglect.	Anyone can get head lice.	Nolt et al., 2022

Misconception and Myths	Truths	Supporting Reference
If one member of the family has head lice, all members of the family must be treated at the same time.	Only persons with an active infestation (presence of at least one live louse) should be treated for head lice. All family members and close family contacts should be screened for head lice.	Nolt et al., 2022
Head lice spread diseases in schools.	*Head lice are not known to* spread disease.	Nolt et al., 2022 Pollack & Norton, 2022
African-Americans do not get head lice.	While the prevalence rate is significantly lower than other groups, head lice infestations occur among African Americans.	McCall et al., 2022
Agricultural pesticides and veterinary flea and tick products can be safely used on humans.	Agricultural pesticides and veterinary flea and tick products are not formulated or tested on humans and may have impurities not found in pharmaceutical-grade products designed to treat head lice. Agricultural and veterinary products are unsafe for children or adults and should never be recommended or used.	Nolt et al., 2022
Head lice can spread in swimming pools.	Head lice do not spread in swimming pools. In an in vitro study, head lice on persons swimming in chlorinated pools survived immersion. However, there was no lice loss or person-to-person transmission observed.	Canyon & Speare, 2007
There are products available that effectively remove or loosen the fixative bonding head louse nits/ eggs to hair strands.	There is no evidence to suggest that products claiming to loosen the fixative that bonds head louse nits/eggs to hair strands are effective. The most effective way to remove nits/eggs is with a quality nit comb. Empty egg casings may contribute to stigma but do not present a re-infestation risk. Therefore, removal is cosmetic.	Burgess, 2010 Burgess, Brunton & Burgess, 2015 .

IMPLICATIONS FOR SCHOOL NURSE PRACTICE

School nurses are often the first healthcare providers to identify a head lice infestation and assist families with treatment and prevention approaches. Nolt et al. representing the American Academy of Pediatrics [AAP] (2022) and the National Association of School Nurses (NASN) (2020), both recommend head lice management policies and procedures based on the best available evidence. However, there are many challenges in caring for children with head lice infestations in school settings.

Social Perceptions

In the U.S., head lice infestations create strong emotional responses. Responses to head lice include disgust, horror, fear, frustration, anger, embarrassment, guilt, shock, shame, and dismay (Gordon, 2007a; Parison et al., 2013). The most common response is disgust (Parison et al., 2013). Feelings of disgust activate the human behavioral immune system (HBIS), which drives protective actions designed to prevent contact with potentially dangerous toxins, microbes, or parasites. Humans' direct feelings of disgust outward toward those thought to be responsible or dangerous. Fear of head lice transmission elicits contamination-avoidance behaviors, including identifying and avoiding persons with head lice.

Schools have historically used management policies and strategies such as school-based screening and forced exclusion from school for the presence of live head lice and nits (no-nit policy) to control the transmission of head lice. Anecdotally, there is considerable policy variation between states, school districts, and even between schools within individual districts.

Parents have reported concern that once school personnel identify a child with a head lice infestation, they target their children and family, resulting in mandatory school exclusions and retaliatory repeated screening procedures (Gordon, 2007a). Some parents change schools to avoid social stigma or to become disassociated with derogatory labels such as *"licers"*, "frequent flyer" or *"lice family"* (Gordon, 2007a).

School nurses should:
- Provide support and a caring environment in which a trusting relationship develops. Without trust, families may not disclose a diagnosis of head lice or be open to treatment recommendations and follow-up care.
- Design educational programs for parents and school personnel that focus specifically on transmission to allay the fear of transmission and resulting negative social behavior.
- Avoid using derogatory labels when referring to children and families experiencing head lice infestations.
- Advocate for consistent non-exclusionary policies that follow authoritative, national recommendations.

Confidentiality

Because of social perceptions and stigma associated with head lice infestations and the possible negative social ramifications, it is especially important for school nurses to maintain strict confidentiality practices as described in the Health Insurance and Portability and Accountability Act, also known as HIPAA (HIPAA, 1996) and the Family Educational Rights and Privacy Act, also known as FERPA (34 CFR § 99.2, FERPA 1974). While parents may feel they have a right to know if there is a child in the school with head lice, HIPAA and FERPA standards allow personal information to be shared only with persons who have a need to know. A head lice infestation is not considered a health hazard (CDC, 2013); therefore, school nurses are not obligated to warn parents or school personnel (Shah et al., 2013). Parents may file a violation of privacy complaint if someone at the school discloses their child's head louse infestation to others. Letters sent home reporting a case of head lice in the classroom, if used, should be used with caution to avoid inadvertent disclosures.

School nurses should:
- Maintain strict confidentiality practices.
- Train all school staff with access to school health information on the importance of confidentiality practices.
- Report breaches of confidentiality.

Identification of Head Lice

The social stigma associated with head louse infestation contributes to parental hesitancy to disclose the condition inside or outside the family. As a result, parents do not share the presence of head lice with extended family members and treat children an average of 5 times before seeking assistance from a school nurse or other healthcare provider (Meinking et al., 2011; Gordon, 2007a). Hesitancy to disclose may delay diagnosis and contribute to transmission.

"The identification of eggs (nits), nymphs or adult lice with the naked eye establishes the diagnoses" of head lice (Nolt et al., 2022, p. 2). However, school nurses should not recommend treatment unless the infestation is active (CDC, 2019c; Nolt et al., 2022). Diagnostic confusion centers on distinguishing active infestation (presence of at least one live louse) from inactive infestation (presence of eggs, nits, and pseudo nits such as dandruff, hair casts, hair debris, etc.). A false negative diagnosis may delay treatment and increase the probability of transmission. False positive diagnoses often lead to unnecessary treatment, increased exposure to chemical pesticides, and forced absences from school and work. In extreme cases, frustrated parents may resort to unsafe treatment approaches such as agricultural and veterinarian treatment products, gasoline, and kerosene (Gordon, 2007a). Unfortunately, diagnostic confusion is common given the size of newly hatched head lice, louse adaptive mechanisms, and lack of evidence-based screening techniques and training programs (Pollack et al., 2000).

The first step in identifying and treating head lice is to screen the head and hair of individuals for the presence of live lice. Therefore, effective, evidence-based screening techniques are essential in determining treatment recommendations and treatment efficacy.

In a study by Gordon (2007a) exploring caring for children with persistent head lice, 100% of the primary caregiver participants reported never receiving instruction on when and how to screen family members for the presence of head lice. Without an effective screening technique, parents had no reliable way of knowing if their child had an active head lice infestation or if an infestation was successfully treated. Parental confidence in effectively screening family members for the presence of live lice may significantly influence caregiver strain and perceived shared vulnerability.

To date, no research studies describe effective screening techniques or educational programs for parents/ family caregivers. Screening methods presented in the literature represent methods developed by researchers for product evaluation studies or for determining participant inclusion criteria. The lack of studies focusing on developing parental screening programs presents a significant challenge to school nurses charged with educating family caregivers.

The school nurse should:
- Establish personal competency and confidence in identifying the presence of live lice (active infestation).
- Document assessment outcomes, including the integrity of the scalp and secondary infection, if present.
- Request educational training if needed.
- Notify, educate, and support family caregivers.
- Train family members to effectively screen for the presence of live lice.
- Encourage family caregivers to check/screen all household members and other close contacts at the same time to identify potential transmission sources.
- Maintain strict confidentiality practices.

Treatment Recommendations

Treatment strategies should be safe, effective, readily accessible, and affordable (CDC, 2019c; Nolt et al., 2022). The AAP periodically publishes a review of recommended treatment approaches (Nolt et al., 2022). Common active ingredients in current over-the-counter products include permethrin 1% and pyrethrins plus piperonyl butoxide. Prescription products include malathion 0.5%, benzyl alcohol 5%, spinosad 0.9%, and ivermectin 0.5%. "Lindane is no longer recommended by the American Academy of Pediatrics or the Medical Letter for use as treatment of pediculosis capitis" (Nolt et al., 2022, p. 6).

No treatment product is 100% ovicidal (kills all eggs). Researchers report emerging pediculicide resistance around the world and anticipate increasing resistance in response to regional use of pediculicides over time (Nolt et al., 2022).

Care should be taken during all product applications to avoid eye contact and limit absorption through the skin by using warm water to rinse products over the sink. Parents may confuse common topical reactions (itching and burning of the scalp) from pediculicides with ongoing infestation resulting in unnecessary, potentially harmful retreatment of their children (Gordon, 2007b; Nolt et al., 2022). Inflammatory responses can also cause flaking and scabbing on the scalp, contributing to ongoing diagnostic confusion. Therefore, careful adherence to application instructions and limiting treatment to active infestations is essential.

Other treatment methods include manual removal (nit comb), natural products (essential oils), occlusive agents, and desiccation (high volume, warm air device). See the AAP review of treatment approaches for additional information and recommendations for use (Nolt et al., 2022).

Treatment strategies such as flammable agents (including gasoline and kerosene), agricultural pesticides, and products designed for use on animals are considered unsafe and should never be recommended for use on humans (Nolt et al., 2022). In addition, in most instances, experts do not recommend prophylactic treatment with pediculicides (Mumcuoglu et al., 2019).

The school nurse should:
- Maintain up-to-date knowledge of available treatment approaches.

- Obtain and document a complete treatment history.
- Recommend treatment only if an active infestation is present.
- Respectfully review safe, effective, readily accessible, affordable treatment options and safety issues with family caregivers.
- Encourage family caregivers to follow manufacturers' guidelines when applying head lice treatment products.
- Document treatment recommendations and follow-up care.
- Report unsafe treatment approaches following appropriate state and district requirements.
- Maintain strict confidentiality practices.

Screening and Mandatory Exclusion from School

The AAP (Nolt et al., 2022) and the NASN (2020) do not support school-wide screening programs and policies designed to exclude children from school for the presence of nits or live lice as methods for reducing transmission in schools. While *there is no evidence that screening reduces the incidence of head lice,* these organizations support **limited screening of children demonstrating symptoms conducted by trained personnel**. To adequately train personnel, they would need to be instructed on the use of microscopic evaluation of the specimens*, as identification of a live louse by microscope is the gold standard for entomologists.* However, symptom-focused school screenings should not take the place of screening by parents and other caregivers (Nolt et al., 2022; Mumcuoglu et al., 2020).

Background for the recommendation: Researchers have challenged the effectiveness of school-wide screening programs and "no-nit" policies in reducing head louse transmission in school settings (Meinking et al., 2011). In one study, the number of nits in a child's hair and distance from the scalp were significant factors in predicting which children with "nits only" would convert to a live infestation (Hootman, 2002). Only 18% of children with "nits only" converted to live infestation. Children with *five* nits within ¼ inch from the scalp were most likely to develop a live infestation. Therefore, schools following a strict no-nit policy would send 82% of the children with nits-only home unnecessarily.

School nurses are required to protect the privacy of students during screening procedures. In school settings, the act of screening a child for head lice may, in itself, be a stigmatizing event. School nurses should be familiar with the head lice policies in place at their school(s). Procedural safeguards include:

- Following the policy/procedure without discriminating against individual students or groups of students.
- Periodic policy/procedure review and update based on evidence as needed.
- Availability of the policy to parents and family caregivers.

Consideration of special protections that may apply to students who fall under the Americans with Disability Act. School nurses should:

- Know their school and/or district head lice policies/procedures.
- Avoid school-wide and classroom-wide screening programs.
- Limit screening to children demonstrating symptoms.

- Support the use of trained personnel for screening.
- Maintain strict confidentiality practices.
- Follow procedural safeguards.
- Advocate for consistent, non-exclusionary policies that follow authoritative, national recommendations.

Storage of Pediculicides in School Settings

Chemicals in pediculicides (treatment products for head lice) can enter the body through absorption, inhalation, and ingestion. In addition, some head lice treatment products are flammable. As potentially hazardous chemicals, pediculicides fall under the Occupational Safety and Health Administration's (OSHA) Hazard Communication Standard [HCS] (OSHA, 2017). The HCS intends to protect employees in the work setting. Employers are required to notify employees of the presence and potential exposure of all hazardous chemicals and train employees to handle products safely. Safety Data Sheets (SDS) have a standard 16-section format and are available for all potentially hazardous chemicals from the manufacturer. SDS includes warnings for flammability, reactivity, health warnings, and required personnel protection equipment. Many SDS can be located on the OSHA website or by searching the internet by product name or chemical name.

School nurses who store and distribute head lice treatment products within the school setting should:
- Maintain up-to-date SDSs and advise personnel of the location of these documents.
- Train all personnel who come in contact with pediculicides to safely handle the products.
- Store all treatment products safely by following manufacturer recommendations.
- Keep products out of the reach of children to avoid accidental exposure or ingestion.

In addition, school nurses who treat children with pediculicides within the school setting should:
- Obtain parental consent for treatment.
- Be familiar with the specific product, its properties, potential side effects, and potential interactions.
- Assess the child's health history, allergy, and immune status prior to applying a pediculicide.
- Ensure that the application process is followed, including appropriate follow-up.

Advocating for Change

School nurses play an important role in advocating for policy change. Long-standing policies based on fear of transmission are especially difficult to change. Pontius (2011) provides a successful exemplar depicting how one state moved from a no-nit exclusionary head lice policy to a non-exclusionary policy. Key elements of success were:

- Use of authoritative, evidence-based supporting materials.
- Documenting the impact of the current policy/procedure.
- Enacting small policy changes
- Documenting the impact of the change to allay fear.
- Ongoing communication with teachers, principals, school board members, and parents regarding the impact of policy changes.

CONCLUSION

Head louse infestations are a highly stigmatized communicable condition. While most transmissions occur in family and community settings, school nurses are often the first to identify the presence of an active infestation. School nurses play an important role in decreasing stigma, promoting safe treatment strategies, allaying the fear of transmission, and advocating for non-exclusionary head lice management policies in school settings.

RESOURCES

Centers for Disease Control and Prevention. (2015). Head lice information for schools.
http://www.cdc.gov/parasites/lice/head/schools.html

National Association of School Nurses. (2020). *Head lice management in schools.* (Position Statement)..
https://www.nasn.org/nasn-resources/professional-practice-documents/position-statements/ps-head-lice

National Association of School Nurses. (2021). NASN Code of Ethics.
https://www.nasn.org/nasn-resources/resources-by-topic/codeofethics

National Association of School Nurses. (2022). School nursing: Scope and standards of practice (4th ed.).

REFERENCES

Burgess, I.F. (2010). Do nit removal formulations and other treatments loosen head louse eggs and nits from hair? *Medical and Veterinary Entomology, 24*(1), 55-61. https://doi.org/10.1111/j.1365-2915.2009.00845.x

Burgess, M.N., Brunton, E. R., & Burgess, I. F. (2016). A novel nit comb concept using ultrasound actuation: Preclinical evaluation. *Journal of Medical Entomology, 53*(1), 152–156. https://doi.org/10.1093/jme/tjv176

Burkhart, C.N. & Burkhart, C.G. (2007). Fomite transmission in head lice. *Journal of the American Academy of Dermatology, 56(6), 1044-1047.* https://doi.org/10.1016/j.jaad.2006.10.979

Canyon, D., & Speare, R. (2007). Do head lice spread in swimming pools? *The International Society of Dermatology, 46,* 1211-1213https://doi.org/10.1111/j.1365-4632.2007.03011.x

Canyon, D., & Speare, R. (2016). Lice---head/body/public (Pediculosis, phthirus infestation, lousiness). *Clinical Advisor.* http://www.clinicaladvisor.com/dermatology/lice-headbodypubic-pediculosis-phthirus-infestation-lousiness/article/589056/

Centers for Disease Control and Prevention. (2013). *Parasites-lice- Index.* https://www.cdc.gov/parasites/lice/head/index.html

Centers for Disease Control. (2015). *Parasites: Life Cycle [Online Image].* https://www.cdc.gov/parasites/lice/head/biology.html

Centers for Disease Control and Prevention. (2019a). *Biology.* www.cdc.gov/parasites/lice/head/biology.html

Centers for Disease Control and Prevention. (2019b). *Epidemiology and risk factors.* https://www.cdc.gov/parasites/lice/head/epi.html Centers for Disease Control and Prevention.

Centers for Disease Control and Prevention. (2019c). *Parasites – lice – head lice - treatment.* http://www.cdc.gov/parasites/lice/head/treatment.html

Centers for Disease Control and Prevention. (2020). Head lice - General Information - *Frequently asked questions*. https://www.cdc.gov/parasites/lice/head/gen_info/faqs.html

Chunge, R.N., Scott, F.E., Underwood, J.E., & Zavarella, K.J. (1991). A review of the epidemiology, public health importance, treatment and control of head lice. *Canadian Journal of Public Health*, *82(3),* 196–200. http://www.ncbi.nlm.nih.gov//pubmed/1884315

Drisdelle, R. (2010). *Parasites: Tales of humanity's most unwelcome guests.* University of California Press.

Family Educational Rights and Privacy Act (FERPA). U.S. Department of Education. (20 U.S.C.§ 1232g; 34 CFR Part 99. https://ed.gov/policy/gen/guid/fpco/ferpa/index.html

Gordon, S.C. (2007a). Shared vulnerability: A theory of caring for children with persistent head lice. *The Journal of School Nursing*, *23*(5), 283-292. http://ezproxy.fau.edu/login?url=http://search.proquest.com/docview/213134889?accountid=10902

Gordon, S.C. (2007b). [Itching as a stigmatizing characteristic]. Unpublished raw data.

Gordon, S.C. (1999). Factors related to the overuse of chemical pesticides in children experiencing persistent head lice. *Journal of School Nursing*, *15*(5), 6-10. https://doi.org/10.1177/105984059901500502

Gordon, S.C. (2015). *Itch-Treatment cycle*. [Unpublished document]. Nursing, Florida Atlantic University.

Gur, I. & Schneeweiss R. (2009). Head lice treatments and school policies in the U.S. in an era of emerging resistance: A cost-effectiveness analysis. *PharmacoEconomics*, *27*(9), 725–734. https://link.springer.com/article/10.2165/11313740-000000000-00000

Health Insurance Portability and Accountability Act of 1996, 45 C.F.R. § § 160, 162 and 164

Hodgdon, H.E., Yoon, K.S., Previte, D.J., Kim, N.J., Aboelghar, G.E., Lee, S. H., & Clark, J.M. (2010). Determination of knock down resistance allele frequencies in global human head lice populations using the serial invasive amplification reaction. *Pest Management Science*, *66*,1031-1040. https://doi.org/10.1002/ps.1979

Hootman, J. (2002). Quality improvement projects related to pediculosis management. *The Journal of School Nursing*, *18*(2), 80–86. https://doi.org/10.1177/10598405020180020401

Juranek, D. D. (1977). Epidemiologic investigations of pediculosis capitis in schoolchildren. In M. Orkin, H.I. Maibach, I.C. Parish, et al. (Eds.). *Scabies and pediculosis,* (p. 168 -173). Lippincott.

Launay, Bardoulat, I., Lemaitre, M., Blanchon, T., & Fardet, L. (2022). Effects of the COVID-19 pandemic on head lice and scabies infestation dynamics: a population-based study in France. *Clinical and Experimental Dermatology*, *47*(5), 867–872. https://doi.org/10.1111/ced.15054

Marks, J. G., Miller, J. J., & Lookingbill, D. P. (2019). *Lookingbill and Marks' Principles of Dermatology* (Sixth edition.). Saunders Elsevier.

Maunder, J.W. (1985). Human lice: Some basic facts and misconceptions. *Bulletin of the Pan American Health Organization*, 1985,*19(2)*,194–197. www.ncbi.nlm.nih.gov/pubmed/4052692?tool=bestpractice.bmj.com

McCall, E. Torpey, M.E., Contento, M., & Cline A. Racial factors regarding diagnosis and treatment of head lice in pediatric patients. *Journal of the American Academy of Dermatology,* 2022; *87*(3) Supplement: AB99. https://doi.org/10.1016/j.jaad.2022.06.430

Meinking, T. L. (1999). Infestations. *Current problems in dermatology*, *11*(3), 73-120. https://www.sciencedirect.com/science/article/pii/S1040048699900054

Meinking, T, Taplin, D. & Vicaria, V. (2011). Infestations. In L. A. Schachner & R.C. Hansen (Eds.). *Pediatric Dermatology* (4th ed.) pp.1535-1583. Mosby Elsevier.

Mumcuoglu, K.Y., Barker, Burgess, I.F, Combescot-Lang, C. Dalgleish, R.C. Larsen, K.S. Miller, J. Roberts, R.J. &

Taylan-Ozkan, A. (2007). International guidelines for effective control of head louse infestations. *Journal of Drugs in Dermatology*, 6(4), 409-414. http://www.lusfrinorge.no/documents/Internasjonale%20retningslinjer,%20hodelus.pdf

Mumcuoglu, K.Y., Hoffman, T. & Schwartz, E. (2022). Head louse infestations before and during the COVID-19 epidemic in Israel. *Acta tropica*, (232), 106503-106503

Mumcuoglu, K.Y., Pollack, R.J. Reed, D.L. Barker, S.T., Gordon, S.C., Toloza, A.C., Picollo, M.I., Taylan-Ozkan, T.,

Chosidow, O., Habedank, B, Ibarra, J. Meinking, T.L., & Vander Stichele, R. (2020) International recommendations for an effective control of head louse infestations. *International Journal of Dermatology, 60*(3), pp. 272-280. https://doi.org/10.1111/ijd.15096

Mumcuoglu, K.Y, Meinking, T.A., Burkhart, C.N., & Burkhardt, C. G. (2006). Head louse infestations: The "no nit" policy and its consequences. *International Journal of Dermatology, 45*(8), 891-896. https://doi.org/10.1111/j.1365-4632.2006.02827.x

Mumcuoglu, K.Y. & Zias, J. (1989). How the ancients deloused themselves. *Biblical Archaeology Review, 15*, 66 – 69. http://phthiraptera.info/content/how-ancients-de-loused-themselves

National Association of School Nurses (NASN). (2020). *Head lice management in schools.* (Position Statement). Author. https://www.nasn.org/nasn-resources/professional-practice-documents/position-statements/ps-head-lice

National Center for Education Statistics. (2022). Public school enrollment. *Condition of Education*. U.S. Department of Education, Institute of Education Sciences. https://nces.ed.gov/programs/coe/indicator/cga

Nolt, D., Moore, S. Albert C. Yan, A.C., Melnick, L., Committee On Infectious Diseases, & Committee On Practice And Ambulatory Medicine, Section On Dermatology. (2022). Head lice. *Pediatrics* 150 (4), e2022059282. https://doi.org/10.1542/peds.2022-059282

Occupational Safety and Health Administration (OSHA). (2017). *Hazard communication standard* (HCS). https://www.osha.gov/dsg/hazcom/

Parison, J., Speare, R. & Canyon, D. (2013). Head lice: The feelings people have. *International Journal of Dermatology*, 52(2), 169-171.https://doi.org/10.1111/j.1365-4632.2011.05300.x

Perez, M., Vinod, B., & Gandham, S. (2022). More than an itch: An unusual cause of severe anemia in a 5-year-old. *Clinical Pediatrics*, 61(12), 879-882. https://doi.org/10.1177/00099228221106630

Pollack, R. (2014, February 24). *Re: Selfies (probably) not spreading lice among teens, expert says.* [Online comment]. http://www.nbcnews.com/science/weird-science/selfies-probably-not-spreading-lice-among-teens-expert-says-n37651

Pollack, R. J., Kiszewski, A.E. & Spielman, A. (2000). Overdiagnosis and consequent mismanagement of head louse infestations in North America. *Pediatric Infectious Disease Journal*, *19*(8), 689–693. https://www.ncbi.nlm.nih.gov/pubmed/10959734

Pollack, R. J. & Norton, S. A. (2022). Ectoparasite infestations and arthropod injuries. In Loscalzo, J., Fauci, A., Kasper, D., Hauser, S., Longo., D., and Jameson, L. (Eds.), *Harrison's principles of internal medicine, 21e.* (pp. 3608-3616). McGraw Hill Medical.

Pontius, D. (2011). Hats off to success. Changing head lice policy. *NASN School Nurse*, (November), *26*(6),357-362. https://doi.org/10.1177/1942602X11421349

Shah, S.K., Hull, S.C., Spinner, M.A., Berkman, B. E., Sanchez, L.A., Abdul-Karim, R., Hsu, A.P., Claypool, R. & Holland, S.M. (2013). What does duty to warn require? The American Journal of Bioethics, *13*(10), 62-63, https://doi.org/10.1080/15265161.2013.828528

Speare, R., Thomas, G., & Cahill, C. (2002*).* Head lice are not found on floors in primary school classrooms. *Australian & New Zealand Journal of Public Health*, *26*(3), 207-208. https://www.ncbi.nlm.nih.gov/pubmed/12141614

Speare, R., Cahill, C., & Thomas, G. (2003). Head lice on pillows, and strategies to make a small risk even less. *International Journal of Dermatology*, *42*(8), 626-629. https://doi.org/10.1046/j.1365-4362.2003.01927.x

Yoon, K.S., Previte, D.J., Hodgdon, H.E., Poole, B.C., Kwon, D.H., El-Ghar, G.E., Lee, S.H. & Clark, J.M. (2014). Knockdown resistance allele frequencies in North American head louse populations. *Journal of Medical Entomology, 51*(2), 450–457. https://www.ncbi.nlm.nih.gov/pmc/articles/PMC4007213/

APPENDIX: Life Cycle of Head Louse

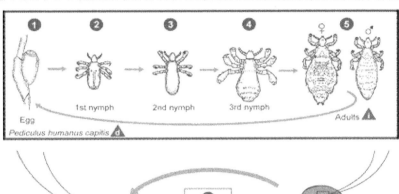

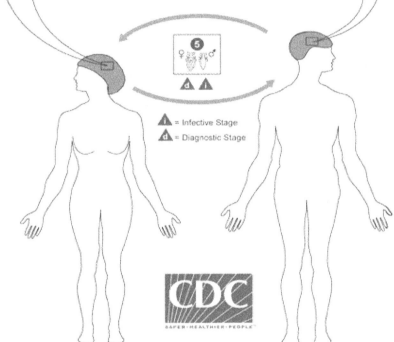

The life cycle of the head louse has three stages: egg, nymph, and adult.

Eggs: Nits are head lice eggs. They are hard to see and are often confused for dandruff or hair spray droplets. Nits are laid by the adult female and are cemented at the base of the hair shaft nearest the scalp❶. They are 0.8 mm by 0.3 mm, oval, and usually yellow to white. Nits take about 1 week to hatch (range 6 to 9 days). Viable eggs are usually located within 6 mm of the scalp.

Nymphs: The egg hatches to release a nymph❷. The nit shell then becomes a more visible dull yellow and remains attached to the hair shaft. The nymph looks like an adult head louse but is about the size of a pinhead. Nymphs mature after three molts❸❹ and become adults about 7 days after hatching.

Adults: The adult louse is about the size of a sesame seed, has 6 legs (each with claws), and is tan to grayish-white❺. In persons with dark hair, the adult louse will appear darker. Females are usually larger than males and can lay up to 8 nits per day. Adult lice can live up to 30 days on a person's head. To live, adult lice need to feed on blood several times daily. Without blood meals, the louse will die within 1 to 2 days off the host.

Life cycle image and information courtesy of <u>DPDx</u>. Centers for Disease Control and Prevention. (2019a). Life Cycle [Online Image].

Chapter 30

HIV AND THE LEGAL IMPLICATIONS FOR SCHOOLS
Alicia Mezu, MSN/Ed, BSN, BS, RN

DESCRIPTION OF ISSUE

HIV, also known as human immunodeficiency virus, is the virus that attacks the body's immune system, specifically the CD4 cells, also known as T cells, causing the body to become ineffective in fighting off infections. If left untreated, the HIV infection can lead to AIDS–acquired immunodeficiency syndrome. There is no effective cure for HIV; however, the development of effective HIV medicines called antiretroviral therapy (ART) is available for treatment. ART is a combination of HIV medicines taken every day. ART is recommended for everyone who has HIV, and it is recommended to start taking it as soon as possible. When ART is taken as prescribed, these medicines are effective in reducing the amount of HIV circulating in the blood, also known as viral load, and reduce the risk of HIV transmission. When the viral load is very low to the point where it becomes undetectable in standard HIV laboratory testing, this is referred to as an undetectable viral load. Thus, individuals infected with HIV who take the prescribed HIV medications and maintain an undetectable viral load can live long and healthy lives. (World Health Organization, [WHO], n.d.).

Adolescents (13–19 years old) and young adults (20–24 years old) with HIV consistently account for about one-fifth of new infections in the United States (Centers for Disease Control and Prevention [CDC], 2022; Kapogiannis et al.,2020). According to the National Institutes of Health, some adolescents in the United States may have acquired HIV infection through perinatal transmission. However, HIV acquired among adolescents later in life may result from infection through sexual transmission.

Comprehensive Health Education curricula taught in schools help to increase awareness and prevention education about HIV and AIDS among school-age children.

BACKGROUND

As of 2022, the CDC reports that 35 states have implemented laws that criminalize HIV exposure (CDC, 2023c). The CDC also reports that in the early years of the HIV epidemic, many states implemented HIV-specific criminal exposure laws to discourage actions that might lead to transmission, promote safer sex practices, and receive funding to support HIV prevention activities. The initial laws were passed when the information about HIV was limited, including how HIV is transmitted, treated, and prevented. After 40 years, HIV research has progressed significantly, including biomedical advancements for treating and preventing HIV transmission. However, many state laws may be outdated as they may not reflect the current understanding of HIV and the effectiveness of treatment options.

School nurses have a valuable role in providing access to health services for students in the school setting. The school nurse's role includes improving student health and wellness, leading to increased student attendance. The availability of school nursing services:
- may range from general health care to treating and providing chronic disease management,
- increased health promotion, prevention education/preventative care, and
- healthcare prevention counseling for the students in the school setting.

Thus, student access to school health services/school nursing services supports increased academic success for all students. School nursing is an extension of public health nursing. School nurses have the expertise to identify, assess, plan, implement, and evaluate students and the school community's health needs. School nurses also provide services for students and families that lead to the promotion of optimal health and academic success in the school setting. School nurses also understand the importance of the three levels of prevention, e.g., primary, secondary, and tertiary prevention.

- Primary prevention in the school health services setting related to primary HIV prevention focuses on health promotion and wellness activities, including promoting and referring students to get tested for HIV, especially since many individuals infected with HIV may not have symptoms. Primary HIV prevention also focuses on reducing the incidence of HIV transmission.
- Secondary prevention strategies in the school health services setting related to HIV prevention may include the availability of HIV testing/HIV screening in the school setting, referrals to healthcare providers/school-based health care programs, and follow-up care.
- Tertiary prevention strategies for HIV prevention in the school health services setting can involve linkage to pre-exposure prophylaxis (PrEP) services which assist in reducing the chance of getting HIV, counseling for behavioral risk reduction, or reminders to test regularly. PrEP prescription is available in pill form (Truvada and Descovy) or injection form (Apretude). The healthcare provider authorized to prescribe PrEP will determine the type of PrEP based on the route of risk of HIV infection Note: If an individual tests positive for HIV, the individual is offered information and resources for linkage to HIV care and treatment, including wrap-around services and support.

According to the National Conference of State Legislators (NCSL), all states are involved in sexual health education in public schools. Thus, sexual health and HIV education is taught in schools across the United States. According to the NCSL, as of October 1, 2020, 39 states in the United States and the District of Columbia have implemented requirements for students to receive HIV instruction in the classroom, including basic sexual health education related to teen pregnancy rates and prevention efforts and information related to sexually transmitted disease (STD) affecting young people ages 15-24 who account for 25 percent of the sexually active population. Most states have current policies. The Guttmacher Institute (2023) provides an overview of the U.S. Sexual Health Education Laws by state.

Adolescents and young adults living with HIV are defined as those who acquired HIV in the first decade of life and those who acquired HIV in or after the second decade of life (HIV.gov,2021). These individuals may receive a broad category of combined treatment regimens with the expectation of reducing the plasma virus levels below the HIV limits of detection, also referred to as undetectable levels of the virus. It is also recommended that pediatric and adolescent health care providers prepare adolescents and young adults for the transition into adult care settings for continued youth engagement in health care and successful transition to adult HIV providers. It is also important to note the social-emotional effects of HIV and the stigma of the disease on adolescents and young adults. Thus, positive communication with school-age children living with HIV/AIDS is necessary to support adherence to the retroviral therapy and treatment plan. Motivators related to viral suppression can serve to support improved HIV/AIDS health, and evidence of undetectable status helps to reduce the stigma of HIV/AIDS and improve medication adherence for adolescents and young adults living with HIV.

The National Association of School Nurses (NASN) (2022), comprehensive health education should begin upon entry into school, continuing through grade 12, and should be inclusive and equitable. The National Health Education Standards provide a framework for schools to facilitate the knowledge and skills related to health topics, including promoting healthy behaviors and health outcomes for school-age youth (CDC, 2023d).

The Whole School, Whole Community, Whole Child (WSCC) Model (CDC, 2023a) is a framework developed collaboratively between the CDC and the Association for Supervision and Curriculum Development (ASCD). The WSCC model focuses on establishing healthy behaviors during childhood and engages schools in promoting health and safety behaviors among school-age children and young people to help establish lifelong health behaviors. The WSCC model also engages schools, families, and communities to improve student health and learning in various settings, i.e., at home, in school, in out-of-school programs, and in the community. The WSCC Model informs HIV, STD, and Pregnancy prevention by monitoring sexual health behaviors, policies, and practices among adolescents.

The Youth Risk Behavior Survey, the School Health Profiles Survey, and the School Health Policies and Practices Study provide important data related to health risk behaviors among youth, including health policies and health practices in the school setting. Additionally, the partnership efforts and communication resources serve as support among school leaders, community agencies, and community groups. They can engage schools in meaningful ways to provide resources for student health education. Additionally, increased learning through implementing the health education curriculum increases the opportunity to address health in schools.
The CDC (2023b) promotes health education in the school setting as helpful to adolescents to acquire and learn about functional health knowledge. Health education helps strengthen and increase the attitudes, beliefs, and opportunities for school-age children and young people to practice health education skills necessary to maintain consistent healthy behaviors throughout life.

IMPLICATIONS FOR SCHOOL NURSE PRACTICE

School nurses promote health and wellness to keep students safe in the school setting. School nurses also help students, families, and the school community to understand prevention education and health promotion. School nurses and schools have a critical role in promoting health and safety in the school setting. HIV prevention education is necessary in schools to provide knowledge, skills, and resources needed to prevent HIV during adolescence and into adulthood. Primary prevention includes health education, availability of adequate school health services, and supportive school environments for youth to be healthy, safe, and connected, which leads to academic success for all students. The CDC, Division of Adolescent and School Health (DASH) is a unique support to schools for HIV, STD, and unintended pregnancy prevention efforts in schools throughout the nation. The CDC and DASH implement an adolescent and school health program focusing on primary prevention for youth in schools. The CDC funding to state and local education agencies further assists in promoting school-based HIV, STD, and pregnancy prevention education. Through the CDC's funded opportunities to state education agencies, states can implement effective health education curricula and build the capacity to connect students to school-based and community-based health services. Additionally, the CDC funding supports establishing safe environments for students to experience school connectedness with support from adults in the school setting. School nurses have various resources to assist students and families in the education of health, wellness and provision of adequate school health services.

School nurses are key in providing adequate school health services for students, which may occur in person or remotely via telehealth services.

School nurses continue to serve as a liaison to assist students and families, promote healthy and safe school environments, and promote and coordinate health care and wellness in the school setting. School nurses are critical in:
- Their membership in the coordinated school health programs in schools
- The management of healthy school environments
- Promoting health and wellness in the school environment
- Promoting health, wellness, and academic achievement

School nurses may experience challenges in the care of students with HIV and AIDS, which may include limited resources, increased health caseloads, and budgetary concerns. School nurses may experience communication challenges to facilitate effective communication with the school administration, parents, guardians, and healthcare providers, and limitations related to available health resources.

School nurses must be mindful and aware of the nursing code of ethics and the legal implications of maintaining confidentiality and understanding the importance of legal and ethical issues related to HIV and AIDS in the school setting. According to the NASN (June 2021), school nurses function under regulatory frameworks for both education and health. Thus, school nurses must have the skills to communicate in both health and education arenas, including the knowledge and skills to interpret and understand the laws, regulations, and professional nursing standards that govern nursing practice. The Family Educational Rights and Privacy Act (FERPA) and the Health Insurance Portability and Accountability Act of 1996 (HIPPA) Privacy Rule are federal laws that regulate privacy and the exchange of specific types of information. These two federal laws also apply to records maintained on students. FERPA is the federal law that protects the privacy of student's education records maintained by public and private schools, including compliance by any state or local education agency. The HIPPA Privacy Rule establishes national standards that protect sensitive patient health information from being disclosed without the patient's consent or knowledge. The main goal of the Privacy Rule is to ensure the proper protection of an individual's health information.

According to the Americans with Disabilities Act (ADA), the provision for federal civil rights protections for individuals with disabilities, especially confidentiality laws, testing issues/concerns/access, applies to individuals living with HIV or AIDS. This aligns with the protections provided to individuals based on race, color, sex, national origin, age, and religion. Persons living with HIV or AIDS, whether symptomatic or asymptomatic, have physical impairments related to HIV or AIDS have the physical impairments that substantially limit one or more major life activities, including major bodily functions, e.g., the immune system becomes prone to opportunistic infections and gradually weakens the body's natural defenses, are protected by the ADA law. The ADA law also protects people discriminated against because they have or may have HIV. The ADA law also protects persons who are discriminated against because they have a known association/relationship with an individual with HIV. The ADA law applies to all State and local governments, and a local education agency/ public school system may not prohibit a child with HIV or AIDS from attending school. School nurses should be aware of the ADA law to best support students and families affected by HIV and AIDS.

CONCLUSION

In summary, school nurses must use the nursing process to develop a plan of care for managing students in the school setting diagnosed with HIV and AIDS. In planning for the care of students with HIV/AIDS in the school setting, school nurses will be able to help the students and their families, as well as teachers and school officials who need to know about the student's health diagnosis to understand the nursing care plan goals and prevention efforts to manage symptoms, including risk factors related to HIV and AIDS, medication and treatment plans, and most importantly to provide emotional and social support for the students, families, and the legal implications/confidentiality concerns related to school personnel who have a need to know about the student's diagnosis.

RESOURCES

American Nurses Association, Teresa A. Savage. (2017). Ethical Issues in school nursing. *OJIN: The Online Journal of Issues in Nursing, 22*(3), Manuscript 4. https://doi.org/10.3912/OJIN.Vol22No03Man04

Centers for Disease Control and Prevention. Guidelines for Effective School Health Education to Prevent the Spread of AIDS. (1988, January 29). *MMWR, 37*(S-2),1-14. https://www.cdc.gov/mmwr/preview/mmwrhtml/00001751.htm

Centers for Disease Control and Prevention. (2022). Health Information & Privacy: FERPA and HIPPA. https://www.cdc.gov/phlp/publications/topic/healthinformationprivacy.html#:~:text=The%20Family%20Educational%20Rights%20and,of%20specific%20types%20of%20information

Centers for Disease Control and Prevention, Division of HIV Prevention, National Center for HIV, Viral Hepatitis, STD, and TB Prevention**. (2022). *HIV basics.* https://www.cdc.gov/hiv/basics/index.html

Centers for Disease Control and Prevention. (2023). Adolescent Health: What Works in Schools. https://www.cdc.gov/healthyyouth/whatworks/index.htm

Guttmacher Institute, U.S. Sex Education – Laws by State (April 2023). Sex and HIV Education. https://www.guttmacher.org/state-policy/explore/sex-and-hiv-education

National Association of School Nurses. (2022). Student Access to School Nursing Services. https://www.nasn.org/nasn-resources/professional-practice-documents/position-statements/ps-access-to-services" https://www.nasn.org/nasn-resources/professional-practice-documents/position-statements/ps-access-to-services

National Association of School Nurses. (2022). Comprehensive Health Education in Schools. https://www.nasn.org/nasn-resources/professional-practice-documents/position-statements/ps-health-education

National Association of School Nurses. (2020). Code of Ethics. https://www.nasn.org/nasn-resources/resources-by-topic/codeofethics

National Center for State, Tribal, Local, and Territorial Public Health Infrastructure and Workforce, Public Health Law Program. (February 21, 2023) https://www.cdc.gov/about/leadership/leaders/ncstltphiw.html

National Conference of State Legislatures
https://www.ncsl.org/health/state-policies-on-sex-education-in-schools

HIVinfo@NIH.gov. (2021). HIV and Children and Adolescents. https://hivinfo.nih.gov/understanding-hiv/fact-sheets/hiv-and-children-and-adolescents#:~:text=How%20do%20adolescents%20get%20HIV,know%20they%20are%20HIV%20positive

HIVinfo@NIH.gov. (2023). HIV and AIDS: The Basics. https://hivinfo.nih.gov/understanding-hiv/fact-sheets/hiv-and-aids-basics

National Institutes of Health, Office of AIDS Research. (2021). Guidelines for the Use of Antiretroviral Agents in Adults and Adolescents with HIV, Clinical Info HIV.gov. https://clinicalinfo.hiv.gov/en/guidelines/hiv-clinical-guidelines-adult-and-adolescent-arv/adolescents-and-young-adults-hiv

Society of Health and Physical Educators (SHAPE America). (n.d.). National Health Education Standards (NHES) https://www.shapeamerica.org/standards/health/default.aspx

UNESCO International Bureau of Education, International Academy of Education. (2002). Preventing HIV/AIDS in Schools. (2002 http://iaoed.org/downloads/prac09e.pdf

U.S. Department of Justice, Civil Rights Division - Disability Rights Section. (2020). Questions and Answers: The Americans with Disabilities Act and Persons with HIV/AIDS. https://archive.ada.gov/hiv/ada_qa_hiv.htm#:~:text=The%20ADA%20applies%20to%20all,AIDS%20from%20attending%20elementary%20school

Case Law

Bragdon v. Abbott (1998)
The first case to address HIV in the United States Supreme Court was Bragdon v. Abbott. The court ruled five to four in this case. It determined that under the existing federal law, the Americans with Disabilities Act (ADA) prohibits discrimination against people living with HIV, regardless of whether they show any visible symptoms or are diagnosed with AIDS. The 1998 U.S. Supreme Court's decision proved a significant victory for individuals living with HIV because the ADA and other similar state disability discrimination statutes proved to be the only legal source to fight against discrimination related to HIV in jobs, housing, and healthcare. (GLBTQ Legal Advocates & Defenders. n.d.)

REFERENCES

Centers for Disease Control and Prevention. (2022). *HIV in the United States by age.*
https://www.cdc.gov/hiv/group/age/index.html?CDC_AA_refVal=https%3A%2F%2Fwww.cdc.
gov%2Fhiv%2Fgroup%2Fage%2Fyouth%2Findex.htm

Centers for Disease Control and Prevention. (2023a). *Whole school, whole community, whole child (WSCC).*
https://www.cdc.gov/healthyschools/wscc/index.htm

Centers for Disease Control and Prevention. (2023b). *Adolescent and school health. Health education.*
https://www.cdc.gov/healthyyouth/health-education/index.htm

Centers for Disease Control and Prevention. (2023c). *HIV and STD criminalization laws.* https://www.cdc.gov/
hiv/policies/law/states/exposure.html" https://www.cdc.gov/hiv/policies/law/states/exposure.html

Centers for Disease Control and Prevention. (2023d). *Standards for health education.*
https://www.cdc.gov/healthyschools/sher/standards/index.htm

GLBTQ Legal Advocates and Defenders. (n.d.). *Bragdon v. Abbott – GLAD.* https://www.glad.org/cases/bragdon-v-
abbott/#:~:text=AIDS%20HIV%2FAIDS-,Overview,or%20have%20an%20AIDS%20diagnosis

HIV.gov. (2021, June 3). *Guidelines for the use of antiretroviral agents in adults and adolescents with HIV.*
https://clinicalinfo.hiv.gov/en/guidelines/hiv-clinical-guidelines-adult-and-adolescent-arv/adolescents-and-young-
adults-hiv

Kapogiannis, B.G., Koenig, L.J., Xu, J., Mayer, K.H., Loeb, J., Greenberg, L., Monte, D., Banks-Shields, M., Fortenberry, J.D.
(2020). Adolescent medicine trials network for HIV/AIDS interventions. The HIV continuum of care for adolescents
and young adults attending 13 urban US HIV care centers of the NICHD-ATN-CDC-HRSA SMILE collaborative.
Journal of Acquired Immune Deficiencies Syndrome, *84*(1),92-100. https://pubmed.ncbi.nlm.nih.gov/32267659/

National Association of School Nurses. (2022). *Comprehensive health education in schools* (Position Statement).
https://www.nasn.org/nasn-resources/professional-practice-documents/position-statements/ps-health-education

U.S. Department of Justice, Civil Rights Division, Disability Rights Section. (2020, February 25). Questions and Answers:
The Americans with Disabilities Act and Persons with HIV/AIDS
https://archive.ada.gov/hiv/ada_qa_hiv.htm

World Health Organization. (n.d.). HIV. Retrieved om June 21,2023 from https://www.who.int/health-topics/hiv-
aids#tab=tab_1

Chapter 31

LIFE-THREATENING EMERGENCIES: ANAPHYLAXIS, ASTHMA, AND ALLERGIES

Mariann F. Cosby, DNP, MPA, RN, PHN, CEN, NE-BC, LNCC, CLCP, CCM, MSCC, CSN, FAEN

DESCRIPTION OF ISSUE

Globally there is a need to implement school-wide food allergy safety and undesignated or stock epinephrine programs to treat anaphylaxis. Why? Because anaphylaxis can occur without warning, can strike those with or without a previous history of an allergy, and may result in a fatal outcome (Cardona et al., 2020; Muraro et al., 2022). When symptoms of possible anaphylaxis are recognized, rapid administration of epinephrine; the first-line treatment for anaphylaxis; can be lifesaving (Russell et al., 2023).

In 2013, federal legislation raised awareness of the importance of unassigned non-student specific or stock epinephrine availability in U.S. public schools (School Access to Emergency Epinephrine Act, 2013). As of 2018, all 50 states and the District of Columbia have laws that allow for stock epinephrine to be on-hand for emergency administration in public schools (Volerman et al., 2022). However, ten years later, there continue to be challenges and barriers to operationalizing emergency preparedness plans that are vital to dealing with food allergies and the successful implementation of access to stock epinephrine in schools (Russell et al., 2023; Volerman et al., 2022). Since not all states legally mandate K-12 public schools to stock epinephrine, those states with laws that allow schools to stock epinephrine instead voluntarily can opt out (Russell et al., 2023).

The following discussion points out potential legal implications for the school nurse and district to consider regarding implementation delays, inadequate program planning, and other allergy and emergency medication-related issues. A list of resources is provided to assist the reader in locating additional educational materials on this topic.

BACKGROUND

Anaphylaxis Overview

Anaphylaxis is a life-threatening emergency defined as a serious systemic hypersensitivity reaction that is usually rapid in onset and may cause death (Cardona et al., 2020). Identified as a global health problem, the World Allergy Organization provides key anaphylaxis assessment and management information. Specifics include information on those who are vulnerable, risk factors for severe or fatal episodes, co-factors that amplify anaphylaxis, and recommendations for managing allergens such as food allergies (Cardona et al., 2020; Murano et al., 2022).

Triggers or causes of anaphylaxis in the pediatric population include exposure to food allergens. In 2021, sesame was added as the ninth food to the U.S. list of food allergens that the Food Allergen Labeling and Consumer Protection Act of 2004 codified. The nine foods now identified as major allergens are: milk, eggs, fish, Crustacean shellfish, tree nuts, peanuts, wheat, soybeans, and sesame (U.S. Food and Drug Administration, 2023).

The occurrence of anaphylaxis after ingestion is typical, with skin and inhalation exposure as less likely causes (Huddleston et al., 2020). In addition to foods, other anaphylaxis triggers and mechanisms include venoms from stinging insects, drugs/medication and biological agents, or reactivity to latex, chemicals, or other allergens and cofactors or co-causes such as exercise, and idiopathic: when no trigger can be identified (Cardona et al., 2020; Volerman et al., 2022).

The severity and clinical presentation of anaphylaxis can vary. Acute onset can occur within minutes or several hours of exposure or precipitating event. Presentation of anaphylaxis can mimic disorders such as acute asthma, acute generalized urticaria (rash), aspiration of foreign body, vasovagal episode, and anxiety or panic attacks (see APPENDIX for comparison of anaphylaxis and asthma symptoms and triggers) (Sicherer et al., 2017). An individual's concomitant severe or uncontrolled asthma can increase hypersensitivity and risk of a fatal episode, especially in adolescence (Bird & Burks, 2009; Sicherer et al., 2017). Cofactors such as exercise, upper respiratory tract infections, fever, nonsteroidal anti-inflammatory drugs or ethanol ingestion, emotional distress, and perimenstrual status can lower the threshold at which the triggers can cause anaphylaxis (Sicherer et al., 2017).

Since simultaneous occurrence is possible, an anaphylactic reaction that may present as an asthma attack should be considered and treated with epinephrine (Barrett & Moore, 2019). The outcome can be fatal when an allergic reaction is not recognized, and instead of epinephrine, antihistamines or inhaled bronchodilators are provided (Huddleston et al., 2020).

Life-Saving Epinephrine

Epinephrine is the first-line medication of choice for the first-aid treatment of anaphylaxis (Russell et al., 2023). Once possible anaphylaxis is recognized, epinephrine can be life-saving due to its rapid onset of action that prevents and relieves airway obstruction, hypotension, and shock (Russell et al., 2023). Epinephrine is available in several forms, but in the school setting, a pre-filled syringe of epinephrine known as an epinephrine auto-injector (EAI) is appropriate for use by both school health professionals and lay responders as permitted by state law and school policy (Schoessler & Selekman, 2019). It should be promptly administered via injection into the mid-outer thigh (vastus lateralis muscle) and held for 3 seconds (Russell et al., 2023; Schoessler & Selekman, 2019)

Prompt response is essential, as predicting the student's response to an allergen is impossible. A student could recover spontaneously due to the secretion of endogenous epinephrine or die within minutes without the life-saving treatment. A secondary or biphasic reaction could also occur in which a resurgence of the symptoms occurs after the resolution of the initial symptoms, despite no further exposure or trigger (Schoessler & Selekman, 2019). Since there are no absolute contraindications to epinephrine treatment, the risk of complications and death from anaphylaxis is related to any delay in epinephrine administration (Cardona et al., 2020). Prompt epinephrine injection can curtail the mild symptoms of anaphylaxis from rapidly progressing to a life-threatening systemic allergic reaction (Schoessler & Selekman, 2019).

Antihistamines that may be part of an order set for a student with a known allergy are not lifesaving (Cardona et al., 2020). Antihistamines do not treat anaphylaxis symptoms but may relieve itching, flushing, urticaria (rash), and other allergy-type symptoms and can take one to two hours to provide relief. Therefore, antihistamines should not be substituted for epinephrine when anaphylaxis is suspected, as they are considered second and third-line options (Dodd et al., 2021; Shaker et al., 2020).

Similarly, anaphylaxis treatment is delayed when life-saving epinephrine administration is the first-aid treatment, but a bronchodilator is provided instead (Huddleston et al., 2020). Distinguishing asthma from anaphylaxis can present some challenges. However, with proper training, this hurdle can be mitigated (see APPENDIX).

Since the School-Based Allergies and Asthma Management Act became law in 2021, bronchodilator albuterol has become more accessible in schools as states passed stock albuterol legislation to mitigate access disparities (Asthma and Allergy Network, 2023). Hence the importance of training about the subtle differences between asthma and anaphylaxis becomes even more critical so that school staff reach for the stock epinephrine rather than stock albuterol when anaphylaxis treatment is needed. Albuterol, stock or prescribed, is best reserved for adjunctive asthma therapy for students who experience bronchospasm/ asthma attacks at school and do not have a prescribed albuterol inhaler with them (Asthma and Allergy Network, 2023; Huddleston et al., 2020; McCaughey et al., 2022).

School nurses should advocate for students with healthcare provider orders that direct school staff to administer antihistamines before epinephrine. Antihistamines and corticosteroids may be appropriate as adjuvant therapy for additional symptoms after administering epinephrine, but only epinephrine can treat anaphylaxis (Keller et al., 2023). Clear care plan instructions should accompany such orders to avert epinephrine administration delays (Wang, 2017; Wang et al., 2017).

Managing Anaphylaxis: Food Allergies and Asthma in Public School

Anaphylaxis and the associated life-threatening components of food allergies and asthma that can occur in children while attending school gained national attention and awareness with the passage of the School Access to Emergency Epinephrine Act (2013). This federal law encouraged states to adopt laws requiring schools to have on-hand stock or undesignated epinephrine to be used for any student who is reasonably believed to be having an anaphylactic reaction. Additionally, the law addressed medication administration by trained unlicensed staff and offered limited civil liability protection for those administering the medication.

Nearly simultaneously, in 2013, the Centers for Disease Control and Prevention (CDC) published the required national guidelines developed in response to the Food Safety Management Act (2010). The CDC developed the voluntary federal guidelines in collaboration with the National Association of School Nurses (NASN) and other groups to help schools manage the risk of food allergies, reduce allergic reactions, define the roles of members of the school community, and improve responses to life-threatening reactions such as anaphylaxis.

As of 2018, all 50 states and the District of Columbia have laws that allow undesignated or stock epinephrine for emergency administration in public schools (Volerman et al., 2022). This aligns with the importance for students in the U.S. to have access to life-saving epinephrine at school, as approximately six million school-aged children have food allergies. Not only are children with food allergies at risk for having a reaction by accidentally eating a food allergen while at school, but 25% of anaphylaxis reactions that require treatment with epinephrine at school occur in students who have never been diagnosed with a severe allergy (Gereige et al., 2022). Schools need to be prepared to care for students with known allergies as well as those who experience their first allergic reaction while at school (Cosby, 2015).

IMPLICATIONS FOR SCHOOL NURSE PRACTICE

General Information

School nurses' involvement with food allergy management of students with known food allergies includes becoming cognizant of the comprehensive school and district-wide strategy to manage the risk of food allergy reactions in children (CDC, 2013). Kao et al. (2018) reported the results of a study, thought to be the first of its kind, which characterizes the diversity of the food allergy policies used by schools. The study reported that most schools use a variety of policies on mitigating allergen exposure, training school staff on allergic reactions, and several other anaphylaxis management policy strategies.

By becoming familiar with the accepted local methodology, the food allergy-related needs of a particular student with a food allergy can be addressed in a coordinated manner. Not only does this enhance student safety, but it provides a means so that the legal requirements and considerations related to the applicable federal laws and regulations that address access and prohibit discrimination based on disability are not violated.

Working with the school team, the school nurse can ensure that if the student's food allergy is a disability, the student's entitlements of Section 504 of the Rehabilitation Act of 1973 and the Americans with Disability Amendments Act (2008) are protected (Huddleston et al., 2020; Schoessler & Selekman, 2019). Similarly, if the student has an individualized education program (IEP) in place, which addresses special education and related services under part B of the Individuals With Disabilities Education Improvement Act (IDEA, [2004]), the nurse, as part of the team, can more easily intervene to develop and integrate the individualized healthcare plan/ food allergy action plan, and emergency care plan for the food allergy and epinephrine (CDC, 2013; Huddleston et al., 2020; Schoessler & Selekman, 2019).

The school nurse is the appropriate professional to develop individualized healthcare plans and emergency care plans, as care planning is a standard of school nursing practice (Gereige et al., 2022; NASN, 2022). Care plan creation is a nursing responsibility due to the assessment component of the process and cannot be delegated to unlicensed personnel (NASN, 2020). Although several anaphylaxis plans are available from various organizations, the American Academy of Pediatrics (AAP) recognized that their use by health professionals varied (Wang et al., 2017). As a result, the AAP Allergy and Anaphylaxis Emergency Plan was developed to promote greater familiarity and standardization (Wang, 2017). The customizable plan is the first of its kind from the AAP and is available online in a fillable format with multiple dose options (Wang, 2017).

Challenges Regarding Food Allergy

A challenge that the school nurse may encounter related to efforts to provide a student with an allergen-free or reduced environment is that other students in the school may need ready access to food. School districts must provide a free and appropriate education (FAPE) for all students (Section 504 of the Rehabilitation Act of 1973; IDEA (2004). Therefore, it is important to keep in mind that, for example, students with diabetes may require food snacks to be on their person. Hence, the rights of students who need immediate access to food in the classroom must be balanced with those who want a food-free/allergen-reduced classroom environment. Working with staff on strategies to educate and integrate solutions is part of the school nurse's role and challenges (Gereige et al., 2022).

Legal Implications

There are legal implications for each of these situations. These challenges should be approached by making reasonable team efforts to accommodate both simultaneously, keeping in mind that a completely allergen-free environment may be unreasonable (Russell & Huber, 2013). Depending on the nature of an allergy, food avoidance strategies can vary (Russell & Huber, 2013; Schoessler & Selekman, 2019; Sicherer et al., 2010). Cases involving these types of situations include *Liebau v. Romeo Comm. Schs.,* 2013 Mich. App. LEXIS 1322 (2013) (the court dismissed a lawsuit by a student disgruntled with the district's decision to adopt a "nut-free" policy to protect the health and safety of students with peanut allergies); *T.F. v. Fox Chapel Area Sch. Dist.*, 589 Fed. Appx. 594 (3d Cir. 2014) (the district did not violate a student's rights under Section 504 by refusing to adopt a nut-free policy).

Decisions focus on federal and state law, which can limit the usefulness of a general publication. Many cases are not published or are non-precedential; they can be referenced as secondary authority only, meaning that these decisions do not bind other courts. Here are a few examples:

> *In T.F. v. Fox Chapel Area School District, DC No. 2-12.cv-1066 (September 12, 2014), the Third Circuit Court of Appeals ruled in a food allergy discrimination case finding that the school district was not "deliberately indifferent" to the child's rights.*
> *http://www2.ca3.uscourts.gov/opinarch/134624np.pdf*

> *J.B. & T.B. v. Manalapan-Englishtown Regional Board of Education (SEA NJ 2007). The Administrative Law Judge ordered the school to provide bus transportation to and from school and school-related activities with a trained aide who could monitor the child and administer an epi-pen.*
> *https://www.wrightslaw.com/info/allergy.2007.manalapan.decision.pdf*

> *In Smith v. Tangipahoa Parish Sch. Bd., 2006 U.S. Dist. LEXIS 85377 (U.S. District Court for the Eastern District of Louisiana), the plaintiffs sued the school for alleged discrimination under Section 504 of the Rehabilitation Act and Title II of the ADA. The court dismissed the claims finding that the school complied with healthcare providers' recommendations surrounding reported allergies and did not discriminate by counting absences related to the student's impairment.*

> *In Liebau v. Romeo Cmty. Schs, 2013 Mich. App. LEXIS 1322 (Unpublished), school formulates 504 Plan for Student A who suffers from severe nut allergy and adopts a nut-free environment. Student B complains that she is not on a Section 504 Plan. The court dismissed various claims, including an equal protection claim, finding that the school has the discretion to exercise its obligation to provide for the safety and welfare of other students and that the school-wide ban was arbitrary and irrational.*

Mears v. Bethel School Dist. No. 403, 332 P.3d 1077, 182 Wash. App. 919 (Ct. App. 2014).

This appeal was from a defense verdict in a wrongful death case arising out of the death of Mercedes Mears. She had a history of persistent asthma and had severe life-threatening allergies. Medications for her asthma (Albuterol inhaler) and allergies (Epinephrine) were available in the health office. When she began having difficulty breathing shortly after arriving at school on October 7, 2008, school staff believed she had an asthma attack and not an allergic reaction. No attempt was made to administer the epinephrine for her allergic emergency or to start CPR, and she died. Although the jury verdict found that the defendant was negligent, they found the negligence did not proximately cause the death. The issues with the bifurcation of negligence and the proximate cause of the death were not overturned in the appeal.

Working as a team by including school staff, parents, the student, and legal counsel to work out an amenable solution that minimizes health-related risks while preserving student rights is desired (Santos et al., 2023). Obtaining guidance from the student's clinical team may also help by providing specific information on the nature of the allergy and other circumstances that may be unique to the school or the student's age.

Challenges Related to Stock Epinephrine Program

Other challenges that carry legal implications include the implementation of the state-mandated or recommended stock epinephrine program. Although the legislation is in place in every state and D.C., operationalizing and overcoming implementation challenges can be cumbersome. Each school district must consider state laws and local setting circumstances when establishing their policies. State laws vary on whether the stock epinephrine is mandated or allowed. Implementation policies also differ in many areas, including who is responsible for the development, the types of regulated school systems, locations covered, the relevant stakeholders, procurement processes, maintenance and administration, incident documentation, and liability (Volerman et al., 2022). Other local considerations include a student's right to self-carry epinephrine and the stock albuterol laws (Asthma and Allergy Network, 2021).

The case *Suing for Peanuts* (Bridges, 2000) discusses the potential liability of negligently or failing to administer epinephrine properly. Some challenges include addressing the utilization of unlicensed assistive personnel (UAP) in response to a possible anaphylaxis event in the absence of the school nurse (Tanner & Clarke, 2016). One example is developing and implementing training for non-licensed staff on identifying the signs and symptoms of anaphylaxis without requiring the assessment skills of the registered nurse.

Another includes securing healthcare providers willing to write standing orders for the undesignated or stock epinephrine to obtain the medication (Schoessler et al., 2014). As typically the lead person for preparing for an emergency response to anaphylaxis in schools, developing policies and protocols that provide the structure for the stock epinephrine program that addresses the legal risks and parameters was reported as the greatest struggle for school nurses (Tanner & Clarke, 2016).

When the stock epinephrine program is not in place or fully implemented, other legal implications and ethical dilemmas come into play. For example, school nurses should not be placed in a position of having to choose between the decision to save a life by using someone else's individually prescribed epinephrine that is on campus and the consequences of the decision (Morris et al., 2011). As a licensed healthcare provider, should a school nurse administer medication to a student for which there is no order, the nurse is at risk of practicing outside the permitted scope of practice (Buppert, 2013). License revocation and other disciplinary action against the professional license are at stake in this situation (Mathes & Reifsnyder, 2014). Additionally, by using another student's EAI to rescue the student in need, the student to whom the EAI is legally prescribed is then placed at risk as the EAI is no longer available for that student should it be needed (Schoessler et al., 2014).

Addressing the Challenges

Administrative and operational obstacles that inadequately provide the necessary elements for or delay the implementation of a stock epinephrine program create havoc and undue ethical dilemmas for staff. If this double jeopardy scenario cannot be averted, school nurses should document efforts to apprise key school district administration and legal counsel of the "what if" situation and come to a mutual understanding of what the nurse can or cannot legally do. The school nurse should consider asking for documentation of such a determination from the school administration.

As the school health expert, school nurses can also consider partnering and positioning themselves to advocate for efforts to remedy the obstacles so that mutually agreed-upon solutions can be expeditiously reached (Schoessler et al., 2014; Tanner & Clarke, 2016). Accessing and sharing current literature that provides strategies to overcome common barriers to the stock epinephrine program should be in the mix (Kao et al., 2018; Russell et al., 2023; Santos et al., 2022; Volerman et al., 2022).

Similar conversations should also occur to determine an agreed-upon communication plan with parents who fail to provide the school with student-specific epinephrine or other emergency medication (Sicherer et al., 2010). The school district's administration and legal counsel should provide guidance and direction on how to best address those issues that pose life-threatening risks for the student without impacting a student's civil rights.

As an advocate for student safety and well-being, the school nurse can consider incorporating sense-making strategies as part of the discussions (Sandberg & Tsoukas, 2020; Taylor & Nash, 2023). When people interpret and give meaning to their experiences in the sense-making dialogue, the school nurse should be prepared to discuss the importance of balancing the legal and ethical elements in the decision-making process. Options that might be considered include:

1) student's exclusion from school until medications are on site,
2) informing the parents that calling 911 may be the only option in the absence of them supplying the medication to the school, and
3) implications for notifying child protective services agencies if medical neglect is a consideration.

Utilizing the team approach and because of the legal implications, the school nurse must be clear about the strategies mutually agreed upon to be endorsed and upheld by the district's legal counsel (Mathes & Reifsnyder, 2014).

CONCLUSION

School nurses and other school officials must be aware of the challenges and potential legal implications associated with anaphylaxis, food allergies, and students' access to the life-saving emergency medication epinephrine in schools. Due to these potentially life-threatening conditions, students' safety and well-being can be at risk. By raising awareness through the provided information, it is anticipated that the path will be paved for easier resolution. Reaching mutually agreeable interventions or strategies that can mitigate the legal/ethical issues and barriers that hinder a healthy and safe school environment for students needs to be the ultimate goal.

RESOURCES

AllergyHome.org. (2011) Managing Food Allergies in Schools: Food Allergy Education for the School Communityhttps://www.allergyhome.org/schools/ and https://community.kidswithfoodallergies.org/blog/free-online-food-allergy-training-for-school-staff
This resource was developed in partnership with Kids with Food Allergies, the Asthma and Allergy Foundation of America New England Chapter, the Association of Camp Nurses, and the American Camping Association. It was modified for and approved by the Massachusetts Department of Public Health's School Health Services. It provides practical teaching tools, including presentations with audio to assist nurses, staff, parents, and student education. This resource provides school nurses with tools to assist in training their school community, including students and parents without food allergies. It includes guidance for school nurses who will train staff on the administration of epinephrine by auto-injector. It includes links to other allergy education sites, materials for families of children with food allergies, and materials for others working in childcare and camp programs.

Asthma and Allergy Network (n.d.) https://allergyasthmanetwork.org
Includes access to information, education, and advocacy regarding asthma, allergies, anaphylaxis, and eczema. The School-Based Asthma Management Program (SAMPRO) webinar recordings are accessible from this website. Includes maps of states with school stock albuterol and epinephrine laws.

American Academy of Allergy Asthma and Immunology (n.d.). Food Allergy. www.aaaai.org/conditions-and-treatments/allergies/food-allergies.aspx
This site provides basic information about food allergy diagnosis, treatment, management, and helpful tips for people with food allergies. Resources include a blank and fillable Anaphylaxis Emergency Action Plan (2020), various school tools, and information on the School-Based Allergies and Asthma **Management Program Act** (HR 2468) which amended the Public Health Service Act to revise the conditions under which the Department of Health Services is making asthma-related grants and state preferences.

Asthma and Allergy Foundation of America. https://aafa.org/about-aafa/
Contains resources, research, reports, and advocacy effort information.
https://aafa.org/advocacy/key-issues/access-to-medications/albuterol-in-schools/ Map of state legislation and guidelines for stock albuterol in schools (2021).

HR 2468, the School-Based Allergies and Asthma Management Program Act (2021). https://community.aafa.org/blog/school-based-allergies-and-asthma-management-program-act-h-r-2468-becomes-law?_gl=1*3561o1*_gcl_au*MTk3OTUxODU2Ni4xNjg0OTUwMjMw

Auvi-Q (2022). https://www.auvi-q.com/public-access/state-laws.html Has training and resources. Includes map of the states that allow or mandate stock epinephrine.

Centers for Disease and Prevention Control (CDC). https://www.cdc.gov/healthyschools/foodallergies/pdf/20_316712-A_FA_guide_508tag.pdf
Direct link to the document: Voluntary Guidelines for Managing Food Allergies in Schools and Early Care and Education Programs (2013). https://www.cdc.gov/healthyschools/foodallergies/pdf/20_316712-A_FA_guide_508tag.pdf

Food Allergy Research & Education. (2023). http://www.foodallergy.orgThis site provides information to raise awareness and understanding of food allergies and to help those who support people with food allergies. It contains a link to access FARE's anaphylaxis care plan after submitting a request.

Food Allergy Research & Education (FARE). (n.d.) Keeping Students Safe and Included. http://allergyready.com This free online course, developed by Food Allergy Research & Education (FARE), is designed to help school staff and administrators become better prepared to manage students with food allergies and respond to food allergy emergencies. The information aligns with the CDC's (2013) Voluntary Guidelines for Managing Food Allergies in Schools and Early Care and Education Programs.

Food Allergy Research & Education. (n.d.). https://www.foodallergy.org/our-initiatives/advocacy/know-your-rights/public-access-epinephrine

Food Allergy Research & Education. (2022). School access to epinephrine map: Allow or require. https://www.foodallergy.org/our-initiatives/advocacy/food-allergy-issues/school-access-epinephrine

Food Allergy Research & Education. (n.d.) Early introduction and food allergy prevention. https://www.foodallergy.org/research-innovation/accelerating-innovation/early-introduction-and-food-allergy-prevention

Food Allergy Research & Education. (n.d.) Recognizing and Treating Reaction Symptoms; https://www.foodallergy.org/resources/recognizing-and-treating-reaction-symptoms

Food Allergy Research & Education. (n.d.) Recognizing and Responding to Anaphylaxis. https://www.foodallergy.org/our-initiatives/education-programs-training/fare-training-food-allergy-academy/recognizing

Guidelines for the Nurse in the School Setting, 4th ed. (2021). Ann & Robert H. Lurie Children's Hospital of Chicago. https://www.luriechildrens.org/globalassets/documents/emsc/resourcesguidelines/guidelines-tool-and-other-resources/schoolnurseguidelines_4ed_april2022_final.pdf

Kids With Food Allergies. https://kidswithfoodallergies.org/

National Association of School Nurses (NASN). (2014). Clinical conversations for the school nurse: Food allergy management in the school setting. https://www.nasn.org/nasn-resources/skills-training/conversations-food-allergy and resources at: https://higherlogicdownload.s3.amazonaws.com/NASN/8575d1b7-94ad-45ab-808e-d45019cc5c08/UploadedImages/PDFs/Clinical_Conversations_2014_2015.pdf
This document contains a compendium of articles for school health professionals to initiate discussion.

National Association of School Nurses (NASN). (2019). Allergy and anaphylaxis. https://www.nasn.org/nasn-resources/resources-by-topic/allergies-anaphylaxis
This site provides various tools and templates to educate and help people responsible for managing students with food allergies as an integral part of the delivery of healthcare services in schools. Checklists, sample policy, sample practice forms, school personnel training resources, education resources, and a section with national and additional resources are included.

NASN School Nurse. Swaffield, T. P., & Olympia, R. P. (2022, September). School nurses on the front lines of healthcare: Emergencies associated with sport and physical activities (part 3): Shortness of breath in a pediatric athlete during a track event. *NASN School Nurse, 37*(5), 257–260. https://doi.org10.1177/1942602X221104195

National Council of State Boards of Nursing & the American Nurses Association. (2019). National guidelines for nursing delegation (Position Paper). https://www.ncsbn.org/nursing-regulation/practice/delegation.page https://www.ncsbn.org/Delegation_joint_statement_NCSBN-ANA.pdf

National Education Association. (n.d.) Food Allergies: What School Employees Need to Know http://neahin.org/foodallergies
This booklet is designed to educate school employees about food allergies and how they can help to prevent and respond to allergic reactions in schools. Booklets are available in print and online in both English and Spanish.

National Institute of Allergy and Infectious Diseases. (2010). Guidelines for the diagnosis and management of food allergy in the United States: Report of the NIAID-sponsored expert panel. *Journal of Allergy and Clinical Immunology,* 126(suppl. 6), S1-S58.doi: https://dx.doi.org/10.1016/j.jaci.2010.10.007

National School Board Association. (2012). Safe at school and ready to learn: A comprehensive policy guide for protecting students with life-threatening food allergies (2nd ed.). https://cdn-files.nsba.org/s3fs-public/reports/Safe-at-School-and-Ready-to-Learn.pdf
This guide is designed to help school leaders, especially school boards, make sure that policies at the district and school level support the safety, well-being, and success of students with life-threatening food allergies. It includes a checklist that the school can use to assess the extent to which the guide's components are included in their food allergy policies and used in practice. It also has examples of state and local education policies.

World Allergy Organization. https://doi.org/10.1111/josh.13202

Case Law

TF v. Fox Chapel Area School District, DC No. 2-12.cv-1066

Smith v. Tangipahoa Parish Sch. Bd., 2006 U.S. Dist. LEXIS 85377 (U.S. District Court for the Eastern District of Louisiana)

Liebau v. Romeo Cmty. Schs, 2013 Mich. App. LEXIS 1322

Mears v. Bethel School Dist. No. 403, 332 P.3d 1077, 182 Wash. App. 919 (Ct. App. 2014).

REFERENCES

Americans with Disabilities Amendments Act (ADAA), (Public Law 110-325) (2008), 42 USC 12102 Education for all Handicapped Children, (Public Law 94-142) (1975). 20 USC 1401.

Asthma and Allergy Network. (2021). *State laws*. U.S. Anaphylaxis. https://advocacy.allergyasthmanetwork.org/laws-to-protect-those-with-allergies-and-asthma/state-laws/

Asthma and Allergy Network. (2023). *State laws*. U.S. Albuterol. https://advocacy.allergyasthmanetwork.org/laws-to-protect-those-with-allergies-and-asthma/state-laws/

Barrett, M., & Moore, C. M. (2019). Students with chronic respiratory conditions: Asthma and cystic fibrosis. In J. Selekman, R. A. Shannon, & C. F. Yonkaitis (Eds.), *School nursing: A comprehensive text* (3rd ed., pp. 523-548). F. A. Davis.

Bird, J. A., & Burk, A. W. (2009). Food allergy and asthma. *Primary Care Respiratory Journal, 18*(4), 258-265. http://doi.org/10.4104/pcrj.2009.00036

Bridges, J. (2000, March). Suing for peanuts. *Notre Dame Law Review (75)* 1269. University of Notre Dame. https://scholarship.law.nd.edu/ndlr/vol75/iss3/16

Buppert, C. (2013). Can I use another student's epipen to save a child's life? *Medscape Nurses*. https://www.medscape.com/viewarticle/803235

Cardona, V., Ansotegui, I. J., Ebisawa, M., Gamal, Y.E., Rivas, M. F., Fineman, S., Gelier, M., Gonzalez-Estrada, A., Greenberger, P.A., Borges, M.S., Senna, G., Sheikh, A., Tanno, L. K., Thong, B.Y., Turner, P.J., & Worm, M. (2020). World allergy organization anaphylaxis guidance (Position Paper). *World Allergy Organization Journal, 13*(10), 1-25. http://doi.org/10.1016/j.waojou.2020.100472

Centers for Disease Control and Prevention. (2013). *Voluntary guidelines for managing food allergies in schools and early care and education programs*. U.S. Department of Health and Human Services. https://www.cdc.gov/healthyschools/foodallergies/index.htm

Cosby, M. F. (2015). *School nursing simulation: An evidence-based practice intervention for improved confidence in health-related school emergency first-responder role* (Doctoral dissertation, Capella University). https://sigma.nursingrepository.org/bitstream/handle/10755/581124/Simulation_DNP_Project_Cosby.pdf?sequence=7 https://www.nursinglibrary.org/vhl/bitstream/10755/581124/7/Simulation_DNP_Project_Cosby.pdf

Dodd, A., Hughes, A., Sargant, N., Whyte, A. F., Soar, J. & Turner, P. J. (2021). Evidence update for the treatment of anaphylaxis. *Resuscitation*, *163*, 86–96. https://doi.org/10.1016/j.resuscitation.2021.04.010

Food Allergen Labeling and Consumer Protection Act (2004). 21 U.S. Code 301. https://www.fda.gov/food/food-allergensgluten-free-guidance-documents-regulatory-information/food-allergen-labeling-and-consumer-protection-act-2004-falcpa

Food Safety Modernization Act, Food Allergy and Anaphylaxis Management. Title 21, U.S. Code § 2205 (2010). https://www.govinfo.gov/app/details/USCODE-2010-title21/USCODE-2010-title21-chap27-subchapl-sec2205

Gereige, R. S., Gross, T., Jastaniah, E., & Council on School Health and Committee on Pediatric Emergency Medicine. (2022). Individual medical emergencies occurring at school (Policy Statement). *Pediatrics, 150*(1), 1- 12, e2022057987. https://doi.org/10.1542/peds.2022-057987

Huddleston, C.M., Kloepfer, K.M., Jin, J.J., & Vitalpur, G. V. (2020). Management of food allergy in the school setting. *Journal of Food Allergy, 2*(1), 104- 107. https://doi.org/10.2500/jfa.2020.2.200023

Individuals with Disability Education Improvement Act (2004), 20 USC 1400 et seq. https://www.congress.gov/bill/108th-congress/house-bill/1350

Kao, L. M., Wang, J., Kagan, O., Russell, A., Mustafa, S. S., Houdek, D., Smith, B., & Gupta, R. (2018). School nurse perspectives on school policies for food allergy and anaphylaxis. *Annals of Allergy, Asthma & Immunology, 120*(3), 304–309. http://doi.org/10.1016/j.anai.2017.12.019https://doi.org/10.1016/j.anai.2017.12.019

Keller, A., Morse, B., Conroy, M. (2023). Food allergies and anaphylaxis in the community: The school nurse's role. *NASN School Nurse, 38*(1), 41-46. https://doi.org/10.1177/1942602X221110083

Mathes, M., & Reifsnyder, J. (2014). *Nurse's law questions and answers for the practicing nurse.* Indianapolis, U.S.: Sigma Theta Tau International. http://www.ebrary.com

McCaughey, R.A., McCarthy, A. M., Maughan, E., Hein, M., Perkhounkova, Y., Kelly, M.W., & Kelly, M. W. (2023). Emergency medication access and administration in schools: A focus on epinephrine, albuterol Inhalers, and glucagon. *The Journal of School Nursing, 38*(4):326-335. https://doi.org /10.1177/1059840520934185

Morris, P., Baker, D., Belot, C., & Edwards, A. (2011). Preparedness for students and staff with anaphylaxis. *Journal of School Health, 81*(8), 471-476. https://doi.org/10.1111/j.1746-1561.2011.00616.x

Muraro, A., de Silva, D., Halken, S., Worm, M., Khaleva, E., Arasi, S., Dunn-Galvin, A., Nwaru, B.II, De Jong, N.W., Del Rio, P.R., Turner, P.J., Smith, P., Begin, P., Angier, E., Arshad, H., Ballmer-Weber, B., Beyer, K., Bindslev-Jensen, C., Cianferoni, A.,...Graham, R. (2022). Managing food allergy: GA²LEN guideline 2022. *World Allergy Organization Journal, 15*(9), 1- 25. http://doi.org/10.1016/j.waojou.2022.100687

National Association of School Nurses. (2020). Use of *individualized healthcare plans to support school health services* (Position Statement). http://www.nasn.org/nasn-resources/professional-practice-documents/position-statements/ps-ihps

National Association of School Nurses. (2022). School nursing: *Scope and standards of school nursing practice* (4th ed.). Author.

Rehabilitation Act of 1973, 29 USC § 701

Russell, A. F., Bingemann, R. A., Cooke, A. T., Ponda, R., Pistiner, M., Jean, T., Nanda, A., Jobrack, J., Hoyt, A.E.W., & Young, M. (2023). The need for required stock epinephrine in all schools: A workgroup report of the AAAAI adverse reactions to foods committee. *The Journal of Allergy and Clinical Immunology: In Practice 11*(4), 1068-1083. http://doi.org/10.1016/j.jaip.2022.12.047

Russell A. F., & Huber, M. M. (2013). Food allergy management in elementary school: Collaborating to maximize student safety. *Journal of Asthma & Allergy Educators, 4*(6), 290-304. https://doi.org/10.1177/2150129713486671

Sandberg, J., & Tsoukas, H. (2020). Sense-making reconsidered: Towards a broader understanding through phenomenology. *Organization Theory, 1*(1). http://doi.org/10.1177/2631787719879937

Santos, M.J.L., Merrill, K.A., Gerdts, J.D., Ben-Shoshan, M., & Protudjer, J.L.P. (2022). Food allergy education and management in schools: A scoping review on current practices and gaps. *Nutrients, 14*(4),732. https://doi.org/10.3390/nu14040732

Schoessler, S., Albert, L., Levasseur, S., & Owens, C. (2014). Saving lives at school: School nurses face the challenge of anaphylaxis in the school setting. *NASN School Nurse, 29*(2), 67-70. https://doi.org/:10.1177/1942602X13516866

Schoessler, S., & Selekman, J. (2019). Students with allergies. In J. Selekman, R. A. Shannon, & C. F. Yonkaitis (Eds.), *School nursing: A comprehensive text* (3rd ed., pp. 500-522). F. A. Davis.

School Access to Emergency Epinephrine Act, Public Law 113-48, 113th Congress (2013). https://www.congress.gov/113/plaws/publ48/PLAW-113publ48.pdf

Shaker, M. S., Wallace, D. V., Golden, D. B. K., Oppenheimer, J., Bernstein, J. A., Campbell, R. L., Dinakar, C., Ellis A., Greenhawt, M., Khan, D. A., Lang, D. M., Lang, E. S., Lieberman, J. A., Portnoy, J., Rank, M. A., Stukus, D. R., & Wang J. (2020). Anaphylaxis-A 2020 practice parameter update, systematic review, and grading of recommendations, assessment, development and evaluation (GRADE) analysis. *Journal of Allergy and Clinical Immunology, 145*(4), 1082–1123. http://doi.org/10.1016/j.jaci.2020.01.017

Sicherer, S. H., Mahr, T. & American Academy of Pediatrics Section on Allergy and Immunology. (2010). Clinical report: Management of food allergy in the school setting. *Pediatrics, 126*(6), 1232-1239. https://doi.org/10.1542/peds.2010-2575

Sicherer, S. H., Simons, F. E. R., & American Academy of Pediatrics Section on Allergy and Immunology. (2017). Epinephrine for first-aid management of anaphylaxis. *Pediatrics ,139*(3) e1- e9. https://doi.org/10.1542/peds.2016-4006

Tanner, A. & Clarke, C. (2016). Epinephrine policies and protocols guidance for schools. *NASN School Nurse, 31*(1), 13-22. https://doi.org/10.1177/1942602X1560760

Taylor, J., & Nash, C. (2023). Sense-making for the coach developer. *Coach development.* Routledge;(In Press).

U.S. Food & Drug Administration (FDA) (2023, January 10.) Food allergies. Major food allergies. https://www.fda.gov/food/food-labeling-nutrition/food-allergies#:~:text=Congress passed the Food Allergen,peanuts%2C wheat%2C and soybeans

Volerman, A., Brindley, C., Amerson, N., Pressley, T., & Woolverton, N. (2022). A national review of state laws for stock epinephrine in schools. *Journal of School Health, 92*(2), 209-222. https://doi.org/10.1111/josh.13119

Wang, J. (2017, February 13). Managing allergy, anaphylaxis: AAP releases customizable emergency plan. *American Academy of Pediatrics News.* https://www.congress.gov/113/plaws/publ48/PLAW-113publ48.pdf Access to the form: https://downloads.aap.org/HC/AAP_Allergy_and_Anaphylaxis_Emergency_Plan.pdf

Wang, J., Sicherer, S. H., & American Academy of Pediatrics Section on Allergy and Immunology. (2017). Guidance on completing a written allergy and anaphylaxis emergency plan. *Pediatrics, 139 (3)* e20164005. https://doi.org/10.1542/peds.2016-4005

OTHER REFERENCES CONSULTED

Abrams, E.M. & Greenhawt, M. (2020). The role of peanut-free school policies in the protection of children with peanut allergies. *Journal of Public Health Policy*, 41, 206–213. https://doi.org/10.1057/s41271-019-00216-y

Broas, E., Lowe, A.A., Ivich, K., Garcia, M. Ward, J., Hollister, J, & Gerald, L.B. (2023) The Implementation and evaluation of a stock epinephrine for schools Program in Maricopa County, Arizona. *The Journal of School Nursing* 0(0). https://doi.org /10.1177/10598405231172957

Bock, S.A., Munoz-Furlong, A., & Sampson, H .A. (2007) Further fatalities caused by anaphylactic reactions to food, 2001-2006. *The Journal of Allergy and Clinical Immunology, 119*, 1016–1018. https://doi.org/10.1016/j.jaci.2006.12.622

De Silva, D., Singh C., Muraro, A., Worm, M., Alviani, C., Cardona, V., DunnGlvin, A., Garvey, L. H., Riggioni, C., Angier, E., Arasi, S., Bellou, A., Beyer, K., Bijlhout, D., Bilo, M. B., Brockow, K., Fernandez-Rivas, M., Halken, S., Jensen B., . . . Clinical Immunology Food Allergy and Anaphylaxis Guidelines Group. (2020). Diagnosing, managing, and preventing anaphylaxis: Systematic review. *European Journal of Allergy and Clinical Immunology, 76,* 1493–1506. https://doi.org/10.1111/all.14580

Gregory, N. (2012) The case for stock epinephrine in schools. *NASN School Nurse, 27*(4), 222-225. https://doi.org/10.1177/1942602X12449057

Gupta, R. S., Springston, E. E., Warrier, M. R., Smith, B., Kumar, R., Pongracic, J., & Holl, J. L. (2011). The prevalence, severity, and distribution of childhood food allergy in the United States. *Pediatrics, 128*(1), e9-e17. https://doi.org/10.1542/peds.2011-0204

Halbert, L. & Yonkaitis, C. F, (2019). Federal laws protecting children and youth with disabilities. In J. Selekman, R. A. Shannon, & C. F. Yonkaitis (Eds.), School nursing: A comprehensive text (3rd ed., pp. 154 - 171). F.A. Davis.

Hogue, S.L., Muniz, R., Herrem, C., Silvia, S., & White, M.V. (2018). Barriers to the administration of epinephrine in schools. *Journal of School Health, 88*(5), 396–404. https://doi.org/10.1111/josh.12620

Jackson, V. (2013) School nurse's role in supporting food allergy safe schools. *NASN School Nurse, 28* (2),76-77. https://doi.org/10.1177/1942602X13477

McIntyre, C. L., Sheetz, A. H., Carroll, C. R., & Young, M. C. (2005). Administration of epinephrine for life-threatening allergic reactions in school settings. *Pediatrics, 116*(5), 1134-1140. https://doi.org/10.1542/peds.2004-1475

Neupert, K.B., Huntwork, M.P., Udemgba, C., Carlson, J.C. (2022). Implementation of Stock Epinephrine in Chartered Versus Unchartered Public-School Districts. *Journal of School Health, 92*(8), 812-814. https://doi.org/:10.1111/josh.13159

Pistiner, M. & Lee, J. (2012) Creating a new community of support for students with food allergies. NASN School Nurse, *27*(5), 260-266. https://doi.org/10.1177/1942602X12455247" https://doi.org/10.1177/1942602X12455247

Russell, W. S. & Schoessler, S. (2017). To give or not to give epinephrine – That is (no longer) the question! *NASN School Nurse, 32*(3), 162- 164. http://doi.org/10.1177/1942602X17690402

Sicherer, S.H., Furlong, T.J, DeSimone J. & Sampson. (2001). The U.S. peanut and tree nut allergy registry: Characteristics of reactions in schools and daycare. *Journal of Pediatrics,138*,560–565. https://doi.org/10.1067/mpd.2001.111821

Vokits, K., Pumphrey, I., Baker, D. & Krametbauer, K. (2014). Implementation of a stock epinephrine protocol. NASN School Nurse,22. https://doi.org/10.1177/1942602X14546642

Volerman, A., Woolverton, N., & Amerson, N. (2022). More Work to Do to Achieve Epinephrine Access for All Children in Schools. *Journal of School Health, 92*(8), 824. https://doi.org/10.1111/josh.13202

Wang, J., Bingemann T., Russell A.F., Young, M. C., & Sicherer, S.H. (2018)., The allergist's role in anaphylaxis and food allergy management in the school and childcare setting. *Journal of Allergy Clinical Immunology Practice.* 6:427–435. https://doi.org/10.1016/j.jaip.2017.11.022

APPENDIX

Anaphylaxis

- ❑ Hives, rash
- ❑ Itchiness, redness, swelling of face and/or tongue
- ❑ Stomach pain
- ❑ Vomiting, diarrhea, or cramps
- ❑ Weak pulse, passing out, shock
- ❑ Dizziness or fainting
- ❑ Flushing
- ❑ Metallic taste
- ❑ Stridor
- ❑ Hoarse voice

Anaphylaxis or Acute Asthma

- ❑ Coughing that will not stop
- ❑ Chest pain and/or tightness
- ❑ Wheezing
- ❑ Shortness of breath, difficulty breathing, very rapid breathing
- ❑ Difficulty talking
- ❑ Pallor
- ❑ Blue lips or fingernails
- ❑ Feelings of anxiety or doom
- ❑ Worsening symptoms despite use of medications

Figure 1. Comparison of anaphylaxis and acute asthma symptoms. Schoessler & White. (2013). Reprinted with permission.

Table 1. Comparison of Anaphylaxis and Acute Asthma Triggers.

Anaphylaxis	Asthma
Ingested foods	Respiratory infections
Insect stings	Allergens
	• Pet dander
	• Dust
	• Pollen
	• Mold
Medications	Irritants
	• Air pollution
	• Smoke
	• Chalk dust
	• Strong odors (eg, indelible markers, perfume)
Latex	Environmental
	• Dusty gym mats
	• Old books
	• Cleaning products
	• Fumes
Cleaning agents	Dry, cold air
Exercise	Exercise

Schoessler & White. (2013). Reprinted with permission. Schoessler, S., & White, M. (2013). Recognition and treatment of anaphylaxis in the school setting: The essential role of the school nurse. *The Journal of School Nursing, 29*, 407-415. https://doi.org/10.1177/1059840513506014

Chapter 32

MEDICAL CANNABIS IN SCHOOLS

Joan Edelstein, DrPH, MSN, RN, PHN*
Rachel J. Torres, DNP, RN, PHNA-BC*

DESCRIPTION OF ISSUE

Since the use of medical cannabis on school grounds was legalized in Colorado in April 2016, twelve other states, the District of Columbia, and a school district in Oklahoma City have followed suit (Medical Cannabis Act, 2017; Kelly, 2019; Americans for Safe Access, 2020). Concern regarding the conflict between state and federal law and the impact on the scope of practice is a common dilemma for school nurses nationally. As the use of medical cannabis, laws, and the scope of practice continues to evolve, school nurses must remain knowledgeable of these dynamics to promote patient/student safety.

The National Council of States Boards of Nursing (NCBSN) recognizes that nurses must be knowledgeable and possess the skills to proficiently care for the growing population of patients using medicinal cannabis (2018). The NCBSN identified the following six principles of essential knowledge about cannabis for *all* nurses, starting in the pre-licensure program (2018):

1. The nurse shall have a working knowledge of the current state of legalization of medical and recreational cannabis use.
2. The nurse shall have a working knowledge of the jurisdiction's medical marijuana program.
3. The nurse shall have an understanding of the endocannabinoid system, cannabinoid receptors, cannabinoids, and the interactions between them.
4. The nurse shall have an understanding of cannabis pharmacology and the research associated with the medical use of cannabis.
5. The nurse shall be able to identify the safety considerations for patient use of cannabis.
6. The nurse shall approach the patient without judgment regarding the patient's choice of treatment or preferences in managing pain and other distressing symptoms (p. S19-21).

According to Holmes, Sheetz, and the American Academy of Pediatrics [AAP] (2016), school nurses are the experts in medications and health conditions in the school setting. Parents/caregivers, school staff, and administrators refer to school nurses with questions about the use of medical cannabis in children and the administration of the medication in school. School nurses must be knowledgeable about cannabis, state laws, and policy implications related to their current medication administration policy.

History of the term Cannabis and Marijuana

The American Cannabis Nurses Association [ACNA] (2022) recommends that healthcare professionals, researchers, and governmental agencies use the term "cannabis" instead of "marijuana." In the 1800s, cannabis was a household name used by Americans to treat over 100 illnesses and diseases in the United States (Russell, 2018). Successful propaganda, such as the Reefer Madness campaign in the 1930s, constructed

---

* Original authors: Kathleen Patrick, MA, RN, NCSN & Kathy L. Reiner, MPH, BSN, RN (2017)

the racist origin of the term "Marijuana" (Schlosser, 1994; Green, 2018). During the Great Depression, White Americans used the term "marijuana/marihuana" to associate the plant with deviant behaviors and criminal activity to deter the employment of Mexican workers (Russell, 2018; Clark, 2021). Barrett's (2016) four-and-a-half-minute reporting on the *Racial History of Weed* clearly lays out the intent and impact of the reefer madness campaign. School nurses are strongly encouraged to review Barrett's report to familiarize themselves with the racial history of how U.S. society views cannabis.

The United States government passed the Marijuana Tax Act (MTA) of 1937, opposed by the American Medical Association (Little, 2018), virtually eliminating access to and medicinal use of cannabis. In 1968, President Richard Nixon began America's war on drugs and used the recreational use of cannabis to criminalize Black people and anti-war protestors (Ford, 2021; Ryan et al., 2021). In 1969, the MTA was deemed unconstitutional. However, in 1970 the U.S. Congress passed the Controlled Substance Act (CSA), which classified drugs, chemicals, or substances into categories or schedules based on the drug's acceptable medical use or potential for misuse (Department of Justice, 2012). A drug labeled as "Schedule 1" status signifies that a drug has "... no currently accepted medical use" (Drug Enforcement Administration [DEA] 2018, para. 3). Under the CSA, cannabis was and remains categorized as a Schedule 1 substance.

The policies that criminalize cannabis have disproportionately impacted the Black and Latinx population (Ryan et al., 2021). Awareness of the racist and negative historical attitudes toward the cannabis plant allows school nurses to value the medicinal properties of cannabis separate from the implicit biases common in society. This will broaden the school nurses' ability to gain confidence and competence to provide safe and ethical nursing care to students who require the administration of medical cannabis in schools.

BACKGROUND

The endocannabinoid system (ECS) is a large and complex receptor system responsible for promoting homeostasis. The ECS is composed of endocannabinoids, cannabinoid receptors, and the enzymes that degrade and synthesize endocannabinoids (Clark, 2021; Russell, 2018). Endocannabinoids are substances made within the human body from cell membranes. Anandamide (AEA) and 2-arachidonoylglyerol (2-AG) are the only identified endocannabinoids. There are two primary endocannabinoid receptors, CB1 and CB2. CB1 receptors are predominantly found in the brain but also in central nervous, peripheral nervous, cardiovascular, gastrointestinal, and reproductive tissues. CB2 receptors are found in the peripheral immune system (mast cells, tonsils, thymus, and spleen), microglial, brainstem, and skin cells (Clark, 2021; Russell, 2018).

Cannabis is derived from the flowering plant family Cannabacae and refers to the plant's dried leaves, seeds, and flowers. The three most recognized species are *Cannabis sativa (C. sativa), Cannabis indica (C. indica), and Cannabis ruderalis (C.ruderalis)* (Clark, 2021). Phytocannabinoids are compounds found in cannabis plants that mimic endocannabinoids (Russell, 2018). Over one hundred active cannabinoids and almost 500 chemical compounds have so far been identified in the plant (Webb, 2019). The most well-known phytocannabinoids are delta-9-tetrahydrocannabinol (THC), cannabidiol (CBD), and cannabinol (CBN). THC reacts with CB1 and CB2 receptors, which allows for the psychoactive and intoxicating effects. The amount of THC in any given plant can vary widely depending on the species, strain, or variety used. While the precise mechanism of action is unclear, researchers have found that CBD does not react with CB1 or CB2 receptors; instead, CBD inhibits cellular uptake of endocannabinoids as well as modulates other non-cannabinoid receptors and ion channels (Russell, 2018; Clark, 2021). CBD can enhance the medicinal properties of THC and, at the same time, reduce the psychoactive effects.

Cannabis can be administered via inhalation (smoking or vaporizing), oral intake (food, drink, capsules, tinctures), dermal (lotions, patches), ophthalmic (eye drops), and rectal (suppositories). Cannabis is distributed by the bloodstream and metabolized by the liver (Clark, 2021).

Controlled Substance

All varieties of cannabis are currently classified as Schedule 1 drugs by the DEA. The U.S. Department of Health & Human Services was granted a patent for *Cannabinoids as antioxidants and neuroprotectants*, which has since expired, identifying potential medical use without a change in Schedule I status (Hampton et al., 2003).

Medicinal use has now been established through clinical trial data for both adult and pediatric populations. As research in the U.S. has been hampered due to DEA scheduling and the legality of cannabis, data have mainly come from other countries such as The Netherlands, Israel, Canada, and the Czech Republic (Stamberger & Nunley, 2020).

Note that there are legal differences in cannabis between the state and federal levels. By the action of the Controlled Substances Act (2012), cannabis is illegal at the federal level. In 2009, U.S. Attorney General Eric Holder stated, "It will not be a priority to use federal resources to prosecute patients with serious illnesses or their caregivers who are complying with state laws on medical cannabis, but we will not tolerate drug traffickers who hide behind claims of compliance with state law to mask activities that are clearly illegal" (U.S. Department of Justice, Drug Enforcement Administration, 2012, para. 2). This approach, along with lack of funding for this purpose to the Department of Justice, is upheld at the time of this writing (Congressional Research Service, 2022).

In 2015, the AAP updated its policy statement on the legalization of cannabis for recreational or medical use. The AAP believes that cannabis should be decriminalized, with a focus on prevention and treatment. If cannabis is used medicinally, it should be done carefully with research, using the U.S. Food and Drug Administration (FDA) process rather than medical cannabis laws (American Academy of Pediatrics [AAP], 2023).

Medicinal Use of Cannabis

The medicinal use of cannabis has been documented as far back as 2900 B.C. (Russell, 2019). Currently, cannabis is not legal for medicinal or recreational use under federal law in the U.S. However, the National Council of State Legislatures (NCSL) (2022) reports that as of February 2022, thirty-seven (37) states, three territories, and the District of Columbia have legalized medicinal cannabis. The number of states that have legalized medicinal cannabis continues to increase. Each state that has legalized medical cannabis may regulate the amount the patient or caregiver can possess, the conditions that cannabis can treat, and require registration. Although cannabis use continues to be illegal under federal law, the 114th Congress included an amendment to appropriations bill HR2578 making it clear that the Department of Justice would not be able to use federal funds to prevent states from implementing laws that authorize the use, distribution, possession, or cultivation of medical Cannabis (Commerce, Justice, Science, and Related Agencies Appropriations Act, 2016). The National Council of State Legislatures website lists the states that allow the legal use of medical cannabis along with the provisions of each state law.

Food and Drug Administration (FDA) Approved Medications

The FDA is responsible for conducting studies and clinical trials to determine the benefits and risks of new medications. This drug approval process ensures that medications are safe and effective. The FDA has approved two medications that contain synthetic (man-made) THC. Dronabinol (Marinol) is a schedule III oral medication used to treat AIDS-related wasting and chemotherapy-induced nausea and vomiting. Cesamet (nabilone) is a schedule II oral medication prescribed for spasticity (Ammerman et al., 2015). Because these drugs contain synthetic THC, medication labels list psychoactive side effects.

In June 2018, the FDA approved the first plant-derived cannabinoid prescription medicine, Epidiolex (cannabidiol). Epidiolex contains 99.9 % CBD and 0.1% THC, producing no psychoactive side effects. Epidioloex could not be prescribed as a Schedule I drug until September 2018, when the DEA moved it to Schedule V (DEA, 2018). How this affects current cannabis plant-based drugs in clinical trials remains to be seen, as they may contain more than 0.1% THC. In addition to Epidiolex, clinical trials are currently underway for several cannabis plant-based cannabidiol medications, such as Sativex. Sativex is available by prescription in several countries for treating symptoms related to multiple sclerosis (National Institute on Drug Abuse [NIDA], 2020). In January 2023, the FDA released guidance for clinical research on developing medical cannabis or cannabis-related compounds (Center for Drug Evaluation and Research, 2023).

The NCSBN concluded that "Available moderate- to high-quality research, along with state and federal laws regarding the use of cannabis, is a necessary component of knowledge in the nursing care of a patient using cannabis. Without the usual FDA approval of cannabis that identifies precise indications, dosage, and efficacy for medications, nurses must have a much more nuanced knowledge while caring for the patient using cannabis" (Alexander, 2018, p. S21).

Hemp

Hemp is a variety of the C. sativa plant grown specifically for industrial uses. For thousands of years, it has been used for paper, textiles, food, and rope. Both hemp and cannabis come from the same cannabis species but have distinct genetic properties. Hemp was removed from Schedule I with The Agricultural Act of 2018 [The Farm Bill] (Cadena, 2018). CBD derived from hemp with <0.3% THC is legal under federal law (Clark, 2021).

RESEARCH

Reports of the use of cannabis for medicinal purposes date back several thousands of years throughout the world. In the 1800s, a prominent English neurologist W. R. Gowers reported using a cannabis-based product to treat seizures (Patel, 2016). Many of the products tested were high in THC. Recently, products like Epidiolex have been developed with low THC and high CBD content.

Products with high CBD content can be obtained in various forms but are usually found in an oil or liquid when administered to children. There is also a transdermal patch. CBD oil can contain varying amounts of THC and

CBD. Since there are no manufacturing regulations, it may be difficult to determine accurate percentages of THC or CBD within a product.

CBD specifically has been used to treat neurologic disorders such as epilepsy. Systematic reviews, as well as randomized controlled trials (RCT)and individual studies, have demonstrated the efficacy and safety of cannabis in epilepsy in children (Anderton, 2019; Devinsky et al., 2017; Elliott et al., 2018; Noonan, 2017; Patel & Kiriakopoulos, 2019; Thomas & Cunningham, 2018; Treves et al., 2021). Anecdotal reports from providers and families on the successful treatment of children with seizure disorders such as Dravet's Syndrome and Lennox-Gestaut Syndrome (LGS) using products with high CBD content led to clinical trials by G.W. Pharmaceuticals (FDA, 2018; Center for Drug Evaluation and Research, 2018; Thomas & Cunningham, 2018).

Reviews of Randomized Control Trials and other open-label and expanded access trials (Zhou et al., 2021) have demonstrated the efficacy of CBD on specific types of epilepsy. A dose-related increase in adverse events of CBD compared with placebo was noted, including drowsiness, fever, diarrhea, vomiting, decreased appetite, and upper respiratory tract infection. The authors noted that adverse events were dose-related. They addressed the impact of legal barriers on cannabis research and stigmatization.

Ongoing trials for autism-related behaviors continue to demonstrate the safety and potential use of medical cannabis to alleviate those behaviors to enable students to access social interaction, communication, and education (Bar-Lev Schleider et al., 2019; Bilge & Ekici, 2021; Holdman et al., 2022; Silva Junior et al., 2021).

THC has been demonstrated to have therapeutic benefits when properly dosed in children (Goldstein, 2020). While associations have been found linking short- and long-term effects of cannabis, studies have not established causal relationships in humans for such areas as long-term effects on the brain; psychiatric disorders; interference in school, work, or social life, according to the NIDA (2020). The NIDA (2020) report states that "THC itself has proven medical benefits in particular formulations" (p. 22).

The American Nurses Association (ANA) position statement on the *Therapeutic Use of Marijuana and Related Cannabinoids* notes that "Current federal regulations impede the research necessary to evaluate and determine the therapeutic use of marijuana and related cannabinoids" (ANA Ethics Advisory Board, 2021, para. 2)

IMPLICATIONS FOR SCHOOL NURSE PRACTICE

Medical Cannabis in Schools

As of January 2023, 37 States and the District of Columbia have laws that provide access to the medicinal use of cannabis. Another 11 states provide access to low-THC products for medicinal use (NORML, 2023). As of this writing, there is no legal mandate to allow the administration of medical cannabis in schools. The following allow but do not require the administration of medical cannabis on school grounds: the Oklahoma City School District, the District of Columbia, and the states of California, Colorado, Delaware, Florida, Illinois, Maine, Maryland, New Jersey, New Mexico, Pennsylvania, West Virginia, Washington (Medical Cannabis Act, 2017; Kelly, 2019; Americans for Safe Access, 2020).

Laws vary by state, and school nurses should refer to their state laws to determine the specific provisions in their state. It is important to note that all states allowing the administration of medical cannabis in school exclude the use of vaped or smoked cannabis.

School districts have questioned their liability under federal law prohibiting illegal drugs on school grounds or at school activities, even if it is permitted under state law. In California, *Student v. Rincon Valley Union Elementary School District* (2018), the administrative law judge found no evidence that schools would lose federal funding. To date, no districts in the states or the District of Columbia that allow medical cannabis to be administered have lost federal funding.

Because cannabis is a Schedule I substance, medicinal cannabis products are not written on traditional prescription pads, which require a federal DEA number. Instead, orders are written as recommendations on forms for cannabis dispensaries. Therefore, school nurses must determine how to best meet district medication administration policies. In California, for example, a physician's written order is accepted in lieu of a prescription (*N. Johnson, personal communication 2020*). Cannabis is generally packaged in the same way as traditional medications in labeled vials. Students receiving medical cannabis are generally referred to dispensaries that standardize and test the products to establish consistent content (*B. Goldstein, personal communication 2022*).

School Nurse Essentials

School nurses should understand the federal, state, and municipal laws, and public/private/charter/ County Office of Education policy as they apply to the school nurse. Registered nurses are required to abide by all state and federal laws under their Nurse Practice Act. As noted, the NCSBN provides guidance for all nurses on medical cannabis (2018).

The New Mexico Public Education Department (NMPED) Safe and Healthy Schools Bureau (2019) provides guidance for school nurses in accordance with current law stating that "nurses should provide the same level of education, counseling support, and administrative guidance they would normally provide in situations where FDA-approved medications are administered in the school setting (p. 1). The NMPED (2022) website is an excellent resource for school nurses as it provides the links to N.M. State Senate Bills 204 and 206, which are now laws, a policy framework for schools to implement the medical cannabis laws in the school setting, guidance for school nurses, and a sample Medical Cannabis Treatment Plan.

In 2019, the National Association of School Nurses published a position brief on cannabis; however, the position brief was retired in January 2022 (NASN, n.d.). The National Association of School Nurses (NASN) is developing educational materials for school nurses (Personal Communications, D. Mazyck February 2, 2023).

Scope of Practice

The California Board of Registered Nursing has determined that "… it is within the scope of practice of registered nurses to administer a medication or therapeutic agent, such as medicinal cannabis, that is necessary to implement a treatment plan ordered by and within the scope of licensure of a physician" (California Board of Nursing, 2022, p. 3). School nurses should determine the scope of practice in their states. In states such as Colorado, where medical cannabis has been allowed on school grounds, the laws specifically protect healthcare professionals, school nurses, and school personnel who administer medical cannabis at school (H. Res. 18-1286, 2018).

Medical cannabis use in schools raises several key issues for policymakers and school administrators. Despite the differences in the legal status of cannabis at the state level, it is still listed as a Schedule I drug under federal law. The National Association of School Nurses (2019) states that "All students, including students with special needs, have the right to participate in school-sponsored trips" (para. 1). School nurses must consider federal laws when students receiving medical cannabis have the opportunity to participate in out of state field trips, as possession of any Schedule I substance when crossing state borders is illegal. Further, the Individuals with Disabilities Education Act (IDEA) is a federal law that ensures students with disabilities are provided Free, Appropriate Public Education tailored to each student's needs. Lawsuits and litigation regarding students with disabilities and access to medical cannabis in school are currently in process (J. Adams, personal communication, 2020).

The five principles of the Framework for 21st School Nursing Practice™ are Leadership, Care Coordination, Quality Improvement, Community/Public Health, and Standards of Practice (NASN, 2016). Leadership, Care Coordination, and Standards of Practice are guiding principles for school nurses and administrators when providing care for students with medical cannabis treatment plans. School nurses and administrators provide Leadership to the school site, district, and community through local, state, and national advocacy of students' rights to access medications during school days with minimal disruption to their education. Through Care Coordination, school nurses collaborate with the health care team and interdisciplinary education teams to ensure the student and family are supported, and accommodations are met during the school day within the scope of the state laws. In cases where the nurses are not allowed to administer medical cannabis during the school day, the school nurse or nurse administrator can collaborate with the caregivers, school administrators, the district attorneys, and the medical provider to suggest the best approach to developing a school plan which best supports the student and their health and safety needs. Lastly, remaining current with clinical competence, guidelines, and evidence-based practice surrounding medical cannabis in the pediatric population is a Standard of Practice, the foundation of the Framework for the 21st Century School Nursing Practice™ (NASN, 2016).

CONCLUSION

As laws related to medical cannabis are rapidly changing, every school nurse should review state laws regarding medical cannabis and the nurse practice act in their state and the states in which they are licensed. They should follow the guidance of the NCSBN to ensure they have the knowledge required to care for students with medicinal cannabis orders. School nurses should review laws allowing the use of medical cannabis to ensure liability is waived when properly providing care under medical supervision. As more states legalize medical cannabis, school nurses are responsible for staying informed about current federal and state laws and current research regarding medical cannabis and providing education and advocacy to ensure all students' health needs are met.

RESOURCES

National Center for Complemental and Integrative Medicine. Cannabis and Cannabinoids: What You Need to Know. https://www.nccih.nih.gov/health/cannabis-marijuana-and-cannabinoids-what-you-need-to-know

National Library of Medicine. Medical Marijuana.
https://medlineplus.gov/ency/patientinstructions/000899.htm

Case Law

Student v. Rincon Valley Union Elementary School District (Office of Administrative Hearings State of California 2018, September).

REFERENCES

Alexander, M. (Ed.). (2018). The NCSBN national nursing guidelines for medical marijuana. *Journal of Nursing Regulation, 9*(2). https://doi.org/10.1016/s2155-8256(18)30082-6

Anderton, K. (Ed.). (2019, July). *Researchers study cannabis dosage to reduce seizures in children with severe epilepsy.* https://www.news-medical.net/news/20190708/Researchers-study-cannabis-dosage-to-reduce-seizures-in-children-with-severe-epilepsy.aspx

American Academy Of Pediatrics. (2015). *AAP reaffirms opposition to legalizing marijuana for recreational or medical use.* https://www.aap.org/en-us/about-the-aap/aap-press-room/pages/american-academy-of-pediatrics-reaffirms-opposition-to-legalizing-marijuana-for-recreational-or-medical-use.aspx

American Cannabis Nurses Association (ACNA). (2022, December). *Cannabis terminology - best practices.* Policy/Position Statements of the American Cannabis Nurses Association. https://www.cannabisnurses.org/assets/docs/CannabisTermsPPFinal.pdf

Americans for Safe Access. (2020, October). Pediatric medical cannabis access in schools. *Americans for Safe Access.* https://www.safeaccessnow.org/pediatric_medical_cannabis_access_in_schools

Ammerman S., Ryan S., & Adelman, W. (2015). The impact of marijuana policies on youth: clinical, research, and legal update. *Pediatrics, 135*(3). https://doi.org/10.1542/peds.2014-4147

ANA Ethics Advisory Board. (2022). ANA position statement: Therapeutic use of marijuana and related cannabinoids. *OJIN: The Online Journal of Issues in Nursing*, 27(1).

Bar-Lev Schleider, L., Mechoulam, R., Saban, N., Meiri, G., & Novack, V. (2019). Real life experience of medical cannabis treatment in autism: Analysis of safety and efficacy. *Scientific Reports, 9*(1). https://doi.org/10.1038/s41598-018-37570-y

Barrett, S. H. (2016, April 15). *The racial history of weed*. Latino USA. https://www.latinousa.org/2016/04/15/racial-history-weed/

Battistella, G., Fornari, E., Annoni, J., Chtioui, H., Dao, K., Fabritius, M., Favrat, B., Mall, J., Maeder, P., & Giroud, C. (2014). Long term effects of cannabis on brain structure. *Neuropsychopharmacology, 39*(9): 2041–2048. https://doi.org/10.1038/npp.2014.67

Bilge, S., & Ekici, B. (2021). CBD-enriched cannabis for autism spectrum disorder: An experience of a single center in Turkey and reviews of the literature. *Journal of Cannabis Research, 3*(1). https://doi.org/10.1186/s42238-021-00108-7

California Board of Nursing. (2022). Declaratory Decision: Administration of Medicinal Cannabis by Registered Nurses in Schools Pursuant to Physician's Order (Case No. 2022-BRN-01 May 27, 2022). https://www.rn.ca.gov/pdfs/regulations/pd2022-brn-01.pdf

Center for Drug Evaluation and Research. (2018, July 17). *Drug trials snapshots: Epidiolex*. U.S. Food and Drug Administration. https://www.fda.gov/drugs/drug-approvals-and-databases/drug-trials-snapshots-epidiolex

Center for Drug Evaluation and Research. (2023, January). *Cannabis and Cannabis-Derived Compounds: Quality Considerations for Clinical Research*. U.S. Food and Drug Administration. https://www.fda.gov/drugs/guidance-compliance-regulatory-information/guidances-drugs

Clark, C. (2021). *Cannabis: A handbook for nurses*. Lippincott Williams & Wilkins.

Colorado Department of Public Health and Environment. (2017). *Healthy Kids Colorado Survey*. https://www.colorado.gov/pacific/cdphe/hkcs

Commerce, Justice, Science, and Related Agencies Appropriations Act. H.R. 2578, 114th Cong. (2016). https://www.congress.gov/congressional-record/volume-161/issue-87/house-section/article/H3700-2

Devinsky, O., Cross, J. H., Laux, L., Marsh, E., Miller, I., Nabbout, R., Scheffer, I. E., Thiele, E.A., & Wright, S. (2017). Trial of cannabidiol for drug-resistant seizures in the Dravet syndrome. *New England Journal of Medicine, 376*(21), 2011–2020. https://doi.org/10.1056/nejmoa1611618

Education Commission of the States. (2017). *Medical marijuana in schools: State legislation and policy considerations*. http://www.ecs.org/medical-marijuana-in-schools-state-legislation-and-policy-considerations/

Elliott, J., DeJean, D., Clifford, T., Coyle, D., Potter, B. K., Skidmore, B., Alexander, C., Repetski, A. E., Shukla, V., McCoy, B., & Wells, G. A. (2018). Cannabis-based products for pediatric epilepsy: A systematic review. *Epilepsia, 60*(1), 6–19. https://doi.org/10.1111/epi.14608

Federal Register. (2016). *Establishment of a new drug code for marihuana extract*. https://www.federalregister.gov/documents/2016/12/14/2016-29941/establishment-of-a-new-drug-code-for-marihuana-extract

Ford, S. (2021, September). Review of Our drug laws are racist, and doctors must speak out—an essay by Simon Woolley. *BMJ (Online), 374*, N2147–N2147. https://doi.org/10.1136/bmj.n2147

Gloss, D., & Vickery, B. (2014). Cannabinoids for epilepsy. *Cochrane Database of Systematic Reviews 2014, 3* Art. No. CD009270, https://doi.org/10.1002/14651858.CD009270.pub3

Goldstein, B. (2020). *Cannabis is medicine: How medical cannabis and CBD are healing everything from anxiety to chronic pain*. Little, Brown Spark.

Green, M. (2018, January). *Reefer madness! the twisted history of America's marijuana laws*. KQED. https://www.kqed.org/lowdown/24153/reefer-madness-the-twisted-history-of-americas-weed-laws

H.B. 18-1286, First, 2018 Regular Session, (Colorado, 2018) (enacted). https://leg.colorado.gov/bills/hb18-1286

Hampton, A. J., Axelrod, A., Grimaldi, M. (2003). *Cannabinoids as antioxidants and neuroprotectants*. (U.S. Patent No. 6,630,507). U.S. Patent and Trademark Office. https://www.holistichempextracts.com/wp-content/uploads/2019/10/USPatentNo.6630507B1.pdf

Hill, A. J., Williams, C. M., Whalley, B. J., & Stephens, G. J. (2012). Phytocannabinoids as novel therapeutic agents in CNS disorders. *Pharmacology & Therapeutics, 133*(1), 79–97. https://doi.org/10.1016/j.pharmthera.2011.09.002

Holdman, R., Vigil, D., Robinson, K., Shah, P., & Contreras, A. E. (2022). Safety and efficacy of medical cannabis in autism spectrum disorder compared with commonly used medications. *Cannabis and Cannabinoid Research, 7*(4), 451–463. https://doi.org/10.1089/can.2020.0154

Holmes, B.W., Sheetz, A., & the American Academy of Pediatrics. (2016). Role of the school nurse in providing school health services (Policy Statement). *Pediatrics, 137* (6) e20160852. https://doi.org/10.1542/peds.2016-0852

H.R.2642 - Agricultural Act of 2014. https://www.gpo.gov/fdsys/pkg/plaw-113publ79/html/plaw-113publ79.htm

Kelly, T. (2019). When medical marijuana meets school drug policy, what can states do? *EdNote*. https://ednote.ecs.org/when-medical-marijuana-meets-school-drug-policy-what-can-states-do/9

Kosterman, R., Bailey, J.A., Gurrmannova, K., Jones, T.M., Eisenberg, N., Hill, K.G., & Hawkins, J.D. (2016). Marijuana legalization and parents' attitudes, use, and parenting in Washington State. *Journal of Adolescent Health, 59*(4),450-6. https://doi.org/10.1016/j.jadohealth.2016.07.004

Liptak, K. (2017). *White House: Feds will step up marijuana law enforcement.* http://www.cnn.com/2017/02/23/politics/white-house-marijuana-donald-trump-pot/index.html

Maa, E. (2014). The case for medical marijuana in epilepsy. *Epilepsia, 55*(6),783-786. https://doi.org/10.1111/epi.12610

Medical Cannabis Act (2017). West Virginia Code Section §16A-15-5. https://www.wvlegislature.gov/wvcode/code.cfm?chap=16A&art=15

Meier, M.H., Caspi, A., Ambler, A., Harrington, H., Houts, R., Keefe, R.S., McDonald, K., Ward, A., Poulton, R., & Moffitt, T.E. (2012). Persistent cannabis users show neuropsychological decline from childhood to midlife. *Proceedings of the National Academy of Sciences of the United States of America, 109*(40), E2657-E2664. https://doi.org/10.1073/pnas.120682010

National Association of School Nurses. (2016). Framework for 21st century school nursing practice. NASN School Nurse, *31*, 45-53. https://doi.org/10.1177/1942602X15618644

National Association of School Nurses. (2019). *School-sponsored trips -The role of the school nurse* (Position Statement). Author. https://www.nasn.org/nasn-resources/professional-practice-documents/position-statements/ps-trips

National Association of School Nurses. (n.d.). *Position brief - cannabis/marijuana*. Position Brief - Cannabis/Marijuana - National Association of School Nurses. https://www.nasn.org/nasn-resources/professional-practice-documents/positionbriefs/pb-cannabis

National Conference of State Legislatures (NCSL). (2022, September). *State medical cannabis laws*. https://www.ncsl.org/health/state-medical-cannabis-laws

National Council of State Boards of Nursing. (2018). The NCSBN national nursing guidelines for medical marijuana. *Journal of Nursing Regulation, 9*(2), S3-S59.

New Mexico Public Education Department. (2019, August). Medical cannabis in schools - guidance regarding school nurses in accordance with current law. *NMPED Safe and Healthy Schools*. https://webnew.ped.state.nm.us/wp-content/uploads/2019/08/SHSB_Guidance_School-Nurses_Medical-Cannabis_August-2019.pdf

New Mexico Public Education Department. (2022, December 22). *Medical cannabis in schools*. New Mexico Public Education Department. https://webnew.ped.state.nm.us/bureaus/safe-healthy-schools/medical-cannabis-in-schools/

National Institute on Drug Abuse. (2020, July). *Cannabis (marijuana) research report.* https://nida.nih.gov/download/1380/cannabis-marijuana-research-report.pdf?v=7fc7d24c3dc120a03cf26348876bc1e4

Noonan, D. (2017, May). Marijuana treatment reduces severe epileptic seizures. *Scientific American*. https://www.scientificamerican.com/article/marijuana-treatment-reduces-severe-epileptic-seizures/

NORML. (2023, March). *Medical marijuana laws. State laws.* https://norml.org/laws/medical-laws/" https://norml.org/laws/medical-laws/

Patel, A. (2016). Medical marijuana in pediatric neurological disorders. *Journal of Child Neurology, 31*(3), 388-391. https://doi.org/10.1177/0883073815589761

Patel, A., & Kiriakopoulos, E. (2019, May). Medical marijuana. *Epilepsy Foundation*. https://www.epilepsy.com/treatment/alternative-therapies/medical-marijuana

Russell, K. A. (2019). Caring for patients using medical marijuana. *Journal of Nursing Regulation, 10*(3), 47–61. https://doi.org/10.1016/s2155-8256(19)30148-6

Ryan, J. E., McCabe, S. E., & Boyd, C. J. (2021). Medicinal Cannabis: Policy, Patients, and Providers. *Policy, politics & nursing practice, 22*(2), 126–133. https://doi.org/10.1177/1527154421989609

Schlosser, E. (1994, August). Reefer madness. *The Atlantic*. https://www.theatlantic.com/magazine/archive/1994/08/reefer-madness/303476/

Selekman, J., & Edelstein, J. (2021). Cannabis vs. Marijuana, THC vs. CBD – The State of the Science. *Pediatric Nursing, 47*(2), 59–65.

Silva Junior, E. A., Medeiros, W. M., Torro, N., Sousa, J. M., Almeida, I. B., Costa, F. B., Pontes, K. M., Nunes, E. L., Rosa, M. D., & Albuquerque, K. L. (2021). Cannabis and cannabinoid use in autism spectrum disorder: A systematic review. *Trends in Psychiatry and Psychotherapy*. https://doi.org/10.47626/2237-6089-2020-0149

Stamberger, J., & Nunley, K. (2020, March). Top 4 countries leading in Cannabis Research. *Medical Marijuana News*. https://news.medicalmarijuanainc.com/top-4-countries-leading-in-cannabis-research/

Thomas, R. H., & Cunningham, M. O. (2018). Cannabis and epilepsy. *Practical Neurology, 18*(6), 465–471. https://doi.org/10.1136/practneurol-2018-002058

Treves, N., Mor, N., Allegaert, K., Bassalov, H., Berkovitch, M., Stolar, O. E., & Matok, I. (2021). Efficacy and safety of medical cannabinoids in children: a systematic review and meta-analysis. *Scientific Reports, 11*(1). https://doi.org/10.1038/s41598-021-02770-6

U.S. DepartmentoOf Agriculture. (2018). *The Agricultural Act of 2018*. https://www.usda.gov/farmbill

U.S. Department of Justice, Drug Enforcement Administration, Diversion Control Division. (2012). *Controlled Substances Act*. https://www.deadiversion.usdoj.gov/21cfr/21usc/

U.S. Drug Enforcement Agency). (2018, July 10). *Drug scheduling*. https://www.dea.gov/drug-information/drug-scheduling

U.S. Drug Enforcement Agency. (2018, September 27). *FDA-approved drug Epidiolex placed in schedule V of controlled substance act*. DEA. https://www.dea.gov/press-releases/2018/09/27/fda-approved-drug-epidiolex-placed-schedule-v-controlled-substance-act

U.S. Food And DRUG ADMINISTRATION (2009). *Controlled Substances Act*. https://www.fda.gov/regulatoryinformation/legislation/ucm148726.htm

U.S. Food and Drug Administration. (2013). *Orphan Drug Act*. https://www.fda.gov/RegulatoryInformation/Legislation/SignificantAmendmentstotheFDCAct/OrphanDrugAct

U.S. Food and Drug Administration. (2017). *FDA and marijuana*. http://www.fda.gov/newsevents/publichealthfocus/ucm421163.htm

U.S. Food and Drug Administration. (2018, June 25). *FDA approves first drug comprised of an active ingredient derived from marijuana to treat rare, severe forms of epilepsy*. https://www.fda.gov/news-events/press-announcements/fda-approves-first-drug-comprised-active-ingredient-derived-marijuana-treat-rare-severe-forms

Zhou, D., Dennis, E., Snehal, I., & Swaminathan, A. (2021, October). Cannabinoids in the treatment of epilepsy: A review. *European Medical Journal*. https://www.emjreviews.com/neurology/article/cannabinoids-in-the-treatment-of-epilepsy-a-review/

Chapter 33

MEDICATION ADMINISTRATION IN THE SCHOOL SETTING

Linda Davis-Alldritt, MA, BSN, RN, FNASN, FASHA*

Due to the length of this chapter, the following outline provides an overview of the chapter content:

IMPLICATIONS FOR SCHOOL NURSE PRACTICE

Challenges and Issues

Strategies Addressing the Challenges and Issues with Medication Administration in Schools

- Medication Policies & Procedures

- Delegation of Medication Administration

- Over-the-Counter (OTC) Medications

- Self-Administration of Medication

- Experimental and Off-Label Medications

- Complementary and Alternative Medicines

- Emergency Medication, Including Oxygen

- Medical Marijuana

- Field Trips, Summer Programs, Before and After-School Programs, Camps

- Students Who Fail to Come to Health Office for Medication/Students Who Refuse Medication

- Handling, Storage, and Disposal of Medications

APPENDIX A: History of Medication Administration

APPENDIX B: Literature Review

APPENDIX C: Medication Policy & Procedures

---

*Original authors: Linda Davis-Alldritt, MA, BSN, RN, FNASN, FASHA and Bill Patterson, MPA, BSN, BA, RN (2017)

MEDICATION ADMINISTRATION IN THE SCHOOL SETTING

DESCRIPTION OF ISSUE

Increasing numbers of students with acute and chronic conditions, complex treatment regimens, and large arrays of daily medications have significantly altered the climate of our schools. Approximately 40 percent of children and youth in the United States have one or more chronic health conditions (Centers for Disease Control and Prevention [CDC], 2021). Many students with chronic healthcare needs are only able to successfully participate at school due to the effectiveness of their medication (Bergren, 2013; Lowe et al., 2022). Federal, and corresponding state laws, mandating the inclusion of children with special healthcare needs require local educational agencies (LEA) to provide accommodations to meet the needs of these children and ensure safe and appropriate care. Such accommodations frequently include medication administration or supervision of students authorized to self-administer their medication (Canham et al., 2007; Zirkel et al., 2012).

In today's schools, the management and administration of medications is an unavoidable reality and frequently performed by unlicensed school personnel. School officials must ensure student health by being prepared to manage complex health needs effectively and administer many kinds of medicine. Most states have laws, and many LEAs have developed policies and guidelines denoting medication management practices (Findlaw, 2016). However, laws related to medication administration at school, at federal, state, and local levels, are frequently inconsistent and often create confusion for school staff, including school nurses, as to which law or policy has precedence (Lowe et al., 2022). For schools with a school nurse, the nurse has the expertise to safely administer medication and the skill to assess the effectiveness of the medication on the student but also must have dedicated time to research new treatment regimens (Lowe, et al., 2022). The school nurse also has the education and training necessary to assist the LEA in developing and implementing a district-wide medication management plan. Since not all schools have a school nurse, school secretaries, health aides, teachers, and other school staff are often recruited to assist with medication management and administration.

BACKGROUND

Thirty years ago, no one could have predicted the tremendous increase in the type and range of medications for children. School-age children with a host of conditions, from asthma to diabetes to attention deficit hyperactivity disorder (ADHD), must take medication during the school day to stay healthy and be ready to learn (Findlaw, 2016; Lowe et al., 2022). Now, medication administration for students is the most common component of school health services throughout the nation. Between 2000 and 2022, several hundred articles referencing various aspects of medication administration at school were published in professional journals in the United States (Lowe et al., 2022). Within that group of articles, federal and state laws related to the rights of eligible students to receive medication at school; school policies, procedures, and recommended guidelines on medication administration; medication management; emergency medication; delegation; medication error; medication administration at school-sponsored events, particularly field trips; stock medication, such as rescue inhalers, epinephrine auto-injectors, and over-the-counter (OTC) analgesics; and medical marijuana were the most frequently discussed topics. The concerns about and ramifications related to medication administration are many.

A full history of medication administration in schools and a thorough literature review on the topic are provided in Appendices A and B at the end of this chapter.

442

Non-compliance with medication regimens has been associated with unsuccessful academic achievement and poor behavioral and physical outcomes (Leroy, 2017). School policies related to medication compliance and management must be applied consistently. As the school health professional, the school nurse should review all requests for medication administration, including self-administration requests, in accordance with the LEA's medication policies and NASN's Clinical Practice Guidelines. Compounding medication management and daily medication administration challenges is the fact that only 52 percent of the nation's public schools have a full-time school nurse (U.S. Department of Education (USDE), National Center for Educational Statistics, 2020). As a result, the school administrator often assigns the task to other school staff, who are typically unlicensed and have other full-time jobs at the school. If the school has a part-time school nurse and state law permits, they may delegate medication administration to an unlicensed staff person, also known as unlicensed assistive personnel (UAP) (American Nurses Association [ANA] and National Council of State Boards of Nursing [NCSBN], 2019).

It is critical that LEAs adopt medication administration policies and guidelines that comply with federal and state laws, including state nurse practice acts, and adhere to national school nurse standards of practice, school nursing protocols National Association of School Nurses (NASN) Clinical Practice Guidelines, and district-specific rules. Frequently legislators and other policymakers have no understanding of laws related specifically to nursing yet are responsible for creating state statutes on a wide variety of issues, ultimately impacting nursing practice. Thus, school nurses should be engaged as members of policy development teams when decisions affecting school nursing practice are being made (NASN), 2021).

IMPLICATIONS FOR SCHOOL NURSE PRACTICE

Medication administration is a primary duty for school nurses. Schools have been significantly impacted by the increase in children with complex health conditions who require daily, and in some cases hourly, medication at school. School nurses are well-equipped through their education in pharmacology to coordinate care and manage children's medication needs. However, frequently due to understaffing caused by LEAs' choices of how to expend education dollars, school nurses are forced by school administrators to delegate nursing tasks to unlicensed school staff. The tendency to use UAP in place of school nurses creates risk potential for the student, his/her parents, the LEA, and the delegating nurse. It is well-documented that UAP make more medication errors than registered nurses (Canham et al., 2007; Maughan et al., 2018). It is incumbent on the school nurse to train and clinically supervise the UAP to reduce risk and ensure the health and safety of the student. To further reduce risk, school nurses must stay current and in compliance with relevant pharmacological advances, their professional association's clinical practice guidelines, and with federal and state laws, including the state nurse practice act and LEA policies and procedures.

Challenges and Issues

Key challenges and issues facing the school nurse related to safe medication administration at school include:
- Compliance with applicable federal and state laws and regulations, state nurse practice act, standards of school nurse practice, and NASN Clinical Practice Guidelines
- Adherence to LEA policies and procedures, including:
  o Relevant communication with the student, parent/guardian, healthcare provider, and school staff
  o Review all medication orders

- o Appropriate storage and disposal of medication
- o Monitoring the medication's therapeutic benefits and other reactions
- o Clear and consistent documentation
- Management of prescription, emergency, OTC, and stock medications
- Carrying and self-administration of medication by students
- Use of complementary and alternative remedies and medical marijuana
- Acceptance and use of off-label and experimental medication
- Delegation to, and training and supervision of, UAP for medication administration when allowed
- Identification and reporting factors that contribute to medication errors, such as:
  - o Inadequate training of the UAP
  - o Inadequate staffing to meet workload demand for medication administration
  - o Training that is not evidenced based
  - o Even when trained, UAP lack the ability to problem-solve issues due to a knowledge deficit of essential elements involved in the medication management process
  - o Lack of priority for safe medication administration practices
  - o Unclear or no requirements for reporting medication errors
  - o Lack of medication reconciliation to create an accurate list of all medications the student is taking
  - o Lack of a quality improvement program, including an annual medication audit
- Maintenance of student rights to confidentiality
- Maintenance of current knowledge and/or reliable information on medication, including expected outcomes and possible adverse effects
- Staying current with and providing nursing input on proposed laws, regulations, LEA policies, and other actions potentially affecting school nursing practice

(Adapted from the following sources: AAP, 2013; AAP, 2016; NASN School Nursing Evidence-based Clinical Practice Guideline: Medication Administration in Schools Implementation Toolkit, 2021; New York State Center for School Health, 2022; U.S. Department of Health and Human Services (USDHHS), 2021).

Public school medication administration policies and procedures should comply with federal and state laws and regulations. Medication administration in school is a required related service, under both Section 504 of the Rehabilitation Act of 1973 and the Individuals with Disabilities Education Improvement Act (IDEIA), for protected students who need medication during the school day to safely access educational opportunities in the least restrictive environment. Under these federal laws, medication administration must be provided regularly, intermittently, or in emergency situations unless a healthcare provider is required to administer the medication or be administered in a hospital or clinic. Section 504, IDEIA, and the Americans with Disabilities Act Amendments Act of 2008 (ADAAA) provide protections for individuals with disabilities but do not cover students who may need episodic medication for short-term illnesses (AAP, 2013).

All states have enacted laws, regulations, and guidance on medication administration for students that apply statewide. State laws vary, although medication administration is a licensed function of healthcare providers and nurses in all states. Some states' nurse practice acts authorize RNs to delegate nursing tasks, including medication administration, to licensed practical/vocational nurses (LPN/LVN) and UAP, and other states may not. The school nurse must be aware of and comply with applicable state laws, regulations, and guidance on the delegation of nursing tasks.

The use of UAP to administer medication to students creates liability risks for the LEA and the school nurse and health risks for the student, particularly related to medication errors (AAP, 2013; Lowe, 2022; Maughan et al., 2018). There is an increased liability risk for unlicensed school staff in states that permit UAP to administer medication, particularly if the LEA does not require the UAP to be adequately trained, have ongoing supervision by the school nurse, and work under the direction of the nurse, and in accordance with safe medication administration standards. LEAs that do not provide adequate staffing for safe medication administration practices and do not follow applicable healthcare standards may also be at higher liability risk for medication errors (Hootman et al., 2005; Lowe, 2022).

Local boards of education are responsible for developing policies and procedures for the safe administration of medication to students who need medication at school and at school-sponsored activities. LEA policies should be clear about the purpose of medication administration in schools and the conditions and requirements under which the service will be provided (Phan et al., 2020). LEA policies and procedures should be grounded in applicable state health and education laws and regulations. They should not conflict with these laws or related professional standards in health fields, including dentistry, medicine, nursing, and pharmacology, or federal and state laws on controlled substances. Periodically, there are conflicts between state laws. When this occurs, LEAs are obligated to apply relevant safety standards for medication administration in district schools (Hootman et al., 2005).

Strategies Addressing the Challenges and Issues with Medication Administration in Schools

Medication Policies & Procedures

It is important for LEAs to develop policies, procedures, and guidelines related to medication administration. School nurses "should lead the development of medication administration policies" (NASN, 2021, page 12). Policies are generally broad statements and should include what types of medications may be administered at school and by whom as well as authorizations from allowable prescribers and parents/guardians. At the end of this chapter, Appendix C includes a detailed step-by-step guide for a medication administration procedure. *(For additional information on LEA policy development, refer to Chapter 19.)*

Delegation of Medication Administration

School nurses must be familiar with state laws and regulations related to medication administration and delegation. The ANA defines delegation as *transferring the responsibility of performing a nursing activity to another person while retaining accountability for the outcome* (ANA & NCSBN, 2019; NASN, 2022a). Delegation of nursing tasks must comply with the state's nurse practice act, other state laws and regulations, and professional nursing standards and guidelines.

When state law permits school nurses to delegate medication administration to UAP, it should only be done if it is safe for the student. The possible benefits and risks of delegation need to be considered in each instance. If an assessment of the student's health condition needs to be done prior to medication administration or the student's health condition is not stable or predictable, the task cannot be delegated because it would entail the UAP making a nursing judgment (ANA & NCSBN, 2019; NASN, 2021). Before delegating medication administration, school nurses must consider the stability of the student's condition, the complexity of the administration process, the risk potential from a drug reaction or medication error, the competency, training, and skills of the UAP, and the availability of the nurse to provide guidance and supervision. Even when state law provides liability immunity, school nurses should not delegate medication administration to UAP when there is a reasonable potential of harm to the student. Although the final decision to delegate to a UAP should belong to the school nurse, decisions about delegation should also be made in collaboration with the student, parent/guardian, healthcare provider, and the rest of the school team. When UAPs are to provide medication administration, they must adhere to local education agency (LEA) policies and procedures and the specific student's individualized healthcare plan (IHP), medication plan, or emergency care plan (ECP) (NASN, 2021; Resha, 2010). Using procedure skills checklists and developing an ECP as part of the student's IHP may help reduce risks associated with delegation (NASN, 2021; Shannon & Kubella, 2013a; Shannon & Kubelka, 2013b). (*See also see Chapter 4 for more information on delegation*).

Over-the-Counter (OTC) Medications

The two categories of medication administered in schools are prescription and OTC medications. School nurses, in collaboration with school physicians, should develop safe practices for OTC use in schools, especially in states that do not have laws and regulations inclusive of or specific to OTC medications. Generally, the same policies and procedures for administering prescription medications should apply to OTC medications (NASN, 2021). Both prescription and OTC medications have the potential for untoward side effects, and if over-used or abused, they can increase the risks of morbidity and mortality. In states where education laws permit schools to accept only parent consent for OTC administration to students, school nurses must verify that their practice act permits them to administer OTC medication without a licensed healthcare provider's order (AAP, 2013; Hootman et al., 2005; NASN, 2021).

A primary function of school nursing is keeping students healthy, in school, and ready to learn. The appropriate use of OTC medication may support these priorities. On the other hand, the use of OTC medication to manage complaints that are better managed with other self-care strategies could train students to rely on drugs rather than healthier alternatives, assuming such alternatives are available. Also, OTC medications may mask underlying symptoms of more serious disorders, delay treatment, and have long-term consequences for the student (Hootman et al., 2001/2005). OTC medication use in school should be limited to those medications needed to alleviate acute conditions such as pain or allergies, and their use in school should be limited to the shortest duration possible (Butler et al., 2020).

When indicated and there is no student-specific healthcare provider order for an OTC medication, in many cases, parents must leave work or otherwise arrange to bring their children OTC medications. Often, these children go home with their parents or other caregivers and lose valuable class time (Foster & Keele, 2006). In an effort to keep students in school, some healthcare providers and school nurse teams have developed standing orders and protocols allowing the school to keep OTC medications in stock that school nurses administer to students "as needed" (NASN, 2021). The protocols require a thorough assessment by the school nurse before medication administration. School nurses may identify other health conditions that require a referral through these assessments. UAP does not have the training, education, or license needed to do the pre-administration assessment. Strict adherence to the protocols helps ensure student safety and reduce risk for the school nurse. LEAs typically require annually renewed written permission from parents to permit the school nurse to administer the stock medication. Parents should be notified in writing each time the medication is given (AAP, 2013; NASN, 2021; Wallace, 2016). Despite the interest in and perceived benefits of standing orders for OTC medications, the legal risk may outweigh the benefits of such orders. The NASN Clinical Practice Guidelines (2021) recommend that LEAs require students to have specific medical orders from their own healthcare provider for any medication, including OTC medicine, that is to be administered at school.

Standing orders for emergency medications, such as epinephrine and glucagon, have saved the lives of students and adults. However, if permitted by state law and to increase access to lifesaving emergency medications, it is important to permit trained school staff to administer stock emergency medication to any student who appears to be experiencing a life-threatening event (Butler et al., 2020). Standing orders for individuals as well as stock emergency medications, like glucagon, epinephrine, anti-seizure medication, short-acting bronchodilators, and naloxone, need to be renewed annually. School nurses should ensure that each school health office has a copy of current signed standing orders (Hootman et al., 2005).

Self-Administration of Medication

Federal laws, IDEA, Section 504, and ADAAA, protect the rights of students to carry and self-administer prescribed medications at school (Laubin et al., 2012). Since 2014, laws have been passed in all 50 states and the District of Columbia that permit students with asthma and life-threatening allergies to carry and self-administer emergency medications. With the passage of these laws, consideration has been given to the need for laws related to medications for other diseases that would benefit from similar laws (Butler et al., 2020).

Self-management and self-administration education are fundamental in caring for children with chronic health conditions, such as asthma, severe food allergy, diabetes, and cystic fibrosis. Healthcare experts support self-administration because quick treatment of symptoms helps reduce the disease's effects and may prevent an acute episode (Butler et al., 2020). Additionally, self-administration may lead to student independence, self-care competence, and improved self-esteem (Hootman et al., 2005; Leroy et al., 2017).

School nurses are uniquely positioned to reinforce self-management principles in students with chronic conditions because they can see such students regularly, sometimes daily (Ahmad & Grimes, 2011; Leroy et al., 2017). LEA policies must be clearly written and define when and in what circumstances self-management and self-administration of medication is permitted (Hootman et al., 2005; NASN, 2021). Even with reasonable policies and procedures in place, LEAs may sometimes have to make exceptions for students who may require self-administration of medication to receive equal access to their education under Section 504 of the Rehabilitation Act. To ensure student safety, the policies should also include a requirement for a nursing assessment to determine that the student is capable and competent to perform self-administration (Laubin et al., 2012: NASN, 2021). Policies for authorization from the licensed healthcare provider and parent/guardian consent should be the same as those governing all other medications.

In accordance with federal and state laws, regulations, and standards, a responsible student should be allowed to carry and self-administer medication for urgent or emergent needs if the medication does not require security or refrigeration. Controlled substances and medications with a risk of abuse or sale to others are not candidates for self-administration (AAP, 2013; NASN, 2021). The school nurse should assist in determining when a student is proficient in medication management techniques used during school or, on the other hand, would benefit from supervised self-administration permitted (Hootman et al., 2005). Medication carried by students must not be left unattended and should always be on the student's person or in the care of a supervising adult (AAP, 2013; NASN, 2021). However, the school nurse may need to train staff to help the student in an emergency (Foley, 2013; McClanahan et al., 2019). If students forget to bring their medication to school, there should be a plan to have backup medication in the school health office. This plan is especially important for self-administered emergency medication (Laubin et al., 2012; NASN, 2021).

Experimental and Off-Label Medications

Periodically medications approved for use by the United States Food and Drug Administration (FDA) in treating one type of health problem are prescribed for a different health condition. This practice is known as an off-label use of an FDA-approved medication (AAP, 2021). Experimental medications are those drugs that are the subject of clinical trials to determine their effectiveness and safety; however, they are not currently approved by the FDA. Typically, only RNs or healthcare providers may administer experimental or research medications; however, when questions arise as to who may administer such medications, it is advisable to consult relevant state laws and regulations (NASN, 2021).

Since off-label medications are sometimes used for school-age children, or students may be participating in clinical trials for experimental drugs, LEA medication administration policies should include requirements for administering research medication at school. The following information on the medication should be provided to the school: the function of the medication, possible side effects, allergy potential, administration schedule, proper dosage, storage requirements, and the intended benefit for the student. The school nurse needs this information to support safe administration at school (NASN, 2021). According to the AAP, Council on School Health (2013), and the NASN Evidence-based Practice Clinical Guideline (2021), school nurses do not have to honor requests to administer non-standard medications, such as doses that exceed manufacturer recommendations, alternative, homeopathic, off-label, experimental medications, or nutritional supplements (AAP, 2013; NASN, 2021). However, the nurse should document the request and work to resolve the conflict with the parent, prescriber, and/or the school physician (AAP, 2013).

Complementary and Alternative Medicines

The National Center for Complementary and Integrative Health (NCCIH) defines complementary medicine as using a non-mainstream practice with conventional medicine and alternative medicine as using a non-mainstream practice instead of conventional medicine. Complementary and alternative medicine (CAM) practices include traditional Chinese medicine, naturopathy, homeopathy, dietary supplements, essential oils, and herbal remedies (USDHHS, 2021).

The popularity of CAM treatments and remedies has become an issue for schools as parent/guardian requests for the administration of these remedies at school are increasing (NASN, 2022b). There are many information sources and websites; however, caution is advised as alternative medications are not controlled by the FDA and are not required to adhere to standards for accurate labeling, potency, or purity (NASN, 2021). The lack of data on their effectiveness and lack of safety information for these remedies limits their use at school (AAP, 2013; NASN, 2021). The school nurse is in an excellent position to provide students and their parents/guardians with current information about complementary and alternative therapies.

State laws and regulations typically specify whether school nurses can accept and implement orders from homeopathic and naturopathic practitioners. Consequently, school nurses must look to state laws for guidance on the types of licensed providers from whom to take orders (McClanahan et al., 2019; NASN, 2021). In states that do not permit school nurses to take orders from alternative practitioners, school nurses can advise parents to suggest that the practitioner collaborates with a healthcare provider who might be willing to provide the order or that the practitioner order doses that do not need to be given during the school day. It is important to let the parents know that if school staff administer substances without adequate scientific data regarding safety, it may put the student at risk (Hootman et al., 2005). As with experimental or research medications, requests to administer non-FDA sanctioned medications, including alternative remedies, often cannot be honored by a LEA or a school nurse, especially if prescribed by an unauthorized prescriber per state laws (NASN, 2021). The school nurse should document the decision and explain to the parent/guardian and the provider that alternative remedies must be administered outside of school (New York State Center for School Health, 2015).

Problems exist even in states that permit school nurses to take orders from homeopathic and naturopathic practitioners. As healthcare professionals, for any medications the school nurse administers or delegates, they are accountable for knowing the ingredients, therapeutic effects, potential side effects, contraindications, and safe dosage (NASN, 2022b). For traditional medications that are researched and approved by the FDA, nurses can access the needed information in nursing and medical drug reference books. For alternative remedies, it is typically not possible to find scientific and research-based information to verify appropriate use, safe dose range, and potential therapeutic value or potential side effects that nurses are required to do per the standard of practice before administering any medication (Hootman et al., 2005; NASN, 2021; Wallace, 2016).

School nurses should stay current with the latest laws, research, and standards for alternative therapies and remedies, as well as with the cultural climate of the school community. Hootman et al., (2005) suggest that a school health advisory council and an ethics committee can help the LEA to investigate the issues and develop policies and procedures to successfully address these issues.

Emergency Medication, Including Oxygen

Most states have laws permitting UAP to receive training in recognizing the signs and symptoms of anaphylaxis and administering epinephrine via an auto-injector. Many states permit UAP to be trained to respond to diabetic and/or epileptic emergencies, most states have protocols for stocking epinephrine for anaphylaxis emergencies, and some states require schools to stock albuterol inhalers in case of an asthma emergency. In these states, LEAs that do not train UAP or stock authorized emergency medicine may be liable and found negligent for not being prepared for emergencies.

Several chronic diseases, including asthma, severe allergies leading to anaphylaxis, diabetes, epilepsy, and other seizure disorders, can rapidly evolve into life-threatening emergencies. Immediate access to emergency medication is critical to successful outcomes. Opioid misuse and abuse necessitate the availability of Naloxone at school to temporarily reverse the potentially fatal effects of both legal and illegal opioid drugs (NASN, 2020). Like all medication administration, emergency medication administration is governed by state laws and regulations and LEA policies, protocols, and procedures. Students with medical orders for emergency medications should have an ECP developed by the school nurse specifying the response needed for the student in case of an emergency (Allen et al., 2012; McClanahan et al., 2019; NASN, 2021). McCaughey et al., (2022) recommend that students with prescriptions for emergency medications be allowed to carry their medication and self-administer when needed. When a life-threatening emergency happens, it is crucial that school policies and all school staff provide for the student's well-being, and that access to the student's emergency medication and emergency medication on standing order is immediate (NASN, 2021). To keep the medication safe and secure and administer the medication as quickly as possible, LEA policies and procedures must specify the location where the medication is stored, the staff member responsible for the medication, who replaces outdated medication, and who is responsible for the medication for field trips (AAP, 2013; Butler, et al., 2020). Additionally, school staff should be trained and supervised by the school nurse as emergency UAP and assigned as "first responders" for students who experience medical emergencies (Allen et al., 2012; AAP, 2013; NASN, 2021).

Due to the increasing prevalence of asthma and anaphylaxis in school-age children and youth, there is a corresponding recognition of the advisability of adding oxygen to the list of medications and supplies that are included in school emergency response plans (Goldman, 2015). School nurses should consult with their medical advisor about obtaining a standing order for oxygen for students or staff with unanticipated medical problems. School nurses should work with school administrators and medical directors and state school nurse consultants and review their nurse practice act to determine how to make oxygen part of their school and LEA's emergency response plan (Goldman, 2015).

Medical Marijuana

As of August 2022, Oklahoma City Schools, the District of Columbia, California, Colorado, Delaware, Florida, Illinois, Maine, Maryland, New Jersey, New Mexico, Pennsylvania, Virginia, Washington, and West Virginia permit but do not require, the administration of non-smokable physician ordered medical marijuana in schools with the provision that the parent(s)/legal guardian or professional caregiver possesses and administers the medication when it is to be administered at school or during school-sponsored away from school activities (Bichu, 2022; Calello, 2019; Cannabis Ground, 2019; Education Commission of the States, 2016; Hopper & Rodriguez, 2019; Pennsylvania Medical Marijuana Program, 2023; Virginia NORML, 2019; West Virginia Medical Cannabis Act §16A, 2022). Other than Epidiolex, Marinol, and Syndros, which are FDA approved for very specific therapeutic uses, the FDA has not yet approved any other drug products that contain CBD (FDA, 2023, February 22).

Because the landscape regarding medical marijuana is changing rapidly and school nurses are receiving increasing questions about medical cannabis administration in schools (Jochen & Holben, 2022), it is critical for school nurses to understand their state medical marijuana laws and regulations and the implications of the laws for safe and appropriate practice. School nurses also need to know that, under federal law, marijuana is still illegal. Additionally, federal and many state laws make schools "drug-free zones," which means that it is illegal to have any drug, including marijuana, on or within a specified distance of the school campus (Safe and Drug-Free Schools and Communities Act, 1986). LEAs in the 38 states and the District of Columbia that permit medical marijuana generally (National Organization for the Reform of Marijuana Laws, 2022) and that are considering permitting medical marijuana use in their schools should review related state laws and consult with their legal counsel prior to implementation as marijuana is still classified as a Schedule I drug under federal law. Permitting Schedule I drugs at school may be a violation of the Drug-Free Workplace Act and could put federal education funds at risk (Anthony & Lampe, 2019; National School Boards Association, 2019).

School nurses should also be familiar with the pharmacology of medical marijuana, any clinical indications for its use, and potential side effects that may be observed in a student who possibly receives healthcare provider prescribed/administered marijuana before coming to school and/or prior to school-sponsored events (DeWitt-Parker, 2016; Jochen & Holben, 2022).

As the school health expert, staff, administrators, students, and parents may ask the nurse for help in understanding medical marijuana laws. If state law and district policy permit the use of medical marijuana at school, the school nurse should document the administration of medical marijuana and monitor the student's response to the treatment. In conjunction with the student, his/her parents, and the healthcare provider, the school nurse should develop an IHP that includes measures to take to ensure the student's safety as they return to the classroom, as well as contingency plans if the student has an untoward response to the treatment (DeWitt-Parker, 2016). (*See also Chapter 32 for more information on medical cannabis*).

Field Trips, Summer Programs, Before and After-School Programs, Camps

Increasing numbers of children with special healthcare needs attend school and are entitled by federal law and corresponding state laws to have equal opportunity to participate fully in all school-sponsored activities, including enrichment activities like field trips, special camps, summer programs, and before- and after-school programs. Pursuant to federal law (U.S. Department of Education, Office of Civil Rights, 2016), students with special healthcare needs, including those who need to take medication, may not be excluded, even when ensuring their full participation creates fiscal or logistical challenges. Without regard to the venue or the season of the year, safe medication administration legal and clinical standards apply (NASN, 2019; NASN, 2021; NASN, 2022a;). Students who require nursing or healthcare services at school will require at least the same level of care during school-sponsored activities away from school (Hootman et al., 2005; NASN, 2021). To ensure the health and safety of all students participating in extended day and away from campus activities, planning for these events should begin well ahead of the intended date and include the school nurse in all the planning phases (NASN, 2019).

Out-of-state field trips are particularly challenging due to state-to-state differences in laws pertaining to nursing practice (Erwin et al., 2014). For school nurses in one of the 39 states in the Nurse Licensure Compact (NLC), which permits registered nurses (RN) and LPN/LVNs to practice across certain state lines, these challenges are somewhat reduced. For school nurses working in non-Compact states, navigating practice licensure may be more cumbersome. The NLC does not cover unlicensed school personnel or advanced practice RNs (NCSBN, 2023). Under federal law and corresponding state laws, parents/guardians cannot be required to go on field trips with their student who has special healthcare needs. When no RN, LPN/LVN, or trained UAP is available to administer medication to the student during the field trip, some state laws permit the parent to delegate medication administration to another family member or adult friend. Well before any off-campus activity, and especially well ahead of out-of-state field trips involving children who need health services, school nurses must review applicable state laws and regulations, including those pertaining to delegation in the states to be visited. The U.S. State Department can provide guidance for out-of-country field trips (Erwin et al., 2014).

State laws and regulations do not typically address many of the medication administration issues related to school-sponsored off-campus activities, including field trips, away camps, summer school programs, and worksite experiences. Even so, a thorough review of state laws, regulations, and standards of practice, as well as meticulous planning and creative problem-solving, are required essentials for effective medication management for off-campus activities (Hootman et al., 2005; NASN, 2021). (*See also Chapter 59 for more information on school-sponsored field trips*).

Students Who Fail to Come to Health Office for Medication/Students Who Refuse Medication

To maximize the therapeutic benefits of medication, medicine should be administered according to the schedule established by the healthcare provider's written order. School nurses should interpret and establish a specific time to administer the medication at school to avoid daily re-interpretation of vague label instructions. The Institute of Safe Medication Practices (2011, p.2) provides the following guidance to hospitals: "time-critical scheduled medications at the exact time indicated when necessary or within 30 minutes before or 30 minutes after the scheduled time (or more exact timing when indicated, as with rapid-, short-, and ultra-short-acting insulins)" and for non-time critical medications, ". . .administered more frequently than daily but not more frequently than every 4 hours . . . Administer these medications within 1 hour before or after the scheduled time." An entirely missed medication dose does constitute an error and, depending on the LEA's policy, would require an error report to be filed (NASN, 2021).

When students do not come to the health office for their medication as scheduled, the school nurse or designated school staff remain responsible for administering the medication to the student and should locate the student to administer the medication (NASN, 2021). The school and LEA's acceptance of the written medical order from the healthcare provider and the written parent consent for the school nurse or designated school staff to administer the medication create an obligation for the school/LEA to administer the medication as scheduled (Hootman et al., 2005; NASN, 2021). Failure to administer the medication may have negative or untoward outcomes for the student, and litigation could result.

LEA medication administration policies and procedures should include guidance on what steps the school nurse, and other designated school personnel must take when a student does not arrive in the health office to take a scheduled medication or when a student refuses to take a scheduled medication. LEA policy should specify that each student needing medication at school has a medication plan that includes each of the student's medications, as well as addressing any individual specific issues the student may have with medication, including problems with failing to come to the health office to take scheduled medication or refusing to take an ordered medication. The medication plan may include strategies to help the student remember to come to the health office to take medication or require the school nurse or other staff responsible for medication administration to locate the student. Medication plans that are not achieving the anticipated results may need to be revised (NASN, 2021). However, a punitive response to the student for forgetting to come to the health office, especially for students whose disability is manifested by poor organization or forgetfulness, may be considered discriminatory (Hootman et al., 2005).

For students who refuse to take medication, school nurses and other designated staff should make every reasonable effort to administer the student's medication; however, physical restraint and force are not appropriate, safe, or legal and could be judged as assault and battery. When students refuse to take medication at school, the school nurse should work with the parents/guardian; the school administrator; other school staff, such as a counselor, psychologist, or social worker; and the student's healthcare provider to develop other options (NASN, 2021). While alternative medication options are being explored, the student's educational needs must be served, and the student cannot be excluded from school. If the student's behavior poses a serious risk of harm to self or others, then it may be appropriate for the student to be excluded, referred for a medical or psychiatric assessment, and information about available resources in the school and the community provided to the parents (Hootman et al., 2005).

Handling, Storage, and Disposal of Medications

All medications should be delivered to the school by the parent/guardian(s) in their original containers with the correct prescription label detailing the name of the prescriber, student's name, medication name, dosage, expiration date, and directions for use (Butler et al., 2020; NASN, 2021). All medications should be counted at the time of delivery to the school, and controlled substances should be counted daily or each time they are administered (NASN, 2021). Nurses should report any count discrepancies according to LEA policies and regulations (Missouri Department of Health and Senior Services, 2020).

Store medications in a secure and locked location – in either a locked cabinet or refrigerator, as appropriate. Emergency medication, such as asthma rescue inhalers, glucagon, and epinephrine auto-injectors, must be kept safe but readily available during the school day in an unlocked, secure area. Controlled substances should be secured with double locks (Butler et al., 2020; NASN, 2021).

All medication should be returned to the parents if it is expired or discontinued if the student moves to a different school, or at the end of the school year (Butler et al., 2020; Missouri Department of Health and Senior Services, 2020; NASN, 2021). When medication is returned, the return should be documented with the date, time, and signatures of the school nurse or administrator and the parent. Any medication not picked up by the parent should be disposed of according to applicable local or state laws (Butler et al., 2020; Missouri Department of Health and Senior Services, 2020; NASN, 2021).

CONCLUSION

Every day in our schools, thousands of students with complex chronic and acute conditions need medication. Federal and state laws require schools to accommodate these students' medication administration requirements safely and appropriately at school and during school-sponsored activities outside regular school hours. The school nurse is the safest and most appropriate school staff member to do and manage medication administration.

Proper management of medication administration is a safety issue for all concerned and left undone, can potentially be the grounds for litigation. School nurses have the knowledge, skill, and experience to ensure safe student medication use. School nurses are the logical individuals to evaluate an LEA's medication administration process, ensuring that the LEA has proactive steps in place for student safety (Zirkel et al., 2012), and assist in the development and implementation of any needed changes to the LEA's medication administration policies and procedures (NASN, 2021). Particularly, school nurse-recommended policies and guidelines should clearly identify what comprises safe staffing, who is responsible for medication administration, when and to whom the administration of medication can be delegated as well as the amount and frequency of training for UAP, how medication must be stored, what is appropriate documentation, what are effective strategies to recognize current and avoid future medication errors, the necessary procedures for school-sponsored activities, and what are the essential features of self-administration plans (NASN, 2021; Phan et al., 2020).

To keep students, school staff, and LEAs safe regarding medication administration, there must be an adequate number of school nurses, other school health personnel, and resources housed within an infrastructure supportive of school health services (Knauer et al., 2015; McCaughey et al., 2022; Nadeau & Toronto, 2016). Additionally, school nurses must have reliable sources of medication information, including a respected pediatric drug handbook, and have the dedicated time to stay current with advanced clinical skills and knowledge and to adequately train LPN/LVNs and UAP who may be delegated in accordance with state laws, medication administration tasks (Best et al., 2022).

RESOURCES

American Academy of Pediatrics, Council on School Health and Committee on Pediatric Emergency Medicine. (2022). Individual Medical Emergencies Occurring at School (Policy Statement). *Pediatrics*, 150 (1): e2022057987. https://doi.org/10.1542/peds.2022-057987

Massachusetts Department of Public Health School Health Unit/Essential School Health Services. (2015). *Field trip tool kit*. https://ce.neusha.org/student/programs/attachments/FieldTrip.pdf

Massachusetts Nurses Association Congress on Nursing Practice. (2011). Medication error (Position Statement). Canton, MA: Massachusetts Nurses Association. https://www.massnurses.org/files/file/Nursing-Resources/Nursing-Practice/Medication_Error.pdf

National Association of School Nurses. (2019). National Association of School Nurses. (2019). Emergency Preparedness (Position Statement). Author. Emergency preparedness and response in the school setting -The role of the school nurse (Position Statement). Author. https://www.nasn.org/nasn-resources/professional-practice-documents/position-statements/ps-emergency-preparedness

National Association of School Nurses. (2022). School Nursing Evidence-based Clinical Practice Guideline: Medication Administration in Schools Toolkit. Author. https://www.nasn.org/blogs/nasn-inc/2022/01/31/nasn-toolkit-on-administering-meds-in-schools

National Association of School Nurses. (2018). School-sponsored before, after and extended school year programs: The role of the school nurse (Position Statement). Author. https://schoolnursenet.nasn.org/blogs/nasn-profile/2017/03/13/school-sponsored-before-after-and-extended-school-year-programs-the-role-of-the-school-nurse

National Diabetes Education Program. (2016). *Helping the student with diabetes succeed: A guide for school personnel* (A program of the National Institutes of Health and the Centers for Disease Control and Prevention). https://diabetes.org/sites/default/files/2020-02/NDEP-School-Guide-Full-508.pdf

National Institute of Diabetes and Digestive and Kidney Diseases. (2020). *Helping the student with diabetes succeed.* https://www.niddk.nih.gov/health-information/professionals/clinical-tools-patient-management/diabetes/helping-student-diabetes-succeed-guide-school-personnel

New York State Education Department. (2015). *Guidelines for medication management in schools.* http://www.p12.nysed.gov/sss/documents/MedicationManagement-final2015.pdf

United States Code (Office of the Law Revision Counsel). (2018). Title 21 United States Code (USC) Controlled Substances Act: Subchapter I — control and enforcement: Part B — Authority to control; standards and schedules: §812. Schedules of controlled substances. https://uscode.house.gov/view.xhtml?path=/prelim@title21/chapter13/subchapter1/partB&edition=prelim

U. S. Department of Education, Office for Civil Rights. (2016). Parent and educator resource guide to Section 504 in public elementary and secondary schools. https://www.ed.gov/news/press-releases/us-department-education-releases- guidance-civil-rights-students-disabilities

United States Department of Education, Office for Civil Rights. (2020). *Questions and answers on the ADA Amendments Act of 2008 for students with disabilities attending public elementary and secondary schools.* http://www2.ed.gov/about/offices/list/ocr/docs/dcl-504faq-201109.html

Legal references

- o Americans with Disabilities Act Amendments Act, 42 USCA § 12101 (2008)
- o Asthmatic Schoolchildren's Treatment and Health Management Act (PL 108-377) (2004). https://www.govtrack.us/congress/bills/108/hr2023
- o Controlled Substances Act, 21 U.S.C. 13 § 801 et seq. (1970).
- o Family Education Rights and Privacy Act (FERPA), 20 U.S.C. § 1232g, 34 C.F.R. . §99.1 et seq. (1974).
- o Individuals with Disabilities Improvement Act (IDEIA), 20 U.S.C. §1400 et seq. (2004).
- o Good Samaritan Laws by State from Recreation Law. (2014). https://recreation-law.com/2014/05/28/good-samaritan-laws-by-state/
- o Safe and Drug-Free Schools and Communities Act (SDFSCA), Title IV--21st Century Schools Part A, 20 U.S.C. §7101 et seq. (1986).

- Secure and Responsible Drug Disposal Act, S. 3397 — 111th Congress (2010). https://www.govtrack.us/congress/bills/111/s3397

- School Access to Emergency Epinephrine Act, H.R. 2094 — 113th Congress (2013).

- Section 504 *of the* Rehabilitation Act, 29 U.S.C. § 701 et seq. (1973).

- Title 21 (Food and Drugs) of the Code of Federal Regulations, Chapter II, Drug Enforcement Administration, 21 CFR § 1300.01 et seq. (2005).

- Uniform Controlled Substances Act, 21 U.S.C. §802, 812 (1994). (Schedules of Controlled Substances). https://uscode.house.gov/view.xhtml?path=/prelim@title21/chapter13/subchapter1/partB&edition=prelim

REFERENCES

Ahmad, E., & Grimes, D.E. (2011). The effects of self-management education for school-age children on asthma morbidity: A systematic review. *The Journal of School Nursing, 27*(4), 282–292. https://doi.org/ 10.1177/1059840511403003

Allen, K., Henselman, K., Laird, B., Quiñones, A., & Reutzel, T. (2012). Potential life-threatening events in schools involving rescue inhalers, epinephrine autoinjectors, and glucagon delivery devices: Reports from school nurses. *The Journal of School Nursing, 28(*1), 47-55. https://doi.org/10.1177/1059840511420726

American Academy of Pediatrics, Council on School Health. (2013). Guidance for the administration of medication in school (Policy Statement). *Pediatrics, 124*(4), 1244-1251. https://doi.org/10.1542/peds.2009-1953

American Academy of Pediatrics, Council on School Health. (2016). Role of the school nurse in providing school health services (Policy Statement). *Pediatrics, 137*(6), e20160852. http://pediatrics.aappublications.org/content/pediatrics/early/2016/05/19/peds.2016-0852.full.pdf

American Academy of Pediatrics, Committee on Drugs. (2021). Off-label use of drugs in children (Policy Statement). Pediatrics, 133(3), 563-567. https://doi.org/0.1542/peds.2013-4060

American Nurses Association and National Council of State Boards of Nursing. (2019). *National guidelines for nursing delegation.* https://ncsbn.org/public-files/NGND-PosPaper_06.pdf

Anthony, L.G. & Lampe, D.J. (2019, December 6). Marijuana and CBD considerations for school districts. https://www.bricker.com/industries-practices/education/insights-resources/resource/marijuana-and-cbd-considerations-for-school-districts-1110

Bergren, M.D. (2013). The case for school nursing: Review of the literature. *NASN School Nurse, 28*(1), 48-51. https://doi.org/10.1177/1942602X12468418

Best, N.C., Nichols, A.O., & Hernandez, J. (2022). Exploration of factors associated with reported medication administration errors in North Carolina school districts. *The Journal of School Nursing*, 2022; 0(0). Published online September 21, 2022. https://doi.org/10.1177/10598405221127453

Bichu, A.M. (2022, August 11). Should medical marijuana be allowed in schools? *Education Week.* https://www.edweek.org/leadership/should-medical-marijuana-be-allowed-in-schools/2022/08

Butler, S.M., Boucher, E.A., Tobison, J., & Phan, H. (2020). Medication use in schools: Current trends, challenges, and best practices. *The Journal of Pediatric Pharmacology and Therapeutics, 25*(1), 7-24. https://www.ncbi.nlm.nih.gov/pmc/articles/PMC6938291/

Calello, M. (2019). School nurses to dispense medical cannabis to students bill passes VA senate. *The News Leader.* https://eu.newsleader.com/story/news/2019/02/27/medical-marijuana-virginia-law-allows-school-nurses-store-dispense-medical-cannabis-students/2990829002/

Canham, D.L., Bauer, L., Concepcion, M., Luong, J., Peters, J., & Wilde, C. (2007). An audit of medication administration: A glimpse into school health offices. *The Journal of School Nursing, 23*(1), 21-27. https://doi.org/10.1177/105984 05070230010401

Cannabis Ground. (2019, February 1). Schools in Oklahoma approve students to use medical marijuana, but not the school staff. Author. https://www.cannabisground.com/schools-oklahoma/

Centers for Disease Control and Prevention, Healthy Schools. (2021). *Managing chronic health conditions. U.S.* Department of Health and Human Services, Centers for Disease Control and Prevention. https://www.cdc.gov/healthyschools/chronicconditions.htm

Colorado Department of Education. (2015). *Guidance on delegation for Colorado school nurses & child care consultants.* Author. https://www.cde.state.co.us/healthandwellness/guidance-on-delegation-for-colorado-school-nurses-child-care-consultants-2-2016

DeWitt-Parker, C. (2016). Medicinal use of marijuana: What school nurses need to know. *NASN School Nurse, 31*(3), 170-176. https://doi.org/10.1177/1942602X16638815

Education Commission of the States. (2016*). Medical marijuana in schools: State legislation and policy considerations.* Author. http://www.ecs.org/medical-marijuana-in-schools-state-legislation-and-policy-considerations/

Erwin, K., Clark, S., & Mercer, S.E. (2014). Providing health services for children with special health care needs on out-of-state field trips. *NASN School Nurse, 29*(2), 84-88. https://doi.org/10.1177/1942602X13517005

Findlaw. (2016). *School authority to administer medication.* https://www.findlaw.com/education/school-safety/school-authority-to-administer-medication.html

Fobbs, E. (2015). Addiction trends require states to change school medication policies. *Policy Update, 22*(10). National Association of State Boards of Education. http://www.nasbe.org/policy-update/addiction-trends-require-states-to-change-school-medication-policies/

Foley, M. (2013). Health services management. In J. Selekman (Ed.). *School nursing: a comprehensive text,* (2nd ed., pp. 1190-1215). F.A. Davis Company.

Foster, L.S., & Keele, R. (2006). Implementing an over-the-counter medication administration policy in an elementary school. *The Journal of School Nursing, 22*(2), 108-113. https://doi.org/10.1177/105984050602200208

Goldman, P. (2015). Emergency first aid oxygen response in schools: O2 administration in schools by nurses and lay responders. *NASN School Nurse, 30*(2), 90-94. https://doi.org/10.1177/1942602X14563802

Hootman, J., Schwab, N.C., & Gelfman, M.H.B. (2001, 2005). School nursing practice: Clinical performance issues. In N.C. Schwab, & M.H.B. Gelfman, (Eds.), *Legal issues in school health services: A resource for school administrators, school attorneys, and school nurses,* (pp. 167-230). Sunrise River Press.

Hopper, D. & Rodriguez, A.A. (2019). Medical cannabis in schools. New Mexico Public Education Department. https://www.nmlegis.gov/handouts/LHHS%20102219%20Item%2015%20Medical%20Cannabis%20in%20Schools.pdf

Houtrow, A. J., Larson, K., Olson, L. M., Newacheck, P. W., & Halfon, N. (2014). Changing trends of childhood disability, 2001–2011. *Pediatrics, 134*(3), 530–538. http://doi.org/10.1542/peds.2014-0594

Jochen, A., & Holben, D. (2022). School Nurse Perspectives of Medical Cannabis Policy in K-12 Schools: An Exploratory Descriptive Study. *The Journal of School Nursing.* 0(0). https://doi:10.1177/10598405221136288

Jones, S. E., & Wheeler, L. (2004). Asthma inhalers in schools: Rights of students with asthma to a free appropriate education. *American Journal of Public Health, 94*(7), 1102–1108. http://www.ncbi.nlm.nih.gov/pmc/articles/PMC1448405/

Knauer, H., Baker, D.L., Hebbeler, K., & Davis-Alldritt, L. (2015). The mismatch between children's health needs and school resources. *The Journal of School Nursing, 31*(5), 326-333. https://doi.org/10.1177/1059840515579083

Laubin, M., Schwab, N.C., & Doyle, J. (2012). Understanding the legal landscape. In C. Costante (Ed.), *School nurse administrators: Leadership and management,* (pp. 459-519). National Association of School Nurses.

Leroy, Z.C., Wallin, R., & Lee, S. (2017) The Role of School Health Services in Addressing the Needs of Students With Chronic Health Conditions: A Systematic Review. *The Journal of School Nursing.* 33(1):64-72. https://doi:10.1177/1059840516678909

Lowe, A.A., Gerald, J.K., Clemens, C., Gaither, C., & Gerald, L.B. (2022). Medication Administration Practices in United States' Schools: A Systematic Review and Meta-synthesis. *The Journal of School Nursing*, 38(1), 21-34. http://doi.org/10.1177/10598405211026300

Maughan E. D., McCarthy A. M., Hein M., Perkhounkova Y., & Kelly M. W. (2018). Medication management in schools: 2015 survey results. *The Journal of School Nursing,* 34(6), 468–479. https://doi.org/10.1177/1059840517729739

McCaughey, R.A., McCarthy, A.M., Maughan, E., Hein, M., Perkhounkova, Y., & Kelly, M.W. (2022). Emergency medication access and administration in schools: A focus on epinephrine, albuterol inhalers, and glucagon. *The Journal of School Nursing.* 38(4):326-335. https://doi:10.1177/1059840520934185

McClanahan, R., Shannon, R.A., & Kahn, P. (2019). School health office management. In J. Selekman, R.A. Shannon, & C. Yonkaitis (Eds.), *School nursing: A comprehensive text* (3rd ed., pp. 888-908). F.A. Davis Company.

McClanahan, R., & Weismuller, P.C. (2015). School nurses and care coordination for children with complex needs: An integrative review. *The Journal of School Nursing, 31*(1), 34-43. https://doi.org/10.1177/1059840514550484

Missouri Department of Health and Senior Services. (2020). Medication administration In Missouri schools: guidelines for developing training and practice. Author. https://health.mo.gov/living/families/schoolhealth/pdf/MedicationManual.pdf

Nadeau, E.H., & Toronto, C.E. (2016). Barriers to asthma management for school nurses: An integrative review. *The Journal of School Nursing, 32*(2), 86-98. https://doi.org/10.1177/1059840515621607

National Association of School Nurses. (2019). *School-sponsored trips, role of the school nurse* (Position Statement). Author. https://www.nasn.org/nasn-resources/professional-practice-documents/position-statements/ps-trips

National Association of School Nurses. (2020). *Naloxone in the school setting* (Position Statement). Author. https://www.nasn.org/nasn-resources/professional-practice-documents/position-statements/ps-naloxone

National Association of School Nurses. (2021). *School nursing evidence-based clinical practice guideline: Medication administration in schools.* Author. https://learn.nasn.org/courses/33787

National Association of School Nurses. (2022a). School nursing: Scope and standards of practice (4th ed.). Author.

National Association of School Nurses. (2022b). *Complementary and integrative therapies* (Position Statement). Author. https://www.nasn.org/nasn-resources/professional-practice-documents/position-statements/ps-therapies

National Council of State Boards of Nursing. (2023). *Nursing licensure compacts*. Author. https://www.ncsbn.org/compacts.htm

National Organization for the Reform of Marijuana Laws. (2022). *Medical marijuana laws.* https://norml.org/laws/medical-laws/

National School Boards Association. (2019). *Drugs substance abuse, and public schools*. https://www.nsba.org/-/media/NSBA/File/legal-drugs-substance-abuse-and-public-schools-guide.pdf

New York State Center for School Health. (2022). *Guidelines for medication management in schools.* https://www.p12.nysed.gov/sss/documents/medication-management.pdf

Pennsylvania Medical Marijuana Program, Department of Health. (2023). Guidance for schools and school districts. https://www.health.pa.gov/topics/programs/Medical%20Marijuana/Pages/School.aspx

Phan, H., Butler, S.M., Tobison, J., Boucher, E.A. & for the Advocacy Committee on behalf of the Pediatric Pharmacy Association. (2020). Medication use in schools. *The Journal of Pediatric Pharmacology and Therapeutics*, *25*(2), 163-166. https://www.ncbi.nlm.nih.gov/pmc/articles/PMC7025751/

Resha, C. (2010). Delegation in the school setting: Is it a safe practice? *Online Journal of Issues in Nursing, 15*(2), Manuscript 5. https://doi.org/10.3912/OJIN.Vol15No02Man05

Schwab, N.C., Hootman, J., & Gelfman, M.H.B. (2001/2005). School nursing practice: Professional performance issues. In N.C. Schwab, & M.H.B. Gelfman (Eds.), *Legal issues in school health services: A resource for school administrators, school attorneys, and school nurses*, 123-165. Sunrise River Press.

Shannon, R.A., & Kubelka, S. (2013a). Reducing the risks of delegation: Use of procedure skills checklists for unlicensed assistive personnel in schools, part 1. NASN School Nurse, 28(4), 178-181. https://doi.org/10.1177/1942602X13489886

Shannon, R.A., & Kubelka, S. (2013b). Reducing the risks of delegation: Use of procedure skills checklists for unlicensed assistive personnel in schools, part 2. NASN School Nurse, 28(5), 222-226. https://doi.org/10.1177/1942602X13490030

Texas School Nurses Organization. (2010). *Medication administration in the school setting* (Position Statement). Author. https://higherlogicdownload.s3.amazonaws.com/NASN/b385213b-35e8-49e3-97fe-d6627843f498/UploadedImages/Public%20Documents/tsno_medication_position.pd

United States Department of Health & Human Services, National Institutes of Health, National Center for Complementary and Integrative Health. (2021). Complementary, alternative, or integrative health: What's in a name. https://www.nccih.nih.gov/health/complementary-alternative-or-integrative-health-whats-in-a-name

United States Department of Education, National Center for Educational Statistics. (2020). School nurses in U.S. public schools. *Data Point*. https://nces.ed.gov/pubs2020/2020086.pdf

United States Food and Drug Administration. (2023, February 24). FDA regulation of cannabis and cannabis-derived products, including cannabidiol (CBD). https://www.fda.gov/news-events/public-health-focus/fda-regulation-cannabis-and-cannabis-derived-products-including-cannabidiol-cbd#othercbdapproved

Virginia NORML. (2019). *Marijuana-related legislation in the 2019 Virginia General Assembly - medical cannabis: Public elementary and secondary school students; suspension and expulsion; cannabidiol oil and THC-A oil.* https://www.vanorml.org/2019_legislation

Wallace, A.C. (2016). *Managing use of over-the-counter medications in the school setting: Keeping kids in school and ready to learn. NASN School Nurse, 31*(4), 210-213. https://doi.org/10.1177/1942602X16636123

West Virginia Medical Cannabis Act §16A. (2022). Legislative Rule §126-25A: Standards for basic and specialized care procedures and standards for the possession and use of medical cannabis by a student. https://www.wvlegislature.gov/wvcode/code.cfm?chap=16A&art=15 and https://apps.sos.wv.gov/adlaw/csr/readfile.aspx?DocId=55684&Format=PDF

Wisconsin Department of Public Instruction. (2022). *Administration of medications in Wisconsin schools.* https://dpi.wi.gov/sites/default/files/imce/sspw/pdf/Administration_of_Medications_in_Wisconsin_Schools.pdf

Yin, H.S., Parker, R.M., Sanders, L.M., Dreyer, B.P., Mendelsohn, A.L., Bailey, S., Patel, D.A., Jessica J. Jimenez,J.J., Kim,K-Y.A., Jacobson, K., Hedlund, L., Smith, M.C.J., Harris, L.M., McFadden, T., & Wolf, M.S. (2016). Liquid medication errors and dosing tools: A randomized controlled experiment. *Pediatrics, 138*(4): 1-11. https://doi.org/10.1542/peds.2016-0357

Zirkel, P.A., Granthom, M.F., & Lovato, L. (2012). Section 504 and student health problems: The pivotal position of the school nurse. *The Journal of School Nursing, 28*(6), 423-432. https://doi.org/10.1177/1059840512449358

APPENDIX A - HISTORY OF MEDICATION ADMINISTRATION

Historically, medication administration in all healthcare settings and schools has been a nursing duty (Hughes & Blegen, 2008). However, as increasing numbers of students with disabilities, chronic conditions, and complex healthcare needs enter school, the school community has researched ways to support and promote their academic success, including how to cost-effectively provide medication assistance to keep these students healthy and in school. Because fewer than half of the nation's schools have a full-time school nurse, when state laws permit, school administrators frequently assign medication administration tasks to unlicensed staff (American Academy of Pediatrics [AAP], Council on School Health, 2016; Fauteux, 2010; McClanahan & Weismuller, 2015).

While medication administration to students is now an everyday activity for school staff, until the passage of the Education for All Handicapped Children Act (Public Law 94-142) in 1975, children with chronic health conditions and disabilities were typically institutionalized or kept at home (Dang, 2010; Hughes & Blegen, 2008; McClanahan & Weismuller, 2015). Prior to the enactment of Public Law 94-142, which has evolved into the Individuals with Disabilities Education and Improvement Act (IDEIA) of 2004, some states did have provisions in their education statutes that provided for episodic oral medication, particularly antibiotics, to be administered at school by the school nurse or other school personnel. California, for instance, passed such a law in the mid-1960s.

Overarching federal laws, including Section 504 of the Rehabilitation Act of 1973 (Section 504), the Americans with Disabilities Act of 1990 (ADA), and the Individuals with Disabilities Education and Improvement Act of 2004 (IDEIA), require that children with health needs receive health services at school. The passage of the Americans with Disabilities Amendments Act of 2008 (ADAAA) broadened the scope of both the ADA and Section 504 and overturns earlier case law interpretations that had denied Section 504 eligibility to individuals with impairments that caused substantial limitations at work or school, such as diabetes, life-threatening allergies, and ADHD (United States Department of Education, Office for Civil Rights, 2012). However, federal law leaves medication administration details at school to the states and school districts (Laubin et al., 2012; Zirkel et al., 2012). States have the authority via the Tenth Amendment to the United States Constitution to regulate activities affecting their citizens' health, safety, and welfare (U.S. Department of Health and Human Services [USDHHS], 2010). Consequently, most states have passed laws that authorize LEAs to adopt local policies and regulations on medication management and administration in schools (Canham et al., 2007).

Other federal laws and regulations, including the Controlled Substances (CSA) and Uniform Controlled Substances (UCSA) Acts, and Title 21, Section 1300 of the Code of Federal Regulations (CFR), which deal with controlled substances, may also impact medication administration in schools, particularly for medications that are classified as controlled substances (DeWitt-Parker, 2016; Findlaw, 2016; Laubin et al., 2012). As a key part of federal drug abuse prevention efforts, in 1970, Congress passed the CSA and Title 21 CFR-Part 1300. Thus, they instituted scheduling substances based on their potential for abuse and consequent dependence. Marijuana is included in Schedule 1, along with other substances classified as having a high potential for abuse and no currently accepted medical treatment use in the United States (United States Department of Justice, Drug Enforcement Administration, Office of Diversion Control, 2016).

With the passage of the *Asthmatic Schoolchildren's Treatment and Health Management Act* (PL 108-377) of 2004 and federal level encouragement (American Lung Association, 2014), all states have passed laws permitting students with asthma to carry and use rescue inhalers, as necessary. With the passage of *the School Access to Emergency Epinephrine Act* of 2013, many states have passed laws permitting students with severe allergies to carry epinephrine auto-injectors and self-administer epinephrine when needed (Findlaw, 2016).

REFERENCES

American Academy of Pediatrics, Council on School Health. (2016). Role of the school nurse in providing school health services (Policy Statement). *Pediatrics, 137*(6), e20160852. https://doi.org/10.1542/peds.2016-0852

American Lung Association. (2014). Improving access to asthma medications in schools: Laws, policies, practices, and recommendations (Issue Brief). Author. http://www.lung.org/assets/documents/asthma/improving-access-to-asthma.pdf

Canham, D.L., Bauer, L., Concepcion, M., Luong, J., Peters, J., & Wilde, C. (2007). An audit of medication administration: A glimpse into school health offices. *The Journal of School Nursing, 23*(1), 21-27. https://doi.org/10.1177/105984 05070230010401

Dang, M. (2010). The history of legislation and regulations related to children with developmental disabilities: Implications for school nursing practice today. *The Journal of School Nursing, 26*(4), 252–259. https://doi.org/10.1177/1059840510368162

DeWitt-Parker, C. (2016). Medicinal use of marijuana: What school nurses need to know. *NASN School Nurse, 31*(3), 170-176. https://doi.org/10.1177/1942602X16638815

Fauteux, N. (2010). Unlocking the potential of school nursing: Keeping children healthy, in school, and ready to learn. *Charting Nursing's Future: Reports on Policies That Can Transform Patient Care* (Issue 14). Robert Wood Johnson Foundation. http://www.rwjf.org/content/dam/farm/reports/issue_briefs/2010/rwjf64263

Findlaw. (2016). *School authority to administer medication*. https://www.findlaw.com/education/school-safety/school-authority-to-administer-medication.html

Hughes, R.G., & Blegen, M.A. (2008). Medication administration safety. In R.G. Hughes (Ed.), *Agency for Healthcare Research and Quality (US)*, pp. 2–397 – 2–457. AHRQ. http://www.ncbi.nlm.nih.gov/books/NBK2656/

Laubin, M., Schwab, N.C., & Doyle, J. (2012). Understanding the legal landscape. In C. Costante (Ed.), *School nurse administrators: Leadership and management,* (pp. 459-519). National Association of School Nurses.

McClanahan, R., & Weismuller, P.C. (2015). School nurses and care coordination for children with complex needs: An integrative review. *The Journal of School Nursing, 31*(1), 34–43. https://doi.org/10.1177/1059840514550484

United States Department of Education, Office for Civil Rights. (2012). *Questions and answers on the ADA Amendments Act of 2008 for students with disabilities attending public elementary and secondary schools.* http://www2.ed.gov/about/offices/list/ocr/docs/dcl-504faq-201109.html

United States Department of Health and Human Services, Health Resources and Services Administration. (2010). *Telehealth licensure report: Special report to the Senate Appropriations Committee* (Senate Report No. 111-66). http://www.hrsa.gov/healthit/telehealth/licenserpt10.pdf

United States Department of Justice, Drug Enforcement Administration, Office of Diversion Control. (2016). *Title 21 United States Code (USC) Controlled Substances Act: Subchapter I — control and enforcement: Part B — Authority to control; standards and schedules: §812. Schedules of controlled substances.* http://www.deadiversion.usdoj.gov/21cfr/21usc/812.htm

Zirkel, P.A., Granthom, M.F., & Lovato, L. (2012). Section 504 and student health problems: The pivotal position of the school nurse. *The Journal of School Nursing*, *28*(6), 423-432. https://doi.org/10.1177/1059840512449358

Federal and State Laws

LEAs are required by three federal laws: Individuals with Disabilities Education Act (IDEA), Section 504 of the Rehabilitation Act of 1973 (Section 504), Title II of the Americans with Disabilities Act Amendments Act (Title II of ADAAA), and corresponding state laws to ensure that all students have equal opportunity and access to all academic, nonacademic, and other school-sponsored activities. Students with disabilities and those requiring health services cannot be excluded or denied access to these activities. **All LEAs should have policies and procedures for safe and effective medication administration** (American Academy of Pediatrics [AAP], 2016). Approximately ninety-seven percent of schools report having policies for medication administration to students (CDC, 2016). While all states have laws related to self-management of some chronic conditions (Findlaw, 2016), not all LEAs have adopted policies related to student self-management.

Policies, Procedures, and Protocols

Policies, procedures, and protocols provide school nurses and other school employees with reliable guidance and, when adhered to, reduce the risk of performance errors that could cause harm or even litigation (Allen et al., 2012; AAP, 2016; Kleinschmidt, 2015; Nadeau &Toronto, 2016; NASN, 2021; NASN, 2022a; Shannon & Kubelka, 2013b; Tanner & Clarke, 2016; Taras et al., 2014; Wallace, 2016; Wilt & Foley, 2011). LEA policies and procedures define the scope and standards of nursing practice and outline an expected standard of behavior for school employees (NASN, 2022a; Schwab et al., 2005) and may limit employee and LEA liability (Zadikoff et al., 2014; Zirkel, 2012). School nurses must know and follow their professional standards of practice, state laws and regulations, and their district's policies and procedures and provide leadership when such policies and procedures need to be revised and updated (NASN, 2021; Schwab et al., 2001; Shannon & Kubelka, 2013a).

Children with Special Healthcare Needs

There has been a dramatic increase in the number of school-age children with special physical and mental healthcare needs, including the need for medication each school day (Bergren, 2013; Knauer et al., 2015; Lebrun-Harris et al., 2022; Leroy et al., 2017; Lowe et al., 2022). The prevalence of students with diabetes, both type 1 and type 2, has increased significantly, according to the Centers for Disease Control and Prevention (CDC) and other researchers (CDC, 2021; Divers et al., 2020). Approximately 43 percent of school-age children experience at least one chronic condition requiring medication each year (Butler et al., 2020; Lowe et al., 2022).

Medications

Increased numbers of children with chronic conditions who need medication during the school day translate into increased amounts and types of medications for school personnel to administer. Additionally, many medications administered in school are controlled substances requiring special handling (Bergren, 2016; Canham et al., 2007; NASN, 2021; Taras et al., 2014; Texas School Nurses Organization, 2010). In one study, at the end of the school year in a large school district of 133,000 students, researchers identified 926 separate packages that were left in the school health offices, consisting of medications for asthma, pain (analgesics), allergy, behavioral issues (controlled substances), psychiatric conditions, gastrointestinal conditions, cold and cough, diabetes, epilepsy, cardiovascular conditions, and corticosteroids (Taras et al., 2014). In a study of 10 schools, researchers collected data on 154 medications prescribed for students (Canham et al., 2007). Students with potentially life-threatening conditions, such as asthma, severe allergies, or diabetes, may need emergency medications during the school day or at school-sponsored activities (Allen et al., 2012; Erwin et al., 2014; McCaughey et al., 2022; NASN, 2021; Tanner & Clarke, 2016; Zadikoff et al., 2014), and in some cases, these students may need emergency oxygen (Goldman, 2015).

Medication Management

Medication management is an important school nursing function. Effective medication management at school enables students who need medication during the school day to optimize their academic achievement (Leroy et al., 2017; Lowe et al., 2022). Medication management in schools has many components, all of which need to be consistently documented, including obtaining needed medication or supplies from parents, medication transport to school; medication acceptance by school staff; secure and appropriate medication storage; administration to students in accordance with the six rights of medication administration; observation of the effectiveness of the medication; appropriate delegation to licensed practical/vocational nurses (LPN/LVN) and UAP if permitted; appropriate disposal of medication, including controlled substances, at the school year's end or when expired; appropriate authorizations, including faxed orders and electronic signatures; and reporting and tracking medication errors (Kleinschmidt, 2015; NASN, 2021; Taras et al., 2014). Medication management also involves developing protocols for administering stock medications, OTC medications, and oxygen (Allen et al., 2012; Goldman, 2015; NASN, 2021; Tanner & Clarke, 2016; Wallace, 2016). Medication management further includes the provision of student medication for school-sponsored events, such as field trips (Erwin et al., 2014; NASN, 2021).

Delegation

For various reasons, including several years of reductions in education budgets, slightly over half of all schools in the United States have a full-time school nurse (Fauteux, 2010; Wang et al., 2014; Willgerodt et al., 2018). To meet the need to accommodate students requiring health services at schools, LEAs frequently rely on UAP, typically school office staff, to administer medication if allowed by state law (Butler et al., 2020; Maughan et al., 2018; McCaughey et al., 2022). Consequently, many school nurses must now train and supervise school secretaries and clerks, who already have full-time duties in the school office, to administer student medication (Canham et al., 2007; Nadeau & Toronto, 2016). Prior to delegating medication administration to UAP, the school nurse assesses the student to determine if the task can be delegated and what level of supervision and training the UAP needs to perform the task safely. Competing priorities for these UAP and their lack of medical background increase the possibility for medication errors (Canham et al., 2007). Medication errors are higher when UAP administers medication than when school nurses administer medication. One study found that documentation errors made by a UAP correlated with the potential for missed or double-dosing errors and medication theft (Celik, 2013). The risks of delegation can be reduced using procedure skills checklists, the development of individual healthcare plans (IHP) and emergency action plans (EAP), and the adoption of federal and state agency guidelines and professional organization guidelines (Butler et al., 2020; NASN, 2021; Shannon & Kubelka, 2013b). When permitted by law and appropriately applied, delegation to UAP is an effective tool for the school nurse (ANA & National Council of State Boards of Nursing [NCSBN], 2019).

However, the AAP recommends that when a registered nurse is unavailable to administer any medication at school, the task should be delegated to an LPN/LVN (AAP 2016).

Medication Errors

Medication errors occur in all clinical settings, including school health offices. The 1999 Institute of Medicine (IOM) report, *To Err is Human*, reviewed medication errors by licensed healthcare staff working in clinical settings and found at the time that medication errors caused 7,000 deaths annually (Kohn et al., 1999). The literature revealed that common medication errors, often linked to UAP in schools and more common in elementary schools when the school nurse is responsible for multiple schools, include incorrect medication dose, missed medication doses, expired medication, inconsistent documentation, and poor record keeping, over- and under-dosing, inappropriate and unsafe medicine storage, lack of healthcare provider authorization, transcription inaccuracies, and medication administered to the wrong student (Best et al., 2022; McClanahan, 2019; NASN, 2021).

> *The NASN Clinical Practice Guideline: Medication Administration in Schools, reviewed by content experts and Institute for Safe Medication Practices (ISMP) in 2022, states: "Medication ordered every four hours or more often may be administered 30 minutes before or after the scheduled time. Medications ordered less frequently than every four hours, AND the administration schedule is not deemed critical may be administered an hour before or an hour after the scheduled time."*

REFERENCES

Allen, K., Henselman, K., Laird, B., Quiñones, A., & Reutzel, T. (2012). Potential life-threatening events in schools involving rescue inhalers, epinephrine auto-injectors, and glucagon delivery devices: Reports from school nurses. *The Journal of School Nursing, 28(*1), 47-55. https://doi.org/10.1177/1059840511420726

American Academy of Pediatrics, Council on School Health. (2016). Role of the school nurse in providing school health services (Policy Statement). *Pediatrics, 137*(6), e20160852. http://pediatrics.aappublications.org/content/pediatrics/early/2016/05/19/peds.2016-0852.full.pdf

American Nurses Association and National Council of State Boards of Nursing. (2019). N*ational guidelines for nursing delegation.* https://ncsbn.org/public-files/NGND-PosPaper_06.pdf

Bergren, M.D. (2013). The case for school nursing: Review of the literature. *NASN School Nurse, 28*(1), 48-51. https://doi.org/10.1177/1942602X12468418

Bergren, M.D. (2016). The feasibility of collecting school nurse data. *The Journal of School Nursing.* Published online before print June 5, 2016. https://doi.org/10.1177/1059840516649233

Best, N.C., Nichols, A.O., & Hernandez, J. (2022). Exploration of factors associated with reported medication administration errors in North Carolina school districts. *The Journal of School Nursing*, 2022; 0(0). https://doi.org/10.1177/10598405221127453

Butler, S.M., Boucher, E.A., Tobison, J., & Phan, H. (2020). Medication use in schools: current trends, challenges, and best practices. *The Journal of Pediatric Pharmacology and Therapeutics*, 25(1), 7-24. https://www.ncbi.nlm.nih.gov/pmc/articles/PMC6938291/

Celik, LA (2013). Learning and applying new quality improvement methods to the school health setting. *NASN School Nurse*, 28(6), 306-311. https://doi.org/10.1177/1942602X13496121

Centers for Disease Control and Prevention. (2016). Table 4.6. Percentage of districts that had adopted policies related to student medications—SHPPS 2016. Results from the School Health Policies and Practices Study 2016. https://www.cdc.gov/healthyyouth/data/shpps/pdf/shpps-results_2016.pdf

Centers for Disease Control and Prevention, Healthy Schools. (2021). *Managing chronic health conditions. US* Department of Health and Human Services, Centers for Disease Control and Prevention. https://www.cdc.gov/healthyschools/chronicconditions.htm

Divers, J., Mayer-Davis, E.J., Lawrence, J.M., Isom, S., Dabelea, D., Dolan, L., Imperatore, G., Marcovina, S., Pettitt, D.J., Pihoker, C., Hamman. R.F., Saydah, S. & Wagenknecht, L.E. (2020, February 14). Trends in incidence of Type 1 and Type 2 diabetes among youths — selected counties and Indian reservations, United States, 2002–2015. Centers for Disease Control, *Morbidity and Mortality Weekly Report, 69*(6);161–165. https://www.cdc.gov/mmwr/volumes/69/wr/mm6906a3.htm?s_cid=mm6906a3_w

Erwin, K., Clark, S., & Mercer, S.E. (2014). Providing health services for children with special health care needs on out-of-state field trips. *NASN School Nurse, 29*(2), 84-88. https://doi.org/10.1177/1942602X13517005

Fauteux, N. (2010). Unlocking the potential of school nursing: Keeping children healthy, in school, and ready to learn. *Charting Nursing's Future: Reports on Policies That Can Transform Patient Care* (Issue 14). Robert Wood Johnson Foundation. http://www.rwjf.org/content/dam/farm/reports/issue_briefs/2010/rwjf64263

Findlaw. (2016). *School authority to administer medication.* https://www.findlaw.com/education/school-safety/school-authority-to-administer-medication.html

Goldman, P. (2015). Emergency first aid oxygen response in schools: O2 administration in schools by nurses and lay responders. *NASN School Nurse, 30*(2), 90-94. https://doi.org/10.1177/1942602X14563802

Institute for Safe Medication Practices. (2011). *ISMP acute care guidelines for timely administration of scheduled medications*: Author. http://www.ismp.org/tools/guidelines/acutecare/tasm.pdf

Kleinschmidt, K.A. (2015). Procedure for the disposal of controlled medication in the school setting. *NASN School Nurse, 30*(5), 259-262. https://doi.org/10.1177/1942602X14566467

Knauer, H., Baker, D.L., Hebbeler, K., & Davis-Alldritt, L. (2015). The mismatch between children's health needs and school resources. *The Journal of School Nursing, 31*(5), 326-333. https://doi.org/10.1177/1059840515579083

Kohn, L.T., Corrigan, J.M., & Donaldson, M.S. (Eds.) & Committee on Quality of Health Care in America, Institute of Medicine. (1999). *To err is human: Building a safer health system*. National Academy Press. https://doi.org/10.17226/9728

Lebrun-Harris, L.A., Ghandour, R.M., Kogan, M.D., & Warren, M.D. (2022). Five-year trends in US children's health and well-being, 2016-2020. *Journal of the American Medical Association, Pediatrics, 176*(7): e220056. https://doi:10.1001/jamapediatrics.2022.0056

Leroy, Z.C., Wallin, R., & Lee, S. (2017). The role of school health services in addressing the needs of students with chronic health conditions: A systematic review. *The Journal of School Nursing. 33*(1):64-72. https://doi:10.1177/1059840516678909

Lowe, A.A., Gerald, J.K., Clemens, C., Gaither, C., & Gerald, L.B. (2022). Medication administration practices in United States' schools: A systematic review and meta-synthesis. *The Journal of School Nursing, 38*(1), 21-34. http://doi.org/10.1177/10598405211026300

Maughan, E. D., McCarthy, A. M., Hein, M., Perkhounkova, Y., & Kelly, M. W. (2018). Medication management in schools: 2015 survey results. *The Journal of School Nursing, 34*(6), 468–479. https://doi.org/10.1177/1059840517729739

McCaughey, R.A., McCarthy, A.M., Maughan, E., Hein, M., Perkhounkova, Y., & Kelly, M.W. (2022). Emergency medication access and administration in schools: A focus on epinephrine, albuterol inhalers, and glucagon. The Journal of School Nursing. 38(4), 326-335. http://doi.org/10.1177/1059840520934185

Nadeau, E.H., & Toronto, C.E. (2016). Barriers to asthma management for school nurses: An integrative review. The Journal of School Nursing, 32(2), 86-98. https://doi.org/10.1177/1059840515621607

National Association of School Nurses. (2021). *School nursing evidence-based clinical practice guideline: Medication administration in schools*. Author. https://learn.nasn.org/courses/33787

National Association of School Nurses. (2022a). *School nursing: Scope and standards of practice (4th ed.)*. Author

Schwab, N.C., Hootman, J., & Gelfman, M.H.B. (2001). School nursing practice: Professional performance issues. In NC. Schwab, & M.H.B. Gelfman (Eds.), *Legal issues in school health services: A resource for school administrators, school attorneys, and school nurses*, (pp. 123-165). Sunrise River Press.

Shannon, R.A., & Kubelka, S. (2013a). Reducing the risks of delegation: Use of procedure skills checklists for unlicensed assistive personnel in schools, part 1. NASN School Nurse, 28(4), 178-181. https://doi.org/10.1177/1942602X13489886

Shannon, R.A., & Kubelka, S. (2013b). Reducing the risks of delegation: Use of procedure skills checklists for unlicensed assistive personnel in schools, part 2. *NASN School Nurse, 28*(5), 222-226. https://doi.org/10.1177/1942602X13490030

Tanner, A., & Clarke, C. (2016). Epinephrine policies and protocols guidance for schools: Equipping school nurses to save lives. *NASN School Nurse, 31*(1),13-22. https://doi.org/10.1177/1942602X15607604

Taras, H., Haste, N.M., Berry, A.T., Tran, J., & Singh, R.F. (2014). Medications at school: Disposing of pharmaceutical waste. *The Journal of School Health*, 84(3), 160–167. https://doi.org/10.1111/josh.12132

Texas School Nurses Organization. (2010). *Medication administration in the school setting* (Position Statement). Author. https://higherlogicdownload.s3.amazonaws.com/NASN/b385213b-35e8-49e3-97fe-d6627843f498/UploadedImages/Public%20Documents/tsno_medication_position.pdf

Wallace, A.C. (2016). *Managing use of over-the-counter medications in the school setting: Keeping kids in school and ready to learn. NASN School Nurse*, 31(4), 210-213. https://doi.org/10.1177/1942602X16636123

Wang, L.Y., Vernon-Smiley, M., Gapinski, M.A., Desisto, M., Maughan, E., & Sheetz, A. (2014). Cost-benefit study of school nursing services. *Journal of the American Medical Association, Pediatrics, 168*(7), 642-648. https://doi.org/10.1001/jamapediatrics.2013.5441

Willgerodt, M. A., Brock, D. M., & Maughan, E. D. (2018). Public school nursing practice in the United States. The Journal of School Nursing, 34(3), 232–244. https://doi.org/10.1177/1059840517752456

Wilt, L., & Foley, M. (2011). Delegation of glucagon® in the school setting: A comparison of state legislation. *The Journal of School Nursing*, 27(3), 185-196. https://doi.org/10.1177/1059840511398240

Zadikoff, E.H., Whyte, S.A., DeSantiago-Cardenas, L., Harvey-Gintoft, B., & Gupta, R.S. (2014). The development and implementation of the Chicago public schools emergency Epi-Pen® policy. *Journal of School Health,* 84(5), 342–347. https://doi.org/10.1111/josh.12147View/

Zirkel, P.A. (2012). Liability for student deaths from asthma. *NASN School Nurse, 27*(5), 242-244. https://doi.org/10.1177/1942602X12449058

APPENDIX C - MEDICATION POLICY AND PROCEDURES

While LEA policies and procedures must adhere to state laws to ensure safe medication administration to students, they need to address the following aspects to ensure safe medication administration to students:

- What medications may be administered at school, and by whom?
- All allowed medication (prescription and non-prescription) be delivered to the school by the parent/ guardian or other designated adult in the original container labeled with the student's name, medication name, dosage, route of administration when the medication is to be given, the name of the licensed prescriber, the pharmacy contact information, and the medication expiration date.
- All allowed medication (prescription and non-prescription) requires written orders from an authorized prescriber and written/signed parent/guardian consent for medication administration and exchange of information between the school nurse and the healthcare provider to clarify questions and report outcomes. These written authorizations are filed in the student's health record.
- School personnel are permitted to assume parent consent for administration is given in emergencies, although written and signed consent may not be available.
- Changes in medication orders, or new orders, are written and signed by the authorized prescriber. Changes that need to be implemented immediately may be taken verbally or via email if the LEA has policies regarding such actions that comply with federal and state laws and regulations and healthcare standards. School personnel (school nurses and other staff) must be identified in the policy if legally authorized (by state law or case law) to accept verbal orders. A written and signed order should be obtained within 48 hours of receipt of the verbal or email order.
- Upon receipt, all medication is counted or measured with and signed off by the parent, school nurse, or other designated staff, and the amount received is documented.

> **How should school nurses *measure liquid medication*?**
>
> Measuring liquid medication is challenging. Measuring and documenting controlled liquid medication, even in bottles with volume markings, is even more challenging. Pouring liquid medication into a measuring container is not good nursing practice, as it risks losing medication to spillage and, more importantly, exposes the medication to contamination.
>
> To avoid dosing errors, a recent study recommends that when dosing liquid medication, better accuracy can be obtained using an oral syringe rather than a medicine cup (Yin et al., 2016).

- Controlled medication is counted and documented upon receipt as above, each time it is administered, and weekly or more often with another school staff member, preferably a school nurse or principal.
- Medication never before administered to the student is inappropriate for the first time to be administered at school.
- Before administering any medication, the medication and the medication order are reviewed by the school nurse for the following: correct medication, correct/safe dosage based on the student's age and weight in kilograms, correct amount, administration directions, and expected outcomes and benefits. This information is incorporated into the student's medication plan that, as appropriate, may be inserted into the student's Individualized Healthcare Plan (IHP), Section 504 Plan as part of the student's accommodation plan, or individualized education program (IEP) for IDEA eligible students. All students with orders for emergency medications should have an Emergency Care Plan (ECP).

- Safe medication administration practices are followed by all responsible staff, which include checking the "six rights" of medication administration:
    1. Right individual
    2. Right medication
    3. Right dose
    4. Right time
    5. Right route
    6. Right documentation
- All medication is securely and appropriately stored in locked drawers, locked cabinets, or locked dedicated refrigerators and in accordance with federal and state laws and regulations, and recommendations. A plan is developed to quickly access and retrieve emergency medications, such as glucagon, epinephrine, rescue inhalers, naloxone (for opioid overdose), and seizure control medication. (LEAs considering keeping emergency medications unlocked for quick retrieval should consult their legal counsel).
- Access to medications is restricted and only available to the school nurse and trained staff, currently designated as being responsible for administering medications.
- All OTC and emergency stock medication require standing physician orders and parent/guardian permission to administer to students. Parents should inform the school if an OTC is given before school. When OTCs are administered at school, the parent/guardian may be notified at the school nurse's discretion (NASN, 2021). Who can administer OTC medications given via standing physician orders varies from state to state. In many states, only an RN may administer such medication.
- Medication is not pre-poured for later administration or for someone else to administer.
- Documentation of medication administration is completed promptly and includes a notation of any medication errors made during the administration process.
- All medication errors, which include missed doses, failure to adhere to one or more of the six rights of medication administration, not being called to the office to receive medication, and lost, wasted, dropped, or stolen medication, are recorded on incident forms and reported to the parent/guardian, school nurse (if not the provider), school principal or designee, and the LEA's risk management department.
- Initial and ongoing training and supervision by the school nurse are required and documented for UAP assigned to administer medication. Training includes all general standards of safe medication administration, student-specific medication, and health needs. Training also includes legal and nursing practice standards, when to call the nurse, the importance of attention to detail and focus in all phases of the medication administration process, and the need to observe the student putting the medicine into their mouth and swallowing it. Additionally, training includes the UAP signing an acknowledgment of training, the successful completion of a skill checklist, successful return demonstrations, and which may include a self-assessment of the level of confidence in carrying out the assignment. Medications. Also, see the NASN Clinical Practice Guidelines for an in-depth training list.
- The school nurse provides supervision of LPN/LVNs and UAP assigned to medication administration. There is adequate school nurse staffing to support this safety function. Medication errors increase when school nurses are assigned to multiple schools and consequently have several LPN/LVNs and UAP to supervise.
- LEA policy supports the registered school nurse's option to delegate or not to delegate medication administration for a specific student, in a specific situation, and/or to a specific UAP. While some state laws permit the school principal or other administrator to assign medication administration to UAP, the

school nurse's decisions are based on professional assessment and clinical criteria. They are made in the interest of the student's health and safety.

- Self-administration procedures for students when allowed by state laws and support by parents, providers, and the school nurse.
- All medication is returned to the parent/guardian at the end of the school year, when it is outdated, or at the end of the course of treatment. After appropriate notification to parents, any medication remaining at school is disposed of in accordance with state laws, regulations, and local ordinances. Medications, particularly controlled substances, are disposed of in the presence of another school employee, preferably the school principal or designee. The disposal is documented and signed by both parties.
- All student medication and personally identifiable information is confidential, in accordance with FERPA requirements, and students are entitled to privacy when medication is being administered.
- Parents do not delegate nursing tasks to school personnel.
- Parents do not change the medication dosage prescribed by a licensed provider or a manufacturer's printed dosage on the medication container.
- Parents are informed annually in writing of their rights and responsibilities regarding medication administration at school.
- The school nurse or other qualified staff conduct periodic reviews and annual audits of all procedures associated with medication management.

(The above list of items identified as needing policies and procedures is adapted from the following sources: American Academy of Pediatrics, Council on School Health, 2013; Best et al., 2022; Colorado Department of Education, 2015; Fobbs, 2015; Foley, 2013; Laubin et al., 2012; McClanahan et al., 2019; National Association of School Nurses, 2021; New York State Center for School Health, 2015; Texas School Nurse Organization, 2010; Wisconsin Department of Public Instruction, 2022; and Wilt and Foley, 2011).

REFERENCES

American Academy of Pediatrics, Council on School Health. (2013). Guidance for the administration of medication in school (Policy Statement). *Pediatrics*, *124*(4), 1244-1251. https://doi.org/10.1542/peds.2009-1953

Best, N.C., Nichols, A.O., & Hernandez, J. (2022). Exploration of factors associated with reported medication administration errors in North Carolina school districts. *The Journal of School Nursing*, 2022; 0(0). https://doi.org/10.1177/10598405221127453

Colorado Department of Education. (2015). *Guidance on delegation for Colorado school nurses & child care consultants*. Author. https://www.cde.state.co.us/healthandwellness/guidance-on-delegation-for-colorado-school-nurses-child-care-consultants-2-2016

Fobbs, E. (2015). Addiction trends require states to change school medication policies. *Policy Update*, *22*(10). National Association of State Boards of Education. http://www.nasbe.org/policy-update/addiction-trends-require-states-to-change-school-medication-policies/

Foley, M. (2013). Health services management. In J. Selekman (Ed.). *School nursing: a comprehensive text,* (2nd ed., pp. 1190-1215). F.A. Davis Company.

Laubin, M., Schwab, N.C., & Doyle, J. (2012). Understanding the legal landscape. In C. Costante (Ed.), *School nurse administrators: Leadership and management,* (pp. 459-519). National Association of School Nurses.

McClanahan, R., Shannon, R.A., & Kahn, P. (2019). School health office management. In J. Selekman, R.A. Shannon, & C. Yonkaitis (Eds.), *School nursing: A comprehensive text* (3rd ed., pp. 888-908). F.A. Davis Company.

National Association of School Nurses. (2021). *School nursing evidence-based clinical practice guideline: Medication administration in schools.* Author. https://learn.nasn.org/courses/33787

New York State Center for School Health. (2022). *Guidelines for medication management in schools.* https://www.p12.nysed.gov/sss/documents/medication-management.pdf

Texas School Nurses Organization. (2010). *Medication administration in the school setting* (Position Statement). Author. https://higherlogicdownload.s3.amazonaws.com/NASN/b385213b-35e8-49e3-97fe-d6627843f498/UploadedImages/Public%20Documents/tsno_medication_position.pdf

Wisconsin Department of Public Instruction. (2022). *Administration of medications in Wisconsin schools.* https://dpi.wi.gov/sites/default/files/imce/sspw/pdf/Administration_of_Medications_in_Wisconsin_Schools.pdf

Wilt, L., & Foley, M. (2011). Delegation of glucagon® in the school setting: A comparison of state legislation. *The Journal of School Nursing*, 27(3), 185–196. https://doi.org/10.1177/1059840511398240

Chapter 34
SUPPORTING STUDENTS WITH MENTAL/BEHAVORIAL HEALTH CHALLENGES
Antoinette Towle, EdD, APRN

DESCRIPTION OF ISSUE

Prior to COVID-19, the Centers for Disease Control and Prevention's (CDC) data found that 1 in 5 children had a mental health disorder; however, only 20% of these children received professional care for their disorder (CDC, 2022). As the United States approaches post COVID-19 pandemic, our nation is presently experiencing a mental health crisis, especially among children (Abramson, 2022). These numbers are projected to be much higher than the previous 1 to 5 ratio. The American Academy of Pediatrics (AAP), the American Academy of Child and Adolescent Psychiatry (AACAP), and the Children's Hospital Association (CHA) have joined together to declare a national state of emergency regarding child and adolescent mental health (AAP, 2021). The CDC also reports that during the pandemic, 29% of U.S. high school students had a parent or caregiver who lost their job, 55% of youth were emotionally abused by a parent or caregiver, and 11% were physically abused (Krause et al., 2022). At least 204,000 U.S. children and teens have lost parents and other in-home caregivers to COVID-19, which is more than one in every 360 youth (DeAngelis, 2022).

The stressors brought on by the pandemic included an increase in homelessness, child abuse, violence, suicides as well as suicidal attempts, social isolation, and a lack of educational structure. These stressors and many others have led to a significant increase in childhood and adolescent mental health problems such as depression, anxiety, stress and trauma-related disorders, aggressive behaviors, and suicidal and homicidal actions.

The post Covid school environment, where most students have returned to the classroom, offers a unique opportunity to begin to address present-day mental health crises. Because students are in school most of the day, barriers such as transportation, scheduling conflicts, and the stigma of receiving mental health services are greatly reduced. Schools can provide an excellent environment for early assessment, intervention, and possible treatment for a wide variety of mental health problems (National Alliance on Mental Illness, 2023). For students with serious mental health needs, schools can partner with more intensive community mental health services. They can then work collaboratively to implement a treatment plan to meet the student's emotional, behavioral, and educational needs. This chapter focuses on the legal and ethical responsibilities of the school's interdisciplinary team in supporting students with mental health challenges that impede their ability to learn.

BACKGROUND

According to a recent research study by Moen and Jacobsen (2022), school nurses have stated that they spend more than 50% of their time working with students who have mental health problems. Because the school nurse is often the bridge between mental health and education in the school setting, they are frequently the first to identify and address behavioral health concerns and connect students and families with systems of support. School nurses help educate staff and administration to recognize signs and symptoms of potential mental health issues, and build upon the staff and administrators' ability to address barriers to learning.

School nurses are key members of the interdisciplinary education team. This team may include the school psychologist, guidance counselor, classroom teachers, principal, social worker, the student, as well as their family. Other members may be added to the team as needed. School nurses are uniquely positioned between policymakers and the student body as caregivers, advocates, and experts (Rosvall, 2020). This unique position allows the school nurse to identify and intervene with at-risk students and lead prevention policies and program development.

IMPLICATIONS FOR SCHOOL NURSE PRACTICE

Rights and Protection

A student's emotional, behavioral, or mental health illness often affects their ability to learn and succeed in school. Many of these students require extra support and/or special education services to be successful. Some students suffering with mental health illness are considered "disabled" as defined by the law. There are several federal, state, and local laws and policies that protect the rights of students with disabilities, which include students disabled due to mental illness. Although these policies and laws are very important, the two with the greatest impact in working with students with mental health disabilities are the Individuals with Disabilities Education Act (IDEA) (formerly called P.L. 94-142 or the Education for all Handicapped Children Act of 1975) and accommodations through Section 504 of the Rehabilitation Act (1973) (U.S. Department of Justice Civil Rights Division, 2020).

The Individuals with Disabilities Education Improvement Act (IDEA) mandates that all students with disabilities receive a free and appropriate public education to meet their unique needs and prepare them for further education, employment, and independent living. The most recent version of IDEA was passed by Congress in 2004. It can be referred to as either IDEA 2004 or IDEA. Prior to IDEA, over 4 million students with disabilities were denied appropriate access to public education. Many students were denied entry into public school altogether, while others were placed in segregated classrooms or in regular classrooms without adequate support for their special needs. In the 2020-21 academic school year, under the IDEA mandate, more than 7.5 million eligible infants, toddlers, children, and youth with disabilities received disability-related services (U.S. Department of Education [USDE], 2023a).

IDEA has four parts: A, B, C, and D. Part A of IDEA outlines the basic foundation of IDEA, defines the terms used within the it, and explains the purpose and responsibilities of the Office of Special Education Programs as it relates to IDEA. Part B of IDEA outlines the educational guidelines for school children 3-21 years of age. IDEA provides financial support to states and local school districts. To receive IDEA funding, IDEA requires school districts to comply with these six main principles:

1. Zero Rejection means that schools must educate all children with disabilities regardless of the nature or severity of the disability.
2. Provide *Free Appropriate Public Education* (FAPE) to students who qualify as a student in need of special education services.
3. Evaluate a child to consider if the child is in need of special education services upon request of parent or concerns of school staff.
4. Provide a FAPE to students in the *Least Restrictive Environment*, such that students are presumed able to be educated with their nondisabled peers.

5. Include parents in educational decision-making.
6. Provide information to parents regarding parents' rights to challenge actions taken by the district regarding their child's FAPE.

Part C of IDEA refers to the early identification of and interventions for children with disabilities with children from birth to 2 years of age. This portion of IDEA provides guidelines concerning the funding and services families may be entitled to based on their child's needs. Families receive an Individualized Family Service Plan (IFSP). This plan lays out the family's priorities, resources, and concerns. It also describes the goals for the child, the services to be provided, and steps for the eventual transitioning of the child into formal education. The final section of IDEA, part D, describes national activities, such as grants, projects, and additional resources, to be undertaken to improve the education of children with disabilities.

The Individuals with Disabilities Education Improvement Act (IDEIA) and accommodations through Section 504 of the Rehabilitation Act (1973) require all public schools and private schools that receive federal funding to provide special services for students with disabilities (USDE, 2020). For students with mental health needs to be considered eligible for these special services, a student is eligible under Section 504 if they have a physical or mental impairment that substantially limits one or more of the student's major life activities. Under the IDEIA, a student needs to fall within one of the set disability categories and must need special-designed instruction in order to qualify. If the student's mental health problem meets this criterion, the student may be considered disabled under emotional or other health impairment categories. The student's parent(s), the legally responsible caregiver of the child, or the school system (e.g., classroom teacher or school social worker) can request the student be evaluated for special education services. Once the school system receives this request in writing, the school has 30 days to complete the assessment to determine eligibility for services.

The assessment is usually completed by a team that may include the school or school district's social worker, psychologist, teachers, school nurses, and others, depending on the student's individual needs. The assessment usually consists of a series of psychological tests that help the team learn more about the student's abilities, behavior, and day-to-day functioning at school. The assessment may also include pertinent information about the student's educational and medical history, social and emotional development, and how they function at school in all settings. IDEIA requires that a Functional Behavioral Assessment (FBA) be completed when:

(1) a child with a disability is removed or absent for more than ten school days,

(2) for any misconduct that may or may not be a manifestation of the child's disability or involves weapons, drugs, or serious bodily injury, regardless of the outcome of the manifestation determination review, or

(3) for behavior that interferes with the learning environment (Insource, 2023).

The steps the team would take include:

- After completing the assessment, the Individualized Education Plan (IEP) is created if the student is deemed eligible for services.
- The team, which includes the student (age 13 or older) and their parents, put together the most appropriate educational plan, including any special services for the student.
- Specific goals, along with objective outcome measures, are determined.

- In addition to outlining educational goals and expectations, the FBA is carefully reviewed, and a Behavioral Intervention Plan (BIP), also called a Positive Behavioral Support Plan (PBSP), is developed.
- The BIP/PBSP specifically targets the student's undesirable behaviors with interventions linked to the behavior's functions; each intervention specifically addresses a measurable, clearly stated targeted behavior (Barrington, 2022).
- The BIP includes prevention strategies geared toward stopping undesirable behavior before it begins and appropriate behaviors and strategies to teach the student appropriate ways to deal with the situation. Environmental concerns are key to the student's success.
- After considering all information, such as the IEP, FBA, and BIP/PBSP, the IEP team may determine that a change in a student's schedule or classroom arrangement is necessary and should be part of the BIP.
- Because the BIP is a legal document and part of the student's IEP, it must be adhered to completely, and it cannot be modified without a formal IEP team meeting.
- If a student experiences disciplinary removals resulting in a change of placement for more than ten days, the law requires that the IEP team meet to determine the manifestation of the child's disability, which may require a change in the IEP and/or BIP (Barrington, 2022).
- At the IEP team meeting, the team reviews whether the student's disruptive behavior, which caused him/her to be removed from their class, is a manifestation of their disability and whether the student can safely return to their former classroom.
- Only after the team has reviewed the student's current IEP, FBA, and BIP/PBSP and discussed all possible modifications that may need to be implemented may the student return to their former classroom.
- If the team rules that the student's present learning environment is not safe or meets the student's needs, a change in placement may be required.

Section 504 Plan

A Section 504 Plan is a legal document providing services and accommodations to students with regular education. Section 504 of the Rehabilitation Act of 1973 defines a disability as a "physical or mental impairment that substantially limits a person's ability to participate in a major life activity, such as learning" (USDE, 2020, p. 4, #11). Section 504 has a much broader definition of "disability" than is stated in the specific disabilities listed in IDEA. To be eligible for a Section 504 Plan the only requirement that must be met is that the student has a disability that must interfere with the student's ability to learn in a general education classroom. Therefore, students who may not be eligible for an IEP might be eligible for a Section 504 Plan.

The purpose of the 504 Plan is to help meet a student's physical or emotional needs, enabling them to achieve academic success in school within a regular classroom setting. The student's parents or caregiver may request a Section 504 Plan for their child. The rules regarding who must participate on the Section 504 team are less specific than they are for an IEP. The team usually consists of people who are familiar with the student and understand the evaluation data and the special services options. Unlike an IEP, there is no standard Section 504 Plan, and it doesn't have to be written. The plan usually includes the following:

- list of specific accommodations
- supports or services for the student
- names of who will provide each service
- name of the person responsible for ensuring the plan is implemented

Some examples of accommodations requested may include adjustment to test taking (more time, questions given orally), seating near the blackboard or near the teacher, or being excused from class to get medications. Legally schools are required to notify parents/caregivers if any accommodations are not able to be met or need to be changed; however, unlike the IEP, a formal meeting is not required. Unlike IEPs that must be reviewed at least once a year, each state determines when Section 504 Plans are reviewed and reevaluated. In addition, states do not receive extra funding for Section 504 Plan students as they do for students with an IEP; however, the federal government can take funding away from schools/programs that do not comply with Section 504 Plans and guidelines. *(Please refer to Chapter 13 for more information on IDEA and Section 504).*

Privacy and Confidentiality

The Family Educational Rights and Privacy Act (FERPA) (20 U.S.C. § 1232g; 34 CFR Part 99) is a federal law that protects the privacy of student education records (USDE, 2021). The law applies to all schools that receive funds under an applicable program of the USDE. Under FERPA, parents have access to their child's education record until the child turns 18 years old and is deemed an "eligible student." At 18, these rights transfer to the student unless the student is declared legally incompetent to handle their own affairs.

Schools must have written permission from the parent or eligible student to release any information from a student's education record, except in certain circumstances, as noted below. It is important to note what is considered part of the education record. According to FERPA (34 CFR § 99.2), education records are records directly related to a student and maintained by an educational agency or institution or by a party acting for or on behalf of the agency or institution. These records include but are not limited to grades, transcripts, class lists, student course schedules, health records (at the K-12 level), student financial information (at the postsecondary level), and student discipline files. FERPA allows schools to disclose those records, without consent, to the following parties or under the following conditions (34 CFR § 99.31):
- School officials with legitimate educational interest
- Other schools to which a student is transferring
- Specified officials for audit or evaluation purposes
- Appropriate parties about financial aid to a student
- Organizations conducting certain studies for or on behalf of the school
- Accrediting organizations
- To comply with a judicial order or lawfully issued subpoena
- Appropriate officials in cases of health and safety emergencies
- State and local authorities within a juvenile justice system, pursuant to specific State law

It is important to note that in cases of health and safety emergencies, such as a student potentially harming themselves or others, schools have the right to release confidential information to the proper authorities to ensure safety. Any information so shared during the emergency must be relevant to the situation and appropriately limited to the safety concern at the time. Adherence to confidentiality and privacy should otherwise be maintained.

The Health Insurance Portability and Accountability Act (HIPAA); Pub.L. 104–191, 110 Stat. 1936 (enacted August 21, 1996) is a law created to protect the confidentiality and security of healthcare information

(Edemekong et al., 2022). In most cases, the HIPAA Privacy Rule does not apply to schools because the school is either not a HIPAA-covered entity or is a HIPAA-covered entity but maintains health information only in the student's education records which FERPA protects and, therefore, is not subject to the HIPAA Privacy Rule (Edemekong et al., 2022). However, if a school-based health center (SBHC) provides mental health services, they may be subject to HIPAA rules. (*Refer to Chapter 12 for more information on FERPA and HIPAA and Chapter 47 on SBHCs*).

Psychotropic Medication

Psychotropic medications, which include anticonvulsants, antidepressants, antihypertensives, antipsychotics (neuroleptics), anxiolytics (antianxiety), mood stabilizers, selective norepinephrine reuptake inhibitors, selective serotonin reuptake inhibitors, and stimulants, are often used to treat psychiatric disorders or illnesses in students. No specific laws address the administration of psychotropic medications to students in school settings (Hoover & Bostic, 2020). Therefore, most school settings treat psychotropic medication in the same way as other medications. Under federal law, IDEA (2004), and Section 504, schools that receive federal funding are mandated to provide "required related services," including medication administration. Depending on state law, some states only permit licensed personnel to administer medication to students, while other states allow school personnel to administer medication and consult with parents regarding the efficacy of medications in connection with academic, functional, or behavioral performance in school.

The National Association of School Nurses (NASN) encourages school districts to develop written medication administration policies and procedures focusing on safe and efficient medication administration, including all medication types, including psychotropic (NASN, 2021). It is important that these policies are consistent with federal and state laws, nursing practice standards, and established safe practices in accordance with evidence-based information. The administration of emergency psychotropic medications or as needed medications (PRNs) should adhere to the same state laws, regulations, guidelines, and local school district policies and protocols. The school nurse should have a detailed emergency care plan in place based on the student's prescribing provider's orders regarding medication use.

Psychotropic medications can be very useful medications in treating the student's mental illness, but the student may experience negative side effects. As students begin to feel the positive effects of the medication, they may discontinue them due to the negative side effects (e.g., weight gain) or their belief that they no longer need the medication because they feel so much better. In accordance with IDEA (2004) and the *Prohibition on Mandatory Medication Amendment*, schools are prohibited from requiring a child to take a psychiatric drug as a requisite for attending school. School nurses can encourage, educate, and counsel students to continue their medication by building positive relationships with students.

Through ongoing assessment and careful monitoring, school nurses must communicate and collaborate closely with the underage student's parents and primary healthcare provider. They must be alert to any behavior changes as well as medication refusal. Most psychotropic medications maintain a therapeutic blood level for a period of time; therefore, behavior changes may not be observed after the medication is discontinued. It can take time before the medication is no longer effective. Intervention is indicated if a student discontinues necessary medication without a healthcare provider's order.

Schools cannot force students to take medication as a condition to attend school. Schools are required by federal and state laws and school district policies to provide a safe school environment for all students. If a student is disruptive, resulting in an unsafe environment, or the student demonstrates unsafe behavior that can result in harm to themselves or others, school administration is, in many cases, required to remove the student from the school environment. In the case of a student with mental health illness symptoms, it is not uncommon to be transported to a local emergency room for assessment and evaluation.

Students who are re-entering the school after a hospitalization often need a great deal of support, which requires team communication, collaboration, and flexibility. <u>The team needs to meet prior to the re-entry back to school to create an action plan.</u> The team must review all current and relevant documents and findings that may impact the student's safety and academic success. The student's current IEP and BIP need to be reviewed and modified as needed. An FBA may need to be completed before changing or modifying the BIP. The FBA will review and update any strategies to incorporate in the BIP in the areas of:

- Prevention
- Replacement behavior instruction
- Positive reinforcement
- Planned consequences
- Emergency interventions, if appropriate
- Home/School collaboration

(See Addendum at the end of this chapter for more information on Effective Transitions Back to School).

Safety and Emergencies

Suicide is the third leading cause of death for youth under age 18 (CDC, 2022). Students with mental health disabilities are at increased risk of self-harming, intentional or unintentional behaviors, including suicide. Prevention is the primary goal. Since the COVID-19 pandemic, a great deal of legislative focus has centered on prevention policy, early intervention, and crisis preparedness. For example, the USDE (Department) is announcing awards of more than $188 million across 170 grantees in over 30 states to increase access to school-based mental health services and to strengthen the pipeline of mental health professionals in high-needs districts (2023b).

School districts must have detailed policies and procedures to assess safety in schools. During IEP team meetings and BIP development, school personnel, the student, and the family must discuss safety concerns and develop a plan to manage a psychiatric emergency safely and effectively. This plan needs to be shared with all school personnel working with the student. School districts developing and implementing effective policies and procedures regarding handling psychiatric emergencies increase the safety of their students and their staff.

CONCLUSION

At the present time, there are no universal standards for mental health screening for children, although there are some evidence-based screening tools available, such as Screening, Brief Intervention, and Referral to Treatment (see resources below). Other than IDEA and Section 504 of the Rehabilitation Act, no specific federal laws mandate mental health services for children or adolescents. Individual states have started to implement policies and regulations regarding such services; however, they vary from state to state and are dependent upon funding. Because children/adolescents spend the majority of their day in school, educators play a significant role in early identification and intervention. School nurses are stepping up to take a leading role in educating personnel, families, students, and policymakers on mental illness and its impact on students, families, and communities.

> See Addendum - **Supporting Effective Transitions Back to School Following Behavioral Health Hospitalizations: The Role of the School Nurse**

RESOURCES

Family Educational Rights and Privacy Act (FERPA). (2021)
https://www2.ed.gov/policy/gen/guid/fpco/ferpa/index.html

The Health Insurance Portability and Accountability Act (HIPPA). (2021).
https://www.hhs.gov/hipaa/for-professionals/index.html

Individuals with Disabilities Education Improvement Act.
https://sites.ed.gov/idea/about-idea/#:~:text=The%20Individuals%20with%20Disabilities%20Education,related%20services%20to%20those%20children.

Screening, Brief Intervention, and Referral to Treatment. https://www.samhsa.gov/sbirt

U.S. Department of Health & Human Services, Office for Civil Rights. (2023) Disability Laws, Regulations, and Guidance.
https://www.hhs.gov/civil-rights/for-individuals/disability/laws-guidance/index.html

REFERENCES

Abramson. A. (2022). Children's mental health is in crisis as pandemic stressors continue; kids' mental health needs to be addressed in schools. *2022 Trends report. America Psychological Association, 53*(1), 69. https://www.apa.org/monitor/2022/01/special-childrens-mental-health

American Academy of Pediatrics. (2021). *AAP-AACAP-CHA declaration of a national emergency in child and adolescent mental health.* https://www.aap.org/en/advocacy/child-and-adolescent-healthy-mental-development/aap-aacap-cha-declaration-of-a-national-emergency-in-child-and-adolescent-mental-health/

Barrington, K. (2022). Behavioral intervention plans. *Public school review.* https://www.publicschoolreview.com/blog/behavioral-intervention-plans

Center for Disease Control and Prevention. (2023). *Faststats: Adolescent health*. https://www.cdc.gov/nchs/fastats/adolescent-health.htm#:~:text=Accidents%20(unintentional%20injuries),Suicide

Centers for Disease Control and Prevention. (2022). *Improving access to children's mental health care.* https://www.cdc.gov/childrensmentalhealth/access.html

DeAngelis, T. (2022). Thousands of kids lost loved ones to the pandemic. Psychologists are teaching them how to grieve, and then thrive. *American Psychological Association, 53*(7),69. https://www.apa.org/monitor/2022/10/kids-covid-grief

Edemekong, P.F., Annamaraju, P., & Hayde, M.J. (2022). Health insurance portability and accountability act (HIPPA). *National Library of Medicine.* https://www.ncbi.nlm.nih.gov/books/NBK500019/

Hoover, S., & Bostic, J. (2020). Schools as a vital component of the child and adolescent mental health system. *Psychiatric Services, 72*(1), 37-48. https://ps.psychiatryonline.org/doi/abs/10.1176/appi.ps.201900575

Insource. (2023). Federal laws and legislation. Individuals with disabilities education improvement act. *Special Education Parent Support.* https://insource.org/get-help/resources/federal-laws-and-legislation/

Krause, K.H., Verlenden, J.V., Szucs, L.E., Swedo, E.A., Merlo, C.L., Niolon, P. H., Leroy, Z.C.,x Sims, V.M., Deng, X., Lee, S., Rasberry, C.N., & Underwood, M (2022). Disruptions to school and home life among high school students during the COVID-19 pandemic — adolescent behaviors and experiences survey, United States, January–June 2021. MMWR Suppl 2022, *71*(3), 28–34. http://dx.doi.org/10.15585/mmwr.su7103a5

Moen, Y. &Jacobson, I.C.R. (2022). School nurses' experiences in dealing with adolescents having mental health problems. *Sage Open Nursing Journals, 8.* https://journals.sagepub.com/doi/10.1177/23779608221124411

National Alliance on Mental Illness. (2023). *Mental health in schools.* https://www.nami.org/Advocacy/Policy-Priorities/Improving-Health/Mental-Health-in-Schools

National Association of School Nursing. (2021). *School nursing evidence-based clinical practice guideline: Medication administration in schools.* https://cdn.fs.pathlms.com/eMfakewQq20XiLuoim9w

Rosvall, P. (2020). Perspectives of students with mental health problems on improving the school environment and practice. *Education inquiry, 11*(3), 159-174. https://doi.org/10.1080/20004508.2019.1687394

U.S. Department of Education. (2023a). *About IDEA: the individuals with disabilities education act (IDEA).* https://sites.ed.gov/idea/about-idea/

U.S. Department of Education. (2023b). *U.S. Department of Education announces more than $188 million from the bipartisan safer communities act to support mental health and student wellness.* https://www.ed.gov/news/press-releases/us-department-education-announces-more-188-million-bipartisan-safer-communities-act-support-mental-health-and-student-wellness

U.S. Department of Education. (2021). *Family educational rights and privacy Act (FERPA). Family Policy Compliance Office.* https://www2.ed.gov/policy/gen/guid/fpco/ferpa/index.html

U.S. Department of Education. (2020). *Protecting students with disabilities: Frequently asked questions about section 504 and the education of children with disabilities.* https://www2.ed.gov/about/offices/list/ocr/504faq.html

U.S. Department of Justice Civil Rights Division. (2020). Resources. *ADA.gov.* https://www.ada.gov/resources/disability-rights-guide/#general-sources-of-disability-rights-information

ADDENDUM

Supporting Effective Transitions Back to School Following Behavioral Health Hospitalizations:

The Role of the School Nurse
Suzanne Levasseur, MSN, APRN, CPNP, NCSN

An increasing number of students are hospitalized each year for psychiatric crises such as suicidal ideation, anxiety, depression, eating disorders, substance abuse, and psychosis. Students often return to school after hospitalization with limited follow-up care. Re-hospitalization is common, with up to 50% of students readmitted to the hospital setting within a year (Grunnikoff, 2016). When return to school is warranted, coordinated after-care services, with a strong re-entry plan, can be highly effective for a smooth transition and preventing hospital readmissions. The plan should consider the student's stamina and ability to attend school, any safety concerns, and encourage academic and school engagement. It is important to note that schools are required to provide a free appropriate public education to K-12 students with disabilities, providing the behavioral supports they need. Denying re-entry instead of making a comprehensive plan for the student would be denying the student's right to FAPE (United States Department of Education, Office of Civil Rights, 2010).

A school transition team, including the school nurse, should be formed. This may also include a school psychologist, teacher, principal, family members, and the student. It may also include a case manager, social worker, or outside provider that has been knowledgeable regarding the hospitalization or outside program, as well as the student's needs for re-entering school. A point person, often the school nurse, should be identified as the contact for the hospital and outside agencies. Outside agencies such as DCF and foster parents should also be included if applicable. If the student receives services under Section 504 or special education, a 504 coordinator or special education case manager should be included. This return to school may also necessitate an official 504 or planning and placement team meeting, and the student should be considered for eligibility if not already identified. Confidentiality should be a priority to ensure that all sensitive information is kept private and that only those with a legitimate educational interest are involved in the information sharing. A release of information form should be obtained and signed by the legal parent or guardian or an eligible student over 18 years of age.

This planning should begin prior to the student's discharge from the hospital or program, and the initial re-entry meeting should take place prior to the student's first day back at school. In the initial meeting, hospital recommendations should be reviewed, and immediate supports including any safety issues, should be addressed.

Interventions and levels of support should be decided by the team with specifics such as the intervention needed, how often the intervention should be implemented, the data that should be recorded, and the people responsible for providing the intervention.

Supports may include:

- Partial Day Schedule
- Academic Supports
- Behavioral supports
- Mental Health Supports
- Family Supports
- Social Integration Supports

Action plans and checklists can be useful tools to help maintain data and evaluate progress. It will be important that the plan is specific and measurable.

It is likely that many students will need the support of a transition plan for many weeks or more as they transition back into the school environment. Every student's transition will be different, and an individualized plan will be important. Progress will occur at different rates. During this time, communication should continue with the outpatient team to share progress and continued needs. Key members of the team should check in with each other regularly to monitor how the student is doing and evaluate how well the plan is working. A specific time frame should be determined to formally re-assess progress and make adjustments as necessary.

A comprehensive and multi-faceted plan will be essential for a student's Integration into the school setting after a hospitalization. The school nurse, as part of a multidisciplinary team, including the student and family, will be pivotal in this process. The school nurse can act as a liaison between outside providers, family, and school staff to share prevalent information and monitor progress. The health office can be a welcoming place for the student who may need a respite during the school day. Data on office visits and the student's overall status will be an important part of the process as well. School nurses, with their broad knowledge of mental, physical, and emotional health, will be an essential leader on the school transition team.

RESOURCES

Supporting Hospital-to-School Transitions. (2020). University of Maryland School of Medicine. https://mdbehavioralhealth.com/"https://mdbehavioralhealth.com/

Supporting Students with Disabilities and Avoiding the Discriminatory Use of Student Discipline Under Section 504 of the Rehabilitation Act of 1973. (2022). U.S. Department of Education, Office of Civil Rights [Fact Sheet]. https://www2.ed.gov/about/offices/list/ocr/docs/504-discipline-factsheet.pdf

REFERENCES

Grundnikoff, E. (2016). 3.41 Correlates of psychiatric inpatient readmissions of children and adolescents with mental disorders. Journal of the American Academy of Child and Adolescent Psychiatry. *55* (supplement), S155=S155. https://www.umb.edu/birch/about

U.S. Department of Education, Office for Civil Rights. (2010). *Free Appropriate Public Education for Students With Disabilities: Requirements Under Section 504 of the Rehabilitation Act of 1973.* https://www2.ed.gov/about/offices/list/ocr/docs/edlite-FAPE504.html

Chapter 35

NALOXONE USE IN THE SCHOOL SETTING

Rebecca King, MSN, RN, NCSN-E

DESCRIPTION OF ISSUE

The United States continues to battle the epidemic of opioid drug overdose (poisoning) deaths. Many factors have fueled opioid use disorder (OUD). The Centers for Disease Control and Prevention (CDC), National Center for Injury Prevention and Control reports that from 1999–2020, more than 564,000 people died from an overdose involving any opioid, including prescription and illicit opioids. CDC (2022a) outlines the rise in opioid overdose deaths in three distinct waves:

1. The first wave began with increased prescribing of opioids in the 1990s, with overdose deaths involving prescription opioids (natural and semi-synthetic opioids and methadone) rising since at least 1999.
2. The second wave began in 2010, with rapid increases in overdose deaths involving heroin.
3. The third wave began in 2013, with significant increases in overdose deaths involving synthetic opioids, particularly those involving illicitly manufactured fentanyl. The market for illicitly manufactured fentanyl continues to change, and fentanyl can be found in combination with heroin, counterfeit pills, and cocaine. (CDC, National Center for Injury Prevention and Control, 2022a)

Naloxone, a pure opioid antagonist, can quickly and safely reverse opioid overdose. Now available in all 50 states, naloxone is a life-saving medication that can swiftly counteract an overdose of opioids—including heroin, fentanyl, and prescription opioid medications—when given in time.

BACKGROUND

Data from the CDC's National Center for Health Statistics (NCHS) indicated that approximately 81,230 drug overdose deaths occurred in the United States in the 12 months ending in May 2020. This data represented a worsening of the drug overdose epidemic in the United States and was the largest number of drug overdoses for a 12-month period ever recorded (CDC, 2020). There were 518 deaths among adolescents (2.40 per 100,000 population) in 2010, with rates remaining stable through 2019 with 492 deaths (2.36 per 100,000). Deaths among this population increased to 954 (4.57 per 100 000) in 2020 and to 1146 (5.49 per 100 000) in 2021. Between 2019 and 2020, overdose mortality increased by 94.03% and from 2020 to 2021 by 20.05%. (Friedman et al., 2022). In the social sciences, unintended consequences (sometimes unanticipated consequences or unforeseen consequences) are outcomes of a purposeful action that are not intended or foreseen.

Opioid use disorder remains an epidemic of unintended consequences. Despite many efforts, overdose deaths have continued to rise, especially with the introduction of illicitly manufactured fentanyl, accelerating this already dangerous and deadly epidemic. Anne Milgram, Administrator for the United States Drug Enforcement Administration (U.S. DEA), stated:

"Fentanyl is everywhere. Fentanyl is the single deadliest drug threat our nation has ever encountered. No community is safe from this poison, from large metropolitan areas to rural America. We must take every

opportunity to spread the word to prevent fentanyl-related overdose death and poisonings from claiming scores of American lives every day." (U.S. DEA, 2022, para. 1).

The situation worsened at the end of 2019 when COVID-19 exponentially proliferated. This pandemic upended many everyday aspects of daily life and produced an unparalleled strain on America's healthcare system. Extreme measures, including continued social distancing and coordinated suppression efforts, became required to reduce catastrophic mortality. Although the pandemic threatened everyone, it was of particularly critical risk to the millions of Americans with OUD, who were already vulnerable, marginalized, and heavily dependent on face-to-face healthcare delivery (Alexander et al., 2019). The pandemic created challenges and barriers for individuals seeking treatment.

Implications for Youth

The statistics for substance use disorder (SUD) remain alarming. In 2020, 40.3 million people aged 12 or older (or 14.5 %) had a SUD in the past year, including 28.3 million who had an alcohol use disorder, 18.4 million who had an illicit drug use disorder, and 6.5 million people who had both alcohol use disorder and an illicit drug use disorder (SAMHSA, 2021).

The COVID-19 Pandemic was particularly hard on isolated adolescents (12 or older) who experienced disruption in typical developmental milestones, resulting in pervasive stress and anxiety. Initial findings suggest that fewer teens started using substances during the pandemic, likely influenced by stay-at-home orders that reduced opportunities for social use. However, increased time at home was not beneficial for all adolescents. Furthermore, adolescents who used substances pre-pandemic, experienced material hardship, or reported higher pandemic-related stress tended to intensify substance use during this time (Calihan & Levy, 2022).

According to the National Survey on Drug Use and Health (NSDUH), among people 12 or older in 2020, 58.7 percent (or 162.5 million people) used tobacco, alcohol, or an illicit drug in the past month (also defined as "current use"), including 50.0 % (or 138.5 million people) who drank alcohol, 18.7 % (or 51.7 million people) who used a tobacco product, and 13.5 % (or 37.3 million people) who used an illicit drug (SAMSHA, 2021). Among people aged 12 or older in 2020, 1.2 million people began misusing prescription pain relievers in the past year. Unlike new users of cigarette, alcohol, and marijuana use, nearly two-thirds of past year initiates tried prescription pain relievers for the first time after age 25 (i.e., 774,000 adults aged 26 or older who began prescription pain reliever misuse) (SAMHSA, 2021).

Though the data have indicated stable or declining use of illicit drugs among young people over many years, research has reported a recent dramatic rise in overdose deaths among young people ages 14-18. Beginning in 2020, adolescents experienced a more significant relative increase in overdose mortality than the overall population, largely attributable to fatalities involving fentanyl (Friedman et al., 2022). In the context of decreasing adolescent drug use rates nationally, these shifts suggest heightened risk from illicit fentanyl, which has variable and high potency. Since 2015, fentanyl has increasingly been added to counterfeit pills resembling prescription opioids, benzodiazepines, and other drugs, which adolescents may not identify as dangerous and may play a vital role in these shifts (Friedman et al., 2022).

When asked a range of questions on the Monitoring the Future survey (an ongoing study of the behaviors, attitudes, and values of Americans from adolescence through adulthood) about the perceived harmfulness of occasionally taking specific prescription medications (such as OxyContin or Vicodin), or the risk of "narcotics other than heroin" overall, the percentage of students who reported perceiving a "great risk" ranged from 22.9% among eighth graders to 52.9% among 12th graders, the rate of respondents who reported perceiving a "great risk" associated with occasionally taking Adderall ranged from 28.1% among eighth graders to 39.6% among 12th graders (National Institute on Drug Abuse [NIDA], 2022). Dr. Nora Volkow, Director of the NIDA at the National Institutes of Health states:

> The proliferation of fentanyl in the drug supply is of enormous concern. Though the data indicates that drug use is not becoming more common among young people than in the past, the tragic increase in overdose deaths suggests that drug use is becoming more dangerous than ever before. It is crucial to educate young people that pills purchased via social media, given to someone by a friend, or obtained from an unknown source may contain deadly fentanyl (NIDA, 2022, para 14).

Schools must be attuned to any subset of students who have the potential to misuse opioids. For example, the overall number of participants in high school sports increased for the 29th consecutive year in 2017-18, according to the annual High School Athletics Participation Survey conducted by the National Federation of State High School Associations (NFHS, 2018). The current research builds on a small number of studies that have shown that adolescents involved in competitive sports are more likely to report non-medical use of prescription opioids (NUPO). According to the National College Health Assessment (NCHA II from 2008 to 2011), 8.3% of students reported NUPO, 8.0% identified as a varsity athlete, and 17.4% reported an injury. Looking at factors individually, having an injury, being a varsity athlete, and being male were all significantly associated with NUPO (Ford et al., 2018).

Another subset at risk for SUD includes students with mental health conditions. Among adolescents aged 12 to 17 in 2020, those with a past-year major depressive episode (MDE) were more likely than adolescents without a past-year MDE to be past-year illicit drug users (28.6 vs. 10.7 %) or past-year marijuana users (22.0 vs. 7.9 %) (SAMHSA, 2021).

IMPLICATIONS FOR SCHOOL NURSES

Naloxone

As stated above, Naloxone, a pure opioid antagonist, can quickly and safely reverse opioid overdose. Now available in all 50 states, naloxone is a life-saving medication that can swiftly counteract an overdose of opioids—including heroin, fentanyl, and prescription opioid medications—when given in time. Naloxone reverses the overdose by blocking the effects of opioids. It can restore normal breathing within two to three minutes in a person whose breathing has slowed or even stopped due to an opioid overdose. More than one dose of naloxone may be required when more potent opioids like fentanyl are involved (CDC, 2020).

"Naloxone is easy to use and small to carry. There are currently two available forms of naloxone that anyone can use without medical training or authorization: prefilled nasal spray and injectable. The decision on which form of naloxone to use or carry can depend on many factors, such as cost, availability, and comfort level. Both are safe, effective and can help save a life" (CDC, 2023, para. 1). Although these are national recommendations, there are some states where a person is required to receive training to receive naloxone from specific programs or to receive legal protections. Currently, most states do not explicitly state that possessing naloxone without a prescription is legal. However, in March of 2023, the FDA approved the first over-the-counter, non-prescription nasal spray of naloxone (Food and Drug Administration[FDA], 2023). Due to the rapidly changing and varying laws, school nurses should follow district policies regarding Naloxone administration.

Naloxone will not harm someone if they are overdosing on drugs other than opioids, so it is always best to go ahead and use it if an overdose is suspected. Carrying naloxone is no different than carrying an epinephrine auto-injector (EpiPen) for someone with allergies. It provides an extra layer of protection for those at a higher risk for overdose (CDC, 2023, 3rd paragraph).

Although naloxone is a prescription drug, it is not a controlled substance and has no abuse potential. While it was traditionally used only by first responders, it can now be administered by laypeople with little or no formal training, depending on applicable state laws. Davis (2021) states that because of its ability to reverse an opioid overdose and its ease of use, by July 15, 2017, all 50 states and the District of Columbia had passed legislation to improve a layperson's access to naloxone. Opioid overdose kills tens of thousands of Americans every year. Most of those deaths are preventable through the timely provision of naloxone. As with most public health problems, no magic bullet prevents overdose deaths. The approval of one or more naloxone formulations as an over-the-counter medication will likely increase access to this medication, and a comprehensive solution that includes increased access to evidence-based treatment together with de-stigmatization and de-criminalization of opioid use disorder is necessary to create large-scale, lasting change. However, ensuring that naloxone is always readily available at the scene of an opioid overdose is still one of the cheapest, safest, and most effective ways available to reduce opioid overdose morbidity and mortality (Davis, 2021).

Overdose Management and School Nurse Practice

"This can't happen to me," "not my kid," or "not in our school" are words anyone, any parent or any school or district administrator, can say, but addiction can happen to anyone, anywhere…it does not discriminate. School nurses are first responders in the school setting and are leaders in planning for and managing emergencies in the school setting. School nurses practicing primary prevention also work to prevent potential emergencies by raising awareness, educating students and families on healthy behaviors, and reducing risks. In September 2016, the National Association of School Nurses (NASN) introduced the *Naloxone in Schools Toolkit* as part of the association's proactive efforts to educate school communities about the country's ongoing opioid epidemic. The toolkit followed the release of NASN's first position statement about using naloxone in the school setting, initially created in June 2015 and revised in 2020. The NASN naloxone toolkit, one of many available naloxone resources, is currently being revised (release date 2023). SAMSHA (2018) also has an *Opioid overdose prevention toolkit*. Toolkits and position documents provide valuable resources to help school nurses, school leaders, and community members develop policies and procedures which include the appropriate steps to identify and react to a possible opioid overdose in a school setting and address necessary education and prevention.

Schools are responsible for anticipating and preparing to respond to various emergencies. The school nurse is often the first health professional who responds to an emergency in the school setting. The school nurse possesses the education and knowledge to identify emergent situations, manage the crisis until relieved by emergency medical services (EMS) personnel, communicate the assessment and interventions to EMS personnel, and follow up with the healthcare provider. Thus, school nurses' access to naloxone as part of their school's emergency preparedness will improve opioid overdose response, response preparation, and harm reduction and reduce overdose-related morbidity and mortality. It is the position of the National Association of School Nurses (NASN, 2020) that:

- The safe and effective management of opioid-related overdoses in schools must be incorporated into the school emergency preparedness and response plans.
- The registered professional school nurse provides leadership in all emergency preparedness and response phases.
- Properly managing these incidents at school is vital to positive outcomes when emergencies happen, including drug-related emergencies.
- The school nurse is essential to the school team responsible for developing and implementing emergency response procedures. School nurses in this role should facilitate access to naloxone for quick response in managing opioid-related overdoses in the school setting.

Although most people who experience an opioid overdose are adults, young children suffer opioid overdose from exploratory behavior, and adolescents through opioid misuse or self-harm exposure. Opioid overdose causes respiratory depression, which can progress from respiratory arrest to cardiac arrest. Pediatric opioid overdose management is the same as for adults. For a patient with suspected opioid overdose who has a definite pulse but no normal breathing or only gasping (i.e., a respiratory arrest), in addition to providing standard pediatric basic life support (BLS) or advanced life support (ALS) care, it is reasonable for responders to administer intramuscular or intranasal naloxone. To address this public health crisis, the American Heart Association has presented new algorithms for the management of opioid-associated emergencies, highlighting that lay rescuers and trained responders should not delay activating emergency response systems while awaiting the patient's response to naloxone or other interventions (Merchant et al., 2020).

Other implications for public health and school health practice include the surveillance of overdose and polysubstance use trends and the illicit drug supply to track emerging threats. It is imperative to continue expanding the distribution of naloxone, enhance linkage to treatment, and elicit a multi-sectoral response which is critical for sustaining and expanding preliminary successes in reducing opioid-involved overdose deaths and specifically curtailing synthetic opioid–involved deaths and other emerging threats (Wilson et al., 2020). Early access to naloxone in the event of an opioid overdose can prevent loss of life and often is the first step in recovery from OUD. While outside the scope of this chapter, the school nurse is also involved in the follow-up and surveillance of the incidence and prevalence of substance use in their school/district. *(Please see addendum to Chapter 37, Substance Abuse screenings).*

Additionally, the stigma attached to OUD remains a fundamental hindrance in responding to the overdose crisis and should be compassionately addressed within school communities. The multiple dimensions of stigma (structural, public, enacted, internalized, and anticipated) result in poorer health outcomes. Stigma influences everyday attitudes, agenda-setting, and policymaking. Stigma compromises the financing of care for OUDs, shapes the distribution of access to care, and impinges upon care delivery (Tsai et al., 2019). It is crucial to embrace people with dignity and offer choices to help them find recovery when they are ready. Many people with SUD are from vulnerable populations, have been victims of trauma, or suffer from mental health conditions. Nurses are uniquely positioned to help combat this epidemic because they are often the first to connect with patients. The nurse "uses advocacy, education, and a supportive approach to honor the patient's right to self-determination, autonomy, and dignity" (ANA, 2016, p. 24). As the most trusted direct-care providers on the frontlines of the opioid epidemic, nurses play a vital role in preventing opioid overuse and dependence (ANA, 2018).

RESOURCES

American Heart Association. (2020). Opioid-associated emergency for healthcare providers algorithm. https://cpr.heart.org/-/media/CPR-Files/CPR-Guidelines-Files/Algorithms/AlgorithmOpioidHC_ Provider_200615.pdf

National Association of School Nurses. (2023). Naloxone in Schools Toolkit. https://learn.nasn.org/courses/58011#

Substance Abuse and Mental Health Services Administration (SAMHSA) Opioid Overdose Toolkit. HHS Publication No. (SMA) 18 4742. First printed 2013. Revised 2014, 2016, 2018. https://store.samhsa.gov/sites/default/files/d7/priv/sma18-4742.pdf

REFERENCES

Alexander G., Stoller K., Haffaiee R., & Saloner, B. (2020). An epidemic during a pandemic: Opioid use disorder and Covid-19. *Annals of Internal Medicine*. https://doi.org/10.7326/M20-1141

American Nurses Association and American Society for Pain Management Nursing. (2016). *Scope and standards of practice: Pain management nursing* (2nd ed.). Authors.

American Nurses Association Ethics Advisory Board. (2018, October 29) ANA position statement: The ethical responsibility to manage pain and the suffering it causes. *OJIN: The Online Journal of Issues in Nursing, 24*(1). https://doi.org/10.3912/OJIN.Vol24No01PoSCol01

Calihan J. B., & Levy S. (2022, August 1). Coronavirus disease pandemic and adolescent substance use. *Current Opinion in Pediatrics, 34*(4), 334-340. https://pubmed.ncbi.nlm.nih.gov/35836392/

Centers for Disease Control and Prevention, Emergency Preparedness and Response, Health Alert Network (2020). *Increase in fatal drug overdoses across the United States driven by synthetic opioids before and during the covid-19 pandemic*. No. CDCHAN-00438. https://emergency.cdc.gov/han/2020/han00438.asp

Centers for Disease Control and Prevention, National Center for Injury Prevention and Control. (2022a). *Understanding the opioid overdose epidemic*. https://www.cdc.gov/opioids/basics/epidemic.html

Centers for Disease Control and Prevention, National Center for Injury Prevention and Control, Division of Drug Overdose Prevention. (2023). *Life-saving naloxone*. https://www.cdc.gov/stopoverdose/naloxone/index.html#print

Davis, C. (2021, February). Opioid misuse and overdose prevention, 50-state survey, legal interventions to reduce overdose mortality: Naloxone access laws. *Network for Public Health Law.* https://www.networkforphl.org/wp-content/uploads/2021/05/NAL-Final-4-29.pdf

Food and Drug Administration. (2023). FDA Approves First Over-the-Counter Naloxone Nasal Spray [press release]. https://www.fda.gov/news-events/press-announcements/fda-approves-first-over-counter-naloxone-nasal-spray

Ford, A., Pomykacz, C., Veliz, P., Esteban McCabe, S., & Boyd, C. (2018, January). Sports involvement, injury history, and non-medical use of prescription opioids among college students: An analysis with a national sample. American Journal of Addictions, 27(1),15-22. https://doi.org/10.1111/ajad.12657

Friedman, J., Godvin, M., Shover, C.L., Gone, J.P., Hansen H, Schriger, & D.L. (2022). Trends in drug overdose deaths among US adolescents, January 2010 to June 2021. *JAMA, 327*(14), 1398–1400. https://doi.org/10.1001/jama.2022.2847

Merchant, R., Topjian, A., Panchal, A., Cheng, A., Aziz, K., Betg, K., Lavonas, E., & Magid, D. (2020, October 20). Part 1: Executive summary: 2020 American Heart Association guidelines for cardiopulmonary resuscitation and emergency cardiovascular care, *Circulation, 142*(16), Supp 2. https://www.ahajournals.org/doi/10.1161/CIR.0000000000000918

National Association of School Nurses. (2020). *Naloxone in the school setting* (Position Statement). Author. https://www.nasn.org/nasn-resources/professional-practice-documents/position-statements/ps-naloxone

National Federation of State High School Associations. (2018). *High school sports participation has increased for 29th consecutive year.* https://www.nfhs.org/articles/high-school-sports-participation-increases-for-29th-consecutive-year/

National Institute on Drug Abuse. (2022, December 15). *Most reported substance use among adolescents held steady in 2022.* https://nida.nih.gov/news-events/news-releases/2022/12/most-reported-substance-use-among-adolescents-held-steady-in-2022

Substance Abuse and Mental Health Services Administration. (2018). *Opioid overdose prevention toolkit.* https://store.samhsa.gov/sites/default/files/d7/priv/sma18-4742.pdf

Substance Abuse and Mental Health Services Administration. (2021). Key substance use and mental HHS Publication No. PEP21-07-01-003, NSDUH Series H-56). *Center for Behavioral Health Statistics and Quality, Substance Abuse and Mental Health Services Administration.* https://www.samhsa.gov/data/

Tsai A., Kiang, M., Barnett, M., Beletsky, L., Keyes, K., McGinty, E., Smith, L., Strathdee, S., Wakeman, S., & Venkataramani, A. (2019, November 26). Stigma as a fundamental hindrance to the United States opioid overdose crisis response. *PLoS Medicine, 16*(11). https://doi.org/10.1371/journal.pmed.1002969

United States Drug Enforcement Administration. (2022). *Fentanyl awareness.* https://www.dea.gov/fentanylawareness

Wilson, N., Kariisa, M., Seth, P., Smith, H. IV, & Davis, N.L. (2020). Drug and opioid-involved overdose deaths — United States, 2017–2018 (2020*). Morbidity and Mortality Weekly Report, 69*(11);290–297. http://dx.doi.org/10.15585/mmwr.mm6911a4

Chapter 36

SCHOOL HEALTH SCREENINGS

Kimberly Lacey, DNSc, MSN, RN, CNE, CNL*
Kelly Martinez, EdD, MSN, APRN, FNP-C*

DESCRIPTION OF ISSUE

School health screenings enable the school nurse to uncover potential health issues in students. When conducted at regularly scheduled periods in the student's educational careers, screenings provide the opportunity to support students' health through education and, as necessary, referrals to appropriate health providers. These health inspections are not substitutes for regular health care or intended to diagnose medical problems. They are a secondary public health prevention strategy e used for the early detection of potential health needs and appropriate referrals and prevention of more serious health issues. The American Academy of Pediatrics (AAP) (Holmes et al., 2016) recognizes the school nurse as a collaborative healthcare team member. It supports the comprehensive role of the school nurse in managing chronic health problems, promoting health and well-being, and conducting school health screenings to identify students with health needs at an early phase. While there are specific recommendations for routine screening in schools, the school nurse is also responsible for initiating non-routine screening if a potential problem is suspected.

School health screenings date back to the end of the 19th century (Allensworth et al., 1997). Health care was initially introduced into schools to identify students with communicable diseases and prevent further transmission of these illnesses. Screenings soon expanded to include all students to identify children with vision problems (Allensworth et al., 1997). Over time, although state-specific, these screenings have broadened to include checking hearing, height, weight, blood pressure, dentition, posture, back (scoliosis), and vision. In response to upward trends in mental health issues and suicide among school-age children, screening in these areas has become common practice on an as-needed basis. More recently, during the COVID-19 pandemic, school nurses experienced an increase in their responsibilities in the school community, including implementing strategies for mitigation, screening, testing, and developing educational programs for students and staff. Providing emotional support to school community members as they endured social isolation and increased mental health issues. In addition to direct care, they were involved with data collection, policy development, implementation, and contact tracing (Cook et al., 2023; McIntosh et al., 2023; & Lowe et al., 2023). (*See Chapters 34 & 38 for more information on mental health and suicide*).

The connection between student health and improved academic achievement is well established (Basch, 2011). Because of this connection to increased academic performance and improved student health, screenings should be used to identify health concerns before they escalate into more serious health problems. Health Barriers to Learning (HBLs) refer to health conditions that, if not identified and addressed early, can negatively impact student learning (Gracy et al., 2017, p.5). Based on their high prevalence, the seven conditions identified as HBLs include "uncontrolled asthma, uncorrected vision problems, unaddressed hearing loss, dental problems, persistent hunger, certain untreated mental health and behavioral problems, and effects of lead exposure" (p.5). However, currently, no national school health screening laws or requirements exist;

---

*Original author: Lee-Ann Halbert, EdDc, JD, RN, MSN, CNM, NCSN (2017) rather, they are controlled at the local level, either by state or within each school district, and vary from state to state (Galemore et al., 2019; National Association of State Boards of Education [NASBE], n.d.). Gracy et al. (2018) examined states' screening requirements across the United States and found that none have guidelines that address the seven priority HBLs, and in 29 states screening in schools is inadequate.

The potential for legal issues related to screenings is based on multiple concerns, including knowledge of individual state requirements for screenings, who may perform the screenings, and what to do with the screening results. For example, with the increased presence of unlicensed assistive personnel in schools, school nurses need to understand regulations around delegation versus assignment (*See Chapter 4 for more information on delegation*). Parental refusal of the screening of their child is also a legal consideration. (*See Chapter 22 for more information on parental refusal*).

As a general guideline, school nurses must know their state and school districts' screening requirements. Failure to screen students, as indicated, can harm their educational development (Galemore et al., 2019). Although no examples of case law could be found related to health screenings in schools or parental refusal of screenings, school nurses must be aware of potential legal issues.

BACKGROUND

Failure to screen properly or follow up as necessary raises the possibility of a legal challenge. Compliance with the screening laws, regulations, and policies and performing these examinations with the clinical knowledge of why they were introduced into the school setting can reduce the risk of legal challenges. A separate regulatory issue concerns consent for school health care, including screenings. School nurses are directed to consult their individual state laws, regulations, and school district policies to determine if minor school students may consent to or decline health screens or if parent/guardian consent is required. If permitted under state laws and regulations, a state or individual school district may require parents/guardians and students to opt out of school health care, including screening. Otherwise, it may be assumed that the student and parent/guardian has consented to the screening.

While the laws vary on the state level, on the federal level, the Individuals with Disability Education Improvement Act 2004 (IDEIA, 2004) includes the "Child Find" component (20 U.S.C. 1412(a)(3)). This section requires that a school system locate and identify students eligible for special education services. School health screenings are one element to meeting this requirement.

Although health screenings conducted by school nurses fall under the general umbrella of "screenings," each type has its history, value, recommended schedule, and how it is to be completed. Furthermore, not all health screenings will be required in every state or school district. For these reasons, the background of the individual screenings will be discussed within each screening section.

Vision Screenings

Among the identified variables that affect student performance is vision ability, an area of clinical need that the school nurse can identify. Addressing student vision needs has been identified as one method to improve academic achievement across all student demographic groups (Basch, 2011). According to the Centers for

Disease Control and Prevention (CDC) (2022b, bullet 3), "approximately 6.8% of children younger than 18 years in the United States have a diagnosed eye and vision condition. Nearly 3 percent of children younger than 18 are blind or visually impaired, defined as having trouble seeing even when wearing glasses or contact lenses."

Research demonstrates the direct relationship between vision problems and compromised academic success (Alvarez-Perregrina et al., 2020). Therefore, identifying students with vision needs can lead to higher academic success when coupled with appropriate referrals and follow-up care. Vision screening by the school nurse or trained volunteer, if permitted by state or school district law/policy, is one component of eye care, in addition, to care provided by professional eye specialists. The multiple components of vision screens can include checking visual acuity and inspecting the eye area (American Association for Pediatric Ophthalmology & Strabismus [AAPOS], 2016a). While case law was not located, the multiple components associated with the screenings raise the possibility of a legal challenge if a school nurse fails to perform a scheduled vision screen and referral and any effect this failure may have had on academic achievement.

Hearing Screenings

Auditory acuity is another need for students to achieve academically at optimal levels. "School-age hearing screenings are an integral tool in identifying children with hearing loss who were not identified at birth, lost to follow-up, or who developed hearing loss later" (The American Speech-Language-Hearing Association, 2023, para 1). The link between hearing impairment and lower mathematical achievement is well established (Santos & Cordes, 2021; Shusterman et al., 2022). Easterbrooks & Beal-Alvarez (2012) point to similar findings related to students' hearing loss and reading ability in their study. These authors also point to the historical data correlating that students with lower levels of hearing loss achieved a lower academic level. More recently, Moore et al. (2020) found an association among impaired hearing and auditory perceptions, cognition, and communication among children 6-11 years old with minimal to mild hearing loss. Like vision screens, missing a hearing screen and a student's potential for lower academic achievement may be a cause for concern, although no such cases were located.

Scoliosis Screening

Scoliosis screening in schools dates back to the 1960s (Grivas et al., 2007). Although typically performed to screen for scoliosis, the student's back examinations were previously done for a posture check for disease-related issues (Jakubowski & Alexy, 2014).

Screening for scoliosis remains an unsettled topic among healthcare professionals. Evidence in support of screening is inconclusive, with no clear association with clinical outcomes in adulthood (U.S. Preventive Task Force [USPTF], 2018; Płaszewski et al.,2020), particularly related to costs associated with screening programs and unnecessary exposure of adolescents and teens to radiation (Oetgen et al., 2021). However, recent studies demonstrate the effectiveness of bracing in slowing the progression of the condition and preventing surgery, suggesting that scoliosis screening is still a role for schools (Oetgen et al., 2021).

The manner of completing a scoliosis screening varies among practitioners. A table in the updated clinical practice guidelines developed by the USPTF (2018) provides a summary. Although many states (>50%) presently have laws or regulations for screenings by a school nurse, many do not (USPTF, 2018).

Weight and Body Mass Index (BMI)

Childhood obesity is a serious problem in the United States. The CDC estimated that between 2017 to 2021, obesity affected about 14.7 million children in the U.S. During this timeframe, the prevalence of obesity in children ages 2 to 5 years was 12.7%, 20.7% among 6 -to 11-year-olds, and 22.2% among 12- to 19-year-olds. Obesity leads to hypertension, high cholesterol, type 2 diabetes, asthma, sleep apnea, and joint problems (CDC, 2020b). School nurses can contribute to school-based obesity interventions due to their clinical expertise, accessibility to students, and student and family rapport (Schroeder & Smaldone, 2017).

The AAP has published its first comprehensive obesity guidance in 15 years, discussing moving away from watchful waiting and how obesity treatment is safe and effective. Evidence-based recommendations on medical care for those age two and older are included in the new *Clinical Practice Guideline for the Evaluation and Treatment of Children and Adolescents with Obesity* (Hampl et al., 2023).

BMI screenings at well-child visits are recommended for managing and tracking overweight and obesity in children. Other health visit opportunities can be used to assess BMI outside the well-child visit (Hampl et al., 2023). Key factors in conducting screenings in different settings (including schools) include asking permission from the parents/caregivers and client and avoiding labels such as "obese" in front of the client. Neutral words should be used in patient conversation and education. Even when using non-stigmatizing language, discussions on weight may elicit strong emotional responses that must be validated while keeping the focus on the child's health (Hampl et al., 2023). School nurses are usually responsible for obtaining a BMI, identifying students with potential obesity concerns, and informing parents of their child's weight status (Ruggieri et al., 2020; CDC, 2022b).

Although many schools have a nurse available to conduct BMI screening, there is no assurance that a school nurse is available for all BMI screenings. Among the concerns about conducting BMI screening in schools is the proper use of the data, ongoing evaluation of the BMI screening program, and ensuring the privacy of students screened for BMI (CDC, n.d.). The CDC does not recommend for or against BMI measurement programs in schools. Still, it does suggest that schools consider having certain parameters in place before utilizing a BMI measurement program:
- A safe and supportive environment for students of all body sizes.
- A comprehensive set of strategies to prevent and reduce obesity.
- Use recommendations from the *School Health Guidelines to Promote Healthy Eating and Physical Activity*.
- Safeguards addressing the primary concerns about such BMI measurement programs (CDC, 2022a).

Other concerns about BMI screening include a lack of proper parent knowledge of using the BMI results appropriately and effectively and students being labeled because of any particular BMI result (Jones et al., 2018). To address these risks, the CDC offers additional recommendations that include providing detailed explanations for how to use BMI screening results to parents and ensuring follow-up with a student who receives a referral for high BMI be implemented (CDC, 2022a).

Blood Pressure Screening

According to the CDC and the AAP, there is a high prevalence of children with hypertension (Flynn et al, 2017). Hypertension in the pediatric population is common in those with obesity. In addition to obesity, these children often have other risk factors that could increase the likelihood of developing heart disease, stroke, and other health problems during childhood and later in life (CDC, 2020a; Flynn et al., 2017).

The CDC believes that 2.6% of children (800,000) in the United States have high blood pressure, and about half of these children are obese. Youth ages 18 to 19 make up about half of the increase, with males comprising more than two-thirds of that group. Furthermore, the CDC has estimated that 1.3 million individuals aged 12 to 19, or 1 in 25 youth, have high blood pressure, which is important for the school nurse to appreciate because, as the CDC explains, "in a classroom of 30 youth, one person would have hypertension, and about three more would have elevated blood pressure." (CDC, 2020a, para 5).

Healthy Children (2017) discusses how the AAP and the National Heart, Lung, and Blood Institute recommend that children have yearly screenings for high blood pressure, starting at age 3, at their yearly physical exams. However, school nurses intervene with students to advance their health. Armed with the knowledge of pediatric hypertension, school nurses can screen for high blood pressure and make appropriate recommendations for their students.

Dental Screenings

Oral health is a fundamental component of general health. The National Institutes of Health estimates that 20% to 30% of children and adolescents in the U.S. have chronic health conditions. Most chronic childhood conditions are dental caries, asthma, diabetes, and obesity. Dental is the most common, occurring 5 to 8 times more frequently than asthma, the second most common condition (Jackson et al., 2011). Caries (cavities) are common among children in the United States. Children with poor oral health tend to be absent from school more than those with good dental health (CDC, 2022a). The CDC (2022d) states that more than half of children aged 6 to 8 have had caries in at least one of their primary teeth, and more than half of adolescents aged 12 to 19 have had a carie in at least one of their permanent teeth.

Furthermore, youth aged 5 to 19 years from low-income families are twice as likely to have caries as children from higher-income households (CDC, 2023). In 2022, the World Health Organization (WHO) released *Global Oral Health Status Report: Towards Universal Health Coverage for Oral Health by 2030*. This report discussed how untreated caries often cause infection and dental pain, affect speech and sleep, and may affect how a child eats, which can affect the child's growth and development. Poor dental health affects students' learning and school attendance, affecting educational performance. An estimated 34 million school hours are lost yearly due to unplanned /emergency dental care (Naavaal & Kelekar, 2018).

Caries are preventable. Brushing teeth daily reduces the risk of developing caries, and using fluoride varnish, which can prevent about one-third of caries in primary teeth. Children living in areas where tap water is fortified with fluoride are at a lower risk of developing caries. Dental sealants can also prevent cavities (CDC, 2023). Therefore, school nurses can play a key role in dental education and dental screenings/referrals to promote optimal dental practices and decrease negative outcomes of poor oral health.

Mental Health Screenings

Mental health challenges for students have increased over the years, particularly during the COVID-19 pandemic. School nurses, in collaboration with other school personnel, are often involved in screenings for mental health concerns. Some school nurses are actively engaged in initiatives, such as SBIRT (screening, brief intervention, referral for treatment). (*See Chapter 34 for more information on mental health needs*).

IMPLICATIONS FOR SCHOOL NURSE PRACTICE

As noted, multiple types of screenings may be required in the school setting or are part of an overarching wellness program based on the unique needs of the school community. These screenings may be controlled by state laws, regulations, or school district policies requiring the screens, or they may be silent on the topic. With so many types of screens, the school nurse must become familiar with the state and local school district requirements and the method for performing each screen. Specialty healthcare providers who address each issue have their own training manuals and protocols available to school nurses, or these may be available through a state department or agency. Additionally, the National Association of School Nurses (NASN) offers a variety of resources for many of the screens. The key issue here is to be properly trained in performing the screening correctly. An incorrectly done screen can lead to false findings. A primary point to remember is that if the school nurse performs a screening, the nurse should implement an appropriate intervention with the information gained from the screening, including a referral when indicated or required by the law, regulations, or applicable policy. It is useless or potentially harmful to ignore findings from a screen. A nurse who ignores positive results may lead a parent or guardian to assume the findings are negative.

At the same time, school nurses must also respect the autonomy of the students and their parents/guardians. Not every student – or student's parent/guardian – may want the school nurse to complete a screen. Individual school districts will have their own instructions regarding how permission must be obtained for the screens, whether to require affirmative permission by the parent/guardian, or whether there is an "opt-out" requirement for parents/guardians. The student's desires must also be considered, though they may not be controlling when evaluating whether to complete a screen. Facilitating positive attitudes and an increased awareness of health screenings in community-and school-based settings may influence participation rates (Jones et al., 2019).

When conducting the screens, proper personnel should be used for the screening process. In addition to ensuring that those conducting the screens have the necessary education and training to perform them accurately, confidentiality issues must also be noted. For some screens, such as scoliosis, a screening protocol in the school district may designate physical education teachers as acceptable for screening the students *if they have been properly trained for the role and are permitted under state laws or regulations*. Bear in mind, however, that these non-nursing personnel, and any other volunteers who assist the nurse, may not understand confidentiality issues when conducting screens. The school nurse should be certain to abide by the school district policies and protocols when allowing non-nursing personnel to participate in the screening process, including instruction regarding maintaining the confidentiality of student information. The Family Educational Rights and Privacy Act (FERPA), a federal law, prohibits the disclosure of information obtained in the screenings by the nurse or any individual assisting in the screenings to anyone without a legitimate educational interest in knowing the information (FERPA, 2013).

CONCLUSION

With the overwhelming research pointing to the academic benefits of a healthier student population, screenings benefit the students and are a valuable use of a school nurse's time. Although the students are a "captive audience" for the school nurse's screening efforts, school nurses must also ask the students and families for permission to complete the screenings. Compliance with local school district policies, state laws and regulations, and federal laws should guide the school nurse's practice for performing screens and providing appropriate follow-up. Failure to complete screens as directed, performing them improperly, or failure to notify parents when required may have legal implications for the school nurse and the school district. Finally, school nurses need to advocate for and seek out professional development on conducting screenings to support the implementation of screening programs and the competency of all screeners.

RESOURCES

Screening requirements will be specific to the individual states and, possibly, each school district. In addition to the information provided here, the school nurse should search for support information specific to the state and school district, especially to ensure that information is the most current and up-to-date.

Action for Healthy Kids. https://www.actionforhealthykids.org/

Active School. https://www.activeschoolsus.org/

American Heart Association. Voices for Healthy Kids: making each day healthier for all children! https://voicesforhealthykids.org/

American Heart Association. High Blood Pressure in Children. https://www.heart.org/en/health-topics/high-blood-pressure/why-high-blood-pressure-is-a-silent-killer/high-blood-pressure-in-children
American Association for Pediatric Ophthalmology & Strabismus. AAPOS has summarized vision screenings for all states in a table available at https://www.aapos.org/resources/state_by_state_vision_screening_requirements/

AAPOS (State by state vision screening requirements). It should be noted that individual states may have updated their vision screening requirements since the table was compiled. School nurses are directed to review the information for alignment with current laws and regulations. https://www.asha.org/advocacy/state/school-age-hearing-screening/

Centers for Disease Control and Prevention. Body Mass Index (BMI) | Healthy Weight, Nutrition, and Physical Activity. https://www.cdc.gov/healthyweight/assessing/bmi/index.html

Centers for Disease Control and Prevention: Healthy Schools
https://www.cdc.gov/healthyschools/index.htm

Centers for Disease Control and Prevention School Health Guidelines
https://www.cdc.gov/healthyschools/npao/strategies.htm

Columbia University, School of Public Health. https://www.publichealth.columbia.edu/news/majority-u-s-states-fail-require-adequate-health-screenings-students

National Association of School Nurses has materials available on the individual types of screens available at https://www.nasn.org/home

National Association of School Nurses. (2016). *Vision and eye health*. https://www.nasn.org/ToolsResources/VisionandEyeHealth

National Association of State Boards of Education State Policy Database. https://statepolicies.nasbe.org/health/categories/health-services

Case Law

Parsons v. Mullica Township Board of Education (2016)

In 2016, a New Jersey case, Parsons v. Mullica Township Board of Education, applied that state's Tort Claims Act (TCA) in dismissing a claim against the school nurse for failure to inform parents of the results of a vision screen on their child. This case was not decided on its merits; rather, the case was dismissed based on the immunity of the school district for which the nurse worked. No recent case law was located.

REFERENCES

Allensworth, D., Lawson, E., Nicholson, L., & Wyche, J. (Eds). (1997). *Schools and health: Our nation's investment.* National Academy Press.

Alvarez-Peregrina, C., Sánchez-Tena, M. Á., Andreu-Vázquez, C., & Villa-Collar, C. (2020). Visual Health and Academic Performance in School-Aged Children. *International journal of environmental research and public health*, 17(7), 2346. https://doi.org/10.3390/ijerph17072346

American Academy of Pediatrics (2016). Policy statement: Role of the school nurse in providing school health services. *Pediatrics, 121,* 1052-1056. https://doi.org/10.1542/peds.2008-0382 https://doi.org/10.1542/peds.2016-0852

American Academy of Pediatric Dentistry. (2022). *Policy on school-entrance oral health examinations. The reference manual of pediatric dentistry.* https://www.aapd.org/globalassets/media/policies_guidelines/p_schoolexms.pdf

American Association for Pediatric Ophthalmology and Strabismus. (2016a). *Vision screening recommendations.* https://www.aapos.org/terms/conditions/131

American Association for Pediatric Ophthalmology and Strabismus. (2016b). *State-by-state vision screening requirements*. https://www.aapos.org/resources/state_by_state_vision_screening_requirements/

Basch, C. (2011). Healthier students are better learners: A missing link in school reforms to close the achievement gap. *The Journal of School Health, 81*(10), 593 – 598. http://www.equitycampaign.org/i/a/document/12557_EquityMattersVol6_Web03082010.pdf

Centers for Disease Control and Prevention. (n.d.). *Body mass index measurement in school: BMI executive summary*. https://www.cdc.gov/healthyschools/obesity/bmi/pdf/bmi_execsumm.pdf

Centers for Disease Control and Prevention. (2020a). *High blood pressure in kids and teens*. https://www.cdc.gov/bloodpressure/youth.htm#prin

Centers for Disease Control and Prevention. (2020b). *Childhood obesity facts. Prevalence of childhood obesity in the United States.* https://www.cdc.gov/obesity/data/childhood.html#print

Centers for Disease Control and Prevention. (2022a*). Body mass index (BMI) measurement in schools*. https://www.cdc.gov/healthyschools/obesity/bmi/pdf/bmi_execsumm.pdf

Centers for Disease Control and Prevention. (2022b). *Fast facts about vision loss*. https://www.cdc.gov/visionhealth/basics/ced/fastfacts.htm#:~:text=Approximately%206.8%25%20of%20children%20younger,wearing%20glasses%20or%20contact%20lenses

Centers for Disease Control and Prevention. (2023). *Children's oral health*. https://www.cdc.gov/healthyschools/npao/oralhealth.htm

Flynn, J. T., Kaelber, D. C., Baker-Smith, C. M., Blowey, D., Carroll, A. E., Daniels, S. R., Ferranti, S., Dionne, J.M., Falkner, B., Flinn, S.K., Gidding, S.S., Goodwin, C., Leu, M. G., Powers, M.E., Rea, C., Samuels, J., Simasek, M., Thaker, V.V., Urbina, E.M. & AAP Subcommittee On Screening And Management Of High Blood Pressure In Children. (2017). Clinical practice guideline for screening and management of high blood pressure in children and adolescents. *Pediatrics, 140*(3), e20171904. https://doi.org/10.1542/peds.2017-1904

Galemore, C., Kimel, L., and Tedder, G. (2019). Health Promotion and Screenings for School-age Children. In J. Selekman, R.A. Shannon, & C.F. Yonkaitis. (Eds.), *School Nursing a Comprehensive Text*. C. FA Davis

Gottardis, L., Nunes, T., & Lunt, I. (2011). A synthesis of research on deaf and hearing children's mathematical achievement. *Deafness and Education International, 13*(3), 131-150. http://dx.doi.org/10.1179/1557069X11Y.0000000006

Grivas, T.B., Wade, M.H., Negrini, S., O'Brien, J.P., Maruyama, T., Hawes, M.C., Rigo, M., Weiss, H.R., Kotwicki, T., Vasiliadis, E.S., Sulam, L.N. & Neuhous, T. (2007). SOSORT consensus paper: School screening for scoliosis. Where are we today? *Scoliosis, 2*(17). https://doi.org/10.1186/1748-7161-2-17

Hampl, S. E., Hassink, S. G., Skinner, A. C., Armstrong, S. C., Barlow, S. E., Bolling, C. F., Edwards, K.C., Eneli, I., Hamre, R., Joseph, M.M., Lunsford, D., Mendonca, E., Michalsky, M.P., Mirza, N., Ochoa, E.R., Sharifi, M., Staiano, A.E., Weedn, A. E., Flinn, S.K., Lindros, J. & Okechukwu, K., (2023). Clinical practice guideline for the evaluation and treatment of children and adolescents with obesity. *Pediatrics, 152*(2), *e2022060640*. https://doi.org/10.1542/peds.2022-060640

Healthy Children. (2017). *Screening & treating kids for high blood pressure: AAP report explained*. https://www.healthychildren.org/English/health-issues/conditions/heart/Pages/High-Blood-Pressure-in-Children.aspx

Holmes, A. S., Allison, M., Ancona, R., Attisha, E., Beers, N., De Pinto, C., Gorski, P., Kjolhede, C., Lerner, M., Weiss-Harrison, A., & Young, T., (2016, June). Role of the school nurse in providing school health services. *Pediatrics 137*(6), e20160852. https://doi.org/10.1542/peds.2016-0852

Individuals with Disability Education Improvement Act (2004), Child Find, 20 U.S.C. 1412(a) (3)

Easterbrooks, S.R., & Beal-Alvarez, J.S. (2012). States' reading outcomes of students who are deaf and hard of hearing. *American Annals of the Deaf, 157*, 27-40. https://doi.org/10.1353/aad.2012.1611

Jackson, S., Vann, W.F., Kotch, J.B., Pahel, B.T., & Lee, J. Y. (2011). Impact of poor oral health on children's school attendance and performance. *American Journal of Public Health, 101*(10), 1900 – 1906. https://doi.org/2010.2105/AJPH.2010.200915h

Jakubowski, T. L., & Alexy, E. M. (2014). Does school scoliosis screening make the grade? NASN school nurse, 29(5), 258–265. https://doi.org/10.1177/1942602X14542131

Jones, M., Huffer, C., Adams, T., Jones, L., & Church, B. (2018). BMI health report cards: parents' perceptions and reactions. *Health Promotion Practice, 19*(6), 896-904. https://doi.org/10.1177/1524839917749489

Jones E., Lee, H., Cho, K. (2019). Exploring Parents' Participation Decisions on School-Based Health Screenings in Mountainous Regions. *Korean J Fam Med. 40*(4),220–226. Epub 2019 Jul 15. PMID: 31304691; PMCID: PMC6669384. https://doi.org/10.4082/kjfm.18.0201

Moore, D., Zobay, O. & Ferguson, M. (2020). Minimal and mild hearing loss in children: Association with auditory perception, cognition, and communication problems. *Ear and Hearing, 41*(4), 720-732. https://doi.org/10.1097/AUD.0000000000000802

National Association of State Boards of Education (n.d.). State health policies. https://statepolicies.nasbe.org/

Naavaal, S., & Kelekar, U. (2018). School hours lost due to acute/unplanned dental care. *Health Behavior and Policy Review, 5*(2), 66-73. https://www.aapd.org/globalassets/naaval-school-days-lost-2018.pdf

Oetgen, M.E., Heyer, J. H. & Kelly, S. M. (2021, May1). Scoliosis screening. *Journal of the American Academy of Orthopaedic Surgeons,29*(9),p 370-379. https://doi.org/10.5435/JAAOS-D-20-00356

Płaszewski, M., Grantham, W., & Jespersen, E. (2020). Screening for scoliosis - new recommendations, old dilemmas, no straight solutions. *World Journal of Orthopedics, 11*(9),364 - 379. https://doi.org/10.5312/wjo.v11.i9.364

Ruggieri, D. G., Bass, S. B., Alhajji, M., & Gordon, T. F. (2020). Understanding parents' perceptions of school-based BMI screening and BMI report cards using perceptual mapping: Implications for school nurses. *The Journal* of *School Nursing, 36*(2), 144-156. https://doi.org/10.1177/1059840518789243

Santos, S., & Cordes S. (2022, Jan). Math abilities in deaf and hard of hearing children: The role of language in developing number concepts. *Psychological Review,.;129*(1),199-211. https://doi.org/10.1037/rev0000303

Schroeder, K., & Smaldone, A. (2017). What barriers and facilitators do school nurses experience when implementing an obesity intervention? *The Journal of School Nursing, 33*(6), 456-466.

Schroeder, K., Travers, J., & Smaldone, A. (2016). Are school nurses an overlooked resource in reducing childhood obesity? A systematic review and meta-analysis. *The Journal of School Health, 86* (5), 309-321. https://doi.org/10.1111/josh.12386

Shusterman, A., Peretz-Lange, R., Berkowitz, T., & Carrigan, E. (2022, September).The development of early numeracy in deaf and hard of hearing children acquiring spoken language. *Child Development, 93*(5), e468-e483. https://doi.org/10.1111/cdev.13793

U.S. Preventive Services Task Force. (2018). Screening for adolescent idiopathic scoliosis: U.S. Preventive Services Task Force recommendation statement. *JAMA, Volume 319,* 165-172. https://doi.org/10.1001/jama.2017.19342

World Health Organization. (2022). Global oral health status report: towards universal health coverage for oral health by 2030. *Geneva: World Health Organization.* https://www.who.int/publications/i/item/9789240061484

Chapter 37

CONDUCTING SUBSTANCE ABUSE SCREENINGS

Patricia Endsley, MSN, PhD, RN, NCSN

DESCRIPTION OF ISSUE

As described in Chapter 28, *Examining Children in the School Setting*, physical examination and assessment of children in the school setting presents special challenges and considerations for school nurses and administrators. Legal principles that apply to routine examinations also apply to specialized assessments. School nurses and administrators must understand this when evaluating students for altered mental status or suspicion of substance use. As with a physical exam for illness or injury, the extent of the assessment must be consistent with the student's constitutional rights, state laws, and local policies. Chapter 28 discusses assessment appropriateness, timeliness, referral to emergency treatment, and outside services.

Although legal mandates apply to all examinations, this chapter specifically addresses student rights and school nurse scope of practice issues when screening for substance abuse. Resources have been provided to supplement school district policy, law enforcement, and other applicable practice mandates. Guidelines are provided by the: National Association of School Nurses (NASN), state nursing statutes/regulations, the American Academy of Pediatrics (APA), and the National School Boards Association (NSBA).

In addition to situational substance use assessments, school nurses might also conduct routine screenings. Examples include scheduled or random drug testing for athletes and participation in comprehensive public health student substance use screening programs. The athletic department, guidance counselors, social workers, or community agencies may also conduct these programs. Community members are often stakeholders and provide input into these programs.

BACKGROUND

The 2022 National Center for Drug Abuse Statistics (NCDAS) indicates that one in eight teenagers abused illicit substances, with alcohol being the most common. Each year between 2010 and 2019, approximately 500 teens died from drug overdoses. During the COVID pandemic, teen overdose deaths rose exponentially. In 2020, the rate almost doubled to 954. In 2021, that number was 108,000. The majority of these deaths involved opioids, such as illicitly manufactured fentanyl (IMF) (Ahmed, 2023).

In response, most school districts address assessments of students believed to be impaired through policy or code of conduct (National School Boards Association [NSBA], 2019). In accordance with state law, schools **may require** a student to undergo an impaired assessment during the school day or at school extracurricular activities if there is reasonable suspicion that they may be under the influence of a substance (NSBA, 2019). A comprehensive substance abuse assessment program might include urine, saliva, or hair drug testing.

The Student with Altered Mental Status

Any physical exam or assessment by a school nurse must:

1) assess the imminent health status of the student,

2) assess the level of contagiousness of the student's potential ailment,

3) assess the level of function of the student to determine whether the student can continue within the school setting at that time, and

4) communicate to the student and parent/guardian any current health concerns and recommendations for follow-up care.

(See Chapter 28 for more information on physical exams and Chapter 34 regarding Mental Health.)

A student can present with an altered mental status due to sleep deprivation, illness, injury, consumption of both legally prescribed and illicit substances, medication side effect, or an interaction of any of these factors. Examples include caffeine (energy products), over-the-counter medications (dextromethorphan), inhalants, cannabinoids, opiates, steroids, and alcohol. Social media challenges encouraging adolescents to take substances in extreme amounts often result in emergencies (Deitche & Burda, 2022; Patterson et al., 2017; Siegmund, 2022).

School nurses (and other school staff) who assess students for substance use must be trained in an evidence-based, systematic process such as *Drug Impairment Training for Education Professionals* (DITEP) (International Association of Police Chiefs, 2023). Policies and procedures must be developed to ensure both student and staff safety. This can include, for example, the requirement that another staff member or school resource officer be present during these assessments.

The response to a substance use assessment depends on the clinical presentation. In some evaluations, students can be discharged into the care of a parent or guardian. In other cases, the student must be sent to the Emergency Department. It is necessary to follow up with the student and parent/guardian for intervention and treatment referral (American Academy of Pediatrics [AAP], 2015; Substance Abuse and Mental Health Services Administration [SAMHSA], 2021).

Student Drug Testing and Screening

In Board of Education v. Earls (2002), the United States Supreme Court upheld the earlier *Vernonia School District 47J v. Action* (1995) opinion and ruled that student athletes may be tested randomly for drug use. A school district does not violate the Fourth Amendment when it requires drug testing for students who choose to engage in extracurricular activities there. Since this ruling, some school districts have expanded the testing to include nonathletic extracurricular activities and middle school students. Some districts have considered testing entire student bodies (Chen, 2022). In their reaffirmed 2015 statement, the American Academy of Pediatrics (AAP) discourages formal student drug testing programs as many are punitive and do not provide follow-up or referral to treatment (Levy et al., 2015).

The AAP and SAMHSA recommend an evidence-based screening process that incorporates referral to treatment such as Screening, Brief Intervention, and Referral to Treatment (SBIRT). SBIRT is an "integrated and comprehensive early intervention implemented in primary care and other settings to identify, reduce, and prevent substance use" (SAMHSA, 2021, p.1). SBIRT for adolescents incorporates the CRAFFT questionnaire, a tool validated for adolescents ages 12-18. CRAFFT stands for elements of specific risk factors: *Car, Relax, Alone, Forget, Friends, Trouble* (Boston Children's Hospital, Center for Adolescent Behavioral Health Research [CABHRe], 2018).

Legal Considerations

All children are entitled to certain rights, such as freedom of expression, privacy, freedom from unlawful search and seizure, accommodations for disabilities or pregnancy, freedom of religion, and freedom from discrimination. Those rights are subject to limitations, and the school nurse must be familiar with those rights and their limitations. Federal, state, and local laws and regulations, along with professional practice standards, must be considered when assessing a student believed to be under the influence of a substance (NSBA, 2019).

Consent and Privacy

Chapter 28 provides an overview of consent and privacy for routine physical assessments by the school nurse. The student may refuse to be assessed or participate in routine school population SBIRT screenings. Parents may also opt their child out of SBIRT screenings. In Massachusetts, for example, parents/guardians are sent notices prior to screening and asked to contact the designated school personnel if they wish to opt their child out. As with other routine screenings, consent is presumed g if the parent does not affirmatively opt the student out of that assessment (Massachusetts Department of Public Health [2021a). Minors might not require parental consent or even notification for substance use disorder issues. School nurses must know what the law is in their state.

Individual school policy, state law, parental consent, and law enforcement requirements inform the process. There can be additional considerations for students in the juvenile justice system. SBIRT screenings must take place in a confidential area, and student names should not be placed on written questionnaires (CABHRe, 2018).

Education records are protected under the Family Educational Rights and Privacy Act (FERPA) (U.S. Department of Education [USDE], 2021). Substance abuse screenings or testing conducted by a school-based health center or outside agency are subject to the Health Insurance Portability and Accountability Act of 1996 (HIPAA) (USDHHS, 2021). Federal Public Health law (imposes restrictions on the use and disclosure of substance use disorder patient records. Some conditions under which the records may be shared include:
- The patient has consented to the disclosure,
- Medical emergencies,
- Scientific research subject to regulations,
- Audits and evaluations subject to regulations, and
- Court orders. (Public Health, 42 CFR, §2.1) https://www.ecfr.gov/current/title-42/part-2/subpart-D)

Constitutional Considerations

The school nurse must practice within the confines of a student's federal and state constitutional rights, understanding that no constitutional right is absolute. For example, legitimate government interests, such as public safety or exigent circumstances, can provide exceptions. Each constitutional right must be evaluated within the context of a specific situation. Some rights under the U.S. Constitution include:

- The First Amendment:
  Congress shall make no law respecting an establishment of religion or prohibiting the free exercise thereof, or abridging the freedom of speech, or of the press; or the right of the people peaceably to assemble, and to petition the government for a redress of grievances (U.S. Const. amend. I).

  As with all constitutional rights, school officials must balance a student's right to free speech and assembly with the need to provide an educational environment. The U.S.S.C. noted in a 1969 decision that "*[F]irst Amendment rights, applied in light of the special characteristics of the school environment, are available to teachers and students. It can hardly be argued that either students or teachers shed their constitutional rights to freedom of speech or expression at the schoolhouse gate*" (*Tinker*, 1969, p. 506).

  Fifteen-year-old John Tinker, sixteen-year-old Christopher Eckhardt, and thirteen-year-old Mary Beth Tinker were students opposed to the Vietnam War. They planned to wear black armbands in school during the 1965 holidays. Upon learning of this plan, the principals of their schools adopted a policy that students would be asked to remove their armbands, and if they did not do so, they would be suspended. When the students wore their armbands and refused to remove them, they were suspended until they returned without them. The students' fathers filed a suit in federal court, seeking an injunction to prohibit the schools from disciplining their children and seeking damages. The case went to the U.S.S.C., which held that wearing armbands did not constitute disruption or interfere with the school's operation.

- The Fourth Amendment:
  The right of the people to be secure in their persons, houses, papers, and effects, against unreasonable searches and seizures, shall not be violated, and no Warrants shall issue, but upon probable cause, supported by Oath or affirmation, and particularly describing the place to be searched, and the persons or things to be seized (U.S. Const. amend. IV).

  This amendment protects a student from unreasonable searches and seizures **by the government**. Probable cause must exist **for the government** to search a student's person, car, home, digital information, or property. It does not prevent all searches and seizures – only those considered unreasonable. Generally, search and seizures require a showing of *probable cause*, meaning reasonable grounds. Schools are considered government actors, subject to the Fourth Amendment prohibitions.

  In a landmark 1985 decision, the U.S.S.C held that school officials do not need to obtain warrants before searching students if the search is reasonable under all circumstances. The Court held that a student's Fourth Amendment protections did not only apply to law enforcement personnel but to school officials as well. While recognizing that students have legitimate expectations of privacy at school, it ruled that those privacy expectations must be balanced against the school's need to maintain an educational environment (*New Jersey v. T.L.O., 1985*).

- The Fifth Amendment:

No person shall be held to answer for a capital or otherwise infamous crime, unless on a presentment or indictment of a Grand Jury, except in cases arising in the land or naval forces or the Militia, when in actual service in time of War or public danger; nor shall any person be subject for the same offense to be twice put in jeopardy of life or limb; nor shall be compelled in any criminal case to be a witness against himself, nor be deprived of life, liberty, or property, without due process of law; nor shall private property be taken for public use, without just compensation (U.S. Const. amend. V).

All of us have seen movies and television shows where police capture suspects and "Mirandize" them by saying, "*[Y]ou have the right to remain silent. Anything you say can and will be used against you in a court of law. You have the right to an attorney. If you cannot afford an attorney, one will be provided for you. Do you understand the rights I have just read to you? With these rights in mind, do you wish to speak to me?*" U.S. citizens have the right to legal counsel prior to participating in a criminal investigation and are entitled to these so-called "Miranda rights." "Miranda rights" come from the 1966 U.S.S.C. case, *Miranda v. Arizona (Miranda,* 1966).

On March 13, 1963, 23-year-old Ernesto Miranda was arrested in his home, taken to the police station, and interrogated without counsel. After two hours of questioning, he signed a confession admitting to kidnapping, robbery, and rape. Miranda had never been advised that he did not have to subject himself to interrogation without a lawyer. After his written confession was used as evidence, he was convicted of the charges and sentenced to 55 years in prison for each count. Miranda appealed the conviction, arguing that the confession should not have been admissible because he had not been advised of his rights. The Supreme Court of Arizona held that his rights were not violated because he had not specifically asked for a lawyer.

The U.S.S.C. disagreed, holding that:

> [I]t is clear that Miranda was not in any way apprised of his right to consult with an attorney and to have one present during the interrogation, nor was his right not to be compelled to incriminate himself effectively protected in any other manner. Without these warnings, the statements were inadmissible. The mere fact that he signed a statement that contained a typed-in clause stating that he had "full knowledge" of his "legal rights" does not approach the knowing and intelligent waiver required to relinquish constitutional rights (*Miranda*, 1966, p. 492).

After Miranda, it was unclear if Fifth Amendment rights applied to school students. This issue was addressed in *J. D. B. v. North Carolina* (2011). A thirteen-year-old seventh grader, J.D.B., was taken from his classroom and interrogated by his principal and the police for at least 30 minutes. Juvenile petitions charging him with felonies were contested. The public defender argued that J.D.B.'s statements were not voluntary because he had not been advised of his rights. The court held that his rights had not been violated because he was not in custody at the time he made the statements. He was adjudicated delinquent. The North Carolina Court of Appeals upheld that judgment, reasoning that age was not a factor in determining if a person was in custody.

On appeal, the U.S.S.C. noted that children are not adults. It sent the case back to determine if J.D.B. had been in custody, noting:

> It is beyond dispute that children will often feel bound to submit to police questioning when an adult in the same circumstances would feel free to leave. Seeing no reason for police officers or courts to blind themselves to that commonsense reality, we hold that a child's age properly informs the *Miranda* custody analysis (*J.D.B.*, 2011, p.264).

Zero tolerance policies regarding weapons or illicit substances raise due process concerns when they intersect with law enforcement. Students exposed to potential criminal charges might not know they have the right not to speak with custodial authorities. As noted above, young schoolchildren can feel intimidated by authority figures and incriminate themselves.

Two Fourth Amendment cases are related to student substance possession and use. The first case involves suspicion of an over-the-counter medication, while the second case details a student thought to be under the influence of an illicit substance.

Case #1

Safford Unified School District v. Redding, 557 U.S. 364 (2009)

Based on a tip by another student that she might have ibuprofen on her person in violation of school policy, 13-year-old Savana Redding was strip-searched by school officials. The school nurse participated in the search. Savana's mother subsequently filed suit against the school district, the assistant principal, an administrative assistant, and the school nurse for violating Savana's Fourth Amendment rights. The district court dismissed the case, finding no Fourth Amendment violation. On appeal, the Ninth Circuit used the test set out in *New Jersey v. T.L.O* discussed above and held that the strip search was unjustified. It reversed the dismissal of the assistant principal but upheld the dismissal of the administrative assistant and the school nurse.

The U.S.S.C. agreed that Savana's Fourth Amendment rights had been violated when school officials (including the school nurse) searched her underwear for non-prescription painkillers. The Court found the search unconstitutional as the intrusiveness was unreasonable but ruled that the assistant principal, the administrative assistant, and the nurse were protected by qualified immunity. It sent the case back for a determination of the school district's liability.

Case #2

Hedges v. Musco, 204 F.3d 109, 122 (3d Cir. 2000)

Tara Hedges was a high school student in 1996 when she was required to submit to blood and urine testing. As she entered math class, the teacher observed her to have: a flushed face, red and glassy eyes, and dilated pupils. She also appeared uncharacteristically talkative and outgoing. During class, Tara asked permission to go to the water fountain but was observed by the teacher to be going in the opposite direction. She disappeared around the corner and was gone for about 10 minutes. Her appearance and uncharacteristic behavior made the teacher suspect that she was under the influence of alcohol or a drug.

Per school policy, the teacher notified the school administration and had security escort Tara to the school nurse. The nurse testified that her first impression was that Tara was under the influence of a substance. Although vital signs were within normal limits except for an elevated blood pressure, and her pupils were normal, Tara's eyes were glassy and bloodshot.

She explained to the nurse and the principal that she had been crying. School security searched her locker and bag according to policy. They found some pills which Tara claimed were diet medication. The policy also required a parent or guardian to be notified and a medical examination arranged. When the school nurse asked Tara how to reach her parents, she could not remember her telephone number. The school nurse called her father, asking him to come to the school. When he arrived, the school nurse informed him that Tara was suspected of being under the influence of drugs or alcohol and that, per school policy, she would need drug and alcohol testing before returning to school.

Her father took her to the local urgent care that the school generally used, where she was tested for drugs and alcohol. The urgent care doctor, after examination, determined that she did not appear to be under the influence of a substance. The school nurse spoke with the urgent care center the following day and was overheard expressing surprise that the results were negative.

Tara's parents filed an action alleging that the math teacher, the school nurse, and the school principal violated her New Jersey Constitutional rights and U.S. Constitutional Fourth and Fourteenth Amendment rights when they subjected her to an intrusive search. They alleged that testing of bodily fluids had been conducted without reasonable suspicion. They also alleged that staff violated her state constitutional privacy rights in disclosing the laboratory results.

The district court dismissed the suit, ruling that a state immunity statute protected the defendants from suits. On appeal, the appellate court disagreed that the plaintiffs enjoyed immunity from the suit. They upheld the district court's dismissal, however. Again, referring to the *TLO* analysis discussed above, the court found the suspicions to be reasonable and the searches not excessively intrusive. The blood and urine testing were not excessively intrusive. The decision also found that Tara's privacy rights under the Ninth and Fourteenth Amendments had not been violated. Although the nurse's comments about the lab results had been overheard, disclosure was not intentional. Furthermore, the only disclosure was that she had been tested.

IMPLICATIONS FOR SCHOOL NURSE PRACTICE

Several guiding principles apply to substance use evaluations in protecting students and staff. Establish that there is reasonable suspicion. As discussed above, lack of sleep, seasonal allergies, and prescribed medications can mimic illicit substance use. An experienced practitioner must make the distinction. Cannabis odors can come from exposure rather than use. School nurses might not always have a second person to consult, such as another nurse, administrator, or school resource officer. The following practice recommendations offer guidance in addressing these challenges.

1. Assess the necessity of the substance use evaluation within the context of age and student characteristics. In the *Safford* case discussed above, the suspicion failed to match the degree of

intrusion. The Ibuprofen Savana was accused of hiding presented no danger to students. A strip search of a 13-year-old girl, which exposed her breasts and pelvic areas, was not justified when it involved a non-dangerous substance. Compare that with *Hedges*. Tara's assessment was conducted upon observations from a teacher and school nurse, both with enough training and experience to reasonably suspect illicit substance use. Urine and blood testing were not excessively intrusive in these circumstances.

2. Follow school policy and statutory mandates.   In *Hedges*, the teacher followed both by reporting his observations to an administrator. The teacher, principal, and school nurse were protected from liability for following specific school policies and New Jersey state law.

3. Maintain competence and practice within the legal scope of nursing practice. With *Hedges*, the school nurse had four years of full-time experience in school nursing. She had been trained in substance use assessment. Five out of eight students she referred for further assessment tested positive for substances in the previous school year (*Hedges v Musco*, 2002). The principal and teacher also had substance use training within the scope of their professions as educators. It is paramount to use evidence-based assessment procedures and tools.

4. Maintain confidentiality. Although *Hedges* was decided before HIPAA regulations were implemented, the school nurse was still bound by professional standards. The school nurse's scope and standards of practice address this professional responsibility:
    In order to safeguard student privacy, school nurses maintain confidentiality within the legal, regulatory, and ethical parameters of health and education, and inform others about student health record protection in accordance with the Family Educational Rights and Protection Act (Family Educational Rights and Privacy Act, 1974), Health Insurance Portability and Accountability Act (Health Insurance Portability and Accountability Act, 1996), and other applicable federal and state laws and regulations. (NASN, 2022, Provision 3).

5. Ensure students, parents, and guardians are clear on substance assessment policy and offer an opportunity to clarify questions. Many districts will refer to this policy in their general and athletic parent handbooks.

6. Document the assessment in a timely manner using an established tool. Maintain records according to statutory requirements and school policy.

7. Join professional organizations to obtain current protocols and assessment tools. Offer to be a resource for the school board policy committee. Understand your job description and discuss substance use assessment as recommended by district legal advisors.

CONCLUSION

Adolescent illicit substance use is a growing public health crisis in the United States. The CDC reports that overdose deaths in persons aged 10-19 increased by 109% from July-December 2021. Sadly, nearly two-thirds of these deaths occurred with potential bystanders present but not responding (Tanz, 2022). School nurses can save more lives by educating staff and students on how to respond to overdoses and advocating for naloxone availability.

It is the responsibility of every school staff member to identify students at risk. Everyone must be trained to recognize the signs of substance use and comply with legal mandates and school policies when suspecting it. School nurses can take the lead in this by understanding their scope of practice and ethical responsibilities as defined by nursing boards, certifying bodies, and professional organizations.

RESOURCES

Adolescent Drug Testing Policies in Schools. https://doi.org/10.1542/peds.2015-0055

Code of Federal Regulations. (2016). *Part 2 – Confidentiality of alcohol and drug abuse patient records*. 42 U.S.C. § 2.2 et seq. (2016). https://www.govinfo.gov/content/pkg/CFR-2016-title42-vol1/xml/CFR-2016-title42-vol1-part2.xml

Students: Your Right to Privacy. https://tinyurl.com/25n9rafx
Drug Impairment Training for Education Professionals. https://www.theiacp.org/ditep

Drugs, Substance Abuse, and Public Schools A Legal Guide for School Leaders Amidst Evolving Social Norms. https://tinyurl.com/3dmhdsh8

Family Educational Rights and Privacy Act (FERPA).
https://www2.ed.gov/policy/gen/guid/fpco/ferpa/index.html

HIPAA for Professionals. https://www.hhs.gov/hipaa/for-professionals/index.html

Management of Toxicological Emergencies in the School Setting: An Overview for School Nurses Part 2.
https://doi:10.1177/1942602X221100213

Public Health, 42 C.F.R., §2.1 (2016). https://www.ecfr.gov/current/title-42/part-2/subpart-D

SBIRT in Schools: FAQs https://tinyurl.com/392pv5ha

Screening and Treatment of Substance Use Disorders Among Adolescents. https://store.samhsa.gov/sites/default/files/pep20-06-04-008.pdf

Case Law

Board of Education v. Earls, 122 S. Ct. 2559 (2002). https://supreme.justia.com/cases/federal/us/536/822/

Hedges v. Musco, 204 F.3d 109, 122 (3d Cir. 2000). https://tinyurl.com/jukvzf59

J.D.B. v. North Carolina, 564 U.S. 261 (2011)
https://supreme.justia.com/cases/federal/us/564/261/

Miranda v. Arizona, 384 U.S. 436 (1966). https://supreme.justia.com/cases/federal/us/384/436/

New Jersey v. T.L.O., 469 U.S. 325 (1985). https://supreme.justia.com/cases/federal/us/469/325/

Safford Unified School District v. Redding, 557 U.S. 364 (2009). https://supreme.justia.com/cases/federal/us/557/364/

Tinker v. Des Moines Independent Community School District, 393 U.S. 503 (1969). https://supreme.justia.com/cases/federal/us/393/503/

Vernonia School District 47J v. Acton. (1995). *Oyez.* https://www.oyez.org/cases/1994/94-590

REFERENCES

Ahmad, F.B., Cisewski, J.A., Rossen, L.M., & Sutton, P. (2023). Provisional drug overdose death counts. National Center for Health Statistics. https://www.cdc.gov/nchs/nvss/vsrr/drug-overdose-data.htm

American Civil Liberties Union. (2023). *Students: Your right to privacy.* https://tinyurl.com/25n9rafx"https://tinyurl.com/25n9rafx

Boston Children's Hospital, Center for Adolescent Behavioral Health Research (CABHRe). (2018). *About the CRAFFT.* https://crafft.org/about-the-crafft/

Chen, G. (2022, May 10). Can your child's school test students for drugs? *Public School Review.* https://www.publicschoolreview.com/blog/can-your-childs-school-test-students-for-drugs

Chen, G. (2022, May 10). Can your child's school test students for drugs? *Public School Review.* https://www.publicschoolreview.com/blog/can-your-childs-school-test-students-for-drugs

Deitche, A.L., & Burda, A.M. (2022). Management of toxicological emergencies in the school setting: An overview for school nurses part 2. *NASN School Nurse. 2022;37(5):250-256.* https://doi.org/10.1177/1942602X221100213

International Association of Chiefs of Police. (2023). *Drug impairment training for education professionals.* https://www.theiacp.org/ditep

Levy, S., Schizer, M., & Committee on Substance Abuse American Academy of Pediatrics. (2015). Adolescent drug testing policies in schools. *Pediatrics, 135(4)*, e1107–e1112. https://doi.org/10.1542/peds.2015-0055

Massachusetts Department of Public Health. (2021a) *SBIRT in schools: FAQs.* https://tinyurl.com/392pv5ha

Massachusetts Department of Public Health. (2021b). *SBIRT in schools resource toolkit.* https://cme.bu.edu/sites/default/files/SBIRT%20in%20Schools%20Toolkit--FINAL-8-30-21.pdf

National Association of School Nurses (2022). School Nursing: Scope and Standards of Practice, 4th Edition, https://www.nasn.org/nasn-resources/resources-by-topic/scope-standards

National Center for Drug Abuse Statistics. (2023). *Drug use among youth: Facts & statistics.* https://drugabusestatistics.org/teen-drug-use/

National School Boards Association. (2019). *Drugs, substance abuse, and public schools A legal guide for school leaders amidst evolving social norms.* https://tinyurl.com/3dmhdsh8

Patterson, K., Brady, J., & Olympia, R.P. (2017). School nurses on the front lines of medicine: Uppers and downers: The approach to the student with altered mental status. *NASN School Nurse 2017, 32(6), 350-355.* https://doi.org/10.1177/1942602X17706380

Siegmund, L.A. (2022). Appearance and performance enhancing drugs and substances: The role of the school nurse. *NASN School Nurse, 37(5)*,263-269. https://doi.org/10.1177/1942602X221093938

Tanz, L.J., Dinwiddie, A.T., Mattson, C.L., O'Donnell, J., & Davis, N.L. (2022). Deaths among persons aged 10-19 years: United States July 2019 – December 2021. *Centers for Disease Control and Prevention Weekly*, *71*(50), 1576-1582. http://dx.doi.org/10.15585/mmwr.mm7150a2

United States Department of Education. (2021). *Family Educational Rights and Privacy Act (FERPA)*. https://www2.ed.gov/policy/gen/guid/fpco/ferpa/index.html

United States Department of Health and Human Services. (2021). *HIPAA for professionals*. https://www.hhs.gov/hipaa/for-professionals/index.html

United States Department of Health & Human Services, Substance Abuse and Mental Health Services Administration. (2021). *Screening and treatment of substance use disorders among adolescents*. https://store.samhsa.gov/sites/default/files/pep20-06-04-008.pdf

United States Department of Health & Human Services, Substance Abuse and Mental Health Services Administration. (2022). *Substance abuse confidentiality regulations. https://tinyurl.com/jwvthvwu*

Chapter 38

SUICIDE/THREATENING HARM, THE SCHOOL'S ROLE

Suzanne Levasseur, MSN, APRN, CPNP, NCSN

DESCRIPTION OF ISSUE

In the United States, suicide is the second leading cause of death for 15-19-year-olds (Centers for Disease Control and Prevention [CDC], 2020a). According to the 2019 Youth Risk Behavior Survey (YRBS), data, 18.8 % of youths had seriously considered attempting suicide, 15.7% of youth had made a suicide plan, and 8.9% had made an attempt (CDC, 2020b).

Suicide is especially high among those that have been bullied, those with attention deficit hyperactivity disorder (ADHD), those with mental health disorders, those who abuse drugs or alcohol, and those that identify as lesbian, gay, bisexual, transgender, queer, and questioning (LGBTQ). Suicide is also more prevalent in those that have had a family member attempt suicide. In addition, suicide is increasing among elementary school children (Patterson et al., 2019).

Suicide can have a tremendous impact not only on the school but on the greater community. The school's prevention efforts and immediate and longer-term crisis plan following a suicide can have lasting implications and may help prevent future tragedies.

BACKGROUND

Schools have a legal duty to take reasonable action to maintain a safe environment for students. While schools cannot be held accountable for all accidents or deaths that may occur, parents may believe that a school did not meet its obligation and may bring legal claims for wrongful death or failure to prevent harm in the event of a suicide. In most states, employees of school districts have liability protection, but this immunity may be challenged if their actions were reckless or indifferent to possible harm (Underwood, 2019). The following cases further highlight this risk:

Mikell v. School Admin. Unit #33, 972 A.2d 1050 (N.H. 2009)

> In this case, a middle school student was overheard by a staff member saying that he "wanted to blow his brains out." The staff member notified the school counselor, who met with the student and notified the family. She also had the student sign a safety contract. Two months later, the student had two disciplinary incidents on two consecutive days and was suspended. After the mother picked him up from school and took him home, he died by suicide.

> The family sued the school district, the teacher, and the counselor, stating they had a duty to prevent the student's suicide. The case was dismissed as the school employees, who had a duty of reasonable care in acting, had warned the family about the student's behavior and had not acted recklessly.

Meyers v. Cincinnati Board of Education, 343 F.Supp.3d 714 (S.D. O.H. 2018), *aff'd* 983 F.3d 873 (6th Cir. 2020)

An eight yr. old student hung himself two days after being attacked in the school bathroom and was unconscious for 7 minutes. There were 12 other bullying incidents, many of which the family only learned about after the student's death. The family alleged that these incidents were often concealed, or their severity was misrepresented and that the school violated the student's civil rights by consciously disregarding his safety. The court denied the school district's attempt to dismiss the complaint, finding that the parents had sufficiently alleged that the student's suicide was a reasonably foreseeable consequence of the school bathroom attack and the school employee's misrepresentations about that attack. The court also found that a state immunity statute did not protect the school employees because the family sufficiently pled facts to show that these employees acted in reckless disregard for the student's safety.

Baab v. Medina City School Board of Education, 130 N.E.3d 1106 (O.H. Ct. App. 2019)

In this case, students reported to a counselor that another student had been cutting himself and had threatened suicide on at least one occasion. The counselor spoke to the student and notified the parents, who took the student to the doctor for evaluation. Two weeks later, another student notified the counselor again that the student had threatened suicide via a text message. The counselor took no additional action, and the student died by suicide a few days later. The family sued the school district and the counselor. The Ohio State Court of Appeals found that there was a genuine issue of material fact as to whether the counselor's actions were reckless and thus possibly preventing her from being protected by the state's immunity statute, remanding the case back to the state trial court.

In general, courts have found that schools may be legally responsible in the event of suicide if the following conditions exist:
- Schools have created a special danger of suicide;
- School employees have not acted reasonably to warn parents of the risk of suicide; or
- School employees acted recklessly in carrying out their responsibilities to the student (Underwood, 2019).

Implications for School Nurse Practice

Improving mental health for all students should start with a school climate that supports school connectedness. School connectedness is when students feel that adults and peers care about them as an individual. When students feel connected to their school, they are less likely to have poor mental health (CDC, 2022).

Training

All school staff should have training in suicide risk factors and protective factors and learn how to recognize and respond to the warning signs. Districts should have a comprehensive protocol that all staff are aware of and addresses how to respond to a suicide risk for an adult or a student at school. It should be kept in teachers' handbooks or the school's crisis plans and should be reviewed yearly. Students should be empowered through both student and parent education programming to share concerns with an adult when they are concerned about another student.

All school nurses and other pupil personnel staff, such as school psychologists, school social workers, and counselors, should be trained to screen for suicide risks. It may be beneficial to perform this screening in multi-disciplinary teams immediately following the suspicion of suicide ideation. It will be crucial to develop an individualized plan to ensure the safety of the student and ensure appropriate follow-up. If the student is at risk for suicide, they should not be left alone.

Parents or Guardians

Parents or guardians of a student at risk of suicide should be notified promptly and involved in consequent actions unless it is determined that this may be detrimental to the student. They should be asked to come to school immediately and remove any weapons or dangerous items, such as medication, from the home. In some instances, medical referrals to an emergency room may be made; in other cases, a community referral to a mental health provider may be warranted. A list of area referrals should be part of the comprehensive planning protocol and immediately made available to parents. Parents may need to be supported to come to terms with this information. If the school team feels that the student may be in danger of self-harm and the family is unwilling to seek help, child protective services may need to be called. Under the Federal Educational Rights and Privacy Act (FERPA), parents are generally required to provide consent prior to the school sharing any personally identifiable information from the educational record. Disclosures for health and safety emergencies are allowable (Department of Education, n.d.).

Confidentiality

Maintaining a student's right to confidentiality under FERPA has both legal and ethical implications. Specifics about incidents involving mental health or suicide should be protected and never part of classroom discussions or communications with the school community. Staff should be provided with the information necessary to work with the student and preserve the young person's safety, but do not need clinical information about the student or a detailed history of his or her suicidal risk or behavior.

Documentation

Documentation of the screening, parent notification, and referrals are an important part of the process. The exchange of information forms which allow communication with the outside provider will allow for collaborations and help with the re-entry process. Prior to the student's return, a re-entry meeting should be held with the students, parents, school nurses, counselor, and key staff or administrators. The goal of the meeting is to provide the student with school support and to develop a safety plan for the student. *(See Chapter 34 Addendum, Supporting Effective Transition Back to School Following Behavioral Health Hospitalizations, for more information on re-entry to school).*

Crisis Team

If there is a suicide in the school community, the school's crisis team, including the school nurse, should be mobilized. Postvention goals should be utilized to reduce the likelihood of another tragedy, facilitate healthy grieving, and stabilize the environment by getting back to a normal school day environment. The district's immediate crisis response, helping students and families cope, and communications with staff and families can have an important impact and help prevent future tragedies. After a suicide, the concept of "suicide contagion" is prevalent and refers to the heightened risks for others who may have been considering suicide. High-risk students should be identified and supported through this time. The school should have evidence-based strategies for dealing with the aftermath of suicide. Having readily available resources to help during this tumultuous time will be essential. The Suicide Prevention Resource Center has a helpful document called After a Suicide: A Toolkit for Schools (see Resources), which can guide postvention planning.

Special Education of 504 Implications

When a student makes a threat of suicide or has suicide ideation, a referral to special education for an IEP or a referral for a 504 plan can be made. School nurses or anyone, including the student's parents and guardians, can make this referral. If the student already has an individualized education plan (IEP) or accommodations under Section 504, these teams should be notified of these events, which may warrant a change in services or accommodations.

CONCLUSION

Promoting behavioral health and having an evidenced-based multifaceted suicide prevention program is essential in schools. This should include prevention strategies, early identification of mental health issues, and, if needed, a postvention plan. This comprehensive plan should involve collaboration across partners, including administrators, educators, school psychologists, school social workers, school counselors, school nurses, and other school health professionals.

Schools are legally responsible for taking reasonable action to keep students safe at school. While all suicides will not be prevented, it is critical that schools take appropriate steps, as discussed above. Although schools and school staff have certain liability protections, failure to notify parents and to keep the student safe if there is a concern for suicide can make the school or staff member legally responsible for the suicide.

School nurses, as part of the crisis team and pupil personal team, can be instrumental in policy development, training of school staff, screening, identification, referral, and postvention whenever a mental health emergency arises in the school community.

RESOURCES

American Psychiatric Association. (2020). Suicide and Serious Mental Illness an Overview of Considerations, Assessment, and Safety Planning. https://smiadviser.org/wp-content/uploads/2020/12/SMI-Adviser-Suicide-and-Serious-Mental-Illness.pdf

National Institute of Mental Health. Ask Suicide-Screening Questions (ASQ) Toolkit. https://www.nimh.nih.gov/research/research-conducted-at-nimh/asq-toolkit-materials

National Vital Statistics Reports. (2021, July). Deaths: Leading Causes for 2019,70(9). https://www.cdc.gov/nchs/data/nvsr/nvsr70/nvsr70-09-tables-508.pdf

Rogers, A., Obrien, K. (2021). Emotionally naked: A Teacher's guide to preventing suicide and recognizing students at risk. Jossey-Bass.

Suicide hotline. 988 Suicide & Crisis Lifeline. https://988lifeline.org/

Suicide Prevention Resource Center. (2020). https://sprc.org/settings/schools/

Suicide Prevention Resource Center. (2018). After a Suicide: A toolkit for schools (2nd edition). https://sprc.org/online-library/after-suicide-toolkit-schools

Case Law

Mikell v. School Admin. Unit #33 (N. H. 2009)

Baab v. Medina City School Board of Education (Ohio Ct. App. 2019)

Meyers V. Cincinnati Board of Education (S.D. Ohio 2018)

REFERENCES

Center for Disease Control and Prevention. (2020a). CDC National Center for Health Statistics Mortality Data. https://www.cdc.gov/nchs/nvss/deaths.htm

Center for Disease Control and Prevention. (2020b, August). Youth risk behavioral surveillance survey-United States, 2019. *Morbidity and Mortality Weekly Report*, 69(1). US Department of Health and Human Services. https://www.cdc.gov/mmwr/volumes/69/su/pdfs/su6901-H.pdf

Center for Disease Control and Prevention. (2022). *School connectiveness helps students thrive.* https://www.cdc.gov/healthyyouth/protective/school_connectedness.htm

Patterson, B.K., Bohnenkamp, J., Hoover, S., Bostic, J., Selekman, J. (2019). Students with mental/behavioral health concerns and disorders. In J. Selekman, R.A.Shannon, & C.F. Yonkaitis (Eds.), *School nursing: A comprehensive text* (3rd ed., p.p. 776-778). F. A. Davis Company.

Underwood, J. (2019). Student suicide and school liability. *Phi Delta Kappan, 101*(3), 64-65. Phi Delta Kappa International. https://kappanonline.org/student-suicide-school-liability-underwood/

U.S. Department of Education. (n.d.). *Protecting student privacy.* https://studentprivacy.ed.gov/faq/when-it-permissible-utilize-ferpa%E2%80%99s-health-or-safety-emergency-exception-disclosures

NURSING COORDINATION

The following section of the book is dedicated to the nursing coordination that occurs in the pre-K to 12 educational setting (i.e., schools). Some topics include Management of Chronic Absenteeism, Communicable Disease/Outbreak Management, Immunization Compliance, and Violence/Restraints in the K-12 Setting.

Nursing coordination is one of the pillars of the Framework for 21st Century School Nursing Practice™ and with this standard comes the responsibility to know the various areas for coordination and the potential legal challenges. The most recent pandemic highlighted this role as a coordinator and the diverse and often conflicting guidance. Therefore, it is essential that school nurses have the knowledge needed to mitigate potential conflicts or challenges.

Chapter 39

MANAGEMENT OF CHRONIC ABSENTEEISM

Suzanne Levasseur, MSN, APRN, CPNP, NCSN

DESCRIPTION OF ISSUE

While absenteeism refers to the number of excused and unexcused absences as well as suspensions or expulsions a student experiences, an unexcused absence from school, as determined by state law or policy, is considered truancy (Attendance Works, 2018). Compulsory school attendance laws are determined by state legislation and often district policy. Each state has laws that determine the age at which a child must begin attending school, the age at which a child may legally drop out of school, and the number of unexcused absences in a given timeframe such as a month, a marking period, or a school year, that establishes a student as truant.

According to the U.S. Department of Education, chronic absenteeism can be defined as missing 15 or more school days in a year. In 2015-2016, 1 in 6 students met this definition, with chronic absenteeism rates being the highest in high school. English learners are 1.2 times more likely to be chronically absent than their English-speaking peers, and students with disabilities are 1.2 times more likely to be chronically absent than students without disabilities (U.S. Department of Education [USDE], 2019).

Children living in poverty are often 2-3 times more likely to be chronically absent due to reasons such as lack of a nearby school bus, food insecurity, or a safe way to travel to and from school. Absenteeism is often linked to health problems, including mental health issues, asthma, diabetes, and other chronic diseases (Attendance Works, 2018).

Children who are chronically absent as early as kindergarten and first grade are less likely to achieve grade-level reading by third grade and are four times more likely to drop out of high school (Healthy Schools Campaign, n.d.).

A study of public school students in Utah found that students who were chronically absent for even one year between 8-12 grade had a sevenfold increase in dropping out of high school. Those who drop out of high school are more likely to experience poverty, poor health outcomes, and involvement in the criminal justice system (USDE, 2019).

BACKGROUND

The first compulsory school attendance law was enacted in the state of Massachusetts in 1642. While other states followed, it was not until the 1930s that states were successful in enforcement (Katz, 1976). Schools are responsible for providing notices to families that explain the truancy laws, district policy, and consequences for non-attendance. If a child is considered truant, judicial intervention may be warranted at some point. Parents are responsible for ensuring that their child attends school regularly, and if that responsibility is not met, the parent may be faced with statutory penalties. Educational neglect is often in a state's definition of child abuse or neglect. Therefore, in accordance with some state laws, districts may have to refer a family to the local child welfare agency as part of its response to a student's truancy. Although parents often want their children to attend school, they have run out of strategies to use at home to get their child to attend school.

Truancy cases are complicated and require the school team to determine a cause or underlying reason for the truancy. School teams should consider that the student may have a disability requiring special education services under Section 504. Although absences alone do not determine eligibility, repeated absences may be enough to suspect a disability. In some circumstances, district personnel should consider undertaking a special education evaluation prior to initiating a judicial referral or the involvement of a child welfare agency. Consideration of whether a student has a disability is warranted under the district's child find obligation, which requires districts to identify and evaluate students who may need special education (IDEA, Sec. 300.111). A student with poor attendance due to a chronic or frequent episodic illness may also be eligible for accommodations under Section 504.

On December 10th, 2015, President Obama reauthorized the Elementary and Secondary Education Act through the Every Student Succeeds Act [ESSA] (2015). ESSA requires states to report chronic absenteeism rates for schools. Most states report this data yearly. ESSA is the first national education law that addresses attendance. In addition to reporting requirements, districts are mandated to adopt attendance policies and maintain an accurate daily record of attendance (Kroger Gardis Regas LLP, 2021).

IMPLICATIONS FOR SCHOOL NURSE PRACTICE

School nurses have an important role in the management of a student with poor school attendance, whether there is chronic absenteeism where the student may be frequently out of school due to medical or other reasons or the student meets the legal definition of truancy in the state. Various health conditions may lead to frequent absences, and the school nurse may first note the condition and its effect on school attendance. It is important to document excused and unexcused absences, and the school nurse should be aware of students who may have attendance problems. It may also be the school nurse who determines if the absences are truly illness related. The nurse will be part of the school team to determine which accommodations may be necessary, especially in the case of a student eligible for Section 504 or under the Individuals with Disabilities Education Act (IDEA).

In some cases, homebound instruction may be warranted to provide education to a student who is medically unable to attend school. The student's multidisciplinary team should evaluate each case based on the student's individual needs. (*For more information on Homebound Instruction, refer to Chapter 57.*)

Just as a chronic disease may be a barrier to school attendance, so may many other issues, such as the need to care for siblings or other family members or lack of basic needs such as transportation, food, or clothes. A student may have an aversion to school due to academic or social struggles or feel unsafe at school. Anxiety-based or other mental health disorders may also contribute to school refusal behavior.

In the case of *Bradley v. Arkansas Department of Education, 45 IDELR 149, 443 F.3d 965 (8th Cir. 2006),* the courts found in favor of the district after the parent requested homebound-based education on a diagnosis of school phobia. The district determined that home was not the appropriate educational placement and that engaging in truancy processes was what state law required.

Improving attendance requires the active participation of school administrators, school counselors, social workers, school nurses, and community agencies as needed. Child welfare services and other social service agencies may also be utilized to help address barriers the family may face that prevent regular school attendance. With necessary permission from the parent/guardian, it is also important for the school nurse to engage local healthcare providers to collaborate with schools to address chronic absenteeism or truancy. Healthcare providers are often unaware of a patient's lack of attendance at school when they continue to issue medical excuse notes. Starting a dialogue to address a student's attendance improvement can be helpful, especially when there are frequent "doctor's notes" excusing the absences.

Strategies to Address Chronic Absenteeism

Attendance Monitoring

Although Average Daily Attendance (ADA) data of a school or district can provide valuable data, a system should be put in place to monitor individual student attendance. It may be the school nurse that brings excessive absenteeism or truancy to the administrator's attention, or the administrator may bring this to the attention of the school nurse.

Formation of District and School Attendance Teams

Active engagement of school administrators and school staff, with clear responsibilities and roles to adopt a comprehensive, tiered approach, is needed to improve attendance (Attendance Works, 2018).

Tiered Supports

Tiered support can begin with Tier 1 interventions that start with prevention and focus on all students, clearly articulating and communicating attendance policies while supporting an engaging school climate. Tier 1 interventions should engage students and parents and can include the following:

- Providing an engaging curriculum.
- Recognizing good and improved attendance.
- Providing a breakfast program.
- Organizing health interventions.
- Engaging in a schoolwide approach to wellness through flu clinics and a healthy indoor air quality program.
- Providing parent/guardian and student education for better management of health issues.

Tier 2 interventions provide personalized early intervention for students who are frequently absent through activities such as:

- Conducting a home visit or parent conference.
- Providing outreach by the school nurse, especially related to health issues.
- Engaging the healthcare provider for students with health concerns such as asthma that are impacting attendance.
- Offering counseling or family-based services. If a student qualifies, such services might be offered as a related service through a student's Individualized Education Plan (IEP).

- Identifying barriers such as lack of transportation or inadequate housing and partnering with community agencies to obtain needed resources.
- Developing a student attendance success plan to develop strategies to support improved attendance.

Tier 3 interventions are for students who need intensive case management or coordination with local agencies or law enforcement and can include:

- Referrals to a community agency capable of supporting family needs that may be affecting attendance.
- Referrals to a community court-based program or resource addressing truancy and schools.
- Assignment of a mentor in the school community.
- Consideration of an alternative educational setting, as the law allows.

CONCLUSION

Chronic absenteeism influences educational success, as well as incidences of early delinquency and school drop- out. The academic consequences of lost instructional time can be great. School districts need to develop a comprehensive approach— beginning with preventive, universal programming and attendance monitoring for all students. Although students may miss school for understandable reasons such as chronic illness or social issues such as homelessness, determining the reason for the chronic absences is essential to determine targeted strategies for the individual student.

Prior to getting to the point where a student is chronically absent or when a student's truancy has reached thresholds for state laws requiring judicial or agency intervention, a meeting with the parent/guardian should be held, and interventions should be put in place.   Districts and school nurses, in particular, should have policies, procedures, and tiered interventions in place to help prevent and mitigate chronic absenteeism and truancy. Families should also be notified that students' failure to attend school every day on time may require districts to engage in required truancy processes.

In addition, poor school attendance may prompt districts to suspect a disability, and a special education or Section 504 eligibility hearing may be warranted. School nurses will be essential in identifying health and other barriers and leading their school teams in addressing the issue (NASN, 2023).

RESOURCES

See ADDENDUM: Attendance and the School Nurse

Attendance Works (2018).*www.attendanceworks.org*

Case Law

Bradley v. Arkansas Department of Education, 45 IDELR 149, 443 F.3d 965 (8th Cir. 2006)

REFERENCES

Attendance Works. (2018). https://www.attendanceworks.org/chronic-absence/the-problem/

Every Student Succeeds Act (ESSA). (2015). Every Student Succeeds Act of 2015, Pub. L. No. 114-95 § 114 Stat. 1177 (2015-2016).

Healthy Schools Campaign. (n.d.). *Addressing the health-related causes of chronic absenteeism: A toolkit for action.* https://healthyschoolscampaign.org/wp-content/uploads/2017/02/Addressing_Health-Related_Chronic_Absenteeism_Toolkit_for_Action_Full.pdf

Individuals with Disabilities Education Act, Sec. 300.111. https://sites.ed.gov/idea/regs/b/b/300.111

Katz, M. S. (1976). *A history of compulsory education laws.* http://files.eric.ed.gov/fulltext/ED119389.pdf

Kroger Gardis Regas LLP. (2021). *Navigating the legal issues of school attendance and student engagement.* https://kgrlaw.com/laws-of-attendance-engagement-in-schools/

National Association of School Nurses. (2023). *Addressing chronic absenteeism* (Position Statement*).* https://www.nasn.org/nasn-resources/professional-practice-documents/position-statements/ps-absenteeism

U.S. Department of Education. (2019). *Chronic absenteeism in the nation's schools.* https://www2.ed.gov/datastory/chronicabsenteeism.html

ADDENDUM

Attendance and the School Nurse

Reviewed and Updated by Leigh E. Dalton, PhD, Esq*

Q: Is it important for a nurse to identify and follow up on chronic absenteeism issues that are or may be disability-related?

A: Failure to provide accommodations, including flexibilities with attendance procedures, for a student experiencing absenteeism due to a Section 504 or IDEA-eligible disability can result in liability for a public school, and nurses are often on the front lines of the school's defense. If the nurse learns that a student is missing a significant amount of school due to the disability, the school nurse should promptly report this situation to the Special Education Director and/or the Section 504 Director. Notifying pertinent school professionals will allow the school-based team to determine whether to move forward with an assessment for the student and/or reconvene the IEP or Section 504 Team to consider the absenteeism issue. Ensuring appropriate communication channels decreases the chance of a successful complaint against the school and helps defend the school against a claim that it violated the student's right to a Free Appropriate Public Education (FAPE) by failing to identify and/or properly accommodate a student's disability. If a school does not have in place proper policies, protocols, and procedures for evaluating and/or accommodating a student under Section 504 and/or IDEA, the nurse should bring the issue to the attention of building and/or district-level administration and should take steps to assist in the creation of such. Some communities have laws that involve criminal action against parents who do not ensure that their child is coming to school every day on time unless there is a valid reason for the student not being present in school. For example, Kansas City, Missouri, has a compulsory school attendance law. If a student is absent for more than a designated percentage of the time during the school year, the student's parents are reported to the prosecuting attorney, who will then issue a show cause order for the parents to appear before a judge to explain the absences. If, during that legal process, parents provide medical reasons to show a valid reason for their student's absences, the school nurse may need to provide documentation as to whether the nurse received any medical documentation to support the parents' defense and, if so, what the district did to try to accommodate the student's medical needs.

Q: How are student attendance issues and Section 504 related?

A: Section 504 is an anti-discrimination law that prohibits schools receiving federal funding from discriminating against a student because of the student's disability. For example, if a student's Section 504 Plan requires the nurse to administer insulin to a student with diabetes but the nurse fails to do so, and, for this reason, the student's parents elect not to send the student to school, the student's failure to attend school may have been caused by the nurse's failure to follow the student's Section 504 Plan. Accordingly, the school would have violated Section 504. Another example is when a school nurse discovers that the reason for the student's failure to attend school may have been caused when the student was hospitalized after attempting self-harm. The nurse should report such hospitalization to the school's Special Education Director and/or the Section 504 Director. If the student is already identified as a student with a disability under the IDEA or Section 504, those federal laws require action to be taken by the school to allow the student to attend school and receive a FAPE. Furthermore, even if the student, prior to the incident, was not receiving IDEA services or Section 504 accommodations, the school should consider whether such hospitalization merits evaluation for the student to receive IDEA services and/or Section 504 accommodations. The best practice is for the school to require the student's healthcare provider to send a proposed safety plan before the student returns to the school. Such a plan may include medical information or administration of medication information, so such a third-party disclosure would require authorization from parents. Accordingly, the nurse would be a vital component in the student's receipt of a FAPE.

*Original author of addendum: Lawrence Altman, Esq. (2017)

Chapter 40

ACCIDENT AND INJURY REPORTING

Timothy E. Gilsbach, Esquire

DESCRIPTION OF ISSUE

When an accident or injury occurs on school grounds, a school nurse has two roles as a member of the risk management team and the health professional in the school. First, a school nurse is generally expected to take the lead in determining if anyone was injured and, if so, to take steps to treat them and, if needed, get them additional help (NASN, 2019a). Second, sometimes overlooked, the nurse also serves as a historian with the unique perspective of often being the only person present with a medical background to provide a record of what happened and what was done as well as any pertinent history (Davis et al., 2020).

BACKGROUND

School nurses are tasked with keeping students healthy and safe, which includes assessment of risks in the school environment and physical plant as part of the risk management and safety considerations. Accident reports are an important part of risk management documentation and assist in identifying risks that result in or may precipitate illness or injury. When litigation involving schools occurs, one of the first things that likely will occur is that records and documents regarding the incident in question are requested (Habeeb, 2022/1960).

Accident reports should be treated as an internal document, never kept in the health or employee file or referred to in the health record in nursing documentation. The report should be completed as soon as possible, on the same day, and not more than 24 hours later (Hootman et al., 2005). In addition, documentation of events created at or about the time of an event's occurrence and prior to any litigation that may come are typically viewed as far more reliable accounts of what occurred than accounts that are given months or even years later or after litigation is commenced (Habeeb, 2022/1960).

Lastly, it is important to make sure that all information is accurately recorded by individuals who complete the form. As a result, it is *critical that the documentation of* accident reports *is accurate, objective, and factual.* Accident reports, under risk management, provide an assessment of risks, documentation of the need for remediation, insurance coverage, and record for litigation. They are a history of the event, which requires a firsthand report from those who first responded and were responsible for the student *at the time of the event.* In cases of injury, the nursing note in the health record accomplishes the necessary documentation of the nurse's care and responsibility. The accident report does not replace nursing documentation, is not considered part of the student's health record, and should never be mentioned (Hootman et al., 2005).

IMPLICATIONS FOR SCHOOL NURSE PRACTICE

When Does an Accident Report Need to Be Completed?

An accident or injury should be considered school-related when the incident occurs at school during normal school hours, at any school-related activity, or while the student is being transported to or from school (Utah Board of Health [UBOH], 2022). The school nurse, as part of the safety risk management committee, may provide education and instructions to administration and staff on how and when to complete a report, including any additional school and district policies associated with one.   While nurses should review the policy and procedures of their school entity to determine when an accident report should or must be completed, an accident or injury report should, at a minimum, be completed, in any of the following four (4) circumstances (UBOH, 2022; Florida Department of Health [FDOH], 2022):

1. The student misses one-half (1/2) day or more of school due to the injury or, if the injured party is an employee, they miss one-half (1/2) day or more of work.

2. The student or employee seeks medical attention from their healthcare provider, emergency room, or urgent care center due to the injury.

3. The school nurse recommends further evaluation or instructions for home care.

4. EMS or 911 is called due to the injuries or for any reason.

It is important to note that, in addition to an accident or injury report, if the school nurse assessed or treated the student the nurse should also document care provided in the student health record per standard documentation procedures. For events that do not require an accident or injury report, information should be documented in the student's health record or other appropriate forms (Mississippi Nursing Foundation, 2013).

What Needs to And Should Be Included in The Report?

As with all nursing documentation, accident and injury reports should be objective, legible, free of spelling and grammatical errors, free of errors, and accurate (Love et al., 2018). If available, the accident and injury forms should be filled out electronically (UBOH, 2022; NASN, 2019b). The report should include the following information (Love et al., 2018; FDOH, 2022).

-   Name of the injured person and the person's date of birth, and grade, (if a student).

-   For students, the name of the parent or guardian and whether that person was contacted about the incident and, if so, how, what information was provided, the time of notification, and the response from the parent or guardian.

-   Whether nurse provided information about the injury to any other parties, including the school principal, another administrator, or the student's medical provider (if referring) and, in the case of a non-student, if someone else outside the school was notified.

-   The name of the school building the employee or student is assigned. In the event of a visitor to the school building, as noted below, the location where the injury occurred should be included and, if known, the reason why this person was in the school building.

- The location in the school building where the accident or injury occurred, any equipment involved, and a description of any unusual circumstances, such as the-type of flooring or surface where the incident occurred, including cracks, breaks, or obstacles.

- The time and date of the accident or injury, including, where appropriate, whether the time is an estimated or exact time.

- An explanation of the incident, including a list of any witnesses, any contributing factors, and a brief description of the incident presented objectively and using the injured's own words in quotes when provided. Ideally, the report should be completed by the person who witnessed the incident; however, often the report is completed with the school nurse due to the nurse's health expertise. When the nurse relies upon what other individuals reported regarding the incident, the report should clearly identify what was reported and by whom. In addition, to the extent other staff members were involved in the initial treatment of the student or injured party, this should also be noted and co-signed by this individual. In describing the incident, care should be taken to avoid assigning blame or fault to any person or item. Instead, it should be an objective and factual accounting of what happened. If more than one student/staff was injured, a separate report should be completed for each person involved.

- The nature of the injuries, including where the injury is located on the injured party's body and the type of injury. For example, was it a scrape, puncture, cut or burn? Medical terms or diagnoses should not be used, only descriptive terms (e.g., "the arm appears disfigured" as opposed to" arm is broken." Or "the ankle is swollen" as opposed to "sprained ankle").

- Any special circumstances should be noted, including if a vehicle was involved, whether specific substances such as chemicals were involved, or if drugs or alcohol were involved if known. Descriptions of special circumstances should be as factual as possible. For example, if the individual in question appears to be under the influence of drugs or alcohol, the symptoms that are seen should be noted and described and, only if professionally appropriate, that this could be a sign of intoxication. No prior history of substance abuse should be included.

- Whether medical assistance was provided to the injured party, including any medication provided, dose, time, and route.

- Whether future medical assistance was recommended, and how this information was provided to the injured party or, if a student, to the student's parent or guardian.

- Whether the student or injured party's care was transferred to someone else, including parent or guardian, medical provider, urgent care, or EMS, as well as the condition of the student or injured party when this transfer occurred; Name of who accompanied the injured party; the instructions provided to the person to whom the injured party's care was transferred; and the name of the facility or person, the time notified, and the time transfer occurs.

ACCIDENT AND INJURY REPORTING

Who May See the Information in the Report?

For students, any educational entity that receives federal funds is subject to the Family Educational Rights and Privacy Act (FERPA) and any state law or regulations relating to handling and sharing student records. FERPA requires that records to which it applies be kept confidential and not disclosed unless permitted under FERPA (U.S. Department of Education [USDE], 2010). FERPA applies to student records handled by school nurses regardless of whether they are employed directly by the school or by an agency with which the school contracts. In addition to FERPA, school nurses must be aware of and comply with school district policy regarding the confidentiality of the information they obtain in their role as school nurses and other state laws related to privacy, such as the Nurse Practice Acts.

FERPA applies to all records maintained by the school district that are directly related to a student (USDE, 2010). Such records include all health records maintained by the school district, including treatment and immunization records (USDE, 2010). This would include accident and injury reports about students.

Generally speaking, *maintenance* includes any records kept by the school district, although some courts have suggested there must be an intent to keep it (*Owasso Independent School District v. Falvo*, 2002; *Bryner v. Canyons School. District,* 2015). **However, when unsure if FERPA applies, school staff are advised to presume it does apply and keep the records confidential**. With respect to *directly related to a student*, this requirement is met if it includes the student's name, initials, and identification number or if it provides information from which someone could identify the student (*Letter to Doe*, 2011). FERPA has even been found to apply to information if it permits the identity of the student by "face, body shape, clothing or otherwise" (*Bryner v. Canyons School District*, 2015).

Disclosure of FERPA records or the information contained in those records is limited to those circumstances provided for under FERPA and its implementing regulations (USDE, 2010). There are several provisions that permit disclosure that are applicable to accident and injury records (USDE, 2010):

- The records or information may be disclosed to the parent and student.

- The information or records can be disclosed if the parent or guardian or student over the age of 18 gives consent in writing to release the information. This consent must state what information can be disclosed and to whom it may be disclosed.

- The information may be disclosed if it qualifies as directory information, which should be defined with specificity in the District's Policy and Annual Notification to Parents. In addition, a school nurse should be aware that a parent or guardian may opt out of the directory information disclosure and, if the parent or guardian does, the disclosure under this provision is not permissible.

- The school district may disclose the information in response to a lawful subpoena or court order but typically must notify the parent or guardian or student over the age of 18 of the same prior to the release unless the subpoena or court order provides that the parent or guardian are not to be notified.

ACCIDENT AND INJURY REPORTING

Who May See the Information in the Report?

For students, any educational entity that receives federal funds is subject to the Family Educational Rights and Privacy Act (FERPA) and any state law or regulations relating to handling and sharing student records. FERPA requires that records to which it applies be kept confidential and not disclosed unless permitted under FERPA (U.S. Department of Education [USDE], 2010). FERPA applies to student records handled by school nurses regardless of whether they are employed directly by the school or by an agency with which the school contracts. In addition to FERPA, school nurses must be aware of and comply with school district policy regarding the confidentiality of the information they obtain in their role as school nurses and other state laws related to privacy, such as the Nurse Practice Acts.

FERPA applies to all records maintained by the school district that are directly related to a student (USDE, 2010). Such records include all health records maintained by the school district, including treatment and immunization records (USDE, 2010). This would include accident and injury reports about students.

Generally speaking, *maintenance* includes any records kept by the school district, although some courts have suggested there must be an intent to keep it (*Owasso Independent School District v. Falvo*, 2002; *Bryner v. Canyons School. District,* 2015). **However, when unsure if FERPA applies, school staff are advised to presume it does apply and keep the records confidential**. With respect to *directly related to a student*, this requirement is met if it includes the student's name, initials, and identification number or if it provides information from which someone could identify the student (*Letter to Doe*, 2011). FERPA has even been found to apply to information if it permits the identity of the student by "face, body shape, clothing or otherwise" (*Bryner v. Canyons School District*, 2015).

Disclosure of FERPA records or the information contained in those records is limited to those circumstances provided for under FERPA and its implementing regulations (USDE, 2010). There are several provisions that permit disclosure that are applicable to accident and injury records (USDE, 2010):

- The records or information may be disclosed to the parent and student.

- The information or records can be disclosed if the parent or guardian or student over the age of 18 gives consent in writing to release the information. This consent must state what information can be disclosed and to whom it may be disclosed.

- The information may be disclosed if it qualifies as directory information, which should be defined with specificity in the District's Policy and Annual Notification to Parents. In addition, a school nurse should be aware that a parent or guardian may opt out of the directory information disclosure and, if the parent or guardian does, the disclosure under this provision is not permissible.

- The school district may disclose the information in response to a lawful subpoena or court order but typically must notify the parent or guardian or student over the age of 18 of the same prior to the release unless the subpoena or court order provides that the parent or guardian are not to be notified.

- The information may be disclosed if there is "an articulable and significant threat to the health or safety or other individual" that such information is necessary to protect. However, it is expected that when applying this provision for disclosure it is necessary that the information be disclosed so quickly that there is no time to get a subpoena or court order. Under these circumstances, such information is typically requested by law enforcement, public health officials, or trained medical personnel.

- The information may be released to other school officials if it is educationally relevant to that person and typically a staff member who does or will be working with the student, consistent with *"need to know."*

Lastly, it is important to note that under FERPA, the district is required to maintain a record of any such disclosures with the student's records (USDE, 2010). The disclosure should include to whom the information was disclosed and the educational reason information is shared.

For non-students, such as staff and school visitors, school nurses need to protect the confidentiality of the information they obtain consistent with the legal and ethical obligations of their nurse practice act and with federal and state law requirements regarding the confidentiality of employment records. Accident reports should be stored separately, not in health or employee files. As a result, school nurses should generally take steps to keep information in such records confidential and only disclose the same if permissible. Typically, disclosure of this information is only permitted if the person whom it is about consents, a provision of law or the rules of ethics would permit disclosure, or if ordered to do so by court order or subpoena. **When in doubt, school nurses should not disclose the information and seek guidance from legal counsel or your professional organization about confidentiality requirements.**

CONCLUSION

Schools use accident reports to document and review events and circumstances for risk management and safety. Given that the record of accidents or injuries at school may become evidence in litigation and such information is needed to provide further care to the student or school employee, it is essential that school nurses or other school personnel make sure such reports are accurate, objective, and comprehensive. School nurses should take the lead in providing policy, procedures, and staff training in the completion of accident reports. In addition, school nurses need to be aware of the legal limits regarding the disclosure of such records because they qualify as educational records under FERPA and may be subject to other federal and state laws, including privacy laws. Lastly, it is essential that school nurses become aware of and comply with any additional applicable district guidelines and policies, as well as state and federal laws and regulations.

RESOURCES

National Association of School Nurses Website – http://www.nasn.org/

Your state School Nurses Association or Organization Website

U.S. Department of Education - Family Educational Rights and Privacy Act (FERPA) Website -
https://www2.ed.gov/policy/gen/guid/fpco/ferpa/index.html

Virginia Student Injury Report Form – available at
https://www.dcjs.virginia.gov/sites/dcjs.virginia.gov/files/publications/law-enforcement/student-injury-report-form.pdf

Student Injury Report Form Utah Department of Health – available at
https://sir.health.utah.gov/pdf/Student_Injury_Report_Form.pdf

Case Law

Bryner v. Canyons School District, 351 P.3d 852 (UT Ct. App. 2015)

Letter to Doe, 111 LRP 64583 (FPCO 2011)

Owasso Independent School District v. Falvo, 534 U.S. 426 (2002)

REFERENCES

Davis, C. R., Lynch, Erik J., & Davis, Patti A. (2020). The principal and the school nurse: Conditions and conceptual model for building a successful and vital professional relationship. *Planning and changing, 50*(1/2), 95-110. https://education.illinoisstate.edu/downloads/planning/Davis_50.1-2.pdf

Habeeb, W. R. (2022/1960). *Admissibility of report of police or other public officer or employee, or portions of report, as to cause of or responsibility for accident, injury to person, or damage to property*, 69 A.L.R.2d 1148 (1960) (Updated 2022).

Hootman, J., Schwab, N.C., Gelfman, M.H.B., Gregory, E.K., & Pohlman, K.J. (2005), School nursing practice: Clinical performance issues. In N. Schwab & M.H.B. (Eds.), *Legal Issues in School Health Services: A Resource for School Nurses, Administrators and Attorneys, p. 186-187.*

Florida Department of Health. (2022). *Student injury report form guidelines.* https://www.floridahealth.gov/provider-and-partner-resources/emsc-program/_documents/fl-injury-rpt.pdf

Love, T., & Roy, K., (2018, Nov.). Completing accident/incident reports: Recommendations to avoid legal pitfalls *Technology and Engineering Teacher, 78*(3), 20–23. https://www.iteea.org/Publications/Journals/TET/TETNov2018/SafetyNov2018.aspx#publicationContent

National Association of School Nurses. (2019b). *Electronic health records: An essential tool in keeping students healthy* (Position Statement). https://www.nasn.org/nasn-resources/professional-practice-documents/position-statements/ps-electronic-health-records

National Association of School Nurses. (2019a*). Emergency preparedness* (Position Statement). https://www.nasn.org/nasn-resources/professional-practice-documents/position-statements/ps-emergency-preparedness

U.S. Department of Education. (2010). *Family Educational Rights and Privacy Act (FERPA) and the disclosure of student information related to emergencies and disasters.* https://studentprivacy.ed.gov/resources/ferpa-and-disclosure-student-information-related-emergencies-and-disasters

Utah Board of Health. (2023). *Student injury report.* https://sir.health.utah.gov/

Chapter 41

ACTIVE SHOOTER

Emily Poland, MPH, RN, NCSN

DESCRIPTION OF ISSUE

School violence is one of the greatest challenges in the United States. The topic of active shooters can cause a visceral reaction of sorrow in those working to provide a healthy, safe, and effective learning environment for children. School staff, including school nurses, should be able to focus on the learning and development of children. Parents want their children to be safe while learning in school. They do not want to worry that their child's school will become yet another setting for these recurrent active shooter incidents. School administrators and staff must spend time preventing and preparing for this possibility. This chapter will provide a brief overview of gun violence in schools, discuss gun violence as a public health issue, prevention efforts in schools, and the potential legal implications for the school nurse.

Many nurses transition into the school setting, expecting to focus on health promotion and maintaining wellness among the pediatric population. Schools have traditionally been seen as safe havens where children are supported by educators and other staff dedicated to educating and supporting young people's development into productive citizens in a global society. The view that schools are safe havens has eroded over the past few decades with each act of gun violence the media reports.

BACKGROUND

For this discussion, an active shooter at a K-12 school is defined as any incident where a firearm is fired, or a bullet hits school property for any reason, regardless of the number of victims or the time of day (Riedman, 2022). Regardless of why a gun is fired in a school setting, there will be a sense of danger to many who are present on campus and family members who experience it off-site. Not all data surrounding active shooters in schools are defined similarly, making it difficult to have consistent information or compare statistics. According to the CHDS's School Shooting Compendium (2022), in the past fifty years, there have been approximately 2069 shootings in schools with 684 related deaths and almost 2000 injuries. The relatively new K-12 School Shooting Database counted fifty-eight (58) school shootings in 2017. In every year since 2017, there have been over one hundred. In 2022, that number climbed to 302 (Riedman, 2022).

According to the U.S. Centers for Disease Control and Prevention (CDC) statistics, fire-arm related homicide in 2016 was the second leading cause of death for children ages 5-18, second to motor vehicles (CDC, 2021). Though by itself is extremely alarming, less than 2% of these fire-arm related deaths occurred on school property (CDC, 2021). However, gun violence is now the number one cause of death in children (Goldstick et al., 2022).

There were 98,577 public K-12 schools in 2020-21 (National Center of Educational Statistics [NCES], 2023). Millions of children and staff spend at least 6 hours per day, five days a week, in schools. While the individual risk of dying by shooting in schools is very low, the alarming trend of increased frequency of school shootings in recent years causes nationwide trauma for school communities. The shooting at Columbine was in 1999.

Since then, there has been a marked increase in the number of shootings per year, with a dramatic increase starting in 2018, as illustrated in the table below (Reidman, 2022).

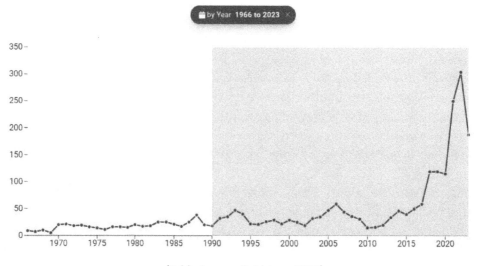

(Table Source: Reidman, 2022)

In the United States, we must consider active shooters in schools as a public health issue that potentially affects a large portion of the population (i.e., school-age children and school staff). Worldwide, this topic is included in the larger context of preventable injuries. The World Health Organization [WHO] lists three of the top five causes of death among those aged five through 29 years as related to injuries defined as homicide, suicide, and traffic accidents (WHO, 2023). In the World Population Review, the United States holds the number one spot for school violence. Between 2009 and 2019, there were 288 school shootings in the United States compared to the second highest, Mexico, which had eight [8] (World Population Review, 2023). We have a long road ahead in prevention. Identifying the issue is the first step to improving outcomes.

In addition to the devastating loss of life, active shooter incidents can have legal implications for schools. Following the 2021 Oxford High School shooting (Oxford, Michigan), where four students were killed and seven injured, a family of one surviving victim sued the school district. They claimed the school did not adequately respond to warning signs or threats. This case also claimed negligence by the gun dealer (Mueller v. Oxford Community School District, 2022). A recent $130 million financial settlement by the U.S. Justice Department to victims of the 2018 Marjory Stoneman Douglas High School shooting is evidence that not responding to threats may pose huge financial implications for those with knowledge of threats or concerning behavior (Wolfe, 2021).

Since the 1999 shooting at Columbine High School in Littleton, Colorado, laws have been passed and policies implemented to prepare for school shootings. Temkin et al. (2020) revealed that the highest number of laws were passed following the 2012 Sandy Hook Elementary School (Newtown, Connecticut) and the 2018 Marjory

Stoneman Douglas High School (Parkland, Florida) shootings. These laws focused on school preparedness efforts such as building security and lockdown drills. Lawmakers have responded to active shooters with legislation at both the federal and state levels. The 1990 Gun-Free School Zone Act, for example, made the knowing possession of firearms in a school zone a crime under federal law. (U.S.C. 101-647). This statute was challenged in court as being unconstitutional. Since then, it has been amended to limit its application to firearms related to interstate commerce (United States v. Lopez, 2019).

Twenty-eight states allow teachers or other school staff to carry a firearm, although there is no evidence that there is any impact on the frequency or lethality of school shootings (Rand, 2023). Some states have passed additional legislation to increase the number of school staff who carry firearms. Missouri school districts, for example, can designate staff as school protection officers, allowing them to carry firearms (Mo. Title 38, §571.107 (10)).

Florida enacted the so-called guardian program that allows teachers to enroll in special training to carry a firearm (Trotta, 2019). The National Education Association opposes increasing the number of firearms in schools (Walker, 2018). Public health research and scientific data should inform gun safety laws, but the politically divisive nature of the issue hinders such an approach.

Despite limited evidence of its effectiveness, active shooter drills were conducted in 95% of U.S. schools during the 2015-16 school year (Musu-Gillette et al., 2017). It is unclear when lockdown drills got their start, but since the Columbine shooting in 1999, they have become the norm in K-12 schools. There is evidence that suggests active shooter drills, required in 40 states, are harmful to the mental health of students and school staff (Everytown Research & Policy, 2021). Well-meaning lawmakers may be contributing to mental health problems.

The Bipartisan Safer Communities Act (BSCA) was signed into law in 2022. The BSCA expands community mental health services for children by increasing access to school health care services through Medicaid and CHIP. The BSCA funds schools to expand mental health and supportive services and institute evidence-based safety measures. Importantly, the law prohibits the use of funds under the Elementary & Secondary Education Act to train or equip any person with dangerous weapons in schools and makes straw purchasing and trafficking of firearms a criminal offense (U.S.C. 117-159).

IMPLICATIONS FOR SCHOOL NURSE PRACTICE

School nurses can assist in active shooter preparation. As part of the multidisciplinary team, the school nurse provides medical/health expertise, critical decision-making skills, knowledge of student health needs, and emergency medical response expertise. The principles in the Framework for 21st Century School Nursing Practice™ are all utilized in emergency planning: standards of practice, care coordination, leadership, quality improvement, and community/public health (National Association of School Nurses [NASN], 2016). As addressed by McIntosh & Brelage (2020), the school nurse is well-positioned to understand and advocate for the needs of children with special needs, whether mobility, sensory, or behavioral challenges, that must be considered in planning.

As noted by the NASN in its position statement on emergency preparedness,

> "...the school nurse is a leader and integral partner with school staff and outside agencies in developing comprehensive school plans/procedures for injury prevention, and first aid, facilitating evacuation, caring for students with special needs, performing triage, educating and training staff, providing surveillance, reporting, and assisting survivors with their immediate psychological and emotional needs, and referral to appropriate mental health services for long-term support" (NASN, 2019).

School nurses have a professional duty to respond to emergencies within the school. The school nurse must be actively engaged and prepared. McIntosh & Brelage (2020) discussed the limitations of published preparedness resources for school staff related to students with disabilities. The school nurse must be included in emergency operations planning as a critical partner.

School Culture

Preventing an active shooter incident in a school must begin with the school's culture. Although the U.S. Department of Homeland Security (DHS) covers school culture within its prevention plan, it is included as the last step in prevention as part of creating a targeted violence prevention program. As noted in the K-12 School Shooting Database, over 40% of all school shootings are related to an escalated dispute, anger related to grades or discipline, and bullying (Riedman, 2022). These situations are all related to the culture within a school. Therefore, a school must proactively create and promote a culture of safety, mutual respect, and emotional support. Staff should encourage and support students when information is shared regarding conflicts and bullying incidents (U.S. Cybersecurity & Infrastructure Security Agency [CISA], n.d.). Building this climate must be among the first steps a school takes, not an afterthought, and must continually be addressed. School nurses can lead in developing this culture of safety and respect.

Bullying has been recognized as a public health problem. U.S. CDC Youth Risk Behavior Surveillance Survey shows that 19.5% of students have been bullied at school (CDC, 2020). Bullying has both short and long-term consequences. The school nurse is vital in creating a supportive culture that recognizes high-risk students. Once recognized, violent threats can be reduced. The school nurse's leadership enhances safety and implements evidence-based interventions that can prevent or mitigate the effects of bullying (NASN 2018).

School Teams

A school may call its multidisciplinary team by different names, such as Emergency Operations or Crisis Team. The team's purpose is to address all risks that might affect their school community. This includes active shooters. By using Federal Emergency Management Agency (FEMA) emergency operations planning resources, schools can form a collaborative team, understand the potential situation, establish goals, and develop a plan. Implementation of the plan can prevent, protect, respond, recover, and mitigate harm (FEMA, 2021).

As part of the multidisciplinary team, the school nurse must stay current with the best emergency response, management, and recovery practices. Because actual incidents create unsafe environments, mobility can be limited or prohibited in the building. If an active shooter is at large, the school nurse might not be able to respond immediately to an injury. School nurses, therefore, must focus on prevention and preparation.

In an active shooter situation, school staff must have already received training and have the tools needed to respond. The school nurse is well-positioned to coordinate and provide the necessary training for school staff in first aid, bleeding cessation, and cardiopulmonary resuscitation (CPR). Response teams must be trained in first aid and CPR. There is no national standard for a minimum number or ratio of school staff to be trained in CPR. The American Heart Association's Hands-Only CPR training can enable school staff to respond to life-threatening situations. School nurses can implement training specific to bleeding, such as STOP THE BLEED®, and advocate for placing emergency kits in each classroom. Emergency tools such as tourniquets and bandages should be readily available in all locations.

Communication

Staff must be trained to recognize and report warning signs (Fielder, 2019). Threats of violence against self or others should never be taken lightly. Safety prevails over a student's free speech rights. Any potential threat should be reported. The United States Supreme Court has held that true threats are not protected under the first amendment right to free speech (Virginia v. Black, 2003).

Safety also prevails over a student's privacy rights. The Federal Education Rights and Privacy Act (FERPA) does not prohibit sharing information regarding a student's conduct that can threaten the well-being of that student or others (U.S. Dept. of Education, n.d.). Failure to understand FERPA can lead to decreased information sharing and unintentionally encourage a culture of secrecy within a school (Goodrum et al., 2022).

Following the 2001 attack on New York City, the New York Metropolitan Transportation Authority initiated an "If you See Something, Say Something®" project. The Department of Homeland Security adopted it as a national campaign to raise public awareness of the signs of terrorism and terrorism-related crime and educate the public on reporting suspicious activity to law enforcement (DHS, 2023). Many schools have implemented some of these practices. The creation of an anonymous reporting system allows anyone to report and for that information to be shared with the appropriate people. The school's multidisciplinary team can follow through with a threat assessment (Stein-Seroussi et al., 2021). Examples of these reporting systems can be found in the resources.

Threat Assessment

A school should implement a comprehensive and systematic way of assessing threats of violence. A behavioral threat assessment and management team can be part of the larger emergency operations planning team. The team must:
- be well-trained and have defined the concerning behavior to be reported,
- be knowledgeable of the process for reporting threats of violence,
- determine the threshold to involve law enforcement,
- establish assessment procedures,
- identify risk management steps, and
- promote a safe school climate and conduct training for all stakeholders (National Association of School Psychologists [NASP], 2021a).

Systematic threat assessment teams reduce suspensions and expulsions and decrease the racial disparities of such actions (National Institute of Justice, 2021). The "team should consider all data, including risk and protective factors, and identify the level of concern (low, moderate, high, imminent), which will guide the team in directive actions and supports to be taken. It is important to note that levels of concern are not to be used to predict human behavior or to determine a change of educational placement automatically but are to be used to design interventions and supports" (NASP, 2021). The Commonwealth of Virginia was the first U.S. state to require threat assessments to be conducted at K-12 schools; since 2019, at least five other states have followed (National Institute of Justice, 2021; Sawchuck, 2019). The Virginia model of Comprehensive School Threat Assessment Guidelines (CSTAG) is an evidence-based model for schools to implement. More information can be found in the resources section.

Drills

When practicing emergency procedures, such as fire drills, evacuations, or lockdowns, school staff must account for students with disabilities, including providing students with any necessary adaptive equipment. "Since reactions of students with special needs during crises are unpredictable, advanced forethought and correspondence with police and first responders are vital. This must be done to ensure that police will not mistake a child who is not following protocol as a threat" (McIntosh & Brelage, 2020, p. 162). Drills must easily identify a student with special needs who cannot follow the same directions as their peers.

Over the past thirty years, different models of school emergency response plans for active shooters have been introduced. Early models included locking doors and stay-in-place procedures. Schools are increasingly using more detailed, multi-option responses like ALICE® (Alert, Lockdown, Inform, Counter, Evacuate). As school violence has escalated, managing school safety has become considerably more complicated. This has prompted research to offer solutions and improve safety. Jonson et al. (2020) designed a simulation study that compared traditional lockdown response (locking the door and sitting quietly out of sight until police arrive or the all-clear is announced) and the multi-option response such as that used in ALICE®. The study supported using a multi-option approach, "In essence, doing something active is better than hiding in a dark room" (Jonson et al., 2018, p. 162). It must be noted that studying the effectiveness of active shooter countermeasures is difficult, and there is no consensus on the best approach. School staff must collaborate with local emergency partners to develop a local emergency response plan.

Other Considerations

In addition to direct prevention and response, schools should consider proactive approaches such as training in emotional intelligence and social-emotional skills. Training to increase self-awareness, stress management skills, and empathy is vital in creating a school culture of safety and respect. Social and emotional intelligence is beneficial for adults as well as for children. Trainers with social and emotional skills are better equipped to implement social and emotional learning techniques with students.

Staff and student survivors of active shooter incidents have increased anxiety, depression, and other mental health challenges. As reported by CNN, an eleven-year-old student survivor from Uvalde, Texas, "dipped her hands in the blood of a classmate – who lay next to her, already dead – and then smeared the blood all over herself to play dead…" (Neus et al., 2022). School staff must be prepared and equipped to recognize, respond to, and support the mental health of survivors and school community members, including themselves, as they return to the classroom.

The framework for behavior, mental health, and health services can be found in a multi-tiered system of support (MTSS). MTSS is a philosophy that organizes and leverages the systems that likely already exist in a school (NASP, 2021b). MTSS analyzes and organizes all available resources within the school context, such as people, facilities, time, data, curriculum and instruction, and additional resources. Direct instruction for all students, starting in PreK, can set students up for success in the long term. Health education can assist students in being better consumers of information, managing the complex world around them, and being more inclusive of others.

Through an effective skills-based health education curriculum, students can practice skills that protect, promote, and enhance lifelong health. Similarly, improving foundational social-emotional skills such as self-awareness, self-regulation, social awareness (empathy, compassion & respect for self and others), relationships, and critical thinking help address risk factors for behavior and potential mental health issues. Educational programs which complement a positive school culture and climate can-create a safer school community.

CONCLUSION

Preventing and responding to active school shooters requires a whole-school approach and the participation of a multidisciplinary team. School nurses have a professional duty to respond to emergencies. To protect students, the school nurse must be actively engaged and prepared. The school nurse must maintain current emergency response certifications and competency in Basic Cardiac Life Support (BCLS), Stop the Bleed, and first aid. The school nurse must implement best practices and actively engage in school and district-level planning and preparations.

RESOURCES

ALICE® Training
https://www.alicetraining.com/our-program/alice-training/

Children's Hospital of Philadelphia, Center for Violence Prevention
https://violence.chop.edu/youth-violence-prevention

Comer, B. (2022). Supreme Court Jurisprudence and School Shooting Threats: A Legal Review. *Journal of Criminal Justice and Law, 5 (2).* https://jcjl.pubpub.org/pub/v5i210ctq8d7

National Association of School Psychologists. Behavior Threat Assessment and Management for Schools Best Practice Considerations for K-12 Schools https://www.nasponline.org/resources-and-publications/resources-and-podcasts/school-safety-and-crisis/systems-level-prevention/threat-assessment-at-school/behavior-threat-assessment-and-management-(btam)-best-practice-considerations-for-k%E2%80%9312-schools

National Child Traumatic Stress Network Resources for Schools.
https://www.nctsn.org/trauma-informed-care/trauma-informed-systems/schools/nctsn-resources

Nevada Department of Education, Safe Voice Nevada http://safevoicenv.org/

Sandy Hook Promise, Say Something Anonymous Reporting https://www.sandyhookpromise.org/our-programs/say-something-anonymous-reporting-system/

U.S. Centers for Disease Control and Prevention, Division of School and Adolescent Health, School Preparedness Unit https://www.cdc.gov/healthyyouth/school-preparedness/index

Case Law

Mueller v. Oxford Community School District, (2022) https://brady-static.s3.amazonaws.com/01-PL-Complaint.pdf

Tinker v. Des Moines Independent Community School District, 393 U.S. 503 (1969) https://supreme.justia.com/cases/federal/us/393/503/

United States v. Lopez, 514 U.S. 549 (1995) https://supreme.justia.com/cases/federal/us/514/549/

Virginia v. Black, 538 U.S. 33 (2003) https://supreme.justia.com/cases/federal/us/538/343/

REFERENCES

Centers for Disease Control and Prevention. (2020). Adolescent and School Health, *Trends in the Prevalence of Behaviors that Contribute to Violence National YRBS: 1991—2019.* https://www.cdc.gov/healthyyouth/data/yrbs/factsheets/2019_violence_trend_yrbs.htm

Centers for Disease Control and Prevention. (2021). Violence Prevention, *School associated violent death study.* https://www.cdc.gov/violenceprevention/youthviolence/schoolviolence/SAVD.html

Center for Homeland Defense and Security. (2022, June). *Data map for shooting incidents at k-12 schools, Jan 1970-2022.* https://k12ssdb.org/all-shootings

Diaz, Jaclyn. (2022, June 29). The dealer that sold the gun used in the Oxford High School shooting is being sued. *National Public Radio.* https://www.npr.org/2022/06/29/1108698652/oxford-high-school-shooting-gun-dealer-sued

Everytown Research & Policy. (2021). *The impact of active shooter drills in schools: Time to rethink reactive school safety strategies.* Originally published September 3, 2020; updated December 29, 2021. https://everytownresearch.org/report/the-impact-of-active-shooter-drills-in-schools/

Federal Emergency Management Agency. (2021). *Developing and maintaining emergency operations plans, version 3.0.* https://www.fema.gov/sites/default/files/documents/fema_cpg-101-v3-developing-maintaining-eops.pdf

Fiedler, N., Sommer, F., Leuschner, V., & Scheithauer, H. (2020). Student crisis prevention in schools: The NETWorks against school shootings program (netwass) – an approach suitable for the prevention of violent extremism? *International Journal of Developmental Science, 13(3-4), 109-122.* https://content.iospress.com/articles/international-journal-of-developmental-science/dev190283

Goldstick, J. Cunningham, R., & Carter, P. (2022). Current causes of death in children and adolescents in the United States. *New England Journal of Medicine 2022, (386), 1955-1956.* https://www.nejm.org/doi/full/10.1056/NEJMc2201761

Goodrum, S., Slepicka, J., Woodward, W., & Kingston, B. (2022). Learning from error in violence prevention: A school shooting as an organizational accident. *Sociology of Education, 95(4), 257–275.* https://doi.org/10.1177/00380407221120431l

Jonson, C.L., Moon, M., & Hendry, J. (2020). One size does not fit all: traditional lockdown versus multi-option responses to school shootings. *Journal of School Violence., 19(2),154-166).* https://doi.org/10.1080/15388220.2018.1553719

McIntosh, C. & Brelage, P. (2020). School nurses' roles in preparing special needs students for active school shootings. *NASN School Nurse,35(3),* pp. 158–164. https://doi.org/10.1177/1942602X19885363

Missouri Revised Statute. (2014). Title 38, §571.107 (10) https://revisor.mo.gov/main/OneSection.aspx?section=571.107&bid=29721

Mueller v. Oxford Community School District. (2022). https://brady-static.s3.amazonaws.com/01-PL-Complaint.pdf

Musu-Gillette, L., Zhang, A., Wang, K., Zhang, J., Kemp, J., Diliberti, M., & Oudekerk, B.A. (2018). *Indicators of school crime and safety: 2017.* National Center for Education Statistics, U.S. Department of Education, and Bureau of Justice Statistics, Office of Justice Programs, U.S. Department of Justice. https://nces.ed.gov/pubsearch/pubsinfo.asp?pubid=2018036

National Association of School Nurses. (2016). Framework for 21st century school nursing practice: National Association of School Nurses. *NASN School Nurse, 31(1),* 45-53. https://doi.org/ 10.1177/1942602X15618644

National Association of School Nurses. (2018). *Bullying and cyberbullying— Prevention in schools* (Position Statement). https://www.nasn.org/nasn-resources/professional-practice-documents/position-statements/ps-bullying

National Association of School Nurses. (2019). *Emergency preparedness* (Position Statement). https://www.nasn.org/nasn-resources/professional-practice-documents/position-statements/ps-emergency-preparedness

National Association of School Psychologists. (2021a). Behavior threat assessment and management for schools best practice considerations for k-12 schools. https://www.nasponline.org/resources-and-publications/resources-and-podcasts/school-safety-and-crisis/systems-level-prevention/threat-assessment-at-school/behavior-threat-assessment-and-management-(btam)-best-practice-considerations-for-k%E2%80%9312-schools

National Association of School Psychologists. (2021b). *ESSA and multi-tiered systems of support for decision-makers.* https://www.nasponline.org/research-and-policy/policy-priorities/relevant-law/the-every-student-succeeds-act/essa-implementation-resources/essa-and-mtss-for-decision-makers

National Center for Education Statistics. (2023). Fast Facts. https://nces.ed.gov/fastfacts/display.asp?id=84

National Institute of Justice. (2021, May 12). *Student threat assessment: Virginia study finds progress, areas to improve.* https://nij.ojp.gov/topics/articles/student-threat-assessment-virginia-study-finds-progress-areas-improve

Neus, N., Alonso, M., & Colbert, C. (2022). She smeared blood on herself and played dead: 11-year-old reveals chilling details of the massacre. *CNN.* June 8, 2022. https://www.cnn.com/2022/05/27/us/robb-shooting-survivor-miah-cerrillo/index.html

Rand Corporation. (2023). *The effects of laws allowing armed staff in k–12 schools.* April 22, 2020, updated January 10, 2023. https://www.rand.org/research/gun-policy/analysis/laws-allowing-armed-staff-in-K12-schools.html#fn1

Riedman, David (2022). K-12 School Shooting Database. https://k12ssdb.org/all-shootings

Sawchuck, S. (2019). What schools need to know about threat assessment techniques. *Education Week. 9(03).* https://www.edweek.org/leadership/what-schools-need-to-know-about-threat-assessment-techniques/2019/09

Stein-Seroussi, A., Hanley, S., Grabarek, M., & Woodlif, T. (2021). Evaluating a statewide anonymous reporting system for students and multidisciplinary response teams: Methods for a randomized trial. *International Journal of Educational Research*, *110*, (2021), 101862. https://doi.org/10.1016/j.ijer.2021.101862

Temkin, D., Stuart-Cassel, V., Lao, K., Nuñez, B., Kelley, S., & Kelley, C. (2020, February 12). The evolution of state school safety laws since the Columbine school shooting. *Child Trends*. https://www.childtrends.org/publications/evolution-state-school-safety-laws-columbine

Trotta, D. (2019, May 1). Florida teachers can arm themselves under new gun bill. *US News*. https://www.reuters.com/article/us-usa-guns-florida/florida-teachers-can-arm-themselves-under-new-gun-bill-idUSKCN1S74GZ

U.S. Department of Education (n.d.) Are there situations in which school officials may non-consensually disclose personally identifiable information from education records of students who have been disciplined for conduct that posed a significant risk to the safety of the school community? Retrieved on 7-8-23 from https://studentprivacy.ed.gov/faq/are-there-situations-which-school-officials-may-non-consensually-disclose-personally

U.S. Department of Homeland Security. (2023). *See something, say something campaign.* https://www.dhs.gov/see-something-say-something

United States Government, Cybersecurity & Infrastructure Security Agency. (n.d.). *School safety and security.* https://www.cisa.gov/school-safety-and-security#

United States Code 101-647, November 29, 1990. https://www.govinfo.gov/content/pkg/STATUTE-104/pdf/STATUTE-104-Pg4789.pdf

United States Code 117-159, June 25, 2022. https://www.congress.gov/117/plaws/publ159/PLAW-117publ159.pdf

Walker, T. (2018, March 3). Arming teachers is not the answer. *NEA Today*. March 3, 2018. https://www.nea.org/advocating-for-change/new-from-nea/arming-teachers-not-answer

Wolfe, J. (2021, November 22). U.S. to pay $130 million to resolve claims over 2018 Parkland school shooting. *Reuters*. https://www.reuters.com/world/us/us-pay-130-million-resolve-claims-over-2018-parkland-school-shooting-2021-11-22/

World Health Organization. (2023). Estimates of homicide rates (per 100,000 population). *Global Health Observatory*. https://www.who.int/data/gho/data/indicators/indicator-details/GHO/estimates-of-rates-of-homicides-per-100-000-population

World Population Review. (2023). *School shootings by country.* https://worldpopulationreview.com/country-rankings/school-shootings-by-country

Chapter 42

COMMUNICABLE DISEASE/OUTBREAK MANAGEMENT

Sandra J. Delack, MEd, BSN, RN, NCSN-E, FNASN

DESCRIPTION OF ISSUE

School nurses are public health's eyes and ears for the nation's children and families. Their position within schools and their understanding of the social environment surrounding the school offer access to care that can extend the reach of public health. Collaboration between school nursing and public health helps to address emerging challenges within the healthcare and education sectors. It proactively supports students' ability to be healthy and ready to learn (National Association of School Nurses [NASN], n.d.)

Once expected to be eliminated as a public health problem, infectious diseases continue to have a significant impact as a cause of death and disability-adjusted life years (DALYs) worldwide, particularly in low- and middle-income countries (World Health Organization, 2020). Although there has been a global decline in communicable diseases, the recent Covid-19 pandemic has demonstrated the need to remain vigilant. When developing preventative strategies many years ago, the Centers for Disease Control and Prevention (CDC) speculated that dramatic changes in society, technology, and the environment, together with the diminished effectiveness of certain approaches to disease control, would usher in an era wherein the spectrum of infectious diseases would expand, and many infectious diseases once thought to be controlled or even eradicated would be increasing (CDC, 1994). The picture has been further complicated by increased global travel, population densities, and thawing permafrost in recent years. Vaccine-preventable diseases and emerging threats, such as the SARS-CoV-2 virus (COVID-19), demonstrate the need for robust infectious disease prevention and control programs (National Association of City and County Health Officials, n.d.) and challenge schools to develop safe and effective public health policies within the educational environment.

BACKGROUND

School nursing's roots are steeped in the realm of public health. Compulsory school attendance led to increased rates of communicable infections among students, creating a problem of chronic absenteeism (Wolfe, 2019). In the early 1900s in the U.S., Lillian Wald, founder of both public health nursing and school nursing, had the vision to mitigate this problem by placing nurses in schools in New York City. The goal was to assess and treat common communicable conditions and provide education related to treatment, obtaining medication, and hygiene issues to families in their homes. School attendance drastically improved as a result of these efforts, allowing previously excluded students, some excluded for years, to be allowed back in school.

In a 1908 American Journal of Nursing article, Supervising School Nurse Lina Rogers noted, "It was seen that the work of the nurses connected the efforts of the Department of Health with the homes of the children, thus supplying the link needed to complete the chain of medical inspection" (Rogers, 1908, p. 966).

Since its inception, the practice of school nursing has become increasingly comprehensive. It has evolved to incorporate the care of students with chronic health conditions and special needs, as well as a myriad of other functions. However, the school nurse's focus on community health promotion and disease prevention remains a critical role. Community/Public Health is identified as one of the five major principles of NASN's 21st Century Framework for School Nursing Practice, including Disease Prevention and Population-Based Care (Maughan et al., 2016). School nurses are responsible for maintaining current knowledge of local and state Department of Health policies related to communicable diseases and work with school district administration to ensure district policies are updated and consistent with health department recommendations.

School nurses intervene via tiered prevention efforts to keep the entire school population and the larger community healthy (NASN, 2022, page 15). Primary prevention describes interventions aimed at preventing occurrences of disease, injury, or disability. Secondary prevention describes initiatives aimed at early detection and treatment of disease before signs and symptoms occur. Tertiary prevention includes interventions aimed at preventing further morbidity, limiting disability, and avoiding mortality and rehabilitation from disease, injury, or disability (University of Maryland, School of Nursing, 2022). The importance of the school nurse's community/public health role was heightened dramatically during the COVID-19 pandemic, cementing the crucial role of school nurses in communicable disease surveillance, intervention, and prevention (Combe, 2020).

Throughout their history of being placed in schools, school nurses have routinely served as sentinels for communicable disease outbreaks. It was a school nurse, Mary Pappas, in Queens, New York, who first recognized the H1N1 outbreak in her school and alerted public health officials (Molyneux, 2009). School nurses collaborate with multiple local and state agencies, such as education departments and health and human services. Local and state health departments are essential partners in guiding and directing school health programs, especially during outbreaks. They provide regulations and guidelines that direct school health policies, recommendations for when students need to be excluded for illness, and form letters to send when there is a communicable disease outbreak at school (Selekman et al., 2019).

Based on guidance from CDC, state and local health departments coordinate lists of reportable diseases and provide a process for reporting and responding. At the national level, CDC maintains the National Notifiable Disease Surveillance System (NNDSS), a collaborative to share information about state and nationally reportable infectious and noninfectious diseases and outbreaks.

The federal government derives its authority for isolation and quarantine from the Commerce Clause of the U.S. Constitution. The authority for carrying out these functions on a daily basis has been delegated to the CDC. States have police power functions to protect persons' health, safety, and welfare within their borders. To control the spread of disease within their borders, states have laws to enforce the use of isolation and quarantine. These laws can be specific or broad from state to state (CDC, 2021). However, a state's authority to mandate quarantine has been challenged in court with a foundation in *Compagnie Francaise &c. v. Board of Health* (186 U.S. 380) in 1902. During a significant outbreak, response activities are organized into a team structure in accordance with the National Incident Management System. These teams have different focus areas, including but not limited to surveillance, laboratory issues, communications, at-risk populations, antiviral medications, vaccines, and traveler's health issues (CDC, 2021). Compulsory vaccinations have been challenged in court with a foundation in *Jacobsen v. Massachusetts* (197 U.S. 11) in 1905.

COVID-19 Pandemic

The World Health Organization (WHO) declares a pandemic when a disease's growth is exponential, with each day resulting in case growth higher than the previous day. In being declared a pandemic, the virus has nothing to do with virology, population immunity, or disease severity; it means a virus covers a wide area, affecting several countries and populations. This wide geographical reach is what makes pandemics lead to large-scale social disruption, economic loss, and general hardship (Columbia University, Mailman School of Public Health, 2021).

In the early months of 2020, large numbers of cases of a novel coronavirus began to circulate across the U.S. Schools were left to respond with little guidance as health experts were scrambling to learn more about the impact of the virus, mode of transmission, and health consequences. WHO declared an international pandemic on March 11, 2020. Schools across the nation's initial response in early March was to take a "pause" from in-school learning to allow time to take stock of the situation and plan for potential extended school closures. In the interim, state and local school authorities began to investigate the option of remote learning in the short term and consider how to safely re-open schools in the future. The media scrambled to report any information they could glean, and school districts struggled to get their arms around an elusive but potentially costly challenge: risk management in the age of coronavirus (Sawchuk, 2020).

Most, if not all, school districts purchase liability insurance to protect against potential lawsuits, some of which exclude communicable diseases from coverage (Sawchuk, 2020). Once the pandemic's extent and impact were realized, most insurance companies informed districts that they would not cover claims stemming from the pandemic. This resulted in many districts having no protection to cover legal costs and damages stemming from a civil lawsuit from a parent or student alleging that they contracted COVID-19 due to a district's failure to protect them against exposure to infection (Sawchuk, 2020). As 2020 progressed, some insurance companies began to offer additional coverage and riders, at an additional cost, for coverage for COVID-19 claims.

One of the many challenges to districts, and school nurses, revolved around the standard of care, which became a moving target as research and recommendations provided by the CDC and local/state health departments evolved. Failure to meet the standards meant a district could be sued for negligence or even recklessness. The American Nurses Association [ANA] (n.d.) issued guidance for nurses and institutions *if and when* standards of crisis may be recommended. Standards of crisis focus on "a utilitarian framework usually guides practice decisions and actions with special emphasis on transparency, protection of the public, proportional restriction of individual liberty, and fair stewardship of resources" (ANA, n.d., para 1). Essentially, depending on resources, it can mean shifting priorities in providing care to the community rather than the individual and, at the same time, ensuring the safety of the nurse.

In general, civil claims related to COVID-19 may be hard to prove. "In the realm of suing a district because your child contracts coronavirus, it is going to be difficult to prove those claims," per Morgan M. Masters, an associate at Albeit Weiker LLP, a Columbus, Ohio-based law firm that offers comprehensive legal services to students and educators. "Because you're going to have to show causation and proving where your child contracted it may not be easy" with so much community spread. Despite that difficulty, districts will still incur significant costs to pay the legal fees to defend against the suits (Sawchuk, 2020).

As the pandemic progressed, the majority of states began to pass laws that protected schools from liability for COVID-19. However, school districts continued to have an obligation to demonstrate that they followed the active federal, state, and local COVID-19 recommendations, a challenging endeavor as recommendations shifted frequently (Lieberman, 2021).

Additional issues related to COVID-19 emerged as students began to return to the classroom in the fall of 2020. By this time, state and local health departments had organized COVID-19 response teams. They utilized the majority of their manpower to digest the enormous amount of information based on current science and trends and filter that information into recommendations for the public, resulting in continually changing guidance to communities, schools, and other stakeholders. Complicating the situation, state and local governments, health authorities, and school district superintendents began to wrestle with the pros and cons of mandates related to masking, isolation and quarantine policies, testing, and potential vaccine mandates.

IMPLICATIONS FOR SCHOOL NURSE PRACTICE

The COVID-19 pandemic amplified school nurses' essential role as guardians of public health during communicable disease outbreaks and their importance in implementing mitigation strategies. As a novel disease with vast outreach and implications, the recent pandemic also exposed the need for state, local, and district plans and policies to address future outbreaks and improved communication systems between state/local health and education hierarchy. Schools are part of a larger public health team, and school nurses are critical to that team (Hansen, 2021). Many health departments were straining to develop guidance for communities, schools, businesses, and healthcare facilities, while so little was known about the epidemiology of this novel virus. Although schools across the nation paused to allow health experts to catch up, as students and staff returned to the classroom, policies and protocols remained ambiguous. School nurses cited several major issues that contributed to lessons learned related to liability issues, most of which they had little control. School nurses are uniquely positioned to integrate student health and education; however, maintaining or optimizing this balance is not the exclusive purview of the school nurse; it requires a team approach, including public health partners, school system administrators, parents, and the community all playing pivotal roles (Bullard et al., 2020).

Evolving Recommendations

During an outbreak of communicable disease, school districts and school health staff must maintain current knowledge of national, state, and local guidelines for case definition, isolation, and quarantine protocols. Additionally, they must develop and adopt mitigation policies, including visitor policies, ventilation, hand hygiene, screening, testing, cleaning/disinfection of high-touch surfaces, cohorting, and PPE use. Schools and early childhood care and education programs are an important part of the infrastructure of communities. They provide safe, supportive learning environments for students and children and enable parents and caregivers to be at work (CDC, 2022).

Legal exposure is significantly reduced if there is evidence that the school district is following the recommendations provided by state and local authorities related to isolation, quarantine, social distancing, ventilation, and masking. It is challenging, however, when a novel virus is the cause of the outbreak and health experts are continually updating and modifying recommendations based on new information. Not only does it create confusion, leading to potential liability, but the frequent changes may also create suspicion and doubt about the science behind the changes. Adding to the confusion of continually changing recommendations by the CDC and local/state health departments, elected state and local officials frequently entered the fray. They used their authority over public health decisions in schools to further confuse the issue.

Regarding often conflicting or confusing guidance, one school nurse shared, "It is only a matter of days before someone challenges us on our ability/authority to require close contacts to quarantine" (Combe, 2020, p.309). As the COVID-19 pandemic entered a second school year, there was much frustration on the part of parents, teachers, coaches, and administrators. School nurses were often left out of the policy development conversations, and interpretation of quarantine protocols was sometimes left to coaches or individual teachers. This often resulted in misinterpretation and potential increased spread of the virus.

School nurses, as subject matter experts with substantial knowledge of public health practice, are essential to the policy and implementation teams from the beginning and throughout an outbreak. As we look to future communicable disease outbreaks, school nurses must be included on leadership teams and utilize their public health expertise to guide decisions.

Ethical Concerns

Ethical and legal concerns arise during a time of uncertainty in an outbreak or pandemic. Despite extensive planning, challenges will arise that cannot be anticipated. Staffing and supply shortages and surges in patient load require nurses to make decisions that may not align with standard care but are necessary under the circumstances (Webster & Wocial, 2020). Shifting guidance, interrupted school health room routines, scarce availability of supplies, triaging limited resources, working in unfamiliar circumstances, and uncertainty about disease progress and transmission are only a few of the potential sources of moral distress (Webster & Wocial, 2020). Scope of practice changes become stressful but necessary, as the goal is not what is best for an individual patient/student but what is best for the *population*.

As students returned to schools in the fall of 2020, most school nurses were charged with screening, testing, and identifying positive cases of COVID-19, as well as contact tracing to quarantine potential contacts. Shifting priorities from acute and chronic individualized care to supporting public health initiatives may cause significant ethical concerns. Because the school nurse is most often the only healthcare professional in the school, there is a need for re-prioritization and balancing the workload. School nurses need to meet the demands of disease surveillance, reporting, contact tracing, masking, and managing excessive amounts of phone, email, and written communication, while still providing the essential services of acute and chronic healthcare for students and meeting objectives described in Individualized Healthcare Plans.

Students who are well still require access to the school health room for chronic condition management in a well area; symptomatic students must be assessed in an ill area; students who meet the criteria for presumptive positive illness must be supervised in an isolation area while awaiting dismissal (Combe, 2020). Creating such an environment requires sound clinical judgment by the school nurse and support from the administration.

Additional ethical and legal challenges may be presented when relying on accurate communication with parents/ guardians, staff, and the community at large. Early in the COVID-19 pandemic, public health departments recommended temperature and symptom screening to promote early identification of ill students/staff members before entering the school building. Many districts required a daily attestation form to be completed by parents/guardians and staff members stating that those entering the school building did not exhibit any signs of illness. It is incumbent upon school districts to weigh the value of daily infectious disease screening tools such as symptom attestation forms or temperature measurements during an outbreak. These actions may lead to conflict and doubt unless implemented with fidelity by all parties.

Information Sharing

Information sharing in the school community environment during an outbreak of communicable disease presents complex legal concerns. In a public health emergency, such as the COVID-19 pandemic, the Family Educational Rights and Privacy Act (FERPA) and, when appropriate, the Health Insurance Portability and Accountability Act (HIPAA) rules still apply. Limited waivers and exceptions may allow for increased sharing of information. In 2008, the U.S. Department of Health and Human Services revised FERPA regulations to clarify the "health or safety emergency exception," which allows educational agencies and institutions to disclose personal identifiable information (PII) from student education records, without prior written consent, to appropriate parties in the event of a health or safety emergency (Baker et al., 2020).

In 2020, the U.S. Department of Education (USDE) provided guidelines for disclosing PII during a health emergency when such disclosure is necessary to protect a student's or other individual's health or safety. This "health or safety emergency" exception to FERPA's general consent requirement is limited in time to the period of the emergency. Generally, it does not allow for a blanket release of PII from student education records. It emphasized that disclosure decisions should be made on a case-by-case and rational basis. This decision indicates that disclosing PHI to a public health department without prior written consent is permissible when the school believes that the COVID-19 virus poses a serious risk to the health and safety of an individual student who attends their school. Also, the school may disclose that a student in a particular classroom has tested positive for COVID-19 to other students and their parents/guardians without consent, as long as the information is in a non-personally identifiable form. The disclosure must be done so that it "does not disclose other information that, alone or in combination, would allow a reasonable person in the school community to identify the students who are absent due to COVID-19 with reasonable certainty" (USDE, 2020). This was particularly challenging as school nurses conducted contact tracing and provided notification of possible exposures and required careful planning on how and what information is shared. The 2020 guidance developed as a result of the COVID-19 pandemic can be instructive in planning for future outbreaks or pandemics.

Masking

Mandates for public health measures such as vaccines and universal masking have long created an opportunity for a public challenge. During the COVID-19 pandemic, school districts have faced lawsuits for requiring masks, as well as for failure to require masks. Those opposed to masks cited the following concerns: decreased oxygen levels or difficulty breathing, inability to be heard or to hear others, headaches, exhaustion, depression, withdrawal, and lack of enthusiasm (Hall, 2021). Parents who brought litigation when the universal masking mandate was lifted expressed concern for their medically fragile students' health or that students would bring the virus home to vulnerable family members, as described in this chapter's *Some Examples of Recent Case Law* section. School nurses were frequently put in the position to defend or refute the science of masking and the district masking policy. Following state and local policies during the height of an outbreak and the subsequent trajectory of the outbreak can help school districts/school nurses in policy decisions on mandatory or voluntary masking.

Classroom or school closures

There has been extensive discussion related to the impact of school closures and intermittent but frequent protracted absences due to the COVID-19 isolation and quarantine policy. Considerations when deciding to quarantine a classroom or close a school must be made with the far-reaching impact on students in mind. Extensive research continues to assess the impact of prolonged school closure on students, especially those most vulnerable. It remains a focal point of legal discussions at the district and state levels.

School districts must comply with federal and civil rights laws, despite remote learning or graduated re-opening of schools. If a school had to comply with Section 504 before the pandemic, it still must meet Section 504's requirements during and after the pandemic. To meet the requirements of Section 504, school districts must make decisions that consider the health, safety, and well-being of all their students and staff, as well as their obligations to ensure that eligible students with disabilities are receiving a free appropriate public education (FAPE) under Section 504 and the Individuals with Disabilities Act (IDEA) (USDE, Office of Civil Rights, 2021). During classroom and school closures, school nurses must also consider transferring medication or medical supplies between home and school and remotely providing health and mental health services. Per NASN (2020), not all care is appropriate via a virtual method, and it requires critical nursing judgment to make this determination. This virtual interaction also requires specific consideration of state laws, board of nursing regulations, and district policies surrounding delegation of nursing duties.

Examples of Recent Case Law or Legal cases

Many of the lawsuits filed nationwide during the COVID-19 pandemic were in reference to universal masking. The two cases cited below are examples of language used by opponents and proponents of the required wearing of masks in school.

Case 1: *Southwell v. McKee*

A group of 16 families in northern RI sought an injunction against Rhode Island's school mask mandate and extended emergency orders. The complaint alleged that the governor lacked constitutional authority to enforce the mandate and included personal stories from parents and grandparents on the effects the face coverings have had on children. While some cited concerns consistently refuted by medical professionals, many also focused on less measurable changes in children, including depression, withdrawal, and a loss of enthusiasm.

Many noted they had difficulty explaining to their children why they must follow a strictly enforced mask policy at school while the same children spend time together mask-free outside the classroom. The 26-page complaint also questioned the efficacy of masking and cited concerns over changes in oxygen levels. Studies have found that wearing a face mask has a negligible negative effect on oxygen and carbon dioxide levels. Moreover, while estimates on the amount of protection a mask provides may vary, health experts widely agree that face coverings reduce the spread of the virus.

The request was ultimately denied as the court found that "the DOH has the legal authority to promulgate an emergency rule as long as the statutory requirements of § 42-35.2.10 are met." The decision stated that "the Court cannot ignore that the DOH did not act in a vacuum when promulgating the rule (*Southwell v. McKee*, C. A. PC-2021-05915 (R.I. Super. November 12, 2021).

Case 2: *L.E., B.B., A.Z. & C.S. v. Cobb County*

Parents of four medically fragile students in the Cobb County School District in GA filed a federal lawsuit in 2021 to impose a mask mandate and other COVID-19 mitigation measures. The 11ᵗʰ Circuit Court of Appeals reversed an original ruling that would have allowed an injunction against a mask mandate and other precautions for affected medically fragile students to safely attend classes in person. The ruling stated that the school district failed to make "reasonable modifications or accommodations" under guidelines issued by the CDC for those students to attend classes at their home schools. The lawsuit claimed the student's educational rights under the Americans with Disabilities Act were being denied when the school district dropped its mask mandate for the 2021-2022 school year. One of the parents filing suit stated that her 13-year-old son was unable to attend classes because he had leukemia.

After requiring masks the previous school year, the Cobb School District, which had previously been sued by parents opposing the mandates, made them optional but offered parents a virtual learning program. The Cobb District Superintendent stated that mandated masks in school did not appear to result in fewer staff and students infected with COVID-19, and he wanted parents to decide what is best for families. In response to the suit, the Cobb District stated that the parents were "simply complaining about not receiving their preferred educational services – not a deprivation of access to education altogether." In rejecting the Cobb District claim, the appeals court stated the issue is about more than a mask mandate and sent it back to the district court to "analyze whether virtual schooling is a reasonable accommodation for in-person schooling, not education in general."

Attorneys for the plaintiffs hold that "school districts cannot relegate students with disabilities to home virtual programs because of their disabilities. Instead, schools must make reasonable accommodations and modifications so students with disabilities can safely and meaningfully access their schools in person. The 11ᵗʰ Circuit court reversed the district court's decision and sent the case back to the district court for re-evaluation. (U.S. District Court, Northern District of GA, USCA 11 Case: 21-13980, 2022)

CONCLUSION

School nurses can and must be welcomed as key members of the emergency planning, response, and community policy development team, where they can leverage their population health knowledge and expertise. Public health will not be the same as before COVID-19. New health priorities, approaches, and agendas will be on the global platforms and initiatives table. The normalization of the public health and social measures introduced during the COVID-19 pandemic are expected to be seen in the future (Bashier et al., 2021). It will be incumbent upon school nurses to remain ever-vigilant in their surveillance of potential outbreaks and current public health reporting procedures and outbreak guidelines. The school nurse is uniquely positioned as the health expert who is able to understand the process of communicable disease transmission and interpret and implement common-sense policies in an ever-changing environment while assuring that policies are congruent with public health and legal principles.

RESOURCES

Centers for Disease Control and Prevention (2022, October 5). Operational guidance for K12 schools and early care and education programs to support safe in-person learning. https://www.cdc.gov/coronavirus/2019-ncov/community/schools-childcare/k-12-childcare-guidance.html

National Association of School Nurses (n.d.). Working with local public health officials, state and local authorities https://schoolnursenet.nasn.org/covid19ref/glossary/working-with-local-public-health-officials-state-and-local-authorities

U.S. Department of Education, Office of Civil Rights. (2021, May 13). *Questions and answers on civil rights and school re-opening in the Covid-19 environment.* https://www2.ed.gov/about/offices/list/ocr/docs/qa-reopening-202105.pdf" https://www2.ed.gov/about/offices/list/ocr/docs/qa-reopening-202105.pdf

Case Law

Compagnie Francaise &c. v. Board of Health {186 U.S. 380](1902). https://supreme.justia.com/cases/federal/us/186/380/

Jacobsen v. Massachusetts [197 U.S. 11] (1905). https://supreme.justia.com/cases/federal/us/197/11/

Southwell v. McKee, C. A. PC-2021-05915 (R.I. Super. November 12, 2021). https://casetext.com/case/southwell-v-mckee

U.S. District Court, Northern District of GA, USCA 11 Case: 21-13980 (December 16, 2022) https://www.splcenter.org/sites/default/files/21-13980_-_opinion.pdf

REFERENCES

American Nurses Association (n.d.). *Crisis standard of care: COVID-19 pandemic*. Retrieved on 7/31/23 https://www.nursingworld.org/~496044/globalassets/practiceandpolicy/work-environment/health--safety/coronavirus/crisis-standards-of-care.pdf

Baker, C., Galemore, C. A., & McGowan Lowrey, K. (2020). Information sharing in the school setting. *NASN School Nurse*, *35*(4), 198-202. https://doi.org/ /10.1177/1942602X20925031

Bashier H, Ikram A, Khan MA, Baig M, Al Gunaid M, Al Nsour M, Khader Y. 2021, June 18). The anticipated future of public health services post covid-19: Viewpoint. *JMIR Public Health Surveill*, *7*(6), e26267. https://doi.org/ 10.2196/26267

Bullard, J. S., McAlister, B. S., & Chilton, J. M. (2020). Covid-19: planning and postpandemic partnerships. *NASN School Nurse*, *36*(2), 80–84. https://doi.org/10.1177/1942602x20962213

Centers for Disease Control and Prevention. (1994, September 17). *Addressing emerging disease threats: A preventative strategy for the United States executive summary.* https://www.cdc.gov/mmwr/preview/mmwrhtml/00031393. htm

Centers for Disease Control and Prevention. (2022, October 5). *Operational guidance for K-12 schools and early care and education programs to support safe in-person learning.* https://www.cdc.gov/coronavirus/2019-ncov/community/ schools-childcare/k-12-childcare-guidance.html

Centers for Disease Control and Prevention. (2021, September 17). *Legal authorities for isolation and quarantine.* https://www.cdc.gov/quarantine/aboutlawsregulationsquarantineisolation.html

Columbia University, Mailman School of Public Health. (2021, February 19). Epidemic, endemic, pandemic: What are the differences? https://www.publichealth.columbia.edu/news/epidemic-endemic-pandemic-what-are-the-differences

Combe, L. G. (2020). Re-opening schools during COVID-19: School nurse ethical conflicts and moral dilemmas. *NASN School Nurse, 35*(6), 308–312. https://doi.org/10.1177/1942602x20963522

Hall, S. (2021, September 18). Parent from Glocester, North Smithfield, sign onto lawsuit over mask mandate. *NRI NOW.* https://nrinow.news/2021/09/18/parents-from-glocester-north-smithfield-sign-on-to-lawsuit-over-mask-mandate/

Hansen, T. L. (2021). The silver lining of COVID-19. *NASN School Nurse, 36*(3), 142–143. https://doi.org/10.1177/1942602x211005680

Lieberman, M. (2021, November 30). Schools in most states are shielded from Covid lawsuits. It may not help. *Education Week.* https://www.edweek.org/policy-politics/schools-in-most-states-are-shielded-from-covid-lawsuits-it-may-not-help/2021/11

Maughan, E. D., Bobo, N., Butler, S., & Schantz, S. (2016). Framework for 21st Century school nursing practice. *NASN School Nurse, 31*(1), 45–53. https://doi.org/10.1177/1942602x15618644

Molyneux, J. (2009, April 29). AJN speaks with Mary Pappas, school nurse who alerted CDC to Swine Flu outbreak. *AJN Off the Charts* [blog]. https://ajnoffthecharts.com/mary-pappas-school-nurse-just-carrying-on-despite-swine-flu-outbreak/

National Association of County and City Health Officials. (n.d.). *Infectious disease.* https://www.naccho.org/programs/community-health/infectious-disease

National Association of School Nurses. (2022). *School nursing: Scope and standards of practice* (4th ed., p. 15). Author.

National Association of School Nurses. (n.d.). *Working with local public health officials, state and local authorities.* https://schoolnursenet.nasn.org/covid19ref/glossary/working-with-local-public-health-officials-state-and-local-authorities

National Association of School Nurses. (2020, July 30). Considerations for school nurses when providing virtual care. https://higherlogicdownload.s3.amazonaws.com/NASN/3870c72d-fff9-4ed7-833f-215de278d256/ UploadedImages/PDFs/2020_05_13_Considerations_for_School_Nurses_When_Providing_Virtual_Care.pdf

Parker, W., Holmes, E., & Gavin. (2023, January 4). Parents in Cobb schools mask mandate lawsuit win appeal. *East Cobb News.* https://eastcobbnews.com/parents-in-cobb-schools-mask-mandate-lawsuit-win-appeal/

Rogers, L. C. (1908). Some phases of school nursing. *American Journal of Nursing, 8*(12), 966–974. https://doi.org/10.1097/00000446-190809000-00012

Sawchuk, S. (2020, September 3). Schools may get sued over covid-19. 7 things to know about managing that risk. *Education Week*. https://www.edweek.org/leadership/schools-may-get-sued-over-covid-19-7-things-to-know-about-managing-that-risk/2020/09

Selekman, J., Chewey, L., Cogan, R., & Conway, S. (2019). School nurse collaboration with community partners. In J. Selekman, R. A. Shannon, & C. F. Yonkaitis (Eds.), *School nursing: A comprehensive text* (3rd ed., p. 126). F.A. Davis Company. U.S. Department of Education. (2020, March). *FERPA & Coronavirus disease 2019 (COVID-19): Frequently asked questions (FAQs) March 2020*. https://studentprivacy.ed.gov/sites/default/files/resource_document/file/FERPA%20and%20Coronavirus%20Frequently%20Asked%20Questions.pdf

U.S. Department of Education, Office of Civil Rights. (2021, May 13). *Questions and answers on civil rights and school re-opening in the Covid-19 environment*. https://www2.ed.gov/about/offices/list/ocr/docs/qa-reopening-202105.pdf

University of Maryland, School of Nursing. (2022). Module 4: Primary, Secondary, and Tertiary Prevention [MOOC]. In the University of Maryland, School of Nursing, Nur 780 Health Promotion and Population Health. https://cf.son.umaryland.edu/NRSG780/module4/subtopic1.htmWebster, L., & Wocial, L. D. (2020, Sept.). Ethics in a pandemic: Nurses need to engage in self-care to reduce moral distress. *American Nurse Journal, 15* (9), pp. 18-23. https://www.myamericannurse.com/wp-content/uploads/2020/09/an9-Pandemic-ETHICS-902.pdf

World Health Organization. (2020, December 9). WHO reveals leading causes of death and disability worldwide: 2000-2019. https://www.who.int/news/item/09-12-2020-who-reveals-leading-causes-of-death-and-disability-worldwide-2000-2019.Wolfe, L. C. (2019). Historical perspectives of school nursing. In J. Selekman, R. A. Shannon, & C. F. Yonkaitis (Eds.), *School nursing: A comprehensive text* (3rd ed., p. 4). F.A. Davis Company.

Chapter 43

DISASTER PREPAREDNESS FOR SCHOOL HEALTH SERVICES
Linda S. Kalekas, MSN, RN, NCSN, PHTLS

DESCRIPTION OF ISSUE

Key Components of Disaster Preparedness for School Health Services include:

1. Understanding of overarching federal, state, territorial, tribal, county, and local laws or policies that influence disaster preparedness requirements for schools;
2. Knowledge of the National Incident Management System (NIMS) and Incident Command System (ICS) and how it impacts the disaster preparedness cycle for schools;
3. Knowledge of emergency and disaster preparedness planning and the physical plans for schools using the Threat and Hazard Identification and Risk Assessment (THIRA) approach;
4. Participation of school health services personnel in emergency operations planning, training, and exercises to include prevention, planning, response, recovery, and mitigation phases of emergency management;
5. Knowledge of the school nurse's role in emergency and disaster preparedness and response in the school setting, including potential Incident Command System (ICS) roles;
6. Ability to demonstrate competency in performing emergency and disaster response duties such as communications, the chain of command, integration into the incident command system on-scene, and coordination of casualty care with other first responder agencies on-scene;
7. Ability to ensure first responder safety, appropriate use of personal protective equipment, and safe use of all emergency equipment and supplies as provided by school health services or schools for use during events; and,
8. Awareness of the school nurse's professional liability related to education, training, and skills competency for disaster preparedness.

The Federal Emergency Management Agency (FEMA) and the Robert T. Stafford Disaster and Emergency Assistance Act (2013) define a major disaster as

> "any natural catastrophe (including any hurricane, tornado, storm, high water, wind-driven water, tidal wave, tsunami, earthquake, volcanic eruption, landslide, mudslide, snowstorm, or drought) or, regardless of cause, any fire, flood, or explosion, in any part of the United States, which in the determination of the President causes the damage of sufficient severity and magnitude to warrant major disaster assistance under this Act to supplement the efforts and available resources of States, local governments, and disaster relief organizations in alleviating the damage, loss, hardship, or suffering caused thereby. " (FEMA, 2023, para. 1).

A disaster will usually occur with little or no forewarning. The size of a disaster is measured relative to the onset, duration, magnitude, and geographical scope of its impact. There is usually significant loss of human life, extensive damage to physical property and critical infrastructure, and large economic or environmental losses. The ability to manage the disaster sequelae depends on the extent to which essential personnel and resources can respond to the type of disaster that has occurred.

The U.S. National Preparedness Goal is to ensure the American public "a secure and resilient with the capabilities required across the whole community to prevent, protect against, mitigate, respond to, and recover from the threats and hazards that pose the greatest risk" (FEMA, 2023, para. 1). Existing legal precepts for federal emergency authority and immunity are based upon laws and policies which provide an overarching framework for disaster preparedness in all state, territorial, tribal, county, and local jurisdictions. Schools are an integral part of the communities where they reside, and school districts may overlap with multiple government and non-government entities. Schools are essential partners in the ability of the local community to effectively engage in all phases of emergency management, including "prevention, preparedness, response, recovery and mitigation," as defined by the Federal Emergency Management Agency (FEMA, 2023, p.2). Successful outcomes during and after a disaster are often the product of excellent collaboration among all stakeholders prior to a real-world event.

School crisis and emergency preparedness plans are developed in accordance with state statutes derived from federal laws and policies (FEMA, 2021). It is essential for school nurses to become familiar with legal directives and school plans governing emergency preparedness, school safety, and school health in the state where they are licensed. The Education Commission of States (2022) conducted state-by-state research and compiled statutes that address school safety plans' core elements nationwide. Nurses must become familiar with the residential state, county, and local statutes that define the difference between crisis, emergency, or disaster conditions. State laws will govern the authorized acts of a licensed nurse under emergency or special conditions, such as disasters occurring within the state.

School nurses have a unique role to protect and serve the nation's children whenever disaster strikes during the school day. According to the National Association of School Nurses (NASN), "[S]school nurses are a vital part of the school team responsible for developing emergency response procedures for the school setting [using an all-hazards approach which includes full range of potential threats]; … while emergencies in the school setting are often unpredictable, those involved in the care of students should prepare to meet the needs of those students before, during, and after an event." (NASN, 2019, para 1). Once a disaster has occurred, school nurses will:
- have either a direct or supportive role in conducting medical and psychological triage;
- implement life-saving interventions;
- provide pre-hospital emergency care;
- coordinate the transfer of care of victims to emergency medical services; and
- provide support for on-scene fatality management.

It is important to know if local, county, or state laws would compel a public or non-public school nurse to serve in disaster relief or disaster service worker status. Once an emergency or disaster declaration has been issued, public healthcare employees in many states may be legally mandated to work in response to a disaster. For example, in California, "as a city, county, or state agency or public district employee, you may be called upon as a disaster service worker in the event of an emergency" (California Government Code, Section 3101-3109, 2016).

Disaster planning for at-risk school populations includes identifying students who are medically fragile and those students who require specialized nursing procedures or emergency medications. Furthermore, the school nurse assists in identifying students who have access or functional needs to confirm that safety accommodations are in place and appropriate adult assistance is available during emergencies. In a policy statement provided by the American Academy of Pediatrics, part of being prepared for a disaster means, "Children with special healthcare needs must be identified and have valid emergency care plans in place, including plans for managing both individual emergencies related to the child's illness and plans to manage the complex medical needs of the student in the event of a larger community emergency" (AAP, 2012, para. 18).

Due to the unique role of the school nurse in disasters, education and training are needed to establish competency as a first responder in extreme medical casualty or public health disaster situations. While specific training or certification in these aspects of care may not be legally mandated or employer-required, there are educational programs available that could enhance the school nurses' competence in disaster response. Additionally, many school districts will mandate annual education, training, practice drills, or exercises for employees who might respond to acts of violence, terrorism, and man-made or natural disasters.

BACKGROUND

Historical Perspective

Disasters have occurred throughout time and are memorialized in some of the earliest recordings of American history. United States (US) disasters have included tragedies such as shipwrecks, railroad accidents, bridge and dam failures, flooding, fires, droughts, airplane crashes, explosions, tornados, hurricanes, blizzards, coal mine accidents, earthquakes, volcanic eruptions, avalanches, bombings, stampedes, military strikes, hazardous material spills, terrorism and much more. These events may adversely impact schools in a community affected by the disaster.

Schools are sometimes targets for man-made disasters, and the school nurse may be confronted with these disasters at any time. School disasters have included school shootings, weather-related incidents, bus accidents, tainted water supply, and other forms of school violence.

School disasters occur overseas as well and may represent acts of terrorism. The Beslan No. 1 School siege in the Russian Federation of North Ossetia lasted three days and involved the capture of over 1,100 students, parents, and staff taken as hostages on the first day of the school year. The siege ended with the death of at least 385 people. With the tragedy at Beslan No.1 School, an alarm was sounded for American communities to recognize that schools in the US might also become a target for terrorism. On December 2, 2015, 14 people were killed, and 22 were seriously injured in a terrorist attack at the Inland Regional Center in San Bernardino, California. The Inland Regional Center, while not a school, provided care for children and adults with severe disabilities. *(See Chapter 52 for more information on school violence and Chapter 41 on Active Shooter.)*

Federal Emergency Authority and Immunity

Following the terrorism events of September 11, 2001, the United States government issued a series of new or revised federal laws and policies (Figure 1) designed to direct national emergency preparedness and response activities. Presidential directives set overarching policy for homeland security in the wake of the horrific events and loss of life in New York, Virginia, and Pennsylvania, that fateful day. Among all the Homeland Security Policy Directives (HSPDs) and Presidential Policy Directives (PPDs) issued, the tenets of HSPD-5 (management of domestic incidents), HSPD-21 (public health and medical preparedness), and PPD-8 (national preparedness) have the greatest influence upon disaster preparedness for school districts and school nurses.

The National Emergencies Act (NEA) (Pub. L. 94–412, 50 U.S.C. § 1601-1651) authorizes the US President to declare a national emergency, and subsequent federal and state authorizations provided by other federal legislation are activated upon that declaration. The Robert T. Stafford Disaster and Emergency Assistance Act (Public Law 93-288, as amended, 42 U.S.C. 5121 et seq.), widely known as the Stafford Act, authorizes the federal government to provide financial, technical, and logistical disaster relief to states and other US localities during disasters. Each state has legislation authorizing its governor to declare a "major disaster" or "state of emergency" whenever state resources become overwhelmed in response to a disaster scenario. Once a governor makes such a declaration, FEMA will begin providing disaster relief and assistance to the state or locality in distress.

If federal buildings are involved or multiple states are impacted, the Stafford Act may authorize federal assistance even without a formal governor's request. Additionally, there are federal laws in place to enhance inter-state cooperation during disasters. States have adopted language in their emergency management statutes to conform to federal guidelines so that they may benefit from state-to-state assistance under the Emergency Management Assistance Compact (EMAC) (Pub. L. No. 104-321, 1996). EMAC provides a framework for one state to assist another state and be reimbursed; it also ensures liability, compensation, and licensure protections when personnel or other resources cross state lines to help.

Following the terrorist attacks on September 11, 2001, the President called for all government and non-government entities to develop a model for emergency preparedness planning that aligned with a national template. In accordance with the guidelines provided by the DHS (2015), the template used by all entities is the *Comprehensive Preparedness Guide* (CPG) 101 document. According to the DHS (2015), the "CPG 101 is the foundation for state, territorial, tribal, and local emergency planning in the United States. Planners in other disciplines, organizations, and the private sector, as well as other levels of government, may find this Guide useful in the development of their [emergency operation plans] EOPs" (FEMA, 2010, Fugate Letter)
Tenets of emergency management are derived from the National Response Framework (NRF) and the National Incident Management System (NIMS). On-scene emergency and disaster first responders (including school nurses and other school staff) utilize the Incident Command System (ICS) to operationalize NIMS's planning, operations, logistics, finance, administration, and intelligence functions. State legislation drives the development of inter-connected emergency operation plans (EOP) across all jurisdictions, including government and non-government organizations (NGOs) within a state. Regional trauma systems further direct and influence the management of medical surge victims to acute-care facilities and the delivery of emergency medical services in the field and across a large disaster-impact area.

Figure 1: Federal Emergency Authority and Immunity Laws & Policies

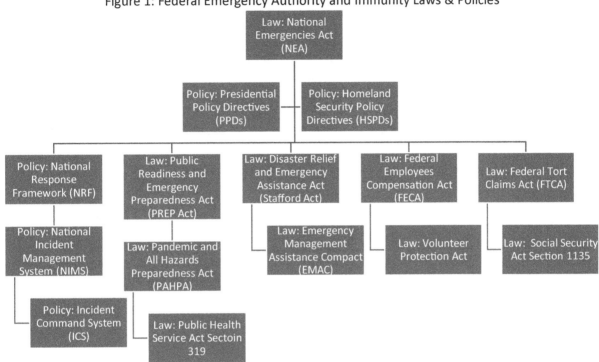

IMPLICATIONS FOR SCHOOL NURSE PRACTICE

While educational leadership focuses primarily on academic goals and objectives for student learning, a host of potential natural and man-made or technological hazards may adversely affect school, student, and staff safety at any moment. Acts of school violence, severe weather and hazards, and global terrorism may contribute to the risks and liability for students and school staff. The public's traditional perception that schools are safe havens for children is challenged whenever disaster strikes.

Following a disaster, a school district may be on its own for some time before assistance becomes available through traditional means from the Emergency Medical System (EMS) and law enforcement (LE) agencies. Thus, each school district will benefit from developing an EOP and school-based emergency response plans encompassing long-term mass care capability. Mass care within a school district often involves a memorandum of understanding (MOU) with the American Red Cross or other NGOs to use school facilities, buses, and staff. School district EOPs and school-based plans might also plan for mass casualty incident (MCI) response capability. MCI management may be the duty of a school nurse (by virtue of nursing licensure and training) until help arrives, so the school district/school should have a plan for this function that involves the school's emergency response team helping with triage at the direction of the school nurse. School nurses trained to initiate triage, provide pre-hospital care, and ready victims for transport during an MCI may be the weakest link in the school nurse's level of preparedness. For schools to build an effective disaster preparedness coalition with other jurisdictions, EOPs must be developed based on collaboration with all appropriate stakeholders. It is critical that school administrators and faculty are fully informed about and trained on the school's emergency plans and can understand their role during all phases of the FEMA Preparedness Cycle (Figure 2).

Area hospitals, health and medical facilities, and emergency medical services may not be able to sustain full operational capacity during a disaster due to adverse impacts on personnel, facilities, or critical infrastructure. Additionally, EMS and local acute care facilities may simply be overwhelmed dealing with the excessive volume of the medical surge. School districts may need to activate the district emergency operations centers (DOC/ EOC) or municipal EOC to facilitate the high demand for personnel, equipment, and supplies to deal with the disaster impact. Health services administrators may be part of the team responding to the EOC to assist the school district with planning, operations, and logistics demands throughout the disaster. The EOC will collaborate with on-scene school personnel and other jurisdictions to provide support.

Figure 2: FEMA Preparedness Cycle- *Federal Emergency Management Agency (2016)*.

Schools will implement emergency plans using the principles of the Incident Command System (FEMA, 2017). An initial communication to staff will alert them to implement appropriate protective measures based on the emergency plan guidelines. Using an all-hazards approach to planning and implementing emergency plans enables schools to set guidelines for four or five specific response capabilities that are well-defined and easy to learn. With practice, staff and students will know how to implement evacuation, reverse evacuation, shelter-in-place, lockdown, and reunification procedures in response to an emergency or disaster event at their schools.

School districts generally have many resources in communications, transportation, facilities, food services, maintenance personnel, emergency managers, police or security monitors, school nurses, health aides, counselors, and psychologists. Mutual aid agreements and pacts established prior to a real-world event are essential to ensuring strong, reliable response and recovery capabilities in an actual disaster. School districts and their respective health services personnel are further challenged to develop and implement continuity of operations plans (COOP) for staff and students that provide a framework for resuming the school district's primary goal of educating students as soon as possible.

School Nurse Role as First Responder

By governor's order or state law or policy, many states may require public school nurses to serve as disaster service workers during a state of emergency or disaster declaration. Their nursing expertise may be required to help restore essential health and medical services for a disaster-impact area within or overlapping the school district. Any school nurse who performs medical triage, life-saving interventions, and emergency treatment within their scope of practice and when performed in good faith during a disaster will likely have immunity from civil liability, but laws vary from state to state. Therefore, knowing the laws, including the Good Samaritan law, in the jurisdiction where the nurse practices is very important.

Statistical data from a nurses' professional liability company, the Nurses Service Organization (NSO, 2020), revealed that frequent reasons that nurses are sued for malpractice are due to "improper technique or negligent performance of treatment" (56%), "failure to follow facility procedures and provide a safe environment" (14.3%) and "acting outside scope of practice" (3.3%). Additionally, among the top six most common injuries resulting in lawsuits naming nurses are _fracture_ (6.4%) and _abrasion/bruise/contusion/ laceration_ (2.9%) (NSO, 2020), all of which are injuries commonly encountered by school nurses when providing first aid and emergency care of students.

According to Brent (2001), "The area of school nursing which holds the most potential for professional liability is that of acute and emergency care" (p. 410). School nurses must be capable of coordinating health and medical services on school district property to reduce the risk of death and injury during emergency situations. Case law illustrates that school nurses must exercise professional judgment to demonstrate competency in injury assessment, to provide appropriate emergency care, and to determine which injuries require medical referral. "Even though nurses who are employees of public-school districts are granted certain immunities from lawsuits based upon ordinary professional negligence, school nurses must be certain to provide nursing care to students consistent with established standards of school nursing practice" (Brent, 2001, p. 412). _(See Chapter 2 for more information on malpractice/legal liability.)_

School-based emergency operations planning must address the need for multiple methods of communication so that school nurses can access school administration, staff, nursing supervisors, police, fire, and emergency medical services during emergencies. School nurses must be capable of implementing and responding to evacuation, reverse evacuation, shelter-in-place, lockdown, and reunification procedures at their schools. Knowing how and when to implement these response actions is paramount to self-survival, especially during active assailant or active shooter situations.

Due to the risk of exposure to chemical, biological, radiological, nuclear, and high-yield explosives (CBRNE) materials, school nurses should receive hazardous materials awareness level training to minimize the risk of exposure. School nurses must be knowledgeable about first responder safety and the appropriate levels of personal protective equipment (PPE) needed to care for disaster victims safely. Available PPE might include gowns, gloves, and masks, including N95 masks, goggles, and shields. Decontamination of victims requires specialized training and should not be attempted unless the school nurse is knowledgeable and trained in the performance of dry doff and wet doff procedures.

During mass casualty incidents (MCIs), school nurses are first responders on their school campuses, providing disaster triage and life-saving care. Conducting triage during a disaster requires transitioning from everyday health office triage when the nurse would first give her attention to the most seriously injured or ill students. In an MCI, the school nurse will be forced to consider which victims are viable based on the number of personnel, equipment, and available resources. Those victims with the most serious injuries or illnesses may not receive immediate care in a disaster with mass casualties. For example, cardio-pulmonary resuscitative measures may not be initiated for anyone arrested during the incident as the focus may be on using resources for those who can be saved.

School nurses may want to seek additional training to learn field triage protocols which explain how to categorize victims based on the severity of the injury. Various tagging systems are available, and nurses are advised to contact their local EMS facilities to see which type of tag system is being used in their local community. The ability of school nurses to make death pronouncements differs state-to-state, so school nurses should seek guidance from their State Board of Nursing. A local source of information regarding fatality management could be obtained from the local coroner's office. If the mass casualty incident is a potential crime scene, preservation of evidence will take precedence over school nurses moving deceased victims.

School Nurse Role in a Public Health Disaster

School nurses routinely monitor student populations for signs and symptoms of communicable diseases and serve as sentinels for actual or potential public health outbreaks. Public health emergency operation plans for infectious diseases will include mobilization and demobilization of pre-determined points of dispensing (PODs), which are often located at public schools. PODs are used to provide mass vaccine prophylaxis and medication treatment to the public due to biological terrorism or widespread communicable disease outbreaks such as influenza. Schools may also be identified as locations for isolation and quarantine during an epidemic or pandemic.

The COVID-19 Pandemic created new challenges for school nurses across the U.S., especially upon the reopening of schools for in-person education in the fall of 2021. Focusing on student health and safety, the school nurse had a magnified responsibility to implement COVID-19 mitigation strategies in schools, including handwashing, mask-wearing, and monitoring all students (and staff) for signs or symptoms of potentially contagious illness. Health services policies and procedures had to be developed per public health and government directives for COVID-19 management, which required frequent revisions to stay consistent with new public health information and guidelines. School administrators looked to health services personnel for COVID-19 guidance and expected the school nurse to manage COVID-19 symptomatic cases, implement quarantine and isolation procedures, perform contact tracing, and conduct COVID-19 testing. School health services moved from a one-room health office to having multiple rooms to serve as a well room, sick room, and a room for performing aerosol-generating procedures such as suctioning and nebulizer treatments. This created a need to triage symptomatic students from the classroom

> "The individual school nurse is in a unique position to help people within their districts to navigate the physical health, emotional well-being, and social challenges COVID-19 has presented to be better educated and make appropriate personal health decisions based on scientific facts" (McIntosh et al., 2022).

to ensure minimal risk of infection transmission. Eventually, the school nurse also referred students and staff for COVID-19 vaccination.

As school nurses experienced the COVID-19 Pandemic in the workplace, its impact created many ethical and legal challenges that should inform future nursing practice in the school setting relative to public health disasters. National and state disaster declarations will have an impact on the delivery of services rendered by all licensed nurses and may include an expansion of their scope of practice during a pandemic to meet staffing shortages. For example, school nurses were permitted to collect COVID-19 lab specimens and perform COVID-19 testing in schools as an expanded role. However, nurse malpractice insurance may not cover a nurse in this or another form of an expanded role even if supported by a legal mandate issued by the governor's order or the state board of education when the expanded role is not customary. State boards of nursing should be consulted if school nurses are expected to perform duties during a pandemic that are not typical of their scope of practice or professional standards of care under ordinary circumstances to ensure legal mandates for an expanded role of the nurse are reasonable and prudent. (*See Chapter 42 for more information on communicable disease outbreak management.*)

School Nurse Competency for Disaster Preparedness

School nurses must demonstrate competency in emergency response during drills, exercises, and emergencies. Opportunities to practice and demonstrate an understanding of the chain of command and communication responsibilities are essential for rapid reporting and response during emergencies. Awareness of school nurses' limitations in skills, knowledge, and authority in response to disasters is essential to minimize legal risks when performing disaster response actions. School nurses have a responsibility to help schools plan, organize, equip, train, exercise, evaluate, and improve response and recovery capabilities for the continued provision of school health services during disasters. Further, the preparedness cycle can be utilized to ensure school nurses can shift from everyday crisis or emergency operations to a disaster-level response capability when necessary.

Education and training of school nurses should emphasize the following:
- NIMS and ICS,
- Knowledge of the school EOP and the nurse's role(s),
- Use of emergency communication systems,
- Donning and doffing of personnel protective equipment,
- Disaster triage,
- Life-saving interventions, and
- Pre-hospital treatment for both children and adults.

Mental health triage and first aid training are essential and should be provided to all school staff who volunteer to assist. School nurses need the ability to identify immediate personnel, equipment, and supply needs. They must know how to utilize available resources wisely, recognizing that management of resources may shift from those whose death is imminent to those with a possible chance of survival.

Conducting drills and exercises for a shelter-in-place due to a Chemical, Biological, Radiological, Nuclear, and high yield Explosives (CBRNE) event response would result in the ability to minimize potential exposure to hazardous materials for everyone involved should an actual CBRNE event occur. School nurses require education and training about mass sheltering and medical surge procedures established for their local communities. Schools may serve as alternative collection sites during mass migration events or as mass shelters for victims displaced from their homes during a disaster. Knowledge of preserving crime scene evidence, providing post-mortem care, and transferring bodies to mortuary personnel is also warranted.

Developing a certification program specifically designed for school nurses in disaster preparedness is appropriate. The NASN developed the School Emergency Triage Training (SETT) Program® to assist school nurses with basic disaster triage knowledge and training. School nurses may also benefit from a program that provides education and training for pre-hospital trauma and treatment skills. Most of the existing nursing certifications address the needs of patients in the acute care hospital or emergency room setting. School nurses may function as first responders in the field, like emergency medical services personnel such as emergency medical technicians (EMTs) or paramedics. Restrictions on nursing scope of practice and licensure may prohibit school nurses from performing many life-saving functions entrusted to paraprofessionals in the field setting.

A widely accepted life-saving intervention during mass casualty incidents is bleeding control, the basis for a nationally recognized training entitled the Stop-the-Bleed® program (n.d.). Participants learn to identify significant bleeding injuries and provide essential life-saving treatment interventions such as wound packing and applying pressure dressings and tourniquets. Schools and school districts should seek this certification for school nurses and other district employees to ensure a rapid response for bleeding control to save lives during mass casualty incidents.

EMTs and paramedics have field guidelines for triage and follow medically approved standing orders for initiating intravenous therapy and administering emergency drugs. Most school nurses are not performing these duties in schools and may not have standing orders for these actions. School nurses may seek additional certifications such as Basic Disaster Life Support (BDLS) or Pre-Hospital Trauma Life Support (PHTLS) to gain the knowledge and skills needed for mass casualty care. Along with other certification programs, these will teach triage, intubation, intravenous therapy, emergency medication administration, and other life-saving interventions; however, individual state laws and the nurse practice act may not permit the school nurse to perform some duties in the school setting. Additionally, the school or district by which a nurse is employed may not be willing to support the liability associated with performing some of these procedures in the school health setting. Nurses need to be assured they have medical-legal support for advanced practice roles, and documentation of such support is prudent.

Funding is needed to support school nursing personnel's planning, operations, equipping, education, training, and exercises. School districts must assert their value to the local community before a real-world event and participate actively in the local, county, and statewide planning and exercises. School nurses benefit their school staff and students in any potential disaster. They can perform better if allowed to participate in tactical and operational disaster tabletops exercises, basic drills, and functional or full-scale exercises involving multi-jurisdictional entities prior to a real-world event.

CONCLUSION

School nurses have an ethical and professional duty to respond to public and mental health emergencies, to protect the public during public health disasters, and to be prepared to respond to mass casualty incidents involving school campuses during disasters. Minimizing loss of life and limb is the number one priority for school nurses as they actively engage in disaster response. School nurses must be educated, trained, and practiced and have appropriate equipment and supplies to respond safely during natural and man-made or technological disasters.

RESOURCES

American Academy of Pediatrics. (2022). *Disaster and Emergency Preparedness in Schools.* https://www.aap.org/en/patient-care/school-health/disaster-and-emergency-preparedness-in-schools/

American College of Surgeons. (2023). *Stop-the-Bleed®*. https://www.stopthebleed.org/training/

Centers for Disease Control and Prevention. (2020). Flint Water Crisis. https://www.cdc.gov/nceh/casper/pdf-html/flint_water_crisis_pdf.html

Federal Emergency Management Agency. (2010). Developing and maintaining emergency operations plans: comprehensive preparedness guide (CPC) 101, version 2.0. https://www.fema.gov/sites/default/files/2020-05/CPG_101_V2_30NOV2010_FINAL_508.pdf

Federal Emergency Management Agency (FEMA). (2011). *Fact Sheet: Disaster Declaration Process*. https://www.fema.gov/pdf/media/factsheets/dad_disaster_declaration.pdf

Federal Emergency Management Agency. (2016). Preparedness cycle. https://www.fema.gov/media-library/assets/images/114295

Federal Emergency Management Agency. (2020). Guide for developing high-quality school emergency operations plans. https://www.fema.gov/sites/default/files/2020-07/guide-developing-school-emergency-operations-plans.pdf

Federal Emergency Management Agency (FEMA), Emergency Management Institute. (2022). *Courses for Independent Study*. This includes courses for National Incident Management System (NIMS) and Incident Command System (ICS). https://training.fema.gov/is/

Federal Emergency Management Agency. (2018). Threat and hazard identification and risk assessment (THIRA) and stakeholder preparedness review (SPR) guide, comprehensive preparedness guide (CPG) 201, 3rd Edition. https://www.fema.gov/sites/default/files/2020-07/threat-hazard-identification-risk-assessment-stakeholder-preparedness-review-guide.pdf

International Council of Nurses (2019). *Core Competencies in Disaster Nursing, Version 2.0.* https://www.icn.ch/sites/default/files/inline-files/ICN_Disaster-Comp-Report_WEB.pdf

National Center for Injury Prevention and Control, Division of Violence Prevention. (2021). *Fast Facts: Preventing School Violence*. https://www.cdc.gov/violenceprevention/youthviolence/schoolviolence/fastfact. html#print

Pew Research Center. (2023). *What the data says about gun deaths in the U.S.* https://www.pewresearch.org/fact-tank/2022/02/03/what-the-data-says-about-gun-deaths-in-the-u-s/

The Nelson A. Rockefeller Institute of Government. (2022). *Mass Shooting Factsheet*. *https://rockinst.org/gun-violence/mass-shooting-factsheet/*

REFERENCES

American Academy of Pediatrics, Council on School Health. (2012). *Disaster planning for schools. Pediatrics, 122*(4). (2ⁿᵈ ed.). W.B. Saunders Company. https://doi.org/10.1542/peds.2008-2170

California Government Code. (2016). *California Legislative Information. CHAPTER 8. Oath or affirmation of allegiance for disaster service workers and public employees [3100 - 3109]* (Heading of Chapter 8 amended by Stats. 1972, Ch. 590.) https://leginfo.legislature.ca.gov/faces/codes_displaySection. xhtml?sectionNum=3100.&nodeTreePath=2.6.7&lawCode=GOV

Chartoff; S.E., Kropp, A.M., Roman, P. (2022). Disaster planning. *StatPearls Publishing LLC*. https://www.ncbi.nlm. nih.gov/books/NBK470570/#:~:text=The%20basic%20structure%20for%20disaster,preparedness%2C%20 response%2C%20and%20recovery

Emergency Assistance Justice Center, New York. (2014). *School safety plans: A snapshot of legislative action*. https://csgjusticecenter.org/wp-content/uploads/2020/02/NCSL-School-Safety-Plans-Brief.pdf

Department of Homeland Security. (2015). *National preparedness goal (2ⁿᵈ Ed)*. https://www.dhs.gov/national-preparedness-goal

Education Commission of States. (2022). *50-state comparison: K-12 school safety*. https://www.ecs.org/50-state-comparison-k-12-school-safety-2022/

Emergency Management Assistance Compact. (1996), *PUBLIC LAW 104–321*. https://www.congress.gov/104/plaws/publ321/PLAW-104publ321.pdf

Federal Emergency Management Agency. (2021). *National response framework, list of authorities, and references*. https://www.fema.gov/pdf/emergency/nrf/nrf-authorities.pdf

Federal Emergency Management Agency. (2022). *Emergency operations center how-to-quick reference guide*. https://www.fema.gov/sites/default/files/documents/fema_eoc-quick-reference-guide.pdf

Federal Emergency Management Agency (2023). *Glossary: Terms frequently used by FEMA*. https://www.fema.gov/about/glossary/m

McIntosh, C.E., Brelage, P.K., Thomas, C.M., Wendel, J.M., & Phelps, B.E. (2022, April). School nurse and COVID-19 response. *Psychology in* the Schools, 60(5), 1532-1543. https://doi.org/10.1002/pits.22708

National Association of School Nurses. (2019). *Emergency preparedness* (Position Statement).   Author. https://www.nasn.org/nasn-resources/professional-practice-documents/position-statements/ps-emergency-preparedness

National Association of School Nurses. *School Emergency Triage Training (SETT)*. (2023). https://www.nasn.org/education-events/sett

National Emergencies Act. (1976). Pub. L. 94–412, 90 Stat. 1255, codified at 50 U.S.C. § 1601-1651

Nurses Service Organization (NSO). 2020. Infographic – Medical Malpractice 101
https://www.nso.com/malpractice-insurance/Individuals/Nurses?Profession=Nurse

Robert T. Stafford Disaster and Emergency Assistance Act. (2013). Public Law 93-288, as amended, 42 U.S.C. 5121 et seq.

Stop the Bleed. (n.d.). Get trained! HTTPS://WWW.STOPTHEBLEED.ORG/TRAINING/

Chapter 44

IMMUNIZATION COMPLIANCE

Linda Davis-Alldritt, MA, BSN, RN, FNASN, FASHA

DESCRIPTION OF ISSUE

School immunization laws have a long history in the United States and have substantially reduced the incidence of communicable and vaccine-preventable diseases throughout the country (Orenstein & Hinman, 1999). Reduction or elimination of vaccine-preventable diseases included smallpox, polio, measles, rubella, mumps, diphtheria, pertussis, and varicella (Boyer-Chu & Yonkaitis, 2019; Salmon et al., 2005). While vaccines have significantly contributed to many worldwide public health achievements and have been acclaimed as one of the ten great public health achievements of the 20th century (Centers for Disease Control and Prevention [CDC], 1999; CDC, 2011), they have also been the basis of legal and ethical controversy (The College of Physicians of Philadelphia, 2022a).

Challenges related to state and local vaccination requirements for schools are particularly complex. For example, questions regarding individual civil liberties versus public health and welfare, parent and staff misperceptions of vaccine safety and disease risk, access disparities to vaccines, and an organized anti-vaccine movement (The College of Physicians of Philadelphia, 2022a) have contributed to declining vaccination rates in many areas in the country. Serious outbreaks of vaccine-preventable diseases have been fueled by decreased uptake of vaccines, misinformation, and falsified research data, resulting in increased absenteeism and subsequent loss of school revenue (Poland & Jacobson, 2011). The global Covid pandemic, 2020-2022, recently fueled the largest decrease in vaccination uptake in over 30 years (United Nations Children's Fund [UNICEF], 2022). Additional challenges to compliance with school immunization laws include missing or incomplete vaccination records, parent, and healthcare provider buy-in, school nurse staffing issues, and due to competing priorities, school administration adherence to school vaccination laws (Mazyck, 2010). The threat of exclusion for non-compliance typically helps enforce school law (Paquette, 2021).

BACKGROUND

Every child in every school in this country is entitled to safety (Association of Supervision and Curriculum Development & CDC, 2014). School immunizations ensure that school-age children have healthy and safe learning environments. Further, reducing the threat of communicable illnesses overall reduces school absenteeism, and families and communities incur less risk of morbidity and mortality (Orenstein & Hinman, 1999).

Schools play an important role in community transmission of vaccine-preventable diseases. The concept of "herd immunity" implies that the risk of disease is lowered in susceptible individuals if a large percentage of the general population is immune to specific diseases and supports school immunization efforts (Association for Professionals in Infection Control and Epidemiology, 2021). However, while proven successful in protecting the public's health, vaccines remain controversial for some individuals and groups.

The United States has no national vaccination requirement for school entry or attendance. The framers of the Constitution seemed to favor the rights of individuals as set forth in the Bill of Rights. The Tenth Amendment states that those powers not specifically delegated to the federal government are reserved for the states, including developing and enforcing school immunization mandates. All 50 states and the District of Columbia (D.C.) have school immunization laws and regulations that generally reflect the Advisory Committee on Immunization Practices (ACIP) recommendations (National Conference of State Legislatures, 2021), and all states and D.C. allow medical exemptions from mandated school immunizations (National Conference of State Legislatures, 2022). Medical exemptions may be permanent or temporary. As of 2022, forty-four states and D.C. allow religious exemptions, and fifteen allow philosophical or personal belief exemptions. California, Connecticut, Maine, Mississippi, New York, and West Virginia only allow medical exemptions (National Conference of State Legislatures, 2022; The College of Physicians of Philadelphia, 2022d). All 50 states, D.C., and all U.S. territories have some immunization registry, either statewide, regional, or local. As of 2015, according to the CDC, 92 percent of children aged six and under were part of a registry (National Conference of State Legislatures, 2021).

This chapter uses the terms "vaccination" and "immunization" interchangeably. While all vaccinations can lead to immunization, immunizations are not the same as vaccines. Vaccines are a type of artificial immunization.

IMPLICATIONS FOR SCHOOL NURSE PRACTICE

Since 1902, when Lina Rogers was hired by the New York City Board of Education as the nation's first school nurse to reduce absenteeism related to infectious diseases, school nurses have been at the forefront of disease surveillance, prevention, and management. School nurses have repeatedly demonstrated their worth in keeping children healthy, safe, in school, and ready to learn. For instance, during the 2009 H1N1 influenza pandemic, a school nurse, Mary Pappas, in New York City recognized and alerted the CDC (CDC) to an outbreak of flu-like symptoms at her school (Fauteux, 2010). School nurses provide important public health services, including health education, immunization surveillance by maintaining student health records and reporting immunization compliance to state departments of public health, and organizing and staffing immunization clinics (Luthy et al., 2011; Maughan et al., 2016; Schaffer et al., 2016).

School nurses are often referred to as "gatekeepers" regarding communicable disease prevention. Parents, healthcare providers, and communities rely on school nurses to keep children safe and healthy while at school. School administrators rely on school nurses to provide guidance to staff, parents, and students about school immunization requirements, compliance, and enforcement. School nurses are a trusted source of health information for students and families. They are well-positioned to educate students, families, and school staff about the importance of immunizations, including addressing safety concerns (National Association of School Nurses [NASN], 2020a).

Every school day in the United States, approximately 50 million students and 7.0 million teachers, administrators, and other school personnel gather in the nation's nearly 130,000 schools (National Center for Educational Statistics, 2022), placing the nation's approximately 96,000 school nurses on the frontlines of disease surveillance (Willgerot et al., 2018). School nurses promote healthy habits, address students' episodic and chronic health conditions, and play an important role in preventing, managing, and containing communicable disease outbreaks in the school and community (Fauteux, 2010). Schools with school nurses tend to have better vaccine coverage and fewer non-medical exemptions than schools without school nurses (Baisch et al., 2011). School nurses correctly identify students out of compliance with state immunization laws and effectively communicate with administrators and parents what is needed to bring students into compliance. School nurses communicate with parents, school staff, and students, addressing concerns and providing information about immunizations that may improve compliance. Charles Basch makes the case that disparities experienced by low-income and urban minority youth can be reduced when student health issues are prioritized and partnerships are developed between education and health (Basch, 2010). School nurses build partnerships with healthcare providers and local health departments to improve vaccine access and overall health for all students (Holmes et al., 2016; NASN, 2020a).

Immunization Compliance Review

As communicable disease "gatekeepers," an important part of the school nurse's role is to review, or train other school staff to correctly review student immunization records for school entry and school attendance. Notifying parents early and often, in writing and via various media sources, of school entry and attendance requirements well ahead of the start of school enables families to collect needed immunization records. It reduces the possibility of attendance denial or exclusion (Sadaf et al., 2013). To be most effective, notifications should be distributed in the language and reading level of the target population. Similar suggestions apply to notifying parents and older students about the passage and implementation of new school immunization laws (Boyer-Chu & Yonkaitis, 2019). Boyer-Chu & Yonkaitis (2019) found success in achieving compliance with a new immunization law through a partnership between the school district and the local health department, buy-in from school district administration, a well-publicized and implemented exclusion policy, electronic data monitoring, low-cost and free immunization clinics, and use of media to publicize the new law.

Deciphering immunization records, especially those of immigrant or foreign exchange students, may be challenging. APPENDIX B of the CDC's Epidemiology and Prevention of Vaccine-Preventable Diseases (14th ed.), also known as the "Pink Book," referenced in the resource section of this chapter, includes translations of foreign language terms and vaccines.

All 50 states and D.C. have a statewide Immunization Information System (IIS) (CDC, 2022b), formerly known as "immunization registries." State IISs are available for clinicians, and other authorized users, to enter and retrieve immunization data from the IIS. Depending on the state and the school district, school nurses or other school staff may have full or partial access to their state's IIS. While the current level of access for school nurses is not available, in 2013, Bobo et al. (2013) reported that only 15 percent of school nurses surveyed had full IIS access; in other words, they were able to both read and enter data. In that same study, approximately half of the school nurses had read-only access, and over 20 percent reported being unable to use their state's IIS. School nurses can access information about their state's IIS on the CDC webpage at https://www.cdc.gov/vaccines/programs/iis/contacts-locate-records.html.

Increasing access to state IISs will ultimately improve immunization record-keeping, guide public health activities that improve immunization rates, and reduce the incidence of vaccine-preventable diseases (Bobo et al., 2013; NASN, 2020a). Other benefits of IIS access and use for all school-related users – school and public health nurses, other school staff, parents, students, healthcare providers, and school-located vaccination clinic (SLVC) staff – include standardized vaccination records, enhanced continuity of care, reduced costs for immunization management (Bobo et al., 2013; NASN, 2020a; Davis et al., 2016), and prevention of convenience non-medical exemptions due to unavailable vaccination records (Luthy et al., 2012).

Since all states require immunizations for school entry and attendance, parents must be encouraged to keep personal copies of their children's immunization records. School nurses and other school staff can use opportunities presented at kindergarten registration, back-to-school nights, parent-teacher meetings, and similar school events to educate parents about the value of vaccination and the importance of keeping copies of immunization records available at home (Hootman et al., 2005). In a few states, parents can directly access the state IIS to retrieve their children's immunization records; however, this access may not be available in all states (CDC, 2022b).

Some parents may not know that school health records, including immunization records, are part of the student's educational record and, as such, are confidential. School nurses can reassure parents that the Family Educational Rights and Privacy Act (FERPA) ensures the privacy of educational records and requires written parental consent prior to sharing student information. School nurses, and other school staff, need parental consent prior to sharing school immunization information with the state and local public health agencies and healthcare providers and prior to inputting student-specific data into a state or regional electronic IIS. Federal laws, such as FERPA, preempt state laws that would allow information sharing of immunization status.

Non-Compliance

For parents who do not comply with immunization laws, the school nurse needs to determine if non-compliance is due to missing or lost vaccination records, lack of access to healthcare, not having time for preventive care due to work schedule(s), being uninsured or underinsured, being illiterate or lacking English language skills, or holding religious or philosophical beliefs against vaccinations (Boyer-Chu & Wooley, 2008). When there are language barriers, it may be possible to bring in an interpreter from the school district office or a local hospital – it is not generally advisable to use children to translate (Boyer-Chu & Wooley, 2008). If the parent expresses concern or beliefs against immunization, it may be an opportunity to clarify their misperceptions and dispel false information about vaccines (Luthy et al., 2012). Once the cause(s) of non-compliance is identified, the school nurse can begin to address the barriers.

If the parent cannot locate the student's vaccination record, and unless the record can be found or retrieved from the student's healthcare provider(s) or other sources, the student may need to be revaccinated. Some healthcare providers have been and may be reluctant to release the student's immunization record directly to the school nurse, citing the Health Insurance Portability & Accountability Act (HIPAA) Privacy Rule as the rationale for their position. In 2013, HIPAA, Section 164.512(b), was modified to permit providers to release student immunization records to school personnel with the oral consent of the parent or guardian.

All 50 states, D.C., and all U.S. territories have laws identifying mandated reporters, that is, persons required to report suspected child abuse and neglect to local child protective services or law enforcement. If a school nurse has a reasonable suspicion that the reason a child is out of compliance with school immunization requirements is due to neglect, then the child abuse and neglect reporting law requires the nurse to report suspected medical neglect to the appropriate agency in that state. There is precedent (as referenced in the resource case law section of this chapter) *in The Matter of Spencer Stratton* that non-compliance with state immunization law could be considered medical neglect.

Access

Access for many children and teens to vaccination services is challenging, and access is particularly problematic for nearly five million children under age eighteen with no healthcare insurance (Mykyta, 2022). Since about 95 percent of our nation's children and teens attend school, there is no doubt that schools, in partnership with public health agencies, are logical places to provide this population with required school immunizations and annual vaccinations, such as against influenza (ASCD & CDC, 2014; Mazyck, 2010; NASN, 2022a). School-based health centers (SBHC) and SLVC, many of which can deliver vaccines at no cost through the federal Vaccines for Children program, reduce barriers for uninsured and under-insured students, deliver vaccinations in a familiar setting, and make it possible for parents not to miss work (Federico et al. 2010;). SLVCs offer opportunities to provide access for children and teens who, without these clinics, may otherwise remain unvaccinated. SLVCs can also be effectively used during communicable disease outbreaks to target students and their families in mass community immunization programs (Fiala et al., 2013). The recent COVID-19 Pandemic has reinforced the importance of SLVs and providing vaccines at school to mitigate the risk of vaccine-preventable diseases (CDC, 2022c; CDC, 2022a; NASN, 2022a). (*See Chapter 48 for more information on SLVC*).

Provision of Vaccines at School

To provide immunizations at school, pre-planning and preparation are critical. The CDC's (2022a) webpage on Considerations for Planning School-Located Vaccination Clinics, as referenced in the resource section of this chapter, has links to information and materials needed to run a successful SLVC. To provide immunizations at school, there needs to be a supportive district policy; partnership with the local health department and local healthcare providers; access to, and proper storage for, vaccines; a funding source to pay for supplies and clinic staffing; medical orders and protocols authorizing nurses to administer immunizations; written informed parent consent or informed student consent for those over eighteen years; and appropriate vaccine information statements (VIS), in multiple languages, from the CDC (Boyer-Chu & Wooley, 2008; CDC, 2022d; Lott & Johnson, 2012a/b). (*See Chapter 48 for more information on SLVCs).*

Failure to follow medical and nursing protocols and standards of practice while administering immunizations, as well as failure to obtain written informed consent either from the parent(s), guardian, or students over eighteen years, could be grounds for disciplinary action against the school nurse and legal action against the school district (Hootman et al., 2005). The National Vaccine Injury Compensation Program (VICP), as referenced in the resource section of this chapter, provides compensation for persons who have adverse reactions to covered vaccines. Qualified healthcare providers who administer vaccines included in the National Childhood Vaccine Injury Act (NCVIA) are afforded liability coverage through that Act. The NCVIA may not protect providers who are negligent when administering immunizations, and a negligence claim could be filed if a provider fails to follow the standard of practice and an injury results. Individual states and some municipalities may have laws or ordinances that provide immunity for government officials. Local school districts generally have liability insurance for administrators and employees that may provide protection if negligence is not involved. It is generally advised that school nurses carry their own malpractice insurance, regardless of their school district's liability protection for employees. Caution should be used if district policy permits taking parental consent to treat or administer any medication via telephone. If telephone consent must be taken, it is advisable to have two school employees listen and clearly document the parent's oral consent or refusal (Hootman et al., 2005). (*See Chapter 48 for more information on SLVS*).

Unvaccinated Children or Vaccine Refusal

National childhood vaccination programs and state school immunization laws have successfully reduced the incidence of vaccine-preventable diseases that, in the past, caused major morbidity and mortality in children (NASN, 2020a). As an example, endemic measles, which prior to the introduction of the measles vaccine in 1963 (The College of Physicians of Philadelphia, 2022c), sickened millions and killed thousands of children each year, was eliminated in the U.S. by 2000 (Buttenheim et al., 2012). However, the risk of disease remains as some children remain unimmunized due to medical contraindications, religious beliefs, or philosophical beliefs. An example of ongoing risk for unvaccinated individuals was the 2015 measles outbreak linked to a California amusement park that sickened 173 people from 24 states and Washington D.C. (Yox et al., 2015). By 2019 the disease had resurged with more confirmed cases than when it was thought to be eliminated in 2000 (NASN, 2020a).

Some parents are vaccine-hesitant. Studies have identified several concerns that parents have with required vaccinations, including vaccine efficacy versus vaccine risk, adverse reactions, mistrust of traditional healthcare providers and involvement with alternative medicine practitioners, distrust of government, and privacy concerns (Federico et al. 2010; Luthy et al., 2012; Siddiqui et al., 2013;). Additionally, some vaccine-hesitant parents, who have never experienced or observed a vaccine-preventable disease, believe there is low susceptibility and low risk to vaccine-preventable diseases and that otherwise healthy children and teens do not need any or more immunizations. These parents may believe that there is more risk to receiving the vaccine than not being vaccinated (NASN, 2020a). Other parents erroneously believe that giving multiple vaccines simultaneously to infants and toddlers will overwhelm or weaken the child's immune system. These parents may request alternate immunizations, which are not evidence-based and leave children at risk for disease for long periods of time (Yox et al., 2015). Some parents have the misconception that natural immunity derived from having the disease is more effective and safer than vaccination, hence the interest in some communities in exposing young children to the disease at "chickenpox parties" (CDC, 2021).

School nurses have a vital role in protecting the health of all students by dispelling the many myths about immunizations and helping parents overcome vaccine hesitancy by providing evidence-based information about vaccine safety and effectiveness. The controversy over the safety of childhood immunizations, particularly the Measles/Mumps/Rubella (MMR), considering the fraudulent data linking the vaccine to autism that Andrew Wakefield published in 1998, which was retracted by The Lancet in 2010, has caused many parents to be hesitant about immunizations and in some cases to refuse to have their children vaccinated (Buttenheim et al., 2012). Even though Wakefield's fraudulent study was retracted, and studies have repeatedly shown that licensed vaccines have very high safety ratings, many parents continue to have vaccine safety concerns that they try to deal with in a variety of ways, including delaying vaccinations or relying on herd immunity, to protect their individual child (Constable et al., 2014; NASN, 2020a).

The whole population absorbs the risk that intentionally unvaccinated individuals pose for the community (Constable et al., 2014). Intentionally unvaccinated children with non-medical exemptions not only are at high risk for vaccine-preventable diseases themselves but also may infect others who are not old enough to be vaccinated, have medical exemptions, or have unknowingly experienced a vaccine failure (Salmon et al., 2005). It is critical that the school nurse track these students, be vigilant in the surveillance of potential disease outbreaks, and in following exclusion procedures when outbreaks occur. For intentionally unimmunized American children, those with personal belief exemptions (PBE), one study revealed that the average risk of measles infection was 22 and 35 times more than those vaccinated against the disease. In that same study, for daycare, preschool, and primary school-age children with PBEs, who are more susceptible than older children, the risk of measles infection was 62 times greater (Feikin et al., 2000).

Availability of School Nurses

When schools have adequate school nurse staffing (NASN, 2020b), they can provide accurate, scientifically based information in language that parents can understand to help parents make informed decisions about immunizing their children. By familiarizing themselves with common and more challenging questions parents may ask about vaccinations, school nurses can readily discuss vaccine issues with parents, individually and in groups (CDC, 2021; Luthy et al., 2012) and via school newsletters and social media sites. *(See Chapter 7 for more information on safe staffing).*

In schools and districts without adequate school nurse staffing, questions arise. Procedures need to be in place regarding who is responsible for monitoring compliance to immunization requirements, who trains school staff on how to review student immunization records, who answers parent and student questions about the vaccine-preventable disease, and who educates hesitant parents on the safety and efficacy of modern vaccines.

Exemptions

The exemption is either permanent or temporary for children who are medically exempted. Permanent exemptions are typically granted because the healthcare provider has determined that it would be unsafe for the child to receive a specific vaccine. Reasons for temporary exemptions include chemotherapy and other temporary medical conditions – most states require that such exemptions be renewed yearly. Typically, state laws also require that the healthcare provider specifies in writing the reason for the medical exemption and, in the case of temporary exemptions, that the estimated duration of the exemption is stated. Regarding religious and philosophical exemptions, it is important for school districts and school personnel, including school nurses, to know the criteria used in their state for granting or denying such exemptions. Forty-four states permit religious exemption, and fifteen permit philosophical or personal belief exemptions (National Conference of State Legislatures, 2022). Some parents request convenience immunization exemptions because, over time, their child's vaccination record has been misplaced or lost or is incomplete for some reason. Luthy et al. (2012) found that more than 25 percent of parents felt that filling out an exemption request was easier than retrieving their child's vaccination record.

As rates of non-medical exemptions rise in specific schools or communities, clusters of intentionally unvaccinated individuals grow, and herd immunity, which remains intact as long as most group members are vaccinated or immune, is threatened (American Academy of Pediatrics [AAP], 2016; Buttenheim et al.,

2012; Salmon et al., 2005). States with fewer requirements for non-medical immunization exemptions have significantly higher rates of exemptions than states with more requirements, and there is a corresponding increase of vaccine-preventable diseases in states with higher rates of non-medical exemptions (Blank et al.,2013). There is no doubt of the need for social and policy change to stem this trend (Blank et al., 2013). State laws for non-medical exemptions must balance restricting the number of such exemptions to maintain adequate vaccination rates and ensure that adopted exemptions are fair (Salmon et al., 2005). Some states have legislatively mandated annual vaccine discussions with healthcare providers or school nurses for parents seeking non-medical exemptions (Blank et al., 2013; Hendrix et al., 2016) as one way to ensure that exemptions are not requested just for convenience (Constable et al., 2014). These education efforts should include print and online information about vaccine safety and information that dispels anti-vaccination misinformation (Poland & Jacobson, 2011). Additionally, messaging should be tailored to address the specific concerns of individual parents to enhance parent discussions and improve vaccine acceptance (AAP, 2016; Siddiqui et al., 2013).

Whenever exemptions are granted, school nurses must keep track of unimmunized students and provide surveillance in anticipation of disease outbreaks. Additionally, parents or guardians and older students need to be notified, preferably by the school nurse and in writing, of the health risks associated with vaccine refusal and of the school or district procedures that exclude and permit the re-entry of unvaccinated students when a disease outbreak occurs. It is reasonable to ask the parent(s) to sign the notice acknowledging that they received the information – the signed notice can then be filed with the exemption request. Many districts also send immunization and exclusion information, along with other annual notifications, in writing to all parents at the beginning of each school year and require that parents return a signed acknowledgment of the notifications.

State laws vary regarding the exclusion of unvaccinated exempted students when there is a disease outbreak. In 2022, twelve states allowed exempted students to be excluded during a disease outbreak (CDC, 2022c). While there have been legal challenges to exclusion practices, in Phillips v. City of New York (2015), the Court upheld the right of school districts to exclude unvaccinated students during disease outbreaks temporarily. When exempted students are excluded from school during a disease outbreak, the length of the exclusion may vary depending on the disease incubation period, state law, and school district policy (Hootman et al., 2005).

CONCLUSION

Overall, school immunization laws have improved compliance rates and dramatically reduced the incidence of vaccine-preventable diseases and associated morbidity and mortality. Despite these successes, there is still resistance and hesitancy on the part of some individual parents and within some population groups. Improved school nurse staffing, parent education about the risks and benefits of vaccines, overcoming access barriers with free vaccine and school-located vaccination clinics, better record keeping through immunization information systems, and reducing immunization exemptions should eventually overcome vaccine-hesitancy and resistance.

It is well established that schools with school nurses generally have higher immunization compliance rates than those schools without school nurses (Baisch et al., 2011). When there are school nurses in the school, they bridge the gap between education and health and promote vaccinations as one means of keeping students safe, healthy, in school, and ready to learn. School nurses are trusted professionals and can effectively remove immunization uptake and compliance barriers.

PLEASE See Appendix A- HISTORY OF IMMUNIZATIONS and Appendix B- LITERATURE REVIEW for additional information.

RESOURCES

Legal references

- o Family Educational Rights and Privacy Act. Pub L No. 93-380 (1974)

- o Health Insurance Portability and Accountability Act of 1996 (HIPAA). Pub.L. 104–191, 110 Stat. 1936.

- o Individuals with Disabilities Improvement Act (IDEIA), 20 USC et seq., 64 (2004)

- o National Vaccine Childhood Injury Act (NCVIA) - 42 U.S.C. § 300aa-26 (1986)

- o Rehabilitation Act of 1973, 29 USC ch. 16; 34 CFR sec. 104.4(a) (1994)

- o Vaccination Assistance Act of 1962

Case law

- o In the Matter of Stratton, No. 563P02. 573 S.E.2d 512 (2002) 356 N.C. 436 – [Upheld a trial court order to immunize children who had been adjudicated dependent and neglected by their parents, appellants, and their legal custody resided with the Mecklenburg County Department of Social Services] https://www.nccourts.gov/documents/appellate-court-opinions/in-the-matter-of-stratton-0

- o Jacobson v. Massachusetts, 197 US 11, 25 S. Ct. 358, 49 L. Ed. 643 - Supreme Court, 1905

- o Lynch v. Clarkstown Central School District, 155 Misc.2d 846 (1992). [Upheld district decision denies a medical exemption due to lack of credible medical evidence for the exemption]

- o Phillips v. City of New York, 775 F. 3d 538 - Court of Appeals, 2nd Circuit (2015). [Upheld school immunization law and right of schools to exclude unvaccinated students during disease outbreaks temporarily]

- o Prince v. Massachusetts, 321 U.S. at 166–7, 64 S.Ct. at 442 – U.S. Supreme Court, 1944. [Neither rights of religion nor rights of parenthood are beyond limitation. Acting to guard the general interest in youth's well-being, the state as *parens patriae* may restrict the parent's control by requiring school attendance, regulating, or prohibiting the child's labor, and in many other ways. Its authority is not nullified merely because the parent grounds his claim to control the child's course of conduct on religion or conscience. Thus, he cannot claim freedom from compulsory vaccination for the child more than for himself on religious grounds. The right to practice religion freely does not include liberty to expose the community or the child to a communicable disease or the latter to ill health or death.]

- o Seubold v. Fort Smith Special Sch. Dist., 237 S.W.2d 884, 887 (Ark. 1951) [mandatory school vaccination does not deprive individuals of liberty and property interests without due process of law]

- o Zucht v. King, 260 U.S. 174, 176 (1922) [the Supreme Court upheld a local ordinance requiring vaccinations for schoolchildren. The Court invoked Jacobson for the principle that states may use their police power to require vaccinations. It noted that the ordinance did not bestow "arbitrary power, but only that broad discretion required for the protection of the public health."

Resources, such as position papers, clinical guidelines

- o Centers for Disease Control and Prevention. (2021, April 28). *Epidemiology and Prevention of Vaccine-Preventable Diseases* (14th ed.). (Hall, Wodi, Hamborsky, Morelli, & Schillie, Eds.) Public Health Foundation. This reference is also known as the "Pink Book." https://www.cdc.gov/vaccines/pubs/pinkbook/front-matter.html

- o Committee on Infectious Diseases; American Academy of Pediatrics. (2021). *Red Book 2021-2024: Report of the Committee on Infectious Diseases* (32nd ed.). Author. https://publications.aap.org/redbook/book/347/Red-Book-2021-2024-Report-of-the-Committee-on

- o National Association of School Nurses. (2020c). Immunizations (Position Statement). Author. https://www.nasn.org/nasn-resources/professional-practice-documents/position-statements/ps-immunizations

- o National Association of School Nurses. (2022a). School-located vaccination (Position Statement). Author. https://schoolnursenet.nasn.org/blogs/nasn-profile/2017/03/13/school-located-vaccination

- o National Association of School Nurses. (2020b). School nurse workload: Staffing for safe care (Position Statement). Author. https://www.nasn.org/nasn-resources/professional-practice-documents/position-statements/ps-workload

- o National Association of School Nurses [NASN]. (2016). Framework for 21st century school nursing practice: National Association of School Nurses. *NASN School Nurse, 31*(1), 45-53. https://www.nasn.org/nasn-resources/framework

- o Offit, P.A. and Moser, C.A. (2011). *Vaccines and your child: Separating fact from fiction.* Columbia University Press. http://cup.columbia.edu/book/vaccines-and-your-child/9780231153072

- o Taliaferro, V. & Resha, C. (Eds.). (2020). *School nurse resource manual: Evidence-based guide to practice* (10th ed.). School Nurse.com

- o Schwab N.C. & Gelfman M.H.B. (Eds.). (2001/2005). *Legal issues in school health services: A resource for School Administrators, School Attorneys, School Nurses.* Authors Choice Press.

Additional Resources

- o American Immunization Registry Association. (2022). http://www.immregistries.org/

- o Centers for Disease Control and Prevention. (2022, December 27). Considerations for planning school-located vaccination clinics. https://www.cdc.gov/vaccines/covid-19/planning/school-located-clinics.html

- ○ Centers for Disease Control and Prevention. (2016). For Immunization Managers: Requirements and Laws. http://www.cdc.gov/vaccines/imz-managers/laws/

- ○ Centers for Disease Control and Prevention. (2023). Recommended Immunization Schedules for Persons Aged 0 Through 18 Years. http://www.cdc.gov/vaccines/schedules/downloads/child/0-18yrs-child-combined-schedule.pdf

- ○ Centers for Disease Control and Prevention. (2021). Vaccines & Immunizations. http://www.cdc.gov/vaccines/index.html

- ○ Centers for Disease Control and Prevention. (2022, November 16). Vaccine Information Statements (VIS). http://www.cdc.gov/vaccines/hcp/vis/

- ○ U.S. Department of Health and Human Services, Health Resources and Services Administration. (2023). National Vaccine Injury Compensation Program (VICP). http://www.hrsa.gov/vaccinecompensation/

REFERENCES

American Academy of Pediatrics, Committees on Practice and Ambulatory Medicine, Infectious Diseases, and State Government Affairs, Council on School Health, and Section on Administration and Practice Management. (2016). Medical versus non-medical immunization exemptions for child care and school attendance (Policy Statement). *Pediatrics*, 138(3), 1-5. https://doi.org/10.1542/peds.2016-2145

Baisch, M.J., Lundeen, S.P., & Murphy, M.K. (2011). Evidence-based research on the value of school nurses in an urban school system. *The Journal of School Health*, 81(2), 74–80. https://doi.org/10.1111/j.1746-1561.2010.00563.x

Basch, C.E. (2010). Healthier students are better learners: A missing link in school reforms to close the achievement gap [Research Review No. 6]. *Equity Matters.* New York, New York: Columbia University. https://equitycampaign.org/i/a/document/12557_EquityMattersVol6_Web03082010.pdf

Blank, N.R., Caplan, A.L., & Constable, C. (2013). Exempting schoolchildren from immunizations: states with few barriers had highest rates of non-medical exemptions. *Health Affairs*, 32(7), 1282-1290. https://www.healthaffairs.org/doi/10.1377/hlthaff.2013.0239

Bobo, N., Etkind, P., Martin, K., Chi A, & Coyle R. (2013). How school nurses can benefit from immunization information systems: information exchange to keep students in school and ready to learn. *NASN School Nurse, 28*(2), 100-109. https://doi.org/10.1177/1942602x12467

Boyer-Chu, L. & Wooley, S.F. (2008*). Give It a shot! Toolkit for nurses and other immunization champions working with secondary schools* (2nd ed.). American School Health Association. https://files.eric.ed.gov/fulltext/ED501888.pdf

Boyer-Chu, L. & Yonkaitis, C.F. (2019). Disease prevention in schools. In J. Selekman, R.A. Shannon, & C.F. Yonkaitis (Eds.), *School nursing: A comprehensive text* (3rd ed., p.p. 313-334). FA Davis Company.

Buttenheim, A., Jones, M., & Baras, Y. (2012). Exposure of California kindergartners to students with personal belief exemptions from mandated school entry vaccinations. *American Journal of Public Health*, 102(8), e59-e67. https://ajph.aphapublications.org/doi/full/10.2105/AJPH.2012.300821

Centers for Disease Control and Prevention. (1999). Impact of vaccines universally recommended for children—United States, 1900-1998. *Morbidity and Mortality Weekly Report*, 48(12), 243-248. https://www.cdc.gov/mmwr/preview/mmwrhtml/00056803.htm

Centers for Disease Control and Prevention. (2011). Ten Great Public Health Achievements—United States, 2001-2010. *Journal of the American Medical Association, 306*(1), 36-38. https://jamanetwork.com/journals/jama/fullarticle/1104063

Centers for Disease Control and Prevention. (2021, August). *Provider resources for vaccine conversations with parents.* https://www.cdc.gov/vaccines/hcp/conversations/index.html

Centers for Disease Control and Prevention. (2022a). *Considerations for planning school-located vaccination clinics.* https://www.cdc.gov/vaccines/covid-19/planning/children/6-things-to-know.html?CDC_AA_refVal=https%3A%2F%2Fwww.cdc.gov%2Fvaccines%2Fcovid-19%2Fplanning%2Fschool-located-clinics.html

Centers for Disease Control and Prevention. (2022b). *Immunization information systems (IIS): Contacts for IIS immunization records.* https://www.cdc.gov/vaccines/covid-19/planning/children/6-things-to-know.html?CDC_AA_refVal=https%3A%2F%2Fwww.cdc.gov%2Fvaccines%2Fcovid-19%2Fplanning%2Fschool-located-clinics.htmlhttps://www.cdc.gov/vaccines/covid-19/planning/school-located-clinics.html

Centers for Disease Control and Prevention. (2022c). *State school immunization requirements and vaccine exemption laws.* https://www.cdc.gov/phlp/docs/school-vaccinations.pdf

Centers for Disease Control and Prevention. (2022d). *Vaccine information statements (VIS).* https://www.cdc.gov/vaccines/hcp/vis/

Constable, C., Blank, N.R., & Caplan, A.L. (2014). Rising rates of vaccine exemptions: Problems with current policy and more promising remedies. *Vaccine, 32*(16), 1793–1797. https://doi.org/10.1016/j.vaccine.2014.01.085

Davis, W.S., Varni, S.E., Barry, S.E., Frankowski, B.L., & Harder, V.S. (2016). Increasing immunization compliance by reducing provisional admittance. *The Journal of School Nursing, 32*(4), 246-257. https://doi.org/10.1177/1059840515622528

Fauteux, N. (2010). Unlocking the potential of school nursing: Keeping children healthy, in school, and ready to learn. *Charting Nursing's Future: Reports on Policies That Can Transform Patient Care* (Issue 14). Princeton, NJ:

Robert Wood Johnson Foundation. http://www.rwjf.org/content/dam/farm/reports/issue_briefs/2010/rwjf64263

Federico, S.G., Abrams, L., Everhart, R.M., Melinkovich, P., & Hambidge, S.J. (2010). Addressing adolescent immunization disparities: A retrospective analysis of school-based health center immunization delivery. *American Journal of Public Health, 100*(9), 1630–1634. https://ajph.aphapublications.org/doi/full/10.2105/AJPH.2009.176628

Feikin, D.R., Lezotte, D.C., Hamman, R.F., Salmon, D.A., Chen, R.T., & Hoffman, R.E. (2000). Individual and community risks of measles and pertussis associated with personal exemptions to immunization. *Journal of the American Medical Association, 284*(24), 3145-3150. https://doi.org/10.1001/jama.284.24.3145

Fiala, S.C., Cieslak, P.R., DeBess, E.E., Young, C.M., Winthrop, K.L., & Stevenson, E.B. (2013). Physician attitudes regarding school-located vaccination clinics. *Journal of School Health, 83*(5), 299–305. https://doi.org/10.1111/josh.12031

Harvard Law Review Association. (2008). Toward a twenty-first-century Jacobson v. Massachusetts. *Harvard Law Review, 121*(7). https://harvardlawreview.org/print/vol-121/toward-a-twenty-first-century-jacobson-v-massachusetts/

Hendrix, K.S., Sturm, L.A., Zimet, G.D., & Meslin, E.M. (2016). Ethics and childhood vaccination policy in the United States. *American Journal of Public Health, 106*(2), 273-278. https://ajph.aphapublications.org/doi/10.2105/AJPH.2015.302952

Hinman, A.R., Orenstein, W.A., & Schuchat, A. (2011). Vaccine-preventable diseases, immunizations, and MMWR --- 1961—2011. [Supplements]. *Morbidity and Mortality Weekly Report, 60*(04), 49-57. https://www.cdc.gov/mmwr/preview/mmwrhtml/su6004a9.htm

Holmes, B.W., Sheetz, A., & AAP Council on School Health (2016). Role of the school nurse in providing school health services [Policy statement]. *Pediatrics*, *137*(6). e20160852. https://doi.org/10.1542/peds.2016-0852

Hootman, J., Schwab, N.C., Gelfman, M.H.B. (with Gregory, E.K. & Pohlman, K.J.) (2005). School nursing practice: Clinical performance issues. In N.C. Schwab N.C. & M.H.B. Gelfman (Eds.), *Legal issues in school health services: A resource for school administrators, school attorneys, school nurses* (pp. 167-230). Authors Choice Press.

Katz, J.A., Capua, T., & Bocchini, J.A. (2012). Update on child and adolescent immunizations: selected review of US recommendations and literature. In H.H. Bernstein (Ed.), *Current Opinion in pediatrics*: *Office pediatrics*, *24*(3)407–421. https//doi.org/10.1097/MOP.0b013e3283534d11

Lear, J.G. (2007). Health at school: A hidden health care system emerges from the shadows. *Health Affairs*, 26(2), 409-419. https://doi.org/10.1377/hlthaff.26.2.409

Lieu, T.A., Ray, G.T., Klein, N.P., Chung, C., & Kulldorff, M. (2015). Geographic clusters in under immunization and vaccine refusal. *Pediatrics, 135*(2), 280-289. ttps://doi.org/10.1542/peds.2014-2715

Lott, J., & Johnson, J. (2012a). Promising practices for school-located vaccination clinics—Part I: Preparation. *Pediatrics*, 129, S75-S80. https://doi.org/10.1542/peds.2011-0737F

Lott, J., & Johnson, J. (2012b). Promising practices for school-located vaccination clinics––: Part II: Clinic operations and program sustainability. *Pediatrics*, *129*, S81-S87. https://doi.org/10.1542/peds.2011-0737G

Luthy, K.E., Beckstrand, R.L., Callister, L.C., & Cahoon, S. (2012). Reasons parents exempt children from receiving immunizations. *Journal of School Nursing*, *28*(2), 153-160. https://doi.org/10.1177/1059840511426578

Luthy K.E., Thorpe A., Dymock L. C., & Connely, S. (2011). Evaluation of an intervention program to increase immunization compliance among school children. *The Journal of School Nursing*, 27(4), 252–257. https://doi.org/10.1177/1059840510393963

Maughan, E.D., Bobo, N., Butler, S., & Schantz, S. (2016). Framework for 21st century school nursing practice. *NASN School Nurse, 31*(1), 45-53. https://doi.org/10.1177/1942602X15618644

Mazyck, D. (2010). School-located vaccination clinics: Then and now [Supplement]. *The Journal of School Nursing*, *26*. https://journals.sagepub.com/toc/jsnb/26/4_suppl

Mykyta, L., Keisler-Starkey, K., & Bunch, L. (2022). *More children were covered by Medicaid and CHIP in 2021.* United States Census. https://www.census.gov/library/stories/2022/09/uninsured-rate-of-children-declines. html#:~:text=Medicaid%20Expansion%20and%20Children's%20Health%20Insurance&text=In%202021%2C%20 about%2050%20million,health%20coverage%20(Figure%203)

National Association of School Nurses. (2020a). *Immunizations* (Position Statement). Author. https://www.nasn.org/nasn-resources/professional-practice-documents/position-statements/ps-immunizations

National Association of School Nurses. (2020b). *School nurse workload: Staffing for safe care* (Position Statement). Author. https://www.nasn.org/nasn-resources/professional-practice-documents/position-statements/ps-workload

National Association of School Nurses. (2022a). School-located vaccination (Position Statement). Author. https://www.nasn.org/nasn-resources/professional-practice-documents/position-statements/ps-slv

National Association of School Nurses (2022b). Scope and standards of practice: School nursing (4th ed.). Author.

National Center for Educational Statistics. (2022c). Fast facts: back-to-school statistics. https://nces.ed.gov/fastfacts/display.asp?id=372

National Conference of State Legislatures. (2021). *Routine child vaccination*. https://www.ncsl.org/health/routine-child-vaccination

National Conference of State Legislatures. (2022). States with religious and philosophical exemptions from school immunization requirements. https://www.ncsl.org/health/states-with-religious-and-philosophical-exemptions-from-school-immunization-requirements

Orenstein, W.A. & Hinman, A.R. (1999). The immunization system in the United States - the role of school immunization laws [Supplement]. *Vaccine*, *17*(3), S19-24. https://doi.org/10.1016/S0264-410X(99)00290-X

Paquette, E. T. (2021). In the wake of a pandemic: revisiting school approaches to non-medical exemptions to mandatory vaccination in the US. *The Journal of Pediatrics*, 231: 17-23. https://doi.org/10.1016/j.jpeds.2021.01.022

Perman, S. Simon Turner, S., Ramsay, A.I.G., Baim-Lance, A., Utley, M., & Fulop, N.J. (2017). School-based vaccination programmes: a systematic review of the evidence on organisation and delivery in high income countries. https//doi.org/ 10.1186/s12889-017-4168-0 https://www.ncbi.nlm.nih.gov/pmc/articles/PMC5348876/

Poland, G.A., & Jacobson, R.M. (2011). The age-old struggle against the anti-vaccinationists. *New England Journal of Medicine*, *364*(2), 97-99. https://www.nejm.org/doi/10.1056/NEJMp1010594" https://www.nejm.org/doi/10.1056/NEJMp1010594

Sadaf, A., Richards, J.L., Glanz, J., Salmon, D.A., & Omer, S.B. (2013). A systematic review of interventions for reducing parental vaccine refusal and vaccine hesitancy. *Vaccine*, *31*(40), 4293–4304. https://doi.org/10.1016/j.vaccine.2013.07.013

Salmon, D.A., & Omer, S.B. (2006). Individual freedoms versus collective responsibility: immunization decision-making in the face of occasionally competing values. *Emerging Themes in Epidemiology, 3*(13). https://doi.org/10.1186/1742-7622-3-13

Salmon, D.A., Sapsin, J.W., Teret, S., Jacobs, R.F., Thompson, J.W., Ryan, K., & Halsey, N.A. (2005). Public health and the politics of school immunization requirements. *American Journal of Public Health*, *95*(5), 778–783. https://ajph.aphapublications.org/doi/10.2105/AJPH.2004.046193

Schaffer, M.A., Anderson, L.J.W., & Rising, S. (2016). Public health interventions for school nursing practice. *The Journal of School Nursing*, 32(3), 195-208. https://doi.org/10.1177/105984051560536

Siddiqui, M., Salmon, D.A., & Omer, S.B. (2013). Epidemiology of vaccine hesitancy in the United States. *Human Vaccines & Immunotherapeutics*, *9*(12), 2643-2648. https://www.tandfonline.com/doi/full/10.4161/hv.27243

The College of Physicians of Philadelphia. (2022a). *The history of vaccines: Ethical issues and vaccines*. https://historyofvaccines.org/vaccines-101/ethical-issues-and-vaccines

The College of Physicians of Philadelphia. (2022b). *The history of vaccines: History of anti-vaccination movements*. https://historyofvaccines.org/vaccines-101/misconceptions-about-vaccines/history-anti-vaccination-movements

The College of Physicians of Philadelphia. (2022c). *The history of vaccines: Timelines*. https://historyofvaccines.org/history/vaccine-timeline/overview

The College of Physicians of Philadelphia. (2022d). *The history of vaccines: Vaccination exemptions*. https://historyofvaccines.org/getting-vaccinated/vaccine-faq/vaccination-exemptions

United Nations Children's Fund. (2022). *The COVID-19 pandemic fuels the largest continued backslide in vaccinations in three decades.* https://www.unicef.org/press-releases/WUENIC2022release

Willgerodt, M.A., Brock, D. M., & Maughan, E.M. (2018). Public School Nursing Practice in the United States. *The Journal of School Nursing*, *34*(3), 232-244. https://www.nasn.org/research/school-nuse-workforce https://doi.org/10.1177/1059840517752456

Yox, S.B., Scudder, L., & Stokowski, L.A. (2015). *Medscape vaccine acceptance report: Where do we stand?* http://www.medscape.com/features/slideshow/public/vaccine-acceptance-report#page=1

APPENDIX A - HISTORY OF IMMUNIZATIONS

The history of human vaccination against infectious disease goes back centuries. As early as 1000 C.E., the Chinese began inoculating matter from smallpox pustules to prevent the spread of infection. In 1721, during a smallpox epidemic in Boston, a local healthcare provider, at the urging of the influential Puritan minister, Cotton Mather, inoculated 248 people against smallpox. The fatality rate for those who were inoculated was about three percent. For those who caught the disease and were not inoculated was fourteen percent. Despite the lifesaving success of inoculation, Cotton Mather was strongly criticized and received death threats from people opposed to vaccination (The College of Physicians of Philadelphia, 2022c).

In 1796, the news about Edward Jenner's landmark work, using cowpox to create a vaccine to prevent smallpox, spread quickly and resulted in widespread endorsement and adoption of vaccination. In 1813, Congress established the National Vaccine Agency, and in 1855, Massachusetts passed the first school immunization law. Despite the success of vaccination in reducing the incidence of smallpox in the 1800s, some groups continued to be wary of vaccination. Severe smallpox epidemics, such as the one in Montreal, Canada, in 1885, where over 3,000 people died within nine months, resulted from vaccine refusal in the anti-vaccination population (The College of Physicians of Philadelphia, 2022c).

When Britain passed a mandatory vaccination law for all babies in 1853 and another law in 1867 requiring vaccination for all children up to age 14 years, with fines or imprisonment for parents who did not comply, organized resistance began almost immediately (Wolfe & Sharp, 2002). In response to the anti-vaccine movement, Parliament passed a new law in 1898, with a "conscience clause" which permitted the parents to request a vaccine exemption and introduced the term "conscientious objector" (Wolfe & Sharp, 2002, p. 2).

The anti-vaccine movement gained momentum in other European countries and the United States. As a result, in the late 1800s, anti-vaccinationists successfully abolished mandatory vaccination laws in several states (Wolfe & Sharp, 2002). In 1905, when Massachusetts' mandatory smallpox vaccination law was challenged in the U.S. Supreme Court in the case of Jacobson v. Massachusetts, the Court ruled that states, to preserve public health, have the authority to enforce mandatory vaccination laws (Cole & Swendiman, 2014; Harvard Law Review Association, 2008; The College of Physicians of Philadelphia, 2022c).

As more states adopted mandatory school immunization requirements in the early 20th century and required unvaccinated children to be excluded from school attendance, anti-vaccination proponents began challenging school smallpox vaccination requirements. For example, in 1922, Zucht v. King alleged that local school immunization requirements violated student Rosalyn Zucht's Fourteenth Amendment rights. The U.S. Supreme Court dismissed the case by stating that local ordinances are state laws and states have the authority to mandate vaccination (Cole & Swendiman, 2014; Harvard Law Review Association, 2008; The College of Physicians of Philadelphia, 2022c). Routine vaccination in the U.S. against smallpox ended in 1972. In 1980, the World Health Organization (WHO) declared that smallpox had been eradicated worldwide (The College of Physicians of Philadelphia, 2022).

Despite anti-vaccination sentiment in some populations, between Jenner's early work and 1900, four other vaccines for cholera, plague, rabies, and typhoid fever were developed. From 1900 to 1999, 21 additional vaccines against infectious diseases were developed and licensed (CDC, 1999), and since then, many more have been developed and licensed. Vaccination against sixteen communicable diseases/conditions is recommended for all children under the age of eighteen years (Hinman et al., 2011).

By the early 1950s, repeated outbreaks of infectious diseases and the success of disease prevention through vaccination led to increased pressure to support a national immunization program. In 1955, with the introduction of the new polio vaccine, federal funds supported a national campaign to encourage childhood vaccination against this disease (CDC, 1999). Since 1962, the federal Vaccination Assistance Act has provided financial and direct support for local and state vaccination programs that have boosted immunization levels for the country's children. In 1977, the Childhood Immunization Initiative established a comprehensive immunization program that includes vaccinations for needy children, regular review of school-age children's immunization records, and annual reports to local health departments. The Childhood Immunization Initiative of 1993 established the Vaccines for Children (VFC) program, which supports vaccination for both uninsured and underinsured children, and funds vaccinations recommended by the Advisory Committee on Immunization Practices (ACIP) records (Hinman et al., 2011).

REFERENCES

Centers for Disease Control and Prevention. (1999). Impact of vaccines universally recommended for children—United States, 1900-1998. *Morbidity and Mortality Weekly Report, 48*(12), 243-248. https://www.cdc.gov/mmwr/preview/mmwrhtml/00056803.htm

Cole, J.P., & Swendiman, K.S. (2014). *Mandatory vaccinations: Precedent and current laws* (Congressional Research Service Report). https://sgp.fas.org/crs/misc/RS21414.pdf

Harvard Law Review Association. (2008). Toward a twenty-first-century Jacobson v. Massachusetts. *Harvard Law Review, 121*(7). https://harvardlawreview.org/print/vol-121/toward-a-twenty-first-century-jacobson-v-massachusetts/

Hinman, A.R., Orenstein, W.A., & Schuchat, A. (2011). Vaccine-preventable diseases, immunizations, and MMWR --- 1961—2011. [Supplements]. *Morbidity and Mortality Weekly Report, 60*(04), 49-57. https://www.cdc.gov/mmwr/preview/mmwrhtml/su6004a9.htm

The College of Physicians of Philadelphia. (2022). *The history of vaccines: Timelines.* https://historyofvaccines.org/history/vaccine-timeline/overview

Wolfe, R. M., & Sharp, L. K. (2002). Anti-vaccinationists past and present. *British Medical Journal, 325*(7361), 430–432. https://doi.org/10.1136/bmj.325.7361.430

LITERATURE REVIEW

There is no doubt that vaccines have dramatically improved global public health (American Academy of Pediatrics [AAP], 2016; CDC, 1999; CDC, 2011; Hinman et al., 2011; Katz et al., 2012; The College of Physicians of Philadelphia, 2022a). Data supports that school immunization requirements improve attendance and overall community health (Association for Supervision and Curriculum Development and CDC, 2014; Findlaw, 2020; Association for Professional in Infection Control and Epidemiology, 2021; Lott & Johnson, 2012a/b; Orenstein & Hinman, 1999). Earlier studies reported that vaccine delivery through school-located vaccination (SLV) programs is a viable and cost-effective option to improve coverage for vaccine-preventable diseases (Federico et al.,2010; Fiala et al., 2013; National Association of School Nurses [NASN], 2022a; Paul & Fabio, 2013), although some studies have questioned the cost-effectiveness of SLV programs (Yoo et al., 2019; Perman et al., 2017).

Mandatory Vaccination

In response to mandatory vaccination and exclusion for unvaccinated or incompletely vaccinated students, some populations resist complying with immunization laws (The College of Physicians of Philadelphia, 2022b; Wolfe & Sharp, 2002). The issues of concern for those opposed to mandatory vaccination center around individual rights, fear about vaccine safety, false information, mistrust of government, and religious or philosophical objections (Dubé et al., 2021; Luthy et al., 2012;_Poland & Jacobson, 2011; The College of Physicians of Philadelphia, 2022b). In recent years, the development of hepatitis B and HPV vaccines against diseases that are different from other vaccine-preventable diseases and subsequent legislative attempts to mandate these vaccines have prompted new anti-vaccine protests from parents who oppose just these two vaccines (Harvard Law Review Association, 2008). Of prime concern for public health advocates is finding and using effective strategies to address the threat of vaccine hesitancy and refusal (Dubé et al., 2021; Sadaf et al., 2013; Salmon & Omer, 2006; Siddiqui et al., 2013).

Exemptions to School Immunizations

All states have adopted exemptions to school immunization laws (NCSL, 2022). There are three types of exemptions:

- Medical, which all states permit;
- Religious, which all states except California, Connecticut, Maine, Mississippi, New York, and West Virginia permit; and
- Philosophical (due to personal, moral, or other beliefs), which fifteen states permit (Cole & Swendiman, 2014; Findlaw, 2020; The College of Physicians of Philadelphia, 2022d).

While allowing for medical need or individual preference, there are risks associated with the exemptions to school immunization laws, including geographical clustering of unimmunized individuals and the weakening of herd immunity, which contribute to disease outbreaks in schools and communities (American College of Obstetricians and Gynecologists, 2022; Blank et al., 2013; Buttenheim et al., 2012; Feikin et al., 2000; Lieu et al., 2015; NASN, 2020a; Salmon et al., 2005). In response to serious concerns about the risk that exemptions present, alternative strategies to reduce the negative impact of exemptions have been suggested. The alternatives include raising financial liability for parents who refuse to vaccinate their children through reforms in tax law, updating vaccination laws to differentiate between practical and medical necessity, increasing health insurance costs, tightening requirements for non-medical exemptions, and reducing public funding (i.e., vouchers and tax credits) for private and charter schools that permit intentionally unvaccinated students to attend those schools (Bednarczyk et al., 2019; Harvard Law Review Association, 2008; Hendrix et al., 2016). Many parents who seek exemptions rely on herd immunity to protect their children from disease. It is argued that these parents should share some of the substantial financial burden resulting from their decisions (Constable et al., 2014). Recently, the AAP issued a policy statement encouraging all states to only permit medical exemptions from school immunization requirements (AAP, 2016). A recent study found that eliminating non-medical exemptions can effectively increase vaccination rates (Nyathi, 2019).

School Nurse's Role

Since the inception of school nursing in New York City in 1902, school nurses have played vital roles in keeping children healthy and safe at school. School nurses provide both individual and population-based services in the schools; they are on the front lines against infectious disease and are part of the public health infrastructure of the United States; they remove barriers and positively impact immunization compliance; and they are key players in immunization surveillance and reporting, and in planning and coordinating school-located immunization programs (Boyer-Chu & Yonkaitis, 2019; Holmes et al., 2016; Maughan et al.,2016; NASN, 2020c; 2022a; and 2022b.).

REFERENCES

American Academy of Pediatrics, Committees on Practice and Ambulatory Medicine, Infectious Diseases, and State Government Affairs, Council on School Health, and Section on Administration and Practice Management. (2016). Medical versus non-medical immunization exemptions for child care and school attendance (Policy Statement). *Pediatrics, 138*(3), 1-5. https://doi.org/10.1542/peds.2016-2145

American College of Obstetricians and Gynecologists. (2022). Vaccines and non-medical exemptions (Position Statement). https://www.acog.org/clinical-information/policy-and-position-statements/statements-of-policy/2022/vaccines-and-nonmedical-exemptions

Association for Professionals in Infection Control and Epidemiology. (2021). Herd Immunity. https://apic.org/monthly_alerts/herd-immunity/

Association for Supervision and Curriculum Development & Centers for Disease Control and Prevention. (2014). *Whole school, whole community, whole child: A collaborative approach to learning and health.* https://www.cdc.gov/healthyschools/wscc/wsccmodel_update_508tagged.pdf

Bednarczyk, R.A., King, A.R., Lahijani, A. & Omer, S.B. (2019). Current landscape of non-medical vaccination exemptions in the United States: impact of policy changes. https://doi.org/ 10.1080/14760584.2019.1562344

Boyer-Chu, L. & Yonkaitis, C.F. (2019). Disease prevention in schools. In J. Selekman, R.A. Shannon, & C.F. Yonkaitis (Eds.), *School nursing: A comprehensive text* (3rd ed., p.p. 313-334). FA Davis Company.

Buttenheim, A., Jones, M., & Baras, Y. (2012). Exposure of California kindergartners to students with personal belief exemptions from mandated school entry vaccinations. *American Journal of Public Health, 102*(8), e59-e67. https://ajph.aphapublications.org/doi/full/10.2105/AJPH.2012.300821

Centers for Disease Control and Prevention. (1999). Impact of vaccines universally recommended for children—United States, 1900-1998. *Morbidity and Mortality Weekly Report, 48*(12), 243-248. https://www.cdc.gov/mmwr/preview/mmwrhtml/00056803.htm

Centers for Disease Control and Prevention. (2011). Ten Great Public Health Achievements—United States, 2001-2010. *Journal of the American Medical Association, 306*(1), 36-38. https://jamanetwork.com/journals/jama/fullarticle/1104063

Cole, J.P., & Swendiman, K.S. (2014). *Mandatory vaccinations: Precedent and current laws* (Congressional Research Service Report). https://sgp.fas.org/crs/misc/RS21414.pdf

Dubé, È. Ward, J.K., Verger, P. & MacDonald, N.E. (2021). Vaccine hesitancy, acceptance, and anti-vaccination: Trends and future prospects for public health. *Annual Review of Public Health.* 42, 175-191. https://doi.org/10.1146/annurev-publhealth-090419-102240

Federico, S.G., Abrams, L., Everhart, R.M., Melinkovich, P., & Hambidge, S.J. (2010). Addressing adolescent immunization disparities: A retrospective analysis of school-based health center immunization delivery. *American Journal of Public Health, 100*(9), 1630-1634. https://ajph.aphapublications.org/doi/full/10.2105/AJPH.2009.176628

Feikin, D.R., Lezotte, D.C., Hamman, R.F., Salmon, D.A., Chen, R.T., & Hoffman, R.E. (2000). Individual and community risks of measles and pertussis associated with personal exemptions to immunization. *Journal of the American Medical Association, 284*(24), 3145-3150. https://doi.org/10.1001/jama.284.24.3145

Fiala, S.C., Cieslak, P.R., DeBess, E.E., Young, C.M., Winthrop, K.L., & Stevenson, E.B. (2013). Physician attitudes regarding school-located vaccination clinics. *Journal of School Health, 83*(5), 299–305. https://doi.org/10.1111/josh.12031

Findlaw. (2020). School vaccinations. https://www.findlaw.com/education/school-safety/school-vaccinations.html

Harvard Law Review Association. (2008). Toward a twenty-first-century Jacobson v. Massachusetts. *Harvard Law Review, 121*(7). https://harvardlawreview.org/print/vol-121/toward-a-twenty-first-century-jacobson-v-massachusetts/

Hendrix, K.S., Sturm, L.A., Zimet, G.D., & Meslin, E.M. (2016). Ethics and childhood vaccination policy in the United States. *American Journal of Public Health, 106*(2), 273-278. https://ajph.aphapublications.org/doi/10.2105/AJPH.2015.302952

Hinman, A.R., Orenstein, W.A., & Schuchat, A. (2011). Vaccine-preventable diseases, immunizations, and MMWR ---1961—2011. [Supplements]. *Morbidity and Mortality Weekly Report, 60*(04), 49-57. https://www.cdc.gov/mmwr/preview/mmwrhtml/su6004a9.htm

Holmes, B.W., Sheetz, A., & AAP Council on School Health (2016). Role of the school nurse in providing school health services [Policy statement]. *Pediatrics, 137*(6). e20160852. https://doi.org/10.1542/peds.2016-0852

Katz, J.A., Capua, T., & Bocchini, J.A. (2012). Update on child and adolescent immunizations: selected review of US recommendations and literature. In H.H. Bernstein (Ed.), *Current Opinion in pediatrics: Office pediatrics, 24*(3)407–421. https//doi.org/10.1097/MOP.0b013e3283534d11

Lieu, T.A., Ray, G.T., Klein, N.P., Chung, C., & Kulldorff, M. (2015). Geographic clusters in under immunization and vaccine refusal. *Pediatrics, 135*(2), 280-289. ttps://doi.org/10.1542/peds.2014-2715

Lott, J., & Johnson, J. (2012a). Promising practices for school-located vaccination clinics—Part I: Preparation. *Pediatrics, 129*, S75-S80. https://doi.org/10.1542/peds.2011-0737F

Lott, J., & Johnson, J. (2012b). Promising practices for school-located vaccination clinics--: Part II: Clinic operations and program sustainability. *Pediatrics, 129*, S81-S87. https://doi.org/10.1542/peds.2011-0737G

Luthy, K.E., Beckstrand, R.L., Callister, L.C., & Cahoon, S. (2012). Reasons parents exempt children from receiving immunizations. *Journal of School Nursing, 28*(2), 153-160. https://doi.org/10.1177/1059840511426578

Maughan, E.D., Bobo, N., Butler, S., & Schantz, S. (2016). Framework for 21st century school nursing practice. *NASN School Nurse, 31*(1), 45-53. https://doi.org/10.1177/1942602X15618644

National Association of School Nurses. (2022a). School-located vaccination (Position Statement). Author. https://www.nasn.org/nasn-resources/professional-practice-documents/position-statements/ps-slv

National Association of School Nurses (2022b). Scope and standards of practice: School nursing (4th ed.). Author.

National Center for Educational Statistics. (2022c). Fast facts: back-to-school statistics. https://nces.ed.gov/fastfacts/display.asp?id=372

Nyathi, S., Karpel, H.C., Sainani, K.L., Maldonado, Y., Hotez, P.J., Bendavid, E., & Lo, N.C. (2019). The 2016 California policy to eliminate non-medical vaccine exemptions and changes in vaccine coverage: An empirical policy analysis. https://pubmed.ncbi.nlm.nih.gov/31869328/

Orenstein, W.A. & Hinman, A.R. (1999). The immunization system in the United States - the role of school immunization laws [Supplement]. *Vaccine, 17*(3), S19-24. https://doi.org/10.1016/S0264-410X(99)00290-X

Paul, P., & Fabio, A. (2013). Literature review of HPV vaccine delivery strategies: Considerations for school- and non-school based immunization program. *Vaccine, 32*(3), 320–326. https://doi.org/10.1016/j.vaccine.2013.11.070

Perman, S. Simon Turner, S., Ramsay, A.I.G., Baim-Lance, A., Utley, M., & Fulop, N.J. (2017). School-based vaccination programmes: a systematic review of the evidence on organisation and delivery in high income countries. https//doi.org/10.1186/s12889-017-4168-0

Wolfe, R. M., & Sharp, L. K. (2002). Anti-vaccinationists past and present. *British Medical Journal, 325*(7361), 430–432. https://doi.org/10.1136/bmj.325.7361.430

Poland, G.A., & Jacobson, R.M. (2011). The age-old struggle against the anti-vaccinationists. *New England Journal of Medicine, 364*(2), 97-99. https://www.nejm.org/doi/10.1056/NEJMp1010594

Sadaf, A., Richards, J.L., Glanz, J., Salmon, D.A., & Omer, S.B. (2013). A systematic review of interventions for reducing parental vaccine refusal and vaccine hesitancy. *Vaccine, 31*(40), 4293–4304. https://doi.org/10.1016/j.vaccine.2013.07.013

Salmon, D.A., & Omer, S.B. (2006). Individual freedoms versus collective responsibility: immunization decision-making in the face of occasionally competing values. *Emerging Themes in Epidemiology, 3*(13). https://doi.org/10.1186/1742-7622-3-13

Salmon, D.A., Sapsin, J.W., Teret, S., Jacobs, R.F., Thompson, J.W., Ryan, K., & Halsey, N.A. (2005). Public health and the politics of school immunization requirements. *American Journal of Public Health, 95*(5), 778–783. https://ajph.aphapublications.org/doi/10.2105/AJPH.2004.046193

The College of Physicians of Philadelphia. (2022a). *The history of vaccines: Ethical issues and vaccines.* https://historyofvaccines.org/vaccines-101/ethical-issues-and-vaccines

The College of Physicians of Philadelphia. (2022b). *The history of vaccines: History of anti-vaccination movements.* https://historyofvaccines.org/vaccines-101/misconceptions-about-vaccines/history-anti-vaccination-movements

The College of Physicians of Philadelphia. (2022c). *The history of vaccines: Timelines.* https://historyofvaccines.org/history/vaccine-timeline/overview

The College of Physicians of Philadelphia. (2022d). *The history of vaccines: Vaccination exemptions.* https://historyofvaccines.org/getting-vaccinated/vaccine-faq/vaccination-exemptions

Wolfe, R.M., Sharp, & L.K. (2002). *Anti-vaccinationists past and present.* BMJ, 325(7361),430–432. https://doi.org/10.1136/bmj.325.7361.430

Yoo, B.K., Schaffer, S.J., Humiston, S.G., Rand, C.M., Goldstein, N.P.N., Albertin, C.S., Concannon, C., & Szilagyi, P.G., (2019). Cost-effectiveness of school-located influenza vaccination programs for elementary and secondary school children. *BMC Health Services Research,19*(1),407. https://pubmed.ncbi.nlm.nih.gov/31234842/

Chapter 45

SUPPORTING LGBTQ+ STUDENTS IN THE SCHOOL SETTING

Suzanne Levasseur, MSN, APRN, CPNP

DESCRIPTION OF ISSUE

Discrimination in education refers to the unfavorable treatment of students based on their membership in a protected class. Federal and state civil rights laws exist to prohibit discrimination by local education agencies and to guarantee equal educational opportunities among students. Local education agencies, however, are constantly challenged by developing social norms that impact the application of these civil rights laws. This chapter focuses on the discrimination against lesbian, gay, bisexual, transgender, queer, or questioning (LGBTQ+) students and on affirming policies that support these students in the school setting.

BACKGROUND

Discrimination against students often manifests in bullying behavior toward the student. Though state definitions of bullying may vary, bullying is generally defined as unwanted, aggressive behavior among school-age children that involves a real or perceived power imbalance. Bullying behavior is repeated or has the potential to be repeated over time (U.S. Department of Health and Human Services, n.d.). Bullying remains a problem among students in the United States. In addition to increased psychological health risks from bullying, LGBTQ+ students also experience health disparities such as physical violence; forced sexual encounters; and higher rates of use of alcohol, tobacco, and other drugs than their heterosexual peers (Kann et al., 2018).

(*See Chapter 52, Violence in the School Setting, for more information on bullying*)

While local education agencies have the initial obligation to ensure that students are not victims of discrimination, the United States Department of Education's Office for Civil Rights (OCR) has the overall responsibility to enforce federal laws that prohibit discrimination on the basis of sex, sexual orientation, gender, race, color, national origin, ancestry, marital status, pregnancy, creed, religion, disability, and age. These laws apply to all local education agencies that receive federal funding. These laws include:
- Title VI of the Civil Rights Act of 1964, which prohibits discrimination on the basis of race, color, and national origin;
- Title IX of the Education Amendments of 1972, which prohibits sex discrimination and harassment;
- Section 504 of the Rehabilitation Act of 1973, which prohibits discrimination on the basis of disability;
- Title II of the Americans with Disabilities Act of 1990, which applies to all public entities and also prohibits discrimination on the basis of a disability; and
- The Individuals with Disabilities in Education Improvement Act (IDEIA) (2004) provides for special education and related services to children with qualifying disabilities.

The U.S. Department of Education (USDE) has clarified that inadequate administrative responses to allegations of bullying can be a violation of federal civil rights law (Blad, 2016). In a *Dear Colleague Letter* issued on October 26th, 2010 (USDE/ OCR, 2010), the OCR explained that harassment could result in the denial of a free and appropriate public education (FAPE).

In June 2020, the Supreme Court ruled (in *Bostock v. Clayton County, Georgia*) that discrimination on the basis of sex "inherently" includes discrimination based on sexual orientation or transgender status. Numerous courts have also held that under this ruling, transgender students are protected from discrimination under Title IX and the Equal Protection Clause of the U.S. Constitution.

LGBTQ+ Students

Attending a safe and supportive school is especially important for LGBTQ+ students because some LGBTQ+ youth are more likely than their heterosexual, cisgender peers to experience difficulties in their lives and school environments.

The U.S. Departments of Justice and Education clarified the rights of transgender students and the corresponding responsibilities of local education agencies in a *Dear Colleague Letter issued* on May 13th, 2016. The Departments explained that the prohibition against sex discrimination under Title IX of the Education Amendments of 1972 encompasses discrimination based on a student's gender identity. As such, discrimination based on a student's transgender status may be a Title IX violation. Importantly, schools are obligated to acknowledge transgender students' identities by granting them access to facilities (i.e., locker rooms and restrooms) that correspond with their gender identities (U.S. Department of Justice [USDOJ]/USDE, 2016). On February 22, 2017, under the Trump administration, the federal Title IX protections were rescinded, and the guidance provided indicated that students' rights should be determined state by state. Many states have continued to follow the guidance provided in the *Dear Colleague Letter* of May 13, 2016.

The 2016 Departments' interpretation of transgender student rights and local education agency responsibilities are aligned with several cases upholding the right of transgender students to use school facilities corresponding to their gender identities.

The Department's Letter also includes guidance for local education agencies regarding:
- Using names and pronouns is consistent with the student's gender identity in student records and academic settings.
- Transgender student participation in single-sex classes is consistent with their gender identity.
- The need for local education agencies to maintain confidentiality in student records regarding birth names and sexes assigned at birth.

In more recent years, the rights of LGBTQ+ students, and specifically transgender students, have been litigated in courts around the country, but many questions still remain.

The more recent Biden administration has returned to the perspectives of the Obama Presidency. One of the administration's first acts was to issue an Executive Order on preventing and combating discrimination on the basis of gender identity or sexual orientation. In accordance with this Executive Order, the Office of Civil Rights (OCR) recently issued guidance, providing public notice that OCR has determined Title IX's prohibition on discrimination "on the basis of sex" encompasses discrimination on the basis of sexual orientation and gender identity.

During the Trump administration, claims of discrimination based on sexual orientation or gender identity were primarily litigated through the federal courts. In its most recent Enforcement Guidance, OCR has made it clear that it will enforce its current interpretation that Title IX prohibits discrimination based on sexual orientation and gender identity in education programs and activities that receive federal financial assistance. As such, public school districts may now see OCR again investigating complaints of discrimination on the basis of sexual orientation or gender identity. In that regard, on June 23rd, 2021, OCR and the U.S. Department of Justice, Civil Rights Division issued a fact sheet, _Confronting Anti-LGBTQ+ Harassment in Schools A Resource for Student and Families_, which includes examples of the kinds of incidents OCR can investigate. School districts should review their policies and procedures for LGBTQ+ students to ensure they are consistent with OCR's current guidance. (Brickman, 2021, para. 1 and 2)

Bathrooms and Locker Rooms:

Courts have consistently supported the rights of transgender students to use facilities that correspond to their biological sex or utilize unisex facilities.   In _Evancho v. Pine-Richland Sch. District_, 237 F. Supp.3d 267,284 (W.D. Pa.2017), the district's requirement that students use bathrooms that correspond to their biological sex or unisex facilities was settled after rescinding the policy and monetary compensation to the students. Other rulings applied the same standard to bathrooms while on field trips.

Sports:

Recent court rulings have indicated that transgender students can join teams that conform to their gender identity and have ruled against laws that limit this right. In the case _A.M. by E.M. v. Indianapolis Pub. School_, 2022 WL 2951430 (S.D. Ind. July 26th, 2022), the court ruled that prohibiting an individual from playing on a team that does not conform to his or her gender identity "punishes that individual for gender non-conformance."

Parental vs. Student's Rights Confidentiality and Student's Records:

This area remains unclear because courts have not set forth clear guidance on parental rights related to schools withholding this information or a student's rights to privacy (Voltz & Tucker, 2022). The Family Educational Rights and Privacy Act (FERPA) is a federal law that protects the privacy of student's education records. Parents and students who are eighteen (18) years of age and older maintain the right to amend their school records "that the parent or eligible student believes to be inaccurate, misleading, or in violation of the student's privacy rights" (FERPA, 1974).   Under FERPA, through official court proceedings or some state regulations and procedures, transgender students may also amend their legal name and gender marker on their education records. However, some laws, such as FERPA and various state name-change legal procedures, require parents of transgender students who are minors to make the amendment request (Seals, 2019). These rights transfer to the student when he or she reaches the age of 18 or attends a school beyond the high school level.

IMPLICATIONS FOR SCHOOL NURSE PRACTICE

As a school team member, the school nurse is in a key position to advocate for all students, especially LGBTQ+ students. School nurses understand physical and psychological development and also have knowledge of the educational system, family systems, and community resources. They are often able to bridge the gap between schools, families, and healthcare providers. The school nurse can be a leader in drafting policies and guidelines that support a safe and inclusive school environment and in educating all staff on best practices and the appropriate use of terminology. Often, a school health office is where students feel safe and welcome. School nurses, thus, have the opportunity to provide a confidential, culturally sensitive, and supportive environment where the needs of the student can be assessed and addressed as needed, taking into account confidentiality. School nurses should not disclose a student's sexuality or gender identity to others without permission from the student (Human Rights Campaign, 2019).

In addition, school nurses can:

- Provide resources to families to aid students with unique needs.
- Assess for signs and symptoms of violence, family rejection, bullying, depression, suicidal ideation, and self-harm.
- Encourage reporting of any acts of bullying.
- Assess students with somatic complaints of bullying and stress.
- Refer students and families as needed to outside agencies or healthcare providers.
- Support policies that address bullying.
- Collaborate with school teams and administrators to implement appropriate interventions to address bullying concerns.
- Educate school staff regarding the rights of LGBTQ + youth and students with disabilities.
- Help school staff learn and utilize proper terminology in addressing LGBTQ+ youth.
- Promote clubs or organizations such as Best Buddies or the Gay Straight Alliance that encourage students' physical and psychological health.

Lawrence Altman, Esquire (2017)

Q: What is the school nurse's role in Title IX issues?

A: Title IX makes all staff mandatory reporters of sexual harassment or sexual violence. It is not uncommon for a school nurse to be the first to learn that a child they are seeing has been subjected to sexual harassment or sexual violence. The school nurse may also learn that the child is staying away from school because of fear or the trauma caused by the attacks. Upon learning of this from the child, the school nurse is legally required to promptly inform the Title IX Coordinator of the district of the alleged incident. Hopefully, the school will have proper Title IX policies, protocols, and procedures in place. If not, the nurse should bring the policy issue to the attention of the school or district administration.

CONCLUSION

Federal and some state civil rights laws exist to protect students from discrimination based on their membership in certain groups. These laws are increasingly interpreted to protect historically marginalized students, including those in the LGBTQ+ community and people with disabilities. However, legal issues involving transgender students are still evolving and being challenged, with some issues having no clear guidance. Districts should consult with their own legal counsel when there is a lack of clarity with present statutes and laws.

School nurses are positioned to be leaders within their school communities, promoting respect for diversity and helping to identify those students who may be victims of bullying or other discrimination. Safe and supportive school environments are accomplished when all school staff are familiar with current LGBTQ best practices and are aware of potential issues.

Preventive strategies should be implemented through a comprehensive model that protects all students from bullying.

RESOURCES

See Chapter 52, Violence in the School Setting, for more information on bullying.

Brill, S. & Pepper, R. (2022). The transgender child. Cleis Press Publications.

Gay, Lesbian, Straight Education Network (GLSEN) (2020). GLSEN Model District Policy for Transgender and Gender Nonconforming Students. https://www.glsen.org/sites/default/files/2020-11/Model-Local-Education-Agency-Policy-on-Transgender-Nonbinary-Students.pdf

Human Rights Campaign. (n.d.). *Anti-transgender legislation spreads nationwide, and bills targeting transgender children surge.* https://www.hrc.org/resources/unprecedented-onslaught-of-state-legislation-targeting-transgender-american

Human Rights Campaign. (2022, December 13TH). Historic victory: The respect for Marriage Act is law. https://www.hrc.org/press-releases/historic-victory-the-respect-for-marriage-act-is-law

Lambda Legal. (N.D.). Legal victories for youth. HTTPS://WWW.LAMBDALEGAL.ORG/KNOW-YOUR-RIGHTS/ARTICLE/YOUTH-LEGAL-VICTORIES

National Association of School Nurses. (2021). *LGBTQ students: The role of the school nurse* (Position Statement). https://www.nasn.org/nasn-resources/professional-practice-documents/position-statements/ps-lgbtq

U.S. Department of Education, Office for Civil Rights. *Know Your Rights.* https://www2.ed.gov/about/offices/list/ocr/know.html

Case Law

Doe v. Regional School Unit 26, 2014 ME 11, 86 A.3d 600 (ME 2014)

Bostock v. Clayton County, Georgia, June 2020

Evancho v. Pine-Richland Sch. District, 237 F. Supp.3d 267,284 (W.D. Pa.2017)

A.M. by E.M. v. Indianapolis Pub. School, 2022 WL 2951430 (S.D. Ind. July 26th, 2022)

REFERENCES

Americans with Disabilities Act of 1990, 42 U.S.C. §§ 12101-12213.

Blad, E. (2016, May 31st). School civil rights took spotlight under Obama. *Education Week, 35*(32), 1, 14-15. https://www.edweek.org/policy-politics/school-civil-rights-took-spotlight-under-obama/2016/05

Brickman, J.W. (2021, July 6th). Yet another guidance document? Understanding the back and forth on OCR's transgender guidance. *Pepples and Waggoner, Attorneys at Law.* https://www.pepple-waggoner.com/yet-another-guidance-document-understanding-the-back-and-forth-on-ocrs-transgender-guidance/

Education Rights and Privacy Act (FERPA). 20 U.S.C. & 1232g; 34 CFR Part99 (1974).

Human Rights Campaign. (2019). *2018 LGBT youth report.* https://www.hrc.org/resources/2018-lgbtq-youth-report

Kann, L., McManus, T., Harris, W.A., Shanklin, S.L., Flint, K.H., Queen, B., Lowry, R., Chyen, D., Whittle, L., Thornton, J., Lim, C., Bradford, D., Yamakawa, Y., Leon, M., Brener, N., & Ethier, K.A. (2018). Youth risk behavior surveillance — United States, 2017. *MMWR Surveillance Summary 2018*; *67* (SS-8):1–114. https://www.cdc.gov/mmwr/volumes/67/ss/ss6708a1.htm

Individuals with Disability Education Improvement Act of 2004, 20 U.S.C. §§ 1400 *et seq.*

Pfrommer, J. (2019). *Disability-based bullying and harassment in the schools: Legal requirements for identifying, investigating and responding.* LRP publications.

Rehabilitation Act of 1973, 29 U.S.C. §§ 701 et seq.

Ring. T. (2019, March 12TH). 10 more states sue Obama administration over trans student guidance. *advocate.com.* https://www.advocate.com/transgender/2016/7/08/10-more-states-sue-obama-administration-over-trans-student-guidance

Seals, A. & Gonzales, M. (2019). Legal rights of transgender students in education. *Diversity, Social Justice, and the Educational Leader, 3*(1), Article 1. https://scholarworks.uttyler.edu/dsjel/vol3/iss1/1/

U.S. Department of Health and Human Services. (2022.) *What is bullying?* https://www.stopbullying.gov/bullying/what-is-bullying

Title VI of the Civil Rights Act of 1964. 42 U.S.C. §§ 2000d *et seq.*

Title IX of the Education Amendments of 1972. 20 U.S.C. §§ 1681 *et seq.*

U.S. Department of Education, Office for Civil Rights. (2010). *Dear colleague letter: Harassment and bullying.* https://www2.ed.gov/about/offices/list/ocr/letters/colleague-201010.html

U.S. Department of Justice/U.S. Department of Education. (2016). *Dear colleague letter: Transgender students.* https://www2.ed.gov/about/offices/list/ocr/letters/colleague-201605-title-ix-transgender.pdf

Voltz, C. & Tucker, A. (2022). *Legal issues involving transgender students.* https://www.jdsupra.com/legalnews/legal-issues-involving-transgender-6514097/

Chapter 46

PRIVATE DUTY NURSES IN THE SCHOOL SETTING

Bill Patterson, MPA, BSN, BA, RN

DESCRIPTION OF ISSUE

There has been an unprecedented increase in the number of children in the United States surviving and thriving despite complex health conditions associated with prematurity, birth complications, severe congenital anomalies, and acquired health conditions. Increasingly, pediatric patients are surviving conditions that were untreatable decades ago (Foster et al., 2019). The home of the pediatric patient can be appropriate and is often the preferred site for providing healthcare services to address a wide range of serious and complex medical needs or developmental disabilities (Simpser et al., 2017). School districts are challenged with how to meet the educational needs of children with complex health conditions and how to provide and pay for necessary healthcare services while the child is at school.

Following the conclusion of *Cedar Rapids v. Garrett F.* (1999) and *Irving v. Tatro* (1984), the U.S. Supreme Court determined that under the Individuals with Disabilities Education Act (IDEA) of 2004 "related services" provision, school districts are required to provide "school health services," including one to one care or continuous nursing services, if those services are "related" to enabling a child with a disability to remain in school and "make such access meaningful." School districts were tasked with providing what is primarily known as private duty nursing, typically provided in home and community settings via public and private health insurance or private pay. School health services are mandated under federal law and defined as related services when required to assist a child with a disability to benefit from special education programs outlined in the child's individual education program [IEP](IDEA, 2004). Private duty nurses may be utilized under the provision of the related services in IDEA or Section 504 of the Rehabilitation Act of 1973 if insufficient school nursing personnel meet the needs of students' complex condition(s) (Rehabilitation Act of 1973, 29 U.S.C. § 504). For clarity and consistency, private duty nurse is the term utilized in this chapter to denote a nurse assigned to care for a specific student or students instead of a school nurse serving the entire school population.

Understanding the role of the school nurse (if available) is essential to ensure that private duty nurses are not operating separately and out of compliance with respective state and federal laws, rules, and regulations pertaining to education. As an increasing number of children with complex healthcare procedures/needs receive healthcare in various settings with multiple providers, there is an urgent need to identify best practices to promote successful integration into the community (Sobotka et al., 2019). Collaboration and understanding of roles and relationships between school nurses, school-level personnel, and private duty nurses are crucial to ensuring the health and safety of the student(s) while attending school.

BACKGROUND

It may be generally assumed that private duty nursing is a recent job creation. It is not; rather, we are witnessing a return to the origins of private duty nursing. Throughout antiquity, the preferable, and often safest, nursing care was provided in one's home, where one was cared for by family members, clansmen, or friends (Egenes, 2017). Skilled, trained, and competent nurses were used in the homes of those with the resources to afford such care. These private duty nurses were needed because most infants were delivered at home. In addition, some surgical procedures were performed at home. The sick who lacked families to tend to their needs were warehoused in almshouses and municipal hospitals, overseen by attendants who lacked any knowledge of nursing care (Egenes, 2017).

A change in payment structure for private duty nursing services has evolved over time, shifting to primarily private and public health insurance plans. However, there are still some private pay arrangements. Fee-for-service payment systems have shifted to managed care plans involving case managers to mitigate increasing healthcare-related costs. For children with disabilities receiving services under the IDEA with an Individualized Education Program (IEP) or Individualized Family Service Plan (IFSP) [legal plan of services under Part C of IDEA], Medicaid is the primary payer to the Department of Education (Centers for Medicare and Medicaid Services, 1997). Recent changes in some states and some school districts allow payment for students with 504 plans per clearly defined criteria.

Respective state Medicaid programs have generated policies, rules, and regulations for Medicaid reimbursement for school-based health-related services in the school setting. Collaboration and mutual understanding with respective state departments of health, human services, and education is essential. States such as Arkansas, New York, Minnesota, Ohio, Texas, Kentucky, Maryland, Missouri, and Indiana have meticulously defined private duty nursing or personal nursing services and delineated roles and responsibilities not only in the provision of nursing services but also in the areas of, finance, payment, and liability.

Delivery of Services Using Private Duty Nurses

Under the IDEA, school teams are comprised of those who know the student's needs best (IDEA, 2017a). The school conducts an evaluation to determine eligibility for special education and related services to be provided for the student to access a free appropriate public education [FAPE] (IDEA, 2017b). "It is the position of the National Association of School Nurses (NASN) that the registered professional nurse (hereinafter referred to as the school nurse) is an essential member of multidisciplinary educational teams participating in the identification, evaluation, and monitoring of students who may be eligible for services through the Individuals with Disabilities Education Improvement Act [IDEIA] (2004) and Section 504 of the Rehabilitation Act of 1973, as amended through the Americans with Disabilities Amendment Act (ADAA) in 2008." (NASN 2023, para. 1). The school nurse can provide a holistic view of the student's needs in the context of health-related services in school and associated settings.

Service Delivery Models

States and school districts utilize various delivery models to meet the school health and related services needs mandated under IDEA and 504. There are pros and cons to each. To further complicate understanding of the mandate, there are related services and accommodations under the mandates of Section 504 of the Rehabilitation Act of 1973 and the Americans with Disabilities Act Amendments Act of 2008 that must also be considered. The most common service delivery models of nursing services are: 1) employee based and 2) third-party contracted private duty nurses (Shannon & Minchella, 2015). School districts must consider the benefits and risks associated with both models in relation to their constituency.

Employee-Based

The benefits of employee-based service provision are that the school district has more control over the following:

1) job description
2) supervision
3) nursing and educational duties (may include nursing delegation)
4) accountability of nursing care;
5) the flexibility of scheduling; and
6) communication protocols between the private duty nurse and school nurse, parents, school personnel, and medical provider(s).

The disadvantages are:

1) the school district must hire and supervise the nurse (i.e., including liability); and
2) there may be limited availability of nurses to provide backup coverage when the private duty nurse is out sick or otherwise absent from work.

Third Party or Contracted Private Duty Nurse

The advantages of utilizing third-party or contracted private duty nurses are:

1) either the family or agency hires the nurse;
2) the agency provides backup nursing coverage, with clear provisions built into the contract;
3) decreased or shared liability between the private duty nurse/agency and the school district;
4) family's comfort with a nurse who is often-familiar with their child; and
5) continuity of nursing care between home and school.

The negatives of the third-party or contracted private duty nurse model are:

1) the private duty nurse's inability to provide care to other students (including delegation)
2) federal funding limitations
3) lack of involvement of the nurse in student's educational needs; and
4) the lack of direct accountability to school personnel for nursing care

(Minang, 2020; North Carolina School Health Program Manual, 2022; Shannon & Minchella, 2015; Rhode Island Health & Human Services, 2021; Wisconsin Department of Public Instruction, n.d.)

There may be situations in which the private duty nurse may be employed by an agency from a different state other than the state in which the services will be provided. This model creates a new set of challenges for school health staff and school administration. Contracts must be carefully written in all cases. However, the out-of-state agreement must be carefully crafted and may require legal or board of nursing guidance.

IMPLICATIONS FOR SCHOOL NURSE PRACTICE

Staffing Determination

Determination of the level of nursing care for students is the responsibility of the IEP team. In the school setting, the school nurse is the professional qualified to conduct a comprehensive health evaluation. The school nurse identifies necessary health accommodations, outlines the plan of care, provides nursing services, and evaluates the effectiveness of the health services provided to students (NASN, 2018). Licensed primary medical care provider (i.e., a healthcare provider with prescriptive authority) orders are required for nursing services as an IEP Team cannot prescribe health/medical services for a nurse to follow. School nurses deliver skilled healthcare to students, provide referrals to other providers, and assist families in gaining access to specialized medical care (Maughan et al., 2018). While some students may need the support of a full-day (continuous) one-to-one nurse to receive a free appropriate public education (FAPE), for other students, based on their specific health needs, assignment of a full-day (continuous) one-to-one nurse may not be necessary (Suriano, 2019). There may be situations where several students in a classroom may require continuous monitoring with multiple treatments and procedures, and one nurse may be able to meet their needs (Shannon & Minchella, 2015). The licensed Registered Nurse (RN) or school nurse is the most qualified member of the IEP team to address these needs and help the team make the most informed decision for appropriate staffing to meet the health and safety needs of the student(s).

Determination of the provider's qualifications necessary to meet the student(s) needs is within the realm of the school nurse. Whether another RN (e.g., private duty nurse or school/district employed nurse), a licensed practical/vocational nurse (LPN/LVN), or an unlicensed assistive aide (UAP) who is delegated appropriate task(s) is determined by the school nurse. Nursing delegation is dependent on individual state nurse practice acts. School nurses must know their respective and potentially neighboring state laws regarding delegation. School health service delivery models and staffing formulas may vary within and across school districts. Staffing depends on the number and distance between schools, the different types of employees, and how school districts are funded (Combe & Clark, 2019). The school nurse must factor in safety and fiscal accountability into decision-making as they relate to the school and family. School nurses may need to educate other school team members that insurance companies have defined benefits and use of the plans in a school setting and may exhaust a family or student's benefits under that defined health plan. *(See Chapters 4 and 7 for more information on delegation and safe staffing).*

Bear in mind that, as the most qualified member of the IEP team to address students' health and nursing needs, a higher level of accountability and responsibility falls upon the school nurse. The school nurse should consult with their state nursing organization or school nursing organization regarding insurance or liability protection coverage. Personal malpractice insurance is strongly recommended for all nurses, regardless of specialty. *(For more information on malpractice and professional liability, see Chapters 1 and 2).*

Liability and Private Duty/Personal Nurses

With the ever-increasing litigious nature of our country, it is understandable (and wise) that school districts, administrators, school nurses, and private duty nurses be aware of potential liabilities in the decision-making and provision of school health services for students. To ensure the school district is covered, contracts and memoranda of understanding with agency nurses must be specifically detailed regarding all services rendered and the responsibilities of all parties involved. County, city, and other local laws affect school nurse practice. Local ordinances, health laws, and school board policies and procedures should be readily available for reference. Job descriptions and the requirements to hold a position as a school nurse can be evidence of the standard of care and must also be adhered to (Combe & Clark, 2019).

These concepts may be new to a school nurse and private duty nurse, so it is best to approach this issue like the IEP process - as a team. It is important to work with the district procurement and contracts specialist, school attorney, and other legal and financial professionals in the school district to ensure that the educational, fiscal, and medicolegal liabilities are considered and mitigated to best meet the needs of the student(s) and the school district. If issues arise, it is more than likely that they will be decided on a case-by-case basis, making it extremely important that they are carefully considered and included in the documents.

As the school nurse with specialized health expertise, know your practice (i.e., respective state nurse practice act[s]). Ensure that your scope of work aligns with your scope of practice. School nurses are the link between the healthcare and educational communities and are valuable resources to students, families, staff, and communities (NASN, 2018). If in doubt or uncertain about areas in the nursing field, consult your nursing organization and national and state school nursing organization, along with respected colleagues and mentors in school nursing. Research and become familiar with all school health and school nursing-related statutes, administrative policies, procedures, and local (if any) and state laws, regulations, and guidelines. This will help in the development of durable contracts and memoranda of understanding and protect the school nurse and private duty nurse when providing school health and school nursing services in school and the community.

Private duty nurses require specialized training and experience to provide nursing services in the community. The demand for qualified, trained pediatric nurses able to care for children with complex medical needs in the home setting is great (Weaver, 2018). With the nationwide nursing shortage, policymakers and leaders must consider how to best meet the needs of children with complex medical conditions in the community and attending school. This highlights the need to grow the workforce and consider addressing the need by increasing the skillset of nurses already practicing in the school and community setting through training or refresher courses. Considering the shortage of nurses, and even more specifically, specialty nurses, telehealth modalities may be a future solution (e.g., specialty nurses clinically supervising trained aides or technicians remotely). Additional training and/or refresher courses should include using information technology (IT) and modalities.

Roles/Relationships

As school nurses are nurses for the health of all students and whole school communities, it can become confusing when private duty nurses enter as service providers within a school community. Clear delineation and understanding of roles, as well as responsibilities, must take place. It may be too late to ask questions after a student with a private duty nurse has entered a school campus. The school nurse needs to work with the school administration and fiscal and legal professionals to address all ambiguities to ensure that the student(s), school nurse, school personnel, and school district are covered when the student(s) is in school.

Communication protocols, policies and procedures, training, orientation, health procedures or protocols, emergency procedures, development and implementation of Individualized Healthcare Plans (IHPs), documentation, schedules, the chain of command, and personnel rules are some of the items that should be covered in a checklist when working with contracted private duty nurses in school (North Carolina School Health Program Manual, 2022; Shannon & Minchella, 2015). When working with a contracted LPN/LVN, it is imperative to clarify the role between the school nurse and the contracted LPN/LVN. When developing the IEP or Section 504 Plan, the roles and responsibilities for developing the IHP for the LPN/LVN must be clarified. Clinical supervision and delegation for the LPN/LVN must also be clear.

A proactive approach by school nurses prior to entry, including collaboration with school administration-and district legal and fiscal professionals, is strongly recommended. It may also be necessary to seek clarification from the respective state Board of Nursing or State Department(s) of Education and Health on any ambiguities related to nursing delegation and supervision.

CONCLUSION

Private duty nurses are not new; they are a return to the roots of nursing care. The inclusion of private duty nurses in the school setting is a more modern nursing care model. As school districts have come to understand, based upon case law and U.S. Supreme Court decisions, the provision of FAPE to some IDEA and Section 504 eligible students may include continuous nursing care delivered to one or more students. One such delivery model of these services is the use of private duty nurses, either contracted or employee-based. Regardless of the nursing services delivery model, creating clear and delineated policies, contracts, memoranda of understanding, guidelines, job descriptions, and protocols/procedures is necessary. In the absence of anything clearly and specifically written, the potential for litigation is possible. In the absence of anything written, anything goes, and mitigating potential litigation is nearly impossible for the individual school nurse or the school district.

With the increase in the population of children with special healthcare needs due to advances in medical science and technology, increases in fiscal and legal costs will logically correlate. It behooves school districts to include school nurses in strategically planning and coordinating how to mitigate these areas of concern to ensure the health and safety of students with special healthcare needs.

RESOURCES

Kentucky Board of Nursing. (2022). *Private duty nursing (P.D.N.) – P.T. 18*. https://www.chfs.ky.gov/agencies/dms/provider/Pages/PDN.aspx

Missouri Department of Social Services. (2023). *Chapter 95 – Private duty nursing care under the healthy childrenand youth program*. https://www.sos.mo.gov/cmsimages/adrules/csr/current/13csr/13c70-95.pdf

Missouri Department of Social Services. (2023). Private duty nursing for children. https://dss.mo.gov/mhd/pdf/pdn-for-children.pdf

National Council of State Boards of Nursing [NCSBN] (2023). *Practice.*
https://www.ncsbn.org/nursing-regulation/practice.page

Ohio Department of Medicaid. (2023). *Private duty nursing.*
https://medicaid.ohio.gov/families-and-individuals/srvcs/pdn

Petersen, O. H., Hjelmar, U., & Vrangbæk, K. (2018). Is contracting out of public services still the great
panacea? A   systematic review of studies on economic and quality effects from 2000 to 2014. *Social
Policy & Administration*, *52*(1), 130-157. https://doi.org/10.1111/spol.12297

Wang, L. Y., Vernon-Smiley, M., Gapinski, M. A., Desisto, M., Maughan, E., & Sheetz, A. (2014). Cost-benefit
study of school nursing services. *JAMA pediatrics*, *168*(7), 642-648. https://jamanetwork.com/journals/
jamapediatrics/fullarticle/1872779

Case Law

U.S. Education Law, Law and Higher Education. (2022a). Cedar rapids community school district v. Garret f.
https://usedulaw.com/205-cedar-rapids-community-school-district-v-garret-f.html

U.S. Education Law, Law and Higher Education. (2022b). Irving independent school district v. Tatro.
https://usedulaw.com/350-irving-independent-school-district-v-tatro.html

REFERENCES

Centers for Medicare and Medicaid Services. (1997). *Medicaid and school health: A technical assistance guide.*
https://www.hhs.gov/guidance/document/medicaid-and-school-health-technical-assistance-guide

Combe, L. & Clark, Y. (2019). Management of school health staff. In J. Selekman, R.A. Shannon, & C. F. Yonkaitis (Eds.),
School nursing: A comprehensive text (3rd ed., p. 946). F.A. Davis Company.

Egenes, K. J. (2017). History of nursing. In G.Roux & J.A. Halstead (Eds.), *Issues and trends in nursing: Essential
knowledge for today and tomorrow*, (p.p.1-26). Jones & Bartlett Publishers.

Foster, C. C., Agrawal, R. K., & Davis, M. M. (2019). Home health care for children with medical complexity: Workforce
gaps, policy, and future directions. *Health Affairs*, *38*(6), 987-993.
https://doi.org/10.1377/hlthaff.2018.05531

Individuals with Disability Education Improvement Act (2004), 20 U.S.C. 1400 et seq.

Individuals with Disability Education Improvement Act. (2017a). Sec. 300.321 *IEP team.*
https://sites.ed.gov/idea/regs/b/d/300.321

Individuals with Disability Education Improvement Act. (2017b). Sec. 300.304 *Evaluation procedures.*
https://sites.ed.gov/idea/regs/b/d/300.304

Maughan, E. D., Cowell, J., Engelke, M. K., McCarthy, A. M., Bergren, M. D., Murphy, M. K., Barry, C., Krause-Parello, C.A.,
Luthy, K.B., Kinter, E.K., & Vessey, J. A. (2018). The vital role of school nurses in ensuring the health of our nation's
youth. *Nursing Outlook*, *66*(1), 94-96. https://doi.org/10.1016/j.outlook.2017.11.002

Minang, D. S. M. (2020). *Evaluating the quality of home health care for individuals with complex medical needs
receiving private duty nursing services in the Maryland rare and expensive case management program.* (Doctoral
dissertation, University of Maryland, College Park).

National Association of School Nurses. (2023). *IDEIA and Section 504 teams - the school nurse as an essential team member* (Position Statement).
https://www.nasn.org/nasn-resources/professional-practice-documents/position-statements/ps-ideia

North Carolina School Health Program Manual. (2022). *When a student needs continuous, one-on-one care at school: Guidelines for school nurses.*
https://publichealth.nc.gov/wch/cy/docs/school-health-manual/E3OnetoOne.pdf

Rhode Island Health & Human Services. (2021). *Pediatric private duty nursing policy guidance document.*
https://eohhs.ri.gov/sites/g/files/xkgbur226/files/2021-11/pediatric-pdn-policy-guidance-document-final-10.21.2021.pdf

Rehabilitation Act of 1973, 29 U.S.C. § 504

Shannon, R. A., & Minchella, L. (2015). Students requiring personal nursing care in school: Nursing care models and a checklist for school nurses. *NASN School Nurse*, *30*(2), 76-80. https://doi.org/10.1177/1942602X15569781

Simpser, E., Hudak, M. L., Okun, A. L., Langley, J., Lin, E., Maynard, R., McNeal, D., Sajous, & Thornburg, J. B. (2017). Financing of pediatric home health care. *Pediatrics*, *139*(3). https://doi.org/10.1542/peds.2016-4202

Sobotka, S. A., Gaur, D. S., Goodman, D. M., Agrawal, R. K., Berry, J. G., & Graham, R. J. (2019). Pediatric patients with home mechanical ventilation: the health services landscape. *Pediatric pulmonology*, *54*(1), 40-46. https://doi.org/ 10.1002/ppul.24196

Suriano.C. State Education Department of New York. (2019). *Guidelines for determining a student with a disability's (sic) need for a one-to-one nurse.*
https://www.p12.nysed.gov/specialed/publications/1-1-nurse.html

Weaver, M. S., Wichman, B., Bace, S., Schroeder, D., Vail, C., Wichman, C., & Macfadyen, A. (2018). Measuring the impact of the home health nursing shortage on family caregivers of children receiving palliative care. *Journal of Hospice and Palliative Nursing*, *20*(3), 260. https://doi.org/10.1097/NJH.0000000000000436

Wisconsin Department of Public Instruction. (n.d.). *School nursing and health services.*
https://dpi.wi.gov/sspw/pupil-services/school-nurse

Chapter 47

SCHOOL-BASED HEALTH CENTERS AND THE SCHOOL NURSE

Lynnette Ondeck, MEd, BSN, RN, NCSN*

DESCRIPTION OF ISSUE

School-Based Health Center (SBHC) providers and school nurses collaborate to monitor and enhance students' health, overall well-being, and academic success. Privacy, confidentiality, and a sense of well-being for students play a key role in both SBHC and school nurse services. However, SBHCs and school nurses are typically governed by separate entities regarding oversight, fiscal responsibility, and relationships with the local education agency (LEA). In addition, schools and healthcare providers operate under different privacy guidelines, SBHCs operate under HIPAA and school nurses operate under FERPA, and local school districts and states have different policies and interpretations of these guidelines. It is prudent for school nurses and SBHCs to understand the various laws protecting student and health information to work more effectively together. Defining the roles and responsibilities of school nurses and the SBHC team is important to ensure compliance with privacy laws and to provide a seamless and comprehensive care protocol for students and their families.

BACKGROUND

School nursing in the United States (U.S.) has existed for many decades. However, it has become increasingly more complex as student health needs have escalated, and the role has expanded in the scope of practice and care delivery. Historically, the primary purpose of school nursing was to promote student attendance, thereby improving students' educational achievement. School nursing has evolved to include chronic disease management, emergency preparedness, case management, behavioral health assessments, and much more (AAP, 2016 & NASN, 2022).

School-based health centers (SBHC) were developed to support student success and remove barriers to medical and mental health needs. SBHCs provide convenient access for students to health education, social services; primary care, including immunizations and other preventive care; behavioral health care, including screening, assessment, diagnosis, treatment, and referral; oral health; adolescent reproductive healthcare, including pregnancy testing, sexually transmitted infection (STI) testing and treatment. Collaboration between SBHC providers, community-based providers, and school nurses enhances student well-being, improves academic outcomes, and ensures better attendance (Gardiner, 2020; Arenson et al., 2019). SBHCs cannot replace the school nurse's role and instead should complement school nurse services. SBHCs should work cooperatively with school nurses to remove barriers to student care, increase communication with community-based physicians, coordinate treatment plans, and support data collection related to educational outcomes (Gardiner, 2020; Maughan, 2018).

SBHCs are typically staffed by a multi-disciplinary team that can include community health workers. registered nurses, medical assistants, behavioral health clinicians, medical providers (including advanced registered nurse practitioners, physician assistants, or physicians), drug and alcohol counselors, and other healthcare providers.

---

* Original authors: Sara Rigel, MPH, CHES & Mary Newell, PhD, RN, NCSN (2017)

They can diagnose and treat common acute health problems, help manage chronic health conditions such as diabetes or asthma and identify and treat mental health conditions. School nurses and SBHCs share a critical mission – "protecting and advancing the health and well-being of school–age children" (National Association of School Nurses [NASN] & School-Based Health Alliance [SBHA], 2022). The interface between SBHCs and school nurse programs is essential for their success. (*Please see APPENDIX for more background and information on how the programs can successfully co-exist to advance student well-being and academic achievement.*)

IMPLICATIONS FOR SCHOOL NURSE PRACTICE IN CO-LOCATED OFFICES WITH SBHCS

Sharing of Information

Schools and healthcare providers are essential partners in facilitating care and protecting children and adolescents from health threats. In some instances, sharing data between schools and healthcare entities (including SBHCs) is the only realistic and reliable method for getting the information necessary for achieving these goals and conducting public health activities, such as tracking student immunization records, including any vaccinations administered by SBHCs.

The federal Health Insurance Portability and Accountability Act (HIPAA, Pub. L. 104–191, 110 Stat. 1936, [1996], as amended) applies to "covered entities" such as SBHCs. HIPAA generally prohibits covered entities from disclosing **protected health information** (PHI) to any third parties unless the individual (in this case, the student who is the subject of the information or the individual's personal representative) authorizes it in writing or HIPAA otherwise permits the disclosure. Protected health information includes any information in a written or electronic healthcare record, including treatment plans and patient information. For example, a student over the age of 13 has the right to have the SBHC not disclose mental health information and treatment plans to the school (HIPAA, 1996). Medical providers in SBHCs must usually abide by the policies and rules spelled out by HIPAA guidelines.

HIPAA allows for sharing of medical information to coordinate patient care, such as monitoring for communicable disease outbreaks and administering required childhood vaccinations. For the smooth and quick transference of information to occur in critical situations, SBHC and school nurses should consider including a release of information in the initial packet of information sent home at the beginning of the school year. Of note, sharing sensitive health care information needs to be specified on the release of information.

School nurses, however, as employees of a public school district or contracted to provide services in a public school system, are not bound by HIPAA because they are not covered entities. School nurses are bound by The Family Educational Rights and Privacy Act (FERPA) which prevents disclosure of **personally identifiable information** (PII) in a student's education record without the consent of a parent or eligible student (aged 18 or older) unless an exception to the law's general consent requirement applies, such as health emergency or safety (20 U.S.C. § 1232g; 34 CFR Part 99). This restriction on disclosure includes school immunization records, Individualized Education Programs (IEPs), Individualized Healthcare Plans (IHPs), medication administration records, incident/ accident reports, educational needs records, and other specialized medical records such as sports physicals, and documentation of specialty care visits held by the school nurse.

The U.S. Department of Health and Human Services and the U.S. Department of Education (2019) have offered joint guidance on applying HIPAA and FERPA specifically to student health records. Though this guidance helps provide examples where disclosure of health and education records may be appropriate, interpretations by states and school districts still vary widely (The Network for Public Health Law, 2020). Except where allowed by law, disclosure of personally identifiable information between the SBHC and the school nurse should occur only after obtaining appropriate authorization to release information.

FERPA has created confusion and difficulties for public health efforts to conduct ongoing and emergency public health activities in schools, such as monitoring for infectious diseases or influenza outbreaks (United States Department of Education, 2023). Therefore, this inability to disclose information may interfere with monitoring efforts.

Additionally, school nurses need to inform the parents how much access the school does or does not have to the school-based health center records. This is imperative since a parent may believe that they do not need to inform the school about a particular condition or medical need that a child has because the school-based health center is already aware of it. Generally, SBHCs maintain their own records, separate from school health records generated by the school nurse.

Under FERPA guidelines, a school may disclose directory information about a student, such as name, address, telephone number, and date of birth, without parental permission. However, it does not allow disclosure of vaccination status if it is part of the educational record. Additionally, schools must give parents and eligible students a reasonable period to request that this information cannot be disclosed (Surprenant & Miller, 2022). For example, to support vaccination compliance for school entry, it could be useful to share vaccination status with the SBHC healthcare provider so that the provider could conduct outreach and complete vaccines for those students who need certain immunizations. Even though the purpose of sharing would be the care coordination followed by (and allowed) HIPAA, many districts do not allow this information to be shared and consider it protected by FERPA. (*See Chapter 12 for more information on FERPA and HIPAA*).

Consent to Treat

Where possible, in parallel to the consent-to-treat process, both school nurses and SBHCs should encourage the use of appropriate release of information forms and consent language to facilitate referrals and coordinate the care of students. Consent refers to permission for care to be given to a student and should be collected annually per SBHC policy. There should be coordination between the SBHC and the school nurse, including delineation of roles and responsibilities. This should include the development of protocols defining permission to share medical information. SBHCs should ensure confidentiality regarding the sharing of medical information under state and federal laws. In addition, the SBHC should annually document acknowledgment from enrolled students and parents informing them of their rights and responsibilities, confidentiality, informed consent, release of information, and financial responsibilities.

Student access to school nursing services generally requires no consent from parents. A student may only access SBHC services with the required permission and consent from the parent(s). The healthcare provider in a SBHC must obtain the student's or student's representative informed consent prior to performing any test, procedure, or treatment. The law requires parental consent for the health care of a minor (under 18 years of age). The law also recognizes that some minors are competent to understand the potential implications of medical procedures. Some states permit certain minors to give consent to their own medical care. This may include emancipated minors, mature minors, married minors, minor parents, pregnant minors, minors in the military, runaway minors, homeless youth, high school graduates, and minors or age specified by law (Centers for Disease Control [CDC], 2022). In some states, minors can self-consent and present unaccompanied for certain services outlined by state laws.

There are additional situations where minors can self-consent to medical treatment without parental consent (including but not limited to minors who fall in the categories previously listed). These particular services are permitted as it is believed that if minors had to seek parental consent for medical care or treatment for these conditions, they might not follow through due to fear of parental reactions. Although these situational conditions vary from state to state, they may include the right to contraceptive care, testing and treatment for STDs, HIV/AIDs, treatment for substance abuse, and outpatient mental healthcare services (CDC, 2022). *(See Chapter 26 for more information on consent for treatment and Chapter 15 for Minor's Rights).*

Confidentiality

Confidentiality refers to the student's right not to have health records disclosed to others without consent. FERPA laws protect school health and educational records. Federal laws stipulate who has the right to access records. FERPA provides access for parents to their student's school health and educational records. Please note that the protections related to minor confidential services provided by the SBHC that protect the information in the medical record from being shared with the parent do not transfer to the academic record. Whereas the medical records of a SBHC, in some instances, are held to stricter standards of confidentiality. For example, suppose the student received medical care for a sexually transmitted infection. In that case, the minor can consent, and in most states, the SBHC cannot share the information with the parent. Sharing of this sensitive health information can be determined at the state level, and SBHC staff need to follow laws as written. Health records maintained by the SBHC are governed by HIPAA laws (AAP, 2022).

When the SBHC is not run by school staff, a clear distinction must be made to determine which records are to be maintained by the school or the SBHC. Policies and procedures must be developed to distinguish between records that can and cannot be accessible to parents or guardians. Record-keeping and information disclosure procedures for a SBHC and the school nurse must be formalized, preferably with legal counsel, to protect student confidentiality (The Network for Public Health Law, 2020). Again, this distinction is essential and related to child find under the Individuals with Disabilities Education Act (IDEA) or Americans with Disabilities Act (ADA). If a student needs accommodations and parents share the information only with the SBHC, the school may not have access to the information, and accommodations may not occur in a timely fashion. Educating parents on the need to share information with both parties is key to good communication between school nurses and SBHC. *(See Chapter 10 for more information regarding school health records).*

Collaboration

Role of the school nurse in relation to the SBHC staff:

It is recommended that school nurses:
- Function as part of the multi-disciplinary healthcare team that develops the rational and design plan for the SBHC.
- Collaborate with health and education staff to develop a system of care for students functioning at its full potential.
- Refer and coordinate care for students who are enrolled for care in the SBHC.
- Facilitate the *Release of Information* and FERPA consents where necessary and beneficial to continuity of care between the school nurse and medical provider within the SBHC.

Role of the SBHC staff in relation to the school nurse:

It is recommended that the staff of the SBHC:
- Collaborate with the school nurse as part of the design team and in all phases of planning, implementing, and evaluating a SBHC.
- Collaborate with the school nurse as a member of a team that provides health services for shared clients utilizing a holistic health approach.
- Facilitate the *Release of Information* and FERPA consents where necessary and beneficial to continuity of care between the school nurse and medical provider within the SBHC.

In partnership:

It is recommended that the school nurse and SBHC staff:
- Coordinate nursing and treatment compliance care plans for clients who require follow-up care.
- Partner with each other to create a culture of health within the school community.
- Work together to document services that will allow data collection to study care outcomes, the cost-effectiveness of care, and other identified outcomes using an evidence-based system of care.
- Develop policies and systems that support the quality and confidentiality of care received by students.
- Jointly plan and implement health promotion, disease prevention, and management programs to improve health outcomes for all school and community members.
- Within the parameters of confidentiality, notify school staff of students with health needs that may require accommodation during the school day.
- Partner with each other and the school's multi-tiered systems of support team to determine a referral plan and system of care for students who seek healthcare services within the school and those returning from a hospital stay or extended period of absence,
- Jointly monitor student grades and attendance patterns.

This integration of school nursing services and the services of the SBHC ensures that students will have access to the health and behavioral health services they may require.

CONCLUSION

Due to the varying social determinants of health and root causes of inequities, communities recognize the emergent need to implement low-barrier access to comprehensive healthcare services for children and families. Changes in disease patterns, growth in medical technology, and an increase in the number of working parents have resulted in more healthcare services being delivered in school. Students who use SBHCs have been shown to have better grades and attendance (NASN, n.d.), and it can be viewed as an integral strategy to help students succeed in school.

School nurses are the leaders in the school, providing oversight for the health and safety of students. Licensed Registered Nurses need to be present in the schools to advocate for school nursing services for every child. SBHCs contribute to providing comprehensive health care and wrap-around services to students. SBHCs contribute by providing low-barrier and accessible physical and behavioral health care by qualified medical and behavioral health professionals who are able to provide diagnosis, prescription management, case management, care coordination, and referrals. Through collaboration between the school nurse and the SBHC with community providers, primary care, behavioral health, health education, and oral health care services can be provided to students and their families. Ultimately this collaboration will improve student outcomes, attendance patterns, academic achievement, and success.

RESOURCES

See Appendix: Interface between SBHCs and School Nurses

National Association of School Nurses: https://www.nasn.org/

National Association of School Nurses: School Nursing & School-Based Health Centers in the United States, Working Together for Student Success. https://www.sbh4all.org/wp-content/uploads/2021/05/SBHA_JOINT_STATEMENT_FINAL_F.pdf

National Clearinghouse for Educational Facilities:
https://www2.ed.gov/programs/edfacclearinghouse/index.html

School-Based Health Alliance: https://www.sbh4all.org/

School-Based Health Alliance: Redefining Health for Kids and Teens (sbh4all.org)

REFERENCES

American Academy of Pediatrics, Council on School Health. (2016). *Role of the school nurse in providing school health services*. http://pediatrics.aappublications.org/content/early/2016/05/19/peds.2016-0852

American Academy of Pediatrics (2022). *HIPAA and FERPA basics*. https://www.aap.org/en/patient-care/school-health/hipaa-and-ferpa-basics/

Arenson, M., Hudson, P.J., Lee, N., & Lai, B. (2019) The evidence on school-based health centers: A review. *Global Pediatric Health, 137*(6), 1-10. https://doi.org/10.1177/2333794X19828745

Center For Disease Control. (2022). *State Laws that Enable a Minor to Provide Informed Consent to Receive HIV and STD Services.* https://www.cdc.gov/hiv/policies/law/states/minors.html

Family Educational Rights and Privacy Act of 1974, 20 U.S.C. § 1232g (1974).

Gardiner, T. (2020). Supporting health and educational outcomes through school-based health centers. *Pediatric Nursing, 46*(6), 292-299, 307. https://www.proquest.com/openview/93b17fb4f263623f6616bb1bec4158cb/1?pq-origsite=gscholar&cbl=47659

Health Insurance Portability and Accountability Act of 1996, Pub. L. No. 104-191 (1996).

Maughan, E.D. (2018). School nurses: An investment in student achievement. *Phi Delta Kappan, 99* (7), 8-14. https://kappanonline.org/maughan-school-nurses-investment-student-achievement/

National Association of School Nurses. (n.d.). *Five ways a school nurse benefits the school.* https://higherlogicdownload.s3.amazonaws.com/NASN/3870c72d-fff9-4ed7-833f-215de278d256/UploadedImages/PDFs/Advocacy/advocacy_FiveWays.pdf

National Association of School Nurses. (2022). *Student access to school nursing services* (Position statement). Author.

National Association of School Nurses and School-Based Health Alliance. (2022). *School nursing & school-based health centers in the United States-working together for student success.* https://higherlogicdownload.s3.amazonaws.com/NASN/8575d1b7-94ad-45ab-808e-d45019cc5c08/UploadedImages/PDFs/Advocacy/School_Nursing_and_School-Based_Health_Centers.pdf

The Network for Public Health Law. (2020). *Data sharing guidance for school nurses.* https://www.google.com/url?sa=t&rct=j&q=&esrc=s&source=web&cd=&cad=rja&uact=8&ved=2ahUKEwiGyfy0kq3-AhVFHjQIHf_RAxgQFnoECA8QAQ&url=https%3A%2F%2Fwww.networkforphl.org%2Fwp-content%2Fuploads%2F2020%2F01%2FData-Sharing-Guidance-for-School-Nurses-with-Appendices-1-23-2020.pdf&usg=AOvVaw2IxPKkzzfQMZTjPf67l32f

Surprenant, K.S., Miller, F. (2022). *IDEA and FERPA Crosswalk A side-by-side comparison of the privacy provisions under Parts B and C of the IDEA and FERPA.* U.S. Department of Education Student Privacy Policy Office IDEA and FERPA Crosswalk (ed.gov)

U.S. Department of Education (2023) *Family Educational Rights and Privacy Act guidance for school officials on student health records.* https://www.google.com/url?sa=t&rct=j&q=&esrc=s&source=web&cd=&cad=rja&uact=8&ved=2ahUKEwjV2eS8mK3-AhVSKH0KHTmzAZ4QFnoECBoQAQ&url=https%3A%2F%2Fstudentprivacy.ed.gov%2Fresources%2Ffamily-educational-rights-and-privacy-act-guidance-school-officials-student-health-records&usg=AOvVaw3BtYDMhHLq7a0n8mbWj7pZ

U.S. Department of Education & U.S. Department of Health and Human Services. (2019). *Joint Guidance on the Application of the Family Educational Rights and Privacy Act (FERPA) And the Health Insurance Portability and Accountability Act of 1996 (HIPAA) To Student Health Records.* https://studentprivacy.ed.gov/sites/default/files/resource_document/file/2019%20HIPAA%20FERPA%20Joint%20Guidance%20508.pdf

APPENDIX: Interface between SBHCs and School Nurses

What is a School-Based Health Center?

School-Based Health Centers (SBHC) began in the early 1970s due to the increasing number of children and adolescents lacking healthcare access. This need included cultural and age-sensitive healthcare delivery suited to their developmental needs. SBHCs may provide comprehensive medical and mental health care to students. This may include services such as well-child exams, immunizations, family planning, and individualized mental health therapy (Love et al., 2019a).

A broad array of research and a recent systematic review has found that SBHCs are effective in improving a variety of education and health-related outcomes. Increasingly SBHCs use telehealth to provide care to students; this is especially useful in rural settings (Love et al., 2019b). Substantial educational benefits associated with SBHCs include reductions in rates of school suspension or high school non-completion and increases in grade point averages and grade promotion (Gardiner, 2020).   It has been shown that when a school-based health center and the school nurse work together, student well-being, ability to self-manage chronic health conditions, and their general knowledge of health improves (National Association of School Nurses [NASN] & School-Based Health Association [SBHA], 2022). Access to SBHCs, where students spend their time, allows for equitable access to health care, reduces out-of-school time for students, out of work time for families, and enables integration of school success goals into students' medical and mental health treatment. SBHCs can help students address a variety of unhealthy behaviors that can create long-term health risks, such as sexually transmitted diseases and substance abuse (Arenson et al., 2019)

Multiple health professionals in a school setting may have distinctive and complementary roles; their student-based objectives are met effectively through open communication and professional collaboration. Working as partners, school nurses and staff of the SBHC can increase access to needed health and mental health care for underserved communities, monitor outcomes of care, uniformly document care, collect data about health needs and outcomes of care, and provide case management – all necessary for improving the quality of health care and academic outcomes for our students (Gardiner, 2020).

Services are available to eligible students who enroll to receive care in the SBHC. While SBHCs do exist in schools that have limited nursing services, they do not take the place of the role of the school nurse School nurses and SBHC staff work in collaboration to develop policies, collect data, and evaluate health outcomes for students (NASN & SBHA, 2022).

Collaboration between healthcare providers in the SBHC and the school nurse will enhance students' health, academic outcomes, and lifelong, overall well-being. The challenge is to define and delineate the roles and responsibilities of school nurses and members of the SBHC team to provide seamless and comprehensive care for students and their families in an evidence-based system of care without duplication of services.

Role of the School Nurse

As the role of school nurses has expanded, they have continued to positively impact the schools they serve. NASN (n.d.) reports that having a school nurse in the building saves an hour a day for the principal, 20 minutes for teachers, and 45 minutes for clerical staff. In addition, school nurses have significantly impacted attendance for students with asthma and allowed students with other chronic conditions to spend more time in class.

After the child's home, the school represents the second most influential environment in a child's life. Teachers, school administrators, and parents know that a student who arrives at school fed, rested, healthy, and engaged is ready to learn. The Centers for Disease Control (CDC) and Prevention (2020) identified that the academic success of youth is strongly linked to their health. In turn, academic success is a primary indicator of the overall well-being of youth and is a primary predictor and determinant of adult health outcomes (American Academy of Pediatrics, 2016). The role of the school nurse encompasses both health and educational goals. School nurses must be prepared to provide equitable access to care for increasingly complex health needs in a school setting where academic success is considered a top priority (NASN, 2022).

Today's professional school nurse has a diverse and challenging role. This is even more amplified due to the increasing number of students with complex health issues (National Academies of Sciences, Engineering, and Medicine, 2021). The school nurse must assess each student's health status, identify social determinants of health that may create a barrier to educational progress, and develop a healthcare plan to manage the problems in the school setting. The nurse is a vital part of the educational team, identifying the health issues that may impact the student's learning (NASN & SBHA, 2022).

Advanced technology has impacted the practice of school nursing. Information on diseases and care measures can now be quickly accessed online. The student health record and the daily health room log of visits have become electronic. Health data on a specific student can easily be retrieved, reviewed, and shared with the student's health provider as part of telemedicine. Parents appreciate the ease of nurse–healthcare provider communication, as it keeps their student in school, not in a waiting room. Advances in patient care technology have also improved disease management and quality of life. Examples include insulin pumps, vagal nerve stimulators, and cardiac monitoring devices (NASN, 2019). School nurses provide effective evidence-based case management for chronic diseases such as asthma, diabetes, and anaphylactic food allergies (NASN, 2017).

School nurses will continue to see an increase in acute and chronic health conditions impacting students. Consistent nursing interventions implemented early will decrease health complications. More students can stay in the classroom and stay healthy through support and education by the nurse and medical management from the SBHC. Teachers and administrators are not health professionals and have other important duties to fulfill during the school day. They identify the nurse as the healthcare expert in the school setting.

REFERENCES

American Academy of Pediatrics, Council on School Health. (2016). Role of the school nurse in providing school health services. *Pediatrics*, *137*(6), e20160852. https://doi.org/10.1542/peds.2016-0852

Arenson, M., Hudson, P.J., Lee, N., & Lai, B. (2019). The evidence on school-based health centers: A review. *Global Pediatric Health, 137*(6), 1-10. https://doi.org/10.1177/2333794X19828745

Centers for Disease Control and Prevention. (2020). *Why schools?* https://www.cdc.gov/healthyyouth/about/why_schools.htm

Gardiner, T. (2020). Supporting health and educational outcomes through school-based health centers. *Pediatric*

Nursing, 46(6), 292-299, 307. https://www.proquest.com/openview/93b17fb4f263623f6616bb1bec4158cb/1?pq-origsite=gscholar&cbl=47659

Love, H.E., Schlitt, J., Soleimanpour, S., Panchal, N., & Behr, C. (2019a). Twenty years of school-based healthcare growth and expansion. *Health Affairs, 38*(5), 755-764. https://doi.org/101377/hlthaff.2018.05472

Love, H.E., Panchal, N., Schlitt, J., Behr, C., & Soleimanpour, S. (2019b). The use of telehealth in school-based health centers. *Global Pediatric Health, 6.* https://doi.org/10.1177/2333794X19884194

National Academies of Sciences, Engineering, and Medicine. (2021). *The future of nursing 2020-2030: charting a path to achieve health equity*. The National Academies Press. https://doi.org/10.17226/25982

National Association of School Nurses. (n.d.) *Five ways a school nurse benefits the school.* https://higherlogicdownload.s3.amazonaws.com/NASN/3870c72d-fff9-4ed7-833f-215de278d256/UploadedImages/PDFs/Advocacy/advocacy_FiveWays.pdf

National Association of School Nurses. (2017). *Definition of school nursing.* https://www.nasn.org/about-nasn/about

National Association of School Nurses. (2019). *Electronic health records: An essential tool in keeping students healthy* (Position Statement). Author. https://www.nasn.org/nasn-resources/professional-practice-documents/position-statements/ps-electronic-health-records

National Association of School Nurses. (2022). *Student access to school nursing services* [Position statement]. Author.

National Association of School Nurses and School-Based Health Alliance. (2022). *School nursing & school-based health centers in the United States-working together for student success.* https://higherlogicdownload.s3.amazonaws.com/NASN/8575d1b7-94ad-45ab-808e-d45019cc5c08/UploadedImages/PDFs/Advocacy/School_Nursing_and_School-Based_Health_Centers.pdf

Chapter 48

SCHOOL-LOCATED VACCINATION CLINICS

Lynne P. Meadows, MS, BSN, RN

Deborah D'Souza Vazirani, DrPH, MHSA

DESCRIPTION OF ISSUE

School-located vaccination clinics provide an opportunity for school-required vaccinations and other vaccinations to be administered in schools. The Centers for Disease Control and Prevention's (CDC) document Flu SLV: Information for Planners defines a school-located vaccination clinic as "a vaccination that is administered on school grounds via temporary clinics which are primarily designed to vaccinate enrolled students and held before, during, and/or after school hours, or when schools are not in session (i.e., during summer break). These clinics typically involve collaboration between public health departments and public and private schools/school districts, and sometimes other public or private entities" (CDC, n.d., para #4). The National Association of School Nurses (NASN) has expanded the definition to include "any vaccine clinic done in partnership with a K-12 school or school nurse, regardless of the location where the clinic is held (i.e., on or off school property) and regardless of the target population of the clinic [i.e., a clinic for school staff or clinic to vaccinate community members] (NASN, 2022b). The Association of Immunization Managers (AIM) and NASN agree that school nurses are valued and trusted leaders in the provision of school health services and a champion for vaccination (NASN/AIM, 2021). School-located vaccination clinics are commonly referred to as school-located vaccination clinics (SLVs) or school-located vaccination events (SLVe). For the purposes of this chapter, SLVs are used as found in the literature and work done on SLVs by NASN.

SLVs are part of an established strategy for increasing vaccination rates for students and staff. SLVs reduce vaccine-preventable disease and absenteeism, increase public perception of the importance of vaccinations, and increase equitable access to vaccines (NASN School Nurse, 2022). SLVs have been shown to positively impact the health of students, staff, and the broader community (Park et al., 2021; NASN School Nurse, 2022a).

With the increase in states' requirements for school vaccinations and the promotion of recommended vaccines like influenza, SLVs became a critical public health entity that expanded during the SARS-CoV-2 (COVID-19) pandemic to include offering COVID-19 vaccines. The focus on utilizing SLVs increased during the pandemic and pushed SLVs into the spotlight, reinforcing their significance in public health practice (CDC, 2022b). The positive as well as significant impact that SLVs have on community health warrants careful and thorough planning, and several factors must be considered when organizing and executing SLVs.

BACKGROUND

SLVs have a long history in the United States since the 1850s and have successfully contributed to lower morbidity and mortality due to vaccine-preventable diseases (Park et al., 2021). In 1875, New York City used schools to deliver the smallpox vaccine. Schools were again utilized in the 1950s to deliver the Salk polio vaccine. In 1969, schools held vaccine clinics to administer the rubella vaccine; Hepatitis B catch-up clinics were held in the 1990s and again in 2009 for varicella and H1N1 vaccines (Perman et al., 2017).

SCHOOL-LOCATED VACCINATION CLINICS

In 2008 the Advisory Committee on Immunization Practices (ACIP) recommended an annual influenza vaccination for all children six months through 18 years of age (Immunize.org, 2022), which would substantially increase the number of individuals recommended to have an annual vaccination. The ability to administer this vast number of vaccinations may be beyond the capacity of primary care providers, leaving schools as an attractive venue for mass influenza immunization clinics (Perman et al., 2017).

According to the CDC, "While children in the United States are vaccinated primarily in their pediatrician's or family doctor's office, schools provide unique opportunities for getting children vaccinated (specifically for influenza) for the following reasons:
- Children are already present in schools.
- Schools are conveniently located throughout communities, and communities are generally familiar with and trust schools.
- School nurses, if present, may be available to assist in vaccination activities and may be familiar with the health of individual students, and school staff have access to parental contact information, which could facilitate communications (e.g., for announcing clinic dates, obtaining parental consent for vaccination)." (CDC, n.d.)

The school is the ideal place to reach the 55.5 million children in the United States who attend school daily and come from diverse cultures, socioeconomic backgrounds, and age groups. Furthermore, the school is conveniently located in a familiar and trusted community environment (NCES, 2022a; NCES, 2022b).

There is ample evidence indicating that school-based vaccination clinics are impactful and increase vaccination rates (Park et al., 2021; Szilagyi et al., 2019). Studies show that SLVs are key for adolescents who have significantly lower vaccination rates due to lower office-based primary care visits (Benjamin-Chung et al., 2020; Bernstein & Bocchini, 2017). SLVs at school play an important role in improving student vaccination coverage rates by improving student and community access and reducing parents' need for time away from work (Perman et al., 2017). Research has also shown that SLV programs for the influenza vaccine have reduced influenza rates and decreased school absenteeism (Wilson et al., 2022).

The COVID-19 pandemic has highlighted the value of SLVs and administering vaccines in schools as a primary mitigation strategy to protect against communicable diseases. A decline in routine vaccination occurred in children due to the pandemic, related to healthcare provider office closures, stay-at-home orders, caregiver fears in accessing primary care related to COVID-19 exposure, and virtual schools' lack of exclusion from non-compliance with state and territorial mandates (Patel et al., 2020).

The literature indicates that the keys to a successful SLV include planning with trusted partners (Park et al., 2021). Public health departments have traditionally led SLV efforts, but other public or private entities could serve as the lead alternatively. Neither schools nor school districts tend to lead SLV efforts unless there is a school-based health center (permanent health clinics often located on school grounds that deliver primary care to enrolled students) affiliation. School districts providing SLVs must have support from the school administration and may require additional staffing to facilitate this effort. School nurses can lead the effort but not in isolation and must have the support of the school leadership and key partners. Establishing partnerships is essential regardless of which entity leads or initiates the SLV effort (CDC, 2022a and b).

IMPLICATIONS FOR SCHOOL NURSE PRACTICE

Because of their role, education, public health experience, and advocacy for health, school nurses are essential team members in the planning and execution of SLVs (Wilson et al., 2022). School nurses are "ideally positioned to initiate this process and provide accurate information, dispelling myths about vaccines. Because they are considered a trusted source of health information by the school community, they can provide valuable education on the impact of vaccination on student and staff attendance" (Park et al., 2021, page 1).

However, determining whether and when to offer SLVs should be made in consultation with the various appropriate/applicable stakeholders (school district, local public health, etc.) as well as utilization of school vaccination data. Decisions about whether to offer an SLV should be made at the local (individual school, school district) level because the feasibility and appropriateness will vary greatly by state, county, school district, and even from school to school. The main factors to be considered include the availability of vaccination providers in the community and community support for vaccinations, including support from the school leadership (NASN School Nurse, 2022b).

SLV programs must ensure they are conducted in accordance with federal, state, and local laws and regulations. Entities should consult their legal counsel for advice concerning the applicability of legal immunity, licensure, medical consent, and privacy laws that may exist with respect to persons involved in vaccination programs. CDC outlined several legal issues (CDC 2022a & b) related to minors, school staff, and volunteers that should be considered before planning and executing SLVs, but the list is not intended to be exhaustive. Some of these legal considerations include establishing memorandum of understanding (MOUs) with community partners, obtaining parental consent, staff training, managing aspects of vaccine administration, delivery, and storage, reporting and information technology (IT) support, observation, and ensuring confidentiality as outlined in the Family Education Rights and Privacy Act (FERPA) and Health Insurance Portability and Accountability Act (HIPAA). Additionally, written guidance resources, including checklists (CDC, 2022 a & b; NASN/AIM, 2021), should be reviewed when planning SLVs. These resources could include culturally specific tools, including the need for interpreters for diverse populations and those with disabilities, traffic management, protocols for adverse reactions, communications ahead of time, etc. *(Please refer to Chapter 12 for more information on FERPA/HIPAA).*

CDC and NASN provide resources and toolkits to assist with the planning and preparation of SLVs which should be designed and executed in accordance with state and local laws and regulations. School nurses need to take account of the following key considerations and legal concerns when helping plan an SLV program: (See Table 1 – School-Located Vaccination Clinics: Key/Important Considerations).

1. Review of state laws governing immunization and vaccination administration (training, procurement, etc.).
2. Permission/approval from the school system (superintendent buy-in and other school staff (school nurses, principals, school board, IT, facilities, communications, security, etc.).
3. Planning – partnerships or school nurses to administer vaccines (if school nurses – appropriate training must be conducted and proper administration parameters for vaccine maintenance and storage, etc.).

- If including partnerships ensuring MOUs and other required certifications and training documentation (if applicable) are in place;
- Budgeting - funding and cost parameters and resources;
- Billing processes and IT considerations (if applicable/required by vaccine providers);
- Determining when to schedule the vaccinations clinics and follow-up dates;
- Consent from parents; advertisement/notices;
- Data tracking and sharing /documentation of vaccines and HIPAA/FERPA compliance with data requirements.

4. Management of post-vaccination concerns and adverse incidents (side effects). (NASN School Nurse, 2022b)

NASN, in partnership with AIM, recently conducted an environmental scan on SLV programs and examined state and local issues surrounding SLV programming. A round table with school nurses was hosted to examine the school nurse's role in planning and implementing SLVs. The resulting report "The Landscape of State and Local School-Located Vaccination Clinics: Practices, Policies, and Lessons Learned for Providing COVID-19 and Routine Vaccinations" provides a plethora of available resources (from national organizations as well as state-specific and local resources) that school nurses can use to plan and implement an SLV. These resources include toolkits and checklists for planning and implementation (NASN School Nurse, 2022b).

CONCLUSION

SLV programs have had a significant impact on providing access to vaccinations and immunizations to students and have provided the opportunity to improve overall school and community health, where they can reach children, school personnel, and families in the school environment. The effectiveness of SLVs has been further highlighted, and their significance has been deemed an important public health strategy during the current pandemic. The need to fully understand the parameters of SLVs and consider the legal ramifications are critical to their success. School nurses and School Health Services can play a significant role in the successful planning and execution of SLVs and often are the primary lead in the SLV planning and execution. NASN believes that immunizations are essential to the primary prevention of disease from infancy through adulthood and continues to support the efforts of school nurses in developing SLV opportunities.

RESOURCES

- National Association of School Nurses (NASN) and Association of Immunization Managers (AIM). School-Located Vaccination School Nurse Planning Checklist. (2021). https://www.immunizationmanagers.org/content/uploads/2021/10/School-Vaccination-Nurse-Plan-Checklist.pdf

- Building Family Confidence in the COVID-19 Vaccine, Framing Strategies for School Nurses (Toolkit) https://www.frameworksinstitute.org/toolkit/building-family-confidence-in-the-covid-19-vaccine/

- COVID-19 Vaccine Administration in Schools https://schoolnursenet.nasn.org/covid19ref/glossary/covid-19-vaccine-administration-in-schools

REFERENCES

Benjamin-Chung, J., Arnold, B.F., Kennedy, C.J., Mishra, K., Pokpongkiat, M., Nguyn, A., Jilek, W., Holbrook, K., Pan, E., Kirley, P.K., Libby, T., Hubbard, A.E., Reingold, A., & Colford, J.M. (2020). Evaluation of a city-wide school-located influenza vaccination program in Oakland, California, with respect to vaccination coverage, school absences, and laboratory-confirmed influenza: A matched cohort study. *PloS Medicine, 17(8),* e1003238. https://doi.org/10.1371/journal.pmed.1003238

Bernstein, H.H., & Bocchini, J.A. (2017). Practical approaches to optimize adolescent immunization. Pediatrics, 139(3), e1-e14. https://doi.org/10.1542/peds.2016-4187

Centers for Disease Control and Prevention. (n.d.). *School-location vaccination: Information for planners.* Retrieved 7-31-23 from www.cdc.gov/flu/pdf/school/SLV_information.pdf

Centers for Disease Control and Prevention. (2022a). *Guidance for planning vaccination clinics held at satellite, temporary or off-site locations.* www.cdc.gov/vaccines/hcp/admin/mass-clinic-activities/index.html

Centers for Disease Control and Prevention. (2022b). *What to consider when planning to operate a COVID-19 vaccine clinic.* www.cdc.gov/vaccines/covid-19/planning/considerations-operating-vaccine-clinic.html

Centers For Disease Control and Prevention. (2021). *Support of health care providers, forms, vaccine information statements, school-located vaccination (slv): information for planners.* www.cdc.gov/flu/school/slv/support.htm

Immunize.Org: Vaccine Timeline- Historic dates and events related to vaccines and immunizations. December 9, 2022. www.imunize.org/timeline/ (viewed March 23, 2023)

NASN School Nurse. (2022a). The landscape of state and local school-located vaccination clinics: practices, policies, and lessons learned for providing covid-19 and routine vaccinations. *NASN School Nurse, 37*(1_suppl), 3S-14S. https://doi.org/10.1177/1942602X211064750

NASN School Nurse. (2022b). Key challenges and opportunities for implementing school-located vaccination clinics for covid-19 and influenza: Roundtables with school nurses and immunization programs. *NASN School Nurse, 37*(1_suppl), 15S-23S. https:/doi.org/10.1177/1942602X211064752

National Association of School Nurses. (2021). *School-located vaccination clinics for covid-19 and influenza.* Roundtable Report, September 13, 2021. https://higherlogicdownload.s3.amazonaws.com/NASN/3870c72d-fff9-4ed7-833f-215de278d256/UploadedImages/PDFs/Roundtable_Report_School-Located_Vaccination_Clinics_for_COVID-19_and_Influenza.pdf

National Association of School Nurse and Association of Immunization Managers. (2021). *School-located vaccination school nurse planning checklist.* (2021). https://www.immunizationmanagers.org/content/uploads/2021/10/School-Vaccination-Nurse-Plan-Checklist.pdf

National Center for Education Statistics (NCES). (2022a). Common core of data (CCD), state nonfiscal survey of public elementary/secondary education, 2019-20, provisional version 1a. *U.S. Department of Education.* https://nces.ed.gov/ccd/tables/201920_summary_2.asp

National Center for Education Statistics (NCES). (2022b). Private school universe survey (PSS), 2019–20. U.S. *Department of Education.* https://nces.ed.gov/surveys/pss/tables/TABLE01fl1920.asp

Park, K., Cartmill, R., Johnson-Gordon, B., Landes, M., Malik, K., Sinnott, J., Wallace, K., & Wallin, R. (2021) Preparing for a school-located covid-19 vaccination clinic. *NASN School Nurse, 36*(3), 156-163. https://doi.org/10.1177/1942602X21991643

Patel, B., Zell, E., Kirtland, K., Jones-Jack, N., Harris, L., Sprague, C., Schultz, J., Le, Q., Bramer, C., Kuramoto, S., Cheng, I., Woinarowicz, M., Robison, S., McHugh, A., Scheuer, S., & Gibbs-Scharf, L. (2020). Administration of selected routine childhood and adolescent vaccinations. 10 U.S. jurisdictions, March-September, 2020. *Morbidity and Mortality Weekly Report, 70*(23), 840-845. http://dx.doi.org/10.15585/mmwr.mm7023a2

Perman, S., Turner, S., Ramsay, A.I.G., Baim-Lance, A., Utley, M., & Fulop, N.J. (2017) School-based vaccination programmes: a systematic review of the evidence on organisation and delivery in high income countries. *BMC Public Health, 17*, 252. https://doi.org/10.1186/s12889-017-4168-0

Szilagyi, P.G., Schaffer, S., Rand, C.M., Goldstein, N.P., Hightower, A.D., Younge, M., Albertin, C.S., DiBitetto, K., Yoo, B.K., & Humiston, S.G. (2019). School-located influenza vaccination: Do vaccine clinics at school raise vaccination rates? *Journal of School Health, 89*(12), 1004-1012. https://doi.org/10.1111/josh.12840

Wilson, O.F., Mote, S.L., & Morse, B.L. (2022). Addressing vaccine hesitancy among students and families: Interventions for school nurses. NASN School Nurse. 38/(3), 146–154. https://doi.org/10.1177/1942602X221106945

Table 1- School-Located Vaccination Clinics: Key/Important Considerations

Considerations for Developing, Planning and Execution of SLVs	Potential Legal Considerations	Literature/Resources
State and local laws governing immunization requirements, administration, training, etc.	1. Explore and review state and local laws/ regulations regarding immunization and vaccination administration (training, procurement, etc. is paramount). 2. All SLV partners should consult legal counsel regarding authority to act, licensure, consents, training, confidentiality, immunity, etc. Clarify the training and certifications required for all critical and mandatory functions of an SLV, such as authority to access and distribute the vaccine, data collection, protecting the vaccine cold chain,	1. CDC Guidance for Planning Vaccination Clinics Held at Satellite, Temporary, or Off-Site Locations, and a Satellite, Temporary, and Off-site Vaccination Clinic Supply Checklist. https://www.cdc.gov/vaccines/hcp/admin/mass-clinic-activities/index.html 2. Checklist - https://www.cdc.gov/vaccines/hcp/admin/mass-clinic-activities/vaccination-clinic-supply-checklist.html
Permission/approval/ support from key stakeholders	1. Prior to planning, document the need, determine the feasibility of holding SLV, and specify what discussions should be conducted among potential partners. 2. Identify and engage key stakeholders: school administration (superintendent, principals, and school board), school personnel (school nursing team/health services, support staff, and others), and local health authorities (local health department and other community healthcare providers). 3. Ensure Confirm that potential partners and stakeholders support the SLV. 4. Make certain that appropriate resources are available to plan, staff, and execute the SLV.	1. CDC Guidance for Planning Vaccination Clinics Held at Satellite, Temporary, or Off-Site Locations, and a Satellite, Temporary, and Off-site Vaccination Clinic Supply Checklist. https://www.cdc.gov/vaccines/hcp/admin/mass-clinic-activities/index.html 2. Checklist - https://www.cdc.gov/vaccines/hcp/admin/mass-clinic-activities/vaccination-clinic-supply-checklist.html

Considerations for Developing, Planning and Execution of SLVs	Potential Legal Considerations	Literature/Resources
Planning the SLV	1. Determine the population in need - who is eligible to participate (students, staff, parents/siblings (family members)/ community members). This may dictate additional planning and considerations. 2. Decide where (which schools) and when (before, during, or after school hours) to host SLVs, which vaccines to offer, and who will participate. 3. Partnerships – delineate roles and responsibilities and establish Memoranda of Understanding (MOUs) for - budget, funding, and billing - site operation logistics -planning, set-up, traffic management, tear-down, IT - acquisition of supplies, equipment including vaccine management - staffing, training, and other certifications - communication with students, staff, parents, and community members 4. Obtain medical orders for vaccines and emergency response procedures; clarify liability, insurance, and coverage. 5. Schools and/or public health may require background checks for partners and volunteers present on school property – check district/school policy and guidelines. 6. Establish the billing processes (Medicaid, third-party payors, etc.) and communicate this appropriately with parents and participants: who will bill, when, and how.	1. School Nurse Plan Checklist: School-Vaccination-Nurse-Plan-Checklist.pdf (immunizationmanagers.org) 2. School Nurse Planning Checklist – www.nasn.org

Considerations for Developing, Planning and Execution of SLVs	Potential Legal Considerations	Literature/Resources
	7. Plan for the unique needs of different populations served: – students without parents present: elementary vs secondary – families with young children -- community members with language differences -- visual and hearing communication differences -- individuals with disabilities – physical, cognitive, emotional 8. Develop a communication plan for who will handle critics of the SLV and how, 9. Post-Clinic Concerns and Management: Although some minor side effects are not uncommon for people (including children and adolescents) after receiving the vaccine/s, SLV staff should develop/have in place protocols for contacting parents/guardians, accessing emergency services, and sending students home early if they are feeling ill post-vaccination which may include protocols for school absences. Make sure trained medical personnel (school nurse, EMS, and/or trained medical provider) are on-site and emergency medications like EpiPens, etc., are readily available in the event of a medical emergency or allergic reaction. Post clinic: Evaluation of impact: - Summarize the population targeted and served. - Cost/benefit analysis. Communicate with partners: School admin/school board, health services staff; - Effort vs. benefit to partners - Improvements	

Considerations for Developing, Planning and Execution of SLVs	Potential Legal Considerations	Literature/Resources
Consent forms for students and other participants, and compliance change of health information (HIPAA/FERPA).	1. Consult with local counsel to help determine when consent is required from a parent, the format of required consent, including possible verbal consent, and the process for obtaining consent. 2. Generally, the federal government does not have medical consent requirements. Requirements for medical consent are legislated and regulated by each state or jurisdiction; these requirements may include the circumstances under which minors can consent to their own medical treatment, including vaccination. Federal law (as well as state law) may regulate the vaccinator's use or disclosure of individually identifiable health information regarding the child. Student information contained in the vaccine consent form may be protected by state or federal privacy laws or regulations. Requesting such authorization may be recommended or necessary, depending on local needs and/or laws. 3. The Family Education Rights and Privacy Act (FERPA) applies to the educational agency or institutions receiving Department of Education funding and/or other Federal or state laws. 4. The Health Insurance Portability and Accountability Act (HIPAA) Privacy Rule may allow the use or disclosure of a minor's health information with signed authorization of the parent/guardian using a form that meets HIPAA requirements. 5. Secure consent documents and ensure confidentiality. 6. As appropriate, involve the IT school department for internet usage/access, student records, and connection with state immunization information systems (registries).	1. Consent forms: www.cdc.gov/flu/school/slv/support.htm 2. FERPA and HIPAA: Family Educational Rights and Privacy Act (FERPA) HIPAA Home | HHS.gov 3. The Family Education Rights and Privacy Act (FERPA) applies to educational agencies or institutions receiving Department of Education funding and/or other Federal or state laws. 4. The Health Insurance Portability and Accountability Act (HIPAA) Privacy Rule may allow the use or disclosure of a minor's health information with signed authorization of the parent/guardian using a form that meets HIPAA requirements. 5. Joint Guidance on the Application of HIPAA and FERPA to Student Health Records (hhs.gov) 6. School Nurse Planning Checklist – www.nasn.org

624

Considerations for Developing, Planning and Execution of SLVs	Potential Legal Considerations	Literature/Resources
Communication and advertisement before the SLV	1. Plan for information about the SLV to be communicated to communication with students, staff, parents, and the community. 2. Establish that communication and messaging forums (flyers, emails, social media, etc.) are utilized appropriately and in concert with district communications policies and guidelines. 3. Consider culturally appropriate educational material and health literacy needs.	1. Customizable Content for School and Childcare-Located Vaccinations Clinics. Customizable Content for School and Childcare-Located Vaccination Clinics | CDC 2. School Nurse Planning Checklist – www.nasn.org
Data, Reporting, and Record-Keeping during the event and after the event	Establish processes to track and collect data to document the number of vaccines administered, other demographic information, etc., and make sure they are utilized. Ensure that the confidentiality and integrity of the patient data collected is maintained. If school nurses administer vaccines, ensure that state department of health regulations and any other federal administration rules to document vaccine lot numbers, doses given, etc. are followed. Additionally, ensure that vaccines administered are appropriately and accurately entered in state immunization registries.	

Chapter 49

SERVICE ANIMALS IN THE SCHOOL SETTING

Antoinette Towle EdD, MSN, APRN, PPCNP-BC, SNP-BC

DESCRIPTION OF ISSUE

Evidence-based research has demonstrated that service animals have measurable effects on an individual with disabilities' psychosocial health, thus positively impacting their quality of life (Rodriguez et al., 2020). These service animals, which are mainly dogs, are individually and specifically trained to perform specific work or tasks for individuals with disabilities. Such work or tasks may include:

- guiding a student who is legally or completely blind.
- alerting a hearing-impaired or deaf student.
- pulling a wheelchair.
- alerting and protecting a student with medical concerns, such as seizure or diabetes symptoms.
- reminding a student to take medication.
- stop or interrupt sudden, impulsive, out-of-control running episodes or self-harm behaviors of a student with a behavioral health issue.
- calming a student who might be suffering from a mental health diagnosis, for example, Post-Traumatic Stress Disorder (PTSD), during an anxiety attack.

A request to bring a service animal into the school setting can cause a great deal of apprehension for school administrators, staff, and students. School administrators must comply with complex disability discrimination laws enacted by local and federal agencies. They must also ensure all school students' and staff's health, safety, and well-being. Protecting students and staff with severe allergies to animal dander or a fear of animals and, at the same time, accommodating a service animal for an individual with disabilities requires a great deal of teamwork and planning. School nurses can be leaders in this area because of their unique role in the school setting. In addition to their skill and expertise in assessing, planning, and implementing care for all students, especially those with special healthcare needs. It is the position of the National Association of School Nurses (NASN) that school nurses play an integral role in helping to facilitate the team planning process necessary to successfully integrate "service animals" into schools (2019).

The Americans with Disabilities Act (ADA) mandates that local buildings, including schools, must accommodate service animals, which usually refers to a trained dog (U.S. Department of Justice (DOJ), 2020). On the other hand, "emotional support" or "therapy" animals are treated differently under the ADA because these emotional support and therapy animals do not receive the same level of training as service animals; and therefore, do not have the same right to public access.

BACKGROUND

In 2010, the DOJ issued revised regulations under the ADA because, in part, of uncertainty regarding what types of animals qualified as a "service animal" under the ADA. The revisions clarified that the service animal must be a dog or, in specific circumstances, a miniature horse (DOJ, 2020). Note that a school is not automatically required to allow a miniature horse in the building. Instead, the school must determine whether it can reasonably modify its policies, practices, or procedures to allow a miniature horse into the building (28 C.F.R. § 35.136). Therefore, no other animal, wild or domestic, is permitted to be a service animal under the ADA. School nurses should consult with their local attorney to determine if state law allows other types of animals as "service animals."

The DOJ's regulatory revisions further explained and clarified that a service animal must be required for the individual with disabilities and specifically trained to do work or a task for such an individual. As a general rule, service animals must be allowed in government agencies, businesses, profit and nonprofit organizations, and schools (DOJ, 2020). As such, schools are generally required to permit service animals to accompany students with disabilities in all areas that students have access to within the school or school-related activities. Other federal laws, such as Section 504 of the Rehabilitation Act of 1973 (29 U.S.C. §794) and the Individuals with Disabilities in Education Act (IDEA) (20 U.S.C. §1400 et seq), further reinforce the use of service animals in the school setting. In addition to federal mandates, many states require additional rules and regulations regarding the use of service animals within that state (U.S. Department of Education [USDE], 2023). Therefore, it is important to research state laws when dealing with a request for a service animal.

In accordance with the ADA, service animals must be harnessed, leashed, or tethered unless those devices interfere with the service animal's work or the individual's disability prevents using those devices (DOJ, 2020). If a device is not used, the individual must have the ability to always control the animal, such as by voice, signal command, or other effective methods. School administrators and staff must be careful about inquiring into the disabled person's need for a service dog. School staff may ask only about the work or task that the animal has been trained to perform. (DOJ, 2020). The law prohibits school staff from requiring medical documentation regarding the student's disability and documentation regarding the service animal's identification card or training. It is also prohibited to ask that the animal demonstrate its ability to perform the work or task. School districts that tend to be aggressive in the enforcement of service animals could be subject to a lawsuit. *See, e.g., K.D. v. Villa Grove Cmty. Unit Sch. Dist. No. 302 Bd. of Educ.,* 403 Ill. App. 3d 1062 (Ill. App. Ct. 4th Dist. 2010) involving a district wrongly removing a student with autism's service dog; *Kalbfleisch v. Columbia Cmty. Unit Sch. Dist. Unit No. 4*, 396 Ill. App. 3d 1105 (Ill. App. Ct. 5th Dist. 2009).

Case Studies:

Case 1: *Hunter, an 11-year-old 6th-grade boy, who was once healthy, energetic, and athletic, suddenly had a stroke. The stroke damaged the left temporal lobe of his brain, causing him to have speech, memory, and learning delays. The damage also caused him to start having seizures. His seizures are frequent, come without warning, and are very difficult to control even while on medication. Hunter is always at risk of hurting himself. He had to quit sports because the seizures were too frequent. He requires someone to be with him at all times, even at night, just in case a seizure occurs and he suffers an injury or needs emergency medication. Classmates were afraid to be around him after witnessing his seizure activity. Hunter went from living a "normal" active life to a life with no privacy, no independence, and no friends.*

At age 13, Hunter was introduced to Argos, a Yellow Labrador service dog. Argos's service is to alert Hunter about 5 minutes before each seizure, giving him time to sit down safely. Argos will rub his entire face on Hunter's thigh and will not stop until Hunter sits down. Once the seizure occurs, Argos will lick Hunter's face attempting to wake him up. If Hunter does not wake up, Argos is trained to find help. The school nurse was the person designated for Argus to alert. Thanks to the services provided by Argos, Hunter has regained his independence and privacy. Argos has not only been a safety net for Hunter but also for his classmates, who are no longer afraid to be around him, and for the school nurse as well.

Case 2: Andrew, a typical six-year-old first-grade student, enjoys riding his bike and playing with his toy construction vehicles or video games. But Andrew also lives with the life-threatening challenges of Type 1 Diabetes. Diagnosed at just three years of age, Andrew only knows daily life with a dozen or more finger-poke blood glucose checks, counting carbohydrate intake, and night-time blood glucose checks. Blood glucose levels that are too high or too low are life-threatening events for children with Type 1 diabetes. Molly, a diabetic alert service animal, provides Andrew with another tool to monitor his diabetes anytime and anywhere he is, especially during his busy school day.

Molly's service is to continually monitor specific smells or scents on Andrew's breath that indicate rapidly dropping or low blood sugar levels. She is trained to "alert" Andrew, usually by pawing or nudging him. Molly is taught to be alert and persistent to the point where she will go get help if Andrew does not respond. Additionally, Molly is trained to retrieve essentials needed such as Glucose tablets, Glucagon, insulin, juice boxes, and testing meters or retrieve medication from a designated spot in the classroom or student's home. Molly has also been trained to go to the school nurse's office to summon emergency medical help if needed. Molly is an extremely valuable tool in keeping Andrew safe and healthy at home and school. A four-legged helper to the school nurse as well!

IMPLICATIONS FOR SCHOOL NURSE PRACTICE

School nurses are leaders in developing and evaluating school health policies and programs that address students' health and safety needs in the school environment (NASN, 2019). School nurses work in inter-professional teams to help identify student health issues and special needs that are pertinent to students' academic success. As the health leader of the team, the school nurse's role is to ensure that students are healthy and safe, enhancing their ability to learn and achieve academic success. A student with a service animal requires an interdisciplinary team approach with open communication, planning, and ongoing coordination to succeed in the school environment. This team needs to collaboratively assess, plan, implement, and evaluate how the service animal can be successfully integrated into the school setting. Additionally, IDEA requires *schools* to prepare Individualized *Education* Plans (*IEP*) or 504 plans. They also need to provide education to school staff, students, school community- parents and families as well as demonstrate advocacy and support to the student and the service animal.

School nurses can take the lead in completing the initial health and safety assessment for a request for a service animal to accompany a child in school. Some initial questions to ask upon receiving a request may include the following:
- Is the service animal required because of a defined disability?
- How will the animal impact the student's academic and behavioral functions to support his or her education?
- Does the student need the service animal for equal access to educational services and programs?

- What work or task has the service animal been trained to perform?
- How will the service animal alert its handler/student to an impending incident, such as an oncoming seizure or low blood glucose?
(Karetnick, 2022)

In addition to these questions, the school nurse must assess the following:
- How will having a service animal in a building affect students/staff who may have an allergy to the service animal or a distinct fear of the animal?
- Federal and state laws mandate that a student with disabilities (with or without a service animal) be granted the same educational opportunities as their non-disabled peers. The school administrators must determine how the school will provide care to the student who is allergic to animal dander/fur or who is afraid of animals.
(Karetnick, 2022)

Following school district policy and procedure is essential when it is determined that a service animal should be incorporated into a student's educational plan. Staff should also contact the district's attorney to ensure the district complies with all applicable local, state, and federal requirements. School districts are required to make "reasonable accommodations" in their policies and procedures to conform with the DOJ's ADA regulations (USDE, 2023). A district's policies should include the following:
- Evidence of compliance with current federal, state, and local laws.
- Requirement for written documentation from a licensed veterinarian that the service animal is in good health and appropriately vaccinated.
- Guidelines regarding education and training of staff and general population students about the role of Service Animals, the laws permitting them access to public places, and the rules regarding student and staff interactions with Service Animals.
- Guidelines about how the service animal will be controlled in the educational setting, according to the DOJ, "Service animals must be harnessed, leashed, or tethered unless these devices interfere with the service animal's work or the individual's disability prevents using these devices. In that case, the individual must maintain control of the animal through voice, signal, or other effective controls" (2020).

These policies should also address compliance with the following:
- Regulations state that the service animal is not permitted to stay at school if it is out of control; the animal's handler does not take effective action to control it; or is not housebroken (DOJ, 2020).
- Regulations state that the school district is not responsible for the care, including elimination needs, food, or a special location for service animals (DOJ, 2020). The animal's owner/family is responsible for the "care and supervision of the service animal" (DOJ, 2020).
- Regulations state that if the disabled student cannot provide care for the service animal at school, a documented plan should be in place stating who is responsible for caring for the animal while the student is in school (DOJ, 2020).
- Regulations state that if there is more than one service animal in a school building at one time, appropriate arrangements to socialize the animal must be made in a controlled environment before or after school hours.

- Regulations state that if the service animal is a miniature horse, the school district needs to evaluate the type, size, and weight of the miniature horse and determine whether the school can safely accommodate the service animal (DOJ, 2020).
- Federal requirements do not require a service animal to wear a vest or harness identifying them as a service animal. Some states may require identification; thus, review your individual state's requirements to determine specific regulations.

CONCLUSION

In today's economic and legally sensitive environment, School nurses are being required to care for not only larger numbers of students but more medically and mentally complex students. They also must ensure the health, safety, and well-being of all students and staff in their schools. Service animals in the school setting need to be thought of as a positive tool, a second set of eyes that helps the school nurse care for that particular student. School nurses must be leaders in helping school staff, and students understand and value the purpose and functions of a service animal. As leaders, school nurses must facilitate Interprofessional collaboration between the school, the student's family, and the student to ensure that the maximum benefits are being obtained from the service animal.

As research continues to discover and uncover new strategies to help enhance and enrich the lives of students, especially students with disabilities, school nurses will continue to be challenged by the need to implement these strategies. With the advancement in the work and tasks that service animals can provide to students with disabilities, the use of a service animals has opened a whole new world of challenges for schools. School nurses need to embrace this new four-legged "tool" and utilize his/her services to the fullest to positively impact the lives of our students and their families.

RESOURCES

Service, Therapy, and Working Dogs (2023). The American Kennel Club (AKC).
https://www.akc.org/public-education/resources/general-tips-information/service-therapy-work-dogs/

Frequently Asked Questions about Service Animals and the ADA: U.S. Department of Justice Civil Rights Division Disability Rights Section. https://www.ada.gov/resources/service-animals-faqs/

Service Animal Resource Hub (2023). National Network: Information, guidance, and training on the American disabilities act. https://adata.org/service-animal-resource-hub

Case Law

K.D. v. Villa Grove Cmty. Unit Sch. Dist. No. 302 Bd. of Educ., 403 Ill. App. 3d 1062 (Ill. App. Ct. 4th Dist. 2010) (district wrongly removed a student with autism's service dog)

Kalbfleisch v. Columbia Cmty. Unit Sch. Dist. Unit No. 4, 396 Ill. App. 3d 1105 (Ill. App. Ct. 5th Dist. 2009).

REFERENCES

Karetnick, J. (2022). Service dogs 101—everything you need to know. *The American Kennel Club.* https://www.akc.org/expert-advice/training/service-dog-training-101/

National Association of School Nurses. (2019). *Service animals in schools* (Position Statement). Author. https://higherlogicdownload.s3.amazonaws.com/NASN/8575d1b7-94ad-45ab-808e-d45019cc5c08/UploadedImages/PDFs/Position%20Statements/2019-ps-animals.pdf

Rodriguez, K.R., Bibbo, J., & O'Haire, M.E. (2020). The effects of service dogs on psychosocial health and wellbeing for individuals with physical disabilities or chronic conditions. *Disability and rehabilitation, 42*(10), 1350–1358. https://doi.org/10.1080/09638288.2018.1524520

U.S. Department of Education. (2023). Individuals with Disabilities Educational Act (IDEA): Statute and Regulations. https://sites.ed.gov/idea/statuteregulations/

U.S. Department of Justice. (2020). *ADA requirements: Service animals.*https://www.ada.gov/resources/service-animals-2010-requirements/

Chapter 50

THE SCHOOL NURSE AND SEXUAL HEALTH EDUCATION

Wendy L. Sellers, RN, MA, CSE, FASHA*

DESCRIPTION OF ISSUE

Sexual health education is a vital topic for schools to include in the curriculum due to the impact that sexual behaviors of youth can have on their success in school and into adulthood. Students who are bullied, sexually harassed, assaulted, pregnant, parenting, or infected with sexually transmitted infections/diseases may be unable to reach their goals compared to students who do not experience these challenges. Comprehensive, inclusive sexual health education and HIV prevention programs can reduce these negative outcomes (Centers for Disease Control and Prevention [CDC], 2023a; Goldfarb & Lieberman, 2021; Kolbe, 2019).

For these reasons and more, schools are intent on providing quality sexual health education that equips students with the knowledge, skills, and attitudes that will allow them to enjoy academic success, adopt healthful behaviors, and develop into sexually healthy adults. At the same time, many schools are hesitant to teach sexual health education because of the sensitivity of the subject matter and the recent increases in controversy. Some schools fear negative parental responses to sex education. The debate over teaching abstinence-only versus comprehensive sex education may erupt. Disagreements about which topics to include, what to teach at each grade level, and what, if any, values to include in sex education can result in schools implementing sex education that is ineffective and irrelevant to students.

School nurses may be called upon to deliver sexual health education directly or may be advocates and supports for sexual health education delivered by health education classroom teachers. School nurse participation in school sexual health education can enhance the efficacy of instruction by exercising their role as public health professionals to advocate for policy changes that enhance the sexual health and well-being of their students. (Best et al., 2018; Rabbitte & Enriquez, 2019).

BACKGROUND

Students of all ages are influenced by sexual messages and modeling from adults, peers, and media, originating in their homes, schools, and communities. Sexual messages can be misleading and misunderstood, and some modeling can be negative. As a result, students may act out sexually in harmful, illegal, and developmentally inappropriate ways. Puberty affects students as young as eight and continues through age 17 or later (Breehl & Caban, 2022; Healthline, 2023). Although students may become reproductively mature at young ages, their emotional, social, and cognitive development takes much longer. The influence of hormones and a highly sexualized society can result in students who are confused, scared, precociously sexual, and at heightened risk of negative outcomes related to sexual activity. Students who experience early or precocious puberty have an increased risk of adolescent anxiety and depression; they are often sexualized as if they are older than their age. (Maron, 2015; Richburg et al., 2021).

---

*Original authors: Wendy L. Sellers, RN, MA, CSE, FASHA & Patricia K. Bednarz, RN, MN, FNASN (2017)

The CDC reports that 30% of U.S. high school students have *ever had* sex. Of the 21% of high school students who are currently sexually active, only 52% reported the use of a condom; 33% reported the use of an effective hormonal birth control (defined as birth control pills, an IUD or implant, a shot, a patch, or a birth control ring) during most recent sexual intercourse. Only 10% of currently sexually active high school students reported the use of both a condom and another contraceptive method during most recent sexual intercourse (CDC, 2023c).

Schools are charged with educating all students in a safe and productive setting that provides all students with the optimal conditions for success. This requires schools to teach in a way that considers the impact of trauma and prevents re-traumatizing students. Schools must ensure that instruction is relevant to students with the diversity of disabilities, races, ethnicities, gender identities, and sexual orientations. Communications and education strategies that meet the needs of English Language Learners and their families also ensure the inclusion of all students. To support teaching sex education that includes all students, access the materials on the Resource List at the end of this chapter.

Because of the sensitive nature of sexual health education and the potential for controversy, schools may be hesitant to teach sexual health education in an effective, inclusive, and comprehensive manner. As a result, only 14% of middle schools and 38% of high schools teach all 19 critical sex education topics identified by the CDC (Brener et al., 2017). Yet, surveys of parents across the U.S. reveal that most support sexual health education in schools and want more sexual health education topics taught in schools (SIECUS, 2018a). A meta-analysis of 23 surveys revealed overwhelming support for sexual health education delivered in schools by 90% of parents (Szucs et al., 2022). Support for sex education is overwhelming regardless of political party. Both Republicans and Democrats support sex education in middle and high school, which includes these topics: abstinence, birth control, STIs, healthy relationships, sexual orientation, and puberty (Kantor & Levitz, 2017).

Parents' rights are protected, allowing parents to decide whether their children participate in sex education classes in school. All but ten states have laws giving parents the right to opt-in or out. Thirty-two states require schools to have sex education curriculum materials available to preview (SIECUS, 2018b).

Federal law does not require that sexual health education be taught in schools. Laws in 30 states and the District of Columbia require sexual health education in public schools (National Conference of State Legislatures [NCSL], 2020); thirty-nine states and the District of Columbia require HIV instruction. However, very little guidance or enforcement is provided, even when required. In this void, local school districts are left to make their own decisions regarding what, if any, sexual health education is taught. School nurses are often called upon to lead or support local efforts to implement sex education in schools.

IMPLICATIONS FOR SCHOOL NURSING PRACTICE

The National Association of School Nurses (NASN) believes the school nurse plays a vital role in the development and implementation of instructional programs that utilize evidence-based strategies to prevent unintended pregnancies and sexually transmitted infections, including HIV. School nurses must be fully aware of their state laws and school district policies concerning sexual health education and current research about effective strategies to implement sexual health education programming. By doing so, school nurses can ensure that their schools are in compliance with their state guidelines and school policies. *Public Health, Care Coordination*, and

Leadership are three of the five key principles of the NASN *Framework for the 21st Century* (NASN, 2016) that provide the foundation for school nursing practice and can guide school nurses to advocate for sexual health education and reduce the risk for school populations. The NASN position statement, *Comprehensive Health Education in Schools* (2022a), and the *School Nursing: Scope and Standards of Practice* (2022b) also provide foundational guidance for the nursing role in enabling school districts to provide sexual health education to students. The NASN position statement, *LGBTQ Students* (2021), calls on school nurses to ensure that sex education is medically accurate, inclusive, and diverse. The CDC (2017) emphasizes the need to pay particular attention to the needs of LGBTQ students in sexual health programs.

Leadership

School nurses must understand the laws within their state for providing sexual health education as they vary across the country. School nurses need to determine the following to ensure sexual health education programming is functioning within state law:

- Mandates: Thirty-eight states and the District of Columbia (DC) mandate both sex education and HIV education; two states mandate only sex education, and 11 states mandate only HIV education.
- General requirements for sexual health education: Some state laws delineate specific requirements for sexual health education, such as 17 states that require sexual health education to be medically, factually, or technically accurate (Guttmacher Institute, 2022; NCSL, 2020). Twenty-six states and DC require sex education instruction to be age appropriate. Other general state requirements may include prohibiting religion or that sexual health education must not be biased against any race, sex, or ethnicity (Guttmacher Institute, 2022).
- Parental rights: Some states allow or mandate parental involvement in sexual health education programming. Currently, four states require parental consent to opt-in for sexual health education instruction (active consent), 35 states and the District of Columbia allow parents to opt-out on behalf of their children (passive consent), two states allow both opt-in and opt-out, and ten states have no requirement for consent (Guttmacher Institute, 2022; NCSL, 2020; SIECUS, 2018b).
- Content requirements for sexual health education: content requirements can differ across the country; however, they may include requirements for instruction about contraception information, abstinence information, the importance of engaging in sexual activity only within marriage, discussion of sexual orientation and gender identity, the inclusion of information on the negative outcomes of teen sex and pregnancy, provision of information about skills for healthy sexuality, healthy decision making and family communication (Guttmacher Institute, 2022).
- Content requirements for HIV education: Currently, 19 states require information on condoms or contraception, and 37 states and DC require that information about abstinence be included when HIV education is taught (Guttmacher Institute, 2022).
- Content requirements for relationship skills: Thirty-five states and DC require skills for healthy romantic and sexual relationships to be taught. Teen dating violence and sexual violence prevention must be taught in 40 states and DC (Guttmacher Institute, 2022).

School policies support and provide guidance to school nurses as they address children's health issues. Therefore, school nurses are required to navigate the policy worlds of both health and education as they teach sexual health education (Dickson & Brindis, 2019). School nurses may be in the position to collaboratively develop or revise sexual health education program policies. The *National Sex Education Standards* [NSES] (Future of Sex Education, 2020) provide guidance on the essential minimum core content for sexuality education that is developmentally and age-appropriate for students in grades K–12. School nurses can use the NSES to identify gaps in sex education content and topics.

Some states provide model policies for sexual health education that can also provide direction for sexual health education programming. States may also define who can teach sexual health education and the required professional development. The U.S. Department of Education (USDE), Office for Civil Rights (2015) provides information about Title IX and single-sex education for schools. Title IX protects people from discrimination based on sex, including sexual orientation and gender identity, in education programs or activities that receive federal financial assistance. School districts need to comply with Title IX obligations when planning for sexual health education policies and programming. This has implications for how sex education classes are taught, such as teaching all students the same information without separating the content into boys-only or girls-only topics. It also has implications for whether classes can be taught in gender-segregated groups.

The Whole School, Whole Community, Whole Child model (CDC, 2018; Kolbe, 2019) may assist school districts in developing policies and practices for sexual health education programming. By utilizing this model, school nurses can engage additional advocacy partners and stakeholders from the school and community to ensure research-based policies are in place for students to receive a comprehensive sexual health education program. Key partners may include parents, educators, students, community health professionals, and faith leaders to advocate for the adoption and implementation of effective programs of instruction. The CDC (2021c) provides the rationale for exemplary sexual health education that can assist school nurses in their advocacy role of helping students make healthy decisions now and in their future. Success stories and evidence-based programs provide examples and resources for providing effective sexual health education and sexual health services for students (CDC, 2021a; CDC, 2021c; CDC, 2022c; CDC, 2022f).

School Health Advisory Councils (SHACs) or Sex Education Advisory Boards (SEABs) may be required by some states' laws. Even without a requirement, these advisory groups are an effective tool to plan, support, and monitor the implementation of sexual health education programming in a school district. The role of the SEAB could include the following:
- Review and recommend curricula and other materials for classroom instruction.
- Ensure sexual health education programming adheres to state law and school policy.
- Evaluate, measure, and report on program goals.
- Ensure individuals teaching the curriculum have the appropriate credentials, certifications, professional development, and professional disposition (Sex Education Collaborative, 2018).
- Ensure diversity and representation among the decision-makers for sexual health education programming (parents, students, teachers, cultural and ethnicity, community).
- Provide oversight to parent communication and notification about sexual health education programming.
- Recommend resources for parents, teachers, and students.

Public Health

Surveillance

School nurses should utilize state and local data to plan, implement, and evaluate sexual health education programming. The Youth Risk Behavior Survey (YRBS) (CDC, 2023b) reports on trend data that show youth risk behaviors and is available at the state and national levels. State and local public health data can identify sexually transmitted infection (STI) rates and teen pregnancy rates that may support the need for sexual health education programming. The CDC (2022c) provides national data describing risk behaviors and current strategies to reduce teen pregnancy rates and STIs. School nurses can also review the *School Health Profiles* (CDC, 2022d) that provide information about school health policies and practices from individual states and territories.

Surveys that assess parental views about sexual health education in their children's school, specific topics to be taught, and when they should be introduced can also inform school policy and practice. Surveys of students' sexual behavior and attitudes may be implemented, but they require parental consent prior to administration (USDE, 2020a; 2020b).

The Protection of Pupil Rights Act [PPRA] (USDE, 2020a, 2020b) and the Family Educational Rights and Privacy Act [FERPA] (USDE, 2012, 2021) are federal laws that establish specific parental rights regarding the use of surveys in public schools that receive federal funding. School nurses need to be familiar with these because schools that violate these laws are subject to financial penalties.

Under the PPRA, schools are legally required to notify parents before surveying students on one or more topics. That notice must inform parents that they have the right to see the survey before it is given and to opt their child out of the survey. *See Addendum for more information on PPRA.*

Access to Care

One of the most important roles for school nurses in healthy sexual development and HIV/STI and pregnancy prevention is facilitating student access to sexual health services within the boundaries of school district policies and state and federal law. School nurses need to assess their state's minor consent laws, state laws for sexual health education, school policy, and federal confidentiality laws, including the Family Educational Rights and Privacy Act [FERPA] (USDE, 2012) and the Health Insurance Portability and Accountability Act [HIPAA] (U.S. Department of Health and Human Services, 1996). Establishing partnerships with adolescent-friendly providers of sexual health services (e.g., contraception services; PrEP; testing for HIV, other STIs and pregnancy; HPV vaccinations, etc.) in the community to facilitate access for students is an important prevention strategy. Collaboration with the local health department and community-based organizations can help identify providers and resources in the community. The CDC (2019, 2021c, 2022a) provides tips and program guidance for linking students to sexual health services.

Outreach

Transparency and open communication with all stakeholders is fundamental to successful sexual health education programming. School nurses must follow state law and school district policy regarding parental notification. Parent communication about the sexual health education program is especially important to help parents understand the following:

- Program mission, goals, and objectives
- Curriculum objectives and topics of discussion
- Protocol for requesting a preview of the curricula
- School policy regarding sexual health education
- State law regarding sexual health education
- Methods of parent notification prior to the curriculum being taught
- Parental rights related to sexual health education, including passive or active consent
- Qualifications of individuals teaching sexual health education
- Where to go in the school district with questions or concerns
- Resources for parents on how to talk to their child about sexual development and their expectations for sexual behavior
- Resources in the community that serve adolescents

Certain states require public hearings to gain input from stakeholders regarding the sexual health education curriculum. Public hearings provide an opportunity to share the goals and objectives of the sexual health education program. They are also an excellent venue to connect with parent groups, school groups, and community agencies and to develop trust and support.

Health Education

When school nurses provide sexual health education in the classroom, they must follow state law regarding any required credentialing, certifications, or professional development. Sexual health education is most often taught within health education courses. Therefore, any sexual health education instruction should be aligned with the *National Health Education Standards: Model Guidance for Curriculum and Instruction, 3rd edition* (National Consensus for School Health Education, 2022) and the state health education standards. The required content for sexual health education and identification of topics prohibited from being discussed in sexual health education may be delineated in state law and school policy.

Many topics related to sexual behavior might best be treated as safety issues rather than being included in sexual health education. These include sexting, sexual harassment, human trafficking for sex, and child sexual abuse. Most states' laws may allow parents to opt out or remove their children from sexual health education (Guttmacher Institute, 2022; NCSL, 2020; SIECUS, 2018b). If safety issues related to sexual behavior are included as part of sex education instruction, the children who need this instruction the most are likely to be removed from the lessons that would equip them to protect themselves. By teaching these vital topics outside the sexual health education curriculum, the opt-out option is not required. Also, sexual health education messaging should be positive, not fear-based. If sexual health education instruction is filled with legal issues and frightening messages, time is taken away from positive messaging and skill development, such as healthy relationship skills, that young people need to develop into sexually healthy adults. Wherever instruction about sexting and other legal topics is included, school nurses should know their state laws and school policies to comply with reporting requirements and access available resources to seek help for young people affected.

In addition to following state laws and district policy, school nurses need to advocate for the use of evidence-based, age-appropriate, culturally relevant, inclusive, and theory-driven sexual health education curricula that have been developed and evaluated by experts in that field rather than creating lessons. The Future of Sex Education (2020) recommends a planned and sequential K-12 curriculum that is part of a comprehensive school health education program. Tools are available to assess the effectiveness of an existing curriculum (Kirby et al., 2014). State departments of education or health might offer resources to guide the selection of new curricula; one example is the curriculum review conducted by the Washington Office of Superintendent of Public Instruction (2022). Lists of evidence-based interventions (EBIs) used to be posted on federal funding websites in the past; however, they have been removed. They focused exclusively on STI and teen pregnancy prevention rather than on comprehensive, inclusive sexual health education that promotes positive sexual development and healthy relationships. In the absence of a list of EBIs, the CDC has identified what works in sexual health education programs in schools which can be found at https://www.cdc.gov/healthyyouth/whatworks/what-works-sexual-health-education.htm.

Measuring, evaluating, and reporting on program goals is a necessary component to monitor the success of the sexual health education program, as well as provide feedback to key stakeholders. Use of student pre- and post-tests can be used to assess gains in student knowledge and skills. Curriculum pacing guides help ensure that sufficient time is allocated to teaching the sexual health education curriculum and that all sex educators are implementing the lessons at the same time across multiple buildings. Teacher implementation logs are also helpful in determining if the lessons are being taught with fidelity and what if any, modifications have occurred. Utilizing student risk behavior surveys, such as the YRBS, can provide insight into changes in student behavior regarding sexual risk-taking (Kirby et al., 2014; CDC, 2023b).

Direct Care

School nurses may be charged with responding to questions and providing resources for students and parents individually about sexual behavior, growth and development, and reproductive health. For this reason, school nurses need to be aware of their state law requirements about topics that can be discussed or topics that are prohibited. Brewen et al. (2014) point out that laws governing confidentially rules and consent for care vary by state. While all states and the District of Columbia allow minors to consent to sexually transmitted infection (STI) testing and treatment without parental permission, other laws vary widely (American College of Obstetricians and Gynecologists, 2020). School nurses need to be aware of their state's minor consent laws and state laws concerning reportable incidents.

School nurses are mandated reporters. Therefore, it is important not to promise students that conversations will be kept confidential. Instead, students should be assured that conversations will not be shared with anyone unless it becomes apparent that the student is in danger of harming themselves or someone else or if someone is harming them. In that case, the school nurse would need to talk to someone who can provide the needed help.

> **Confidentiality vs Privacy**
>
> School nurses should assure students that they will not share the conversations with anyone (privacy) unless it becomes apparent that the student is in danger of harming themselves or someone else or if someone is harming them. In that case, the school nurse would need to talk to someone who can provide the needed help; and, therefore, cannot keep this information confidential.

Providing a private space for students to share questions and concerns is essential. School nurses address a broad scope of health concerns from students. Similar to other health concerns, questions about sexual behavior or reproductive health need to be documented to meet the standard of practice and comply with the NASN standards of school nursing practice. Documentation is the legal requirement for nursing care in any practice environment.

At times, students younger than the age of legal consent may disclose that they are having sexual intercourse. School nurses and teachers often wonder if this is a reportable incident. If the sexual behavior is between students of similar age and is consensual, this is not, in general, a reportable incident. For example, the case of People v Beardsley (People v. Beardsley 263 Mich. App 148) found this based on the statutory language in that state.   However, school nurses must be aware of state laws regarding criminal sexual contact, sexual assault, and age discrepancies. It is important to access authoritative sources of information rather than relying on commonly held beliefs regarding adolescent sexual behaviors.

Developing a guideline for answering student questions may help the individuals implementing the curriculum to stay within the limits of the state law and school district policy. At a minimum, answers to student questions should be accurate, affirming, positive, and age and developmentally appropriate. For any questions that cannot be answered at school, students should be pointed to another source to find the answer.

If asked to initiate STI testing of students at school, school nurses will need to work with their state and local health departments to adhere to state laws related to parent notification, partner notification, and students' confidentiality, as well as the clinical protocols required. The American Academy of Pediatrics (2022) offers guidance on conducting school-located STI testing.

Social Determinants of Health and Health Equity

The CDC (2020a) defines health equity as achieved when "everyone has an equal chance to be healthy regardless of their background. This includes a person's race, ethnicity, income, gender, religion, sexual identity, and disability." The CDC (2020) continues to emphasize that research shows there is a higher rate of STIs among some racial or ethnic minority groups compared to whites. These "higher rates are not caused by ethnicity or heritage, but by social conditions that are more likely to affect minority groups. Factors such as poverty, large gaps between the rich and the poor, fewer jobs, and low education levels can make it more difficult for people to stay sexually healthy." The CDC offers resources for improving sexual health and cultural competence to reduce these disparities (CDC, 2022e). Other disproportionately at-risk school populations include sexual minority youth (CDC, 2017; GLSEN, 2022) and students with disabilities (Schaafsma et al., 2017; SIECUS, 2021; Szydlowski, 2018).

School nurses can advocate for health equity within their student population by:
- Utilizing risk behavior trend data,
- Collaborating with community stakeholders who serve diverse populations,
- Engaging parents, students, and educators from diverse backgrounds,
- Communicating effectively to school boards, school administrators, and school staff,
- Increasing personal and staff allyship for disenfranchised students, and
- Ensuring parent materials are easy to understand and translated when appropriate.

WARNING

As highly respected members of the school community, school nurses are positioned to develop trust and support for sexual health education in schools. To do so, school nurses need to be aware of potential red flags for sexual health education programming, including the following:

- Use of inappropriate or offensive terms and language;
- Lack of transparency with parents, students, teachers, school administrators, and the community;
- Not honoring parents' roles;
- Missed opportunities to amplify the voices of the majority of parents who support sex education;
- Lack of diversity on the sexual health education advisory committee or other decision-making bodies; and
- Lack of support from the school district administration or school board.

CONCLUSION

School nurses are in an ideal position to advocate for all students to receive sexual health education that is current, inclusive, relevant, and addresses the needs of all students. Research supports the need for comprehensive, inclusive, research-based, or evidence-based curriculum that provides the skills and support needed for students to make healthy decisions that impact their current and future health. State laws regarding sexual health education vary across the country and may impact the role of school nurses in providing or advocating for sexual health education. School nurses must understand and follow school district policies and state laws when planning and implementing sexual health education programming. Utilizing local, state, and national data and following best practice is imperative to develop effective policies and interventions for school populations. (*For more information on Minor's Rights, see Chapter 15*).

RESOURCES

A Call to Action: LGBTQ Youth Need Inclusive Sex Education. Human Rights Campaign. (2021). https://hrc-prod-requests.s3-us-west-2.amazonaws.com/Call-to-Action-LGBTQ-Sex-Ed-Report-2021.pdf This resource provides guidance for sex education that includes LGBTQ+ students.

An Overview of Consent to Reproductive Health Services by Young People. Guttmacher Institute. (2022). https://www.guttmacher.org/state-policy/explore/overview-minors-consent-law This resource provides state laws on minors' consent.

Comprehensive Sex Education for Youth with Disabilities: A Call to Action. (2021). SIECUS. https://siecus.org/wp-content/uploads/2021/03/SIECUS-2021-Youth-with-Disabilities-CTA-1.pdf This resource provides guidance for sex education that includes students with disabilities.

Guide to Trauma-Informed Sex Education. Cardea Services. (2018). https://cardeaservices.org/resource/guide-to-trauma-informed-sex-education/ This resource provides guidance for sex education using trauma-informed strategies.

Keep It Simple: Linking Teens to Sexual Health Care Facilitator's Guide. Healthy Teen Network. (2013). https://www.healthyteennetwork.org/wp-content/uploads/Keep-It-Simple-Facilitators-Guide.pdf. This facilitator's guide includes a free lesson that teaches teens how to access sexual health care.

National Health Education Standards: Model Guidance for Curriculum and Instruction, 3rd edition. National Consensus for School Health Education (NCSHE). (2022). https://www.schoolhealtheducation.org/standards/ These standards guide health education nationally.

National Sex Education Standards: Core Content and Skills, K–12, Second Edition. Future of Sex Education (FoSE). (2020). https://www.advocatesforyouth.org/resources/health-information/future-of-sex-education-national-sexuality-education-standards/ These are the minimum recommended standards for sex education as developed by national experts.

Power to Decide. https://powertodecide.org/ This organization offers many resources to support sexual health education.

PPRA Model Notice & Consent Opt-Out for Specific Activities. U.S. Department of Education. (2017). https://studentprivacy.ed.gov/resources/ppra-model-notice-consent-opt-out-specific-activities This sample parent notification form meets the federal requirements for Pupil Rights Amendment (PPRA).

Promoting positive adolescent health behaviors and outcomes: Thriving in the 21st century. National Academies of Sciences, Engineering, and Medicine. (2020). https://nap.nationalacademies.org/catalog/25552/promoting-positive-adolescent-health-behaviors-and-outcomes-thriving-in-the This report describes what is important to the development of optimal health for adolescents.

Role of the COVID-19 Pandemic on Sexual Behaviors and Receipt of Sexual and Reproductive Health Services Among U.S. High School Students — Youth Risk Behavior Survey, United States, 2019–2021. CDC (2023). https://www.cdc.gov/mmwr/volumes/72/su/pdfs/su7201a7-H.pdf This resource identifies the impact of the COVID pandemic on youth sexual behaviors.

School Nursing: Scope & Standards of Practice, 4th Edition. National Association of School Nurses and the American Nurses Association (2022). https://www.nasn.org/blogs/nasn-inc/2022/07/28/school-nursing-scope-and-standards-of-practice-4th This resource provides guidance for school nurses.

Sex and HIV Education. Guttmacher Institute. (2022). https://www.guttmacher.org/state-policy/explore/sex-and-hiv-education This resource outlines state policies related to sex education.

Sex ed state law and policy chart. SIECUS. (2022). https://siecus.org/wp-content/uploads/2021/09/2022-Sex-Ed-State-Law-and-Policy-Chart.pdf This report summarizes state laws and policies into an easy-to-read format. Note: This report is updated yearly.

Sex, Etc. Answer. https://sexetc.org/ This monthly newsletter is written by and for adolescents and published by a national organization that provides and promotes unfettered access to comprehensive sexuality education for young people and the adults who teach them.

Sex, Race, and Politics in the U.S.: A Call to Action to Address Racial Justice in Sexuality Education. (2022). SIECUS. https://siecus.org/wp-content/uploads/2022/06/2022-Racial-Justice-Resource.pdf This resource provides guidance for sex education that is racially and ethnically inclusive.

Sexual Health Education Curriculum Assessment Tool (SHECAT). Centers for Disease Control and Prevention. (2021). https://www.cdc.gov/healthyyouth/hecat/pdf/2021/hecat_module_sh.pdf This module focuses on providing guidance in assessing sexual health education curriculum and is part of the Health Education Curriculum Assessment Tool (HECAT) https://www.cdc.gov/healthyyouth/hecat/index.htm.

State Policies on Sex Education in Schools. National Conference of State Legislatures. (2020). https://www.ncsl.org/health/state-policies-on-sex-education-in-schools This resource outlines state policies related to sex education.

State Profiles. SIECUS. (2021). https://siecus.org/the-siecus-state-profiles-2021/ These profiles provide an in-depth and up-to-date look at the state of sex education in all 50 states, the District of Columbia, Puerto Rico, and the outer United States territories and associated states.

The 2021 National School Climate Survey: The Experiences of Lesbian, Gay, Bisexual, Transgender, and Queer Youth in Our Nation's Schools. (2022). https://www.glsen.org/research/2021-national-school-climate-survey The survey reports on the school experiences of LGBTQ youth and makes recommendations for improvement.

Three decades of research: The case for comprehensive sex education. Future of Sex Education. (2021). https://www.advocatesforyouth.org/wp-content/uploads/2021/03/Three-Decades-One-Pager.pdf This set of fact sheets summarizes the research about the effectiveness of sex education.

Trends in the Prevalence of Sexual Behaviors and HIV Testing, National YRBS: 1991-2019. Centers for Disease Control and Prevention. (2020). https://www.cdc.gov/healthyyouth/data/yrbs/factsheets/2019_sexual_trend_yrbs.htm This fact sheet provides trend data from the National Youth Risk Behavior Survey.

Case Law

People v. Beardsley, 688 N.W.2d 304 (Mich. Ct. App.) (2004). https://www.courtlistener.com/opinion/2206051/people-v-beardsley/

REFERENCES

American Academy of Pediatrics. (2022). *Considerations for hosting a school-located sexually transmitted infection (STI) testing event.* https://downloads.aap.org/AAP/PDF/Publication_%20STI%20testing%20pop%20up.pdf

American College of Obstetricians and Gynecologists. (2020). *Confidentiality in adolescent health care.* https://www.acog.org/clinical/clinical-guidance/committee-opinion/articles/2020/04/confidentiality-in-adolescent-health-care

Best, N. C., Oppewal, S., & Travers, D. (2018). Exploring school nurse interventions and health and education outcomes: An integrative review. *The Journal of School Nursing, 34*(1), 14-27. https://doi.org/10.1177/1059840517745359

Breehl, L. & Caban, O. (2022). Physiology, Puberty. StatPearls Publishing. https://www.ncbi.nlm.nih.gov/books/NBK534827/

Brener, N. D., Demissie, Z., McManus, T., Shanklin, S. L., Queen, B., & Kann, L. (2017). *School Health Profiles 2016: Characteristics of health programs among secondary schools.* Centers for Disease Control and Prevention.

Brewen, D., Koren, A., Morgan, B., Shipley, S., & Hardy, R.L. (2014). Behind closed doors: School nurses and sexual education. *The Journal of School Nursing, 31*(1), 31–41. https://doi.org/10.1177/1059840513484363

Centers for Disease Control and Prevention. (2017). *LGBTQ programs at-a-glance.* https://www.cdc.gov/lgbthealth/youth-programs.htm

Centers for Disease Control and Prevention. (2018). *Whole school, whole community, whole child.* https://www.cdc.gov/healthyyouth/wscc/index.htm

Centers for Disease Control and Prevention. (2019). *PS18-1807 program guidance: Guidance for school-based HIV/STD prevention (component 2) recipients of PS18-1807.* U.S. Department of Health and Human Services.

Centers for Disease Control and Prevention. (2020). *STD health equity.* https://www.cdc.gov/std/health-disparities/default.htm

Centers for Disease Control and Prevention. (2021a). *Adolescent and school health. Funded programs.* https://www.cdc.gov/healthyyouth/fundedprograms/

Centers for Disease Control and Prevention. (2021b). *Adolescent health: What works in schools.* https://www.cdc.gov/healthyyouth/whatworks/index.htm

Centers for Disease Control and Prevention. (2021c). *Health services for teens.* https://www.cdc.gov/healthyyouth/healthservices/index.htm

Centers for Disease Control and Prevention (2022a). HIV information and youth. https://www.cdc.gov/healthyyouth/youth_hiv/hiv-information-and-youth.htm

Centers for Disease Control and Prevention. (2022b). *Program Performance and Evaluation Office (PPEO).* https://www.cdc.gov/evaluation/

Centers for Disease Control and Prevention. (2022c). *Reproductive health: Teen pregnancy.* https://www.cdc.gov/teenpregnancy/

Centers for Disease Control and Prevention. (2022d). *School health profiles.* https://www.cdc.gov/healthyyouth/data/profiles/index.htm

Centers for Disease Control and Prevention. (2022e). *Sexual health cultural competence resources.* https://www.cdc.gov/std/health-disparities/cultural-competence-resources.htm

Centers for Disease Control and Prevention. (2022f). *Success stories.* https://www.cdc.gov/healthyyouth/stories/index.htm

Centers for Disease Control and Prevention. (2023a). *What works in schools:* Sexual health education. https://www.cdc.gov/healthyyouth/whatworks/what-works-sexual-health-education.htm

Centers for Disease Control and Prevention. (2023b). *Youth risk behavior surveillance system (YRBS).* https://www.cdc.gov/healthyyouth/data/yrbs/results.htm

Centers for Disease Control and Prevention. (2023c). *Youth risk behavior survey data summary & trends report: 2011-2021.* https://www.cdc.gov/healthyyouth/data/yrbs/pdf/YRBS_Data-Summary-Trends_Report2023_508.pdf

Dickson, E. & Brindis, C. D. (2019). The double bind of school nurses and policy implementation: Intersecting the street-level bureaucracy framework and teaching sexual health education. *Journal of School Nursing 37*(4), 1-12. https://escholarship.org/uc/item/35k4z293

Future of Sex Education. (2020). *National sex education standards core content and skills, K–12.* https://www.advocatesforyouth.org/resources/health-information/future-of-sex-education-national-sexuality-education-standards/

GLSEN. (2022). *The 2021 national school climate survey: The experiences of lesbian, gay, bisexual, transgender, and queer youth in our nation's schools*. https://www.glsen.org/research/2021-national-school-climate-survey

Goldfarb, E. S. & Lieberman, L. D. (2021). Three decades of research: The case for comprehensive sex education. *Journal of Adolescent Health, 68*(1), 13-27. https://www.jahonline.org/article/S1054-139X(20)30456-0/fulltext

Guttmacher Institute. (2022). *Sex and HIV education.* https://www.guttmacher.org/state-policy/explore/sex-and-hiv-education

Healthline. (2023). *Navigating Puberty: The Tanner stages.* https://www.healthline.com/health/parenting/stages-of-puberty#tanner-stages

Kantor, L. & Levitz, N. (2017) Parents' views on sex education in schools: How much do Democrats and Republicans agree? PLoS One. 2017 Jul 3;12(7),e0180250. https://doi.org/10.1371/journal.pone.0180250. PMID: 28672027; PMCID: PMC5495344. https://www.ncbi.nlm.nih.gov/pmc/articles/PMC5495344/

Kirby, D., Rolleri, L. A. & Wilson, M. M. (2014). *Tool to assess the characteristics of effective sex and STD/HIV education programs.* https://pages.etr.org/tool-to-assess-17-characteristics?_ga=2.106669891.156549838.1672437296-1772602941.1670440913

Kolbe L. J. (2019). School health as a strategy to improve both public health and education. *Annual Review of Public Health, 40*, 443–463. https://www.annualreviews.org/doi/pdf/10.1146/annurev-publhealth-040218-043727

Maron, D. F. (2015). Early puberty; Causes and effects. *Scientific American.* https://www.scientificamerican.com/article/early-puberty-causes-and-effects/

National Association of School Nurses. (2016). Framework for the 21st century school nursing practice. *NASN School Nurse, 31*(1), 45-53. https://www.nasn.org/nasn-resources/framework

National Association of School Nurses. (2021). *LGBTQ students* (Position Statement). https://www.nasn.org/nasn-resources/professional-practice-documents/position-statements/ps-lgbtq

National Association of School Nurses. (2022a). *Comprehensive health education in schools* (Position Statement). https://www.nasn.org/nasn-resources/professional-practice-documents/position-statements/ps-health-education

National Association of School Nurses and the American Nurses Association (2022b). *School Nursing: Scope & Standards of Practice, 4th Edition.* https://www.nasn.org/blogs/nasn-inc/2022/07/28/school-nursing-scope-and-standards-of-practice-4th

National Conference of State Legislatures. (2020). *State policies on sex education in schools.* https://www.ncsl.org/health/state-policies-on-sex-education-in-schools

National Consensus for School Health Education. (2022). *National health education standards: Model guidance for curriculum and instruction* (3rd ed.). https://www.schoolhealtheducation.org/standards/

Rabbitte, M. & Enriquez, M. (2019). The role of policy on sexual health education in schools: Review. *The Journal of School Nursing*, 35(1), 27-38. https://doi.org/10.1177/1059840518789240

Richburg, A. G. & Kelly, D. P. & Davis-Kean, P. E., (2021) Depression, anxiety, and pubertal timing: Current research and future directions, *University of Michigan Undergraduate Research Journal* 15. https://doi.org/10.3998/umurj.1383

Schaafsma, D., Kok, G., Stoffelen, J. M. T. & Curfs. L. M. G. (2017) People with intellectual disabilities talk about sexuality: Implications for the development of sex education. *Sexuality and Disability, 35*, 21-38. https://doi.org/10.1007/s11195-016-9466-4

Sex Education Collaborative. (2018). *Professional Learning Standards for Sex Education* (PLSSE). https://sexeducationcollaborative.org/resources/plsse

SIECUS, (2018a). *On our side: Public support for sex education.* https://siecus.org/wp-content/uploads/2018/08/On-Our-Side-Public-Support-for-Sex-Ed-2018-Final.pdf

SIECUS. (2018b) *Policy Brief: Sex Ed & Parental Consent: Opt-In vs. Opt-Out.* https://siecus.org/wp-content/uploads/2018/09/Policy-Brief-Opt-in-v.-Opt-out-Redesign-Draft-09.2018.pdf

SIECUS, (2021). *Comprehensive Sex Education for Youth with Disabilities.* https://siecus.org/wp-content/uploads/2021/03/SIECUS-2021-Youth-with-Disabilities-CTA-1.pdf

Szucs, L. E., Harper, C. R., Andrzejewski, J., Barrios, L. C., Robin, L., Hunt, P. (2022). Overwhelming support for sexual health education in U.S. schools: A meta-analysis of 23 surveys conducted between 2000 and 2016. *Journal of Adolescent Health, 70*(4). 598-606. https://doi.org/10.1016/j.jadohealth.2021.05.016

Szydlowski, M. B. (2018) *Sexual health education for young people with disabilities – Research and resources for educators.* Advocates for Youth. https://www.advocatesforyouth.org/resources/fact-sheets/sexual-health-education-for-young-people-with-disabilities/

U.S. Department of Education (2012). *Family Educational Rights and Privacy Act Regulations (34 CFR Part 99.31).* https://www2.ed.gov/policy/gen/reg/ferpa/index.html

U.S. Department of Education, Office for Civil Rights. (2015). *Title IX and sex discrimination.* https://www2.ed.gov/about/offices/list/ocr/docs/tix_dis.html

U.S. Department of Education. (2020a). *Protection of pupil rights amendment (PPRA) general guidance.* https://studentprivacy.ed.gov/resources/protection-pupil-rights-amendment-ppra-general-guidance

U.S. Department of Education. (2020b). *PPRA Model general notice of rights.* https://studentprivacy.ed.gov/resources/ppra-model-general-notice-rights

U.S. Department of Education. (2021). *Family and Educational Rights and Privacy Act (FERPA)* https://www2.ed.gov/policy/gen/guid/fpco/ferpa/index.html

U.S. Department of Health and Human Services, Office of the Assistant Secretary for Planning and Evaluation (1996). *Health insurance portability and accountability act of 1996.* https://aspe.hhs.gov/reports/health-insurance-portability-accountability-act-1996

Washington Office of Superintendent of Public Instruction. (2022). *2022 Sexual health education curriculum review.* https://www.k12.wa.us/student-success/resources-subject-area/sexual-health-education/instructional-materials-review-reports-and-tools/2022-sexual-health-education-curriculum-review

Q & A - Protection of Pupil Rights Act

Carol Marchant, Esquire *

Q: Are there any laws that might impact educational programs provided by school nurses?

The Protection of Pupil Rights Act, or the PPRA, is a federal law that may impact a school nurse's practice. Atty. Carol Marchant, Deputy Division Counsel with the Prince William County Public Schools in Manassas, VA, highlights the importance of this law.

"It is very important that nurses have a good understanding of the requirements of the PPRA, particularly if they are going to be teaching a class or addressing groups of students. Like FERPA, the PPRA applies to all schools that receive federal funding, and it establishes specific parental rights regarding the use of surveys in public schools."

So what types of surveys are covered under the PPRA?

Atty Marchant explains.
"The PPRA governs surveys, analyses, or evaluations given to students under the age of 18 that involve any of eight specific topics. The eight topics identified under the PPRA are:
1. Political affiliations or beliefs of students or their parents
2. Mental or psychological problems of students or their families
3. Sexual behavior or attitudes
4. Illegal, anti-social, self-incriminating, or demeaning behavior
5. Critical appraisals of other individuals with whom the students have close family relationships
6. Legally recognized privileged relationships (lawyers, healthcare providers, ministers, etc.)
7. Religious practices, affiliations, or beliefs of students or their parents
8. Income (other than questions required by law related to financial assistance for a program)"

Atty. Marchant cautioned that nurses should be aware that some states have enacted laws similar to the PPRA. These state laws may expand upon the eight specific topics set forth in federal law and may impose additional requirements or student protections. it is increasingly important for nurses to be aware not only of the federal requirements set by the PPRA and the U.S. Department of Education but also of additional relevant state student privacy laws that may impact surveys or lessons they present to students.

Atty. Marchant emphasizes that nurses need to be aware not only of the topics identified by the PPRA but also of the parental rights afforded under the law. "Because there are a number of topics in this list that might be addressed by a school nurse in a class or when speaking with a group of students, nurses need to be aware of the parameters of the law. Under the PPRA, schools are legally required to provide notice to parents before surveying students on one or more of the topics. That notice has to inform parents that they have the right to see the survey before it is given and/or to opt their child out of the survey.

The law is enforced by the U.S. Department of Education's Student Privacy Protection Office (SPPO), which is the same office designated by law to address FERPA violations."

As with FERPA, there is no private cause of action for PPRA violations, which means that it can't be enforced through individual lawsuits, but the SPPO does have the authority to withhold federal funding for schools that violate its provisions. "Because of this," Atty. Marchant adds, "It is imperative that schools, including school nurses, understand their obligations and responsibilities under the PPRA."

For more information about the PPRA, please refer to *Protection of Pupil Rights Amendment (PPRA) | Protecting Student Privacy* (ed.gov).

* Original author: Carol A. Marchant, Esquire & Erin D. Gilsbach, Esquire (2017)

Chapter 51

SOCIAL MEDIA AND TECHNOLOGY: IMPLICATIONS FOR SCHOOL HEALTH
Jane Boyd, MSN, RN, NCSN*

DESCRIPTION OF ISSUE

While social media and digital communication technologies offer many opportunities for school nurses to communicate quickly and effectively, school nurses must exercise caution and follow professional guidelines to minimize the risk of breaching student privacy and confidentiality. Concerns of boundary issues and the blurring between personal and professional life can also be challenges of social media. It is the responsibility of the professional school nurse to understand the potential benefits of engaging with others on social media platforms and their use of digital technology, as well as the possible risks and steps that can be taken to reduce those risks.

Despite the growth of social media use in nursing, the ambiguity surrounding the use of social media in nursing remains. Nursing codes exist to guide ethical obligations and duties; however, professional guidelines and ethical and legal frameworks focusing on how nurses interact on these platforms are still needed to support nurses. While the guidelines and frameworks will aid the nurse in using better judgment while interacting with social media, they will not solve the issue of incorrect use (González-Luis et al., 2022). Enforcement of standardized and clearly communicated policies will create a culture of safeguarding students' rights and protecting the nurse.

BACKGROUND

Overview of Digital Technology

Nurses use many forms of technology for planning, delivering, and documenting nursing care. School nurses are increasingly using technology in the school nurse office to provide better care to students. Electronic Health Records (EHRs) and mobile devices can improve healthcare quality and coordination of care by allowing quick access to records, clinical alerts/reminders, and providing real-time reporting (USDHHS, 2023). School nurses can use EHRs to monitor and track student information, including health histories, health screenings, immunizations, allergies, medications, and health office visits, document nursing care, and track trends in student health. Health monitoring devices (e.g., blood pressure monitors, pulse oximeters, and glucose meters) and wearable applications[apps] (e.g., to monitor biomedical systems) are being utilized to manage student health conditions, identify potential health issues, and provide care.

Telehealth offers remote consultations, assessments, and even some treatments by school nurses, especially in rural and underserved areas. Online educational resources and communication tools can be powerful tools for educating students, promoting health, and keeping families and school staff updated on policies and events. Videos and interactive apps can offer an engaging and effective way to present educational content, such as health and wellness information. Online communication, such as email, blogs, messaging apps, and social media, can disseminate information regarding school policies and events to a larger audience and

---

Original author: Jessica Porter, BSN, RN, NCSN (2017)

promote a sense of community. Using digital technology such as smartphones, social networks, the internet, and software applications enhances communication and provides innovative ways for health monitoring and gathering information (U.S. Food and Drug Administration, 2020). Technology provides the school nurse with an effective way to inform parents, staff, and healthcare providers about student health issues. Social media is defined as an online resource (internet-based tools) that allows sharing, collaboration, discussion, and curation of information among individuals through private or public networks (Moss, 2021; Ventola, 2014).

While social media continues to evolve, social media is being embraced and utilized by healthcare professionals to enhance communication, share information, and educate peers and the public (Vukusic et al., 2021; Ventola, 2014). Social media also allows school nurses to debate healthcare policy and practice issues and provide health education/information (Ventola, 2014). The number and variety of social media apps and platforms continue to increase, but the most common formats utilized by school nurses are Facebook®, Twitter®, Instagram®, LinkedIn®, YouTube®, school health websites, blogs, and podcasts.

Social Media

According to the Pew Research Center, around seven-in-ten Americans use social media to connect. In 2021, 72% of U.S. adults reported they use at least one social media site (Pew Research Center, 2021a). In 2021, 97% of Americans owned a cell phone, three-quarters of U.S. adults owned a desktop or laptop computer, and roughly half owned a tablet (Pew Research Center, 2021b).

A significant limitation of social media includes the lack of quality and reliability of the information found in online sources. Nurses using social media need to steer their audience to credible peer-reviewed websites where information is validated and subject to quality control (Ventola, 2014). A credible source of health information is defined as "a source that is likely to offer high-quality information and employ processes to reduce conflict of interest and promote transparency and accountability" (Kingston et al., 2021, p.7). Suggested foundational principles to guide the identification of credible sources of health information on social media include the following attributes:

- Science-based: Sources should include information about the scientific evidence that is consistent and available for the time, including the date of content, links to other credible sources, citations from multiple sources, and use of peer or content review before being vetted.
- Objective: Sources should include evidence that no financial influence, bias, or conflict of interest exists that might compromise the information (e.g., independence from financial, political, or ideological messages or sources, separate or no engagement in lobbying, and does not include advertisements with relevant health information).
- Transparent and Accountable: Sources should disclose limitations, conflicts of interest, and content errors related to messages provided (e.g., disclosure of financial, lobbying, and policy conflicts, providing public feedback mechanism, and posts public corrections or retractions) (Kingston et al., 2021).

Examples of credible sources per Kingston, et al., (2021) include accredited organizations (e.g., health professional schools and other educational institutions (schools of medicine, nursing, public health, dentistry, pharmacies and universities), nonprofit health plans, public health departments, health care organizations, academic health and medical journals, health industry groups (e.g., the American Hospital Association), independent organizations or advisory panels (e.g., U.S. Preventive Services Task Force), professional associations or societies (e.g., NASN), government organizations (e.g., U.S. Department of Health and Social Services), advisory organizations/think tanks (e.g., the RAND Corporation), nongovernmental organizations (e.g., Partners in Health), foundations (e.g., Robert Wood Foundation), patient or disease advocacy groups (e.g., the Cystic Fibrosis Foundation), community health organizations (e.g., DC Health Matters) and news organizations (e.g., National Public Radio).

Another challenge for nurses with content shared via social media is the perception of offering medical advice to individuals. Caution is necessary when sharing health advice, and it is best to share general educational tips rather than specific medical advice (Nguyen et al., 2020). It is recommended that the nurse encourage the student and family to consult with their medical providers prior to making any changes to medications, diets, exercise plans, or medical routines (Advent Health University, 2020).

Ethical and Legal Considerations

Appropriate professional use of social media as a school nurse includes maintaining privacy and confidentiality. These two terms are related but not synonymous. The American Nurses Association (ANA) Code of Ethics (2015) states, "privacy is the right to control access to, and disclosure or nondisclosure of, information pertaining to oneself and to control the circumstances, timing, and extent to which information may be disclosed" while "confidentiality pertains to the nondisclosure of personal information that has been communicated within the nurse-patient relationship" (p. 9). Additionally, because many school nurses live and work in the same community, there is frequent overlap between friends, family, neighbors, families, and even work colleagues. This presents an additional challenge to maintaining the privacy and confidentiality of student health information. Through social media, nurses can connect and communicate with their school nurse colleagues and share information about best practices; the nurse should be aware of the possible risks of inappropriate use of social media and the consequences of such inappropriate use. It is crucial for nurses to remember that the internet culture is different from the professional healthcare culture, creating ethical issues related to privacy and boundaries. Equally important for the trust of the public and individuals, nurses need to understand the limits and risks of disclosure of sensitive information online (Ahmed et al., 2020).

The Family Education Rights Privacy Act (FERPA) is a federal law that controls the confidentiality and sharing of information in student health records by schools, and the Health Insurance Portability and Accountability Act (HIPAA) regulates health care professional data privacy and sharing (Network for Public Law, 2020). Since HIPAA excludes education records, nurses practicing in school settings are most frequently subject to FERPA laws. HIPAA "regulations are intended to protect patient privacy by defining individually identifiable information and establishing how this information may be used, by whom, and under what circumstances. The definition of individually identifiable information includes any information that relates to the past, present, or future physical or mental health of an individual or provides enough information that leads someone to believe the information could be used to identify an individual" (National Council of State Boards of Nursing [NCSBN], 2018, p.7). Ethical concerns related to social media include confidentiality breaches or HIPAA violations.

Along with concerns about the ethical and legal implications of social media misuse, the potential for deterioration in the quality of patient care exists. The NCSBN (2018) describes possible "lateral violence" or cyberbullying and intimidation resulting from posting negative online comments about co-workers. While interpersonal conflict and bullying behaviors have always been part of the nursing work environment, social media tools have enabled more of this behavior due to the ease and speed of posting information and the illusion of anonymity. These types of comments and behaviors can impact the interpersonal relationships among team members, ultimately affecting student safety. "Breaches in patient confidentiality, lateral violence between co-workers, personal and professional boundary violations, and conflicts in the representation of employers are challenges associated with social media usage in the nursing landscape" (Lefebvre et al., 2020, p. 137).

Another issue to consider is the distraction and interruption created by using portable devices during nursing care and the impact on concentration and nursing activities (Doucette, 2018). Discussion of nurses and social media is complex because nurses' interface with social media as both individuals and as professionals, and sometimes on behalf of their institutions. "Social media policy and instruction may assist users in recognizing the potential pitfalls of blurred social and professional identities online. When institutional policy is in place, departures from acceptable social media practice within a healthcare paradigm may be explained by a lack of policy awareness" (Lefebvre et al., 2020, p. 139).

Digital Communication Technologies

Separate from social media but related are the digital communication technologies of email and texting, EHRs, videoconferencing, and monitoring devices. Like social media, these modes of communication offer faster and more efficient methods of contact with colleagues, families, and students but pose unforeseen risks to privacy and confidentiality. Emailing health information has its risks if appropriate safeguards are not in place. Email messages can be intercepted, forwarded, and accessed by unauthorized individuals. Strict Information Technology (IT) oversight and security measures must be implemented to mitigate this. This includes using secure email systems that require encryption, password protection, limiting access to authorized personnel, and email policies. Software built for secure texting is a way to keep protected health information private. However, pitfalls can exist with access due to the complexity of the application or device, such as the network's reliability resulting in nurses using unsecured cellular network texting features on their personal cell phones (Collins, 2019).

Concerns arise that once a text message is sent over a realm the agency does not control; it becomes under the domain of the wireless carrier. Sometimes, the end user may not password-protect their mobile phone, allowing the text messages to become available to unauthorized persons (Karaz, 2013). Similarly, school nurses are increasingly using discussion forums and live streams for virtual meetings/video conferencing, phone calls, and webinars to collaborate with colleagues regarding best practices and share healthcare information about students. Platforms such as Zoom®, GoTo Meetings®, and Microsoft Teams® along with video calling via FaceTime® and WhatsApp® are widely utilized by school teams for multidisciplinary meetings and collaboration. Considering technical issues and the meeting space is crucial with online meetings and videoconferencing applications.

The nurse needs to be mindful of how to handle technical issues that may arise, such as bandwidth, audio feedback, and connectivity issues. Using a unique link with a password to access the meeting and locking the meeting once all participants have joined is recommended to prevent hackers or unwelcome participants from gaining access to the meeting. Attention to the physical meeting space is vital when participating in and facilitating online meetings to allow for private discussion (Sherrod & Holland, 2021). Choosing a quiet room with carpet to prevent extraneous noises is recommended, wearing a headset to facilitate communication and keeping the webcam at eye level to mimic sitting across from the other participants.

Cloud computing through Google Apps®, Dropbox®, and iCloud® is used to store and manage school-related documents remotely with access from any device with an internet connection. This is helpful for collaboration and ensures that important documents are not lost due to hardware failures or other storage issues. School health websites and podcasts are other tools frequently used by school nurses to share school health-related information. "Professional practice websites provide the school nurse with the opportunity to increase their visibility, inform stakeholders of their multifaceted role in the health of our country's youth, and positively influence the public narrative of school nursing" (Moss, 2021, p.53). Risks and challenges associated with these digital platforms include poor quality of information, confidentiality, and legal issues (e.g., privacy, reliability, and security) (Hazzam & Lahrech, 2018).

School nurses can use telehealth technology to coordinate student healthcare, provide education, and increase access to health services in the school setting. This ultimately reduces disparities, provides equitable access to healthcare, reduces absenteeism, decreases hospitalizations and emergency care, and lessens the financial burden for families and healthcare costs (NASN, 2022b). Telehealth "is the use of electronic information and telecommunication technologies to support long-distance clinical health care, patient and professional health-related education, health administration, and public health" (HRSA, 2022, para 1). Telehealth encompasses the use of the internet, video conferencing, store-and-forward imaging (the electronic transmission of information for evaluation to a specialist outside of real-time or live interaction), streaming media, and land and wireless communications (HRSA, 2022). By "utilizing sound telehealth delivery principles and complying with relevant regulations such as FERPA, HIPAA, and other federal, state, and local laws, public schools can be ideal locations to implement telehealth" (NASN, 2022b, para 4). Schools are encouraged to work with experienced telehealth providers to ensure that the telehealth services comply with laws and regulations.

Benefits of Social Media and Digital Technology

There are many benefits to nurses being active on social media and using digital technology. Social media is not just limited to personal time on personal devices. Benefits include:
- strengthening of support systems,
- fostering professional networking,
- promoting timely communication,
- disseminating knowledge for better decision-making, and
- impacting health behaviors (Miller, 2018).

As individuals and for personal reasons, school nurses utilize a variety of social media platforms to connect and communicate with friends and family. School nurses frequently connect with teachers and other school staff on social media as school team members, supporting one another and building community. As health professionals, school nurses are increasingly using social media to network, share strategies and best practices with other school nurses nationwide. Some school nurses use social media platforms like Twitter® to share health promotion messaging campaigns with families. Some school nurses represent their professional organizations on social media platforms and communicate with other health organizations to advocate for nursing and to raise awareness about issues. Nurses are using social media for political activism and participation to facilitate and garner support for nurses. As an educational resource, social media can effectively disseminate conference findings and share insights (Geraghty et al., 2021).

The benefits of digital technology, including video conferencing, EHRs, monitoring via mobile devices, and access to online resources, are transforming school nursing and promoting engagement. Video conferencing in real-time makes it easier for school nurses to collaborate and communicate with school staff, families, students, and other healthcare professionals. Sharing EHR information provides easy access to the individual health record, which improves care coordination. Monitoring via mobile devices (smartphones and tablets) can be useful for school nurses to remotely monitor student health and provide more effective care. Mobile devices can allow school nurses to receive real-time updates on student health and track health data.

Lack of Case Law

Social media misuse can impact the nurse, employer, and even patient safety and care (NCSBN, 2018). Data is starting to emerge from state boards of nursing (BONs) on the numbers and nature of complaints of inappropriate social media use by nurses from employers, patients, and families. If a complaint is filed, the BON may investigate on the grounds of unprofessional conduct, moral turpitude, unethical conduct, mismanagement of patient records, revealing privileged nurse-patient communication, or breach of confidentiality (NCSBN, 2018). If the BON finds the allegations true, the nurse may face disciplinary action that could entail reprimand or sanction, monetary fine, or temporary or permanent loss of licensure (NCSBN, 2018).

Inappropriate social media by nurses may violate state and federal laws that exist to protect patient privacy and confidentiality. These violations could be deemed both civil and criminal penalties, resulting in fines and potential incarceration. The nurse may face termination if the conduct violates employer policies (NCSBN, 2018). Regarding the impact of social media misuse on patient care, online comments by a nurse about co-workers may fall under lateral violence. Lateral violence entails intimidation and cyberbullying, and this sort of behavior negatively affects team-based care, which can cause patient safety issues (NCSBN, 2018). Concerns about the issue of speech protected by labor law, the First Amendment, and if the employer can impose rules related to personal time outside of work still have not been resolved (NCSBN, 2018).

What are the Standards?

The use of social media is subject to the same professional standards that guide all aspects of nursing practice. Part of those standards is the application of *professional filters* when considering the implications of social media. These filters include the following:

- **State and federal laws include the Health Insurance Portability and Accountability Act (HIPAA) and the Family Educational Rights and Privacy Act (FERPA).** While most information gathered and maintained by the school nurse is regulated by FERPA (U.S. Dept. of Education [USDE] & U.S. Dept. of Health and Human Services [USDHHS], 2019) rather than HIPAA, both laws protect the privacy and confidentiality of student records (USDHHS, Office of Civil Rights Headquarters, 2013). Parents/guardians who feel the school nurse has divulged confidential student health records could lodge a FERPA complaint with the USDE.

- **Nurse regulators.** State and regional bodies, including BONs, set standards for nursing practice. If a school nurse misuses social media, a parent/guardian or the school nurse's employer may file a complaint with the state BON. These complaints may result in an investigation by the BON and possible disciplinary action (NCSBN, 2018).

- **Employers.** Employers put policies in place regarding how a nurse functions at work and how an employee's actions outside the workplace can affect the institution. School nurses should know that employers monitor not only social media activity carried out on employer-owned computers from work, but also can monitor an employee's personal social media postings. Inappropriate social media posting, even outside the workplace, can result in serious consequences, employer sanctions, and even termination of employment (NCSBN, 2018).

- **Professional standards.** The school nurse's education, licensure, and nursing standards set professional practice expectations. For school nurses, their nursing standards are:
    - ANA's *Nursing Scope and Standards of Practice* (2021)
    - ANA's *Code of Ethics for Nurses with Interpretive Statements* (2015)
    - NASN's *School Nursing: Scope and Standards of Practice* (2022a)

These professional organizations do not play a direct regulatory role. However, their nursing standards comprise the broader definition of standard of care against which possible cases of negligence or nursing malpractice are compared. "These bodies have a duty of care to the reputation and continued development of the nursing profession" (González-Luis et al., 2022, p. 2380).

Misconceptions and Misunderstandings about Social Media

Although there are rare cases of intentional breaches of patient confidentiality on social media, most breaches of patient privacy and confidentiality by nurses on social media have been unintentional, often due to myths and mistaken beliefs about the nature of social media. NCSBN (2018) has summarized these common myths and factors that may lead a nurse to commit an inadvertent breach of privacy and confidentiality on social media in a 2018 brochure:
- A mistaken belief that the communication or posting is private and accessible only by the intended recipients.
- A mistaken belief that the content deleted from a site is no longer accessible.
- A mistaken belief that disclosing private or confidential information about patients is harmless if the communication is accessed only by the intended recipient.
- A mistaken belief is that discussing or referring to patients is acceptable if they are not identified by name but by a nickname, room number, diagnosis, or condition.

- Confusion regarding a patient's right to disclose personal information (or a healthcare organization's right to disclose otherwise protected information with a patient's consent) and the need for healthcare providers to refrain from disclosing patient information without a care-related need for disclosure.
- The ease of posting and the commonplace nature of sharing information via social media.

IMPLICATIONS FOR SCHOOL NURSE PRACTICE

The ANA (2021) and the NCSBN (2018) have developed guidelines to assist nurses in utilizing social media while minimizing the risks.

- Nurses must not share individually identifiable patient health information online.
- Nurses must not transmit via electronic media any patient-related image.
- Nurses must not take photos or videos on personal cell phones or other digital devices. Any treatment-related photos or videos should be taken following employer guidelines and on employer equipment.
- Nurses must maintain professional boundaries with patients on social media.
- Nurses should report any patient privacy or confidentiality breaches they observe to their nursing supervisor/administrator.
- Nurses must remove all patient identifiers (e.g., name or other information that may lead to the identification of the patient).
- Never mention a patient's name – neither first nor last- to someone not part of the care team. Under FERPA guidelines, the care team in the school setting includes teachers and other school officials with "legitimate educational interests" (USDE, 2019).
- Avoid indirect identifiers by removing any reference to the dates care was provided or the location where care was provided. For example, a prudent school nurse might talk about "students with diabetes I've cared for over the years" instead of "a third grader we have in my school this year with diabetes."
- Know and adhere to the employer's social media policy across all social media platforms.
- Share only credible and reliable information. Reliable and evidence-based resources must be utilized. Information from official medical and healthcare entities is recommended (Wysocki, 2015).
- Secure one's personal media profile using privacy settings for social media platforms.
- Avoid lateral violence and cyberbullying via negative comments about colleagues and co-workers.
- Be aware that social media posts are discoverable long after they are deleted.

Digital Communications

As with social media, the courts have yet to weigh in on how digital communications, such as email and text communications between families and school staff, are to be handled (Franczek, 2023.) In some jurisdictions, the courts have said that the FERPA regulations never intended every family teacher email to be made part of the student's educational record. School nurses need again to remember that they should exercise even greater caution than teaching staff because FERPA regulations do spell out that communication, including student health information, is part of the educational record and, as such, is subject to privacy, security, and archiving guidelines. School nurses must be aware of their school district's record retention policy and any specific district or state guidelines on the retention of medical records and parent communications related to student health.

EHRs

Electronic Health Records (EHRs) are defined as "real-time patient-centered records that make information available instantly and securely to authorized users" (Rowland et al., 2022, p. 3). EHRs are digital/electronic versions of the paper chart that include health-related information on an individual. The use of EHRs has been adopted by many states and school nurses to maintain comprehensive, accurate documentation and to collect data to identify trends to make decisions related to school nursing care. "EHRs are the standard for collecting and managing large student caseloads, for analyzing data, and for producing reports" (Bergren & Maughan, 2019, p.110). For data collection and research purposes, school nurses need to use standardized data points and document accurately (Bergren & Maughan, 2019). Access to up-to-date health information, assessments, evaluations, and treatment allows for more coordinated and efficient care. Collaboration and communication can be improved with health information being readily available and accessible. Despite the quick access, organization, and retrieval of health information, challenges persist with EHRs.

A lack of integration of systems makes a comprehensive EHR difficult (Rowland et al., 2022). For the end user (the nurse), there may be issues with a lack of training and navigating the EHR efficiently. This can result in the EHR contents being inaccurate or incomplete due to burdensome, rigid document requirements (Rowland et al., 2022). Topaz et al. (2017) found that poor usability of the EHR can significantly affect how well it supports the nurses' work. Usability refers to how easy and efficient the system is to use. If the system is slow or unresponsive and has too many keystrokes or drop-down options, it can impact the nurse's time to complete their work and lead to frustration. These navigation issues can increase the risk of errors or omissions in information.

Similarly, if the EHR was developed for other disciplines, such as education, it may not include the specific features and functionality for nursing resulting in workarounds or manual processes to complete work. Also, EHRs may affect the nurse-student relationship due to the perception that the nurse focuses too much on the computer rather than the student. *(See Chapter 10 on School Health Records for more information).*

Mobile Technology

Mobile technology includes cellular communication, such as 4G/5G networking, Wi-Fi, and Bluetooth connections. Smartphones, tablets, and laptops are the most popular devices used. Text messaging, also known as short message service (SMS), is a medium of digital communication that offers the potential benefits of speed of communication and greater access to clients (Liu et al., 2019). School nurses and families have expressed eagerness to use texting since it is often easier to respond quickly to text from virtually any location and in situations like meetings or waiting rooms where phone communication is impossible. Instant messaging allows audio, video, images, and file attachments to be easily shared. SMS texting is utilized in many clinical settings since it is the most widely adopted, least expensive, and offers a means of simplicity for a connection delivering "just-in-time" information to individuals without any effort on the part of the individual (Wilcox et al., 2019). While texting has great potential, healthcare providers must be aware of privacy and security concerns. End-to-end encryption often does not allow data to be intercepted; messages inadvertently be sent to the wrong individual or viewed by unauthorized individuals (Texting in Healthcare, 2019).

Mobile health uses technological (tech) devices and applications (apps) to monitor health, gather data, and provide remote care to improve care and overall health. Smart devices are being used to monitor biomedical systems (e.g., blood pressure monitoring, data gathering for diabetic monitoring, and wearable tech/mobile apps (e.g., fitness trackers, health monitoring, mindfulness, and nutritional). School nurses must be aware of privacy and security risks when using mobile tech devices, policies for obtaining medical orders and caregiver consent, and ensure that apps are secure, reliable, and compliant with privacy laws and regulations.

Concerns about privacy, confidentiality, and archiving of student health records all underscore the importance of carrying out work-related digital communication **only on school-issued devices** (e.g., work computers, laptops, iPad®, and cell phones). Using school-issued devices maintains student health records' confidentiality and security, and the school can properly archive and manage the records. Using only school-issued devices and accounts gives the school control over the information. It prevents unauthorized access to sensitive information and reduces the risk of data or security breaches from using a vulnerable personal account or device, which is often vulnerable to security issues (DeJong et al., 2020).

School Health Websites

Social media and school nurse websites can be utilized to increase school nurse visibility and change the public narrative of school nursing regarding the role, training, and value of the school nurse (Moss et al., 2019). The National Association of School Nurses (NASN) has a School Nurse Toolkit educational toolkit that is available for school nurses. This toolkit suggests that school nurses acquire district website space, identify content and design the site (NASN, 2019). School health websites are excellent for nurses to connect with families, students, and staff and provide access to school contact information, health promotion and wellness content, and evidence-based resources. Audio, video files, images, and other file attachments must adhere to the employer's policies regarding content. It is advised to use the school or district's-maintained website to create a school health-specific website.

CONCLUSION

Social media and other digital communication technology offer many potential benefits to school nurse practice. To safely incorporate these platforms into their practice, professional school nurses must educate themselves about the benefits and risks of these modes of communication. Even if specific social media regulations are not yet in place in some work settings, school nurses can utilize critical thinking skills and their professional filters, as well as guidance from professional nursing organizations regarding how to mitigate any risk to student privacy and confidentiality.

Social media platforms and applications will continue to evolve and expand rapidly. The platforms and risks will evolve; however, the school nurse's commitment to protecting privacy and confidentiality remains paramount. School nurses are responsible for working with regulatory agencies and their employers to develop policies and guidelines for the safe and appropriate utilization of social media and other digital communication technology.

RESOURCES

American Nurses Association. (n.d.). *Social media principles.* https://www.nursingworld.org/social/

Center for Disease Control and Prevention. (2023). *Social media at CDC. CDC social media tools, guidelines, and best practices.* https://www.cdc.gov/socialmedia/tools/guidelines/index.html

National Association of School Nurses. (2019). *School nurse website toolkit.* https://learn.nasn.org/courses/13405

REFERENCES

Advent Health University (2020, July 8). *Social media and nursing: Tips for nurses to promote health online.* Advent Health University. https://www.ahu.edu/blog/social-media-and-nursing

Ahmed, W., Gutheil, T., & Katz, M. (2020). Public disclosure on social media of identifiable patient information by health professionals: Content analysis of Twitter data. *Journal of Medical Internet Research, 22*(9). https://doi.org/10.2196/19746. PMID: 32870160; PMCID: PMC7492977

American Nurses Association. (n.d.). *Social media principles.* https://www.nursingworld.org/social/

American Nurses Association. (2015). *Code of ethics for nurses with interpretive statements.* Author.

American Nurses Association. (2021). *Nursing scope and standards of practice.* Author.

Bergren, M., & Maughan, E. (2019). The school nurse's role in evidence-based practice, quality, improvement and research. In J. Selekman, R. A. Shannon, & C.F. Yonkaitis (Eds.) *School nursing: A comprehensive text* (pp. 96-116). FA Davis.

Center for Disease Control and Prevention. (2023.). *CDC social media too). FAA guidelines and best practices.* Social media at CDC. https://www.cdc.gov/socialmedia/tools/guidelines/index.html

Collins, R. (2019). Nurses' perceived usefulness of secure texting applications for the purpose of patient care. *Online Journal of Nursing Informatics, 23*(1). https://www.himss.org/resources/nurses-perceived-usefulness-secure-texting-applications-purpose-patient-care

DeJong, A., Donelle, L., & Kerr, M. (2020). Nurses' use of personal smartphone technology in the workplace: Scoping review. *JMIR mHealth and uHealth, 8*(11), e18774. https://doi.org/10.2196/18774

Doucette, J. (2018). When staff members won't stop texting. *Nursing Management 49*(2). https://journals.lww.com/nursingmanagement/fulltext/2018/02000/when_staff_members_won_t_stop_texting.12.aspx

Franczek, P.C. (2023). *Are emails, texts, tweets, and other digital communications student records under FERPA and state law?* https://www.jdsupra.com/legalnews/are-emails-texts-tweets-and-other-dig-60950/

Geraghty, S., Hari, R., & Oliver, K. (2021). Using social media in contemporary nursing: risks and benefits. *British Journal of Nursing., 30*(18), 1078–1082. https://doi.org/10.12968/bjon.2021.30.18.1078

González-Luis, H., Azurmendi, A., Santillan-Garcia, A., & Tricas-Saura, S. (2022). Nurses' freedom of expression: Rights, obligations and responsibilities. *Journal of Nursing Management, 30*(7), 2379-2382. https://doi.org/10.1111/jonm.13839

Hazzam, J. & Lahrech, A. (2018). Health care professionals' social media behavior and the underlying factors of social media adoption and use: quantitative study. *Journal of Medical Internet Research 20*(11). https://doi.org/10.2196/12035

Health Resources Services Administration. (2021). *What is telehealth?* https://www.hrsa.gov/rural-health/telehealth/what-is-telehealth

HIPAA Journal. (n.d.). *Text messaging in healthcare.* https://www.hipaajournal.com/text-messaging-in-healthcare/

Karasz, H., Eiden, A., & Bogan S. (2013). Text messaging to communicate with public health audiences: How the HIPAA security rule affects practice. *American Journal of Public Health.103*(4). 617-622. https://doi.org/10.2105/AJPH.2012.300999

Raynard S. Kington, R.S., Arnesen, S., Chou, W-Y.S., Curry, S.J., Lazer, D. & Villarruel, A.M. (2021). Identifying credible sources of health information in social media: Principles and attributes. *NAM Perspectives.* Discussion Paper, National Academy of Medicine, Washington, DC. https://doi.org/10.31478/202107a

Lefebvre, C., McKinney, K., Glass Cline, D., Franasiak, R., Husain, I., Pariyadath, M., Roberson, A., McLean, A., & Stopyra, J. (2020). Social media usage among nurses, *The Journal of Nursing Administration*, *50*(3), 135–141. https://doi.org/10.1097/nna.0000000000000857

Liu, X., Sutton, P., McKenna, R., Sinanan, M., Fellner, B., Leu, M., & Ewell, C. (2019). Evaluation of secure messaging applications for a health care system: A case study. *Applied Clinical Informatics,10*(1), 140-150. https://doi.org/10.1055/s-0039-1678607

Miller, L. A. (2018). Social media savvy: risk versus benefit. *The Journal of Perinatal & Neonatal Nursing*, *32*(3), 206-208. https://doi.org/10.1097/JPN.0000000000000346

Moss, E. (2021). Enhancing your virtual footprint: The school nurse's professional health office website. *NASN School Nurse,36*(1), 52–57. https://doi.org/10.1177/1942602X20937337

Moss, E., Bergren, M. D., & Maughan, E. D. (2019). School Nurse websites: What do they tell us about school nurses? *The Journal of School Nursing*, *35*(6), 395-400. https://doi.org/10.1177/1059840519843315

National Association of School Nurses. (2022a). *School nursing: Scope and standards of practice* (4th ed.). National Association of School Nurses.

National Association of School Nurses. (2019). *School nurse website toolkit.* https://learn.nasn.org/courses/13405

National Association of School Nurses. (2022b). *Telehealth: Equitable student access to health services* [Position Statement]. Author.

National Council of State Boards of Nursing. (2018). *A nurse's guide to the use of social media* (Brochure). https://www.ncsbn.org/public-files/NCSBN_SocialMedia.pdf

Network for Public Law. (2020, January 23). *Data sharing guidance for school nurses*. Network for Public Health Law. https://www.networkforphl.org/resources/data-sharing-guidance-for-school-nurses/

Nguyen, B. M., Lu, E., Bhuyan, N., Lin, K., & Sevilla, M. (2020). Social media for doctors: Taking professional and patient engagement to the next level. *Family Practice Management*, *27*(1), 19–14.

Pew Research Center. (2021a). *Social media fact sheet.* https://www.pewresearch.org/internet/fact-sheet/social-media/

Pew Research Center. (2021b). *Mobile fact sheet.* https://www.pewresearch.org/internet/fact-sheet/mobile/

Rowland, S.P., Fitzgerald, J.E., Lungren, M. *et al.* Digital health technology-specific risks for medical malpractice liability. *npj Digital. Medicine 5*, 157 (2022). https://doi.org/10.1038/s41746-022-00698-3

Sherrod, D. & Holland, C. (2021). Facilitating successful online meetings in healthcare. *Nursing Management ,52*(4), 40–45. https://doi.org/10.1097/01.NUMA.0000737616.61710.39

Topaz, M., Ronquillo, C., Peltonen, L. M., Pruinelli, L., Sarmiento, R. F., Badger, M. K., Ali, S., Lewis, A., Georgsson, M., Jeon, E., Tayaben, J. L., Kuo, C. H., Islam, T., Sommer, J., Jung, H., Eler, G. J., Alhuwail, D., & Lee, Y. L. (2017). Nurse informaticians report low satisfaction and multi-level concerns with electronic health records: Results from an international survey. *AMIA Annual Symposium proceedings. AMIA Symposium, 2016*, 2016–2025.

U.S. Department of Education and U.S. Department of Health. (2019, December). *Joint guidance on the application of the family educational rights and privacy act (FERPA) and the health insurance portability and accountability act of 1996 (HIPAA) to student health records. Protecting student privacy.* https://studentprivacy.ed.gov/sites/default/files/resource_document/file/2019%20HIPAA%20FERPA%20Joint%20Guidance%20508.pdf"

U.S. Department of Health & Human Services, Office for Civil Rights Headquarters. (2013). *Does the HIPAA privacy rule apply to an elementary or secondary school* ?https://www.hhs.gov/hipaa/for-professionals/faq/513/does-hipaa-apply-to-an-elementary-school/index.html" https://www.hhs.gov/hipaa/for-professionals/faq/513/does-hipaa-apply-to-an-elementary-school/index.html

U.S Department of Health & Human Services, Office of the National Coordination for Health Information Technology. (2023). *Benefits of EHRs.* HealthIt.gov. https://www.healthit.gov/topic/health-it-and-health-information-exchange-basics/improved-patient-care-using-ehrs

U.S. Food and Drug Administration. (2020). *What is digital health?* https://www.fda.gov/medical-devices/digital-health-center-excellence/what-digital-health#benefits

Ventola C. L. (2014). Social media and health care professionals: benefits, risks, and best practices. *P & T: A Peer-Reviewed Journal for Formulary Management, 39*(7), 491–520.

Vukušić Rukavina, T., Viskić, J., Machala Poplašen, L., Relić, D., Marelić, M., Jokic, D., & Sedak, K. (2021). Dangers and benefits of social media on E-professionalism of health care professionals: Scoping review. *Journal of Medical Internet Research, 23*(11), e25770. https://doi.org/10.2196/25770

Willcox, J., Dobson, R, & Whittaker, R. (2019). Old-fashioned technology in the era of "bling": Is there a future for text messaging in health care? *Journal of Medical Internet Research, 21*(12). https://doi.org/10.2196/16630

Chapter 52

VIOLENCE IN SCHOOLS

Kathleen A. Hassey, DNP, MEd, BSN, BA, RN
Jenny M. Gormley, DNP, BA, RN, NCSN, FNASN

DESCRIPTION OF ISSUE

The topic of violence in schools in the United States can generate great concern for adults who seek to provide safe and effective learning environments for students. School nurses, educators, and administrators focus on student growth and achievement. The concept of intentional harm challenges the school community. Nonetheless, school staff must understand the issue of violence in schools to help prevent harm and provide appropriate responses based on the best evidence available. This chapter is organized to:

- Define violence in schools
- Present the incidence, prevalence, and impact of different types of school violence
- Highlight relevant legal cases and policies
- Identify school violence as a public health issue
- Describe school violence prevention efforts
- Share implications for school nursing practice

BACKGROUND

Definitions: How is violence in schools generally defined?

As with other phenomena involving student behaviors and attitudes, school violence must be defined clearly to facilitate discussion of the issue, track the problem, and measure the impact of efforts to prevent and improve response to violence. According to the World Health Organization (WHO), violence is the "intentional use of physical force or power, threatened or actual, against oneself, another person, or against a group or community, which either results in or has a high likelihood of resulting in injury, death, psychological harm, mal-development, or deprivation" (WHO, 2017, para. 2). For this chapter, the more specific definition from the Centers for Disease Control and Prevention (CDC) is used: "School violence is youth violence that occurs on school property, on the way to or from school or school-sponsored events, or during a school-sponsored event. A young person can be a victim, a perpetrator, or a witness of school violence. School violence may also impact adults" (CDC, 2016, p. 1). Examples of school violence include bullying, physical fighting, use of weapons, electronic aggression, and gang violence (CDC, 2021a). It also includes dating violence and restraint, and seclusion. Interactions involving violent behavior occur between individuals/groups such as student on student, student on staff, staff on student, staff on staff, and outside perpetrators on students and staff. Depending on the situation, the school district may face liability for violence that occurs on school grounds. *See Doe v. Claiborne County, Tenn.,* 103 F.3d 495 (6th Cir. 1996) generally holding that "a school system has an unmistakable duty to create and maintain a safe environment for its students" (Doe v Claiborne County, 1996, para. 74).

Incidence, Prevalence, and Impact: How Serious Is the Issue of Violence in Schools?

The CDC, the United States Justice Department, and the U.S. Department of Education (USDE) have collaborated on collecting and analyzing data about violence in schools, including violent deaths, since the early 1990s. According to the CDC, violent death in school is "a fatal injury (e.g., homicide, suicide or legal intervention) that occurs on school property, or during or on the way to/from school-sponsored event" (CDC, 2021b, para. 2). Regarding school homicides, the CDC's School Associated Violent Death Study (CDC, 2016b) shows between 14 and 34 school-age children are victims of homicide on school grounds on their way to and from school - every year. The following facts provide more detail about violent school deaths:

- Most school-associated violent deaths occur during transition times – immediately before and after the school day and during lunch.
- Violent deaths are more likely to occur at the start of each semester.
- Nearly 50 percent of homicide perpetrators gave a warning signal, such as making a threat or leaving a note, prior to the event.
- Firearms used in school-associated homicides and suicides came primarily from the perpetrator's home or from friends or relatives.
- Homicide is the second leading cause of death among youth aged 5-18. Data from the CDC study (2021b) indicate that between 1% and 2% of these deaths happen on school grounds or on the way to or from school. "These findings underscore the importance of preventing violence at school and in communities" (CDC, 2021b, para 2).

The CDC has also collected data on non-fatal violence in schools since 1991. In 2021, CDC's nationwide Youth Risk Behavior Survey (YRBS) was administered to U.S. high school students who were asked to report incidences of violence in the previous 30 days for the CDC. Many factors contributing to school violence remain stable or increased, as seen in Figure 1 (CDC, 2023b). The two factors that increased were "Threatened or injured with a weapon on school property" and "Did not go to school because of safety concerns."

Figure 1. CDC National Youth Risk Behavior Survey Data (2023b) (p. 47)

In 2021, 9% of high school students did not go to school because they felt unsafe either at school or on their way to or from school at least once during the past 30 days. Female students were more likely than male students to miss school because of safety concerns. Black and Hispanic students were more likely than Asian, White, and multiracial students to miss school because of safety concerns. LGBQ+ students and students who had any same-sex partners were more likely than their peers to miss school because of safety concerns.

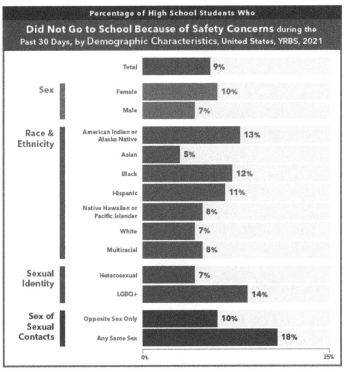

Gun violence in schools

As of 2020, firearm injury became the leading cause of death for children 0-19 years of age in the United States, surpassing motor vehicle accidents (Goldstick et al., 2022). For firearm injuries occurring in schools, "Since 2015, there have been approximately 275 intentional shootings (shootings where there was intent to harm someone else) in K-12 schools across the nation" (Rajan et al. (2022, para 1).

In a national study of firearm injuries tracked by the Gun Violence Archive, researchers found an increase in the risk of fatal and non-fatal firearm injuries in children during the first six months of the COVID-19 pandemic as compared to similar time periods prior to the pandemic (Cohen et al., 2021). Furthermore, these "firearm injuries were correlated with increased firearm purchases during the COVID-19 pandemic period when compared to corresponding pre-pandemic months in 2016–2019." (Cohen et al., 2021, p.1)

Figure 2. School shootings 1970 - 2022

2022 had the most K-12 school shootings

School shootings have increased 163% since 2020 and 1,900% since 2010.

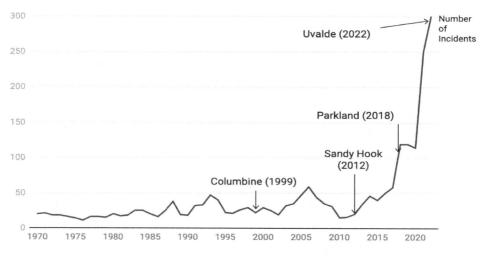

2022 data updated as of Dec. 20 at 3:30 p.m. ET.

Chart: Kara Arundel/K-12 Dive · Source: K12 School Shooting Database · Get the data · Created with Datawrapper

The K-12 School Shooting Database, https://k12ssdb.org/, updates information on school shootings in the U.S. Washington Post reporters track and periodically publish how many students have been exposed to gun violence during school hours, beginning with the Columbine massacre in 1999. According to John Woodrow Cox and his colleagues, "Beyond the dead and wounded, children who witness the violence or cower behind locked doors to hide from it can be profoundly traumatized" (Cox et al., 2022, para 1) and have the ripple effect among children exposed to gun violence at school. Firearm intentional and unintentional injuries have increased to the number one cause of death for youth in the U.S. ages 0-24 (Goldstick et al., 2022). *A database maintained by the* Washington Post *provides the most updated numbers of injuries.* Click on this link:https:// www.washingtonpost.com/graphics/2018/local/school-shootings-database/

(See Active Shooter Chapter 41 for more information on school shootings)

Dating Violence

According to the CDC, teen dating violence is a type of intimate partner violence and is considered an adverse childhood experience, impacting one in 12 adolescents in the US. Dating violence includes the following:

- **Physical violence** is when a person hurts or tries to hurt a partner by hitting, kicking, or using another type of physical force.
- **Sexual violence** is forcing or attempting to force a partner to take part in a sex act or sexual touching when the partner does not consent or is unable to consent or refuse. It also includes non-physical sexual behaviors like posting or sharing sexual pictures of a partner without their consent or sexting someone without their consent.
- **Psychological aggression** is verbal and non-verbal communication with the intent to harm a partner mentally or emotionally and exert control over a partner.

- **Stalking** is a pattern of repeated, unwanted attention and contact by a current or former partner that causes fear or safety concerns for an individual victim or someone close to the victim (CDC, 2023a, para. 1).

Students most at risk for dating violence are female or students who identify as lesbian, gay, bisexual, transgender, queer (LGBTQ), or questioning their gender identity (CDC, 2023a, para. 4).

Gang Violence Impacting School Safety

According to the U.S. Office of Juvenile Justice and Delinquency, "Gangs have an adverse impact on youth and communities across America. Over the years, youth gangs have become increasingly complex, lethal, and resistant to control" (OJJDP, 2022, para #2). The presence of gangs in schools is related to increased violence. Gang members may be victimizing other students in the school, which impacts their ability to be in a safe learning environment. One student referred to in the Carson article said:

> "I would come home crying…like when I would see people fighting, like one time, **I even had to go the nurse, because I think I got an anxiety attack** like I started shaking a lot like 'cause there was like blood everywhere and it was raining, so it kinda made the blood look worse." (Carson et al., 2017)

School nurses may be involved in injury response and become aware of gang violence in their schools. School administrators, school nurses, counselors, and local law enforcement should coordinate the approach to the gang issue. The Office of Justice National Gang Center has an excellent resource for schools, listed in the resource section, that includes prevention and interventions.

Restraint and Seclusion

In 2012, The USDE issued a Resource Document (Restraint and Seclusion) to provide guidance and describe fifteen principles that state, school districts, school staff, parents, and other stakeholders may find helpful to consider when states, localities, and districts develop practices, policies, and procedures on the use of restraint and seclusion in schools (USDE, 2012, p.1). According to this resource,

> There is no evidence that using restraint or seclusion effectively reduces the occurrence of the problem behaviors that frequently precipitate the use of such techniques. Physical restraint or seclusion should not be used except in situations where the child's behavior poses an imminent danger of serious physical harm to self or others, and restraint and seclusion should be avoided to the greatest extent possible without endangering the safety of students and staff. Schools should never use mechanical restraints to restrict a child's freedom of movement (USDE, 2012, p.1).

Regarding restraint and seclusion, the USDE Office of Civil Rights (OCR) announced that the annual *Civil Rights Data Collection* (CRDC) would include questions on using these controversial behavior techniques in public schools. The latest data publicly available *is* from the 2017-2018 school year *and* includes every public school and district in the nation, with 99.5% of schools and 50.9 million students represented (USDE, 2020). As seen in Figure 4, more than 101,000 students were reported to be physically restrained or secluded, including more than 70,000 students with disabilities in special education served by the Individual Disabilities Education Act (IDEA).

Figure 4. Numbers of students subject to restraint and seclusion

Figure 1. The total number of students enrolled vs. the total number of students who were subjected to restraint or seclusion

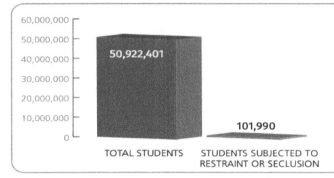

Figure 1 illustrates the total number of students enrolled vs. the total number of students who were subjected to restraint or seclusion. During the 2017-18 school year, 101,990 students of the over 50.9 million students enrolled across the nation's public schools were subjected to physical restraint, mechanical restraint or seclusion — including 70,833 students who were subjected to physical restraint, 3,619 students who were subjected to mechanical restraint, and 27,538 students who were subjected to seclusion.[4]

Figure 2. Students who were subjected to restraint or seclusion nationally

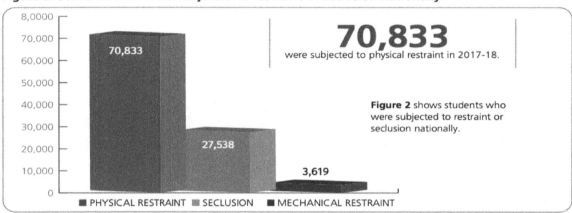

70,833 were subjected to physical restraint in 2017-18.

Figure 2 shows students who were subjected to restraint or seclusion nationally.

The use of restraints, seclusion, and corporal punishment in school is controversial. While no federal laws prohibit staff use of these techniques to control student behavior, many states have statutes, policies, and guidelines regarding their use (see next section). School nurses may witness and be asked to assess students during and after using these techniques; a discussion of restraint, seclusion, and corporal punishment is warranted in this chapter. As with violence in schools, definitions are provided.

Physical restraint refers to the following:

> A personal restriction that immobilizes or reduces the ability of a student to move his or her torso, arms, legs, or head freely. The term physical restraint does not include a physical escort. Physical escort means a temporary touching or holding of the hand, wrist, arm, shoulder, or back to induce a student who is acting out to walk to a safe location (USDE, 2012, p.10).

Mechanical restraint refers to:

> The use of any device or equipment to restrict a student's freedom of movement. This term does not include devices implemented by trained school personnel or utilized by a student that has been prescribed by an appropriate medical or related services professional and are used for the specific and approved purposes for which such devices were designed (USDE, 2012, p.10).

Seclusion refers to:

The involuntary confinement of a student alone in a room or area from which the student is physically prevented from leaving. It does not include a timeout, a behavior management technique that is part of an approved program. It involves the monitored separation of the student in a non-locked setting and is implemented to calm the student (USDE, 2012, p.10).

Corporal punishment refers to the following:

A discipline method in which a supervising adult deliberately inflicts pain upon a child in response to a child's unacceptable behavior or inappropriate language. The immediate aims of such punishment are usually to halt the offense, prevent its recurrence and set an example for others. The purported long-term goal is to change the child's behavior and to make it more consistent with the adult's expectations. In corporal punishment, the adult usually hits various parts of the child's body with a hand or with canes, paddles, yardsticks, belts, or other objects expected to cause pain and fear (American Academy of Child & Adolescent Psychiatry, 2014, para. 1).

While support for using these techniques varies in U.S. schools, it is important to note the similarities in definitions of violence in that the intent of the adult initiating physical interaction with the student is to cause emotional and behavior changes in that student.

Corporal Punishment in Schools

Physical force against students as a form of discipline or punishment has declined over the past four decades. However, the following 17 states still allow it: Alabama, Arizona, Arkansas, Florida, Georgia, Indiana, Kansas, Kentucky, Louisiana, Mississippi, Missouri, North Carolina, Oklahoma, South Carolina, Tennessee, Texas, and Wyoming (Figure 5). Example of Texas Education Code Chapter 37

Code Section	Texas Education Code Chapter 37: Discipline; Law and Order.
Corporal Punishment Defined	Deliberate infliction of physical pain by hitting, paddling, spanking, slapping, or any other physical force used as a means of discipline. The following activities are excluded from the definition of corporal punishment: • Physical pain caused by reasonable athletic training, competition or physical education; or • Confinement, restraint, seclusion, and time-out (which are addressed separately by state law).
Circumstances When Corporal Punishment is Allowed	If permitted by the board of trustees of a school district, a district educator may use corporal punishment to discipline a student. The exception to this rule is when a parents or guardians with custody or control of a child have previously provided a written, signed statement forbidding the use of corporal punishment to discipline the child. A new written statement must be provided each year to the board of trustees of the district where the child attends school. At any point during the school year a parent or guardian may revoke the statement by providing a written, signed revocation.

Figure 5. Use and legality of corporal punishment by state
(School Corporal Punishment in the United States, 2023)

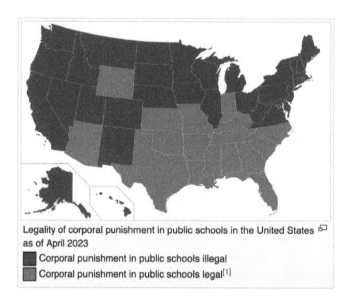

Legality of corporal punishment in public schools in the United States
as of April 2023
- Corporal punishment in public schools illegal
- Corporal punishment in public schools legal[1]

Although the percentage of students in the U.S. hit as punishment dropped from 4% to less than .5% between 1978 and 2015, more than 70,000 school students were hit or spanked during the 2017-18 school year, the last for which statistics are available (Dahl, 2022). As seen with violence statistics, the incidence of corporal punishment varies by race and disability status. The USDE reports

> that what is more alarming is that the Civil Rights Data Collection (CRDC) shows that corporal punishment is used overwhelmingly on male students and is much more commonly administered to African American students of all genders. In nearly all of the states where the practice is permitted, students with disabilities were subjected to corporal punishment at a higher rate than students without disabilities. (USDE, 2016b, para 8.)

Three states - Mississippi, Arkansas, and Alabama - account for 71% of the total number of Black students who experienced corporal punishment in the U.S. in 2018. Incidentally, they also account for more than half of the corporal punishment of white students. Texas and Georgia are the other states where the largest number of Black children are corporally punished. As of 2018, Texas has a high rate of corporal punishment, but the rate is slightly higher for white than for Black students. "Black children are almost 50% more likely than white children to be punished in Georgia schools, but it is noteworthy that the rates of corporal punishment for both races have dropped by a factor of three in the state since our last look at the data" (Startz, 2022, para 8). It is important to note that the usage of **corporal punishment in private schools** is legally permitted **in** nearly every state except Iowa and New Jersey. (School Corporal Punishment in the United States, 2023).

Figure 6. The practice of corporal punishment with discrepancies by race and disability

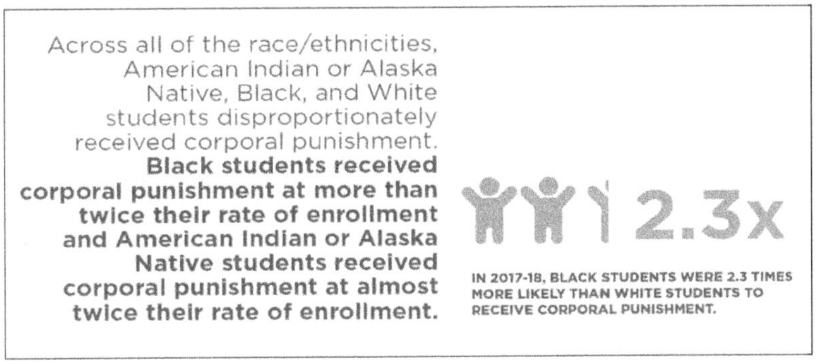

Across all of the race/ethnicities, American Indian or Alaska Native, Black, and White students disproportionately received corporal punishment. **Black students received corporal punishment at more than twice their rate of enrollment and American Indian or Alaska Native students received corporal punishment at almost twice their rate of enrollment.**

2.3x

IN 2017-18, BLACK STUDENTS WERE 2.3 TIMES MORE LIKELY THAN WHITE STUDENTS TO RECEIVE CORPORAL PUNISHMENT.

(USDOE, Office of Civil Rights, 2023)

Select Legal Cases and Policies

Aside from the practical aspect of not wanting students to be harmed, school officials have a duty to ensure that the school environment is reasonably free from the risk of harm.

- See *William G.*, 40 Cal. 3d 550, 221 Cal. Rptr. 118 (1985) for the school's role in maintaining a safe environment for all students.
- Several court cases have addressed a school district's liability after a student's death. For instance, in *Maness v. City of New York*, 607 N.Y.S.2d 325, 325 (N.Y. App. Div. 1st Dept 1994), a 13-year-old student was shot to death near the junior high school during the lunch hour. The school allowed students to leave the building during the lunch hour. On the day in question, the student left the building, waited near a parked car, and was shot after an argument erupted. The student's mother filed a negligence action against the student, alleging that the district was negligent in not providing adequate supervision over the students outside the school building during lunch. The court held that there was no evidence to establish a sufficient causal connection between the student's actions outside of the school building and the resulting gunshot wound.
- Other court cases have addressed similar issues and arrived at opposite conclusions. See *Mirand v. City of New York*, 84 N.Y.2d 44, 46 (N.Y. 1994) (sufficient evidence existed to hold the school district liable for negligent supervision when a student fight occurred after the district knew of a prior altercation and death threat to students). As a result, district staff should be careful to ensure appropriate supervision in the school building to prevent violence.

A summary of school safety laws since the violence of the Columbine shooting in 1999 is included in the resource section (Temkin et al., 2020).

Regarding restraint and seclusion, the National Association of School Nurses (NASN) 2021 position statement on the *Use of Restraint and Seclusion in the School Setting* states:

> It is the position of the National Association of School Nurses (NASN) that restraint and seclusion should not be used in the school setting as a routine form of discipline...the registered professional

school nurse (hereinafter referred to as the school nurse) is in a position to promote positive behavioral supports in the school setting. NASN believes that the school nurse is an essential advocate for the health and well-being of all students (NASN, 2021a, para. 1)

Some inconsistent policies regarding corporal punishment arise because individual state guidelines regulate it. Within a school district, schools can have different policies on paddling, spanking, and physical discipline (Sparks & Harwin, 2016). In some school systems, parents can opt out of corporal punishment. Students can be injured during staff use of restraint and seclusion in schools. Following a review of legal cases of students injured or died during restraint or seclusion, a 2014 U.S. Senate Majority Committee of the Health, Education, Labor, and Pensions Committee issued six major recommendations regarding the use of restraint and seclusion, the first of which was the passing of legislation that would "limit the use of restraints to emergency situations only, when there is an imminent threat of serious harm to students themselves or to others" (U.S. Senate, Health, Education, Labor, and Pensions Committee, 2014, p. 5).

In a November 2016 letter sent to states, U.S. Education Secretary John B. King Jr. urged states to "to end the use of corporal punishment in schools, a practice repeatedly linked to harmful short-term and long-term outcomes for students" (USDE, 2016a). Secretary King suggests a "safe, supportive school environment being critical to support effective teaching and learning" (USDE, 2016a). Many professional groups such as NASN, the American Academy of Pediatrics (AAP), the National Education Association, the American Psychological Association, the American Federation of Teachers, and many more want legislation in all states to ban corporal punishment for all students. Head Start programs do not allow corporal punishment (Gundersen Center for Effective Discipline, n.d.).

Public Health Issue: Why is it important to view school violence, including seclusion, restraint, and corporal punishment, as a public health issue?

Violence is more than a law enforcement or justice system problem. Violence has been recognized as a public health problem by the CDC (2022a, January 18), the National Institutes of Health (NIH) (n.d.), and the American Public Health Association (APHA, 2018). The AAP refers to school violence as a public health emergency (2022). Victims and witnesses of violence in schools experience short and long-term impacts, including exacerbation of chronic illness, such as asthma, and physical disabilities from injuries sustained. Additionally, according to the Substance Abuse & Mental Health Services Administration (SAMHSA),

> "studies have shown that the use of seclusion and restraint can result in psychological harm, physical injuries, and death to both the people subjected to and the staff applying these techniques. Injury rates to staff in mental health settings that use seclusion and restraint are higher than injuries sustained by workers in high-risk industries. Restraints can be harmful and often re-traumatizing for people with trauma histories. Beyond the physical risks of injury and death, it has been found that people who experience seclusion and restraint remain in care longer and are more likely to be readmitted for care." (SAHMSA, 2022, para. 7)

The *Adverse Childhood Event Study* (ACES) conducted by Kaiser in the mid-1990 has demonstrated a dose-response relationship between the number of negative childhood events within the family, e.g., abuse and neglect, and subsequent development of chronic physical and mental/behavioral health conditions (CDC, 2023c).

According to the CDC (2022a), a public health approach uses an evidence-based, four-step process for effective outcomes that includes:

1. defining the problem
2. identifying risk and protective factors
3. developing and testing prevention strategies
4. assuring widespread adoption

A public health approach to this significant health and safety issue impacting school student and adult populations involves many disciplines, including education, law enforcement, nursing, and psychology. School nurses are recognized as essential participants in public health as they work directly and indirectly, individually, and collaboratively, to prevent health problems, including those caused by experienced or witnessed violence (AAP, 2016; USDE, 2016b).

> As school nurses have an essential role in promoting the population health of children and staff in the school setting, they must be knowledgeable and confident in their abilities to prevent school violence.

Prevention Efforts: How are Prevention Efforts Categorized?

The CDC identifies four levels of strategies for preventing school violence (CDC, 2021c).

- **Individual Level Strategies**: include programs available for all students that address "emotional self-awareness, emotional control, self-esteem, positive social skills, social problem-solving, conflict resolution, and teamwork" (para. 2).
- **Relationship Level Strategies:** "include programs that generate positive connections between students, teachers and families" (para. 3).
- **Community Level Strategies:** includes "supporting effective classroom management practices, promoting cooperative learning techniques, providing educators with train and support to meet the diverse needs of students, providing opportunities to actively engage families and creating open communication and decision-making processes" (para. 4).
- **Societal Level Strategies:** includes "addressing social norms about the acceptability of violence in schools and ensuring that educational systems promote strong education growth for all students are additional strategies" (para. 5).

School nurses can use this concept of strategy levels to prioritize efforts and to understand the various efforts their school communities may be making to reduce violence. An excellent compilation of strategies based on the best available evidence can be found in the CDC (2016), *A Comprehensive Technical Package for the Prevention of Youth Violence and Associated Risk Factors*, listed in the Resource section.

CDC has developed a resource *Preventing Intimate Partner Violence Across the Lifespan: A Technical Package of Programs, Policies, and Practices.* The resource includes multiple strategies that can be used in combination to prevent intimate partner violence and teen dating violence. School nurses can assist students by utilizing the following strategies.

Figure 7. School nurses' strategies

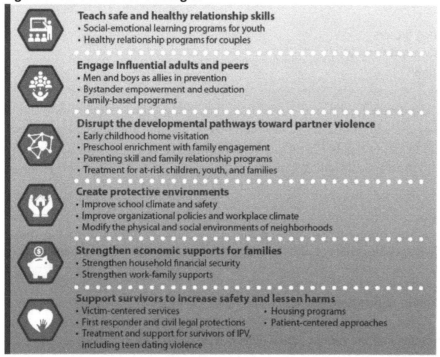

Centers for Disease Control and Prevention. (2016).

School nurses must also be aware of the discipline policies in their schools and how they may especially impact students of color. Much research shows that severe discipline, expulsion, and referrals to law enforcement play into the School to Prison Pipeline. The "...school to prison pipeline...refers to a process by which youth who experience punitive punishment in schools are increasingly enmeshed with the criminal justice system" (Hemez et al., 2020, p. 2). According to New York Civil Liberties Union, "... the practices put into place in many of America's schools 'disproportionately' impact students and youth of color, those with disabilities, and LGBTQ students. Citing zero-tolerance policies in schools as the driver for these school-to-prison pipeline statistics, there is a general sense among many that the prison numbers and those being incarcerated yearly are a direct result, or at least untowardly influenced by the rules put in place within the educational system" (Norrie, 2022, para. 13).

IMPLICATIONS FOR SCHOOL NURSE PRACTICE

School nurses should be aware of their role in providing a safe and supportive school environment as described at the federal level. School nurses should also prioritize students' mental and behavioral health, including safety, by familiarizing themselves with the NASN position statement, *The Behavioral Health and Wellness of Students* (NASN, 2021b). School nurses can and should take a leading, if not contributing, role in supporting the adoption and implementation of evidence-based programs to support improved prevention and response to violence in schools. They should be knowledgeable about federal legislation that directs policy and funding. For example, in June 2022, President Biden signed into law the Bipartisan Safer Communities Act (BSCA) legislation that:

> expands vital mental health services and provides additional support for States and districts to design and enhance initiatives that will promote safer, more inclusive, and positive school environments for all students, educators, and school staff...The BSCA includes funding through Title IV, Part A of the Elementary and Secondary Education Act (ESEA) for SEAs to competitively award subgrants to high-need LEAs to establish safer and healthier learning environments, and to prevent and respond to acts of bullying, violence, and hate that impact our school communities at individual and systemic levels, among other programs and activities. The Department has designated this component of the BSCA the Stronger Connections Grant Program (APHA, 2018, paragraphs 1-2).

NASN issued "*ESSA Talking Points for School Nurses*" in July 2016, which highlights the increased opportunity for school nurses to make an impact at their school and local levels on indicators such as data collected for ESSA-required report cards on incidences of violence, bullying, harassment, and chronic absenteeism (NASN, 2016). NASN had previously issued several statements about the school nurse's role related to school violence, including preventing school violence (NASN, 2018a), bullying (NASN, 2018b), and the use of restraints, seclusion, and corporal punishment in the school setting (NASN, 2021a).

The school nurse's role related to violence in schools includes:
- assessment of school climate and student reports of bullying and violence;
- gain and share knowledge about preventing and responding to violence;
- communication with school colleagues and safety teams about students at risk; and
- responding as effectively as possible during and after a violent event and practicing self-care in the face of violence in schools (NASN, 2018).

The following guidelines are found in these statements as well as other referenced resources:

1. **Assess the school climate and student reports of bullying and violence.**
   School nurses should seek out Youth Risk Behavior Survey data to understand students' reports of violence, bullying, mental health, and perception of adult support at school and home. School nurses should also determine how his/her school or district level data compares to other like communities and if the data shows a trend over time. For example, the percentage of students reporting carrying a weapon on school property may be lower than in similar communities; however, data from the past three surveys may demonstrate an increase, suggesting a need for a closer look at why more students are reporting weapon-carrying.

   Other risk factors identified by the CDC Division of Violence Prevention, which may contribute to violence in youth, are listed in Figure 8 (adapted from CDC, 2022c):

Figure 8. CDC Risk factors for violence

Individual	Family	Peer and Social	Community
History of violent victimization	Harsh, lax, or inconsistent disciplinary practices	Association with delinquent peers	Diminished economic opportunities
History of early aggressive behavior	Parental substance abuse or criminality	Involvement in gangs	High concentration of poor residents
Involvement with drugs, alcohol, or tobacco	Poor monitoring and supervision of children	Social rejection by peers	High level of transiency
Deficits in social, cognitive, or information processing abilities	Low parental involvement	Poor academic performance	High level of family disruption
Anti-social beliefs and attitudes	Low parental education and income	Low commitment to school and school failure	Low levels of community participation
High emotional distress			Socially disorganized neighborhoods

School nurses should also be aware of protective factors, as nurses can have a direct positive impact by supporting attitudes and behaviors that reduce the risk of violence. Based on multiple studies, the CDC has proposed protective factors, including the following listed in Figure 9 (adapted from CDC, 2022c):

Figure 9. Protective factors for violence

Individual	Family	Peer and Social
High academic achievement	Connectedness to family or adults outside the family	Close emotional relationships with those at school
Positive social orientation	Ability to discuss problems with parents	Commitment to school
Highly developed social skills/competencies	High parental expectations about school performance	Close relationship with non-deviant peers
Highly developed skills for realistic planning	Frequent shared activity with parents	Exposure to positive school climates
Religiosity	Parental modeling of constructive strategies for coping with problems	

School nurses may contribute to developing and maintaining a positive climate by supporting supervision, clear behavior rules and consequences, and prioritizing interest and engagement in student activities. School nurses must partner with other school staff, family, and community members to reduce the stigma of mental illness and support struggling families (Rollins, 2013).

2. **Communicate with school colleagues and safety teams about students at risk.**
   School nurses should share concerns about students at risk for violence during student assistance and crisis intervention team meetings with administrators and counselors. School nurses should know that

even though deaths from mass shootings account for a small fraction of total deaths, "most people who commit a mass shooting are in crisis leading up to it and are likely to leak their plans to others, presenting opportunities for intervention" (Gramlich, 2022; National Institute of Justice; 2022, para. 2). It is important for school nurses to be present during these meetings to advocate for students about whom they may have concerns. For students exhibiting escalating behaviors, verbalizations of access to weapons, and intent to harm, the school nurse would notify the administration and law enforcement to protect the safety of the student and others.

School nurses should be aware that, although student records are generally confidential under the *Family Education Rights and Privacy Act* ("FERPA"), FERPA provides an exception for the disclosure of otherwise-confidential information "to protect the health or safety of the student or other persons" in connection with an emergency (20 U.S.C. § 1232g(b)(1)(i)). In determining whether such an emergency exists, the district "may take into account the totality of the circumstances pertaining to a threat to the health or safety of a student or other individuals" 34 C.F.R. § 99.36(c).

School nurses should be familiar with individual state laws pertaining to schools and bullying and stay abreast of any changes to state statutes. Most states have laws requiring schools to adopt bullying prevention policies or programs. *See, e.g.,* Ariz. Rev. Stat. § 15-2301 (requiring hazing prevention policy), Fla. Ed. Code. § 1006.135 (requiring hazing policy); Mo. Rev. Stat. § 160.775.1 (requiring anti-bullying policy); Ohio Rev. Stat. § 3301.22 (requiring harassment prevention policy). For questions, always consult the school board attorney and follow district policy on school violence and bullying. If necessary, nurses should determine the procedures for contacting district counsel so that the school nurse can access school attorneys to seek legal advice.

3. **Gain and share knowledge about preventing violence in schools.**
    School nurses should assess if their schools have violence prevention programs, which often involve social-emotional curricula across multiple grades which focus on building healthy relationships and managing challenging emotions such as anger, frustration, disappointment, and sadness. These programs have been shown to be successful in helping prevent violence at the individual and community levels (CDC, 2021c). Additionally, school nurses can advocate for a welcoming physical environment that contributes significantly to a positive school climate, such as adequate natural lighting, cleanliness, and artwork. School nurses can promote safe storage of firearms; New Jersey school nurse Robin Cogan has provided free gun locks to her school community to promote safe storage using the harm reduction model of access and education (Cogan, 2021).

4. **Respond effectively as possible during and after a violent event.**
    According to the USDE, nurses and other school personnel have essential responsibilities related to school violence: "Learn the signs of a potentially volatile situation and ways to prevent an incident. Learn the best steps for survival when faced with an active shooter situation. Be prepared to work with law enforcement during the response" (USDE, 2013, p. 59). School nurses should know their school district policies about engaging law enforcement. If possible, school nurses should learn and practice de-escalation practices through crisis intervention training. According to the NASN, school nurses can be active members of crisis intervention teams, participate on school safety committees and assist with implementing violence

prevention programs (NASN, 2018a). School nurses can learn more about responding to a violent person in school from government and private organizations offering information and online videos listed under Resources, such as the U.S. Department of Homeland Security (2016), USDE (2013), Indiana State Police (2016), and ALICE Training Institute (2023). However, the school nurse should know that some students may be traumatized by simulations or active shooter drills, and increasingly, educators and parents are questioning the risk-benefits of such drills, especially on student mental health (Cogan, 2019; Moore-Petinak et al., 2020; Simonetti, 2020).

As with most emergency situations, being prepared for potential violence may lead to a more effective response. School nurses should collaborate as needed with key stakeholders, such as parents/guardians, teachers, school counselors, principals, and local fire and police departments, to plan for students with special healthcare needs. For example, students with diabetes should always have access to necessary medications, testing supplies, and food, especially if a lockdown might last more than several hours. When developing the Individual Healthcare Plan at the start of the school year, the school nurse should discuss with family members how medical needs might be addressed during a prolonged lockdown. Parents of students with special healthcare needs are encouraged to bring additional supplies to school in case their child is separated from them beyond the school/workday (AAP, 2015). The district should plan for special education students needing certain health services in the event of a lockdown. "School health services and school nurse services means health services that are designed to enable a child with a disability to receive FAPE as described in the child's IEP" (34 C.F.R. § 300.34(c) (13). An individualized plan should be developed and shared with school staff in accordance with FERPA. School nurses can participate with other school staff in lockdown tabletop simulations to identify gaps or updates needed to plan for students with special healthcare needs.

5. **Practice self-care in the face of violence in schools.**
   During and after an episode of school violence, the school nurse must be aware of how they respond to the trauma. After the event, students and staff may look to the school nurse for support. Being patient and recognizing the impact of the violence on all involved will help the nurse cope effectively. It is important to debrief after an event with those who were involved. Outside agencies and their experienced, professional staff (Emergency Medical System [EMS], local mental health organizations, etc.) will often lead a debriefing to assist those who witnessed a traumatic event. Getting enough quality sleep, healthy food, physical activity, and relaxation activities are essential for helping to heal after trauma.

Figure 10. Summary of School Nurse Responses to Violence Types

TYPE	SCHOOL NURSE ACTIONS AND PRIORITIES
Bullying	Assess the student, refer to administration/guidance, and provide student support.
Cyber-bullying	Identify student(s), notify administration/guidance, and provide student support.
Mental Health Crisis	Assess student. Follow district protocol (e.g., crisis response team) for de-escalation and contact behavioral health emergency services or activate EMS.
Physical assault	Assess and treat any physical injuries, including activating emergency medical services (EMS) if needed, report to administration, and report to parents.
Sexual assault	Assess and treat student/staff, report to police, call Sexual Assault Nurse Examiner, and activate EMS.
Student on Student	Assess and treat any physical injuries, including activating emergency medical services (EMS) if needed, report to administration, and report to parents.
Student on Staff	Assess and treat staff, report to administration, and activate emergency medical services (EMS) if needed.
Staff on Student	Assess and treat the student, including activating emergency medical services (EMS) if needed, and report to administration and child protective services.
Escalating Violence/ Violent Intruder	Follow pre-planned district procedures, including lockdown, barricade, evacuation, and defensive/counter procedures. Make sure students with chronic conditions have access to what they will need. Maintain access to emergency equipment, student information, and communication devices. In a lockdown, remain in place until cleared by authorities according to district protocols.

6. **Build resilience.**

School nurses should understand the importance of supporting the capacity of youth to recover from difficulties. According to the AAP, "Resilience is critical to a child's ability to navigate through stressful events – even those that are traumatic – successfully. Resilience provides a buffer between the child and the traumatic event, mitigating the negative effects that could result, such as physical, emotional, and behavioral health issues that can last even into adulthood" (APA, 2017, para. 3). School nurses promoting the development of protective factors will assist students in building resilience even in the event of a violent incident.

CONCLUSION

The national survey data show that different types of violence in school have decreased over the past 25 years. However, there has been an increase in school shootings, and more students are reporting not attending school due to safety concerns. A small percentage of students continue to report carrying weapons, and even more admit to engaging in physical fighting at school. Tragically, violence from individuals known and unknown to schools continues to take its toll on the physical and emotional well-being of school community members. As challenging as it may be to prepare, respond, and recover from violence in schools, the school nurse has the responsibility and capacity to save lives and support the primary mission of schools: helping students learn to be active, engaged citizens.

RESOURCES

ALICE Training Institute. (2023). *ALICE Training K-12 program*. https://www.alicetraining.com/our program/alice-training/k12-education/

American Academy of Pediatrics. (2021) https://www.aap.org/traumaguide - trauma toolbox

American Academy of Pediatrics. (2023). Corporal Punishment in Schools. Policy Statement. https://doi.org/10.1542/peds.2023-063284

American Psychological Association for Parents & Educators. http://www.apa.org/helpcenter/resilience.aspx

Centers for Disease Control and Prevention. About the CDC-Kaiser ACE Study . https://www.cdc.gov/violenceprevention/acestudy/about.html

Centers for Disease Control and Prevention. Intimate Partner Violence: Prevention Strategies https://www.cdc.gov/violenceprevention/intimatepartnerviolence/prevention.html

Centers for Disease Control and Prevention. School-Associated Violent Death Study. https://www.cdc.gov/violenceprevention/youthviolence/schoolviolence/savd.html

Centers for Disease Control and Prevention. Understanding School Violence: Fact Sheet http://www.cdc.gov/violenceprevention/pdf/School_Violence_Fact_Sheet-a.pdf

Centers for Disease Control and Prevention. School Violence: Prevention http://www.cdc.gov/violenceprevention/youthviolence/schoolviolence/prevention.html

Centers for Disease Control and Prevention. (2016). A Comprehensive Technical Package for the Prevention of Youth Violence and Association Risk Behaviors. https://www.cdc.gov/violenceprevention/communicationresources/pub/technical-packages.html

Center for Disease Control and Prevention (2023). YRBS Survey: Data Summary and Trends 2011-2021 https://www.cdc.gov/healthyyouth/data/yrbs/yrbs_data_summary_and_trends.htm

Indiana State Police. (2016). Unarmed Response to an In-School Active Shooter Event, https://www.youtube.com/watch?v=zeoZmsXpc6k

PTA: Checklist to Help Prevent Violence in Schools. (n.d.). http://www.pta.org/content.cfm?ItemNumber=984

Service Learning: A School Violence Prevention Strategy. (n.d.). http://www.crf-usa.org/school-violence/school-violence-prevention-strategy.html

School Shootings Reach Unprecedented High In 2022. (2022, December 21). https://www.k12dive.com/news/2022-worst-year-for-school-shootings/639313/?utm_source=Sailthru&utm_medium=email&utm_campaign=Issue:%202022-12-21%20K-12%20Dive%20%5Bissue:46914%5D&utm_term=K-12%20Dive

National Association of School Nurses. (2021). *The Behavioral Health and Wellness of Students* (Position Statement) https://journals.sagepub.com/doi/abs/10.1177/1942602X211066656

National Center for Education Statistics. https://nces.ed.gov/fastfacts/display.asp?id=49

National Gang Center. *National Youth Gang Survey Analysis.* https://nationalgangcenter.ojp.gov/survey-analysis

The Evolution of State School Safety Laws since the Columbine School Shooting. Temkin, D., Stuart-Cassel, V., Lao, K., Nunez, B., Kelley, S., Kelley, C. (2020, February 12). ChildTrends, https://www.childtrends.org/publications/evolution-state-school-safety-laws-columbine

U.S. Department of Education. (2013). *Guide for developing high quality school emergency operations plans*. http://www2.ed.gov/about/offices/list/oese/oshs/rems-k-12-guide.pdf

U.S. Department of Homeland Security. (2016). *Active shooter preparedness*. https://www.cisa.gov/topics/physical-security/active-shooter-preparedness

Case Law

Doe v. Claiborne County, Tenn., 103 F.3d 495 (6th Cir. 1996) https://caselaw.findlaw.com/court/us-6th-circuit/1201384.html

Maness v. City of New York, 607 N.Y.S. 2d 325, 325 (N.Y. App. Div. 1st Dep't 1994). https://www.leagle.com/decision/1994548201ad2d3472373

Mirand v. City of New York, 84 N.Y.2d 44,46 (N.Y. 1994). http://law.justia.com/cases/new-york/court-of-appeals/1994/84-n-y-2d-44-0.html

William G., 40 Cal. 3d 550, 221 Cal. Rptr. 118 (1985). http://scocal.stanford.edu/opinion/re-william-g-23395

REFERENCES

20 USC 1232g: Family educational and privacy rights. http://uscode.house.gov/view.xhtml?req=granuleid:USC-prelim-title20-section1232g&num=0&edition=prelim

ALICE Training Institute (2013-2016). *ALICE training K-12 program.* https://www.alicetraining.com/our-program/alice-training/k12-education/

American Academy of Child & Adolescent Psychiatry. (2014). *Corporal punishment in schools* (Position Statement). https://www.Aacap.Org/Aacap/Policy_Statements/1988/Corporal_Punishment_In_Schools.Aspx

American Academy of Pediatrics. (2016). *Role of the school nurse in providing school health services.* https://doi.org/10.1542/peds.2016-0852

American Academy of Pediatrics (2022, October 8). *Firearm violence prevention demands a public safety approach like regulation of motor vehicles.* https://www.aap.org/en/news-room/news-releases/conference-news-releases/american-academy-of-pediatrics--firearms-violence-prevention-demands-a-public-safety-approach-like-regulation-of-motor-vehicles

American Psychological Association. (2013). *Gun violence: Prediction, prevention, and policy.* https://www.apa.org/pubs/reports/gun-violence-report.pdf

American Public Health Association (2018, November 13). *Violence is a public health issue: Public health is essential to understanding and treating violence in the U.S.* https://apha.org/policies-and-advocacy/public-health-policy-statements/policy-database/2019/01/28/violence-is-a-public-health-issue

Carson, D., and Esbensen, F.A., (2017). *Gangs in School: Exploring the Experiences of Gang Involved Youth.* https://journals.sagepub.com/doi/10.1177/1541204017739678

Centers for Disease Control and Prevention. (2016a). *Understanding school violence (Fact Sheet).* https://www.cdc.gov/violenceprevention/pdf/school_violence_fact_sheet-a.pdf

Centers For Disease Control and Prevention. (2021a, September 2). *Fast fact: Preventing school violence.* https://www.cdc.gov/violenceprevention/youthviolence/schoolviolence/fastfact.html

Centers for Disease Control and Prevention. (2021b, September 2). *School associated violent death study.* https://www.cdc.gov/violenceprevention/youthviolence/schoolviolence/SAVD.html

Centers for Disease Control and Prevention. (2021c, September 2). *School violence: Prevention.* https://www.cdc.gov/violenceprevention/youthviolence/schoolviolence/fastfact.html

Centers for Disease Control and Prevention. (2022a, January 18). *The public health approach to violence prevention.* https://www.cdc.gov/violenceprevention/about/publichealthapproach.html

Center for Disease Control and Prevention (2022b, January 18). *Timeline of violence as a public health issue.* https://www.cdc.gov/violenceprevention/about/timeline.html

Centers for Disease Control and Prevention. (2022c, April 21). *Youth violence: Risk and protective factors.* https://www.cdc.gov/violenceprevention/youthviolence/riskprotectivefactors.html

Center for Disease Control. (2023a, January 27). *Fast facts: Preventing teen dating violence.* https://www.cdc.gov/violenceprevention/intimatepartnerviolence/teendatingviolence/fastfact.html

Center for Disease Control and Prevention (2023b, April 27). YRBS Survey: Data Summary and Trends 2011-2021 https://www.cdc.gov/healthyyouth/data/yrbs/yrbs_data_summary_and_trends.htm

Centers for Disease Control and Prevention. (2023c, June 29). *Fast Facts: Preventing Adverse Childhood Experiences.* https://www.cdc.gov/violenceprevention/aces/fastfact.html

Cogan, R. (2019, November 21). *The relentless school nurse: "Active-shooter drills in schools may do more harm than good."* https://relentlessschoolnurse.com/2019/11/21/the-relentless-school-nurse-active-shooter-drills-in-schools-may-do-more-harm-than-good/

Cogan, R. (2021, December 16). *The relentless school nurse: More guns locked up, equals fewer school lock downs.* https://relentlessschoolnurse.com/2021/12/16/the-relentless-school-nurse-more-guns-locked-up-equals-fewer-school-lock-downs/

Cohen, J. S., Donnelly, K., x Patel, S.J., Badolato, G. M., Boyle, M. D., McCarter, R., & Goyal, M.K. (2021). Firearms injuries involving young children in the United States during the covid-19 pandemic. *Pediatrics* July 2021; 148 (1), e2020042697. https://doi.org/10.1542/peds.2020-042697

Cox, J.,Rich, S., Chong, L., Trevor, LL., Muyskens, J., Ulmanu, M., 2022. *Students have experience gun violence*. https://www.washingtonpost.com/education/interactive/school-shootings-database/

Dahl, R. (September 2022). *Is corporal punishment legal in schools?* https://www.findlaw.com/legalblogs/law-and-life/is-corporal-punishment-legal-in-schools/

Findlaw. Texas Corporal Punishment in Public Schools (2018) https://www.findlaw.com/state/texas-law/texas-corporal-punishment-in-public-schools-laws.html#:~:text=In%20Texas%2C%20corporal%20punishment%20in%20public%20schools%20is,in%20public%20schools%20laws%20in%20the%20table%20below.

Gersohff, E., & Font, S. (2016). Corporal punishment in U.S. public schools: Prevalence, disparities in use, and status in state and federal policy. *Society for Research in Child Development, 30*(1). https://srcd.onlinelibrary.wiley.com/doi/10.1002/j.2379-3988.2016.tb00086.x

Goldstick, J.E., Cunningham, R.M., Carter, P.M. (2022, May 19). *Current causes of death in children and adolescents in the United States. New England Journal of Medicine*, 386(20), 1955-1956 https://www.nejm.org/doi/full/10.1056/NEJMc2201761

Gramlich, J. (2022, Feb 3). *What the data says about gun deaths in the U.S.* Pew Research Center. https://www.pewresearch.org/fact-tank/2022/02/03/what-the-data-says-about-gun-deaths-in-the-u-s/

Hemez, P., Brent, J. J., & Mowen, T. J. (2020). Exploring the school-to-prison pipeline: how school suspensions influence incarceration during young adulthood. *Youth Violence and Juvenile Justice, 18*(3), 235–255. https://doi.org/10.1177/1541204019880945

Indiana State Police. (2016). *Unarmed response to an in-school active shooter event.* https://www.youtube.com/watch?v=zeoZmsXpc6k

K-12 School Shooting Database. https://k12ssdb.org/

Moore-Petinak, N., Waselewski, M., Patterson, B. A., & Chang, T. (2020). Active shooter drill in the United States: a national study of youth experiences and perceptions. North American Primary Care Research Group 2019 Annual Meeting. *Journal of Adolescent Health, 67*(4), 509-513. https://www.jahonline.org/article/S1054-139X(20)30320-7/fulltext

National Association of School Nurses (2016). *ESSA talking points for school nurses.* https://www.nasn.org/portals/0/advocacy/2016_ESSA_Talking_Points.pdf

National Association of School Nurses (2021a). *Use of restraints, seclusion and corporal punishment in the school setting* (Position Statement). https://www.nasn.org/nasn-resources/professional-practice-documents/position-statements/ps-restraints

National Association of School Nurses. (2021b). *The behavioral health and wellness of students* (Position Statement). https://www.nasn.org/nasn-resources/professional-practice-documents/position-statements/ps-behavioral-health

National Institute of Justice [NIJ]. (2022, August 22). Five Facts about K-12 School Shootings. https://nij.ojp.gov/topics/articles/five-facts-about-mass-shootings-k-12-schools

Norrie, Doug, (2022), *School-to-prison pipeline statistics – Are educational policies leading to incarceration. https://go2tutors.com/school-to-prison-pipeline-statistics-2/*

Office of Justice and Juvenile Delinquency. (2019). Preventing intimate partner violence across the lifespan: a technical package of programs, policies, and practices. www.cdc.gov/violenceprevention/pdf/ipv-factsheet508.pdf

Rollins, J.A. (2013). The aftermath of December 14, 2014. *Pediatric Nursing, 39*, 10-11. https://www.researchgate.net/publication/236091467_The_aftermath_of_December_14_2012

School Corporal Punishment in the United States. (2023, April 1). In *Wikipedia*. https://en.wikipedia.org/wiki/School_corporal_punishment_in_the_United_States

Simonetti, J.A. (2020). Active shooter safety drills and US students-should we take a step back? *JAMA Pediatrics*, 174(11), 1021-1022. https://doi.org/10.1001/jamapediatrics.2020.2592

Startz, D. (2022, January 14). Corporal punishment, schools, and race: an update. Brookings Institute Brown Center Chalkboard. https://www.brookings.edu/blog/brown-center-chalkboard/2022/01/14/corporal-punishment-schools-and-race-an-update/

Substance Abuse & Mental Health Services Administration. (2022). *Alternatives to seclusion and restraint.* https://www.samhsa.gov/trauma-violence

Rajan, S., Reeping, P. M., Ladhani, Z., Vasudevan, L. M., & Branas, C. C. (2022). Gun violence in K-12 schools in the United States: Moving towards a preventive (versus reactive) framework. *Preventive medicine*, *165*(Pt A), 107280. https://doi.org/10.1016/j.ypmed.2022.107280

Sparks, S., & Harwin, A. (2016). Corporal punishment use found in schools in over 21 states. *Education Week*. http://www.edweek.org/ew/articles/2016/08/23/corporal-punishment-use-found-in-schools-in.html

U.S. Department of Education. (2012). *Restraint and seclusion: Resource document.* https://www2.ed.gov/policy/seclusion/index.html

U.S. Department of Education. (2013). *Guide for developing high quality school emergency operations plans*. https://www.samhsa.gov/resource/dbhis/guide-developing-high-quality-school-emergency-operations-plans

U.S. Department of Education. (2016a). King sends letter to states calling for an end to corporal punishment in schools https://safesupportivelearning.ed.gov/news/king-sends-letter-states-calling-end-corporal-punishment-schools

U.S. Department of Education. (2016b). *2013-2014 Civil rights data collection: A first look*. https://www2.ed.gov/about/offices/list/ocr/docs/2013-14-first-look.pdf" pdf

U.S. Department of Education. (2023, January 19). *Bipartisan Safer Communities Act*. https://oese.ed.gov/bipartisan-safer-communities-act/

U.S. Department of Education, Office for Civil Rights. (2023). *Corporal Punishment in Public Schools*. https://ocrdata.ed.gov/assets/downloads/Corporal_Punishment_Part4.pdf

U.S. Department of Homeland Security. (2016). *Active shooter preparedness*. https://www.cisa.gov/topics/physical-security/active-shooter-preparedness

U.S. Senate, Health, Education, Labor, and Pensions Committee. (2014). Dangerous use of seclusion and restraints in schools remains widespread and difficult to remedy: A review of ten cases. https://files.eric.ed.gov/fulltext/ED544755.pdf

World Health Organization. (2017). *Violence*. http://www.who.int/topics/violence/en/

SCHOOL STAFF INTERACTIONS

The following section of the book is dedicated to the School Staff Interactions in the school setting. The topics include the Provision of Health Services for School Staff, School Staff Training, and Employment Issues and Conflict Resolution.

Although the main focus of school nursing practice is directed at the student and their family, school nurses interact with various school staff and administrators on a daily basis. These chapters will provide a framework for the school nurse to train school staff when appropriate, intervene for emergent or urgent health concerns, and assist in the development of policies to guide safe practice.

Chapter 53

SCHOOL STAFF: PROVISION OF HEALTH SERVICES

Brenna L. Morse, PhD, FNP-BC, NCSN, CNE, PMGT-BC, FNASN, FAAN*

DESCRIPTION OF ISSUE

Schools employ adult workers who may request care from the school nurse. School nurses, and their employers, must comply with laws, regulations, and policies concerning worker health and safety; especially when such policies conflict with or go beyond the school nurse's scope of practice and established duties. Schools may have motivations beyond regulatory compliance to support teacher and staff wellness via the provision of school nursing care. For example, teachers' health is associated with students' academic achievement (Madigan & Kim, 2021). Staff days out of work due to illness may leave students with too few staff members to care for them. Health plan providers (also known as health insurance companies) may incentivize subscribers to improve their health status to lower insurance costs for school districts. School staff members may also become injured while at work, and schools may need to determine the extent and nature of the injury and the need for compensation while the staff member is unable to work (Division of Federal Employees' Compensation [DFEC], 2016). The COVID-19 pandemic presented a need for many school nurses to discuss symptoms, test, assess, and exclude school staff from work (Morse et al., In Press; Lee et al., 2021). As a result, school nurses are being asked to provide care to adult staff members. It is imperative for the school nurse to understand the legal requirements and practice implications of providing health services to staff.

BACKGROUND

Over the last 15 years, the National Institute for Occupational Safety and Health (NIOSH) *Total Worker Health Program* has provided guidance and programming to employers to protect the safety and health of workers and to advance their well-being by creating safer and healthier work and work environments (Schill et al., 2019). Workers across industries may face health risks at work, such as contracting communicable illnesses, musculoskeletal injuries, chemical exposures, occupational dust inhalation, or mental illness secondary to workplace bullying. Teachers and other staff members generally value the professional opinion of the school nurse and often turn to this trusted expert for health information, health monitoring, first aid care, illness assessment, and injury evaluation. In fact, during the COVID-19 pandemic, teachers felt safer in schools when the school nurse was present and able to support their health (Santana-López et al., 2023). School administrators may ask a nurse to determine an employee's fitness for duty or question if a staff person should be excluded from contagion or engage the school nurse in other aspects related to staff health.

In industry, occupational health nurses engage in injury assessments and health-promoting activities with employees, evaluate the work area and procedures to reduce health risks, and address episodic concerns (American Association of Occupational Health Nursing, 2023). For example, an occupational health nurse may provide over-the-counter (OTC) medications for employees with minor ailments to address pain and minimize unnecessary absence. While all of these activities are within the scope of practice of registered nurses, the school nurse and occupational health nurse fill two substantially separate professional roles. Like school nursing,

---

*Original author: Linda Caldart Olson, MS, BSN, RN, FASHA (2017)

occupational health nursing is a distinct specialty with its own national certification exam, national association, and scope and standards. There are many common denominators in current school nursing practice, but also many differences in settings, roles, state laws, and school employment practices. Although school nursing and occupational and environmental health nursing are very similar, the most obvious differences between school nurses and occupational nurses are in the target population and organizational mission. School nurses work in educational settings where the primary focus is the health and well-being of students. Occupational health nurses work in a variety of workplaces, generally employing adults, e.g., factories and offices, with a focus on the health and safety of workers. While school nurses generally want to help and are often willing to use their expertise to support the health of all people, including adult staff members, such professional generosity presents questions of capacity, roles, responsibilities, and liability. Ultimately, a decision to involve school nurses in providing care to adult staff members should be based on a thorough assessment of their capacity, training, legal considerations, documented job description, and collaboration with other clinicians. Both students and adult staff members should be safe and healthy in the school; however, the school nurse must be able to effectively fulfill their professional obligations to the students first and foremost.

IMPLICATIONS FOR SCHOOL NURSE PRACTICE

While student health is the primary focus of school nursing practice, caring for the entire school community is an important part of the professional role. Whether caring for the whole school community includes providing direct care to employees (e.g., assessments, medication administration) depends on local regulations, the school nurse's job description, and the policies of specific schools and districts. When providing nursing care to any member of the population, nurses are at risk for liability and/or negligence. An increasing focus on providing more comprehensive school staff health services, including general wellness programs, presents many legal quandaries. It has also raised the issue of the school nurse's capacity to accomplish all that is needed of the students and their families while also serving staff health needs. *(See Chapter 3 for more information on scope and standards).*

Liability, Negligence, and Duty

Liability is in part determined by the standard of care, which is what an ordinary prudent professional with the same qualifications would provide under the same or similar circumstances. Professional negligence is failure to act to the standard. To be negligent, it must be proven that a nurse had a duty to provide care, the nurse failed to accomplish the duty, the failure caused harm, and a person was harmed or injured. The school nurse must be aware of the duty the school has in providing staff services and the role, if any, the school nurse is specifically expected to take on. Importantly, the nurse must determine if what might be asked is within the scope of practice, can be safely accomplished, is in their job description, represents ethical practice, and is what the law requires. The job description should include the specific language of the school nurse's role and purpose in the provision of staff health services and a listing of specific job functions. Functions that may or may not be in a school nurse's job description but are common health care requests from staff, including over-the-counter medications, emergency care for staff, chronic condition monitoring, and wellness program provision. Other documents that may provide guidance to the school nurse when determining the appropriateness of a request for staff care include the code of ethics, specific state nurse practice act, requirements of the nurse's professional malpractice insurance carrier, professional organization position papers, and resolutions, staff contracts, the employee handbook, school policies, health plan policies, as well as state health and labor laws.

School nurses are well advised to ensure they are up to date on the proper standard of care for circumstances they are likely to see in their practice. In the event that the school nurse's role does include the provision of employee health services, the nurse is encouraged to engage in nursing continuing professional development specific to the care of the adult client. For example, the nurse may enroll in seminars or courses reviewing adult metabolic conditions, addressing injuries in the adult population, or other primary care topics with a focus on the worker. Such continuing education should be in excess of that relevant to the health and care of schoolchildren.

Additionally, the school nurse, school administrators, and district legal team must also come to an agreement on episodic services that will be provided and specific procedures, medical orders, documentation, and reporting activities relevant to the care of school staff. For example, if the staff has authorized access to over-the-counter medication, but the school nurse will not dispense medication to staff, a policy to that effect should be written. Generally, the school nurse should encourage adult staff members and administrators to self-obtain and self-administer medications as they see fit, given their health context and current condition.

> Of note, school nurses who are trained and licensed as nurse practitioners **may not prescribe medication**, even over-the-counter medication, in the school setting **unless they are employed by the school as an advance practice registered nurse.**

Specific to emergency situations, it is crucial for school nurses to maintain basic life support (BLS) certification, including essential life-saving techniques, such as cardiopulmonary resuscitation (CPR), automated external defibrillator (AED) use, and basic airway management. School nurses should maintain and are strongly encouraged to seek certification in a method that allows for hands-on training and testing. This will allow the school nurse to respond effectively to emergency situations and render basic life support to a staff member in the school building as needed. Regarding emergencies other than those of a cardiopulmonary nature (e.g., anaphylaxis or overdose), school nurses may provide care in support of sustaining life while emergency transport is on the way to the school building.

Other State and Federal Provisions for Employee Health

The Occupational Safety and Health Administration (OSHA) is a regulatory agency in the United States that supports safe or healthful employment and places of employment. One example of an OSHA safety requirement is blood-borne pathogen training. The organization requires employees who may be exposed to blood-borne pathogens and other infectious materials in the workplace to undergo training on how to prevent such exposures and what to do in the event of an exposure. While teachers and other staff may not routinely work with needles and sharps as many healthcare workers do, there are risks such as human bites in the school setting (Collins et al., 2019). The standard contains specific requirements for training content, targeted staff, frequency, documentation, and listing of to whom an employee should report an exposure and from whom to seek first aid care (Denault & Gardner, 2023).

All employers are required to provide worker compensation insurance (U.S. Department of Labor [DOL], 2023a, 2023b). When an employee has a job-related injury, an employer must follow specific steps in reporting the injury, recording the injury, and determination of fitness for duty. If a school nurse is to be involved in any of these aspects, the role must be clearly documented in the job description. When components such as employee exams following a worksite injury be a part of the school nurse's role, assigning this duty must not exceed local laws and regulations or the policies of the worker's compensation insurance. For example, the school nurse would typically be the first person to provide care and initial disposition to an injured or ill worker and determine the need to seek further medical care or be sent home. However, if there is any question as to how long an employee must stay home when they should return, or if they can return earlier, that disposition should be left to a medical or appropriately licensed healthcare professional.

Workers' compensation claims involve complex processes and potential legal proceedings, which can result in expenses for both the injured worker and the employer. Open communication is essential for all parties involved to minimize potential costs or workers' compensation disputes. School nurses are encouraged to work with district leaders to remove responsibility for these exams from their job description and expectations, as the school nurse should be permitted to focus professional time on and is an expert in the comprehensive, community-based health care of children and adolescents. Adult teachers and staff members are best served following a worksite injury by seeking an evaluation from their established primary care provider, an urgent care center treating adults, or a local emergency room, depending on the severity and acuity of the injury.

Wellness Programs

School nurses may be asked to coordinate employee wellness programs encompassing various activities and initiatives aimed at promoting the well-being of staff members. Per the interest of the school nurse and availability to do so, providing timely and topical evidence-based health promotion information that school staff members may elect to consume is well within the scope of practice of a school nurse with few legal risks. For example, the school nurse may select topics such as tick bite prevention, the importance of sunscreen use, hydration, or sleep hygiene as monthly health promotion/disease prevention topics to write about in the employee newsletter. School nurses may consider surveying staff members for topics of interest and collaborating with other school clinicians (e.g., counselors) or providers in the district (e.g., pediatricians, dentists) when determining the topics and content of health promotion information.

Wellness programs that focus on gains (e.g., steps taken by each employee per week, servings of fruits and vegetables consumed) and losses (e.g., weight loss, smoking cessation) present an opportunity for discrimination and stigma among the staff. Staff with mobility limitations or chronic conditions that may not be able to follow a specific exercise plan or diet will be excluded. Additionally, wellness programs focused on weight loss may be traumatic or triggering to employees with a history of or current eating disorders (Eikey, 2021). Even seemingly harmless steps-per-day challenges or challenges using wellness phone applications can be upsetting or the antecedent of a relapse for a staff member with a history of a harmful focus on diet and exercise metrics (Hahn et al., 2021; Motyl, 2020). Further, workplace wellness challenges have failed to demonstrate long-term differences in clinical measures of health, health spending and utilization, or employment outcomes (Song & Baicker, 2019; Jones et al., 2019; Reif et al., 2020). Issues of privacy, security, information abuse, and employee autonomy are also present (Fleming, 2020). School nurses are strongly discouraged from developing, coordinating, collecting measurements for, or encouraging participation in such workplace wellness challenges.

CONCLUSION

Providing health services to school staff can be within the standards of school nurse practice. The extent of services is dependent on multiple variables, including the capacity of the school nurse (e.g., workload, available resources, time constraints, and the nurse's specific skills and expertise) to meet the demand for staff health needs and, importantly, the documented job description. The school nurse must examine a number of issues to know if requests for staff care are achievable and safe. The individual circumstances of employment will help determine what duty the nurse has to provide staff health services. Federal and state employment laws, nurse practice acts, employment contracts, policies, handbooks, and roles of others in the school will guide the nurse, but the individual nurse is the best judge of capacity.

To establish responsibilities and for clarity, it is imperative to gather data and meet with administrative decision-makers, safety officers, human resource directors, and other relevant stakeholders. Involving the school's wellness team and collaborating with them, if available, can provide valuable input. Documenting discussions and decisions is important to protect the nurse's practice and maintain a record of agreed-upon responsibilities. By considering these variables, engaging in necessary discussions, and documenting decisions, school nurses can navigate the complexities of providing health services to school staff while upholding their professional responsibilities and ensuring the safety and well-being of all involved.

RESOURCES

Legal References

- o Amendment of Americans with Disabilities Act Title II and Title III Regulations to Implement ADA Amendments Act of 2008, 29 CFR, Subtitle B, Chapter 14, Part 1630, § 1630.14
- o Americans with Disabilities Act, 42 U.S.C. § 12101 (1990)
- o Americans with Disabilities Act Amendments Act, 42 USCA § 12101 (2008)
- o Equal Employment Opportunity Act of 1972, 42 U.S.C. §§2000e et seq. (1972)
- o Family and Medical Leave Act of 1993 (FMLA), 29 U.S.C. §2601 et seq. (1993)
- o Family Education Rights and Privacy Act (FERPA), 20 U.S.C. § 1232g, 34 C.F.R. (1974)
- o Genetic Information Nondiscrimination Act of 2008 (GINA)
- o Health Insurance Portability & Accountability Act of 1996 (HIPAA), 26 U.S.C. § 294, 42 U.S.C. §§ 201, 1395-b, (1996)
- o Individuals with Disabilities Improvement Act (IDEIA), 20 USC et seq., 64 (2004)
- o Occupational Safety and Health Act (OSHA) (1970)
- o Regulations to implement the Equal Employment (EEOC) provisions of the Americans with Disabilities Act, 29 CFR, subtitle B, Chapter 14, part 1630, §1630.14(c) (2015, July)
- o Section 504 *of the* Rehabilitation Act, 29 U.S.C. § 701 et seq. (1973)

Position Papers, Clinical Guidelines

- United States Department of Health and Human Services, Center for Disease Control and Prevention, National Institute for Occupational Safety and Health. (2021). *Let's get started with Total Worker Health approaches.* https://www.cdc.gov/niosh/twh/letsgetstarted.html

- United States Department of Labor, Occupational Safety and Health Administration. (2023). *Medical and first aid.* https://www.osha.gov/medical-first-aid

- United States Department of Labor, Occupational Safety and Health Administration. (2023). *Workplace violence.* https://www.osha.gov/workplace-violence

- United States Department of Labor, Occupational Safety and Health Administration. (2023). *Bloodborne pathogens and needle stick prevention. https://www.osha.gov/bloodborne-pathogens*

REFERENCES

American Association of Occupational Health Nurses. (2023). *Occupational health nursing as a career* https://www.aaohn.org/Practice/Become-an-Occupational-Health-Nurse

Americans with Disabilities Act, 42 U.S.C. § 12101 (1990).

Americans with Disabilities Act Amendments Act, 42 USCA § 12101 (2008).

Collins, R., Wallin, R., & Park, K. (2019). School nursing protocol for the management of human bites. *NASN School Nurse, 34*(6), 351–356. https://doi.org/10.1177/1942602X19844261

Denault, D., & Gardner, H. (2023). OSHA bloodborne pathogen standards. In *StatPearls.* StatPearls Publishing. http://www.ncbi.nlm.nih.gov/books/NBK570561/"http://www.ncbi.nlm.nih.gov/books/NBK570561/

Eikey, E. V. (2021). Effects of diet and fitness apps on eating disorder behaviours: Qualitative study. *BJPsych Open, 7*(5), e176. https://doi.org/10.1192/bjo.2021.1011

Fleming, H. K. (2020). Navigating workplace wellness programs in the age of technology and big data. *Journal of Science Policy & Governance, 17*(01). https://doi.org/10.38126/JSPG170104

Hahn, S. L., Linxwiler, A. N., Huynh, T., Rose, K. L., Bauer, K. W., & Sonneville, K. R. (2021). Impacts of dietary self-monitoring via MyFitnessPal to undergraduate women: A qualitative study. *Body Image, 39*, 221–226. https://doi.org/10.1016/j.bodyim.2021.08.010

Jones, D., Molitor, D., & Reif, J. (2019). What do Workplace Wellness Programs do? Evidence from the Illinois Workplace Wellness Study. *The Quarterly Journal of Economics, 134*(4), 1747–1791. https://doi.org/10.1093/qje/qjz023

Lee, R. L. T., West, S., Tang, A. C. Y., Cheng, H. Y., Chong, C. Y. Y., Chien, W. T., & Chan, S. W. C. (2021). A qualitative exploration of the experiences of school nurses during COVID-19 pandemic as the frontline primary health care professionals. *Nursing Outlook, 69*(3), 399–408. https://doi.org/10.1016/j.outlook.2020.12.003

Madigan, D. J., & Kim, L. E. (2021). Does teacher burnout affect students? A systematic review of its association with academic achievement and student-reported outcomes. *International Journal of Educational Research, 105*, 101714. https://doi.org/10.1016/j.ijer.2020.101714

Morse, B., Meoli, A., Samuel, C., & Carmichael, A. (In Press). School nurse experiences and changes to practice during the COVID19 pandemic. *Journal of School Nursing.*

Motyl, K. (2020). Compulsive self-tracking: When quantifying the body becomes an addiction. In U. Reichardt & R. Schober (Eds.), *Laboring bodies and the quantified self* (pp. 167–187).

Reif, J., Chan, D., Jones, D., Payne, L., & Molitor, D. (2020). Effects of a Workplace Wellness Program on Employee Health, Health Beliefs, and Medical Use: A Randomized Clinical Trial. *JAMA Internal Medicine*, *180*(7), 952. https://doi.org/10.1001/jamainternmed.2020.1321

Santana-López, B. N., Bernat-Adell, M. D., Santana-Cabrera, L., Santana-Cabrera, E. G., Ruiz-Rodríguez, G. R., & Santana-Padilla, Y. G. (2023). Attitudes and feelings towards the work of teachers who had a school nurse in their educational center during the COVID-19 pandemic. *International Journal of Environmental Research and Public Health*, *20*(4), 3571. https://doi.org/10.3390/ijerph20043571

Schill, A. L., Chosewood, L. C., & Howard, J. (2019). The NIOSH Total Worker Health® vision. In H. L. Hudson, J. A. S. Nigam, S. L. Sauter, L. C. Chosewood, A. L. Schill, & J. Howard (Eds.), *Total worker health.* (pp. 29–45). American Psychological Association. https://doi.org/10.1037/0000149-003

Song, Z., & Baicker, K. (2019). Effect of a workplace wellness program on employee health and economic outcomes: A randomized clinical trial. *JAMA*, *321*(15), 1491. https://doi.org/10.1001/jama.2019.3307

United States Department of Labor, Occupational Safety and Health Administration. (2023a). *Safety and health topics, occupational health professionals.* https://www.osha.gov/occupational-health-professionals

United States Department of Labor, Occupational Safety and Health Administration. (2023b). OSH Act of 1970. https://www.osha.gov/laws-regs/oshact/completeoshact

United States Department of Labor, Office of Workers' Compensations Programs, Division of Federal Employees' Compensation (DFEC). (2016). *State Workers' Compensation Offici*als. https://www.dol.gov/owcp/dfec/regs/compliance/wc.htm

Chapter 54

SCHOOL STAFF TRAINING

Ingrid Hopkins Duva, PhD, RN*

DESCRIPTION OF ISSUE

School nurses are responsible for various staff training 1) student-specific training due to the student's health condition and medical concerns for the staff involved with the child, and 2) training for school staff as necessary on population-based and employee issues such as universal precautions and Occupational Safety and Health Administration (OSHA) issues, and disaster and emergency plans for the safety of the school, its employees, and the student population.

Federal law generally mandates that students receive the healthcare they need to safely participate in school activities (U.S. Department of Education [USDE], 2010). As the number of students with health conditions requiring daily management increases and health, education, and social needs become increasingly complex, so does the school nurse's work (Denke & Winkleblack, 2020). Staff, including teachers, participate in the delivery of health services, and it is usually the school nurse's responsibility to train them. According to the Centers for Disease Control and Prevention (CDC), approximately 40% of children in the United States have one or more chronic health conditions, contributing to the increasing need for health care at school (National Center for Chronic Disease Prevention and Health Promotion [NCCDPHP], 2021). The 2020-2021 Child and Adolescent Health Measurement Initiative reported that almost 35% of school-age children have health concerns that moderately affect their daily activities at least some of the time (Data Resource Center for Child and Adolescent Health, 2023). This is in addition to the requirement for schools to prepare for potential health emergencies and address students' acute health needs.

A clear need exists for non-medical personnel working in school districts to have basic training about students' chronic and other health conditions. The school nurse must provide ongoing support to the school to optimize how students have their healthcare needs met and to make certain staff are trained to perform necessary tasks in students' care. Serving as a bridge between health and education, school nurses promote appropriate accommodations for students, explaining to teachers and administrators the impact health conditions have on a student's academic performance, classroom behavior, and attendance. Student health contributes to academic success, and healthy schools are environments where youth can focus on learning and can grow into healthy and successful adults (Centers for Disease Control and Prevention, [CDC], 2018; Willergodt et al., 2018).

As in healthcare in general, assuring safe care in schools is a challenge. Staff training is necessary to provide safe care for students, especially as school nurses are presented with new challenges. Global concerns are implicating the health of our society and youth in particular: emerging infectious diseases, increasing mental health illness, and climate change, to name a few. An increasing number of students with chronic conditions, combined with legislation, such as the Americans With Disabilities Act, Section 504, adverse childhood experiences, social determinants of health, and mental health issues, have expanded the breadth of school

---

*Original author: Mary Blackborow, MSN, RN, NCSN (2017)

health services, raising the complexity of student health management overall (NASN, 2016). Training staff allows for task sharing, increasing school nurse capacity and increasing the prospect for school nurses to provide more consult, leadership, and training for staff in this setting (NASN, 2016).

BACKGROUND

School nurses have population health responsibilities such as screening, prevention of communicable diseases, prevention of injury, and health promotion. School nurses are also responsible for delivering individual health services. Medical technology advancements and legislation have allowed children with severe disabilities to live longer and attend schools in their communities. The Civil Rights Movement gave rise to two federal initiatives regarding children with disabilities. Requirements for special education were first enacted in Public Law 194-92, The Education of All Handicapped Children of 1975, which was amended in 1990, 1991, and 2004 as the Individuals with Disabilities Education Improvement Act (IDEIA) (2004).

The second set was Section 504 of the Vocational Rehabilitation Act of 1973 and the Americans with Disabilities Act of 2004 (amended in 2008). These require schools to provide a free, appropriate public education (FAPE) for all children in the least restrictive environment (NASN, 2020a). These requirements contributed to the shift in focus of school nursing from screening for infectious disease, a renewed emphasis since COVID-19, to also managing acute and chronic conditions. Care management and collaboration with school staff for up to 40% of children with chronic conditions (behavioral, mental, physical) over the growing number of students at risk for new medical conditions has become a dominating focus for the school nurse (NCCDPHP, 2017).

The Patient Protection and Affordable Care Act (ACA, 2010) and Every Student Succeeds (ESSA, 2015) are two broader federal laws promoting the role of nurses in the school setting. The ACA encouraged more care coordination, invested in preventative health care, increased coverage for low-income children, and provided a payment source for more screenings (ACA, 2010). ESSA promoted more support roles for education, such as nurses, and included federal funding in recognition that student success depends on more factors than academics (ESSA, 2015). More recently and specifically, *The Future of Nursing 2020-2030* report emphasizes nurses' unique position in addressing health inequities. There is value to the upstream insight school nurses have into the social determinants of health, as this is an opportunity to work with the school population and individual students and families to address health concerns earlier (NASEM, 2021).

Despite these growing and serious school health concerns, large student-to-school nurse ratios exist. Professional recommendations are for every student to have access to a Registered Nurse every day (NASN, 2020a). Unfortunately, approximately 18% of schools report that no nurse is available. Almost 48% have part-time coverage, and of those with a nurse available, 5% staff only with a Licensed Practical Nurse (Willergodt et al., 2018). In situations of high workload or when there is no nurse on site, redistributing and delegating tasks to lower-skilled healthcare personnel are necessary to ensure that Registered Nurses have the capacity to provide more complex care, planning, and oversight. When healthcare tasks are shared, or nursing responsibility delegated, the Registered Nurse is still accountable for the student's care and training staff to provide that care; this may mean training other licensed nurses, unlicensed assistive personnel (UAPs) who may or may not be non-healthcare professionals, for example, teachers or coaches. Task shifting involves a reallocation of responsibility to a different staff member but may still require the nurse to train staff so that safe care is delivered in the school setting. The exact approach by the nurse depends on the healthcare need, the type of staff available to the student, the nurse's scope of practice, and federal and state laws. (*See Chapter 4 for more information on the delegation*).

Factors Influencing Staff Training

Teachers, coaches, and other school staff are particularly well-suited to facilitate individual student health and well-being because they have more direct contact with students (Biag et al., 2015). However, even in schools with a Registered Nurse on-site, teachers or other school staff can become overwhelmed by their students' individual health needs if they have not been properly trained.

Individual Student Needs

Individualized healthcare plans (IHP), developed by school nurses, are based on the nursing process and guide nurses' healthcare for students and staff training. Portions of the IHP may be used to communicate how to manage a student's healthcare needs and make certain all staff have the necessary information to work with these students and manage their classrooms. Emergency care plans (ECPs) are short, succinct plans in a "see this, do this' format to help teachers and staff recognize when their students are having a medical emergency and describe how to intervene (NASN, 2020b). Serious conditions such as asthma, diabetes, seizures, or anaphylaxis may call for the closest staff member's immediate, life-saving response. Staff need to be educated to recognize signs and symptoms when a student with a known condition is in distress in addition to responding to an emergent condition. Staff need to be trained if expected to provide any health service or task as part of this plan.

Nurse Scope of Practice

School nurse scope of practice is regulated by the applicable state nurse practice act, which governs what nurses can delegate to non-medical personnel and affects what is taught to school staff. Professional standards, such as the *School Nursing: Scope and Standards of Practice* (NASN, 2022) are also relevant, assuring that practice is current and based on the best evidence. Nursing codes of ethics (ANA, 2015; NASN, 2021) also advise school nurses to stay current with knowledge, act to maintain student safety, and advocate for student health.

Policy

Federal, state, and local school policies largely determine the health topics that require staff training. School nurses need to be familiar with these legislative requirements and the disease-specific legislation in their individual states as this varies. For example, under federal law, diabetes is classified as a disability. So, any school that receives federal funding or any facility that is open to the public must reasonably accommodate the special needs of children with diabetes. In addition to having an IHP, these students may require accommodations documented in a written plan developed under the applicable federal law, such as a Section 504 Plan or an Individualized Education Program (IEP). The school nurse should be a part of the Section 504 team and participate in writing the plan. Related to Section 504, the school nurse should educate staff on aspects of the student's routine and emergency care as well as explain the student's ability to self-manage. The school nurse may also train staff in tasks related to diabetes, such as carbohydrate counting and insulin administration, where allowable by state law. National resources that provide guidance on the training required for school staff are available in the resources section. (*See Chapter 13 for more information on Section 504 and 504 teams*).

State laws vary, as do staff training obligations. Requirements may be in health or education statutes, nursing regulations, or teacher training regulations. For example, some states require that all staff be trained in asthma and allergy management. In Georgia, if a school has a student attending with diabetes, state law requires at least two school personnel, not necessarily a Registered Nurse, to be trained to care for the student, and one of those staff must always be available to the student. In contrast, some states limit insulin administration to RNs only, so staff training would vary accordingly. States have specific regulations but may also provide training resources and guidelines for school staff so that students are safe and receive appropriate care, meeting federal law requirements.

Local school policies and administration will also influence the priorities for staff training. As any additional requirements are considered, the school nurse's planning for staff training is still best served by adhering to the general rule of public safety, and this may depend on school district policies, expectations, and needs specific to the school community or even the age and composition of the student body. School nurses can assess these context-specific factors and train staff accordingly (NASN, 2021). For instance, all staff would benefit from training to recognize the signs and symptoms of diabetes or life-threatening allergies. However, not all staff would need training in how to administer emergency glucagon or an epinephrine auto-injector.

Case Law

Case law interprets law based on the specific facts of the case.

> In *Irving Independent School District v. Tatro (1984),* the Supreme Court ruled that a related service must be provided if it will assist the medically fragile student to be able to learn. In the Tatro case, the related service was clean intermittent catheterization (CIC) that did not require the services of a healthcare provider, which are subject to a medical services exclusion. The court ruled that CIC could be performed by a nurse or a qualified layperson and were deemed as school health services. In the *Cedar Rapids Community School District v. Garret F. (1999)*, the Supreme Court ruled that the district must pay for continuous nursing services for the ventilator-dependent student. In this case, Garret could not attend school unless the services were provided during the school day.

Both these decisions resulted in school districts being required to provide nursing services, when needed, to support a medically fragile student being able to attend school and learn. This has also led schools to the expanded use of unlicensed assistive personnel (UAP), and delegation to help support students with complex healthcare needs due to the lack of nursing staff in many school districts.

Confidentiality

As the need for training increases, there becomes a legitimate education need to share information about students' health needs with school staff. The Family Educational Rights and Privacy Act of 1974 (FERPA) (20 U.S.C. § 1232g; 34 (CFR Part 99) and the United States Department of Education guidance provided guidelines about the confidentiality of student records. The 1996 Health Insurance Portability and Accountability Act (HIPAA)

(Pub. L. 104–191, 110 Stat. 1936) created an additional layer of confidentiality when sharing information. The publication "Joint Guidance on the Application of the Family Educational Rights and Privacy Act (FERPA) and the Health Insurance Portability and Accountability Act of 1996 (HIPAA) to Student Health Records" provides detailed information and answers to frequently asked questions about privacy records (U.S. Department of Health and Human Services & U.S. Department of Education, 2019). As discussed in other chapters of this book, school nurses must be knowledgeable about sharing confidential medical information about students within both the healthcare and school settings. State laws and guidelines may include other obligations or restrictions.   As student advocates, school nurses are responsible for protecting the rights of all students in their care (NASN, 2016). The school nurse should take the lead by explaining or training school staff to follow these guidelines as well.

Common Staff Training

Standard Precautions:

One basic component of staff training includes education on how staff can protect themselves from infectious diseases while safely working with their students. As employers, schools are required by OSHA to provide training and have available protective equipment for staff that may be exposed to bloodborne pathogens standards (BBP, 29 CFR 1910.1030). School nurses can take the lead in training staff in broader standard precautions to protect from other transmissible diseases, as recommended in healthcare settings by the Centers for Disease Control and Prevention (CDC) (OHSA, n.d.). Some states have specific mandates regarding protection from infectious diseases while others do not; therefore, the school nurse's role in training may vary from state to state and district to district. There is no better illustration of the wide policy variation that existed between schools than guidance during COVID-19. School nurses can help navigate differences and communicate local guidelines to teachers, staff, students, and families. At times, explaining healthcare policies that may be challenging to understand and designing training to promote the implementation of and adherence to safe practices. Any training on the protective practices schools and school districts implement should include the intent of the guidelines. The implementation of any policy or procedure, particularly infectious disease guidelines at the local school level, will only be effective if properly followed. This is more likely with understanding how these procedures benefit staff and students.

Emergency Training:

School staff may require additional training to respond to individual emergencies as well as population-based emergencies or disasters at school. Preparation/mitigation, preparedness, response, and recovery are the steps used in emergency management (USDE, 2013) that help provide a uniform response to emergencies. Identification of emergency plans, practice drills, and the development and communication of individual and emergency healthcare procedures for students are all necessary to evaluate the effectiveness of response (NASN, 2019). According to NASN (2019), schools that are prepared to handle individual emergencies are more likely to be prepared for community disasters. For instance, sudden cardiac arrest is a rare but fatal emergency most common in schools with high school-age athletes. Some states require training for staff in the recognition and response to this event. Defibrillator implementation programs assist the school nurse and staff in providing necessary life-saving services for Sudden Cardiac Arrest (SCA) victims of all ages. A similar approach can be used for school-wide emergencies or mass casualty training, such as implementing "Stop the

Bleed" programs. The school nurse can train or facilitate staff training to use a tourniquet to stop bleeding and save lives. School staff should be prepared and trained to meet the needs of students before, during, and after an event. School-sponsored before and after-care programs also need a plan for recognizing and responding to health-related emergencies and disasters; training in first aid, CPR, signs and symptoms of trauma, and disaster management should also be extended to these staff (NASN, 2019).

Emergencies that may occur at school include:
- Student, staff, and visitor health-related emergencies or injuries
- Mass casualty incidents
- Weather-related emergencies; and
- Hazardous materials emergencies (NASN 2019).

IMPLICATIONS FOR SCHOOL NURSE PRACTICE

Staff training related to health issues is a nursing duty unique to the school setting. Adequate staff training is likely necessary to meet the federal requirements for student inclusion, critical to assure students are safe while at school. It helps the rest of the school team function optimally. Many factors impede the ability of school nurses to provide staff training, such as workload or varying school priorities. The conflict between professional standards of care, local/state educational regulations, and ethical dilemmas can also be challenging. Clearly, this is a complex responsibility that calls for high-level nursing skills such as critical thinking, leadership, supervision of others, and effective teaching.

Framework

The nursing process universally guides practice as outlined in the *School Nursing: Scope and Standards of Practice* (NASN 2022): assessment, diagnosis, outcomes identification, planning, implementation, and evaluation. Utilizing the *Scope and Standards* enables each school nurse to customize the staff training program for their school community. The principles in the *Framework for 21st Century School Nursing Practice* (2016) provide a focus for the school nurse and will inform the training needs assessment. The principles may also apply during content development and training delivery. Once information on the need for training is collected, the planning can begin, and a training goal can be developed. Training goals should be documented, and after implementation, evaluated. Staff training needs will evolve over time, so maintaining a structure that includes documentation and evaluation will facilitate quality improvement efforts (NASN, 2016).

There needs to be collaboration with other members of the school team. One consideration to make before planning is the context; there should be an understanding of the school community and resources available to meet staff training needs. The size of the school, the acuity of students, and the number of students, school nurses, and staff are factors to consider when planning for training. Other considerations may include but are not limited to:
- Are there before and after school programs, clubs, and athletics taking place in the school or off school grounds?
- Are the bus drivers, cafeteria workers, or after-school programs district employees contracted outside the school district?

The Every Student Succeeds Act (ESSA,2015) recognized the school nurse as the care manager for students with chronic medical conditions at school. This care manager role requires that school nurses be knowledgeable about the health conditions of students and factors that can exacerbate or mitigate the impact on academic achievement. The NASN *School Nursing: Scope and Standards of Practice* (2022) Standard 13 states: "The school nurse seeks knowledge and competence that reflects the current nursing practice and promotes innovative, anticipatory thinking" (p.86). School nurses as educators should attend professional development programs, read evidence-based peer-reviewed journals, and seek feedback on performance which help them remain current on the latest trends and developments that can impact school health (NASN, 2021; NASN, 2022).

School Nurse as Leader

School nurses must be life-long learners and effective communicators with teaching skills to be able to train staff on the most current evidence-based care for their students. In the school setting, the school nurse is viewed as an expert in student health and, therefore, an informal, if not formal, leader. Exercising command communication, demonstrating the art of negotiating, and enhancing collaborative efforts by pulling in team members as needed will improve student outcomes. There are several aspects of school health that pertain to staff training where the school nurse can demonstrate leadership if appropriately able to communicate the issue.

Confidentiality

FERPA permits the sharing of confidential student individual health information when necessary for "legitimate educational purposes" (2012). However, one way to minimize the sharing of student-specific confidential information is with generalized training for all staff on how to handle potential emergencies that might arise in the school setting (McClanahan et al., 2019). Staff members need to know how to intervene in an emergency, such as recognizing the specific health condition and how to help maintain a safe environment for students and staff (McClanahan et al., 2019). Therefore, all school staff should have training in how to recognize and respond to cardiac events, drug/opioid overdoses/, respiratory distress, and seizures. (*See Chapter 12 for more information on HIPPA and FERPA).*

Unlicensed Assistive Personnel

Unlicensed assistive personnel (UAP), where laws allow, have a valuable role in assisting the school nurse in providing health services to students according to an Individualized Healthcare Plan (NCSBN &ANA, 2019). Nurses are responsible for knowing about the nurse practice act in their state and what nursing activities may be delegated. On occasion, there is a conflict between educational and health law, resulting in legal litigation to resolve the issues, such as the California case with insulin delegation (Zirkel, 2014). The California Supreme Court decision stated, "California law does permit trained, unlicensed school personnel to administer prescription medications, including insulin, in accordance with written statements of individual students' treating healthcare providers, with parental consent" (pp. 1-2), which overrode the ANA's position that per the California Nurse Practice Act, only nurses could administer insulin (American Nurses Association v. Torlakson, 2013).

Delegation

The ANA defines delegation as transferring the responsibility of performing an activity to another person while retaining accountability for the outcome (ANA & National Council of State Boards of Nursing [NCSBN], 2019). Federal and state laws, rules and regulations, employer policies and procedures/agency regulations, and professional school nursing practice standards hold school nurses accountable when delegating care in the school setting (NASN, 2018). It is imperative that school nurses understand their state nurse practice act when delegating a nursing activity to a UAP. Delegation can help schools fulfill their obligations under Section 504, the Americans with Disabilities Act (ADA), and the IDEA (Bobo, 2018).

School administrators and parents may not understand that school nurses are required to have and follow medical orders and are held to higher practice standards than parents when delivering care to students at school (Resha, 2010). The assessment for delegation accounts for the needs and condition of the student, the complexity of the task, the potential for harm, the predictability of outcome, the competence of the UAP, the degree of supervision, and parental consent (ANA, 2019).

The school nurse uses critical thinking and professional judgment when following the Five Rights of Delegation. This is necessary to be sure that the delegation or assignment is:
1. The right task
2. Under the right circumstances
3. To the right person
4. With the right directions and communication; and
5. Under the right supervision and evaluation. (NCSBN & ANA, 2019)

Despite delegation being so widely called for in nursing, school nurses often express concerns about the extent and type of delegation that occurs in this setting (Schofield, 2018). Educating nurses on delegation can reduce concerns and improve effectiveness and safe delegation. There are benefits to delegation in the school setting that can only be achieved once the school nurse trains, verifies, and documents staff competence. A critical step for delegation is supervision, which allows for the evaluation of the staff training. It is important that school nurses understand their local requirements

---

Strategies to Manage Staff Training

Be knowledgeable about current nursing practice and your student population.

Understand the state nurse practice act.

Understand the ethical implications of nursing practice.

Know the federal, state, and local statutes that pertain to both the educational and healthcare framework.

Use the *School Nursing: Scope and Standards of Practice* to guide practice.

Stay informed on school district policy as it pertains to nursing delegation issues and staff training.

Understand state delegation rules.

Utilize evidence-based guidelines for practice.

Develop standards of practice for staff training across the school district to promote best practice.

Learn how to use technology to help staff receive training and ask questions.

Educate stakeholders (teachers, administrators, parents/guardians) about delegation, the school nurses' role, and accountability.

Incorporate practice drills into emergency and crisis planning and training.

Collaborate with relevant stakeholders across disciplines to develop solutions to difficult problems.

Document all staff training.

Document unsafe staffing and unsafe practices in writing.

Understand Good Samaritan Laws in your state and other pertinent legal protections for acting in good faith.

Look to professional organizations to provide resources to promote optimal care of students.

for supervision (on-site or not) and ensure that the evaluation of delegated activities is documented and consistent.

(See Chapter 4 for more information on safe, effective delegation).

Refusal to Accept Task

In the California Supreme Court decision, "volunteered" could mean assigned with the necessary training to administer the medication and may subject the refusing staff to discipline for insubordination (Zirkel, 2014). The "right" of the teacher to refuse has emerged in teacher contract negotiations through collective bargaining, but many issues have not been decided judicially or legislatively (American Federation of Teachers, 2009; Zirkel, 2014). After the court's decision in California, the refusal of a school nurse to provide training may also result in insubordination unless collective bargaining or local policy protects the school nurse in these circumstances (Zirkel, 2014). Collaboration is important to help resolve difficult issues.

School Nurse as an Educator

As previously noted, ESSA (2015) recognized the school nurse as the care manager for students with chronic medical conditions at school. In the school setting, the nurse is viewed as the health expert, and so the expectation is that the school nurse's knowledge base remains current. Based on the *Scope and Standards of Practice* (2022), Standard 13 states: "The school nurse seeks knowledge and competence that reflects the current nursing practice and promotes innovative, anticipatory thinking" (p.86). School nurses as educators should attend professional development programs, read evidence-based peer-reviewed journals, and seek feedback on performance which help them remain current on the latest trends and developments that can impact school health (NASN, 2021; NASN, 2022).

There are resources available to ensure that health education and services the school nurse provides are proactive, based on current evidence, and follow regulatory requirements. State public health departments focus on population health and provide expert guidance on student health issues. In some states, the public health department provides the school nursing services, ensuring schools follow their latest guidelines. The CDC is also a resource on broad aspects of school health and student well-being teaching and professional development (CDC, 2023). Topics range from content ready to use for training to process strategies to manage training across individual schools or large school systems, such as e-learning or "How to build a training Cadre" (CDC, 2023).

Adult learning principles are addressed in these resources and are important to consider when designing training. School nurses should attend to the characteristics of adult learners related to self-concept, experience, orientation to learning, and readiness to learn (CDC, 2018). School staff are adults who learn best when their current knowledge and experience can be validated and if they perceive the education or training will help them perform or cope effectively with a current or immediate situation. As far as learning style, active participation should be encouraged whenever possible.

More information about school health, professional development, adult learning, and tactics can be found on the CDC website https://www.cdc.gov/healthyschools

CONCLUSION

Staff training is an identified need to manage students with chronic health conditions, address federal mandates such as blood-borne pathogen training, and address the social determinants of health to keep students healthy, safe, and ready to learn (NASN, 2016a). The school nurses are part of an educational team that can promote student success through collaboration and communication with students, families, administrators, educators, specialized instructional support staff, and paraprofessionals.

School teachers want their students to succeed and therefore view school nurses as a positive factor in helping them meet the needs of their students (Biag et al., 2015). Staff may require disease-specific information, planning for emergencies, and specific training as UAPs when care is delegated for a specific student. Communicating and collaborating with staff is important to recognize how school nurses can meet the staff and students' identified concerns and to discover any unrecognized or unmet needs.

School nurses are generally expected to know federal, state, and local laws and policies that mandate training and to be compliant with these regulations. In addition, school nurses need to understand their state nurse practice act, FERPA and HIPAA confidentiality guidelines, evidence-based practice guidelines, delegation practices, and the specific needs of their school community. There are many additional areas in which school nurses may contribute to educating staff about issues that impact student success, including but not limited to bullying, violence prevention, social determinants of health, and mental health. Effective staff training by school nurses will help ensure the health and safety of all students.

RESOURCES

American Diabetes Association. (2023). *Safe at school state laws: Training resources for school staff.* https://diabetes.org/tools-support/know-your-rights/safe-at-school-state-laws/training-resources-school-staff

Federal Emergency Management Agency. (2011). *Sample school emergency operations plan.* https://training.fema.gov/programs/emischool/el361toolkit/assets/sampleplan.pdf
NOTE: FEMA is rolling out a new training resource in July 2023. Until then, REMS has more up-to-date resources.

National Association of School Nurses. (2022). *Asthma.* https://www.nasn.org/nasn-resources/resources-by-topic/asthma

National Association of School Nurses. (2023). *IDEIA and Section 504 teams - The school nurse as an essential team member* (Position Statement). https://www.nasn.org/nasn-resources/professional-practice-documents/position-statements/ps-ideia

National Center for Chronic Disease Prevention and Health Promotion, Division of Population Health. (n.d.). *Healthy schools, Training, and professional development*. Centers for Disease Control and Prevention. Retrieved 6-1-23 from *https://www.cdc.gov/healthyschools/trainingtools.htm*

National Center for Chronic Disease Prevention and Health Promotion, Division of Population Health. (2013). *Voluntary guidelines for managing food allergies in schools and early care and education programs*. Centers for Disease Control and Prevention. *http://www.cdc.gov/healthyyouth/foodallergies/ pdf/13_243135_a_food_allergy_web_508.pdf*

National Center for Chronic Disease Prevention and Health Promotion Division of Population Health. (2022, May 23). *Chronic disease fact sheet: Healthy Schools* [Fact Sheet]. Centers for Disease Control and Prevention. https://www.cdc.gov/chronicdisease/resources/publications/factsheets/healthy-schools.htm

National Council of State Boards of Nursing & American Nurses Association. (2019). *Joint statement on delegation*. https://www.nursingworld.org/practice-policy/nursing-excellence/official-position-statements/ id/joint-statement-on-delegation-by-ANA-and-NCSBN/

National Council of State Boards of Nursing. (2023). *Nurse practice act toolkit*. https://www.ncsbn.org/npa-toolkit.htm

Office for Civil Rights. (2016). Parent and Educator Resource Guide to Section 504 in Public Elementary and Secondary Schools. U.S. Department of Education. https://www2.ed.gov/about/offices/list/ocr/docs/504-resource-guide-201612.pdf

Office of Civil Rights. (2020). *Protecting students with disabilities: Frequently asked questions about section 504 and the education of students with disabilities*. U.S. Department of Education, http://www2.ed.gov/about/offices/list/ocr/504faq.html

Office of Safe and Supportive Schools. (2023, January 17). Readiness and Emergency Management for Schools (REMS) Technical Assistance (TA) Center. US Department of Education. https://rems.ed.gov/AboutUs.aspx

Selekman, J., Shannon, R. A. & Yonkaitis, C. F. (Eds.). (2019). *School nursing: A comprehensive text* (3rd ed.). F.A. Davis Company.

Stroud, L. M., & Roy, K. R. (2014). OSHA Training and Requirements and Guidelines for K-14 Schools. Science & Safety Consulting Services for National Science Teachers Association. https://static.nsta.org/pdfs/stroudroy-osharequirementsfork-14schools.pdf

Taliaferro, V. & Resha, C. (Eds.). (2020). *School nurse resource manual: A guide to practice* (10th edition). School Health Alert.

U.S. Department of Health and Human Services & U.S. Department of Education. (2019). *Joint Guidance on the Application of the Family Educational Rights and Privacy Act (FERPA) and the Health Insurance Portability and Accountability Act of 1996 (HIPAA) to Student Health Records*. https://studentprivacy.ed.gov/resources/ joint-giudance-application-ferpa-and-hipaa-student-health-records

Wilt, L., & Jameson, B. (2021). School nursing evidence-based clinical practice guideline: Students with Type 1 Diabetes. *NASN Learning Center*. https://learn.nasn.org/courses/37660

Case Law

American Nurses Association v. Torlakson (2013).http://www.cde.ca.gov/ls/he/hn/documents/anavtorlakson2013.pdf

Cedar Rapids Community School District v. Garret F. (1999). https://www.oyez.org/cases/1998/96-1793

Irving Independent School District v. Tatro (1984). https://www.oyez.org/cases/1998/96-1793

REFERENCES

American Federation of Teachers. (2009). *The medically fragile child.* https://www.aft.org/sites/default/files/medicallyfragilechild_2009.pdf

American Nurses Association. (2015). *Code of ethics for nurses.* American Nurses Publishing.

Biag, M., Srivastava, A., Landua, M., & Rodriguez, E. (2015). Teachers' perceptions of full- and part-time nurses at school. *The Journal of School Nursing, 31*(3), 183-195. https://doi.org/10.1177/1059840514561863

Bobo, N. (2018). *Nursing delegation to unlicensed assistive personnel in the school setting: Principles of practice.* National Association of School Nurses.

Centers for Disease Control and Prevention. (2018). *How to captivate and motivate adult learners: A guide for instructors providing in-person public health training.* https://www.cdc.gov/training/development/pdfs/design/adult-learning-guide-508.pdf

Data Resource Center for Child and Adolescent Health. (2021). *Child and Adolescent Health Measurement Initiative, 2020-2021 National Survey of Children's Health (NSCH) data query.* https://www.childhealthdata.org/browse/survey/results?q=9329&r=1

Denke, N., Winkleblack, L. K. (2020). Challenges and opportunities in population health, The role of school nurses as complexity leaders. *Nursing Administration Quarterly, 44*(2), 136-141. https://doi.org/10.1097/NAQ.0000000000000411

Every Student Succeeds Act, 20 U.S.C. § 6301 (2015). https://www.congress.gov/114/plaws/publ95/PLAW114publ95.pdf

Family Educational Rights and Privacy Act, 20 U.S.C. § 1232g (1974 & rev 2012). https://www.govinfo.gov/content/pkg/CFR-2013-title34-vol1/pdf/CFR-2013-title34-vol1-part99.pdf

Gormley, J. M., Hassey, K. (2019). The school nurse's role as health educator. In J. Selekman, R. A Shannon, & C. F. Yonkaitis (Eds.), *School nursing: A comprehensive text* (3rd ed., pp. 75–95). F.A. Davis Company.

Health Insurance Portability and Accountability Act, Pub. L. No. 104-191 110 Stat. 1938 (1996).

Individuals with Disability Education Improvement Act (2004), 20 U.S.C. 1400 et seq.

McClanahan, R., Shannon, R. A., & Kahn, P. (2019). School health office management. In J. Selekman, R. A. Shannon, & C. F. Yonkaitis (Eds..), School *nursing: A comprehensive text* (3rd ed., pp. 88–908). F.A. Davis Company.

National Academies of Sciences, Engineering, and Medicine. (2021). *The future of nursing 2020–2030: Charting a path to achieve health equity*. The National Academies Press. https://doi.org/10.17226/25982

National Association of School Nurses. (2016). Framework for 21st century school nursing practice: National Association of School Nurses. *NASN School Nurse, 31*(1), 45-53. https://doi.org/10.1177/1942602X15618644

National Association of School Nurses. (2018). *School-sponsored before, after and extended school year programs: The role of the school nurse* (Position Statement). https://www.nasn.org/nasn-resources/professional-practice-documents/position-statements/ps-before-after-programs

National Association of School Nurses. (2019). *Emergency preparedness* (Position Statement). https://www.nasn.org/nasn-resources/professional-practice-documents/position-statements/ps-emergency-preparedness

National Association of School Nurses. (2020a). *School nurse workload: Staffing for safe care* (Position Statement). https://www.nasn.org/nasn-resources/professional-practice-documents/position-statements/ps-workload

National Association of School Nurses. (2020b). *Use of individualized healthcare plans to support school health services* (Position Statement). https://www.nasn.org/nasn-resources/professional-practice-documents/position-statements/ps-ihps

National Association of School Nurses. (2021). *Code of ethics.* https://www.nasn.org/nasn-resources/resources-by-topic/codeofethics

National Association of School Nurses. (2022). *School nursing: Scope and standards of practice* (4th ed.). https://www.nasn.org/blogs/nasn-inc/2022/07/28/school-nursing-scope-and-standards-of-practice-4th

National Center for Chronic Disease Prevention and Health Promotion Division of Population Health. (2021). *Healthy school. Managing chronic health conditions.* Centers for Disease Control and Prevention. https://www.cdc.gov/healthyschools/chronicconditions.htm

National Center for Chronic Disease Prevention and Health Promotion Division of Population Health. (2017). *Research brief: Chronic health conditions and academic achievement.* Centers for Disease Control and Prevention. https://www.cdc.gov/healthyschools/chronic_conditions/pdfs/2017_02_15-how-schools-can-students-with-chc_final_508.pdf

National Council of State Boards of Nursing & American Nurses Association. (2019). *National guidelines for nursing delegation* (Position Statement). https://www.ncsbn.org/public-files/NGND-PosPaper_06.pdf

Patient Protection and Affordable Care Act (2010). Pub.L. No.111-148, 124 Stat. 119

Resha, C. (2010). Delegation in the school setting: Is it a safe practice? *Online Journal of Issues in Nursing, 15*(2). https://doi.org/10.3912/OJIN.Vol15No02Man05

Schofield, S. L. (2018). *"A qualitative case study on delegation of school nursing practice: school nurses, teachers, and paraprofessionals perspectives."* Theses and Dissertations. 2491. https://rdw.rowan.edu/etd/2491

U.S. Department of Education. (2016). *Dear colleague letter school officials at institutions of higher education.* https://studentprivacy.ed.gov/sites/default/files/resource_document/file/DCL_Medical%20Records_Final%20Signed_dated_9-2.pdf

Office of Safe and Healthy Students. (2013). *Guide for developing high-quality school emergency operations plans.* U.S. Department of Education, Office of Elementary and Secondary Education. https://rems.ed.gov/docs/School_Guide_508C.pdf

Office for Civil Rights. (2010). *Free appropriate public education for students with disabilities: Requirements Under Section 504 of the Rehabilitation Act of 1973.* U.S. Department of Education, https://www2.ed.gove/about/offices/list/ocr/docs/edlite-FAPE504.html

U.S. Department of Health and Human Services, & U.S. Department of Education. (2019). *Joint guidance on the application of the Family Educational Rights and Privacy Act (FERPA) and the Health Insurance Portability and Accountability Act of 1996 (HIPAA) to student health records.* https://studentprivacy.ed.gov/resources/joint-guidance-application-ferpa-and-hipaa-student-health-records

Occupational Safety and Health Administration. (n.d.). *Worker protection against occupation exposure to infectious disease*. United States Department of Labor. Retrieved 6-1-23 from https://www.osha.gov/bloodborne-pathogens/worker-protections" https://www.osha.gov/bloodborne-pathogens/worker-protections

Vocational Rehabilitation Act of 1973, 29 U.S.C. § 504

Willergodt, M. A., Brok, D. M., & Maughan, E. D. (2018). Public school nursing practice in the United States. *The Journal of School Nursing, 34*(3), 232-244. https://doi.org/10.1177/1059840517752456

Zirkel, P. A. (2014). Unlicensed administration of medication: The California Supreme Court decision. *NASN School Nurse, 29*(5), 248-52. https://doi.org/10.1177/1942602X14540412

APPENDIX

Examples of School Nurse Trainings*

Audience	Topic	May Include:
All school staff	To respond to student or staff needs	Basic lifesaving (CPR, AED); response to seizure, diabetes, asthma, and anaphylaxis emergencies; other issues per state law and policy (e.g., peanut/tree nut allergies, opioid overdose, suicide risk)
	Worker protections	Universal precautions for communicable diseases, BBP (OSHA requirements)
	To maintain good health	Wellness programs per state law and policy or teachers' contract
Teaching staff (and leaving information for substitute teachers)	For the individual student's health condition	• About the condition, daily needs – health office visits and classroom activities (example: diabetes monitoring), (portions of IHP) • Effect on learning, behavior, and attendance • 504 Plan and IEP: legal obligations
	Urgent conditions for the entire school population (i.e., cardiac arrest, choking, seizures)	Signs and symptoms, emergency response procedures (ECP)
	Emergency Disaster Plan	Evacuation plan, shelter-in-place plan
Special education and related services staff for individual students	For the individual student's health condition: Same as teaching staff depending on services provided.	• Effect of condition on learning and behavior and special education needs • Collaboration and support
Ancillary staff for individual children (e.g., bus driver, school food service, school safety officer)	Health condition Urgent condition	• About the condition and only information that staff need to know (ex., food allergy – food service only) • Signs/symptoms and emergency response procedures for that staff (e.g., bus procedures for seizure)

Audience	Topic	May Include:
Health office staff	Role of staff and responsibilities	• Health office procedures, climate, student privacy, expectations for RN consultation if licensed practical nurses or UAPs work in health office
	Individual student needs	• Documentation for all visits – legal record, confidentiality
	Role of RN and responsibilities	• Medical orders – procedures, legal record; parent permission for meds/treatment
		• Nursing authority to assess and determine action plans for students, including delegating certain tasks.
		• Nursing decisions on assigning/delegating health care tasks
Registered Nurse/ School Nurse	Provided by supervisor or School Nursing Program during orientation and ongoing professional development	• Nurse Practice Act
		• Public health principles, processes, conditions, and partners
		• Health and mental health pediatric/adolescent conditions – up-to-date knowledge
		• Federal and state laws regarding worker safety, teacher/ staff health in-service requirements
		• Federal and state laws regarding student rights, safety, and reporting, including 504, IEP, FERPA, HIPPA

* **Note: These are examples, and it is not an inclusive list.**

Chapter 55

EMPLOYMENT ISSUES AND CONFLICT RESOLUTION

Timothy E. Gilsbach, Esquire

DESCRIPTION OF ISSUE

School nurses are pulled in different directions, being called to serve as health professionals and educators. In addition, school nurses are often called upon to serve in leadership roles in the school environment, especially in situations involving medical issues. However, they may not be in the formal chain of command (each school nurse should consult formal board policy for the specific chain of command process). As a result, school nurses may have conflicts with other colleagues and supervisors about their respective obligations.

BACKGROUND

School nurses' role differs from other school staff in several respects, and those differences can create conflict (Savage, 2017; Davis, 2020). First, school nurses are often isolated from others in the healthcare profession and isolated from other school employees (Isler, 2021; Savage, 2020). They are usually the only nurse in the building and often travel during the day because they cover multiple schools.

Unlike most other staff in school buildings, school nurses are bound by two sets of laws, educational and health-related laws (National Association of School Nurses [NASN], 2021; Savage, 2017; Davis et al., 2020). These legal obligations and potential conflicts between professional nursing standards and school district policy can create challenging dilemmas for school nurses, which may result in conflict with other staff and employees (Savage, 2017; Davis et al., 2020).

IMPLICATIONS FOR SCHOOL NURSE PRACTICE

What Guides the Nature of the Employment Relationship?

School nurses may be employed by a school entity in several different arrangements depending upon how they are hired, which impacts their employment terms. In some circumstances, the school entity employs the school nurse through a direct contract that dictates the nurse's working conditions and duties. In other districts, school nurses may be part of a collective bargaining unit that negotiates the terms of employment, which are then memorialized in a collective bargaining agreement between the union or bargaining agent and the school entity. Given the unique role of the school nurse compared to other nurses who may be part of the bargaining unit, the agreement may lack specificity in terms of the school nurse's duties. Finally, school nurses may be employed by an agency that contracts with the school or district to provide school nursing services. Under those circumstances, the employment relationship is controlled by the terms of employment between the school nurse and the agency. However, the service contract between the school or district and the agency also impacts what obligations the school expects the nurses to perform.

Regardless of the nature of the individual employment relationship and contractual obligations, the school nurse must still be guided by their profession's ethical guidelines and best practices (Savage, 2017; NASN, 2021b). In addition, to the extent that school entity actions put a student's health or safety at risk, a school nurse may have a legal or ethical duty to speak up that does not apply to other staff members (Savage, 2017). When contractual obligations, or directions provided by supervisors, with best practices or the school nurse's legal or ethical obligations, the nurse should raise that concern. When indicated, the nurse should also seek further guidance from outside professional sources, consistent with confidentiality obligations and each state's ethical guidelines. Written documentation should reflect those concerns and, when necessary, information or guidance received from those outside sources. Guidance may come from legal counsel, state or national professional associations, or other licensed practitioners (Savage,2017). Memberships in professional organizations, especially those that focus on school nurses, allow nurses to discuss concerns with others in their profession who may have experience with similar issues.

Issues with Respect to Working Conditions

Given the unique role that school nurses play in the education agencies and schools that they serve, they are often treated differently than other employees. This is especially true given that school nurses are expected to meet ever-increasing needs but, given a lack of any uniform standards for the student-to-nurse ratio, may not have a reduced load of students (Savage, 2017). School nurses should carefully review their employment agreement with their school or agency to determine their rights and obligations with respect to their employment. In addition, if the employee is a collective bargaining unit or union member, they should be familiar with their union contract and discuss possible concerns with their union representative. Nurses should also review and provide input on board policy and handbook provisions that relate specifically to the nurse's duties and obligations. However, school nurses should be careful in understanding that their contractual obligations do not alter their obligations under applicable ethical rules or state law related to the practice

> **Denise Herrmann, DNP, RN, CPNP, FNASN**
>
> Q: What things might help the school nurse prepare for conflicts?
>
> A: The school nurse can prepare by
>
> (1) Become familiar with the nurse practice act in the state, specifically the nurse's scope of practice and all other applicable laws, rules, and regulations.
>
> (2) Review the professional nursing standards for school nursing practice, including ethical standards by the National Association of School Nurses (NASN) and state professional school nurse organizations.
>
> (3) Finally, if the nurse's position is covered by a union contract, connect with union leadership to ensure s/he understands their contractual obligations and privileges.

of nursing and, to the extent these conflicts, should comply with their nursing ethical obligations first and foremost (NASN, 2021a). In addition, if such a conflict is found to exist, a school nurse should raise the issue with their supervisor before it impacts direct practice to avoid more significant conflicts and do so in writing when necessary.

Means of Addressing Issues with Other Staff

While typically not administrators or supervisors, school nurses play such a unique role in the school district that they are often called upon as leaders to provide direction and expertise in healthcare (NASN, 2021b; Davis, 2020). Some examples of this include:

- Providing direction to the school and staff regarding medically fragile students, which is on the increase (Davis, 2020).

- Providing direction regarding students with a disability, who are mainstreamed into the least restrictive environment, and drafting the health components of Individualized Education Plans (IEP) or Section 504 Plans for such students (NASN, 2021b).

- Working in schools that are becoming, at least in part, healthcare providers (Davis, 2020).

- Advocating for the needs of individual students (NASN, 2021b; Savage, 2017).

- Advocating for systematic change in safety plans, promoting education, and healthcare reform (NASN, 2021b; Savage, 2017).

- Training other school staff members to provide tasks that a nurse would have done in the past, including medication administration (Savage, 2017).

- Providing education to staff on the health needs of students, both individual students and the student body as a whole (NASN, 2016). These various roles may create some potential conflict between the school nurse and other staff in the school setting (Davis, 2020). One example is the dispute over provisions in a student's IEP or Section 504 Plan, with the school nurse and administrator taking opposing positions. Another example is when a staff member asks the school nurse for a student's medical information that they are not entitled to under the Family Education Rights and Privacy Act (U.S. Department of Education [USDE], 2010).

> **Strengthening Your Response to Conflicts**
> **Sharonlee Trefry, MSN, RN, NCSN**
>
> Q: How might you, as a school nurse, increase your skills in responding to conflicts?
>
> A: Consider taking a structured approach that you could apply to any conflict. Take the time to ask yourself if you have done your nursing assessment of the situation that led to the conflict; what might be missing from your assessment? What is your nursing diagnosis, who are the appropriate stakeholders, what is the desired outcome and your plan of action for reaching that outcome? You are then ready to meet with the right people and discuss how you can implement steps for addressing the concerns together. Did you include plans for how you will document your actions and sustain a successful resolution?

As a result, school nurses may have to work carefully to defuse such potential situations with staff. However, in doing so, school nurses must simultaneously comply with their ethical and legal obligations under their state's nurse practice act and any other applicable codes, laws, rules, and regulations. (NASN, 2021; Savage, 2017). To the extent that a school nurse is being asked to act inconsistent with those professional/ethical/legal obligations or conflicts with other staff members, they should also involve supervisors and follow their chain of command. In addition, school nurses should consider discussing such disputes or ethical concerns, consistent with their confidentiality obligations, with other school nurses who may be able to help in addressing such concerns (Savage, 2017). School nurses may wish to explore possible means to proactively address such concerns before conflict arises. Examples include developing sound communication and conflict negotiation skills, using opportunities to train and educate staff on school nurses' obligations, and determining the school or district chain of command through which to voice concerns about such issues. (Davis, 2020). Finally, school nurses should consider networking with other school nurses and their professional organizations (local and national) who can provide advice and support when such issues arise.

CONCLUSION

School nurses play an important but unique role in the school setting and, as a result, may have situations in which their obligations to the health profession and their obligation to education conflict, as well as situations in which those duties cause conflict with other staff members. School nurses should remember that based on their nursing license, their priority is their legal and ethical duties regarding the care of their students/patients. In addition, school nurses should be familiar with and ready to use the process available to them to work to reduce conflict when it arises and involve their local, statewide, or national professional organizations in supporting them to use best practices as they do so.

RESOURCES

Historic Leadership: One Courageous School Nurse's Heroic Journey
Ellen F. Johnsen, BA; Katherine J. Pohlman, MS, JD, RN
NASN School Nurse, Vol 32, Issue 1, pp. 19-24, January 2017
https://doi.org/10.1177/1942602X166777

Historic Leadership: One Courageous School Nurse's Heroic Journey, Part 2
Ellen F. Johnsen, BA, Katherine J. Pohlman, MS, JD, RN
NASN School Nurse ,32(2), pp. 94 - 99 March-01-2017
https://journals.sagepub.com/doi/10.1177/1942602X16688322

Individual State School Nurses Association or Organization Website

National Association of School Nurses Website - http://www.nasn.org/

REFERENCES

Davis, C. R., Lynch, E. J., Davis, P. A. (2020). The principal and the school nurse: Conditions and conceptual model for building a successful and vital professional relationship. *Planning and Changing, 50*(1/2), 95–110. https://education.illinoisstate.edu/downloads/planning/Davis_50.1-2.pdf

Isler, A. (2021, January 29). *This is how COVID has changed my job as a school nurse.* https://nurse.org/articles/school-nurse-pandemic/

National Association of School Nurses. (2021a). *Code of ethics.* https://www.nasn.org/nasn-resources/resources-by-topic/codeofethics

National Association of School Nurses. (2021b). Framework for 21st century school nursing practice: National Association of School Nurses. *NASN School Nurse, 31*(1), 45-53. https://doi.org/10.1177/1942602X15618644

Savage, T.A. (2017, September 30). Ethical issues in school nursing. *OJIN: The Online Journal of Issues in Nursing, 22*(3). https://doi.org/10.3912/OJIN.Vol22No03Man04

U.S. Department of Education. (2010). *Family Educational Rights and Privacy Act (FERPA) and the disclosure of student information related to emergencies and disasters.* https://studentprivacy.ed.gov/sites/default/files/resource_document/file/ferpa-disaster-guidance.pdf

BEYOND THE PUBLIC SCHOOL WALLS

The following section of the book is dedicated to activities that occur beyond the pre-K to 12 educational setting (e.g., school-sponsored field trips). Some topics include Homebound Education, School Sponsored Field Trips, Non-public Schools, and Transportation for Students with Health Concerns.

The nuances associated with activities that occur outside the physical space of a school building can be daunting. Being equipped with knowledge and potential concerns will assist school nurses engage in activities that support these situations. It is critical that school nurses recognize that their role and responsibilities extend beyond the physical location of the school buildings.

Chapter 56

SCHOOL-SPONSORED BEFORE, AFTER, AND EXTENDED SCHOOL YEAR PROGRAMS

Jo Volkening, MSEd, BSN, RN, PEL/IL-CSN, NCSN*

DESCRIPTION OF ISSUE

Local education agencies (LEAs) across the United States provide a variety of before and after-school programs, extracurricular activities in athletics and the performing arts, and summer extended school year programs to support students' academic achievement, educational progress, health, and wellness. In accordance with the American Disabilities Act (ADA) and Section 504 of the Rehabilitation Act of 1973 (Section 504), all students, including those with identified disabilities, must have **equal opportunity** to participate in (or equal access to) school-sponsored activities. The Individuals with Disabilities Education Improvement Act (IDEIA) (2004) mandates that a free appropriate public education (FAPE), which includes participation in before and after-school programs, be provided for students with Individualized Education Programs. State and local anti-discriminatory laws may provide further protection. School nurses need to be actively involved in supporting the health needs of students enrolled in these programs to enable this legal access and opportunity by understanding their legal responsibility for providing support.

BACKGROUND

Several factors have created the need for school nurses to understand their role in addressing the health needs of students in activities beyond the regular school day. In 2002, The No Child Left Behind Legislation created the 21st Century Community Learning Center (21st CCLC), which included before, after, and summer school programs to improve low-performing students' academic performance. In 2015, another law, the Every Student Succeeds Act (ESSA), authorized continuing funding for the 21st CCLC (After School Alliance, n.d.). According to the After-school Alliance (2022), there are currently 1.6 million students participating in these programs across the US. In addition, the After-school Alliance reports that students receive academic support and health education, art, counseling, music, and recreational programs. The American Institute for Research (2021) also notes that students participating in these programs show improvements in attendance, classroom behavior, math, reading achievement, and social-emotional development.

More students than ever have chronic health needs while attending school. The Centers for Disease Control and Prevention (CDC) 2020 statistics revealed that 7.2 % of students had asthma, and Type I Diabetes was diagnosed in 187,000 students under 20. Food allergies in children have increased in prevalence over the last two to three decades, as reported by Seth et al. (2020). The CDC's 2015 report estimated that 470,000 children have a diagnosis of epilepsy in the US (Zack & Korbau, 2017). The 2017-2018 National Survey of Children's Health (NSCH) showed 13.6 million US children affected with special health needs (Health Resources & Services Administration, 2020). Pageet et al. report that significant advances in critical care interventions have allowed many children to improve enough to be discharged to home and who may not have survived their complex medical needs in the past to improve enough to be discharged to home (2020). Many of these students require specific nursing interventions while attending school, such as medication administration,

---

*Original author: Elizabeth Clark, MSN, RN, NCSN (2017)

gastrostomy tube feedings, catheterizations, and respiratory care, including suctioning, oxygen administration, and tracheostomy care. The National Association of School Nurses [NASN] (2023) conveys the school nurse's role in the management of health care both during the school day and at extracurricular activities, field trips, and athletics, including direct nursing services; nursing accommodations; nutrition and food safety support; behavioral health care; environmental management; intervention in medical emergencies; and preparedness planning.

Federal law governs a school's provision and support of school-sponsored events, before and after school programs, extended school year programs, and extracurricular activities, such as intramurals, sports, and the performing arts, as they must be offered to students regardless of race, economic status, or disability. Legal protections and standards are mandated for accommodations, support, equal access, and inclusion of students with disabilities in school-sponsored activities. State laws and regulations may supplement these federal requirements. The United States Department of Education, Office of Civil Rights states that students with disabilities, such as a severe life-threatening allergy or diabetes, may not be denied access to school-sponsored events or services offered to other students (2022). Section 794 of the ADA states that LEAs receiving federal funds must provide reasonable accommodations for student participation in school activities (2004). The Americans with Disabilities Act Amendments Act (ADAA) of 2008 revised the definition of disability to establish broader coverage for students with disabilities. In addition, IDEIA (2004) mandates a free appropriate public education (FAPE) in which school staff develop Individualized Education Programs for students that may require access to extended school day or school year activities under state-specific guidelines.

IMPLICATIONS FOR SCHOOL NURSE PRACTICE

School nurses are essential school employees to support the health needs of students participating in extracurricular activities. They are leaders in providing health services and in the training and support of educational professionals educating these students. School nurses have the knowledge, skills, and expertise to assess, plan, and evaluate the health needs of students in programming and activities beyond the regular school day. They create individualized healthcare plans and emergency care plans for students and serve as expert health resources for accommodations to meet student health needs (NASN, 2020). School nurses not only manage complex health needs, including chronic disease management for students but participate in writing policies and procedures for these needs (McCabe et al., 2022).

Clear and timely communication within the local educational system is necessary as students enroll in extracurricular activities. For school-sponsored programs and activities beyond the regular school day, communication of a student's health needs may be compromised due to a different group of staff and administrators from those in the regular school day. Program leaders, coaches, and administrators should have a system with well-defined protocols in place in place to exchange health information for enrolled students. Parental consent should be obtained with respect to FERPA and HIPAA compliance for access to health records by those with a legitimate educational interest. School nurses are able to assist in the creation of these protocols to provide a seamless process for enrollment and health service provision.

Additionally, the school nurse should implement and evaluate nursing care coordination. This healthcare implementation depends on the individual state nurse practice act, which provides the guidelines for nursing tasks, training, and delegation of nursing tasks to unlicensed assistive personnel (UAP) if permitted. School nurses should continually monitor changes in local policies and state and federal laws, regulations, and codes that may impact nursing practice.

LEAs should provide adequate financial compensation for school nurses required to provide nursing services beyond the regular school day or calendar year contract. The compensation for school nurses should be comparable to teachers and other professional school staff providing services in these settings. School nurses, particularly those serving minority and underserved communities, are critical components in a framework to advance health equity (Centers for Medicare and Medicaid Services, 2023). An additional registered nurse position may be created for direct nursing care, emergency response, or supervising delegated medication administration. Nursing services may be met by a nurse available on site or on call in a location nearby for a phone consultation, depending on the assessment by the school nurse of the student's health needs. A contract with a community nursing agency is also an option to meet this mandated support requirement for equal opportunity and access for students to participate in activities outside of the regular school day.

Various before and after-school, extracurricular, and extended school-year activities and programs have been developed nationwide. These programs not only provide childcare for elementary and middle school students, but they also provide supervised academic support. They include school clubs and community and private programs located in school buildings and often occur on non-contact student days, such as holidays and summer vacation. The programs focus on academics, enrichment activities, clubs, social-emotional learning, physical education, and sports (After School Alliance, 2022). Programs may be district, community, or privately sponsored. Many programs fall under state childcare rules and regulations, and school nurses must know the requirements, which may differ from school regulations in their state or territory. School nurses should determine if the LEA sponsors the extended school day activities or are community or private agency sponsored with the activity located within or on the LEA's property. The LEA's legal counsel will be a valuable resource to assist in the determination of whether an activity is school sponsored versus community or privately sponsored. Community and privately sponsored activities located on the school district property are not the responsibility of the LEA. Therefore, the school nurse ordinarily may not be required to provide health services under this circumstance, and the duty of care would typically remain the responsibility of the parent and the community agency.

Medication administration, including safe medication storage, is a significant issue that school nurses often address when children participate in before and after-school programs. Registered nurses (RNs) are strongly endorsed as professionals with the knowledge and skills required to safely deliver medication (American Academy of Pediatrics, 2009/2013). The nurse should administer the medication following the five "rights," supplemented by modern technology such as warning prompts in electronic health records (Hanson & Haddad, 2022). If medication processes are delegated to UAPs, the delegation should generally be limited to no more than three UAPs and not usually more than three school sites. School nurse staffing must be adequate for the school nurse to supervise the UAPs appropriately (NASN, 2021). According to NASN (2022), policies and procedures for medication administration requirements should be based on state rules and regulations and include medications being provided in the original pharmacy-labeled containers accompanied by consent forms signed by the primary care provider and parent(s) and stored correctly in a secure/locked cabinet. A parent or legal guardian may be requested to submit duplicate medication consent forms to follow childcare licensing requirements for before and after-school programs as well as the consent forms received by the school nurse for the regular school day. This request could potentially be a hardship for families, and school nurses may need to consider health equity in addressing medication access issues for programs and sports beyond the school day.

Some states allow trained, non-medical employee volunteers to be designated and trained to provide specific medical care, such as diabetes care, including the administration of medication (ADA, n.d.). Other initiatives have been followed to seek the same provision of care for students with epilepsy (Epilepsy Foundation, 2022) and other chronic health conditions. These employee volunteers for diabetes, seizures, etc., should be included in the staffing matrix for school-sponsored programs. Ideally, medication for after-school programs should be used exclusively by the program and stored for the program. For example, nurses can request that parents obtain a separate labeled bottle of medication for the extended school program from the pharmacy. If shared medication between programs is the only available option, then it is important that nurses set up procedures for returning medications to the school health room (i.e., medications stored in the health room during the school day and securely stored in the after-school location during that program). A mechanism for proper back-and-forth transfer is needed so that a nurse is not faced with failing to implement a medical order due to a lack of medication available during the school day. If the before and after school staff have access to the school nurse's medication storage location, then procedures are needed to separate school day meds from before and after school meds. Controlled substances should be stored using a double-locked system (NASN, 2022). The school nurse is paramount to ensuring that state rules and regulations are followed for medication and other health issues, as the school nurse may be the only school, licensed staff knowledgeable of healthcare policies and regulations.

CONCLUSION

School nurses advocate for the health needs of their students in programs and activities beyond the regular school day. It is within nurses' scope and practice to determine students' health needs and accommodations (NASN, 2021). Legal requirements to meet the accommodation standards are set forth in IDEA, Section 504, ADA, and other state and federal anti-discrimination laws. School nurses are necessary to address the health needs of students with identified nursing or health needs in activities and programs outside the regular school day.

School nurses are the experts who determine, in conjunction with a healthcare provider, the needed nursing care for students with identified health needs participating in before, after, and extended school year activities. The legal requirements of state and federal laws, such as IDEA, Section 504, and ADA, mandate that students are not denied access to programs and activities based on their disability.

> Please see Appendix: Legal Responsibilities for Accommodating Children with Special Needs in After School and Summer Programs.

RESOURCES

U.S. Department of Education US, Office for Civil Rights. (2013). Dear Colleague Letter. January 25, 2013. https://www2.ed.gov/about/offices/list/ocr/letters/colleague-201301-504.pdf

American Diabetes Association. (2022). Helping the student with diabetes succeed: A guide for school personnel. https://diabetes.org/sites/default/files/2022-11/School-guide-final-11-10-22.pdf

U.S. Department of Education, Office for Civil Rights. (2020). *Protecting students with disabilities. Frequently asked questions about Section 504 and the education of children with disabilities*. https://www2.ed.gov/about/offices/list/ocr/504faq.html

REFERENCES

After School Alliance. n.d. *ESEA legislation overview.* http://www.afterschoolalliance.org/policyESEALegOverview.cfm

After School Alliance. (2022, May). *21st century community learning centers.* http://afterschoolalliance.org/documents/21st-CCLC-Overview-2022.pdf

American Academy of Pediatrics. (2009/2013). Policy statement: Guidance for the administration of medication in school. *Pediatrics*. 2009;*124*(4),1244–1251. Reaffirmed February 2013. https://doi.org/10.1542/peds.2009-1953

Americans With Disabilities Act of 1990, 42 USC § 12101 *et seq.* (1990).

Centers for Disease Control and Prevention. (2020). *2020 National diabetes statistics report.* https://www.cdc.gov/diabetes/pdfs/data/statistics/national-diabetes-statistics-report.pdf

Centers for Disease Control and Prevention. (2020). *Most recent asthma data.* https://www.cdc.gov/asthma/most_recent_national_asthma_data.htm

Centers for Medicare and Medicaid Services. (2023). *Framework for health equity.* https://www.cms.gov/about-cms/agency-information/omh/health-equity-programs/cms-framework-for-health-equity

Epilepsy Foundation (2022). *Advocacy: Seizure safe schools.* https://www.epilepsy.com/advocacy/priorities/seizure-safe-schools https://www.epilepsy.com/sites/default/files/2022-10/Seizure_Safe_Schools_Position_Statement_October2022.pdf

Every Student Succeeds Act, 20 USC § 6301 (2015). congress.gov/114/plaws/publ95/PLAW-114publ95.pdf

Hanson A., & Haddad L.M. (2022, Jan.). Nursing rights of medication administration. StatPearls [Internet]. StatPearls Publishing. https://www.ncbi.nlm.nih.gov/books/NBK560654/

Health Resources & Services Administration. (2020, July). *Children with special healthcare needs.* https://mchb.hrsa.gov/sites/default/files/mchb/programs-impact/nsch-cshcn-data-brief.pdf

McCabe, E.M., Jameson, B.E., & Strauss, S.M. (2022). School nurses matter: Relationship between school nurse employment policies and chronic health condition policies in US school districts. *The Journal of School Nursing, 38*(5):467–477. https://doi.org/10.1177/1059840520973413

Merriam-Webster. (2008). Braggadocio. In *Merriam-Webster's Advanced Learner's English Dictionary*. Merriam-Webster.

National Association of School Nurses. (2020). *Use of individualized healthcare plans to support school health services* (Position Statement). Author. https://www.nasn.org/nasn-resources/professional-practice-documents/position-statements/ps-ihps

National Association of School Nurses. (2021). *Medication administration clinical practice guidelines in the school*. Author. https://learn.nasn.org/courses/33787#

National Association of School Nurses (2022). *School nursing: Scope and standards of practice* (4th ed.). NASN.

National Association of School Nurses. (2023). *School-sponsored before, after, and extended school year/out of school time programs* (Position Statement). Author. https://www.nasn.org/nasn-resources/professional-practice-documents/position-statements/ps-before-after-programs

Page, B.F., Hinton, L., Harrop, E., & Vincent, C. (2020). The challenges of caring for children who require complex medical care at home: 'The go between for everyone is the parent and as the parent that's an awful lot of responsibility.' *Health Expect.* 2020; *23*(5), 1144– 1154. https://doi.org/10.1111/hex.13092

U.S. Department of Education. Individuals with Disabilities Education Act of 2004. https://www.govinfo.gov/content/pkg/PLAW-108publ446/html/PLAW-108publ446.htm

U.S. Department of Education, Office for Civil Rights, Free Appropriate Public Education for Students with Disabilities: Requirements Under Section 504 of the Rehabilitation Act of 1973, 2010.

Zack, M. & Kobau, R. (2017). National and state estimates of the numbers of adults and children with active epilepsy — United States, 2015. *Morbidity and Mortality Weekly Report, 66*(31), 821–825. http://dx.doi.org/10.15585/mmwr.mm6631a1

APPENDIX

Legal responsibilities for accommodating children with special needs in after school & summer programs

Responsibilities under the Law	Public School	After school program operated or funded by a public school	After school program operated by a private organization (non-profit or for-profit) or public entity other than school	After school or summer program operated by a religious organization	Summer Programs
Individuals with Disabilities Education Act of 2004 (IDEA)	Makes determination of eligibility. Meets with parents to develop goals, services & accommodations in an IEP (Individualized Education Program).	Must follow IEP goals and provide accommodations although services may be different.	May follow IEP if the parent, school and provider agree to goals, services & accommodations. Parent-initiated.	May follow IEP if the parent, school and provider agree to goals, services & accommodations. Parent-initiated.	School programs must comply with ESY* services in the IEP. Non public school programs, if agree, must comply.
Americans with Disabilities Act (ADA) Title II - Public entities	All schools have an ADA compliance officer under Title II.	Must comply.	Only programs operated by government entities must comply.	Does not apply.	Must comply if operated by a public entity.
Americans with Disabilities Act (ADA) Title III -Public Accommodation	Does not apply.	Applies to places of public accommodation including after school programs.	Applies to places of public accommodation including after school programs.	Only applies if the organization accepts state or federal funding.	Applies to summer programs serving the general public, not to religious organizations.
Section 504 of the Rehabilitation Act of 1973	Makes determination of eligibility. Meets with parents to set accommodations in a 504 Plan.	Must follow school 504 Plan but services &/or accommodations may be different.	Must make accommodations but not required to follow the school 504 Plan.	Only applies if the organization accepts state or federal funding.	Must make accommodations but not required to follow the school 504 plan.
New Jersey Law Against Discrimination Broader than ADA or IDEA	Must comply.	Must comply.	Must comply.	Exempt unless required by contract or regulation.	Must comply unless a religious organization- see box at left.

Fees and/or waiting lists for after school program may apply.
Afterschool programs operated by municipal governments must comply with Title II and III of ADA and must be licensed in NJ.
*ESY- Extended School Year, breaks in school calendar (i.e. summer or holidays)

Chapter 57

HOMEBOUND INSTRUCTION FOR REGULAR EDUCATION STUDENTS AND CHILDREN WITH DISABILITIES

Suzanne Levasseur, MSN, APRN, CPNP, NCSN

DESCRIPTION OF ISSUE

"Homebound instruction" refers to the process of providing instruction to a student in the home, hospital, institution, or other setting. Students may be eligible for homebound instruction when the student is unable to attend school due to a medical or emotional condition. It can allow a student to stay current on their schoolwork and minimize the negative educational effects of a serious or long-term illness. Homebound instruction can be provided for all students, including students who are eligible under the Individuals with Disabilities Education Act (IDEA) and Section 504 of the Rehabilitation Act of 1973 (Section 504).

A distinction should be made between homebound instruction and home schooling. Often these two terms are confused by parents and staff. Homeschooling refers to parents who provide education to their children by themselves or through tutors in the home, outside of the public education system.

BACKGROUND

In November of 1975, Congress passed the *Education of All Handicapped Children Act* (Public Law 94-142 1975), which mandated that all school-aged children with disabilities receive a free appropriate public education (FAPE). Federal law and regulations provide minimal information about homebound instruction. When students cannot attend school due to a verified medical or mental health condition, homebound or hospital-based instruction may be required for the student to receive a FAPE under the IDEA or Section 504. Homebound instruction may also be appropriate for a medically complex student who has a serious, ongoing illness or chronic condition that may result in frequent absences or hospitalizations. It also may be provided for a student who is pregnant or has given birth and, for extenuating medical reasons, cannot attend school. (*For more information on IEPs and Section 504, please see Education Laws for Children with Disabilities Chapter 13*).

Homebound instruction is determined by state law and regulations and local education authority (LEA) policies and procedures if any exist. These laws, regulations, policies, and procedures vary among states and LEAs. State education agencies (SEAs) often issue guidance documents for the provision of homebound instruction. In general, a parent may request homebound instruction, and documentation is required from the treating healthcare provider (refer to state law for who can authorize treatment plans), which typically includes the medical condition or diagnosis, the anticipated duration of the absence, and the impact on the student's ability to receive educational services. The school team or homebound instruction office would consider the request. If the student has an individualized education program or Section 504 plan, then that team would meet to discuss the student's services and support. Homebound instruction is a highly restrictive placement for a student with a disability because students receiving homebound instruction do not have access to their peers. Students with disabilities must be educated in the least restrictive environment with their nondisabled peers to the maximum extent appropriate. The instruction should enable the student to continue participating in the general education curriculum and progress toward the student's IEP goals and objectives. If a student does not receive special education or related services, the need for homebound instruction may prompt staff to review whether the student may have a disability and may require referral evaluation of eligibility under the IDEA or Section 504.

CONSIDERATIONS

Location and Scheduling

Although the term "homebound" implies that the instruction is given in the home, it can be provided at other places such as the public library, the school itself, or other locations. In general, students, families, and the tutoring staff can determine the appropriate time when the tutoring can take place. State law, regulation, or local education agency policy may determine the minimum number of hours. If a student is in the hospital, the district may provide tutors to go to the hospital to give instruction, or in some cases, the hospital would provide the tutoring and bill the district for those services. There may be time limits on how long a student with a disability may receive homebound instruction.

Staff Safety and Presence of an Adult

Although there is no legal mandate, most districts require the presence of an adult in the home when the instruction is taking place. There may also be challenging situations where staff do not feel safe during instruction. Other alternatives, such as distance learning, could be considered. There should be documentation to support the perceived threat, and it may be necessary for the LEA to provide compensatory services.

Related Services

The IEP team should consider what related services (e.g., counseling services, speech-language pathology services, occupational therapy services, medical services, nursing services, etc.) are required for the student to continue to make progress in the general education curriculum and advance toward achieving their IEP goals. The IEP team should also consider whether the student is available for related services. The IEP team may need to consider additional related services to address the condition that requires homebound instruction.

Parent Cooperation

Parents need to be part of the process for homebound instruction to be successful. The parent must provide medical documentation for the school district to determine whether the student requires homebound instruction. Documentation can include releases of information so that the school can talk to the medical provider. It is important that parents keep schedules and appointments and make an adult available if instruction is delivered in the home. A local education agency cannot be held accountable if a parent does not make the student available for instruction. Districts should maintain documentation of attempts to provide homebound instruction.

Disputes

Occasionally disputes arise when the local education authority may question the basis on which the treating healthcare provider has asserted the need for homebound instruction. The school nurse should utilize the district medical advisor if available for a case review and may also utilize other qualified healthcare providers to review and assess the information at the district's expense. Consent for the exchange of information should be obtained prior to the consultation. Consultation may include a review of the educational and medical records and, where appropriate, a review of accommodations and school health services that can be provided so the student can attend school safely.

Mental Health Conditions

Homebound instruction may be required for students with mental health conditions or school refusal; however, it may not be appropriate in some circumstances. Homebound instruction does not allow students to interact with their peers during the school day and has implications related to LRE. An extended homebound instruction period may make it more difficult for the student to return to school, particularly when the student has difficulty attending school due to anxiety or school refusal and does not provide the student with the full experience of coming to school.

In the case of *Bradley v. Arkansas Department of Education, 45 IDELR 149, 443 F.3d 965 (8th Cir. 2006)*, the court found in favor of the district after the parent requested homebound instruction on a diagnosis of school phobia and the district determined that home was not the appropriate placement and that the principal followed state law by initiating the truancy process.

IMPLICATIONS FOR SCHOOL NURSE PRACTICE

The school nurse will have an integral role in the homebound process. As the leader for health issues in the school setting, school nurses will be part of the team of professionals to help determine if a student has a disability or a diagnosis that prevents the student from attending school. An essential role of the school nurse is to be the liaison between the treating healthcare provider and the school team. Often the healthcare provider or parent may be unaware of the many accommodations that can be offered during the school day to allow the student to attend at least part of the school day. This may include but is not limited to frequent rest periods, modified school days, medication administration, or intermittent classes.

Since homebound instruction is a very restrictive environment, all accommodations should be explored prior to initiating the homebound instruction. The school nurse also helps determine if the student is ready to receive homebound instruction. For example, a student recovering from a surgical procedure may not be well enough to access instruction immediately after returning from the hospital. The nurse should assess and plan for the homebound instruction to be implemented as soon as the student is medically ready. As indicated, this plan should be incorporated into the Section 504 plan, IEP, or individualized healthcare plan (IHP).

Students with long-term or complex healthcare needs who may have repeated frequent absences can be especially challenging. The school nurse can be the case manager in these cases to monitor the student's attendance and quickly alert the school staff of absences. As part of these students' IEPs, homebound or hospital-based instruction may begin after a minimum time of missed school. State statute, regulation, or local education authority policy may dictate this minimum time.

Although rare, a request may be made for homebound instruction based on the presence of a communicable disease such as tuberculosis. School nurses should work closely with their medical advisor and local public health authorities to ascertain the risk to others and the necessity of the restrictive environment.

When the student is ready to transition or return to school, the school team should implement a return plan. Some states require that a student's IEP team develop a plan for the student's return to school when the IEP team develops the student's IEP that will be implemented during homebound instruction. The school team, with the parents and student as appropriate, should determine what accommodations or services need to be put in place for the student's safe return. This may include counseling or arrival monitoring with a pupil personnel or student services staff member for students with mental health conditions. For a child with a medical condition, it may include attendance for a partial day or rest periods during the day.

CONCLUSION

Providing a FAPE when a student requires homebound or hospital-based instruction requires careful consideration of the whole team and especially the expertise of the school nurse. Many states offer guidance on homebound instruction, and many local education authorities develop their own policies and procedures. Home is the most restrictive environment in which a student can be provided instruction. The whole team must evaluate all aspects of the request. If the student is eligible for an IEP or Section 504 plan, the IEP or Section 504 plan should be revised to reflect the homebound instruction. If the student has not been previously identified, the request itself may trigger a referral to evaluate eligibility.

Communication and collaboration among the healthcare providers, school team, and parents will be essential. The school nurse will often be the liaison between the stakeholders. With knowledge of healthcare and an understanding of education and educational laws, the school nurse can help provide a better understanding to all parties and be instrumental in assuring appropriate placement for a student with a medical or mental health condition.

RESOURCES

Selekman, J. (Ed.) (2019). School nursing: A comprehensive text (3rd ed). F.A. Davis Company.

Case Law

Bradley v. Arkansas Department of Education, 45 IDELR 149, 443 F.3d 965 *(8th Cir. 2006)*

REFERENCES

Graff, H. (2018). *Homebound services under the IDEA and Section 504: An overview of legal issues* (p.vii). LRP Publications.

Individuals with Disability Education Act (2004), 20 U.S.C. 1400 et seq.

Rehabilitation Act of 1973, 29 U.S.C. § 794

United States Department of Education. (n.d.). *Building the legacy: IDEA 2004.* http://idea.ed.gov/

Zettel, J., & Ballard, J. (1979). The Education for All Handicapped Children Act of 1975 PL 94-142: Its history, origins, and concepts. *The Journal of Education, 161*(3), 5-22. http://www.jstor.org/stable/42772958

Chapter 58

NONPUBLIC SCHOOLS

Cheryl Blake, MSN, RN, NCSN*

DESCRIPTION OF ISSUE

Questions concerning legal issues are recurring in discussion posts for private, independent, and parochial school nurses. To comply with current laws and regulations, nonpublic school nurses must be aware of standards that relate to school health within educational settings, and with an increase in the number of medically fragile children attending all schools, legal acumen has become more important than ever.

School health issues are governed by federal, state, and district laws, and as such, can be formidable to navigate, even for those with some expertise in the legal arena. In most situations, the nonpublic school nurse is employed in a school where the legal advisor may have little or no knowledge of health mandates or the conflicts that can occur between federal and state laws. With or without direct and regular communication from their state or district department of health, the nonpublic school nurse must become acquainted with laws, regulations, policies, and standards that affect the delivery of healthcare to their students. This chapter provides a brief overview of the five most frequently discussed topics, along with websites for additional exploration.

BACKGROUND

In the 2019-2020 academic year, 4.7 million elementary and secondary students were enrolled in private and parochial schools (National Center for Education Statistics [NCES], 2019). The first known record of collecting data on private schools goes back to 1890 (NCES, 2019), which coincides with a time when English and American nurses were entering schools to check on infectious diseases (Stanhope & Lancaster, 2019). In the 1920s, nurses were assigned by community health departments to go into schools, but by the 1940's, school districts began to employ their own school nurses (Stanhope & Lancaster, 2019). In 1974 the *Child Abuse Prevention and Treatment Act (CAPTA)* was enacted, marking the beginning of legislation affecting child health (Child Welfare Information Gateway, 2019).

Today, the two Acts that afford the greatest challenge to the nonpublic school nurse are the Family Education Rights and Privacy Act (FERPA), and the Health Insurance Portability and Accountability Act (HIPAA). These and their associated documents are addressed in the next section, along with topics that have become of particular concern to nurses working in nonpublic school settings – health screenings, immunizations, the support of a school physician, and the administration of medications.

FERPA AND HIPAA IMPLICATIONS FOR SCHOOL NURSE PRACTICE

Health mandates govern all public schools, and nonpublic schools should adhere to the directives that govern the jurisdiction in which their school is located. Using these mandates as the acceptable standard of care

---

*Original author: Elizabeth Chau, SRN (UK), RN (2017)

and incorporating current evidence-based practice, the nonpublic school nurse is well-equipped to develop and implement policies and procedures applicable to their unique nonpublic school setting. Unfortunately, nonpublic school nurses rarely have direct access to these local or regional public school health guidelines and must resort to navigating an overwhelming maze of complex legislative material relating to child health. Yet, knowing these regulations is essential to establishing school policies, procedures, and protocols that align with federal, state, and district laws.

Supplemental to the laws that apply to the health and education of students in nonpublic schools, nonpublic school nurses must be aware of the regulations that apply to their nursing license. Disputes have arisen when practice standards have conflicted with regulations governing education. Therefore, thorough knowledge of the state nurse practice act (NPA) is crucial. Working outside of the usual realm of a healthcare institution means administrative supervisors (often educators) and school lawyers are not well-versed in laws that apply to child health and nursing. Therefore, having ready access to the state NPA is essential. Some state NPAs have a section on the duties of a school nurse. Thus, be aware of legislative changes that may be under consideration by subscribing to updates offered by your state board of nursing. The National Council of State Boards of Nursing (NCSBN) lists all states and their websites (see Resources below).

There is a long history of the United States providing healthcare services to its citizens, particularly to those in need. Federal laws are established and implemented through state statutes and regulations (Stanhope & Lancaster, 2019). Over time, and with the introduction of electronic communication, concerns regarding confidentiality have emerged, particularly the privacy of health information. Two regulations that directly affect school nurses are the Family Educational Rights and Privacy Act (FERPA) and the Health Insurance Portability and Accountability Act (HIPAA. There has been – and continues to be – much confusion over how FERPA and HIPAA pertain to school health records. The National Association of School Nurses (NASN) has amassed a collection of facts about these that may be accessed on their website (www.nasn.org). Below is a brief overview of FERPA and HIPAA affect nonpublic school nurses:

- FERPA - a federal law originally enacted in 1974, which is intended to protect the privacy of the students' educational records, and limits access to those records, except for parents, students of legal age, emancipated minors, or school officials with a justifiable interest in a student's educational record (U.S. Department of Education [USDE], 2021). However, this applies only to schools that receive federal funds from any program managed by the (USDE, 2021). As nonpublic schools generally do not receive such funding, they are not subject to these rules. Nevertheless, if a school district places a student with a disability in a nonpublic school, the records of that student *are* subject to FERPA; the records of the other students attending that school are not (U.S Department of Health and Human Services [USDHHS] & USDE, 2019).

- HIPAA – a privacy rule enacted in 1996 that prevents covered entities from disclosing protected health information (PHI) to others without written consent. Covered entities under HIPAA are individuals or entities that transmit PHI for transactions. Transactions include transmission of healthcare claims, payment and remittance advice, healthcare status, coordination of benefits, enrollment and disenrollment, eligibility checks, healthcare electronic fund transfers, and referral certification and authorization.

Covered entities under HIPAA compliance rules include health plans, healthcare providers, and healthcare clearinghouses (HIPAA Journal, 2022).Generally, nonpublic school settings are not considered "covered entities", but to be certain, contact your school administration to confirm that none of your enrolled students fall within the HIPAA and FERPA guidelines. Even though HIPAA or FERPA may not pertain to the nonpublic school setting, the nonpublic school nurse should continue to follow evidence-based nursing documentation procedures and confidentiality standards.

- Obtaining immunization records from a student's healthcare provider remains problematic for some nonpublic school nurses. In 2021, because of the confusion and restrictions placed upon schools caused by the original HIPAA legislation, modifications were made to "increase flexibility" of HIPAA, one of which applied to immunizations (USDHHS Federal Register, 2021). In this revision, a parent may give verbal permission (instead of written permission) for the healthcare provider to share their child's immunization records. It was communicated to the USDHHS that healthcare providers were unable to consistently obtain *written* permission from parents and guardians, thus causing a delay in sharing immunization records. Now, permission may be received verbally, and a written note made by the person receiving the verbal directive placed in the student's health file at the time (USDHHS) (Federal Register, 2021). However, in states where immunizations are required for school entry, no such permission is necessary to provide this information to the state immunization registry. Permission, whether verbal or written, is considered ongoing until a parent revokes such approval (USDHHS Federal Register, 2021).

- Nevertheless, school nurses continue to encounter healthcare providers who will not share information, citing the HIPAA ruling. As a result, many nonpublic school nurses have successfully avoided this complication by asking for parents' signatures on their annual emergency information form to give permission for the school nurse to exchange healthcare information with their healthcare provider (Brous, 2019). Alternative placement for this permission can be in the school's general consent form or in a statement on the school's annual medical forms, such as the annual physical exam or health history update.

Health Assessments and Screenings

In keeping with legislation, another frequent dilemma encountered by nonpublic school nurses is the topic of student health assessments or examinations. Each state specifies how often health assessments should be completed and contacting the state department of education (DOE) or department of health (DOH) will furnish this information. The approved health assessment forms or health certificates are often available for download at the state website. Providing the link to families will ensure that the correct documentation is completed when they take their child to their healthcare provider. Families of students from out-of-state or overseas will also benefit by having this information before arrival. A general list of state regulations may be found using the Centers for Disease Control and Prevention (CDC) website *Public Health Professionals Gateway* (CDC, 2023). In addition to health assessments and physicals, screening mandates or guidelines may be written into state law, state regulations, or determined by a school district. These school health screenings may include vision, hearing, dental, anthropometric measurements, and scoliosis. Contact your DOE or DOH to determine if these mandates apply to the nonpublic school setting.

Immunizations

Each state mandates immunizations required for entry into school, and the schedule of vaccinations to be administered along with the type of exemptions permitted may be found on each State DOH or DOE website. These sites include exclusion policies and, if allowed, how long a student may stay in school without an immunization record (e.g., District of Columbia permits ten days, North Carolina, 30 days). Even for those states that allow a "grace period", there are policies and procedures for student exclusion if the school feels there is a health risk. Once retrieved, it is advisable that a printed copy of these mandates is kept for use as a reference for clarification or in the event of a dispute when a student lives in one state but attends school in another and immunization laws may differ.

Electronic access to immunization records is becoming more frequent using state immunization registries. Access to these registries, along with their primary contact personnel, may be reached through the Immunization Information Systems (IIS) located at the Centers for Disease Control and Prevention (CDC) website (CDC, 2023). It is advisable to register with the state agency not only to verify the immunization history of a student but to alert the parent or guardian to any discrepancies that may be present.

The promotion of immunizations as essential to preventing disease throughout life is a core tenet of the NASN (NASN, 2020), and the school nurse is in a prime position to provide access to evidence-based, medically accurate information, and to dispel myths that continue to circulate about the dangers of vaccines. Philosophical beliefs were the most common reason parents wished to have their children exempt (AAP, 2016), and discussing these concerns will serve as an opportunity for the school nurse to educate parents on the importance of immunizing their children. One excellent resource on the history, signs and symptoms, schedule, and adverse reactions to all vaccine-preventable diseases may be found in the publication *The 14th Edition Epidemiology and Prevention of Vaccine-Preventable Diseases* (fondly known as "The Pink Book") published by the CDC. This may be purchased as a bound copy or downloaded in its entirety from the CDC website (CDC, 2021). For those schools that enroll students from overseas, this book also contains a section to help translate foreign immunization records. The USDHHS is an additional resource for precise translations of foreign immunization records.

States establish their immunization requirements for both public and nonpublic schools, and most allow exemptions (CDC, 2017). In the event of a vaccine exemption, it is important for the school nurse to apprise these families and the student of the school policy in the event of an outbreak of a communicable disease for which the student has not been immunized, as most states require unvaccinated (or incompletely vaccinated) students to remain at home for a specific length of time. The applicable state immunization department will provide details, along with the procedure for reporting a communicable disease outbreak.

Medications

Most states will have written policies and statutes on the administration of over-the-counter (OTC) and prescription medications, along with identifying individuals who are permitted to administer such medications

(National Association of State Boards of Education [NASBE], 2022). Many states now allow students to carry asthma inhalers and epinephrine auto-injectors with written permission from the student's healthcare provider, a completed individualized healthcare plan (IHP), and an emergency care plan (ECP). However, be sure to check with your state DOE (or DOH) for the most current information.

The management of short-term prescription medications is generally straightforward, and schools should have written policies outlining the requirements for access and administration of these during the school day. Forms should be completed and signed by both the student's healthcare provider and the parent or guardian and should specify a definitive beginning and end date. If it is a medication that the student will require additional doses taken at home, it is recommended that the parent obtain two prescription bottles from the pharmacy – one for home and one for school. This eliminates the need for the parent to come in twice daily to deliver and collect the medication and prevents the temptation for a "baggie" to be used – a practice that should not be permitted in school and discouraged at home. Upon receipt of any medication, the best practice is to note the amount received - and request the parent confirm and co-sign. All medications (except emergency medications such as asthma inhalers, Naloxone, and epinephrine auto-injectors) should be kept in a locked cabinet in the school nurse's office. Ideally, a separate double-locked metal cabinet for controlled substances should be used and kept in the school nurse's office. If a medication needs to be refrigerated, the temperature should be monitored on a regular basis and the refrigerator should be locked (McClanahan et al., 2019). Medication should also be located in the school nurse's office and be a medication-only refrigerator, not one that also stores drinks and snacks.

Student asthma inhalers, epinephrine auto-injectors, and diabetic supplies should be stored in easily retrievable containers with the student's name, photograph, date of birth, ECP, and expiration date of the medication clearly visible in the school nurse's office. Prior to the start of school, it is advisable for the school nurse to meet with the student (and family) to show where his or her medication is kept, and to ensure the student knows how to correctly use their medication. This would also be a suitable time to review school-wide policy and procedures, including staff training, and the student's individual ECP with the student and parent or guardian.

Providing OTCs to manage minor discomforts has been shown to benefit students by keeping them in school (NASN, 2021), yet their use continues to be controversial. The oversight of a healthcare provider in creating policies and procedures for their administration is strongly encouraged, where permitted by federal, state, and district regulations. In addition, federal, state, and district laws must be considered when creating guidelines for the administration of medications, along with state NPA regulations, established safety procedures, and evidence-based practice (NASN, 2021). When determining what stock OTC medication to keep on hand, an historical evaluation of the medications that were most requested over the past three years should be made, then, after discussion and written authorization from the school physician, appropriate supplies may be ordered (NASN, 2021). Annually, all students and their families should be provided with a health form indicating what OTC medications may be administered at the school nurse's discretion during the school day. This form must be signed by the student's healthcare provider and parent. No OTC medication should be administered without these authorizations.

There will be instances (when permitted by state NPAs and state and district regulations) that administration of OTCs may be provided by unlicensed assistive personnel (UAP). The school nurse has the knowledge and necessary expertise to decide whether a UAP is competent to perform this task after taking into consideration the acuity and general status of the student to whom the medication will be given (NASN, 2021). Once all relevant criteria have been met, the school nurse will create a student IHP that provides clear guidelines on the scope and limitations within which the UAP may function (NASN, 2018). The school nurse delegation process to a UAP should encompass the training and oversight of UAP.

These same standards apply in the event of on-and-off-campus school-sponsored field trips. If it is determined that care cannot safely (or legally) be delegated to a UAP during these events, the school nurse should, in conjunction with school administration, arrange for a substitute nurse to be brought in to either cover the health room while the school nurse accompanies the student on the trip (NASN, 2019), or escort the field trip in lieu of the school nurse. If the trip occurs in another state, the school nurse must verify whether that state is a member of the Nurse Licensure Compact (NLC), an interstate alliance that permits RN's located in one state to practice in another (NCSBN, 2022). If the school nurse does not practice in an NLC or the state to be visited is not a NLC member, the school nurse must receive permission from that state board of nursing to practice and establish that permission to practice will include the ability to delegate to UAPs (NCSBN, 2019). In the event of an overseas trip, it is advised that communication with the host country's embassy is made to determine their laws and guidelines regarding prescription and OTC medications.

School Physician

One of the more difficult aspects of working as a registered nurse in a nonpublic school is the lack of interprofessional collaboration, with the absence of a consulting school physician presenting the greatest challenge. In general, many of the students are cared for by a localized group of pediatricians, and with permission from parents, nonpublic school nurses are able to confer with these health professionals on individual students. Some school districts and local governments employ physicians to oversee school health services, but there is no national requirement to make such provisions available (Devore & Wheeler, 2016). To have such a partnership would be invaluable to the nonpublic school nurse. Apart from advising on policies and serving as a consultant on the crisis management team, school physicians can collaborate on written standing orders for the administration of stock emergency medications and emergency treatment protocols, as well as provide confidential consultation on issues of school health that may occur during the school year.

Finding a healthcare provider may be daunting for those new to nonpublic school nursing. Seasoned school nurses propose the following options:

- Advise your school administration of your need and ask if you may be in touch with alumni who have entered the medical field for advice/referrals.
- Approach a parent of an enrolled student who is a pediatrician to ask if they would be willing to serve as a consultant.
- Contact pediatricians who regularly see your enrolled students to ask if they would be willing to serve as a school consultant.
- Be in touch with other nonpublic school nurses in your jurisdiction to ask whom they use.

- Get in touch with your state school nurse consultant to ask for referrals; if your state has no such person, make a direct call to your DOE.
- Contact the American Academy of Pediatrics, the Society for Adolescent Medicine, and the American Academy of Family Physicians for local affiliates that may be able to help.

In some instances, and where federal, state, and local laws permit, a pediatric or family advanced practice registered nurse (APRN) may act as a school health consultant. These advanced nurse practitioners are registered nurses with master's or doctoral degrees in pediatrics or family practice. They provide several clinical practice resources for healthcare providers and families, and work in pediatric offices, departments of health, state boards of nursing, and outpatient clinics.

In either situation, retaining a consulting medical provider or an APRN, the school should develop a contract or Memorandum of Understanding with that provider to establish a professional relationship that would allow for the sharing of confidential information as needed.

CONCLUSION

In the 2019-2020 school year, almost 9% of students in the U.S. were enrolled in nonpublic schools (NCES, 2019). The percentage of those students who have chronic health conditions or are medically fragile is increasing (CDC, 2022) and many nonpublic school nurses will have these students in their school communities. As the sole healthcare provider in their educational setting, knowledge of laws pertaining to education, school health, and nursing must be implemented. For those who have no access to administrative help (indeed the confidential nature of their role within the school makes such help challenging), the task of searching for legislative rulings falls to the nonpublic school nurse. Membership in the Private, Independent, and Parochial School Nurses (PIPSN), a Special Interest Group of NASN, will provide immeasurable help, advice, and support, and in many cases, easy access to legislative materials made available by other nonpublic school nurses. Find out more at www.nasn.org.

RESOURCES

See APPENDIX: Are private schools required to comply with federal laws e.g., ADA?

See ADDENDUM: Tort Claims Liability

Agency for Healthcare Research and Quality - http://www.ahrq.gov

American Academy of Pediatrics – https://www.aap.org

American Academy of Pediatrics – Healthy Children – https://www.healthychildren.org

American Nurses Association - http://www.nursingworld.org/

Asthma & Allergy Foundation of America - http://www.aafa.org/

Centers for Disease Control and Prevention - http://www.cdc.gov

Centers for Disease Control and Prevention Immunization Information Systems (2023). https://www.cdc.gov/vaccines/programs/iis/

Centers for Disease Control and Prevention Morbidity and Mortality Weekly Report (MMWR) - http://www.cdc.gov/mmwr/index.html

Centers for Disease Control and Prevention National Notifiable Diseases Surveillance System (NNDSS) - https://wwwn.cdc.gov/nndss/

Food Allergy and Research Education - https://www.foodallergy.org/

Healthy People 2030 - https://www.cdc.gov/nchs/healthy_people/hp2030/hp2030.html

Institute for Safe Medication Practices - http://www.ismp.org

National Association of Pediatric Nurse Practitioners - https://www.napnap.org

National Association of School Nurses - www.nasn.org

National Association of School Nurses HIPAA and FERPA - https://www.nasn.org/nasn-resources/resources-by-topic/school-health-documentation/hipaa-ferpa

National Council of State Boards of Nursing - https://www.ncsbn.org

U.S. Department of Education - http://www.ed.gov

U.S. Department of Health and Human Services - https://www.hhs.gov

U.S. Department of Justice - https://www.justice.gov

U.S. Department of Justice Civil Rights Division - https://www.justice.gov/crt

United States Office of the Executive Branch Web Sites - http://www.loc.gov/rr/news/fedgov.html

U. S. Department of Justice, Civil Rights Division - https://www.justice.gov/crt

REFERENCES

American Academy of Pediatrics. (2016). Countering vaccine hesitancy. *Pediatrics, 138* (3), e20162146. https://doi.org/10.1542/peds.2016-2146

Brous, E. (2019). The law and school nursing practice. In J. Selekman, R.A. Shannon, & C.F. Yonkaitis (Eds.), *School nursing. A comprehensive text* (3rd ed., pp. 136–153). F.A.Davis.

Centers for Disease Control and Prevention. (2017). *State school immunization requirements and vaccine exemption laws.* https://www.cdc.gov/vaccines/imz-managers/coverage/schoolvaxview/requirements/

Centers for Disease Control and Prevention. (2021). *Epidemiology and prevention of vaccine-preventable diseases. The pink book* (14th ed.) https://www.cdc.gov/vaccines/pubs/pinkbook

Centers for Disease Control and Prevention. *(2022). Healthy schools.* https://www.cdc.gov/chronicdisease/resources/publications/factsheets/healthy-schools.htm

Centers for Disease Control and Prevention. (2023). *Public health professionals gateway: State and territorial health department websites.* https://www.cdc.gov/publichealthgateway/healthdirectories/healthdepartments.html

Child Welfare Information Gateway. (2019). *About CAPTA: A legislative history.* U.S. Department of Health and Human Services, Children›s Bureau. https://www.childwelfare.gov/pubs/factsheets/about/

Devore, C. & Wheeler, L. (2016). Role of the school physician. In American Academy of Pediatrics Council on School Health (Eds.). *School health policy and practice* (7th ed.). https://doi.org/10.1542/9781581108453-ch03_sub01_sect04

HIPAA Journal. (2022). *What are covered entities under HIPAA.* https://www.hipaajournal.com/covered-entities-under-hipaa

McClanahan, R., Shannon, R. A., & Kahn, P. (2019). School health office management. In J. Selekman, Shannon, R. A.& Yonkaitis, C. F. (Eds.), *School nursing: A comprehensive text* (3rd ed.) F. A. Davis.

National Association of School Nurses. (2018). *Nursing delegation to unlicensed assistive personnel in the school setting* (Position statement). https://www.nasn.org/nasn-resources/resources-by-topic/delegation

National Association of School Nurses. (2019). *School-sponsored trips, role of the school nurse* (Position Statement). https://www.nasn.org/nasn-resources/professional-practice-documents/position-statements/ps-trips

National Association of School Nurses. (2020). *Immunizations* (Position statement). -https://www.nasn.org/nasn-resources/professional-practice-documents/position-statements/ps-immunizations

National Association of School Nurses. (2021). *School nursing evidence-based clinical practice guidance: Medication administration in schools implementation toolkit.* http://www.pathlms.com/nasn/courses/36927

National Association of State Boards of Education . (2022). *Enhancing school-based health services.* https://nasbe.nyc3.digitaloceanspaces.com/2022/11/Blanco_School-Based-Health-Final.pdf

National Center for Education Statistics. (2019). *Private school enrollment.* https://nces.ed.gov/programs/coe/indicator/cgc/private-school-enrollment

National Council of State Boards of Nursing . (2019). *National guidelines for nursing delegation.* https://www.ncsbn.org/public-files/NGND-PosPaper_06.pdf

National Council of State Boards of Nursing. (2022). *Nurse licensure compact.* https://www.ncsbn.org/compacts/nurse-licensure-compact.page

Stanhope, M., and Lancaster, J. (Eds). (2019). *Public health nursing: Population-centered health care in the community* (8th ed.). Elsevier.

U.S. Department of Education. (2021). *Family Education Rights and Privacy Act.* http://www2.ed.gov/policy/gen/guid/fpco/ferpa/index.html)

U.S. Department of Health and Human Services. (2021). *HIPAA for professionals.* http://www.hhs.gov/hipaa/for-professionals/index.html

U.S. Department of Health and Human Services & U.S. Department of Education. (2019). *Joint guidance on the application of the Family Educational Rights and Privacy Act (FERPA) and the Health Insurance Portability and Accountability Act of 1966 (HIPAA) to student health records.* https://studentprivacy.ed.gov/resources/joint-guidance-application-ferpa-and-hipaa-student-health-records

U.S. Department of Health and Human Services, Federal Register. (2021). *Modification to the Health Insurance Portability and Accountability Act., 86(12),* pp.6447-6450. https://www.federalregister.gov/documents/2021/01/21/2020-27157/proposed-modifications-to-the-hipaa-privacy-rule-to-support-and-remove-barriers-to-coordinated-care

APPENDIX

Are nonpublic schools required to comply with federal laws e.g., ADA?

Privately-run childcare centers -- like other public accommodations such as nonpublic schools, recreation centers, restaurants, hotels, movie theaters, and banks -- must comply with Title III of the ADA. Childcare services provided by government agencies, such as Head Start, summer programs, and extended school day programs, must comply with Title II of the ADA. Both Titles apply to a childcare center's interactions with the children, parents, guardians, and potential customers that it serves. The exception is childcare centers that are actually run by religious entities such as churches, mosques, or synagogues. Title III does not cover activities controlled by religious organizations) (U. S. Department of Justice, Civil Rights Division).

When schools are religious-based - i.e., a religious organization controls all aspects of the school's governance - they ARE exempt from federal laws. Having said that, of course, the school will need to check with their attorney, who should know the specifics of their school, as even one child receiving any type of federal assistance will nullify that exemption.

Exemptions also apply to transportation. For example, if a completely run religious school owns the transportation, it does not have to comply with ADA requirements (i.e., a pneumatic lift or ramp to load a wheelchair). However, again, the school must check with their attorney (and it is advisable that the school nurse get the attorney's response in writing to keep on file as they are the ones who initially deal with parents).

RESOURCES

- **Overview from USDE on the role of Federal Government in Education**: https://www2.ed.gov/policy/landing.jhtml?src=pn

- **10 Facts about K-12 Education Funding:** https://www.ed.gov/category/keyword/K-12

- ADA & Private Schools: https://study.com/academy/lesson/ada-private-schools.html

- **Architectural and Transportation Barriers Compliance Board**: http://uscode.house.gov/statviewer.htm?volume=104&page=363

ADDENDUM: Tort Claims Liability

Erin D. Gilsbach, Esquire, 2017
Reviewed by Herbert Z. Rosen, Esquire, 2023

The possibility of tort claims and malpractice actions, from which public schools are largely immune in most states, heightens the professional risk for school nurses and results in the need for additional protections for nurses. All states have some form of sovereign limitation for immunity tort claims I. The National Council of State Legislatures provides a helpful table of authority listing tort claims legislation by state. That resource can be found at: http://www.ncsl.org/research/transportation/state-sovereign-immunity-and-tort-liability.aspx

In most states, public schools fall within the full protection of their state's sovereign immunity laws due to the fact that they are local governmental entities. Sovereign immunity does not protect school officials against cases involving intentional harm, but they do provide varying degrees of protection for negligence and other non-intentional torts. Private and parochial schools, however, are not afforded this protection. While this fact is significant for the schools themselves, it is even more important to the non-public school nurses. Medical malpractice or professional liability deals with professional negligence and is a subset of tort law from which public school nurses generally have immunity. The same is not true for a nurse in a nonpublic school setting. This type of liability has the potential to be very costly, and a legal finding of professional negligence can result in the loss of employment, difficulty obtaining future employment in that field due to the fact that court documents are public records and potential action by the state against the nurse's license. The latter is, perhaps, the most damaging because the loss of licensure for a nurse equates to the complete loss of any potential employment in the field of nursing.

Due to the potential for liability, nonpublic school nurses need to take steps to ensure that they are protected from devastating loss. The first thing that they should do is determine whether the school's insurance policy would cover a professional liability claim. Most insurance companies require schools to take out additional and specific professional liability policies (sometimes called "Errors and Omissions" policies). Where the school does have coverage for professional liability claims, the nurse should also verify whether such policies specifically include coverage for medical professional liability claims. In addition to determining whether coverage exists and is applicable to the nurse, it is also a good idea to determine the policy limitations, such as the amount of coverage and any specific exclusions. Where no coverage exists, or where the existing coverage is not sufficient, nonpublic school nurses will need to consider obtaining their own professional liability coverage. Where coverage does exist, school nurses should review the coverage to determine whether it provides licensure protection and will cover the costs of a nurse if they are required to defend their actions before the board of nursing or other licensure-issuing body.

Chapter 59

SCHOOL-SPONSORED FIELD TRIPS

Maria D. Krol, DNP, RNC-NIC, ACUE*
Frances Penny, PhD, RN, MPH, MSN, IBCLC, CNL*

DESCRIPTION OF ISSUE

School-sponsored field trips enhance the student's educational experience but may also create many challenges for the school nurse if the student requires health services during the field trip. Federal law generally requires equal access to school attendance and school-sponsored activities, which may require the provision of health services. Including the Nurse Licensure Compact (NLC) states, discussed later in this chapter, nursing practice laws and regulations vary from state to state. A critical issue of concern is delegating nursing healthcare services to unlicensed assistive personnel (UAP) on school-sponsored trips. A review of state laws, regulations, and nursing scope of practice for school health services in both the state of residence and the state where the field trip occurs is critical when planning and problem-solving for students requiring school health services on field trips.

Field trips offer a wonderful learning opportunity for students. The school and the teacher determine the number of field trips offered to enhance learning during a school year. However, students attending school today include an increasing number of children with special healthcare needs. For these students to attend school or participate in school-sponsored activities, the delegation of school health services may be necessary when a shortage of school nurses exists. Nursing practice laws differ from state to state and may not allow for the delegation of school health services to UAP. Additionally, the home or destination state may have restrictions or mandates relative to the possession or administration of medications, particularly controlled drugs. For example, does the destination state nursing scope of practice allow for administering or delegating intranasal Midazolam (Versed) or medical marijuana? An understanding of state laws, regulations, and nursing scope of practice is essential when planning for the delivery of necessary student health services on both in-state and out-of-state field trips.

BACKGROUND

For students to participate fully on field trips, schools are usually obligated by law to provide any health service accommodation necessary for the student to have full access to the activity. The location of the field trip may vary from a local site to a different city, state, or country. Laws that protect students with special healthcare needs include 1) Section 504 of the Rehabilitation Act of 1973, 2) Title II of the American Disabilities Act of 1990 (ADA), and 3) the Individuals with Disability Education Improvement Act (IDEIA) reauthorized in 2004. All students, regardless of disability or special healthcare needs, have a right to attend and have full access to all school-sponsored activities (including field trips) (US Department of Education [USDE],2020). School nurses must be included in the planning process for school-sponsored field trips that may include accommodations for healthcare needs, required medications or treatments and potential emergency care. It is also important

---

*Original authors: Karen Erwin, RN, MSN & Sandra Clark, RN (2017)

that school nurses collaborate with other staff to ensure all needs are met; however, the role of the school nurse is critical, as stated within the NASN position statement (NASN, 2019).

School nurses who provide healthcare to students should know their state's laws governing nursing. However, when a field trip occurs out-of-state or out-of-country, it is equally important to know and understand the laws and regulations for nursing practice in the state or countries where the care will be administered. School nurses should be particularly aware of the nursing practice regulations regarding delegation, medications, treatment, and emergency care.

In-State, Out-of-State, or Out-of-Country Field Trips and Nursing Scope of Practice

Federal law generally requires equal access to school-sponsored activities and field trips, including providing school health services on field trips (USDE, 2020). Students may usually not be denied access to these activities. While the school nurse is familiar with the nursing scope of practice in the state of residence, it is essential that the school nurse also understand the nursing practice laws where the field trip occurs. Nurses providing health services on out-of-state field trips must adhere to the state nursing law of the state they visit. If the field trip occurs out-of-country, the U.S. Embassy can provide information on whom to contact for that country.

Nurse Licensure Compact States

The Nurse Licensure Compact (NLC) is a mutual recognition model of licensure, similar to a driver's license, that provides the privilege of driving in another state without requiring another driver's license. The NLC is based on the nurse's license from their state of residence but provides the privilege to practice in another NLC member state. Nurses in a participating NLC member state do not have to obtain another nursing license to administer care. However, the nurse is obligated to follow the nurse practice laws of the destination state. Like a driver's license, the licensee must know and follow the rules for that particular state and not the state of residence.

Figure 1- *Map of NLC membership*

Note. This map shows the Nurse Licensure Compact (NLC). Copyright 2023 National Council of State Boards of Nursing, Inc. (Reprinted with Permission). Visit https://www.nursecompact.com/

Not all states are NLC members that provide a Multi-State License (MSL). A nurse in a NLC non-member state has a single-state license that limits practice to that specific state. Furthermore, a nurse whose primary state of residence is a non-compact state and who applies for a license in a compact state is issued a single-state license.

The NLC and the APRN Compact allow nurses to practice in other compact states with a single multi-state license. The NLC provides multi-state rights for registered nurses (RN) and licensed practical/vocational nurses (LPN/LVN) who reside in a member state. The APRN Compact provides the same rights to advanced practice registered nurses. When considering an out-of-state field trip, the school nurse must clearly understand the nursing scope of practice and delegation regulations in the state where care will be provided. Some states do not allow for delegating nursing tasks to UAP, while others may limit the nursing tasks that may be delegated. The school nurse is responsible for complying with the nurse practice laws where care will be administered. If the nurse may delegate a task that is permissible in the nurse's home licensing state but not in the state where the field trip occurs, the nurse's actions are accountable to both state boards of nursing (National Council of State Boards of Nursing [NCSBN], 2019).

Considerations to include when planning an out-of-state field trip include:
- Do I hold a MSL?
- Is the state to be visited a member of the Nurse Licensure Compact?
- Does the state where the field trip will occur have the same scope of nursing practice? If not, what are the differences? Contacting the board of nursing in the state where the field trip will occur may be necessary to clarify the nursing scope of practice.
- Are RNs permitted to delegate school health nursing services to UAPs in the state to be visited?
- If delegation is permitted, are there limitations to the delegation?
- If delegation is allowed, is training and competency verification required for the UAP?

IMPLICATIONS FOR SCHOOL NURSE PRACTICE

Not every school has a school nurse; not all state nursing laws and regulations are the same, and not all state laws allow for the delegation of nursing school health services to UAP. Therefore, when organizing plans for a field trip, the school nurse should be consulted for any health services that may be required.

Nursing health service considerations should include, but not be limited to:
- What health services accommodations are required by the students participating in the field trip (i.e., equipment needs, availability of privacy for medication or treatments, nursing assessment? see below)
- Storage or refrigeration of medications
- Are accommodations specified in Individual Health Plan (IHP), Individual Education Plan (IEP) or Section 504 Plan? Consider the activity and the student's limitations.
- Does the student have an Emergency Action Plan (EAP)?
- Food allergies or special dietary considerations, or other allergies
- What are the school's policies and procedures for providing school health services while on a school-sponsored field trip?
- What is the availability of trained staff to provide healthcare services?

- Availability of Emergency Medical Services (EMS)
- Handicap accessibility needs, including accessible transportation
- Where will the field trip occur (in-state, out-of-state, out-of-country)?
- If out-of-state, what are the nursing practice laws of the state the students will visit?
- Does the state where the field trip occurs allow for the delegation of nursing health services to UAP?
- If out-of-state, is the state a Nurse Compact Licensure State? If not, what does the state where the field trip will take place require for the licensed registered nurse to provide care in that state? Is there a different requirement for LPN or LVN?
- Are there restrictions related to the storage, possession, or administration of particular medications or substances if out-of-state?
- What options are available for alteration of the trip if not all students can be reasonably accommodated?

Use of Nursing Assessment

What is the level of care required for the student? Will medications or clinical procedures be required to be provided during the time of the field trip? Can the student provide self-care, self-monitoring, and self-administration of medication? Regardless of the location of the field trip, the nurse must assess the healthcare needs of the students who will be participating in the field trip.

Student Accommodations

Does the student have an IHP, IEP, or Section 504 Plan? What are the accommodations within the student's specific plan that must also be provided on the field trip? Are the accommodations reasonable, or can the accommodations be revised for the trip, e.g., MDs may write orders to forego glucagon on a day trip and use glucose gel and 911 depending on the location? Costs associated with any accommodation specified in the student's plan are the school's responsibility and must be considered during the planning of any field trip.

The school nurse is familiar with the healthcare services and accommodations the student requires to participate fully in school-sponsored functions. This familiarity gives the school nurse the unique position to coordinate the individual student's care needs on a field trip. Planning and coordination of what the student health services requirements may include:

- Assessing the method of transportation for the field trip, consulting with school food service personnel on the food to be served, determining the staff who will be present, the layout of the planned site, the duration of the trip, and emergency medical care proximity.
- Determining the medication and healthcare treatments or procedures that must be provided during the field trip and the potential for health emergencies (NASN, 2019).

Emergency Action Plan (EAP)

Does the student have asthma, diabetes, seizures, or a risk for anaphylaxis? A student Emergency Action Plan (EAP) is written by a registered professional school nurse based on the Individual Health Plan (IHP) or is sometimes used instead of an IHP. Using succinct terminology, the EAP should be written in clear action steps that school UAP can understand. The EAP should include how to treat the emergency, the name of the student's healthcare provider, phone number, and parent or legal guardian contact information. Does the school provide the medication for emergency treatment for the student who may have an undocumented risk of anaphylaxis? (NASN, 2020). The EAP may have to be adjusted during the school day based on individual circumstances during the field trip. EMS may have to be activated if the school nurse cannot access emergency medications.

Considerations for out-of-country field trips:

- Obtain permission for emergency treatment as determined by chaperones/school trip coordinators.
- Determine if the district requires students to have an insurance policy for medical care, including emergency transport back to U.S. if needed.
- Determine if any immunization requirements exist for the destination country.
- Determine if any Health Alerts exist for the destination country.
- Have copies of all prescriptions for prescription medication. Carry all medication on the plane, do not pack in luggage (Wisconsin Department of Public Instruction, 2019).

School Policies and Procedures

Does the school have specific policies and procedures/protocols in place for all students to participate in school-sponsored activities? Does the school have a system to ensure that all school field trip responsible personnel have been consulted on the upcoming field trip? Furthermore, does the school allow students to self-carry and self-administer their medications while on the field trip? Some schools use a checklist that also includes the signature of the school nurse to ensure that all student accommodations have been arranged for the field trip and according to any existing accommodation plans of care.

Trained Staff Availability

Before the school field trip occurs, it is essential that the school nurse determine the availability of school staff to provide the necessary healthcare services during the field trip. What medications or supplies must be provided on the field trip? If the school nurse is not attending the field trip, are there trained staff who can safely perform the health service?

"The level of nursing or healthcare services required for a student in the classroom is, at a minimum, the same level of care that the student requires during school programs outside the classroom" (Hootman et al., 2005, p. 223). School districts should have procedures/protocols in place for the provision of health services, including acquiring medications and supplies from the student's parents or legal guardians, well in advance of the date of the trip so that the provision of health services for students while they are away from the school building is the same level of care received in the school building (Wisconsin Department of Public Instruction, 2019). Parents may be invited to attend the trip to provide care for their child. However, schools may not mandate parents to accommodate their child (NASN, 2020).

Delegation of School Health Services

Delegation of nursing tasks in the school setting can be a valuable tool for school nurses, especially during field trips. Delegation of nursing services is defined as transferring the responsibility of performing a nursing activity to another person while retaining accountability for the outcome (American Nurses Association [ANA] & NCSBN, 2019. The nursing scope of practice in any state, including the delegation of nursing health services, is typically governed by the state's board of nursing and varies from state to state. State nurse practice acts, or equivalent state statutes, define the legal parameters for nursing practice, which may include delegation (ANA, 2019). Professional organizations such as the ANA and the National Association for School Nurses (NASN) have developed standards of practice and policy statements to provide guidance on daily nursing practice. They are utilized and referred to in a court of law (Erwin et al., 2014).

Delegation of school nursing services is a complex skill requiring clinical judgment and final accountability of the client (ANA & NCSBN, 2019). The RN determines when a nursing service is appropriate to delegate to a UAP. The licensed nurse cannot delegate nursing judgment or any activity involving nursing judgment or critical decision-making (ANA & NSCBN, 2019, p.2).

Determination of whether the delegation of a specific nursing task is appropriate in the school setting or on a field trip includes:
- RN assessment of the student health services needed
- Determined on a case-by-case basis
- Stability and acuity of the student's condition
- Potential for harm
- Complexity of task
- Predictability of outcomes
- Availability/competency of UAP
- Type and frequency of supervision required for UAP (ANA, 2019)

The decision to delegate and supervise a nursing task in schools is the responsibility of the registered nurse. For more guidance on determining the appropriateness of delegating a school nursing health service, please refer to the ANA's *Principles for Delegation by Registered Nurses to Unlicensed Assistive Personnel (UAP)* and *Chapter 4,* including a nursing delegation decision tree (ANA, 2019). Not all nursing practices are appropriate to delegate, and some states do not allow for the delegation of nursing health services to a UAP. Therefore, when planning a field trip, particularly if out-of-state or out-of-country, the RN must determine the nursing laws for the state or country where the field trip will occur, including clarifying with the state's board of nursing whether alternative, natural medications are allowed.

According to NCSBN, the school nurse will need to contact the boards of nursing in the states where the field trips occur to determine the practice allowances for the licensed nurse related to the delegation of nursing function (NCSBN, 2019).

CONCLUSION

School-sponsored trips provide an opportunity for the student to expand their learning potential. Many variables must be considered when planning the field trip so that the student's healthcare needs are continued to be provided. The school nurse's knowledge and expertise to provide safe, optimal healthcare services is critical to the planning and collaboration with key school personnel, school administrators, families, and students attending the field trip. Pre-planning is of utmost importance, including reviewing state nursing laws, regulations, and nursing scope of practice to identify potential problems and ensure the safe delivery of school health services to each student participating in the field trip.

RESOURCES

See Appendix: School Nurse Field Trip Checklist

Field Trips: Guidance for School Nurses. (2014). Connecticut State Department of Education, APPENDIX A Sample letters to out-of-state boards of nursing. Downloadable from http://www.sde.ct.gov/sde/cwp/browse.asp?A=2663&BMDRN=2000&BCOB=0&C=21291

Massachusetts Field Trip Tool Kit. (2015). ESHS CQI Project. Downloadable from https://neushi.org/student/programs/attachments/FieldTrip.pdf

Wisconsin Department of Public Instruction (2019). *Meeting student health needs while on field trips tool kit for Wisconsin schools.* https://dpi.wi.gov/sites/default/files/imce/sspw/pdf/Meeting_Student_Health_ Needs_While_on_Field_Trips_Tool_Kit.pdf

National Council of State Boards of Nursing: Resources on Nurse Licensure Compacts https://www.ncsbn.org/compacts.page

REFERENCES

American Nurses Association. (2019). *Principles for delegation by registered nurses to unlicensed assistive personnel (UAP).* Author.

American Nurses Association & National Council of State Boards of Nursing. (2019). *Joint statement on delegation.* https://www.ncsbn.org/nursing-regulation/practice/delegation.page

American with Disabilities Act of 1990 (ADA) (2000). 42 U.S.C §§ 12101-12213

Erwin, K., Clark, S., & Mercer, S. (2014). Providing health services for children with special health care needs on out-of-state field trips. *NASN School Nurse, 29*(2), 85-88. https://doi.org/10.1177/1942602X13517005

Hootman, J., Schwab, N.C., Gelfman, M.H.B., Gregory, E.K. & Pohlman, K.J. (2005). School nursing practice: Clinical performance issues. In M.H. Gelfman & N.C. Schwab (Eds.). *Legal issues in school health services* (pp. 167-229). Authors Choice Press.

Individuals with Disability Education Improvement Act (2004). 20 USC 14 et seq.

National Association of School Nurses. (2020*). Use of Individualized healthcare plans to support school health services* (Position Statement). (Position Statement). Author. https://www.nasn.org/nasn-resources/professional-practice-documents/position-statements/ps-ihps

National Association of School Nurses. (2019). *School-sponsored trips, role of the school nurse* (Position Statement Author. https://www.nasn.org/nasn-resources/professional-practice-documents/position-statements/ps-trips

National Council of State Boards of Nursing. (2023). *Nursing license compact.* http://www.ncsbn.org/nurse-licensure-compact.htm

Rehabilitation Act of 1973, USC § 504

U. S. Department of Education. (2020). Protecting *students with disabilities: Frequently asked questions about Section 504 and the education of children with disabilities.* https://www2.ed.gov/about/offices/list/ocr/504faq.html

Wisconsin Department of Public Instruction (2019). M*eeting student health needs while on field trips tool kit for Wisconsin schools.* https://dpi.wi.gov/sites/default/files/imce/sspw/pdf/Meeting_Student_Health_Needs_While_ on_Field_Trips_Tool_Kit.pdf

SCHOOL-SPONSORED FIELD TRIPS

APPENDIX

SCHOOL NURSE FIELD TRIP CHECKLIST

Trip Destination _____   Date of Field Trip: _____

Field Trip Coordinator: _____

_____1) Review school district policy and follow the plan accordingly.

_____2) Review the district/school filed trip request form and develop a list of all attending students.

_____3) Identify all health-related issues and concerns, including students with food allergies and accessibility for attending students.

_____4) Review Individual Healthcare Plans, Individual Education Plans, Section 504 Accommodation Plans, and Emergency Action Plans (EAP) for attending students.

_____5) Evaluate to determine whether the parent/guardian of the student with medical needs plans to accompany the field trip.

_____6) Review nursing scope of practice and applicable state laws and regulations for in-state, out-of-state, and out-of-country field trips, including whether delegation to UAP and who may delegate (RN, LPN). Is the destination state a MLS state?

_____7) Determine what emergency/medical services are available at the destination site as necessary

_____8) Notify the Field Trip Coordinator if a nurse is required for the field trip.

_____9) Prepare any necessary forms for documentation of medication administration, special healthcare procedures/treatments, copies of EAPs, licensed prescribed orders, and parent and physician contact information is to be included.

_____10) Prepare necessary equipment, medications, and first aid supplies, including medications to be refrigerated, care plans, and treatment plans.

_____11) Review medical concerns, medication administration, treatment plans, and emergency protocols with the nurse or staff member attending the field trip.

_____12) Provide current cell phone number to attending nurse/staff/chaperone for ongoing consultation for student health concerns if needed.

_____13) If a nurse is **NOT** accompanying the field trip:
  - Notify parent/guardian of the names of staff personnel who will be administering student's medications and or/treatments. Obtain parenteral/guardian written consent.
  - Train staff members in medication administration, epinephrine, glucagon medication administration (as state practice act allows), Cardio Pulmonary Resuscitation, and necessary healthcare treatments as indicated and document all training.

_____14) When the field trip is completed, ensure all medications, equipment, care plans, first aid supplies, and other confidential information/forms are returned to the school nurse.

CHECKLIST COMPLETED: School Nurse: _____   DATE: _____

Chapter 60

TRANSPORTATION OF STUDENTS WITH HEALTH CONCERNS

Suzanne Levasseur, MSN, APRN, CPNP, NCSN

DESCRIPTION OF ISSUE

Since 1939, school transportation safety experts have developed and revised safety standards for school buses (National Congress on School Transportation, n.d.). Currently, it is estimated that approximately 25 million children ride school buses to and from school (National Center for Education Statistics, 2021). For school nurses, legal issues arise in bus accidents, transporting students via ambulances following an illness or injury at school, and transporting students with disabilities.

Transporting all students requires planning and often is monitored by the school transportation coordinator. Transporting students with disabilities requires more careful planning and preparation by the school team, including special education administrators. The school nurse can also play a pivotal role. Together, they are equipped to understand the various considerations involved in a transportation plan. Traveling to and from school daily is only one component of the plan. Consideration must also be given to traveling between schools, traveling within a school building, any specialized equipment needed to accomplish transportation (such as ramps, wheelchairs, or lifts), specially trained staff, and transportation modes and means. The unique needs of the student must be addressed on a case-by-case basis.

BACKGROUND

Millions of students ride on school buses every day. Thanks to safety standards and regulations, bus accidents are less common than other vehicular accidents. In fact, buses are cited as the safest vehicles on the road (National Association of State Directors of Pupil Transportation Services [NASDPT], 2023). Nonetheless, school districts should have policies and procedures to address transportation concerns.

In most districts, the district provides transportation to and from school for students who do not live within walking distance, but this service remains up to the district policy and state law. The IDEA regulations promulgated at 34 CFR 300.34(c) (16) (United States Department of Education [USDE], n.d.) lists transportation as a related service. Transportation is provided as a related service for a student with a disability if the student requires transportation to benefit from special education and related services. When the school district provides transportation to all students, if a special education student requires specialized transportation beyond that provided to the general education population, specialized transportation may be provided as a related service in the Individual Education Program (IEP).

A student may live a short distance from school but because of a disability, be unable to ambulate or may need specialized transportation such as a wheelchair-accessible van. IDEA would consider whether the child requires transportation as a related service to benefit from special education. If a disability does not allow the student to get to school like their non-disabled peers, the local educational agency (LEA) must provide the related service of transportation (Pfrommer, 2022). In addition, if a school district does provide transportation to the general school population, it must also provide transportation to the student with a disability in any special education program where the district has placed the student. It should also include any transportation needs for transition training or community placements that prepare the student for postsecondary needs.

Under Section 504 of the Rehabilitation Act of 1973 (29 USC § 794), districts must provide transportation if necessary to allow students with disabilities the same access to transportation as their non-disabled peers. Additionally, the same legal standard may require specialized transportation if the student's disabilities require it to ensure equal access to school. A student with health needs may require more specialized care in school and may require that care during transportation. For example, a student's disability may require someone trained to provide emergency medication during transport to accompany them.

Specialized transportation should also be considered for a student with a temporary disability, such as a broken leg or after surgery.

Because of Section 504 nondiscrimination principles, students with disabilities must have access to and opportunity to participate in extracurricular activities and field trips the same as their non-disabled peers. If the IEP team has determined that extracurricular activities or community placements are necessary to allow the student an equal opportunity for participation, and if that access requires specialized transportation, then the school district must provide this service (Pfrommer, 2022).

IMPLICATIONS FOR SCHOOL NURSE PRACTICE

School nurses are a vital part of the school team when a child requires their health needs to be addressed during transport and in deciding on transportation for disabled or medically complex students. As part of the general education team, IEP Team, and Section 504 team, the school nurse is instrumental in developing a plan related to transportation. For children with special healthcare needs, the nursing process should start with a comprehensive health assessment that includes a functional nursing diagnosis and identification of student health status and any developmental issues. This assessment should be done with input from the healthcare provider, parent(s), and community resources involved with the student. After the assessment phase is complete, the school nurse can identify outcomes to begin to plan for the student's transportation needs, which should be included in an individualized healthcare plan (IHP) and/or individualized transportation plan (ITP) (often cited within a Section 504 plan or IEP). Collaborating with the transportation department and the school team and educating the bus driver about the needed accommodations are also an important role of the school nurse.

Any recommendations for necessary modifications, aids, and nursing interventions involved in transportation should be shared with the school IEP or Section 504 team, decided on during the evaluation process of the meeting, and should be reflected in the student's IEP or Section 504 plan, respectively. Some states have developed a separate plan to be utilized in conjunction with a Section 504 plan or IEP, to further outline the specifics of care required for transportation. *See* Pennsylvania Department of Health. *Individual Transportation Plan.*

TRANSPORTATION OF STUDENTS WITH HEALTH CONCERNS

Considerations for Students with Health Concerns

Mode of Transportation

The school administration should make decisions regarding the type of vehicle needed in conjunction with the transportation coordinator, school nurse, and parent(s). Safe transportation of the student is the highest priority. Many different types of vehicles can be used, including regular school buses, private cars, minibuses, taxis, and, when necessary, ambulances with trained emergency personnel. This may be dictated by state law/regulations or LEA policy/rules. IDEA's least restrictive environment (LRE) requirement requires school districts to transport students with a disability with their non-disabled peers as appropriate relative to this student's needs. For a student with a wheelchair, a bus with a ramp that can safely transport a wheelchair will be necessary. In addition, the time a student with disabilities is on the bus or other transportation should be comparable to their non-disabled peers.

Sometimes, timing accommodations are necessary because of the student's needs; a student may be the last to be picked up or the first dropped off.

Required Personnel

The Section 504 team or IEP team, in conjunction with the school nurse, will determine if school health services or school nurse services during transportation are required to ensure the provision of a Free Appropriate Public Education (FAPE)and to avoid discrimination. School nurses should be knowledgeable about their state statutes, nurse practice acts and standards, and scope of practice regarding delegation to determine if the student's health services needs can be safely met by unlicensed assistive personnel (UAP) on transportation. This delegation requires appropriate training and supervision by the school nurse if permissible. It may also be determined that the student's needs require a licensed nurse to accompany the student on the bus. Sometimes, the school district may contract with an outside agency to provide the necessary personnel. The school nurse or nursing supervisor would be the appropriate person to communicate the student's needs to the outside agency to ensure the appropriate care level is provided. A backup plan, including training of additional staff, should also be in effect for the possibility of staff illness or absence.

Effective communication with transportation providers is essential. Any potential problems or concerns of any student should be shared with transportation providers, monitors, or any other staff members involved with the care of students on transportation. Training of transportation staff may also be indicated as a supplemental support or service. Transportation workers that receive personally identifiable information about the student (protected under the Family Educational Rights and Privacy Act) should also receive training to protect that information's confidentiality. The school nurse may be the most qualified school personnel to share that information with transportation staff, along with other special education or Section 504-responsible administrators.

Safety during transportation must be addressed in the student's IHP and ITP. Emergency equipment, such as oxygen, epinephrine, or suctioning equipment, must be with the student during transportation. Equipment, and any emergency medications, should be safely stored and secured but accessible in an emergency and have fully charged batteries. If necessary, communication methods should be established between the bus driver, aide, school nurse, and Emergency Medical Service (EMS). Walkie-Talkies or cell phones should be available.

The comprehensive training program for the personnel responsible for the student on the bus should include training on any implements or equipment required for the student.

In School Transportation

The definition of transportation also involves moving in and around the school building. The school nurse should be part of the planning for needed equipment such as ramps, lifts, and wheelchairs. The school district is responsible for providing the needed equipment to navigate the school at no cost to the student and family (Norlin et al., 2015). For some students, an aide may also be required in this process.

Field Trips/School Sponsored Trips

A student with a disability cannot be denied access to a field trip/school-sponsored trip due to transportation issues (Pfrommer, 2022) or nursing service issues. The student's individualized transportation needs must be met in the same way as transportation to and from school. School nurses should incorporate field trip planning in the student's IHP and ITP. *(See Chapter 59 for more information on school-sponsored field trips).*

Considerations for General Education Students

Because only a few laws govern transportation for general education students, school district policy is generally the guiding principle. Therefore, as health experts in the school, school nurses should be consulted in policy development for their school district. *McKinney-Vento,* a federal law, contains transportation provisions that require local educational agencies (LEAs) to provide students experiencing homelessness with transportation to and from the school at the request of a parent/guardian (McKinney-Vento Homeless Assistance Act, 2004). *McKinney-Vento* is one example of a federal mandate that requires multiple school departments to work together to properly implement required transportation for certain students. *(See Chapter 14 for more information on Mc-Kinney-Vento Act Homeless Assistance Act).*

Bus Accidents

Some school nurses have been asked to respond to bus accidents. While the nurse may also feel it constitutes part of his/her emergency duties, other matters should be considered. In an area with a quick emergency response time, the Emergency Medical Services (EMS) provider would be the person in authority for medical care at their time of arrival and, therefore, may not necessitate the need for the school nurse to go to the scene. Although a comforting person from the school the children know may be warranted, a school administrator may be a better choice. If the school nurse leaves the building when EMS providers are available at the scene, there could be an issue of who would be available to address other health concerns or possible emergencies of children in the building.

Transportation of Students in Employee-Owned Cars

All school staff should avoid using personally owned vehicles to transport pupils to and from school-related activities for liability and safety concerns unless specifically allowed by school district policy and auto liability insurance. Permission to use private vehicles should be obtained in writing from the administration and based on school district policy. Additionally, school districts should have an established policy that limits any school staff from being alone with a singular student on transportation, except in an emergency. On occasion, parents may be unable to pick up a sick child from school. The use of taxis, ride-share programs, or an unscheduled bus may be utilized per school policy, but only with serious consideration of the legal implications. Transportation arrangements outside of school district-controlled transportation should only be utilized with express parent consent, in an emergency, or in accordance with school district policy. *See* New Jersey School Boards Association, *Policy Update: Uber Cautious (2017).* There are legal implications when a school district, which stands *in loco parentis** to a student, releases a student to another adult's custody for transportation purposes. Taxis, ride-share programs, and unscheduled buses may not have an adult with clearances operating them. A student's age, maturity, and needs are also strong considerations for utilizing alternative transportation.

Minor Injuries on the Bus

Occasionally, a student will arrive at school with an injury that occurred during the bus ride. Documentation of how and why the injury occurred should be thorough and shared with the building administrator for any reason, including if the injury was a result of an altercation with another student, as a result of misbehavior, or due to a safety issue on the bus. Parents should be notified, and an incident report should be completed. Videos of the transportation incident may be secured to provide further clarification.

Transportation via Ambulance

School nurses are often at the forefront when an ambulance is called for an injured or ill student. When EMS providers arrive, healthcare responsibilities transfer from the school nurse to the paramedic/ Emergency Medical Technician (EMT). If the student is transported to the hospital, one question that frequently emerges is who should accompany the student in the ambulance if a parent is unavailable. While school district policy should dictate that responsibility, in general, someone from the school district who knows the student and can offer reassurance should accompany the student until the parent/guardian is united with them. Again, school districts should avoid assigning the school nurse for this responsibility, as they maintain responsibilities for other health concerns or emergencies within the building.

*the legal responsibility of some person or organization to perform some of the functions or responsibilities of a parent

CONCLUSION

For a student with medical needs or a disability to have equal access to the school district's programs and services, it may be necessary for the school district to provide transportation or even specialized transportation. This obligation can include transportation to and from school, between schools, transportation within the school building, and any specialized equipment needed. School teams, including IEP and Section 504 teams, should carefully consider the needed accommodations when developing the student's IEP or Section 504 Plan. The school nurse will be essential in this planning and in developing any IHP or ITP to be shared with the school team and other staff involved with the student's transportation needs.

RESOURCES

Centers for Disease and Prevention: Safe Routes to School (SRTS).
https://www.cdc.gov/policy/opaph/hi5/saferoutes/

Do Long Bus Rides Drive Down Academic Outcomes? https://doi.org/10.3102/01623737221092450

National Council on State Boards of Nursing. Nurse Practice Act Toolkit.
https://www.ncsbn.org/npa-toolkit.htm

Transporting Students with Disabilities (2022). Legalities of Transporting Students with Special Needs.
https://tsdconference.com/2022/11/16/legalities-of-transporting-students-with-special-needs-discussed-at-tsd-conference/

United States Department of Education. (2020). Protecting Students with Disabilities.
http://www2.ed.gov/about/offices/list/ocr/504faq.html

U.S. Department of Transportation: Safe Routes to School Programs
https://www.transportation.gov/mission/health/Safe-Routes-to-School-Programs

Youth. Gov: Safe Routes to School (SRTS). https://youth.gov/feature-article/safe-routes-school-srts

Case Law

Section 504 Compliance Advisor, November 2019, *23*(9)

Letter to McKaig, 211 IDELR 161 (EHLR 211:161) (OSEP 1980)

Letter to Stohrer, 213 IDELR 209 (EHLR 213:209) (OSEP 1989)

Macomb County Intermediate School District vs. Joshua S., 715 F. Supp. 824 (E.D. Mich. 1989)
http://www.leagle.com/decision/19891539715FSupp824_11367/MACOMB%20COUNTY%20INTERMEDIATE%20SCHOOL%20D.%20v.%20JOSHUA%20S

REFERENCES

Individuals with Disability Education Improvement Act (2004), 20 USC 1400 et seq.

McKinney-Vento Homeless Assistance Act. (2004). (Subtitle B – Section 725 [42 U.S.C. 11431 et seq.] as reauthorized by Title X, Part C of the Elementary and Secondary Education).

National Association of State Directors of Pupil Transportation Services. (2023).https://nasdpts.org/

National Congress on School Transportation. (n.d.) *History of NCST*. Retrieved on 5-27-23.
https://nasdpts.org/history-of-ncst

National Center for Education Statistics. (2021). *National digest of education statistics*.
https://nces.ed.gov/programs/digest/d21/tables/dt21_236.90.asp

Norlin, J., Pfrommer, J., & Pitasky, V. (2015). Transportation. In *The complete OSEP handbook* (2nd ed., pp.1-20). (Citation included biannual updates, 2022).

Pfrommer, J. (2022). *Serving students with medical needs: Achieving legal compliance with 50)*. (Citation included pamphlet, 2022)

Section 504 of the Rehabilitation Act of 1973, 29 USC § 794.

INDEX

www.ingramcontent.com/pod-product-compliance
Lightning Source LLC
Chambersburg PA
CBHW061304190825
31336CB00027B/120